Microsoft

Microsoft® Access® 2010 Inside Out

Jeff Conrad
John Viescas

Published with the authorization of Microsoft Corporation by:
O'Reilly Media, Inc.
1005 Gravenstein Highway North
Sebastopol, California 95472

Printed and bound in the United States of America.

1 2 3 4 5 6 7 8 9 QGT 5 4 3 2 1 0

Microsoft Press titles may be purchased for educational, business or sales promotional use. Online editions are also available for most titles (*http://my.safaribooksonline.com*). For more information, contact our corporate/institutional sales department: (800) 998-9938 or *corporate@oreilly.com*. Visit our website at *microsoftpress.oreilly.com*. Send comments to *mspinput@microsoft.com*.

Acquisitions and Development: Juliana Aldous and Kenyon Brown
Production Editor: Rachel Monaghan
Editorial Production: Custom Editorial, Inc. and Nancy Kotary
Technical Reviewers: Andrew Couch and Jim Bailie
Indexing: Potomac Indexing, LLC
Cover: Karen Montgomery
Compositor: Nellie McKesson
Illustrator: Robert Romano

978-0-735-62685-0

For my family, Cheryl, Amy, Aaron, and Arica, for your love and support. You are the reason I have written this book and I couldn't have done it without you.

—Jeff Conrad

To Jeff, who adopted my book and made it his own.

—John Viescas
Paris, France
June 2010

Contents at a Glance

Part 7: Working with the Web

Bonus Content on the Companion CD

Part 8: Automating an Access Application Using Visual Basic

Part 9: After Completing Your Application

Table of Contents

Part 3: Building Queries

Part 4: Creating Forms

Part 5: Working with Reports

Part 6: Automating an Access Application Using Macros

Part 7: Working with the Web

Bonus Content on the Companion CD

Part 8: Automating an Access Application Using Visual Basic

Acknowledgments

Nearly every member of the Microsoft Access development team provided invaluable technical support as I worked through the finer details in Microsoft Access 2010. The program managers, developers, and test engineers on the team helped with suggestions, tips and tricks, and reviewing my material. Special thanks to program manager Ric Lewis, who helped write the Business Connectivity Services chapter. You folks make an author's job so much easier. But any errors or omissions in this book are ultimately mine.

A book this large and complex requires a top-notch team to get what I put into Microsoft Word documents onto the printed pages you are now holding. I had some of the best in the business at both Microsoft Press and O'Reilly Media to get the job done. Many thanks to Kenyon Brown at O'Reilly Media for serving as Acquisitions and Development Editor and to Juliana Aldous as Acquisitions Editor for Microsoft Press. Special thanks also to Linda Allen and Rachel Monaghan for handling copy and production editing and to Andrew Couch and Jim Bailie for technical reviewing. I couldn't have done it without you!

And last, but certainly not least, I thank my wife and soulmate, Cheryl. She not only patiently stood by me as I cranked through 1,800 pages of manuscript, but also helped behind the scenes reviewing and editing what I did.

—Jeff Conrad
Redmond, Washington
July 2010

About the CD

The companion CD that ships with this book contains many resources to help you get the most out of your Inside Out book.

What's on the CD

Your Inside Out CD includes the following:

- **Sample client and web database applications.** Includes query, form, and report examples.
- **Four bonus chapters.** Here you'll find coverage of Visual Basic fundamentals, adding the finishing touches, and distributing your application.
- **Six technical articles.** This section includes an overview of SQL, exporting data, a function reference, color names and codes, and macro actions.
- **Complete eBook.** In this section, you'll find the entire electronic version of this title.

Sample Applications

Throughout this book, you'll see examples from four sample Access applications included on the sample CD:

- *Back Office Software System Restaurant Management Application (BOSS.accdb).* This application is a hybrid Access application designed for use in both client and web. It demonstrates how a restaurant might manage food orders, maintain employee records, and create weekly work schedules. This application can be published to a server running SharePoint 2010 and Access Services and then used within a web browser. You'll also find BOSSDataCopy.accdb and BOSSDataCopy2.accdb files that contain many of the query, form, and report examples.
- *Conrad Systems Contacts (Contacts.accdb and ContactsData.accdb).* This application is both a contacts management and order entry database—two samples for the price of one! This sample database demonstrates how to build a client/server application using only desktop tools as well as how to "upsize" an application to create an Access project and related SQL Server tables, views, stored procedures, and functions. You'll also find a ContactsDataCopy.accdb file that contains additional query, form, and report examples.

- *Housing Reservations (Housing.accdb)*. This application demonstrates how a company housing department might track and manage reservations in company-owned housing facilities for out-of-town employees and guests. You'll also find HousingDataCopy.accdb and HousingDataCopy2.accdb files that contain many of the query, form, and report examples.

- *Wedding List (WeddingMC.accdb and WeddingList.accdb)*. This application is an example of a simple database that you might build for your personal use. It has a single main table where you can track the names and addresses of invitees, whether they've said that they will attend, the description of any gift they sent, and whether a thank-you note has been sent. Although you might be tempted to store such a simple list in an Excel spreadsheet or a Word document, this application demonstrates how storing the information in Access makes it easy to search and sort the data and produce reports. The WeddingMC database is automated entirely using macros, and the WeddingList database is the same application automated with Visual Basic.

You can find these databases on the companion CD provided with this book. Please note that the person names, company names, email addresses, and web addresses in these databases are fictitious. Although we pre-loaded all databases with sample data, the Housing Reservations and Conrad Systems Contacts databases also include a special form (zfrmLoadData) that has code to load random data into the sample tables based on parameters that you supply.

The examples in this book assume you have installed the 32-bit version of Microsoft Office 2010, not just the 32-bit version of Access 2010. The sample databases included with the companion CD have not been modified to work with the 64-bit version of Access 2010. Several examples also assume that you have installed all optional features of Access through the Office 2010 setup program. If you have not installed these additional features, your screen might not match the illustrations in this book or you might not be able to run the samples from the companion CD. A list of the additional features you will need to run all the samples in this book is included in the Appendix.

System Requirements

Following are the minimum system requirements neccessary to run the CD:

- A Pentium 500 megahertz (MHz) or faster processor (Pentium III is recommended as a minimum), and 1 gigahertz (GHz) is required for Microsoft Outlook with Business Contact Manager.

- Microsoft Windows XP with Service Pack (SP) 3 (32-bit), Windows Vista with SP1 (32-bit or 64-bit), Windows Server 2003 R2 (32-bit or 64-bit) with MSXML 6.0 installed,

Windows Server 2008 (32-bit or 64-bit), or Windows 7 (32-bit or 64-bit). Terminal Server and Windows on Windows (WOW), which allows installing 32-bit versions of Office 2010 on 64-bit operating systems, are supported.

- At least 256 megabytes (MB) of random access memory (RAM); 512 MB is recommended.
- A hard drive with at least 527 MB of free space for a minimum installation when your network administrator has set up an install package for you on a server. When you perform a local installation, you need up to 3.5 gigabytes (GB) on your primary hard drive for the installation files and programs. At the end of the Office system install, you have the option to leave some of the installation files on your hard drive, which requires up to an additional 240 MB of free space.
- A CD-ROM or DVD-ROM drive. (A DVD-ROM is recommended.) If you are installing over a network, no disc drive is required.
- A mouse or other pointing device.
- A 1024 × 768 or greater monitor display.

Other options required to use all features include the following:

- A multimedia computer for sound and other multimedia effects.
- Dial-up or broadband Internet access.
- Certain inking features require running Windows XP Table PC edition or later. Speech recognition functionality requires a close-talk microphone and an audio output device. Information Rights Management features require access to a Windows Server 2003 with SP1 or later running Windows Rights Management Services.
- Connectivity to Microsoft Exchange 2000 Server or later is required for certain advanced functionality in Outlook 2010. Instant Search requires Windows Desktop Search 3.0. Dynamic Calendars require server connectivity.
- Microsoft Internet Explorer 6 or later, 32-bit browser only. Internet functionality requires Internet access (fees might apply).
- Connection to an Internet service provider or a local copy of Microsoft Internet Information Services (IIS) installed.
- 512 MB of RAM or higher recommended for Outlook Instant Search. Grammar and contextual spelling in Microsoft Word 2010 is not turned on unless the computer has 1 GB memory.

Note
An internet connection is necessary to access the hyperlinks on the companion CD. Connect time charges may apply.

Support Information

Every effort has been made to ensure the accuracy of the contents of the book and of this CD. As corrections or changes are collected, they will be added to a Microsoft Knowledge Base article. Microsoft Press provides support for books and companion CDs at the following website: *www.microsoft.com/learning/support/books/*.

If you have comments, questions, or ideas regarding the book or this CD, or questions that are not answered by visiting the site above, please send them via e-mail to *mspinput@microsoft.com*.

You can also click the Feedback or CD Support links on the Welcome page. Please note that Microsoft software product support is not offered through the above addresses.

If your question is about the software, and not about the content of this book, please visit the Microsoft Help and Support page or the Microsoft Knowledge Base at *http://support.microsoft.com*.

Conventions and Features Used in This Book

This book uses special text and design conventions to make it easier for you to find the information you need.

Text Conventions

Convention	Meaning
Abbreviated menu commands	For your convenience, this book uses abbreviated menu commands. For example, "Click Tools, Track Changes, Highlight Changes" means that you should click the Tools menu, point to Track Changes, and click the Highlight Changes command.
Boldface type	**Boldface** type is used to indicate text that you enter or type.
Initial Capital Letters	The first letters of the names of menus, dialog boxes, dialog box elements, and commands are capitalized. Example: the Save As dialog box.
Italicized type	*Italicized* type is used to indicate new terms.
Plus sign (+) in text	Keyboard shortcuts are indicated by a plus sign (+) separating two key names. For example, Ctrl+Alt+Delete means that you press the Ctrl, Alt, and Delete keys at the same time.

Design Conventions

INSIDE OUT **This Statement Illustrates an Example of an "Inside Out" Heading**

These are the book's signature tips. In these tips, you'll get the straight scoop on what's going on with the software—inside information about why a feature works the way it does. You'll also find handy workarounds to deal with software problems.

Sidebars

Sidebars provide helpful hints, timesaving tricks, or alternative procedures related to the task being discussed.

TROUBLESHOOTING

This statement illustrates an example of a "Troubleshooting" problem statement.

Look for these sidebars to find solutions to common problems you might encounter. Troubleshooting sidebars appear next to related information in the chapters. You can also use the Troubleshooting Topics index at the back of the book to look up problems by topic.

Cross-references point you to other locations in the book that offer additional information about the topic being discussed.

Note

Notes offer additional information related to the task being discussed.

CAUTION!

Cautions identify potential problems that you should look out for when you're completing a task or problems that you must address before you can complete a task.

When an example has a related file that is included on the companion CD, this icon appears in the margin. You can use these files to follow along with the book's examples.

Syntax Conventions

The following conventions are used in the syntax descriptions for Visual Basic statements in Chapter 24, "Understanding Visual Basic Fundamentals," Chapter 25, "Automating Your Application with Visual Basic," SQL statements in Article 2, "Understanding SQL," and any other chapter where you find syntax defined. These conventions do not apply to code examples listed within the text; all code examples appear exactly as you'll find them in the sample databases.

You must enter all other symbols, such as parentheses and colons, exactly as they appear in the syntax line. Much of the syntax shown in the Visual Basic chapter has been broken into multiple lines. You can format your code all on one line, or you can write a single line of code on multiple lines using the Visual Basic line continuation character (_).

<table>
<tr><th>Convention</th><th>Meaning</th></tr>
<tr><td>Bold</td><td>Bold type indicates keywords and reserved words that you must enter exactly as shown. Microsoft Visual Basic understands keywords entered in uppercase, lowercase, and mixed case type. Access stores SQL keywords in queries in all uppercase, but you can enter the keywords in any case.</td></tr>
<tr><td>Italic</td><td>Italicized words represent variables that you supply.</td></tr>
<tr><td>Angle brackets < ></td><td>Angle brackets enclose syntactic elements that you must supply. The words inside the angle brackets describe the element but do not show the actual syntax of the element. Do not enter the angle brackets.</td></tr>
<tr><td>Brackets [ ]</td><td>Brackets enclose optional items. If more than one item is listed, the items are separated by a pipe character (|). Choose one or none of the elements. Do not enter the brackets or the pipe; they're not part of the element. Note that Visual Basic and SQL in many cases require that you enclose names in brackets. When brackets are required as part of the syntax of variables that you must supply in these examples, the brackets are italicized, as in [MyTable].[MyField].</td></tr>
<tr><td>Braces { }</td><td>Braces enclose one or more options. If more than one option is listed, the items are separated by a pipe character (|). Choose one item from the list. Do not enter the braces or the pipe.</td></tr>
<tr><td>Ellipsis ...</td><td>Ellipses indicate that you can repeat an item one or more times. When a comma is shown with an ellipsis (,...), enter a comma between items.</td></tr>
<tr><td>Underscore _</td><td>You can use a blank space followed by an underscore to continue a line of Visual Basic code to the next line for readability. You cannot place an underscore in the middle of a string literal. You do not need an underscore for continued lines in SQL, but you cannot break a literal across lines.</td></tr>
</table>

Introduction

Microsoft Access 2010 is just one part of Microsoft's overall data management product strategy. Like all good relational databases, it allows you to link related information easily—for example, customer and order data that you enter. But Access 2010 also complements other database products because it has several powerful connectivity features. As its name implies, Access can work directly with data from other sources, including many popular PC database programs (such as dBASE), with many SQL (Structured Query Language) databases on the desktop, on servers, on minicomputers, or on mainframes, and with data stored on Internet or intranet web servers. Access also fully supports Microsoft's ActiveX technology, so an Access application can be either a client or a server for all the other 2010 Microsoft Office system applications, including Word, Excel, PowerPoint, Outlook, Publisher, and OneNote.

Access provides a very sophisticated application development system for the Microsoft Windows operating system. This helps you build applications quickly, whatever the data source. In fact, you can build simple applications by defining forms and reports based on your data and linking them with a few macros or Microsoft Visual Basic statements; there's no need to write complex code in the classic programming sense. Because Access uses Visual Basic, you can use the same set of skills with other applications in the Microsoft Office system or with Visual Basic.

For small businesses (and for consultants creating applications for small businesses), the Access desktop development features are all that's required to store and manage the data used to run the business. Access coupled with Microsoft SQL Server—on the desktop or on a server—is an ideal way for many medium-size companies to build new applications for Windows quickly and inexpensively. To enhance workgroup productivity, you can use Access 2010 to create an Access Services web application running on a server with SharePoint 2010. Users of your application can view, edit, and delete data from your application directly in their web browser. For large corporations with a big investment in mainframe relational database applications as well as a proliferation of desktop applications that rely on personal computer databases, Access provides the tools to easily link mainframe and personal computer data in a single Windows-based application. Access 2010 includes features to allow you to export or import data in XML format (the lingua franca of data stored on the web).

Getting Familiar with Access 2010

If you have never used a database program—including Access—you'll find Access 2010 very approachable. Using the results of extensive productivity lab tests, Microsoft has revamped the user interface in all the Microsoft Office programs. The Backstage view and ribbon technology makes it much easier for novice users to get acquainted with Access and easily discover its most useful features. To get a new user jump-started, Microsoft has provided over a dozen local client and web database templates that load onto your hard disk when you install Access. In addition, you'll find many additional database templates available for easy download from the Microsoft Office website directly from within Access. Microsoft plans to continue to add templates after Access 2010 is released to further enhance your productivity.

But if you have used any version of Access prior to 2007, you're in for a big surprise. Menus and toolbars are gone—all replaced by the Backstage view and ribbon. The Database window has been replaced by the Navigation pane. When you first start using Access 2010, you'll probably notice a decrease in productivity, but it won't take you long to get comfortable with the new interface. You'll probably soon discover features that you didn't know were there. Nearly all the old familiar objects are around—tables, queries, forms, reports, macros, and modules, and you'll find that the standard design and data views you've come to know and love are still around. You'll also quickly learn that the Layout and Report views and macro Logic Designer rapidly increase your productivity.

About This Book

If you're developing a database application with the tools in Access 2010, this book gives you a thorough understanding of "programming without pain." It provides a solid foundation for designing databases, forms, and reports and getting them all to work together. You'll learn that you can quickly create complex applications by linking design elements with macros or Visual Basic. This book will also show you how to take advantage of some of the more advanced features of Access 2010. You'll learn how to build an Access web database that you can then publish to a server running SharePoint 2010 and Access Services. You'll also learn about new data macros that allow you to attach business logic to your tables and how to work with the revamped Logic Designer to design macros.

If you're new to developing applications, particularly database applications, this probably should not be the first book you read about Access. We recommend that you first take a look at *Microsoft Access 2010 Plain & Simple* or *Microsoft Access 2010 Step By Step*.

Microsoft Access 2010 Inside Out is divided into nine major parts:

- Part 1 provides an overview of Access 2010 and provides you with a detailed look at the user interface, including the new Backstage view.
  - Chapter 1 explains the major features that a database should provide, explores those features in Access, and discusses some of the main reasons why you should consider using database software.
  - Chapter 2 thoroughly explores the user interface introduced in the Office 2010 release. The chapter also explains content security, working with the Backstage view, ribbon, and the Navigation pane, and setting options that customize how you work with Access 2010.
  - Chapter 3 describes the architecture of Access 2010, gives you an overview of the major objects in an Access database by taking you on a tour through two of the sample databases, and explains the many ways you can use Access to create an application.
- Part 2 shows you how to create your desktop or web database and tables.
  - Chapter 4 teaches you how to design client databases and tables.
  - Chapter 5 shows you the ins and outs of modifying tables even after you've already begun to load data and build other parts of your application.
  - Chapter 6 focuses on designing tables for use in a web database.
  - Chapter 7 discusses the new feature of table data macros and how to work with the new Logic Designer to create your macro logic.
  - Chapter 8 explains how to link to or import data from other sources.
- Part 3 focuses on how to build queries to analyze and update data in your tables.
  - Chapter 9 shows you how to build simple queries and how to work with data in Datasheet view.
  - Chapter 10 discusses how to design client and web queries to work with data from multiple tables, summarize information, build queries that require you to work in SQL view, and work with the PivotTable and PivotChart views of queries.
  - Chapter 11 focuses on modifying sets of data with queries—updating data, inserting new data, deleting sets of data, or creating a new table from a selection of data from existing tables.

- Part 4 discusses how to build and work with forms in client and web applications.
    - Chapter 12 introduces you to forms—what they look like and how they work.
    - Chapters 13, 14, and 15 teach you all about form design in client and web applications, from simple forms you build with a wizard to complex, advanced forms that use embedded forms and navigation and web browser controls. You'll also learn how to use Layout view to design web forms that you can open in a web browser using Access Services.
- Part 5 explains how to work with reports in client and web applications.
    - Chapter 16 leads you on a guided tour of reports and explains their major features.
    - Chapters 17 and 18 teach you how to design, build, and implement both simple and complex reports in your client or web application.
- Part 6 shows you how to make your client and web applications "come alive" using macros.
    - Chapter 19 discusses the concept of event processing in Access, provides a comprehensive list of events, and explains the sequence in which critical events occur.
    - Chapter 20 covers macro design for client applications in depth and explains how to use error trapping and embedded macro features.
    - Chapter 21 focuses on how to create web macros, work with web forms and control events, and perform actions in a web browser.
- Part 7 is all about using Access tools and working with the web.
    - Chapter 22 teaches you how to publish your web database to an Access Services site and use your application in a browser. It discusses making changes to a web application, synchronizing your changes with the server, working in offline mode, and instantiating a web template.
    - Chapter 23 covers features in Access that handle XML and how to use Business Connectivity Services.
- The Appendix explains how to install the Office 2010 release, including which options you should choose for Access 2010 to be able to open all the samples in this book.

- Part 8, on the companion CD, shows you how to use the programming facilities in Microsoft Visual Basic to integrate your database objects and automate your application.
  - Chapter 24 is a comprehensive reference to the Visual Basic language and object models implemented in Access. It presents two complex coding examples with a line-by-line discussion of the code. The final section shows you how to work with the new 64-bit Access Visual Basic.
  - Chapter 25 thoroughly discusses some of the most common tasks that you might want to automate with Visual Basic. Each section describes a problem, shows you specific form or report design techniques you must use to solve the problem, walks you through the code from one or more of the sample databases that implements the solution, and discusses calling named data macros.

- Part 9, on the companion CD, covers tasks you might want to perform after completing your application.
  - Chapter 26 teaches you how to automate custom ribbons, create a custom Backstage view, and how to set Startup properties.
  - Chapter 27 teaches you tasks for setting up your application so that you can distribute it to others. It also shows you how to create your own custom Data Type Parts, Application Parts, and application templates.

- The CD provides an additional six Articles that contain important reference information:
  - Article 1 explains a simple technique that you can use to design a good relational database application with little effort. Even if you're already familiar with Access or creating database applications in general, getting the table design right is so important that this article is a "must read" for everyone.
  - Article 2 is a complete reference to SQL as implemented in desktop databases. It also contains notes about differences between SQL supported natively by Access and SQL implemented in SQL Server.
  - Article 3 discusses how to export data and Access objects to various types of other data formats from your Access application.
  - Article 4 lists the functions most commonly used in an Access application categorized by function type. You'll also find a list of functions that you can use with web databases.
  - Article 5 lists the color names and codes you can use in Access.
  - Article 6 lists the macro actions for both client and web applications you can use in Access.

PART 1

Understanding Access

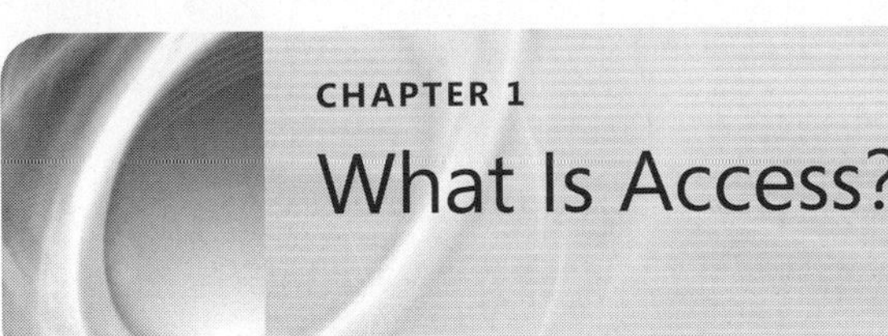

CHAPTER 1

What Is Access?

If you're a serious user of a personal computer, you've probably been using word processing or spreadsheet applications to help you solve problems. You might have started a long time ago with character-based products running under MS-DOS but subsequently upgraded to software that runs under the Microsoft Windows operating system. You might also own some database software, either as part of an integrated package such as Microsoft Works or as a separate program.

Database programs have been available for personal computers for a long time. Unfortunately, many of these programs have been either simple data storage managers that aren't suitable for building applications, or complex application development systems that are difficult to learn and use. Even many computer-literate people have avoided the more complex database systems unless they have been handed a complete, custom-built database application. The introduction of Microsoft Access nearly two decades ago represented a significant turnaround in ease of use. Many people are drawn to it to create both simple databases and sophisticated database applications.

Now that Access is in its ninth release and has become an even more robust product in the seventh edition, designed for 32-bit versions of Windows and the first edition designed for 64-bit versions of Windows, perhaps it's time to take another look at how you work with your personal computer to get the job done. If you've previously shied away from database software because you felt you needed programming skills or because it would take you too much time to become a proficient user, you'll be pleasantly surprised at how easy it is to work with all the new features rolled into Microsoft Access 2010.

Access 2010 comes loaded with many existing database templates to solve business and personal needs. These templates are fully functioning applications that can be used as is, without having to make any modifications. For users who do want to modify the templates or even start from scratch, this latest version of Access comes with new application and data type parts, improved form and report What You See Is What You Get (WYSIWYG) authoring tools, data macros to control your business logic, new database level themes, and expanded conditional formatting options. You also can now publish your application to a Microsoft SharePoint Server 2010 site using Access Services and view your forms and reports in a web browser.

But how do you decide whether you're ready to move up to a database system such as Access? To help you decide, let's take a look at the advantages of using database application development software.

What Is a Database?

In the simplest sense, a *database* is a collection of records and files that are organized for a particular purpose. On your computer system, you might keep the names and addresses of all your friends or customers. Perhaps you collect all the letters you write and organize them by recipient. You might have another set of files in which you keep all your financial data—accounts payable and accounts receivable, or your checkbook entries and balances. The word processor documents that you organize by topic are, in the broadest sense, one type of database. The spreadsheet files that you organize according to their uses are another type of database. Shortcuts to all your programs on your Windows Start menu are a kind of database. Internet shortcuts organized in your Favorites folder are a database.

If you're very organized, you can probably manage several hundred spreadsheets or shortcuts by using folders and subfolders. When you do this, *you're* the database manager. But what do you do when the problems you're trying to solve get too big? How can you collect information about all customers and their orders easily when the data might be stored in several document and spreadsheet files? How can you maintain links between the files when you enter new information? How do you ensure that data is being entered correctly? What if you need to share your information with many people but don't want two people to try updating the same data at the same time? How do you keep duplicate copies of data from proliferating when people can't share the same data at the same time? Faced with these challenges, you need a *database management system* (DBMS).

Relational Databases

Nearly all modern database management systems store and handle information using the *relational* database management model. In a relational database management system, sometimes called an *RDBMS,* the system manages all data in *tables*. Tables store information about a single subject (such as customers or products) and have *columns* (or *fields*) that contain the different kinds of information about the subject (for example, customers' addresses or phone numbers) and *rows* (or *records*) that describe all the attributes of a single instance of the subject (for example, data on a specific customer or product). Even when you *query* the database (fetch information from one or more tables), the result is always something that looks like another table.

The term *relational* stems from the fact that each table in the database contains information related to a single subject and only that subject. If you study the relational database management model, you'll find the term *relation* applied to a set of rows (a table) about a single subject. Also, you can manipulate data about two classes of information (such as customers and orders) as a single entity based on related data values. For example, it would be redundant to store customer name and address information with every order that the customer places. In an RDMS, the information about orders contains a field that stores data, such as a customer number, which can be used to connect each order with the appropriate customer information.

You can also *join* information on related values from multiple tables or queries. For example, you can join company information with contact information to find out the contacts for a particular company. You can join employee information with department information to find out the department in which an employee works.

Some Relational Database Terminology

- **Relation** Information about a single subject such as customers, orders, employees, products, or companies. A relation is usually stored as a table in a relational database management system.
- **Attribute** A specific piece of information about a subject, such as the address for a customer or the dollar amount of an order. An attribute is normally stored as a data column, or field, in a table.
- **Instance** A particular member of a relation—an individual customer or product. An instance is usually stored in a table as a record, or row.
- **Relationship** The way information in one relation is related to information in another relation. For example, customers have a one-to-many relationship with orders because one customer can place many orders, but any order belongs to only one customer. Companies might have a many-to-many relationship with contacts because there might be multiple contacts for a company, and a contact might be associated with more than one company.
- **Join** The process of linking tables or queries on tables via their related data values. For example, customers might be joined to orders by matching customer ID in a customers' table and an orders table.

Database Capabilities

An RDBMS gives you complete control over how you define your data, work with it, and share it with others. The system also provides sophisticated features that make it easy to catalog and manage large amounts of data in many tables. An RDBMS has three main types of capabilities: data definition, data manipulation, and data control.

- **Data definition** You can define what data is stored in your database, the type of data (for example, numbers or characters), and how the data is related. In some cases, you can also define how the data should be formatted and how it should be validated.
- **Data manipulation** You can work with the data in many ways. You can select which data fields you want, filter the data, and sort it. You can join data with related information and summarize (total) the data. You can select a set of information and ask the RDBMS to update it, delete it, copy it to another table, or create a new table containing the data.
- **Data control** You can take advantage of features that help ensure that the right type of data goes into the correct places. In many cases, you can also define how data can be shared and updated by multiple users using the database.

All this functionality is contained in the powerful features of Access. Let's take a look at how Access implements these capabilities and compare them to what you can do with spreadsheet or word processing programs.

Access as an RDBMS

An Access desktop database (.accdb or .mdb) is a fully functional RDBMS. It provides all the data definition, data manipulation, and data control features you need to manage large volumes of data.

You can use an Access desktop database (.accdb or .mdb) either as a stand-alone RDBMS on a single workstation or in a shared client/server mode across a network. A desktop database can also act as the data source for data displayed on web pages on your company intranet. When you build an application with an Access desktop database, Access is the RDBMS. You can also use Access to build applications in a project file (.adp) connected to Microsoft SQL Server, and you can share the server data with other applications or with users on the web. When you create an Access project file (.adp), SQL Server (or the Microsoft SQL Server Desktop Engine—MSDE) is the RDBMS.

Note

Access 2000, Access 2002 (XP), and Access 2003 databases use the .mdb file format, but beginning with Access 2007, Microsoft introduced a new file format with an .accdb extension. To maintain maximum backward compatibility, Access 2010 can still open, run, and save .mdb databases created in the Access 2000 or Access 2002–2003 .mdb format, but to take advantage of all the new features in Access 2010, you need to use the .accdb file format. If you have to create an Access application that will be run by users with previous versions of Access, you should use the Access 2000 or Access 2002–2003 .mdb file format. You'll need to take extra precautions, however, to only use features in Access 2010 that are supported in earlier versions of Access.

Data Definition and Storage

As you work with a document or a spreadsheet, you generally have complete freedom to define the contents of the document or each cell in the spreadsheet. Within a given page in a document, you might include paragraphs of text, a table, a chart, or multiple columns of data displayed with multiple fonts. Within a given column on a spreadsheet, you might have text data at the top to define a column header for printing or display, and you might have various numeric formats within the same column, depending on the function of the row. You need this flexibility because your word processing document must be able to convey your message within the context of a printed page, and your spreadsheet must store the data you're analyzing as well as provide for calculation and presentation of the results.

This flexibility is great for solving relatively small, well-defined business problems. But a document becomes unwieldy when it extends beyond a few dozen pages, and a spreadsheet becomes difficult to manage as the amount of data grows. If you design a document or spreadsheet to be used by others, it's difficult (if not impossible) to control how they will use the data or enter new data. For example, on a spreadsheet, even though one cell might need a date and another a currency value to make sense, a user might easily enter character data in error.

Some spreadsheet programs allow you to define a "database" area within a spreadsheet to help you manage the information you need to produce the desired result. However, you are still constrained by the basic storage limitations of the spreadsheet program, and you still don't have much control over what's entered in the rows and columns of the database area. Also, if you need to handle more than number and character data, you might find that your spreadsheet program doesn't understand such data types as pictures or sounds.

An RDBMS allows you to define the kind of data you have and how the data should be stored. You can also usually define rules that the RDBMS can use to ensure the integrity of your data. In its simplest form, a *validation rule* might ensure that the user can't accidentally store alphabetic characters in a field that should contain a number. Other rules might define valid values or ranges of values for your data. In the most sophisticated systems, you can define the relationship between collections of data (usually tables or files) and ask the RDBMS to ensure that your data remains consistent. For example, you can have the system automatically check to ensure that every order entered is for a valid customer.

With an Access desktop database (.accdb or .mdb), you have complete flexibility to define your data (as text, numbers, dates, times, currency, Internet hyperlinks, pictures, sounds, documents, and spreadsheets), to define how Access stores your data (string length, number precision, and date/time precision), and to define what the data looks like when you display or print it. You can define simple or complex validation rules to ensure that only accurate values exist in your database. You can request that Access check for valid relationships between files or tables in your database. When you connect an Access project (.adp) to an SQL Server database, SQL Server provides all these capabilities.

Access 2010 includes an Attachment data type that can store images and other file types within the record. The Attachment data type can handle multiple attachment files per record via the use of a concept called *Complex Data*. In previous versions of Access using the .mdb file format, storing images and files through OLE Object data types caused significant bloat of the database file, but in version 2010, Access compresses these files to minimize the size overhead. Examples of files that could be attached to a record using the Attachment data type could be a cover letter created in Microsoft Word for each business contact, a bitmap picture of the contact person, or various sales worksheets created in Microsoft Excel. Figure 1-1 shows an example of a form using the Attachment data type to display a contact picture in the Contacts Map.accdb sample web database. (You can find the Contacts Map.accdb database loaded with sample data on the companion CD.)

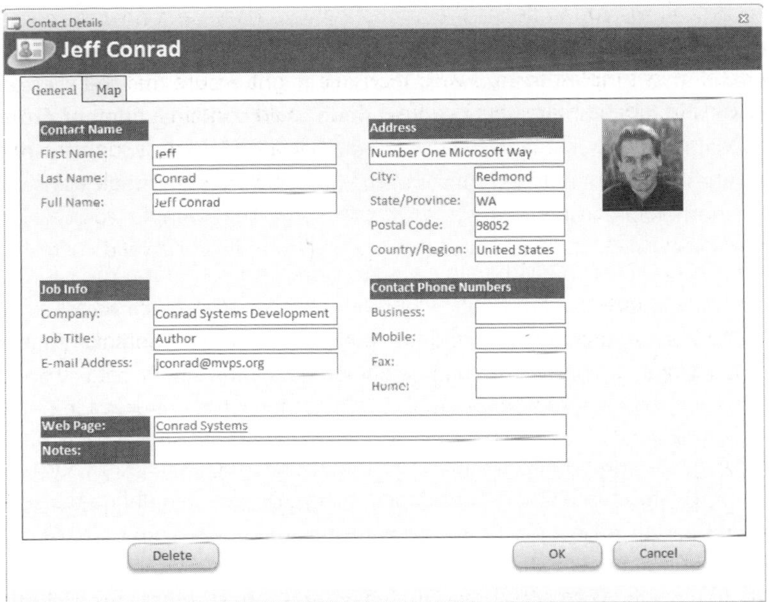

Figure 1-1 The Attachment data type displays a picture in a form.

Access can also understand and use a wide variety of other data formats, including many other database file structures. You can export data to and import data from word processing files or spreadsheets. You can access dBASE III, dBASE IV, Microsoft FoxPro, and other database files directly. You can also import data from these files into an Access table. In addition, Access can work with most popular databases that support the Open Database Connectivity (ODBC) standard, including SQL Server, Oracle, and DB2. Access 2010 has added enhanced functionality to work with SharePoint Server 2010.

Data Manipulation

Working with data in an RDBMS is very different from working with data in a word processing or spreadsheet program. In a word processing document, you can include tabular data and perform a limited set of functions on the data in the document. You can also search for text strings in the original document and, with ActiveX controls, include tables, charts, or pictures from other applications. In a spreadsheet, some cells contain functions that determine the result you want, and in other cells, you enter the data that provides the source information for the functions. The data in a given spreadsheet serves one particular purpose, and it's cumbersome to use the same data to solve a different problem. You can link to data in another spreadsheet to solve a new problem, or you can use limited search capabilities to copy a selected subset of the data in one spreadsheet to use in problem solving in another spreadsheet.

An RDBMS provides you with many ways to work with your data. You can, for example, search a single table for information or request a complex search across several related tables. You can update a single field or many records with a single command. You can write programs that use RDBMS commands to fetch data you want to display and allow the user to update.

Access uses the powerful SQL database language to process data in your tables. (SQL is an acronym for Structured Query Language.) Using SQL, you can define the set of information that you need to solve a particular problem, including data from perhaps many tables. But Access simplifies data manipulation tasks. You don't even have to understand SQL to get Access to work for you. Access uses the relationship definitions you provide to automatically link the tables you need. You can concentrate on how to solve information problems without having to worry about building a complex navigation system that links all the data structures in your database. Access also has an extremely simple yet powerful graphical query definition facility that you can use to specify the data you need to solve a problem. Using pointing and clicking, dragging, and a few keystrokes, you can build a complex query in a matter of seconds.

Figure 1-2 shows a complex query used in the Conrad Systems Contacts application. You can find this query in the Contacts.accdb sample database on the companion CD included with this book. Access displays field lists from selected tables in the upper part of the window; the lines between field lists indicate the automatic links that Access will use to solve the query.

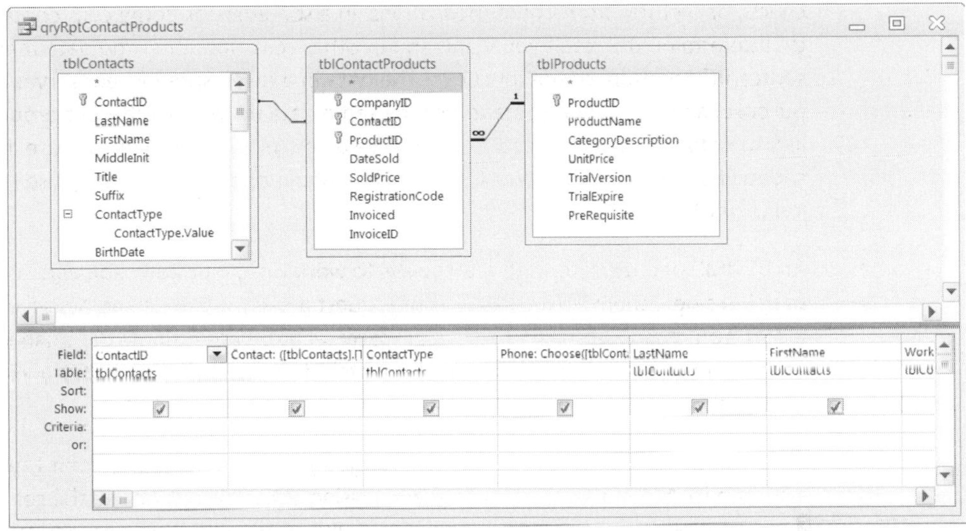

Figure 1-2 This query will retrieve information about products owned by contacts in the Conrad Systems Contacts sample application.

To create the query, you add the tables containing the data you need to the top of the query design grid, select the fields you want from each table, and drag them to the design grid in the lower part of the window. Choose a few options, type in any criteria, and you're ready to have Access select the information you want.

You don't need to be an expert to correctly construct the SQL syntax you need to solve your problem, but you can learn a lot about SQL in the article "Understanding SQL," found on the companion CD. For certain advanced types of queries, you'll need to learn the basics of SQL.

Figure 1-3 shows the result of asking the query to return its data.

qryRptContactProducts

Contact ID	Contact	Contact Type	Phone	Last Name	First Name	Work City	State/Provinc	Ho
5	Mr. Paul West	Customer	(456) 555-0146	West	Paul	Kalamazoo	MI	Kala
12	Mr. Harry Lingg	Customer	(567) 555-0146	Linggoputro	Harry	Yorktown	VA	Yorl
16	Mr. John Smith	Customer	(789) 555-0137	Smith	John	Easton	CA	Fres
23	Mr. Eugene Zab	Customer	(456) 555-0135	Zabokritski	Eugene	Riverside	ND	Wal
26	Dr. Peter Villads	Customer	(234) 555-0138	Villadsen	Peter	Grandy	NC	Fris
27	Mr. Adam Truka	Customer	(567) 555-0113	Trukawka	Adam	Irrigon	OR	Imn
3	Mr. Tom Micha	Customer	(456) 555-0114	Michaels	Tom	Youngsville	PA	Ken
6	Mr. Mario Kresr	Customer	(234) 555-0140	Kresnadi	Mario	Grosse Pointe	MI	Gro
12	Mr. Harry Lingg	Customer	(567) 555-0146	Linggoputro	Harry	Yorktown	VA	Yorl
15	Mrs. Shengda Y	Customer	(789) 555-0137	Yang	Shengda	Easton	CA	Fres
16	Mr. John Smith	Customer	(789) 555-0137	Smith	John	Easton	CA	Fres
17	Mr. Douglas Cur	Customer	(789) 555-0137	Curran	Douglas	Easton	CA	East
22	Mr. Mikael Sanc	Customer	(456) 555-0110	Sandberg	Mikael	Conway	MA	Colr
28	Dr. Mark Hanso	Customer	(567) 555-0113	Hanson	Mark	Irrigon	OR	Imb
6	Mr. Mario Kresr	Customer	(234) 555-0140	Kresnadi	Mario	Grosse Pointe	MI	Gro
8	Mr. Joseph Mat	Customer	(234) 555-0140	Matthews	Joseph	Grosse Pointe	MI	Det
12	Mr. Harry Lingg	Customer	(567) 555-0146	Linggoputro	Harry	Yorktown	VA	Yorl
16	Mr. John Smith	Customer	(789) 555-0137	Smith	John	Easton	CA	Fres
19	Mr. Dániel Kocz	Customer	(678) 555-0137	Koczka	Dániel	Elias	KY	San
24	Dr. Mindy Marti	Customer	(234) 555-0138	Martin	Mindy	Grandy	NC	Gra
25	Mr. Markus Zule	Customer	(234) 555-0138	Zulechner	Markus	Grandy	NC	Har
28	Dr. Mark Hanso	Customer	(567) 555-0113	Hanson	Mark	Irrigon	OR	Imb
5	Mr. Paul West	Customer	(456) 555-0146	West	Paul	Kalamazoo	MI	Kala

Record: 1 of 92 No Filter Search

Figure 1-3 The query returns a list of contacts and the products they own.

Data Control

Spreadsheets and word processing documents are great for solving single-user problems, but they are difficult to use when more than one person needs to share the data. Although spreadsheets are useful for providing templates for simple data entry, they don't do the job well if you need to perform complex data validation. For example, a spreadsheet works well as a template for an invoice for a small business with a single proprietor. But if the business expands and several salespeople are entering orders, the company needs a database. Likewise, a spreadsheet can assist employees with expense reports in a large business, but the data eventually must be captured and placed in a database for corporate accounting.

When you need to share your information with others, true RDMSs give you the flexibility to allow multiple users to read or update your data. An RDBMS that is designed to allow data sharing also provides features to ensure that no two people can change the same data at the same time. The best systems also allow you to group changes (a series of changes is sometimes called a *transaction*) so that either all the changes or none of the changes appear in your data. For example, while confirming a new order for a customer, you probably want to know that both the inventory for ordered products is updated and the order confirmation is saved or, if you encounter an error, that none of the changes are saved. You probably also want to be sure that no one else can view any part of the order until you have entered all of it.

Because you can share your Access data with other users, you might need to set some restrictions on what various users are allowed to see or update. Access 2010 has greatly improved the ability to share data with secured SharePoint lists to ensure data security. With SharePoint-to-Access integration, users can take advantage of improved workflow support, offline SharePoint lists, and a Recycle Bin to undo changes. Access 2010 also has strong data encryption with tougher encryption algorithms. Access automatically provides locking mechanisms to ensure that no two people can update an object at the same time, and Access also understands and honors the locking mechanisms of other database structures (such as FoxPro and SQL databases) that you attach to your database.

Access as an Application Development System

Being able to define exactly what data you need, how it should be stored, and how you want to access it solves the data management part of the problem. However, you also need a simple way to automate all the common tasks you want to perform. For example, each time you need to enter a new order, you don't want to have to run a query to search the Customers table, execute a command to open the Orders table, and then create a new record before you can enter the data for the order. After you've entered the data for the new order, you don't want to have to worry about scanning the table that contains all your products to verify the order's sizes, colors, and prices.

Advanced word processing software lets you define templates and macros to automate document creation, but it's not designed to handle complex transaction processing. In a spreadsheet, you enter formulas that define what automatic calculations you want performed. If you're an advanced spreadsheet user, you might also create macros or Microsoft Visual Basic procedures to help automate entering and validating data. If you're working with a lot of data, you've probably figured out how to use one spreadsheet as a "database" container and use references to selected portions of this data in your calculations.

Although you can build a fairly complex application using spreadsheets, you really don't have the debugging and application management tools you need to construct a robust data management application easily. Even something as simple as a wedding guest invitation and gift list is much easier to handle in a database. (See the Wedding List sample database on the companion CD included with this book.) Database systems are specifically designed for application development. They give you the data management and control tools that you need and also provide facilities to catalog the various parts of your application and manage their interrelationships. You also get a full programming language and debugging tools with a database system.

When you want to build a more complex database application, you need a powerful RDMS and an application development system to help you automate your tasks. Virtually all database systems include application development facilities to allow programmers or users of the system to define the procedures needed to automate the creation and manipulation of data. Unfortunately, many database application development systems require that you know a programming language, such as C or Xbase, to define procedures. Although these languages are very rich and powerful, you must have experience working with them before you can use them properly. To really take advantage of some database systems, you must learn programming, hire a programmer, or buy a ready-made database application (which might not exactly suit your needs) from a software development company.

Fortunately, Access makes it easy to design and construct database applications without requiring that you know a programming language. Although you begin in Access by defining the relational tables and the fields in those tables that will contain your data, you will quickly branch out to defining actions on the data via forms, reports, macros, and Visual Basic.

You can use forms and reports to define how you want to display the data and what additional calculations you want to perform—very much like spreadsheets. In this case, the format and calculation instructions (in the forms and reports) are separate from the data (in the tables), so you have complete flexibility to use your data in different ways without affecting the data. You simply define another form or report using the same data.

When you want to automate actions in a simple application, Access provides a macro definition facility to make it easy to respond to events (such as clicking a button to open a related report) or to link forms and reports. Access 2010 makes using macros even easier by letting you embed macro definitions in your forms and reports. When you want to build something a little more complex (like the Housing Reservations database included with this book), you can quickly learn how to create simple Visual Basic event procedures for your forms and reports. If you want to create more sophisticated applications, such as contact tracking, order processing, and reminder systems (see the Conrad Systems Contacts sample database), you can employ more advanced techniques using Visual Basic and module objects.

Access provides advanced database application development facilities to process not only data in its own database structures but also information stored in many other popular database formats. Perhaps Access's greatest strength is its ability to handle data from spreadsheets, text files, dBASE files, FoxPro databases, and any SQL database that supports the ODBC standard. This means you can use Access to create a Windows-based application that can process data from a network server running SQL Server or from a mainframe SQL database.

For advanced developers, Access provides the ability to create an Access application in a project file (.adp) that links directly to SQL Server (version 7.0 and later). You store your tables and queries (as views, functions, or stored procedures) directly in SQL Server and create forms for data entry and reports for data output in Access.

Deciding to Move to Database Software

When you use a word processing document or a spreadsheet to solve a problem, you define both the data and the calculations or functions you need at the same time. For simple problems with a limited set of data, this is an ideal solution. But when you start collecting lots of data, it becomes difficult to manage in many separate document or spreadsheet files. Adding one more transaction (another contact or a new investment in your portfolio) might push you over the limit of manageability.

If you need to change a formula or the way certain data is formatted, you might find that you have to make the same change in many places. When you want to define new calculations on existing data, you might have to copy and modify an existing document or create complex links to the files that contain the data. If you make a copy, how do you keep the data in the two copies synchronized?

Before you can use a database program such as Access to solve problems that require a lot of data or that have complex and changing requirements, you must change the way you think about solving problems with word processing or spreadsheet applications. In Access, you store a single copy of the data in the tables you design. Perhaps one of the hardest concepts to grasp is that you store only your basic data in database tables.

You can use the query facility to examine and extract the data in many ways. This allows you to keep only one copy of the basic data, yet use it over and over to solve different problems. In a sales database, you might create one form to display vendors and the products they supply. You can create another form to enter orders for these products. You can use a report defined on the same data to graph the sales of products by vendor during specified time periods. You don't need a separate copy of the data to do this, and you can change either the forms or the report independently, without destroying the structure of your database. You can also add new product or sales information easily without having to worry about the impact on any of your forms or reports. You can do this because the data (tables) and the routines you define to operate on the data (queries, forms, reports, macros, or modules) are completely independent of each other. Any change you make to the data via one form is immediately reflected by Access in any other form or query that uses the same data.

Reasons to Switch to a Database

Reason 1: You have too many separate files or too much data in individual files. This makes it difficult to manage the data. Also, the data might exceed the limits of the software or the capacity of the system memory.

Reason 2: You have multiple uses for the data—detailing transactions (invoices, for example), and analyzing summaries (such as quarterly sales summaries) and "what if" scenarios. Therefore, you need to be able to look at the data in many different ways, but you find it difficult to create multiple "views" of the data.

Reason 3: You need to share data. For example, numerous people are entering and updating data and analyzing it. Only one person at a time can update a word processing document, and although an Excel 2003 and later spreadsheet can be shared among several people, there is no mechanism to prevent two users from updating the same row simultaneously on their local copies of the spreadsheet, requiring the changes to be reconciled later. In contrast, Access locks the row of a table being edited by one person so that no conflicting changes can be made by another user, while still permitting many other users to access or update the remaining rows of the database table. In this way, each person is working from the same data and always sees the latest saved updates made by any other user.

Reason 4: You must control the data because different users access the data, because the data is used to run your business, and because the data is related (such as data for customers and orders). This means you must control data values, and you must ensure data consistency.

If you're wondering how you'll make the transition from word processing documents and spreadsheets to Access, you'll be pleased to find features in Access to help you out. You can use the import facilities to copy the data from your existing text or spreadsheet files. You'll find that Access supports most of the same functions you have used in your spreadsheets, so defining calculations in a form or a report will seem very familiar. Within the Help facility, you can find "how do I" topics that walk you through key tasks you need to learn to begin working with a database, and "tell me about" and reference topics that enhance your knowledge. In addition, Access provides powerful wizard facilities to give you a jump start on moving your spreadsheet data to an Access database, such as the Import Spreadsheet Wizard and the Table Analyzer Wizard to help you design database tables to store your old spreadsheet data.

INSIDE OUT **Design Considerations When Converting from a Spreadsheet to a Database**

You can obtain free assistance from us and many other Microsoft Most Valuable Professionals (MVPs) in the Access newsgroups. Some of the most difficult problems arise in databases that have been created by copying spreadsheet data directly into an Access table. The typical advice in this situation is to design the database tables first, then import and split up the spreadsheet data.

You can access the newsgroups using Windows Mail, or you can go to *http://support.microsoft.com/communities/newsgroups/default.aspx*, and in the Community Newsgroups column on the left, expand the Office category and then the Access category to see the available newsgroups. Click one of the links to go to that newsgroup within your web browser, where you can post questions and read answers to questions posted by others.

Extending the Power of Access to the Web

The World Wide Web, built from simple low-cost servers and universal clients, has revolutionized computing. Not so long ago, the very concept of a common global information network was unthinkable. Today, the concept of living *without* the web is just as unthinkable. Database applications were among the last to appear on the web, but today, they are arguably the fastest growing type of web application. The prospect of distributing data to or collecting it from literally a world of clients, working on disparate computers and operating systems, and not requiring software distribution other than the ubiquitous browser, is simply too compelling to resist for long.

As Microsoft looked at the long-term direction of Access, it was clear that the Access development team needed a way to make it easier for Access developers to move their applications to the web—a *cloud*. In the new global economy we are in, Access developers need an easier way to share their databases and still maintain a single point of maintenance. In fact, if you look at the types of questions Access developers post into newsgroups and support forums, one of the most common questions in the last few years has been: "How do I move my database to the web so that users who do not have Access can use my application?"

Access 2007 laid the foundation of using SharePoint lists as a data platform for Access databases; however, there were still many limitations of using SharePoint lists to store your data. Access developers wanted better data integrity—relationships, validation rules, and the ability to enforce required uniqueness for fields. Developers also wanted better performance when running against large data sets in SharePoint and the ability to design forms and reports that run in a web browser.

Access 2010 includes an exciting new feature set to make it easy to provide access to your data and objects over your company's local intranet or on the web using SharePoint Server 2010, Enterprise Edition. You can publish your database to a server running SharePoint Server 2010 and Access Services to make a fully functional web application. Access Services is a set of features and services running on top of the SharePoint Server platform. After you publish your database to a server running SharePoint Server and Access Services, your forms and reports can be viewed in a web browser. You can edit and view data from your web browser, in addition to editing your data from within Access 2010. Creating an Access Services web application with your data and objects stored in a SharePoint site allows you to tap into the security, backup, and collaboration capabilities built into the SharePoint Server platform.

In Figure 1-4, you can see an example of an Access Services web application, created entirely within Access 2010, published to a server running SharePoint Server, and running in a web browser. The data for the application lives in SharePoint lists, macros which control the logic of the application are converted to SharePoint workflows, and Access forms and reports are converted to objects that can be viewed in a web browser.

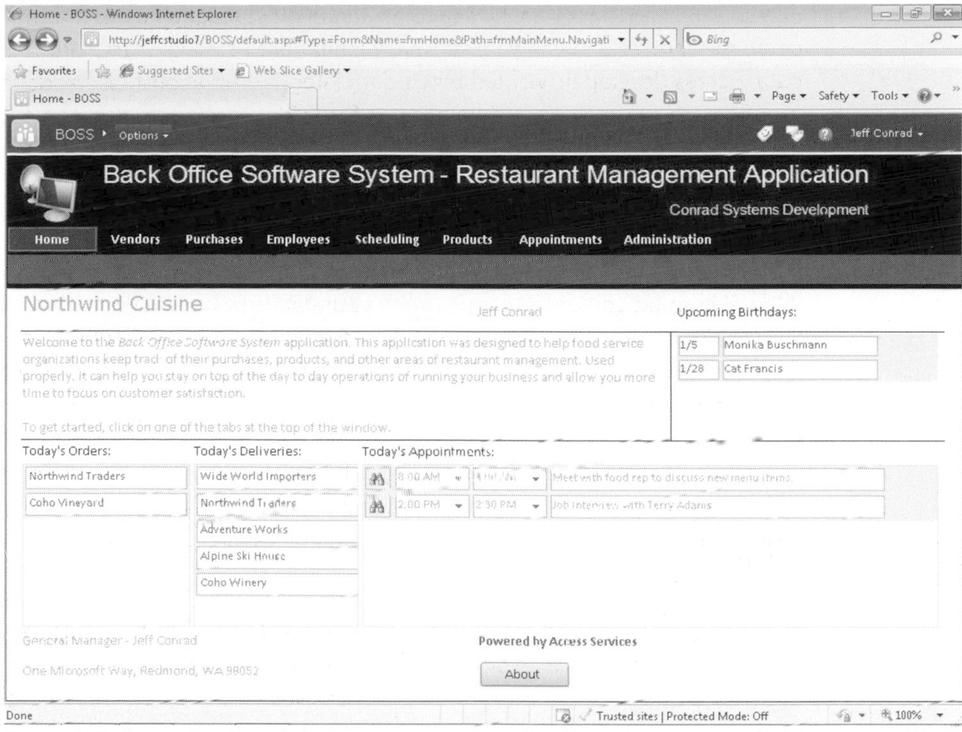

Figure 1-4 Access Services, running on a server running SharePoint Server, allows you to publish your web database and view it in a web browser.

Take a long look at the kind of work you're doing today. The sidebar, "Reasons to Switch to a Database," on page 16, summarizes some of the key reasons why you might need to move to Access. Is the number of files starting to overwhelm you? Do you find yourself creating copies of old files when you need to answer new questions? Do others need to share the data and update it using only a web browser? Do you find yourself exceeding the limits of your current software or the memory on your system? If the answer to any of these is *yes,* you should be solving your problems with an RDMS like Access.

In Chapter 2, "Exploring the Access 2010 Interface," you'll learn about all the new user interface changes in Access 2010. You'll also open some of the built-in Access web template databases and explore the new Microsoft Office Backstage view for Access 2010. Finally, you'll learn about using the Navigation pane to interact with all your various database objects.

CHAPTER 2

Exploring the Access 2010 Interface

Before you explore the many features of Microsoft Access 2010, it's worth spending a little time looking it over and "kicking the tires." Like a new model of a favorite car, this latest version of Access has changes to the body (user interface) as well as new functionality under the hood. In this chapter and the next, we'll explore the changes to the user interface, show you how to navigate through Microsoft's new replacement for the File menu called the Microsoft Office Backstage view, and discuss the various components of an Access database and how they interact.

Opening Access for the First Time

The first time you open Access 2010, you are presented with the Privacy Options dialog box shown in Figure 2-1. This dialog box lists three radio buttons, which are not selected by default. Note that you must have an active connection to the Internet to use the first two options. The Use Recommended Settings radio button, when selected, turns on several features of your Microsoft Office 2010 installation. Your computer will periodically check Microsoft's website for any product and security updates to your Office, Windows, or other Microsoft software. If any updates are detected, your computer will install these updates automatically for you. Selecting this radio button also allows Access to search Office.com's vast resources for content relevant to your search. Access downloads this information to your local computer for faster searching when you search for items in the Help section. Selecting this option means you will have the latest Help information at your disposal. When you choose Use Recommend Settings, Office downloads a special diagnostic tool that interfaces with the Office 2010 system. You can use this tool to help identify problems with your Office installation. Although not required to run the Office 2010 release or Access 2010, this tool might assist you with locating the cause of any unforeseen system crashes. Selecting Use Recommend Settings also allows you to sign up for Microsoft's Customer Experience Improvement Program. This utility tracks various statistics while you use Access 2010 and the Office 2010 release and sends that information to Microsoft. By tracking how customers are using their products, Microsoft can improve its Office line of products for future releases. Note that this option does not send any personal information to Microsoft. Click the Read Our Privacy Statement link in the lower-left corner to read Microsoft's privacy statement.

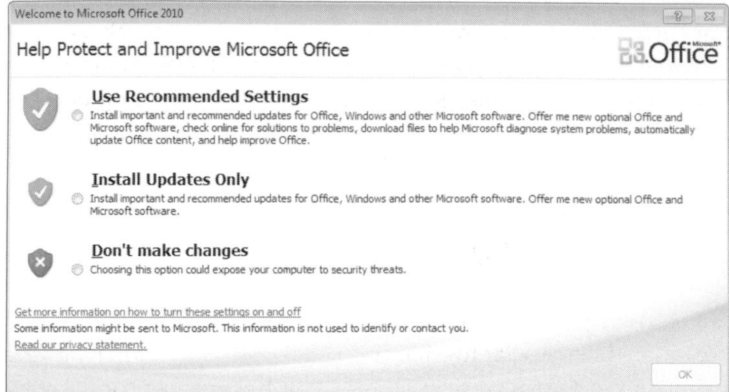

Figure 2-1 You can choose Privacy Options when you first start Access 2010.

The second radio button in the Privacy Options dialog box, Install Updates Only, performs a subset of the features for Use Recommend Settings. When you select this option, your computer will check Microsoft's website only periodically for any product and security updates to your Office, Windows, or other Microsoft software and install them. The last radio button, Don't Make Changes, makes no changes to your Office 2010 installation. Selecting this option could leave your computer at risk, however, because your computer will not download and install product or security updates. After you make your selection in the Privacy dialog box, click OK to start using Access 2010.

Note

The dialog box shown in Figure 2-1 is what we saw when opening Access for the first time using Windows 7. You might see a slightly different sequence of prompts if you install Office on Windows Vista.

After selecting your options in the Privacy Options dialog box, you can always alter these settings later. For more information on changing these settings, see "Modifying Global Settings via the Access Options Dialog Box," on page 112.

CAUTION!

If you are in a corporate network environment, you should check with your Information Technology (IT) department to determine whether your company has established guidelines before making selections in the Privacy Options dialog box.

Getting Started with Access 2010

If you are a seasoned developer with the 2007 version of Access, the user interface of Access 2010 should be familiar to what you've been working with. If however, you have been working only in Access versions before 2007, be prepared for quite a shock when you first open Access 2010. Microsoft revamped the entire look and feel of the user interface in Access 2007 and made additional changes in Access 2010 and the other products in the Office 2010 release. To some degree, users of versions before Access 2007 will have a challenging task adjusting to all the changes the development team has incorporated into Access 2007 and Access 2010. If you are one of these users, you might even experience a short-term decrease in productivity as you become accustomed to where commands and tools are located on the new user interface elements called the Backstage view and the ribbon. (See "Exploring the Microsoft Office Backstage View," on page 27, for details about the Backstage view, and "Understanding the Office Fluent Ribbon," on page 57, for details about the ribbon.) For first-time users of Access, Microsoft continues to spend a great deal of development effort trying to make the "Access experience" easier and more intuitive in this version. With a new Getting Started screen, a host of ready-to-use client and web database applications available, and a context-driven, rich graphical ribbon and Backstage view, users will have an easier and quicker time creating professional-looking database applications.

On first starting Access, you see a new Getting Started screen on the New tab of the Backstage view, as shown in Figure 2-2. We will discuss all the elements of this New tab and the Backstage view in great detail in "Exploring the Microsoft Office Backstage View," on page 27.

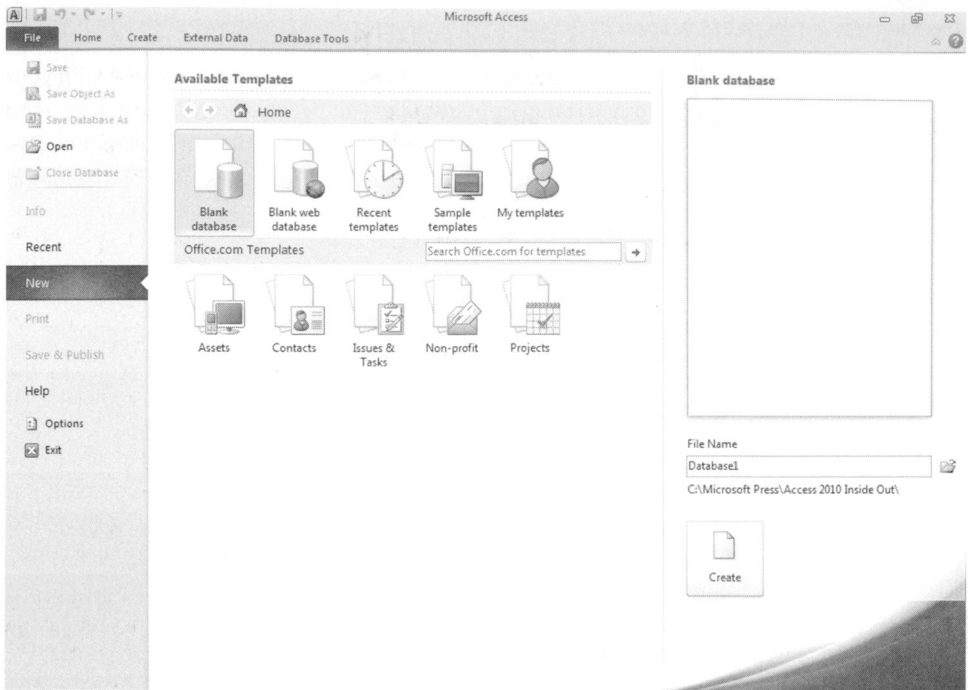

Figure 2-2 When you first open Access 2010, you can see the new Backstage view.

Opening an Existing Database

To showcase the user interface, let's take one of the template databases out for a test drive. Using the TasksSample.accdb database on the companion CD, based on the Microsoft Tasks template, we will highlight some specific areas of Access 2010. First, follow the instructions at the beginning of this book for installing the sample files on your hard drive. Click the Open button on the left side of the Backstage view to see the Open dialog box shown in Figure 2-3.

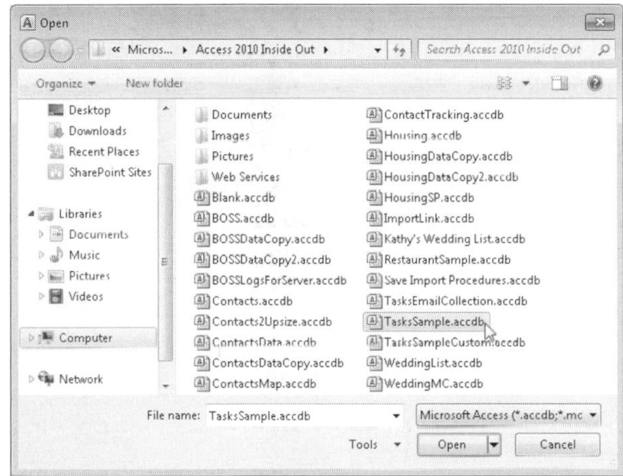

Figure 2-3 You can use the Open dialog box to find and open any existing database file.

In the Open dialog box, select the TasksSample.accdb file from the folder in which you installed the sample databases, and then click OK. You can also double-click the file name to open the database. (If you haven't set options in Windows Explorer to show file name extensions for registered applications, you won't see the .accdb extension for your database files.) The Tasks sample application will start, and you'll see the startup form for the Tasks Sample database along with all the various database objects listed on the left side, as shown in Figure 2-4.

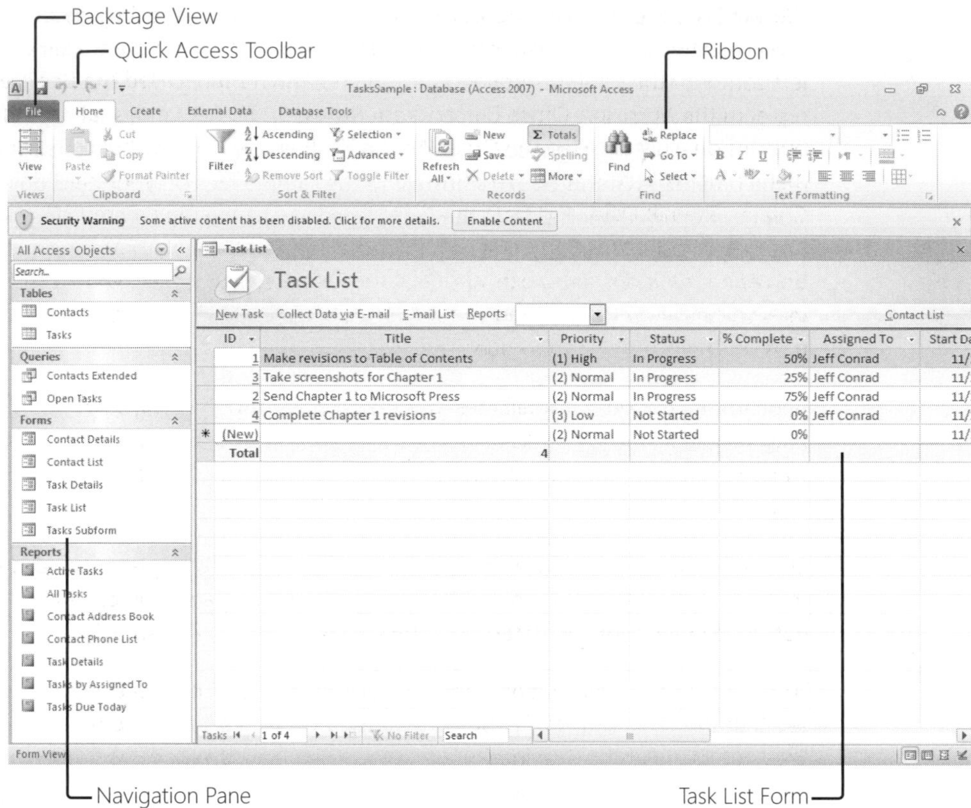

Figure 2-4 When you open the Tasks Sample database, you can see the user interface for Access 2010.

Note

If you installed the sample files for this book in the default location from the companion CD, you can find the files in the Microsoft Press\Access 2010 Inside Out folder on your C drive.

We will discuss each of the Access 2010 user interface elements in greater detail in the following sections, but for now, here is a brief overview of the different elements. The upper-left corner of the screen contains a tab called File. This tab, called the Backstage view, replaces the Microsoft Office Button from Access 2007. Above this tab are a few smaller buttons on what is called the Quick Access Toolbar. This toolbar holds frequently used commands within Access 2010. Beneath the Quick Access Toolbar is a series of four tabs (Home, Create, External Data, and Database Tools) that contain many commands, options, and drop-down list boxes. These tabs are on what Microsoft refers to as the Office Fluent Ribbon and it replaces menu bars and toolbars from versions of Access before 2007. You will interact heavily with the ribbon when developing and using Access 2010 databases because most of the commands you need are contained on it.

Beneath the ribbon is a small message that says "Security Warning." This Message Bar informs you if Access has disabled potentially harmful content in this database. See "Understanding Content Security," on page 47, to learn what this message means and what you can do to avoid it.

On the left side of the screen is the Navigation pane, which replaces the Database window from versions of Access before 2007. In the Navigation pane, you can find all the various database objects for this database (tables, queries, forms, and so on).

To the right of the Navigation pane is where your database objects open. In Figure 2-4, you see that the Task List form is open. All possible views of your database objects appear in this area. Just beneath the Navigation pane and main object window is the status bar. The status bar displays text descriptions from field controls, various keyboard settings (Caps Lock, Num Lock, and Scroll Lock), and object view buttons.

Exploring the Microsoft Office Backstage View

The new Microsoft Office Backstage View in Access 2010 replaces the Microsoft Office Button from Access 2007, and you can display its collection of commands by clicking the File tab from within any database. Figure 2-5 shows you the available commands on the Info tab of the Backstage view.

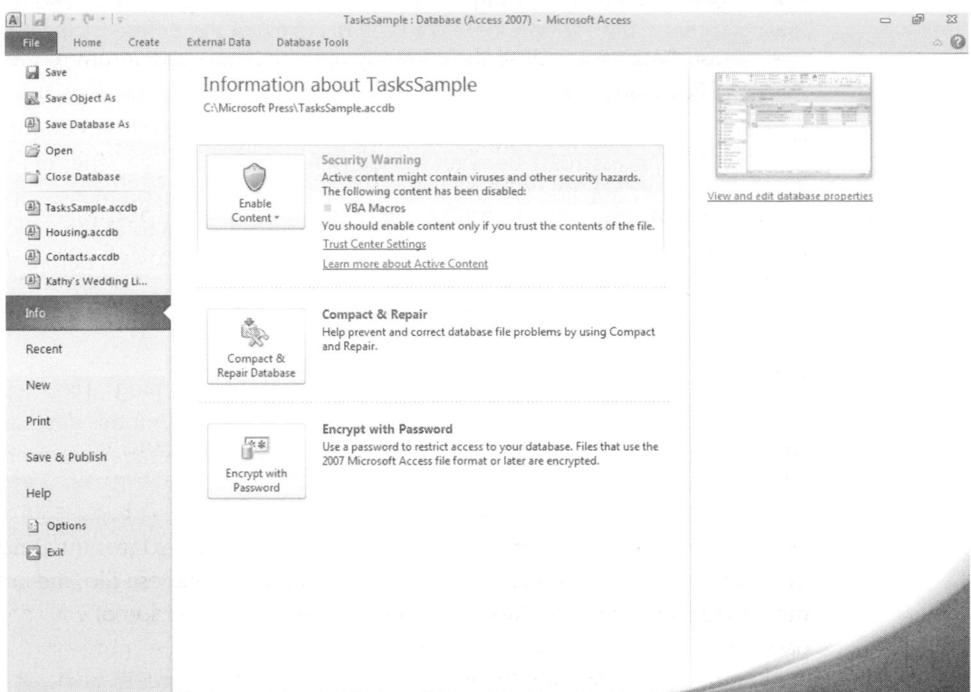

Figure 2-5 You can view many commands by clicking the File tab to open the Backstage view.

The Backstage view contains information and commands that apply to an entire database, as well as commands that were on the Microsoft Office Button in Access 2007. If you used versions of Access before 2007, the Backstage view contains commands that were on the File menu. At the upper-left section of the Backstage View, you'll see five commands that show at all times—Save, Save Object As, Save Database As, Open, and Close Database.

Using these commands, you can do any of the following:

- **Save** Save design changes for the database object that is open and has the focus in the Navigation pane.
- **Save Object As** Save a copy of the current open object that has the focus or the object that has the focus in the Navigation pane.
- **Save Database As** Save a copy of the current database. Note that if you click this command, Access closes the database that you have open so that it can create the copy.

- **Open** Open any existing database file on your computer or network.
- **Close Database** Close the currently open database and return to the New tab in the Backstage view.

Listed below the first five commands on the Backstage view, Access, by default, displays the file names of the last four databases you recently opened. To open any of these databases quickly, click the file name in the list. The six main tabs of the Backstage view—Info, Recent, New, Print, Save & Publish, and Help—are beneath the list of recently opened databases. Commands and information displayed on these tabs can change depending upon the current state of your database or if you are using a client versus a web database.

Info Tab

Let's first explore the Info tab previously shown in Figure 2-5. The Info tab displays the name of your database and the full path to its location. Beneath the file path, you'll see an Enable Content button and security information about your database. You'll learn more about these settings in "Understanding Content Security," on page 47. The button below it, Compact & Repair Database, compacts and repairs your database file. The last button on the Info tab, Encrypt With Password, creates an encrypted version of your database with a password. On the far right of the Info tab, you'll see a thumbnail preview of your database in its current state. Beneath the preview picture, is the View And Edit Database Properties link. Click this link to open the Database Properties dialog box to review and change properties specific to this database.

Recent Tab

The Recent tab, shown in Figure 2-6, displays a list of the databases you previously opened. If the number of databases you open exceeds the space to display them, Access provides a scroll bar for you to scroll up and down to see the complete list. At the bottom of the Recent tab, you'll see a check box called Quickly Access This Number of Recent Databases, which is selected by default. Clear this check box if you do not want to show a list of recent databases you have opened above the Info tab on the Backstage view. You can also customize the number of databases you want to display above the Info tab by changing the default value of four databases in the text box at the bottom of the screen.

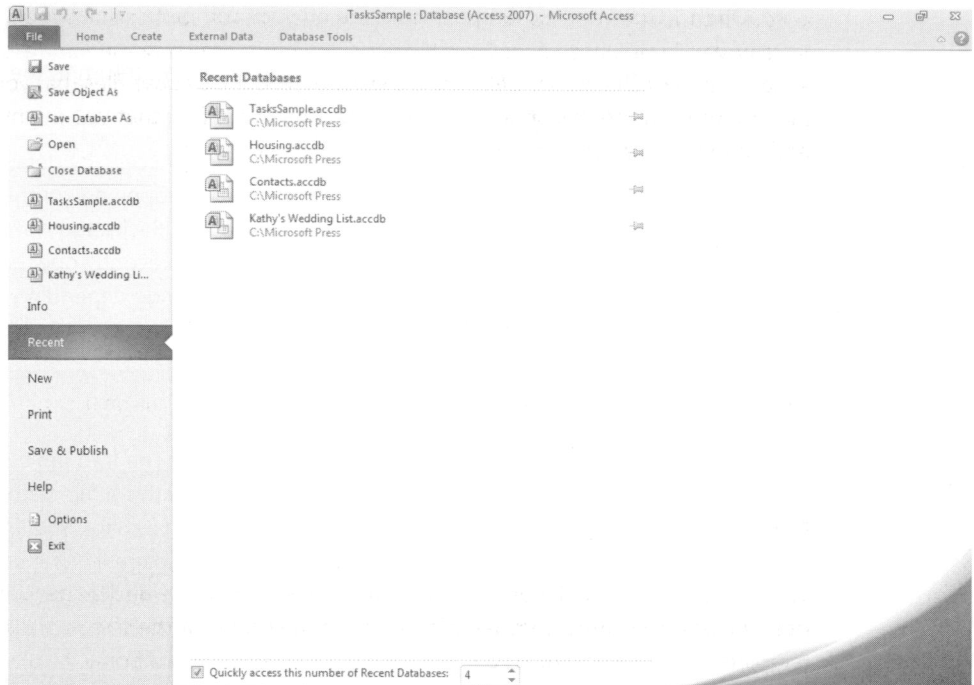

Figure 2-6 The Recent tab of the Backstage view displays a list of recent database files you opened.

To the right of each database file name, you'll see a pushpin button. Click this button to pin that specific database file to the displayed list of recent databases. Right-click any of the recent databases displayed, and Access provides a shortcut menu with four options, as shown in Figure 2-7. Select Open from the list, and Access opens the highlighted database. When you select the Pin To List option, Access pins that specific database file to the displayed list of recent databases. When you select the third option, Remove From List, Access removes that database file from the list of recent databases. Note that when you remove the database file from the list, you're not deleting the database from your computer; you are only removing it from this list on the Backstage view. When you select the last option on the list, Clear Unpinned Items, Access prompts you for confirmation that you want to remove all unpinned items from the list. Click Yes in the confirmation dialog box, and Access removes all database files from the list of recent database files that you have not pinned. You can use this option to quickly clear database files that you might have deleted and no longer wish to use from your list of recent databases.

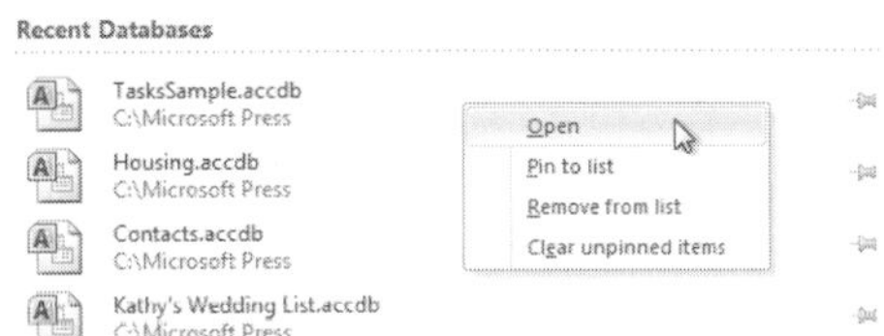

Figure 2-7 Right-click a database file to see additional options you can use to manage your list of recent databases.

New Tab

The New tab, shown in Figure 2-8, is the first tab shown in the Backstage view when you open Access. The Office.com Templates area in the center of the screen displays different template categories grouped by subject. Click one of these categories to change the display in the center of the screen to a list of templates that you can download from the Office.com website. Note that you must be connected to the Internet to see and download any templates in each of these categories. These templates were created by the Access development team and developers in the Access community. The templates represent some of the more common uses for a database and are therefore presented to you first. Microsoft is continually adding and modifying the selections available in the Office.com categories, so the list you see might be different from that shown in Figure 2-8. Be sure to check these groups from time to time to see if a new template exists for your specific needs. You can also search for a template on the Office.com website by typing your search criteria in the Search Office.com for Templates text box.

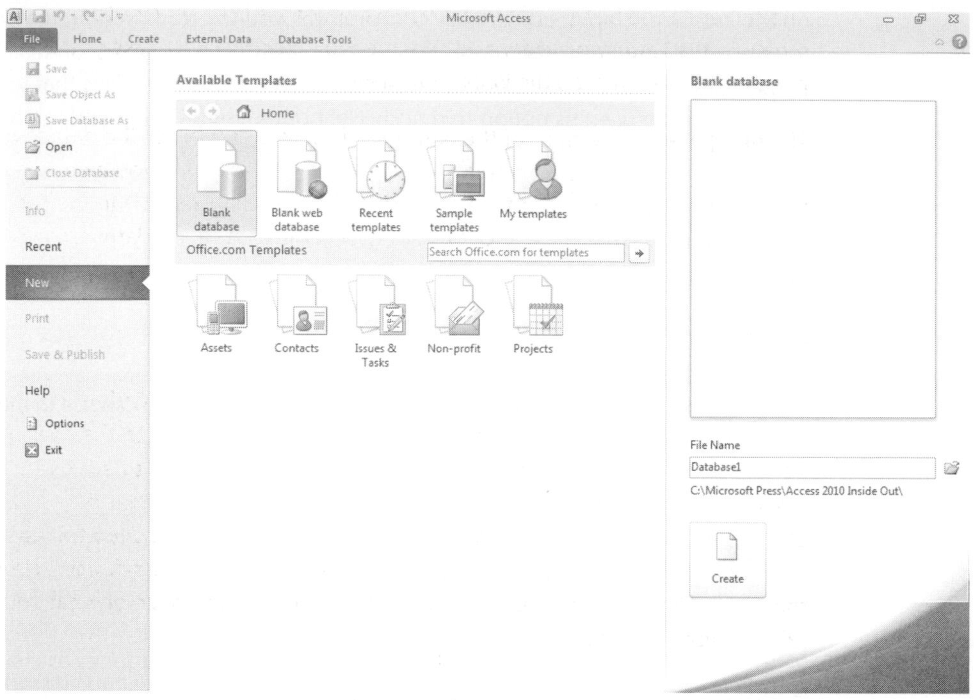

Figure 2-8 You can create a database from a template, create a new blank or web database, or search for a database file to open on the New tab of the Backstage view in Access 2010.

Just above Office.com Templates in the middle of the screen are five buttons under Available Templates. The first button on the left is labeled Blank Database. You use this button to start the process of creating a new empty client database with no objects. See Chapter 4, "Designing Client Tables," for details on how to create a new blank client database. The next button to the right, Blank Web Database, starts the process of creating a new empty web database with no objects. See Chapter 6, "Designing Web Tables," for details on how to create a new blank web database. When you click Recent Templates, Access displays a list of database templates that you recently created from this New tab. To view the list of database templates available on your local drive that were installed with Access, click Sample Templates. Five of the sample templates listed under Sample Templates are web-compatible templates—Assets, Charitable Contributions, Contacts, Issues, and Projects. The last button under Available Templates, My Templates, lists any database templates that you created and saved locally to your computer. See Chapter 26, "The Finishing Touches," on the companion CD, for details on how to create your own database template.

Just beneath the Available Templates text at the top of the screen you'll see three navigation buttons. The Back, Forward, and Home buttons function like web browser buttons. As you navigate between the various template screens, you can click Back to move you back one screen in the history of screens you've opened. Click Forward to move you forward one screen in the history of screens you've opened. Click Home to take you back to the main page of the New tab on the Backstage view.

The task pane on the right of the New tab displays a graphic of the database template you select from the list of templates. For new blank databases you create, Access leaves this graphic empty. You can type the name of a new database file in the File Name text box beneath this graphic and browse to a location to save the database using the Browse button.

Print Tab

The Print tab, shown in Figure 2-9, displays three commands—Quick Print, Print, and Print Preview. Click Quick Print to send the selected database object to the printer immediately. Be careful here, because the object that has the focus might not be the one currently on the screen. If the focus is on an object in the Navigation pane, that object is printed instead of the object currently open. When you click Print, Access opens the Print dialog box to print whatever object currently has the focus. Here again, be careful about which object has the focus. Click Print Preview to preview the printed appearance of what you are about to print on your monitor.

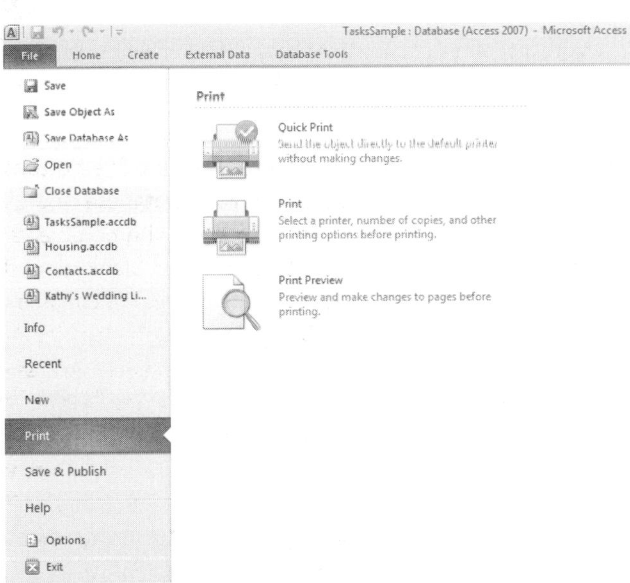

Figure 2-9 The Print tab of the Backstage view displays commands to print objects in your database.

Save & Publish Tab

The Save & Publish tab, shown in Figure 2-10, displays commands to save your database and objects in other formats and to publish your application to Access Services. In the center of the Save & Publish tab, you'll see two categories—File Types and Publish—and three commands—Save Database As, Save Object As, and Publish To Access Services. If you click one of these commands, additional commands appear in a submenu to the right. Click Save Database As and you'll see two categories for this option—Database File Types and Advanced. Under Database File Types, you can choose to save a copy of your entire database in 2007/2010 (.accdb), 2002/2003 (.mdb), or 2000 (.mdb) Access format. Note that if you choose to save the entire database, Access closes the database you have open so that it can create the copy. You can use the last option under Database File Types, Template (.accdt), to save your database as an Access database template. To start these commands, you can either double-click the command you want or highlight the command and then click the Save As button at the bottom of the screen. Under the Advanced category, the first option, Package And Sign, packages your database as a Cabinet file (CAB) and digitally signs it. Double-click the Make ACCDE command to make an execute-only version (.mde or .accde) of your database. When you double-click the Back-up Database command, Access creates a complete backup of your database file with the current date in the file name. You can choose the last command under the Advanced category, SharePoint, to publish your database to a document manager server.

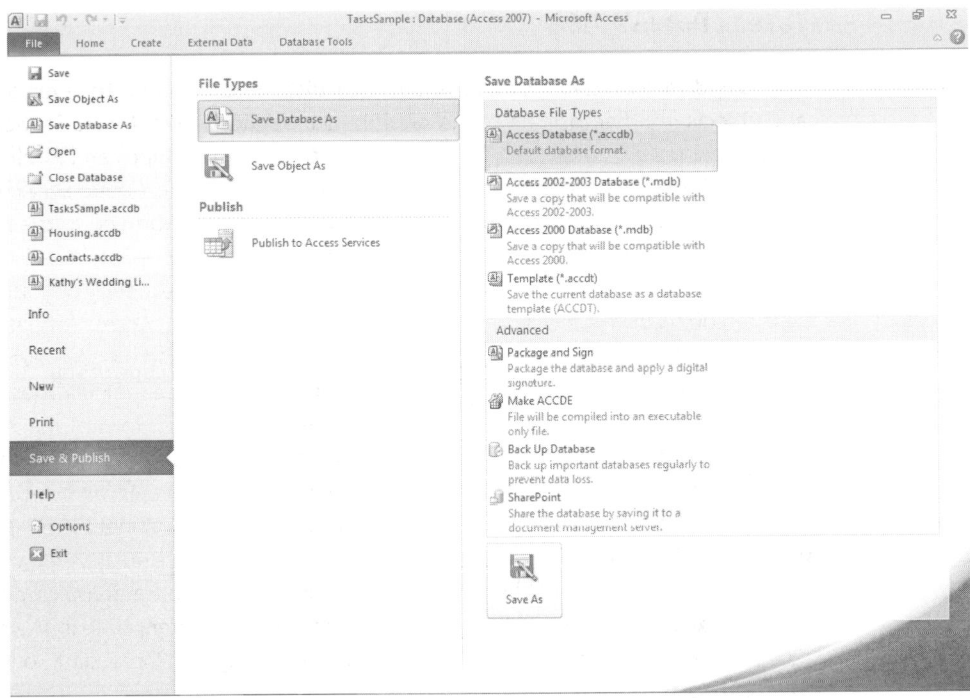

Figure 2-10 The Save & Publish tab contains commands to save your objects and database in different formats and to publish your application to Access Services.

Click Save Object As under File Types on the Save & Publish tab, and Access displays a different set of commands on the right, as seen in Figure 2-11. When you double-click Save Object As on the right side, the default is to save a copy of the current open object that has the focus or the object that has the focus in the Navigation pane. Double-click PDF Or XPS to publish a copy of the current open object as a Portable Document Format (PDF) or XML Paper Specification (XPS) file. The last command for Save Object As, Save As Client Object, saves a copy of the current open web object to a client object format. See Chapter 6 for details on how to create a web database and work with web objects.

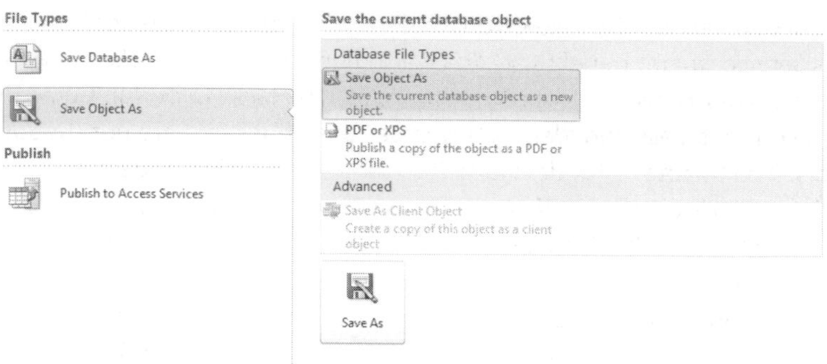

Figure 2-11 You can use the Save Object As command to save a copy of your database objects into different formats.

Click Publish To Access Services under the Publish category on the Save & Publish tab, and Access displays commands and information on the right concerning the new Access Services feature in Access 2010, as seen in Figure 2-12.

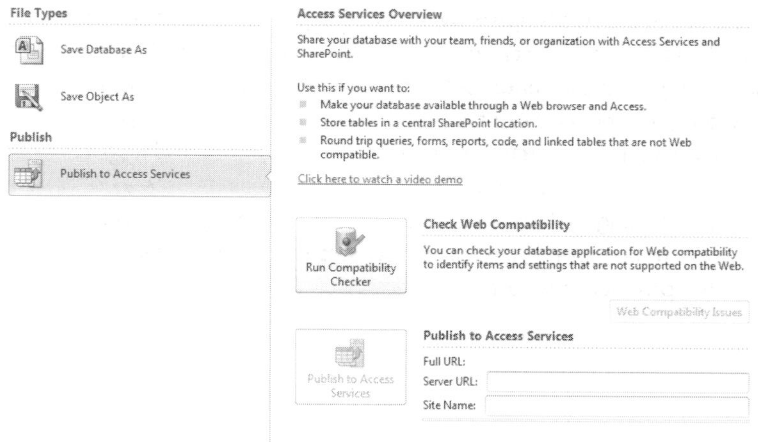

Figure 2-12 You can publish your database to Access Services from the Save & Publish tab of the Backstage view.

Under Access Services Overview, you'll see information and bullet points on when using Access Services might benefit you. You'll also find a link you can click to watch a prepared video demo of Access Services on the Office.com website. Click Run Compatibility Checker to scan your database and identify any issues or settings that are not supported for Access Services. (See Chapter 6 for details on how to create a web database and working with the Web Compatibility Checker.) If any issues are found during the web compatibility scan, Access enables the Web Compatibility Issues button. Click that button to open a table that lists all the issues found. If you are currently using a web database, the Publish To Access Services button is enabled. Clicking this button starts the process of publishing your web database to a Microsoft SharePoint site to become an Access Services application. To the right of the Publish To Access Services button, you'll see two text boxes—Server URL and Site Name. Enter the full Uniform Resource Locator (URL) to the SharePoint server that you want to publish to in the Server URL text box and the name of the site you want to create in the Site Name text box. You'll learn more about all the Access Services features later in this book, beginning in Chapter 6.

Help Tab

The Help tab of the Backstage view, shown in Figure 2-13, displays commands and links to helpful information concerning Access 2010 and the Office 2010 software. Under the Support category in the center of the screen, you'll see three commands—Microsoft Office Help, Getting Started, and Contact Us. Click Microsoft Office Help to open the Access Help system where you can search Access topics for assistance building your database. Click Getting Started to open a link on Office.com where you can see a list of new features and resources pertaining to Access 2010. Click Contact Us to go to a website where you can find links to support options, go to online support communities, or submit suggestions to improve the product or report a problem.

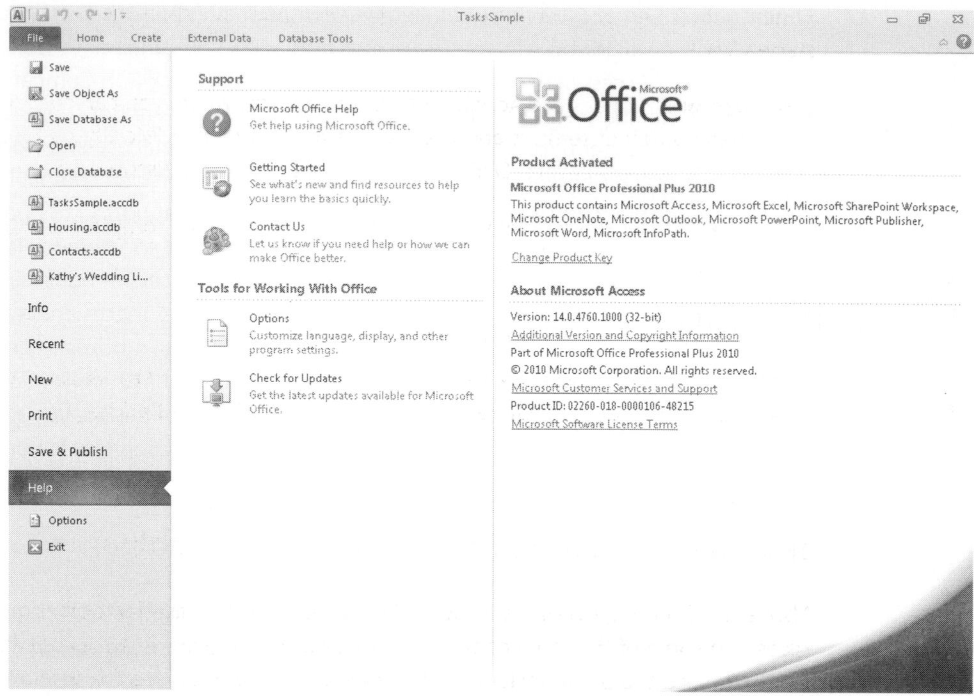

Figure 2-13 The Help tab on the Backstage view displays links to resources, help, and support for Access 2010.

Under the Tools For Working With Office category in the center of the screen, you'll see two commands—Options and Check For Updates. Click Options to open the Access Options dialog box, where you can choose different settings and preferences for your Access installation. Click Check For Updates to go to a website where you can run a program that verifies that you have the latest updates for your Office system.

On the right side of the Help tab, you'll see information about your Access 2010 and Office 2010 installed programs. Click the Change Product Key link to open the Microsoft Office setup dialog box to change your product key for your installation. Click the Additional Version and Copyright Information link to open the Access About dialog box to view the copyright information of your Access and Office installations. Click the last link on this tab, Microsoft Software License Terms, to view and print the licensing terms for your Office installation.

Beneath the Help tab, you can also find these two commands at the bottom of the Backstage view:

- **Options** Opens the Access Options dialog box, where you can choose and define many different settings and preferences for Access. See "Modifying Global Settings via the Access Options Dialog Box," on page 112, for a discussion of these options.
- **Exit** Closes the currently open database file as well as completely exits Access.

INSIDE OUT **Closing the Backstage view**

You can close the Backstage view quickly by pressing the Esc key. When you do this, Access returns focus to where you were before opening the Backstage view.

Taking Advantage of the Quick Access Toolbar

Above the Backstage view is the Quick Access Toolbar. This special toolbar gives you "quick access" to some of the more common commands you will use in Access 2010, and you can customize this toolbar to include additional commands. Here are the default commands available on the Quick Access Toolbar:

- **Save** Saves any changes to the currently selected database object
- **Undo** Undoes the last change you made to an object or a record
- **Redo** Cancels the last Undo change you made to an object or a record

At the right end of the Quick Access Toolbar is a small arrow. Click that arrow, and you'll see the Customize Quick Access Toolbar menu, as shown in Figure 2-14.

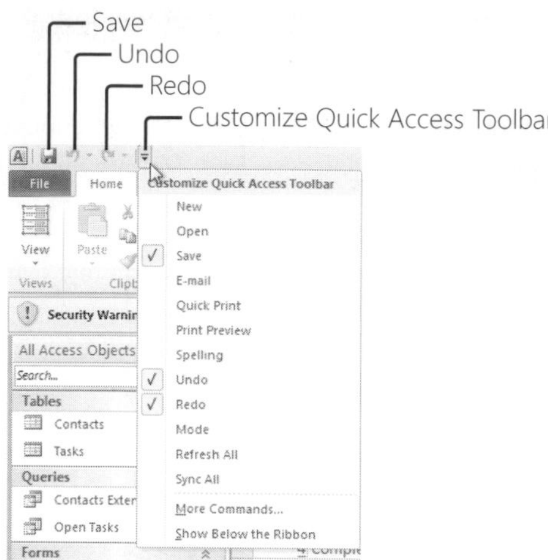

Figure 2-14 The default Quick Access Toolbar contains the Save, Undo, and Redo commands for the current object, and the command to customize the toolbar.

The upper section of the menu displays common commands that you might want to add to the Quick Access Toolbar. Note that the three default commands—Save, Undo, and Redo—have check marks next to them. You can click any of these to clear the check mark and remove the command from the Quick Access Toolbar. You can click any of the other nine commands (New, Open, E-Mail, Quick Print, Print Preview, Spelling, Mode, Refresh All, and Sync All) to add them to the right end of the Quick Access Toolbar. Near the bottom of this menu is More Commands, which allows you to fully customize what commands are available and how those commands appear on the Quick Access Toolbar. The Show Below The Ribbon option on the menu allows you to move the Quick Access Toolbar above or below the ribbon, depending on your preference.

To customize the Quick Access Toolbar, click the arrow on the right end and click More Commands near the bottom of the list. The Access Options dialog box appears, with the Quick Access Toolbar category selected, as shown in Figure 2-15.

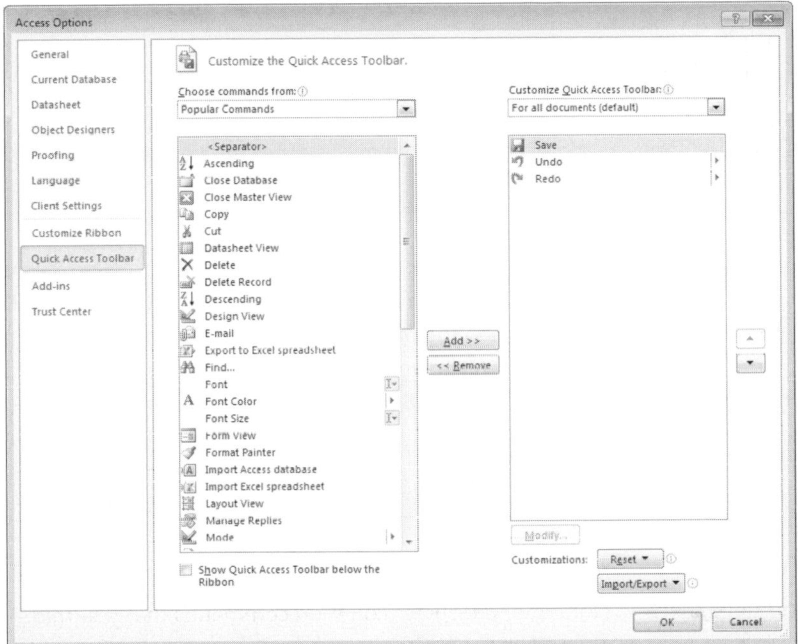

Figure 2-15 You can add or remove commands on the Quick Access Toolbar and change their sequence using the Customize category in the Access Options dialog box.

On the left, you can see a list of built-in Access commands that you can select to add to the Quick Access Toolbar. By default, the list shows commands from the Popular Commands category—commands that are used very frequently. You can change the list of commands by selecting a different category from the Choose Commands From list. The All Commands option displays the entire list of Access commands available in alphabetical order. Just below the list of available commands is a check box that you can select to show the Quick Access Toolbar below the ribbon. Clear the check box to show the Quick Access Toolbar above the ribbon.

The list on the right side of the screen by default displays what options are available on every Quick Access Toolbar for all your database files. If you add, remove, or modify the commands shown in the list on the right when you have chosen For All Documents (Default) in the Customize Quick Access Toolbar list, the changes are reflected in every database you open with Access 2010. To customize the Quick Access Toolbar for only the specific database you currently have open, click the arrow in the drop-down list and select the database file path for your current database from the list, as shown in Figure 2-16.

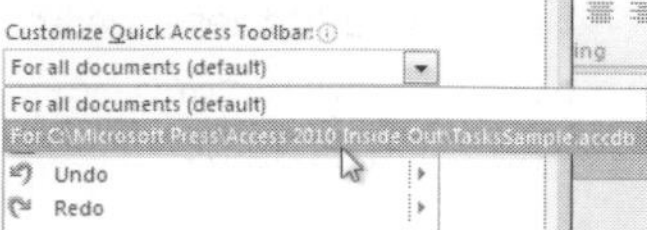

Figure 2-16 You can add or remove commands on the Quick Access Toolbar for the current database by selecting your database from the Customize Quick Access Toolbar list.

When you select the current database, the command list below it is now empty, awaiting the changes you request. Find a command in the list on the left, and then either double-click it or click the Add button in the middle of the screen to add this command to your custom Quick Access Toolbar, as shown in Figure 2-17. If you make a mistake and select the wrong command, select the command in the list on the right and click Remove to eliminate it from your custom list.

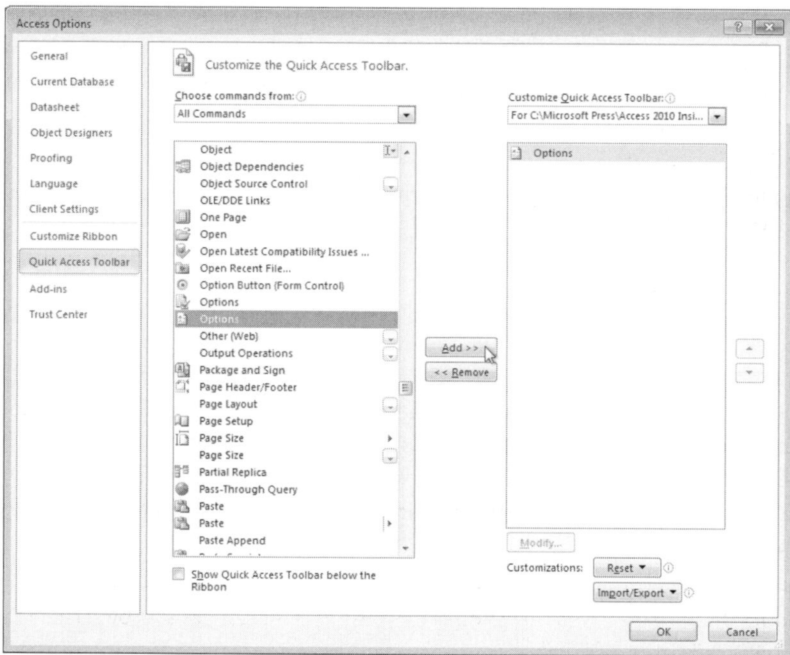

Figure 2-17 Add a command to the Quick Access Toolbar by selecting it in the list on the left and then clicking Add.

In addition to the built-in commands, you can select any macros you have defined in this current database. To do this, select Macros in the Choose Commands From list on the left.

A list of all your saved macro objects appears, and you can add these macros directly to your custom Quick Access Toolbar, as shown in Figure 2-18. We added one macro called mcrSample to this Tasks Sample database to illustrate the next steps.

CAUTION!

Do not add a macro to your Quick Access Toolbar when you have selected the option to customize the Quick Access Toolbar for all documents. Access displays an error if you try to click your custom macro command in a database that does not contain the macro you selected.

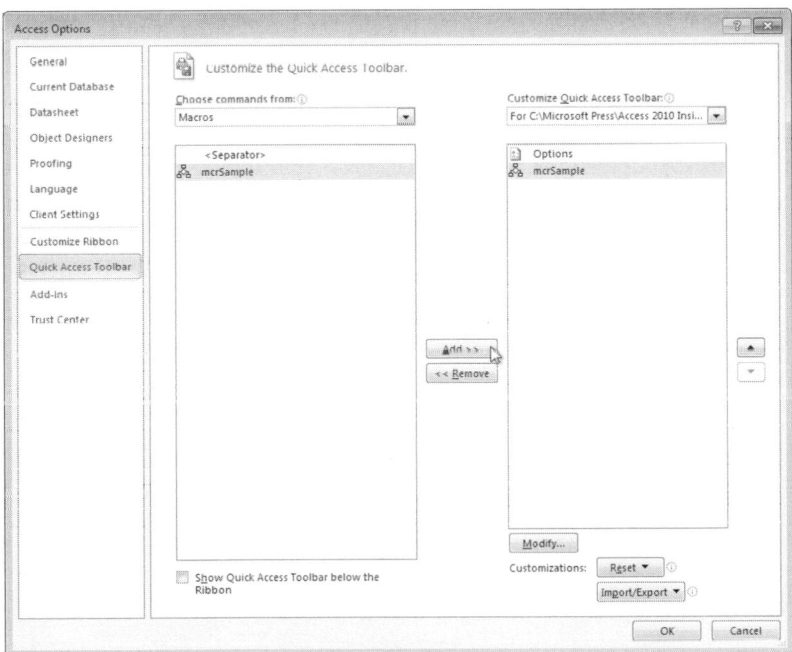

Figure 2-18 Add a saved macro object to the Quick Access Toolbar by selecting it in the list on the left and then clicking Add.

You can also assign custom button images to the macro objects you select. To do so, select one of your macros in the list on the right, and then click the Modify button to open the Modify Button dialog box shown in Figure 2-19. From here, you can choose one of the predefined button images available and also change the display name for this option on your custom Quick Access Toolbar.

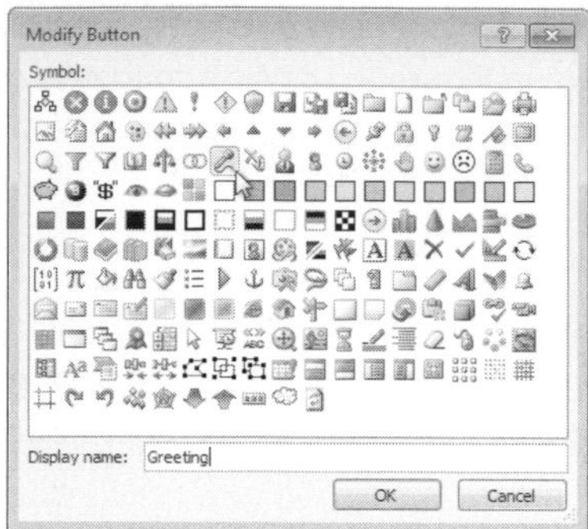

Figure 2-19 You can change the button face and the display name in the Modify Button dialog box.

After you have all the commands and macros that you want on your custom Quick Access Toolbar, you might decide that you do not like the order in which they appear. Access 2010 allows you to modify this order easily using the Move Up and Move Down arrow buttons at the far right of the dialog box. (You can rest your mouse pointer on either button to see the button name.) Select a command you want to move in the list on the right and click the up arrow to move it up in the list, as shown in Figure 2-20. Each successive click moves that command up one more place in the custom list. Likewise, the down arrow shifts the selected command down in the list. In Figure 2-20, you can see that we have moved the macro titled Greeting above the Options command.

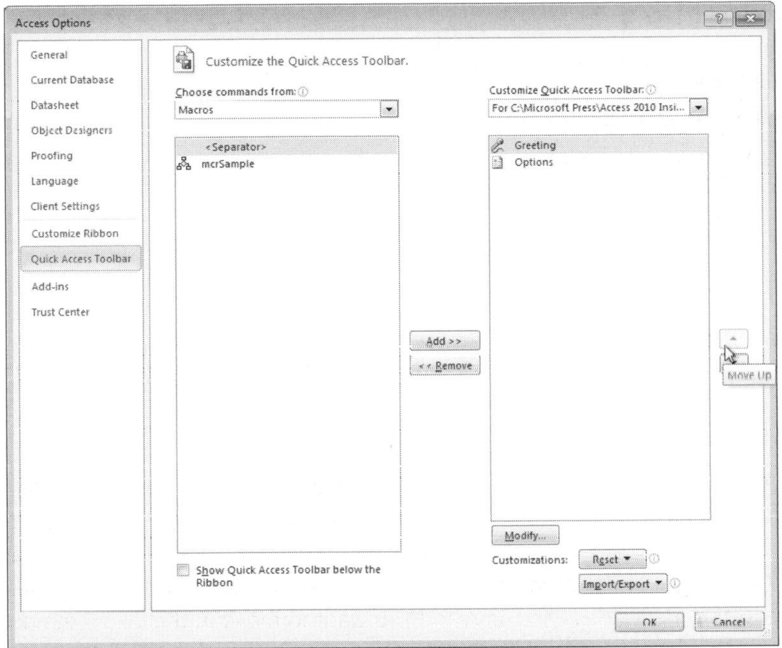

Figure 2-20 You can change the order of the commands on your Quick Access Toolbar by clicking the Move Up and Move Down arrow buttons.

From top to bottom in the list on the right, the commands appear from left to right on the Quick Access Toolbar after the commands assigned to all databases. When you are completely satisfied with your revisions, click OK to save your changes. Observe that your custom Quick Access Toolbar now appears on the screen above or below the ribbon, depending on the choice you have selected. Figure 2-21 shows our completed changes to the Quick Access Toolbar for this specific database.

Note

You might have noticed the <Separator> option in the list on the left. Adding <Separator> to your custom Quick Access Toolbar places a small space below the command currently selected in the list on the right. You can add as many separators as you want to your custom Quick Access Toolbar to separate groups of commands visually.

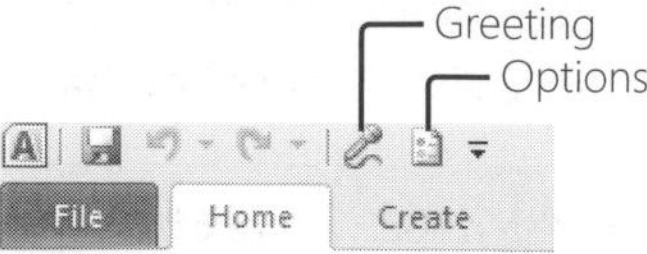

Figure 2-21 Our two additional commands now appear on the Quick Access Toolbar for this database.

To remove an item from your custom Quick Access Toolbar, reopen the Access Options dialog box with the Quick Access Toolbar category selected again by clicking the arrow on the Quick Access Toolbar and then clicking More Commands. To remove an item, select it in the list on the right and click Remove, and Access removes it from your list of commands. If you inadvertently remove a command that you wanted to keep, you can click the Cancel button in the lower-right corner to discard all changes. You can also find the command in the list on the left and add it back. Keep in mind that you can remove commands for all databases, or for only the current database.

If you want to restore the Quick Access Toolbar for all databases to the default set of commands, select For All Documents (Default) in the Customize Quick Access Toolbar list, click the Reset button in the lower-right corner of the screen, and then click Reset Only Quick Access Toolbar from the drop-down list. To remove all custom commands for the current database, select the database path in the Customize Quick Access Toolbar list, click Reset, and then click Reset Only Quick Access Toolbar. Before removing any commands on the Quick Access Toolbar, Access displays the warning message shown in Figure 2-22. If you click Yes to this Reset Customizations message, Access resets the Quick Access Toolbar for this current database back to the defaults.

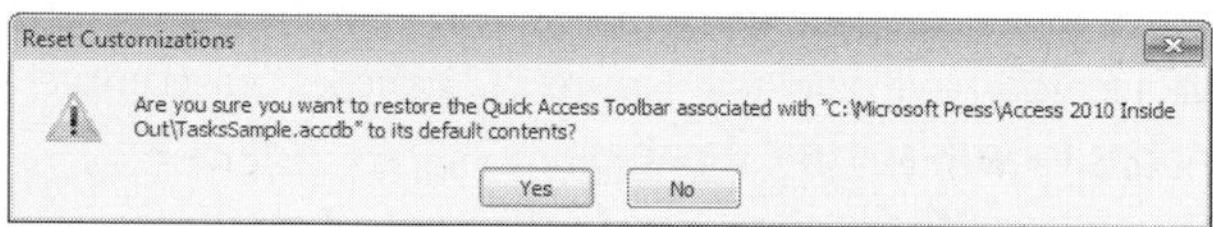

Figure 2-22 Access asks you to confirm resetting the Quick Access Toolbar back to the default commands.

INSIDE OUT **Adding a Command to the Quick Access Toolbar with Two Mouse Clicks**

If you notice that you are using a command on the ribbon quite often, Access 2010 provides a very quick and easy way to add this command to the Quick Access Toolbar. To add a command on the ribbon to the Quick Access Toolbar, right-click the command and click Add To Quick Access Toolbar. This adds the command to the Quick Access Toolbar for all databases. Alternatively, you can remove an item from your custom Quick Access Toolbar quickly by right-clicking the command and clicking Remove From Quick Access Toolbar.

If you modify the Quick Access Toolbar for all databases, you can export your customizations to a file that can be imported to another computer running Access 2010. Click the Import/Export button at the lower-right corner of the screen and then click Export All Customizations, as shown in Figure 2-23. You can choose a location to save this customization file for use on other computers. To import the Quick Access Toolbar customizations onto another computer, open Access 2010 on the second computer, reopen the Access Options dialog box with the Quick Access Toolbar category selected, click the Import/Export button at the bottom of the screen, and then click Import Customization File. Your custom Quick Access Toolbar options for all databases created on the first computer now appear in the Access program installed on the second computer.

Figure 2-23 You can export and import your custom Quick Access Toolbar commands to other computers.

Understanding Content Security

In response to growing threats from viruses and worms, Microsoft launched a security initiative in early 2002, called Trustworthy Computing, to focus on making all its products safer to use. In an email sent to employees, Bill Gates summed up the seriousness of the initiative:

"In the past, we've made our software and services more compelling for users by adding new features and functionality, and by making our platform richly extensible. We've done a terrific job at that, but all those great features won't matter unless customers trust our software. So now, when we face a choice between adding features and resolving security issues, we need to choose security. Our products should emphasize security right out of the box, and we must constantly refine and improve that security as threats evolve."

Prior to Access 2003, it was quite possible for a malicious person to send you a database file that contained code that could damage your system. As soon as you opened the database, the harmful code would run—perhaps even without your knowledge. Alternatively, the programmer could embed dangerous code in a query, form, or report, and your computer would be damaged as soon as you opened that object. In version 11 (Access 2003), you were presented with a series of confusing dialog boxes when you opened an unsigned database file if you had left your macro security level set to Medium or High. After wading through the various dialog boxes, you could still be left with a database you were unable to open.

Access 2007 improved upon the security model by adding a component to the Access interface called the Trust Center. This security interface is far less confusing and intrusive than the Access 2003 macro security feature. With a security level set to High in Access 2003, you would not be able to open any database files because all Access databases could have some type of macros, Visual Basic for Applications (VBA) code, or calls to unsafe functions embedded in their structure. Access 2010 further improves upon the Access 2007 security model by adding Trusted Documents. Any database with queries is considered unsafe by Access 2010 because those queries could contain expressions calling unsafe functions. In Access 2010, each database file opens without presenting you with a series of dialog boxes as in Access 2003. Depending on where your file is located on the local computer drive or network share, Access silently disables any malicious macros or VBA code without any intrusive dialog box messages.

Note

The sample databases included on the companion CD are not digitally signed, because they will become unsigned as soon as you change any of the queries or sample code. We designed all the sample applications to open successfully, but each displays a warning dialog box if the database is not trusted. If you have installed the database in an untrusted location, the application displays instructions in the warning dialog box that you can follow to enable the full application. See "Enabling Content by Defining Trusted Locations," on page 55, for information about defining trusted locations.

Enabling a Database That Is Not Trusted

When you open an existing database or template, you might see a Security Warning message displayed in the Message Bar, just below the Quick Access Toolbar and ribbon, as shown in Figure 2-24. This message notifies you that Access has disabled certain features of the application because the file is not digitally signed, the file is not a trusted document, or the file is located in a folder that has not been designated as trusted.

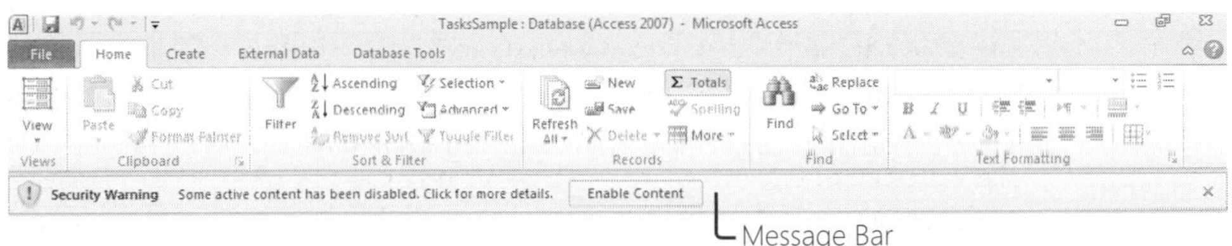

Figure 2-24 The Message Bar alerts you if Access has disabled certain content.

To ensure that any restricted code and macros function in this database, you must manually tell Access to enable this content by clicking the Enable Content button on the Message Bar. After you click this button, Access closes the database and then reopens the file to enable all content. Access does not display the Message Bar after it reopens the file, and all functions, code, and macros are now allowed to run in this specific database. Access also adds this database to its list of trusted documents.

If your database is not currently trusted, Access displays the Security Warning information on the Info tab of the Backstage view, as shown in Figure 2-25. Note that if you have enabled the content of the database you are viewing or if the file is located in a folder that has been designated as trusted, Access does not display the Security Warning information on the Info tab of the Backstage view.

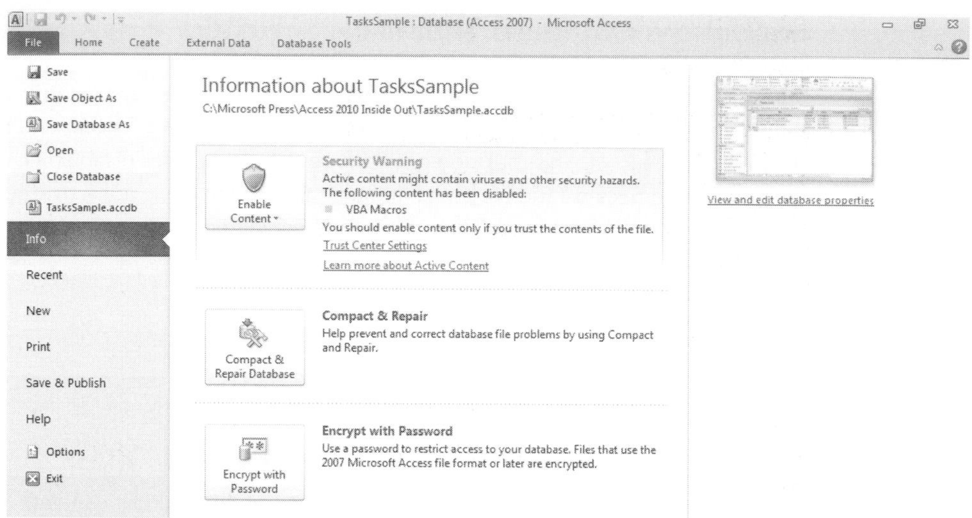

Figure 2-25 If your database is not trusted, Access displays the Security Warning on the Backstage view.

When you click the Enable Content button under Security Warning, Access displays two options—Enable All Content and Advanced Options, as shown in Figure 2-26. When you click Enable All Content, Access adds this database to its list of trusted database files. Each time you open this database from this point on, Access does not disable the content for that database. Note that if you move this database to a different file location on your computer, Access disables the content again when you open the database.

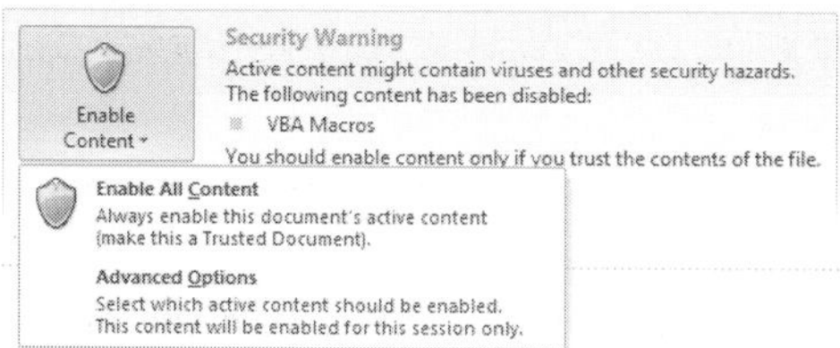

Figure 2-26 Click Enable Content to enable all the content of your database or open advanced security options.

Click Advanced Options under Enable Content, and Access opens a dialog box, called Microsoft Office Security Options, as shown in Figure 2-27. This dialog box warns you that this file's content cannot be verified because a digital certificate was not found.

Figure 2-27 You can enable blocked content from the Microsoft Office Security Options dialog box.

You can choose to have Access 2010 continue to block any harmful content by leaving the default option set to Help Protect Me From Unknown Content (Recommended). By having Access block any harmful content, you can be assured that no malicious code or macros can execute from this database. However, you also have to realize that because Access blocks all Microsoft Visual Basic code and any macros containing a potentially harmful command, it is quite possible that this application will not run correctly if you continue to let Access disable potentially harmful functions and code. To have Access discontinue blocking potentially harmful content, you must select the option Enable Content For This Session. After you select that option and click OK, Access closes the database and then reopens the file to enable all content. Access does not display the Message Bar after it reopens the file, and all functions, code, and macros are now allowed to run in this specific database.

Note

When you enable content after opening an untrusted database, the database becomes trusted only for the current session. If you close the database and then attempt to reopen it, Access displays the warnings again on the Message Bar.

Understanding the Trust Center

You might have noticed a link to the Trust Center in the lower-left corner of the Microsoft Office Security Options dialog box. You can also open the Trust Center from the Info tab of the Backstage view by clicking the Trust Center Settings link beneath Security Warning, as discussed earlier. We will discuss the Access Options dialog box later in this chapter; see "Modifying Global Settings via the Access Options Dialog Box," on page 112.

Click Open The Trust Center in the Microsoft Office Security Options dialog box to view the advanced security settings. If the Security Warning on the Info tab of the Backstage view is not currently available, click the File tab and then click Options on the Backstage view. In the Access Options dialog box, click the Trust Center category on the left and then click Trust Center Settings. In the Trust Center dialog box, shown in Figure 2-28, you see nine categories of security settings.

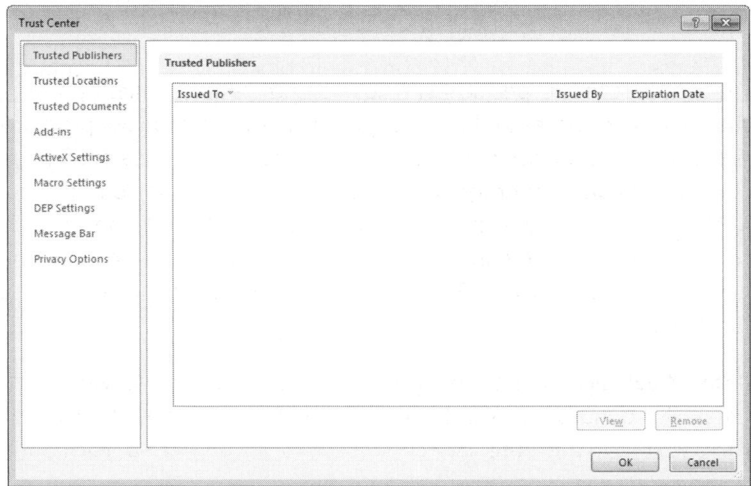

Figure 2-28 The Trust Center dialog box displays various categories, from which you can select trust and privacy options.

Briefly, the categories are as follows:

- **Trusted Publishers** Use to view and remove publishers that you have designated as being trustworthy. When applications are digitally signed by one of these trusted publishers, Access does not disable any content within the database and the Message Bar does not display any warning. By default, digitally signed applications from Microsoft are trusted. You might see one or more additional trusted publishers if you have ever tried to download and run a signed application and have indicated to Windows that you trust the publisher and want to save the publisher's certificate. See

Chapter 27, "Distributing Your Application," on the companion CD, for information about digitally signing your own applications.

- **Trusted Locations** Use to designate specific folders and subfolders as trusted locations. Access considers any database files within this folder as trustworthy, and all content in these folders is enabled. In the Trusted Locations dialog box, each designated trusted folder is listed with the file path, an optional description, and the date the entry was last modified. See "Enabling Content by Defining Trusted Locations," on page 55, for details about using the options in this category.

- **Trusted Documents** Use to allow databases on a network share to be trusted, disable the Trusted Documents feature, or clear all trusted databases. By default, Access allows you to trust database files on a network share. Clearing this check box disables your ability to trust individual database files on network shares. If you select the option to disable trusted documents, Access disables all content in databases that you previously designated as trusted. If you click Clear, Access removes all database files from its internal list of trusted documents.

- **Add-Ins** Use to set specific restrictions on Access add-in files by selecting or clearing the three check boxes in this category. An add-in is a separate program or file that extends the capabilities of Access. You can create these separate files or programs by using VBA or another programming language such as C#. You can require that add-in files be signed by a trusted publisher before Access will load and run them. If you select the option to require that add-ins be signed, you can disable notifications for add-ins that are unsigned. For added security, you can disable all application add-in functionality.

- **ActiveX Settings** Use to configure how Access handles ActiveX controls in databases. Five options are available with this feature, only one of the first four options can be active at any time. Table 2-1 discusses the purpose of each option.

Table 2-1 ActiveX Settings

Option	Purpose
Disable All Controls Without Notification.	Access disables all harmful ActiveX controls but does not notify you through the Message Bar.
Prompt Me Before Enabling Unsafe For Initialization (UFI) Controls With Additional Restrictions And Safe For Initialization (SFI) Controls With Minimal Restrictions.	If a VBA project is present, Access disables all ActiveX controls and displays the Message Bar. If no VBA project is present, Access enables SFI and disables UFI ActiveX controls. In this case, Access displays the Message Bar. If you enable the content for a UFI ActiveX control, they will be initialized, but with restrictions.

Option	Purpose
Prompt Me Before Enabling All Controls With Minimal Restrictions.	This is the default option for new installations of Access. If a VBA project is present, Access disables all ActiveX controls and displays the Message Bar. If no VBA project is present, Access enables SFI and disables UFI ActiveX controls. In this case, Access displays the Message Bar. If you enable the content for a UFI ActiveX control, they will be initialized, but with restrictions.
Enable All Controls Without Restrictions And Without Prompting (not recommended; potentially dangerous controls can run)	Access enables any and all potentially harmful ActiveX controls with minimal restrictions without prompting you. Setting this option could leave your computer at risk.
Safe Mode (helps limit the control's access to your computer)	This option, selected by default, enables SFI ActiveX controls in safe mode.

- **Macro Settings** Use to configure how Access handles macros in databases that are not in a trusted location. Four options are available with this feature, only one of which can be active at any given time. Table 2-2 discusses the purpose of each option.

Table 2-2 Macro Settings

Option	Purpose
Disable All Macros Without Notification	Access disables all harmful content but does not notify you through the Message Bar.
Disable All Macros With Notification	Access disables all harmful content but notifies you through the Message Bar that it has disabled the content. This is the default option for new installations of Access. This is equivalent to the Medium macro security level option available in Access 2003.
Disable All Macros Except Digitally Signed Macros	Access allows only digitally signed macros (code in digitally signed databases). All other potentially harmful content is disabled. This is equivalent to the High macro security level option available in Access 2003.
Enable All Macros (not recommended, potentially dangerous code can run)	Access enables any and all potentially harmful content. In addition, Access does not notify you through the Message Bar. This is equivalent to the Low macro security option available in Access 2003.

- **DEP Settings** Use to enable or disable Data Execution Prevention (DEP) mode for your Access installation. This option, selected by default, helps prevent poorly written code from running on your computer. If, for example, an add-in that was not designed to run in a DEP setup tries to execute on your computer, Access might crash to prevent the add-in from damaging your computer. You can view the Add-ins category of the Trust Center to see if DEP is preventing any add-ins from running on your computer.

- **Message Bar** Use to configure Access either to show the Message Bar when content has been disabled or not to display the bar at all.
- **Privacy Options** Use to enable or disable actions within Access regarding computing privacy, troubleshooting system problems, and scanning suspicious website links. The first check box under Privacy Options tells Access to scan Microsoft's Office.com help site when you are connected to the Internet. If you clear this check box, Access scans only your local hard drive when you conduct a search in Help. Selecting the second check box instructs Access to download and activate a special file from Microsoft's site that helps you troubleshoot Access and Office program installation and program errors. The third check box allows you to sign up for the Customer Experience Improvement Program. Microsoft uses this program to track statistics of the features you use most frequently and gather information about your Office system configuration. These statistics help determine changes in future program releases. The fourth check box, Automatically Detect Installed Office Applications To Improve Office.com Search Results, helps to narrow your search results on Office.com to programs you currently have installed. The fifth check box under Privacy Options allows Access to scan Office documents automatically for possible links to and from suspicious websites. This option is turned on by default to help safeguard your computer against documents containing harmful web links. The final check box, Allow The Research Pane To Check For And Install New Services, allows Access to automatically check for new updates to research services and install them.

Enabling Content by Defining Trusted Locations

You can permanently enable the content in a database that is not trusted by defining a folder on your hard drive or network that is trusted and then placing the database in that folder. Alternatively, you can define the folder where the database is located as trusted. You define trusted locations in the Trust Center dialog box.

CAUTION!

If you are in a corporate network environment, you should check with your IT department to determine whether your company has established guidelines concerning enabling content on Access databases.

To define a trusted location, click the File tab on the Backstage view and then click Access Options. In the Access Options dialog box, click the Trust Center category and then click Trust Center Settings. Access displays the Trust Center dialog box. Click the Trusted Locations category to see its options, as shown in Figure 2-29.

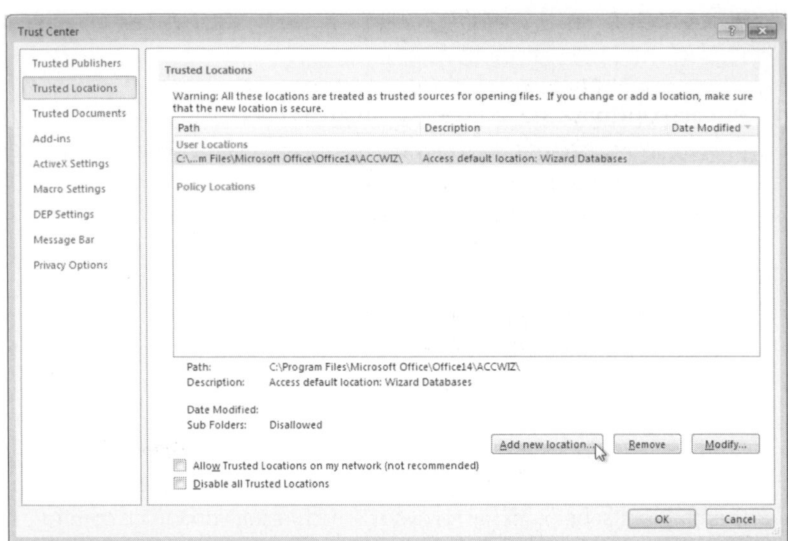

Figure 2-29 The Trusted Locations category in the Trust Center dialog box shows you locations that are currently trusted.

Click Add New Location. Access now displays the Microsoft Office Trusted Location dialog box, as shown in Figure 2-30.

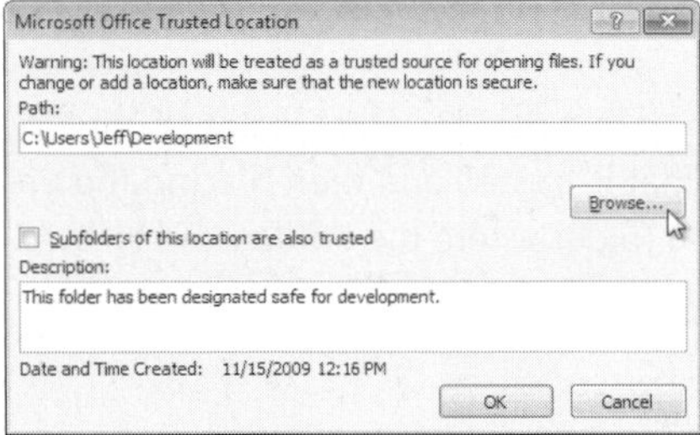

Figure 2-30 Creating a new trusted location from the Microsoft Office Trusted Location dialog box.

Click Browse and locate the folder that you want to designate as trusted. You have the option of designating any subfolders in that directory as trusted without having to designate each individual folder within the hierarchy. Enter an optional description you want for this folder, and click OK to save your changes. The new location you just specified now appears in the list of trusted locations. Microsoft recommends you do not designate the root folder for your Windows installation (for example, C:\ on a standard installation) as a trusted location. You should instead designate only the individual folders you want trusted.

If you later decide to remove this folder as a trusted location, select that location, as shown in Figure 2-29, and then click Remove. Any Access databases in that folder are now treated as unsafe. Figure 2-29 also shows two check boxes at the bottom of the dialog box. The first check box allows you to define network locations as trusted locations. Microsoft recommends you not select this check box because you cannot control what files others might place in a network location. The second check box disables all Trusted Location settings and allows content only from trusted publishers.

> **Note**
>
> **To ensure that all the sample databases from the companion CD operate correctly, add the folder where you installed the files (the default location is the Microsoft Press\ Access 2010 Inside Out folder on your C drive) to your Trusted Locations.**

Understanding the Office Fluent Ribbon

The Office Fluent Ribbon, shown in Figure 2-31, is a strip that contains all the functionality of the older menu bar options (File, Edit, View, and so on) and the various toolbars from versions of Access before Access 2007, condensed into one common area in the application window. Microsoft's usability studies revealed that most users failed to discover many useful features that were previously buried several levels deep in the old menu structure. The ribbon is a context-rich environment displaying all the program functions and commands, with large icons for key functions and smaller icons for less-used functions. Access displays a host of different controls on the ribbon to help you build and edit your applications. Lists, command buttons, galleries, and Dialog Box Launchers are all on the ribbon and offer a rich user interface for Access 2010 and the other Office 2010 system products.

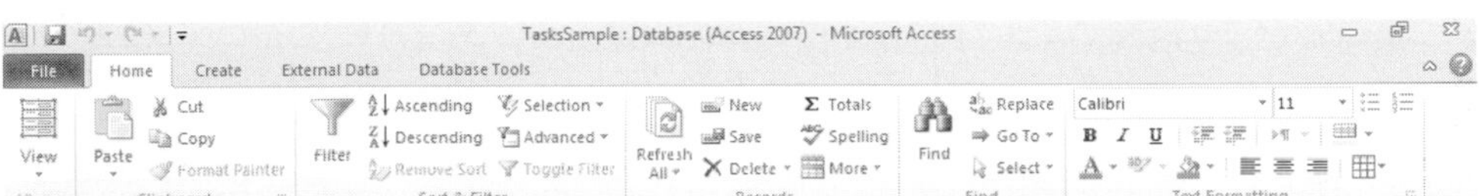

Figure 2-31 The ribbon interface replaces menu bars and toolbars from versions before Access 2007.

The ribbon in Access 2010 consists of four main tabs—Home, Create, External Data, and Database Tools—that group together common tasks and contain a major subset of the program functions in Access. These main tabs are visible at all times when you are working in Access 2010 because they contain the most common tools you need when working with any database object. Other tabs, called contextual tabs, appear and disappear to the right of the Database Tools tab when you are working with specific database objects and in various views. (In the following chapters, we will discuss in detail the various database objects and the contextual tabs that appear when working with each.)

> **INSIDE OUT** **Scrolling Through the Ribbon Tabs**
>
> **If you click one of the ribbon tabs, you can then scroll through the other tabs using the scroll wheel on your mouse.**

Each tab on the ribbon has commands that are further organized into groups. The name of each group is listed at the bottom, and each group has various commands logically grouped by subject matter. To enhance the user experience and make things easier to find, Microsoft has labeled every command in the various groups. If you rest your mouse pointer on a specific command, Access displays a ScreenTip that contains the name of the command and a short description that explains what you can do with the command. Any time a command includes a small arrow, you can click the arrow to display options available for the command.

Home Tab

Let's first explore the Home tab, shown in Figure 2-32.

Figure 2-32 The Home tab provides common commands for editing, filtering, and sorting data.

The Home tab has the following groups:

- **Views** Most objects in an Access database have two or more ways to view them. When you have one of these objects open and it has the focus, you can use the View command in this group to switch easily to another view.
- **Clipboard** You can use the commands in this group to manage data that you move to and from the Clipboard.
- **Sort & Filter** You can use these commands to sort and filter your data.

- **Records** Use the commands in this group to work with records, including deleting records and saving changes.
- **Find** The commands in this group allow you to search and replace data, go to a specific record, or select one or all records.
- **Window** Use the commands in this group to resize windows or select one of several windows that you have open. Note that Access displays this group only when you have set your database to display Overlapping Windows rather than Tabbed Documents. For more details, see "Using the Single-Document vs. the Multiple-Document Interface" on page 107.
- **Text Formatting** You can change how Access displays text using the commands in this group. You can also design fields in your database to contain data formatted in Rich Text. (See Chapter 4 for more details about data types.) You can use the commands in this group to format text in a Rich Text field.

INSIDE OUT **Adding a Group to the Quick Access Toolbar with Two Mouse Clicks**

If you notice that you are using commands found in a group on the ribbon quite often, Access 2010 provides a very quick and easy way to add the entire group to the Quick Access Toolbar. To add a group on the ribbon to the Quick Access Toolbar, right-click the group and click Add To Quick Access Toolbar. This adds the group, including all commands, to the Quick Access Toolbar for all databases. Alternatively, you can quickly remove a group from your custom Quick Access Toolbar by right clicking on the group and clicking Remove From Quick Access Toolbar.

Create Tab

The Create tab, shown in Figure 2-33, contains commands that let you create new database objects. Each group on this particular tab arranges its specific functions by database object type.

Figure 2-33 The Create tab provides commands for creating all the various types of database objects.

The Create tab contains the following groups:

- **Templates** Use the commands in this group to create new templates parts such as fields, tables, forms, and other objects. You can learn more about template parts in Chapter 4, "Designing Client Tables."
- **Tables** Use the commands in this group to create new tables or link to a SharePoint Services list. You can learn more about SharePoint Services in Chapter 22, "Using Web Applications in a Browser."
- **Queries** Use the commands in this group to create new queries. You can learn more about creating queries beginning in Chapter 9, "Creating and Working with Simple Queries."
- **Forms** You can create new forms using the commands in this group, including PivotChart, PivotTable, and web forms. For more details about PivotCharts, see Chapter 15, "Advanced Form Design." For more details about web forms, see Chapter 12, "Using Forms in an Access Application."
- **Reports** The commands in this group allow you to create new reports using available wizards, start a new report design from scratch, or build web reports.
- **Macros & Code** Use the commands in this group to build macros or modules to automate your application.

External Data Tab

The External Data tab, shown in Figure 2-34, provides commands to import from or link to data in external sources or export data to external sources, including other Access databases or SharePoint lists.

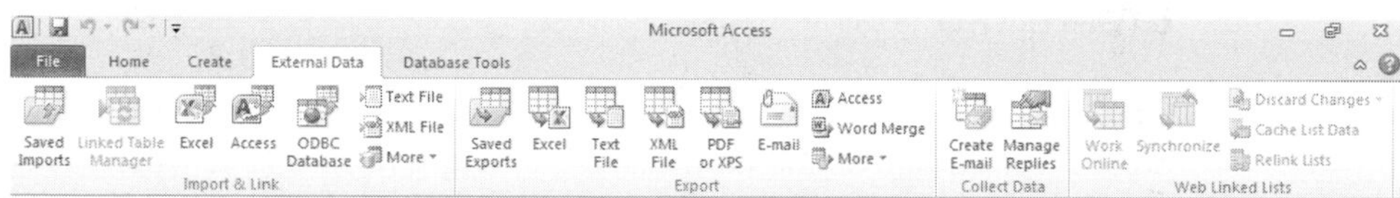

Figure 2-34 The External Data tab provides commands for working with external data sources.

This tab has the following groups:

- **Import & Link** The commands in the Import group let you link to data or import data or objects from other sources such as other Access databases, Microsoft Excel spreadsheets, Windows SharePoint Services lists, and many other data sources such as Microsoft SQL Server and dBase.
- **Export** You can use these commands to export objects to another Access database or to export data to Excel, SharePoint, Microsoft Word, and more.
- **Collect Data** These two commands allow you to update data in your Access 2010 database from special email options using Microsoft Outlook 2010. See Chapter 8, "Importing and Linking Data," for details about using these features.
- **Web Linked Lists** Commands in this group allow you to synchronize offline data with an active SharePoint site, cache list data, and relink SharePoint lists.

Database Tools Tab

The last tab that is always available on the ribbon is the Database Tools tab, shown in Figure 2-35. The upper part of Figure 2-35 shows the Database Tools tab when using an Access 2010 database (.accdb) and the lower part shows the Database Tools tab when using Access 2000, 2002, or 2003 databases (.mdb).

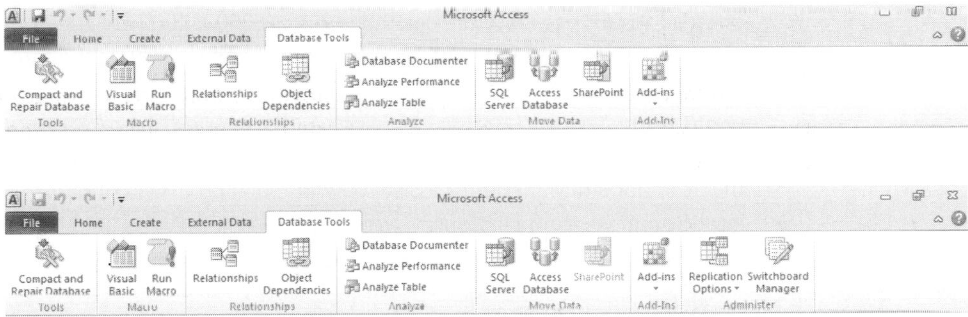

Figure 2-35 The Database Tools tab gives you access to miscellaneous tools and wizards.

The Database Tools tab on the ribbon includes the following groups:

- **Tools** This group has one command: Compact And Repair Database. Use this command to compact and repair your database file.
- **Macro** Commands in this group let you open the Visual Basic Editor or to run a macro.
- **Relationships** Commands in this group activate useful information windows. Use the Relationships command to view and edit your table relationships. (See Chapter 4 for details.) Click the Object Dependencies command to see which objects are dependent on the currently selected object.
- **Analyze** Use the commands in this group to print a report about your objects or run one of the two analysis wizards.
- **Move Data** The three wizards available in this group allow you to either move some of or all your tables to SQL Server, move all your tables to a separate Access database and create links to the moved tables in the current database, or move some or all of your tables to a SharePoint site.
- **Add-Ins** You can manage add-ins from this group or start the Add-In Manager to install new add-ins for your Access installation.
- **Administer** Access displays this group on the Database Tools tab only when you open an Access database file created in Access 2000, 2002, or 2003 (.mdb). The Replication Options let you manage the legacy replication features that are no longer supported in Access 2007 format database files. For more information on these features, see *Running Microsoft Access 2000* (Microsoft Press, 1999) or *Microsoft Office Access 2003 Inside Out* (Microsoft Press, 2004). The Switchboard Manager command starts the Switchboard Manager to assist you with building a switchboard form for navigating through your application.

INSIDE OUT Collapsing the Entire Ribbon

If you need some additional workspace within the Access window, you can collapse the entire ribbon by double-clicking any of the tabs. All the groups disappear from the screen, but the tabs are still available. You can also use the keyboard shortcut Ctrl+F1 to collapse the ribbon or click the Minimize The Ribbon button next to the Help button in the upper-right corner of the application window. To see the ribbon again, simply click any tab to restore the ribbon to its full height, press Ctrl+F1 again, or click the Expand The Ribbon button.

Customizing the Ribbon

In Access 2010 and the other Office 2010 products, Microsoft introduces a new feature that allows you to customize the ribbon easily through an interface similar to customizing the Quick Access Toolbar. If you do not like the order of the groups on the four default ribbon tabs, for example, you can easily change the order to your liking. To customize the ribbon, click the File tab and then click the Options button on the Backstage view to open the Access Options dialog box. Now click the Customize Ribbon category on the left to begin customizing the ribbon, as shown in Figure 2-36.

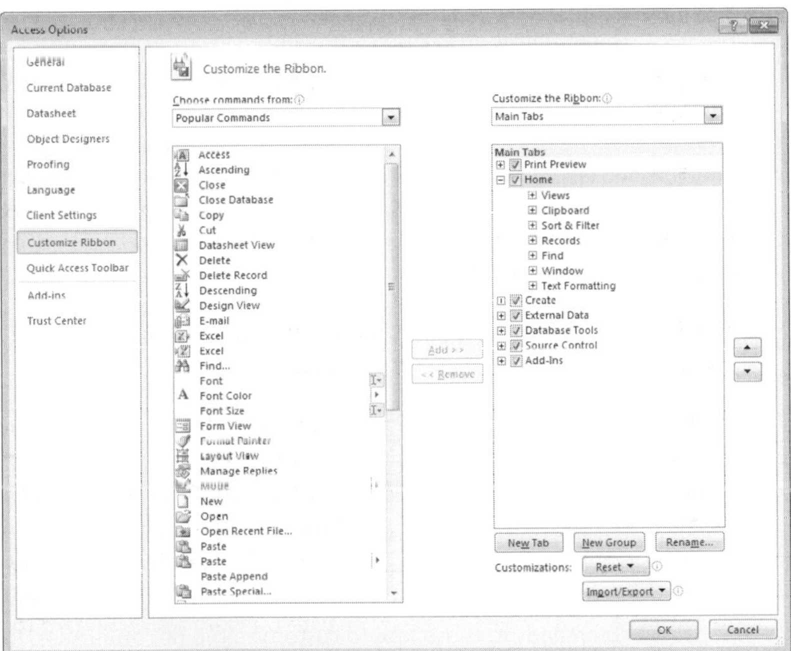

Figure 2-36 You can add new tabs, groups, or commands to the ribbon and change their sequence using the Customize Ribbon category in the Access Options dialog box.

On the left, you can see a list of built-in Access commands that you can select to add to groups on the ribbon. By default, the list shows commands from the Popular Commands category—commands that are used very frequently. You can change the list of commands by selecting a different category from the Choose Commands From list. The All Commands option displays the entire list of Access commands available in alphabetical order.

INSIDE OUT **Opening the Access Options Dialog Box Quickly to Customize the Ribbon**

Right-click any part of the ribbon and then click Customize The Ribbon to open the Access Options dialog box quickly with the Customize Ribbon category selected.

The list on the right side of the screen by default displays a list of the built-in Access ribbon tabs—Print Preview, Home, Create, External Data, Database Tools, Source Control, and Add-Ins. You can change the list of tabs by selecting a different category from the Customize The Ribbon list. The All Tabs option displays the entire list of Access ribbon tabs, and the Tool Tabs option displays only the list of Access contextual ribbon tabs. Next to the name of each tab in the list below Customize The Ribbon is a plus symbol. Click the plus symbol, and Access expands the list beneath the tab to show you all the groups and commands within that specific tab. Click the minus symbol, and Access collapses the list to show you only the name of the tab itself. Similarly, you'll see a plus symbol next to each of the group names underneath the tab name. Click the plus symbol here, and Access expands the group to show you all the commands on that specific group. Click the minus symbol to collapse the group. Next to the plus and minus symbols for each tab, you'll see a check box. Clear this check box to not display that tab on the ribbon. Note that clearing this check box does not delete the tab and all its contents; it merely tells Access not to show this tab on the ribbon. Select the check box, and Access displays that tab in the ribbon.

You'll notice that all the commands listed on the default tab groups are dimmed. You cannot rename or reorder the commands listed on the default tab groups; however, you can rename and reorder the group names on the default tabs, rename and reorder the names of the default tabs, add new custom groups to the default tabs, and add commands to these custom groups on the default tabs. You can also create your own custom tabs and add groups and commands to those tabs to customize the ribbon further. To create a new custom tab, click the New Tab button near the lower-right corner of the screen. Access adds a new tab to the list on the right called New Tab (Custom) and a new group beneath that tab called New Group (Custom), as shown in Figure 2-37. All custom tabs and custom groups have (Custom) after the name. However, Access does not show (Custom) on the ribbon.

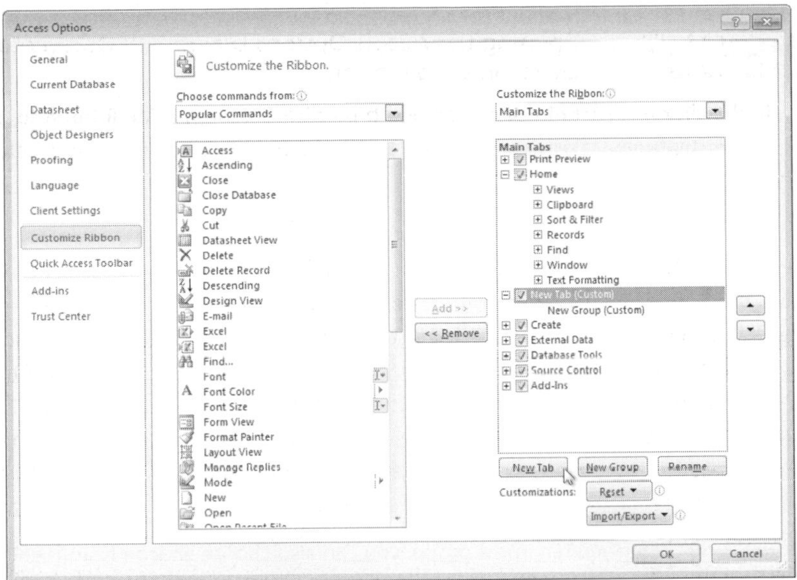

Figure 2-37 Click New Tab to create a new custom tab on the ribbon.

To change the name of your custom tab, highlight it and then click Rename. Access opens the Rename dialog box, as shown in Figure 2-38. Type in a new name for your custom tab in the Display Name text box and then click OK. Access displays your new tab name in the tab list followed by (Custom). Remember that (Custom) appears only in the Customize Ribbon category of the Access Options dialog box.

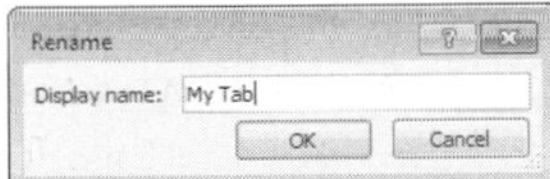

Figure 2-38 You can change the display name of a custom tab on the Rename dialog box.

To change the name of your custom group, highlight it in the list of groups and then click Rename. Access opens the Rename dialog box for group names, as shown in Figure 2-39. On this dialog box, you can type in a new name for your custom group and you can choose an icon to represent the group. If you add this entire group to your Quick Access Toolbar, Access displays your custom icon for this group instead of a default green ball icon.

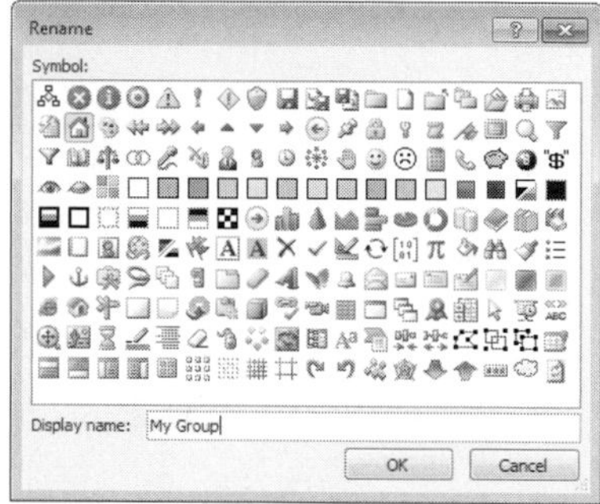

Figure 2-39 When you rename a group, you can also choose an icon from the Rename dialog box to display for your group.

To add a command to your custom group, find a command in the list on the left, and then either double-click it or click the Add button in the middle of the screen to add this command to your custom ribbon group, as shown in Figure 2-40. If you make a mistake and select the wrong command, select the command in the list on the right and click Remove to eliminate it from your custom group.

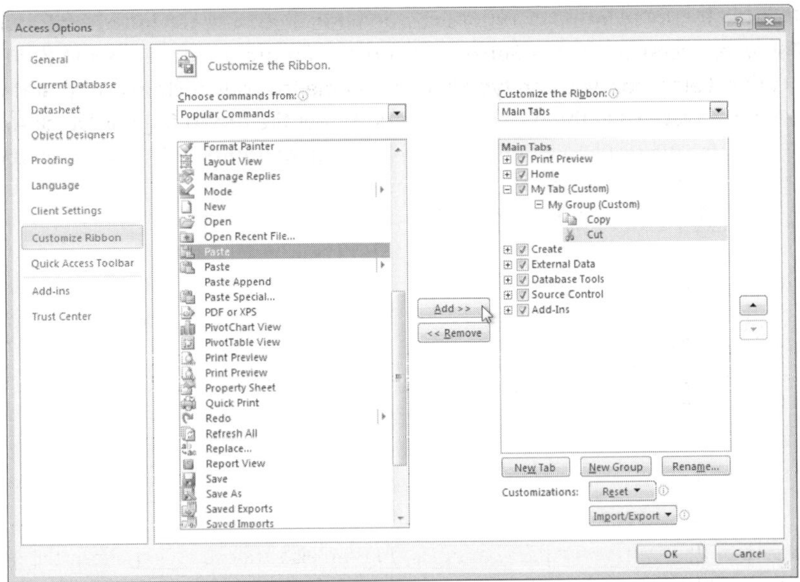

Figure 2-40 To add a command to your custom group, highlight a command on the left and then click Add.

After you have all the commands and macros you want on your custom group, you might decide that you do not like the order in which they appear. Access 2010 allows you to easily modify this order using the Move Up and Move Down arrow buttons at the far right of the dialog box. (You can rest your mouse pointer on either button to see the button name.) Select a command that you want to move in the list on the right and click the up arrow to move it up in the list. Each successive click moves that command up one more place in the group. Likewise, the down arrow shifts the selected command down in the group. Alternatively, you can right-click a command and then click Move Up or Move Down on the shortcut menu, as shown in Figure 2-41.

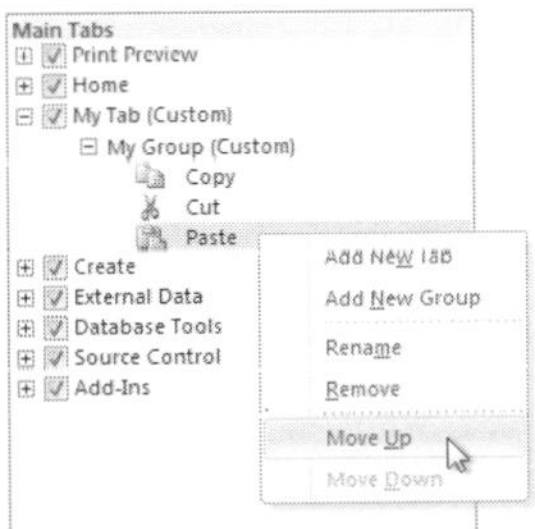

Figure 2-41 Right-click a command, and Access displays a shortcut menu that you can use to rename, remove, or move commands up and down the group list.

To add additional groups to your custom tab or to one of the built-in ribbon tabs, click the New Group button at the bottom of the screen, or right-click a tab and then click Add New Group. You can continue customizing the ribbon by adding more commands to these additional groups, renaming the groups and commands, and changing their display order. By default, Access displays labels next to your custom commands on the ribbon. If you don't want to display these labels, right-click your custom group and click Hide Command Labels. To see how your custom ribbon looks, click OK at the bottom of the screen to save your work. In Figure 2-42, you can see the custom ribbon tab and group we created. The upper part of Figure 2-42 shows our custom ribbon tab and group with command labels showing, and the bottom part of Figure 2-42 shows our custom ribbon tab and group with command labels hidden.

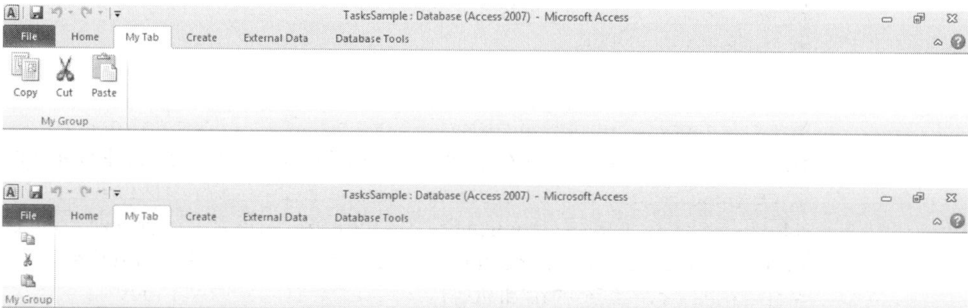

Figure 2-42 You can choose to display or hide the labels for your commands in a custom group.

If you want to remove a custom group from your custom ribbon tab or from one of the default tabs, highlight the group in the list on the right side and then click the Remove button in the middle of the screen. Alternatively, you can right-click a custom group name and then click Remove from the shortcut menu. If you want to remove an entire custom tab from the ribbon, highlight the tab name in the list on the right side and then click Remove. Alternatively, right-click a custom tab name and then click Remove from the shortcut menu, as seen in Figure 2-43.

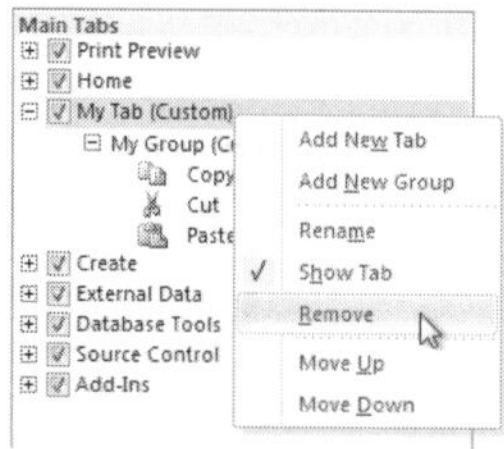

Figure 2-43 Right-click a custom tab and click Remove if you want to remove the entire tab from your ribbon.

If you want to restore one of the built-in ribbon tabs to the default set of groups and commands, highlight the tab name in the list on the right, click the Reset button in the lower-right corner of the screen, and then click Reset Only Selected Ribbon Tab from the drop-down list. To remove all ribbon customizations, click Reset, and then click Reset All Customizations. Before removing all ribbon customizations, Access displays the warning message shown in Figure 2-44. If you click Yes to this Reset Customizations message, Access resets the ribbon, as well as the Quick Access Toolbar, back to the defaults.

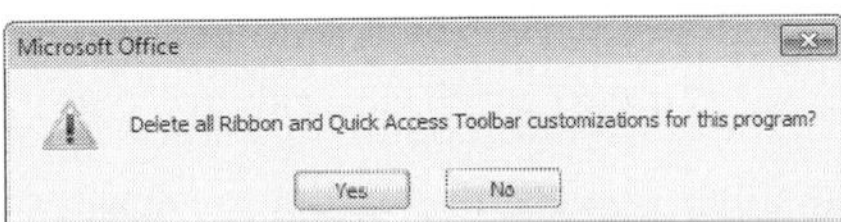

Figure 2-44 Access asks you to confirm resetting the ribbon and Quick Access Toolbar back to the default commands.

You can export your ribbon customizations to a file that can be imported to another computer running Access 2010. Click the Import/Export button at the lower-right corner of the screen, and then click Export All Customizations, as shown in Figure 2-45. You can choose a location to save this customization file for use on other computers. To import the ribbon customizations onto another computer, open Access 2010 on the second computer, reopen the Access Options dialog box with the Customize Ribbon category selected, click the Import/Export button at the bottom of the screen, and then click Import Customization File. Your Access ribbon customizations that you created on the first computer now appear in the Access program installed on the second computer.

Figure 2-45 You can export and import your ribbon customizations to other computers.

> **Note**
>
> **When you choose to export ribbon customizations, Access also exports any Quick Access Toolbar customizations you created for all databases.**

Understanding the Navigation Pane

In versions of Access before Access 2007, you navigated among the various database objects through the Database window. Access grouped all database objects together by type and displayed various properties of each object alongside the object name depending on the view you chose. Beginning with Access 2007, Microsoft replaced the Database window with the Navigation pane, shown in Figure 2-46. Unlike the Object bar in the old Database window that you could position anywhere in the Access workspace, the Navigation pane is a window that is located permanently on the left side of the screen. Any open database objects appear to the right of the Navigation pane instead of covering it up. This means you still have easy access to the other objects in your database without having to shuffle open objects around the screen or continually minimize and restore object windows. In contrast to the Database window, the Navigation pane lets you view objects of different types at the same time. If the list of objects in a particular group is quite extensive, Access provides a scroll bar in each section so that you can access each object.

To follow along in the rest of this section, open the Tasks Sample database (TasksSample.accdb) from the companion CD. Unless you have previously opened this database and changed the Navigation pane, you should see the Navigation pane on the left side of the screen, exactly like Figure 2-46.

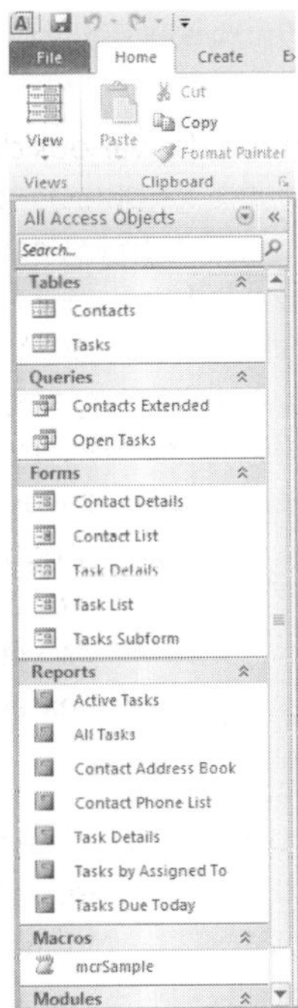

Figure 2-46 The Navigation pane replaces the Database window from Access versions before Access 2007.

INSIDE OUT Jumping Quickly to a Specific Object in the Navigation Pane

Click an object in one of the groups in the Navigation pane to highlight it and then press a letter key to jump quickly to any objects that begin with that letter in that particular group.

Shutter Bar Open/Close Button

You can expand or contract the width of the Navigation pane easily by positioning your pointer over the right edge of the Navigation pane and then clicking and dragging the edge in either direction to the width you want. Keep in mind that the farther you expand the width, the less screen area you have available to work with your database objects because all objects open to the right of the Navigation pane. To maximize the amount of screen area available to work with open objects, you can collapse the Navigation pane completely to the far-left side of the application window by clicking the double-arrow button in the upper-right corner, called the Shutter Bar Open/Close button. When you do this, the Navigation pane appears as a thin bar on the left of your screen, as shown in Figure 2-47.

After you have "shuttered," click the button again to reopen the Navigation pane to its previous width. Access 2010 remembers the last width that you set for the Navigation pane. The next time you open an Access database, the width of the Navigation pane will be the same as when you last had the database open. Pressing the F11 key alternately toggles the Navigation pane between its collapsed and expanded views.

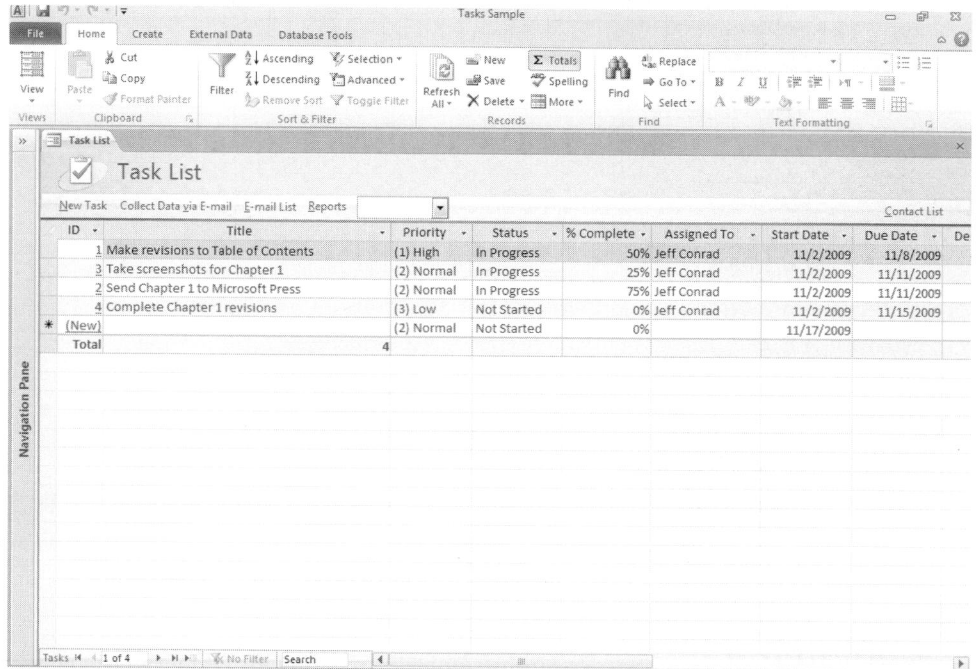

Figure 2-47 You can collapse the Navigation pane to give yourself more room to work on open objects.

We will discuss the various database objects and their purposes within an Access database in Chapter 3, "Access 2010 Overview."

Exploring Navigation Pane Object Views

When you first open the TasksSample.accdb sample database, the Navigation pane shows you all the objects defined in the database grouped by object type and sorted by object name. You can verify this view by clicking the menu bar at the top of the Navigation pane, as shown in Figure 2-48, which opens the Navigation Pane menu. Under Navigate To Category, you should see Object Type selected, and under Filter By Group, you should see All

Access Objects selected. This is the view we selected in the database before saving it on the companion CD. By default, all new blank databases created in the Access 2007/2010 format display the object list in the Navigation pane in this view.

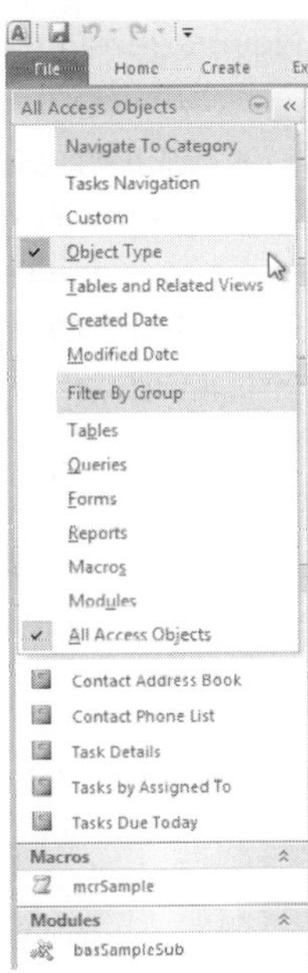

Figure 2-48 You can change the display in the Navigation pane by selecting a different category or filter from the Navigation Pane menu.

This view closely matches the Database window in previous versions of Access, where you could select tabs to view each object category, and each object type was sorted by object name. The objects in each of the six object types—Tables, Queries, Forms, Reports, Macros, and Modules—are grouped together. When the list of objects is longer than can be displayed within the height of the Navigation pane, Access provides a scroll bar.

You can customize the Navigation pane to display the object list in many different ways. Access 2010 provides a set of predefined categories for the Navigation pane that you can access with a few mouse clicks. You can see these available categories by clicking the top of the Navigation pane to open the menu, as shown in Figure 2-48.

Notice that this Tasks Sample database lists six categories under Navigate To Category: Tasks Navigation, Custom, Object Type, Tables And Related Views, Created Date, and Modified Date. The first category in the list, Tasks Navigation, is a custom category specific to this database. We'll show you how to create and modify custom categories later in this section. Access always provides the other five categories in all databases to allow you to view objects in various predefined ways. We will discuss the Custom and Tasks Navigation categories in "Working with Custom Categories and Groups," on page 78.

INSIDE OUT Collapsing an Entire Group in the Navigation Pane

If you click the header of each object type where the double arrow is located, Access collapses that part of the Navigation pane. For example, if you want to hide the tables temporarily, you can collapse that section by clicking the double arrow next to the word Tables. To bring the table list back to full view, simply click the double arrow that is now pointing downward, and the tables section expands to reveal all the table objects.

The Navigation pane menu also provides commands under Filter By Group to allow you to filter the database object list. The filter commands available change depending on which Navigate To Category command you select. Notice in Figure 2-48, where Navigate To Category is set to Object Type, that the Filter By Group section in the lower half of the Navigation Pane menu lists each of the object types that currently exist in your database. When you have the menu categorized by object type, you can filter the list of objects further by selecting one of the object types to see only objects of that type. Click one of the object types (Forms, for instance), and Access hides all the other object types, as shown in Figure 2-49. This feature is very useful if you want to view and work with only a particular type of database object. Click the All Access Objects filter command to see all objects by object type again.

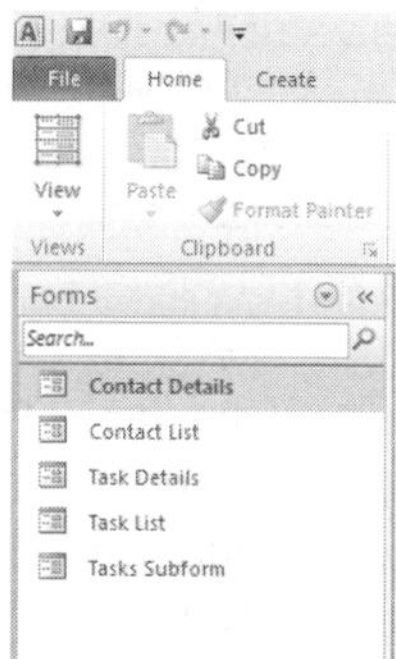

Figure 2-49 You can display only the Forms group of objects in the Object Type view by applying a filter in the Navigation Pane menu.

By default, new blank databases created in the Access 2007/2010 format also include a Navigation Pane category called Tables And Related Views. You can switch the Tasks Sample database to this category by opening the Navigation Pane menu that contains categories and filters, and then clicking the Tables And Related Views command, as shown in Figure 2-50.

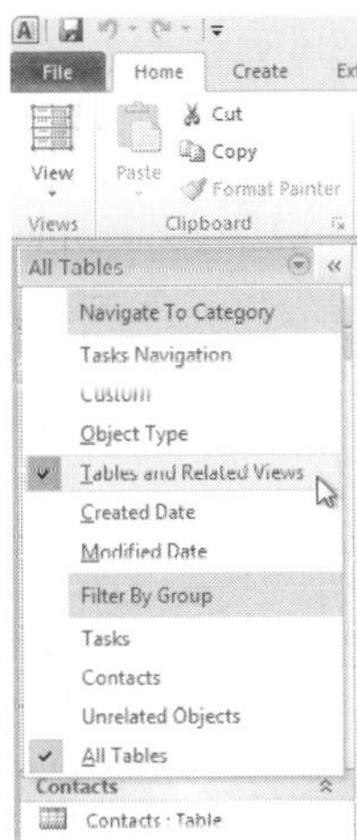

Figure 2-50 The Tables And Related Views category on the Navigation Pane menu offers a different way to view your database objects.

After you click Tables And Related Views, the Navigation pane should look similar to Figure 2-51. This particular view category groups the various database objects based on their relation to a common denominator—a table. As you can observe in Figure 2-51, each group of objects is the name of one of the tables. Within each group, you can see the table as the first item in the group followed by all objects that are dependent on the data from the table. Therefore, Access lists all database objects dependent on the Tasks data table together in the Tasks group, and similarly, it lists all objects dependent on the Contacts table in the Contacts group. At first glance, you might be a bit confused as to the purpose of each object, but notice that the various types of objects each have their own unique icon to help you differentiate them. The Tasks table, for example, is listed first with the icon for a table before the name and the word Table next to it. The remaining objects in the group are the various objects that are dependent on the Tasks table in alphabetical order by name, and each object has an icon before the name that identifies the type of object.

You can find more details about the various object types and related icons in Chapter 3.

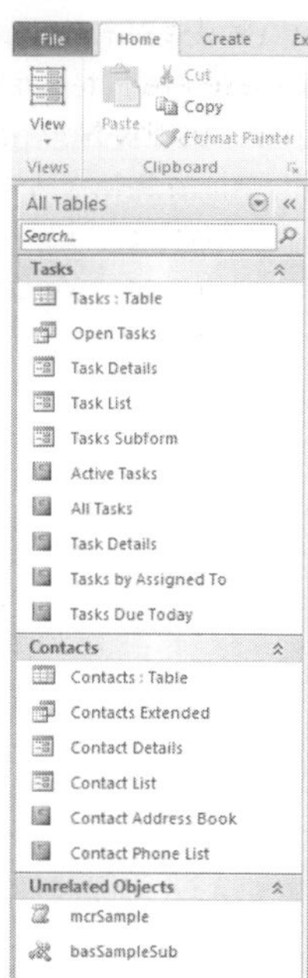

Figure 2-51 The Tables And Related Views category in the Navigation pane groups objects under a table.

Some objects appear in a category called Unrelated Objects, such as the macro called mcrSample and the module called basSampleSub, in this Tasks Sample database. Macros and modules contain code that you can reference from any object in your database. They always appear in the Unrelated Objects category of Tables And Related Views because Access does not search through the macro arguments and module code to see if any table references exist.

INSIDE OUT When to Use the Tables And Related Views Category

This particular view category can be quite useful if you are making some changes to a table and want to see what objects might be affected by the change. You can check each query, form, and report that is related to this table one at a time in this view to ensure that no functionality of the database is broken after you make a change to the underlying table.

Now that you have changed to Tables And Related Views, open the Navigation Pane menu again. Notice that the names of both data tables in this database are listed beneath Filter By Group, as shown in Figure 2-50. Click Tasks, and Access reduces the Navigation pane to show only the objects related to the Tasks table, as shown in Figure 2-52. By filtering the Navigation pane to one table, you have reduced the number of objects displayed and can focus your attention on only a small subset of database objects. You can open the Navigation Pane menu again and click All Tables to restore the complete list.

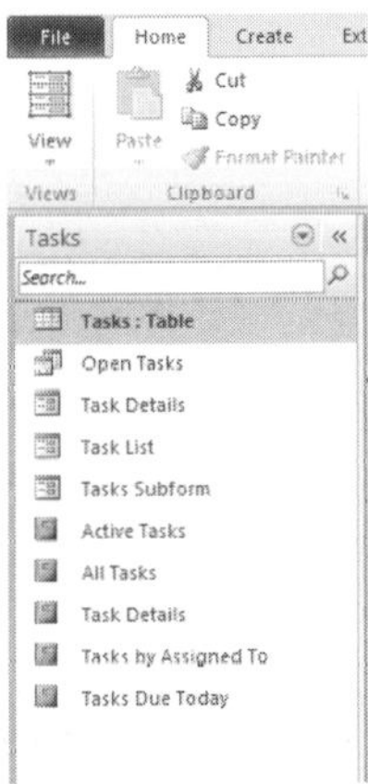

Figure 2-52 You can filter Tables And Related Views to show only the database objects dependent on one table.

Access provides two related types of object view categories on the Navigation Pane menu called Created Date and Modified Date, as shown in Figure 2-53. These categories list all the objects in descending order based on when you created or last modified the object. These views can be quite useful if you need to locate an object that you created or last modified on a specific date or within a range of dates. When you click either of these commands, the Filter By Group options on the Navigation Pane menu offers to filter by Today, Yesterday, one of the five days previous to that (listed by day name), Last Week, Two Weeks Ago, Three Weeks Ago, Last Month, Older, or All Dates.

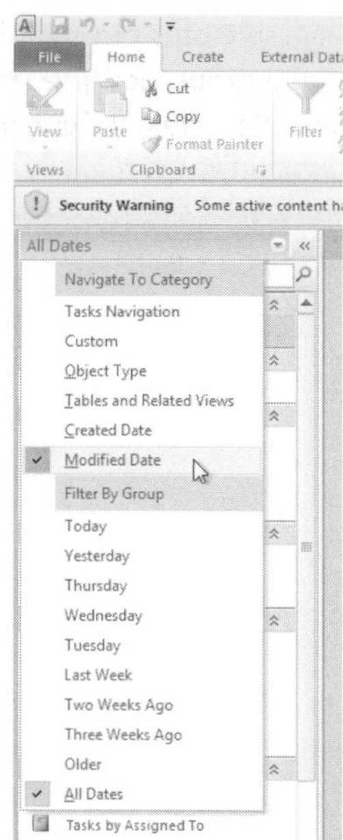

Figure 2-53 The Created Date and Modified Date categories display objects in the order you created or last modified them.

> ### Note
> **You will not see the same options listed in Figure 2-53 when you open your copy of Tasks Sample, because all the Modified dates will be older than three weeks. The only two options you will see are Older and All Dates.**

Working with Custom Categories and Groups

We have not yet discussed the remaining two object categories available in the Navigation Pane menu of the Tasks Sample database: Custom and Tasks Navigation, as shown in Figure 2-54. Whenever you create a new database, Access creates the Custom category that you can modify to suit your needs. Initially, the Custom category contains only one group, Unassigned Objects, containing all the objects defined in your database. As you'll learn later, you can change the name of the Custom category, create one or more custom groups, and assign objects to those groups.

When you create a new database using one of the many templates provided by Microsoft, nearly all these databases contain an additional predefined group designed to make it easier to run the sample application. We created the Tasks Sample database using the Tasks template, and the Tasks Navigation category is predefined in that template. As with any custom category, you can create new groups, modify or delete existing groups, assign additional objects to the groups within the custom category, or delete the category and all its groups altogether.

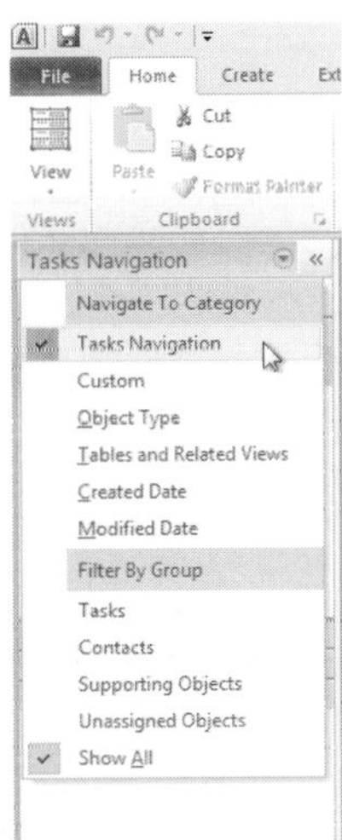

Figure 2-54 Both Custom and Tasks Navigation are custom categories available in the Tasks Sample database.

To see an example of a finished custom category in this database, open the Navigation Pane menu and select Tasks Navigation. The Navigation pane changes to display the object list shown in Figure 2-55. This custom category contains three custom groups called Tasks, Contacts, and Supporting Objects. There is actually a fourth group called Unassigned Objects, which you cannot see. In the following sections, you'll learn how to hide one or more groups.

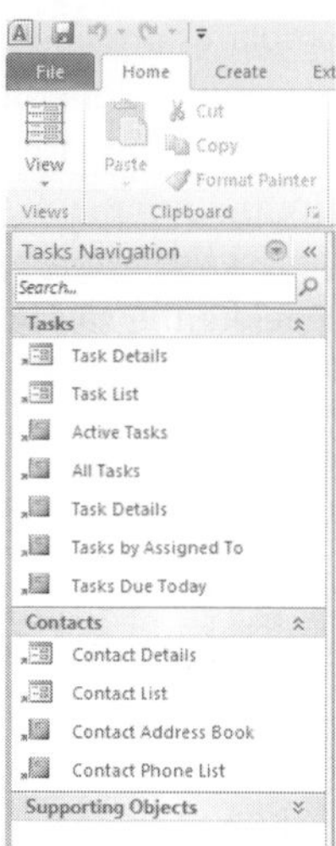

Figure 2-55 The Tasks Navigation category displays a custom view of the various database objects.

In Figure 2-55, notice that each object icon has a small arrow in the lower-left corner. This arrow indicates that you are looking at a shortcut or pointer to the actual object. These shortcuts act similarly to shortcuts in Windows—if you open the shortcut, you're opening the underlying object to which the shortcut points. When you view custom categories and groups in the Navigation pane, you are always looking at shortcuts to the objects. If you delete one of these shortcuts, you are deleting only the pointer to the object and not the object itself. We'll discuss more about working with these object shortcuts in "Hiding and Renaming Object Shortcuts," on page 93.

Exploring the Navigation Options Dialog Box

Now that you have seen how a completed custom view category looks in the Navigation pane, you can create your own new category and groups within that category in this Tasks Sample database for the Tasks forms and reports and the Contacts forms and reports. If any database objects are currently open, close them so that they do not interfere with the following steps. First, let's create a custom category and then some groups within that category to hold our designated database objects. To begin this process, right-click the menu bar at the top of the Navigation pane and click Navigation Options on the shortcut menu, as shown in Figure 2-56.

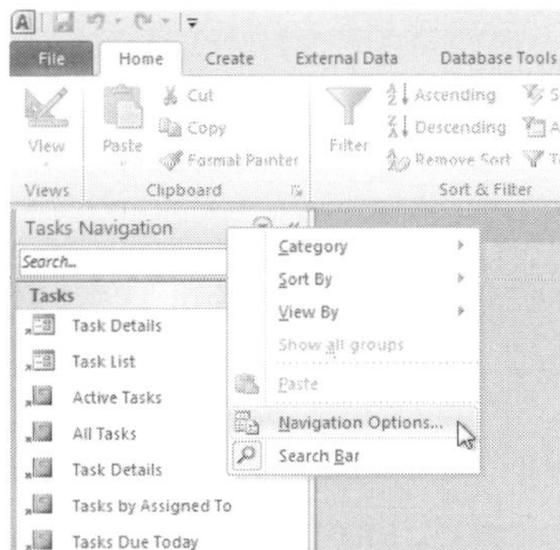

Figure 2-56 Right-click the top of the Navigation pane and click Navigation Options to open the Navigation Options dialog box.

Access opens the Navigation Options dialog box, as shown in Figure 2-57.

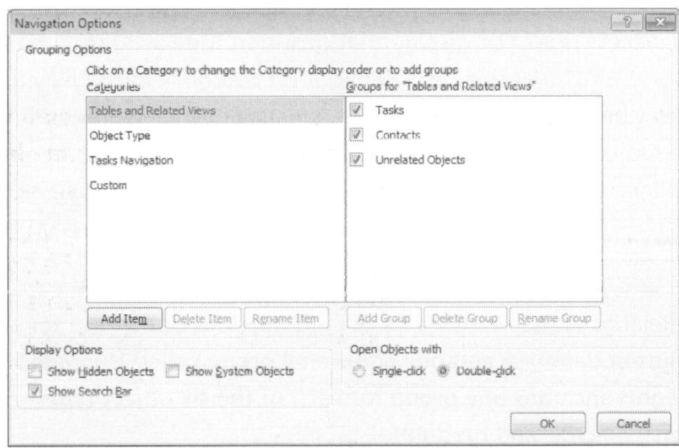

Figure 2-57 The Navigation Options dialog box lets you create and edit grouping and display options.

The Categories list under Grouping Options lists all the categories that have been defined in this database. In this list, you can see two built-in categories—Tables And Related Views and Object Type—that you cannot delete. The list also shows the Tasks Navigation category that was defined in the template and the Custom category that Access defines in all new databases. When you select a different category in the list on the left, the list on the right displays the groups for that category. For example, click the Tasks Navigation category on the left and notice that Access changes the list at the right to show the four groups defined in that category—Tasks, Contacts, Supporting Objects, and Unassigned Objects, as shown in Figure 2-58.

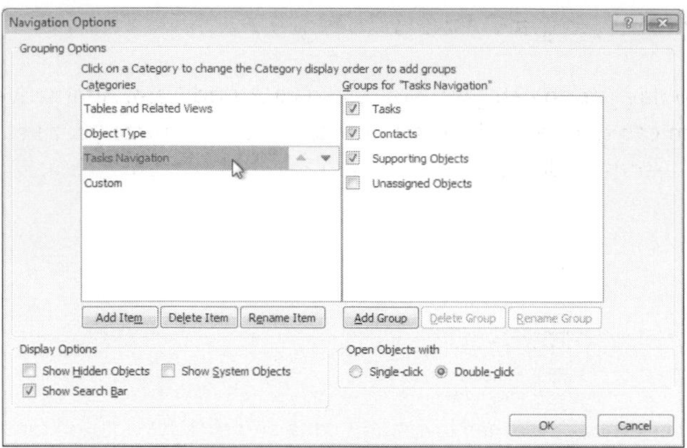

Figure 2-58 Four groups have been defined in the Tasks Navigation category.

Next to each of the four groups for Tasks Navigation is a check box. All but the last check box, next to Unassigned Objects, is selected. When you clear the check box next to any group on the right, Access does not display that group in the Navigation pane. As you might recall, when you looked at the Tasks Navigation category in the Navigation pane, you could see only Tasks, Contacts, and Supporting Objects. Because we cleared the check box next to Unassigned Objects in the Navigation Options dialog box, you are unable to view it in the Navigation pane.

Note

The Tables And Related Views category by default includes one group for each table defined in the current database and one additional group called Unrelated Objects. The Object Type category includes one group for each of the six object types—tables, queries, forms, reports, macros, and modules.

In the lower-left corner of this dialog box, the Display Options section contains three check boxes—Show Hidden Objects, Show System Objects, and Show Search Bar. We'll discuss these options in detail in "Hiding and Renaming Object Shortcuts," on page 93, and "Searching for Database Objects," on page 102. The last section in the lower right of the Navigation Options dialog box is called Open Objects With. When you select the Single-Click option, each object listed in the Navigation pane acts like a hyperlink, so you need only one click to open the object. Double-Click, the default option, opens objects in the Navigation pane with a double click.

Creating and Modifying a Custom Category

To create your new navigation category, you could click Add Item. Alternatively, because the unused Custom category already exists, you can use it to create your new category. Start by clicking Custom under Categories and then click Rename Item, as shown in Figure 2-59.

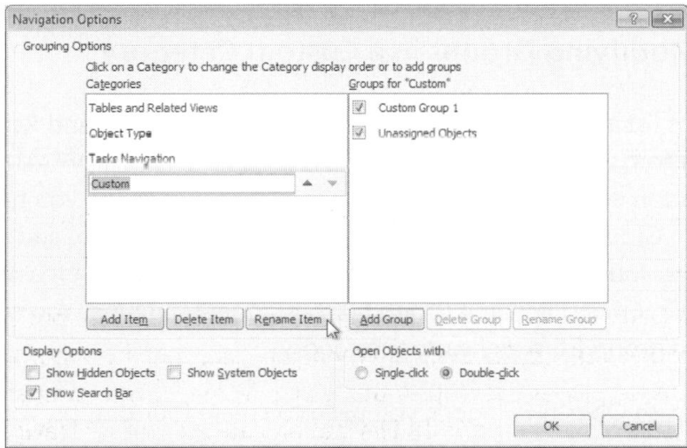

Figure 2-59 Click Rename Item when Custom is selected to rename that category.

After you click Rename Item, Access unlocks the Custom field in the Categories list so you can change the name. Delete the word Custom using the Backspace or Delete key and type **Tasks Database Objects** for your new name, as shown in Figure 2-60.

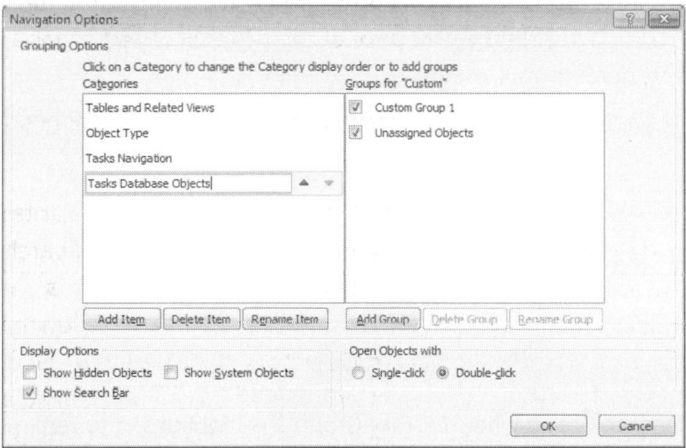

Figure 2-60 You can rename the Custom group by typing a new name in the field.

Under Groups For "Custom," for the Tasks Database Objects category, you can see Custom Group 1 and Unassigned Objects, as shown in Figure 2-60. The Custom Group 1 group is an empty placeholder that Access defines in the Custom category in all new Access 2010 database files. By default, no objects are placed in this group for new databases. The Unassigned Objects group is also a built-in Access group for the Custom category. Access places all objects that are not assigned to any other groups in the Unassigned Objects group for display in the Navigation pane.

Creating and Modifying Groups in a Custom Category

Beneath the Groups list are three buttons: Add Group, Delete Group, and Rename Group. When you click Custom Group 1 in the list, you can see that all these buttons are available. The Add Group button creates another group under whichever group you have currently selected; the Delete Group button deletes the currently selected group; and the Rename Group button allows you to rename the current group. If you click the Unassigned Objects group, the Delete Group and Rename Group buttons appear dimmed. You cannot delete or rename this built-in group from any custom category.

For the Tasks Database Objects category, you need to create four groups. You can rename the Custom Group 1 group to a name of your choice, but you also need to create three additional groups. Let's start by renaming Custom Group 1 to Tasks Forms. Click Custom Group 1 to highlight it and then click Rename Group. Access unlocks the name of this group so you can change it. Delete the words Custom Group 1 and type **Tasks Forms** for your new name, as shown in Figure 2-61.

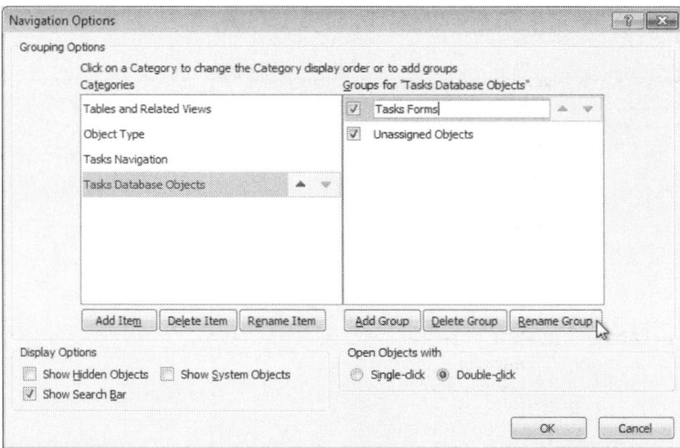

Figure 2-61 Click Rename Group when Custom Group 1 is highlighted to rename that group.

You cannot change the name of the Unassigned Objects group, so you'll need to create additional groups. To create a new group, click Add Group. Access creates another group called Custom Group 1 below Tasks Forms and unlocks it for you to enter a name, as shown in Figure 2-62. Type **Tasks Reports** for your new name and press Enter.

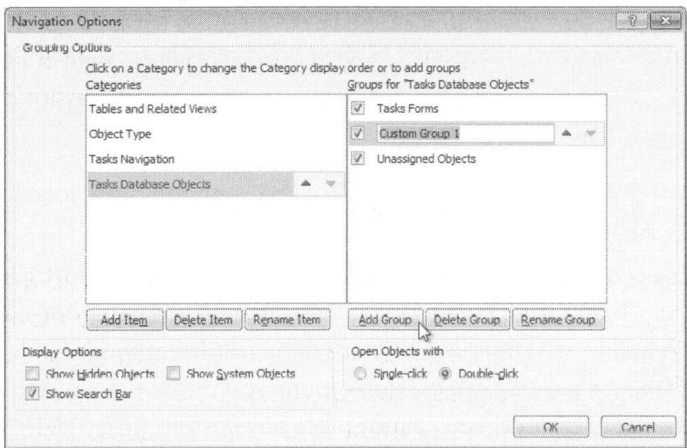

Figure 2-62 When you click Add Group, Access creates another Custom Group 1 group.

Follow the preceding steps to create two additional new groups for the Tasks Database Objects category called Contact Forms and Contact Reports. In each case, start by clicking Add Group to have Access create another Custom Group 1. Type over that name and enter **Contact Forms** and **Contact Reports** for the two names. Your completed changes should now look like Figure 2-63, with your new custom category, four custom groups, and the Unassigned Objects group.

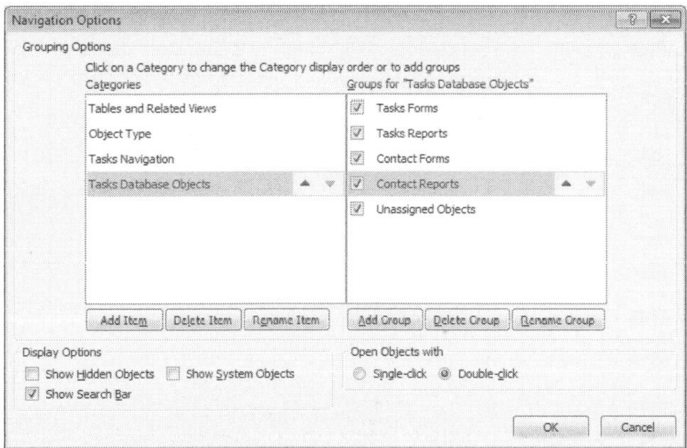

Figure 2-63 The completed Tasks Database Objects category now contains five groups.

Next to whichever custom group is selected on the right are a Move Up arrow and a Move Down arrow, which you can click to change the display order of the groups in this category.

When you select this category from the Navigation Pane menu, Access displays the groups in the Navigation pane based on the display order that you set in the Navigation Options dialog box. In Figure 2-63, you can see arrow buttons next to the Tasks Database Objects category and the Contact Reports group within that category. For now, keep the display order of the custom groups and categories as they are. Click OK to save your current changes.

INSIDE OUT Understanding Display Order Rules for Categories and Groups

In the Categories list of the Navigation Options dialog box, you cannot change the display order of the Tables And Related Views and Object Type categories. All custom categories you create must appear below these two built-in categories.

The Unassigned Objects group in all custom groups you create can be displayed only at the bottom of the list of groups. You cannot place any custom groups below this built-in group. Similarly, the Unrelated Objects group within the Tables And Related Views category always appears at the bottom of the list.

To see how your changes appear in the Navigation pane, click the top of the Navigation pane to open the menu and select your new Tasks Database Objects category, as shown in Figure 2-64.

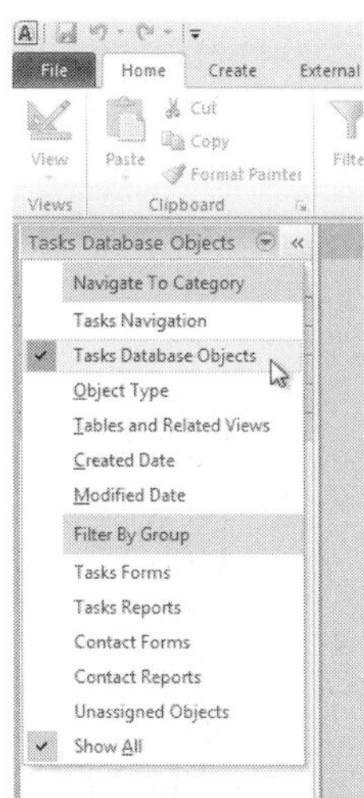

Figure 2-64 After you select the new Tasks Database Objects category, the Navigation pane displays the custom groups you defined.

The Navigation pane now displays each of your four custom group names along with the Unassigned Objects category, as shown in Figure 2-65. Note that Access placed all your objects into the Unassigned Objects group and listed no database objects in any of the four custom groups. (In Figure 2-65, we collapsed the ribbon to show you all the objects.)

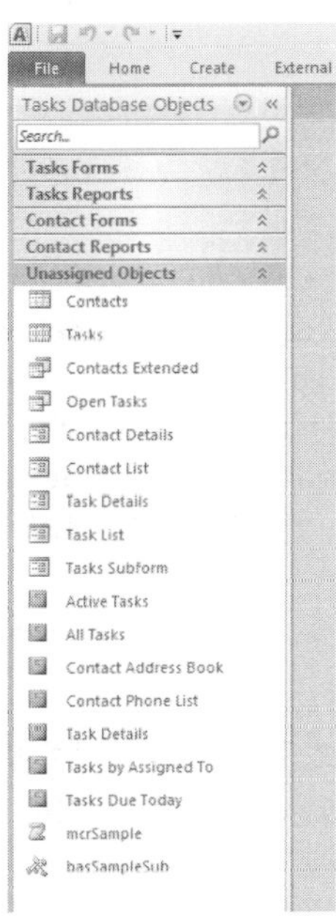

Figure 2-65 Access initially places all objects into the Unassigned Objects group after you create a custom category.

Creating Object Shortcuts in Custom Groups

Now that you have finished creating the category and group structure, it's time to move the objects into the groups you set up. You can move the forms that display or edit Tasks into the new group called Tasks Forms. To accomplish this task, hold down the Ctrl key and single-click each of the three forms that focus on Tasks: Tasks Details, Task List, and Tasks Subform. This action causes Access to highlight all these objects. If you make a mistake by selecting an incorrect object, continue holding down the Ctrl key and single-click the incorrect object to unselect it. After you have selected all three form objects, right-click one of them and, on the shortcut menu that appears, click Add To Group and then Tasks Forms to move the three selected form objects to that group, as shown in Figure 2-66.

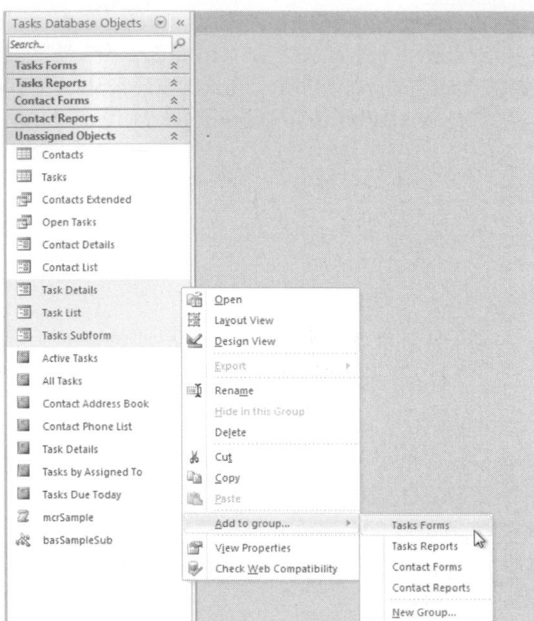

Figure 2-66 You can move several objects to your custom group at the same time by selecting them and clicking Add To Group from the shortcut menu.

Access creates a shortcut to each of the three objects in the first group, as shown in Figure 2-67. Each of the icons now has a small arrow next to it to indicate that it is actually a shortcut to the respective database object and not the actual object itself, as we discussed earlier. If you delete a shortcut, you are deleting only the shortcut or pointer to the object, not the object itself.

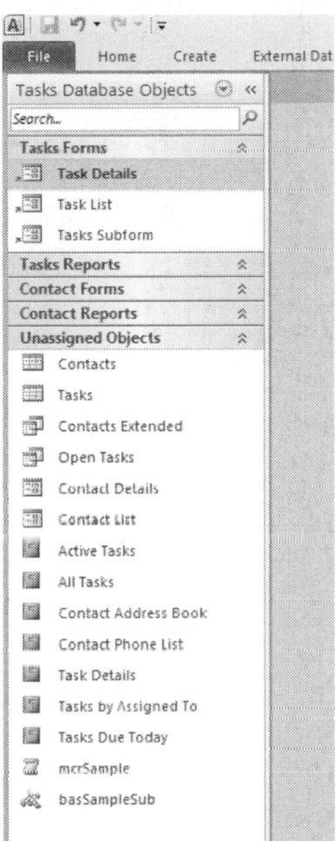

Figure 2-67 After you move your objects to the first custom group, Access creates a shortcut to each object.

With the first set of objects assigned to a group, let's continue moving the other forms and reports. Hold down the Ctrl key and single-click each of the following five reports: Active Tasks, All Tasks, Task Details, Tasks by Assigned To, and Tasks Due Today. After you have selected these reports, right-click and click Add To Group. Click the group called Tasks Reports, and again note how Access creates a shortcut to each of these reports in our custom group, as shown in Figure 2-68.

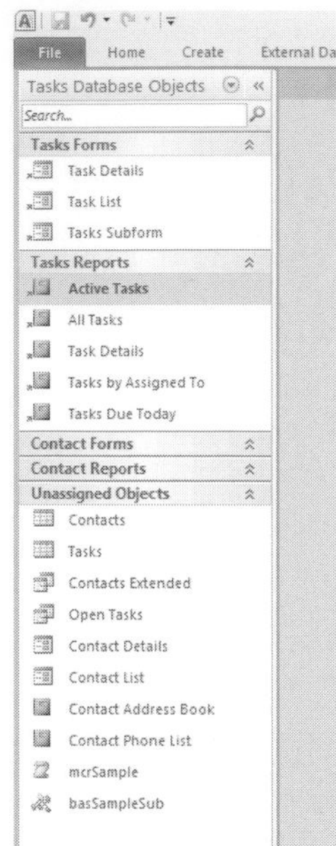

Figure 2-68 Group all your tasks reports together under Tasks Reports by selecting them and clicking Add To Group from the shortcut menu.

INSIDE OUT Dragging and Dropping Objects into Custom Groups

You can also select objects you want to add to a custom group and drag them into the group with your mouse. If you want a shortcut to appear in more than one group, add it to the first group, select it with your mouse, and while holding down the Ctrl key, drag it into the second group. Holding down the Ctrl key tells Access that you want to copy the shortcut, not move it. (Release the mouse button before releasing the Ctrl key to be sure the copy feature works correctly.)

Now repeat this process for the two contact forms called Contact Details and Contact List and move them to the group called Contact Forms. Similarly, move the two contact reports called Contact Address Book and Contact Phone Book to the group called Contact Reports. The Navigation pane should now look like Figure 2-69.

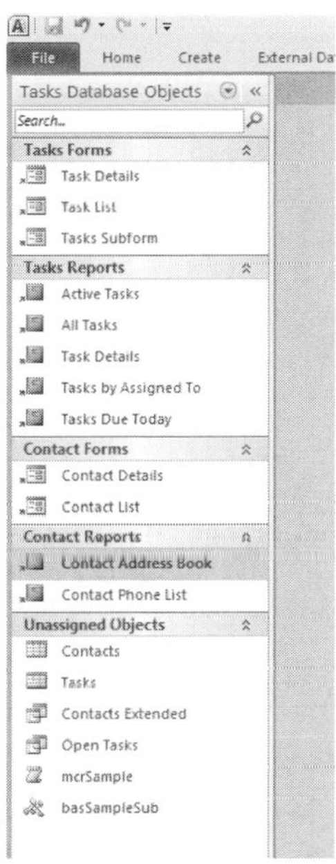

Figure 2-69 All the form and report objects now have shortcuts in custom groups in the Navigation pane.

Hiding Custom Groups in a Category

With the previous steps completed, you should now see only six objects in the Unassigned Objects group—a collection of data tables, queries, one macro, and one module. For now, assume that we do not want to have the users of this database application view these objects. We can hide this entire Unassigned Objects group of objects from the users by going back to the Navigation Options dialog box. Right-click the top of the Navigation pane, and then click Navigation Options to open the Navigation Options dialog box again. In the Categories list, click the Tasks Database Objects category to display our custom groups. Clear the Unassigned Objects check box to tell Access to hide this particular group when showing our custom Tasks Database Objects view in the Navigation pane, as shown in Figure 2-70.

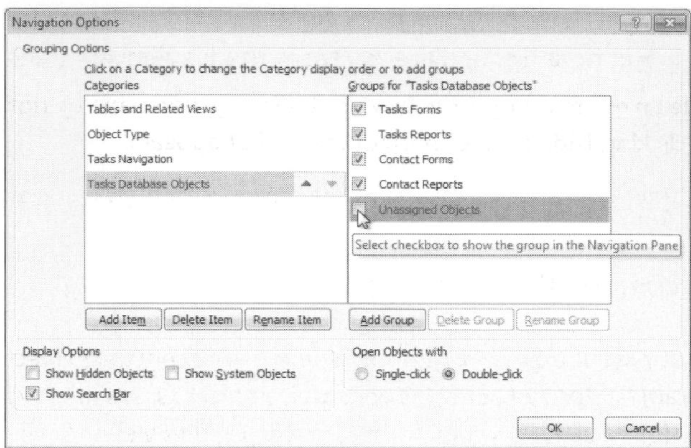

Figure 2-70 Clear the check box next to Unassigned Objects to hide this group in the Navigation pane.

Click OK in the Navigation Options dialog box, and Access completely removes this group from view in the Navigation pane. We are now left with a concise list of form and report objects separated into logical groups, as shown in Figure 2-71.

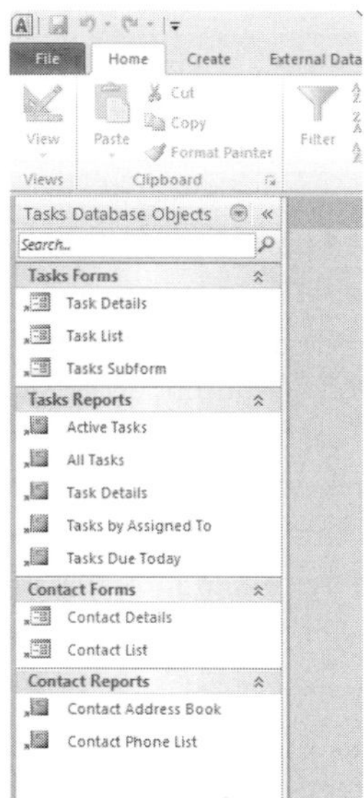

Figure 2-71 The completed changes to the Navigation pane now display only form and report object shortcuts in four custom groups.

INSIDE OUT Hiding a Group Directly from the Navigation Pane

You can also hide an entire group from view in the Navigation pane by right-clicking that group and clicking Hide on the shortcut menu that appears.

Hiding and Renaming Object Shortcuts

We can customize our list of objects further by hiding object shortcuts directly in the Navigation pane. For example, for illustration purposes right now, assume that you want to hide the data entry form called Tasks Subform from the current view. (You'll learn in Part 3, "Building Queries," that a subform is a form designed to be embedded in another form. A user normally won't need to open subforms directly.) There are two methods for accomplishing this task, both of which you can access directly from the Navigation pane. For the first method, right-click the Tasks Subform in the Navigation pane and click Hide In This Group from the shortcut menu, as shown in Figure 2-72.

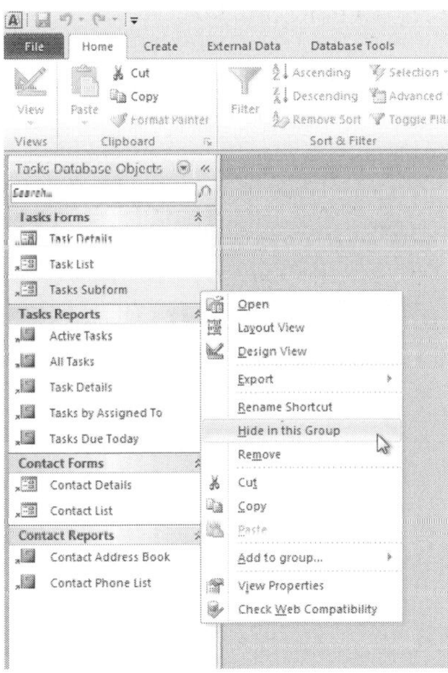

Figure 2-72 To hide an object in a specific group, right-click it and click Hide In This Group from the shortcut menu.

Access hides this object shortcut from view in the Navigation pane, but it does not in any way delete or alter the existing form itself. Alternatively, you can right-click that object in the Navigation pane and click View Properties from the shortcut menu, shown in Figure 2-72, to open the Properties dialog box for this object, shown in Figure 2-73.

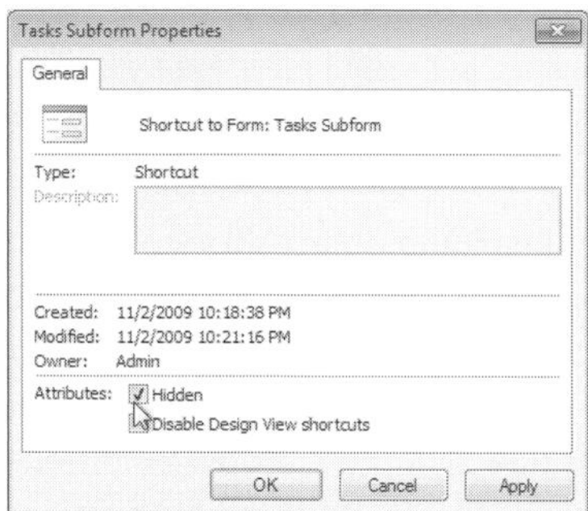

Figure 2-73 You can hide a database object or an object shortcut from view in the Navigation pane by selecting the Hidden check box in the Properties dialog box.

The Properties dialog box displays the name of the object and whether this is a shortcut to an object. In the middle of the dialog box, you can see any description inherited from the original object (which you can't modify), the date the object was created, date the object was last modified, and the owner of the object. The Attributes section has two check boxes called Hidden and Disable Design View Shortcuts. (We will discuss Disable Design View in Chapter 26.) In the Attributes section, select the Hidden check box and then click OK. In the Navigation pane, you will see the Tasks Subform disappear from view. Remember that you have hidden only the shortcut for this object and have not affected the actual form itself in any way.

You now know how to hide objects or object shortcuts from view in the Navigation pane, but what if you want to rename the object shortcuts? Access 2010 allows you to easily rename the shortcuts to database objects without affecting the underlying names of the objects. To illustrate this procedure, let's rename one of the report object shortcuts. Right-click the Tasks Details report and click Rename Shortcut from the shortcut menu, as shown in Figure 2-74.

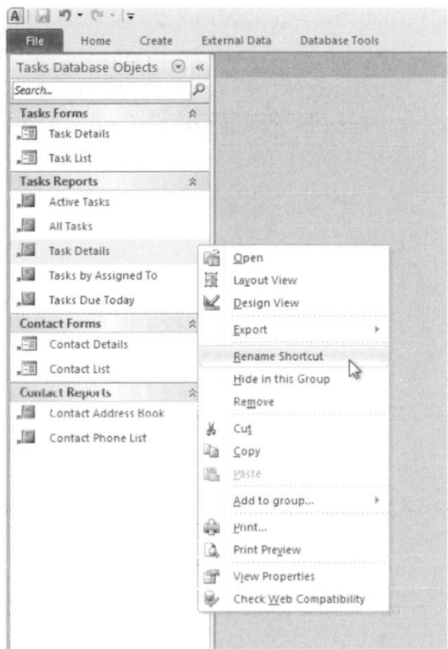

Figure 2-74 To rename an object shortcut in the Navigation pane, right-click it and click Rename Shortcut.

Access sets the focus on this report in the Navigation pane and unlocks the name of the shortcut. Enter a new name for this object by typing **All Task Details Report** and then pressing Enter, as shown in Figure 2-75. Access saves the new name of this report shortcut, but it does not change the name of the actual report object to which the shortcut points.

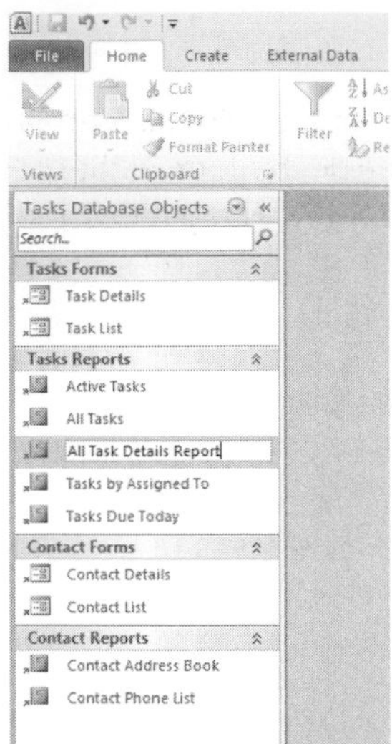

Figure 2-75 After you click Rename Shortcut, Access unlocks the object shortcut name so that you can change it.

The final custom Navigation pane with all your modifications should now look like Figure 2-76. Behind the scenes, all the database objects are still present and unchanged, but you customized the display view for users of your database. You are now showing only a list of form and report shortcuts, while other objects are hidden from view.

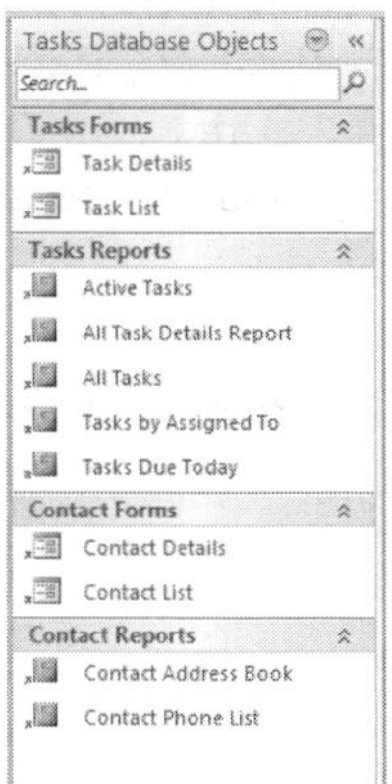

Figure 2-76 The customized Navigation Pane category and groups now display only form and report shortcuts.

Revealing Hidden Shortcuts

If you have followed along to this point, remember that you hid the form Tasks Subform from the current view in the Navigation pane. To unhide this form, right-click the top of the Navigation pane and click Navigation Options to open the Navigation Options dialog box. Select the Show Hidden Objects check box, as shown in Figure 2-77. Click OK to save this change and close the Navigation Options dialog box.

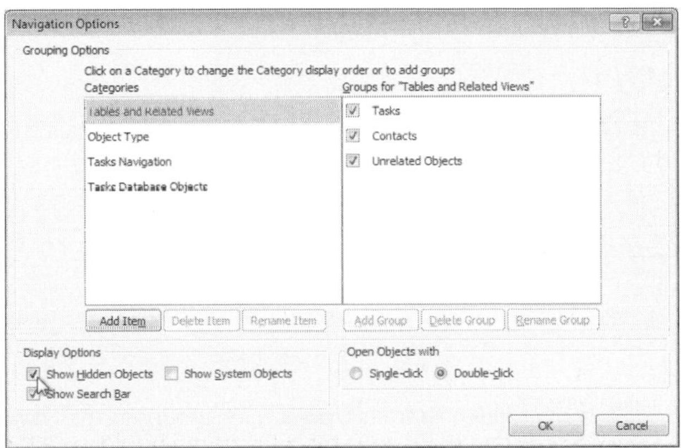

Figure 2-77 Selecting the Show Hidden Objects check box causes Access to display any hidden object shortcuts in the Navigation pane.

When you return to the Navigation pane, Access displays the shortcut to the form Tasks Subform in the Tasks Forms group, as shown in Figure 2-78. If you look closely in Figure 2-78, you can see that Access displays the object dimmed compared to the other object shortcuts. This dimmed state is a visual cue that Access uses to indicate object shortcuts that are hidden. In Figure 2-78, you can also see that Access now shows the hidden group Unassigned Objects and all the objects contained within it. All the objects in the Unassigned Objects group, along with the group name itself, also appear dimmed in the Navigation pane.

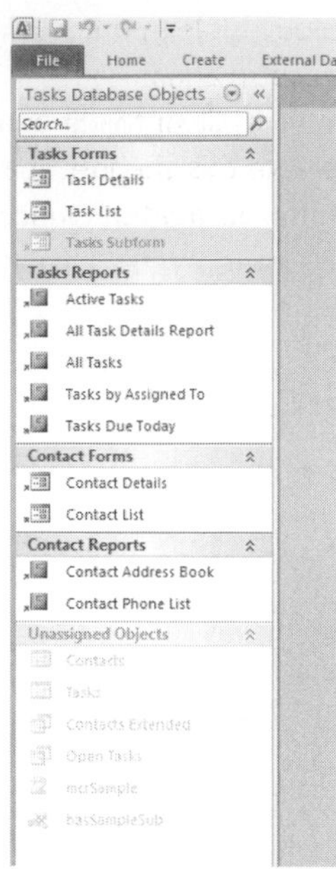

Figure 2-78 Access displays any hidden shortcuts, objects, or groups in the Navigation pane when you select the Show Hidden Objects check box.

To change the Hidden property of the form Tasks Subform, right-click that object in the Navigation pane and click View Properties to open the Properties dialog box for this object, as shown in Figure 2-79. In the Attributes section, clear the Hidden check box and then click OK. You can see that the Tasks Subform no longer appears dimmed in the Navigation pane.

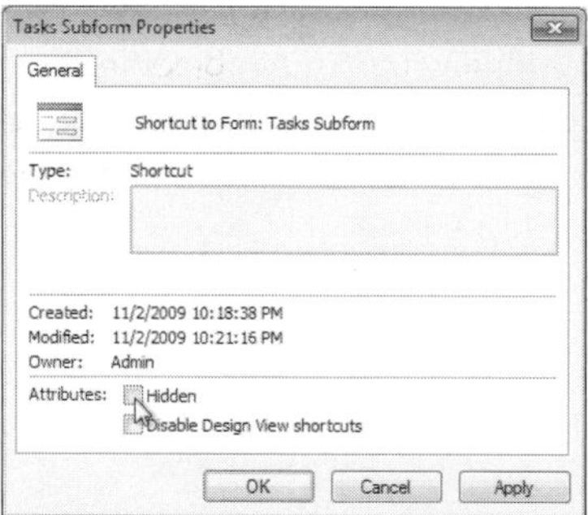

Figure 2-79 You can unhide a database object or an object shortcut from view in the Navigation pane by clearing the Hidden check box in the Properties dialog box for the object or shortcut.

Now that you have changed the form Tasks Subform to be visible in the Navigation pane, you need to tell Access to hide the Unassigned Objects group again. To do this, right-click the top of the Navigation pane and click Navigation Options. Clear the Show Hidden Objects check box, as shown in Figure 2-80. Click OK to save this change, and Access once again hides the Unassigned Objects group from view in the Navigation pane.

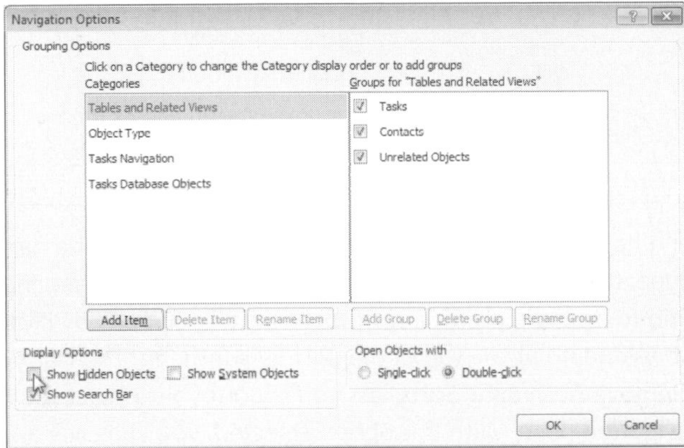

Figure 2-80 Clear the Show Hidden Objects check box to have Access hide any hidden object shortcuts, objects, or groups in the Navigation pane.

On the companion CD, you can find a database file called TasksSampleCustom.accdb, which has all the changes from the steps we completed in the preceding sections. If you would like to compare your Tasks Database Objects category and groups to our completed sample, open this file from the folder where you installed the sample files.

Sorting and Selecting Views in the Navigation Pane

By default, Access sorts the objects in the Navigation pane by object type in ascending order. The Navigation pane allows for several other types of object sorting. Right-click the menu at the top of the Navigation pane and move the mouse pointer over Sort By, as shown in Figure 2-81.

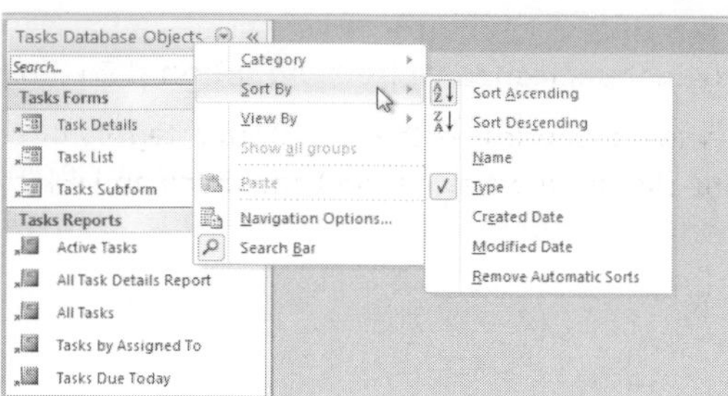

Figure 2-81 The Sort By submenu in the Navigation Pane menu allows for further Navigation pane sorting.

The Sort By submenu has options to sort the Navigation pane list by the name of the object, the object type, the created date, and the modified date. You can change the sort order from ascending to descending for any of these Sort By options by clicking Sort Ascending or Sort Descending at the top of the Sort By submenu. The last option on the Sort By submenu, Remove Automatic Sorts, lets you lay out your object list in any order you want within the Navigation pane. With this option selected, you can click and drag your objects within their respective groups into any order, and Access will not re-sort them in alphabetical, type, created date, or modified date order after you have repositioned your objects in the list.

The View By submenu has three choices available—Details, Icon, and List—as shown in Figure 2-82. The Details view displays in the Navigation pane the name of each object, its type, and the creation and modified dates, as well as a large icon next to each name. The Icon view displays only the name of the object (or the shortcut name) next to a large icon of the object type. The List view similarly displays only the name of the object or shortcut, but the object icon is smaller than in the other two views.

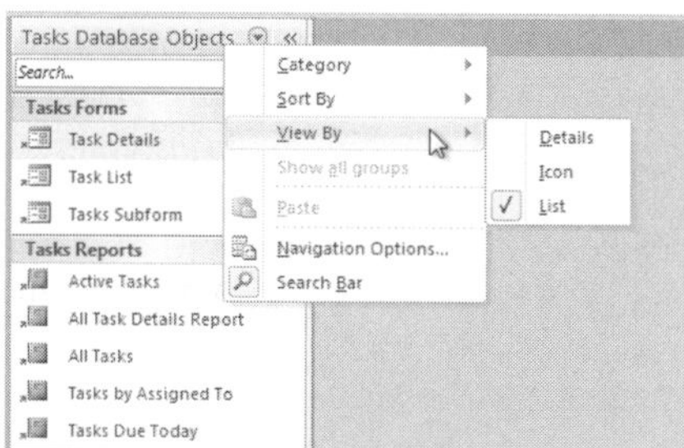

Figure 2-82 The View By submenu lists commands to view the Navigation pane objects by Details, Icon, or List.

INSIDE OUT **Viewing Categories from the Navigation Pane Submenus**

You can choose one of the view categories—either a custom category or one of the built-in categories—by right-clicking the Navigation Pane menu and selecting the Category submenu.

In Figure 2-83, you can see what the Navigation pane looks like with the view set to Details. Notice that more information is displayed about each object, but you see fewer objects. To see the remaining objects, you have to use the vertical scroll bar. If you changed your view to Details to test this, go back to the View By submenu and change the view back to List before continuing.

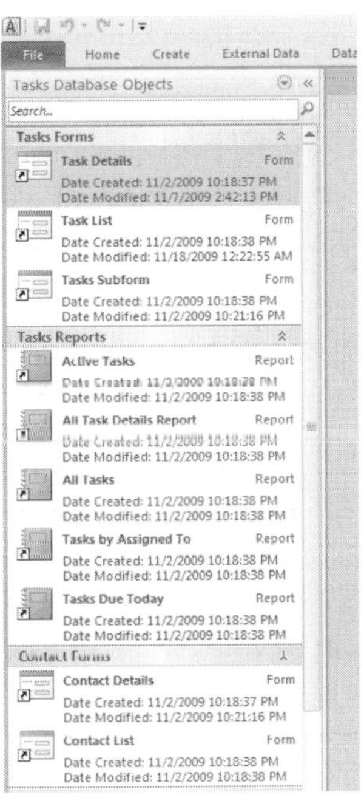

Figure 2-83 The Details view displays more information about each object in the Navigation pane than Icon or List view.

Manually Sorting Objects in the Navigation Pane

So far, we have seen how Access can sort the list of objects and object shortcuts in the Navigation pane automatically for you. Access also allows you to sort the object lists manually so that you can further customize the display order. You must first tell Access to stop automatically sorting your objects. Right-click the top of the Navigation pane, click Sort By, and then click Remove Automatic Sorts, as shown in Figure 2-84.

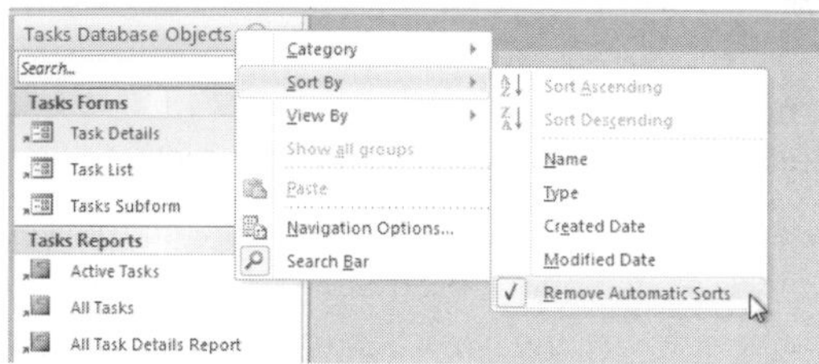

Figure 2-84 Click the Remove Automatic Sorts command to sort your object list manually in the Navigation pane.

Now you can click and drag your objects and object shortcuts around into different positions in the Navigation pane. For example, click and drag the Task Details form shortcut in the Navigation pane until you have your cursor between the Task List and Tasks Subform forms. An I-beam pointer will appear while you drag to help you position the object, as shown in Figure 2-85. After you release the mouse, Access drops the form shortcut into the new position.

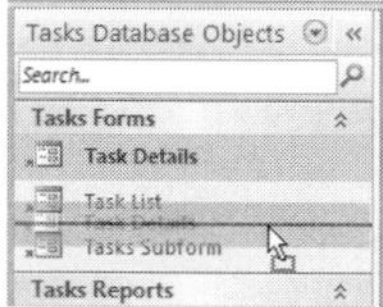

Figure 2-85 Click and drag your form shortcut into a new position within the Tasks Forms category.

To have Access automatically sort the object list again, select any of the four available sort options above Remove Automatic Sorts from the Display Options menu.

Searching for Database Objects

In databases with a large number of objects, locating a specific object can be difficult, so Access 2010 includes the Search Bar feature to make this task easier. By default, this feature is turned on; however, if the feature is turned off for your Access installation, you must turn it on through the Navigation pane. You can enable this feature in one of two ways. For the first method, right-click the top of the Navigation pane and then click Search Bar, as shown in Figure 2-86.

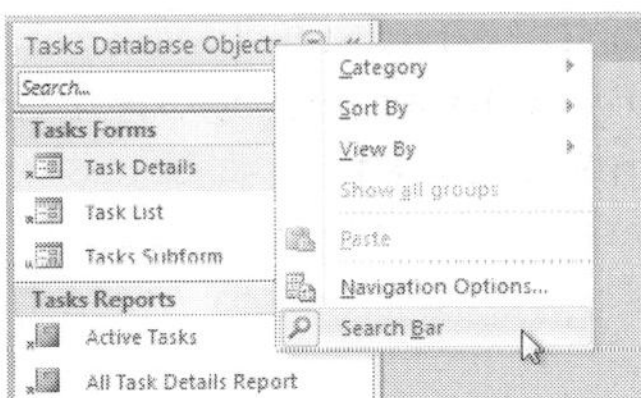

Figure 2-86 Click the Search Bar command on the Display Options menu to display the Search Bar.

Alternatively, you can right-click the top of the Navigation pane and then click Navigation Options from the shortcut menu to open the Navigation Options dialog box, shown in Figure 2-87.

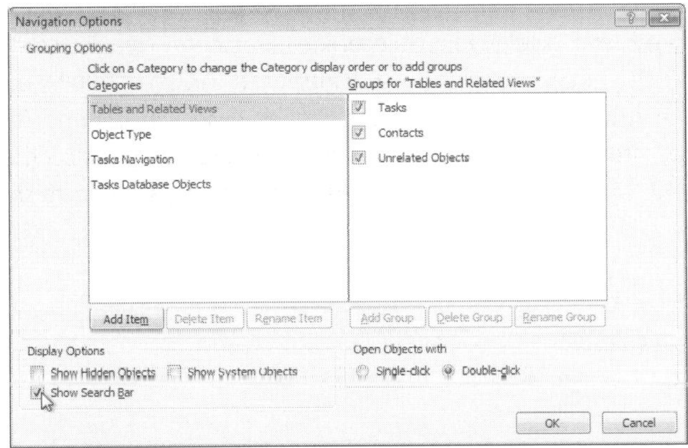

Figure 2-87 Select the Show Search Bar check box in the Navigation Options dialog box to display the Search Bar.

Select the Show Search Bar check box and then click OK. Access displays a Search Bar near the top of the Navigation pane, as shown in Figure 2-88.

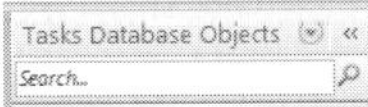

Figure 2-88 The Search Bar in the Navigation pane helps you find specific database objects.

We think the Search Bar is misnamed. Rather than "search" for objects that match what you type in the search box, Access filters the list in the Navigation pane. As you begin to type letters, Access filters the list of objects to those that contain the sequence of characters you enter anywhere in the name. For example, if you want to find an object whose name contains the word Today, type the word **today** in the Search Bar. As you enter each letter in the Search Bar, Access begins filtering the list of objects for any that contain the characters in your entered search string. With each successive letter you type, Access reduces the list of objects shown in the Navigation pane because there are fewer objects that match your search criteria. Notice that as soon as you have typed the letters to, Access has reduced the list to two objects—Tasks by Assigned To and Tasks Due Today. The names of both objects contain the letters to.

After you finish typing the entire word today in the Search Bar, the Navigation pane should look like Figure 2-89. Access collapses any group headers if it does not find any objects (or object shortcuts if you're using a custom category) that meet your search criterion. In this case, Access located one object, Tasks Due Today, with the word today in its name. To clear your search string if you need to perform another object search, either delete the existing text using the Backspace key or click the Clear Search String button on the right side of the Search Bar. Clearing the search box or clicking the Clear Search String button restores the Navigation pane to show all displayable objects.

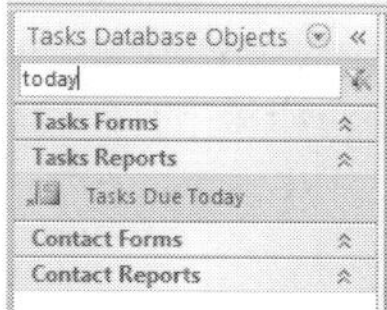

Figure 2-89 The Search Bar collapses any groups if it does not find any objects in that group that meet your search criterion.

INSIDE OUT Moving Focus to the Search Bar with a Keyboard Shortcut

You can quickly move the focus to the Search Bar from anywhere within the application window by pressing Ctrl+Alt+F.

Note that Access searches for objects only in categories and groups that are currently displayed in the Navigation pane. If Access cannot find an object that you know exists in the database, it is possible that the view you have selected in the Navigation pane is interfering. For example, suppose you conduct the same search as described previously, but this time you have only one group showing. Clear the Search Bar of any text by using the Backspace key or clicking the Clear Search String button. Now click the menu bar at the top of the Navigation pane and select Tasks Forms in the Filter By Group section of the Navigation Pane menu, as shown in Figure 2-90. The only group now displayed in the Navigation pane is Tasks Forms, with three object shortcuts.

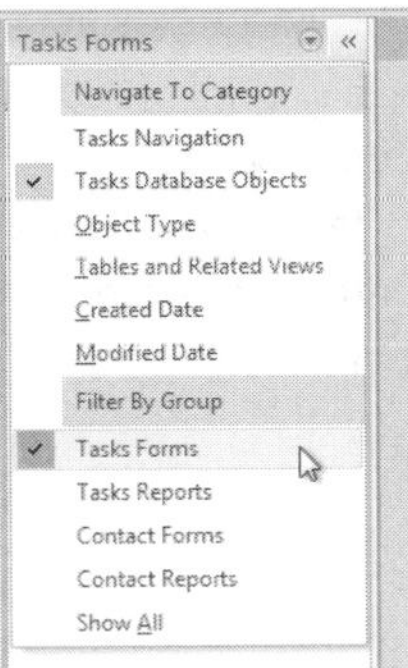

Figure 2-90 Select Tasks Forms from the Navigation Pane menu to show only that group in the Navigation pane.

Enter the word **today** again in the Search Bar, and notice that Access cannot locate any objects that meet your criterion. In Figure 2-91, you can see that Access shows an empty Navigation pane because none of the three form object shortcuts in the Tasks Forms groups has the word today in its name. This does not mean that no objects in the entire database have the word today in their name; it means only that Access could not locate any objects with that search criterion in the current view selected in the Navigation pane.

Figure 2-91 Access might not be able to find any objects that meet your criterion if your chosen display view is too restrictive.

If you know the exact name of the object you want to find and the type of object as well, you can save some additional searching through object types that you might not be interested in. For example, suppose you want to find a form that has the word list in its name. First, open the Navigation Pane menu and click Object Type. Open the menu again and click Forms under Filter By Group to restrict the list of objects to display only forms, as shown in Figure 2-92.

INSIDE OUT Using the Shortcut Menu to Display Only One Category

You can also right-click the Forms group header and click Show Only Forms so that only forms show in the Navigation pane.

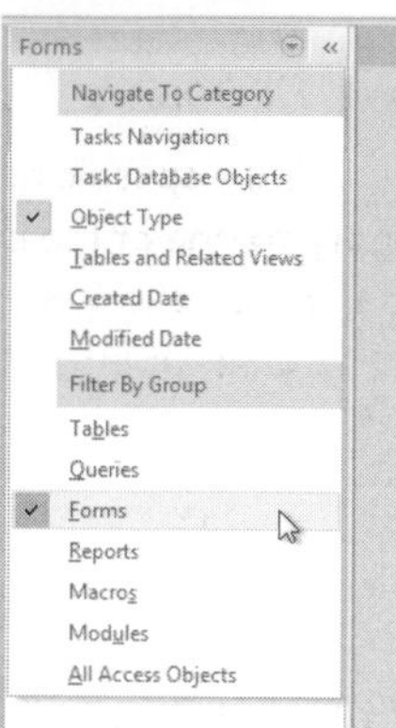

Figure 2-92 You can limit your search to form objects by selecting the Object Type category and Forms group from the Navigation Pane menu.

Type the word **list** in the Search Bar, and Access searches through only data entry forms until it finds a match. In Figure 2-93, Access has found two forms that have the word list in their name—Contact List and Task List.

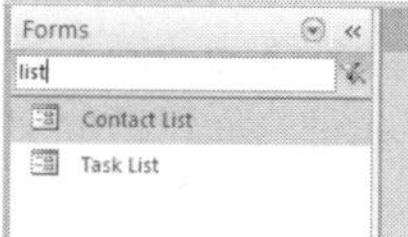

Figure 2-93 After restricting the Navigation pane to show only forms, text you enter in the Search Bar searches only in the Forms group.

INSIDE OUT **Maximizing Your Search to Include All Objects**

If you need to search through all your database objects to find a specific named object, we recommend that you set the Navigation Menu category to one of the built-in categories such as Object Type or Tables And Related Views. Also check to see that all groups are visible in the Navigation pane for that category to ensure that Access does not miss any objects when it conducts the search.

Using the Single-Document vs. the Multiple-Document Interface

In versions of Access before Access 2007, all objects opened in their own windows where you could edit, view, or print them. This type of interface, multiple-document interface (MDI for short), was the cornerstone for working with objects in Access. Office Access 2007 introduced a new interface model called single-document interface (SDI). In the SDI model, all objects open in a series of tabs along the top of the object window to the right of the Navigation pane. In the older MDI model, switching between open objects usually meant constantly minimizing, resizing, and maximizing the various objects to work with them. In Figure 2-94, you can see two forms, one table, and one report open using MDI format. To switch among these objects, you must move the objects around or minimize some of them, as shown near the bottom of the screen.

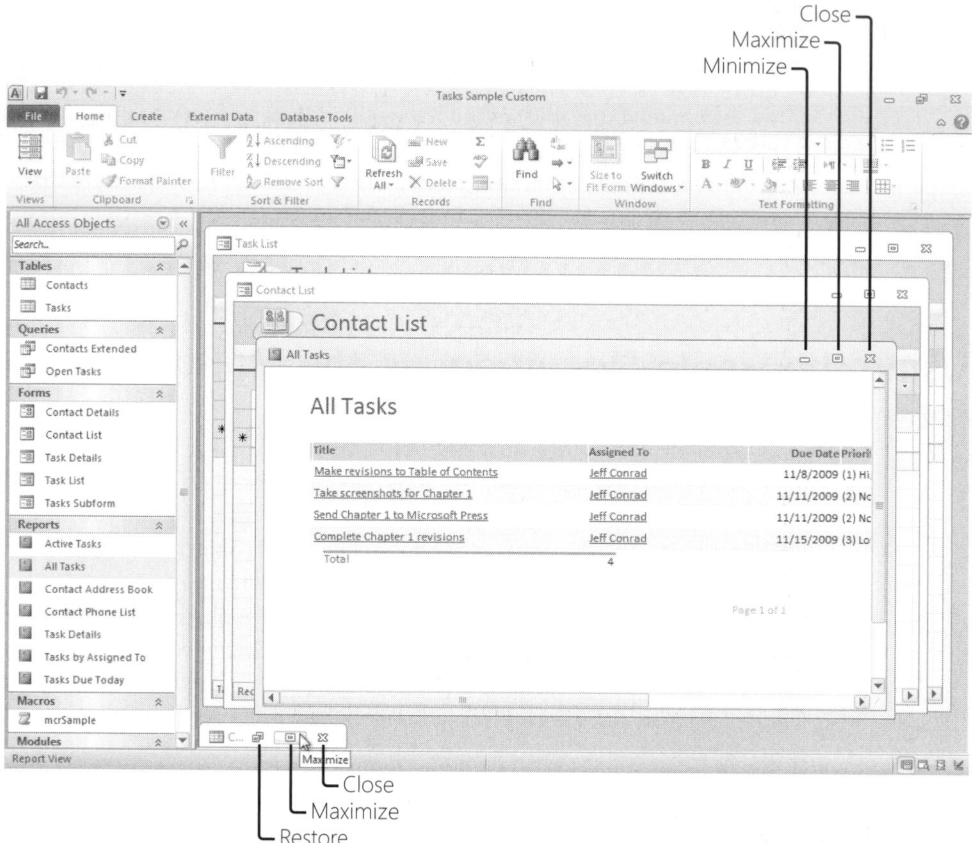

Figure 2-94 All open objects appear in their own separate windows when using the MDI.

In the SDI model, each open object appears on a tab to the right of the Navigation pane. In Figure 2-95, you can see the same four objects open as before, but here each open object has its name listed at the top of a tab next to an icon for that particular type of database object. Switching among open objects is as simple as clicking on a different tab. The end result of this interface is that you can easily see the names of all open objects and find the ones that you need to work with much faster.

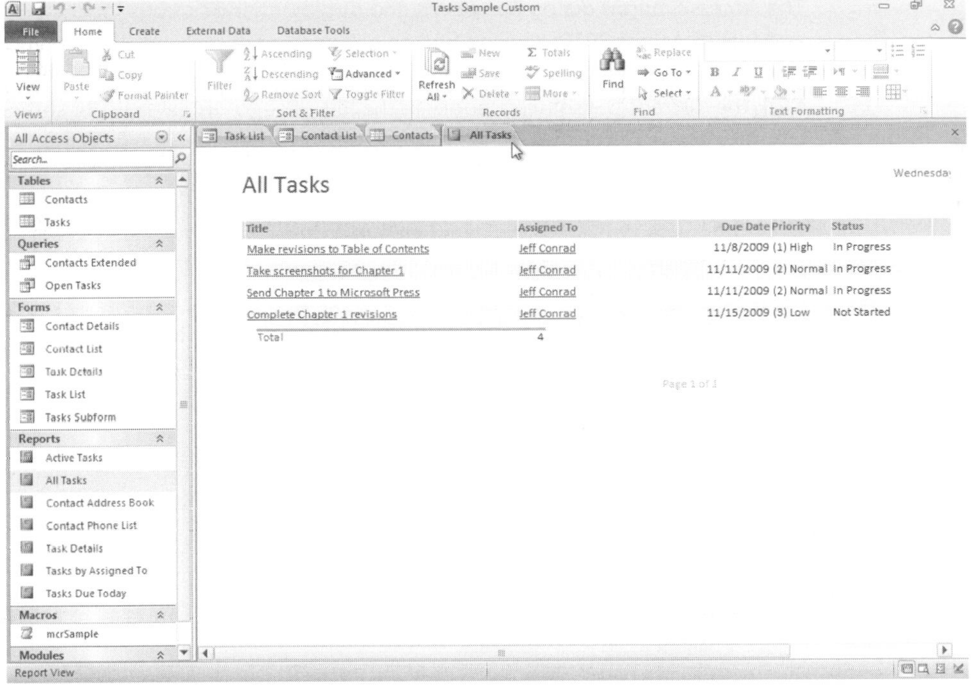

Figure 2-95 All open objects appear on their own tabs when using the SDI.

> **INSIDE OUT** **Closing Objects with One Click**
>
> **If you are using the SDI, you can close any window with a middle-click. Click the mouse wheel on the object tab at the top of the application window, even if the tab is not currently selected, and Access closes that object.**

For new databases created in the Access 2007/2010 format, Access uses the SDI by default, but for older databases in the MDB/MDE type format, Access 2010 still opens those files in MDI mode. Access easily allows you to change the interface mode for any database through the Access Options dialog box. Click the File tab on the Backstage View, and then click Options.

The Access Options dialog box opens and displays many options for customizing the look and feel of Access 2010. You can find an explanation of more of the various options on these tabs in "Modifying Global Settings via the Access Options Dialog Box," on page 112. Click the Current Database category in the left pane to display a list of settings to tailor this current database. In Figure 2-96, note the section called Document Window Options in the Current Database category of the Access Options dialog box.

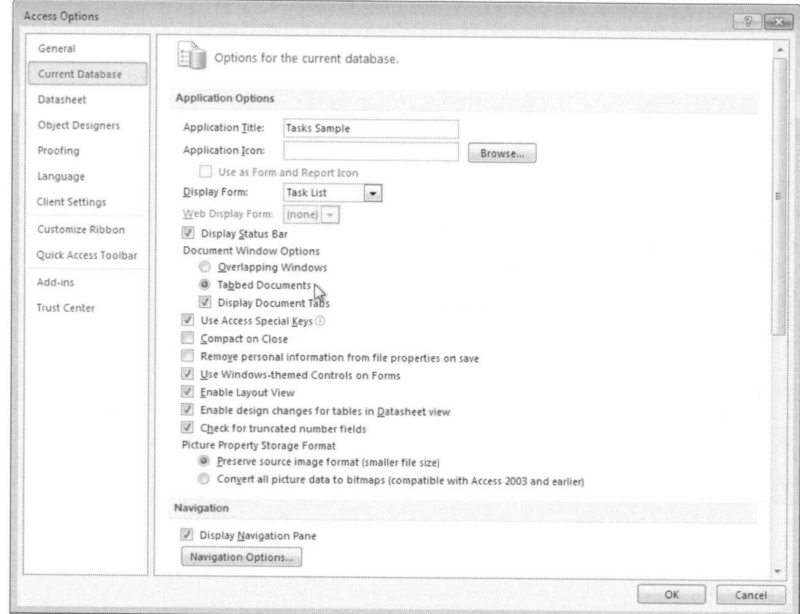

Figure 2-96 The Document Window Options section in the Current Database category of the Access Options dialog box controls the interface mode.

To work in MDI mode, select Overlapping Windows. For the SDI interface, with each object on its own tab, select Tabbed Documents. Under these two options is a check box called Display Document Tabs. You can select this check box only in conjunction with the Tabbed Documents option. When you select the Display Document Tabs check box, each object has a tab across the top of the object window with the object's name and an icon for the object type, as shown in Figure 2-95. If you clear Display Document Tabs, you do not see any tabs for open objects, nor do you see any Restore, Minimize, Maximize, or Close buttons for open objects.

In Figure 2-97, we have two forms, one table, and one report open, but you can see only the report because no object tabs are visible. Notice that you do not see the Restore, Minimize, Maximize, or Close button along the top of the object window, which means it is more difficult to switch among various open objects. It is possible, but awkward, to switch from one object to another by pressing Ctrl+F6.

After you make your selections in the Access Options dialog box, click OK to save your changes. Access applies these interface settings to this current database the next time you open the file. To see the interface change, you need to close and reopen the database.

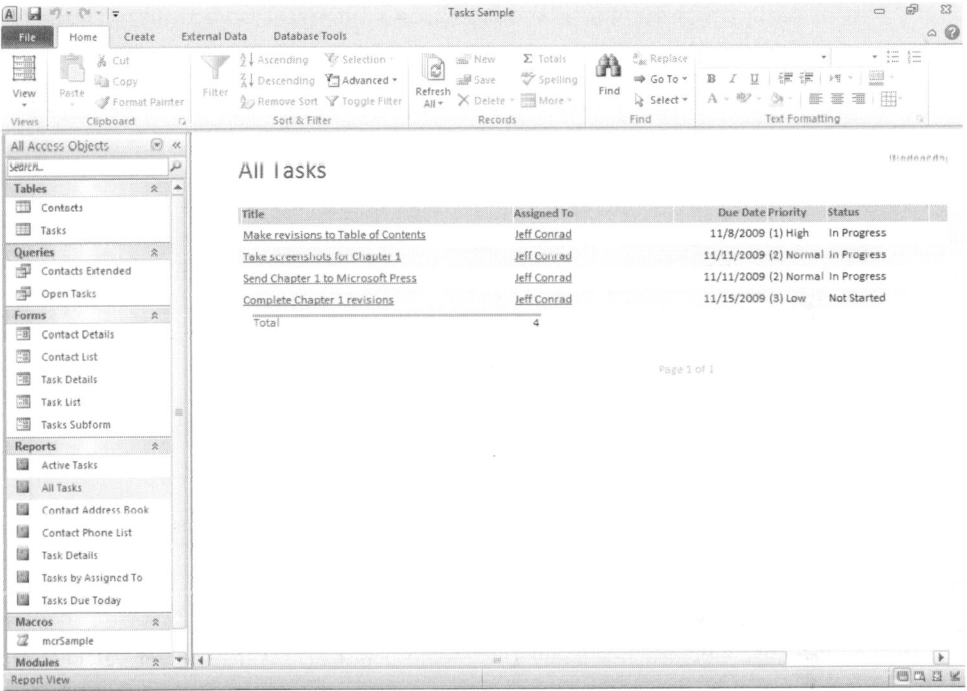

Figure 2-97 With Tabbed Documents selected and the Display Document Tabs check box cleared, no tabs for open objects appear at the top of the object window.

INSIDE OUT Why You Might Want to Use the Tabbed Documents Setting with No Tabs Visible

If you're creating an application for novice users, you might want to set up the application so that the user can work with only one object at a time. Presenting a single object minimizes the choices for the user. However, you will have to be sure to include a method to allow the user to navigate to other objects, perhaps with command buttons that execute VBA code or macros to open and set the focus to other objects. You must design such an application carefully so the user never gets "trapped" in one object, unable to get to others.

Modifying Global Settings via the Access Options Dialog Box

In addition to all the various commands and options available on the Backstage view, ribbon, and in the Navigation pane, Access 2010 has one central location for setting and modifying global options for all your Access database files or for only the database currently open. This location is the Access Options dialog box. To open the Access Options dialog box, click the File tab on the Backstage view and then click Options, as shown in Figure 2-98.

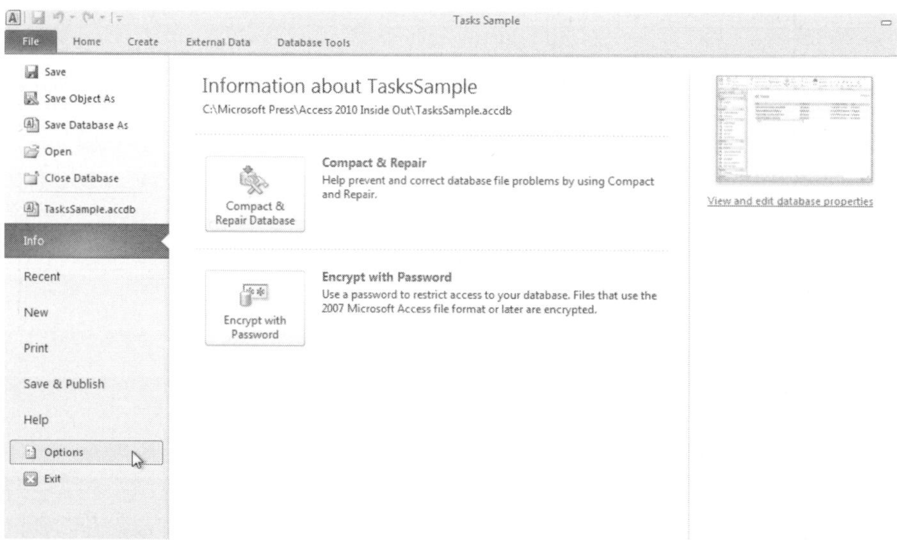

Figure 2-98 Click the File tab on the Backstage view and then click Options to open the Access Options dialog box.

The Access Options dialog box contains 11 categories in the left pane to organize the various options and settings. The first category, General, has settings that apply not only to Access 2010, but also any other Office 2010 system programs you might have installed.

From here, you can choose to enable Live Preview, display ScreenTips, select a color scheme for the application window, and enter a user name for use in all your Office 2010 system applications. In the Creating Databases section, you can choose a default file format for new databases that you create in Access 2010. By default, the file format is set to create all new databases in Access 2007 format. The Default Database Folder box displays the folder where Access will save all new database files unless you select a different folder when creating the database. Figure 2-99 shows the General category of the Access Options dialog box.

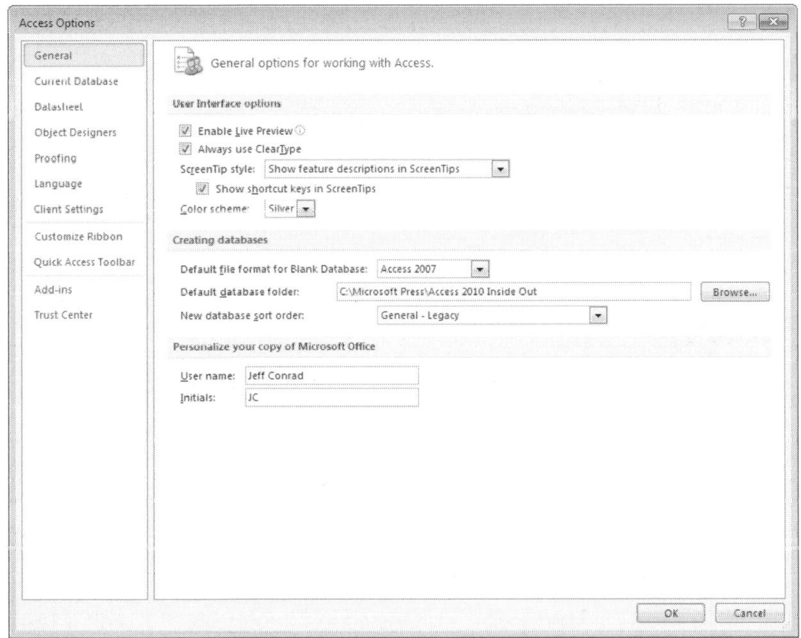

Figure 2-99 The General category has general settings for your Office system applications.

The Current Database category, shown in Figure 2-100, has many settings that apply only to the database currently open. This category groups the options into these areas: Application Options, Navigation, Ribbon And Toolbar Options, Name AutoCorrect Options, Filter Lookup Options, and Caching Web Service And SharePoint Tables.

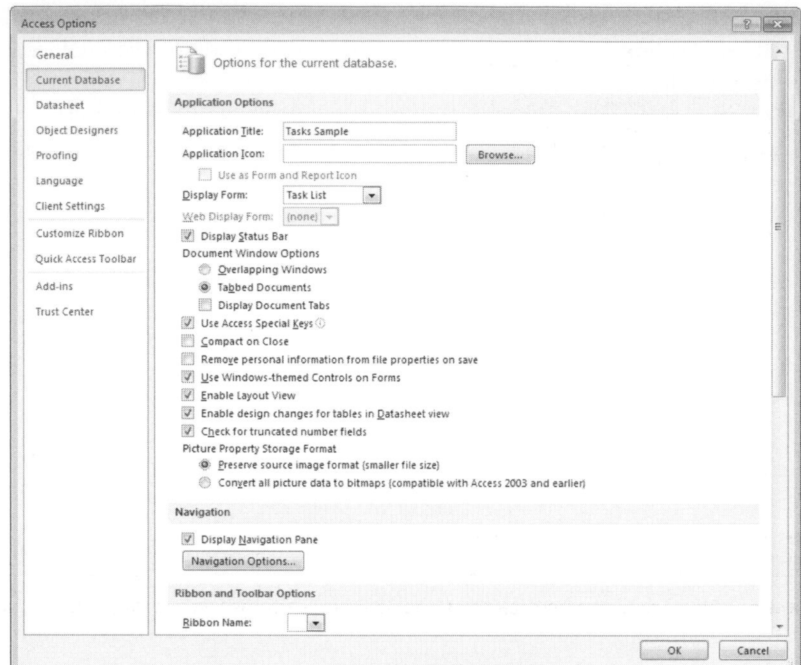

Figure 2-100 The Current Database category has general settings for the database currently open.

The Document Window Options section in this category was discussed previously in "Using the Single-Document vs. the Multiple-Document Interface," on page 107. Use Windows-Themed Controls On Forms will be discussed in Chapter 13, "Building a Form," and Chapter 14, "Customizing a Form." The remaining options in the Current Database category will be discussed in Chapter 26, "The Finishing Touches."

The Datasheet category, shown in Figure 2-101, has settings that control the appearance of the datasheet views in your database. This category has options grouped in the following sections—Gridlines And Cell Effects and Default Font—which allow you to modify the look of your datasheets with different colors, gridlines, and cell effects. You can also select a default font and size under Default Font. You'll learn more about applying these settings to datasheets in "Working in Query Datasheet View," on page 589, and in Chapter 12, "Using Forms in an Access Application," and Chapter 13, "Building a Form."

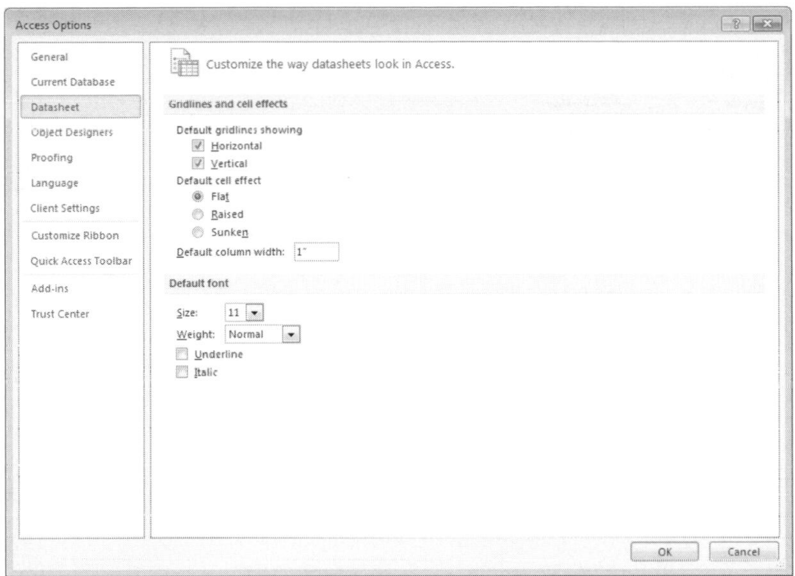

Figure 2-101 The Datasheet category has general settings to control the look of datasheets.

The Object Designers category, shown in Figure 2-102, includes settings for creating and modifying database objects in all databases. The Object Designers category is divided into four sections: Table Design View, Query Design, Form/Report Design View, and Error Checking In Form And Report Design View. The Table Design View section has settings for Default Field Type, Default Text Field Size, and Default Number Field Size. You'll learn more about the impact of these settings in Chapter 4, "Designing Client Tables." The Query Design section lets you select a default font and size for working in the query design grid. You'll learn more about the impact of these settings in Chapter 10, "Building Complex Queries." The Form/Report Design View section has options that allow you to use the existing form and report templates or choose a custom template that you have created. You'll learn more about these settings in Chapter 13, "Building a Form." The Error Checking In Form And Report Design View section has several default options that Access looks for when checking for errors in your database file. You'll learn more about these settings in Chapter 24, "Understanding Visual Basic Fundamentals," on the companion CD.

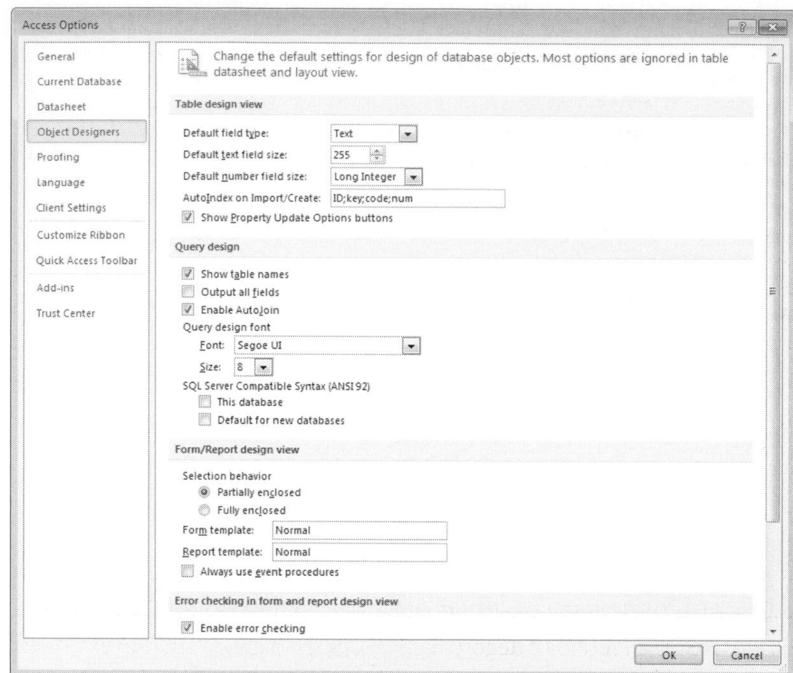

Figure 2-102 The Object Designers category has settings for working with database objects.

The Proofing category, shown in Figure 2-103, includes options for controlling the spelling and AutoCorrect features. You can click AutoCorrect Options to customize how Access helps you with common typing mistakes. You can also click Custom Dictionaries to select a custom dictionary to use when working with Access 2010 and the other Office 2010 system applications. See Chapter 26 for more information on these options.

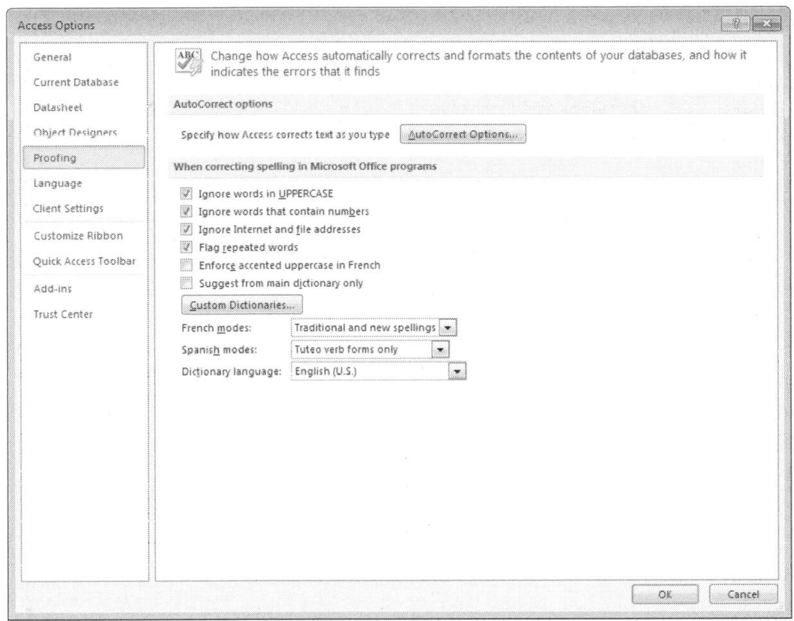

Figure 2-103 The Proofing category has settings for checking spelling and AutoCorrect.

The Language category, shown in Figure 2-104, contains options for controlling the language settings for your Access 2010 and Office 2010 installed programs. Under Choose Editing Languages, you can select a default editing language for Access 2010. If you have installed additional language packs, you can choose to change your default language to a different language. Under Choose Display and Help Languages, you can change what display language and Help language to use when working with Access 2010. Note that you will need to close your current session of Access and reopen to see these changes. If you click the arrow next to View Display Languages Installed for each Microsoft Office Program, a list expands beneath the arrow that lists all of the Office applications that you have installed and their display languages.

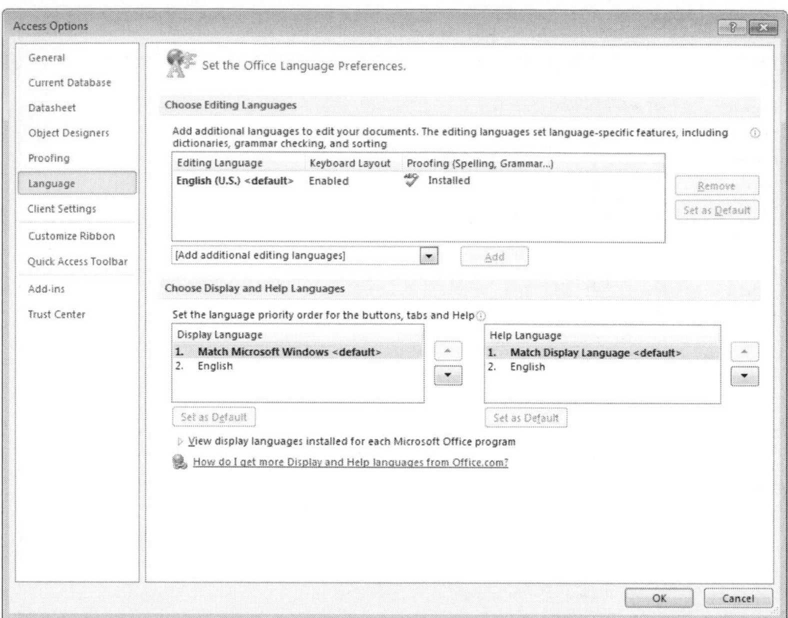

Figure 2-104 The Language category has settings for changing your editing, display, and Help language for Access 2010 and other Office 2010 programs.

The Client Settings category, shown in Figure 2-105, contains a wide variety of settings for Access 2010. This category has options grouped in the following sections: Editing, Display, Printing, General, Advanced, and Default Theme. Each of the settings on this category applies to all client database files that you use in Access 2010. Many of these settings are discussed later in various parts of this book. See Chapter 8, "Importing and Linking Data," and Chapter 9, "Creating and Working with Simple Queries," for more information.

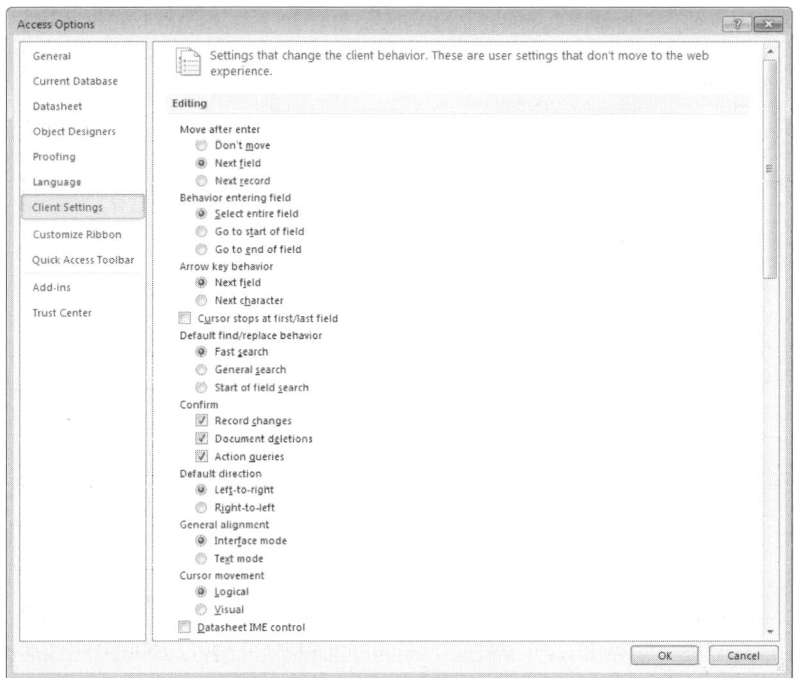

Figure 2-105 The Client Settings category has options for controlling editing, display, and printing.

The Customize Ribbon category, shown in Figure 2-106, was discussed previously in "Customizing the Ribbon," on page 63. This category is where you customize the ribbon. You can make modification to the built-in ribbon tabs or create your own custom ribbon tabs and groups.

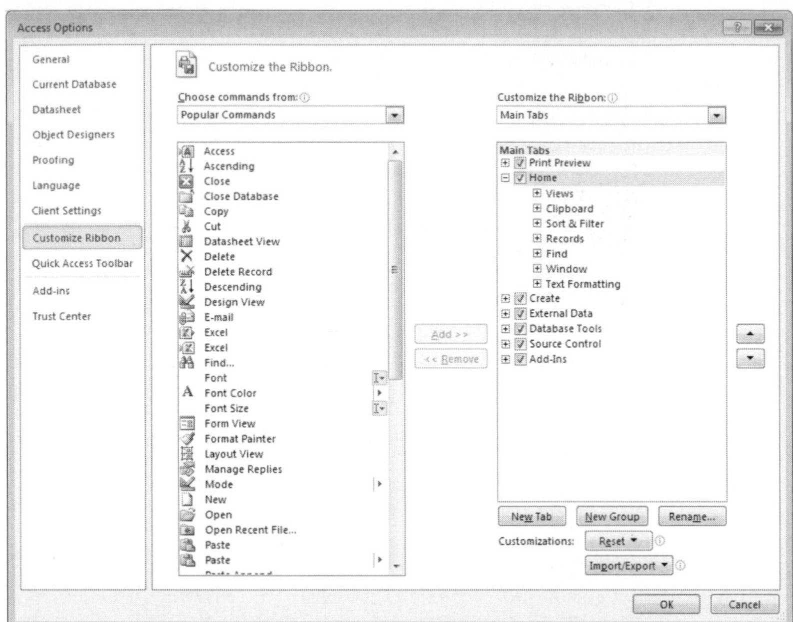

Figure 2-106 The Customize Ribbon category allows you to customize the ribbon.

The Quick Access Toolbar category, shown in Figure 2-107, was discussed previously in "Taking Advantage of the Quick Access Toolbar," on page 39. This category is where you customize the Quick Access Toolbar. You can make modifications to the Quick Access Toolbar for this specific database only or to the Quick Access Toolbar for all Access databases.

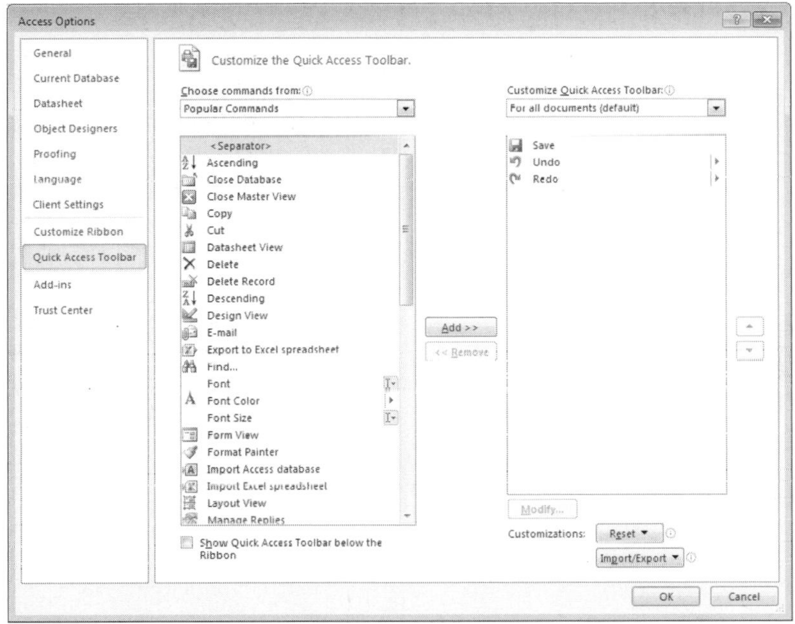

Figure 2-107 The Quick Access Toolbar category allows you to customize the Quick Access Toolbar.

The Add-Ins category, shown in Figure 2-108, lists all the various Access add-ins that might be installed on your computer. You can manage COM add-ins and Access add-ins from this area, and each add-in has its various properties listed. COM add-ins extend the ability of Access and other Office system applications with custom commands and specialized features. You can even disable certain add-ins to keep them from loading and functioning.

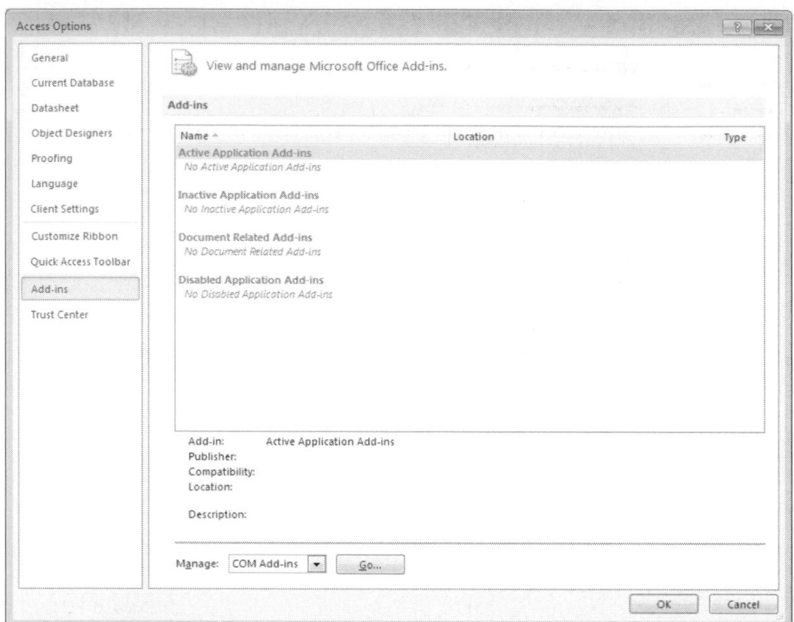

Figure 2-108 The Add-Ins category lists any installed Access add-ins and COM add-ins.

The Trust Center category, shown in Figure 2-109, is the last category in the Access Options dialog box. This category is where you access all Trust Center options for handling security. As we discussed earlier in "Understanding Content Security," on page 47, you can open the Trust Center Settings dialog box, which controls all aspects of macro security. This category also has links to online privacy and security information.

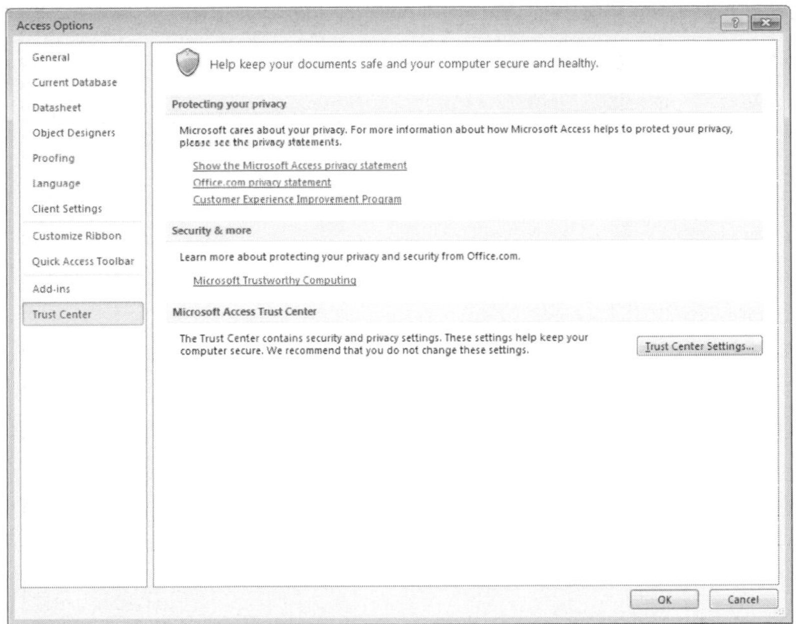

Figure 2-109 The Trust Center category has links to privacy and security information and the Trust Center Settings button, which allows you to view more options.

In the next chapter, you'll learn about the internal architecture of an Access 2010 application. You'll also open the Housing Reservations and Conrad Systems Contacts sample databases to explore some of the many features and functions of Access. Finally, you'll discover some of the ways that you can use Access as an application solution.

CHAPTER 3

Access 2010 Overview

Now that you are more comfortable with the user interface in Microsoft Access 2010, it's time to dig deeper into exactly what makes up an Access database. This chapter helps you understand the relationships among the main components in Access and shows you how to move around within the database management system.

The Architecture of Access

Access calls anything that can have a name an *object*. Within an Access database, the main objects are tables, queries, forms, reports, macros, and modules.

If you have worked with other database systems on desktop computers, you might have seen the term *database* used to refer to only those files in which you store data. In Access, however, a desktop database (.accdb) also includes all the major objects related to the stored data, including objects you define to automate the use of your data. You can also create an Access application using a project file (.adp) that contains the objects that define your application linked to a Microsoft SQL Server database that stores the tables and queries. Here is a summary of the major objects in an Access database:

- **Table** An object that you define and use to store data. Each table contains information about a particular subject, such as customers or orders. Tables contain *fields* (or *columns*) that store different kinds of data, such as a name or an address, and *records* (or *rows*) that collect all the information about a particular instance of the subject, such as all the information about a department named Housing Administration. You can define a *primary key* (one or more fields that have a unique value for each record) and one or more *indexes* on each table to help retrieve your data more quickly.

- **Query** An object that provides a custom view of data from one or more tables. In Access, you can use the graphical query by example (QBE) facility or you can write SQL statements to create your queries. You can define queries to select, update, insert, or delete data. You can also define queries that create new tables from data in one or more existing tables. When your Access application is a project file connected to an SQL Server database, you can create special types of queries—functions and stored procedures—that can perform complex actions directly on the server.

- **Form** An object designed primarily for data input or display or for control of application execution. You use forms to customize the presentation of data that your application extracts from queries or tables. You can also print forms. You can design a form to run a macro or a Microsoft Visual Basic procedure in response to any of a number of events—for example, to run a procedure when the value of data changes.

- **Report** An object designed for formatting, calculating, printing, and summarizing selected data. You can view a report on your screen before you print it.

- **Macro** An object that is a structured definition of one or more actions that you want Access to perform in response to a defined event. For example, you might design a macro that opens a second form in response to the selection of an item on a main form. You can include simple conditions in macros to specify when one or more actions in the macro should be performed or skipped. You can use macros to open and execute queries, to open tables, or to print or view reports. You can also run other macros or Visual Basic procedures from within a macro.

- **Module** An object containing custom procedures that you code using Visual Basic. Modules provide a more discrete flow of actions and allow you to trap errors. Modules can be stand-alone objects containing functions that can be called from anywhere in your application, or they can be directly associated with a form or a report to respond to events on the associated form or report.

For a list of events on forms and reports, see Chapter 19, "Understanding Event Processing."

INSIDE OUT What Happened to Data Access Pages?

Access 2010 no longer supports designing or executing *data access pages* (DAPs). Usability studies conducted by Microsoft show that DAPs are not a widely used feature within Access, and Microsoft is focusing more of their efforts on publishing Access databases to Microsoft SharePoint Services as Access Services applications for sharing data in corporate environments. To maintain backward compatibility with previous versions, Access 2010 will continue to display DAPs in the Navigation pane for existing .mdb applications that contain DAPs, but you cannot create new data access pages, modify existing pages, or execute existing pages from within Access 2010.

Figure 3-1 shows a conceptual overview of how objects in Access are related. Tables store the data that you can extract with queries and display in reports or that you can display and update in forms. Notice that forms and reports can use data either directly from tables or from a filtered view of the data created by using queries. Queries can use Visual Basic functions to provide customized calculations on data in your database. Access also has many built-in functions that allow you to summarize and format your data in queries.

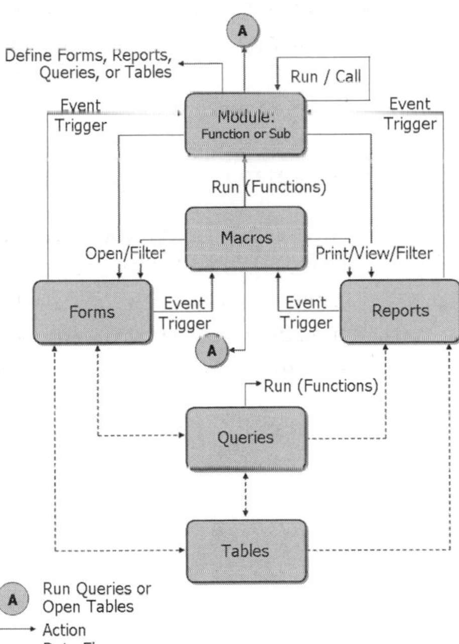

Figure 3-1 In an Access application, you can design queries to extract data from or update data in tables; you can build forms or reports on tables or queries, and you can write code in macros or modules to automate your application.

Events on forms and reports can trigger either macros or Visual Basic procedures. An event is any change in the state of an Access object. For example, you can write macros or Visual Basic procedures to respond to opening a form, closing a form, entering a new row on a form, or changing data either in the current record or in an individual control (an object on a form or report that contains data). You can even design a macro or a Visual Basic procedure that responds to the user pressing individual keys on the keyboard when entering data. In Access 2010, you can now also trigger macros to run on table events such as before committing data or after entering new data.

For more information about using data macros, see Chapter 7, "Creating Table Data Macros." For more information about using Visual Basic within Access, see Chapter 24, "Understanding Visual Basic Fundamentals," and Chapter 25, "Automating Your Application with Visual Basic," on the companion CD.

Using macros and modules, you can change the flow of your application, build new tables, run queries, and open, filter, and change data in forms and reports. Using Visual Basic, you can manipulate data in your database row by row or column by column, handle exceptional conditions, and create, modify, and delete any Access object. Using module code, you can even call Windows application programming interface (API) routines to extend your application beyond the built-in capabilities of Access.

Exploring a Desktop Database—Housing Reservations

Now that you know something about the major objects that make up an Access database, a good next step is to spend some time exploring the Housing Reservations database (Housing.accdb) on the companion CD that accompanies this book. First, follow the instructions at the beginning of this book for installing the sample files on your hard drive. When you start Access, it displays the New tab on the Microsoft Office Backstage view, as shown in Figure 3-2.

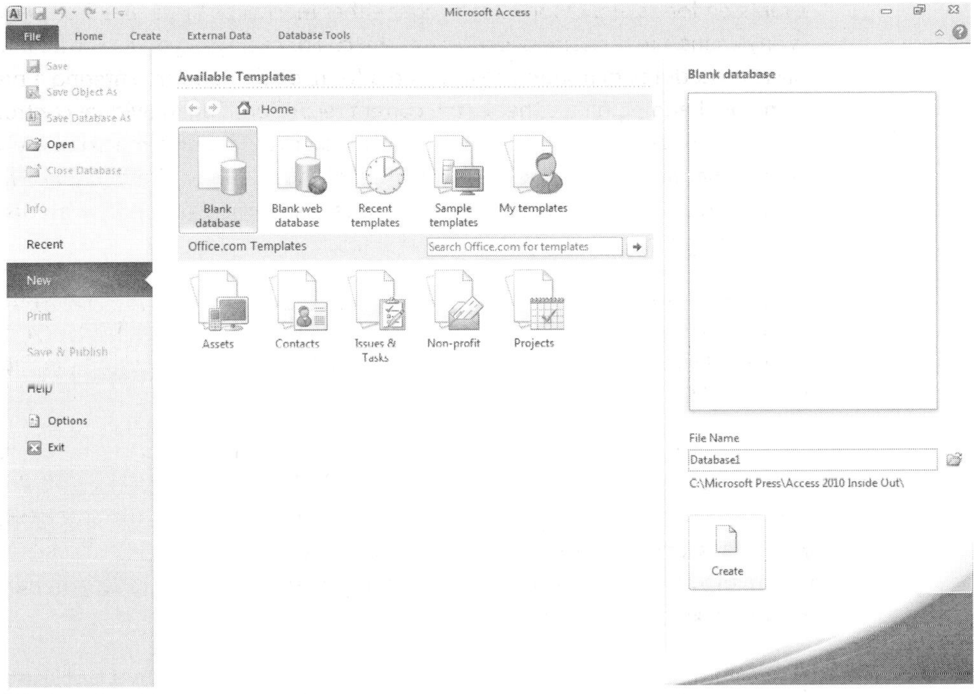

Figure 3-2 Access 2010 displays the New tab on the Backstage view every time you start the program.

Click the Open button on the left side of the window to see the Open dialog box shown in Figure 3-3. In the Open dialog box, select the file Housing.accdb from the folder in which you installed the sample databases, and then click Open. You can also double-click the file name to open the database. (If you haven't set options in Windows Explorer to show file name extensions for registered applications, you won't see the .accdb extension for your database files.)

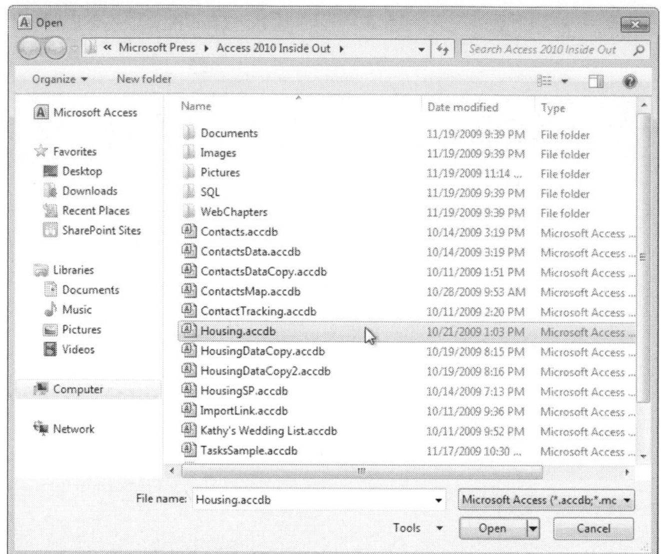

Figure 3-3 Use the Open dialog box to locate the database that you want to open.

When you open the Housing Reservations application, it displays a Not Trusted dialog box if you have not followed the instructions in Chapter 1, "What Is Access?" to define the location of the sample files as trusted. If this happens, click the Close button to close the dialog box. The application also briefly displays a copyright information notice and then displays a message box instructing you to open the frmSplash form. Click OK to dismiss this message box, and then Access puts the focus on the frmSplash form in the Navigation pane. (You can open the frmSplash form if you want to run the application, but for now, we'll just explore the interface.) Your Access window should look similar to Figure 3-4.

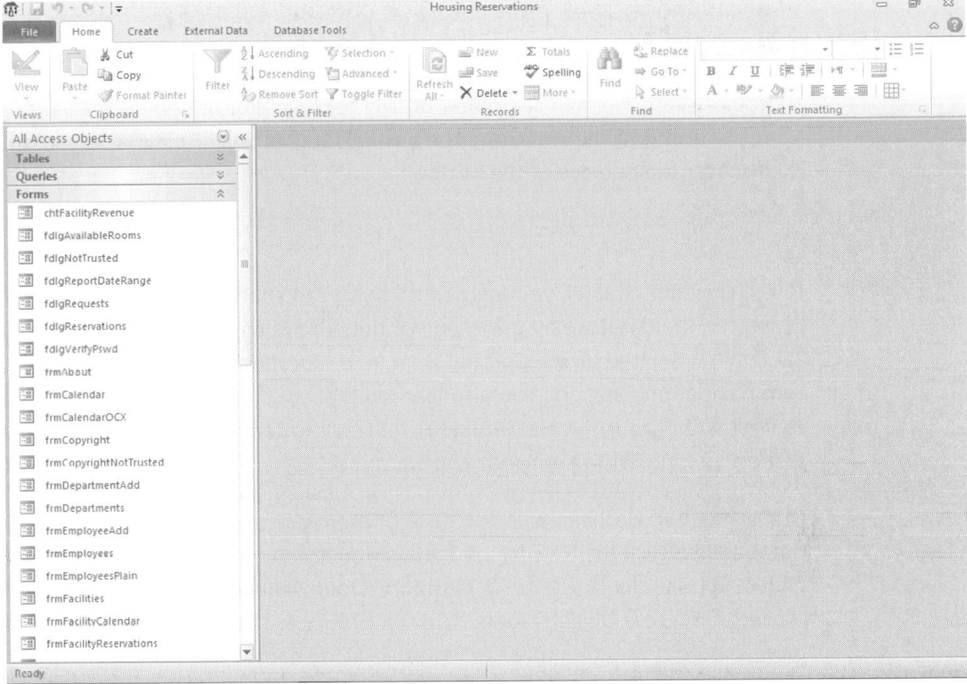

Figure 3-4 The Navigation pane displays the objects defined in the Housing Reservations sample database.

For an existing database, the Navigation pane is always the same width as it was when you last set it. The title bar of the window normally shows the name of the database that you have open. As you'll learn in Chapter 26, "The Finishing Touches," on the companion CD, you can set options in the database to change the title bar of the main Access window to show the name of your application instead of Access—we modified the sample database to display the title Housing Reservations on the title bar.

As we discussed in the previous chapter, the ribbon has four main tabs that are displayed at all times. As you explore Access 2010, you'll see that the ribbon provides several contextual tabs that appear and disappear as you work with specific database objects and areas of the program. These contextual tabs make available commands that are useful only within the context of the object that has the focus and that object's current view. For example, it wouldn't make sense to show you form design commands when you have a query open in Design view. We'll explain the various contextual tabs in more detail as we explore the database objects and other areas of Access in the following chapters.

INSIDE OUT Viewing ScreenTips

You can rest your mouse pointer on any command or option on the various ribbon tabs for a second (without clicking the button), and Access displays a ScreenTip to help you discover the purpose of the button.

In the previous chapter, you learned that you can change how Access displays the list of objects in the database by using one of the built-in navigation categories (Object Type, Tables And Related Views, Created Date, and Modified Date) or by defining your own custom navigation category. You also learned that you can filter each navigation category to limit what group Access displays within each category so that you don't have to wade through a long list to find what you want.

In this chapter, we'll be exploring each of the types of objects in the Housing Reservations database, so click the Navigation Pane menu at the top of the Navigation pane and click Object Type under Navigate To Category. Open the menu again and be sure that you have clicked All Access Objects under Filter By Group, as shown in Figure 3-5. Your Navigation pane should now look similar to Figure 3-4. You can collapse an entire group of objects by clicking the group's header bar. If you open the Navigation Pane menu, you can see the names of some custom groups we have defined under Navigate To Category to help organize your work. You'll learn how to work with groups later in this chapter.

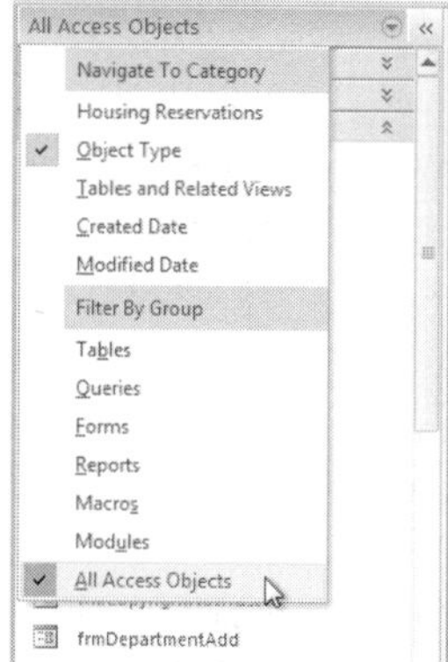

Figure 3-5 Select Object Type under Navigate To Category, and then select All Access Objects under Filter By Group to see all objects organized in groups by object type.

Tables

Click the menu bar at the top of the Navigation pane and select Object Type under Navigate To Category. Open the menu again and select Tables under Filter By Group to display a list of tables available in the Housing Reservations database, as shown in Figure 3-6.

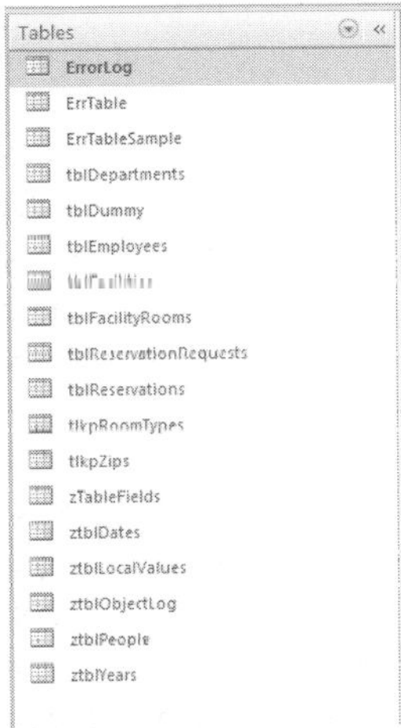

Figure 3-6 After filtering the Object Type category in the Navigation pane, you can see only the tables in the Housing Reservations database.

You can open a table in Datasheet view to see the data in the table by double-clicking the table name in the Navigation pane; or you can open the table in Design view by highlighting the table name, holding down the Ctrl key, and then pressing the Enter key. If you right-click a table name, Access displays a shortcut menu, as shown in Figure 3-7, that lets you perform a number of handy operations on the item you selected. Click one of the commands on the shortcut menu, or click anywhere else in the Access window to dismiss the menu.

INSIDE OUT Turning on Single Click

If you want to make it easier to open objects from the Navigation pane, you can right-click the menu bar at the top of the Navigation pane and select Navigation Options on the shortcut menu. In the lower-right corner of the Navigation Options dialog box, select Single-Click under Open Objects With and click OK. The examples in this chapter assume you are using the default Double-Click setting.

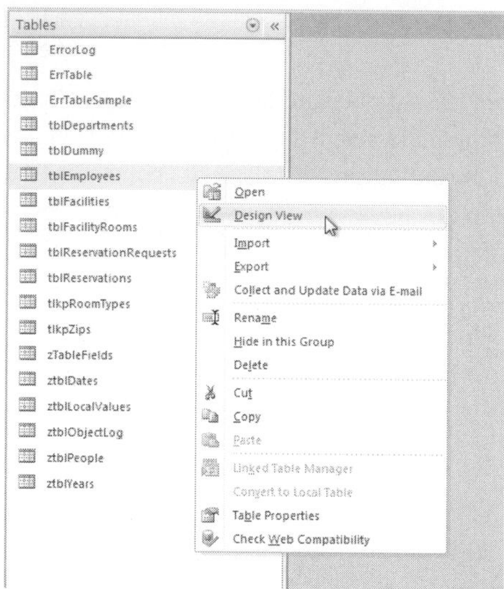

Figure 3-7 You can access many commands from the shortcut menu for a table in the Navigation pane.

Table Window in Design View

When you want to change the definition of a table (the structure or design of a table, as opposed to the data in a table), you generally must open the table in Design view. As you'll learn in Chapter 6, "Designing Web Tables," you can also make definition changes in Datasheet view while you are designing the table. For now, we will concentrate on changing the table definition in Design View. With the Housing Reservations database open, right-click the tblEmployees table and select Design View from the shortcut menu; this opens the tblEmployees table in Design view, as shown in Figure 3-8. (Collapse the Navigation pane to be able to see the entire width of the design area.) You'll learn about creating table definitions in Chapter 4, "Designing Client Tables."

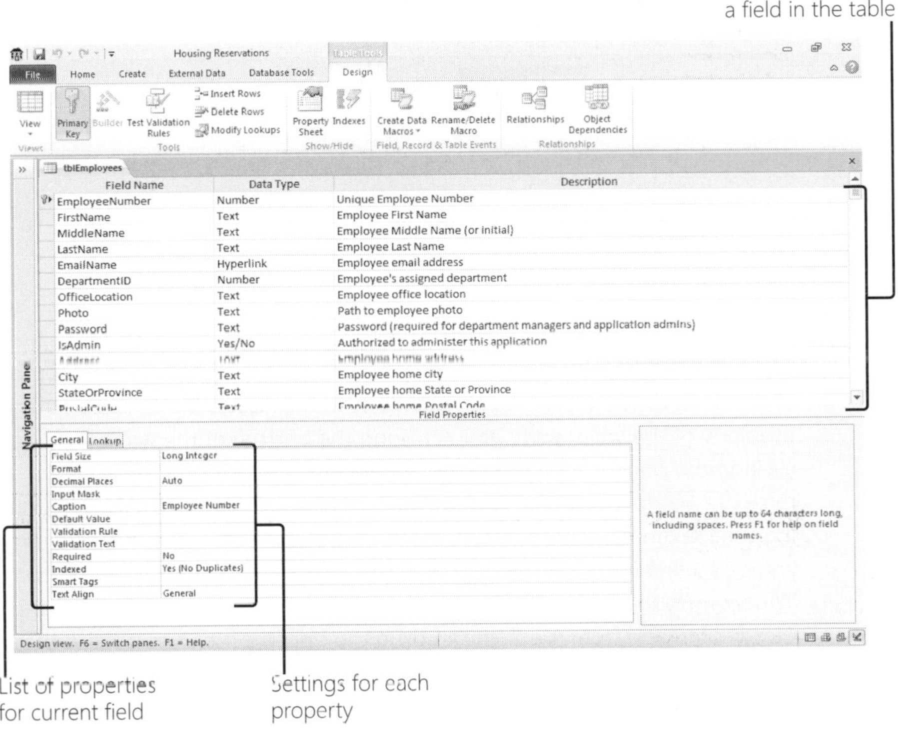

Figure 3-8 Open a table in Design view to change its structure.

In Design view, each row in the top portion of the Table window defines a different field in the table. You can use the mouse to select any field that you want to modify. You can also use the Tab key to move from left to right across the screen, column to column, or Shift+Tab to move from right to left. Use the Up and Down Arrow keys to move from row to row in the field list. As you select a different row in the field list in the top portion of the window, you can see the property settings for the selected field in the bottom portion of the window. Press F6 to move between the field list and the field property settings portions of the Table window in Design view. Unlike versions of Access before Access 2007, pressing F6 again does not immediately move the focus back to the field list. If you press F6 repeatedly, the focus goes to the Navigation pane, to the ribbon, and then finally back to the field list.

Access has many convenient features. Wherever you can choose from a limited list of valid values, Access provides a list box to assist you in selecting the proper value. For example, when you tab to the Data Type column in the field list, a small arrow appears at the right of the column. Click the arrow or press Alt+Down Arrow to see the list of valid data types, as shown in Figure 3-9.

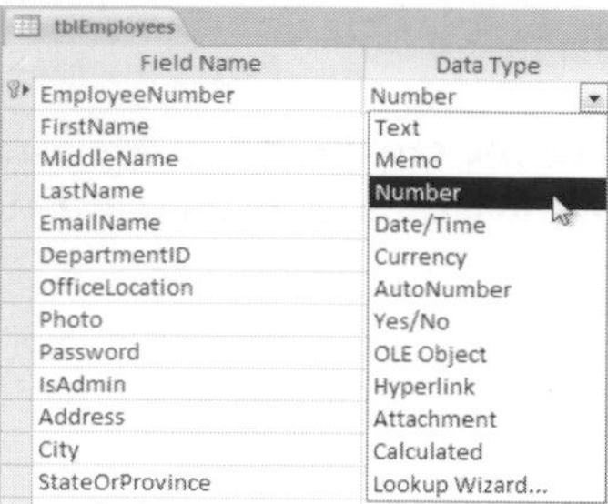

Figure 3-9 The Data Type list box shows you the available data types.

You can open as many as 254 tables (fewer if you are limited by your computer's memory). If you have selected Overlapping Windows in the Access Options dialog box, you can minimize any of the windows to an icon along the bottom of the Access workspace window by clicking the Minimize button in the upper-right corner of the window. You can also maximize the window to fill the Access workspace to the right of the Navigation pane by clicking the Maximize/Restore button in that same corner. If you don't see a window you want, you can select it from the list of active windows in the Switch Windows command in the Window group on the Home tab on the ribbon to bring the window to the front. Click the Close command from the Control Box in the upper-left corner, or click the window's Close button in the upper-right corner to close any window.

TROUBLESHOOTING

Why can't I see the Maximize/Minimize buttons on my table?

If you are using the Tabbed Documents interface (the setting used in the Housing Reservations sample database), each open object has its own tab to the right of the Navigation pane. This option is the default for new databases you create in Access 2010. However, when you open older database files created in earlier versions of Access before Access 2007, the Document Window Options setting in the Access Options dialog box defaults to Overlapping Windows. With the Tabbed Documents setting, there is no need to constantly minimize and maximize object windows to switch views because each open object has an individual tab at the top of the Access workspace (the area below the ribbon and to the right of the Navigation pane). Clicking on these object tabs enables you to switch easily among any open objects, so Access 2010 does not provide the Maximize/Minimize buttons. To set your database to Overlapping Windows or Tabbed Documents, see "Using the Single-Document vs. the Multiple-Document Interface," on page 107.

Table Window in Datasheet View

To view, change, insert, or delete data in a table, you can use the table's Datasheet view. A datasheet is a simple way to look at your data in rows and columns without any special formatting. You can open a table's Datasheet view by double-clicking the name of the table you want in the Navigation pane or by right-clicking on the table name and selecting Open from the shortcut menu. When you open a table in Design view, such as the tblEmployees table shown in Figure 3-8, you can switch to the Datasheet view of this table, shown in Figure 3-10, by clicking the arrow in the Views group on the ribbon and clicking Datasheet View from the list of available views. Likewise, when you're in Datasheet view, you can return to Design view by clicking the arrow in the Views group and clicking Design View from the available options. You can also switch views for the table by clicking the various view buttons on the status bar located in the lower-right corner of the Access window. You'll read more about working with data in Datasheet view in Chapter 9, "Creating and Working with Simple Queries."

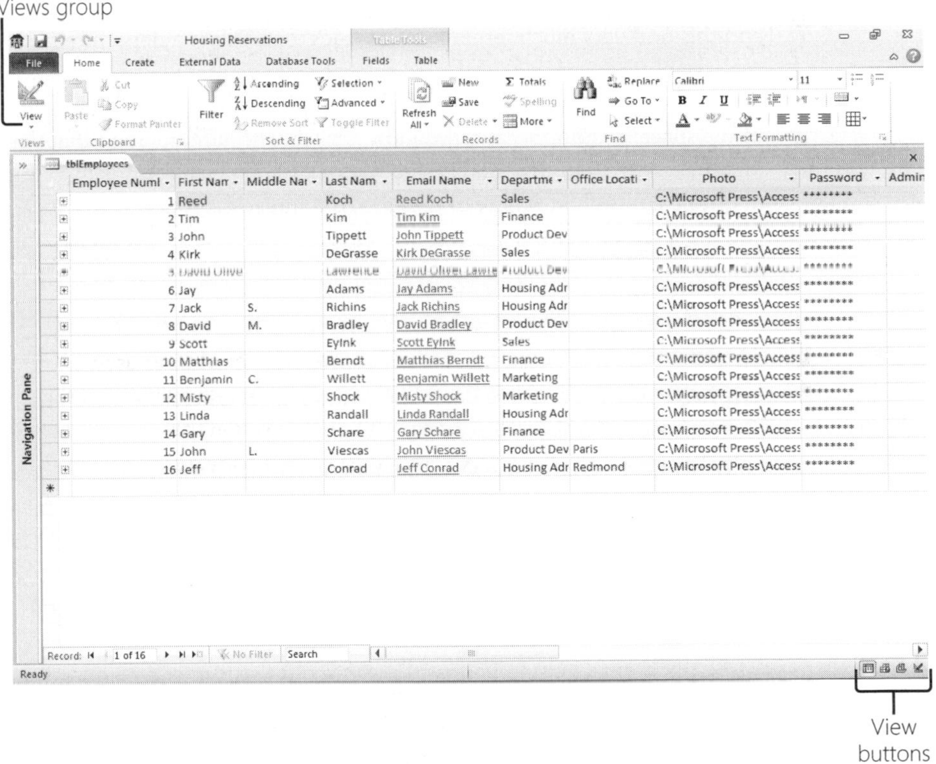

Figure 3-10 Use the Views button on the ribbon or the individual view buttons on the status bar to switch from Design view to Datasheet view.

As in Design view, you can move from field to field in the Table window in Datasheet view by pressing Tab, and you can move up and down through the records using the arrow keys. You can also use the scroll bars along the bottom and on the right side of the window to move around in the table. To the left of the horizontal scroll bar, Access shows you the current record number and the total number of records in the currently selected set of data. You can select the record number with your mouse (or by pressing Alt+Shift+F5), type a new number, and then press Enter to go to that record. You can use the arrows on either side of this record number box to move up or down one record or to move to the first or last record in the table. You can start entering data in a new record by clicking the New (Blank) Record button on the right.

TROUBLESHOOTING

Why does my table have extra rows in the lower half of the screen like a spreadsheet?

You might notice in Figure 3-10 that there are extra rows beneath our existing records, and this grid very much resembles a spreadsheet. This is a departure from versions of Access before Access 2007, which displayed only one row for each record in that table, plus one for a new record. For tables in Datasheet view in Access 2010, the remainder of the space in the application window is filled with dummy rows that you cannot click into. In essence, these extra rows are simply placeholders for possible future records. It might be confusing to think of this grid as a spreadsheet because of its appearance, but you must remember that Access is not a spreadsheet. What you see is only a visual aid and does not denote actual records in the tables.

Queries

You probably noticed that the Datasheet view of the tblEmployees table gave you all the fields and all the records in the table. But what if you want to see only the employee names and addresses? Or maybe you would like to see in one view information about employees and all their confirmed room reservations. To fill these needs, you can create a query. To do this, open the Navigation Pane menu, click Object Type under Navigate To Category if it isn't already selected, and then click Queries under Filter By Group to display a list of queries available in the Housing Reservations database, as shown in Figure 3-11.

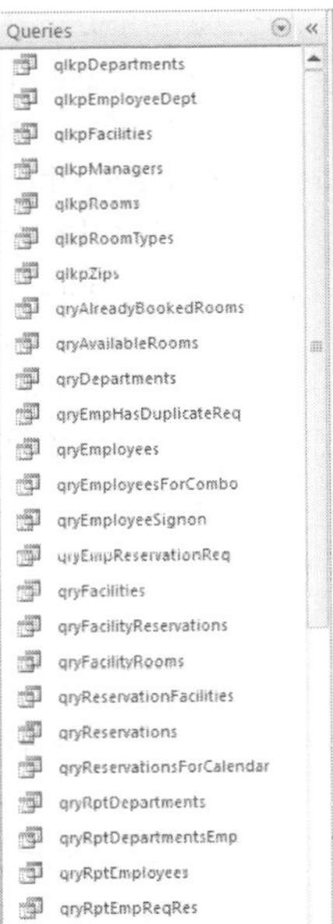

Figure 3-11 When you filter object types by queries in the Navigation pane, Access displays a list of only the queries in the Housing Reservations database.

You can open a query in Datasheet view by double-clicking the query name, or you can open it in Design view by clicking the query to select it, and then pressing Ctrl+Enter. You can also right-click a query and click the Open or Design View command from the shortcut menu.

Query Window in Design View

When you want to change the definition of a query (the structure or design, as opposed to the data represented in the query), you must open the query in Design view. Take a look at one of the more complex queries in the Housing Reservations query list by scrolling to the query named qryFacilityReservations. Select the query and then press Ctrl+Enter to display the query in Design view, as shown in Figure 3-12. Collapse the Navigation pane to see more of the width of the query design.

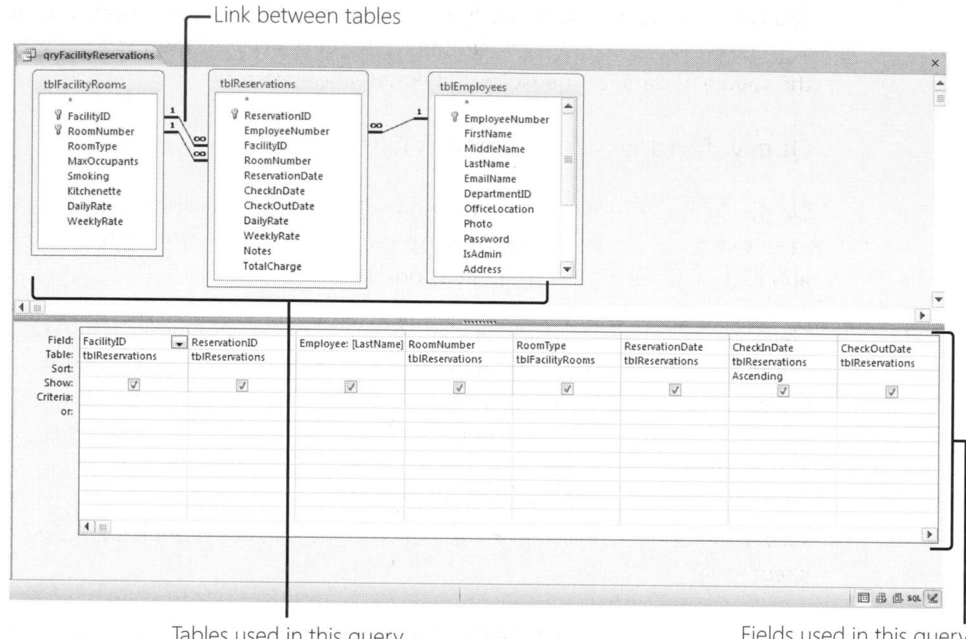

Figure 3-12 The qryFacilityReservations query in Design view shows data from three tables being linked.

In the upper part of a Query window in Design view, you see the field lists of the tables or other queries that this query uses. The lines connecting the field lists show how Access links the tables to solve your query. If you define relationships between two tables in your database design, Access draws these lines automatically when you include both tables in a query design. See Chapter 4 for details. You can also define relationships when you build the query by dragging a field from one field list to another field list.

In the lower part of the Query window, you see the design grid. The design grid shows fields that Access uses in this query, the tables or queries from which the fields come (when you select Table Names in the Show/Hide group on the ribbon's Design tab), any sorting criteria, whether fields show up in the result, and any selection criteria for the fields. You can use the horizontal scroll bar to bring other fields in this query into view. As in the Design view of tables, you can use F6 to move between the upper and lower portions of the Query window, but the F6 key also cycles through the Query window, the Navigation pane, and the ribbon.

You can learn how to build this type of complex multiple-table query in Chapter 10, "Building Complex Queries." You can find this query used in the Housing Reservations database as the source of data for the fsubFacilityReservations form.

Query Window in Datasheet View

On the Design or Home tab on the ribbon, click View to run the query and see the query results in Datasheet view, as shown in Figure 3-13. You can also right-click the query tab and click Datasheet View from the shortcut menu.

The Query window in Datasheet view is similar to a Table window in Datasheet view. Even though the fields in the query datasheet shown in Figure 3-13 are from three different tables, you can work with the fields as if they were in a single table. If you're designing an Access application for other users, you can use queries to hide much of the complexity of the database and make the application simpler to use. Depending on how you designed the query, you might also be able to update some of the data in the underlying tables simply by typing new values in the Query window as you would in a Table window in Datasheet view.

qryFacilityReservations

Facility	Reservation	Employee	Room	Type	Reservation	Check-In	Ch
South Campus Housing C	7	Koch, Reed	501	2BR Suite - 1 King, 2 Queen, Kitchenette	8/18/2010	8/24/2010	
Main Campus Housing A	1	Richins, Jack S.	810	Studio - Queen Sofa	8/2/2010	8/30/2010	
North Satellite Housing D	3	Lawrence, Davi	305	1BR Suite - 2 Queen Beds	8/9/2010	9/13/2010	
Main Campus Housing B	2	Richins, Jack S.	111	2BR Suite - 1 King, 2 Queen, Kitchenette	8/6/2010	9/17/2010	
Main Campus Housing A	12	Tippett, John	207	Room - King bed	9/7/2010	9/18/2010	
Main Campus Housing B	11	Lawrence, Davi	301	1BR Suite - 2 Queen Beds	9/6/2010	9/10/2010	
Main Campus Housing B	5	Tippett, John	214	Room - 2 Queen beds	8/11/2010	9/19/2010	
Main Campus Housing A	6	Berndt, Matthi	902	2BR Suite - 1 King, 2 Queen beds	8/15/2010	9/25/2010	
Main Campus Housing A	13	Bradley, David	111	1BR Suite - 1 King Bed, Kitchenette	9/16/2010	9/28/2010	
Main Campus Housing B	15	Adams, Jay	206	1BR Suite - 1 King Bed, Kitchenette	9/20/2010	9/28/2010	
Main Campus Housing A	4	Tippett, John	502	2BR Suite - 1 King, 2 Queen beds	8/10/2010	10/8/2010	
Main Campus Housing A	8	Bradley, David	509	Room - 2 Queen beds	8/21/2010	10/10/2010	
Main Campus Housing B	9	Kim, Tim	504	1BR Suite - 1 King Bed	8/21/2010	10/14/2010	
Main Campus Housing A	14	Richins, Jack S.	708	Studio - Queen Sofa, Kitchenette	9/17/2010	10/21/2010	
South Campus Housing C	17	DeGrasse, Kirk	101	2BR Suite - 1 King, 2 Queen, Kitchenette	9/26/2010	10/25/2010	
Main Campus Housing A	10	Tippett, John	707	Room - King bed	9/1/2010	10/26/2010	
South Campus Housing C	22	Bradley, David	103	1BR Suite - 1 King Bed	10/18/2010	10/27/2010	
Main Campus Housing A	20	Lawrence, Davi	309	Room - 2 Queen beds	10/3/2010	10/29/2010	
North Satellite Housing D	21	Bradley, David	402	1BR Suite - 1 King Bed, Kitchenette	10/6/2010	11/2/2010	
South Campus Housing C	16	Richins, Jack S.	111	Studio - Queen Sofa	9/20/2010	11/13/2010	
Main Campus Housing A	18	Bradley, David	702	2BR Suite - 1 King, 2 Queen beds	9/30/2010	11/16/2010	
Main Campus Housing B	19	Lawrence, Davi	610	2BR Suite - 1 King, 2 Queen, Kitchenette	10/2/2010	11/16/2010	
Main Campus Housing A	24	Tippett, John	207	Room - King bed	10/25/2010	11/18/2010	
Main Campus Housing B	28	Bradley, David	403	2BR Suite - 1 King, 2 Queen beds	10/31/2010	11/18/2010	
Main Campus Housing A	27	Willett, Benjan	505	Room - King bed	10/30/2010	11/26/2010	

Record: 1 of 58 No Filter Search

Figure 3-13 The Datasheet view of the qryFacilityReservations query shows you fields from three related tables.

Forms

Datasheets are useful for viewing and changing data in your database, but they're not particularly attractive or simple to use. If you want to format your data in a special way or automate how your data is used and updated, you need to use a form. Forms provide a number of important capabilities:

- You can control and enhance the way your data looks on the screen. For example, you can add color and shading or add number formats. You can add controls such as list boxes and check boxes. You can display ActiveX objects such as pictures and graphs directly on the form. And you can calculate and display values based on data in a table or a query.
- You can perform extensive editing of data using macros or Visual Basic procedures.
- You can link multiple forms or reports by using macros or Visual Basic procedures that are run from buttons on a form.

Click the menu bar at the top of the Navigation pane, click Object Type under Navigate To Category, and then click Forms under Filter By Group to display a list of forms available in the Housing Reservations database, as shown in Figure 3-14.

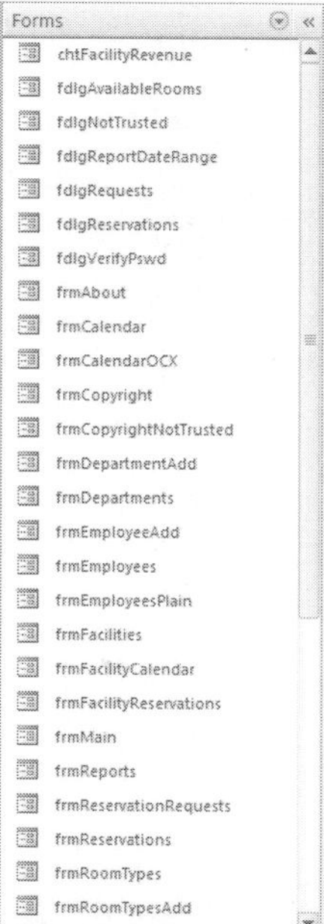

Figure 3-14 When you filter Object Type by Forms, Access displays a list of only the forms in the Housing Reservations database.

You can open a form in Form view by double-clicking the form name in the Navigation pane. You can also open the form in Design view by clicking the form to highlight it, and then pressing Ctrl+Enter. Finally, you can right-click a form name and click a command from the shortcut menu. To create a new form, use the commands in the Forms group of the Create tab on the ribbon.

Form Window in Design View

When you want to change the definition of a form (the structure or design, as opposed to the data represented in the form), you generally must open the form in Design view. As you'll learn in Chapter 14, "Customizing a Form," you can also set a form property to allow you to make changes in Layout view while you are designing the form. Take a look at the frmEmployeesPlain form in the Housing Reservations database. To open the form, scroll through the list of forms in the Navigation pane to find the frmEmployeesPlain form, click the form to select it, then press Ctrl+Enter. This form, shown in Figure 3-15, is designed to display all data from the tblEmployees table. Don't worry if what you see on your screen doesn't exactly match Figure 3-15. In this figure, we opened the field list on the right so that you can see some of the main features of the Form window in Design view.

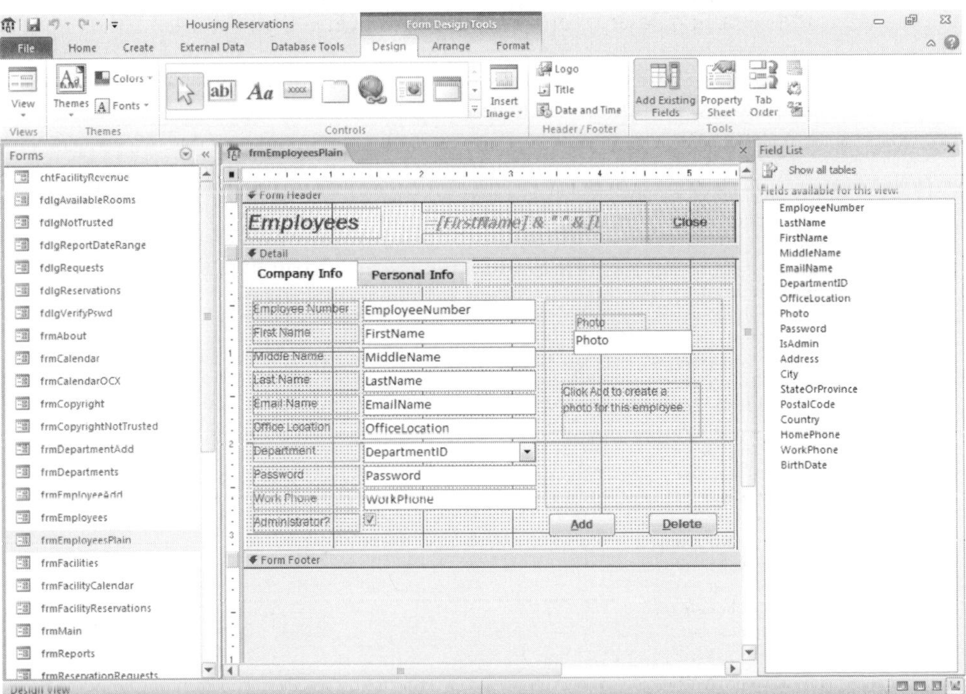

Figure 3-15 When you open the frmEmployeesPlain form in Design view, you can modify its design.

The large window in the center is the form design window where you create the design of the form. When you first open this form in Design view, you should see the Form Design Tools collection of three contextual tabs, Design, Arrange, and Format, on the ribbon just to the right of Database Tools. These tabs are the action centers of form design—you'll use the tools here to add and arrange the design elements of your form.

On the right side of the window shown in Figure 3-15, you can see a field list for this form, called the Data Source Task Pane. This form gets its information from a query called qryEmployees that selects all the fields in the tblEmployees table and then sorts the rows by last name and first name. If you don't see the field list, click the Add Existing Fields command in the Tools group of the Design contextual tab. You can resize this window by clicking on the far-left edge of the box and dragging it to a new width toward the left side of the screen. When your mouse pointer is positioned over the title bar, it changes to cross arrows. Click the title bar and drag it to the left and down to undock the window from the right side and position it where you like. When you undock the Field List window, it becomes a window that floats on top of the design area. When you read about form design in Chapter 13, "Building a Form," you'll see that you can drag a field from the field list to place a control on the form that displays the contents of the field.

After you place all the controls on a form, you might want to customize some of them. You do this by opening the property sheet displayed in Figure 3-16. To see the property sheet, click the Property Sheet button in the Tools group of the Design tab. In Figure 3-16, we collapsed the Navigation pane to show more of the property sheet.

The property sheet always shows the property values for the control selected in the form design. (The property sheet can also display the properties for the form or any section on the form.) Click the tabs at the top of the property sheet to display all properties or to display only properties for formats, data, or events. In the example shown in Figure 3-16, we clicked the text box named EmployeeNumber, near the top of the form, to select it. If you click this text box and then scroll down the list of properties for it, you can see the wide range of properties you can set to customize this control. As you learn to build applications using Access, you'll soon discover that you can customize the way your application works by simply setting form and control properties—you don't have to write any code.

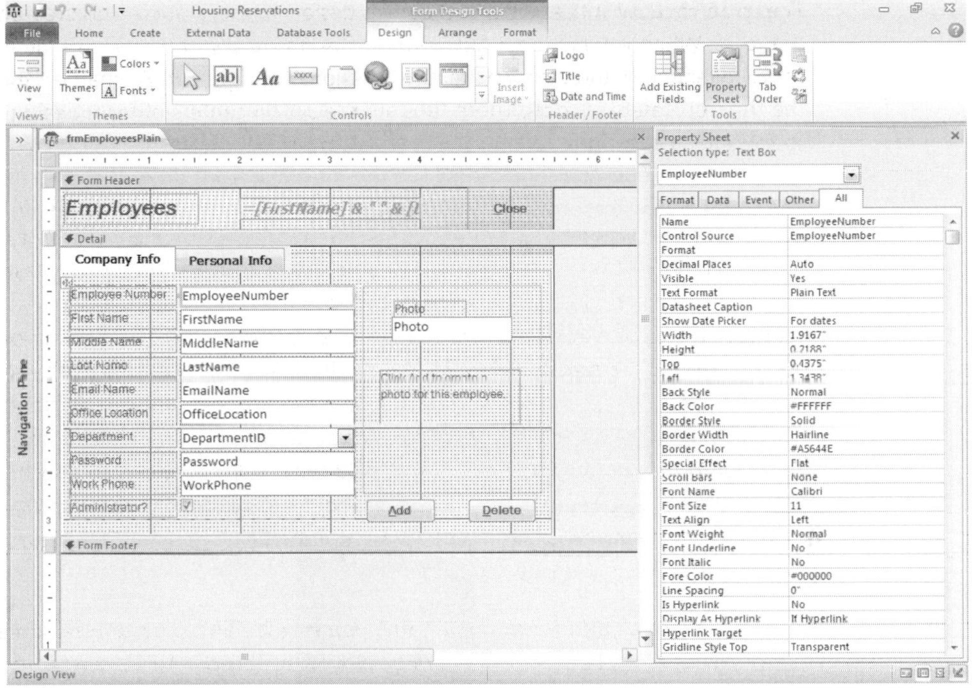

Figure 3-16 The property sheet lets you set individual properties for a form, form sections, or form controls.

If you scroll to the bottom of the property list or click the Event tab, you'll see a number of properties that you can set to define the macros or Visual Basic procedures that Access runs whenever the associated event occurs on this control. For example, you can use the Before Update event property to define a macro or procedure that performs additional validation before Access saves any changes typed in this control. You can use the On Click or On Dbl Click event properties to perform actions when the user clicks the control. If you need to, you can even look at every individual character the user types in a control with the On Key event properties. As you'll discover later, Access provides a rich set of events that you can detect for the form and for each control on the form.

Form Window in Layout View

In Access 2007, Microsoft introduced a new view for forms called Layout view. If you have the frmEmployeesPlain form from the previous section open in Design view, you can switch to Layout view by right-clicking the frmEmployeesPlain tab and clicking Layout View from the shortcut menu. You should now see the form in Layout view, as shown in Figure 3-17. This unique view for forms gives the developer a fast and easy way to create and modify form designs.

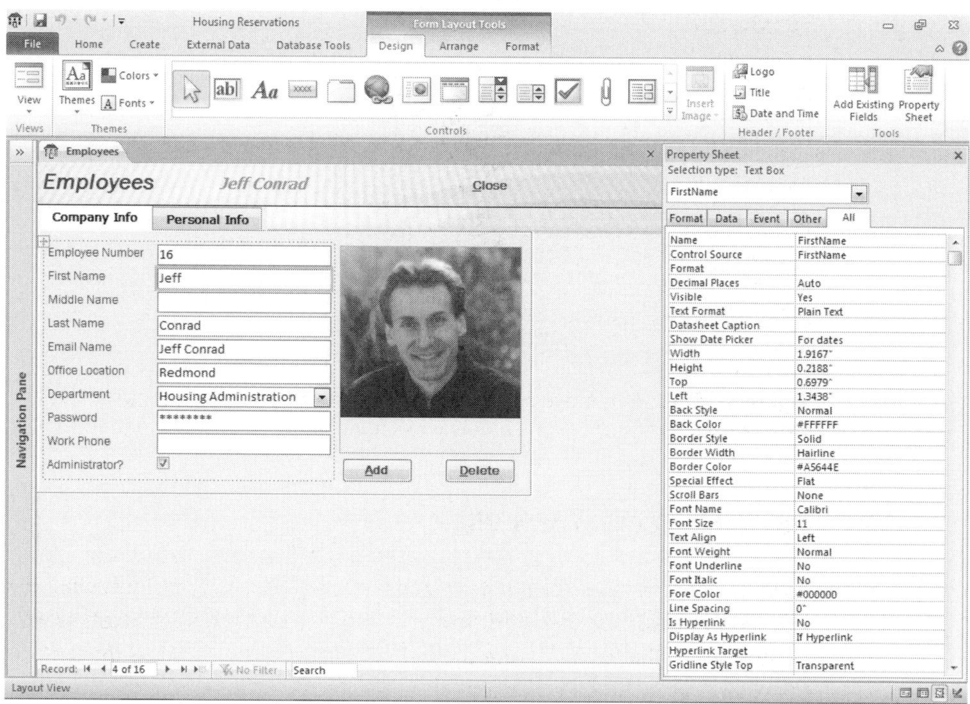

Figure 3-17 Layout view lets you see your data and also modify the design of the form.

Unlike Design view, Layout view enables you to work with the various control elements and form sections using existing live data. If, for example, you need to resize a text box to fit the available data, you do not have to switch back and forth continually between Form view and Design view to see if your size change works effectively—you actually see data in the text box while resizing the control. This What You See Is What You Get (WYSIWYG) form-authoring view provides the best of both worlds by combining the ability to change the structure of the data entry form at the same time you're accessing actual data.

If you have grouped a set of controls in Layout view, you can move the controls around the form design grid together to maintain their proximity and orientation to one another. In this sample form, we grouped all the controls in the first column in a stacked layout. In Figure 3-18, you can see that we're dragging the Email Name field down below the Office Location field. A horizontal bar designates where Access will place the control after you release the mouse button. Because these controls are grouped, Access places the Email Name field below the Office Location field and aligns it perfectly.

Figure 3-18 You can move a control within a group in Layout view, and Access keeps all the controls perfectly aligned.

Form Window in Form View

To view, change, insert, or delete data via a form, you can use Form view. Depending on how you've designed the form, you can work with your data in an attractive and clear context, have the form validate the information you enter, or use the form to trigger other forms or reports based on actions you take while viewing the form. You can open a form in Form view by right-clicking the form's name in the Navigation pane and clicking Open from the shortcut menu. If you still have the frmEmployeesPlain form from the previous section open in Layout view, you can go directly to Form view by clicking the arrow in the Views group and then clicking Form View.

Figure 3-19 shows a complex form that brings together data from three tables and loads the related employee picture from a file on your hard drive into a screen that's easy to use and understand. This form includes all the fields from the tblEmployees table. You can tab or use the arrow keys to move through the fields. You can click the Personal Info tab to see additional information about the current employee. You can experiment with filtering by selection to see how easy it is to select only the records you want to see. For example, you can click in the Department field, select the department name, click the Selection button in the Sort & Filter group on the Home tab, and then click Equals "Selected Department" (where "Selected Department" is the department name you highlighted) to display records only for the current department.

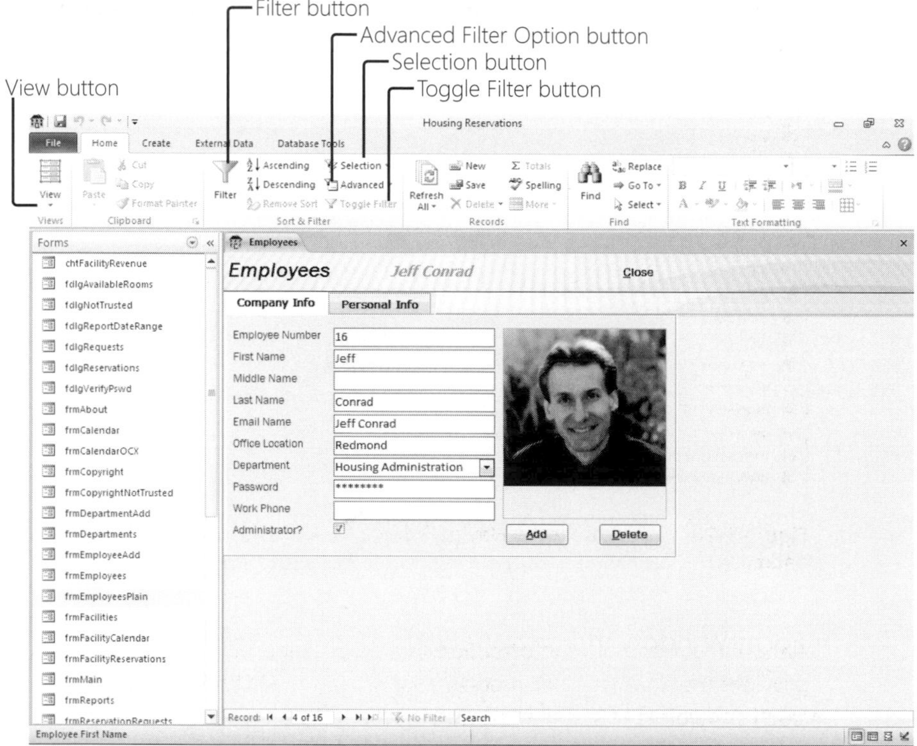

Figure 3-19 The frmEmployeesPlain form in Form view lets you view and edit employee data.

There are four other ways to look at a form: Datasheet view, PivotTable view, PivotChart view, and Print Preview. You can select the Datasheet view by clicking the arrow in the Views group and clicking Datasheet View to see all the fields in the form arranged in a datasheet, similar to a datasheet for a table or a query. When a form has been designed to display data in a PivotTable (similar to a spreadsheet) or graphed in a PivotChart, you can also select these views with the View button. You can click the File tab on the Backstage view, click Print, and then click Print Preview to see what the form will look like on a printed page. You'll read more about Print Preview in the next section.

Reports

If your primary need is to print data, you should use a report. Click the menu bar at the top of the Navigation pane to open the Navigation Pane menu and click Object Type under Navigate To Category. Then open the menu again and click the Reports option under Filter By Group to display a list of reports available in the Housing Reservations database, as shown in Figure 3-20.

Figure 3-20 You can filter the Navigation pane to show only a list of the reports in your database.

Although you can print information in a datasheet or a form, neither of these formats provides the flexibility that reports do when you need to produce complex printed output (such as invoices or summaries) that might include many calculations and subtotals. Formatting in datasheets is limited to sizing the rows and columns, specifying fonts, and setting the colors and gridline effects. You can do a lot of formatting in a form, but because forms are designed primarily for viewing and entering data on the screen, they are not suited for extensive calculations, grouping of data, or multiple totals and subtotals in print.

Report Window in Design View

When you want to change the definition of a report, you generally must open the report in Design view. As you'll learn in Chapter 17, "Constructing a Report," you can also make changes in Layout view while you are designing the report. In the report list for Housing Reservations, click the rptEmployeesPlain report to highlight it, and then press Ctrl+Enter to see the design for the report, as shown in Figure 3-21. Don't worry if what you see on your screen doesn't exactly match Figure 3-21. We clicked the Add Existing Fields command on the Design tab under Report Design Tools to display the Field List window.

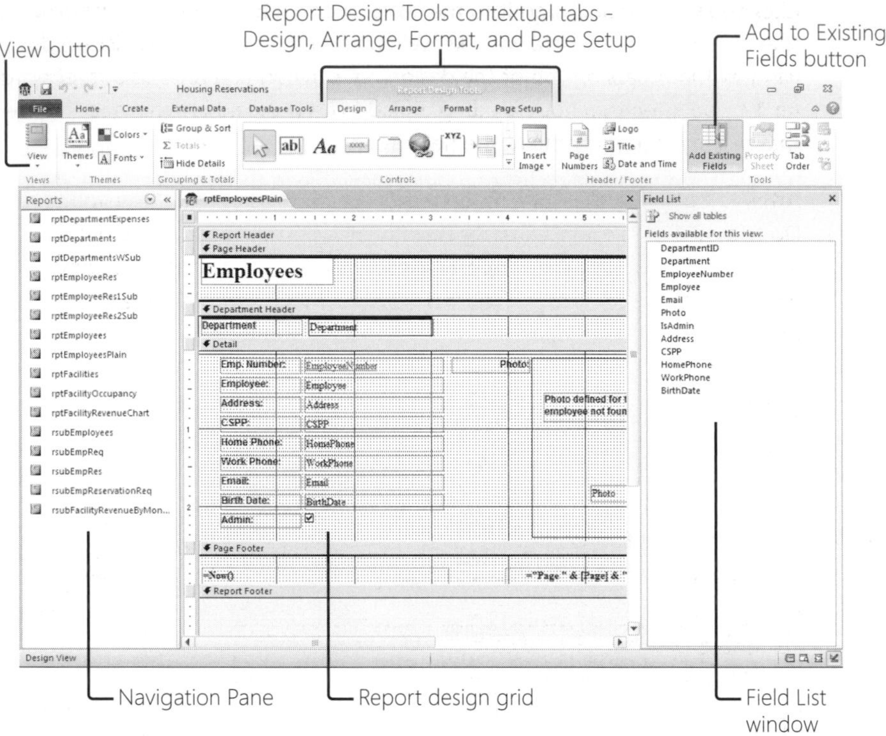

Figure 3-21 Open the rptEmployeesPlain report in Design view to modify its design.

The large window in the center is where you create the design of the report. This report is designed to display all the information about employees by department. Notice that Design view for reports is similar to Design view for forms. (For comparison, see Figure 3-15 on page 143.) Reports provide additional flexibility, allowing you to group items and to total them (either across or down). You can also define header and footer information for the entire report, for each page, and for each subgroup on the report. When you first open this report in Design view, you should see four new contextual tabs appear on the ribbon just to the right of Database Tools under Report Design Tools: Design, Arrange, Format, and Page Setup. These contextual tabs are the action centers of report design—you'll use the tools here to add the design elements you want.

On the right side of the window shown in Figure 3-21, you can see the field list for this report. This list shows all the fields returned by the record source for the report, the saved query qryRptEmployees. If you don't see the field list, click the Add Existing Fields command from the Tools group on the Design contextual tab. You can resize this window by clicking the far-left edge and dragging it toward the left side of the screen to a new width. When your mouse pointer is positioned over the title bar, it changes to cross arrows.

Click the title bar and drag it to the left and down to undock the window from the right side and position it where you like. When you undock the Field List window, it becomes a window that floats on top of the design area. When you read about report design in Chapter 17, you'll see that you can drag a field from the field list to place a control on the report that displays the contents of the field.

After you place all the controls on a report, you might want to customize some of them. Do this by opening the property sheet, which you can see on the right side of the screen in Figure 3-22. To see the property sheet, click the Property Sheet command in the Tools group of the Design tab. In Figure 3-22, we collapsed the Navigation pane so you can see more of the property sheet.

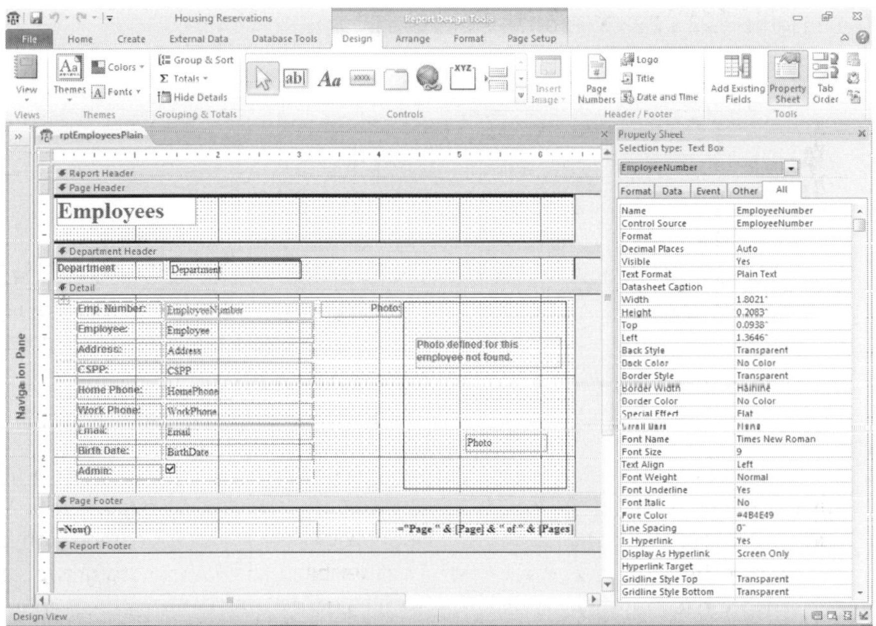

Figure 3-22 The property sheet lets you set individual properties for a report, report sections, or controls on the report.

The property sheet always shows the property settings for the control selected in the Report window. (The Property Sheet pane can also display the properties for the entire report or any section on the report.) In the example shown in Figure 3-22, we clicked the text box named EmployeeNumber to select it. If you click this text box, you can see that Access displays the EmployeeNumber field from the tblEmployees table as the control source (input data) for this control. You can also specify complex formulas that calculate additional data for report controls.

Reports can be even more complex than forms, but building a simple report is really quite easy. Access provides report wizards that you can use to automatically generate a number of standard report layouts based on the table or query you choose. You'll find it simple to customize a report to suit your needs after the Report Wizard has done most of the hard work. You'll learn how to customize a report in Chapter 17, "Constructing a Report," and Chapter 18, "Advanced Report Design."

Report Window in Print Preview

To see what the finished report looks like, click the arrow in the Views group and then click Print Preview when you're in the Report window in Design view. You can also right-click the report name in the Navigation pane and then click Print Preview from the shortcut menu. Figure 3-23 shows a report in Print Preview.

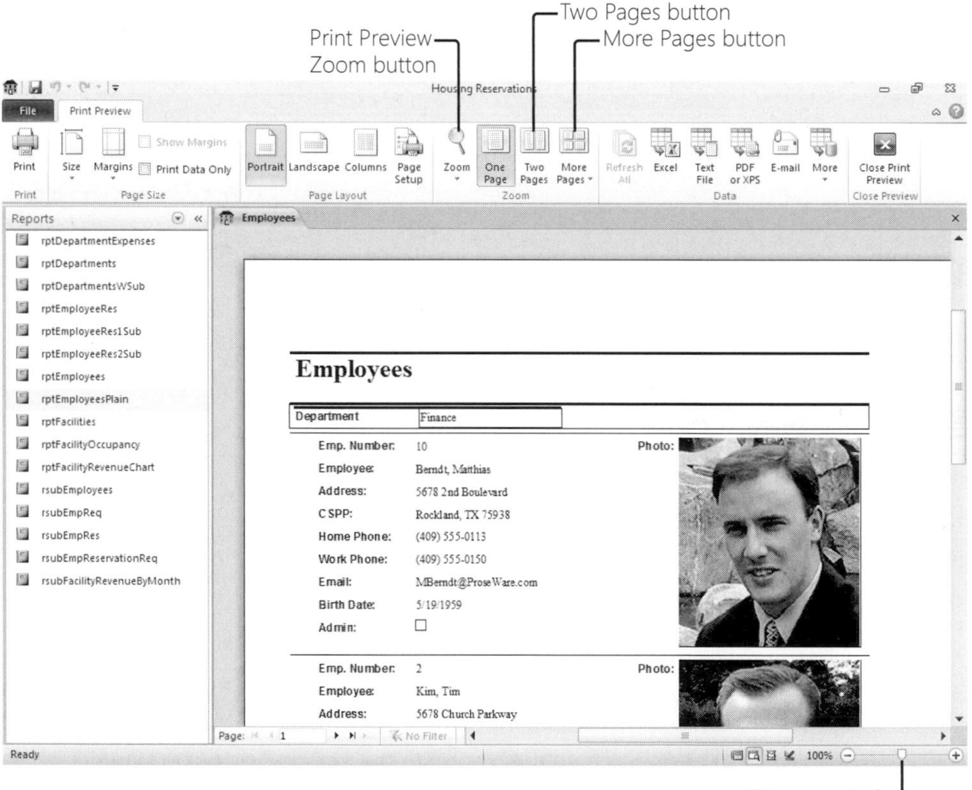

Figure 3-23 When you open a report in Print Preview, Access shows you how the report will look when you print it.

Access initially shows you the upper-left corner of the report. To see the report centered in full-page view in Print Preview, click the Zoom control in the lower-right corner of the status bar, where it says 100%. Clicking that button automatically adjusts the zoom level percent so that you can see a full page of the report. To see two pages side by side, click the Two Pages button in the Zoom group of the Print Preview contextual tab. This gives you a reduced picture of two pages, as shown in Figure 3-24, and an overall idea of how Access arranges major areas of data on the report. Unless you have a large monitor, however, you won't be able to read the data. Click More Pages and then click an option (Four Pages, Eight Pages, or Twelve Pages) to see more than two pages. When you move the mouse pointer over the window in Print Preview, the pointer changes to a magnifying glass icon. To zoom in, click over an area that you want to see more closely. You can then use the scroll bars to move around in the magnified report. Use the Zoom control on the status bar to magnify or shrink your view. Access also provides several output options such as Word or Excel in the Data group of the Print Preview tab.

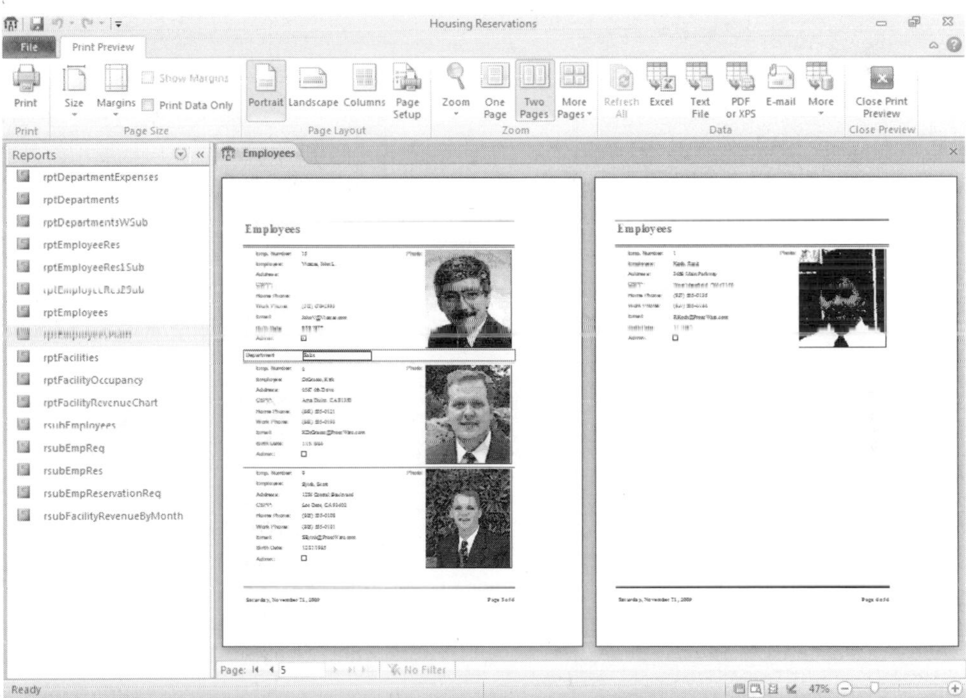

Figure 3-24 Click Two Pages to see two pages side-by-side in Print Preview.

Report Window in Layout View

In Access 2007, Microsoft introduced a new view for reports called Layout view. This unique view for reports gives the developer a fast and easy way to create and modify report designs. Unlike Design view, Layout view enables you to work with the various control elements and report sections using existing live data. Similar to Layout view for forms, this WYSIWYG report-authoring view provides the best of both worlds by giving you the ability to change the structure of the report as you're accessing the data.

To open the rptEmployeesPlain in Layout view, find the report in the Navigation pane, right-click the report name, and click Layout View from the shortcut menu. Figure 3-25 shows the report in Layout view. In Figure 3-25, we collapsed the Navigation pane so you can see more of the report design grid.

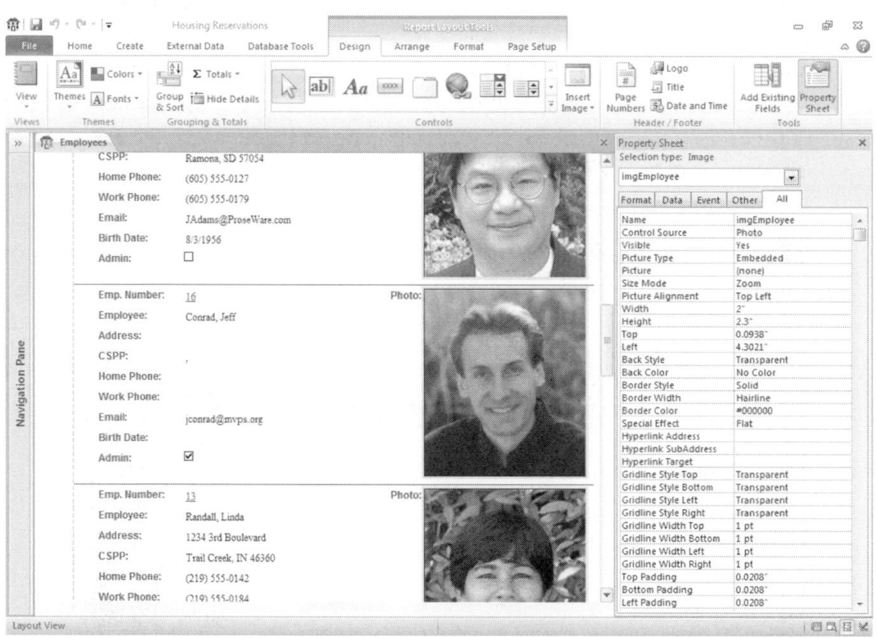

Figure 3-25 Similar to Layout view for forms, Layout view in reports lets you adjust design elements while looking at the data from your database.

Just like Layout view for forms, if you have grouped a set of controls, you can move them around the report grid together to maintain their orientation to one another. In Figure 3-26, you can see that we're dragging the Birth Date field above the Email field. A horizontal bar designates where Access will place the control after you release the mouse button. Because these controls are grouped, Access places the Birth Date field above the Email field. The two controls align perfectly.

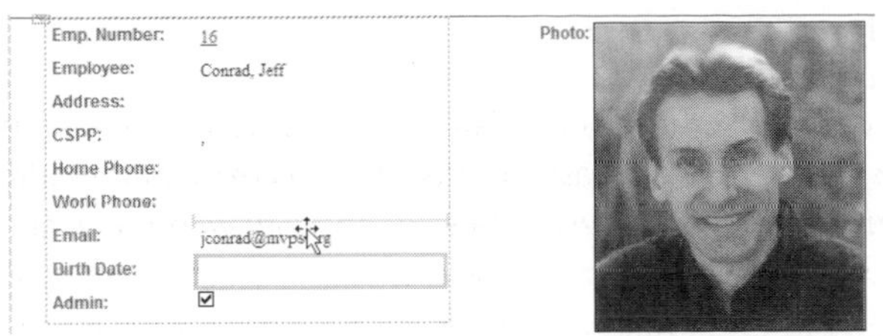

Figure 3-26 Access makes it easy to move controls around within a group in Layout view in a report.

Report Window in Report View

Beginning in Access 2007, Microsoft introduced another new view for reports, called Report view. This is an interactive view for reports that can respond to control events, much like data entry forms. If you have the rptEmployeesPlain report from the previous section open in Layout view, you can switch to Report view by right-clicking the Employees tab and clicking Report View from the shortcut menu. You should now see the report in Report view, as shown in Figure 3-27.

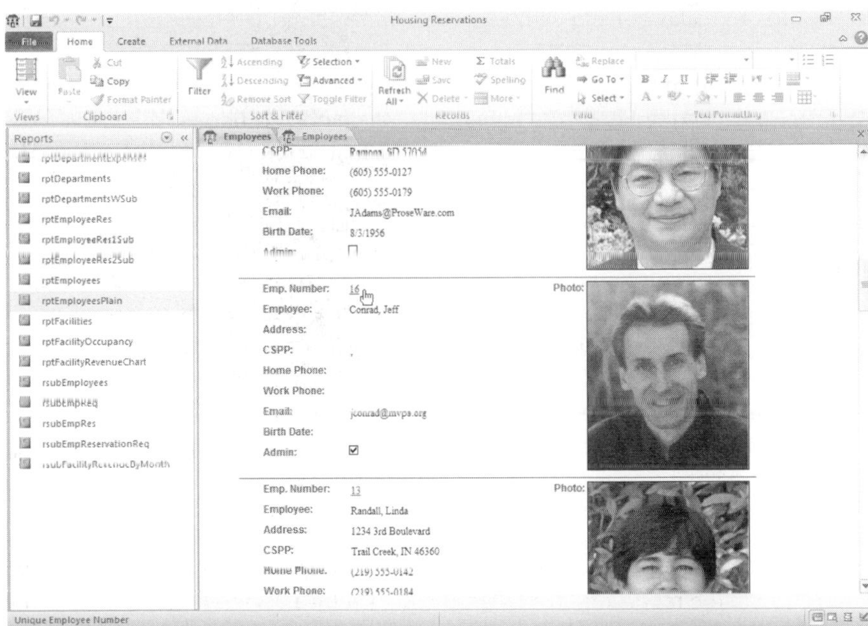

Figure 3-27 When a report is in Report view, you can program controls to respond to mouse clicks to open a related form.

Versions of Access before 2007 treat reports on screen as static. After you open a report on the screen, you can only view the report or print it. Report view in Access 2010 gives you the ability to interact with the report through filters to show specific records and then print only this smaller group of records. You can include command buttons on your reports with Access 2010 and program the buttons to respond to a mouse click in Report view. In Report view, you can designate controls that respond to events as hyperlinks to provide a visual cue that an event occurs when clicking that control. In Figure 3-27, for example, observe that the Employee Number field looks like a hyperlink with a blue line underneath the data. (In Figure 3-27, we have scrolled down the records to show Jeff's information.) Clicking the Employee Number field opens the frmEmployeesPlain form to display all information for that specific employee so that you can make any necessary changes. After closing the form and returning to the report, click the Refresh All command in the Records group of the Home tab on the ribbon to see any changes you made to the data using the form reflected in the report. In Figure 3-27, you can see that the frmEmployeesPlain form opens on a new tab because we are using a tabbed interface.

Close the Form window and the Report window to return to the Navigation pane.

Macros

You can make working with your data within forms and reports much easier by triggering a macro action. Access 2010 provides more than 80 actions that you can include in a macro. They perform tasks such as opening tables and forms, running queries, running other macros, selecting options from menus, and sizing open windows. You can also group multiple actions in a macro and specify conditions that determine when each set of actions will or will not be executed by Access.

Open the Navigation Pane menu and make sure that Object Type is selected under Navigate To Category. Then open the menu again and click Macros under Filter By Group to display a list of macros available in the Housing Reservations database, as shown in Figure 3-28. You can run a macro by right-clicking the macro name in the Navigation pane and clicking Run on the shortcut menu. To open a macro in Design view, right-click the macro name and click Design View from the shortcut menu. To create a brand new macro, click the Macro button in the Macros & Code group of the Create tab on the ribbon.

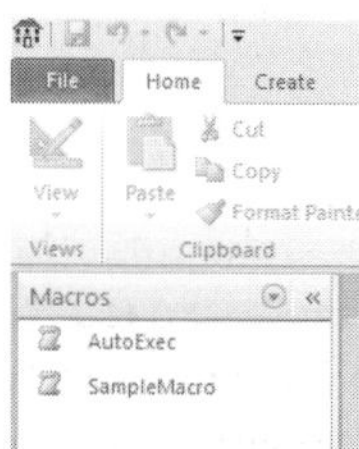

Figure 3-28 You can filter the Navigation pane to show the Macros list in the Housing Reservations database.

Macros are a great way to learn about the basics of responding to events and automating actions in an Access database. As you'll learn later in Chapter 7, if you want to respond to table events such as after inserting new records or before committing new records, you'll need to create macros for this purpose. If you are creating an Access Services application that you intend to publish to the web using Microsoft SharePoint Server, you can only use macros to automate your application. It is a good idea, then, to become familiar with how to create and use macros. For complex client applications that you intend to distribute to others, you'll probably find that you need to use Visual Basic to handle events and automate actions. Nearly all the sample databases use Visual Basic exclusively. You can take a look at the design of a macro example in the Housing Reservations database by selecting the SampleMacro macro in the Navigation pane, and then pressing Ctrl+Enter. Access opens the Macro window (also called the Logic Designer) in Design view, as shown in Figure 3-29.

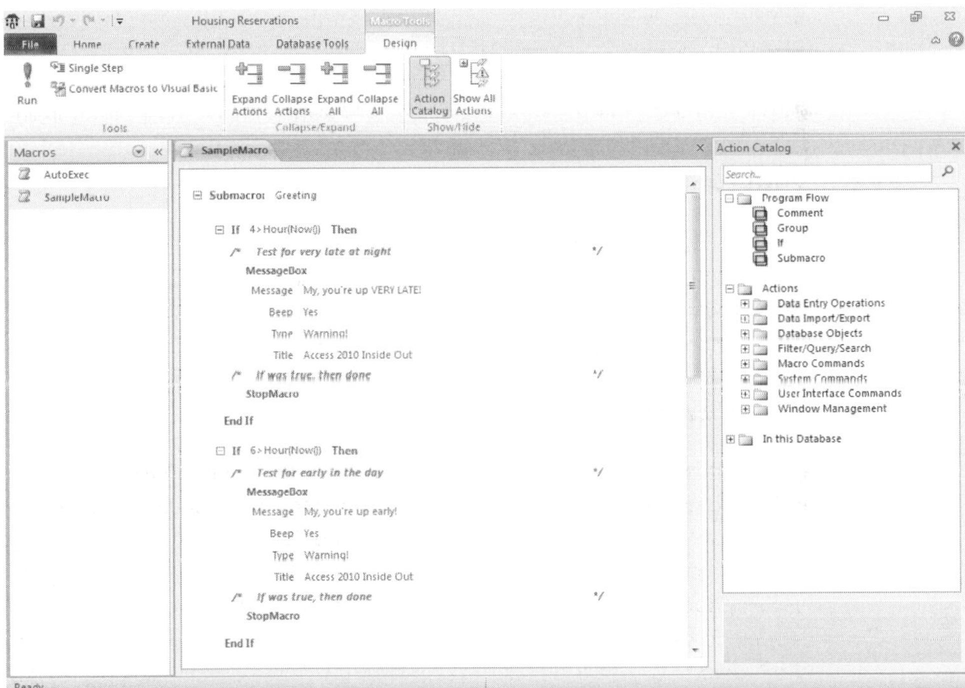

Figure 3-29 Open the SampleMacro macro object in the Housing Reservations database in Design view to examine and modify its definition.

In Access 2010, Microsoft has completely redesigned the macro design surface. In previous versions of Access, the macro design surface resembled more of a table datasheet. Each line or row in the macro window represented an action for the macro to execute. The columns in the older macro window designated the name, conditions, macro actions, and comments about that specific action to execute. In Access 2010, the macro designer surface resembles more of a Visual Basic Editor. As you can see in Figure 3-29, Access indents the lines of the macro for easier readability of the program logic. You'll also notice that the new macro designer supports using If/Else/Else If/End If constructs. In previous versions of Access, you needed to use a continuation indicator (...) on subsequent lines to specify additional commands that should execute when a condition was true. With the new design surface in Access 2010, however, it is much easier for you to see what actions will execute and under what conditions. The Action Catalog on the right side of the macro designer lists all the macro actions grouped by subject. You can add macro actions directly within the design surface or drag actions from the Action Catalog. You'll learn more about all the new changes in the macro designer in Chapter 7, "Creating Table Data Macros."

If you want to see what the SampleMacro macro does, click the Run button in the Tools group of the Design contextual tab to execute it. You should see a greeting message appropriate to the time of day appear on your screen. To learn more about events and the macro design facility, see Chapter 7, "Creating Table Data Macros," Chapter 20, "Automating a Client Application with Macros," and Chapter 21, "Automating a Web Application with Macros." You can find one sample application on the companion CD that is automated entirely using macros—WeddingListMC.accdb.

Close the Macro window now to return to the Navigation pane.

Modules

You might find that you keep coding the same complex formula over and over in some of your forms or reports. Although you can build a complete Access application using only forms, reports, and macros, some actions might be difficult or impossible to define in a macro. If that is the case, you can create a Visual Basic procedure that performs a series of calculations and then use that procedure in a form or report.

If your application is so complex that it needs to deal with errors (such as two users trying to update the same record at the same time), you must use Visual Basic. Because Visual Basic is a complete programming language with complex logic and the ability to link to other applications and files, you can solve unusual or difficult programming problems by using Visual Basic procedures.

Version 2 of Access introduced the ability to code Basic routines in special modules attached directly to the forms and reports that they support. You can create these procedures from Design view or Layout view for forms or reports by requesting the Code Builder in any event property. You can edit this code behind forms and reports by clicking View Code from the Tools group on the Design contextual tab when you have a form or report open in Design view. See Chapters 24 and 25 for details. In fact, after you learn a little bit about Visual Basic, you might find that coding small event procedures for your forms and reports is much more efficient and convenient than trying to keep track of many macro objects. You'll also soon learn that you can't fully respond to some sophisticated events, such as KeyPress, in macros because macros can't access special additional parameters (such as the value of the key pressed) that are generated by the event. You can fully handle these events only in Visual Basic.

Open the Navigation Pane menu and click Object Type under Navigate To Category. Open the menu again and click Modules under Filter By Group to display a list of modules available in the Housing Reservations database, as shown in Figure 3-30. The Housing Reservations database has several module objects that contain procedures that can be called from any query, form, report, or other procedure in the database. For example, the modMedian module contains a function to calculate the median value of a column in any table or query. The modUtility module contains several functions that you might find useful in your applications.

Figure 3-30 You can filter the Navigation pane to display only the Visual Basic modules in the Housing Reservations database.

From the Navigation pane, you can create a new module by clicking the Module button in the Macros & Code group of the Create tab on the ribbon, or you can open the design of an existing module by double-clicking the name of the module in the Navigation pane. In addition, you can right-click the module name in the Navigation pane and click Design View from the shortcut menu. In a module, you can define procedures that you can call from a macro, a form, or a report. You can also use some procedures (called *functions*) in expressions in queries and in validation rules that you create for a table or a form. You'll learn about how to create procedures in Chapter 24.

Right-click the modUtility module in the Navigation pane, and then click Design View to open the Visual Basic Editor window containing the Visual Basic code in the module. Use the Procedure list box (in the upper-right section of the Code window) to look at the procedure names available in the sample. One of the functions in this module, IsFormLoaded, checks all forms open in the current Access session to see whether the form name, passed as a parameter, is one of the open forms. This function is useful in macros or in other modules to direct the flow of an application based on which forms the user has open. You can see this function in Figure 3-31.

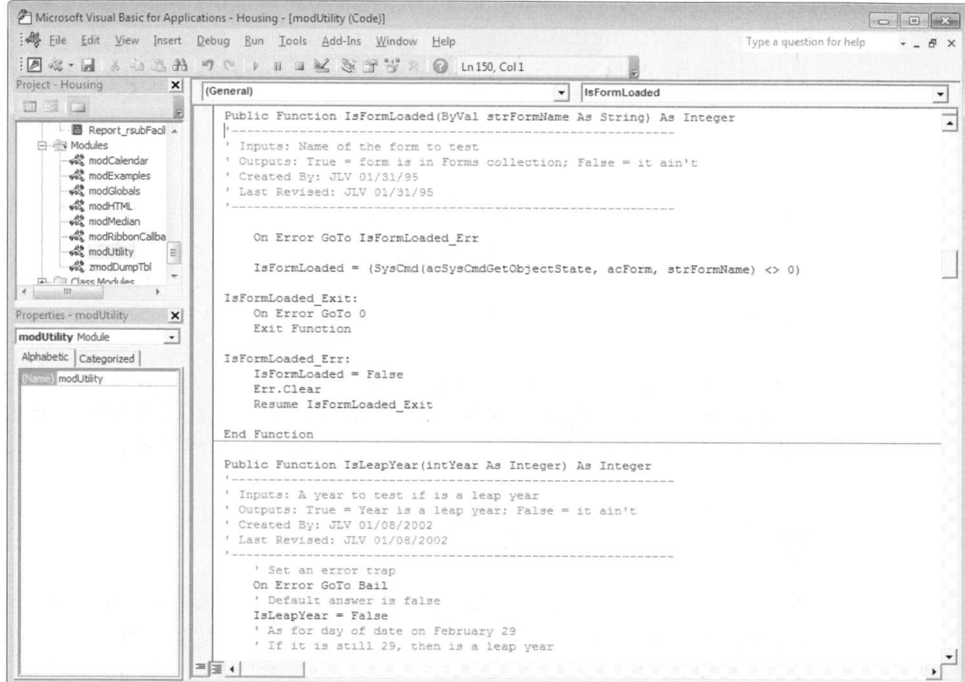

Figure 3-31 The Visual Basic Editor window displays the IsFormLoaded function in the modUtility module.

Note that the Visual Basic Editor runs in an entirely different application window from Access, and it still uses the classic menus and toolbars found in earlier versions of Access. Click the View Microsoft Office Access button on the far-left side of the toolbar to return to the Access window easily.

This completes the tour of the objects in the Housing Reservations sample database. Close the Visual Basic Editor window (if you still have it open), return to the Access window, and close the database.

What Happened to Project Files (ADP)?

Access 2000 introduced an advanced facility that allows you to create a project file (with an .adp extension) that contains only your forms, reports, macros, and modules. When you create a new project file, you can specify an SQL Server database to support the project. SQL Server stores the tables and queries you use in the application that you design in the project. You can connect your project file to a database in SQL Server version 7.0 or later, on a server or on your desktop. You can download a special edition of SQL Server 2008, SQL Server Express Edition, which you can install to run on your desktop computer from the following location on Microsoft's website: *http://www.microsoft.com/sqlserver/2008/en/us/express.aspx*

Access Data Projects (ADPs) still exist in Access 2010; however, Microsoft did not add a lot of new functionality to them for the 2010 release besides adding support for connection to SQL Server 2008 and support for a few more data types. For the Access 2010 product cycle, most of the Access team's development resources were focused in other areas, most notably the new Access Services functionality. In deciding what features to cover for this edition of the "Inside Out" series, there simply was not enough space to include a full discussion of ADPs along with all the new features included in Access 2010. For more information on ADPs, see *Microsoft Office Access 2007 Inside Out* (Microsoft Press, 2007).

The Many Faces of Access

Access is not only a powerful, flexible, and easy-to-use database management system, but it is also a complete database application development facility. You can use Access to create and run, under the Microsoft Windows operating system, an application tailored to your data management needs. Access lets you limit, select, and total your data by using queries. You can create forms for viewing and changing your data. You can also use Access to create simple or complex reports. Forms and reports inherit the properties of the underlying table or query, so in most cases, you need to define such properties as formats and validation rules only once. Figure 3-32 gives you an overview of all the ways you can use Access to implement an application.

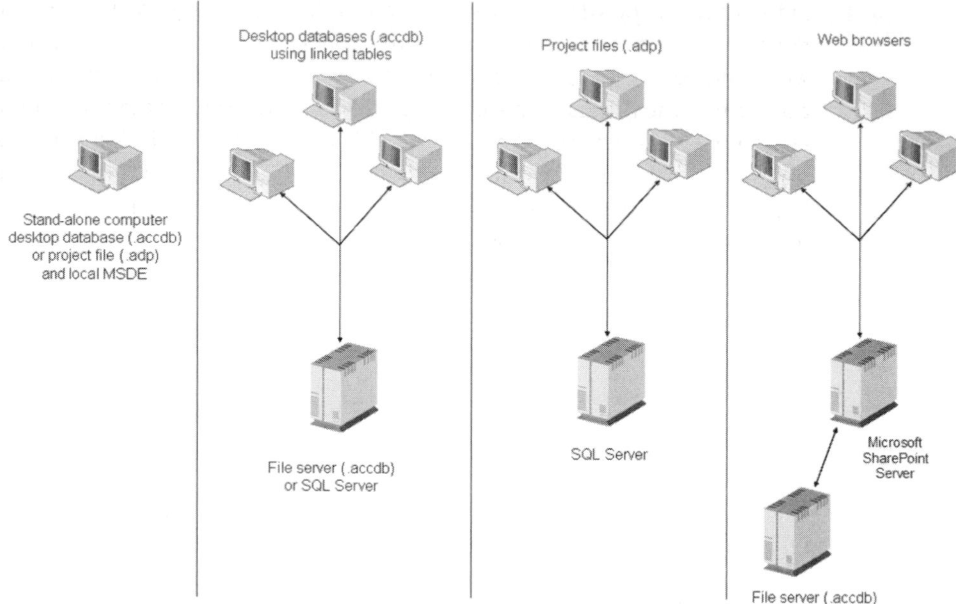

Figure 3-32 Although Access is primarily a desktop database system, you can use Access to build client/server applications.

The four panes in the figure illustrate ways you can implement an Access application, as follows:

- Using the desktop database facility or an Access project file linked to a local copy of MSDE, you can create a stand-alone application used by a single person.
- You can place a data-only desktop database on a file server or in a database in SQL Server and link the tables over a network into multiple desktop databases so that several users can share the same application.
- You can design your database in SQL Server and connect to the server over a network from multiple Access project files running on different computers.
- Finally, you can create an Access Services application using SharePoint Server that connects to data that you designed using Access.

To borrow a cliché, the possibilities are endless. . . .

In this chapter, you've had a chance to look at the major objects in the Housing Reservations sample database. You've also been introduced to the architecture of Access and the wide range of ways that you can use Access. You should be feeling comfortable that you can learn to use Access at the level appropriate to solve your database application needs. Perhaps the most important aspect of building an application is designing the database that will support your application. Chapter 4 describes how you should design your database application and its data structures. Building a solid foundation makes creating the forms and reports for your application easy.

PART 2

Creating a Database and Tables

CHAPTER 4

Designing Client Tables

Defining tables in a Microsoft Access 2010 desktop database (.accdb file) is incredibly easy. This chapter shows you how it's done. You'll learn how to:

- Create a new database application using a database template
- Create a new empty database for your own custom application
- Create a simple table by entering data directly in the table
- Get a jump start on defining custom tables by using Application Parts
- Create new fields by using Data Type Parts
- Define your own tables from scratch by using Design view
- Select the best data type for each field
- Define the primary key for your table
- Set validation rules for your fields and tables
- Tell Access 2010 what relationships to maintain between your tables
- Optimize data retrieval by adding indexes
- Set options that affect how you work in Design view
- Print a table definition

Note

All the screen images in this chapter were taken on a Windows 7 with the Access color scheme set to Silver.

INSIDE OUT Take Time to Learn About Table Design

You could begin building a database in Access 2010 much as you might begin creating a simple single-sheet solution in a spreadsheet application such as Microsoft Excel—by simply organizing your data into rows and columns and then inserting formulas where you need calculations. If you've ever worked extensively with a database or a spreadsheet application, you already know that this unplanned approach works in only the most trivial situations. Solving real problems takes some planning; otherwise, you end up building your application over and over again. One of the beauties of a relational database system such as Access is that it's much easier to make midcourse corrections. However, it's well worth spending time up front designing the tasks you want to perform, the data structures you need to support those tasks, and the flow of tasks within your database application.

To teach you all you might need to know about table design would require another entire book. The good news is Access 2010 provides many examples of good table design in the templates available with the product and online. If you want to learn at least the fundamentals of table and application design, be sure to read Article 1, "Designing Your Database Application," which you can find on the companion CD.

Creating a New Database

When you first start Access 2010, you see the New tab on the Microsoft Office Backstage view, as shown in Figure 4-1. We explored the New tab in detail in Chapter 2. If you've previously opened other databases, you also see a most recently used list of up to four database selections by default under Close Database on the left.

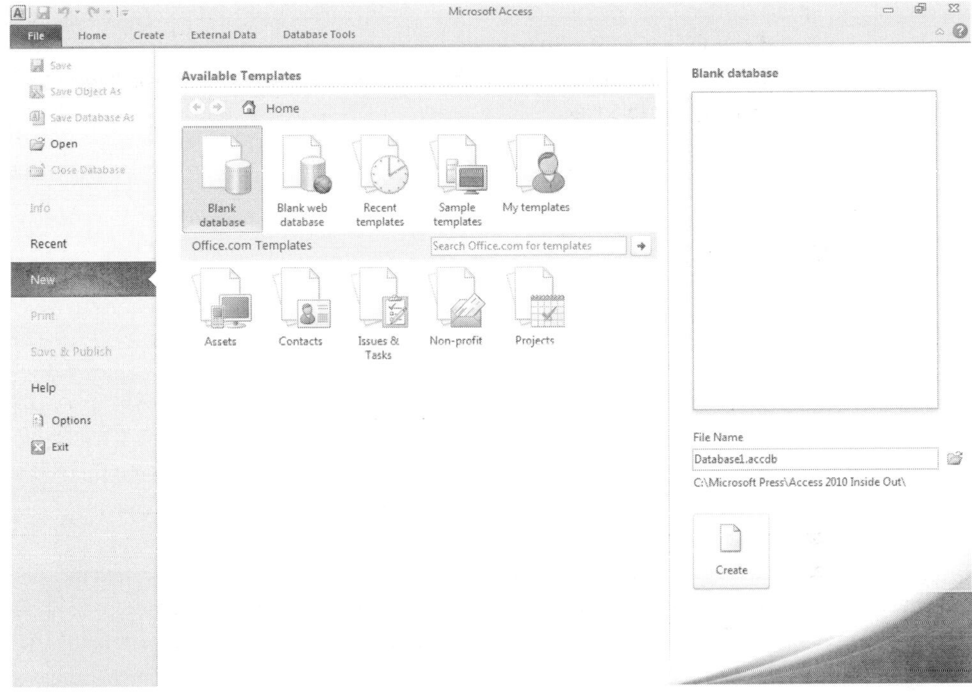

Figure 4-1 When you first start Access 2010, you see the New tab on the Backstage view.

Using a Database Template to Create a Database

Just for fun, let's explore the built-in database templates first. If you're a beginner, you can use the templates included with Access 2010 to create one of several common applications without needing to know anything about designing database software. You might find that one of these applications meets most of your needs right away. As you learn more about Access 2010, you can build on and customize the basic application design and add new features.

Even if you're an experienced developer, you might find that the application templates save you lots of time in setting up the basic tables, queries, forms, and reports for your application. If the application you need to build is covered by one of the templates, the wizard that builds an application with one of the templates can take care of many of the simpler design tasks.

On the New tab of the Backstage view, you can access the built-in local templates by clicking Sample Templates under Available Templates in the center of the screen. You can also choose to download a template from Microsoft's website by clicking one of the options under Office.com Templates. When you click one of the options under Sample Templates or Office.com Templates, the center section of the New tab changes to show a graphic representing each of the database templates available in that category. Click the Non-Profit category under Office.com to see the list of nonprofit template options, as shown in Figure 4-2.

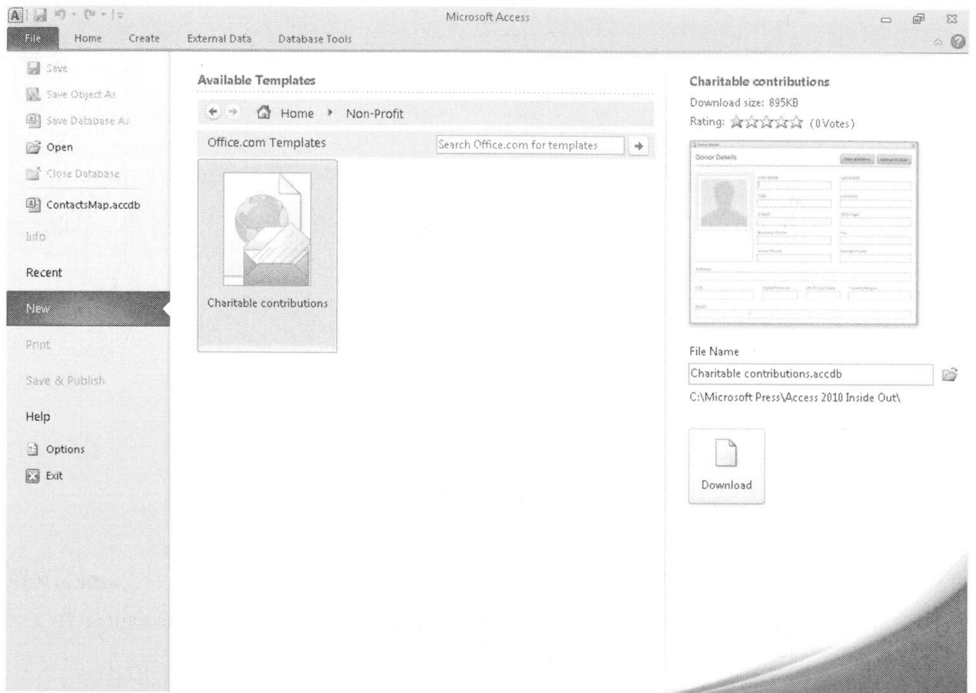

Figure 4-2 You can access templates from Office.com by selecting one of the categories to see a list of database templates for that category.

When you click one of the template graphics in the center of the New tab, Access 2010 displays additional information about the purpose of the database in the right task pane. Click the Home button near the top of the screen to return to the main Home page of the New tab. Click Sample Templates to see a list of templates installed locally on your computer. Click the Tasks template in the middle of the screen to see detailed information about the Tasks database template, as shown in Figure 4-3. You can work with all templates from the New tab in the same way. This example will show you the steps that are needed to build a Tasks database.

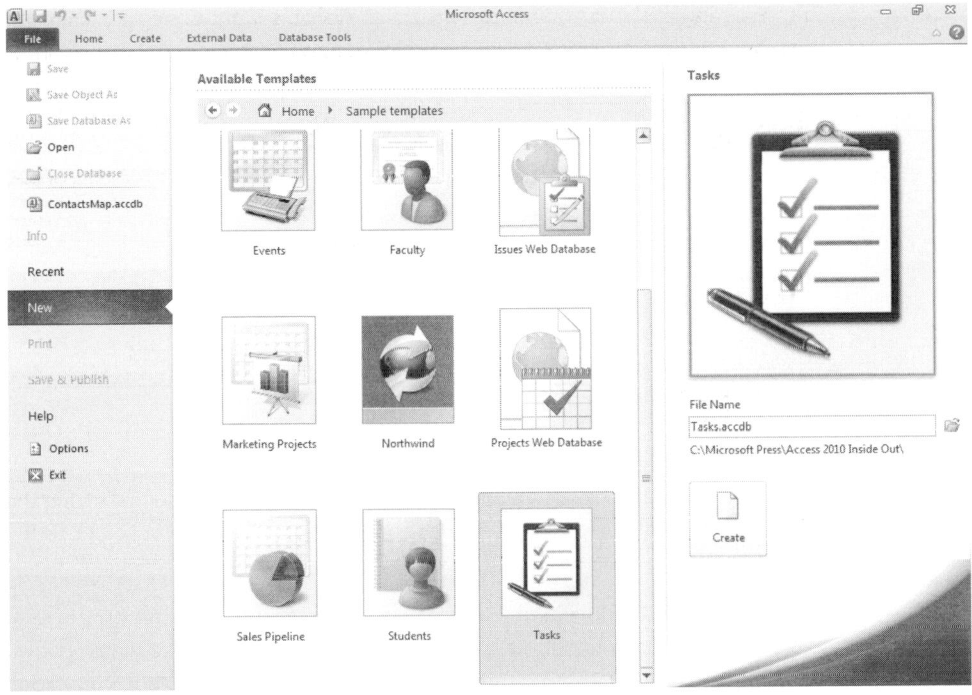

Figure 4-3 When you choose one of the database templates in the center of the screen, Access shows you a larger graphic in the right task pane.

Access 2010 displays a larger graphic in the right task pane when you click a specific database template. Note that when you have selected an online template, Access 2010 also shows you the template size and the rating given this template by other users. Access 2010 suggests a name for your new database in the File Name text box and a location to save the file beneath the File Name text box. You can modify the name of this database by typing in the File Name text box. If you want to change the suggested save location, click Browse to open the File New Database dialog box, as shown in Figure 4-4.

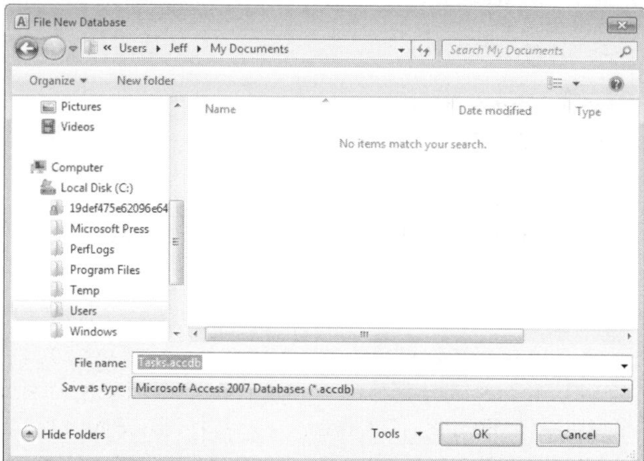

Figure 4-4 Use the File New Database dialog box to select a folder for saving the new local database template.

You can select the drive and folder you want by clicking the links on the left and browsing to your destination folder. After you select the specific folder to which you want to save this new database, click OK to return to the New tab on the Backstage view. Your new folder location is shown beneath the File Name text box. If you decide at this point not to create the database, click the Home button near the top of the screen to return to the main Home page of the New tab to stop the process. Click Download when working with an online template or Create when working with a local template, and Access 2010 begins the process of creating this new database template.

The first time you choose to download an online template, Access 2010 might display the Microsoft Office Genuine Advantage confirmation dialog box, as shown in Figure 4-5. Each time you download a template, Access 2010 confirms that you have a valid and registered copy of the Microsoft Office 2010 system. If you do not want to see this dialog box again, select the Do Not Show This Message Again check box. Click Continue to proceed with the download and creation of your sample database.

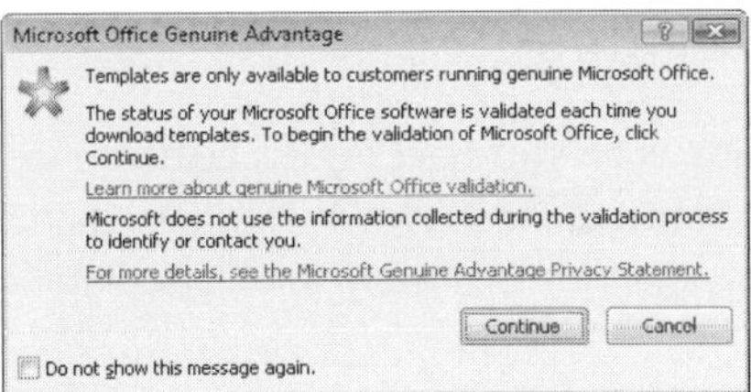

Figure 4-5 When you ask to download a template, Access verifies that you have a genuine copy of the Office 2010 release.

A progress bar appears on the screen asking you to wait while Access 2010 creates the template. After a few seconds of preparation, Access opens the new Tasks database and displays the Task List form, as shown in Figure 4-6. Close this new database for now by clicking the File tab on the Backstage view and then clicking Close Database to return to the New tab. Note that when you browse or download Access templates from Office.com, you might see additional folders on the New tab of the Backstage view under Office.com Templates.

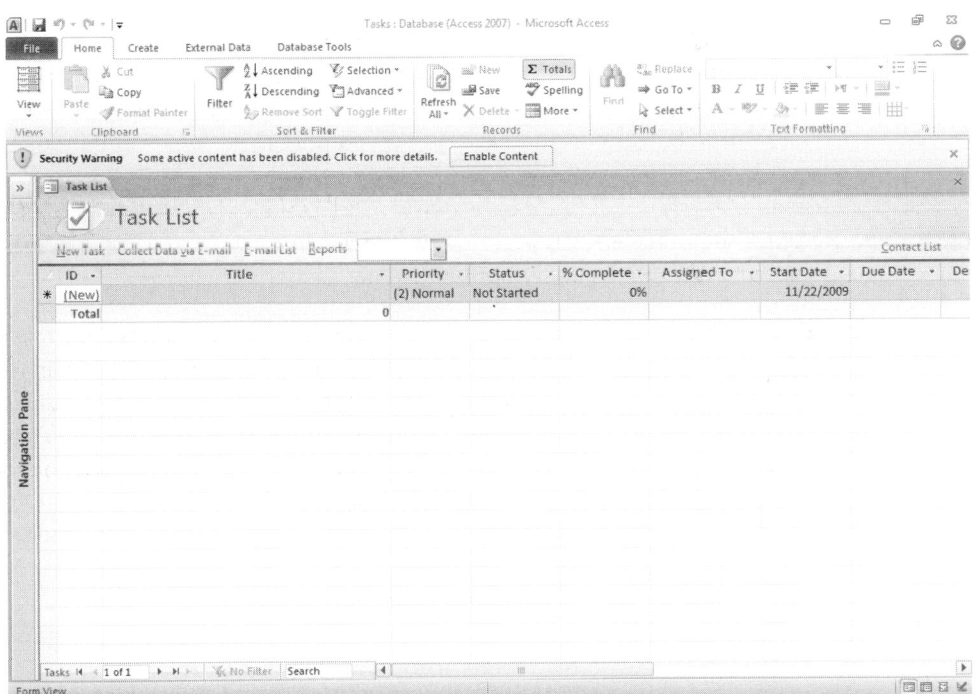

Figure 4-6 After you create the Tasks database from a template, Access opens the database and displays the Task List form.

Creating a New Empty Database

To begin creating a new empty database when you start Access 2010, go to the Available Templates section in the middle of the New tab (as shown in Figure 4-1) and click Blank Database. The right side of the New tab changes to display the Blank Database task pane, as shown in Figure 4-7.

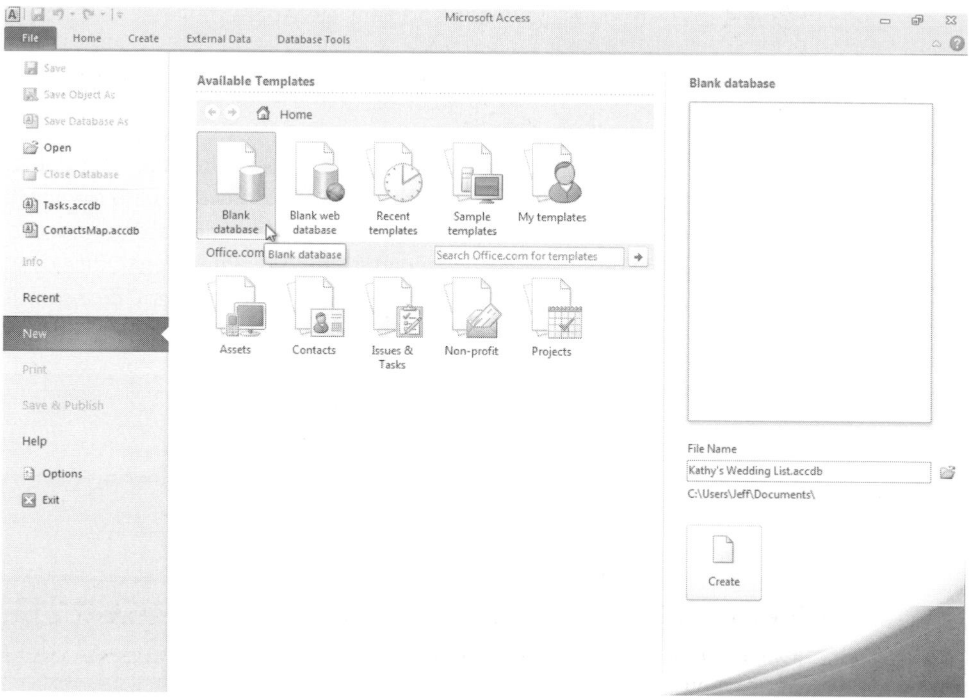

Figure 4-7 From the New tab on the Backstage view, click Blank Database in the center to open the Blank Database task pane on the right.

You can click Browse to open the File New Database dialog box, shown in Figure 4-4, to select the drive and folder that you want. In this example, we selected the Documents folder in Windows 7 for the current user. Next, type the name of your new database in the File Name text box—Access 2010 appends an .accdb extension to the file name for you. Access 2010 uses a file with an .accdb extension to store all your database objects, including tables, queries, forms, reports, macros, and modules. For this example, let's create a database with a table containing names and addresses—something you might use to track invitees to a wedding. Type **Kathy's Wedding List** in the File Name box and click Create to create your database.

Access 2010 takes a few moments to create the system tables in which to store all the information about the tables, queries, forms, reports, macros, and modules that you might create. Access then displays the Navigation pane for your new database and opens a new blank table in Datasheet view, as shown in Figure 4-8.

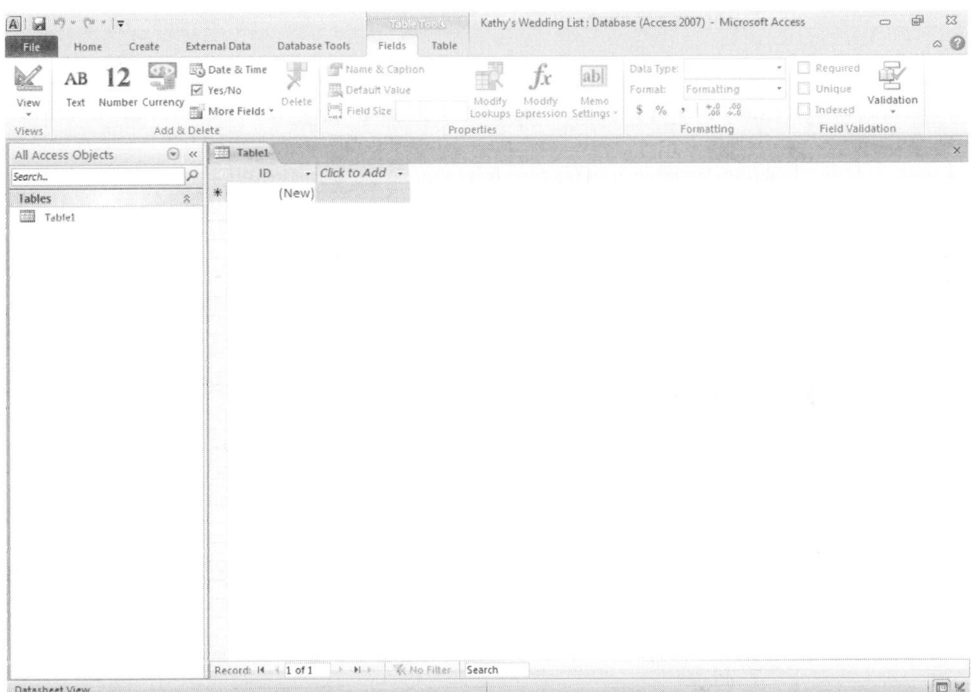

Figure 4-8 When you create a new blank database, Access 2010 opens a new table in Datasheet view for you.

When you open a database (unless the database includes special startup settings), Access 2010 selects the object you last chose in the Navigation pane for that database. For example, if you worked on a table the last time you opened this database, Access highlights that object (a table) in the Navigation pane. Access also remembers the view and filters you applied to the Navigation pane. For example, if Tables And Related Views was the last selected view applied to the Navigation pane, Access will remember this the next time you open the database.

Because this is a new database and no objects or special startup settings exist yet, you see a Navigation pane with only one object defined. For new databases, Access, by default, creates a new table in Datasheet view called Table1 with an ID field already defined. However, Access has not saved this table, so if you do not make any changes to it, Access will not prompt you to save the table if you close it. The following sections show you various methods for creating a new table.

Creating Your First Simple Table by Entering Data

If you've been following along to this point, you should still have your new Kathy's Wedding List database open with Table1 open in Datasheet view, as shown in Figure 4-8. (You can also follow these steps in any open database.) What you see is an empty datasheet, which looks quite similar to a spreadsheet. Access 2010 automatically created the first field, called ID, in the left column. Leave this field intact for now. In the second column, Access has placed another field with the Add New Field heading. You can enter just about any type of data you want in this field—text, dates, numbers, or currency. But unlike a spreadsheet, you can't enter any calculated expressions in a datasheet. As you'll see later in this chapter, you can easily display a calculated result using data from one or more fields by entering an expression in a Calculated data type.

Because we're starting a list of wedding invitees, we'll need columns containing information such as title, last name, first name, middle initial, street address, city, state, postal code, number of guests invited, number of guests confirmed, gift received, and a gift acknowledged indicator. Be sure to enter the same type of data in a particular column for every row. For example, enter the city name in the seventh column (named Field6 by Access) for every row.

You can see some of the data entered for the wedding invitee list in Figure 4-9. When you start to type in a field in a row, Access 2010 displays a pencil icon on the row selector at the far left to indicate that you're adding or changing data in that row. Press the Tab key to move from column to column. When you move to another row, Access 2010 saves what you typed. If you make a mistake in a particular row or column, you can click the data you want to change and type over it or delete it. Notice that after you enter data in a column, Access 2010 guesses the most appropriate data type and displays it in the Data Type box on the Fields tab on the ribbon.

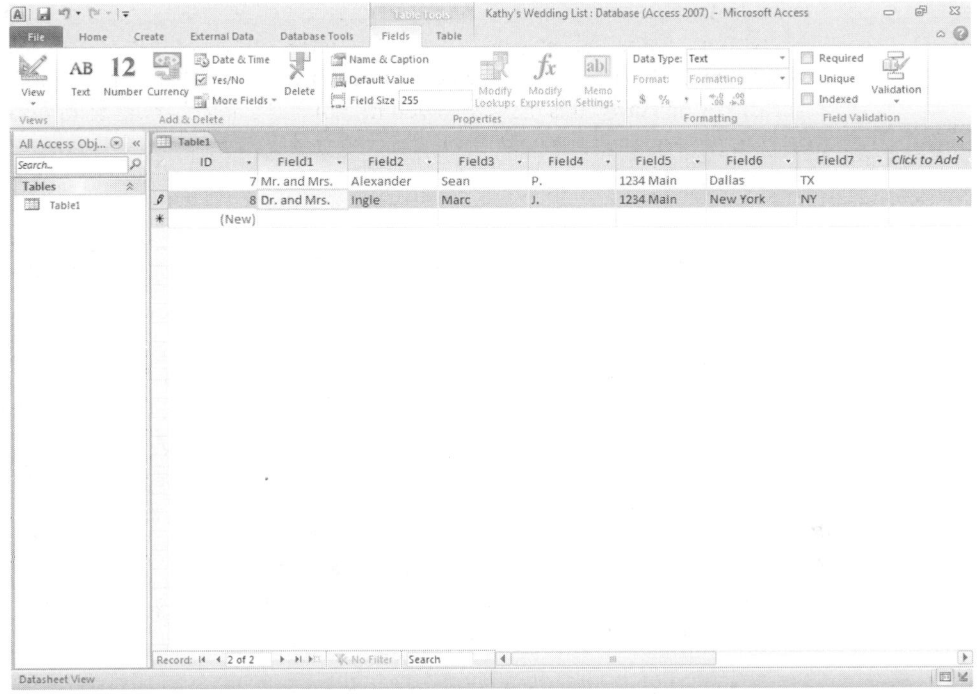

Figure 4-9 You can create the wedding invitee list table by entering data.

If you create a column of data that you don't want, click anywhere in the column and click Delete in the Add & Delete group of the Fields contextual tab on the ribbon. Click Yes when Access asks you to confirm the deletion. If you want to insert a blank column between two columns that already contain data, right-click the column header to the right of where you want to insert the new column and then click Insert Field from the shortcut menu that appears. To move a column to a different location, click the field name at the top of the column to select the entire column, and then click again and drag the column to a new location. You can also click an unselected column and drag your mouse pointer through several adjacent columns to select them all. You can then move the columns as a group.

You probably noticed that Access 2010 named your columns Field1, Field2, and so forth—not very informative. You can enter a name for each column by double-clicking the column's field name. You can also right-click a column header and then click Rename Field from the shortcut menu that appears. In Figure 4-10, we have already renamed one of the columns and are in the process of renaming the second one.

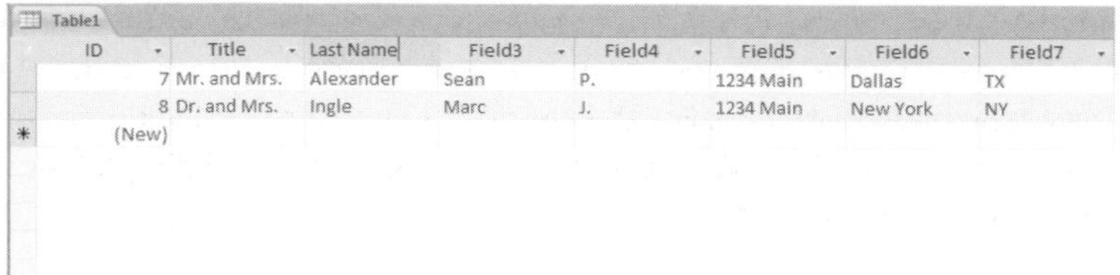

Table1

ID	Title	Last Name	Field3	Field4	Field5	Field6	Field7
7	Mr. and Mrs.	Alexander	Sean	P.	1234 Main	Dallas	TX
8	Dr. and Mrs.	Ingle	Marc	J.	1234 Main	New York	NY
(New)							

Figure 4-10 Double-click the column heading to rename a column in Datasheet view.

Save

After you enter several rows of data, it's a good idea to save your table. You can do this by clicking the Save button on the Quick Access Toolbar or by clicking the File tab and then click Save. Access 2010 displays a Save As dialog box, as shown in Figure 4-11. Type an appropriate name for your table, and then click OK. If you deleted the ID field by mistake, Access 2010 displays a message box warning you that you have no primary key defined for this table and offers to build one for you. If you accept the offer, Access adds a field called ID and assigns it a special data type named AutoNumber that automatically generates a unique number for each new row you add. See "Understanding Field Data Types," on page 190, for details about AutoNumber. If one or more of the data columns you entered would make a good primary key, click No in the message box. In Chapter 5, "Modifying Your Table Design," you'll learn how to use Design view to define your own primary key(s) or to change the definition of an existing primary key. In this case, Access 2010 should not display a message box because it already generated the field called ID to serve as the primary key.

Figure 4-11 Access 2010 displays the Save As dialog box when you save a new table so that you can specify a table name.

Creating a Table Using Application Parts

If you look in the Wedding List sample database (WeddingList.accdb) included on the companion CD, you'll find it very simple, with one main table and a few supporting tables for data such as titles, cities, and groups. Most databases are usually quite a bit more complex. For example, the Proseware Housing Reservations sample database contains six main tables, and the Conrad Systems Contacts sample database contains more than a dozen tables. If you had to create every table manually, it could be quite a tedious process.

Fortunately, Access 2010 comes with a new feature called Application Parts to help you build a few common tables and other database objects. Let's move on to a more complex task—building tables like those you find in Conrad Systems Contacts. To do this, click the File tab on the Backstage view and then click New. This returns you to the New tab, ready to define a new blank database. For this exercise, create a new blank database and give it the name "Contact Tracking." We'll use this database to start building tables like some of those you saw in Chapter 3, "Access 2010 Overview."

To build a table using one of the Application Parts, close the table that Access 2010 created when you opened the database (Table1), click the Create tab on the ribbon, and then click the Application Parts button in the Templates group. Access displays a list of 10 form types under the Blank Forms category and five Application Parts under the Quick Start category, as shown in Figure 4-12. Microsoft also uses the term *Models* to refer to this one-click object creation feature. You'll learn more about using the 10 form Application Parts in Chapter 13, "Building a Form."

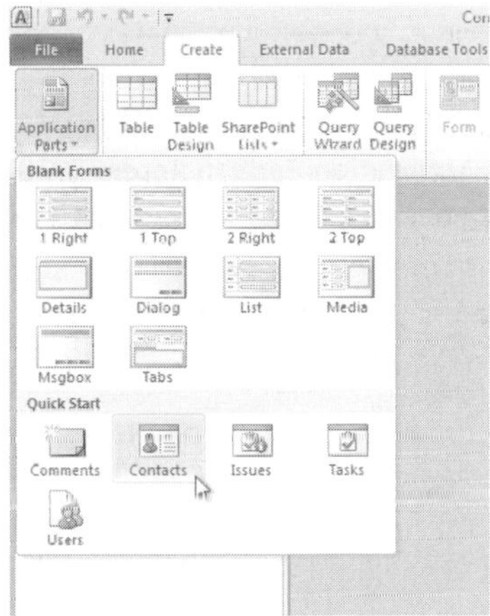

Figure 4-12 Application Parts help you create common types of database objects.

The five Application Parts under Quick Start, which represent some of the more common types of table structures and objects found in databases, are as follows:

- **Comments** Use this Application Part when you need a table to track various comments. Clicking this option creates one table with a comment date and comment fields.

- **Contacts** Use this Application Part when you need to track your personal or business contacts. Clicking this option not only creates a Contacts table, but it also creates a query, three forms, and four reports to work with that Contacts table. With one click, you are well on your way to creating a functional application to track your contacts. Key fields in the Contacts table include the contact's company, job title, and phone numbers.

- **Issues** Use this Application Part for recording various personal or business issues. Clicking this option creates an Issues table as well as two forms to work with that table. Some key fields in the Issues table include the title of the issue and the issue status.
- **Tasks** Use this Application Part for keeping track of various tasks and projects needing completion. Clicking this option creates a Tasks table as well as two forms to work with that table. Key fields in the Tasks table include start and due dates for the task and percentage complete.
- **Users** Use this Application Part for maintaining a list of users for your database. Clicking this option creates a Users table as well as two forms to work with that table. Key fields in the Users table include the email, full name, and login information.

INSIDE OUT **What Happened to the Table Templates?**

The five Table Templates from Access 2007 do not exist in Access 2010. Microsoft replaced the Table Templates with various Application Parts in Access 2010 so you can quickly build fields, tables, and other database objects commonly found in most databases.

Click Contacts in the Quick Start list, and Access 2010 builds a complete table structure for a contacts table as well as other supporting objects, as shown in Figure 4-13. Access creates a total of 20 fields to identify the data elements for this contacts table. Use the horizontal scroll bar or press Tab to see the field names to the right. This contacts table Application Part includes fields such as Company, First Name, Last Name, E-mail Address, Job Title, and so on to identify a single subject—a contact. The Quick Start command also automatically defines a data type for each of these fields.

See Table 4-1, on page 190, for a full discussion of the various data types available within Access 2010.

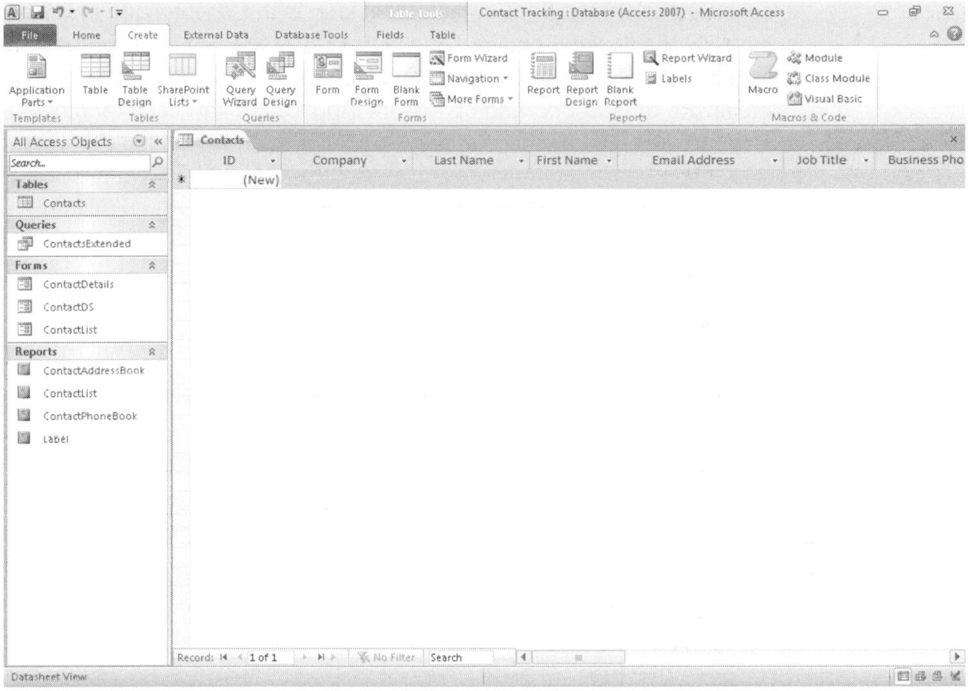

Figure 4-13 The Quick Start command builds a complete table with appropriate field types and supporting objects.

By default, Access 2010 assigned the name ID to the first field in this Contacts table. This field name is not very descriptive, so we will rename this field ContactID. There are several ways to rename a field using Access 2010, but for now we will focus on one of the easiest methods—renaming the field directly from Datasheet view. Double-click the heading of the ID field and then type **ContactID,** as shown in Figure 4-14. After you press Enter, Access immediately renames the field. Save the change to this table now by clicking the Save button on the Quick Access Toolbar.

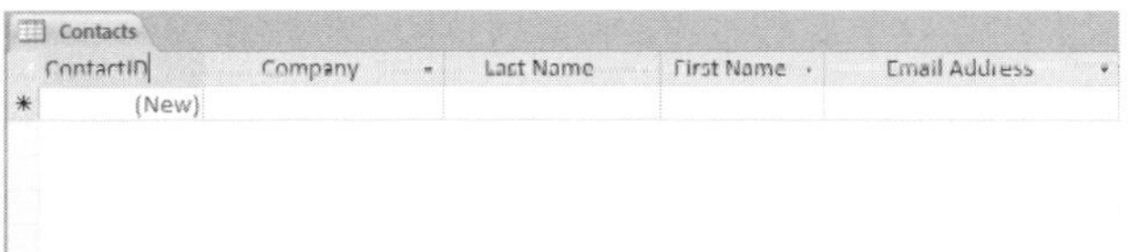

Figure 4-14 You can double-click a column heading in Datasheet view to change the name of the field.

You will further change this Contacts table later in this chapter and in Chapter 5 so that it is more like the final tblContacts table in the Conrad Systems Contacts database. For now, close the Table window so that you can continue building other tables you need. Also, let's delete all the other supporting objects the Application Part command created so we can concentrate just on the tables for now. Highlight the query called ContactsExtended in the Navigation pane and then press Delete. Click OK in the confirmation dialog box when Access prompts you to delete the object. Continue deleting the remaining three forms and four reports until you are left with just the Contacts table in the Navigation pane.

Creating a Table Using Data Type Parts

Access 2010 includes another new feature, called Data Type Parts, to assist you with creating tables and fields. Application Parts, as you just learned, help you build complete tables and other database objects, but Data Type Parts help you create individual fields or groups of fields. As you design more databases, you might find yourself needing to create similar field structures in your tables. For example, you'll probably find yourself needing to have fields in at least one table that tracks address information such as street address, city, state, and ZIP code. With Access 2010, you can now add a group of fields to track address information easily using Data Type Parts. You can also save your own custom field or groups of fields to be used in other Access applications that you create.

If you've been following along to this point, you should still have your new Contact Tracking database open with just the Contacts table in the Navigation pane. (You can also follow these steps in any open database.) To build a table using one of the Data Type Parts, you first need to have a table opened in Datasheet view. Click the Create tab on the ribbon and then click the Table button in the Tables group. Access creates a new table called Table1 with one field called ID and displays it in Datasheet view. Click the More Fields button in the Add & Delete group on the Fields tab and Access displays a large list of field types grouped by category, as shown in Figure 4-15.

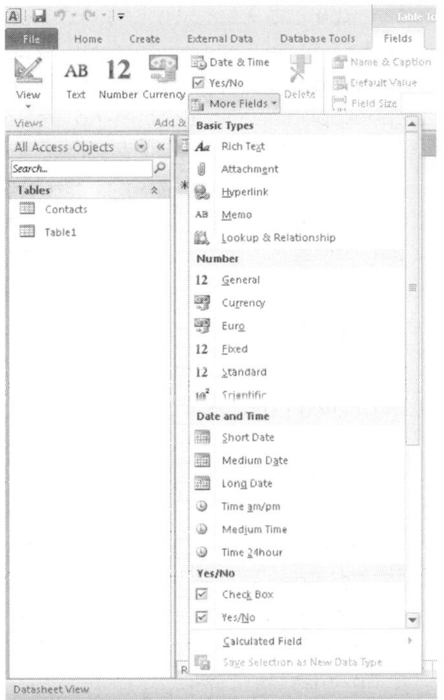

Figure 4-15 Click More Fields to see many field types and formatting choices you can use in your table.

Under the Basic Types, Number, Date and Time, and Yes/No categories, Access displays many options for different field types and field formats you can use in your table. You can click any of the options in these categories and Access creates a new field in your table. You'll learn more about the different field types and formats later in this chapter. Scroll down to the bottom of the list under the More Fields button, and Access displays a list of nine Data Type Parts under the Quick Start category, as shown in Figure 4-16.

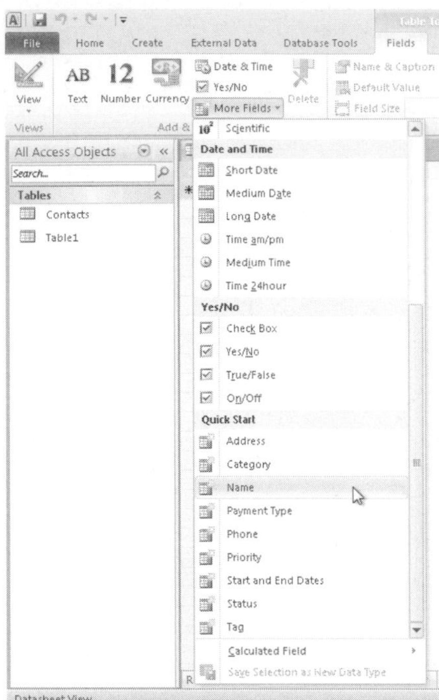

Figure 4-16 Data Type Parts help you create common types of fields.

The nine Data Type Parts under Quick Start, which represent some of the more common types of fields used in a database, are as follows:

- **Address** Use this Data Type Part when you need fields to list address information. Clicking this option creates the following five fields—Address, City, State Province, Zip Postal, and Country Region.
- **Category** Use this Data Type Part when you need to create a list of categories. Clicking this option creates a list box with three generic category names.
- **Name** Use this Data Type Part to create fields to store the names of people. Clicking this option creates the following fields—Last Name, First Name, Contact Name, and File As.

- **Payment Type** Use this Data Type Part when you need a list of payment types for order tracking or contribution tracking purposes. Clicking this option creates a list box called Payment Type with four options—Cash, Credit Card, Check, and In Kind.
- **Phone** Use this Data Type Part when you need to create fields to store phone numbers. Clicking this option creates the following fields—Business Phone, Home Phone, Mobile Phone, and Fax Number.
- **Priority** Use this Data Type Part when you need to create a list of priority levels. Clicking this option creates a list box with three generic priority levels—(1) High, (2) Normal, and (3) Low.
- **Start and End Dates** Use this Data Type Part when you need fields to track start dates and end dates. Clicking this option creates two Date/Time fields.
- **Status** Use this Data Type Part when you need to create a list of status levels. Clicking this option creates a list box with five generic status levels—Not Started, In Progress, Completed, Deferred, and Waiting.
- **Tag** Use this Data Type Part when you need to create a list that allows you to select multiple items. Clicking this option creates a multi-value list with three generic items—Tag 1, Tag 2, and Tag 3.

See Table 4-1, on page 190, for a full discussion of the various data types available within Access 2010.

Click Name under the Quick Start category and Access creates four fields ready for you to use to track names of your contacts, as shown in Figure 4-17. You can add more Data Type Parts to this table by clicking another option under the Quick Start category.

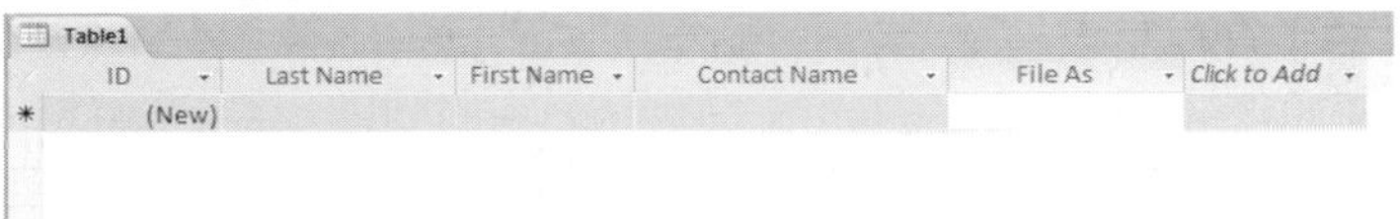

Figure 4-17 Use the Name Data Type Part when you need to create fields to record the names of people.

To add the Address Data Type Part to this table, first click the Click To Add entry to move the focus to the right of the File As field in the table Datasheet view. Access always adds new fields to the left of where the current focus is located in the Datasheet view grid. Now click the More Fields button in the Add & Delete group on the ribbon and then click Address under the Quick Start category. Access creates five more fields in your table, as shown in Figure 4-18. Your table now has fields to track the address information for your contacts.

Figure 4-18 You can add fields to hold address information by clicking the Address Data Type Part.

Using Data Type Parts can save you time when you're designing your tables in Access 2010 by giving you a jump start on creating common field types. Close the Table window now, and do not save the changes to this table when Access prompts you to save the changes.

Creating a Table in Design View

You could continue to use Application Parts and Data Type Parts to build some of the other tables in the Contact Tracking database to mimic those in Conrad Systems Contacts. However, you'll find it very useful to learn the mechanics of building a table from scratch, so now is a good time to explore Design view and learn how to build tables without using Application Parts or Data Type Parts. Application Parts offer only a few choices for sample tables, and there is no way to pick and choose which fields to include or exclude. By working in Design view, you'll see many additional features that you can use to customize the way your tables (and any queries, forms, or reports built on these tables) work when creating a table from scratch.

To begin creating a new table in Design view, click the Create tab on the ribbon and then click the Table Design button in the Tables group. Access 2010 displays a blank Table window in Design view, as shown in Figure 4-19.

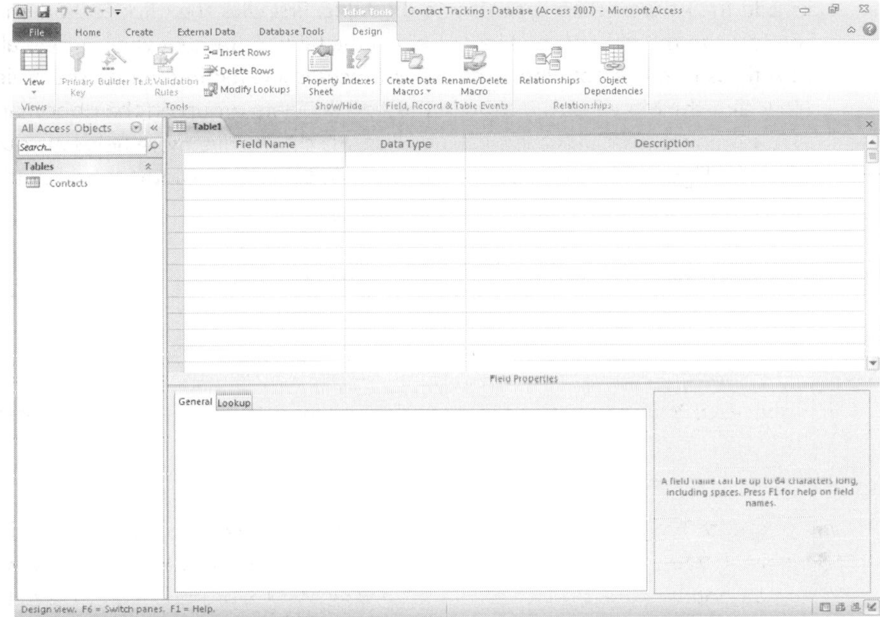

Figure 4-19 The Table Design command opens a new table in Design view.

In Design view, the upper part of the Table window displays columns in which you can enter the field names, the data type for each field, and a description of each field. After you select a data type for a field, Access 2010 allows you to set field properties in the lower-left section of the Table window. In the lower-right section of the Table window is a box in which Access displays information about fields or properties. The contents of this box change as you move from one location to another within the Table window.

For details about data type values, see "Understanding Field Data Types," on page 190.

Defining Fields

Now you're ready to begin defining the fields for the Companies table that mimics the one you can find in the Conrad Systems Contacts sample database (Contacts.accdb). Be sure the insertion point is in the first row of the Field Name column, and then type the name of the first field, **CompanyID**. Press Tab once to move to the Data Type column. A button with an arrow appears on the right side of the Data Type column. Here and elsewhere in Access 2010, this type of button signifies the presence of a list. Click the arrow or press Alt+Down Arrow to open the list of data type options, shown in Figure 4-20. In the Data Type column, you can either type a valid value or select from the values in the list. Select AutoNumber as the data type for CompanyID.

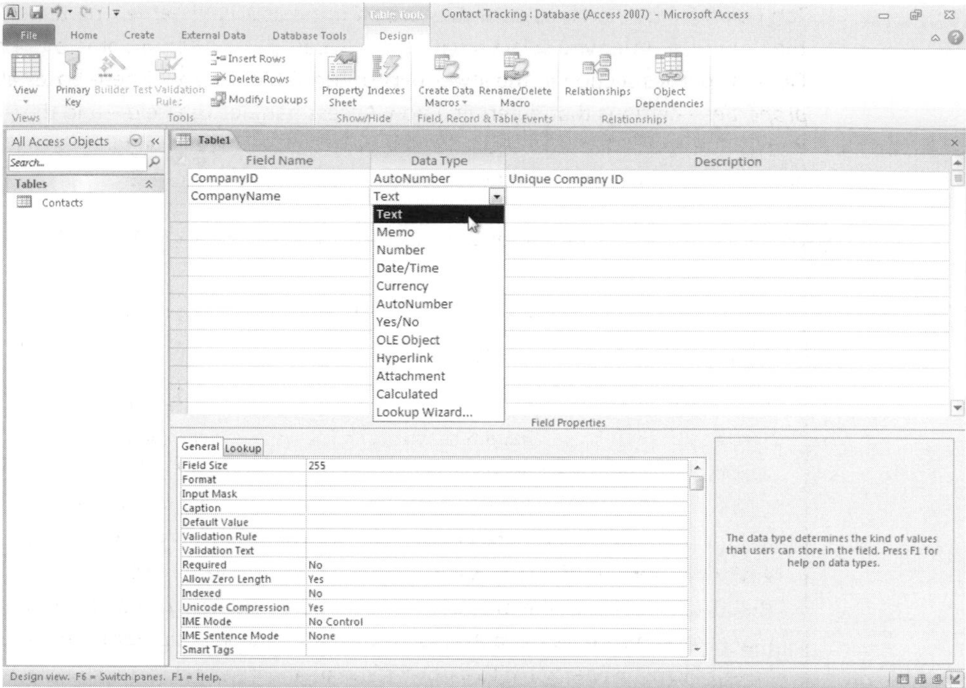

Figure 4-20 You can choose the data type of a field from a list of data type options.

In the Description column for each field, you can enter a descriptive phrase. Access 2010 displays this description on the status bar (at the bottom of the Access window) whenever you select this field in a query in Datasheet view or in a form in Form view or Datasheet view. For example, enter **Unique Company ID** in the Description column for the CompanyID field.

INSIDE OUT

Why Setting the Description Property Is Important

Entering a Description property for every field in your table helps document your application. Because Access 2010 also displays the description on the status bar, paying careful attention to what you type in the Description field can later pay big dividends as a kind of mini-help for the users of your database. Also, because this data propagates automatically, you probably don't want to type something nonsensical or silly. Typing "**I don't have a clue what this field does**" is probably not a good idea—it will show up later on the status bar!

Tab down to the next line, enter **CompanyName** as a field name, and then choose Text as the data type. After you select a data type, Access 2010 displays some property boxes in the Field Properties section in the lower part of the Table window. These boxes allow you to set *properties*—settings that determine how Access handles the field—and thereby customize a field. The properties Access displays depend on the data type you select; the properties appear with some default values in place, as shown in Figure 4-20.

For details about the values for each property, see "Setting Field Properties," on page 193.

Choosing Field Names

Access 2010 gives you lots of flexibility when it comes to naming your fields. A field name can be up to 64 characters long, can include any combination of letters, numbers, spaces, and special characters except a period (.), an exclamation point (!), an accent grave (`), and brackets ([ ]); however, the name cannot begin with a space and cannot include control characters (ANSI values 0 through 31). In general, you should give your fields meaningful names and should use the same name throughout for a field that occurs in more than one table. You should avoid using field names that might also match any name internal to Access or Microsoft Visual Basic. For example, all objects have a Name property, so it's a good idea to qualify a field containing a name by calling it CustomerName or CompanyName. You should also avoid names that are the same as built-in functions, such as Date, Time, Now, or Space. See Access Help for a list of all the built in function names.

Although you can use spaces anywhere within names in Access 2010, you should try to create field names and table names *without* embedded spaces. Many Structured Query Language (SQL) databases to which Access can link (notably Oracle and Ingres) do not support spaces within names. Although Microsoft SQL Server does allow spaces in names, you must enclose such names in brackets, or use quotes and execute a Set Quoted Identifier On command. If you ever want to move your application to a client/server environment and store your data in a SQL database such as SQL Server or Oracle, you'll most likely have to change any names in your database tables that have an embedded space character. As you'll learn later in this book, table field names propagate into the queries, forms, and reports that you design using these tables. So any name you decide to change later in a table must also be changed in all your queries, forms, and reports. See "Setting Table Design Options," on page 226, for details about options to propagate changes automatically.

If you use reserved words or function names for field names, Access 2010 catches most of these and displays a warning message. This message warns you that the field name you chose, such as Name or Date, is a reserved word and you could encounter errors when referring to that field in other areas of the database application. Access still allows you to use this name if you choose, but take note of the problems it could cause. To avoid potential conflicts, we recommend you avoid using reserved words and built-in functions for field names.

Understanding Field Data Types

Access 2010 supports 11 types of data, each with a specific purpose. You can see the details about each data type in Table 4-1. Access also gives you a 12th option, Lookup Wizard, to help you define the characteristics of foreign key fields that link to other tables. You'll learn about the Lookup Wizard in Chapter 6, "Designing Web Tables."

Table 4-1 Access Data Types

Data Type	Usage	Size
Text	Alphanumeric data.	Up to 255 characters.
Memo	Alphanumeric data—sentences and paragraphs.	Up to about 1 gigabyte (GB), but controls to display a memo are limited to the first 64,000 characters.
Number	Numeric data.	1, 2, 4, 8, or 16 bytes.
Date/Time	Dates and times.	8 bytes.
Currency	Monetary data, stored with 4 decimal places of precision.	8 bytes.
AutoNumber	Unique value generated by Access for each new record.	4 bytes (16 bytes for ReplicationID).
Yes/No	Boolean (true/false) data; Access stores the numeric value zero (0) for false, and –1 for true.	1 byte.
OLE Object	Pictures, graphs, or other ActiveX objects from another Windows-based application.	Up to about 2 GB.

Data Type	Usage	Size
Hyperlink	A link "address" to a document or file on the Internet, on an intranet, on a local area network (LAN), or on your local computer.	Up to 8,192 (each part of a Hyperlink data type can contain up to 2048 characters).
Attachment	You can attach files such as pictures, documents, spreadsheets, or charts; each Attachment field can contain an unlimited number of attachments per record, up to the storage limit of the size of a database file.	Up to about 2 GB.
Calculated	You can create an expression that uses data from one or more fields. You can designate different result data types from the expression.	Dependent on the data type of the Result Type property. Text data type result can have up to 243 characters. Memo, Number, Yes/No, and Date/Time should match their respective data types.
Lookup Wizard	The Lookup Wizard entry in the Data Type column in Design view is not actually a data type. When you choose this entry, a wizard starts to help you define either a simple or complex lookup field. A simple lookup field uses the contents of another table or a value list to validate the contents of a single value per row. A complex lookup field allows you to store multiple values of the same data type in each row.	Dependent on the data type of the lookup field.

For each field in your table, select the data type that is best suited to how you will use that field's data. For character data, you should normally select the Text data type. You can control the maximum length of a Text field by using a field property, as explained later. Use the Memo data type only for long strings of text that might exceed 255 characters or that might contain formatting characters such as tabs or line endings (carriage returns).

When you select the Number data type, you should think carefully about what you enter as the Field Size property because this property choice will affect precision as well as length. (For example, integer numbers do not have decimals.) The Date/Time data type is useful for calendar or clock data and has the added benefit of allowing calculations in seconds, minutes, hours, days, months, or years. For example, you can find out the difference in days between two Date/Time values.

INSIDE OUT

Understanding What's Inside the Date/Time Data Type

Use the Date/Time data type to store any date, time, or date and time value. It's useful to know that Access 2010 stores the date as the integer portion of the Date/Time data type and the time as the fractional portion—the fraction of a day, measured from midnight, that the time represents, accurate to seconds. For example, 6:00:00 A.M. internally is 0.25. The day number is actually the number of days since December 30, 1899 (there will be a test on that later!) and can be a negative number for dates prior to that date. When two Date/Time fields contain only a date, you can subtract one from the other to find out how many days are between the two dates.

You should generally use the Currency data type for storing money values. Currency has the precision of integers, but with exactly four decimal places. When you need to store a precise fractional number that's not money, use the Number data type and choose Decimal for the Field Size property.

The AutoNumber data type is specifically designed for automatic generation of primary key values. Depending on the settings for the Field Size and New Values properties you choose for an AutoNumber field, you can have Access 2010 create a sequential or random long integer. You can include only one field using the AutoNumber data type in any table. If you define more than one AutoNumber field, Access displays an error message when you try to save the table.

Use the Yes/No data type to hold Boolean (true or false) values. This data type is particularly useful for flagging accounts paid or not paid, or orders filled or not filled.

The OLE Object data type allows you to store complex data, such as pictures, graphs, or sounds, which can be edited or displayed through a dynamic link to another Windows-based application. For example, Access 2010 can store and allow you to edit a Microsoft Word document, a Microsoft Excel spreadsheet, a Microsoft PowerPoint presentation slide, a sound file (.wav), a video file (.avi), or pictures created using the Paint or Draw application.

The Hyperlink data type lets you store a simple or complex "link" to an external file or document. (Internally, Hyperlink is a memo data type with a special flag set to indicate that it is a link.) This link can contain a Uniform Resource Locator (URL) that points to a location on the World Wide Web or on a local intranet. It can also contain the Universal Naming Convention (UNC) name of a file on a server on your LAN or on your local computer drives. The link can point to a file that is in Hypertext Markup Language (HTML) or in a format that is supported by an ActiveX application on your computer.

The Attachment data type, introduced in Access 2007, is very similar to the OLE Object data type in that you can use it to store complex data. However, unlike the OLE Object data type, you can store *multiple* attachments in a single record. These files are stored in a binary field in a hidden system table. OLE objects usually result in database bloat because the files are not compressed, and Access also stores a bitmap thumbnail of the embedded file that can often be larger than the original file. For the Attachment data type, Access compresses each file, if it isn't already, and uses the original file rather than a generated thumbnail to minimize the amount of database bloat.

The Calculated data type, newly introduced in Access 2010, allows you to create a calculated result using an expression. The expression can include data from one or more fields. If you have a number field, for example, that holds quantity information for products purchased and a currency field that holds the price of a product, you can create a calculated field that multiplies the quantity and price fields and stores it with a result type of currency. You could also create a calculated field that concatenates first name, middle name, and last name fields and stores it with a result type of text for a field called Full Name. Access recalculates the value of the calculated field any time the dependent fields are changed.

CAUTION!

You can use the Attachment and Calculated data types only with databases in the .accdb file type. If you plan to create a database in the older .mdb format and have users with previous versions of Access use this database, you cannot define any fields as Attachment or Calculated.

Setting Field Properties

You can customize the way Access 2010 stores and handles each field by setting specific properties. These properties vary according to the data type you choose. Table 4-2 lists all the possible properties that can appear on a field's General tab in a table's Design view, and the data types that are associated with each property.

Table 4-2 Field Properties on the General Tab

Property	Data Type	Options, Description
Field Size	Text	Text can be from 0 through 255 characters long, with a default length of 255 characters.
	Number	**Byte.** A 1-byte integer containing values from 0 through 255.
		Integer. A 2-byte integer containing values from –32,768 through +32,767.
		Long Integer. A 4-byte integer containing values from –2,147,483,648 through +2,147,483,647.
		Single.[1] A 4-byte floating-point number containing values from -3.4×10^{38} through $+3.4 \times 10^{38}$ and up to seven significant digits.
		Double.[1] An 8-byte floating-point number containing values from -1.797×10^{308} through $+1.797 \times 10^{308}$ and up to 15 significant digits.
		Replication ID.[2] A 16-byte globally unique identifier (GUID).
		Decimal. A 12-byte integer with a defined decimal precision that can contain values from approximately -7.9228×10^{28} through $+7.9228 \times 10^{28}$. The default precision (number of decimal places) is 0 and the default scale is 18.
New Values	AutoNumber only	**Increment.** Values start at 1 and increment by 1 for each new row.
		Random. Access assigns a random long integer value to each new row.

Chapter 4

Property	Data Type	Options, Description
Format	Text, Memo	You can specify a custom format that controls how Access displays the data. For details about custom formats, see "Setting Control Properties for Client Forms," on page 865, or the Access Help topic "Format Property—Text and Memo Data Types."
	Number (except Replication ID), Currency, AutoNumber	**General Number (default).** No commas or currency symbols; the number of decimal places shown depends on the precision of the data.
		Currency.[3] Currency symbol (from Regional And Language Options in Windows Control Panel) and two decimal places.
		Euro. Euro currency symbol (regardless of Control Panel settings) and two decimal places.
		Fixed. At least one digit and two decimal places.
		Standard. Two decimal places and separator commas.
		Percent. Moves displayed decimal point two places to the right and appends a percentage (%) symbol.
		Scientific. Scientific notation (for example, 1.05E+06 represents 1.05×10^6).
		You can specify a custom format that controls how Access displays the data. For details about custom formats, see "Setting Control Properties for Client Forms," on page 865, or the Access Help topic "Format Property—Number and Currency Types."
	Date/Time[4]	**General Date (default).** Combines Short Date and Long Time formats (for example, 7/1/2010 5:30:10 PM).
		Long Date. Uses Long Date Style from the Regional And Language Options item in Control Panel (for example, Thursday, July 1, 2010).
		Medium Date. 1-Jul-2010.
		Short Date.[5] Uses Short Date Style from the Regional And Language Options item (for example, 7/1/2010).
		Long Time. Uses Time Style from the Regional And Language Options item (for example, 5:30:10 PM).
		Medium Time. 5:30 PM.
		Short Time. 17:30.
	Yes/No	**Yes/No (default)**
		True/False
		On/Off
		You can specify a custom format that controls how Access displays the data. For details about custom formats, see "Setting Control Properties for Client Forms," on page 865, or the Access Help topic "Format Property—Yes/No Data Type."
	Calculated	Format options for calculated fields depend on the Result Type. The format options and defaults for the Result Type align with the other data types.

Property	Data Type	Options, Description
Precision	Number, Decimal	You can specify the maximum number of digits allowed. The default value is 18, and you can specify an integer value between 1 and 28.
Scale	Number, Decimal	You can specify the number of digits stored to the right of the decimal point. This value must be less than or equal to the value of the Precision property.
Decimal Places	Number (except Replication ID), Currency, Calculated	You can specify the number of decimal places that Access displays. The default specification is Auto, which causes Access to display two decimal places for the Currency, Fixed, Standard, and Percent formats and the number of decimal places necessary to show the current precision of the numeric value for General Number format. You can also request a fixed display of decimal places ranging from 0 through 15.
Input Mask	Text, Number (except Replication ID), Date/Time, Currency	You can specify an editing mask that the user sees while entering data in the field. For example, you can have Access provide the delimiters in a date field such as __/__/__, or you can have Access format a U.S. phone number as (###) 000-0000. See "Defining Input Masks," on page 204, for details.
Caption	All	You can enter a more fully descriptive field name that Access displays in form labels and in report headings. (Tip: If you create field names with no embedded spaces, you can use the Caption property to specify a name that includes spaces for Access to use in labels and headers associated with this field in queries, forms, and reports.)
Default Value	Text, Memo, Number, Date/Time, Currency, Hyperlink, and Yes/No	You can specify a default value for the field that Access automatically uses for a new row if no other value is supplied. If you don't specify a Default Value, the field will be Null if the user fails to supply a value. (See also the Required property.)
Validation Rule	All (except OLE Object, Replication ID, Attachment, Calculated, and AutoNumber)	You can supply an expression that must be true whenever you enter or change data in this field. For example, **<100** specifies that a number must be less than 100. You can also check for one of a series of values. For example, you can have Access check for a list of valid cities by specifying **"Chicago" Or "New York" Or "San Francisco"**. In addition, you can specify a complex expression that includes any of the built-in functions in Access. See "Defining Simple Field Validation Rules," on page 201, for details.
Validation Text	All (except OLE Object, Replication ID, Attachment, Calculated, and AutoNumber)	You can specify a custom message that Access displays whenever the data entered does not pass your validation rule.
Required	All (except Calculated and AutoNumber)	If you don't want to allow a Null value in this field, set this property to Yes.
Allow Zero Length	Text, Memo, Hyperlink	You can set the field equal to a zero-length string ("") if you set this property to Yes. See the sidebar "Nulls and Zero-Length Strings," on page 199, for more information.

Property	Data Type	Options, Description
Indexed	All except OLE Object, Calculated, and Attachment	You can ask that an index be built to speed access to data values. You can also require that the values in the indexed field always be unique for the entire table. See "Adding Indexes," on page 222, for details.
Unicode Compression	Text, Memo, Hyperlink	As of version 2000, Access stores character fields in an .mdb and .accdb file using a double-byte (Unicode) character set to support extended character sets in languages that require them. The Latin character set required by most Western European languages (such as English, Spanish, French, or German) requires only 1 byte per character. When you set Unicode Compression to Yes for character fields, Access stores compressible characters in 1 byte instead of 2, thus saving space in your database file. However, Access will not compress Memo or Hyperlink fields that will not compress to fewer than 4,096 bytes. The default for new tables is Yes in all countries where the standard language character set does not require 2 bytes to store all the characters.
IME Mode, IME Sentence Mode	Text, Memo, Hyperlink	On machines with an Asian version of Windows and appropriate Input Method Editor (IME) installed, these properties control conversion of characters in kanji, hiragana, katakana, and hangul character sets.
Smart Tags	All data types except Yes/No, OLE Object, Attachment, and Replication ID	Indicates the registered smart tag name and action that you want associated with this field. When the user views this field in a table datasheet, a query datasheet, or a form, Access displays a smart tag available indicator next to the field. The user can click on the indicator and select the smart tag action to perform. For an example using a smart tag, see Chapter 14, "Customizing a Form."
Text Align	All data types except Attachment	**General (default).** Text aligns to the left, but numbers and dates align to the right.
		Left. All data aligns to the left.
		Center. All data aligns to the center of the field.
		Right. All data aligns to the right.
		Distribute. The data is evenly distributed throughout the field.
Text Format	Memo only	**Plain Text (default).** The text in the Memo field is stored and displayed as plain text.
		Rich Text. You can specify that the data in the Memo field can be formatted as rich text. Access applies HTML formatting tags to your data.
Append Only	Hyperlink and Memo	You can specify to see column history for this field. When you change the field's data, the data change and time stamp are recorded and appended to the version history of the field.

Property	Data Type	Options, Description
Show Date Picker	Date/Time only	**For Dates (default).** Displays the built-in date picker control to select a date when the field receives focus in a table datasheet or query.
		Never. The built-in date picker control is not shown when the field receives focus in a table datasheet or query.
Expression	Calculated	The expression used to calculate the value for this column. The expression can use the value of one or more fields in the same table and can be up to 65,000 characters in length.
Result Type	Calculated	For calculated fields, you need to provide the data type that results from the expression you use for the field. The result type can be Double, Integer, Long Integer, Single, Replication ID, Decimal, Text, Date/Time, Memo, Currency, or Yes/No.

1 Single and Double field sizes use an internal storage format called floating point, which can handle very large or very small numbers, but which is somewhat imprecise. If the number you need to store contains more than 7 significant digits for a Single or more than 15 significant digits for a Double, the number will be rounded. For example, if you try to save 10,234,567 in a Single, the actual value stored will be 10,234,570. Likewise, Access stores 10.234567 as 10.23457 in a Single. If you want absolute fractional precision, use Decimal field size instead.

2 In general, you should use the Replication ID field size only in an Access 2003 format and earlier database that is managed by the Replication Manager.

3 Note that Currency, Euro, Fixed, and Standard formats always display two decimal places regardless of the number of actual decimal places in the underlying data. Access rounds any number to two decimal places for display if the number contains more than two decimal places.

4 You can also specify a custom format in addition to the built-in ones described here. See Chapter 14 for details.

5 To help alleviate problems with dates spanning the start of the century, we recommend that you select the Use Four-Digit Year Formatting check box in Access. To do this, click the File tab on the Backstage view, click Options, and then scroll to the General section in the Client Settings category to find this option. You should also be sure that your Short Date Style in the Regional And Language Options dialog box uses a four-digit year. (This is the default in Windows XP, Windows Vista, and Windows 7; you can double-check your settings by accessing Regional And Language Options within Control Panel.)

INSIDE OUT Don't Specify a Validation Rule Without Validation Text

If you specify a validation rule but no validation text, Access 2010 generates an ugly and cryptic message that your users might not understand:

"One or more values are prohibited by the validation rule '<your expression here>' set for '<table name.field name>'. Enter a value that the expression for this field can accept."

Unless you like getting lots of support calls, we recommend that you always enter a custom validation text message whenever you specify a validation rule.

For details about the properties on the Lookup tab, see "Taking a Look at Lookup Properties," on page 275.

Nulls and Zero-Length Strings

Relational databases support a special value in fields, called a Null, that indicates an unknown value. In contrast, you can set Text and Memo fields to a zero-length string to indicate that the value of a field is known but the field is empty.

Why is it important to differentiate Nulls (unknown values) from zero-length strings? Here's an example: Suppose you have a database that stores the results of a survey about automobile preferences. For questionnaires on which there is no response to a color-preference question, it is appropriate to store a Null. You don't want to match responses based on an unknown response, and you don't want to include the row in calculating totals or averages. On the other hand, some people might have responded "I don't care" for a color preference. In this case, you have a known "no preference" answer, and a zero-length string is appropriate. You can match all "I don't care" responses and include the responses in totals and averages.

Another example might be fax numbers in a customer database. If you store a Null, it means that you don't know whether the customer has a fax number. If you store a zero-length string, you know the customer has no fax number. Access 2010 gives you the flexibility to deal with both types of "empty" values.

You can join tables on zero-length strings, and two zero-length strings will compare to be equal. However, for Text, Memo, and Hyperlink fields, you must set the Allow Zero Length property to Yes to allow users to enter zero-length strings. (Yes became the default value in Microsoft Access 2002.) Otherwise, Access converts a zero-length or all-blank string to a Null before storing the value. If you also set the Required property of the Text field to Yes, Access stores a zero-length string if the user enters either "" (two double quotes with no space) or blanks in the field.

Nulls have special properties. A Null value cannot be equal to any other value, not even to another Null. This means you cannot join (link) two tables on Null values. Also, the question "Is A equal to B?" when A, B, or both A and B contain a Null, can never be answered "Yes." The answer, literally, is "I don't know." Likewise, the answer to the question "Is A not equal to B?" is also "I don't know." Finally, Null values do not participate in aggregate calculations involving such functions as Sum or Avg. You can test a value to determine whether it is a Null by comparing it to the special keyword NULL or by using the IsNull built-in function.

Completing the Fields in the Companies Table

You now know enough about field data types and properties to finish designing the Companies table in this example. (You can also follow this example using the tblCompanies table from the Conrad Systems Contacts sample database.) Use the information listed in Table 4-3 to design the table shown in Figure 4-21.

Table 4-3 Field Definitions for the Companies Table

Field Name	Data Type	Description	Field Size
CompanyID	AutoNumber	Unique Company ID	
CompanyName	Text	Company Name	50
Department	Text	Department	50
Address	Text	Address	255
City	Text	City	50
County	Text	County	50
StateOrProvince	Text	State or Province	20
PostalCode	Text	Postal/Zip Code	10
PhoneNumber	Text	Phone Number	15
FaxNumber	Text	Fax Number	15
Website	Hyperlink	Website address	
ReferredBy	Number	Contact who referred this company	Long Integer

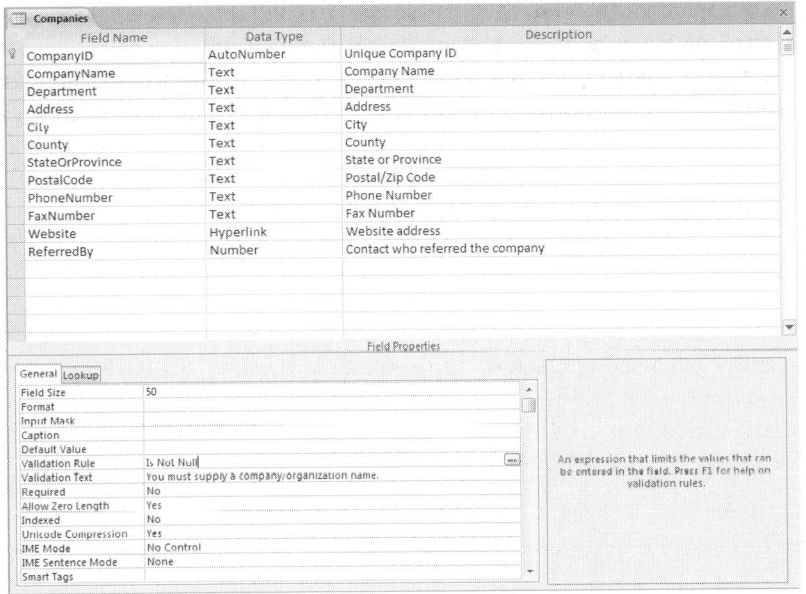

Figure 4-21 Your fields in the Companies table should look like this. You'll learn how to define validation rules in the next section.

Defining Simple Field Validation Rules

To define a simple check on the values that you allow in a field, enter an expression in the Validation Rule property box for the field. Access 2010 won't allow you to enter a field value that violates this rule. Access performs this validation for data entered in a Table window in Datasheet view, in an updateable query, or in a form. You can specify a more restrictive validation rule in a form, but you cannot override the rule defined for the field in the table by specifying a completely different rule in the form. For more information on using validation rules in forms, see Chapter 14.

In general, a field validation expression consists of an operator and a comparison value. If you do not include an operator, Access assumes you want an "equals" (=) comparison. You can specify multiple comparisons separated by the Boolean operators OR and AND.

It is good practice to always enclose text string values in quotation marks. If one of your values is a text string containing blanks or special characters, you must enclose the entire string in quotation marks. For example, to limit the valid entries for a City field to the two largest cities in the state of California, enter **"Los Angeles" Or "San Diego"**. If you are comparing date values, you must enclose the date constants in pound sign (#) characters, as in #07/1/2010#.

You can use the comparison symbols to compare the value in the field to a value or values in your validation rule. Comparison symbols are summarized in Table 4-4. For example, you might want to ensure that a numeric value is always less than 1000. To do this, enter **<1000**. You can use one or more pairs of comparisons to ask Access to check that the value falls within certain ranges. For example, if you want to verify that a number is in the range of 50 through 100, enter either **>=50 And <=100** or **Between 50 And 100**. Another way to test for a match in a list of values is to use the IN comparison operator. For example, to test for states surrounding the U.S. capital, enter **In ("Virginia", "Maryland")**. If all you need to do is ensure that the user enters a value, you can enter the special comparison phrase **Is Not Null**.

Table 4-4 Comparison Symbols Used in Validation Rules

Operator	Meaning
NOT	Use before any comparison operator except IS NOT NULL to perform the converse test. For example, NOT > 5 is equivalent to <=5.
<	Less than
<=	Less than or equal to
>	Greater than
>=	Greater than or equal to
=	Equal to
<>	Not equal to
IN	Test for equal to any member in a list; comparison value must be a comma-separated list enclosed in parentheses
BETWEEN	Test for a range of values; comparison value must be two values (a low and a high value) separated by the AND operator
LIKE	Test a Text or Memo field to match a pattern string
IS NOT NULL	Requires the user to enter a value in the field

INSIDE OUT A Friendlier Way to Require a Field Value

When you set the Required property to Yes and the user fails to enter a value, Access 2010 displays an unfriendly message:

"You must enter a value in the '<tablename.fieldname>' field."

We recommend that you use the Validation Rule property to require a value in the field and then use the Validation Text property to generate your own specific message.

If you need to validate a Text, Memo, or Hyperlink field against a matching pattern (for example, a postal code or a phone number), you can use the LIKE comparison operator. You provide a text string as a comparison value that defines which characters are valid in which positions. Access understands a number of *wildcard characters*, which you can use to define positions that can contain any single character, zero or more characters, or any single number. These characters are shown in Table 4-5.

Table 4-5 LIKE Wildcard Characters

Character	Meaning
?	Any single character
*	Zero or more characters; use to define leading, trailing, or embedded strings that don't have to match any specific pattern characters
#	Any single digit

You can also specify that any particular position in the Text or Memo field can contain only characters from a list that you provide. You can specify a range of characters within a list by entering the low value character, a hyphen, and the high value character, as in [A-Z] or [3-7]. If you want to test a position for any characters *except* those in a list, start the list with an exclamation point (*!*). You must enclose all lists in brackets (*[ ]*). You can see examples of validation rules using LIKE here.

Validation Rule	Tests For
LIKE "#####" or	A U.S. 5-digit ZIP Code
LIKE "#####-####"	A U.S. 9-digit ZIP+ Code
LIKE "[A-Z]#[A-Z] #[A-Z]#"	A Canadian postal code
LIKE "###-##-####"	A U.S. Social Security Number
LIKE "Smith*"	A string that begins with *Smith*[1]
LIKE "*smith##*"	A string that contains *smith* followed by two numbers, anywhere in the string
LIKE "??00####"	An eight-character string that contains any first two characters followed by exactly two zeros and then any four digits
LIKE "[!0-9BMQ]*####"	A string that contains any character other than a number or the letter *B, M,* or *Q* in the first position and ends with exactly four digits

1 Character string comparisons in Access are case-insensitive. So, smith, SMITH, and Smith are all equal.

Defining Input Masks

To assist you in entering formatted data, Access 2010 allows you to define an *input mask* for Text, Number (except Replication ID), Date/Time, and Currency data types. You can use an input mask to do something as simple as forcing all letters entered to be uppercase or as complex as adding parentheses and hyphens to phone numbers. You create an input mask by using the special mask definition characters shown in Table 4-6. You can also embed strings of characters that you want to display for formatting or store in the data field.

Table 4-6 Input Mask Definition Characters

Mask Character	Meaning
0	A single digit must be entered in this position.
9	A digit or a space can be entered in this position. If the user skips this position by moving the insertion point past the position without entering anything, Access stores nothing in this position.
#	A digit, a space, or a plus or minus sign can be entered in this position. If the user skips this position by moving the insertion point past the position without entering anything, Access stores a space.
L	A letter must be entered in this position.
?	A letter can be entered in this position. If the user skips this position by moving the insertion point past the position without entering anything, Access stores nothing.
A	A letter or a digit must be entered in this position.
a	A letter or a digit can be entered in this position. If the user skips this position by moving the insertion point past the position without entering anything, Access stores nothing.
&	A character or a space must be entered in this position.
C	Any character or a space can be entered in this position. If the user skips this position by moving the insertion point past the position without entering anything, Access stores nothing.
.	Decimal placeholder (depends on the setting in the Regional And Language Options item in Control Panel).
,	Thousands separator (depends on the setting in the Regional And Language Options item in Control Panel).
: ; - /	Date and time separators (depends on the settings in the Regional And Language Options item in Control Panel).
<	Converts to lowercase all characters that follow.
>	Converts to uppercase all characters that follow.
!	Causes the mask to fill from right to left when you define optional characters on the left end of the mask. You can place this character anywhere in the mask.

Mask Character	Meaning
\	Causes the character immediately following to be displayed as a literal character rather than as a mask character.
"literal"	You can also enclose any literal string in double quotation marks rather than use the \ character repeatedly.

An input mask consists of three parts, separated by semicolons. The first part defines the mask string using mask definition characters and embedded literal data. The optional second part indicates whether you want the embedded literal characters stored in the field in the database. Set this second part to **0** to store the characters or to **1** to store only the data entered. The optional third part defines a single character that Access 2010 uses as a placeholder to indicate positions where data can be entered. The default placeholder character is an underscore (_).

Perhaps the best way to learn to use input masks is to take advantage of the Input Mask Wizard. In the Companies table of the Contact Tracking database, the PhoneNumber field could benefit from the use of an input mask. Click the PhoneNumber field in the upper part of the Table window in Design view, and then click in the Input Mask property box in the lower part of the window. You should see a small button with three dots on it (called the Build button) to the right of the property box.

Build

Click the Build button to start the Input Mask Wizard. If you haven't already saved the table, the wizard will insist that you do so. Save the table and name it Companies. When Access 2010 warns you that you have not defined a primary key and asks if you want to create a primary key now, click No. We'll define a primary key in the next section. On the first page, the wizard gives you a number of choices for standard input masks that it can generate for you. In this case, click the first one in the list—Phone Number, as shown in Figure 4-22. Note that you can type something in the Try It box below the Input Mask list to test the mask.

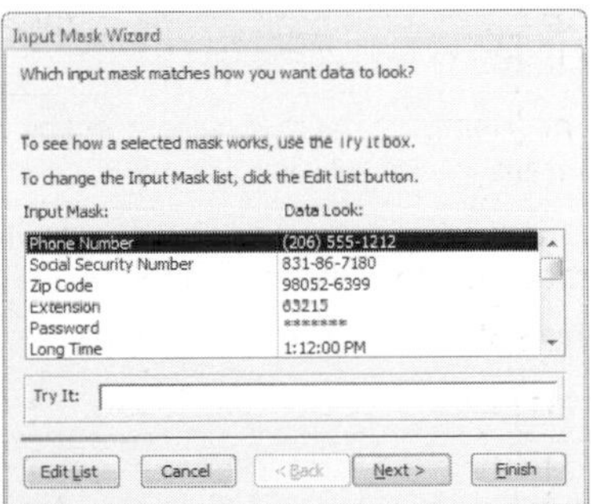

Figure 4-22 You can choose from several built-in input masks in the Input Mask Wizard.

Click Next to go to the next page. On this page, shown in Figure 4-23, you can see the mask name, the proposed mask string, a list from which you select the placeholder character, and another Try It box. The default underscore character (_) works well as a placeholder character for phone numbers.

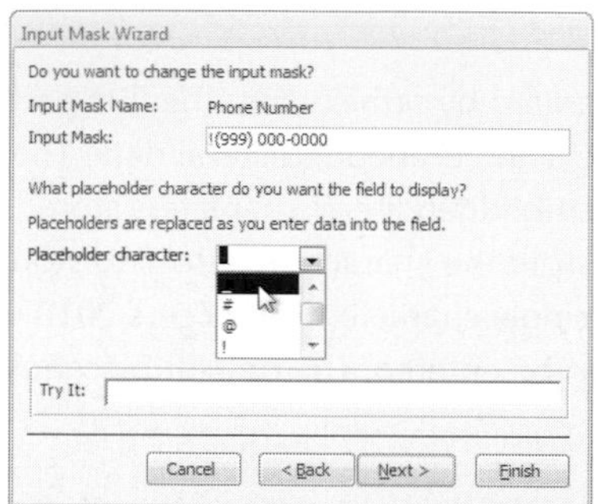

Figure 4-23 You can choose the placeholder character in the Input Mask Wizard.

Click Next to go to the next page, where you can choose whether you want the data stored without the formatting characters (the default) or stored with the parentheses, spaces, and hyphen separator. In Figure 4-24, we're indicating that we want the data stored with the formatting characters. Click Next to go to the final page, and then click the Finish button on that page to store the mask in the property setting. Figure 4-25 shows the resulting mask in the PhoneNumber field. You'll find this same mask handy for any text field that is meant to contain a U.S. phone number (such as the phone number fields in the Contacts table).

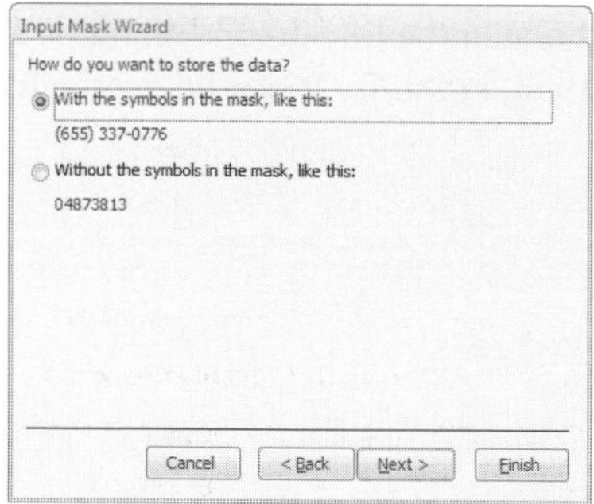

Figure 4-24 You can choose to store formatting characters.

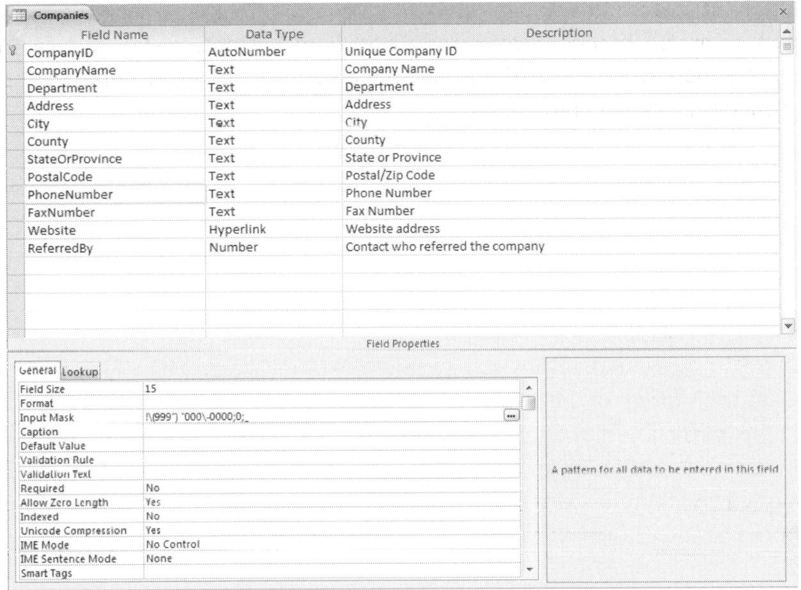

Figure 4-25 The wizard stores the input mask for PhoneNumber based on the criteria you selected.

Note

If you look closely at Figure 4-25, you can see a backslash before the area code and quotation marks around the second parenthesis. When you complete the Input Mask Wizard, Access initially does not display these extra characters. After you click off that field or save the table, Access adds the missing characters. The mask generated by the wizard is incorrect, but the table editor fixes it before saving.

CAUTION !

Although an input mask can be very useful to help guide the user to enter valid data, if you define an input mask incorrectly or do not consider all possible valid values, you can prevent the user from entering necessary data. For example, we just showed you how to build an input mask for a U.S. telephone number, but that mask would prevent someone from entering a European phone number correctly.

Defining a Primary Key

Every table in a relational database should have a primary key. Telling Access 2010 how to define the primary key is quite simple. Open the table in Design view and click the row selector to the left of the field you want to use as the primary key. If you need to select multiple fields for your primary key, hold down the Ctrl key and click the row selector of each additional field that you need.

For details about designing primary keys for your tables, see Article 1, "Designing Your Database Application," on the companion CD.

After you select all the fields you want for the primary key, click the Primary Key button in the Tools group of the Design contextual tab on the ribbon. Access 2010 displays a key symbol to the left of the selected field(s) to acknowledge your definition of the primary key. To eliminate all primary key designations, see "Adding Indexes," on page 222. When you've finished creating the Companies table for the Contact Tracking database, the primary key should be the CompanyID field, as shown in Figure 4-26.

Be sure to click the Save button on the Quick Access Toolbar to save this latest change to your table definition.

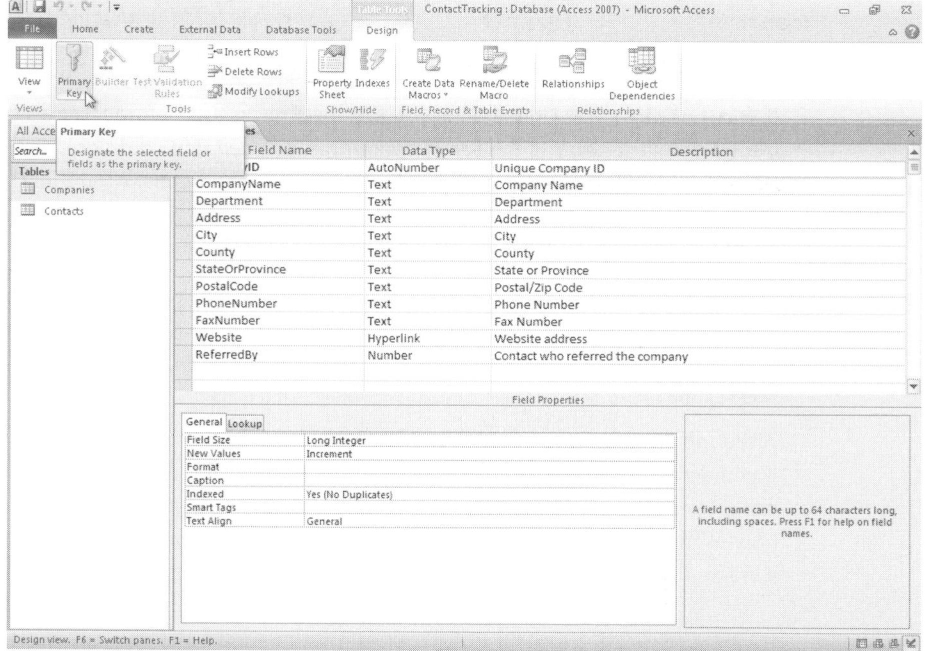

Figure 4-26 You can define the primary key for the Companies table easily by selecting the field in Design view and clicking the Primary Key button on the ribbon.

Defining a Table Validation Rule

The last detail to define is any validation rules that you want Access 2010 to apply to any fields in the table. Although field validation rules get checked as you enter each new value, Access checks a table validation rule only when you save or add a row. Table validation rules are handy when the values in one field depend on what's stored in another field. You need to wait until the entire row is about to be saved before checking one field against another.

One of the tables in the Contact Tracking database—Products—needs a table validation rule. Define that table now using the specifications in Table 4-7. Be sure to define ProductID as the primary key, and then save the table and name it Products.

Table 4-7 Field Definitions for the Products Table

Field Name	Data Type	Description	Field Size
ProductID	AutoNumber	Unique product identifier	
ProductName	Text	Product description	100
CategoryDescription	Text	Description of the category	50
UnitPrice	Currency	Price	
TrialVersion	Yes/No	Is this a trial version?	
TrialExpire	Number	If trial version, number of days before expiration	Long Integer

To define a table validation rule, be sure that the table is in Design view, and then click the Property Sheet button in the Show/Hide group of the Design contextual tab on the ribbon, shown in Figure 4-27.

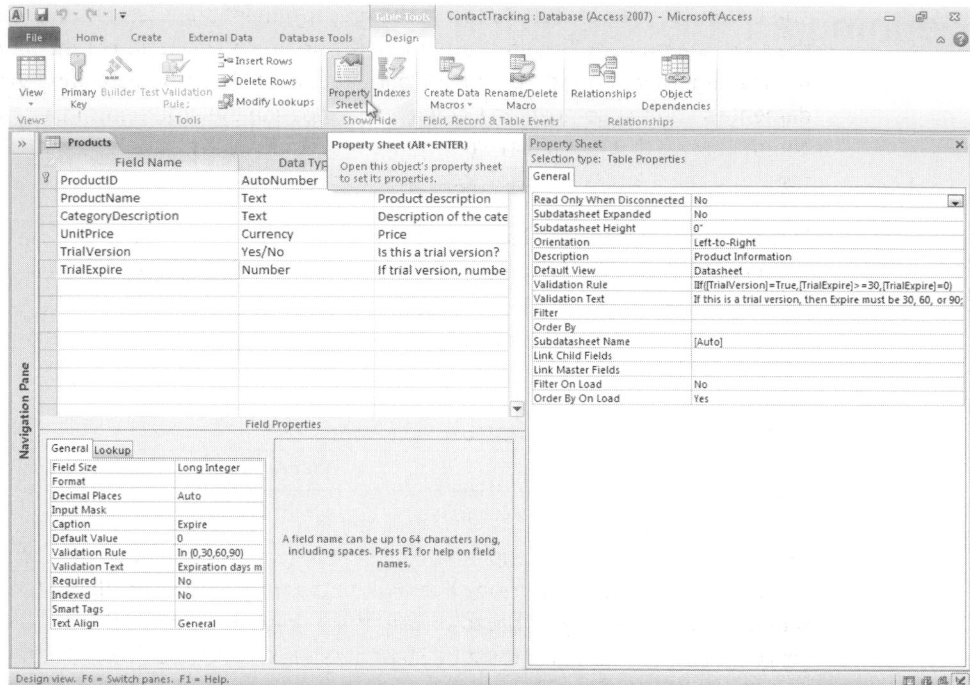

Figure 4-27 You can define a table validation rule in the property sheet for the table.

To learn more about expressions, see "Using the Expression Builder," on page 572.

On the Validation Rule line in the table's property sheet, you can enter any valid comparison expression, or you can use one of the built-in functions to test your table's field values. In the Products table, we want to be sure that any trial version of the software expires in 30, 60, or 90 days. Zero is also a valid value if this particular product isn't a trial version. As you can see in Figure 4-27, we've already entered a *field* validation rule for TrialExpire on the General tab to make sure the TrialExpire value is always 0, 30, 60, or 90—IN (0, 30, 60, 90). But how do we make sure that TrialExpire is zero if TrialVersion is False, or one of the other values if TrialVersion is True? For that, we need to define a *table-level* validation rule in the table's property sheet.

To refer to a field name, enclose the name in brackets (*[ ]*), as shown in Figure 4-27. You'll use this technique whenever you refer to the name of an object anywhere in an expression. In this case, we're using a special built-in function called Immediate If (or IIF for short) in the table validation rule to perform the test on the TrialExpire and TrialVersion fields.

The IIF function can evaluate a test in the first argument and then return the evaluation of the second argument if the first argument is true or the evaluation of the third argument if the first argument is false. As you will learn in Chapter 24, "Understanding Visual Basic Fundamentals," on the companion CD, you must separate the arguments in a function call with commas. Note that we said *evaluation of the argument*—this means we can enter additional tests, even another IIF, in the second and third arguments.

In the Products table, you want to make sure that the TrialVersion and TrialExpire fields are in sync with each other. If this is not a trial version, the TrialExpire field value should be zero (indicating the product never expires), and if it is a trial version, TrialExpire must be set to some value greater than or equal to 30. The expression we used to accomplish this is as follows:

IIf([TrialVersion]=True,[TrialExpire]>=30,[TrialExpire]=0)

Therefore, the first argument uses IIF to evaluate the expression **[TrialVersion] = True**—is the value in the field named TrialVersion True? If this is true (this is a trial version that must have a nonzero number of expiration days), IIF returns the evaluation of the second argument. If this is not a trial version, IIF evaluates the third argument. Now all we need to do is type the appropriate test based on the true or false result on TrialVersion. If this is a trial version, the TrialExpire field must be 30 or greater (we'll let the field validation rule make sure it's exactly 30, 60, or 90), so we need to test for that by entering **[TrialExpire] >= 30** in the second argument. If this is not a trial version, we need to make sure TrialExpire is zero by entering **[TrialExpire] = 0** in the third argument. Got it? If TrialVersion is True, then [TrialExpire] >= 30 must be true or the validation rule will fail. If TrialVersion is False, then [TrialExpire] = 0 must be true. As you might imagine, once you become more familiar with building expressions and with the available built-in functions, you can create very sophisticated table validation rules.

On the Validation Text line of the table's property sheet, enter the text that you want Access to display whenever the table validation rule is violated. You should be careful to word this message so that the user clearly understands what is wrong. If you enter a table validation rule and fail to specify validation text, Access displays the following message when the user enters invalid data: "One or more values are prohibited by the validation rule '< *your validation rule expression here* >' set for '<*table name*>'. Enter a value that the expression for this field can accept."

Not very pretty, is it? And you can imagine what the user will say about your IIF expression!

Understanding Other Table Properties

As you can see in Figure 4-27, Access 2010 provides several additional table properties that you can set in Design view. You can enter a description of the table in the Description property, and you'll see this description in the Navigation pane if you ask for the Details view. For Default View, you can choose from Datasheet (the default), PivotTable, or PivotChart. You can read more about PivotTable and PivotChart views in Chapter 15, "Advanced Form Design."

The Filter property lets you predefine criteria to limit the data displayed in the Datasheet view of this table. If you set Filter On Load to Yes, Access applies the filter that you defined when you open the datasheet. You can use Order By to define one or more fields that define the default display sequence of rows in this table when in Datasheet view. If you don't define an Order By property, Access displays the rows in primary key sequence. You can set the Order By On Load property to Yes to request that Access always applies any Order By specification when opening the datasheet.

Note

If you apply a filter or specify a sorting sequence when you have the table open in Datasheet view, Access 2010 saves the filter in the Filter property and the sorting sequence in the Order By property. If you have Filter On Load or Order By On Load set to Yes, Access reapplies the previous filter or sort sequence criteria the next time you open the datasheet.

You can find five properties—Subdatasheet Name, Link Child Fields, Link Master Fields, Subdatasheet Height, and Subdatasheet Expanded—that are all related. Access 2000 introduced a feature that lets you see information from related tables when you view the datasheet of a table. For example, in the Contacts Tracking database you have been building, you can set the Subdatasheet properties in the definition of Contacts to also show you related information from ContactEvents or ContactProducts. In the Proseware Housing Reservations sample database, you can see Departments and their Employees, or Employees and their Reservation Requests. Figure 4-28 shows you the Departments table in Housing.accdb open in Datasheet view. For this table, we defined a subdatasheet to show related employee information for each department.

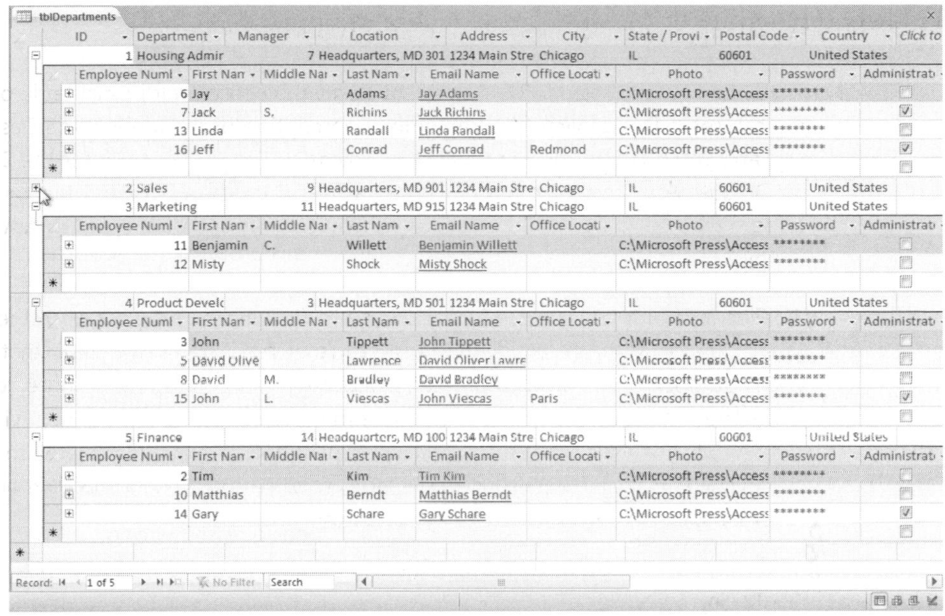

Figure 4-28 The datasheet for the Departments table in the Proseware Housing Reservations sample database shows an expanded subdatasheet.

Notice the small plus and minus signs at the beginning of each department row. Click on a plus sign to expand the subdatasheet to show related employees. Click the minus sign to shrink the subdatasheet and show only department information. Table 4-8 explains each of the Table Property settings that you can specify to attach a subdatasheet to a table.

Table 4-8 Table Properties for Defining a Subdatasheet

Property	Setting	Description
Subdatasheet Name	[Auto]	Creates a subdatasheet using the first table that has a *many* relationship defined with this table.
	[None]	Turns off the subdatasheet feature.
	Table.*name* or Query.*name*	Uses the selected table or query as the subdatasheet.

Property	Setting	Description
Link Child Fields	Name(s) of the foreign key fields(s) in the related table, separated by semicolons	Defines the fields in the subdatasheet table or query that match the primary key fields in this table. When you choose a table or query for the Subdatasheet Name property, Access uses an available relationship definition or matching field names and data types to automatically set this property for you. You can correct this setting if Access has guessed wrong.
Link Master Fields	Name(s) of the primary key field(s) in this table, separated by semicolons	Defines the primary key fields that Access uses to link to the subdatasheet table or query. When you choose a table or query for the Subdatasheet Name property, Access uses an available relationship definition or matching field names and data types to set this property automatically for you. You can correct this setting if Access has guessed wrong.
Subdatasheet Height	A measurement in inches	If you specify zero (the default), each subdatasheet expands to show all available rows when opened. When you specify a nonzero value, the subdatasheet window opens to the height you specify. If the height is insufficient to display all rows, a scroll bar appears to allow you to look at all the rows.
Subdatasheet Expanded	Yes or No	If you specify Yes, all subdatasheets appear expanded when you open the table datasheet. No is the default.

INSIDE OUT Don't Set Subdatasheet Properties in a Table

For a production application, it's a good idea to set Subdatasheet Name in all your tables to [None]. First, when Access 2010 opens your table, it must not only fetch the rows from the table but also fetch the rows defined in the subdatasheet. Adding a subdatasheet to a large table can affect performance negatively.

However, you might find the table and query subdatasheets feature useful in your own personal databases. We'll show you how to build a query with a subdatasheet in Chapter 10, "Building Complex Queries," and a form that uses a subdatasheet in Chapter 15.

You can use the Orientation property to specify the reading sequence of the data in Datasheet view. The default in most versions of Access is Left-to-Right. In versions that support a language that is normally read right to left, the default is Right-to-Left. When you use Right-to-Left, field and table captions appear right-justified, the field order is right to left, and the tab sequence proceeds right to left.

The Read Only When Disconnected property by default is set to No, which means you can still update or add new records to a table that is linked to a Microsoft SharePoint Services site when you are offline. We'll discuss working with data in an Access Services application in Chapter 22, "Using Web Applications in a Browser."

Defining Relationships

After you have defined two or more related tables, you should tell Access 2010 how the tables are related. You do this so that Access 2010 will be able to link all your tables when you need to use them in queries, forms, or reports.

Thus far in this chapter, you have seen how to build the main subject tables of the Contact Tracking database—Companies, Contacts, and Products. Before we define the relationships in this sample database, you need to create a couple of *linking* tables that define the many-to-many relationships between the Companies and Contacts tables and between the Products and Contacts tables. Table 4-9 shows you the fields you need for the Company Contacts table that forms the "glue" between the Companies and Contacts tables.

Table 4-9 Field Definitions for the Company Contacts Table

Field Name	Data Type	Description	Field Size
CompanyID	Number	Company/organization	Long Integer
ContactID	Number	Person within company	Long Integer
Position	Text	Person's position within the company	50
DefaultForContact	Yes/No	Is this the default company for this contact?	

Define the combination of CompanyID and ContactID as the primary key for this table by clicking the selection button next to CompanyID and then holding down the Ctrl key and clicking the button next to ContactID. Click the Primary Key button in the Tools group of the Design tab on the ribbon to define the key and then save the table as CompanyContacts.

Table 4-10 shows you the fields you need to define the Contact Products table that creates the link between the Contacts and Products tables.

Table 4-10 Field Definitions for the Contact Products Table

Field Name	Data Type	Description	Field Size
CompanyID	Number	Company/ organization	Long Integer
ContactID	Number	Related contact	Long Integer
ProductID	Number	Related product	Long Integer
DateSold	Date/Time	Date product sold	
SoldPrice	Currency	Price paid	

The primary key of the Contact Products table is the combination of CompanyID, ContactID, and ProductID. You can click CompanyID to select it and then hold down the Shift key while you click ProductID (if you defined the fields in sequence) to select all three fields. Click the Primary Key button in the Tools group of the Design tab on the ribbon to define the key, and then save the table as ContactProducts.

You need one last table, the Contact Events Table, to define all the major tables you'll need for Contact Tracking. Table 4-11 shows the fields you need. The primary key for this table is the combination of ContactID and ContactDateTime. Note that we took advantage of the fact that a Date/Time data type in Access 2010 can store both a date and a time, so we don't need the two separate date and time fields. Save this last table as ContactEvents.

Table 4-11 Field Definitions for the Contact Events Table

Field Name	Data Type	Description	Field Size
ContactID	Number	Related contact	Long Integer
ContactDateTime	Date/Time	Date and time of the contact	
ContactNotes	Memo	Description of the contact	
ContactFollowUpDate	Date/Time	Follow-up date	

Now, you're ready to start defining relationships. To define relationships, first close any Table windows that are open and then click the Relationships command in the Relationships group of the Database Tools tab on the ribbon to open the Relationships window. If this is the first time you have defined relationships in this database, Access 2010 opens a blank Relationships window and opens the Show Table dialog box, shown in Figure 4-29.

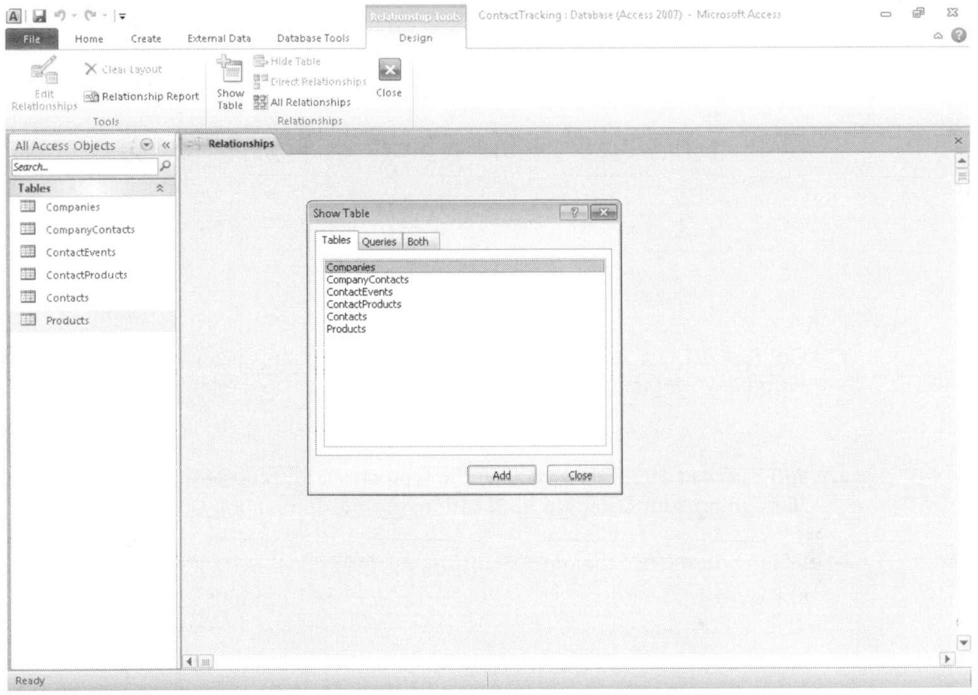

Figure 4-29 Access displays the Show Table dialog box when you open the Relationships window for the first time.

In the Show Table dialog box, select each table and click Add in turn. Click Close to dismiss the Show Table dialog box.

Defining Your First Relationship

A company can have several contacts, and any contact can belong to several companies or organizations. This means that companies have a many-to-many relationship with contacts. Defining a many-to-many relationship between two tables requires a linking table. Let's link the Companies and Contacts tables by defining the first half of the relationship—the one between Companies and the linking table, CompanyContacts. You can see that for the CompanyID primary key in the Companies table, there is a matching CompanyID foreign key in the CompanyContacts table. To create the relationship you need, click in the CompanyID field in the Companies table and drag it to the CompanyID field in the CompanyContacts table, as shown in Figure 4-30.

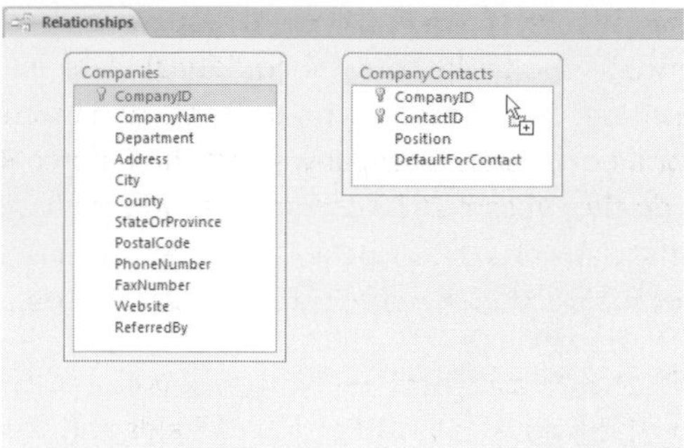

Figure 4-30 Drag the linking field from the "one" table (Companies) to the "many" table (CompanyContacts) to define the relationship between the tables.

You can read about determining the type of relationship between two tables in Article 1, "Designing Your Database Application," on the companion CD.

When you release the mouse button, Access opens the Edit Relationships dialog box, shown in Figure 4-31.

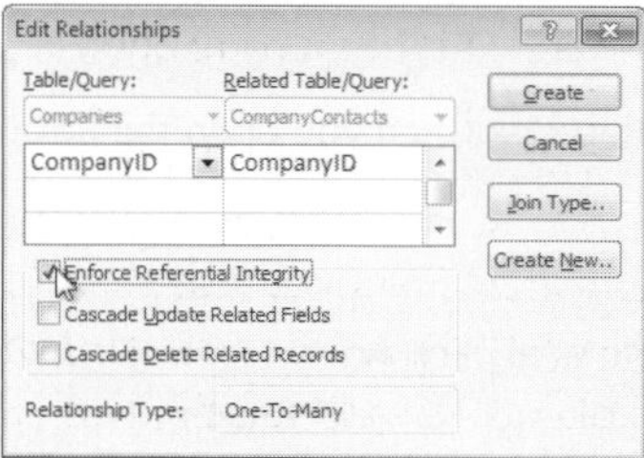

Figure 4-31 The Edit Relationships dialog box lets you specify the linking fields in two tables.

INSIDE OUT Creating Relationships from Scratch

You can also click the Edit Relationships command in the Tools group of the Design contextual tab on the ribbon to create a new relationship, but you have to fill in the table and field names yourself. The dragging operation does some of this work for you.

You'll notice that Access 2010 has filled in the field names for you. If you need to define a multiple-field relationship between two tables, use the additional blank lines to define those fields. (We'll do that in just a second.) Because you probably don't want any rows created in CompanyContacts for a nonexistent company, select the Enforce Referential Integrity check box. When you do this, Access 2010 ensures that you can't add a row in the CompanyContacts table containing an invalid CompanyID. Also, Access won't let you delete any records from the Companies table if they have contacts that are still defined.

Note that after you select the Enforce Referential Integrity check box, Access 2010 makes two additional check boxes available: Cascade Update Related Fields and Cascade Delete Related Records. If you select the Cascade Delete Related Records check box, Access 2010 deletes child rows (the related rows in the *many* table of a one-to-many relationship) when you delete a parent row (the related row in the *one* table of a one-to-many relationship). For example, if you removed a company from the table, Access 2010 would remove the related company contact rows. In this database design, the CompanyID field has the AutoNumber data type, so it cannot be changed once it is set. However, if you build a table with a primary key that is Text or Number (perhaps a ProductID field that could change at some point in the future), it might be a good idea to select the Cascade Update Related Fields check box. This option requests that Access automatically update any foreign key values in the *child* table (the *many* table in a one-to-many relationship) if you change a primary key value in a *parent* table (the *one* table in a one-to-many relationship).

You might have noticed that the Show Table dialog box, shown earlier in Figure 4-29, gives you the option to include queries as well as tables. Sometimes you might want to define relationships between tables and queries or between queries so that Access 2010 knows how to join them properly. You can also define what's known as an *outer join* by clicking the Join Type button in the Edit Relationships dialog box and selecting an option in the Join Properties dialog box. With an outer join, you can find out, for example, which companies have no contacts or which products haven't been sold.

For details about outer joins, see "Using Outer Joins," on page 634.

INSIDE OUT **Avoid Defining a Relationship with an Outer Join**

We recommend that you do not define an outer join relationship between two tables. As you'll learn in Chapter 10, Access 2010 automatically links two tables you include in a query design using the relationships that you have defined. In the vast majority of cases, you will want to include only the matching rows from both tables. If you define the relationship as an outer join, you will have to change the link between the two tables every time you include them in a query.

We also do not recommend that you define relationships between queries or between a table and a query. If you have done a good job of naming your fields in your tables, the query designer will recognize the natural links and define the joins for you automatically. Defining extra relationships adds unnecessary overhead in your database application.

Click the Create button to finish your relationship definition. Access draws a line between the two tables to indicate the relationship. Notice that when you ask Access to enforce referential integrity, Access displays a 1 at the end of the relationship line, next to the *one* table, and an infinity symbol next to the *many* table. If you want to delete the relationship, click the line and press the Delete key.

You now know enough to define the additional one-to-many simple relationships that you need. Go ahead and define a relationship on ContactID between the Contacts and CompanyContacts tables to complete the other side of the many-to-many relationship between companies and contacts, a relationship on ContactID between the Contacts and ContactEvents tables, and a relationship on ProductID between the Products and ContactProducts tables. For each relationship, be sure to select the Enforce Referential Integrity check box.

Creating a Relationship on Multiple Fields

There's one last relationship you need to define in the Contact Tracking database between CompanyContacts and ContactProducts. The relationship between these two tables requires multiple fields from each table. You can start by dragging the CompanyID field from the CompanyContacts table to the ContactProducts table. Access 2010 opens the Edit Relationships dialog box, shown in Figure 4-32.

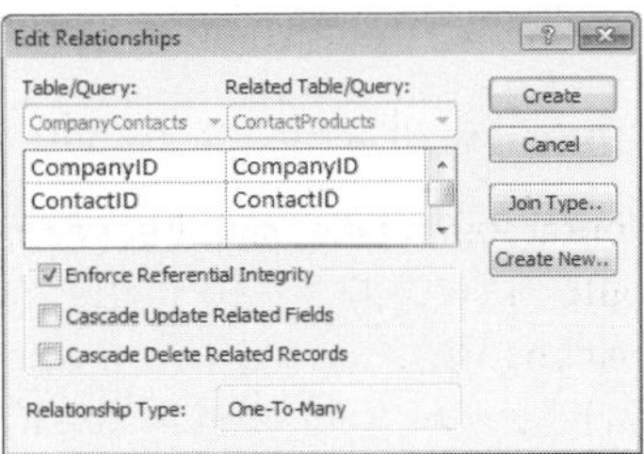

Figure 4-32 Select multiple fields in the Edit Relationships dialog box to define a relationship between two tables using more than one field.

When you first see the Edit Relationships dialog box for the relationship you are defining between CompanyContacts and ContactProducts, Access 2010 shows you only the CompanyID field in the two lists. To complete the relationship definition on the combination of CompanyID and ContactID, you must click in the second line under both tables and select ContactID as the second field for both tables, as shown in Figure 4-32. Select the Enforce Referential Integrity check box, as shown, and click Create to define the compound relationship.

Figure 4-33 shows the Relationships window for all the main tables in your Contact Tracking database. Notice that there are two linking lines that define the relationship between CompanyContacts and ContactProducts.

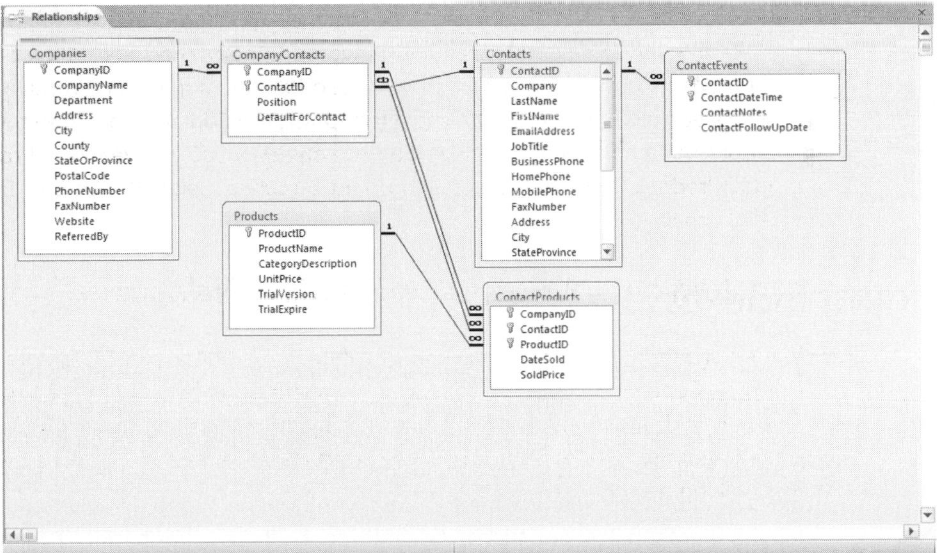

Figure 4-33 The Relationships window shows a graphical representation of all the main tables in your Contact Tracking database.

If you want to edit or change any relationship, double-click the line to open the Edit Relationships dialog box again. If you want to remove a relationship definition, click on the line linking two tables to select the relationship (the line appears highlighted) and press the Delete key. Access 2010 presents a warning dialog box in case you are asking it to delete a relationship in error.

Note that once you define a relationship, you can delete the table or query field lists from the Relationships window without affecting the relationships. To do this, click the table or query list header and press the Delete key. This can be particularly advantageous in large databases that have dozens of tables. You can also display only those tables that you're working with at the moment. To see the relationships defined for any particular table or query, include it in the Relationships window by using the Show Table dialog box, and then click the Direct Relationships button in the Relationships group of the Design contextual tab on the ribbon. To redisplay all relationships, click the All Relationships button in the Relationships group.

When you close the Relationships window, Access 2010 asks whether you want to save your layout changes. Click Yes to save the relationships you've defined. That's all there is to it. Later, when you use multiple tables in a query in Chapter 9, "Creating and Working with Simple Queries," you'll see that Access 2010 builds the links between tables based on these relationships.

INSIDE OUT **Additional Features in the Relationships Window**

You can right-click any table in the Relationships window and then choose Table Design from the shortcut menu to open that table in Design view. You can also click Relationship Report in the Tools group of the Design contextual tab on the ribbon to create a report that prints what you laid out in the window.

Adding Indexes

The more data you include in your tables, the more you need indexes to help Access 2010 search your data efficiently. An *index* is simply an internal table that contains two columns: the value in the field or fields being indexed and the physical location of each record in your table that contains that value. Access 2010 uses an index similarly to how you use the index in this book—you find the term that you want and jump directly to the pages containing that term. You don't have to leaf through all the pages to find the information you want.

Let's assume that you often search your Contacts table by city. Without an index, when you ask Access 2010 to find all the contacts in the city of Chicago, Access has to search every record in your table. This search is fast if your table includes only a few contacts but very slow if the table contains thousands of contact records collected over many years. If you create an index on the City field, Access 2010 can use the index to find more rapidly the records for the contacts in the city you specify.

Single-Field Indexes

Most of the indexes you'll need to define will probably contain the values from only a single field. Access uses this type of index to help narrow the number of records it has to search whenever you provide search criteria on the field—for example, City = Chicago or PostalCode = 60633. If you have defined indexes for multiple fields and provided search criteria for more than one of the fields, Access uses the indexes together (using a technology called Rushmore from Microsoft FoxPro) to find the rows that you want quickly. For example, if you have created one index on City and another on LastName, and you ask for City = Redmond and LastName = Conrad, Access uses the entries in the City index that equal Redmond and matches those with the entries in the LastName index that equal Conrad. The result is a small set of pointers to the records that match both criteria.

Creating an index on a single field in a table is easy. Open the Contacts table (which you created earlier using an Application Part) in Design view, and select the field for which you want an index—in this case, City. Click the Indexed property box in the lower part of the Table window, and then click the arrow to open the list of choices, as shown in Figure 4-34.

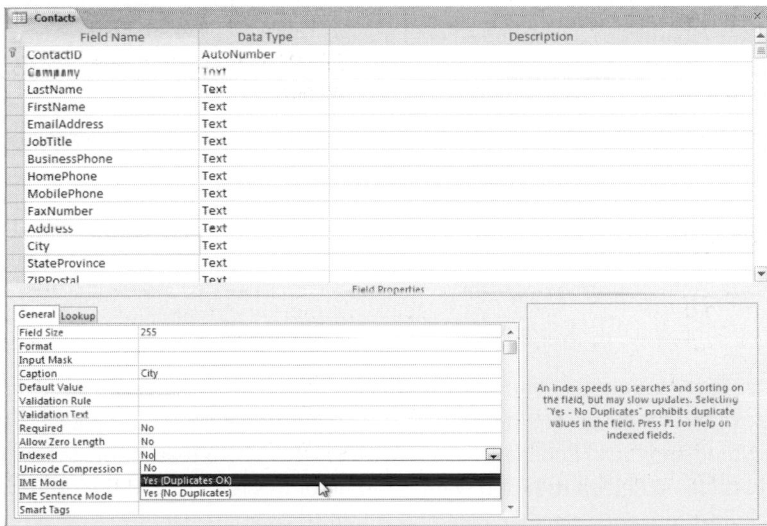

Figure 4-34 You can use the Indexed property box to set an index on a single field.

When you create a table from scratch (as you did earlier in this chapter for the Companies table), the default Indexed property setting for all fields except the primary key is No. If you use an Application Part or a Data Type Part to help create a table (as you did for the Contacts table in this chapter), the Application Part or Data Type Part indexes fields that might benefit from an index. If you followed along earlier using an Application Part to build the Contacts table, you will find that the template built an index only for the ContactID and ZIPPostal fields. Any tables created using an Application Part or Data Type Part could obviously benefit from some additional indexes.

If you want to set an index for a field, Access 2010 offers two possible Yes choices. In most cases, a given field will have multiple records with the same value—perhaps you have multiple contacts in a particular city or multiple products in the same product category. You should select **Yes (Duplicates OK)** to create an index for this type of field. By selecting **Yes (No Duplicates)**, you can have Access 2010 enforce unique values in any field by creating an index that doesn't allow duplicates. Access 2010 always defines the primary key index with no duplicates because all primary key values must be unique.

Note

You cannot define an index using an OLE Object, Attachment, or Calculated field.

Multiple-Field Indexes

If you often provide multiple criteria in searches against large tables, you might want to consider creating a few multiple-field indexes. This helps Access 2010 narrow the search quickly without having to match values from two separate indexes. For example, suppose you often perform a search for contacts by last name and first name. If you create an index that includes both of these fields, Access can satisfy your query more rapidly.

To create a multiple-field index, you must open the Table window in Design view and open the Indexes window by clicking the Indexes button in the Show/Hide group of the Design contextual tab on the ribbon. You can see the primary key index and the index that you defined on City in the previous section as well as the index defined by the Application Part (ZIP_PostalCode index on the ZIPPostal field). Each of these indexes comprises exactly one field.

To create a multiple-field index, move the insertion point to an empty row in the Indexes window and type a unique name. In this example, you want a multiple-field index using the Last Name and First Name fields, so FullName might be a reasonable index name. Select the Last Name field in the Field Name column of this row. To add the other field, skip down to the next row and select First Name without typing a new index name. When you're done, your Indexes window should look like the one shown in Figure 4-35.

INSIDE OUT Inserting New Rows in the Indexes Window

To insert a row in the middle of the list in the Indexes window, right-click in the Index Name column and then choose Insert Rows from the shortcut menu.

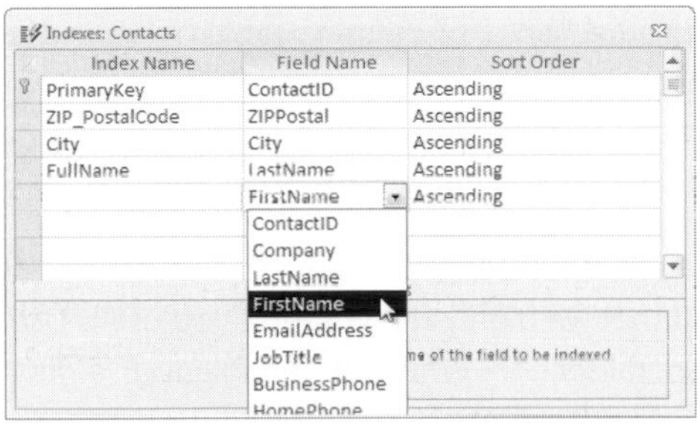

Figure 4-35 The FullName index includes the Last Name and First Name fields.

You can remove an existing single-field index by changing the Indexed property of a field to No on the field's property list. The only way to remove a multiple-field index is via the Indexes window. To remove a multiple-field index, select the rows (by holding down the Ctrl key as you click each row selector) that define the index and then press Delete. Access 2010 saves any index changes you make when you save the table definition.

Access 2010 can use a multiple-field index in a search even if you don't provide search values for all the fields, so long as you provide search criteria for consecutive fields starting with the first field. Therefore, with the FullName multiple-field index shown in Figure 4-35, you can search for last name or for last name and first name. There's one additional limitation on when Access can use multiple-field indexes: Only the last search criterion you supply can be an inequality, such as >, >=, <, or <=. In other words, Access can use the index shown in Figure 4-35 when you specify searches such as these:

Last Name = "Smith"
Last Name > "Franklin"
Last Name = "Buchanan" And First Name = "Steven"
Last Name = "Viescas" And First Name >= "Bobby"

But Access will not use the FullName index shown in Figure 4-35 if you ask for

Last Name > "Davolio" And First Name > "John"

because only the last field in the search (First Name) can be an inequality. Access also will not use this index if you ask for

First Name = "John"

because the first field of the multiple-field index (Last Name) is missing from the search criterion.

Setting Table Design Options

Now that you understand the basic mechanics of defining tables in your desktop database, it's useful to look at a few options that you can set to customize how you work with tables in Design view. Close any open tables so that all you see is the Navigation pane. Click the File tab on the Backstage view and then click Options to see all the custom settings offered.

You can find the first options that affect table design in the Client Settings category, as shown in Figure 4-36. One option that we highly recommend you use is Use Four-Digit Year Formatting, found in the General section. When you enable four-digit year formatting, Access 2010 displays all year values in date/time formats with four digits instead of two. This is important because when you see a value (in two-digit medium date format) such as 15 MAR 12, you won't be able to tell easily whether this is March 15, 1912 or March 15, 2012. Although you can affect the display of some formats in your regional settings in Control Panel, you won't affect them all unless you set four-digit formatting in Access.

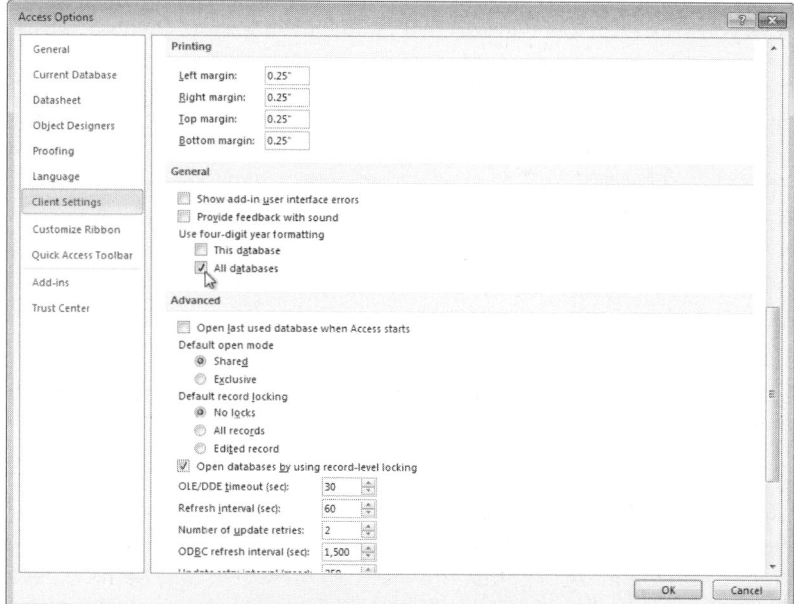

Figure 4-36 You can find settings that affect table design in the General section in the Client Settings category of the Access Options dialog box.

As you can see in Figure 4-36, you have two options under Use Four-Digit Year Formatting in the General section. If you select the This Database check box, the setting creates a property in the database you currently have open and affects only that database. If you select the All Databases check box, the setting creates an entry in your Windows registry that affects all databases that you open on your computer.

In the Current Database category of the Access Options dialog box, you can configure an option that was introduced in Access 2000 called Name AutoCorrect that asks Access to track and correct field name references in queries, forms, and reports. If you select the Track Name AutoCorrect Info check box in the Name AutoCorrect Options section, Access maintains a unique internal ID number for all field names. This allows you to use the Object Dependencies feature explained in Chapter 5. It also allows you to select the next check box, Perform Name AutoCorrect, as shown in Figure 4-37.

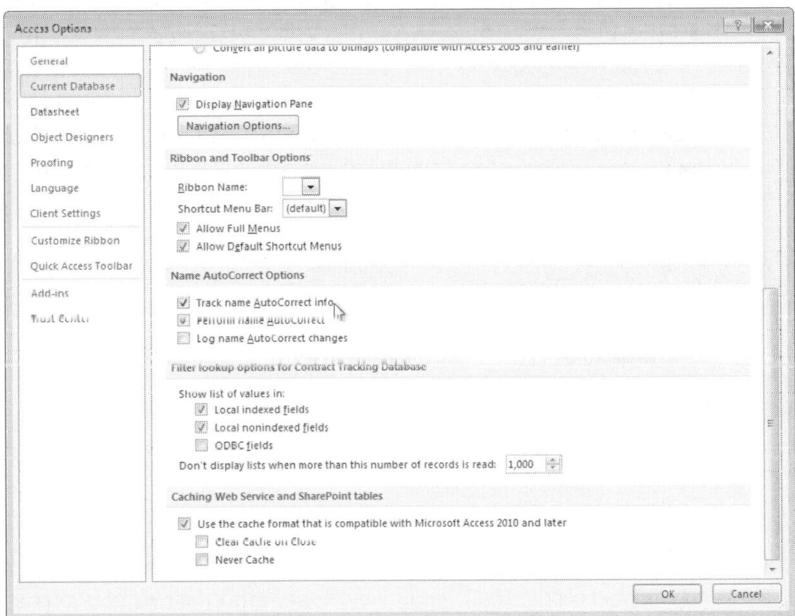

Figure 4-37 You can set Name AutoCorrect options in the Current Database category of the Access Options dialog box.

If you select the Perform Name AutoCorrect check box, when you change a field name in a table, Access 2010 automatically attempts to propagate the name change to other objects (queries, forms, and reports) that use the field. However, Track Name AutoCorrect Info requires some additional overhead in all your objects, so it's a good idea to choose names carefully as you design your tables so that you won't need to change them later. Note that Access does not attempt to propagate the name change to any Visual Basic code you created in your database. Finally, if you select the Log Name AutoCorrect Changes check box, Access 2010 logs all changes it makes in a table called AutoCorrect Log. You can open this table to verify the changes made by this feature. (Access doesn't create the table until it makes some changes.)

The next category that contains useful settings affecting table design is Object Designers. Click that category to see the settings shown in Figure 4-38.

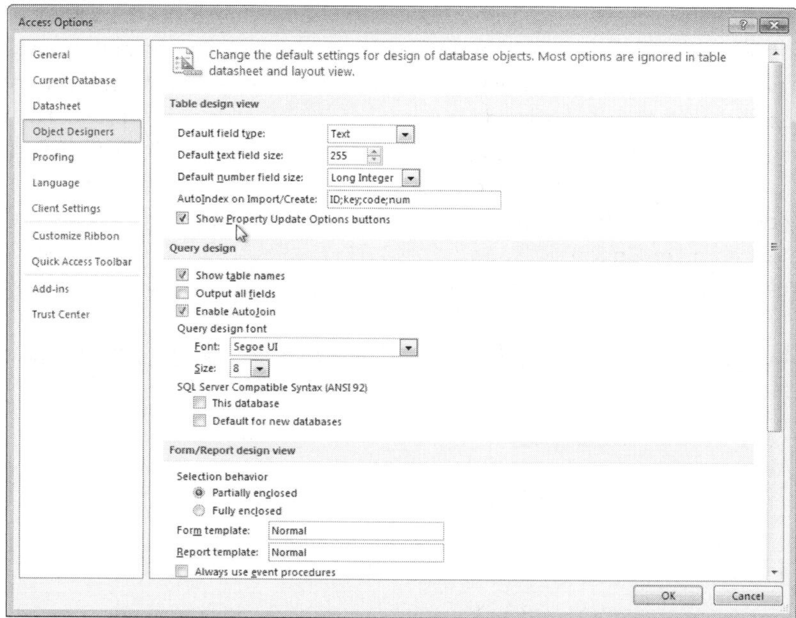

Figure 4-38 You can find settings that affect table design in the Object Designers category of the Access Options dialog box.

In the Table Design View section, you can set the default field type and the default field size for Text and Number fields. The Default Field Type setting allows you to choose the default data type that Access 2010 selects when you type a new field name in table design and then tab to the Data Type column. When you select a data type of Text (either because it is the default data type or you select the Text data type in a new field), Access will automatically set the length you select in the Default Text Field Size box. When you select a data type of Number, Access sets the number size to your choice in the Default Number Field Size box of Byte, Integer, Long Integer, Single, Double, Decimal, or Replication ID. Use the AutoIndex On Import/Create box to define a list of field name prefixes or suffixes for which Access automatically sets the Index property to Yes (Duplicates OK). In the default list, for example, any field that you define with a name that begins or ends with ID will have an index automatically.

If you select the Show Property Update Options Buttons check box, a smart tag appears that offers to update related properties automatically in queries, forms, and reports when you change certain field properties in a table design. You can see more details about this option in the next chapter.

You can find the last option that affects how your tables are stored (and, in fact, all objects in your database) in the General category, as shown in Figure 4-39. When you create a new database in Access 2010, you actually have a choice of three different file formats. These options also appear in the File New Database dialog box, but this setting in the Access Options dialog box controls which file format appears as the default. You should use the Access 2000 format if others with whom you might share this database are still using Access version 9 (2000), or you should use the 2002-2003 format if others sharing this database are still using Access version 10 (2002) or Access version 11 (2003). Selecting the Access 2007 format—used by both Access 2007 and Access 2010—ensures maximum compatibility of what you build in Access with future versions of the product. Note that if you choose to use an older file format, you won't be able to use some of the new features found only in the .accdb file format, such as Attachment, Multi-Value Field, and Calculated data types.

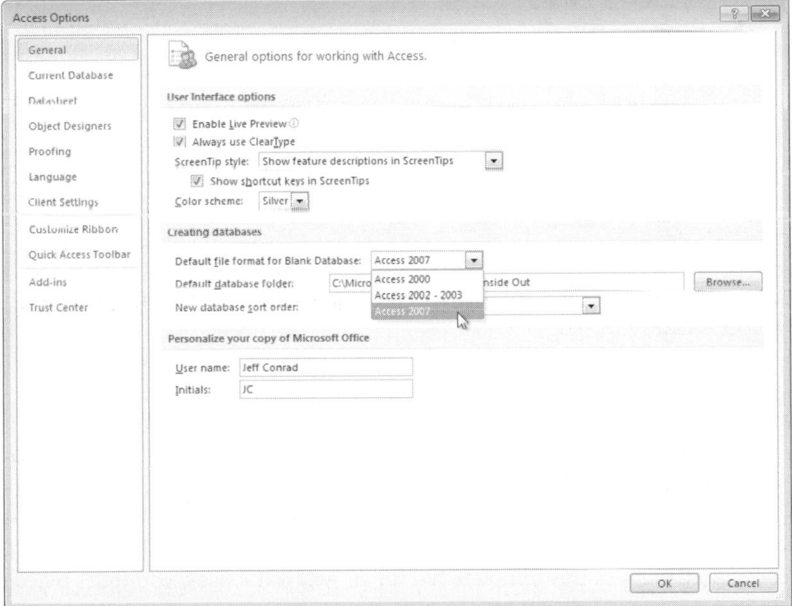

Figure 4-39 You can select your default database file format in the Creating Databases section of the General category in the Access Options dialog box.

Creating a Default Template for New Databases

Access 2007 introduced a new feature that allows you to create your own default database template for use with all new blank databases. Rather than set options for each new database after you create it, you can set your preferred options only one time and have those settings apply to each new database. To accomplish this, you first need to open a new blank database from the Backstage view. Click the File tab on the Backstage view and then click the Blank Database command on the New tab to display the Blank Database task pane on the right, as shown in Figure 4-40.

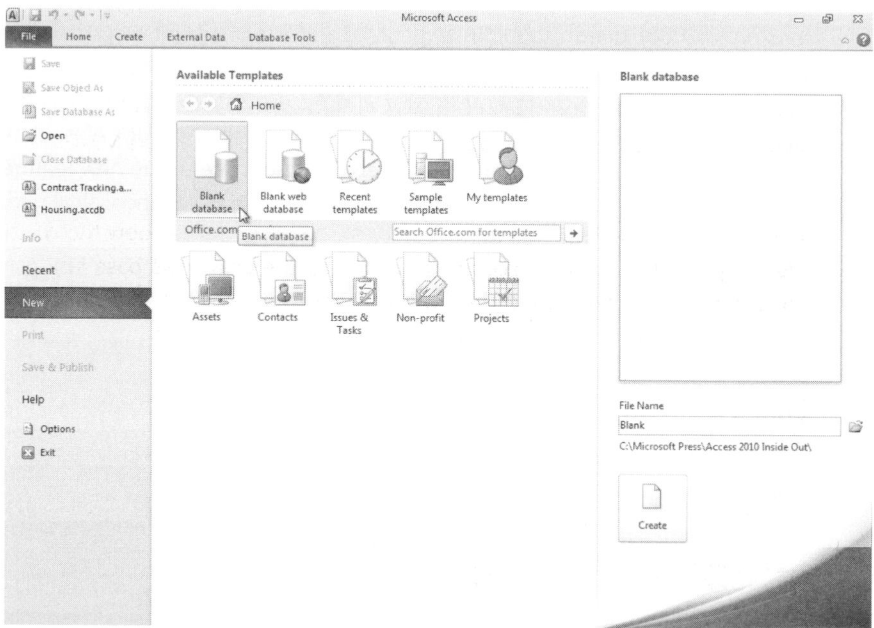

Figure 4-40 The Blank Database task pane appears on the right when you click the Blank Database command.

You must name this new database Blank for this procedure to work. Type **Blank** in the File Name text box, and then click Browse to open the File New Database dialog box. So that Access 2010 will use this template file for all new databases, you must place this file in a specific subfolder in the Microsoft Office folder. Navigate to the following folder on your system drive by clicking the folder icons in the left pane of the File New Database dialog box: \Program Files\Microsoft Office\Templates\1033\Access, as shown in Figure 4-41. This file path assumes a default installation of the Microsoft Office 2010 system on a 32-bit Windows installation, so your exact file path might be different if you chose a custom installation and selected a different installation path.

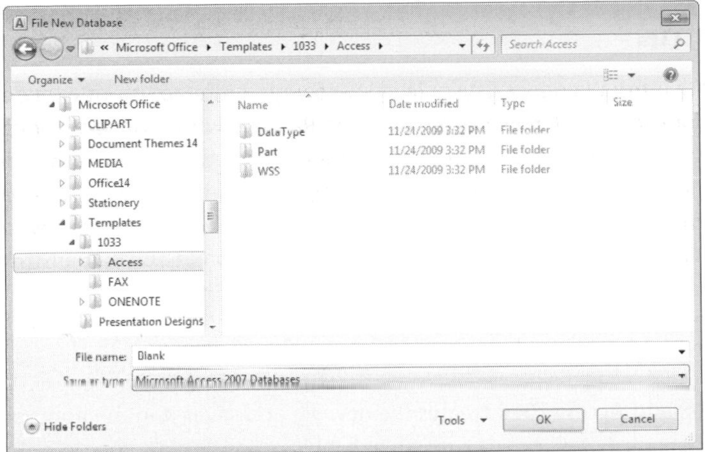

Figure 4-41 Save the Blank.accdb file in the correct subfolder in the Microsoft Office folder.

Click OK in the File New Database dialog box to return to the New tab on the Backstage view. If you followed the preceding instructions, the Blank Database task pane on the right should look like Figure 4-42. The File Name text box says Blank.accdb, and the path to the correct template location is displayed above the Create button.

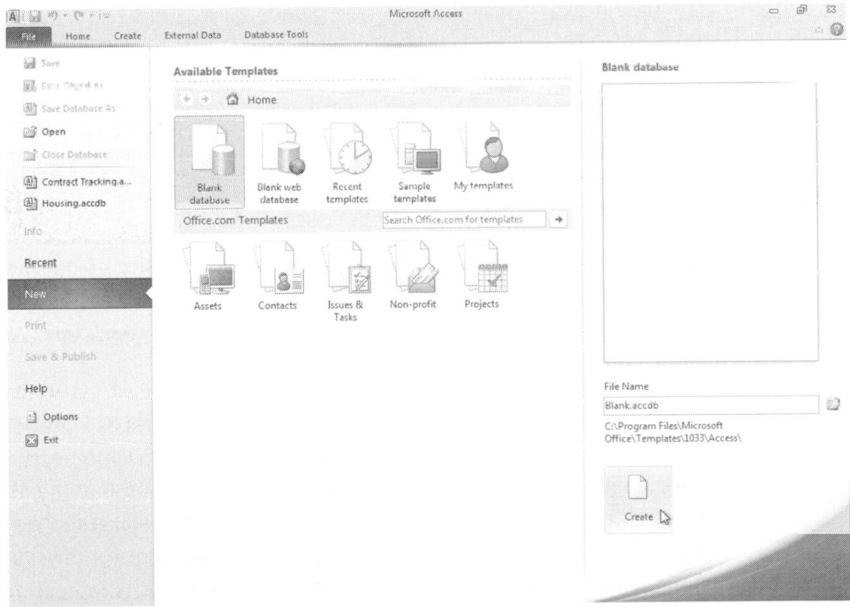

Figure 4-42 After you enter the correct name and select the correct location, you're ready to create your new database template.

CAUTION!

If you are using Windows Vista or Windows 7, you might not be able to save the Blank.accdb database into the needed template folder. Windows Vista and Windows 7 use User Account Control, which protects critical program folders. If your computer is connected to a domain, you get a prompting dialog box and then you can save to the correct folder. You might need to turn off User Account Control temporarily to save the database into the template folder. If you are in a corporate network environment, you should ask your system administrator for assistance with this procedure.

Click Create, and Access 2010 creates the new file and saves it in the appropriate template folder. By default, Access opens a new blank table called Table1. You do not need this table, so close it and do not save it.

Now that you have an empty database with no objects, open the Access Options dialog box by clicking the File tab on the Backstage view and then Options. Select all the options you want to set for any new databases in the various categories of the Access Options dialog box.

Included on the companion CD is a database called Blank.accdb that has the Access Options settings that we recommend for new databases. In the Current Database category, in the Name AutoCorrect Options section, we cleared the Track Name AutoCorrect Info check box. In the General section of the Client Settings category, we selected the Use Four-Digit Year Formatting and This Database check boxes. We left all other options set to the defaults.

Note

You can also open the Visual Basic Editor (VBE) and select Options from the Tools menu to select options that apply to Visual Basic in all new databases. In the sample Blank.accdb database, we selected the Require Variable Declaration check box. We will discuss the VBE Options dialog box in detail in Chapter 24.

After you have defined all the settings you want, close the database and exit Access 2010. Each new blank database you create from the New tab on the Backstage view will now include all the settings you selected for the Blank.accdb file. To make revisions to those settings, open the Blank.accdb file in the template folder and make whatever modifications are necessary. Figure 4-43 shows our Blank.accdb file in the appropriate template folder along with the other local database templates discussed at the beginning of this chapter.

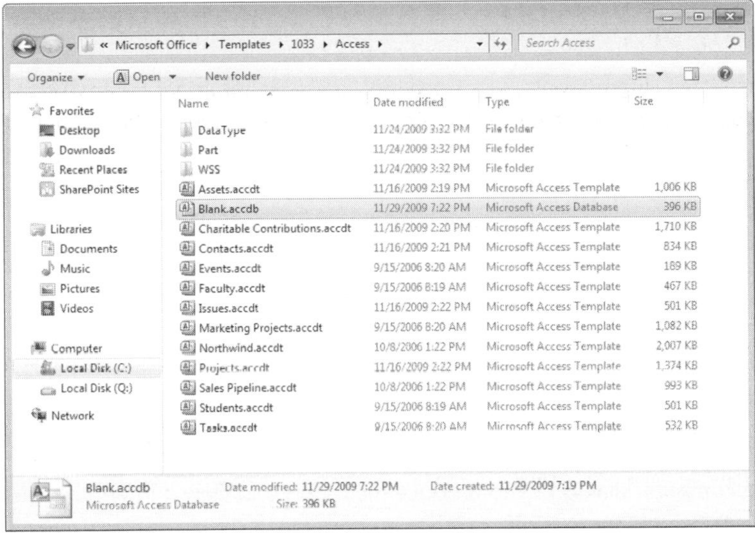

Figure 4-43 The Blank.accdb file must be located in the same folder as the local database templates.

Creating a custom blank database template saves you time by not having to continually set your personal Access options and VBE options each time you create a new database. In addition to this timesaver, you can also include specific code modules, forms, and any other database objects with new databases. If, for example, you have some common functions and procedures stored in standard code modules that you use in all your database files, you can include them in this Blank.accdb file. Instead of having to manually import these modules into all new databases, Access does all the work for you by including them in new databases.

We will discuss creating form templates in Chapter 14. You'll learn about creating public functions in Chapter 24.

Printing a Table Definition

After you create several tables, you might want to print out their definitions to provide a permanent paper record. You can do this by clicking Database Documenter in the Analyze group of the Database Tools tab on the ribbon. Access 2010 displays several options in the Documenter dialog box, as shown in Figure 4-44.

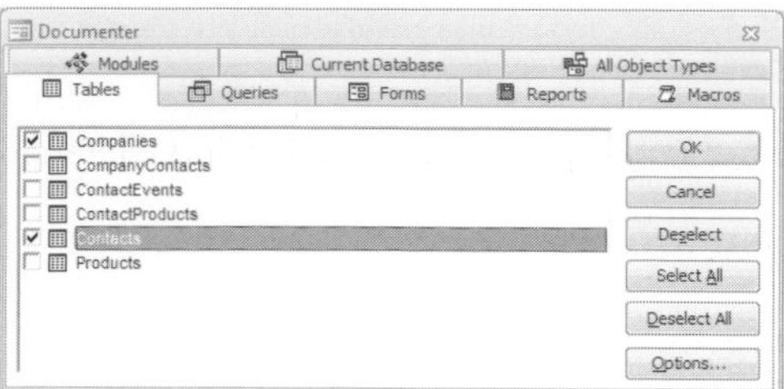

Figure 4-44 You can select the objects you want to document in the Documenter dialog box.

You can select not only the types of objects you want to document but also which objects you want to document. Click Options to select what you want reported. For example, you can ask for the properties, relationships, and permissions for a table; the names, data types, sizes, and properties for fields; and the names, fields, and properties for indexes. Click OK in the Documenter dialog box to produce the report and view it in Print Preview, as shown in Figure 4-45.

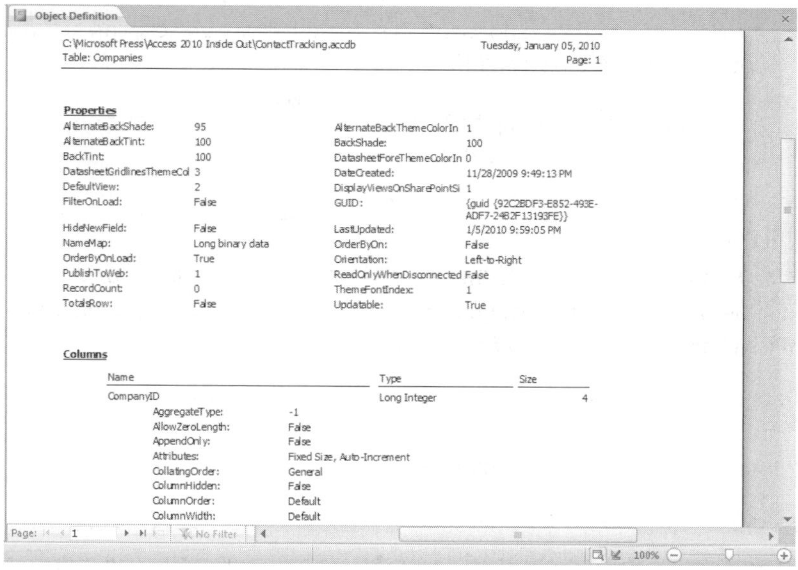

Figure 4-45 The Database Documenter previews its reports on your screen.

Database Limitations

As you design your database, you should keep in mind the following limitations:

- A table can have up to 255 fields.
- A table can have up to 32 indexes.

> **Note**
>
> **Keep in mind that defining relationships with Referential Integrity turned on creates one additional index in each participating table that counts toward the 32-index limit per table.**

- A multiple-field index can have up to 10 fields. The sum of the lengths of the fields cannot exceed 255 bytes.
- A row in a table, excluding memo fields and ActiveX objects, can be no longer than approximately 4 kilobytes (KB).
- A memo field can store up to 1 GB of characters, but you can't display a memo larger than 64 KB in a form or a datasheet.

> **Note**
>
> **Clearly, if you try to store a 1-GB memo (which requires 2 GB of storage because of double-byte character set support) or a 2-GB ActiveX object in your database file, your file will be full with the data from one record.**

- An ActiveX object can be up to 2 GB in size.
- There is no limit on the number of records in a table, but an Access 2010 database cannot be larger than 2 GB. If you have several large tables, you might need to define each one in a separate Access database and then attach it to the database that contains the forms, reports, macros, and modules for your applications. See Chapter 8, "Importing and Linking Data," for details.

Now that you've started to get comfortable with creating databases and tables, you can proceed to Chapter 5 to learn how to make modifications to existing tables in a database.

Database Limitations

CHAPTER 5

Modifying Your Table Design

No matter how carefully you design your database, you can be sure that you'll need to change it at some later date. Here are some of the reasons you might need to change your database.

- You no longer need some of the tables.
- You need to perform some new tasks that require not only creating new tables but also inserting some linking fields in existing tables.
- You need to perform some new tasks that require not only creating new tables but also inserting some linking fields in existing tables.
- You find that you use some fields in a table much more frequently than others, so it would be easier if those fields appeared first in the table design.
- You no longer need some of the fields.
- You want to add some new fields that are similar to fields that already exist.
- You discover that some of the data you defined would be better stored as a different data type. For example, a field that you originally designed to be all numbers (such as a U.S. ZIP Code) must now contain some letters (as in a Canadian postal code).

- You have a number field that needs to hold larger values or needs a different number of decimal places than you originally planned.
- You can improve your database design by splitting an existing table into two or more tables using the Table Analyzer Wizard.
- You discover that the field you defined as a primary key isn't always unique, so you need to change the definition of your primary key.
- You find that some of your queries take too long to run and might execute more quickly if you add an index to your table.

Note

The examples in this chapter are based on the tables and data in Housing.accdb and Contacts.accdb on the companion CD included with this book and the Contact Tracking database you built in Chapter 4, "Designing Client Tables." If you did not create the Contact Tracking database, you can find ContactTracking.accdb in the sample files that you can use to follow along in this chapter. The results you see from the samples you build in this chapter might not exactly match what you see in this book if you have changed the sample data in the files. Also, all the screen images in this chapter were taken on a Windows 7 system with the Access color scheme set to Silver, and Use Windows-Themed Controls on Forms has been turned on in the sample databases.

This chapter takes a look at how you can make these changes easily and relatively painlessly with Microsoft Access 2010. If you want to follow along with the examples in this chapter, you should first create the Contact Tracking database described in Chapter 4.

Note

You might have noticed that the Contacts table you defined for the Contact Tracking database in Chapter 4 is different from the tblContacts table in the Conrad Systems Contacts database on the companion CD. In this chapter, you'll modify the Contacts table you built in Chapter 4 so that it is more like the one on the companion CD. You'll also learn how to use the Table Analyzer Wizard to help you normalize an existing table that contains data from several subjects.

Before You Get Started

Access 2010 makes it easy for you to change the design of your database, even when you already have data in your tables. You should, however, understand the potential impact of any changes you plan and take steps to ensure that you can recover your previous design if you make a mistake. Here are some things to consider before you make changes.

- Access 2010 does not automatically propagate changes that you make in tables to any queries, forms, reports, macros, or modules. You must make changes to dependent objects yourself or configure Access to propagate the changes for you. To do so, click the File tab on the Backstage view, click Options, and then in the Current Database category, select the Perform Name AutoCorrect check box. See "Setting Table Design Options," on page 226, for more details.

- You cannot change the data type of a field that is part of a relationship between tables. You must first delete the relationship and then change the field's data type and redefine the relationship.

- You cannot change the definition of any table that you have open in a query, a form, or a report. You must close any objects that refer to the table you want to change before you open that table in Design view. If you give other users access to your database over a network, you won't be able to change the table definition if someone else has the table (or a query or form based on the table) open.

INSIDE OUT **Access Always Prompts You to Save Your Work**

Before saving any changes that permanently alter or delete data in your database, Access 2010 always prompts you for confirmation and gives you a chance to cancel the operation.

Making a Backup Copy

The safest way to make changes to the design of your database is to make a backup copy of the database before you begin. If you expect to make extensive changes to several tables in your database, you should also make a copy of the accdb file that contains your database. You could use a utility such as Windows Explorer, but Access 2010 includes a handy feature for making backups easily. When you have the database open that you want to back up, click the File tab on the Backstage view, click the Save & Publish tab, and then click Back Up Database, as shown in Figure 5-1. Access offers to create a copy of your database with the current date appended to the file name.

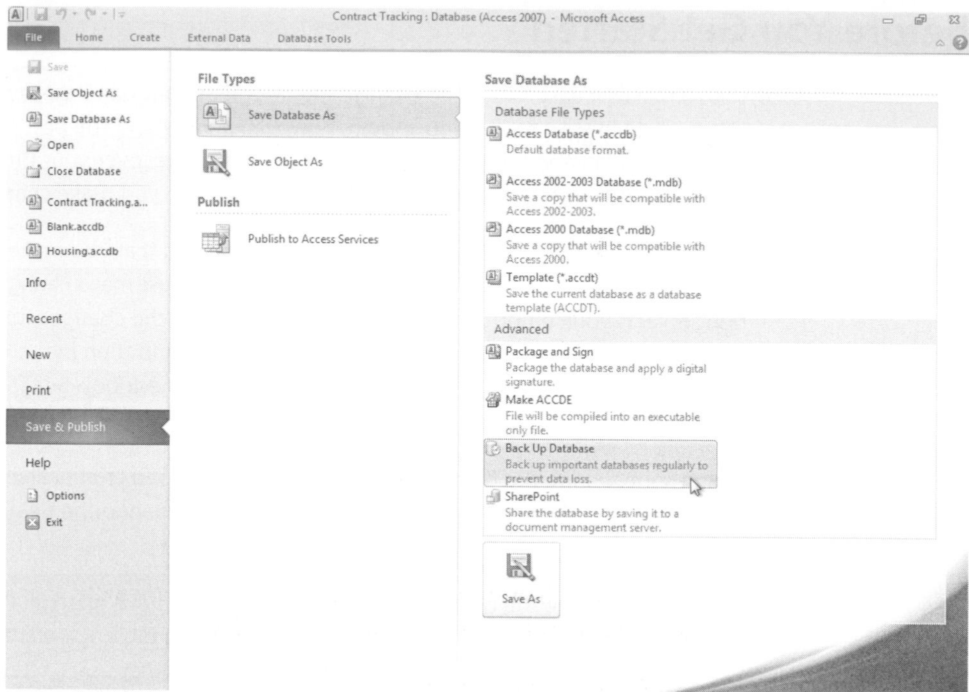

Figure 5-1 The Back Up Database command creates a backup of your entire database file.

If you want to change a single table, you can make a backup copy of that table easily, right in your database. Use the following procedure to copy any table—the structure and the data together.

1. Open the database containing the table you want to copy. If the database is already open, make sure the list of tables is showing in the Navigation pane. Click the top of the Navigation pane to open the Navigation Pane menu and click Object Type beneath Navigate To Category. Click the top of the Navigation pane again and then click Tables under Filter By Group, as shown in Figure 5-2, to display only the tables contained in your database.

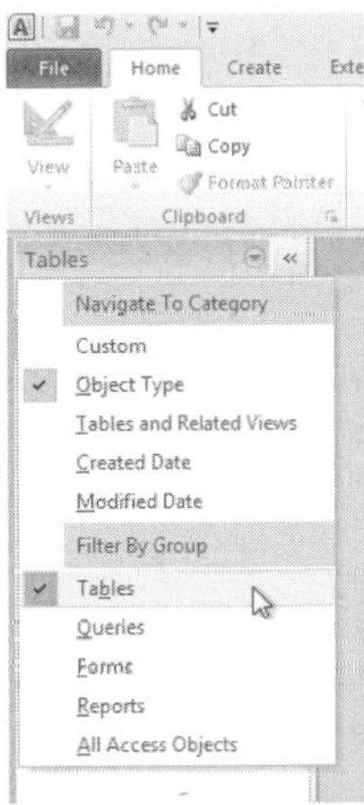

Figure 5-2 Click Object Type and Tables on the Navigation Pane menu to display only the tables in your database.

2. Select the table you want to copy by clicking the table's name or icon in the Navigation pane. The table name will be highlighted.
3. Click the Copy command in the Clipboard group on the Home tab on the ribbon, as shown in Figure 5-3. This copies the entire table (structure and data) to the Clipboard.

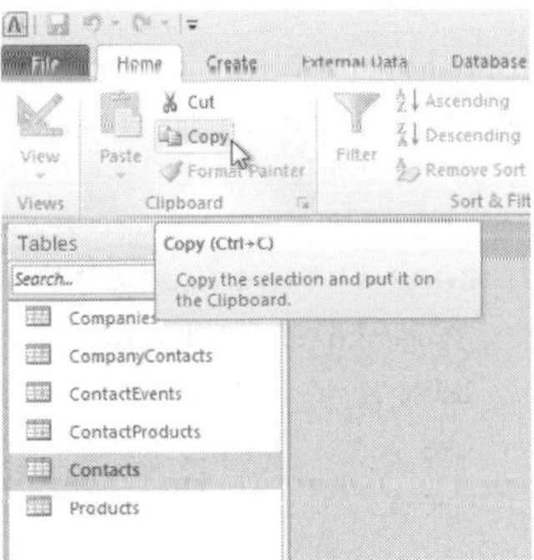

Figure 5-3 Click the Copy command to copy a table from the Tables list.

4. Click the Paste command in the Clipboard group on the Home tab on the ribbon. Access opens the Paste Table As dialog box, shown in Figure 5-4. Type a new name for your table. (When naming a backup copy, you might simply add Backup and the date to the original table name, as shown in Figure 5-4.) The default option is to copy both the structure and the data. (You also have the option of copying only the table's structure or of appending the data to another table.)

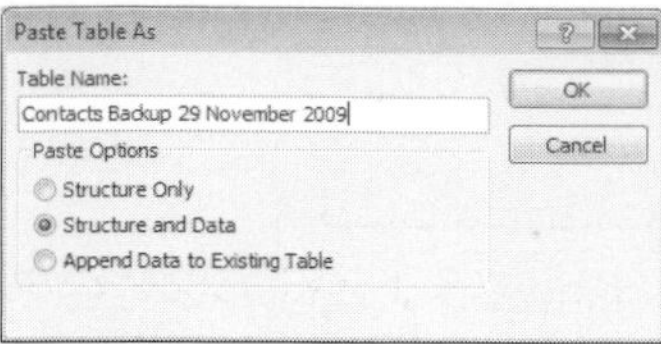

Figure 5-4 Enter the new name for the copied table in the Paste Table As dialog box.

Checking Object Dependencies

If you're just starting out and learning Access 2010 by reading this book from the beginning, you probably haven't built anything but tables yet. In Chapter 3, "Access 2010 Overview," you learned that you can ask Access to show you what queries, forms, and reports are dependent on each table, but the Object Dependencies command in Access won't provide very interesting results in a database with nothing but tables. You'll find this tool invaluable later after you have built dozens of objects and then need to make some changes to your tables.

As you learned in Chapter 4, you can select options to track and perform Name AutoCorrect for objects by clicking the File tab on the Backstage view, clicking Options, and then selecting the check boxes for these features in the Current Database category. Access 2010 uses this AutoCorrect information not only to correct names automatically but also to provide you with detailed information about which objects depend on one another. If you're about to make a change to a field in a table, wouldn't it be good to know which queries, forms, and reports use that table before you make the change? The Perform Name AutoCorrect option will help you if you have selected it, but it can't always detect and fix field names when you have used them in an expression. You'll learn more about creating expressions in Chapter 9, "Creating and Working with Simple Queries," and in the chapters on using Microsoft Visual Basic in Part 8, "Automating an Access Application Using Visual Basic," on the companion CD.

If you would like to see object dependencies in action on your computer, open one of your own databases that contains tables, queries, forms, and reports, or open the Conrad Systems Contacts sample database (Contacts.accdb) that you installed from the companion CD. You can find out which other objects depend on a particular object (such as a table) by selecting the object that you're planning to change in the Navigation pane and then clicking Object Dependencies in the Relationships group on the Database Tools tab of the ribbon. If you haven't selected the Track Name AutoCorrect Info option, Access 2010 shows you the dialog box in Figure 5-5.

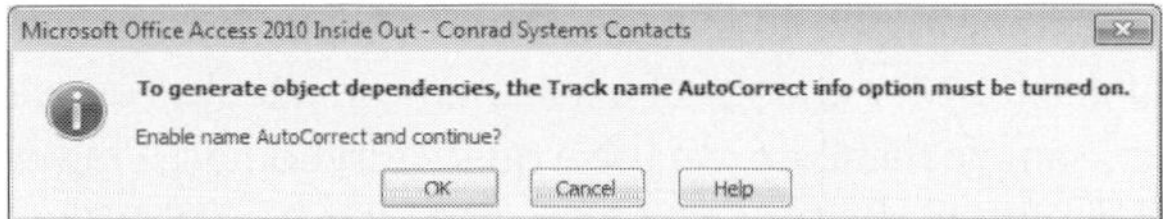

Figure 5-5 The Object Dependencies feature tells you it needs to turn on Track Name AutoCorrect Info and examine all objects in your database.

Click OK to turn on Track Name AutoCorrect Info. The Object Dependencies command will take a few seconds or minutes to examine all your objects depending on the number of objects you have in your database. Access shows you the result in the Object Dependencies pane, as shown in Figure 5-6. At the bottom of the Object Dependencies pane, in Figure 5-6, you can see a warning message that some objects were ignored. Access displays this message if there are macros or modules present in your database because macros and modules are not checked for object dependencies.

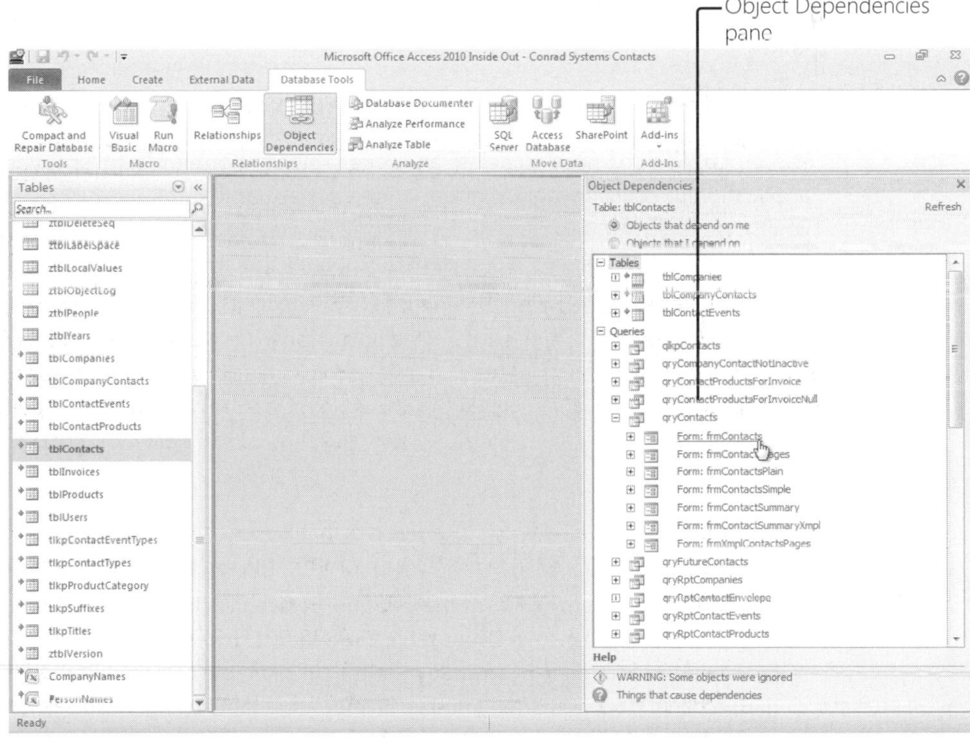

Figure 5-6 The Object Dependencies pane shows you the list of objects that depend on the object you selected in the Navigation pane.

Notice that in many cases, you will have to follow a chain of dependencies to find all the objects that might be affected by the change of a field name in a table. For example, in the Conrad Systems Contacts sample database, we use a query (qryContacts) rather than the table (tblContacts) to provide records to the form that edits contact information (frmContacts). If we were to scroll further down the Object Dependencies pane looking for forms dependent on tblContacts, we would not find the form frmContacts listed.

You can click the plus sign next to any object name to open an expanded list of dependent objects, as we did with qryContacts in Figure 5-6. Notice that we find frmContacts listed there as a dependent object of qryContacts, which is ultimately dependent on the table we're thinking about changing. When you find an object that you want to investigate further, you can click the object name in the Object Dependencies pane to open it in Design view.

As you can imagine, this command can make maintaining your application much easier. Even if you have selected the Perform Name AutoCorrect option, you can use this tool after you have modified your table to verify that the changes you expect were made.

Deleting Tables

You probably won't need to delete an entire table very often. However, if you set up your application to collect historical information—for example, total product sales by year—you'll eventually want to delete information that you no longer need. You also might want to delete a table if you've made extensive changes that are incorrect and it would be easier to delete your work and restore the table from a backup.

To delete a table, select it in the Navigation pane and press the Delete key (or click the Delete command in the Records group on the Home tab of the ribbon). Access 2010 opens the dialog box shown in Figure 5-7, which asks you to confirm or cancel the delete operation.

INSIDE OUT **Access Is Forgiving When You Delete Something by Mistake**

Even if you mistakenly confirm the deletion, you can click the Undo command on the Quick Access Toolbar to get your table back. In fact, you can undo up to the last 20 changes that you made in a window—either in the table's Design view or in the Navigation pane. However, after you save changes to a table design, you will not be able to undo those changes.

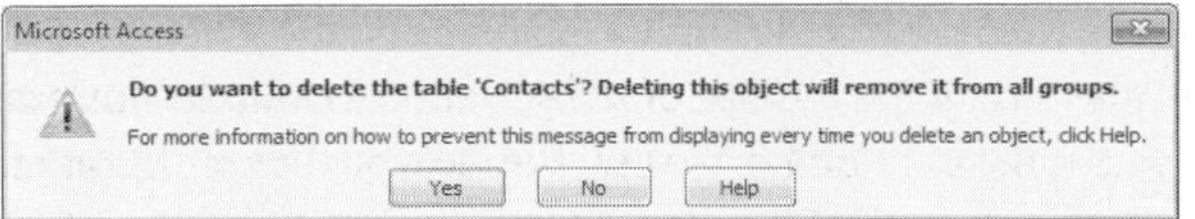

Figure 5-7 This dialog box gives you the option of canceling the deletion of a table.

INSIDE OUT **Using Cut to Move an Object to the Clipboard**

You can use the Cut command in the Clipboard group on the Home tab on the ribbon to delete a table. This method moves a copy of the table to the Clipboard. If you open another instance of Access, you can paste the table into a different database from the Clipboard into it. However, if you close the database you deleted the table from, you cannot paste the table into a different database.

If you have defined relationships between the table you want to delete and other tables, Access 2010 displays another dialog box that alerts you and asks whether you want to also delete the relationships. If you click Yes, Access deletes all relationships between any other table and the table you want to delete and then deletes the table. (You can't have a relationship defined to a nonexistent table.) Even at this point, if you find you made a mistake, you can click Undo on the Quick Access Toolbar to restore both the table and all its relationships.

CAUTION!

When you undo a table deletion, Access 2010 might not restore all the previously defined relationships between the table and other tables. You should verify the table relationships in the Relationships window.

Renaming Tables

If you keep transaction data (such as receipts, deposits, or checks written), you might want to save that data at the end of each month in a table with a unique name. One way to save your data is to rename the existing table (perhaps by adding a date to the name). You can then create a new table (perhaps by making a copy of the backup table's structure) to start collecting information for the next month.

To rename a table, right-click it in the Navigation pane and click Rename on the shortcut menu. Access 2010 places the name in edit mode in the Navigation pane so that you can type in a new name, as shown in Figure 5-8. Type the new name, and press Enter to save it.

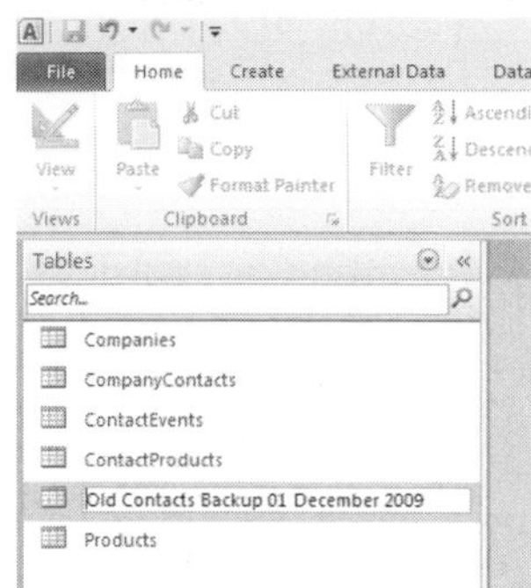

Figure 5-8 After clicking Rename on the shortcut menu, you can rename a table in the Navigation pane.

INSIDE OUT Using the Keyboard to Rename an Object

You can also edit the name of the object by selecting it in the Navigation pane and pressing the F2 key. This puts the object name in edit mode so that you can type a new name.

If you enter the name of a table that already exists, Access 2010 displays a dialog box that asks whether you want to replace the existing table, as shown in Figure 5-9. If you click Yes, Access deletes the old table before performing the renaming operation. Even if you replace an existing table, you can undo the renaming operation by clicking the Undo command on the Quick Access Toolbar.

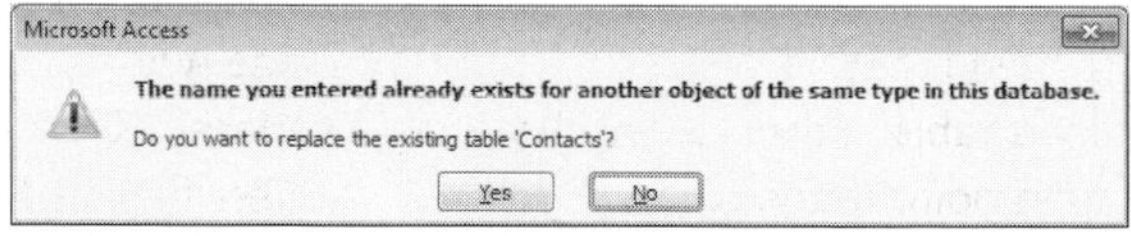

Figure 5-9 This dialog box asks whether you want to replace an existing table with the same name.

INSIDE OUT **Renaming Other Access Objects**

You can use the techniques you just learned for copying, renaming, and deleting tables to copy, rename, and delete queries, forms, reports, macros, or modules.

Changing Field Names

Perhaps you misspelled a field name when you first created one of your tables, or perhaps you've decided that one of the field names isn't descriptive enough. As you learned in Chapter 4, you can change the displayed name for a field by setting its Caption property. But you won't necessarily want the hassle of giving the field a caption every time it appears in a query, a form, or a report. Fortunately, Access 2010 makes it easy to change a field name in a table—even if you already have data in the table.

Note

The next several examples in this chapter show you how to change the Contacts table that you created in the previous chapter to match the tblContacts table in the Conrad Systems Contacts sample database more closely.

You created the first draft of the Contacts table by using an Application Part. Now you need to make a few changes so that it will hold all the data fields that you need for your application. The Contacts Application Part does not give you the option to rename the fields before creating them, but now you decide to rename one of the fields before beginning to work on the rest of your application.

Renaming a field is easy. For example, the Application Part created a field called Address, but you've decided that you want to have two address fields because a contact could have a work address and a home address in this database. It makes sense to change the field name to reflect the actual data you intend to store in the field, so let's change Address to WorkAddress. To do this, open the Contacts table in the Contact Tracking database in Design view, use the mouse to move the insertion point to the beginning of the Address field name, and then type **Work**. You can also click in the field name, use the arrow keys to position the insertion point just before the letter A, and type **Work**. As you learned in Chapter 4, we recommend that you not have any spaces in your field names, so do not put a space between the words Work and Address. Your field should now be called WorkAddress. Press F6 to move down to the Field Properties section of the window, tab down to the Caption property, and change the field caption to **Work Address**. Your result should look like Figure 5-10.

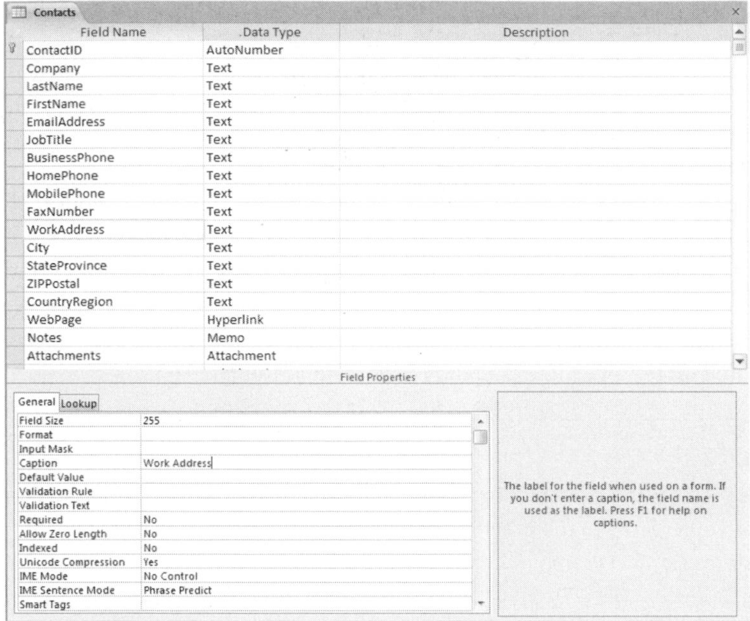

Figure 5-10 You can change a field name and a field caption in Design view.

Comparing the Two Contacts Tables

As you follow along with the examples in this chapter, it might be useful to compare the structure of the Contacts table you built in Chapter 4 and the actual tblContacts table in the Conrad Systems Contacts sample database. If you exactly followed the instructions in Chapter 4, your Contacts table in the Contact Tracking database should look like Table 5-1. You can see the actual design of tblContacts in Table 5-2.

Table 5-1 Contacts

Field Name	Type	Length
ContactID	AutoNumber	
Company	Text	255
LastName	Text	255
FirstName	Text	255

Field Name	Type	Length
EmailAddress	Text	255
JobTitle	Text	255
BusinessPhone	Text	255
HomePhone	Text	255
MobilePhone	Text	255
FaxNumber	Text	255
Address	Text	255
City	Text	255
StateProvince	Text	255
ZipPostal	Text	255
CountryRegion	Text	255
WebPage	Hyperlink	
Notes	Memo	
Attachments	Attachment	
ContactName	Calculated	
FileAs	Calculated	

Table 5-2 tblContacts

Field Name	Type	Length
ContactID	Auto Number	
LastName	Text	50
FirstName	Text	50
MiddleInit	Text	1
Title	Text	10
Suffix	Text	10
ContactType	Text	50
BirthDate	Date/Time	
DefaultAddress	Integer	
WorkAddress	Text	255
WorkCity	Text	50
WorkStateOrProvince	Text	20
WorkPostalCode	Text	20
WorkCountry	Text	50
WorkPhone	Text	30

Field Name	Type	Length
WorkExtension	Text	20
WorkFaxNumber	Text	30
HomeAddress	Text	255
HomeCity	Text	50
HomeStateOrProvince	Text	20
HomePostalCode	Text	20
HomeCountry	Text	50
HomePhone	Text	30
MobilePhone	Text	30
EmailName	Hyperlink	
Website	Hyperlink	
Photo	Attachment	
SpouseName	Text	75
SpouseBirthDate	Date/Time	
Notes	Memo	
CommissionPercent	Number	Double
Inactive	Yes/No	

As you can see, we have a lot of work to do—renaming fields, moving fields, inserting fields, adding new fields, and changing data types and lengths—to make the two tables identical.

Before we go any further, you should rename the remaining fields and add captions so that they more closely match the fields in the tblContacts table in the Conrad Systems Contacts sample database. Following the preceding steps for renaming fields and changing the Caption property, go through each of the fields and change them as follows:

Old Name	New Name	Caption
EmailAddress	EmailName	Email Name
JobTitle	Title	Title
BusinessPhone	WorkPhone	Work Phone
FaxNumber	WorkFaxNumber	Fax Number
City	WorkCity	Work City
StateProvince	WorkStateOrProvince	State/Province
ZIPPostalCode	WorkPostalCode	Postal Code

Old Name	New Name	Caption
CountryRegion	WorkCountry	Work Country
WebPage	Website	Website
Attachments	Photo	

Your table should now look like Figure 5-11. Click the Save button on the Quick Access Toolbar to save the changes to the table.

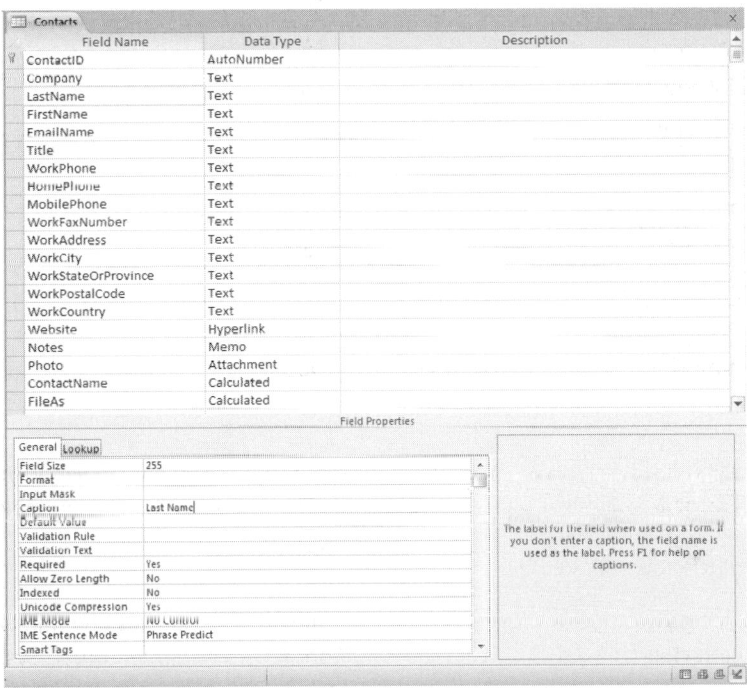

Figure 5-11 After renaming the fields in the Contacts table created from the template, it is beginning to look more like the table in the Conrad Systems Contacts sample database.

Moving Fields

You might want to move a field in a table definition for a number of reasons. Perhaps you made an error as you entered or changed the information in a table, or perhaps you've discovered that you're using some fields you defined at the end of a table quite frequently in forms or reports, in which case it would be easier to find and work with those fields if they were nearer the beginning of your table definition.

INSIDE OUT How Important Is the Sequence of Fields in Your Table?

The actual sequence of field definitions in a table is not all that important. In the relational database model, there really is no defined sequence of fields in a row or rows in a table. Access 2010, like most databases that implement the relational model, does allow you to define a field order when you create a table. This order, or sequence of fields, becomes the default order you see in a table datasheet or in a list of field names when you're designing a query, form, or report.

We like to at least group fields together in some reasonable order so that they're easy to find, and we like to place the primary key fields at the top of the list. There's really no hard and fast rule that you must follow for your database to work efficiently.

You can use the mouse to move one or more rows. Simply follow these steps.

1. To select a row you want to move, click its row selector.

   If you want to move multiple contiguous rows, click the row selector for the first row in the group and scroll until you can see the last row in the group. Hold down the Shift key and click the row selector for the last row in the group. The first and last rows and all rows in between will be selected. Release the Shift key.

2. Click and drag the row selector(s) for the selected row(s) to a new location. A small shaded box attaches to the bottom of the mouse pointer while you're dragging, and a highlighted line will appear, indicating the position to which the row(s) will move when you release the mouse button.

In the design for the tblContacts table in the Conrad Systems Contacts database, the EmailName field appears after all the address fields and before the Website field. It certainly makes sense to place all the web-related fields together. Select the EmailName field by clicking its row selector. Click the row selector again, and drag down until the line between the WorkCountry field and the Website field is highlighted, as shown in Figure 5-12.

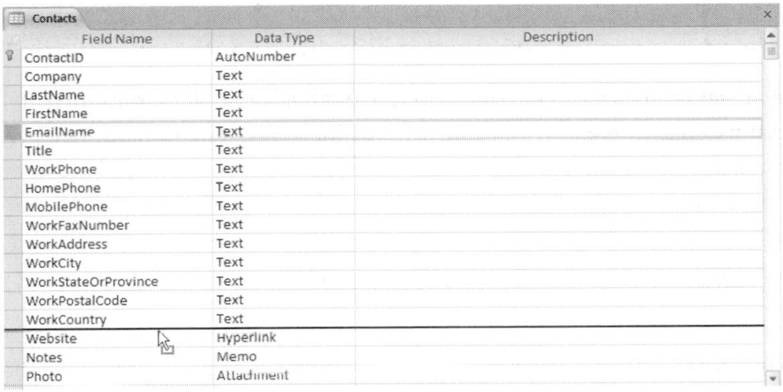

Contacts

Field Name	Data Type	Description
ContactID	AutoNumber	
Company	Text	
LastName	Text	
FirstName	Text	
EmailName	Text	
Title	Text	
WorkPhone	Text	
HomePhone	Text	
MobilePhone	Text	
WorkFaxNumber	Text	
WorkAddress	Text	
WorkCity	Text	
WorkStateOrProvince	Text	
WorkPostalCode	Text	
WorkCountry	Text	
Website	Hyperlink	
Notes	Memo	
Photo	Attachment	

Figure 5-12 You can drag the EmailName field to a new position between the WorkCountry and Website fields.

INSIDE OUT Using the Keyboard Instead of the Mouse in Table Design View

When it comes to moving fields, you might find it easier to use a combination of mouse and keyboard methods in Table Design view. Use the mouse to select the row or rows you want to move. Then activate Move mode by pressing Ctrl+Shift+F8, and use the arrow keys to position the row(s). Press Esc to deactivate Move mode. As you experiment with Access 2010, you'll discover more than one way to perform many tasks, and you can choose the techniques that work the best for you.

In Figure 5-13, the fields are positioned correctly.

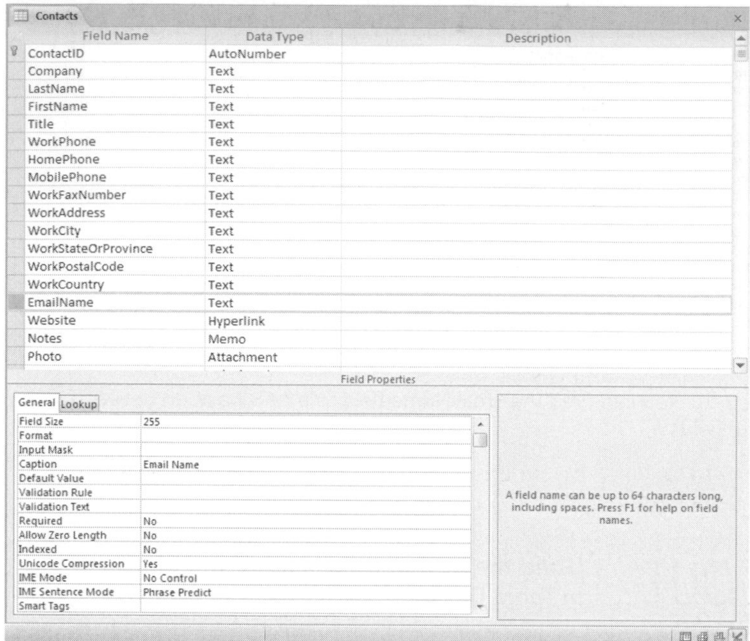

Figure 5-13 The EmailName field now is placed correctly.

In this exercise, we'll move a couple of additional fields to make the design of Contacts more similar to tblContacts. In the tblContacts table, the HomePhone and MobilePhone fields appear just before the EmailName field. Click the row selector for HomePhone, hold down the Shift key, and click the row selector for MobilePhone to select both fields. Drag and drop the two fields before the EmailName field. Now that you've moved HomePhone and MobilePhone out of the way, you can select both WorkPhone and WorkFaxNumber and drag them to where they belong after the WorkCountry field. Finally, move the Notes field after the Photo field. After you've done this, your table should look like Figure 5-14.

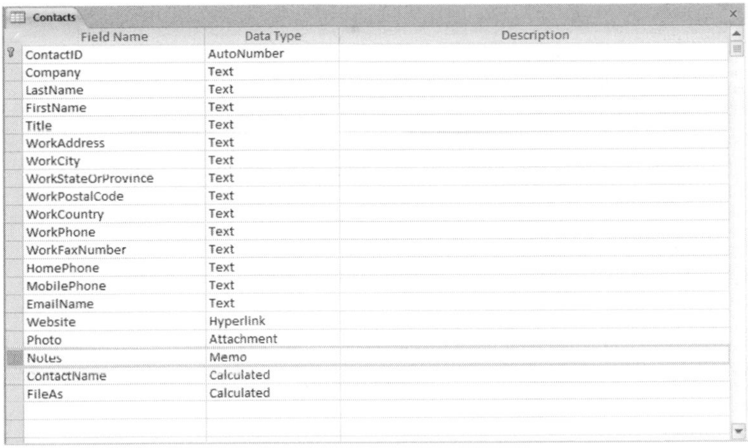

Contacts

Field Name	Data Type	Description
ContactID	AutoNumber	
Company	Text	
LastName	Text	
FirstName	Text	
Title	Text	
WorkAddress	Text	
WorkCity	Text	
WorkStateOrProvince	Text	
WorkPostalCode	Text	
WorkCountry	Text	
WorkPhone	Text	
WorkFaxNumber	Text	
HomePhone	Text	
MobilePhone	Text	
EmailName	Text	
Website	Hyperlink	
Photo	Attachment	
Notes	Memo	
ContactName	Calculated	
FileAs	Calculated	

Figure 5-14 After moving several fields, the sequence of fields in your Contacts table is similar to that in tblContacts.

Inserting Fields

Perhaps one of the most common changes you'll make to your database is to insert a new field in a table. Up until now, we've renamed and moved the available fields to match tblContacts more closely. If you take a look at the comparison of the two tables again (Tables 5-1 and 5-2, on pages 248 and 249), you can see that we need to add several more fields. Now you're ready to insert fields to store the middle initial, suffix, contact type, default address indicator, and more. As you go through adding these new fields, be sure to enter a description for each new field as well as the existing fields.

First, select the row or move your insertion point to the row that defines the field after the point where you want to insert the new field. In this case, if you want to insert a field for the middle initial between the FirstName and Title fields, place the insertion point anywhere in the row that defines the Title field. You can also select the entire row by using the arrow keys to move to the row and then pressing Shift+Spacebar or by clicking the row selector. Next, click the Design contextual tab, which is located below Table Tools on the ribbon. Finally, click the Insert Rows command in the Tools group, as shown in Figure 5-15. (You can also click a field row and press the Insert key to insert a row above your selection.)

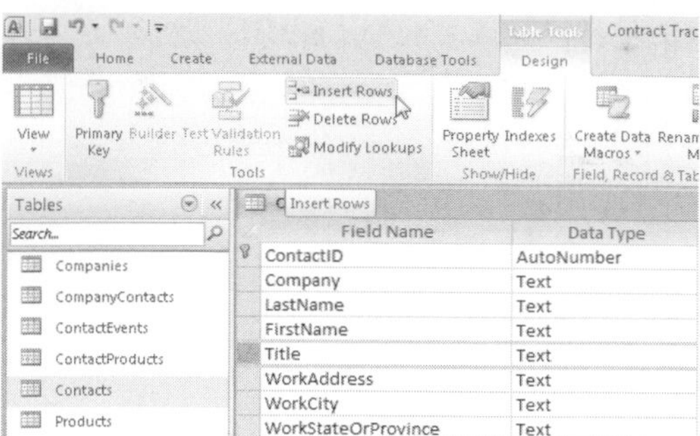

Figure 5-15 The Insert Rows command inserts a new row above a selected row or above the row in which the insertion point is located.

Access 2010 adds a blank row that you can use to define your new field. Type the definition for the MiddleInit field. Choose the Text data type, and set the Field Size property to **1**. Now move down to the WorkAddress field, and insert another row above it. Enter a Suffix field that has the Text data type with a field size of **10**. Do it one more time and insert a ContactType field between Suffix and WorkAddress, set its data type to Text, and set its length to **50**. Insert a field between ContactType and WorkAddress, name it BirthDate, and set its data type to Date/Time. Insert another field between BirthDate and WorkAddress, name it DefaultAddress, set its data type to Number, and set the field size to Integer. The actual Conrad Systems Contacts application uses this field to indicate whether the work or home address is the default mailing address.

Move down to WorkFaxNumber and insert a field above it. Enter a field name of WorkExtension, set its data type to Text, and set the field size to **20**. Now move down to the bottom of the field list and insert another new field above Notes. Enter a field name of SpouseName, set its data type to Text, and set the field size to **75**. Insert another row between the SpouseName and Notes fields, enter a field name of SpouseBirthDate, and set its data type to Date/Time. Move down to the ContactName field and insert a field above it. Create a field named CommissionPercent with a data type of Number and a field size of Double. Finally, insert another new field above ContactName named Inactive and set its data type to Yes/No.

At this point, your Table window in Design view should look something like the one shown in Figure 5-16. (We entered information in the Description properties of all fields we're going to keep. You can change your descriptions to match the figure.) Don't worry about setting other properties just yet. As you can see, we are getting closer to the exact design specifications of tblContacts in the Conrad Systems Contacts database, but we still have more things to change.

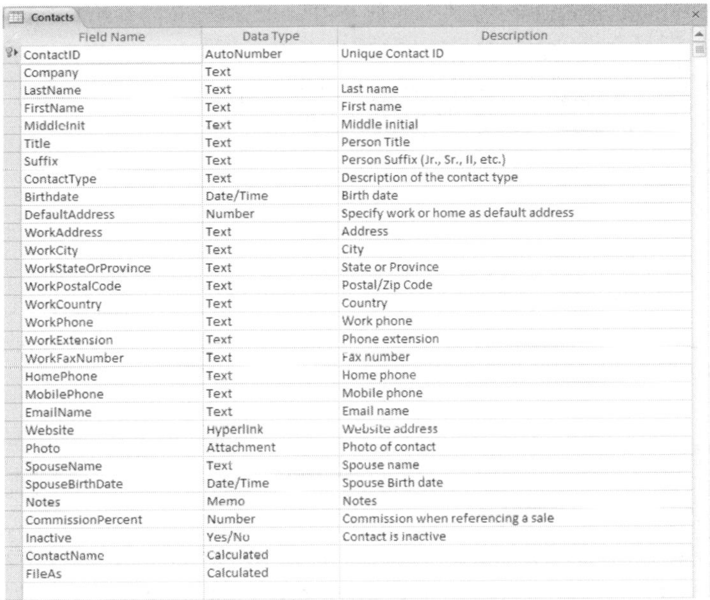

Contacts

Field Name	Data Type	Description
ContactID	AutoNumber	Unique Contact ID
Company	Text	
LastName	Text	Last name
FirstName	Text	First name
MiddleInit	Text	Middle initial
Title	Text	Person Title
Suffix	Text	Person Suffix (Jr., Sr., II, etc.)
ContactType	Text	Description of the contact type
Birthdate	Date/Time	Birth date
DefaultAddress	Number	Specify work or home as default address
WorkAddress	Text	Address
WorkCity	Text	City
WorkStateOrProvince	Text	State or Province
WorkPostalCode	Text	Postal/Zip Code
WorkCountry	Text	Country
WorkPhone	Text	Work phone
WorkExtension	Text	Phone extension
WorkFaxNumber	Text	Fax number
HomePhone	Text	Home phone
MobilePhone	Text	Mobile phone
EmailName	Text	Email name
Website	Hyperlink	Website address
Photo	Attachment	Photo of contact
SpouseName	Text	Spouse name
SpouseBirthDate	Date/Time	Spouse Birth date
Notes	Memo	Notes
CommissionPercent	Number	Commission when referencing a sale
Inactive	Yes/No	Contact is inactive
ContactName	Calculated	
FileAs	Calculated	

Figure 5-16 The Contacts table with additional fields inserted and descriptions defined.

INSIDE OUT **Using the Keyboard to Move Between Windows**

You can move the insertion point between the upper part and the lower part of any Table or Query window in Design view by pressing F6.

Copying Fields

As you create table definitions, you might find that several fields in your table are similar. Rather than enter each of the field definitions separately, you can enter one field definition, copy it, and then paste it as many times as necessary.

To finish defining our Contacts table, we need five additional fields—HomeAddress, HomeCity, HomeStateOrProvince, HomePostalCode, and HomeCountry. You could insert a new row and type all the properties as you just did in the previous section, but why not copy a field that is similar and make minor changes to it?

For this part of the exercise, select the row for the WorkAddress field definition by clicking the row selector at the left of the row. Click the Copy command in the Clipboard group on the Home tab, as shown in Figure 5-17.

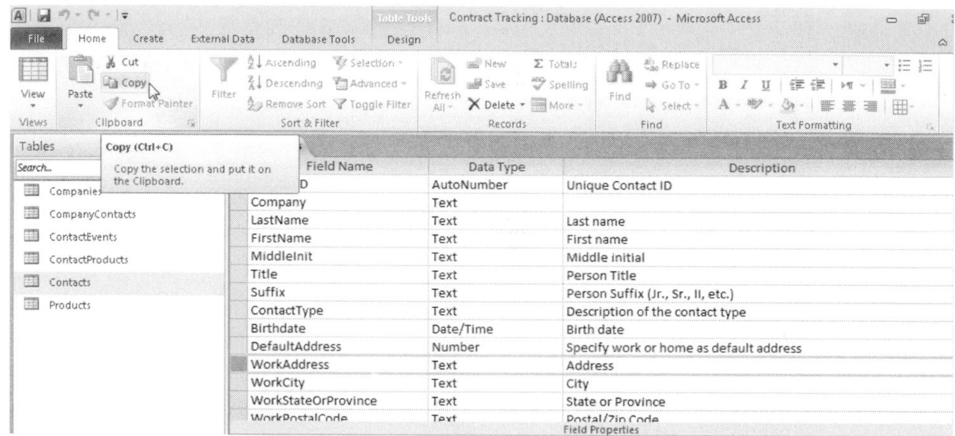

Figure 5-17 Select the WorkAddress field and click the Copy command on the Home tab on the ribbon to copy the field to the Clipboard.

Move the insertion point to the row that should follow the row you'll insert. (In this case, move the insertion point to the HomePhone field, which should follow your new field.) Insert a blank row by clicking Insert Rows in the Tools group of the Design contextual tab below Table Tools on the ribbon. (In this procedure, you switch back and forth between the Home tab and the Design contextual tab.) Select the new row by clicking the row selector. Click the Paste command in the Clipboard group on the Home tab on the ribbon, as shown in Figure 5-18.

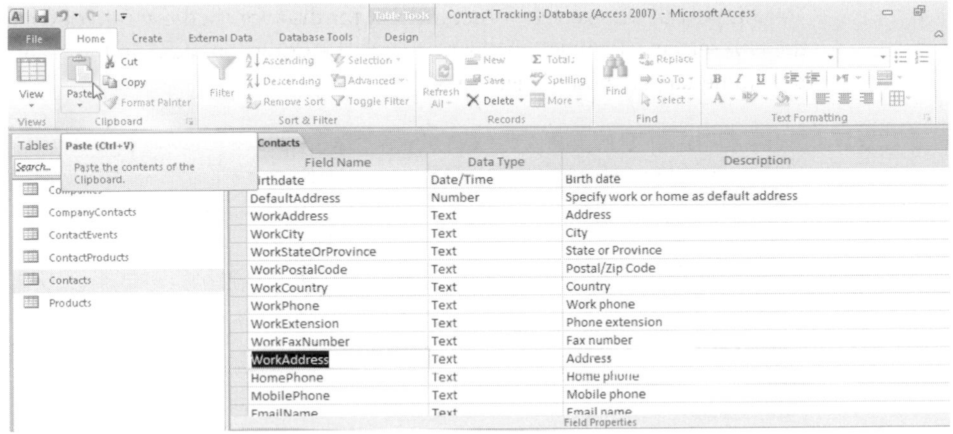

Figure 5-18 You can paste the copied WorkAddress field into a new blank row.

CAUTION!

If you click the Paste command when a row containing data is selected, the copied row will replace the selected row. Should you make this replacement in error, click the Undo command on the Quick Access Toolbar to restore the original row.

You can use the Paste command repeatedly to insert a copied row more than once. Remember to change both the name and the description of the resulting field or fields before you save the modified table definition. In this case, it's a simple matter to change the name of the copied row from WorkAddress to HomeAddress and to correct the description and caption accordingly. Note that this procedure also has the benefit of copying any formatting, default value, or validation rule information.

If you're careful, you don't actually have to insert a blank row to paste a field definition from the Clipboard. You can also copy and paste multiple fields at a time. After you fix the HomeAddress field name in the upper part of the window and caption in the lower part of the window, select the WorkCity field, hold down the Shift key, and select the WorkCountry field. Click the Copy command to copy all four fields to the Clipboard. Move down to the HomePhone field again and click in the row, but *do not select the row*. Click the Paste button in the Clipboard group of the Home tab to insert the four fields just above HomePhone. Change the name of the first one to HomeCity, the second to HomeStateOrProvince, the third to HomePostalCode, and the fourth to HomeCountry, and then correct the captions.

You should now have a table that's almost identical to the tblContacts table in the Conrad Systems Contacts sample database, as shown in Figure 5-19. Be sure to save your changed table.

Contacts

Field Name	Data Type	Description
ContactID	AutoNumber	Unique Contact ID
Company	Text	
LastName	Text	Last name
FirstName	Text	First name
MiddleInit	Text	Middle initial
Title	Text	Person Title
Suffix	Text	Person Suffix (Jr., Sr., II, etc.)
ContactType	Text	Description of the contact type
Birthdate	Date/Time	Birth date
DefaultAddress	Number	Specify work or home as default address
WorkAddress	Text	Address
WorkCity	Text	City
WorkStateOrProvince	Text	State or Province
WorkPostalCode	Text	Postal/Zip Code
WorkCountry	Text	Country
WorkPhone	Text	Work phone
WorkExtension	Text	Phone extension
WorkFaxNumber	Text	Fax number
HomeAddress	Text	Address
HomeCity	Text	City
HomeStateOrProvince	Text	State or Province
HomePostalCode	Text	Postal/Zip Code
HomeCountry	Text	Country
HomePhone	Text	Home phone
MobilePhone	Text	Mobile phone
EmailName	Text	Email name
Website	Hyperlink	Website address
Photo	Attachment	Photo of contact
SpouseName	Text	Spouse name
SpouseBirthDate	Date/Time	Spouse Birth date
Notes	Memo	Notes
CommissionPercent	Number	Commission when referencing a sale
Inactive	Yes/No	Contact is inactive
ContactName	Calculated	
FileAs	Calculated	

Figure 5-19 The Contacts field list is now almost identical to tblContacts.

Deleting Fields

Removing unwanted fields is easy. With the Table window open in Design view, select the field that you want to delete by clicking the row selector. You can extend the selection to multiple contiguous fields by holding down the Shift key and pressing the Up and Down Arrow keys to select multiple rows. You can also select multiple contiguous rows by clicking the row selector of the first row and, without releasing the mouse button, dragging up or down to select all the rows you want. After you select the appropriate fields, click Delete Rows in the Tools group of the Design tab below Table Tools on the ribbon. Or, press the Delete key to delete the selected fields.

We have three extra fields in our current Contacts table that we do not need—the Company, ContactName, and FileAs fields that were created by the Contacts Application Part. (Remember that in Chapter 3, you created a Company Contacts table to link contacts to their respective companies.) To delete the Company field, click the row selector next to the Company field and then click the Delete Rows button in the Tools group of the Design tab on the ribbon. Access prompts you that calculated columns depend on the Company field. Click Yes to confirm that you want to delete the field. Now move down to the last two fields and also delete the ContactName and FileAs fields from your contacts table. Your Contacts table now matches the tblContacts table from the Conrad Systems Contacts database in terms of the correct number of fields and field names. Save these latest changes to the Contacts table by clicking the Save button on the Quick Access Toolbar.

If a table contains one or more rows of data, Access displays a warning message when you delete field definitions in Design view, as shown in Figure 5-20. Click No if you think you made a mistake. Click Yes to proceed with the deletion of the fields and the data in those fields. Keep in mind that you can still undo this change up to the point that you save the table.

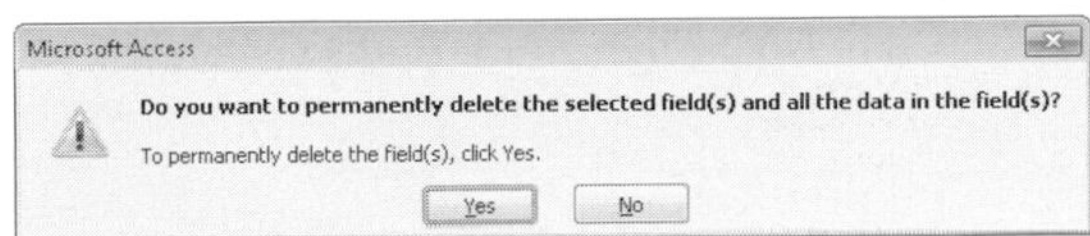

Figure 5-20 This dialog box asks you to confirm a field deletion.

If you want to test this in the sample table you have been building, make sure you have saved your latest changes and then switch to Datasheet view by clicking the small arrow below the View button in the Views group on the Home tab and then clicking Datasheet View. Type your name in the Last Name and First Name fields and switch back to Design view by clicking the small arrow below the View button again. Try deleting any field in the design, and Access will warn you that you may be deleting some data as well.

Changing Data Attributes

As you learned in the previous chapter, Access 2010 provides a number of different data types. These data types help Access work more efficiently with your data and also provide a base level of data validation; for example, you can enter only numbers in a Number or Currency field.

When you initially design your database, you should match the data type and length of each field to its intended use. You might discover, however, that a field you thought would contain only numbers (such as a U.S. ZIP Code) must now contain some letters (perhaps because you've started doing business in Canada). You might find that one or more number fields need to hold larger values or a different number of decimal places. Access allows you to change the data type and length of many fields, even after you've entered data in them.

Changing Data Types

Changing the data type of a field in a table is simple. Open the table in Design view, click in the Data Type column of the field definition you want to change, click the arrow button at the right to see the available choices, and select a new data type. You cannot convert an OLE Object, an Attachment, Calculated, or a ReplicationID data type to another data type. With several limitations, Access can successfully convert every other data type to any other data type, even when you have data in the table. Table 5-3 shows you the possible conversions and potential limitations when the table contains data.

CAUTION!

When the field contents don't satisfy the limitations noted in Table 5-3, Access 2010 deletes the field contents (sets it to Null) when you save the changes.

Table 5-3 Limitations on Converting One Data Type to Another

Convert To	From	Limitations
Text	Memo	Access truncates text longer than 255 characters.
	Hyperlink	Might lose some data if the hyperlink string is longer than 255 characters.
	Number, except ReplicationID	No limitations.
	AutoNumber	No limitations except ReplicationID.
	Currency	No limitations.
	Date/Time	No limitations.
	Yes/No	Yes (–1) converts to Yes; No (0) converts to No.
Memo	Text	No limitations.
	Hyperlink	No limitations.
	Number, except ReplicationID	No limitations.
	AutoNumber	No limitations.
	Currency	No limitations.
	Date/Time	No limitations.

Convert To	From	Limitations
	Yes/No	Yes (–1) converts to Yes; No (0) converts to No.
Hyperlink	Text	If the text contains a valid Hyperlink string consisting of a display name, a # delimiter, a valid link address, a # delimiter, and optional bookmark and ScreenTip, Access changes the data type without modifying the text. If the text contains only a valid link address, Access surrounds the address with # delimiters to form the Hyperlink field. Access recognizes strings beginning with *http://*, *ftp://*, *mailto:*, *news:*, *\\servername*, and *d:* as link addresses. Access also assumes that a text string in the form *text@text* is an email address, and it adds *mailto:* to the beginning of the string before converting it. If Access does not recognize the text as a link, it converts the text to *[text]#http://[text]#*, where *[text]* is the original contents of the field; the result is probably not a valid link address.
	Memo	Same restrictions as converting from Text.
	Number, except ReplicationID	Possible, but Access converts the number to a text string in the form *[number]#http://[number]#*, where *[number]* is the text conversion of the original numeric value; the result is probably not a valid link address.
	AutoNumber	Possible, but Access converts the AutoNumber to a text string in the form *[number]#http://[number]*, where *[number]* is the text conversion of the original AutoNumber; the result is probably not a valid link address.
	Currency	Possible, but Access converts the currency value to a text string in the form *[currency]#http://[currency]*, where *[currency]* is the text conversion of the original currency value; the result is probably not a valid link address.
	Date/Time	Possible, but Access converts the date/time to a text string in the form *[date/time]#http://[date/time]#*, where *[date/time]* is the text conversion of the original date or time value; the result is probably not a valid link address.
	Yes/No	Possible, but Access converts the yes/no to a text string in the form *[yes/no]#- http://[yes/no]*, where *[yes/no]* is the text conversion of the original yes (–1) or no (0) value; the result is probably not a valid link address.
Number	Text	Text must contain only numbers and valid separators. The number value must be within the range for the Field Size property.
	Memo	Memo must contain only numbers and valid separators. The number value must be within the range for the Field Size property.
	Hyperlink	Not possible.

Convert To	From	Limitations
	Number (different field size or precision)	Number must not be larger or smaller than can be contained in the new field size. If you change precision, Access might round the number.
	AutoNumber	The number value must be within the range for the Field Size property.
	Currency	Number must not be larger or smaller than can be contained in the Field Size property.
	Date/Time	If the Field Size is Byte, the date must be between April 18, 1899,[1] and September 11, 1900. If the new Field Size is Integer, the date must be between April 13, 1810, and September 16, 1989. For all other field sizes, there are no limitations.
	Yes/No	Yes (–1) converts to –1; No (0) converts to 0.
AutoNumber	Text	Not possible if the table contains data.
	Memo	Not possible if the table contains data.
	Hyperlink	Not possible.
	Number	Not possible if the table contains data.
	Currency	Not possible if the table contains data.
	Date/Time	Not possible if the table contains data.
	Yes/No	Not possible if the table contains data.
Currency	Text	Text must contain only numbers and valid separators.
	Memo	Memo must contain only numbers and valid separators.
	Hyperlink	Not possible.
	Number, except Replication ID	No limitations.
	AutoNumber	No limitations.
	Date/Time	No limitations, but value might be rounded.
	Yes/No	Yes (–1) converts to $1; No (0) converts to $0.
Date/Time	Text	Text must contain a recognizable date and/or time, such as 18-Jul-10 5:15 PM.
	Memo	Memo must contain a recognizable date and/or time, such as 18-Jul-10 5:15 PM.
	Hyperlink	Not possible.
	Number, except Replication ID	Number must be between –657,434 and 2,958,465.99998843.
	AutoNumber	Value must be less than 2,958,466 and greater than –657,433.
	Currency	Number must be between –$657,434 and $2,958,465.9999.

Convert To	From	Limitations
	Yes/No	Yes (–1) converts to 12/29/1899; No (0) converts to 12:00:00 AM.
Yes/No	Text	Text must contain only one of the following values: Yes, True, On, No, False, or Off.
	Memo	Text must contain only one of the following values: Yes, True, On, No, False, or Off.
	Hyperlink	Not possible.
	Number, except Replication ID	Zero or Null converts to No; any other value converts to Yes.
	AutoNumber	All values evaluate to Yes.
	Currency	Zero or Null converts to No; any other value converts to Yes.
	Date/Time	12:00:00 AM or Null converts to No; any other value converts to Yes.

1 Remember, Access stores a date/time value as an integer date offset and fraction of a day. April 18, 1899, happens to be –256 internally, which is the smallest number you can store in a Byte.

If you want to see how this works in the Contacts table you have been building, open the table in Datasheet view and enter any last name and first name in one or two rows. We want to change the EmailName field from the Text data type that the Contacts Application Part provided to Hyperlink. Scroll right and enter an invalid email address in one of the rows in the form: **Proseware email address**. In another row, add the correct URL prefix in the form: **mailto:jeffc@proseware.com**.

Now, switch to Design view and change the data type of the EmailName field from Text to Hyperlink and save the change. Notice that Access 2010 gives you no warning about any conversion problems because it knows it can store any text field that is not larger than 255 characters in a hyperlink, which can be up to 8,192 bytes. Save this change to the table, switch back to Datasheet view, and scroll to the right to find the changed field. You should see a result something like Figure 5-21.

Figure 5-21 Access 2010 can convert the Text data type to Hyperlink correctly, but only if the text contains a recognizable protocol string.

Both entries look fine. However, if you click the first one, Access 2010 attempts to open your browser because the full text stored in the hyperlink is *Proseware email address#http://Proseware email address#*. Because the link address portion indicates the http protocol, your browser attempts to open instead of your email program. Access displays a message box that says it cannot follow the hyperlink. When you click on the second link, it should open a blank message in your email program with the To: line filled in correctly. Access recognized the *mailto:* prefix and converted the text correctly.

You can read more about working with hyperlinks in Chapter 12, "Using Forms in an Access Application." We show you how to make sure that Access correctly recognizes an email name typed into a hyperlink field in Chapter 25, "Automating Your Application with Visual Basic," on the companion CD.

Changing Data Lengths

For text and number fields, you can define the maximum length of the data that can be stored in the field. Although a text field can be up to 255 characters long, you can restrict the length to as little as 1 character. If you don't specify a length for text, Access 2010 normally assigns the length you specify in the Table Design section in the Object Designers category of the Access Options dialog box. (The default length is 255.) Access won't let you enter text field data longer than the defined length. If you need more space in a text field, you can increase the length at any time; but, if you try to redefine the length of a text field so that it's shorter, you will get a warning message (like the one shown in Figure 5-22) stating that Access will truncate any data field that contains data longer than the new length when you try to save the changes to your table. Note also that it warns you that any validation rules you have designed might fail because of the changed data.

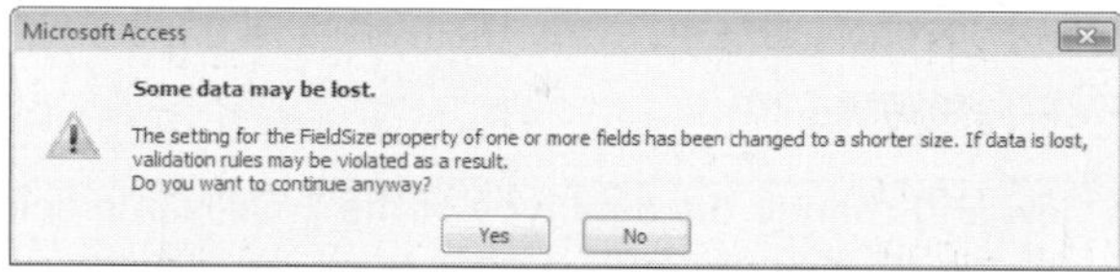

Figure 5-22 This dialog box informs you of possible data truncation problems.

INSIDE OUT Setting Field Defaults Through Access Options

Remember, you can change the default data type for a new field and the default length of new text and number fields by clicking the File tab on the Backstage view, clicking Options, clicking the Object Designers category of the Access Options dialog box, and then selecting your defaults in the Table Design View section.

If you want to try this in your Contacts table, open it in Design view, change the length of the MiddleInit field to **10**, and save the change. Switch to Datasheet view and type more than one character in MiddleInit. Now switch back to Design view and set the length of MiddleInit to **1**. When you try to save the change, you should see the error message in Figure 5-22 (because you're shortening the length of the MiddleInit field). Click Yes to allow the changes and then switch back to Datasheet view. You should find the data you typed truncated to one character in MiddleInit. Review Table 5-2 (on page 249) and verify that each field's length in your Contacts table matches tblContacts in the Conrad Systems Contacts database and make any necessary adjustments before proceeding further.

Sizes for numeric data types can vary from a single byte (which can contain a value from 0 through 255) to 2 or 4 bytes (for larger integers), 8 bytes (necessary to hold very large floating-point or currency numbers), or 16 bytes (to hold a unique ReplicationID or decimal number). Except for ReplicationID, you can change the size of a numeric data type at any time, but you might generate errors if you make the size smaller. Access also rounds numbers when converting from floating-point data types (Single or Double) to integer or currency values.

Dealing with Conversion Errors

When you try to save a modified table definition, Access 2010 always warns you if any changes to the data type or field length will cause conversion errors. For example, if you change the Field Size property of a Number field from Integer to Byte, Access warns you if any of the records contain a number larger than 255. (Access deletes the contents of any field that it can't convert at all.) If you examine Table 5-3, you'll see that you should expect some data type changes to always cause problems. For example, if you change a field from Hyperlink to Date/Time, you can expect Access to delete all data. You'll see a dialog box, similar to the one shown in Figure 5-23, warning you about fields that Access will set to a Null value if you proceed with your changes. Click Yes to proceed with the changes. You'll have to examine your data to correct any conversion errors.

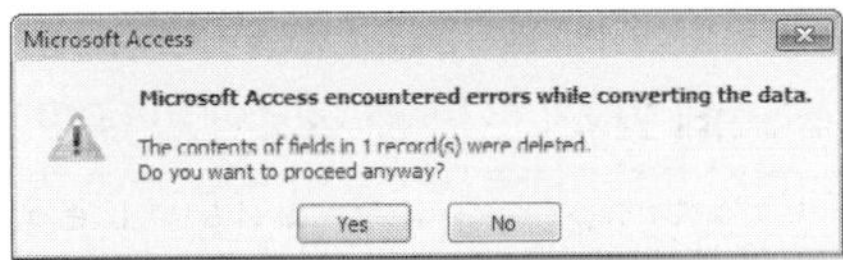

Figure 5-23 This dialog box informs you of conversion errors.

If you click No, Access 2010 opens the dialog box shown in Figure 5-24. If you deleted any fields or indexes, added any fields, or renamed any fields, Access will save those changes. Otherwise, the database will be unchanged. You can correct any data type or field length changes you made, and then try to save the table definition again.

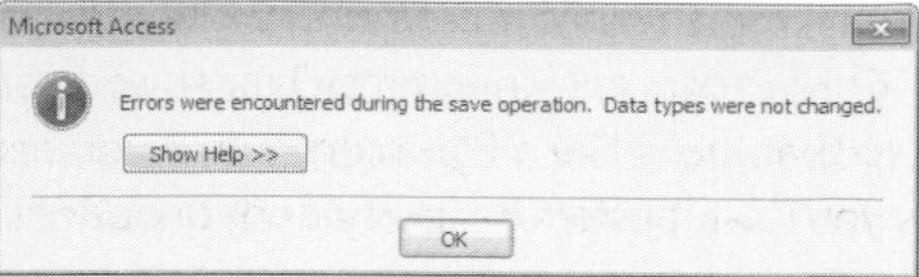

Figure 5-24 This dialog box appears if you decide not to save a modified table definition.

Changing Other Field Properties

As you learned in Chapter 4, you can set a number of other properties that define how Access 2010 displays or validates a field that have nothing to do with changing the data type. These properties include Description, Format, Input Mask, Caption, Default Value, Validation Rule, Validation Text, Required, Allow Zero Length, and Indexed.

If you have data in your table, changing some of these properties might elicit a warning from Access. If you change or define a validation rule, or set Required to Yes, Access offers to check the new rule or requirement that a field not be empty against the contents of the table when you try to save the change. If you ask Access to test the data, it checks all the rows in your table and opens a warning dialog box if it finds any rows that fail. However, it doesn't tell you *which* rows failed—we'll show you how to do that in Chapter 9. If you changed the rules for more than one field, you'll see the error dialog box once for each rule that fails.

As you'll learn later, when you define queries, forms, and reports, these objects inherit several of the properties that you define for your table fields. In previous versions of Access before Access 2007, the catch was that once you defined and saved another object that used table fields, any subsequent change that you made to properties in table design didn't change automatically in other dependent objects. You had to go find those properties yourself and fix them. You would get the new property settings in any new objects you created, but the old ones remained unchanged.

The good news is there's a feature in Access 2010 that takes care of this problem for some properties. To see how this works, you must first make sure that you have this option selected in Access Options as we showed you in the previous chapter. Click the File tab on the Backstage view, click Options, click the Object Designers category, and verify that you have selected the Show Property Update Options Buttons check box. Click OK to close the Access Options dialog box.

Next, open the Contacts table in Design view in the Contact Tracking database you have been building. Remember from the previous chapter that Access displays the description on the status bar when the focus is on the Description field in any datasheet or form.

Click in the Description column next to the ContactID field and change the description from "Unique contact ID" to just "Contact ID," and then press Tab. As soon as you do this, you'll see an AutoCorrect smart tag that looks like a lightning bolt. If you rest your mouse pointer near the smart tag, it tells you that it offers property update options. Click the arrow next to the tag to see the options you can choose from, as shown in Figure 5-25. Access offers you these options whenever you change the Description, Format, or Input Mask properties.

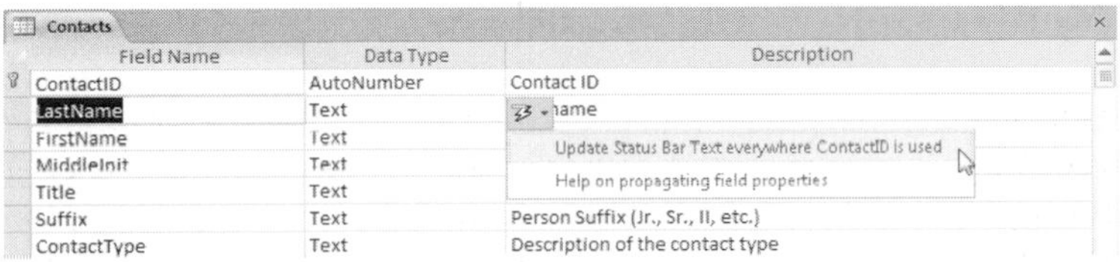

Contacts

Field Name	Data Type	Description
ContactID	AutoNumber	Contact ID
LastName	Text	ame
FirstName	Text	Update Status Bar Text everywhere ContactID is used
MiddleInit	Text	Help on propagating field properties
Title	Text	
Suffix	Text	Person Suffix (Jr., Sr., II, etc.)
ContactType	Text	Description of the contact type

Figure 5-25 When you change a field description, you see a smart tag offering property update options.

You can click Update Status Bar Text Everywhere ContactID Is Used to ask Access to change this property wherever the ContactID field is used in other objects as well. Of course, you don't have anything but tables in your sample database right now, so clicking this command won't do anything. You can select Help On Propagating Field Properties to open the Help window to read how this works.

CAUTION!

You must click the Update Status Bar Text Everywhere ContactID Is Used command immediately after you make the change in your table definition. If you move to another field or move to another property and make another change, the smart tag disappears. You can make it reappear by returning to the property you changed and changing it again. If you choose to make changes, Access opens an Update Properties dialog box that lists all the objects it plans to change. You can reject all changes or selectively apply the change to only some of the objects.

Reversing Changes

If you make several changes and then decide you don't want any of them, you can close the Table window without saving them. When you do this, Access opens the dialog box shown in Figure 5-26. Simply click No to reverse all your changes. Click Cancel to return to the Table window in Design view without saving or reversing your changes.

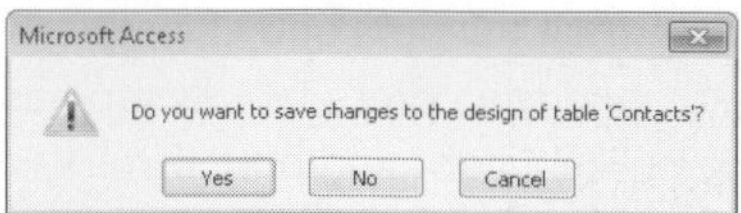

Figure 5-26 This dialog box gives you the option of reversing unsaved changes to a table.

INSIDE OUT **Reversing Multiple Changes**

You can always reverse up to the last 20 changes you made since you last saved the table design by clicking the Undo button. You can also open the list next to the Undo button to undo a series of changes selectively.

Using the Table Analyzer Wizard

Even if you use good design techniques (see Article 1, "Designing Your Database Application," on the companion CD) and build a normalized database, you might not arrive at the best design. In fact, you often cannot fully evaluate a database design until you use the database and store data. Access 2010 includes the Table Analyzer Wizard that can examine data in your tables (or data you import from another source) and recommend additional refinements and enhancements to your database design.

One of the key elements of good database design is the elimination of redundant data. The Table Analyzer Wizard is particularly good at scanning data in your tables, identifying data repeated in one or more columns, and recommending alterations to your design that break out the redundant data into separate tables. You can find an example of such redundant data in the Conrad Systems Contacts database (Contacts.accdb). Imagine that a customer sent you a file containing company and contact information. Sounds like a good, easy place to start collecting or adding to your contact data. However, when you open the file, you see that most companies are listed several times because the original data isn't normalized. You'll find just such a table, saved as tblContacts4TableAnalyzer, in the Conrad Systems Contacts sample database.

You can see how the Table Analyzer Wizard works by using it on the tblContacts4TableAnalyzer table. First, open the Conrad Systems Contacts database. Click the Database Tools tab and then click the Analyze Table command in the Analyze group. Access starts the Table Analyzer Wizard and displays the first window, shown in Figure 5-27.

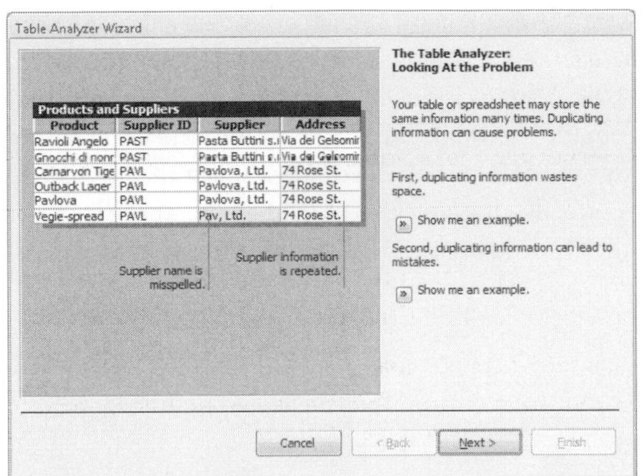

Figure 5-27 The opening page of the Table Analyzer Wizard informs you about the problems it is designed to correct.

This first page is one of two introductory pages that explain what the wizard can do. Click the Show Me An Example buttons to get a better understanding of the kinds of problems the wizard can solve and to see how the wizard works. Click Next twice to get to the first action page in the wizard, shown in Figure 5-28.

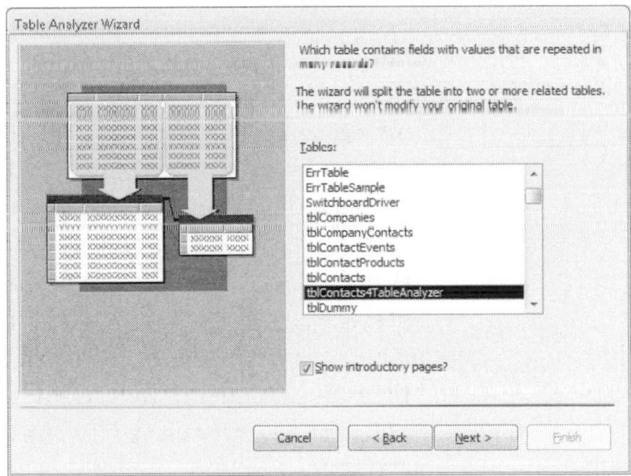

Figure 5-28 Select the table you want to analyze in the Table Analyzer Wizard.

On this page, you select the table you want to analyze. For this exercise, select the tblContacts4TableAnalyzer table. (Note that you have a check box on this page to continue to show the two introductory pages each time you start the wizard. If you think you understand how the wizard works, you can clear the check box to skip the introductory pages the next time you start the wizard.) Click Next.

In the next window, the wizard asks if you want to rearrange the fields in the target table or if you want the wizard to decide the arrangement for you. If you know which fields contain redundant data, you can make the decision yourself. Because the wizard handles all the tedious work of splitting out lookup data, you might choose the latter option in the future to normalize tables in your application further. For now, select the Yes, Let The Wizard Decide option to see how effective it is. Click Next to start the analysis of your table. Figure 5-29 shows the result of the wizard's analysis. (We've shifted the contents of this figure to fit the result in a single window.)

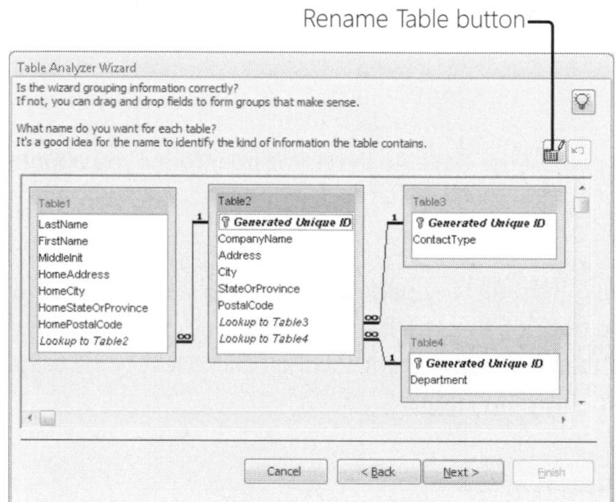

Figure 5-29 The Table Analyzer Wizard examines the data in your table and makes an initial recommendation.

In this case, the wizard did a pretty good job of identifying the separate company and contact information and splitting the fields into two tables. It also recognized that ContactType and Department have lots of repeating values and perhaps should each be in separate lookup tables. There isn't enough data (only 18 rows—and each contact is related to only one company) in the table for the wizard to have noticed a many-to-many relationship between companies and contacts.

We really don't need to do much work to fix this if we're happy with the one-to-many relationships. Click the Lookup To Table3 field in Table2 and drag it to Table1 to relate the contact type lookup information to contacts instead of companies. Now move the Department field from Table4 to Table2 between CompanyName and Address. This last move should remove Table4 from the design window.

After you have adjusted the way the wizard split your tables, the next step is to give each of the new tables a new name. To rename a table, first click the table name and then click the Rename Table button in the upper part of the window. (You can also double-click the table's title bar.) The wizard opens a dialog box in which you can enter a new name. You should change Table1 to **Contacts**, Table2 to **Companies**, and Table3 to **ContactTypes**. Click Next when you are finished.

The next page asks you to verify the primary key fields for these tables. You can select new fields for the primary key of each table or add fields to the primary key. The wizard couldn't identify any naturally occurring unique value, so it generated a unique ID (which will be an AutoNumber in the final tables) for two of the tables. You need to select the Contacts table and click Add Generated Key to create a primary key for that table. Figure 5-30 shows the result of moving fields, assigning new names to the tables, and adding a primary key. Click Next to accept the settings and go on to an analysis of duplicate values in the lookup tables.

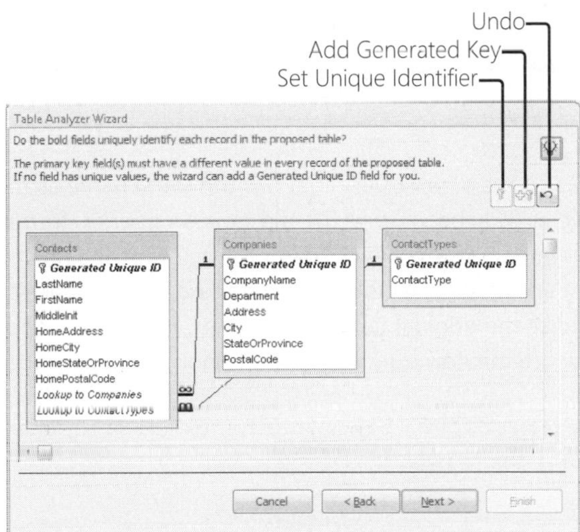

Figure 5-30 After adjusting what the wizard proposed, you're ready to create the new tables.

The Table Analyzer Wizard looks at values in the new tables to try to eliminate any possible duplicates created by typing errors. Figure 5-31 shows the result of this analysis on the sample table. Because the wizard sees several rows with Marketing or Sales in them, it suggests that some of these values might, in fact, be the same. You can use this page to tell the wizard any correct values for actual mistyped duplicates. This could be extremely useful if your incoming data had the same company listed several times but with a slightly different spelling or address. The wizard will store only unique values in the final table. You could, if necessary, tell the wizard to substitute one set of similar values for another to eliminate the near duplicates. In this case, you should tell the wizard to use the original value for all the values listed as duplicates by clicking the arrow in the Correction field and selecting the (Leave As Is) option, as shown in Figure 5-31. Click Next when you are finished to go on to the next page.

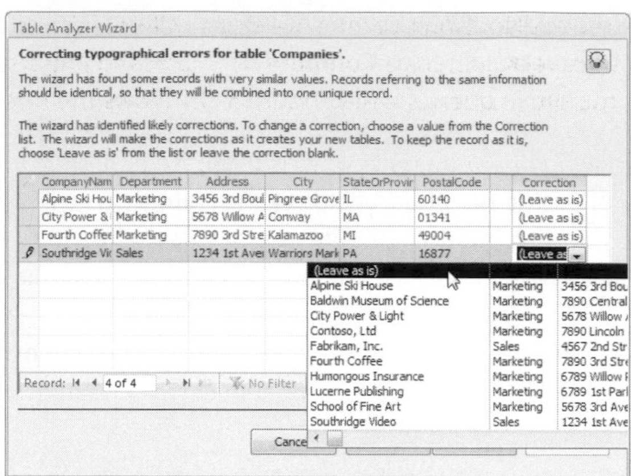

Figure 5-31 The Table Analyzer Wizard gives you the opportunity to fix potentially duplicate lookup values.

Finally, the wizard offers to create a new query that has the same name as the original table (see Figure 5-32). If you've already been using the old table in queries, forms, and reports, creating a new query that integrates the new tables into the original data structure means you won't have to change any other objects in your database. In most cases, the new query will look and operate just like the original table. Old queries, forms, and reports based on the original table will now use the new query and won't know the difference.

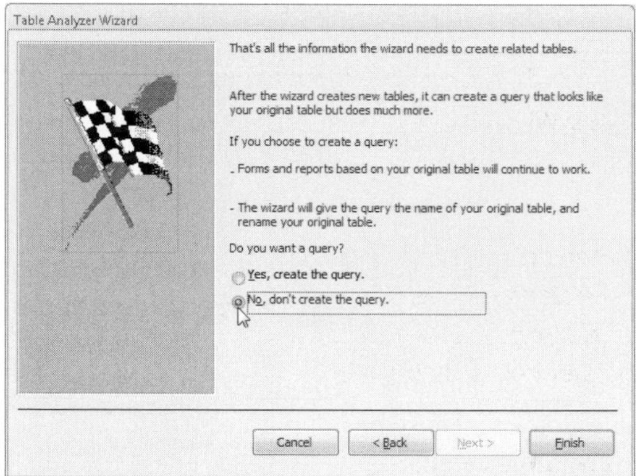

Figure 5-32 The final page of the Table Analyzer Wizard lets you decide whether you want a query to duplicate the original unnormalized data structure.

This is only an example, so select No, Don't Create The Query. Click Finish to build your new tables. The wizard also creates relationships among the new tables to make sure you can re-create the original data structure in queries easily. Figure 5-33 shows the three new tables built by the wizard.

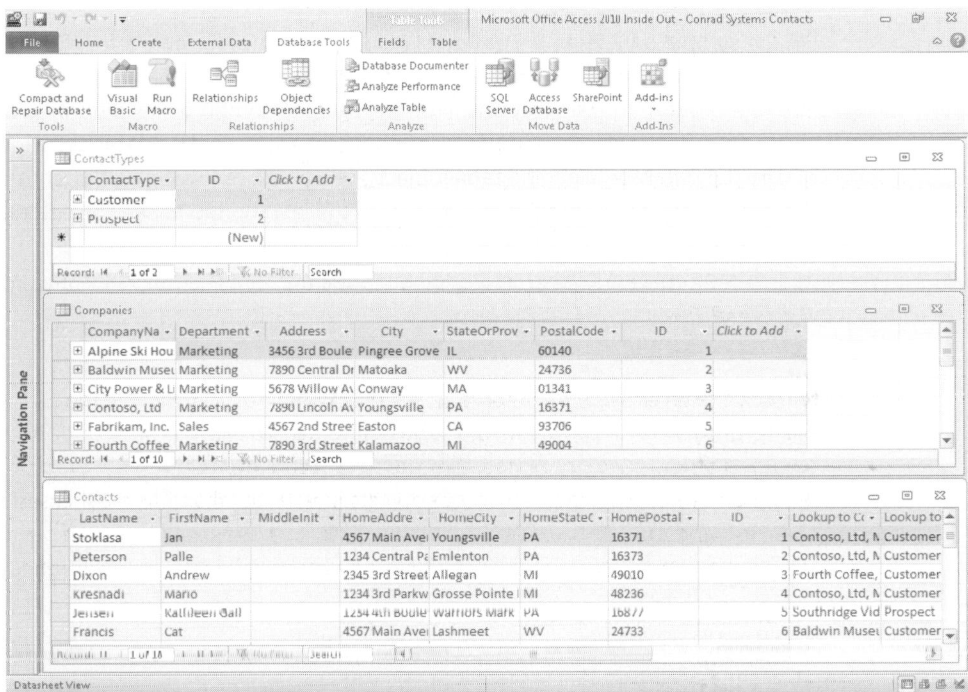

Figure 5-33 The Table Analyzer Wizard automatically separates your old data into the new table structure.

Notice that the wizard left behind an ID field in the Contacts table as a link to the ContactTypes table. The values in the ContactTypes table are actually unique, so there's no reason not to use the actual value as the primary key instead of an artificial ID. We'll show you how to change the primary key later in this chapter.

Taking a Look at Lookup Properties

As you have been working with table design, you've probably noticed that there's a Lookup tab available in the lower part of the Table window in Design view. You might have also noticed that Access 2010 offers you a Lookup Wizard entry in the drop-down list of data types and a Modify Lookups option in the Tools group on the Design tab. This feature allows you to predefine how you want the field displayed in a datasheet, form, or report.

For example, if you have a DepartmentID field in an Employees table that stores the primary key value of the department for which the employee works, you might want to display the department name rather than the number value when you look at the data. If you're displaying a Yes/No field, you might want to provide a drop-down list that shows options for *invoiced* and *not invoiced* instead of *yes* and *no* or *true* and *false*.

In the sample databases, we defined Lookup properties for only a few fields—ones for which we knew that we would later need a combo box with the relevant available choices on one or more forms or reports. (You will also see combo boxes described as drop-down lists.) One such example is in the Housing Reservations sample database (Housing.accdb). Open the database, view the table objects, select tblEmployees, and open it in Design view. Click the DepartmentID field and then click the Lookup tab to see the settings, as shown in Figure 5-34.

tblEmployees

Field Name	Data Type	Description
EmployeeNumber	Number	Unique Employee Number
FirstName	Text	Employee First Name
MiddleName	Text	Employee Middle Name (or initial)
LastName	Text	Employee Last Name
EmailName	Hyperlink	Employee email address
DepartmentID	Number	Employee's assigned department
OfficeLocation	Text	Employee office location
Photo	Text	Path to employee photo
Password	Text	Password (required for department managers and application admin
IsAdmin	Yes/No	Authorized to administer this application
Address	Text	Employee home address
City	Text	Employee home city

Field Properties

General | Lookup

Display Control	Combo Box
Row Source Type	Table/Query
Row Source	qlkpDepartments
Bound Column	1
Column Count	2
Column Heads	No
Column Widths	0";1.5"
List Rows	16
List Width	Auto
Limit To List	Yes
Allow Multiple Values	No
Allow Value List Edits	No
List Items Edit Form	
Show Only Row Source V	No

A field name can be up to 64 characters long, including spaces. Press F1 for help on field names.

Figure 5-34 The DepartmentID field in tblEmployees in the Housing Reservations sample database has Lookup properties defined.

As you can see, we have set the Display Control property to Combo Box. You see combo boxes in Windows applications all the time. It's a box that you can type in with a button on the right that you can click to drop down a list of values to select. In Access, you tell the combo box what type of list you want (Row Source Type) and specify the source of the list (Row Source). Access is a bit unusual because it lets you define a list that contains more than one column that you can display (Column Count), and it requires you to specify which of the columns (Bound Column) actually supplies the value to be stored when you pick an item from the list. This means that you might see a text value, but the combo box stores a number.

You can see this combo box in action by switching to Datasheet view. You can click in the Department field and type a name from the list, or click the arrow on the right and select an item from the list, as shown in Figure 5-35. Remember, DepartmentID is actually a number. If you didn't define the special settings on the Lookup tab, you would see a list of numbers in the Department column. For details about these settings, see Table 5-4 on page 278.

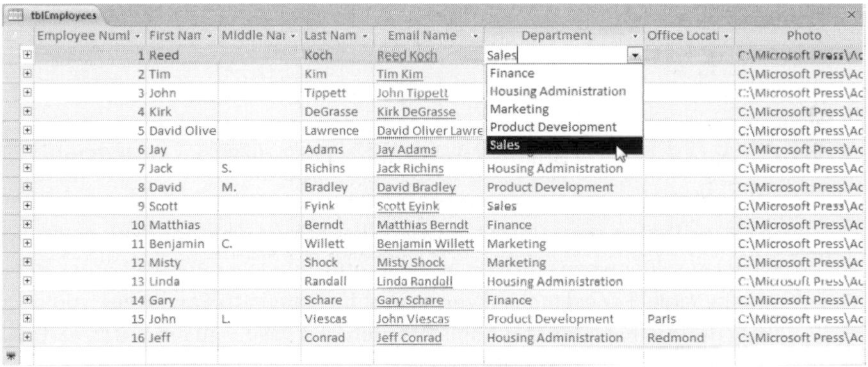
tblEmployees

Employee Numl	First Nam	Middle Na	Last Nam	Email Name	Department	Office Locati	Photo
1	Reed		Koch	Reed Koch	Sales		C:\Microsoft Press\Ac
2	Tim		Kim	Tim Kim	Finance		C:\Microsoft Press\Ac
3	John		Tippett	John Tippett	Housing Administration		C:\Microsoft Press\Ac
4	Kirk		DeGrasse	Kirk DeGrasse	Marketing		C:\Microsoft Press\Ac
5	David Olive		Lawrence	David Oliver Lawre	Product Development		C:\Microsoft Press\Ac
6	Jay		Adams	Jay Adams	Sales		C:\Microsoft Press\Ac
7	Jack	S.	Richins	Jack Richins	Housing Administration		C:\Microsoft Press\Ac
8	David	M.	Bradley	David Bradley	Product Development		C:\Microsoft Press\Ac
9	Scott		Fyink	Scott Fyink	Sales		C:\Microsoft Press\Ac
10	Matthias		Berndt	Matthias Berndt	Finance		C:\Microsoft Press\Ac
11	Benjamin	C.	Willett	Benjamin Willett	Marketing		C:\Microsoft Press\Ac
12	Misty		Shock	Misty Shock	Marketing		C:\Microsoft Press\Ac
13	Linda		Randall	Linda Randall	Housing Administration		C:\Microsoft Press\Ac
14	Gary		Schare	Gary Schare	Finance		C:\Microsoft Press\Ac
15	John	L.	Viescas	John Viescas	Product Development	Paris	C:\Microsoft Press\Ac
16	Jeff		Conrad	Jeff Conrad	Housing Administration	Redmond	C:\Microsoft Press\Ac

Figure 5-35 The Lookup tab settings show you a combo box in Datasheet view.

We decided to go ahead and define these properties in this table because we knew we were probably going to use a combo box in one or more forms that we would build later to display related department information while editing an employee record. By setting the values in the table, we can avoid having to define the combo box settings again when we build the forms. If you want to see how this works on a form, you can open frmEmployeesPlain in the Housing Reservations database. (Although you can open the "production" version of frmEmployees from the Navigation pane, code in that form prevents you from updating any data unless you are signed on to the application.) You can see the result in Figure 5-36.

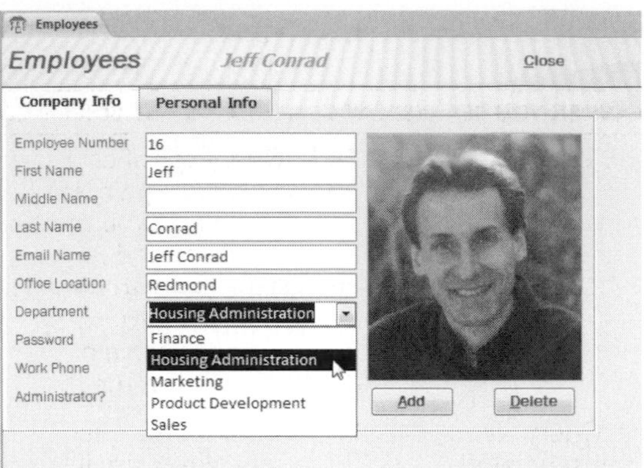

Figure 5-36 The table Lookup tab properties were inherited by the combo box on frmEmployeesPlain.

INSIDE OUT Lookup Tab Settings: For Advanced Users Only

We recommend that only experienced users set the Lookup tab properties of a field in a table's Design view. Unless you are fully aware of what the settings do, you can have problems later when you look at the information in a datasheet or try to build a query on the table. For example, if you look at the data in tblEmployees, you could mistakenly decide that "Housing Administration" is a valid value in the DepartmentID field. If you try to build a query and filter the DepartmentID field looking for that department name, your query won't run.

Table 5-4 gives you an overview of what the lookup settings mean. When you study combo box controls later, in Chapter 13, "Building a Form," you'll see how you can also use lookup properties to display lists from related tables in a form. In Chapter 13, we'll also explore the Combo Box Wizard, which makes it easy to correctly define these settings.

Table 5-4 Lookup Properties

Lookup Property	Setting	Meaning
Display Control	Check Box (Yes/No fields only), Text Box, List Box, or Combo Box	Setting this property to Text Box or Check Box disables lookups. List Box shows a list of values in an open window. Combo Box shows the selected value when closed and shows the available list of values when opened.

Lookup Property	Setting	Meaning
PROPERTIES AVAILABLE WHEN YOU SET DISPLAY CONTROL TO LIST BOX OR COMBO BOX		
Row Source Type	Table/Query, Value List, or Field List	Table/Query specifies that you want rows from a table or query to fill the list. If you select Value List, you must enter the values you want displayed in the Row Source property, separated by semicolons. The Field List setting shows the names of the fields from the table or query you enter in Row Source—not the data in the rows.
Row Source	Table Name, Query Name, or a list of values separated by semicolons	Use a table name, query name, or enter the text of the query in Structured Query Language (SQL) that provides the list values when Row Source Type is Table/Query. See Chapters 9 and 10 for details about building queries, and Article 2 on the companion CD for details about SQL. Enter a list of values separated by semicolons when Row Source Type is Value List. Use a table or query name when Row Source Type is Field List.
Bound Column	An integer value from 1 to the number of columns in the Row Source	Specify the column in the Row Source that provides the value stored by the list box or combo box.
Column Count	An integer value from 1 to 255	This determines the number of columns available to display. (See Column Widths.) When Row Source Type is Value List, this setting determines how many consecutive values that you enter in Row Source make up a logical row.
Column Heads	No (default) or Yes	Choose Yes to display the field name at the top of any displayed column when you open the list.
Column Widths	One width value per column, separated by semicolons	Specify a zero width if you do not want the combo box or list box to display the column. It is common not to display an AutoNumber ID field, but you might need that field in Row Source as the bound column.
Allow Multiple Values	No (default) or Yes	Choose Yes to allow the user to select multiple values from Row Source for each record. Caution: If you set this property to Yes and save the table definition, you cannot change the value back to No later.

Lookup Property	Setting	Meaning
Allow Value List Edits	No (default) or Yes	Choose Yes to allow the user to add and edit items in the underlying Row Source.
List Item Edit Form	Form Name	Specify the name of a form that Access will open for the user to add items to the Row Source when the user enters a new value that is not in the list specified in Row Source.
	PROPERTIES THAT APPLY TO COMBO BOXES ONLY	
List Rows	An integer value between 1 and 255 (default is 16)	Specify how many rows the combo box displays when you open the list. If this setting is less than the number of rows in Row Source, the combo box makes a scroll bar available to move through the list.
List Width	Auto or a specific width	Specify the width of the list when you open it. Auto opens the list the width of the field display.
Limit To List	No (default) or Yes	Choose No to allow the user to enter a value that's not in the list. When the bound column is not the first displayed column, the combo box acts as though Limit To List is Yes regardless of the setting.

INSIDE OUT **Allowing Space for the Scroll Bar**

When we're designing a combo box that displays multiple columns when dropped down, we always specify a List Width value that's the sum of the Column Width values plus 0.25 inch to allow for the vertical scroll bar.

Working with Multi-Value Lookup Fields

In Chapter 1, "What Is Access?" we introduced you to the concept of complex data. Access 2010 includes a feature (first introduced in Access 2007), called Multi-Value Lookup Fields, to handle complex data. The purpose of lookup fields, as you just learned, is to *display* one value in a field but actually *store* a different value. For example, a lookup field could store the company ID in a field for an invoice but display the company name to the user for easier data entry on a form or to show the name on a printed invoice report. Lookup fields in this scenario take the guesswork out of trying to remember a specific company ID number.

Multi-Value Lookup Fields take this concept a step further by allowing you to store multiple values in a single lookup field. When you define a field as a Multi-Value Lookup Field, Access provides a special control in the Datasheet view of the table similar to a combo box to display the list of valid values. When you drop down the combo box list, you'll see what looks like a list box that has a check box next to each of the available value choices. Selecting the check box next to one or more of the values stores the selected values in the field.

Figure 5-37 shows an example of a Multi-Value Lookup Field in the Conrad Systems Contacts database. Open the Contacts.accdb database and then open the tblContacts table in Datasheet view. Any specific contact could be one or more contact types. The Contact Type field is designated as a Multi-Value Lookup Field, so the user can select from any of the contact types in the database and mark them as related to the current record. In Figure 5-37, you can see that John Viescas is both a developer and a distributor. By selecting the check boxes next to the available contact types, you tell Access to store multiple values for this single record. Notice that after you tab away from this field, Access separates the values with commas.

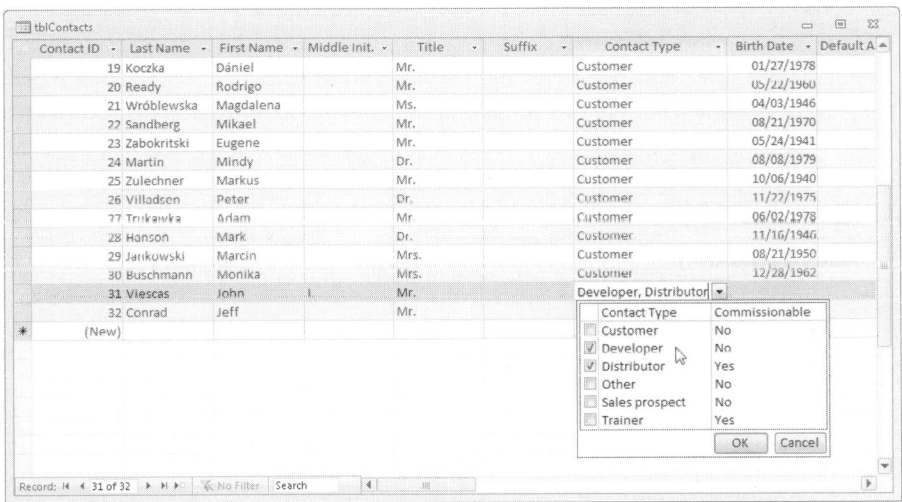

Figure 5-37 A Multi-Value Lookup Field control allows you to select more than one value for a particular field.

Access also provides the list box control you see in a table in Datasheet view on a form in Form view. Close the tblContacts table and then open the frmContactsPlain form in Form view. In Figure 5-38, you can see the Contact Type field, which displays an arrow on the right side. Clicking the arrow drops down the list with the available choices of contact types.

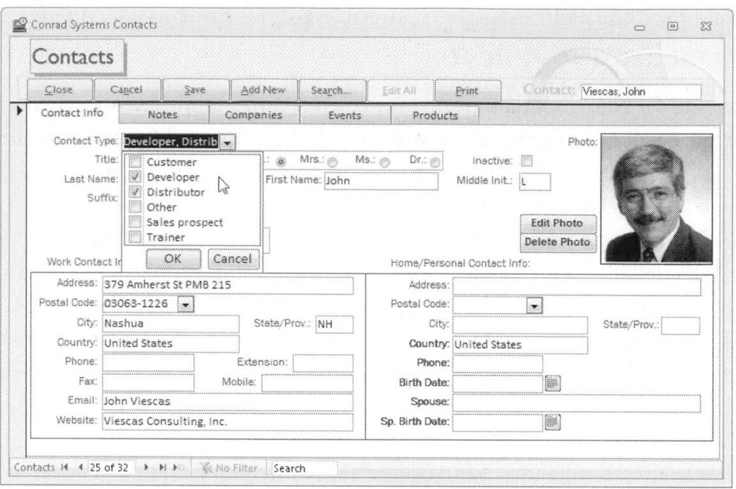

Figure 5-38 Access also provides a Multi-Value Lookup Field control in the frmContactsPlain form of the Conrad Systems Contacts database.

To set up a Multi-Value Lookup Field, you must set the properties in the table in Design view. Close the frmContactsPlain form and then open the tblContacts table in Design view. (Because this is a linked table, Access will warn you that you cannot modify the design. Click Yes in the warning dialog box to open the table design and view the field properties.) Click the ContactType field and then click the Lookup tab under Field Properties to see the settings, as shown in Figure 5-39. The Allow Multiple Values property has been set to Yes, which tells Access that it can store multiple values in this field.

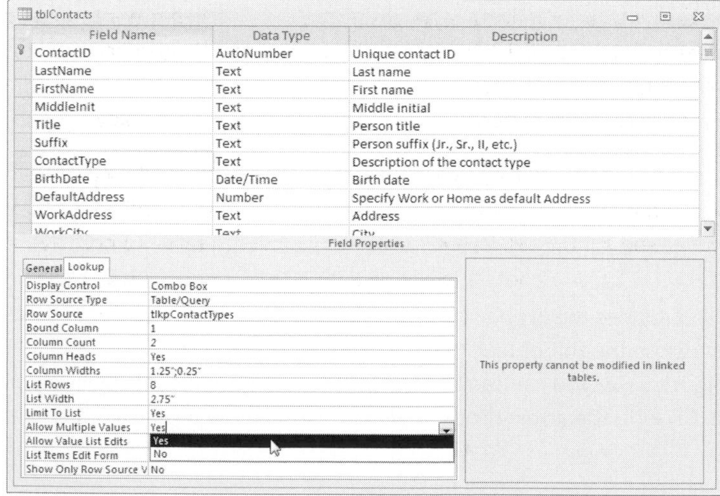

Figure 5-39 Set the Allow Multiple Values property to Yes to enable a field as a Multi-Value Lookup Field.

How Do Multi-Value Lookup Fields Maintain Data Normalization Rules?

If you are familiar with data normalization rules, you might be asking yourself how it is possible to store multiple values into a single field and still follow normalization rules. Under the covers and hidden from the standard user interface, Access 2010 actually creates a many-to-many relationship with a hidden join table. All the work of creating this join table and establishing the relationship rules is handled by Access when you set the Allow Multiple Values property to Yes or choose to allow multiple values in the Lookup Wizard. To ensure that only possible related values can be entered into the Multi-Value Lookup Field, Access displays a combo box or list box control containing only the valid related values for data entry. These Multi-Value Lookup Fields allow for better integration with Microsoft SharePoint complex data structures.

However, you cannot upsize any table that has a Multi-Value Lookup Field to Microsoft SQL Server. Although Multi-Value Lookup Fields can help novice developers create applications that deal with complex many-to-many relationships in a simple way, we recommend that you learn to create such relationships properly when you need them in your database using the appropriate linking table.

Changing the Primary Key

Article 1, "Designing Your Database Application," on the companion CD, discusses the need to have one or more fields that provide a unique value to every row in your table. This field or group of fields with unique values is identified as the primary key. If a table doesn't have a primary key, you can't define a relationship between it and other tables, and Access 2010 has to guess how to link tables for you. Even if you define a primary key in your initial design, you might discover later that it doesn't actually contain unique values. In that case, you might have to define a new field or fields to be the primary key.

Let's go back to the three tables we built earlier with the Table Analyzer Wizard. Suppose you discover that users are becoming confused by the fact that ContactTypes_ID is a number instead of the actual text. You could keep the lookup table to help avoid duplicate values, but there's no reason not to store the actual text value in the Contacts table instead of storing a linking ID.

To fix this, you need to perform the following steps. Be sure to save your work at the end of each step.

1. Open the Contacts table in Design view and insert a new field below ContactTypes_ID named ContactType, data type Text, length 50.
2. Update the new ContactType field with related information from the ContactTypes table. We'll show you how to do this easily with an update query in Chapter 11, "Modifying Data with Action Queries." For now, you can switch to Datasheet view and copy what you see in the Lookup to ContactTypes field to your new ContactType field. (There are only 18 rows, so this shouldn't take you very long.)
3. Open the Relationships window and click the All Relationships button in the Relationships group of the Design tab below Relationship Tools so that you can see the additional relationships that the Table Analyzer Wizard built. Click on the line between Contacts and ContactTypes and press the Delete key to remove the relationship. (You must delete any relationship involving the primary key of a table before you can change the key.) Click Yes to confirm this action.
4. Open the Contacts table in Design view and delete the ContactTypes_ID field.
5. Open the ContactTypes table in Design view and change the primary key from ID to ContactType. (You can also select the ID field and delete it if you like.)

   Access provides several ways for you to accomplish this task. You could open the Indexes window (as you learned in Chapter 4), delete the primary key definition, and build a new one. A simpler way is to select the new field you want as the primary key and then click the Primary Key button in the Tools group of the Design contextual tab below Table Tools, as shown in Figure 5-40.
6. Finally, reopen the Relationships window and define a new relationship between ContactType in the ContactTypes table and your new ContactType field in the Contacts table.

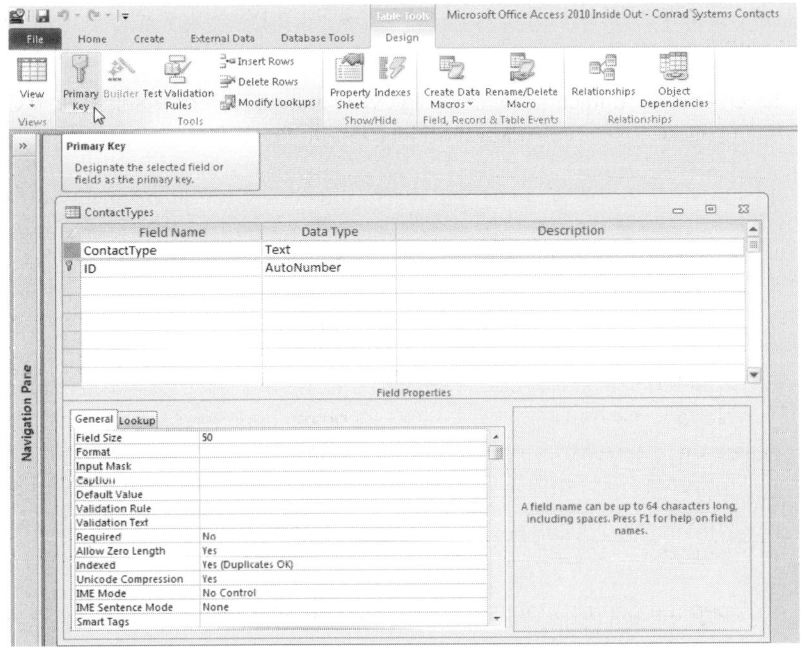

Figure 5-40 Select the new field that will become the primary key and then click Primary Key on the Design tab to define the key.

Keep in mind that you can change the primary key directly for any table that does not have any relationships defined. Also, when the table contains data, the new fields that you choose for a primary key must have unique values in all the rows.

Compacting Your Database

As you delete old database objects and add new ones, the space within your .accdb file can become fragmented. The result is that, over time, your database file can grow larger than it needs to be to store all your definitions and data.

To remove unused space, you should compact your database periodically. No other users should be accessing the database you intend to compact. You can compact the database you currently have open by clicking the File tab on the Backstage view and then clicking Compact & Repair Database on the Info tab. If you want to compact another database, you must close your current database and then click the Compact & Repair Database command in the Tools group on the Database Tools tab. Access 2010 opens the dialog box shown in Figure 5-41.

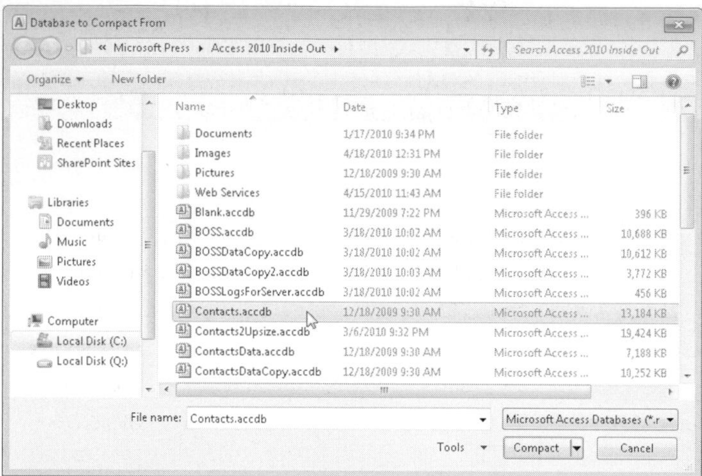

Figure 5-41 Click the Compact & Repair Database button in the Tools group on the Database Tools tab to open the dialog box for specifying a database to compact.

Select the database you want to compact, and then click Compact. Access asks you for a name for the compacted database. You can enter the same name as the database you are compacting, or you can use a different name. If you use the same name, Access warns you that the original database of the same name will be replaced. If you proceed, Access compacts your database into a temporary file. When compaction is completed successfully, Access deletes your old database and gives its name to the new compacted copy.

INSIDE OUT Compacting a Database When You Close It

You can also set an option to compact the database each time you close it. Open your database, click the File tab on the Backstage view, and then click Options. In the Access Options dialog box, select the Current Database category and then select the Compact On Close check box under Application Options. If multiple users are sharing the same database, Access compacts the database when the last user closes it.

You now have all the information you need to modify and maintain your client database table definitions. In Chapter 6, "Designing Web Tables," you'll explore how to create and modify tables for web databases.

CHAPTER 6

Designing Web Tables

The process of defining web tables in a Microsoft Access 2010 web database (.accdb file) is similar to designing client tables in a desktop database. In general, you create the fields you need, assign properties to those fields, and create relationships between the tables. The differences in the process of table creation for web databases lie in the design surface options you can use and the available data types and properties for web fields. In this chapter, we'll show you how to begin creating your first web application by starting with the tables. You'll learn how to:

- Create a new web database application using a web database template
- Create a new empty web database for your own custom application
- Create a simple web table by entering data directly in the table
- Get a jump start on defining custom web tables by using Application Parts
- Create new web fields by using Data Type Parts
- Define your own web tables and web fields from scratch by using Datasheet view
- Create Calculated fields in your web tables
- Set validation rules for your web fields and web tables
- Create lookups to other web fields to define relationships between your web tables
- Run the Compatibility Checker to verify your fields and tables are web-legal
- Prepare a client database for the web

Note

All the screen images in this chapter were taken on a Windows 7 system with the Access color scheme set to Silver.

INSIDE OUT **Take Time to Learn About Table Design**

At the start of Chapter 4, "Designing Client Tables," we mentioned the importance of planning up front the tasks you want to perform, the data structures you need to support those tasks, and the flow of tasks within your client database application. The importance of this planning stage is the same when designing a web application. Proper planning at the start of the web application building process can save you from constantly redesigning your application over and over. If you haven't already, we encourage you to learn at least the fundamentals of table and application design by reading Article 1, "Designing Your Database Application," that you can find on the companion CD.

Working with the Web

The topic of web databases in Access 2010 is a very broad subject—certainly not a topic we can fully cover in just one chapter. In fact, a large portion of the Access development team at Microsoft worked solely on all the various features of web databases during the Access 2010 development cycle. The process of developing a web application is very much the same as developing a client application—you identify the tasks you want to accomplish with the application, chart the flow of tasks, identify the data elements, organize the data elements, design a user interface for the application, construct the application, and then test and refine the application. We've organized this book to closely follow the application building process for both client and web databases. We start by building the fields and tables of an application and then continue with building queries, forms, reports, macros, and modules throughout the various chapters.

This chapter begins the discussion of developing a web database by starting with creating fields and tables—the foundation of your web application. We'll continue the discussion of creating a fully functional web database in subsequent chapters. You'll learn how to create data macros and attach them to table events, create queries to pull out the data you need, create forms and reports that run in a web browser, and how to create macros to automate your web application. In Chapter 22, "Using Web Applications in a Browser," we'll pull everything together and show you how to publish your application to a Microsoft SharePoint 2010 server running Access Services, work with your objects in a web browser, and how to make modifications to your web application.

Before we start the discussion of building tables for web databases, we should first discuss some terminology you'll be hearing throughout this chapter and subsequent chapters to follow. A *web database* (or web application) is a database that has web tables—tables that will successfully publish to a SharePoint server running Access Services. A web database must be in the .accdb file format and created in Access 2010 or later. A *client database* is a standard Access database with client tables that you've been working with for many Access releases. A client database can be in the .mdb or .accdb file format and can be created in Access 2010 or earlier versions.

A web database can have client objects, such as queries, forms, reports, macros, and modules, as well as web objects. Tables are the one exception to this rule. In a web database, you can only have web tables. The tables in a web database, also called the *schema* of the database, must be compatible with SharePoint server lists. You are allowed to have links to other data sources in a web database because they are not local tables. However, linked tables will not work in your web browser—you will not be able to use the data from those external data sources in your queries, forms, and reports that run in the browser. When a web database contains client objects as well as web objects, Microsoft uses the term *hybrid application* to describe this type of database.

It's important to note that you don't need a SharePoint server to use a web database in Access. You can use a web database in Access 2010 and never publish the database to a SharePoint server. The web database will function just fine in Access, and you can continue to modify the application as your needs grow. However, if you want to take advantage of all the extra features that publishing your web database to a server can offer, you'll need to set up a SharePoint server running Access Services within your business. If you are in a corporate domain, your IT department might already have a SharePoint server installed and running Access Services. You should check with your network administrator to see if this is the case. If you do not want to take the time and expense to setup and install a SharePoint server within your business, you can also use a third party that offers SharePoint hosting services. There are many third party companies, including Microsoft, that can host your Access Services applications.

When you publish your web database to a SharePoint server, you can use the application from within Access 2010 and you can use the application within a web browser. When you use or design the database from within Access, Microsoft often uses the term *rich client* in these discussions. Web databases, as you just learned, can contain web objects as well as client objects. The client objects do not run in the browser, but they will run in Access 2010. When you see the term *rich client*, we are referring to designing or using the web database from within Access 2010 where you have all the design facilities available to you, including the ability to work with client objects. Access Services on SharePoint does not have any design facilities to modify your web database and the server cannot run or execute something it doesn't understand. Rich client refers to the fact that Access 2010 has all the rich design and functional capabilities that the server might not have available.

If you're already familiar with creating client databases in previous versions of Access, you're already well on your way to understanding how to create web databases. In general, the server has less functionality than the rich client so when you are designing web objects, Access 2010 presents design surfaces that only show options, properties, controls, and other design mechanisms that will seamlessly move to the server. We use the term *web-legal* to describe those objects, controls, properties, etc. that can move successfully to the server.

Creating a New Web Database

When you first start Access 2010, you see the New tab on the Microsoft Office Backstage view, as shown in Figure 6-1. We explored the New tab in detail in Chapter 2, "Exploring the Access 2010 Interface," and in Chapter 4, "Designing Client Tables."

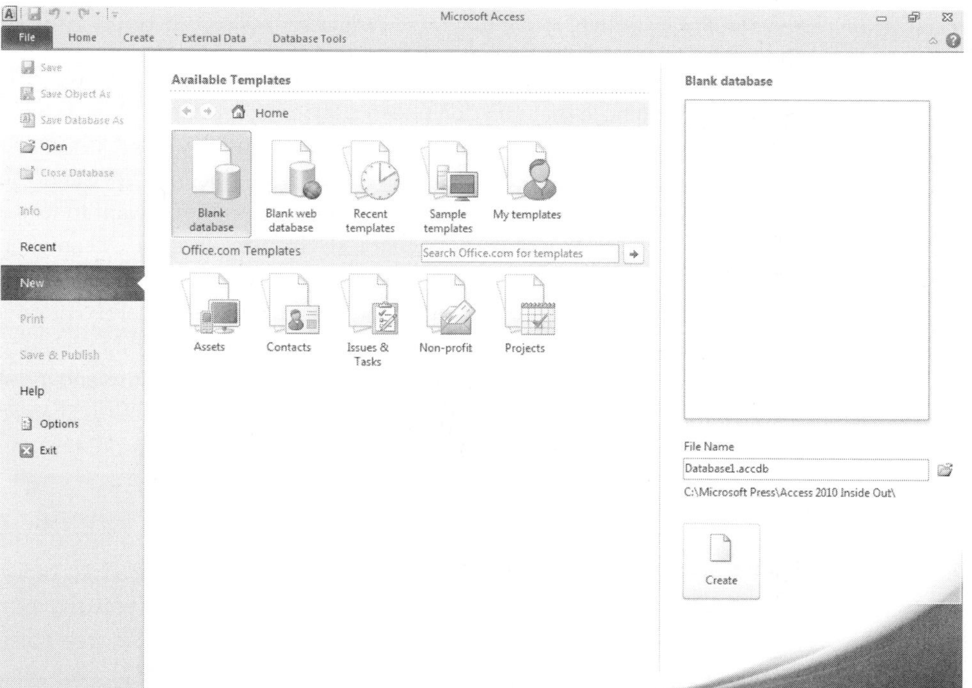

Figure 6-1 You can see the New tab of the Backstage view when you first launch Access 2010.

Using a Database Template to Create a Web Database

Web databases are a new templafeature for Access 2010, so even if you're an experienced developer, you might find that studying the built-in web application templates will help you understand how to design and work with web databases. You might find that one of these applications meets most of your needs without any modifications. You can also build on and customize the basic web application design and add new features as your application needs grow.

On the New tab of the Backstage view, you can access the built-in locally installed web templates by clicking Sample Templates under Available Templates in the middle of the screen. When you click Sample Templates, the center section of the New tab changes to show a graphic representing each of the local database templates available in Access 2010, as shown in Figure 6-2.

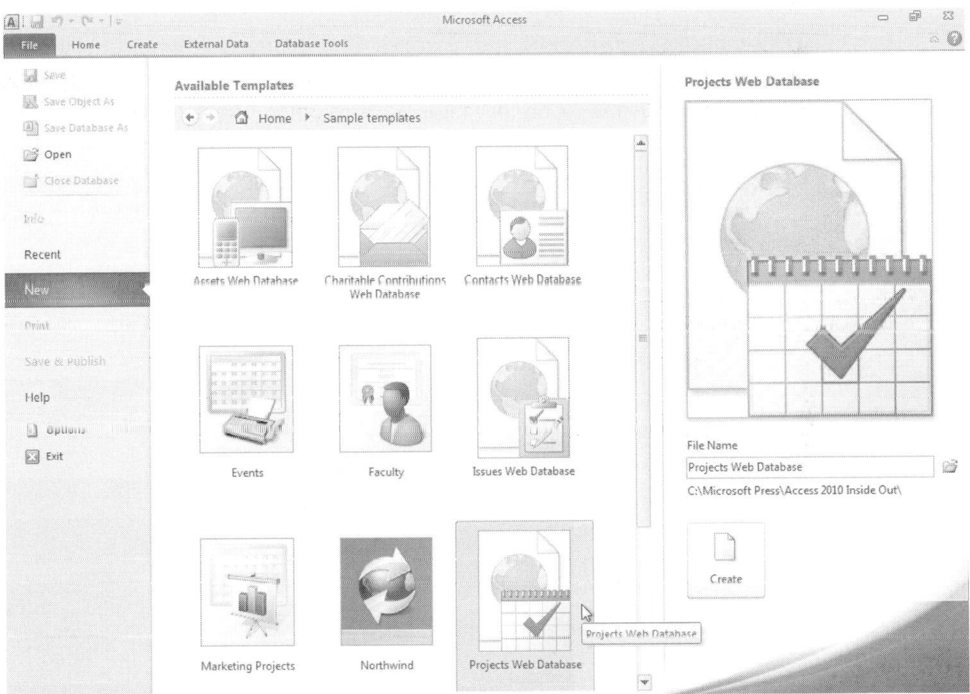

Figure 6-2 You can choose to work with any of the five web templates from the Sample Templates section.

Access 2010 includes over 10 locally installed database templates, five of which are web templates—Assets, Charitable Contributions, Contacts, Issues, and Projects. You can differentiate which templates under Sample Templates are web templates by looking for the world icon in the template graphic and by the word Web included in the file name. When you click one of the web template graphics in the center of the New tab, Access displays the file name and a larger graphic in the right task pane. Click the Projects Web Database template in the middle of the screen to see the file name and graphic for the Projects Web Database Template, as shown in Figure 6-2. You can work with all five local web templates from the New tab in the same way. This example will show you the steps that are needed to build a Projects web database.

Access suggests a name for your new web database in the File Name text box and a location to save the file beneath the File Name text box. You can modify the name of this web database by typing in the File Name text box. If you want to change the suggested save location, click Browse to open the File New Database dialog box, as shown in Figure 6-3.

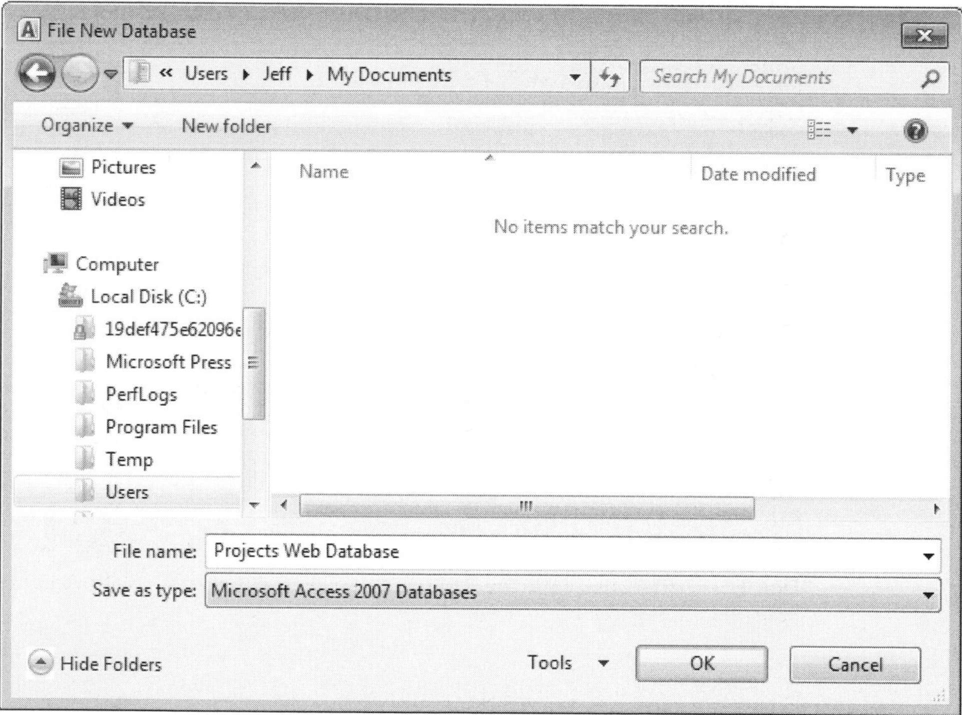

Figure 6-3 Use the File New Database dialog box to select a folder for saving the new local web database template.

You can select the drive and folder you want by clicking the links on the left and browsing to your destination folder. After you select the specific folder to which you want to save this new web database, click OK to return to the New tab on the Backstage view. Your new folder location is shown beneath the File Name text box. If you decide at this point not to create the web database, click the Home button near the top of the screen to return to the main Home page of the New tab to stop the process. Click Create to start the template instantiation process.

A progress bar appears on the screen informing you to please wait while Access creates the web template. After a few seconds of preparation, Access opens the new Projects web database and displays the Login form, as shown in Figure 6-4.

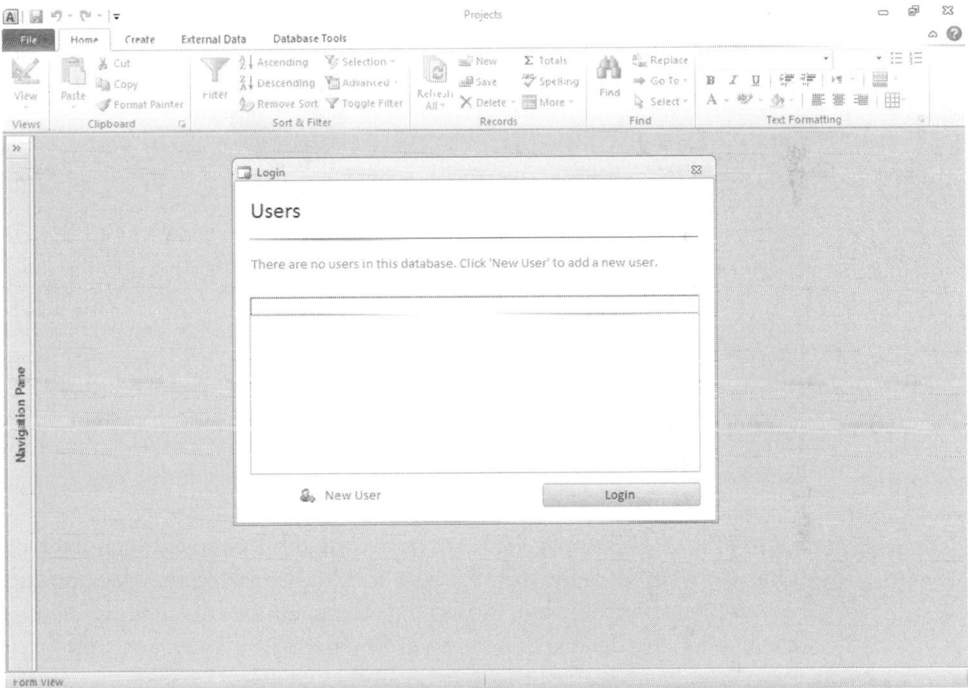

Figure 6-4 After you create the Projects web database from a template, Access opens the database and displays the Login form.

Dismiss this Login form for now by clicking the X button in the upper-right corner of the form window. After you close this form, Access displays the Main navigational form for the Projects web database, as shown in Figure 6-5.

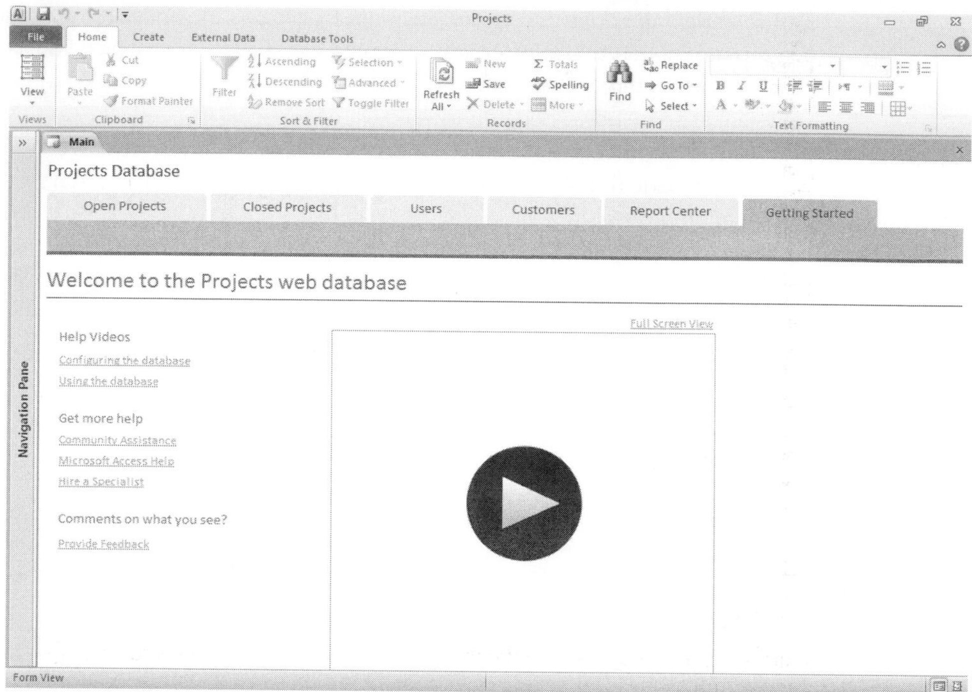

Figure 6-5 When you close the Login form, Access displays the Main navigational form in the Projects web database.

This Projects web database is a complete application that can track the progress of your various projects. The database comes with tables, queries, forms, reports, and macros. We'll discuss all the form elements you are currently looking at beginning in Chapter 12, "Using Forms in an Access Application." For now, close this form by clicking the X button in the upper-right corner of the form window or by right-clicking the Main tab and clicking Close Form on the shortcut menu. Expand the Navigation pane now to see all the various objects contained in this database, as shown in Figure 6-6.

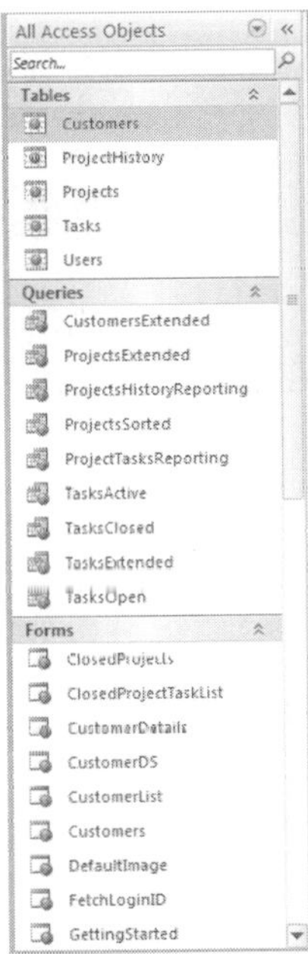

Figure 6-6 The Projects web database contains many web objects to track the status of your various projects.

In a web database, like the Projects one here, any web objects—tables, queries, forms, reports, and macros—have a globe on the object icon to indicate they are web objects. In this Projects web database, as well as the other four built-in local web templates, all objects are web objects which means they will publish and render in a web browser. You can also use this application in Access client if you do not want to publish to a SharePoint server. We'll discuss designing and working with all the various web queries, forms, reports, and macros in later chapters. For now, close this new web database by clicking the File tab on the Backstage view and then clicking Close Database to return to the New tab.

Creating a New Empty Web Database

To begin creating a new empty web database when you start Access 2010, go to the Available Templates section in the middle of the New tab (as shown in Figure 6-1) and click Blank Web Database. The right side of the New tab changes to display the Blank Web Database task pane, as shown in Figure 6-7.

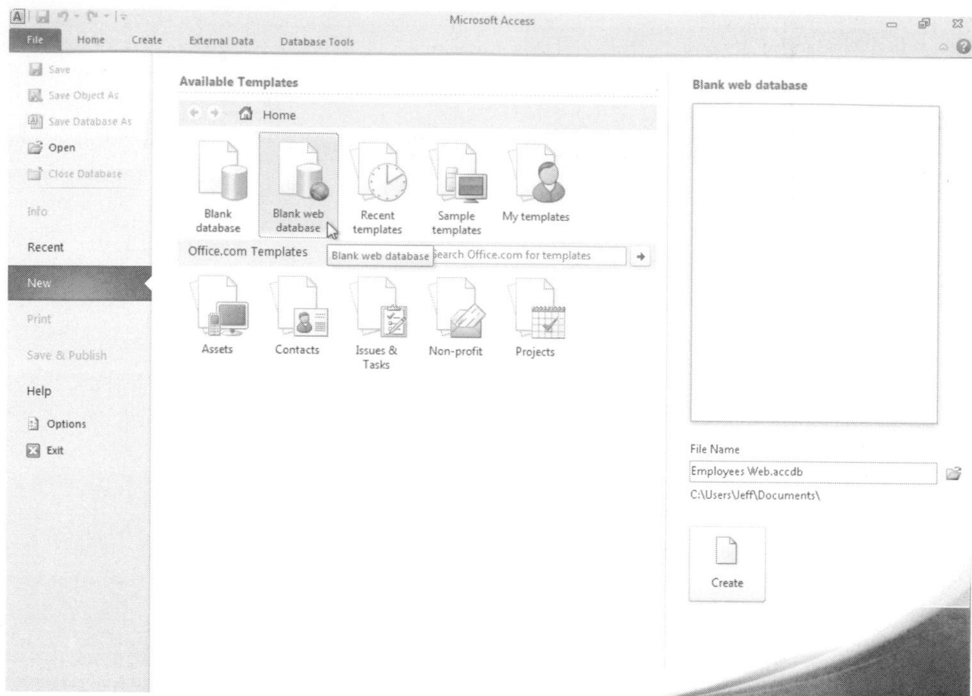

Figure 6-7 From the New tab on the Backstage view, click Blank Web Database to open the Blank Web Database task pane on the right.

You can click Browse to open the File New Database dialog box, shown in Figure 6-3, to select the drive and folder you want. In this example, we selected the Documents folder in Windows 7 for the current user. Next, type the name of your new database in the File Name text box—Access 2010 appends an .accdb extension to the file name for you. For this example, let's create a database with a table containing employee names and addresses. Type **Employees Web** in the File Name box and click Create to create your web database.

Access 2010 takes a few moments to create the system tables in which to store all the information about the tables, queries, forms, reports, and macros that you might create. Access then displays the Navigation pane for your new web database and opens a new blank web table in Datasheet view, shown in Figure 6-8.

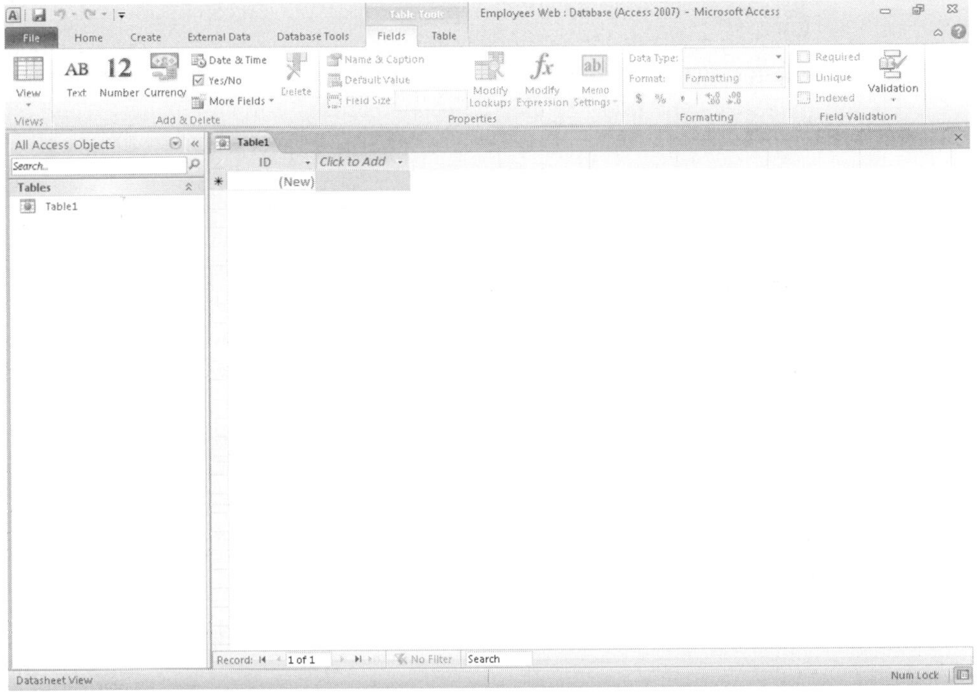

Figure 6-8 Access 2010 opens a new web table in Datasheet view when you create a new blank web database.

Because this is a new web database and no objects or special startup settings exist yet, you see a Navigation pane with only one object defined. For new web databases, Access, by default, creates a new web table in Datasheet view called Table1 with an ID field already defined. However, Access has not saved this table, so if you do not make any changes to it, Access will not prompt you to save the table if you close it. The following sections show various methods for creating a new table.

Creating Your First Simple Web Table by Entering Data

If you've been following along to this point, you should still have your new Employees Web database open with Table1 open in Datasheet view, as shown in Figure 6-8. (You can also follow these steps in any open web database.) Access 2010 automatically created the first web field, called ID, in the left column. Leave this web field intact for now. In the second column, Access has placed another web field with the Add New Field heading. Just like client tables, you can enter just about any type of data you want in this web field—text, dates, numbers, or currency.

Let's start with a simple list of employee names so you can become more comfortable working in Datasheet view with web tables. For this quick example, we'll only need two columns containing the employee's first name and last name. Be sure to enter the same type of data in a particular column for every row. For example, enter Jeff's and John's last names in the third column (named Field2 by Access) for every row.

You can see some of the data entered for the employee list in Figure 6-9. Access behaves the same in this situation for web fields and tables just as it does for client fields and tables. When you start to type in a web field in a row, Access displays a pencil icon on the row selector at the far left to indicate that you're adding or changing data in that row. Press the Tab key to move from column to column. When you move to another row, Access saves what you typed. If you make a mistake in a particular row or column, you can click the data you want to change and type over it or delete it. Notice that after you enter data in a column, Access guesses the most appropriate data type and displays it in the Data Type box in the Formatting group of the Fields tab on the ribbon.

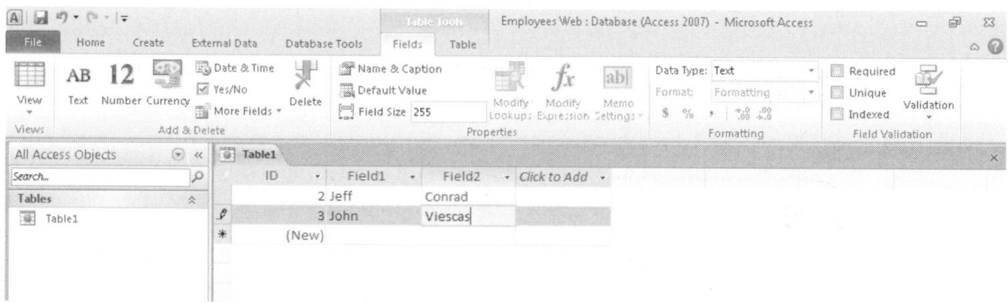

Figure 6-9 You can create the employee list table by entering data.

If you create a column of data that you don't want, click anywhere in the column and click Delete in the Add & Delete group of the Fields contextual tab on the ribbon. Click Yes when Access asks you to confirm the deletion. If you want to insert a blank column between two columns that already contain data, right-click the column header to the right of where you want to insert the new column and then click Insert Field from the shortcut menu that appears. To move a column to a different location, click the field name at the top of the column to select the entire column, and then click again and drag the column to a new location. You can also click an unselected column and drag your mouse pointer through several adjacent columns to select them all. You can then move the columns as a group.

Access named your columns Field1 and Field2 just as it does if you are creating client tables in Datasheet view. You can change the name of a field by highlighting the column and then clicking the Name & Caption command in the Properties group on the Fields tab. Access opens the Enter Field Properties dialog box, as shown in Figure 6-10. In this dialog box, you can enter the field name you want to use in the Name text box, the field caption in the

Caption text box, and the field description in the Description text box. Note that for web tables, the Enter Field Properties dialog box is your only entry point in the user interface to set and update the field caption and field description for your web fields.

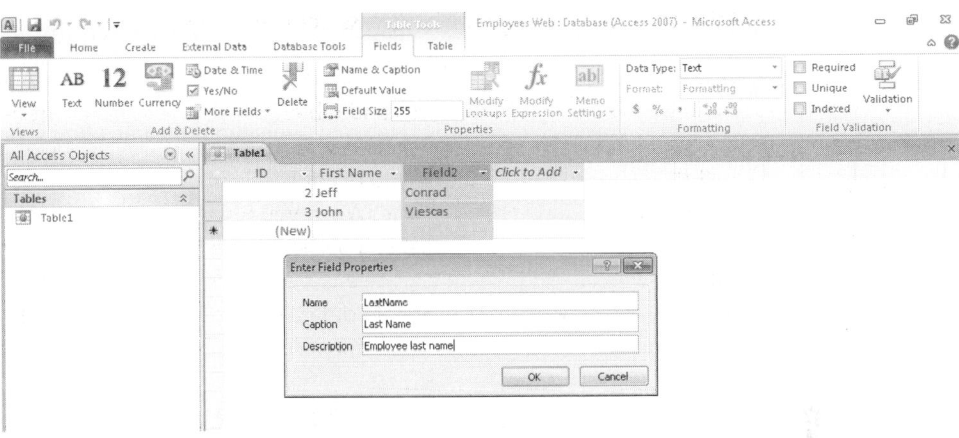

Figure 6-10 The Enter Field Properties dialog box allows you to change the name, caption, and description for your web fields.

Note

Just as with client tables in Datasheet view, you can change the name of a column by double-clicking the column's field name or right-clicking a column header and then clicking Rename Field from the shortcut menu that appears.

After you enter several rows of data, it's a good idea to save your table. You can do this by clicking the Save button on the Quick Access Toolbar or by clicking the File tab and then clicking Save. Access 2010 displays a Save As dialog box, as shown in Figure 6-11.

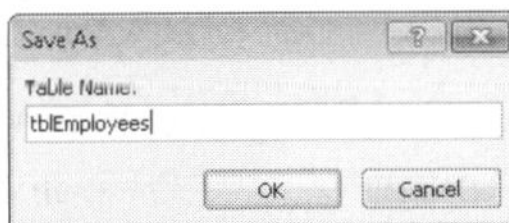

Figure 6-11 Access 2010 displays the Save As dialog box when you first save a new web table so that you can specify a table name.

> **Choosing Web Table Names**
>
> Access 2010 gives you lots of flexibility when it comes to naming your web tables; however, there are some restrictions to be aware of. A web table name can be up to 64 characters long, can include any combination of letters, numbers, spaces, and special characters except a period (.), exclamation point (!), square brackets ([]), leading space, leading equal sign (=), or nonprintable character such as a carriage return. The name also cannot contain any of the following characters: / \ : ; * ? "" < > | # <TAB> { } % ~ &. In general, you should give your web tables meaningful names. You cannot name your web tables the same as any built-in SharePoint list names that Access Services uses to maintain your site. Specifically, you cannot use any of the following web table names: Lists, Docs, WebParts, ComMd, Webs, Workflow, WFTemp, Solutions, Report Definitions, or AppImages.

Creating a Web Table Using Application Parts

If you were to look in the Contacts Map sample web database (ContactsMap.accdb) included on the companion CD, you'll find it to be very simple, with one main table to store contact information. Most databases are usually quite a bit more complex. For example, the built-in Projects sample web template you saw earlier in this chapter contains five main tables, and the Back Office Software System sample web database (BOSS.accdb) included on the companion CD contains nearly two dozen tables. If you had to create every web table manually, it could be quite a tedious process.

Fortunately, Access 2010 comes with a new feature called Application Parts to help you build a few common web tables and other web database objects. In Chapter 4, we first introduced you to this new feature when we discussed creating client tables. The good news with this feature is that you can also use Application Parts when creating web fields, web tables, and other web objects. In this section, we'll show you another feature with Application Parts that we did not discuss in Chapter 4—using Application Parts to create lookup fields with relationships to other web tables.

To complement the simple employee web table you created previously, it would be helpful to create another web table that can track any issues assigned to the employees. To build this second web table using one of the Application Parts, close the employees table if you still have it open, click the Create tab on the ribbon, and then click the Application Parts button in the Templates group. Access displays a list of 10 form types under the Blank Forms category and five Application Parts under the Quick Start category, as shown in Figure 6-12. Microsoft uses the term Models to refer to this one-click object creation feature. You'll learn more about using the 10 form Application Parts in Chapter 13, "Building a Form."

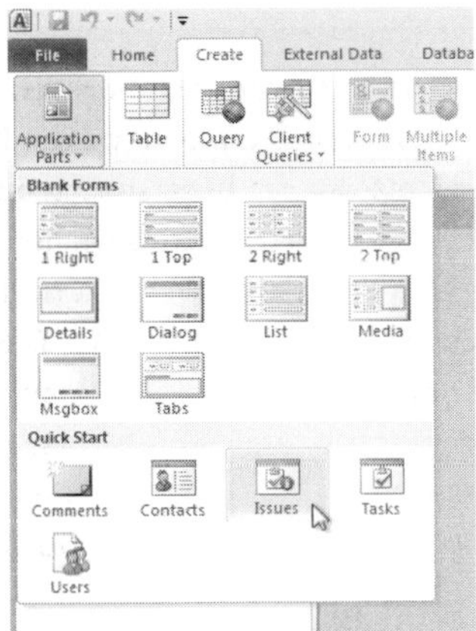

Figure 6-12 Application Parts help you create common types of web database objects.

When you are using the five Application Parts under Quick Start in a web database, Access creates the same fields, tables, and objects as it does for a client database. The only difference when creating these objects in a web database is that Access marks everything as a web object. The five web Application Parts under Quick Start, which represent some of the more common types of web table structures and objects found in databases, are Comments, Contacts, Issues, Tasks, and Users. See "Creating a Table Using Application Parts," on page 178, for a description of each of these Application Parts.

Click Issues in the Quick Start list, and Access opens the Create Relationship wizard, as shown in Figure 6-13. Whenever you select to build an Application Part under Quick Start in a database that already includes at least one existing table, Access displays the Create Relationship wizard to see if you want to create a relationship between one of your existing tables and the new table. In this case, Access identified the existing employees table you created earlier and now asks if you want to build a relationship with the new Issues table Access is about to create.

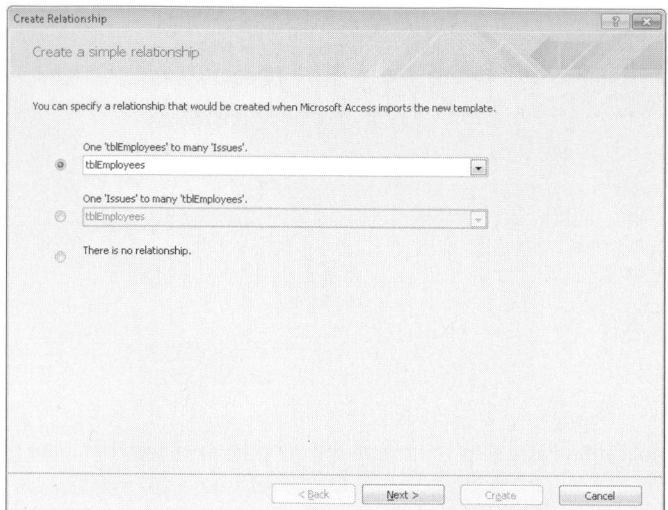

Figure 6-13 Use the Create Relationship wizard to help create relationships between tables through Application Parts.

On the first page of the Create Relationship wizard, Access displays three options. Next to the first two options, Access displays combo boxes that list all the existing saved tables in your database. Above these combo boxes, Access displays text to help identify how it will create the relationship between the two tables. If you select either of these two first options, Access creates a one-to-many relationship between the selected table in the combo box and the new issues table Access will create. Select the first option if you want Access to create a new lookup field in the issues table, representing the many part of the relationship. (We'll discuss more about lookup fields and relationships in web tables later in this chapter.) Select the second option if you want Access to create a new lookup field in the selected table, representing the many part of the relationship. You can choose to select a different table in the combo boxes; by default, Access displays the tables in alphabetical order. Select the third option if you do not want Access to create a relationship between the new issues table and any existing table. Note that if you choose this option, Access does not create an additional lookup field in any tables.

For your example, we want to have the employees table (tblEmployees) represent the one side of the relationship and the issues table represent the many side of the relationship—each employee can have many issues assigned to them. Select the first option and leave the default tblEmployees selected in the combo box. (We only have one existing table in this sample database so you don't need to change any settings on the first page of the wizard.) Click Next to move to the second page of the wizard, as shown in Figure 6-14.

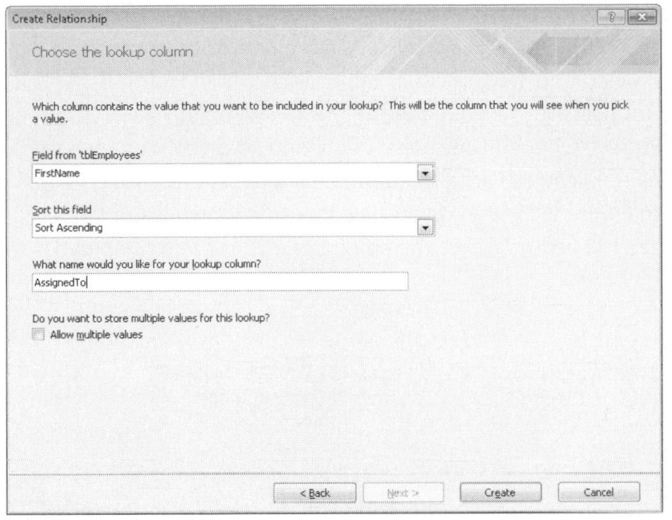

Figure 6-14 Select options for the lookup field on the second page of the wizard.

On the second page of the wizard, Access displays options where you can customize the new lookup field in the issues table. In the first combo box, Access displays a list of field names from the table you selected on the first page of the wizard. Access displays the field you choose here as the drop-down list of options in the new lookup field. Select FirstName in this combo box, selected by default, to display the first name of each employee in the lookup field. The second option, Sort This Field, allows you to sort the values of the field you selected in the first combo box option. You can choose Sort Ascending, Sort Descending, or None (the default) to sort the values. Select Sort Ascending, for this example, to sort the first names in ascending order. In the third option, enter the name of your new lookup field in the text box provided (AssignedTo, for our example). The last option on this page of the wizard—Allow Multiple Values—tells Access to create a Multi-Value Lookup Field. We don't want to assign issues to more than one employee, so leave this option cleared. Note that if you selected There Is No Relationship on the first page of the wizard, you won't see the second page of the wizard.

Note

If you click Cancel on either page of the Create Relationship wizard, Access immediately closes the wizard but does not cancel the creation of the objects associated with the Application Part you selected. Access, in this case, still continues the process of creating the objects but does not create any lookup fields in the tables representing relationships.

Click Create and Access builds a complete table structure for an issues web table, as well as other supporting objects. Open the Issues table and notice Access created 13 fields to identify the data elements for this Issues table, as shown in Figure 6-15. This Issues Application Part includes fields such as AssignedTo (your new lookup field), Summary, Status, Priority, Category, Project, Opened Date, Resolution, and so on to identify a single subject—an issue. The Issues Application Part also automatically defines a data type for each of these fields. Notice, in Figure 6-15, that if you click the drop-down list in the AssignedTo lookup field, you can see the first names of the employees from the tblEmployees table.

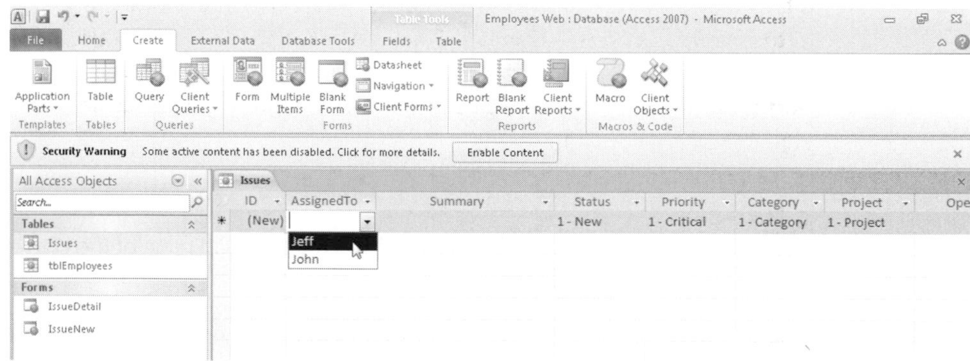

Figure 6-15 The Issues command under Quick Start builds a complete table with appropriate field types and supporting objects.

You can save time creating a web table by using an Application Part even if the table structure Access creates does not exactly match your needs. You can rename fields, add new fields, and delete unneeded fields to customize the table to your specific application needs. When you use an Application Part to help you create a web table, you also get the added benefit of Access creating other supporting objects to work with that table. Close the Issues table window now so you can continue with the next section.

Using Data Type Parts

In Chapter 4, you learned about the new feature in Access 2010, called Data Type Parts, which assist you in creating fields in your tables. Similar to Application Parts, Data Type Parts help give you a jump start on creating your application. Data Type Parts create individual fields or groups of fields in existing tables. As you design more web databases, you might find yourself needing to create similar field structures in your tables. For example, you'll probably find yourself needing to have fields in at least one table that track address information such as street address, city, state, and ZIP code. Fortunately, this new feature in Access 2010 can also be used when you are creating web tables. However, you only have the Quick Start options for Data Type Parts available for web tables.

If you've been following along to this point, you should still have your test web database open with the tblEmployees web table, Issues web table, and supporting two forms in the Navigation pane. To create fields using one of the Data Type Parts, you first need to have a table opened in Datasheet view. Select the tblEmployees web table you created earlier in the Navigation pane, open it in Datasheet view, and then put your cursor in the Click To Add empty field to the right of the LastName field. Click the More Fields button in the Add & Delete group on the Fields tab, and Access displays various field types, as shown in Figure 6-16.

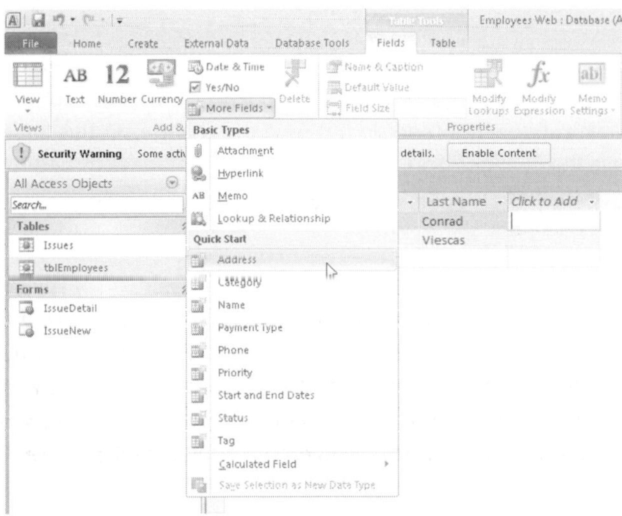

Figure 6-16 Click More Fields to see the Data Type Parts you can use to create groups of web fields.

Under the Basic Types category, Access displays four field types you can use in your web table—Attachment, Hyperlink, Memo, and Lookup & Relationship. You'll be creating these types of fields later in this chapter. Beneath the Quick Start category, you can see a list of the nine Data Type Parts—Address, Category, Name, Payment Type, Phone, Priority, Start And End Dates, Status, and Tag. These are the same Data Type Parts you can use in client tables, except in this case, Access creates web fields because you are using a web database. See "Creating a Table Using Data Type Parts," on page 182, for a description of each of these Data Type Parts.

Click Address under the Quick Start category and Access creates five fields to hold address information ready for you to use in your employees table, as shown in Figure 6-17. You can add additional Data Type Parts to your web table by clicking another option under the Quick Start category. If you want any new Data Type Part fields to appear at the end of your web table (as you saw with the address fields you just created), make sure to set the focus in the Click To Add empty field at the far right. Access always adds new Data Type fields to the left of where the current focus is located in the Datasheet view grid.

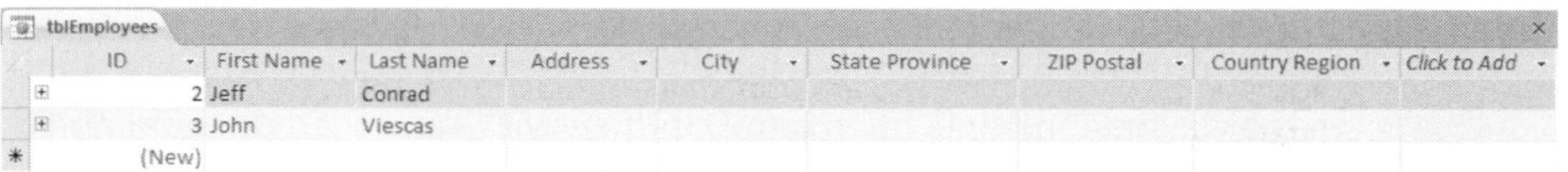

Figure 6-17 Use the Address Type Part when you need to create fields to track address information.

Using Data Type Parts can save you time when you're designing your web tables in Access 2010, just like for client tables, by giving you a jump start on creating common field types. Close the Table window now and do not save the changes to this table when Access prompts you to save the changes. You can now close this database to begin the next section.

Creating Web Tables in Datasheet View

You could continue to use Data Type Parts and Application Parts to build web fields and other web tables. However, you'll find in most cases, you need to create your web schema from scratch to meet your specific application needs. Even if you're already very familiar with creating new client tables in Design View, you'll find it necessary to learn the mechanics of building a web table from scratch in Datasheet view because Design view is not available for web objects. You can only use Datasheet View to design web tables. By learning how to create web tables in Datasheet view, you can also use that knowledge to design client tables in Datasheet view.

To begin creating a new web table in Datasheet view, let's start with a new, empty web database. Click the Blank Web Database button on the New tab of the Backstage view, name your new web database Restaurant Database, and then click Create. Access 2010 displays a blank web Table window in Datasheet view, as shown in Figure 6-18.

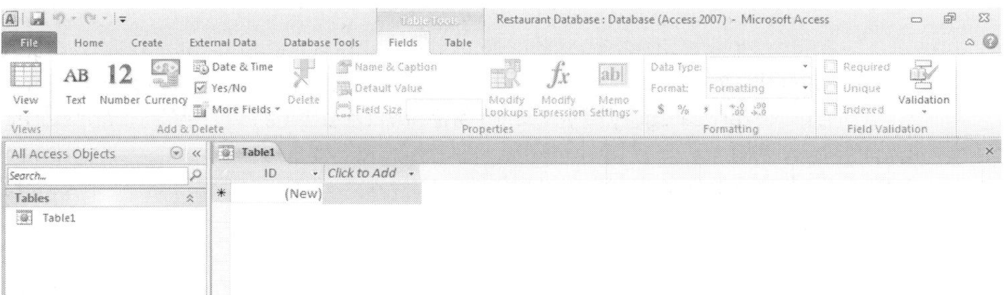

Figure 6-18 Access displays an empty web table in Datasheet view when you create a blank web database.

When you work in Design view with client tables, the upper part of the Table Design window displays columns in which you can enter the field names, the data type for each field, and a description of each field. Access allows you to set various field properties in the lower-left section of the Table Design window. When you design web tables in Datasheet view, however, all your design elements are in the two contextual ribbon tabs—Fields and Table—under Table Tools.

For details about web data type values, see "Understanding Web Field Data Types," on page 311.

Defining Web Fields

Now you're ready to begin defining some of the web fields and web tables in this new empty web database that you can find in the Back Office Software System sample web database (BOSS.accdb). The Back Office Software System sample web application is used to track various facets of a restaurant business such as purchases, employee file maintenance, scheduling, and so forth. To understand how to create web tables like the ones you can find in the Back Office Software System, we'll start by creating a new web table from scratch to use for a vendor list. You should still have your empty Table1 open in Datasheet view that Access created when you opened a new web database. Be sure the insertion point is in the Click To Add field in the first row, and then click the Text command in the Add & Delete group on the Fields contextual tab, as shown in Figure 6-19.

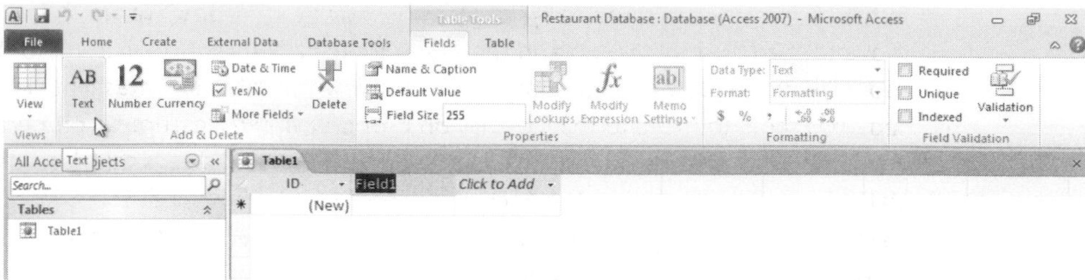

Figure 6-19 You can add new web fields to your table by clicking the various data type commands in the Add & Delete group.

Access creates a new text field called Field1 to the right of the ID field. You'll notice in Figure 6-19 that Access now displays Text in the Data Type list in the Formatting group and sets the default Field Size to 255 in the Properties group. When you are creating and modifying web fields in Datasheet view, you'll need to look at the Properties, Formatting, and Field Validation groups on the Fields contextual ribbon to view and edit the various properties for each field.

Access sets your focus to the top of the new Field1 column where you can change the name. You can change the default name Field1 Access provided by highlighting the existing text and typing in a new field name. We need to also set a caption and description for this new field so we'll set all of these at the same time. Click the Name & Caption button in the Properties group, and Access opens the Enter Field Properties dialog box, as shown in Figure 6-20.

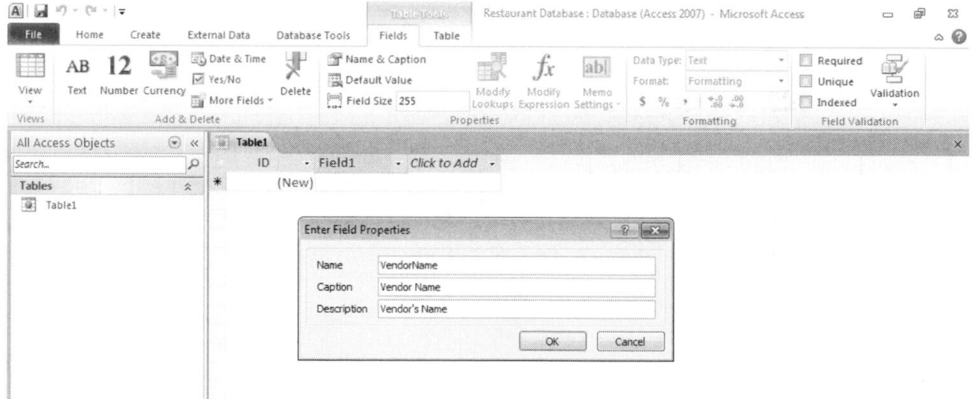

Figure 6-20 Click the Name & Caption command to set the field name, caption, and description properties for your new field.

In the Name field, type the name of this first new field, **VendorName**. Press Tab once to move to the Caption column and then type **Vendor Name**. Access displays this caption property at the top of the column when you view this table in Datasheet view. Finally, press Tab once more to move to the Description property. In the Description property for each web field, you can enter a descriptive phrase. Access 2010 displays this description on the status bar (at the bottom of the Access window) whenever you select this field in a query in Datasheet view or in a form in Form view or Datasheet view. For your new VendorName field, enter **Vendor's Name** in the Description property and then click OK to close the dialog box.

INSIDE OUT Why Setting the Description Property Is Important

In Chapter 4, we discussed the importance of entering a Description property for every field in your client table to help document your application. Access 2010 also displays the description on the status bar, which can serve as a kind of mini-help for the users of your database. Our advice on using the Description property also applies to web fields in web databases. Documenting your web database is just as important for web databases as it is for client databases because it can help you as well as other people who might need to modify your work in the future.

In addition to using the data type commands in the Add & Delete group to create your new web fields, you can also click the column header of the Click To Add empty field to display a list of the data types you can use in web tables, as shown in Figure 6-21. Click Text or press the shortcut key T to create another new text field for your vendor table. Access creates another new text field and gives it the default name of Field1.

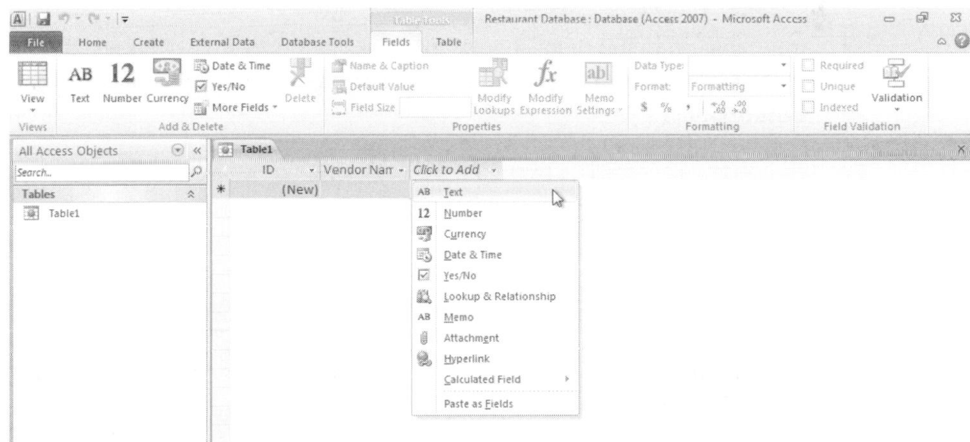

Figure 6-21 Click the column header on the Click To Add empty field to drop down a list of data types to use for your new web field.

You can use the options in the Click To Add empty field for rapid creation of your web fields and then go back through and add captions and descriptions to your fields later. For example, the focus should currently be on the column header of the new text field you just created. Enter **CustomerNumber** as the name of this new text field. (We're using a text data type for this field, because the customer number can contain alphanumeric characters.) Once you've entered the new field name, press Tab and Access moves the focus to the Click To Add empty field and drops down the list of data types again for you, as shown in Figure 6-22. You can press the shortcut key corresponding to the data type you want to create your next field without ever having to use the mouse. Use this technique to create two new text fields called **ContactFirstName** and **ContactLastName**.

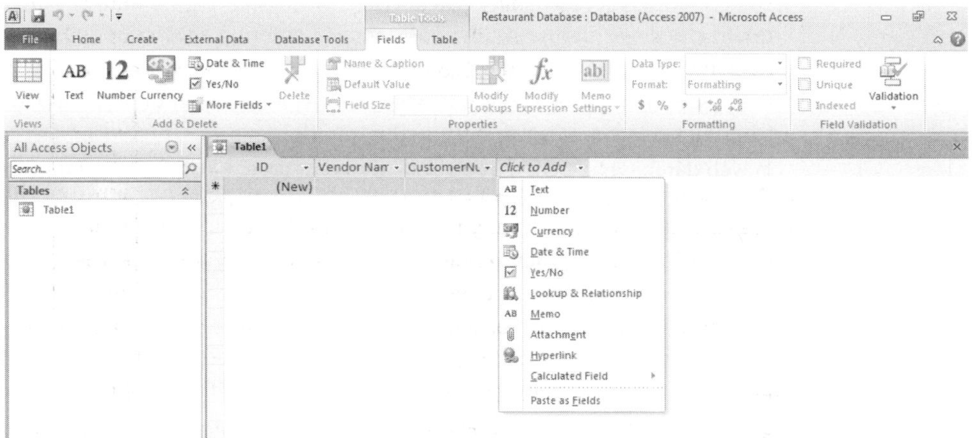

Figure 6-22 Use the shortcut keys for the corresponding data type options in the Click To Add empty field to quickly create new web fields for your table.

Your table up to this point should now look like Figure 6-23. Click the Save button on the Quick Access Toolbar to save this table in its present state and name the new web table **Vendors**.

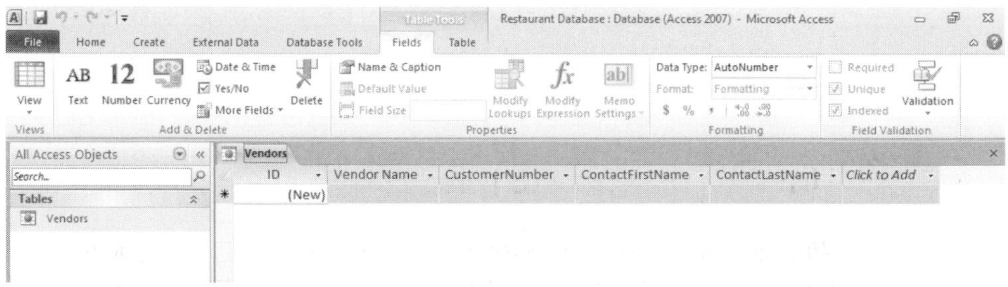

Figure 6-23 Your changes for your new web Vendors table should now look like this.

Choosing Web Field Names

Access 2010 gives you lots of flexibility when it comes to naming your web fields. A web field name can be up to 64 characters long, can include any combination of letters, numbers, spaces, and special characters except a period (.), exclamation point (!), square brackets ([]), leading space, leading equal sign (=), or nonprintable character such as a carriage return. The name also cannot contain any of the following characters: / \ : ; * ? "" < > | # <TAB> { } % ~ &. In general, you should give your fields meaningful names and should use the same name throughout for a field that occurs in more than one table. You should avoid using field names that might also match any name internal to Access or Microsoft Visual Basic. For example, all objects have a Name property, so it's a good idea to qualify a field containing a name by calling it VendorName or CompanyName. You should also avoid names that are the same as built-in functions, such as Date, Time, Now, or Space. See Access Help for a list of all the built-in function names.

Although you can use spaces within your field names in a web database, you should try to create field names without embedded spaces. Many Structured Query Language (SQL) databases to which Access can link (notably Oracle and Ingres) do not support spaces within names. Although Microsoft SQL Server does allow spaces in names, you must enclose such names in brackets or use quotes and execute a Set Quoted Identifier On command. If you ever want to move your web application to a client/server environment and store your data in an SQL database such as SQL Server or Oracle, you'll most likely have to change any names in your web database tables that have an embedded space character. As you'll learn later in this book, table field names propagate into the queries, forms, and reports that you design using these tables. So any name you decide to change later in a table must also be changed in all your queries, forms, and reports.

If you use reserved words or function names for web field names, Access 2010 catches most of these and displays a warning message. This message warns you that the field name you chose, such as Name or Date, is a reserved word and you could encounter errors when referring to that field in other areas of the database application. Access still allows you to use this name if you choose, but take note of the problems it could cause. To avoid potential conflicts, we recommend you avoid using reserved words and built-in functions for web field names.

Understanding Web Field Data Types

When you are creating fields for a web database, Access allows you to use only data types that are supported in SharePoint lists. Access 2010 web databases support 10 types of data, each with a specific purpose. You can see the details about each data type in Table 6-1.

The Lookup & Relationship option helps you define the characteristics of foreign key fields that link to other tables or value lists. You'll learn about the Lookup & Relationship option later in this chapter in "Creating Lookup Fields in a Web Database," on page 337.

Table 6-1 Access Web Data Types

Data Type	Usage	Size
Text	Alphanumeric data.	Up to 255 characters
Number	Numeric data.	All numbers in web tables are 8-byte Double
Currency	Monetary data, stored with four decimal places of precision.	8 bytes
Date/Time	Dates and times.	8 bytes
Yes/No	Boolean (true/false) data; SharePoint stores the numeric value zero (0) for false, and one (1) for true.	1 byte
Lookup & Relationship	When you choose this entry, a wizard starts to help you define either a simple or complex lookup field. A simple lookup field uses the contents of another table or a value list to validate the contents of a single value per row. A complex lookup field allows you to store multiple values of the same data type in each row.	Dependent on the data type of the lookup field
Memo	Alphanumeric data—sentences and paragraphs.	Values are truncated if they contain more than 8,192 characters
Attachment	You can attach files such as pictures, documents, spreadsheets, or charts; each Attachment field can contain an unlimited number of attachments per record, up to the storage limit of the SharePoint list. You can only have one Attachment field per web table.	Varies based on SharePoint list and site settings
Hyperlink	A link "address" to a document or file on the World Wide Web, on an intranet, on a local area network (LAN), or on your local computer.	SharePoint Hyperlink fields can only store 255 characters for the Uniform Resource Locator (URL) and 255 characters for the description
Calculated	You can create an expression that uses data from one or more fields. You can designate different result data types from the expression.	Dependent on the data type of the Result Type property. Text data type result can have up to 243 characters. Memo, Number, Yes/No, and Date/Time should match their respective data types.

For each field in your table, select the data type that is best suited to how you will use that field's data. For character data, you should normally select the Text data type. You can control the maximum length of a Text field by using a field property, as explained later in this chapter. Use the Memo data type only for long strings of text that might exceed 255 characters or that might contain formatting characters such as tabs or line endings (carriage returns).

The Date/Time data type is useful for calendar or clock data and has the added benefit of allowing calculations in seconds, minutes, hours, days, months, or years. For example, you can find out the difference in days between two Date/Time values.

INSIDE OUT Understanding the SharePoint Date/Time Data Type

Use the Date/Time data type to store any date and time value. It's useful to know that SharePoint lists, like Access 2010, store the date as the integer portion of the Date/Time data type and the time as the fractional portion—the fraction of a day, measured from midnight that the time represents. For example, 6:00:00 A.M. internally is 0.25. In SharePoint Date/Time fields, the day number is actually the number of days since January 1, 1900, and cannot display dates prior to that date. The Date/Time data type in Access client tables starts with December 30, 1899, and can be a negative number for dates prior to that date. If you are working in a web database with web tables, however, you cannot store any date values prior to January 1, 1900, because SharePoint Date/Time fields do not support data before that date.

You should generally use the Currency data type for storing money values. Currency has the precision of integers, but with exactly four decimal places.

Use the Yes/No data type to hold Boolean (true or false) values. This data type is particularly useful for flagging accounts paid or not paid or orders filled or not filled. SharePoint Boolean fields store True values as 1, unlike Access Boolean fields, which store True as –1. To work around this disparity, you should only use check boxes to display Boolean fields in web databases so the users of your database are not looking at an integer value for the field. (When you create a Boolean field in a web table, you'll notice Access only gives you the option to display check boxes.) If you attempt to use any restrictions, filters, or comparisons on the integer value of Boolean fields on server forms, you'll see a runtime error. Note that it is still possible to use the integer value of Boolean fields in restrictions, filters, and comparisons in Access client with data published to the server; however, we recommend you always use True and False constants when working with Boolean fields in web databases to ensure consistent behavior in both client and server.

The Hyperlink data type lets you store a simple or complex "link" to an external file or document. (Internally, Hyperlink is a memo data type with a special flag set to indicate that it is a link.) This link can contain a URL that points to a location on the World Wide Web or on a local intranet. It can also contain the Universal Naming Convention (UNC) name of a file on a server on your LAN or on your local computer drives. The link can point to a file that is in Hypertext Markup Language (HTML) or in a format that is supported by an ActiveX application on your computer. If you are using existing data in a Hyperlink field before publishing your database to a SharePoint server, be careful about how many characters are stored in your hyperlinks. Hyperlink fields in client tables (and web tables before publishing to the server) can support more than 255 characters; however, Hyperlink fields in SharePoint lists support only up to 255 characters. Access prevents you from publishing your data to the server if any Hyperlink fields contain more than 255 characters. You need to edit or remove any hyperlinks that contain more than 255 characters before you can successfully publish your web database to the server.

The Attachment data type, introduced in Access 2007, allows you to store multiple attachments in a single record. These files are stored in a binary field in a hidden system table. For the Attachment data type, Access compresses each file, if it isn't already, and uses the original file rather than a generated thumbnail to minimize the amount of database bloat. You are restricted to only having one Attachment field per web table in web databases. Access displays an error message if you try to create more than one Attachment field in a single web table. SharePoint lists have a default size limit of 50 MB for each attachment. If you have attachments larger than 50 MB, you might encounter problems publishing your application to the server or syncing your data to the server. The attachment size limit is an administrative configurable setting. Contact your SharePoint server administrator if you are experiencing issues publishing larger attachments.

The Calculated data type, newly introduced in Access 2010, can also be published to the server. When you publish a web table to the server that includes a Calculated data type, Access creates a Calculated column in the SharePoint list and sets the expression to match what you defined in Access client. Calculated fields allow you to create a calculated result using an expression. The expression you use can include data from one or more fields in the same table. If you have a number field, for example, that holds quantity information for products purchased and a currency field that holds the price of a product, you can create a calculated field that multiplies the quantity and price fields and stores it with a result type of currency. You could also create a calculated field that concatenates a first name, middle name, and last name fields and stores it with a result type of text for a field called Full Name. Access recalculates the value of the calculated field any time the dependent fields are changed.

You might have noticed that you cannot create an AutoNumber field in web tables. All SharePoint lists include an ID field which increments sequentially like Access AutoNumber data types. Whenever you create a new web table, Access automatically creates an ID field for you because SharePoint lists require it. You cannot delete the ID field from your web tables; however, you can rename the field if you choose.

In client databases, you have a hard limit of 255 fields allowed in a table, but for web databases, you have a hard limit of 220 fields (including the ID field) because SharePoint lists have many hidden fields. Unlike Access tables, SharePoint lists have default limits on the number of columns for each data type. SharePoint lists also have a logical row-size limit of 8,000 KB and a configurable limit of physical rows per list item. This means that you might encounter publishing errors if you have more fields of one data type allowed in a web table, you are over the limit of row size for all fields combined, or a combination of the two. As a baseline, you can publish 48 Date/Time fields, 71 Number or Currency fields, 96 Yes/No fields, 191 Hyperlink fields, 191 Memo fields, or 219 Text fields in a single web table with default SharePoint list settings.

Setting Field Properties for Web Databases

You can customize the way Access 2010 stores and handles each field in web databases by setting specific properties. These properties vary according to the data type you choose and are available in the Properties, Formatting, and Field Validation groups on the Fields contextual ribbon tab. Table 6-2 lists all the possible properties that can appear for fields in a web database displayed in Datasheet view, and the data types that are associated with each property.

Table 6-2 Field Properties on the Fields Contextual Tab

Property	Data Type	Options, Description
Field Size	Text	Text can be from 0 through 255 characters long, with a default length of 255 characters.
Format	Number	**General Number (default).** No commas or currency symbols; the number of decimal places shown depends on the precision of the data.
		Standard. Two decimal places and separator commas.
		Percent. Moves displayed decimal point two places to the right and appends a percentage (%) symbol.
	Currency	**Currency.**[1] Currency symbol (from Regional And Language Options in the Control Panel) and two decimal places.
		Euro. Euro currency symbol (regardless of Control Panel settings) and two decimal places.
	Date/Time	**General Date (default).** Combines Short Date and time (for example, 7/1/2010 5:30:10 PM).
		Short Date.[2] Uses Short Date Style from Regional And Language Options (for example, 7/1/2010).
	Calculated	Format property options for calculated fields depend on the Result Type. The format property options and defaults for the Result Type align with the other data types.
Increase/ Decrease Decimals	Number and Currency	You can specify the number of decimal places that Access displays. The default specification is to display two decimal places for the Currency, Standard, and Percent formats and the number of decimal places necessary to show the current precision of the numeric value for General Number format. You can request a fixed display of decimal places by clicking these buttons.
Caption	All	You can enter a more fully descriptive field name that Access displays in form labels and in report headings. (Tip: If you create field names with no embedded spaces, you can use the Caption property to specify a name that includes spaces for Access to use in labels and headers associated with this field in queries, forms, and reports.)
Default Value	Text, Number, Currency, Date/Time, and Boolean	You can specify a default value for the field that Access automatically uses for a new row if no other value is supplied. If you don't specify a Default Value, the field will be Null if the user fails to supply a value. (See also the Required property.)

Property	Data Type	Options, Description
Validation Rule	Text, Number, Currency, and Date/Time	You can supply an expression that must be true whenever you enter or change data in this field. For example, <100 specifies that a number must be less than 100. You can also check for one of a series of values. For example, you can have Access check for a list of valid cities by specifying "Boston" Or "Seattle" Or "Los Angeles". In addition, you can specify a complex expression that includes any of the built-in functions in Access. See "Defining Simple Field Validation Rules," on page 201, for details.
Validation Text	Text, Number, Currency, and Date/Time	You can specify a custom message that Access displays whenever the data entered does not pass your validation rule.
Required	All except Boolean and Calculated	If you don't want to allow a Null value in this field, select this property.
Unique	Text, Number, Currency, and Date/Time	If you don't want to allow duplicates in this field, select this property.
Indexed	Text, Number, Currency, and Date/Time	You can ask that an index be built to speed access to data values.
Memo Settings	Memo	**Plain Text (default).** The text in the Memo field is stored and displayed as plain text.
		Append Only. You can specify to see column history for this Memo field. When you change the memo field's data, the data change and time stamp are recorded and appended to the version history of the field.
		Rich Text. You can specify that the data in the memo field can be formatted as rich text. Access applies HTML formatting tags to your data.
Modify Expression	Calculated	The expression used to calculate the value for this column. The expression can use the value of one or more fields in the same table and can be up to 65,000 characters in length.

[1] Note that Currency and Euro formats always display two decimal places regardless of the number of actual decimal places in the underlying data. Access rounds any number to two decimal places for display if the number contains more than two decimal places.

[2] To help alleviate problems with dates spanning the start of the century, we recommend that you select the Use Four-Digit Year Formatting check box in Access. Click the File tab on the Backstage view, click Options, and then scroll to the General section in the Client Settings category to find this option. You should also be sure that your Short Date Style in the Regional And Language Options dialog box uses a four-digit year. (This is the default in Windows XP, Windows Vista, and Windows 7; you can double-check your settings by accessing Regional And Language Options within Control Panel.)

INSIDE OUT **Don't Specify a Validation Rule Without Validation Text**

If you specify a validation rule but no validation text, Access 2010 generates an ugly and cryptic message that your users might not understand:

"One or more values are prohibited by the validation rule '<*your expression here*>' set for '<*table name.field name*>'. Enter a value that the expression for this field can accept."

Unless you like getting lots of support calls, we recommend that you always enter a custom validation text message whenever you specify a validation rule.

Completing the Fields in the Vendors Web Table

You now know enough about field data types and properties for web databases to finish designing the Vendors table in this example. (If you'd like to compare your work to the Back Office Software System web database, you can take a look at the tblVendors web table in the BOSSDataCopy.accdb sample web database on the companion CD.) Use the information listed in Table 6-3 to complete the web table shown in Figure 6-24.

Table 6-3 Field Definitions for the Vendors Table

Field Name	Data Type	Description	Field Size
VendorID	ID	ID Field (AutoNumber)	
VendorName	Text	Vendor's name	50
CustomerNumber	Text	Customer number used by vendor	50
ContactFirstName	Text	Contact person's first name	50
ContactLastName	Text	Contact person's last name	50
ContactTitle	Text	Contact person's title	50
ContactCellNumber	Text	Contact person's cell phone number	30
Address	Text	Address of vendor	255
Address2	Text	Additional address information of vendor if needed	255
City	Text	City	50
PostalCode	Text	Postal/Zip Code	20
PhoneNumber	Text	Telephone number of vendor	30
PhoneNumberExtension	Text	Telephone extension if applicable	30

Field Name	Data Type	Description	Field Size
FaxNumber	Text	Fax number of vendor	30
EmailAddress	Text	Email address of contact or vendor	100
Notes	Memo-Rich Text	Additional notes for internal use	
Website	Hyperlink	Company website	
Active	Yes/No	Yes/No field whether this is an active vendor	
RelatedFiles	Attachment	Vendor specific files	

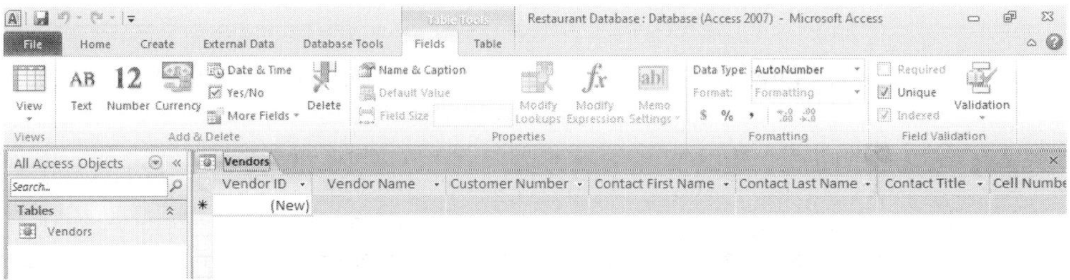

Figure 6-24 Your fields in the Vendors web table should now look like this.

You might have noticed that we did not have you create two fields found in the tblVendors table in the Back Office Software System sample web database—ContactFullName and State. We'll discuss creating these two fields in the next sections.

Creating Calculated Fields

Access 2010 introduces a new data type called Calculated. SharePoint lists already have a Calculated data type, so if you create a Calculated field in a web database, the field and data will move to the server if you publish the database. This new data type can be used in client databases as well as web databases so the steps we show you here to create Calculated fields in web tables can be applied to client tables.

The Calculated data type allows you to create a calculated result using an expression. The expression you use can include data from one or more fields in the same table, but you cannot reference fields in other tables. If you have a number field, for example, that holds quantity information for products purchased and a currency field that holds the price of a product, you can create a calculated field that multiplies the quantity and price fields and stores it with a result type of currency. Access recalculates the value of the calculated field any time the dependent fields are changed. If the calculation for a specific row evaluates to an error, Access stores the error for the Calculated field. For example, if your expression result divides a number by zero, Access displays the error #Div/0 in the Calculated field.

In client databases, you can reference all data types except Multi-Value and OLE Object fields in Calculated field expressions. In web databases, you cannot reference Multi-Value, OLE Object, Memo, Lookup, and AutoNumber fields for Calculated field expressions to maintain parity with SharePoint Calculated columns.

Calculated field expressions can reference functions and use operators that are supported in SharePoint Calculated columns. You cannot use volatile functions, such as Date() and Now(), in Calculated fields, because the stored value of the field would always be incorrect. You cannot use functions that look up outside the current record of the table, such as DSum, DCount, and DLookup, because Access cannot track when field dependencies change in those scenarios. You also cannot create an index or a relationship on a Calculated field. You can, however, use a Calculated field as a display column for a lookup field. You'll learn how to create relationships with lookup fields later in this chapter.

In Access 2010, you can generally use Calculated fields anywhere you can use other data types in your database. You can sort, filter on, and group by Calculated fields in client and web queries, forms, and reports. If your Calculated field evaluates to an error and you are filtering or grouping on that field, your query or report will fail to run. Access sorts Calculated field errors as Null values in table datasheets.

Why Use Calculated Fields?

If you are familiar with data normalization rules, you might be asking yourself why you would use a Calculated field to store a value that is derived from other fields. As you'll learn in Chapter 9, expressions in queries can do everything a Calculated field can do and more. So why would you want to add a Calculated field in your table? Calculated fields in tables can provide potential performance gains when running large queries with the same expression. For a Calculated field, the result of the expression is stored at the time Access saves the record. When you're fetching data from a table using a query, the Calculated field value is fetched just like other data rather than calculated for each record. If you're running large queries against data stored in an Access Services site, you might see performance improvements by storing the value of an expression instead of calculating the value for each row.

However, you cannot upsize any table that has a Calculated field to SQL Server. If you plan to upsize your database in the future to SQL Server, you should consider not creating Calculated fields in your tables.

In the Vendors table you have been building in the Restaurant Database, let's add a Calculated field that concatenates, or combines, the vendor contact's first and last name. Open your Vendors table in Datasheet view, if it isn't already, and tab into the ContactLastName field. (Access creates the new field to the right of the field that currently has focus in Datasheet view so we are starting you off in the last name field.) Next, click the More Fields button in the Add & Delete group on the Fields contextual tab, highlight the Calculated Field option near the bottom of the drop-down list, and then click Text on the shortcut menu, as shown in Figure 6-25.

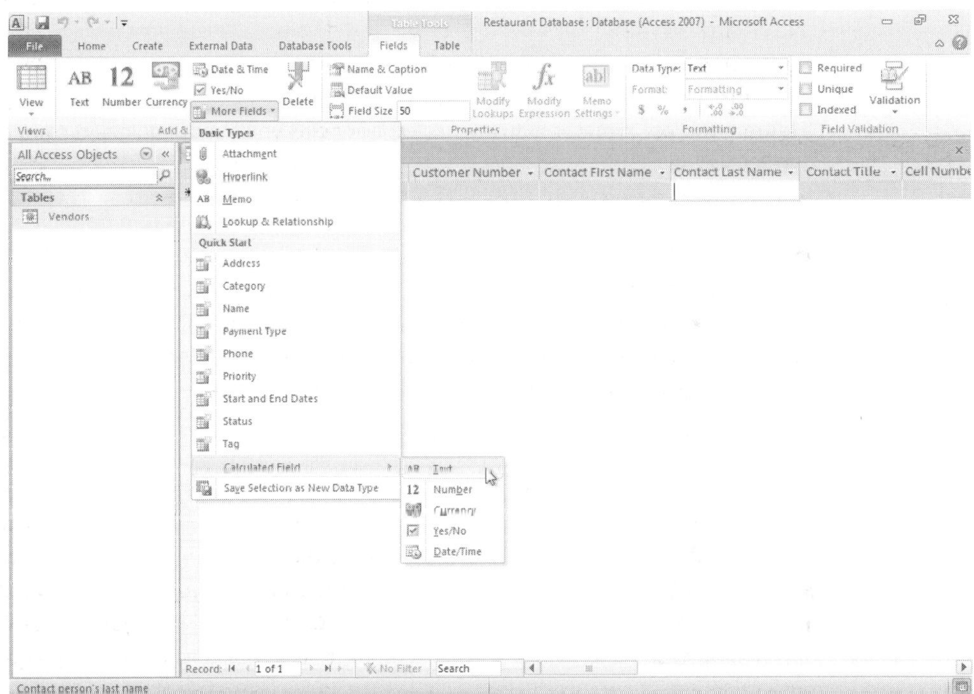

Figure 6-25 Select Text as the result type from the drop-down list for your new Calculated field.

Access opens the Expression Builder dialog box, as shown in Figure 6-26. In the upper part of the dialog box is a blank text box in which you can build an expression. You can type the expression yourself, but it's sometimes more accurate to find field names, operators, and function names in the three panes in the lower part of the dialog box.

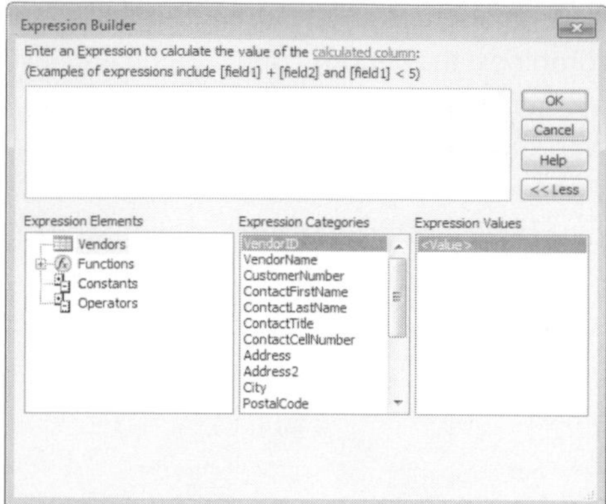

Figure 6-26 The Expression Builder dialog box helps you build simple and complex expressions.

The expression you need to build, which we'll walk you through in detail in just a moment, will look like this:

```
[ContactFirstName] & " " & [ContactLastName]
```

You can use the Expression Builder to help you correctly construct the expression we need for our new Calculated field. The Expression Builder exists in previous of Access, but in Access 2010, Microsoft enhanced the dialog box with some new capabilities. The first major enhancement to the Expression Builder in Access 2010 is a concept called *progressive disclosure*. In previous versions of Access, the Expression Builder showed all available functions, constants, and operators for expressions regardless of context. In Access 2010, the Expression Builder shows you only the elements applicable to the current context. For example, in Figure 6-26, Access only shows you the list of functions, constants, and operators you can use for Calculated fields in web tables under the Expression Elements pane on the far left. The middle pane, Expression Categories, lists all the current fields in your Vendors table that you can refer to in your Calculated field. The right pane, Expression Values, shows you all possible values you can use based on the currently highlighted category selected in the middle pane. In this context, you can only refer to the field value of existing fields for new Calculated fields.

Start by typing the letter **c**, which is the first letter of the ContactFirstName field in the text box at the top of the Expression Builder, as shown in Figure 6-27. Access now shows the second enhancement to the Expression Builder in Access 2010—the addition of *IntelliSense*. IntelliSense helps you create expressions faster by showing you a drop-down list of words that match an object (such as a field or form name), function, or parameter once you type enough characters for Access to filter to the term. You can either accept the suggestion Access provides in the drop-down list by pressing Enter or Tab, or you can continue manually typing the name you want.

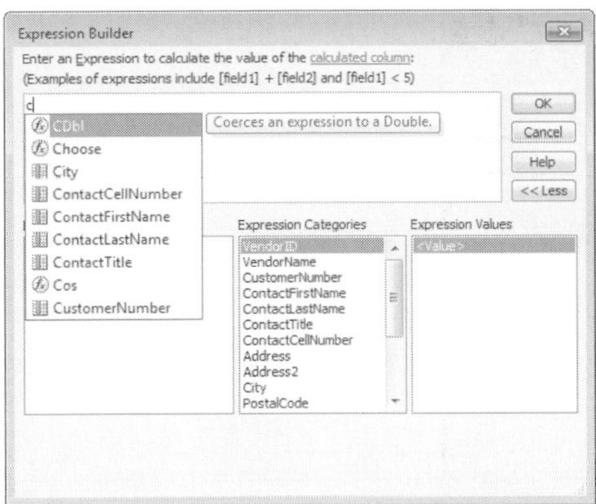

Figure 6-27 IntelliSense helps you create expressions faster by providing a list of drop-down choices as you type to use in your expression.

In Figure 6-27, you'll notice that by typing the letter **c**, Access displays three functions—CDbl, Choose, and Cos—and six fields in your Vendors tables, all of which start with the letter c. If you pressed Enter right now, Access selects the function CDbl and adds that to the text box. You'll also notice in Figure 6-27 that Access displays a tooltip (also called a ScreenTip) for the CDbl function. (You can find a list of the most useful functions and their descriptions in Article 4, "Function Reference," on the companion CD.)

INSIDE OUT Using Keyboard Shortcuts to Display or Hide IntelliSense Options

When you are working in the Expression Builder, you can press Ctrl+Space to show the IntelliSense list of available items based on where your insertion point is located. If no characters precede your insertion point, Access displays all available items. Press the Esc key to dismiss the IntelliSense list at any time.

To select the ContactFirstName field from the drop-down list, you can use the down arrow key to highlight the field and then press Enter or Tab, or you can double-click the field name in the drop-down list. Alternatively, you can continue typing the letters **contactf**, as we did, until that is the only option in the drop-down list, as shown in Figure 6-28. Notice that Access displays the field's description in the tooltip next to the field. Press Enter or Tab now to add the ContactFirstName field to the text box. (You could also choose to simply double-click the field name you want to use in the Expression Categories pane to add the field to the top text box.)

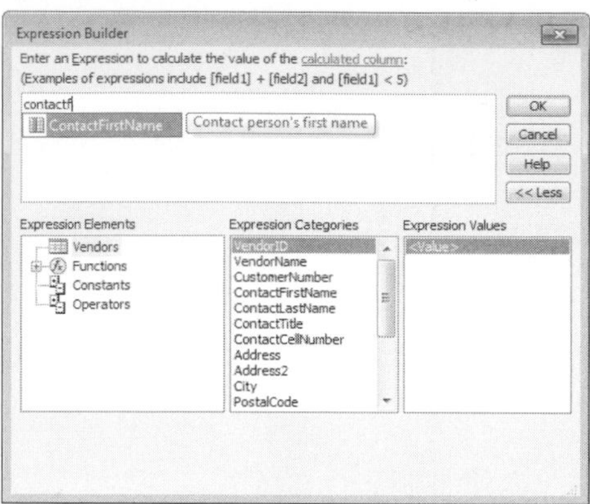

Figure 6-28 Access displays descriptions next to the field names in the IntelliSense drop-down list.

INSIDE OUT Increasing the Font Size in the Expression Builder

If the font size in the upper part of the Expression Builder seems too small for you to read, you can adjust the size of the font by holding down the Ctrl key and then scrolling with your mouse wheel. When you scroll up, Access increases the font size, and when you scroll down, Access decreases the font size. Access returns the font size to the default size whenever you open the Expression Builder dialog box.

You'll notice that after you select the field, the Expression Builder pastes [ContactFirstName] into the expression area, not just ContactFirstName, as shown in Figure 6-29. The Expression Builder adds brackets ([ ]) around all field names in case they might have embedded spaces in their names. If you design your field names without any blank spaces, you can leave out the brackets, but it's always good practice to include them.

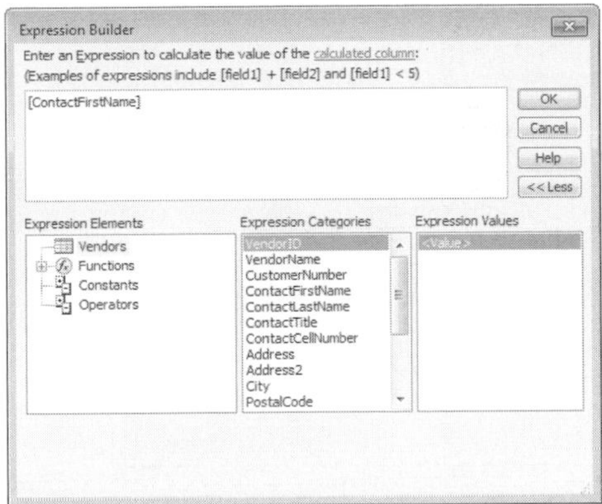

Figure 6-29 The Expression Builder automatically places brackets around field names after you add them to the text box area.

Continue with the rest of the expression we need by typing **& " " &** and then adding the ContactLastName field by typing it manually, using the IntelliSense drop-down list as you type the letters, or double-clicking the field name in the Expressions Categories pane. Your completed expression should now look like Figure 6-30.

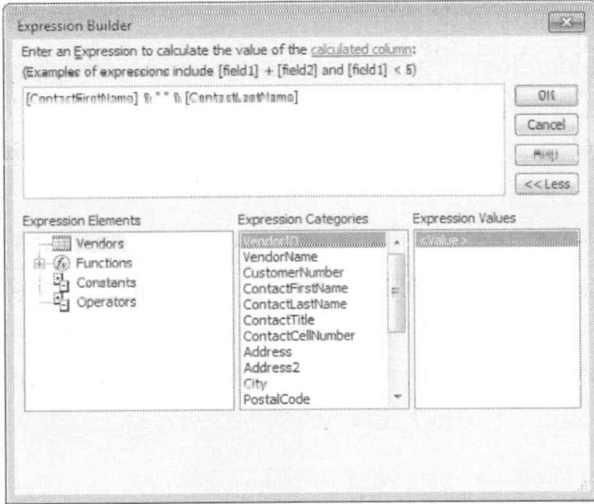

Figure 6-30 Your completed expression for the new Calculated field should now look like this.

Click OK to save your expression changes and dismiss the Expression Builder dialog box. Access returns focus to the Vendor datasheet and names your new Calculated field Field1, by default. Let's give our new Calculated field a proper name. Click the Name & Caption button in the Properties group to open the Enter Field Properties dialog box, as shown in Figure 6-31. Type **ContactFullName** for the Name, **Contact Full Name** for the caption, and **Contact's full name** for the description. Click OK in the dialog box to save your changes.

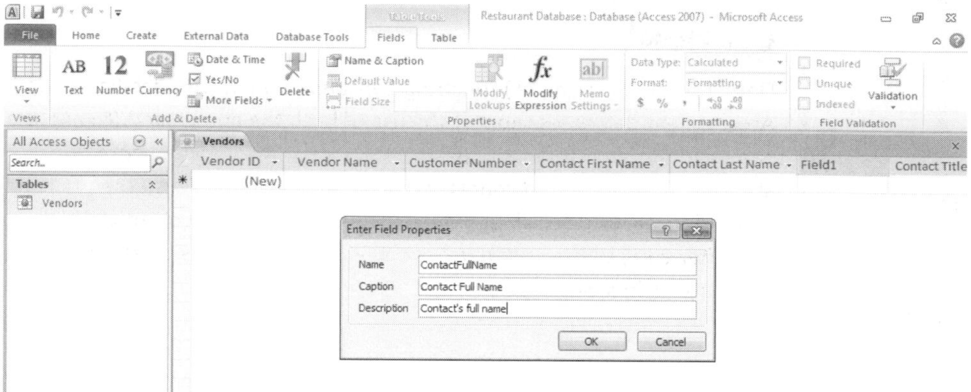

Figure 6-31 You can enter a proper name for the new Calculated field in the Enter Field Properties dialog box.

Your new Calculated field will now concatenate the first and last names of the vendor contact with a space between the two names for each record automatically. For example, if the contact's first name is Jeff and the contact's last name is Conrad, Access displays the text Jeff Conrad in your ContactFullName field. Note that all Calculated fields are read-only—you cannot type anything into these fields, nor can you adjust their data through any other means such as using Visual Basic code. Remember that Access recalculates the Calculated field whenever any dependent field values are changed. If you need to adjust the expression used for your Calculated field, highlight your field in Datasheet view and then click the Modify Expression button in the Properties group, as shown in Figure 6-32. Access opens up the Expression Builder dialog box, where you can adjust the expression to your needs. (Note that if you are using a client database, you can also adjust the expression for Calculated data types on the Expression field property setting in table Design view.) Save your changes to the Vendors table by clicking the Save button on the Quick Access Toolbar.

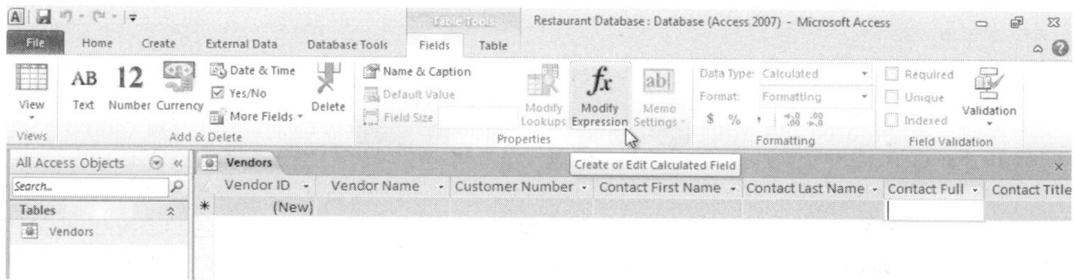

Figure 6-32 Click the Modify Expression button in the Properties group if you need to adjust the expression used for your Calculated field.

CAUTION!

Don't use the plus sign (+) for string concatenation in web databases. Traditional Access client databases support the use of both the ampersand (&) and the plus sign (+) for concatenation of strings. However, the server only supports the use of the ampersand (&) for string concatenation. If you attempt to use the plus sign (+) in an expression with string values, you'll receive an error in any controls that use the expression after you publish your database to a SharePoint server and work with your database objects in a web browser.

Defining Field Validation Rules for Web Databases

To define a simple check on the values that you allow in a field in a web database, you can enter an expression in the Validation Rule property for the field just as you can for client databases. Access won't allow you to enter a field value that violates this rule. Access performs this validation for data entered in a Table window in Datasheet view, in an updateable query, or in a form. If you publish your web database to a SharePoint server, the server will also enforce your field validation rules.

In general, a field validation expression consists of an operator and a comparison value. If you do not include an operator, Access assumes you want an "equals" (=) comparison. You can specify multiple comparisons separated by the Boolean operators OR and AND.

It is good practice to always enclose text string values in quotation marks. If one of your values is a text string containing blanks or special characters, you must enclose the entire string in quotation marks. For example, to limit the valid entries for a City field to two of the largest cities in the state of Washington, enter **"Seattle" Or "Tacoma"**. If you are comparing date values, you must enclose the date constants in pound sign (#) characters, as in #07/1/2010#.

You can use the comparison symbols to compare the value in the field to a value or values in your validation rule. Comparison symbols for web databases are summarized in Table 6-4. (Unlike client databases, you cannot use the Between operator in validation rules in web databases.) For example, you might want to ensure that a numeric value is always a positive number. To do this, enter **>0**. You can use one or more pairs of comparisons to ask Access to check that the value falls within certain ranges. For example, if you want to verify that a number is in the range of 100 through 200, enter either **>=100 And <=200**. Another way to test for a match in a list of values is to use the IN comparison operator. For example, to test for states surrounding California, enter **In ("Oregon", "Nevada", "Arizona")**. If all you need to do is ensure that the user enters a value, you can use the special comparison phrase Is Not Null.

Table 6-4 Comparison Symbols Used in Validation Rules for Web Databases

Operator	Meaning
NOT	Use before any comparison operator except IS NOT NULL to perform the converse test. For example, NOT > 10 is equivalent to <=10.
<	Less than.
<=	Less than or equal to.
>	Greater than.
>=	Greater than or equal to.
=	Equal to.
<>	Not equal to.
IN	Test for *equal to* any member in a list; comparison value must be a comma-separated list enclosed in parentheses.
LIKE	Test a Text field to match a pattern string.
IS NOT NULL	Requires the user to enter a value in the field.

If you need to validate a Text field against a matching pattern (for example, a postal code or a phone number), you can use the LIKE comparison operator in web databases. You can provide a text string as a comparison value that defines which characters are valid in which positions. Access understands a number of *wildcard characters*, characters which you can use to define positions that contain any single character, zero or more characters, or any single number. These characters are shown in Table 6-5 and are identical to what you can use for client databases.

Table 6-5 LIKE Wildcard Characters

Character	Meaning
?	Any single character.
*	Zero or more characters; use to define leading, trailing, or embedded strings that don't have to match any specific pattern characters.
#	Any single digit.

You can also specify that any particular position in the Text field can contain only characters from a list that you provide. You can specify a range of characters within a list by entering the low value character, a hyphen, and the high value character, as in [A-Z] or [3-7]. If you want to test a position for any characters *except* those in a list, start the list with an exclamation point (!). You must enclose all lists in brackets ([ ]). You can see examples of validation rules using LIKE in web databases here.

Validation Rule	Tests For
LIKE "#####" or	A U.S. 5-digit ZIP Code
LIKE "#####-####"	A U.S. 9-digit ZIP+ Code
LIKE "[A-Z]#[A-Z] #[A-Z]#"	A Canadian postal code
LIKE "###-##-####"	A U.S. Social Security number
LIKE "Smith*"	A string that begins with *Smith*[1]
LIKE "*smith##*"	A string that contains *smith* followed by two numbers, anywhere in the string
LIKE "??00####"	An eight-character string that contains any first two characters followed by exactly two zeros and then any four digits
LIKE "[!0-9BMQ]*####"	A string that contains any character other than a number or the letter *B*, *M*, or *Q* in the first position and ends with exactly four digits

1 Character string comparisons in Access and on the server are case-insensitive, so smith, SMITH, and Smith are all equal.

In the Vendors table of the Restaurant Database you've been building, the EmailAddress field could benefit from the use of a validation rule. Open the Vendors table in Datasheet view, if it isn't already open, tab over to the EmailAddress field, click the Validation button in the Field Validation group, and then click the Field Validation Rule option from the drop-down list, as shown in Figure 6-33.

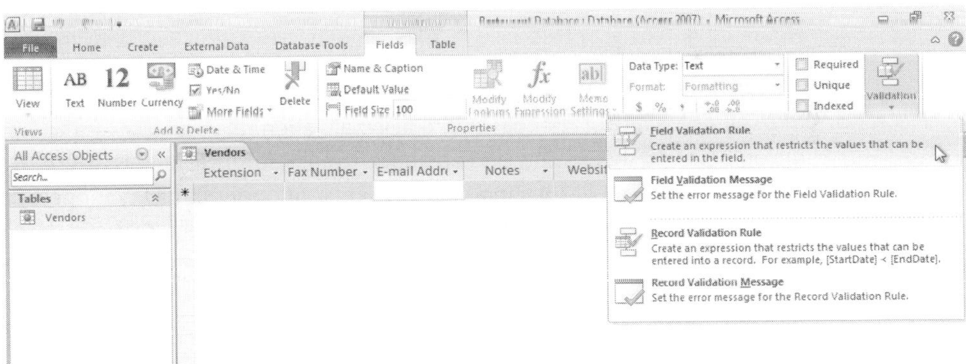

Figure 6-33 Click the Validation button on the Fields contextual tab to add or edit field validation rules.

Access opens the Expression Builder dialog box, as shown in Figure 6-34. In the EmailAddress field, we want to be sure the email address provided by the user appears to be a valid email address. We can verify the email address meets most standards of valid syntax by using a combination of the LIKE operator and wildcard characters in a field validation rule. In the blank text box at the top of the Expression Builder dialog box, type Is Null OR ((Like "*?@?*.?*") AND (Not Like "*[,;]*")) for the field validation rule, as shown in Figure 6-34. This field validation rule ensures that every email address provided by the user starts with at least one character followed by the @ symbol, contains at least one more character following the @ symbol, and contains the dot symbol followed by at least one more character after the dot symbol. Also, this field validation rule does not allow a space, a comma, or a semicolon anywhere in the email address.

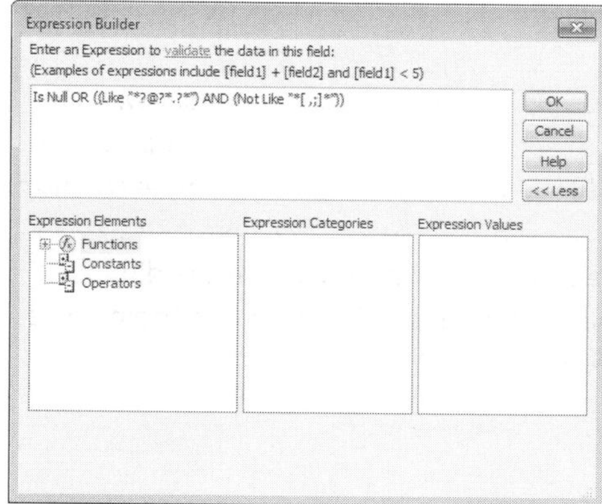

Figure 6-34 Type your field validation rule into the Expression Builder dialog box.

Click OK to save your changes to the field validation rule and dismiss the Expression Builder dialog box. You should now add an appropriate custom validation text to display to users if they provide data to the EmailAddress field that does not pass your new field validation rule. Make sure the focus is still in the EmailAddress field, click the Validation button in the Field Validation group, and then click the Field Validation Message option from the drop-down list, as shown in Figure 6-35. If you look closely at Figure 6-35, you'll notice that Access adds an orange square around the graphic next to the Field Validation Rule option. Access highlights these graphics on the drop-down list as a visual cue if you define a property for that specific option.

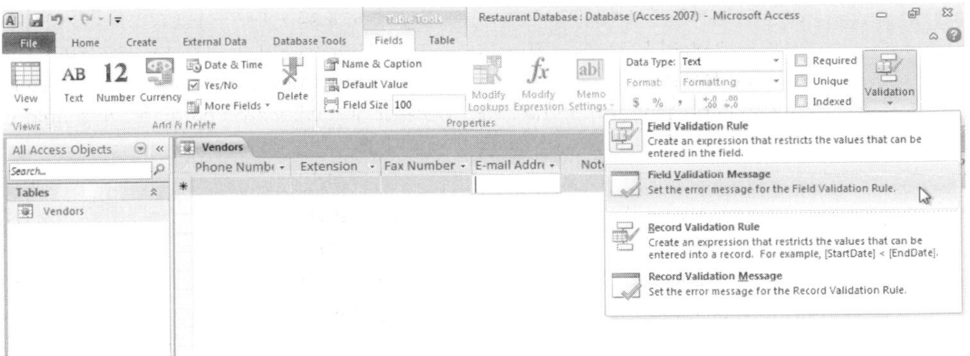

Figure 6-35 Click the Field Validation Message option to add a custom field validation text.

Access now opens the Enter Validation Message dialog box, as shown in Figure 6-36. Type the following custom message into the dialog box—**The email address you provided does not appear to be valid.** Click OK to save your changes to this property and dismiss the dialog box. You now have a completed field validation rule and message for the EmailAddress field that will be enforced whether you use the database in client or on the server. Be sure to click the Save button on the Quick Access Toolbar to save this latest change to your web table definition.

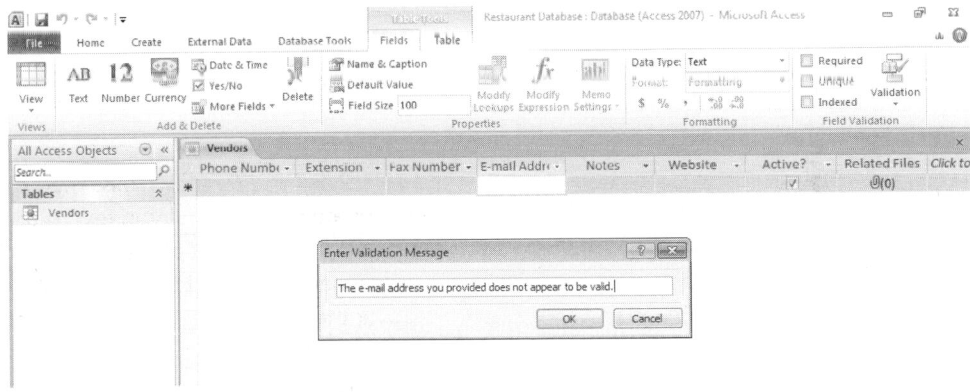

Figure 6-36 Enter your custom validation text into the Enter Validation Message dialog box.

Defining a Table Validation Rule for Web Databases

You can create table validation rules in web databases just like you can for client databases. Although field validation rules get checked as you enter each new value, Access checks a table validation rule only when you save or add a complete record. Table validation rules are handy when the values in one field are dependent on what's stored in another field. You need to wait until the entire row is about to be saved before checking one field against another.

In the Restaurant Database you have been creating, we need an Appointments table to track our day to day appointments of managing the restaurant. This table requires a table validation rule. Click the Table button in the Tables group on the Create Ribbon tab to get started. Define that table now using the specifications in Table 6-6. Be sure to rename the ID field Access provides for you to **AppointmentID** and then save the table and name it **Appointments**. Be sure to also set both the StartTime and EndTime fields as required fields by selecting the Required option in the Field Validation group. You can set the Format property for the fields in the Format text box in the Formatting group on the Fields tab.

Table 6-6 Field Definitions for the Appointments Table

Field Name	Data Type	Description	Field Size	Format
AppointmentID	ID	Unique appointment identifier		
AppointmentDescription	Text	Description of appointment	100	
StartTime	Date/Time	Start time of appointment		General Date
EndTime	Date/Time	End time of appointment		General Date
Notes	Memo	Extended notes from appointment		Rich Text

To define a table validation rule in a web database, open the table in Datasheet view, click the Validation button in the Field Validation group on the Fields contextual tab, and then click the Record Validation Rule option from the drop-down list, as shown in Figure 6-37.

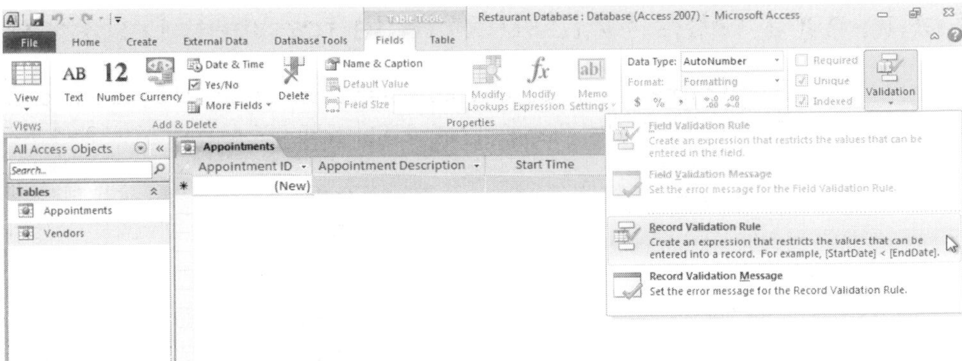

Figure 6-37 You can define table validation rules in web databases by clicking the Record Validation Rule option.

Access opens the Expression Builder dialog box, as shown in Figure 6-38. For this web table, we want to ensure the start time of the appointment provided by the user comes before the end time. (It certainly would not make sense to have an appointment end before it even started.) We can accomplish this by using the less than (<) operator in a table validation rule. In the blank text box at the top of the Expression Builder dialog box, type **[StartTime]<[EndTime]** for the table validation rule, as shown in Figure 6-38. This table validation rule ensures that every record in the Appointments web table contains a start time that comes before the end time.

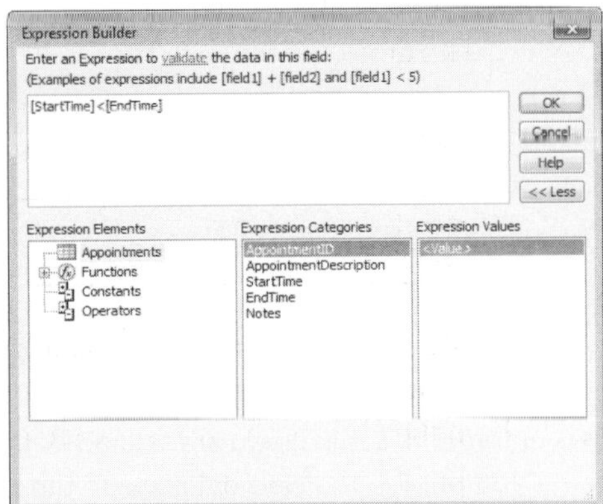

Figure 6-38 Type your table validation rule into the Expression Builder dialog box.

Click OK to save your new table validation rule and dismiss the Expression Builder dialog box. You should now add a descriptive message to display to users if they add data to a record that violates the rule in this web table. You should be careful to word this message so that the user clearly understands what is wrong. If you enter a table validation rule and fail to specify validation text, Access displays the following message when the user enters invalid data: "One or more values are prohibited by the validation rule '< *your validation rule expression here* >' set for '<*table name*>'. Enter a value that the expression for this field can accept." Although the message does include the complete expression, it's not very pretty, is it? If you publish this web table to the server without a validation text, the default message you'll see on the server is, "List Data Validation failed," so we recommend you always add a descriptive validation text to accompany your table validation rules.

To create a table validation message, click the Validation button in the Field Validation group, and then click the Record Validation Message option from the drop-down list, as shown in Figure 6-39. You'll notice that Access adds an orange square around the graphic next to the Record Validation Rule option to indicate that you already defined a property for that specific option.

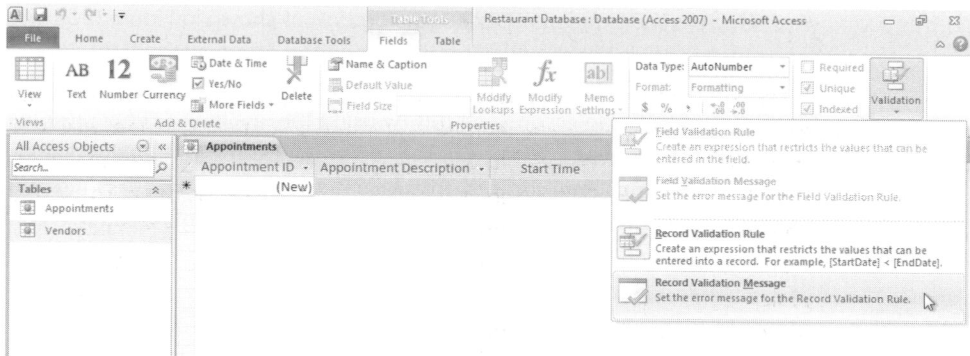

Figure 6-39 Click the Record Validation Message option to add a custom table validation text to your web table.

Access now opens the Enter Validation Message dialog box, as shown in Figure 6-40. Type the following custom message into the dialog box—**The End Time for the appointment cannot be before the Start Time.** Click OK to save your changes to this property and dismiss the dialog box. You now have a completed table validation rule and message for the Appointments web table. Access enforces this rule if you are adding or editing in client, and SharePoint enforces the rule after you publish the web database to the server. Be sure to click the Save button on the Quick Access Toolbar to save this latest change to your web table definition.

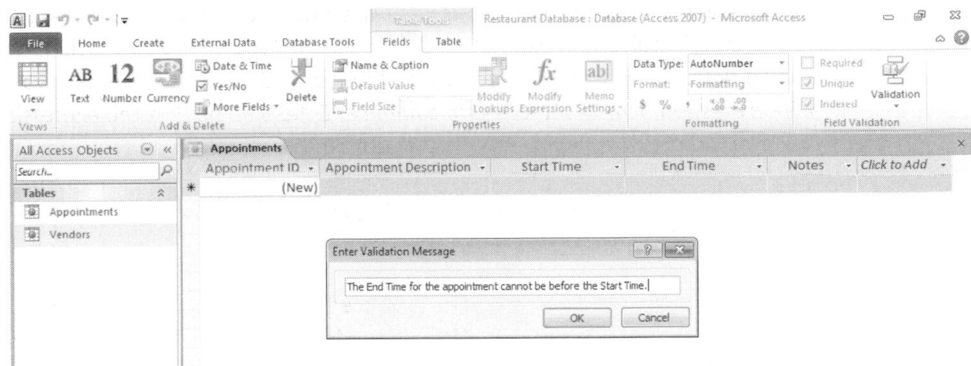

Figure 6-40 Enter your custom validation text into the Enter Validation Message dialog box.

Defining a Primary Key for Web Databases

Every table in a relational database should have a primary key, and web databases are no exception. In Chapter 4, you learned that you have many options available to use for a primary key in client databases. In web databases, however, you must follow the structure of SharePoint lists, which only allows the SharePoint ID field as the primary key. From a certain perspective, this makes defining a primary key in web databases quite simple—Access automatically creates the primary key field, the ID field, for you whenever you create a new web table. You cannot delete this field from your web table, but you can rename the ID field to something more to your liking, such as VendorID or InvoiceID.

If you're an experienced Access developer, you might find the ID primary key restriction to be very limiting. What if you want to create a multi-field primary key and set it to be unique, as you can for client databases? While it's true you cannot define a unique multi-field primary key in SharePoint lists, you can achieve the same functionality by using table events, which is a new feature in Access 2010. In Chapter 7, "Creating Table Data Macros," you'll learn how to create a data macro that can give you the functionality of a multi-field unique primary key for a web table.

Understanding Other Web Table Properties

Access 2010 provides several additional web table properties that you can set in Datasheet view. To edit these properties, open in Datasheet view the Appointments web table you finished creating in the previous section. Click the Table Properties button in the Properties group on the Table contextual tab, as shown in Figure 6-41. Note that we'll discuss the other commands on this contextual tab in Chapter 7, when we discuss data macros.

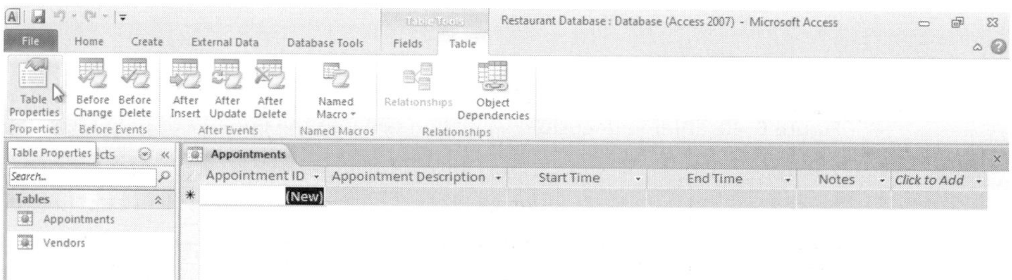

Figure 6-41 Click Table Properties to view the table properties for web tables.

Access opens the Enter Table Properties dialog box, as shown in Figure 6-42. You can use the Order By property to define one or more fields that define the default display sequence of rows in this web table when in Datasheet view. If you don't define an Order By property for web tables, Access displays the rows in primary key sequence. The Filter By property lets you predefine criteria to limit the data displayed in the Datasheet view of this table.

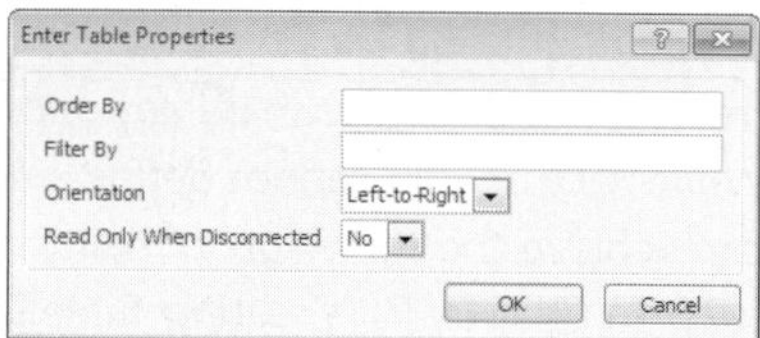

Figure 6-42 You can edit web table properties by using the Enter Table Properties dialog box.

You can use the Orientation property to specify the reading sequence of the data of your web table in Datasheet view. The default in most versions of Access is Left-to-Right. In versions that support a language that is normally read right to left, the default is Right-to-Left. When you use Right-to-Left, field and table captions appear right-justified, the field order is right to left, and the tab sequence proceeds right to left.

The Read Only When Disconnected property by default is set to No, which means you can still update or add new records to a web table that is linked to a Microsoft SharePoint Services site when you are offline. We'll discuss working with data in an Access Services application in Chapter 22.

> **Note**
>
> If you apply a filter or specify a sorting sequence when you have the web table open in Datasheet view, Access 2010 saves the filter in the Filter By property and the sorting sequence in the Order By property. However, Access does not use the Filter By property when you open a web table datasheet in web databases because the Filter On Load table property is set to No for web databases. To apply the filter to your datasheet, click the Toggle Filter button in the Sort & Filter group on the Home tab.

Creating Lookup Fields in a Web Database

If you've been following along in this chapter, creating the Vendors web table in your Restaurant Database, you'll remember we are still missing one more field found in the tblVendors web table in the Back Office Software System sample web database on the companion CD—the State field. If you open the tblVendors web table in the BOSSDataCopy.accdb database in Datasheet view and tab to the State field, you'll notice that Access displays a drop-down list of states, as shown in Figure 6-43.

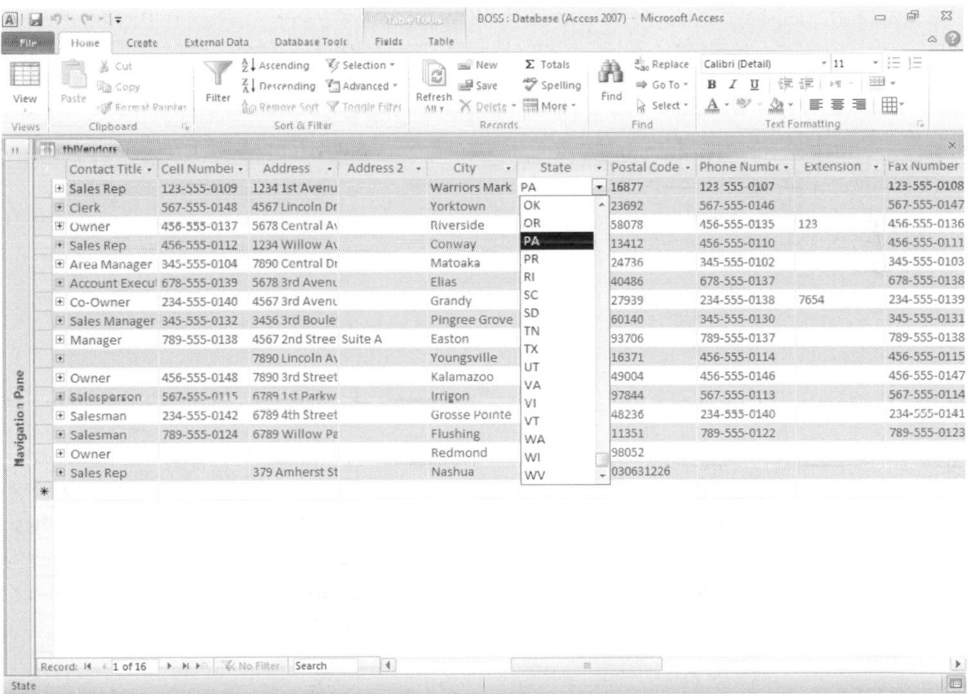

Figure 6-43 The State field in the tblVendors web table is a Lookup Field that displays a list of state abbreviations.

We defined the State field in this web table to be a lookup field. A lookup field can generally be classified as one of two types—a field that "looks up" its data from a predefined list stored with the field itself, or a field that looks up its data from a different table. The State field in the tblVendors web table looks up its data from a pre-defined list we provided when we created the field. Microsoft also uses the term *value list* to describe this type of field because the field gets its data from a list of values.

Let's create this State lookup field in the Vendors table that you've been working on. Open the Restaurant Database file again if you closed it and then open the Vendors web table in Datasheet view. Next, tab over to the City field so the focus is in that field. (Remember that Access creates the new field to the right of the field that currently has focus.) Now click the More Fields button in the Add & Delete group on the Fields contextual tab, and then click Lookup & Relationship from the drop-down list of options, as shown in Figure 6-44.

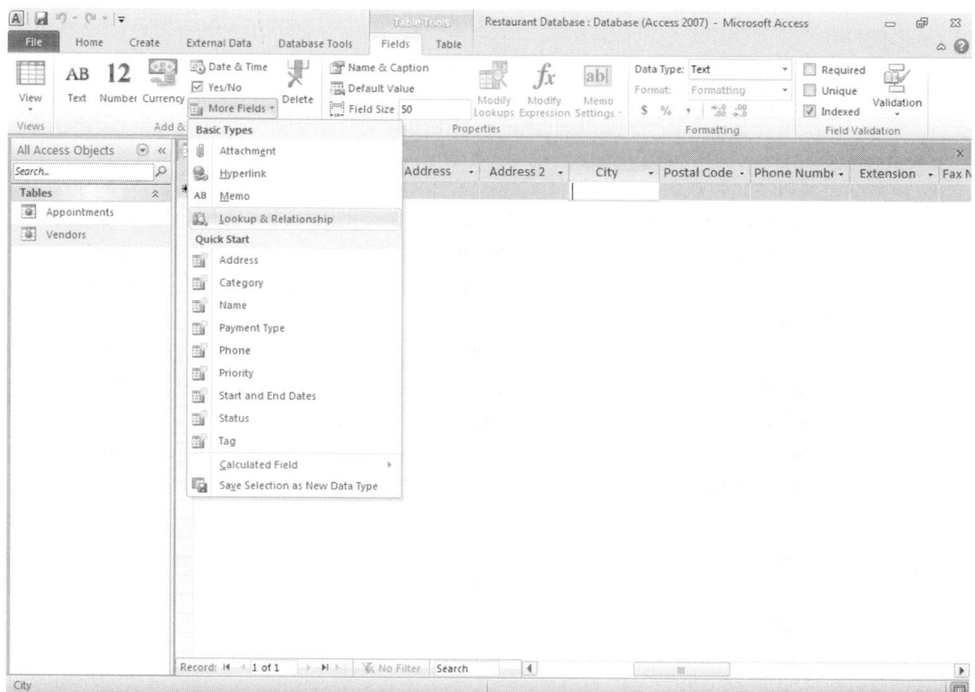

Figure 6-44 Click Lookup & Relationship under the More Fields option to start creating your lookup field.

Access opens the Lookup Wizard, shown in Figure 6-45, and displays the first page. You must use this wizard if you want to create lookup fields in web databases. The first page of the wizard needs to know where you want to get the values for the field. You can either choose to have the values come from another table or type in the values yourself. (We'll discuss the first option in the next section of this chapter.) Select the second option—I Will Type In The Values That I Want—and then click Next to proceed to the next page of the wizard.

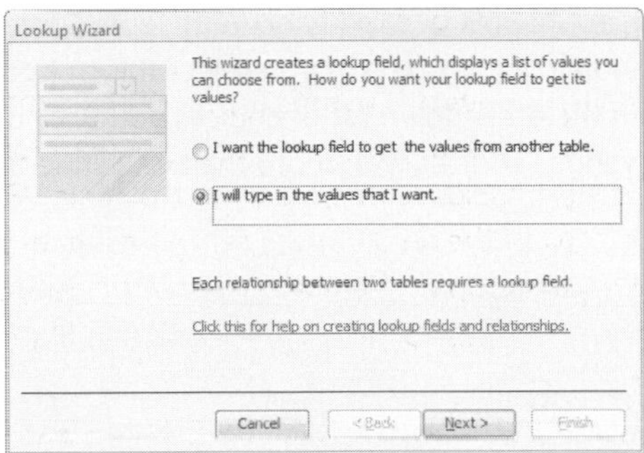

Figure 6-45 The Lookup Wizard walks you through the steps necessary to create a lookup field for your web database.

The second page of the Lookup Wizard, shown in Figure 6-46, now needs to know specifically what values you want displayed for this field. By default, Access shows one column in the drop-down list of choices for the lookup field. If you want to display more than one column, enter the number of columns you want to display in the Number Of Columns text box. In the bottom half of this page, Access displays a datasheet where you can type in the specific values you need—one per row. In Figure 6-46, you'll notice we typed in the first six state abbreviations in alphabetical order. You can resize the column by dragging its right edge to the size you want or you can double-click the right edge of the column and Access adjusts the width to just fit the data you provide. Enter several state abbreviations now and then click Next to proceed to the next page of the wizard.

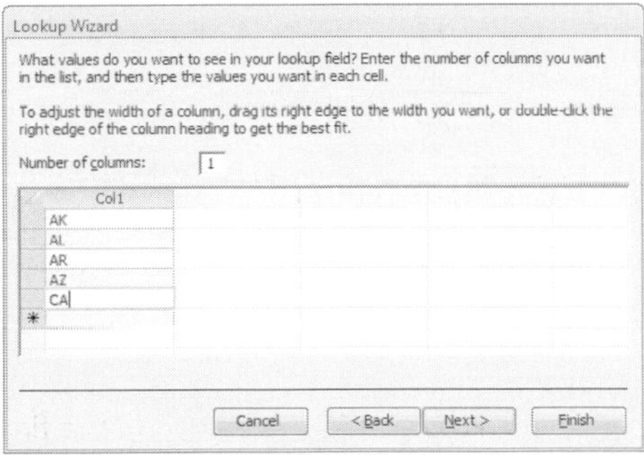

Figure 6-46 Type in the values you want to see displayed for your lookup field on the second page of the Lookup Wizard.

Access now displays the final page of the Lookup Wizard, as shown in Figure 6-47. On this page, you can provide the name you want to use for this lookup field. Type **State** as the name of your new field in the text box. Select the Limit To List check box—cleared by default—if you want Access to not allow users to enter any other data into this lookup field other than the values you provided. The last option—Allow Multiple Values—tells Access to create a Multi-Value Lookup Field. In Chapter 5, "Modifying Your Table Design," you learned that Multi-Value Lookup Fields handle complex data. If you select this option, Access allows you to select multiple options from the drop-down list of choices you provided. In our case, it does not make sense to have a vendor address with more than one state abbreviation, so leave this option cleared.

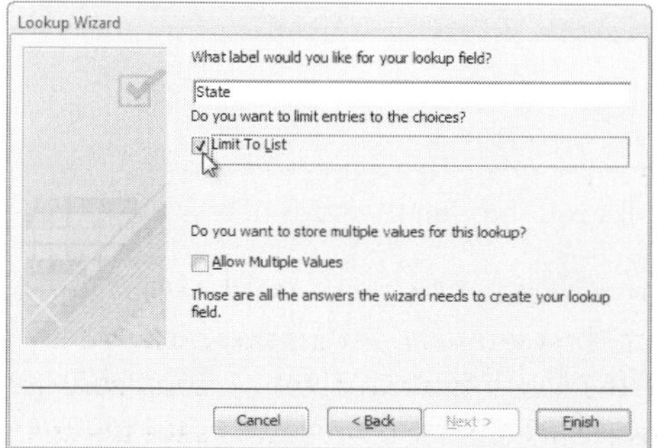

Figure 6-47 On the last page of the Lookup Wizard, you can name your field, decide if you want to restrict the choices, and decide if you want to store multiple values.

Click Finish to save your changes and dismiss the Lookup Wizard. Access creates your new State field to the right of the City field. When you tab or click into the State field, Access displays a down arrow on the right edge of the field. When you click that arrow, Access displays all the state abbreviations you typed into the Lookup Wizard, as shown in Figure 6-48.

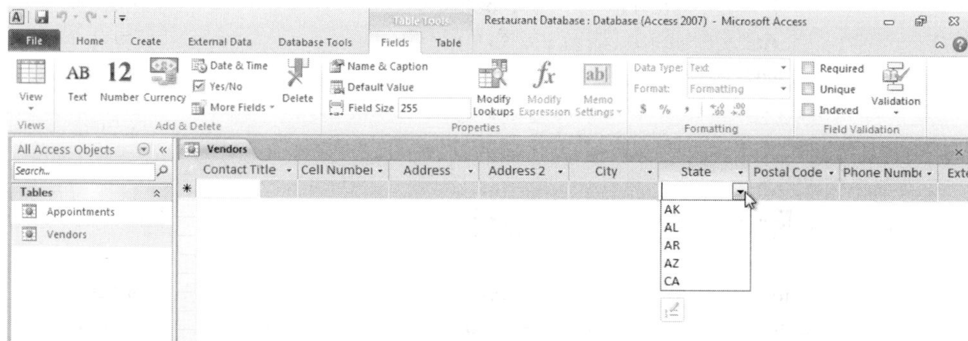

Figure 6-48 Your completed lookup field now displays the list of values you provided in the Lookup Wizard.

In Figure 6-48, you'll notice that just below the drop-down list of state abbreviations is the Edit List Items button. Click this button, and Access opens the Edit List Items dialog box, as shown in Figure 6-49. In this dialog box, you can add, edit, or delete items from this value list lookup field. At the bottom of the dialog box, you can also select a default value to use for this field for all new records.

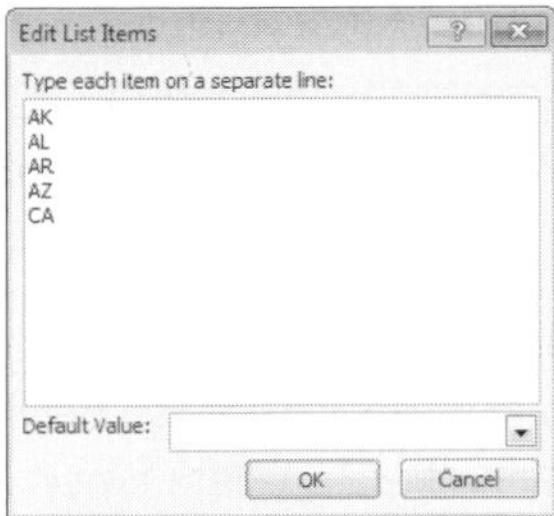

Figure 6-49 You can edit the values in your lookup field in the Edit List Items dialog box.

In addition to using the Edit List Items dialog box to change the values of your lookup field, you can also make changes to the values and settings by clicking the Modify Lookups button in the Properties group on the Fields contextual tab. Access reopens the Lookup Wizard, where you can make adjustments to your settings and save the changes. Be sure to click the Save button on the Quick Access Toolbar to save this latest change to your web table definition.

INSIDE OUT **Value List Lookup Fields Create Choice Data Types in SharePoint**

When you create a value list lookup field in a web database and then publish it to a SharePoint server, Access creates a Choice data type in the SharePoint list for that field. If you create a multi-value lookup field in a web database and publish it to the server, Access creates a Choice data type with the Checkboxes display property set to True to allow multiple selections.

Creating Relationships Using Lookup Fields

The process of creating relationships between tables in web databases is very different from creating relationships in client databases. In client databases, you generally create all the tables and fields you need and then create relationships between the various tables using the Relationship Window. In web databases, however, you do both of these steps at the same time through the Lookup Wizard. What this means to you as an Access developer is that you cannot fully complete child tables before you complete the parent tables. For example, in a client database, you could create a vendor field in a table of invoices to hold the vendor ID even before you created the vendor table itself. After you create the vendors table, you could then link the two tables on the appropriate fields using the Relationship Window. In a web database, the vendor table must exist before you can actually create fields in child tables that you intend to link to the vendor table. You cannot add relationships to existing fields in web databases; you must create the relationship at the time you create the field.

One other important difference between relationships in client and web databases is that client databases allow you to create relationships between tables with data types other than number. You can, for example, create a relationship in a client database between two tables using a Text data type (so long as both fields are defined as Text data types). In a web database, you can create relationships only on the SharePoint ID field.

In versions of SharePoint before SharePoint 2010, you could not create relationships between SharePoint lists. In SharePoint 2010, Microsoft added the ability to create relationships between different lists using the ID field. To ensure that the relationships you create in a web database are compatible with the SharePoint relationship structures, you must use the Lookup Wizard in Access 2010 to create or modify your web table relationships.

Thus far in this chapter, you have seen how to build one of the main subject tables of the Back Office Software System web database—Vendors. You also created a generic Appointments table in your Restaurant Database file. To show you how to create relationships in web databases, we first need to create another main subject table—Report Groups—and then a parent and child table—Invoice Headers and Invoice Details—to track the invoices that list all our food purchases. We'll first create all the fields for these three tables and then add the *linking* field last. Table 6-7 shows you the fields you need to create for the Report Groups table that hold the information for the report groups we use to track all the various expenditures for the restaurant.

Table 6-7 Field Definitions for the Report Groups Table

Field Name	Data Type	Description	Field Size
ReportGroupID	ID	ID Field (AutoNumber)	
ReportGroupName	Text	Report group name	50
AccountNumber	Text	Account number of report group	50
AccountDescription	Text	Optional description for additional information	255

The Report Groups main table has all the fields we need, but the Invoice Details table depends on this table, so you need to create this table first. After you define all the fields, save the table as ReportGroups.

Table 6-8 shows you the fields you need to define for the Invoice Headers table that holds the parent information about each invoice the restaurant receives.

Table 6-8 Field Definitions for the Invoice Headers Table

Field Name	Data Type	Description	Field Size	Format
InvoiceID	ID	ID Field (AutoNumber)		
InvoiceDate	Date/Time	Date of the invoice		Short Date
InvoiceNumber	Text	Invoice number shown on invoice	50	
InvoiceAmount	Currency	Total invoice amount		Currency
Comments	Memo	Any additional comments		Rich Text
Attachments	Attachment	Invoice specific files		
IsBalanced	Yes/No	Invoice balanced?		

The Invoice Headers table needs to know which vendor this invoice came from. We'll create that field and relationship to the Vendors table in just a moment. Save this table as InvoiceHeaders after you create the necessary fields.

You need one last table, the Invoice Details table, to track the invoices for Restaurant Database. Table 6-9 shows the fields you need to create. This table needs the InvoiceID from the Invoice Headers table and the ReportGroupID from the Report Groups table to track the all the line items from the invoice. We'll create those fields in just a moment. Save this last table as InvoiceDetails.

Table 6-9 Field Definitions for the Invoice Details Table

Field Name	Data Type	Description	Format
InvoiceDetailsID	ID	ID Field (AutoNumber)	
ReportGroupAmount	Currency	Amount for this report group	Currency

Defining a Restrict Delete Relationship

Now, you're ready to start defining relationships between these web tables. Each vendor in our Restaurant Database can have more than one invoice. This means Vendors and InvoiceHeaders have a one-to-many relationship. Before you begin, make sure the Vendors table is closed. When you use the Lookup Wizard, Access needs to lock both tables in order to create the new lookup field. If you have the Vendors table open in Datasheet view and try to create a lookup field that uses that table as its source, you'll get an error when Access tries to create the field during the last step. To create the relationship you need, open the InvoiceHeaders table in Datasheet view and place the focus in the InvoiceID field so your new field appears to the right of the ID field. Next, click the More Fields button in the Add & Delete group on the Fields contextual tab and then click Lookup & Relationship from the drop-down list of options. Access opens the Lookup Wizard dialog box, as shown in Figure 6-50.

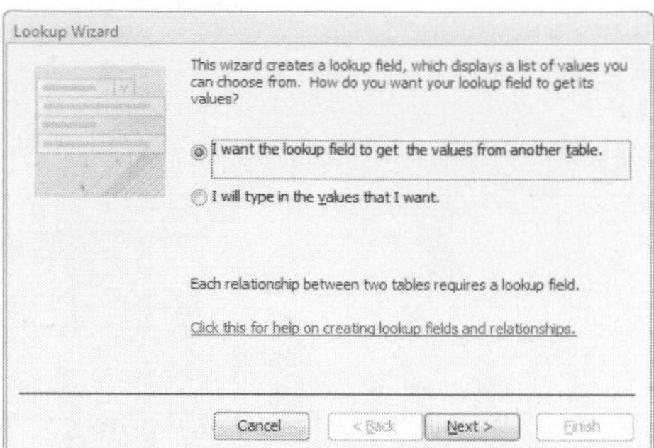

Figure 6-50 To create a new lookup field with a relationship to another web table, you need to select the first option on this page of the Lookup Wizard.

On the first page of the wizard, Access needs to know where you want to fetch the values for this new lookup field. To create a new field that has a relationship between a different web tables, select the first option—I Want The Lookup Field To Get The Values From Another Table. Click Next to proceed to the second page of the wizard, as shown in Figure 6-51.

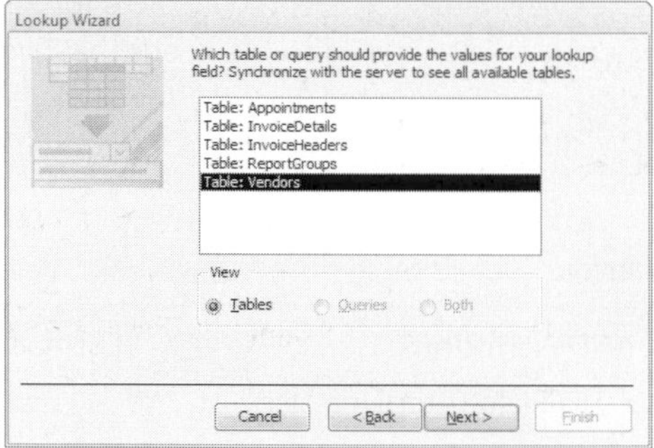

Figure 6-51 Select the Vendors web table to provide a source of data for your new lookup field.

On the second page of the wizard, Access needs to know which web table you want to use to provide the values for your new lookup field. (Note that in web databases, you cannot create relationships between a table and query.) We want to store the vendor who produced the invoice in the InvoiceHeaders web table, so select the Vendors table from the list and then click Next. Access opens the third page of the wizard, as shown in Figure 6-52.

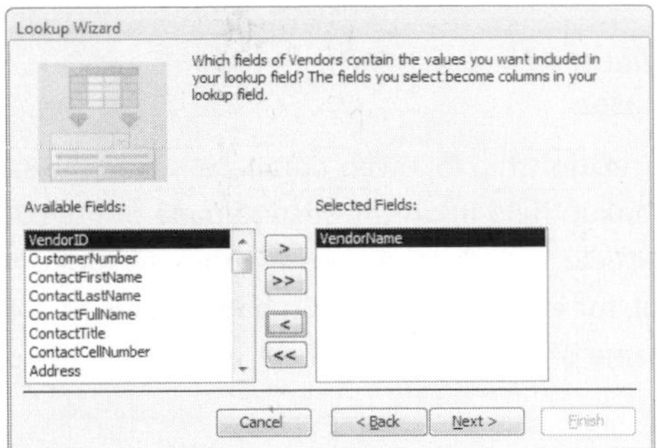

Figure 6-52 You can select more than one column to display in your lookup field by selecting fields from the Available Fields list.

On the third page of the wizard, you can select which field or fields to display in your lookup field. You can select any field in the Available Fields list and click the single right arrow (>) button to copy that field to the Selected Fields list. You can also click the double right arrow (>>) button to copy all available fields to the Selected Fields list. If you copy a field in error, you can select the field in the Selected Fields list and click the single left arrow (<) button to remove the field from the list. You can remove all fields and start over by clicking the double left arrow (<<) button.

INSIDE OUT Using Calculated Fields as Display Values for Lookup Fields

If you want to use a Calculated field as one of the display columns in your Lookup Field for a web database, you can only use Calculated fields that have Text result types. In web databases, Access does not show you any Calculated fields with result types other than Text on the third page of the Lookup Wizard dialog box to choose display columns. However, if you are using a client database, you can use Calculated fields with result types other than text for display values in a Lookup Field.

By default, Access always sets the ID field as the first column in your lookup field. You cannot change this behavior because it is a SharePoint requirement. SharePoint enforces the relationships on the server through the ID field. For your new lookup field, select the VendorName field. (The users of your database will find it much easier to choose a vendor name from a list rather than just a list of vendor ID numbers.) Click Next to proceed to the fourth page of the wizard, as shown in Figure 6-53.

INSIDE OUT Self Join Relationships Are Supported in Web Databases

If you want to create a self join relationship in a web database, select the same table that you are creating the new lookup field in on the second page of the Lookup Wizard. You can then select another field you want to use for your new lookup field. A self join relationship could be useful, for example, when you have a table of employees and one of the fields contains the name of the employee they report to in the organization.

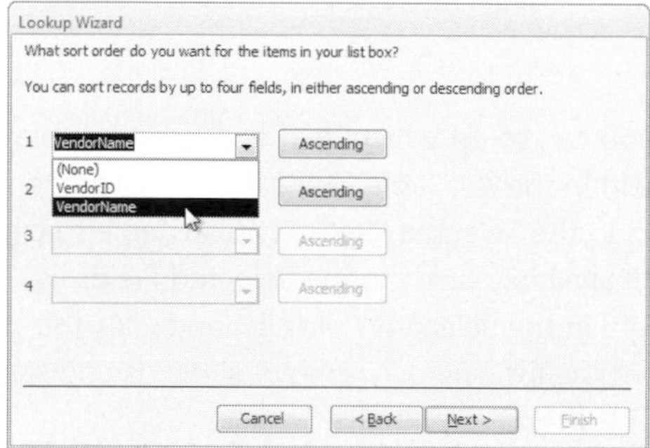

Figure 6-53 Select the VendorName field in the first box to sort the lookup field values in Ascending order.

On the fourth page of the wizard, Access allows you to select up to four fields to sort either Ascending or Descending. Click the arrow to the right of the first field and then select the VendorName field, as shown in Figure 6-53. The button next to the first box indicates *Ascending*. If you click the button, it changes to *Descending*. For now, let's leave it as Ascending. (You can click the button again to set it back.) Click Next to go to the fifth page of the wizard, as shown in Figure 6-54.

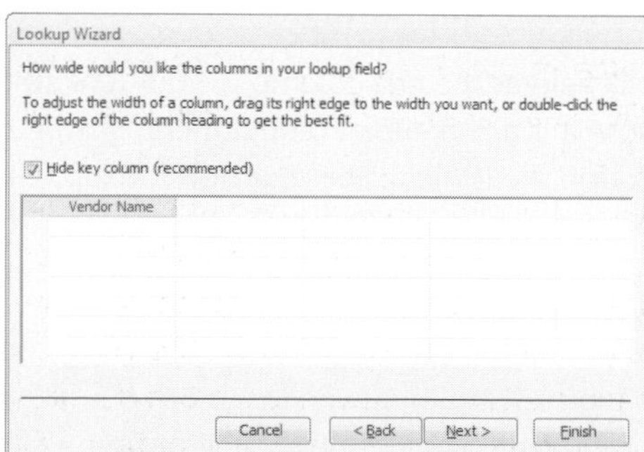

Figure 6-54 On this page of the wizard, you can select to hide the ID column and resize the display columns for your lookup field.

On the fifth page of the wizard, you can choose to hide the key column, which is selected by default. If you clear this option, Access displays the ID field from the Vendors table in your lookup field drop-down list. On the bottom half of the page, you can resize the Vendor Name column by dragging its right edge to the size you want, or you can double-click the right edge of the column and Access adjusts the width to fit the data. Leave these settings as they are and then click Next to proceed to the last page of the wizard, as shown in Figure 6-55. Note that you could click Finish now to exit the Lookup Wizard, but Access would not enforce referential integrity for this field because it is not the default option on the last page of the wizard.

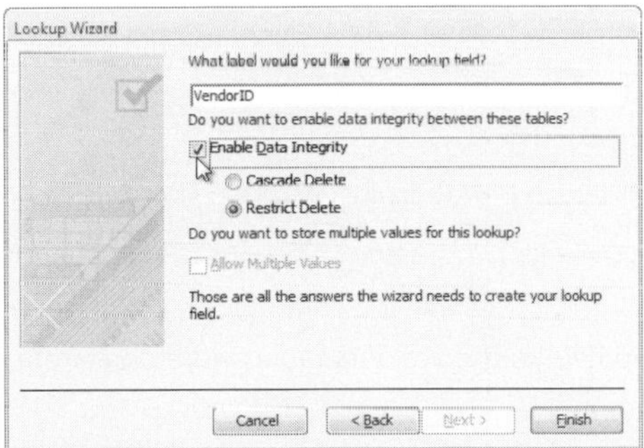

Figure 6-55 Make sure to select the Enable Data Integrity option on the last page of the wizard to maintain referential integrity.

On the last page of the wizard, you can enter a name for your new lookup field. Type **VendorID** for the name of your new lookup field in the text box at the top of the page. Because you probably don't want any rows created in InvoiceHeaders for a nonexistent vendor, select the Enable Data Integrity check box. (Selecting this check box achieves the same functionality as selecting Enforce Referential Integrity in a client database relationship.) When you do this, Access 2010 ensures that you can't add a row in the InvoiceHeaders web table containing an invalid VendorID. Also, Access won't let you delete any records from the Vendors table if they have invoices still defined.

After you select the Enable Data Integrity check box, Access 2010 makes two additional radio buttons available: Cascade Delete and Restrict Delete. If you select the Cascade Delete check box, Access deletes child rows (the related rows in the many table of a one-to-many relationship) when you delete a parent row (the related row in the one table of a one-to-many relationship). For example, if you remove a vendor from the Vendors web table, Access removes all the related InvoiceHeader rows. If you select the Restrict Delete option (the default), Access prevents you from deleting a vendor from the Vendors table if there are invoices in the InvoiceHeaders table that use that vendor. In this design, we don't want to remove all invoices for accounting purposes so leave the default option, Restrict Delete, set.

The last option on this final page of the wizard—Allow Multiple Values—tells Access to create a Multi-Value Lookup Field. You can only select this option if the Enable Data Integrity check box is cleared. Click Finish to complete the steps necessary to create your lookup field with a relationship to the Vendors table. In Figure 6-56, you can see the completed new VendorID lookup field in the InvoiceHeaders web table. Click the Save button on the Quick Access Toolbar to save these latest definition changes.

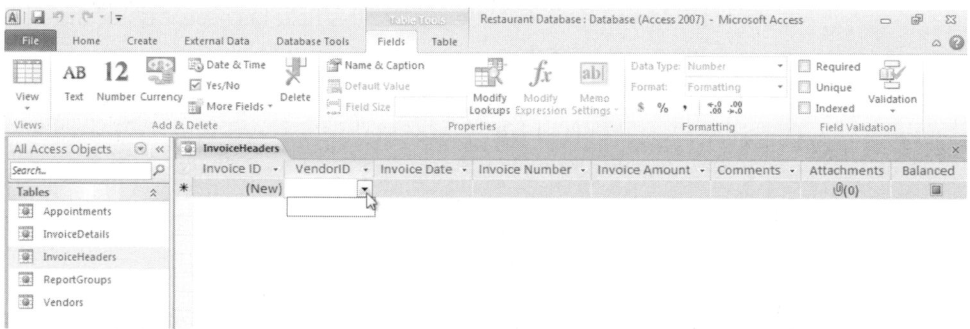

Figure 6-56 You can create a lookup field to the Vendors table and enforce referential integrity for the data.

If you need to modify this lookup field or its relationship, you can highlight the field in Datasheet view, and click the Modify Lookups button in the Properties group on the Fields contextual tab. Access opens the Lookup Wizard to the third page, where you can adjust the field or fields to display in your lookup field. You can adjust the settings for this lookup field on the various wizard pages from this point on and then save the changes. If you want this lookup field to use a different table as its source or use a value list as its source, you'll need to delete the lookup field and recreate a new lookup field by starting over with the Lookup Wizard.

You now know enough to define the additional one-to-many Restrict Delete relationship that you need in the InvoiceDetails web table. You need to include the ReportGroupName field from the ReportGroups web table in the InvoiceDetails web table, so open the InvoiceDetails web table in Datasheet view and set the focus on the InvoiceDetailsID field.

Follow this procedure to build your relationship:

1. Start the Lookup Wizard by clicking More Fields and then clicking Lookup & Relationship.
2. On the first page of the wizard, select the I Want The Lookup Field To Get The Values From Another Table option, and then click Next.
3. On the second page of the wizard, select the ReportGroups web table, and then click Next.

4. On the third page of the wizard, bring over the ReportGroupName field from the Available Fields list to the Selected Fields list, and then click Next.

5. On the fourth page of the wizard, select the ReportGroupName field in the drop-down list to sort Ascending by that field, and then click Next.

6. On the fifth page of the wizard, leave the default options as they are to hide the key column and keep the widths the same. Click Next to go to the final page of the wizard.

7. On the last page of the wizard, name your field **ReportGroupID** and select the Enable Data Integrity option. Leave the default option, Restrict Delete, set, and then click Finish to complete the new field and relationship.

8. Finally, save your changes to the InvoiceDetails web table.

INSIDE OUT **SharePoint Lists Support Only 20 Indexes**

SharePoint lists support a maximum of 20 indexes, so you need to take this into account when deciding which fields to index. The SharePoint ID field and each Lookup Field you create all count toward the 20-index limit. If you attempt to publish a table with more than 20 indexes to a SharePoint site, Access stops the publish process and reports the error.

Defining a Cascade Delete Relationship

There's one last relationship you need to define in the Restaurant Database between InvoiceDetails and InvoiceHeaders. The relationship between these two tables requires a Cascade Delete relationship. We want to ensure that when an invoice is deleted in the InvoiceHeaders web table (the *one* side of the relationship) that all corresponding child records in the InvoiceDetails web table (the *many* side of the relationship) are deleted.

Follow this procedure to build your Cascade Delete relationship:

1. You want to include the InvoiceNumber field in the InvoiceDetails web table, so open the InvoiceDetails web table in Datasheet view and set the focus on the InvoiceDetailsID field. Start the Lookup Wizard by clicking More Fields and then clicking Lookup & Relationship.

2. On the first page of the wizard, select the I Want The Lookup Field To Get The Values From Another Table option, and then click Next.

3. On the second page of the wizard, select the InvoiceHeaders web table, and then click Next.

4. On the third page of the wizard, bring over the InvoiceNumber field from the Available Fields list to the Selected Fields list, and then click Next.

5. On the fourth page of the wizard, select the InvoiceNumber field in the drop-down list to sort Ascending by that field, and then click Next.

6. On the fifth page of the wizard, leave the default options as they are to hide the key column and keep the widths the same. Click Next to go to the final page of the wizard.

7. On the last page of the wizard, shown here, name your field **InvoiceID** and select the Enable Data Integrity option. Select the Cascade Delete option, and then click Finish to complete the new field and relationship.

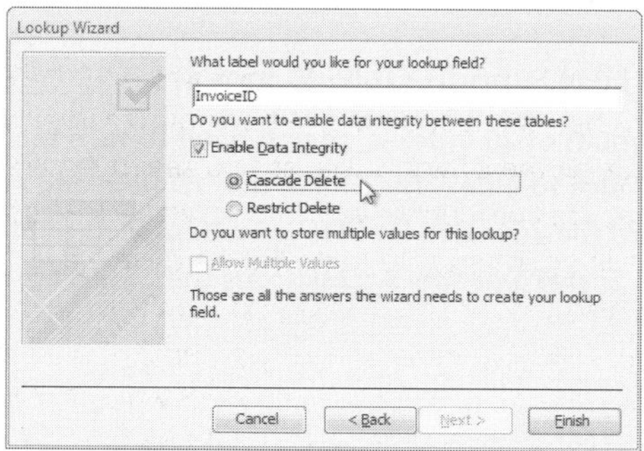

8. Finally, save your changes to the InvoiceDetails web table.

Your completed InvoiceDetails web table should now look like Figure 6-57.

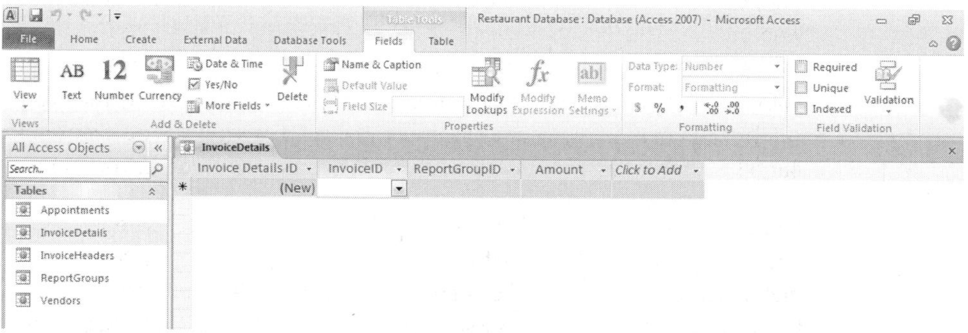

Figure 6-57 You now have two lookup fields to two different web tables in your InvoiceDetails table.

The sample web database, called RestaurantSample.accdb, on the companion CD, contains all the web tables you created in this chapter if you want to compare the results of your work.

INSIDE OUT **Viewing Web Relationships Limitation**

One of the shortcomings of creating relationships in web databases is that you cannot view the Relationships window as you can in client databases. As a result, you cannot run the Relationships Report option to get a nice graphical printout of all the relationships in your web database.

Using the Web Compatibility Checker

Access Services does not support all the data types, relationships, properties, controls, objects, and events that the Access rich client supports. When you create a web database from scratch or use a web template, all the design surfaces you see in Access are designed to show you only the elements that are compatible with the server. Microsoft created these design surfaces for web databases in an attempt to keep Access developers from creating controls, objects, etc. that are not web-legal. It is still possible, however, to create elements in a web database that are not web-legal. If you create an element that is not web-legal and publish it to the server, Access Services does not understand what to do with it and you'll most likely see an error. In more extreme cases, you would be unsuccessful in publishing your database to the server.

To help prevent Access developers from publishing elements to the server that are not supported by Access Services, Access 2010 includes a tool called the Web Compatibility Checker. This tool checks the web compatibility of all the tables in a database as well as any web objects. This tool, however, does not check any data in the tables nor does it attempt to check any client objects other than local tables. If you attempt to run the Web Compatibility Checker on a client object other than a table, you'll actually receive no errors, which can be a bit misleading. The tool, in fact, did not even run on the client object. The Compatibility Checker also does not check any linked tables to other data sources.

You can think of the Web Compatibility Checker tool as a gatekeeper, always making sure your objects are web-legal before you publish your database to the server, import objects into a web database, or make changes to existing objects and try to send those changes to the server. If the tool finds issues during any of those actions, Access aborts the process. You'll learn all about publishing a web database to the server and syncing changes in Chapter 22.

Analyzing the Web Compatibility Issues Table

To run the Web Compatibility Checker on the web database you created, click the File tab on the Backstage view and then click Save & Publish. Next, click Publish To Access Services and then click Run Compatibility Checker, as shown in Figure 6-58.

> **Note**
>
> **All database objects must be closed before the Web Compatibility Checker tool can begin to scan your database. If you have any objects open, the tool displays a message box informing you it needs to close all open objects. Click Yes in this dialog box, and Access closes all open objects and then begins to scan your database.**

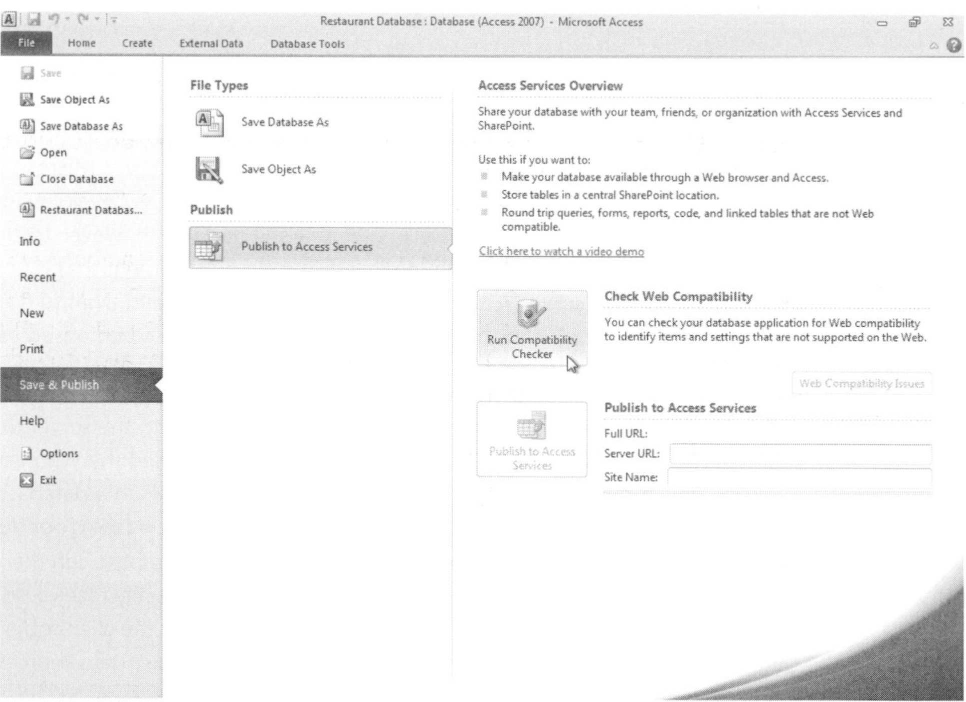

Figure 6-58 You can run the Web Compatibility Checker from the Backstage view.

The Web Compatibility Checker scans each table's schema and every web object, control, and property in your web database. In general, the Web Compatibility Checker checks your database in the following order: table schema, queries, macros, forms, reports, and then relationships. Note, however, that the order can deviate based on the dependencies of the various objects in your database.

If the Web Compatibility Checker tool finds any issues in your database, the tool creates a new table, called Web Compatibility Issues, and lists any incompatibilities found in your web database in this table. Every time you run the Web Compatibility Checker, Access deletes any existing Web Compatibility Issues table and then creates a new table. If the tool does not find any incompatibilities in your web database, Access deletes the Web Compatibility Issues table when it completes the scan of your database. Access then displays the message, "The database is compatible with the Web," below the Run Compatibility Checker button on the Backstage, as shown in Figure 6-59.

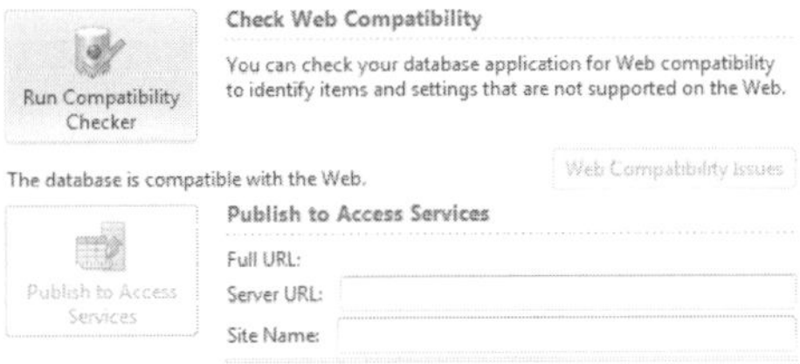

Figure 6-59 Access displays a success message on the Backstage view if the Web Compatibility Checker did not find any issues with your web database.

If the Web Compatibility Checker finds any issues in your web database, Access changes the background color around the Run Compatibility Checker button on the Backstage to red, as shown in Figure 6-60. Access also displays the message, "The database is incompatible with the Web. Press 'Web Compatibility Issues' to see errors," to indicate it found at least one issue. Finally, Access enables the Web Compatibility Issues button on the Backstage view.

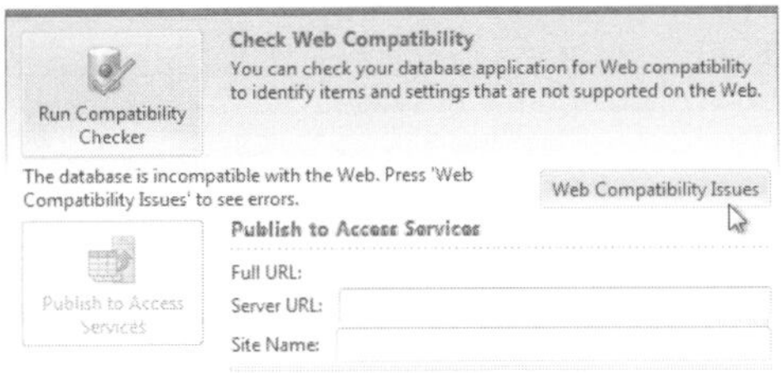

Figure 6-60 Access informs you if the Web Compatibility Checker found any issues in your web database.

Click Web Compatibility Issues on the Backstage view, and Access closes the Backstage view and opens a new table, called Web Compatibility Issues, in Datasheet view, as shown in Figure 6-61.

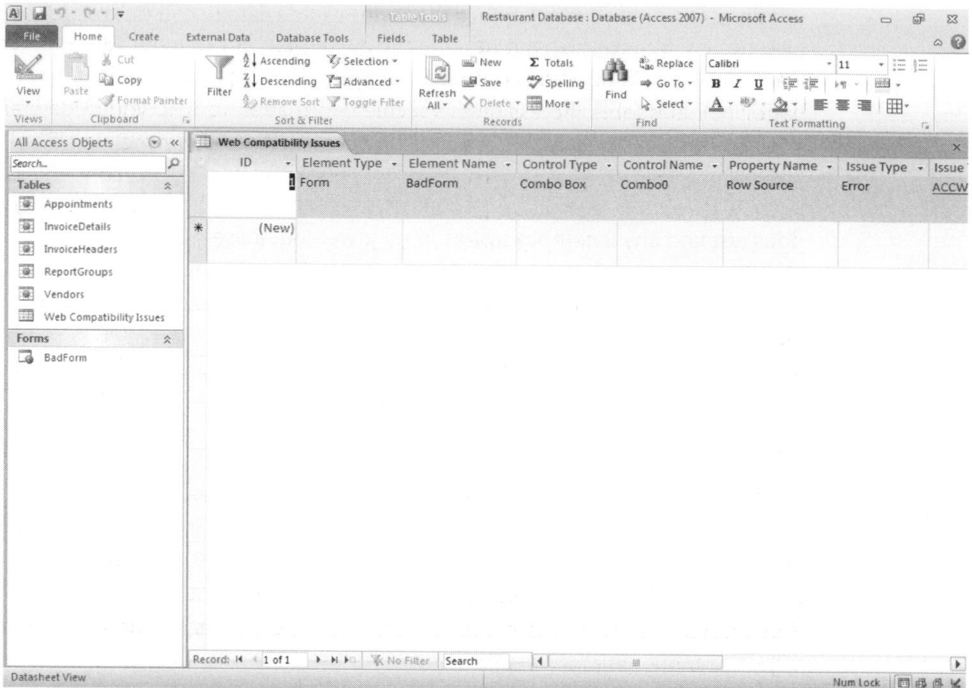

Figure 6-61 The Web Compatibility Issues table list any incompatibilities that the Web Compatibility Checker found in your web database.

The Web Compatibility Issues table contains the following fields: Element Type, Element Name, Control Type, Control Name, Property Name, Issue Type, Issue Type ID, and Description. You cannot see all the information in this table in Figure 6-61, so we've reproduced the information in Table 6-10.

Table 6-10 Sample Web Compatibility Issues Table Results

Field Name	Data
Element Type	Form
Element Name	BadForm
Control Type	Combo Box
Control Name	Combo0
Property Name	Row Source
Issue Type	Error
Issue Type ID	AccWeb103906
Description	The definition of the query is invalid, so the query object cannot be created.

In this example, we created a new web form called BadForm. On this form, we created a new Combo Box control that has a Row Source pointing to a nonexistent web table. (You'll learn all about Combo Box controls in Chapter 12.) If you look at the data in the Web Compatibility Issues table, Access gives specific information to help you understand what you need to fix to make the database web compatible. Access lists the specific object type (a form, in this case), the object name, the control type, the specific control name (Combo0), and the specific property that is causing the error (the Row Source property). The description field lists more detailed information about the specific error.

The Issue Type ID field is a hyperlink that points to a specific error ID assigned to the particular error. When you click on the Issue Type ID hyperlink, Access directs you to a help topic for more information. The help topics concerning web compatibility issues fall into seven categories—General, Schema, Relationships and Lookups, Queries, Forms and Reports, Expressions, and Macros.

You'll need to fix all the errors listed in the Web Compatibility Issues table before your web database can be completely web compatible. You should start by fixing any errors concerning the tables in your database. The reason for fixing table errors first is because the Web Compatibility Checker tool lists an error for any object that depends on another object that is incompatible. For example, suppose you have five forms in a database that all depend on a specific table. Let's also assume that the table is incompatible with the server. When you run the Web Compatibility Checker tool, the Web Compatibility Issues table lists one error for the table as well as one error for each of the five forms because the forms depend on that table. You could be wasting your time trying to fix forms when the real reason for the error is the object the form depends on.

To minimize your time spent trying to fix any errors in the Web Compatibility Issues table, we recommend an iterative process—fix several errors and then run the Web Compatibility Checker tool again. Always start with fixing several table-related errors first and then run the tool again to see the result of your changes. If the tool still finds errors, fix more table issues and then run the tool again. Once you fix all the compatibility errors concerning tables, you might find that everything in your database is now web compatible. If you still have issues remaining, fix any errors concerning query objects next, because forms and reports can depend on queries, and then run the tool again. Finally, move on to fixing any errors concerning forms, reports, and macros.

You can also run the Web Compatibility Checker on a single object in your web database. Right-click a table or web object in the Navigation pane and then click Check Web Compatibility from the shortcut menu, as shown in Figure 6-62.

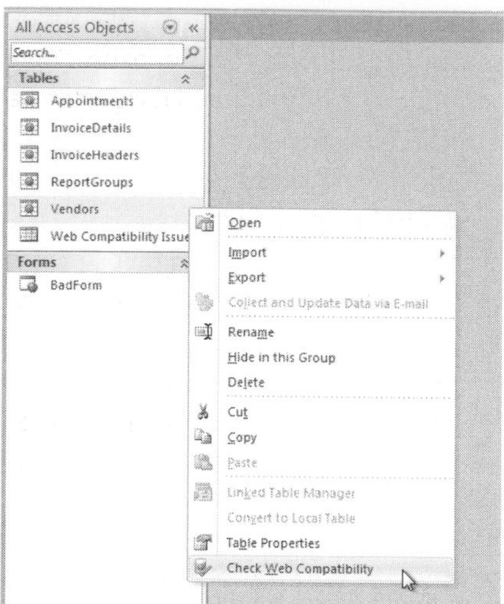

Figure 6-62 You can run the Web Compatibility Checker tool on a single object from the shortcut menu.

If the Web Compatibility Checker finds no issues with the specific object you selected, Access displays a success message, as shown in Figure 6-63.

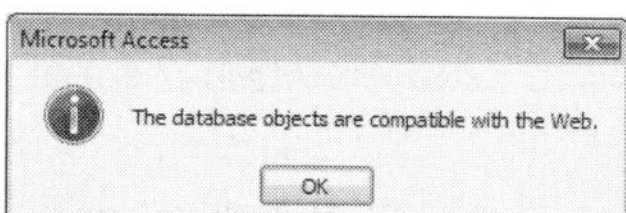

Figure 6-63 The Web Compatibility Checker displays this message if no errors are found in the object you selected to scan.

If the Web Compatibility Checker does find at least one error in the object you selected, Access displays a notification dialog box indicating it found issues with the object, as shown in Figure 6-64. You'll then see a new Web Compatibility Issues table in the Navigation pane, where you can diagnose exactly what the issues are with the object.

Figure 6-64 The Web Compatibility Checker displays this error message if issues are found in the object you selected.

When the Web Compatibility Checker finds no errors in your web database, the tool deletes any existing Web Compatibility Issues table from the Navigation pane. You can also delete this table at any time yourself by highlighting the table in the Navigation pane and pressing Delete.

Preparing a Client Database for the Web

If you create a new web database from scratch or use a web database template, you are less likely to encounter any errors when you run the Web Compatibility Checker tool because you start out within a confined design surface. But what happens if you have an existing client database and want to publish it to a SharePoint server running Access Services to make it a web application? If you have a client database you want to publish to the server, your first step is to run the Web Compatibility Checker.

In the previous section, we mentioned the Web Compatibility Checker checks all local tables and web objects. In a client database, this means the Web Compatibility Checker tool only checks the local tables because the other objects will remain client objects. To publish to the server, you need all the schema in your database to be web compatible. The Web Compatibility Checker tool helps you migrate existing client databases to the server by showing what changes you need to make to your tables for the database to successfully publish to a SharePoint server. (In Chapter 22, you'll learn how to publish databases to a SharePoint server.)

Let's use one of the built-in client database templates to illustrate this process. Close any databases you have open by clicking the File tab on the Backstage view and then click Close Database. Next, click the Sample Templates button on the New tab to show all the built-in local templates, as shown in Figure 6-65. Finally, click the Faculty client template in the center of the screen, select a location to save this new database, and then click Create to create the new client database.

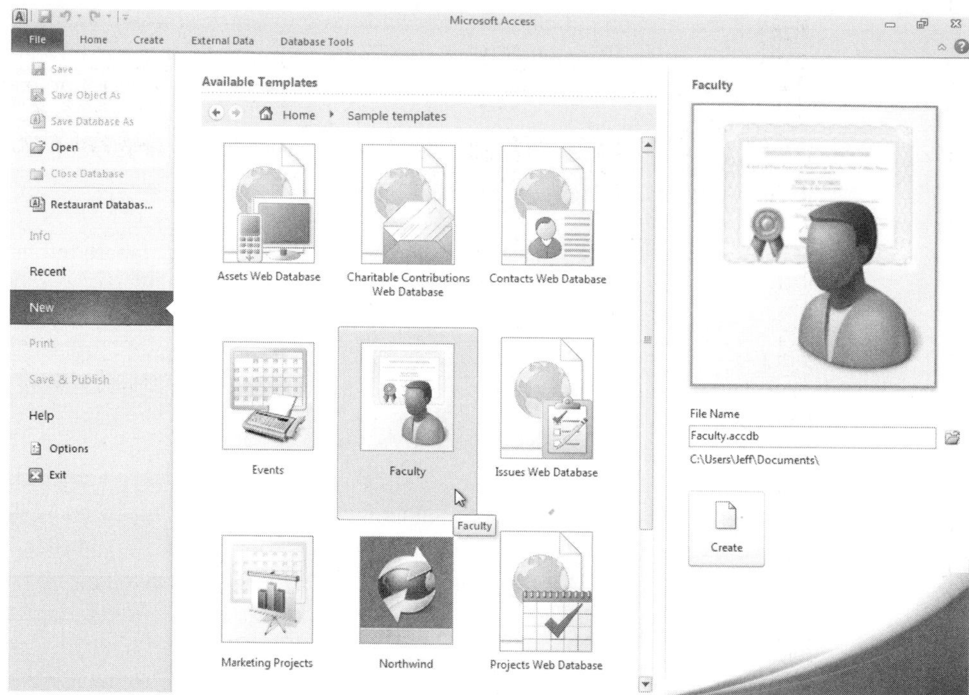

Figure 6-65 Click the Faculty button in the Sample Templates section to create a client database.

Access creates the new client database and displays the startup form for the database—the Faculty List form. To run the Web Compatibility Checker on your client database, click the File tab on the Backstage view and then click Save & Publish. Next, click Publish To Access Services and then click Run Compatibility Checker. Note that Access prompts you to close all open objects before it begins to scan the database. Click Yes on the dialog box prompt, and the Web Compatibility Checker tool now scans your client database. Once it completes the scan, Access reports on the Backstage view that your database is incompatible with the web, as shown in Figure 6-60. Click the Web Compatibility Issues button on the Backstage view and Access opens the Web Compatibility Issues table, shown in Figure 6-66. Note that in Figure 6-66, we resized the columns in the table so you can see all the data.

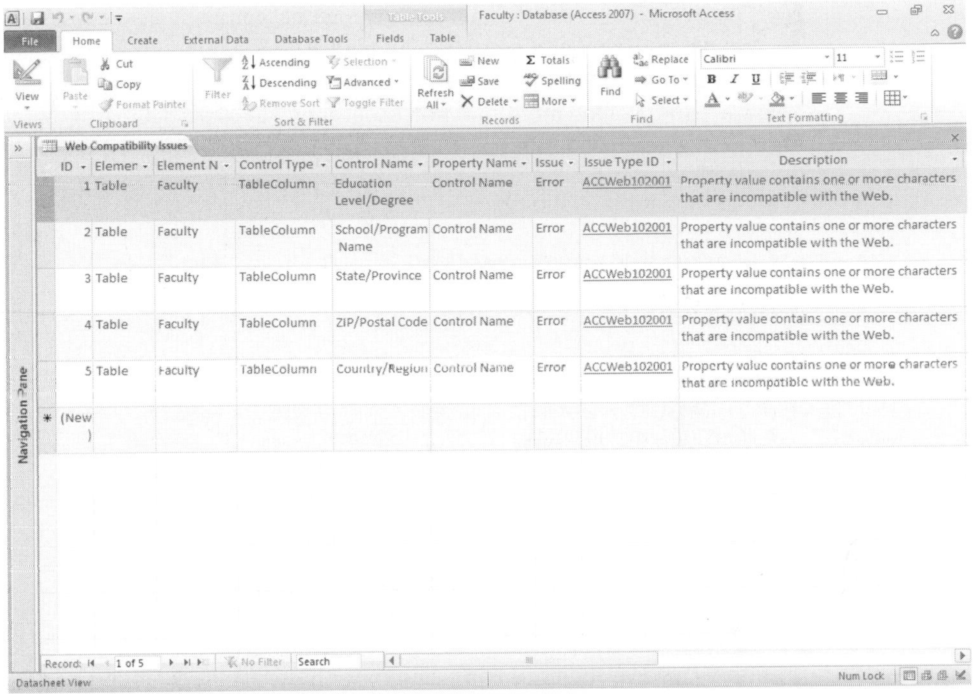

Figure 6-66 The Compatibility Checker reports any issues with tables in client databases.

The Web Compatibility Checker found five issues with the Faculty table in this client database. If you look at the Description field for each error, you'll notice that each error is identical. In this client database, the Web Compatibility Checker found five field names that are incompatible with the server. Specifically, each of these five field names contains the forward slash character (/), which is incompatible with the server. To fix these issues, you can open the Faculty table in Design view or Datasheet view and remove the forward slash character from each of the five field names listed in the Web Compatibility Issues table—Education Level/Degree, School/Program Name, State/Province, ZIP/Postal Code, and Country/Region. After you make these changes to the Faculty table and save your changes, you can run the Web Compatibility Checker tool again. You'll now receive a successful message on the Backstage view that your client database is compatible with the web. Note that because you changed field names in the table, you should verify that the rest of the application still functions.

Most existing client databases have more potential compatibility issues than just invalid column names. The Web Compatibility Checker does a good job of providing specific help topics to inform you what you need to change to make your schema web-legal. Listed below are some of the more common issues found in client databases that you might encounter when trying to prepare your database for the web:

- Incompatible relationships
- Lookup field row sources
- Primary keys that are not Number that have the Field Size property set to Long
- Composite indexes
- Custom field formats
- Subdatasheets
- Other field properties

Before making any changes to your client tables, we recommend creating a backup copy of your database in case you need to refer to the original. In general, most of the issues you'll need to fix involve adding, editing, or removing specific field properties. To fix these issues, you need to open the client table in Design view and make the appropriate changes. For errors concerning relationships, you'll need to take additional steps to fix these errors, especially if you have existing data in your client tables. First, you'll need to open the Relationships window and delete the offending relationships. Next, you'll need to make sure you have an appropriate Primary Key. The simplest solution here is to add a new AutoNumber field to your client table, if one does not already exist, and make that field the Primary Key. You should then use the Lookup Wizard to create relationships to other tables. If you have existing data in your tables, you'll also need to run some action queries to adjust the data so all the parent and child data is mapped correctly. You'll learn all about creating action queries in Chapter 11, "Modifying Data with Action Queries."

In this chapter, you've taken the first steps to learn how to create a web database. You've learned how to create a web database from scratch and create your schema and relationships between different web tables. You've also learned how to use the Web Compatibility Checker tool to verify your tables are web compatible. In Chapter 7, you'll learn how to add logic to tables by creating data macros and attaching them to table events.

CHAPTER 7

Creating Table Data Macros

In Microsoft Access 2010, you can define a data macro to respond to different types of table events that would otherwise require the use of writing Microsoft Visual Basic code or the creation of macros attached to forms and reports. The unique power of data macros in Access 2010 is their ability to automate responses to several types of table events without forcing you to learn a programming language. The event might be a change in the data, the creation of a new record, or even the deletion of an existing record. Within a data macro, you can include multiple actions and define condition checking so that different actions are performed depending on the values in your table fields or criteria you specify.

As you'll learn in Chapter 24, "Understanding Visual Basic Fundamentals," (on the companion CD) you can use Visual Basic to perform any functionality that you can create in a data macro. However, even if you think you're ready to jump right into Visual Basic, you should study all the data macro actions first. Learning data macros is an excellent introduction to programming in Access in general.

Note

The examples in this chapter are based on the backup copy of the Back Office Software System sample web database (BOSSDataCopy.accdb) on the companion CD included with this book. The results you see from the samples in this chapter might not exactly match what you see in this book if you have changed the sample data in the files. Also, all the screen images in this chapter were taken on a Windows 7 system with the Access display theme set to Silver. Your results might look different if you are using a different operating system or a different theme.

In this chapter, you will:

- Learn about the various types of actions that you can define in data macros and the table events that you can use.
- Tour the new logic designer facility and learn how to build both a simple data macro and a data macro with multiple defined actions.
- Learn how to create local variables in data macros to store values temporarily or calculate a result.
- See how to define parameters and use them inside data macro actions.
- Learn how to create return variables in data macros to return data to the calling macro.
- See how to add conditional statements to a data macro to control the actions that Access performs.
- Learn how to create named data macros and execute them from other data macros or table events.
- Understand some of the actions automated with data macros in the Back Office Software System sample web database.

Uses of Data Macros

Access 2010 provides various types of data macro actions that you can attach to table events to automate your application. With data macros, you can:

- Verify that an invoice is balanced with the invoice detail line items before saving the record.
- Mark an employee as inactive after you create a termination record.
- Prevent a record from being saved if it violates a composite key index.
- Send an email to the database administrator if an unexpected error occurs within the application.
- Prevent any data from being edited, added, or deleted from a table.

- Email individual employee schedule details to all employees.
- Create new schedule records based on the previous week's schedule or a labor plan template.
- Delete all schedule records within a specific time frame.

As you'll learn in Chapter 20, "Automating a Client Application Using Macros," and Chapter 21, "Automating a Web Application Using Macros," Access 2010 supports user interface macros to control application flow in your forms and reports and to respond to user actions. You can also utilize user interface macros, as well as Visual Basic, to enforce complex business logic that might not be covered by table relationships, unique properties, validation rules, and required properties. The potential problem with using user interface macros and Visual Basic to enforce complex business logic, however, is that you don't always have complete control over how users interact with the data in your tables. For example, users can add, update, and delete data through queries. Users can also link to the tables in one Access database file from another Access file and add, update, and delete data from that database. In both of these examples, users can bypass your complex business logic rules normally stored in user interface macros and Visual Basic code. (You'll learn all about queries in Part 3, "Building Queries," and linking Access files in Chapter 8, "Importing and Linking Data.")

Access 2010 introduces a new type of macro, called *data macros*, to provide a place for Access developers to centralize all their business logic and rules. Data macros are similar to triggers in Microsoft SQL Server because they allow you to attach business logic directly to table events. However, unlike triggers in SQL Server, data macros are not performed within a transactional context—each operation is separate. Data macros respond to data modifications, so no matter how users edit data in the database, Access enforces those rules. This means you can write business logic in one place, and all the data entry forms and Visual Basic code that update those tables inherit that logic from the data layer. Once you create a data macro for a table event, Access runs the data macro no matter how you change the data.

Data macros in Access 2010 can be used in both client and web databases. In fact, the events, actions, and properties that you can use in data macros are identical between client and web databases, so you can easily reuse data macros that you defined in a client database for use in a web database. The Access database engine enforces data macros when you work with a client database. When you publish a web database to a Microsoft SharePoint 2010 server, Access Services enforces data macros on the server through the use of SharePoint Workflow actions.

INSIDE OUT **Important Considerations Using Data Macros**

When you're adding data macro logic to your client and web tables, you need to be aware of these important issues:

- You cannot call Visual Basic code from a data macro; however, you can call a named data macro from Visual Basic and pass in parameters.
- If you upsize your database to SQL Server, Access cannot upsize the data macro logic.
- Data macros cannot process data from multi-valued fields or attachment fields.
- Access 2007 Service Pack 1 can read but not write data in linked Access 2010 tables that include data macros because the Access 2007 data engine can't execute them.
- You cannot create data macros on linked tables; you must create the data macro logic in the ACCDB that contains the local tables.

The Data Macro Design Facility—An Overview

The following sections explain how to work with the macro design facility in Access 2010.

Redesigning the Macro Window from Previous Versions of Access

In Access 2010, Microsoft has completely redesigned the design surface for creating macros. In Figure 7-1, you can see an example of the macro design window from Access 2007. In the upper part of the older macro window, you defined your macro, and in the lower part, you entered settings, called *arguments*, for the actions that you selected for your macro. The upper part of the macro window showed five columns—Macro Name, Condition, Action, Arguments, and Comment.

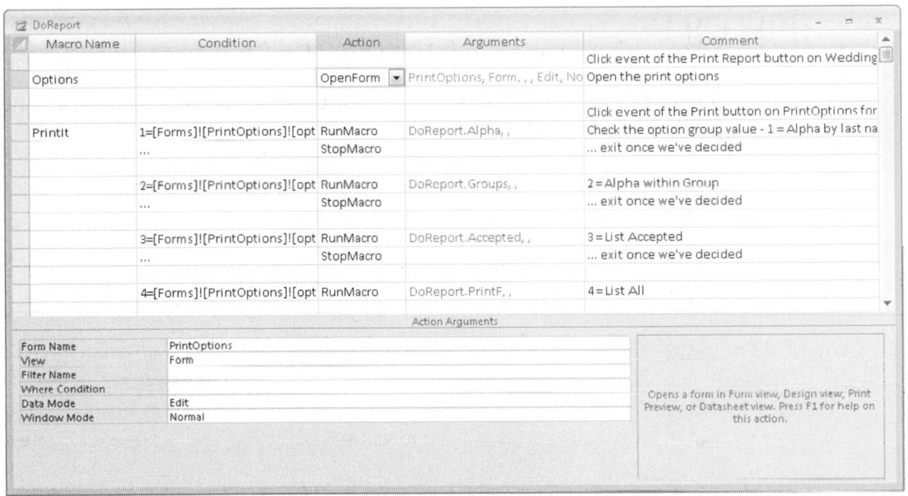

Figure 7-1 This is the macro design window in Access 2007.

Although functional, the older macro design window was not the most intuitive interface to work with. For example, when you wanted to create a new action for a macro, you selected the action in the upper part of the window, but you entered the arguments in the bottom part of the window. The Arguments column in the upper part of the window was read-only, so you constantly needed to switch from the top window to the bottom window. You also could not create complex nested logic conditions for your macro execution, and the readability of the macro elements was difficult to follow.

In Access 2010, Microsoft redesigned the macro design window so that Access developers could be more productive when creating macros in their applications. The Access development team at Microsoft studied user interactions with the older macro design window and came up with five main goals in their redesign:

- Increase productivity of application developers by adding features such as the Action Catalog, IntelliSense for writing expressions, support for copy and paste, and keyboard accessibility improvements.
- Support more complex logic execution with macros by allowing nested `If/Else/Else If` constructs.
- Increase the readability of macros by having the macro design surface display the program flow more like Visual Basic code.
- Create macros faster by reusing existing macros in other parts of the database.
- Support the ability to share macros easily with other users and other applications through the use of Extensible Markup Language (XML).

Touring the New Logic Designer

Open the Back Office Software System backup copy sample web database (BOSSDataCopy.accdb) from the folder where you installed the sample files. As you'll learn in Chapter 20, a special user interface macro called *Autoexec* runs each time you open the database. This user interface macro determines whether the database is trusted, opens an informational form for a few seconds, and then closes the informational form so you can see the Navigation pane.

To create data macros, you first need to open a local client table in Design or Datasheet view, or a web table in Datasheet view. To display all the tables in your BOSSDataCopy.accdb web database, click the bar at the top of the Navigation pane, click Object Type under Navigate To Category and then click Tables under Filter By Group. Double-click the table called tblCompanyInformation to open it in Datasheet view and then click the Table contextual ribbon tab under Table Tools to see the data macro events, as shown in Figure 7-2.

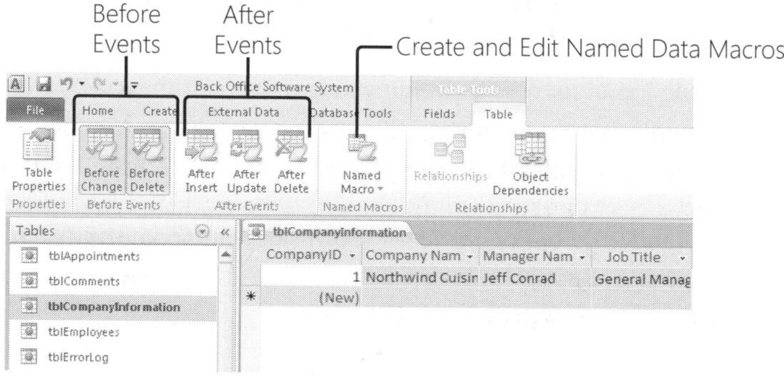

Figure 7-2 Data macro events are listed on the Table contextual ribbon tab in web databases.

If you are working in the client database, you can add and edit data macros from Design view as well. When you have a local client table open in Design View, Access displays a group called Field, Record, & Table Events on the Design contextual ribbon tab. Click the

Create Data Macros button on the Design tab and Access displays a list of the data macro events. In Figure 7-3, you can see an example of a table in the Housing Reservations client database opened in Design view and the table events listed, after clicking Create Data Macros.

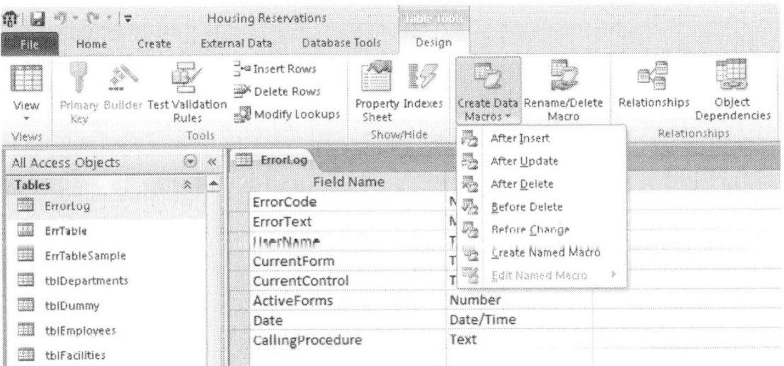

Figure 7-3 Data macro events are listed under the Create Data Macros button on the Design contextual ribbon tab in table Design view for client databases.

You can attach data macros to the Before Change, Before Delete, After Insert, After Update, and After Delete events of tables. In Figure 7-2, with the Back Office Software System sample web database, you can see that Access highlighted the Before Change and Before Delete buttons on the Table contextual ribbon tab. When you create and save a data macro for a table event, Access highlights that event button in the ribbon as a visual cue for you to show that a data macro already exists for that event.

To create a new data macro for a table event or edit an existing one, you click the corresponding event button in the ribbon. Let's explore the existing data macro that we defined for the Before Change event in the tblCompanyInformation table to show you the new Logic Designer for creating macros. Click the Before Change button on the Table contextual ribbon tab, and Access opens the new Logic Designer, as shown in Figure 7-4.

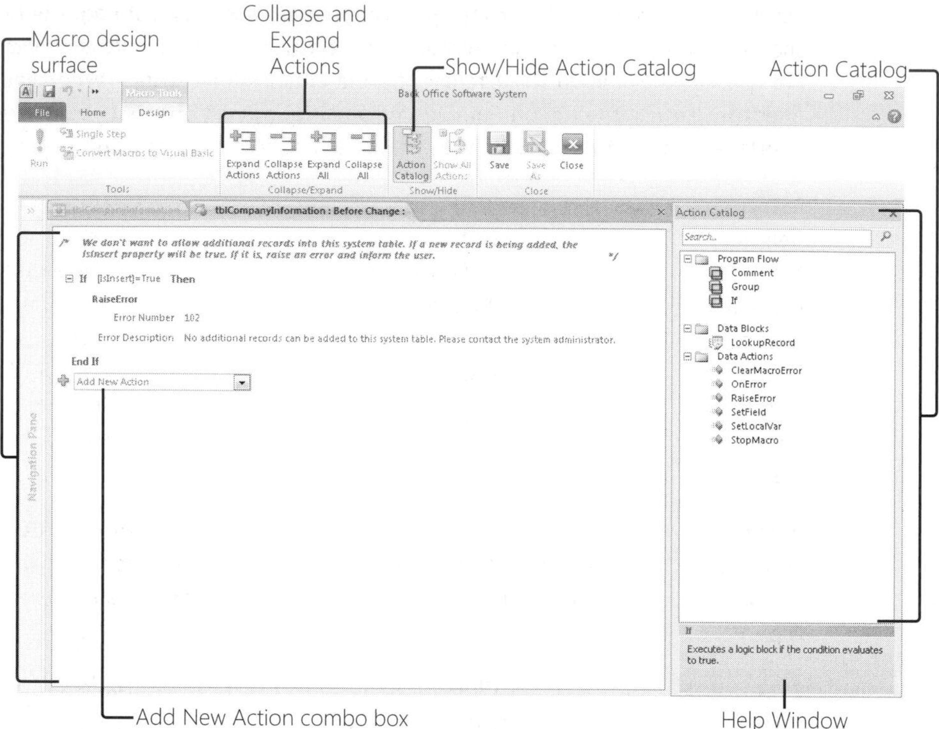

Figure 7-4 This is the new Logic Designer, where you can create data and user interface macros.

Whenever you need to create or edit data macros or user interface macros in Access 2010, this is the design surface that you use. Access selectively enables or disables the buttons on the Design contextual tab under Macro Tools based on whether you are working with data macros or user interface macros. (In Chapters 20 and 21, you'll learn how to work with the Logic Designer to create and edit user interface macros.) You'll notice Access automatically collapsed the Navigation pane to show you more of the macro designer surface. Access also opens the Logic Designer window modally, which means that you cannot open any other database objects until you close the designer window.

As you can see in Figure 7-4, the new Logic Designer layout looks more like a Visual Basic code window. The Expand Actions, Collapse Actions, Expand All, and Collapse All buttons in the Collapse/Expand group selectively expand or collapse the actions listed in the macro designer surface. In the Show/Hide group on the Design tab, you can choose to hide the Action Catalog shown on the right side of the Logic Designer window by clicking the Action Catalog toggle button. In the Close group, you can click Save to save any changes to your data macro. Click Close to close the Logic Designer window for now. Note that if you attempt to close the Logic Designer window with unsaved changes, Access asks if you want to save your changes before closing the window.

On the right side of the Logic Designer window is the Action Catalog. The Action Catalog shows a contextual list of the program flow constructs, data blocks, and data actions that are applicable to the data macro event you are currently viewing. (When you create user interface macros, the Action Catalog similarly displays actions that you can use for user interface macros.) We'll discuss the Action Catalog in more detail in the next section.

In the middle of the Logic Designer window is the main macro designer surface where you define your data macro. You add program flow constructs, macro actions, and arguments to the designer surface to instruct Access what actions to take for the data macro. If you have more actions than can fit on the screen, Access provides a scroll bar on the right side of the macro design surface so you can scroll down to see the rest of your actions. You'll notice in Figure 7-4 that Access displays any arguments directly beneath the action. Access displays a combo box called Add New Action at the bottom of the macro designer surface. This combo box displays a list of all the actions you can use for the type of data macro you are creating.

In the bottom right corner of the Logic Designer window is the Help window. Access displays a brief help message in this window depending upon where the focus is located in the Action Catalog. (Remember, you can always press F1 to open a context-sensitive Help topic.)

Click the Close button in the Close group on the Design contextual tab to return to the Datasheet view of the tblCompanyInformation web table, and then close the table.

Working with Before Events

As we mentioned in the previous section, you can attach data macros to the Before Change, Before Delete, After Insert, After Update, and After Delete events of tables. In the following sections, you'll learn about the Before Change and Before Delete events, create new data macros attached to events, and examine other data macros attached to these events in the Back Office Software System sample web database.

In Before events, you can look at the incoming values in the current record and compare them with a record in other tables using the LookupRecord data block. You can also use the SetField data action to alter data before Access commits the changes, but only on the incoming row of data, not on a record returned from the LookupRecord data block. In Before events, you can also prevent a record from being saved or deleted and display custom error messages to the user using the RaiseError data action. Before events are designed to be fast operations, which means the actions and data blocks that you can use in these events are more limited. For example, you cannot iterate over a collection of records in Before events or call named data macros.

Before Change

The Before Change event fires whenever you add new records to a table or when you update data in an existing record. Let's create a new data macro attached to the Before Change event of the tblWeekDays table to illustrate the process of creating, saving, and testing a new data macro. Open the tblWeekDays table in Datasheet view, click the Table contextual tab under Table Tools, and then click the Before Change button in the Before Events group to open the Logic Designer, as shown in Figure 7-5.

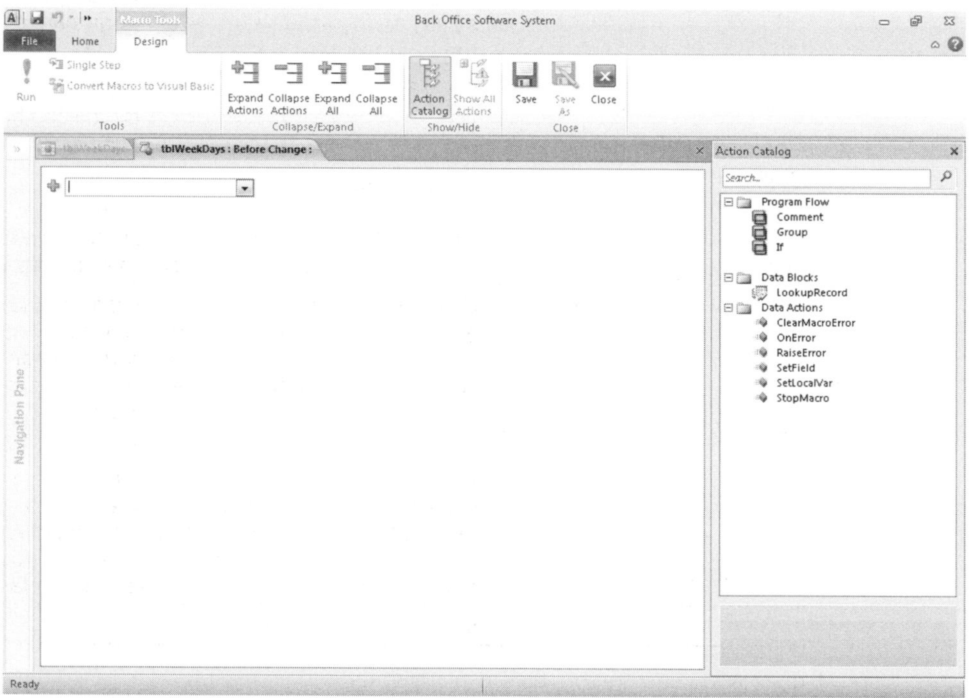

Figure 7-5 Click the Before Change button on the ribbon to begin creating your data macro.

In the Action Catalog on the right side of the Logic Designer, you can see three options under Program Flow, one option under Data Block, and six options under Data Actions. The three program flow options—Comment, Group, and If—are available in all data macro events, but the options under Data Blocks and Data Actions change based on whether you are using a Before event or an After event. Table 7-1 summarizes the data blocks and data actions that you can use in the Before events—Before Change and Before Delete.

Table 7-1 Data Blocks and Data Actions Available to Before Events

Element	Name	Description
Data Blocks	LookupRecord	Instructs Access to look up a record in the same table, a different table, or in a query. In Before events, you can inspect the values in another table or query using the LookupRecord data block, but you cannot change any values in the other table or query.
Data Actions	ClearMacroError	Clears any information stored in the MacroError object, including the error number, error description, macro name, action name, condition, and any arguments. Access resets the error number to 0 after you run this action.
	OnError	Specifies how Access should handle an error when running your data macro. In Before events, you can have the data macro halt execution if an error occurs or you can skip to the next action.
	RaiseError	Displays a custom message to the user interface level and cancels the event changes. You can use this action to manually throw an error and cancel an insert, update, or delete.
	SetField	Changes the value of a field. You can use the SetField action, for example, to change the value of another field in the same record before committing the changes. Note that you cannot use SetField in before events to change values in other tables using the LookupRecord data block.
	SetLocalVar	Creates a temporary local variable and lets you set it to a value that you can reference throughout the data macro execution. The value of the variable stays in memory as long as the data macro runs or until you change the value of the local variable by assigning it a new value. Once the data macro completes, Access clears the local variable.
	StopMacro	Stops the current data macro.

The tblWeekDays table contains seven records, each record listing the name of a day of the week. This table helps build a linking table between the tblVendors table and the tblOrderDays table. Each vendor in the database can have more than one order day and each weekday can be used by more than one vendor. Similarly, the tblWeekDays table also serves as a linking table between tblVendors and tblDeliveryDays. For the purposes of this database, we consider tblWeekDays to be a system table: a table used by other parts of the application, but one in which we don't ever need to add, change, or delete data. (We can't foresee the names of the weekdays changing any time soon.) To prevent new records from being added to this table, we'll create a data macro in the Before Change event that checks to see if Access is inserting a new record and then stop the insert if that condition is met.

Including Comments

To start creating your data macro in the Before Change event of the tblWeekDays table, let's first add a comment to the macro design surface. Comments are useful for documenting the purpose of your data macro and the various data actions within it. Access ignores any comments as it executes the actions within your data macro. Click on the word Comments under the Program Flow node in the Action Catalog, hold the mouse key down, drag the comment onto the macro design surface, and then release the mouse button, as shown in Figure 7-6.

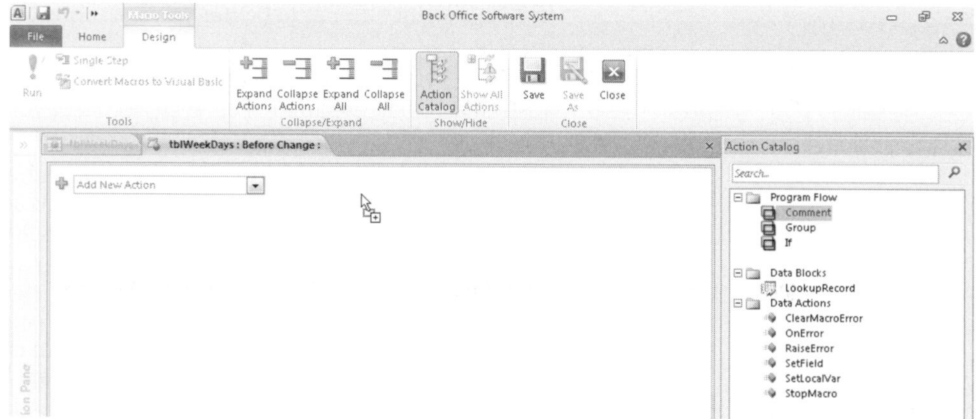

Figure 7-6 Drag the Comment program flow element from the Action Catalog onto the macro design surface.

Access creates a new Comment block on the macro designer surface, as shown in Figure 7-7. If your cursor is not in the Comment block and you do not have any comments typed into the Comment block, Access displays the text Click Here To Type A Comment. You'll notice in Figure 7-7 that Access moved the Add New Action box below the Comment block. You'll also notice that Access places a delete button to the far right of the Comment block. The delete button has a symbol shaped like an X. If you want to remove the Comment block, click the delete button and Access removes the Comment block from the macro design surface. If you deleted the Comment block in error, click the Undo button on the Quick Access Toolbar to restore the Comment block.

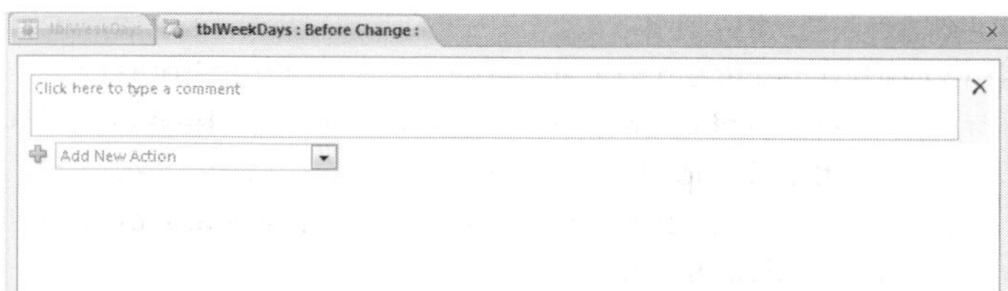

Figure 7-7 Access creates a new Comment block when you drag a Comment program flow onto the macro design surface.

Click inside the Comment block and type the following text:

We don't want to allow additional records into this system table. If a new record is being added, the IsInsert property will be True. In this case, raise an error and inform the user.

Click outside the Comment block onto the macro design surface. Access collapses the size of the Comment block to just fit the text you typed and displays the text in green, as shown in Figure 7-8. The /* and */ symbols mark the beginning and end of a block of comments. Access designates anything written between those symbols as a comment and is there only to provide information about the purpose of the data macro or particular action to follow.

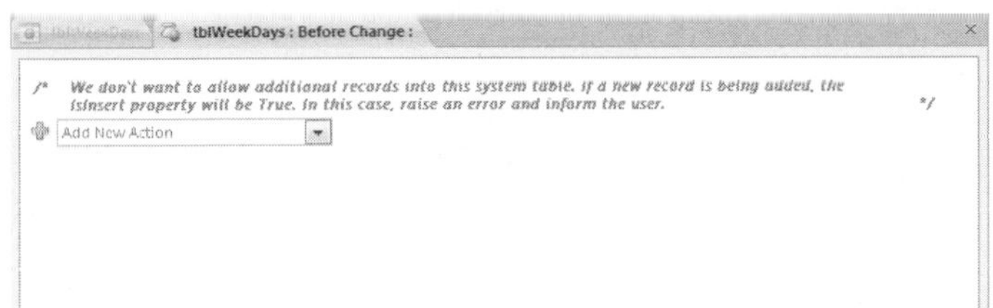

Figure 7-8 Access displays any comments inside comment block characters.

INSIDE OUT Take the Time to Include Comments

You might be asking yourself if it's really worth your time including comments in your data macros. While it's true that it takes additional time to include comments as you're creating your data macros, the investment of your time now pays off in the future. If you need to modify your application at a later date, you'll find it much easier to understand the purpose of your data macros if you include comments. This is especially true if someone else needs to make changes to your application. Trust us; it's worth your time to include comments when you design data macros!

Grouping Macros

When you're creating data macros, you can use a program flow construct called Group. You use a Group construct to group a set of actions together logically to make your data macro actions easier to read. When you group macro actions inside a Group construct, you can also expand or collapse the entire group easily to see more of the macro design surface. It's not required to use the Group construct when you're creating data macros; however, grouping macro actions can be especially helpful if you have many disparate actions inside the same event or named data macro.

To add a Group construct to your data macro, click on the word Group from the Action Catalog, hold down the mouse key, and drag the group just beneath the comment block that you inserted previously. As you get close to the comment block, you'll notice that Access displays a horizontal bar across the macro design surface, as shown in Figure 7-9. This horizontal bar is your insertion point for the new program flow, data block, or data action. If you want to drop your new Group above the comment block, position your mouse pointer above the comment block and Access displays the horizontal bar above the comments to indicate where it will drop your new Group. We want to have this Group positioned below the comment block, so place your mouse pointer below the comment block and then release the mouse.

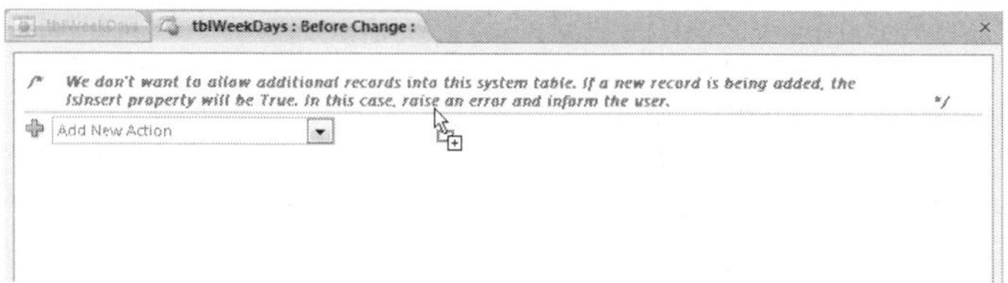

Figure 7-9 Access displays a horizontal bar on the macro design surface when you drag items from the Action Catalog.

Access displays a new Group block on the macro design surface, as shown in Figure 7-10. You need to provide a name for your new Group block, so type **PreventNewRecords** in the text box provided. You are limited to 256 characters, including any spaces, for the name of any Group block. In Figure 7-10, you'll notice that Access denotes the end of the Group block by placing the words End Group at the bottom of the Group block. When you click on the Group block, Access highlights the entire block as a visual cue to indicate where the starting and ending points of the block are. You'll also notice that Access placed another Add New Action combo box inside the Group block when you dropped the Group construct onto the design surface. You can use this combo box to add new actions inside the Group block. (We'll do that in just a moment.) Next to the delete button on the right side of the Group block is a green up arrow button. Click this button if you want to move the entire Group block above the Comment block that you created earlier. For now, leave the Group block where it is.

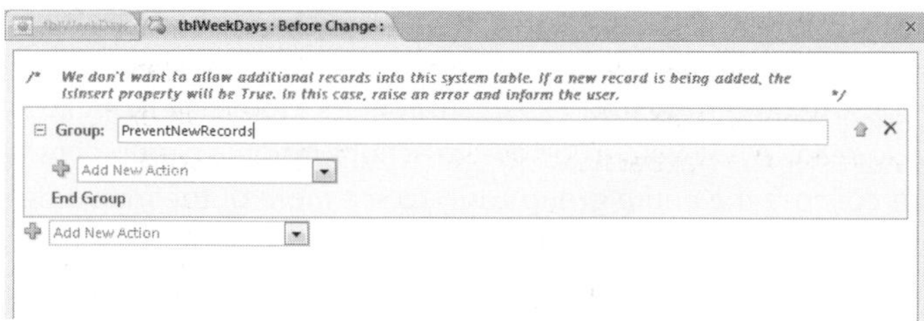

Figure 7-10 You can use a Group block to group a set of actions together logically.

Using If Blocks to Create Conditional Expressions

You might want to execute some actions only under certain conditions depending upon your application needs. For example, you might want to update a field in the same record, but only if a specific field was changed. Or you might want to prevent an update to a record if a value in another field is a higher or lower value than you expect.

To add an If block inside the Group block that you previously created, you could drag the If program flow construct from the Action Catalog onto the macro design surface and place the insertion point inside the Group block. You've already done this type of procedure twice before when creating the Comment and Group blocks, so let's show you an alternative way of adding new elements to the macro design surface. Click the Add New Action combo box inside the Group block, and Access displays a context-sensitive drop-down list of all the program flow constructs, data blocks, and data actions that you can use based on where your insertion point is located. Click the If option from the drop-down list, as shown in Figure 7-11, to add an If block to the macro design surface.

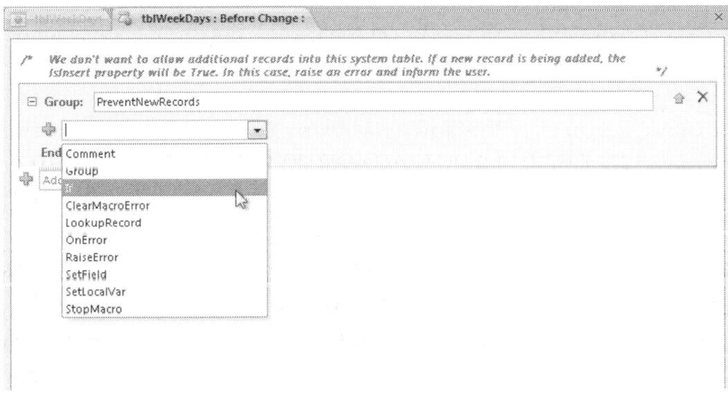

Figure 7-11 Select the If option from the Add New Action combo box inside the Group block.

Access creates a new If block inside the Group block, as shown in Figure 7-12. The text box next to If is where you type your conditional expression. Each condition is an expression that Access can evaluate to True (nonzero) or False (0 or Null). A condition can also consist of multiple comparison expressions and Boolean operators. If the condition is True, Access executes the action or actions immediately following the Then keyword. If the condition is False, Access evaluates the next ElseIf condition or executes the statements following the Else keyword, whichever occurs next. If no Else or ElseIf condition exists after the Then keyword, Access executes the next action following the End If keyword.

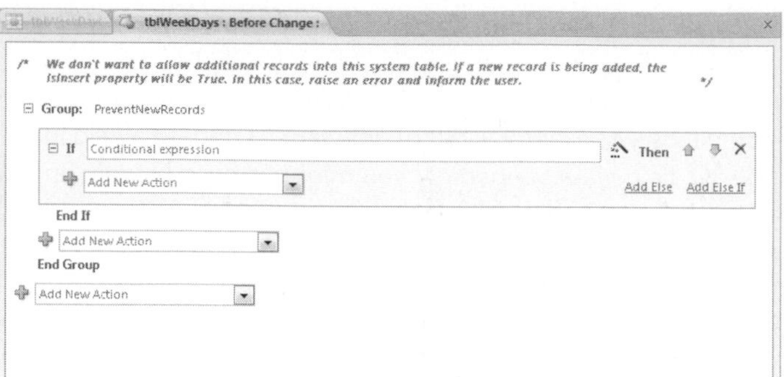

Figure 7-12 Use an If block when you want to execute actions only if a certain condition is met.

If you need help constructing your conditional expression, you can click the button that looks like a magic wand to the right of the expression text box. When you click this button, Access opens the Expression Builder, where you can build your conditional expression. (You learned about the Expression Builder in Chapter 6, "Designing Web Tables.") To the right of the word "Then," Access displays both an up and a down green arrow. You can click these buttons if you want to move the position of the If block. For example, if you click the up arrow once, Access moves the entire If block above and out of the Group block, but below the Comment block. If you click the down arrow once, Access moves the entire If block down and out of the Group block to the bottom of the macro design surface. If you move a block in error, you can click the Undo button on the Quick Access Toolbar. If you want to delete the If block, you can click the Delete button to the right of the down arrow. Below the arrow buttons and the Delete button are two links—Add Else and Add Else If. If you click the Add Else link, Access adds an Else branch to the If block, and if you click the Add Else If link, Access adds an ElseIf branch to the If block. We'll explore these two conditional elements later in this chapter.

We've mentioned previously that the Before Change event fires whenever you add new records to a table or update values in an existing record. In order to differentiate whether you are adding new records, you can use the IsInsert property. The IsInsert property returns True if you are creating a new record in a table and returns False if you are updating values in an existing record. For the Before Change data macro that you have been building, we can use the IsInsert property in our conditional expression to test whether we are adding a new record. In the conditional expression text box in the If block, type the letters **Is** and notice that Access provides IntelliSense options for you, as shown in Figure 7-13.

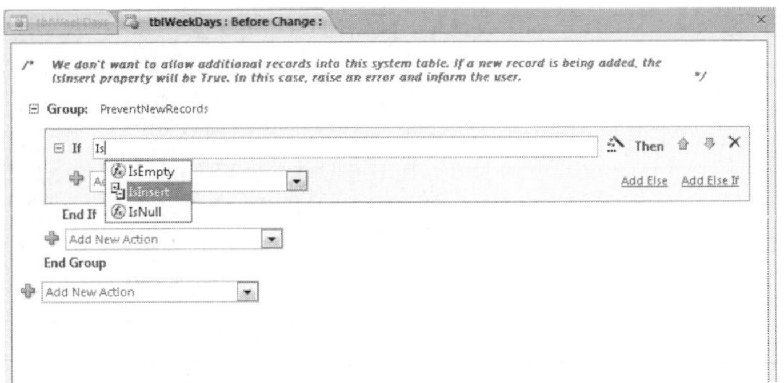

Figure 7-13 Access provides IntelliSense options whenever you are writing expressions in data macros.

You can continue to type IsInsert or use the down arrow to highlight the IsInsert property from the IntelliSense drop-down list and then press Tab or Enter. After you complete typing IsInsert or selecting it with IntelliSense, Access adds brackets around the word IsInsert. Complete the entire expression by adding an equals sign (=) and then type the word **True**. Your completed expression should be **[IsInsert]=True**, as shown in Figure 7-14.

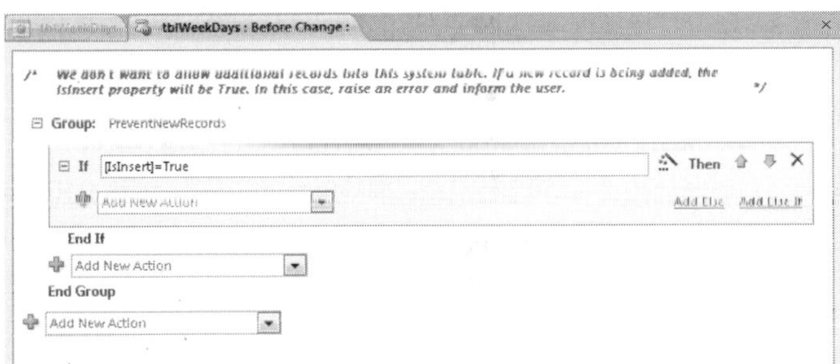

Figure 7-14 Your completed conditional expression should now look like this.

With your completed conditional expression for the If block, Access only executes actions after the Then keyword and before the End If keywords if you are adding new records to this table.

INSIDE OUT Nesting Limitations in the Logic Designer

In Figure 7-14, the If block is *nested*, or inside, the Group block. The Logic Designer supports only 10 levels of nesting program flow constructs and data blocks. In other words, you can nest up to nine additional constructs or data blocks inside a single top-level construct or data block (each one nested deeper inside the previous one).

Raising Errors in Data Macros to Cancel Events

In Chapters 20 and 21, you'll learn that user interface macros can interact heavily with the user's experience working with forms and reports. With user interface macros, you can display message boxes, open forms and reports, and dynamically change properties on a form. Data macros, on the contrary, are limited to the data layer and cannot interact with the user interface level. In a data macro, you cannot, for example, display a custom message box to the user and perform different steps based on how the user responds to your message. The only tool you can use in data macros to display information to the user is the RaiseError data action.

You can use the RaiseError data action whenever you need to force an error to occur and display a non-actionable message to the user manually. When you use the RaiseError action in a data macro, Access cancels the pending insert, update, or delete if it reaches this action during the macro execution. In the Before Change event that you've been building for the tblWeekDays table, we don't want to allow new records to be created in this table. In the previous section, you've already constructed the necessary If block conditional expression to determine when an update is occurring; now, you need to cancel the insert entirely if this condition is met. To do this, tab into the Add New Action combo box just below the If block conditional expression text, type the letter **R**, and then press Enter when Access displays RaiseError in the combo box. Note that this time, instead of clicking the combo box to drop down the list of actions and selecting one, we had you just type in the first letter of the action that you needed. (The macro design surface is flexible to allow you to use the mouse for selecting actions or just the keyboard if you prefer.) After you select RaiseError from the Add New Action combo box, Access displays the RaiseError data action inside the If block, as shown in Figure 7-15.

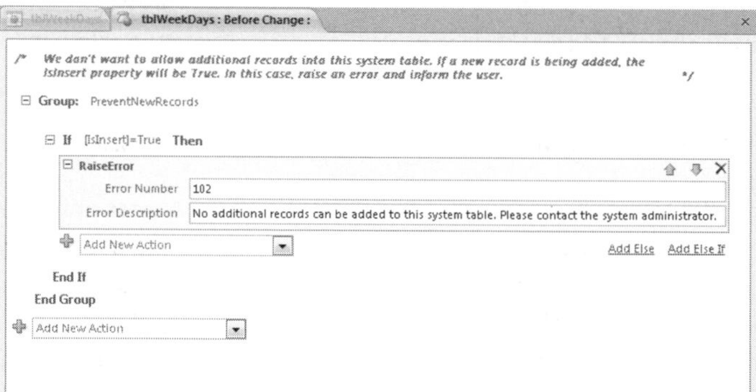

Figure 7-15 Use the RaiseError data action when you need to cancel an insert, update, or delete.

The RaiseError data action has two arguments—Error Number and Error Description. The Error Number argument is required. If you do not provide an Error Number, Access prevents you from saving your changes to the data macro. The number that you provide for the Error Number argument can be any whole number between the range of –2,147,483,648 to 2,147,483,647. (In Chapter 21, you'll learn how you can trap for this error number in a user interface macro.) We chose the number 102 for our example, so type **102** in the Error Number argument text box, as shown in Figure 7-15.

Note

The error number that you choose for the RaiseError action is only for your benefit. You can choose, for example, to reuse the same error number for similar types of error conditions with other data macros or choose different error numbers for each data macro. Although you can use negative numbers for the error number, we recommend you use positive numbers. Most Access internal errors are negative numbers (except for 11 and 13, which are two positive internal error numbers), so it might be easier to distinguish your own error numbers from internal errors if you use positive error numbers.

The Error Description argument is the message displayed to the user if the RaiseError action is hit during execution of the data macro. You can type any custom message you want up to 256 characters in length. You can also use an expression for the Error Description if you want by typing the equals sign (=) as the first character. If you type an equals sign at the beginning of the Error Description argument, Access displays the Expression Builder button on the far right of the text box If you need assistance creating your expression. (We'll show you an example of using an expression in a RaiseError action later in this chapter.) For our example, we'd like to display a simple message to the user informing them that they cannot enter new records into this table. Type the following message into the Error Description argument:

No additional records can be added to this system table. Please contact the system administrator.

If you do not provide an error description in your RaiseError data action, Access displays a generic message if the RaiseError condition is hit, as shown in Figure 7-16. Although the message does indicate something went wrong, your users do not have sufficient information as to the exact cause of the error nor do they have sufficient information to fix the issue. We recommend that you always include a custom message to display to users when you use the RaiseError data action.

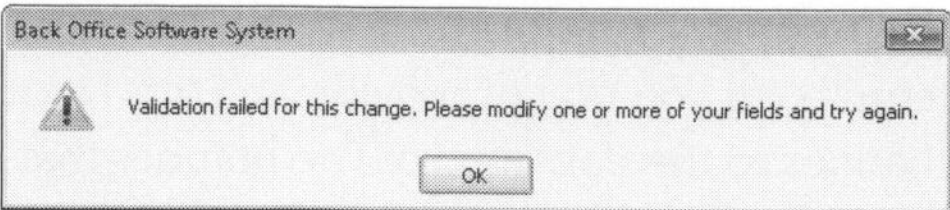

Figure 7-16 Access displays a generic error message if you leave the Error Description argument empty.

INSIDE OUT Hover over Elements to See Help Information

A very useful feature of the Logic Designer window is the ability to view Help information quickly no matter where you are. When you place your mouse over any elements on the macro design surface, Access displays a tooltip with specific Help information covering the program flow, data block, data action, or argument that you are currently on. Similarly, Access displays tooltips with Help information when you hover over the elements displayed in the Action Catalog. This feature is especially useful as you are learning your way around the Logic Designer.

Testing Your Data Macro

You've now completed all the steps necessary to prevent any new records from being added to the tblWeekDays table. To test the data macro that you've created so far, you first need to save your changes to the Before Change event. Click the Save button in the Close group on the Design contextual tab under Macro Tools or click the Save button on the Quick Access Toolbar. Now click the Close button in the Close group to close the Logic Designer window and return to the Datasheet view of the tblWeekDays table. To test this Before Change event, you need to create a new record in this table. Click in the WeekDayText field on the new record line of the datasheet, enter any text other than one of the existing weekday names, and then tab or click outside of the new record line. Access displays the custom error that you created in the RaiseError data action, as shown in Figure 7-17.

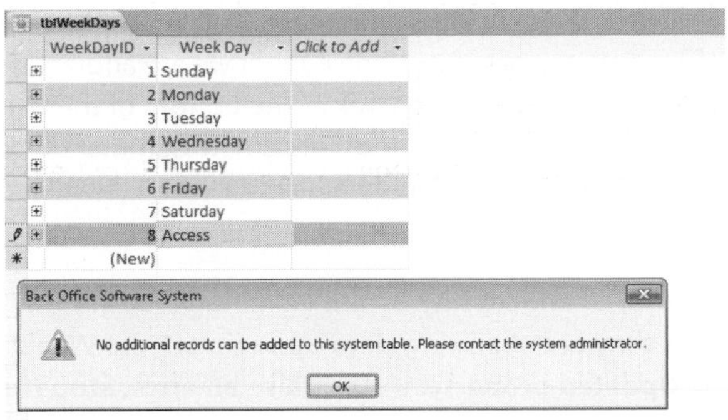

Figure 7-17 Access prevents you from adding new records with the data macro that you created for the Before Change event.

The Before Change event fires because you are inserting a new record into this table. In this event, Access checks to see if a new record is being inserted using the IsInsert property. If the IsInsert property is True, the RaiseError data action fires, Access displays the custom message that you created, and then Access cancels the insert. When you click OK in the message box, Access keeps your focus on the new record that you are trying to insert. You now need to press Esc to undo your changes to the new record. There is no way that you can add records to this table unless you remove the data macro that you defined in the Before Change event of the table. Access enforces this restriction no matter what the entry point is for creating a new record. As you can see, data macros are a very powerful new feature in Access 2010.

Defining Multiple Actions

You can define more than one action within a data macro, and you can specify the sequence in which you want the actions performed. In the preceding section, you designed a data macro in the Before Change event of the tblWeekDays table to prevent new records from being added to the table. Currently, it is still possible for users to change the values in the WeekDayText field for the existing seven records. (Note that you cannot change the data in the WeekDayID field because it is the ID field of the web table.) We can prevent users from changing data in the existing records using data macros by adding additional logic and actions into the Before Change event. Open the tblWeekDays table in Datasheet view, click the Table contextual ribbon tab under Table Tools, and then click the Before Change button in the Before Events group. You should now see the data macro that you created previously for preventing new records from being added to this table.

Before we start adding additional logic to this data macro, let's add a new Comment block and Group block to differentiate the new functionality that we are adding to this Before Change event. Click inside the Add New Action box at the bottom of the macro design surface, type Comments, and then press Enter to create a new Comment block. Type the following text into the Comment block to identify easily the logic that we are going to add to this data macro:

We also don't want the user changing any of the existing values in this table. We can easily check to see if they are changing data by seeing if the WeekDayText field was changed using the Updated property. If it is, raise an error, stop the update, and inform the user.

Your changes to the Before Change event should now look like Figure 7-18.

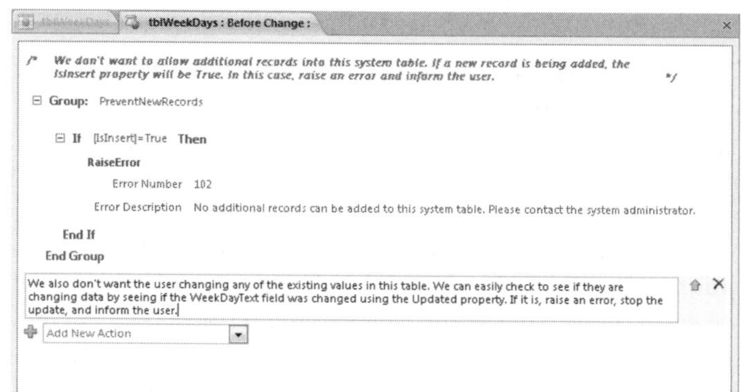

Figure 7-18 Add another Comment block to the macro design surface to document the next set of actions.

INSIDE OUT Shortcut Keys to Adding Comment Blocks

To add a new Comment block onto the macro design surface quickly, you can simply type two backslashes (//) when you are in any Add New Action combo box and press Enter. Alternatively, you can type a single apostrophe (') when you are in an Add New Action combo box and press Enter. In both cases, Access creates a new Comment block on the macro design surface.

Next, tab down to the Add New Action combo box at the bottom of the macro design surface, type **Group**, and then press Enter to create a new Group block. Access creates a new Group block on the macro design surface below the Comment block that you just created. Now type **PreventDataChanges** in the text box to name this new Group block.

To determine if data in a specific field has changed during a Before Change event, you can use the Updated function. The *Updated* function takes one argument, a field name, and returns True if the field is dirty and returns False if the field is not dirty during the record update. For the Before Change data macro that you have been building, we can use the Updated function in a conditional expression to test whether a user is attempting to change the value of the WeekDayText field.

To start, we first need an If block inside the Group block that you just completed. In the Add New Action combo box, between the Group and End Group keywords, type If and press Enter to create a new If block. In the conditional expression text box in the If block, type the expression **Updated("WeekDayText")=True**, as shown in Figure 7-19. When using the Updated function, you must surround the field name with quotation marks even if the field name has no spaces. You cannot put brackets around field names using the Updated function; otherwise, you'll receive a run-time error when the data macro executes.

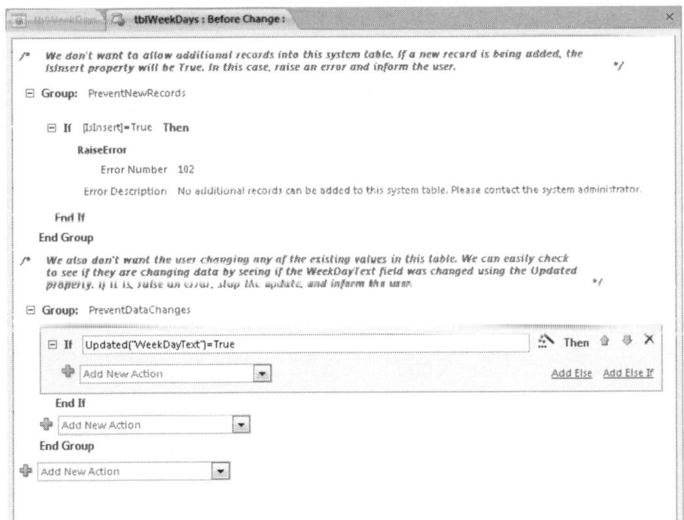

Figure 7-19 Use the Updated function when you need to test if a field is dirty during a record update.

The last step that we need to take is to include another RaiseError data action inside the If block to stop the field update if the condition is met. Tab or click inside the Add New Action box between the If and End If keywords, type **RaiseError**, and press Enter to add the new RaiseError data action to the macro design surface. In the Error Number argument, enter **103**. (Remember, you can use any whole number you want between the range of –2,147,483,648 to 2,147,483,647.) For the Error Description argument, we'd like to display a simple message to users informing them that they cannot edit any of the data in this table. Type the following message into the Error Description argument:

You cannot change the existing data in this system table. Please contact the system administrator.

Remember, if you do not provide an error description in your RaiseError data action, Access displays a generic message if the RaiseError condition is hit. We recommend you always include a helpful message in any RaiseError data actions you create. Your completed changes to the data macro should now match Figure 7-20.

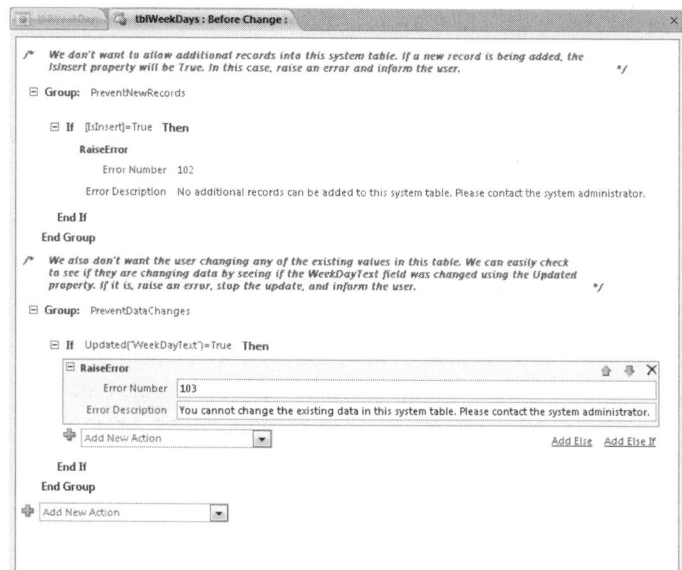

Figure 7-20 Your completed Before Change data macro should now look like this.

Let's try out the additional logic and actions you've added to the Before Change event. Click the Save button in the Close group on the Table tab or click the Save button on the Quick Access Toolbar to save your changes. Now, click the Close button in the Close group to close the Logic Designer window and return to the Datasheet view of the tblWeekDays table. Tab into the WeekDayText field for any of the seven records, change the value to something other than one of the existing seven weekday names, and then move to a different record. Access displays the custom error that you created in the RaiseError data action, as shown in Figure 7-21.

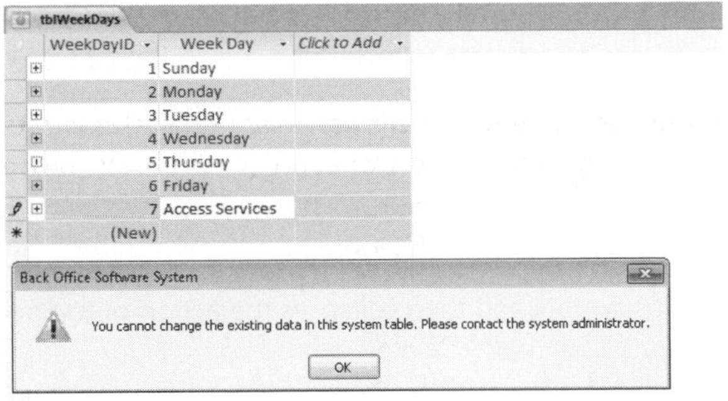

Figure 7-21 Access prevents you from changing any of the data in the existing records with the additional actions that you added to the Before Change event.

When you click OK in the message box, Access keeps the focus on the record that you are trying to edit. You need to press Esc to undo your changes to the existing record. With the completed data macro that you created and attached to the Before Change event, you've now prevented any new records from being added to this table as well as prevented any changes to existing records. The only way to make changes to the data in this table is to remove the data macro that you defined in the Before Change event of the table. Access enforces these restrictions no matter what the entry point is for creating new records or editing existing records.

Collapsing and Expanding Actions

When you have complex data macros with many program flow constructs, data blocks, and data actions, you might find it harder to understand everything happening with the structure of your data macros, especially if you have to scroll the macro design surface to see everything. Fortunately, the Logic Designer includes features that can make these tasks easier.

Open the tblWeekDays table in Datasheet view, click the Table contextual ribbon tab under Table Tools, and then click the Before Change button in the Before Events group. You should now see the data macro that you created previously for preventing new records from being added to this table and changing existing values. To the left of the Group and

If blocks on the macro design surface, you'll notice that Access displays a box with a dash inside. If you place your mouse over the RaiseError data action, you can also see a similar box. (For data actions, Access only shows this box when you hover over the action.) You can use this box to expand and collapse the group or action. By default, the Logic Designer displays all group blocks and data actions in expanded mode so you can see all actions and arguments. To collapse the RaiseError data action, hover over the action until you see the box to the left of the RaiseError action and then click inside the box. Access changes the dash inside the box to a plus symbol and then collapses the action onto one line, as shown in Figure 7-22.

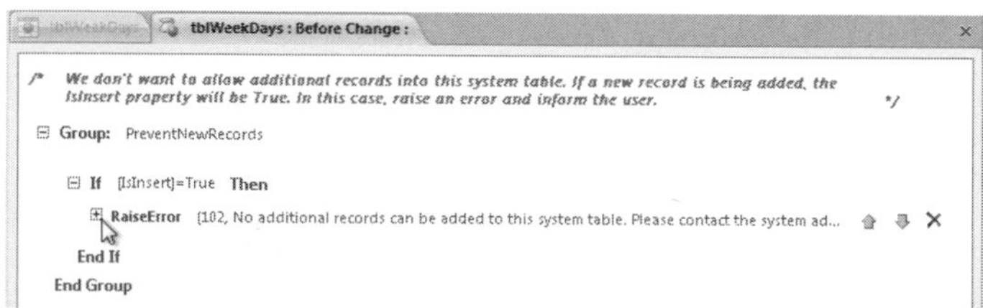

Figure 7-22 Click the box next to an action to collapse it onto one line.

Access now displays the action without the argument names—Error Number and Error Description—and separates the argument values with a comma. By collapsing the action, you can now see more of the macro design surface. To expand the action again, click inside the box, now displaying a plus symbol, and Access expands the RaiseError action. You can also collapse an entire group, such as the PreventNewRecords Group block that you created earlier or any If blocks, by clicking inside the expand/collapse box next to each block. If you want to collapse all data actions showing on the macro design surface at the same time, you can click the Collapse Actions button in the Collapse/Expand group on the ribbon, as shown in Figure 7-23. In Figure 7-23, you can see that Access collapsed both RaiseError data actions onto one line. Click the Expand Actions button in the Collapse/Expand group on the ribbon to expand all data actions showing on the macro design surface.

INSIDE OUT Viewing Super Tooltips

If you hover your mouse over a collapsed data action, Access displays a super tooltip with all the arguments. You can then view all the argument values of the data action easily, without having to expand the data action.

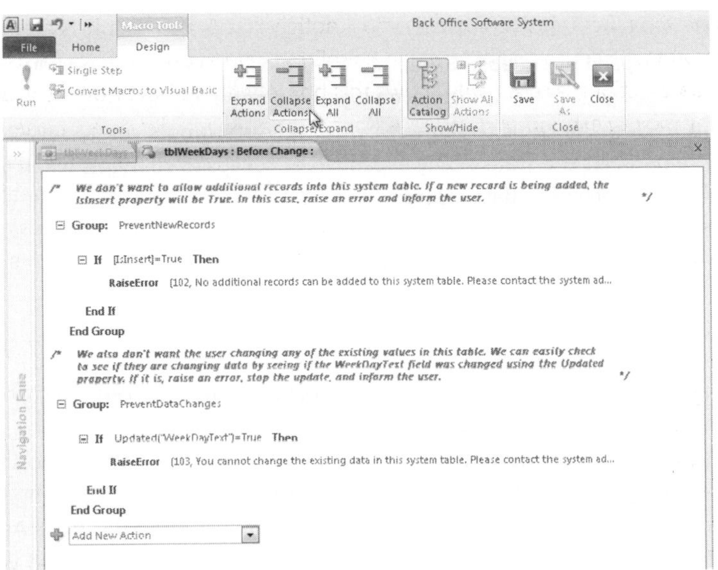

Figure 7-23 Click the Collapse Actions button to collapse all actions on the macro design surface.

For the maximum amount of space on the macro design surface, click the Collapse All button in the Collapse/Expand group on the ribbon. Access collapses all groups onto one line, as shown in Figure 7-24. You can't see very much with this view, of course. However, you can then selectively expand Groups and If blocks one at a time to work on specific parts of the data macro. Click the Expand All button on the ribbon to expand all Group blocks, If blocks, and data actions.

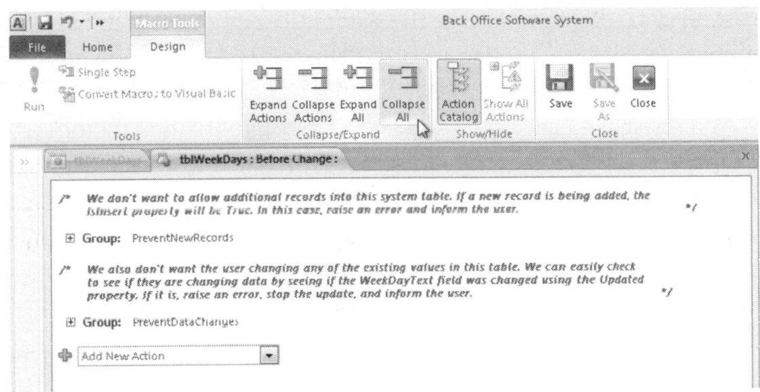

Figure 7-24 Access collapses everything on the macro design surface, except Comment blocks, when you click the Collapse All button.

Note

When you expand or collapse Group blocks, If blocks, or Data Actions, Access marks the macro design surface as dirty even if you did not make any other changes. If you attempt to close the Logic Designer window, Access prompts you to save your changes. Access remembers the state of any expanded or collapsed elements when you save changes and reopen the data macro.

Moving Actions

As you design data macros or user interface macros in the new Logic Designer, you might find that you need to move actions around as the needs of your application change. In the Before Change event for the tblWeekDays table, you created a data macro that prevents new records from being added to the table and existing records from being changed. We had you create two separate Groups and If blocks to accomplish this goal. As with many areas of Access, there is usually more than one way to accomplish a task. If you analyze the logic we created in the Before Change event, you'll realize we could simplify the logic further by using only one If block instead of two. The Logic Designer makes the task of moving actions around the macro design surface very easy.

Open the tblWeekDays table in Datasheet view if you closed it, click the Table contextual ribbon tab under Table Tools, and then click the Before Change button in the Before Events group. You should now see the data macro that you created previously for preventing new records from being added to this table and changing existing values. The first If block tests to see if a new record is being added to the table by using the IsInsert property. The second If block tests to see if the data in the WeekDayText field is being changed. We can simplify this data macro further because if the IsInsert property is False, the user must be trying to change existing data. (Remember that the Before Change event fires only when adding new records or changing data in existing records.) The tblWeekDays table has only two fields—WeekDayID and WeekDayText. WeekDayID is the ID field for the table and is therefore read-only. As a result, we can simply add an Else block to the first If block and not include the conditional test using the Updated function in the first test. To make these changes, you first need to add an Else block to the first If block. Click inside the first If block and then click the Add Else link at the lower-right corner of the If block, as shown in Figure 7-25.

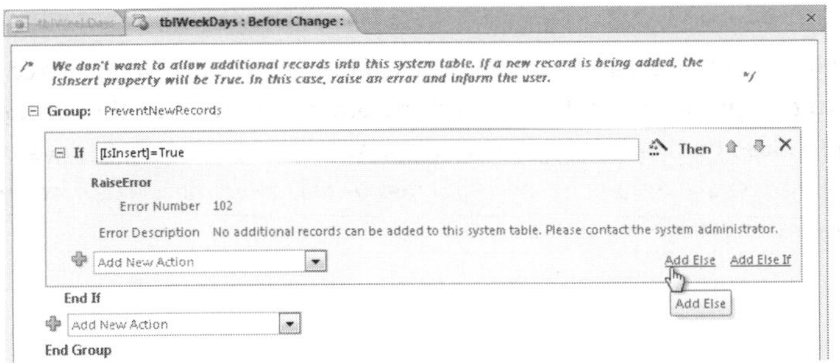

Figure 7-25 Click the Add Else link to add an Else block to the If block.

Access creates an Else block below the RaiseError data action, as shown in Figure 7-26. Access also places an Add New Action combo box inside this Else block. When Access runs this data macro on the Before Change event, it first checks the conditional expression in the If statement. If the IsInsert property is False, Access moves down to the Else block and then executes any actions inside the Else block. Note that if you added an Else If block instead of an Else block, you would need to provide an additional conditional expression for Access to execute actions inside the Else If block.

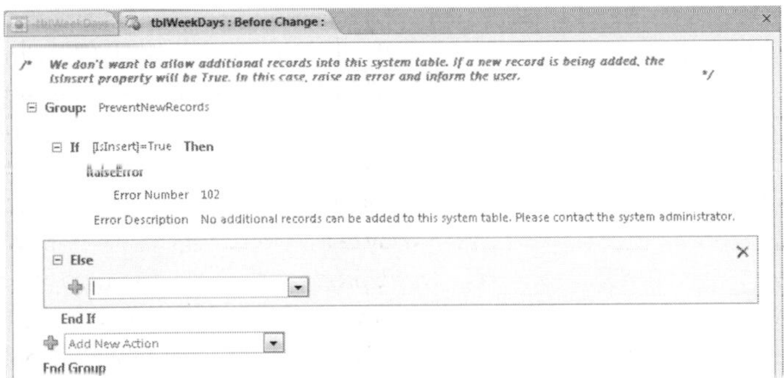

Figure 7-26 Access places the Else block below any actions inside the first part of the If block.

In previous sections, you've already created an appropriate RaiseError data action to handle the condition when a user is trying to change existing data. You could recreate the entire RaiseError data action inside the Else block, but it's much quicker to move the existing RaiseError inside this Else block. To move the RaiseError data action that traps for data changes, click anywhere on the RaiseError data action, hold the mouse key down, drag the action block up to the Else block until the Else keyword is highlighted, and then release the mouse, as shown in Figure 7-27.

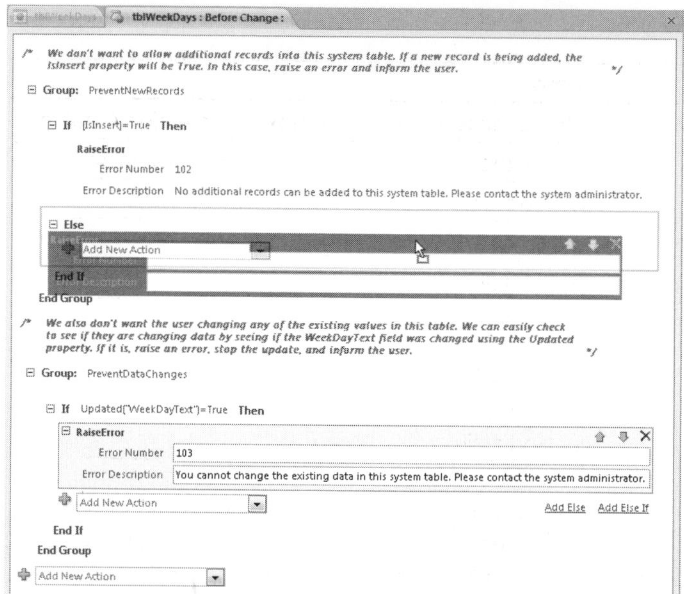

Figure 7-27 Drag the RaiseError data action up into the Else block.

Access places the RaiseError data action inside the Else block. Instead of using the drag technique, you could also click the Up arrow button on the far side of the RaiseError to move it up into the Else block. When you click the Up arrow button, Access moves the selected action up one position in the macro design surface. In our example, it would take five clicks of the Up arrow to move the second RaiseError data action up into the Else block.

INSIDE OUT Creating a Duplicate Copy of Logic

To duplicate any logic on the macro design surface, you can hold the Ctrl key down and then drag to a different location. Access creates an exact copy of the program flow construct, data block, or data action, including any argument information.

You might find it easier to use the keyboard rather than the mouse to move actions around the macro design surface. Table 7-2 lists the keyboard shortcuts for working inside the Logic Designer.

Table 7-2 Keyboard Shortcuts for Logic Designer

Keys	Action
Ctrl+F	Moves focus to the Search box in the Action Catalog
Ctrl+F2	Opens the Expression Builder dialog box if in an expression context
Ctrl+Space	Calls up IntelliSense in expression contexts
Ctrl+Up arrow	Moves selected action up
Ctrl+Down arrow	Moves selected action down
Shift+F2	Opens the Zoom Builder dialog box
Shift+F10	Opens a context-sensitive shortcut menu
Left arrow	Collapse action
Right arrow	Expand action

Now that you've moved the RaiseError data action out of the second Group block in this data macro, we no longer need that Group block or the If block inside it. Highlight the second Group block, called PreventDataChanges, and then click the Delete button on the right side of the block to remove it from the macro design surface. Your data macro should now look like Figure 7-28.

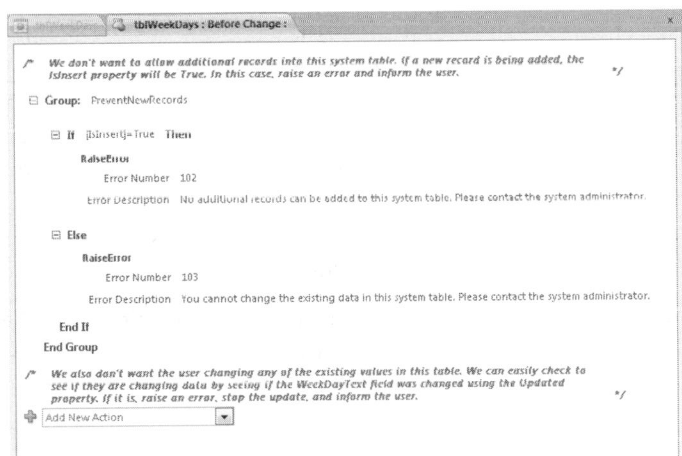

Figure 7-28 Your data macro should now look like this after you remove the second Group block.

We still have the extra Comment block at the bottom of the macro design surface, which we really don't need now that we removed the second Group block. However, we should probably add additional information into the first Comment block to mention that the data macro prevents any existing data from being changed. Click into the first Comment block, move your cursor to the end of the text, and then type the following additional text:

We also prevent any data from being changed in the Else block by raising an error in that condition as well.

Now, highlight the Comment block at the bottom of the macro design surface and then click the Delete button on the far right to remove it. Finally, click in the Group block and rename it from PreventNewRecords to PreventNewRecordsOrDataChanges. Your revised Before Change event for the tblWeekDays table should now match Figure 7-29.

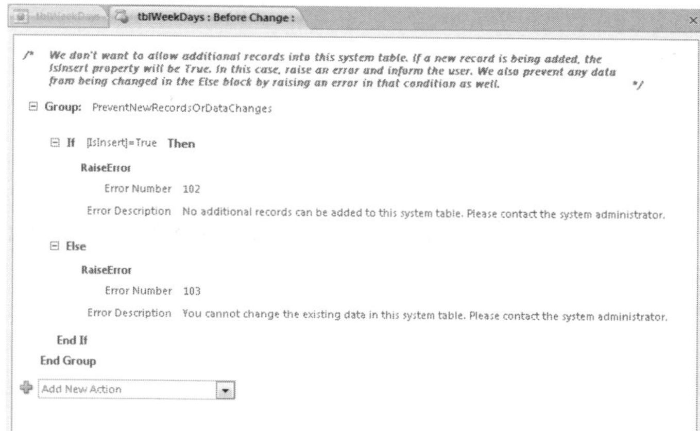

Figure 7-29 Your revised Before Change event should now look like this.

You've now successfully revised the data logic in the If conditional block, moved the second RaiseError data action, and condensed the data macro. Even with the changes you made, the data macro in this Before Change event still functions just as it did before. Save your changes, close the Logic Designer window, and test it by trying to add new records to the table and edit existing data. You'll see that Access prevents you from making these changes, just as it did before you made the design adjustments.

Preventing Duplicate Records Across Multiple Fields

In Chapter 4, "Designing Client Tables," you learned about primary keys and multiple-field indexes in client tables to create composite keys. You learned how you could enforce uniqueness across multiple fields in a record instead of on just one field. In Chapter 6, however, you learned that web tables do not support primary keys other than the ID field, nor do they support multiple-field indexes. To work around this limitation for web tables, you can create a data macro attached to a Before Change event that checks for duplicates across multiple fields. (Note that you can also do the same for client tables; however, it's unnecessary because you can create multiple-field indexes in client tables.)

In the Back Office Software System sample web database data copy (BOSSDataCopy.accdb), several of the web tables use this technique to prevent duplicates across multiple fields. Open the tblVendorDeliveryDays in Datasheet view, click the Table contextual tab under Table Tools, and then click the Before Change button in the Before Events group to open the Logic Designer, as shown in Figure 7-30. Note that in Figure 7-30, we closed the Action Catalog so you could see more of the macro design surface.

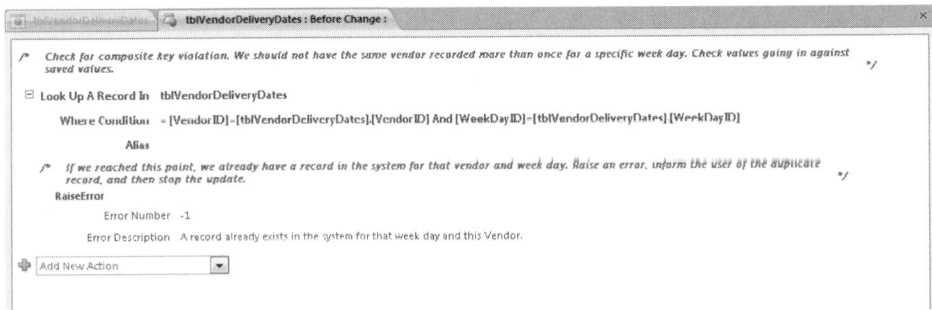

Figure 7-30 The Before Change event of the tblVendorDelieveryDates web table prevents duplicate records across two fields.

Each vendor that delivers products to the restaurant using this database usually delivers more than once during any week, but each vendor delivers only once on the specific delivery day. We don't want users of the database to accidentally enter the same delivery day of the week more than once for the same vendor; if we did, we would have repeating records. We cannot enforce this restriction in web tables unless we use a data macro in the Before Change event to check the *combination* of both the VendorID and the WeekDayID fields for duplicates before committing new or changed data to the table. The data macro logic is as follows:

```
Comment Block: Check for composite key violation. We should not have the same vendor
recorded more than once for a specific weekday. Check values going in against saved
values.
LookUpRecord In tblVendorDeliveryDates
 Where Condition = [VendorID]=[tblVendorDeliveryDates].[VendorID] And
                   [WeekDayID]=[tblVendorDeliveryDates].[WeekDayID]
 Alias
 Comment Block: If we reached this point, we already have a record in the system for
 that vendor and weekday. Raise an error, inform the user of the duplicate record,
 and then stop the update.
 RaiseError
    Error Number: -1
    Error Description: A record already exists in the system for that weekday
                       and this Vendor.
```

The LookupRecord data block takes three arguments:

- **Look Up A Record In** Required argument. The name of a table, query, or SQL statement to look up a record in.
- **Where Condition** Optional argument. The expression that Access uses to select records from the table, query, or SQL statement.
- **Alias** Optional argument. A substitute or shorter name for the table.

When Access enters the LookupRecord block, the default data context is the incoming record. The incoming record is either a new record or changes to an existing record. Access evaluates the Where condition of a data block with the same default context as when you are inside the data block. This means that if you do not use an alias as the table qualifier for field names in the Where condition argument, you are referring to a field within the new default data context that you just created by using the data block.

In the first part of our example Where condition argument, `[VendorID]=[tb]VendorDeliveryDates].[VendorID]`, VendorID refers to the VendorID of the new record being created or changed. We compare that value to a saved VendorID that already exists in the table. Similarly, we do the same type of comparison with the WeekDayID field. Access then tries to see if there is a record currently in the table with the same VendorID and WeekDayID as the new or changed record being committed to the table. If Access finds a match in the LookupRecord block, this means that a record exists for the combination of the two fields. Access then executes the RaiseError action, displays the custom error that we created, and then cancels the update.

If you want to see Access enforce this restriction, you can close the Logic Designer and return to the tblVendorDeliveryDates in Datasheet view. Next, create a new record in the table and select a vendor and weekday that matches an existing record. You'll notice that Access displays the custom error message that we defined in the RaiseError event. You'll see the same error message if you try to change an existing record with values that match a different record.

You can apply this technique of enforcing uniqueness across multiple fields to more than two fields by simply modifying the Where condition argument of the LookupRecord data block to include additional fields with the AND operator. Using data macro logic inside the Before Change event of web tables allows you to achieve the data integrity that multiple field indexes provide in client tables.

The Back Office Software System sample web database includes Before Change events attached to other web tables besides the two examples you've already seen. You can explore the data macros attached to these events for additional examples.

- **tblCompanyInformation** Prevents additional records from being added to the table. Uses IsInsert property to test for new records.
- **tblLaborHours** Prevents duplicates across multiple fields using the LookupRecord data block. Uses the SetLocalVar action to construct a custom message to user that pulls data from other tables.
- **tblSettings** Prevents additional records from being added to the table. Uses IsInsert property to test for new records.
- **tblTimeLookups** Prevents additional records from being added to the table. Also prevents changes to existing data as well. Uses IsInsert property to test for new records.
- **tblVendorDelieveryDays** Prevents duplicates across multiple fields using the LookupRecord data block.
- **tblVendoOrderDays** Prevents duplicates across multiple fields using the LookupRecord data block.
- **tblWeekDays** Prevents additional records from being added to the table and prevents changes to existing datal. Uses the IsInsert property to test for new records.

INSIDE OUT Nesting LookupRecord Blocks in Before Events

If you are working in a client database, you can nest LookupRecord blocks inside each other up to 10 levels deep. If you are using a web database, however, and intend to publish the database to a SharePoint server, you should not nest any LookupRecord data blocks in Before events—Before Change and Before Delete. If you nest LookupRecord data blocks in a Before event, the web table fails to compile on the server. Nesting LookupRecord blocks inside Before events are not supported on the server. To work around this limitation for web databases, you can separate the LookupRecord blocks and use local variables and If blocks to accomplish the same goal as nesting. If you examine the Before Change event in the tblLaborHours web table, you can see we could have simplified the logic by nesting the two LookupRecord blocks. Because of the server limitation on nesting in Before events, we had to use two separate LookupRecord blocks to test for duplicate records and then display the employee name of the duplicate record.

Before Delete

The Before Delete event fires whenever Access attempts to delete a record. There are many entry points for deleting a record when you are working with Access. For example, you can delete a record in a table or query datasheet, you can run a delete action query, you can delete a record when using a form, or you can delete records using user interface macros or Visual Basic code. When you attach a data macro to the Before Delete event, Access runs the data macro logic no matter where the entry point is for deleting a record.

In the previous sections, you created a data macro attached to the Before Change event of the tblWeekDays system table for the Back Office Software System sample web database data copy (BOSSDataCopy.accdb). The data macro you created prevents any additions or changes to the existing data. You can also lock this table down further by preventing any records from being deleted using a data macro attached to the Before Delete event.

Open the tblWeekDays table in Datasheet view, click the Table contextual tab under Table Tools, and then click the Before Delete button in the Before Events group to open the Logic Designer, as shown in Figure 7-31.

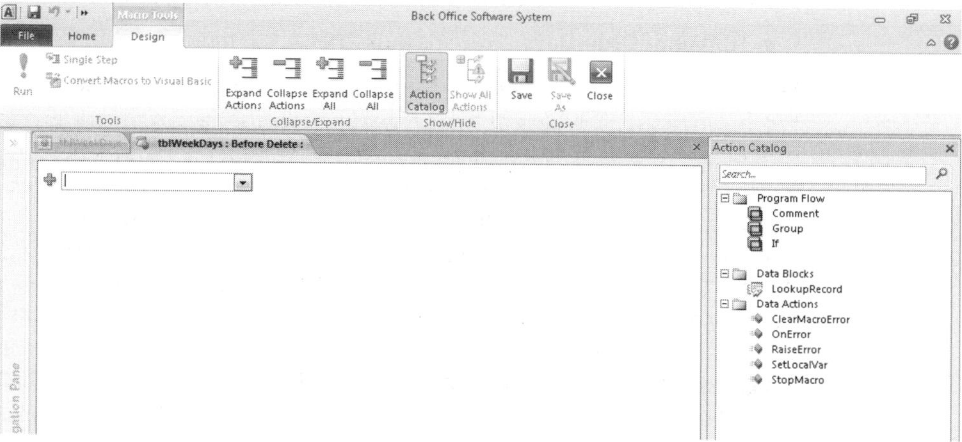

Figure 7-31 Click the Before Delete button on the ribbon to open the Logic Designer.

We should first add a Comment block to this data macro so anyone looking at it can understand the purpose of the logic in this Before Delete event. You should now be familiar with the different methods of adding a new Comment block to the macro design surface. Drop a new Comment block onto the macro design surface and enter the following text:

We do not want to allow the user to delete any records from this system table. If the user attempts to delete any records from this table, raise an error and inform them of the mistake.

Now add a RaiseError data action below the Comment block. In the Error Number argument, enter **104**. For the Error Description argument, enter the following text:

You cannot delete any records from this system table; they are used in other areas of the application.

Your completed changes to the Before Delete event should now match Figure 7-32.

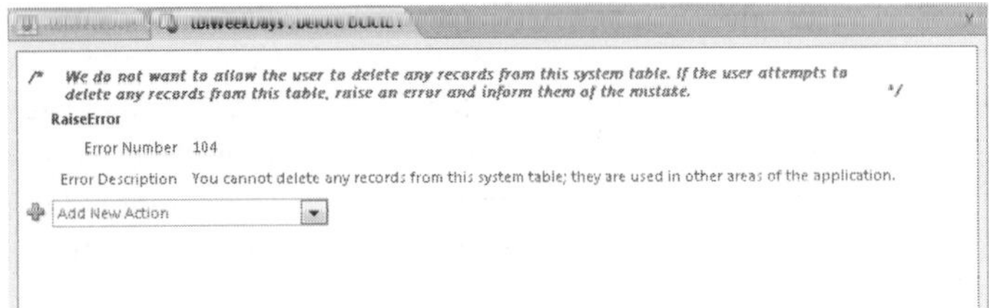

Figure 7-32 Your completed Before Delete event logic should match this.

Seems almost too simple doesn't it? Simple, yes, but completely effective. We don't need to test for any special conditions for our scenario; we just need to throw an error if this event ever occurs. To try this, save the changes to this data macro by clicking the Save button in the Close group or the Save button on the Quick Access Toolbar. Next, close the Logic Designer window by clicking the Close button in the Close group. Finally, click the record selector next to any of the records in the tblWeekDays table in Datasheet view and press Delete. Access displays the custom message in the RaiseError data action, as shown in Figure 7-33.

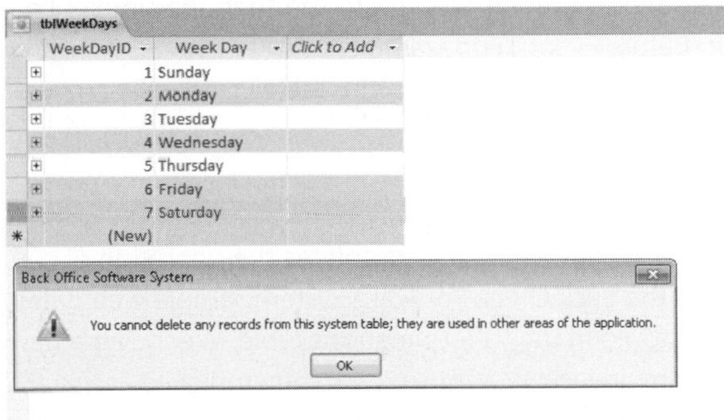

Figure 7-33 When you attempt to delete a record, Access displays your error message.

Note

In the After Delete event example we just discussed, you might be asking why this is even necessary if a Restrict Delete relationship is enforced on any related tables. You are correct that Access prevents deletes in this case; however, it is possible that for a specific record in tblWeekDays, no related records exist in the other tables. In that case, a user could still delete a record from a static table that you don't want modified. Also, you might have other tables in your database that do not have relationships with other tables and want to prevent any records from being deleted. The tblCompanyInformation and tblSettings tables in the Back Office Software System sample web database are two such examples where no relationships exist with other tables, but we want to prevent any record deletions.

The Back Office Software System sample web database includes Before Delete events attached to other web tables that use this same technique to prevent records from being deleted. You can explore the data macros attached to these events for additional examples.

- **tblCompanyInformation** Prevents deletion of existing records.
- **tblSettings** Prevents deletion of existing records.
- **tblTimeLookups** Prevents deletion of existing records.
- **tblWeekDays** Prevents deletion of existing records.

Working with After Events

Access 2010 supports three After events where you can attach data macros. The AfterInsert, AfterUpdate, and AfterDelete events are designed for more extensive operations. In After events, you can use data blocks that take longer to run than the simpler LookupRecord data block available to Before events. For example, in After events, you can iterate over a collection of records, modify other records in other tables, and call named data macros.

After Insert

The After Insert event fires whenever Access completes the operation of committing a new record to a table. In the Back Office Software System sample web database, employee termination records are stored in the tblTerminations table. Whenever a new termination record is created for an employee, we want to mark the employee as inactive automatically. To accomplish this, we can use the After Insert event to look up the employee's record in the tblEmployees table and set the Boolean Active field to False for that specific employee.

If you've closed it, open the Back Office Software System backup copy sample web database (BOSSDataCopy.accdb), and then open the tblTerminations table in Datasheet view. Next, click the Table contextual tab under Table Tools, and then click the After Insert button in the After Events group to open the Logic Designer, as shown in Figure 7-34.

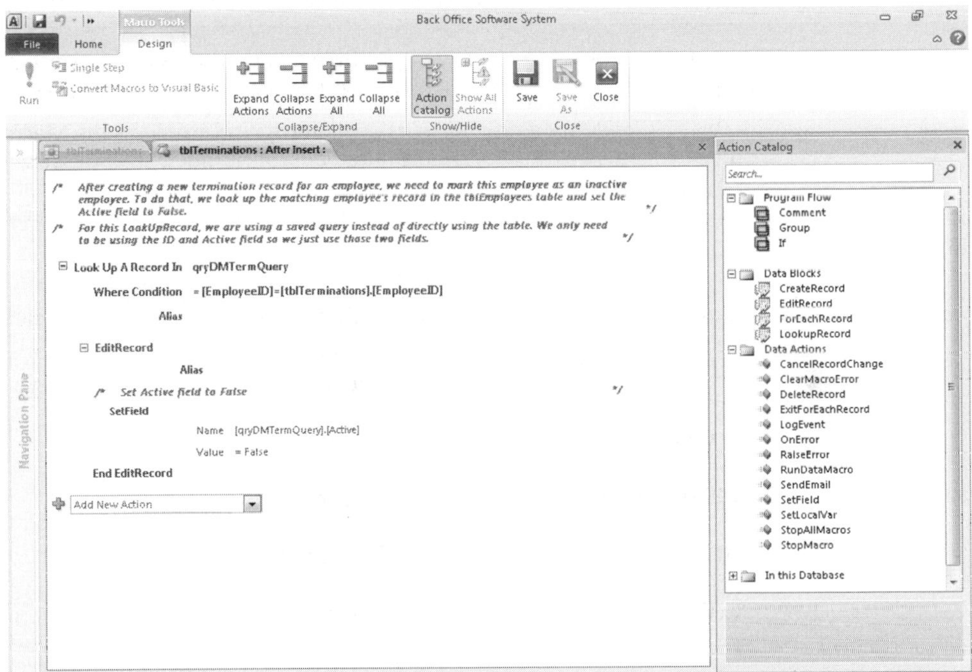

Figure 7-34 Click the After Insert button on the ribbon to examine the After Insert event of the tblTerminations table.

In the Action Catalog on the right side of the Logic Designer, you can see three options under Program Flow, four options under Data Block, and 13 options under Data Actions. The three program flow options—Comment, Group, and If—are available in all data macro events. Table 7-3 summarizes the Data Blocks and Data Actions you can use in the After Events group.

Table 7-3 Data Blocks and Data Actions Available to After Events

Element	Block or Action	Description
Data Blocks	CreateRecord	Creates a new record in a table.
	EditRecord	Allows Access to edit a record. This data block must be used in conjunction with a ForEachRecord or Lookup-Record data block.

Element	Block or Action	Description
	ForEachRecord	Iterate over a recordset from a table, query, or SQL statement.
	LookupRecord	Instructs Access to look up a record in the same table, a different table, or a query.
Data Actions	CancelRecord-Change	Cancels any current record changes currently in progress. You can use this action to break out of CreateRecord or EditRecord changes.
	ClearMacroError	Clears any information stored in the MacroError object, including the error number, error description, macro name, action name, condition, and any arguments. Access resets the error number to 0 after you run this action.
	DeleteRecord	Deletes the current record from the table. Access determines the current record based on the scope of where the action is called. If, for example, you are inside a LookupRecord data block, Access deletes the record found in the Where condition argument.
	ExitForEachRecord	Exits the innermost ForEachRecord loop. You can use this action when you want to break out of a long-running loop if a condition is met.
	LogEvent	Logs an event to the USysApplicationLog table. You can use this action for the purpose of debugging data macros.
	OnError	Specifies how Access should handle an error when running your data macro. In After events, you can have the data macro halt execution if an error occurs, or you can skip to the next action.
	RaiseError	Displays a custom message to the user interface level and cancels the event changes. You can use this action to manually throw an error and cancel an insert, update, or delete.
	RunDataMacro	Runs a saved named data macro attached to any table. You can optionally pass parameters to the named data macro and return values.
	SendEmail	Sends an email message. If you are using an unpublished database, Access sends the email through your local email program. If you are using a published database, the SharePoint server sends the message.
	SetField	Changes the value of a field. You can use the SetField action, for example, to change values in other table using a ForEachRecord or LookupRecord data block.

Element	Block or Action	Description
	SetLocalVar	Creates a temporary local variable and lets you set it to a value that you can reference throughout the data macro execution. The value of the variable stays in memory as long as the data macro runs or until you change the value of the local variable by assigning it a new value. Once the data macro completes, Access clears the local variable.
	StopAllMacros	Stops all macros currently executing.
	StopMacro	Stops the current data macro.

In Figure 7-34, you'll notice there is also an additional node listed at the bottom of the Action Catalog called In This Database. When you expand this node, Access lists all the named data macros attached to the tables in the database, as shown in Figure 7-35. We'll discuss named data macros later in this chapter.

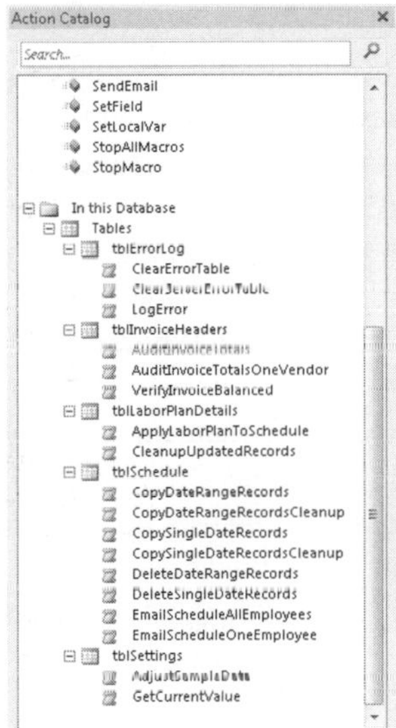

Figure 7-35 Expand the In This Database node in the Action Catalog to see a list of all the named data macros.

The data macro logic for the After Insert event is as follows:

```
Comment Block: After creating a new termination record for an employee, we need to
mark this employee as an inactive employee. To do that, we look up the matching
employee's record in the tblEmployees table and set the Active field to False.
Comment Block: For this LookupRecord, we are using a saved query instead of directly
using the table. We only need to be using the ID and Active field so we just use
those two fields.
LookupRecord In qryDMTermQuery
 Where Condition = [EmployeeID]=[tblTerminations].[EmployeeID]
 Alias
 EditRecord
    Alias
    Comment Block: Set Active field to False
    SetField
       Name: [qryDMTermQuery].[Active]
       Value: False

 End EditRecord
```

The first part of the data macro includes two Comment blocks to indicate the purpose of this event. Next, we use a LookupRecord data block to look up a record in a saved query called qryDMTermQuery. This query returns only two fields from the tblEmployees table—EmployeeID and Active. The tblEmployees table has many fields in it, but we really don't need most of those fields for the purposes of this data macro, so we created just a simple query to return the fields we need. In the Where condition argument for the LookupRecord data block, we want to look up the EmployeeID in the query that matches the EmployeeID field found in the tblTerminations table that Access just finished committing. Once Access finds the matching record, we enter into the EditRecord block. Whenever you want to change data in another table, you must use the SetField action inside an EditRecord block. For our example, we want to change the Active field of the matching employee to False to indicate they are no longer an active employee in the database. The SetField action takes two arguments, Name and Value. In the Name argument, we use the query name that was also used for the LookupRecord block. The context inside the LookupRecord here is the employee record Access found inside the query so we qualify the Active field name with the saved query name.

To test this After Insert event, close the Logic Designer window by clicking the Close button in the Close group. You should now see the tblTerminations table again in Datasheet view. Begin a new record in this table and select Jeff Conrad from the drop-down list of employee names displayed in the EmployeeID field. The LastDayWorked, DateTerminated, and ReasonInDetail fields are all required fields in this table, so enter dates for the two Date/Time fields and then enter some text into the ReasonInDetail field, as shown in Figure 7-36. Now, click or tab off the record and Access saves the record.

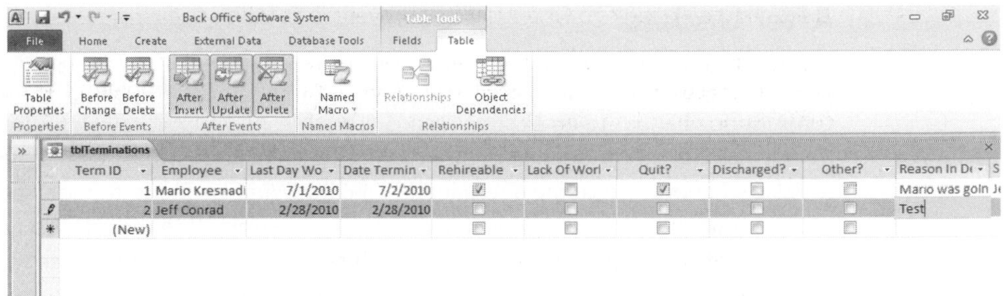

Figure 7-36 Enter a new record into the tblTerminations table and use Jeff Conrad as the employee.

To see the effects of the After Insert event that we defined, you need to open the tblEmployees table. Open the tblEmployees table in Datasheet view and scroll down to the employee record for Jeff Conrad. You'll notice that the Active field for Jeff Conrad is now set to False, as shown in Figure 7-37.

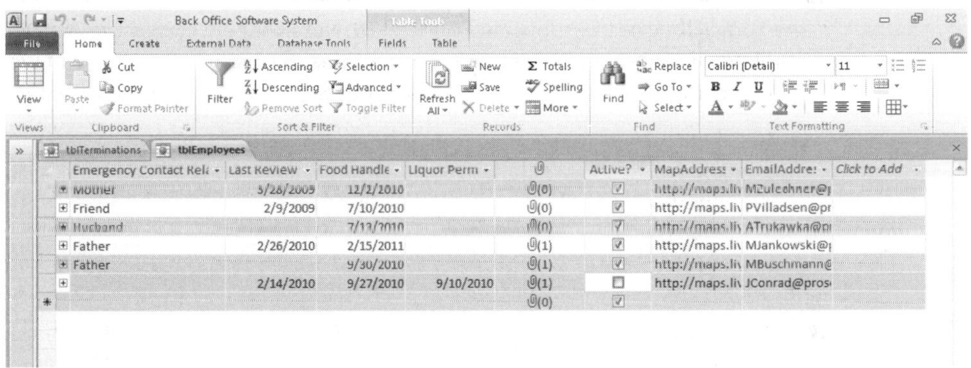

Figure 7-37 The After Insert event of the tblTerminations table set the matching employee's record in the tblEmployees table to False.

In previous versions of Access, you would need to write Visual Basic code to accomplish the same task as the data macro that we defined for the After Insert event using Access 2010. By using a data macro attached to an After Insert event, we are guaranteed that the logic works no matter where the entry point is for creating new records in the tblTerminations table.

After Update

The After Update event fires whenever After Update Access completes the operation of committing changes to an existing record in a table. As you just saw in the previous section, we have a data macro defined in the After Insert event to mark the employee's Active field to False whenever we create a termination record. What happens, though, if we accidentally select the wrong employee when we save the new termination record? We now have a situation where two employee records are inaccurate. We have one employee marked as inactive, which shouldn't be the case, and another employee still marked as active even though he or she should not be active. To fix this discrepancy manually, you would need to change the data in the existing termination record to use the correct employee, change the Active field of the employee's record to True for the employee to whom you first assigned the termination record, and also change the Active field to False for the employee that now has the termination record assigned to him or her. Instead of doing all these steps manually, we can use the After Update event to fix both employee records.

Open the tblTerminations table again in Datasheet view. Next, click the Table contextual tab under Table Tools, and then click the After Update button in the After Events group to open the Logic Designer, as shown in Figure 7-38. Note that we closed the Action Catalog in Figure 7-38 so you can see more of the macro design surface.

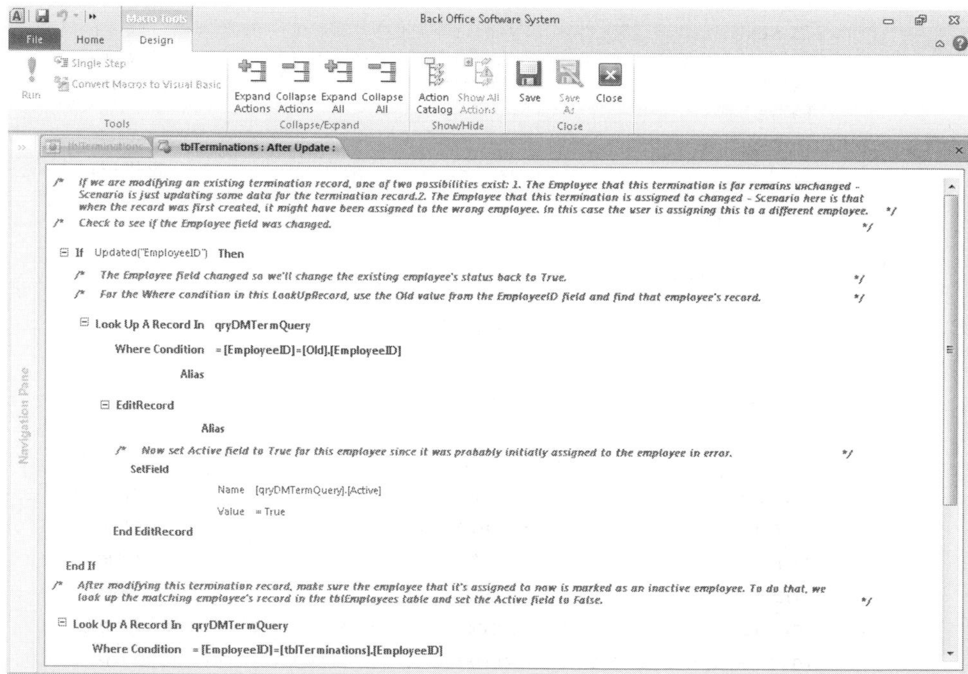

Figure 7-38 Click the After Update button on the ribbon to examine the After Update event of the tblTerminations table.

The data macro logic for the After Update event is as follows:

```
Comment Block: If we are modifying an existing termination record, one of two
possibilities exist: 1. The Employee that this termination is for remains unchanged -
Scenario is just updating some data for the termination record.2. The Employee that
this termination is assigned to changed - Scenario here is that when the record was
first created, it might have been assigned to the wrong employee. In this case the
user is assigning this to a different employee.
Comment Block: Check to see if the Employee field was changed.
If Updated("EmployeeID") Then
 Comment Block: The Employee field changed so we'll change the existing employee's
 status back to True.
 Comment Block: For the Where condition in this LookupRecord, use the Old value from
 the EmployeeID field and find that employee's record.
 LookupRecord In qryDMTermQuery
   Where Condition = [EmployeeID]=[Old].[EmployeeID]
   Alias
     EditRecord
     Alias
       Comment Block: Now set Active field to True for this employee since it was
       probably initially assigned to the employee in error.
       SetField
         Name: [qryDMTermQuery].[Active]
         Value: True

     End EditRecord
End If
Comment Block: After modifying this termination record, make sure the employee that
it's assigned to now is marked as an inactive employee. To do that, we look up the
matching employee's record in the tblEmployees table and set the Active field to
False.
LookupRecord In qryDMTermQuery
   Where Condition = [EmployeeID]=[tblTerminations].[EmployeeID]
   Alias
     EditRecord
     Alias
       Comment Block: Now set Active field to False.
       SetField
         Name: [qryDMTermQuery].[Active]
         Value: False

     End EditRecord
```

The first part of the data macro includes two Comment blocks to indicate the purpose of this event. Next, we use an If condition using the Updated property to see if the EmployeeID field changed. If the EmployeeID field changed, we know the user is assigning this existing termination record to a different employee. We then go into a LookupRecord data block and use the saved query qryDMTermQuery as the source. In the Where condition argument for the LookupRecord data block, we want to look up the EmployeeID in the query that matches the EmployeeID field found in the tblTerminations table that Access just finished committing. Once Access finds the matching record, we enter it into the EditRecord block.

Whenever you want to change data in another table in After events, you must use the SetField action inside an EditRecord block. For our example, we want to change the Active field of the matching employee to False to indicate that he or she is no longer an active employee in the database. The SetField action takes two required arguments, Name and Value. In the Name argument, we use the query name that was also used for the LookupRecord block. The context inside the LookupRecord here is the employee record that Access found inside the query, so we qualify the Active field name with the saved query name. Our Where condition argument for the LookupRecord uses the Old property. The Old property returns the value of the field before Access changed its value and saved the record. Our Where condition argument is therefore the following:

```
[EmployeeID]=[Old].[EmployeeID]
```

To help understand this concept, imagine the value of the EmployeeID is currently 31, the record for Jeff Conrad in the existing termination record. If you change the EmployeeID to John Viescas, EmployeeID of 16, the Old value for that field is 31 and the new value after saving the record is 16. By referencing the Old value of the EmployeeID, we can determine which employee this termination record *used* to be assigned to. (There is no New property available when creating data macros because the new value is simply the committed value of the field, and you can refer to it by using the field name.)

After Access finds the EmployeeID that the termination record used to be assigned to, we use a SetField data action to set the Active status of that employee back to True. It's our assumption that if the user is assigning the termination record to a different employee, we'll error on the side of caution and assume this employee's status should be changed back to True.

The first part of the data macro logic is inside an If block. Based on our logic, if the user did not change the EmployeeID field, Access does not change anything in the first part of the data macro. The second part of the After Update event is outside the If block, which means this part of the data macro logic runs every time a user changes anything about a termination record. We use another LookupRecord data block to look up a different employee record in the saved query. In this case, our Where condition argument is the following:

```
[EmployeeID]=[tblTerminations].[EmployeeID]
```

This time, Access looks for the EmployeeID in the saved query that matches the now-committed value in the EmployeeID field in the tblTerminations table. In our previous example, this means Access looks for the EmployeeID of John's record, which is 16. Finally, we set the Active status of that employee's record to False because this termination record is now assigned to that employee.

To test this After Update event, close the Logic Designer window by clicking the Close button in the Close group. You should now see the tblTerminations table again in Datasheet view. Find the termination record that you created in the previous section—the one assigned to Jeff Conrad. Tab over to the EmployeeID for this record, look at the drop-down list of employee names displayed in the EmployeeID field, and change the value from Jeff Conrad to John Viescas, as shown in Figure 7-36. Now click or tab off the record and Access saves the record with John Viescas's EmployeeID number.

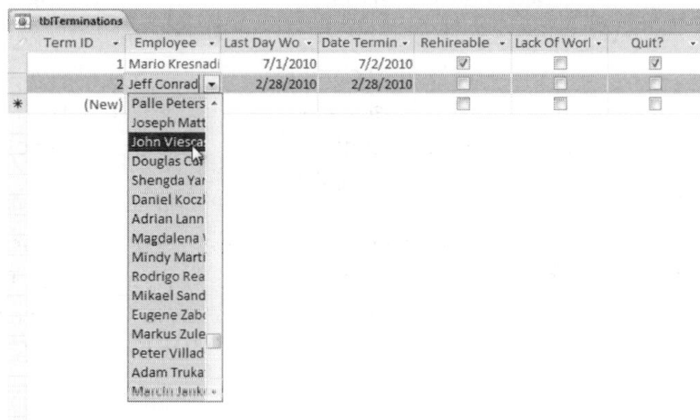

Figure 7-39 Change the EmployeeID field from Jeff Conrad to John Viescas and then save the record.

To see the effects of this After Update event, open the tblEmployees table in Datasheet view and scroll down to the record for the employee record for Jeff Conrad. You'll notice that the Active field for Jeff Conrad is now set to True, as shown in Figure 7-40. You'll also notice that John's record shows his Active status is now set to False. Note that in Figure 7-40, John's record is the record at the top (where the mouse cursor is pointing) and Jeff's record is at the bottom (the highlighted record).

tblTerminations | tblEmployees

	Last Review	Food Handle	Liquor Perm	📎	Active?	MapAddress	EmailAddre	Click to Add
⊞	6/12/2009	6/27/2010	3/29/2010	(1)	☐	http://maps.liv	JViescas@pros	
⊞		11/30/2009		(1)	☑	http://maps.liv	DCurran@pros	
⊞	1/30/2010	1/21/2011	4/28/2011	(1)	☑	http://maps.liv	SYang@prosew	
⊞		10/27/2010		(1)	☑	http://maps.liv	DKoczka@pros	
⊞	9/1/2009	2/3/2010		(1)	☑	http://maps.liv	ALannin@pros	
⊞	6/28/2009	1/13/2010	9/10/2010	(1)	☑	http://maps.liv	MWroblewska	
⊞	5/13/2009	11/9/2010	6/22/2010	(1)	☑	http://maps.liv	MMartin@pros	
⊞	2/26/2010	3/30/2010		(1)	☑	http://maps.liv	RReady@prose	
⊞	8/28/2009	12/17/2010		(1)	☑	http://maps.liv	MSandberg@p	
⊞		10/4/2010		(1)	☑	http://maps.liv	EZabokritski@	
⊞	3/28/2009	12/2/2010		(0)	☑	http://maps.liv	MZulechner@	
⊞	2/9/2009	7/10/2010		(0)	☑	http://maps.liv	PVilladsen@pr	
⊞		7/13/2010		(0)	☑	http://maps.liv	ATrukawka@p	
⊞	2/26/2010	2/15/2011		(1)	☑	http://maps.liv	MJankowski@	
⊞		9/30/2010		(1)	☑	http://maps.liv	MBuschmann@	
⊞	2/14/2010	9/27/2010	9/10/2010	(1)	☑	http://maps.liv	JConrad@pros	
*				(0)	☑			

Figure 7-40 Access changes the Active field for both Jeff's and John's records from the After Update event of the tblTerminations table.

With the data macro logic that we have defined in the After Update event, Access automatically maintains the Active status of the employee records. If the user assigns the termination record to a different employee, Access changes the Active status of two different employees. If the user changed information other than the EmployeeID field, Access marks that employee as inactive again just to be safe.

The Back Office Software System sample web database includes After Update events attached to two other web tables. You can explore the data macros attached to these events for additional examples.

- **tblLaborPlanDetails** Creates new records in the tblSchedule table if the NeedToUpdate field is set to True. This data macro uses the CreateRecord data block to create new records in tblSchedule by copying schedule data from tblLaborPlanDetails to tblSchedule.
- **tblSchedule** Creates new records in the tblSchedule table if the NeedToUpdate field is set to True. This data macro uses the CreateRecord data block to create additional new records in tblSchedule by copying existing schedule data from tblSchedule to the same table but putting in new schedule dates for the appended records.

Note

In After Insert and After Update events, the new record (the one that caused the event to fire) is read-only. This means you cannot have an EditRecord block by itself in these events changing data by using SetField actions on the same record. Ideally, you should be using the Before Change event if you need to be updating data on the same record based on data you are committing. This makes the data updated all at once instead of two separate updates. If you must use an After event, you need to put the EditRecord block inside a LookupRecord block and use a Where condition argument that looks up the record Access just committed in order to make the record not read-only.

After Delete

The After Delete event fires whenever Access completes the operation of deleting a record from the database. As you just saw in the previous two sections, we have data macros defined in the After Insert and After Update events of the tblTerminations table to adjust the employee's Active field whenever we are creating or editing termination records. What happens, though, when you delete an existing termination record? We now have a situation where you need to decide the appropriate logic based on the workflow needs of the application. You could decide to do nothing, which means that the employee to whom the termination record was assigned remains an inactive employee. For our database requirements with this application, we decided that an employee should be changed back to an active employee if a user deletes his or her termination record. In this workflow, a user might have accidentally created a termination record when no record should have been created in the first place.

Open the tblTerminations table again in Datasheet view. Next, click the Table contextual tab under Table Tools, and then click the After Delete button in the After Events group to open the Logic Designer, as shown in Figure 7-41.

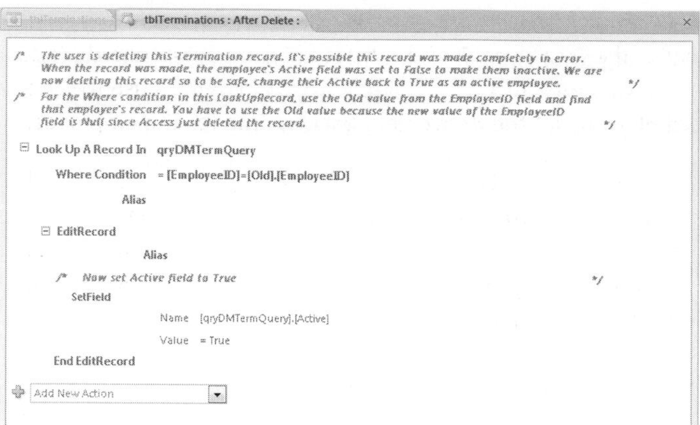

Figure 7-41 Click the After Delete button on the ribbon to examine the After Delete event of the tblTerminations table.

The data macro logic for the After Delete event is as follows:

```
Comment Block: The user is deleting this Termination record. It's possible this
record was made completely in error. When the record was made, the employee's Active
field was set to False to make them inactive. We are now deleting this record so to
be safe, change the Active field back to True as an active employee.
Comment Block: For the Where condition in this LookupRecord, use the Old value from
the EmployeeID field and find that employee's record. You have to use the Old value
because the new value of the EmployeeID field is Null since Access just deleted the
record.
LookupRecord In qryDMTermQuery
 Where Condition = [EmployeeID]=[Old].[EmployeeID]
 Alias
 EditRecord
    Alias
    Comment Block: Now set Active field to True
    SetField
       Name: [qryDMTermQuery].[Active]
       Value: True

 End EditRecord
```

The first part of the data macro includes two Comment blocks to indicate the purpose of this event. Next, we use a LookupRecord data block to look up a record in the saved query called qryDMTermQuery. In the Where condition argument for the LookupRecord data block, we want to look up the EmployeeID in the query that matches the EmployeeID field that Access just finished deleting from the tblTerminations table. When you are using the After Delete event and need to refer to a field value in the record that Access just deleted, you must use the Old property to retrieve the value. The existing field value is Null because Access deleted the record. Our Where condition is as follows:

```
[EmployeeID]=[Old].[EmployeeID]
```

The first half of the Where condition expression is the EmployeeID in the saved query and the second half is the EmployeeID of the deleted termination record. Once Access finds the matching record, we enter into the EditRecord block. We then use the SetField action inside the EditRecord block to set the Active field back to True for the employee.

To see the effects of this After Delete event, open the tblTerminations table in Datasheet view and then delete the termination record that you created and edited earlier—the record currently assigned to John. Now open the tblEmployees table in Datasheet view and scroll down to John's employee record. You'll notice that the Active field for John is now set back to True, as shown in Figure 7-42.

tblTerminations | tblEmployees

	Food Handle	Liquor Perm	(attachment)	Active?	MapAddress	EmailAddres	Click to Add
+	6/27/2010	3/29/2010	(1)	☑	http://maps.li	JViescas@pros	
+	11/30/2009		(1)	☑	http://maps.li	DCurran@pros	
+	1/21/2011	4/28/2011	(1)	☑	http://maps.li	SYang@prosew	
+	10/27/2010		(1)	☑	http://maps.li	DKoczka@pros	
+	2/3/2010		(1)	☑	http://maps.li	ALannin@pros	
+	1/13/2010	9/10/2010	(1)	☑	http://maps.li	MWroblewska	
+	11/9/2010	6/22/2010	(1)	☑	http://maps.li	MMartin@pros	
+	3/30/2010		(1)	☑	http://maps.li	RReady@prose	
+	12/17/2010		(1)	☑	http://maps.li	MSandberg@p	
+	10/4/2010		(1)	☑	http://maps.li	EZabokritski@	
+	12/2/2010		(0)	☑	http://maps.li	MZulechner@	
+	7/10/2010		(0)	☑	http://maps.li	PVilladsen@pr	
+	7/13/2010		(0)	☑	http://maps.li	ATrukawka@p	
+	2/15/2011		(1)	☑	http://maps.li	MJankowski@	
+	9/30/2010		(1)	☑	http://maps.li	MBuschmann	
+	9/27/2010	9/10/2010	(1)	☑	http://maps.li	JConrad@pros	
*			(0)	☑			

Figure 7-42 The After Delete event in tblTerminations changed John's Active field back to True.

Working with Named Data Macros

So far in this chapter, you've been studying data macros attached to specific table events. Access 2010 also supports creating named data macros. A named data macro is a data macro attached to a table, but not to a specific event. Named data macros execute only when called from another data macro, a user interface macro, or from Visual Basic code. Logic that is in a named data macro can interact with data in any table, require parameters before executing, and return data to the calling data macro, user interface macro, or Visual Basic code procedure. You can attach named data macros to any local client table or web table. You could, for example, attach all named data macros to one table or attach different named data macros to different tables based on their purpose. The Back Office Software System sample web database includes more than a dozen named data macros attached to various tables. In the next sections, you'll explore some examples of these named data macros, as well as create a new named data macro.

Creating Named Data Macros

In the Back Office Software System sample data copy web database (BOSSDataCopy.accdb), a table called tblErrorLog is used to record any application errors that might occur during the operation of any client objects in this hybrid application. The database administrator can monitor this table for any errors occurring in the operation of the database and then analyze the information recorded in the fields for debugging purposes. The database administrator would like an easy method to delete all the records in this error table after examining the errors and fixing the underlying issues. We can create a named data macro for this purpose, which can then be called from other areas of the application. To create a new named data macro for this purpose, we'll attach it to the tblErrorLog table for easy reference. Open the BOSSDataCopy.accdb sample web database, and then open the tblErrorLog table in Datasheet view. Next, click the Table contextual ribbon tab under Table Tools. Finally, click the Named Macro button in the Named Macros group and then click the option called Create Named Macro, as shown in Figure 7-43.

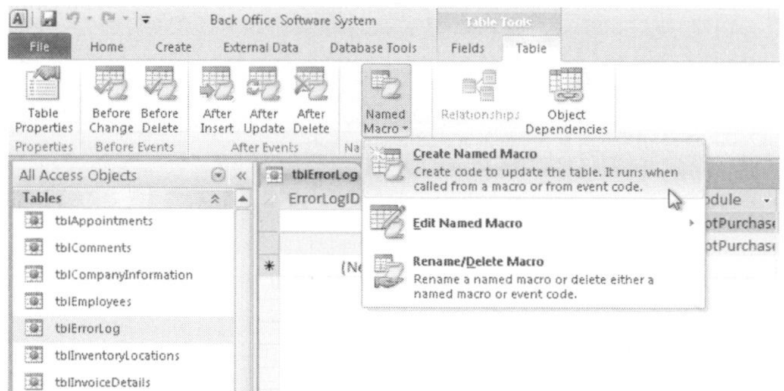

Figure 7-43 Click the Create Named Macro option under the Named Macro button to start creating a new named data macro attached to the tblErrorLog table.

Access opens the Logic Designer with an empty macro design surface, as shown in Figure 7-44. You'll notice one difference immediately on the macro design surface that you did not see when creating data macros attached to table events in the preceding sections. At the top of the macro design surface, you can see a section called Parameters. Named data macros allow you to create parameters, which you can use to pass information into the data macro. Creating parameters for named data macros is optional, but Access always displays the Parameters block at the top of the macro design surface whenever you are working with named data macros. (We'll explore parameters for named data macros later in this chapter.) The list of program flow constructs, data blocks, and data actions that you can use in named data macros is the same for After events except with the addition of one more data action called SetReturnVar. (We'll discuss the SetReturnVar action later in this chapter.) See Table 7-3 on page 399 if you want to review the list of elements available in After events.

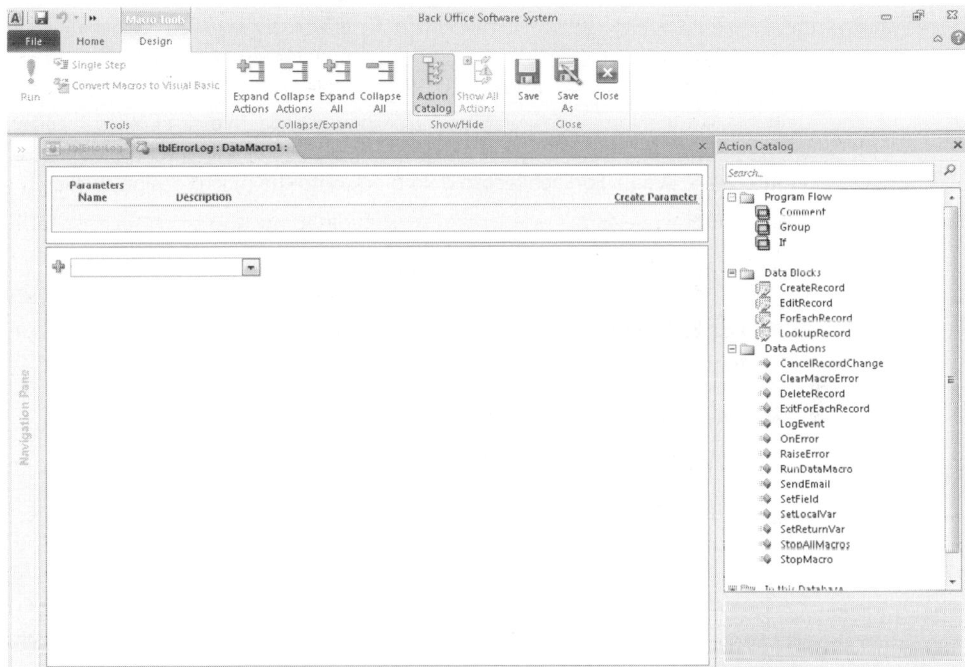

Figure 7-44 When you create named data macros, Access displays a Parameters block at the top of the macro design surface.

Let's first add a Comment block to this named data macro to document its purpose. Drag a Comment block from the Action Catalog onto the macro design surface. Enter the following text into the new Comment block:

Loop through all records in the client error table and delete them.

To delete all the records in the tblErrorLog table, we need to use the ForEachRecord data block. Drag a ForEachRecord data block from the Action Catalog to beneath the Comment block, or select ForEachRecord from the Add New Action box at the bottom of the macro design surface. Access creates a new ForEachRecord block, as shown in Figure 7-45.

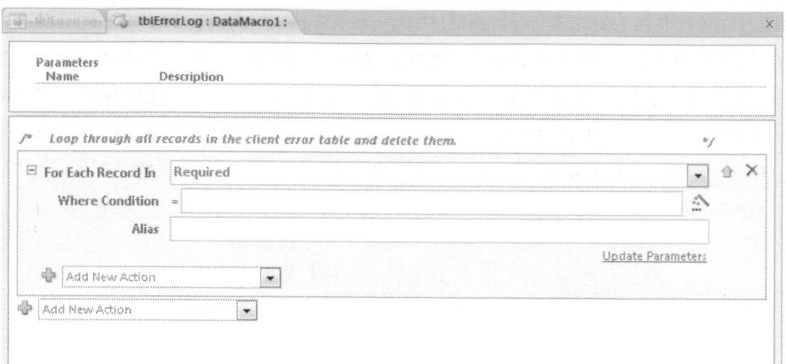

Figure 7-45 Drag a ForEachRecord data block onto the macro design surface.

The ForEachRecord data block takes three arguments:

- **For Each Record In** Required argument. A name of a table, query, or SQL statement to look up a record in.
- **Where Condition** Optional argument. An expression that Access uses to select records from the table, query, or SQL statement.
- **Alias** Optional argument. A substitute or shorter name for the table.

You'll notice in the lower-right corner of the ForEachRecord data block there is an Update Parameters link. If you are using a query for your data source that includes parameters, you can update the parameters using this link. We'll discuss using parameters with named data macros later in this chapter.

INSIDE OUT Creating Records in a ForEachRecord Block

You cannot use the CreateRecord action inside a ForEachRecord block in Access 2010. This is a design limitation that prohibits you from creating many records at one time. You can, however, work around this limitation by using a combination of a ForEachRecord block and an After Update event.

Both the tblLaborPlanDetails and tblSchedule tables in the Back Office Software System web database have an After Update event that checks to see if a Boolean field in the table is True. If the field is True, the After Update event runs a CreateRecord action to create new records in the tblSchedule table. We use a named data macro to loop through the records that we want to copy in the tblSchedule or tblLaborPlanDetails tables and set those Boolean fields to True. The After Update events fire and create new records. We then execute another named macro to reset the Boolean field back to False for all the records that we previously updated. You can study the After Update events and named data macros attached to tblLaborPlanDetails and tblSchedule to see examples of this functionality.

Click the drop-down list on the For Each Record In argument and select the tblErrorLog table. We don't need to provide anything for the Where condition or Alias arguments because we don't need to restrict our logic to a subset of the records in the tblErrorLog table; we want to delete all the records. Now, tab into or click the Add New Action box just beneath the Alias argument and then select the DeleteRecord action from the box. Access creates a DeleteRecord action inside the ForEachRecord block, as shown in Figure 7-46.

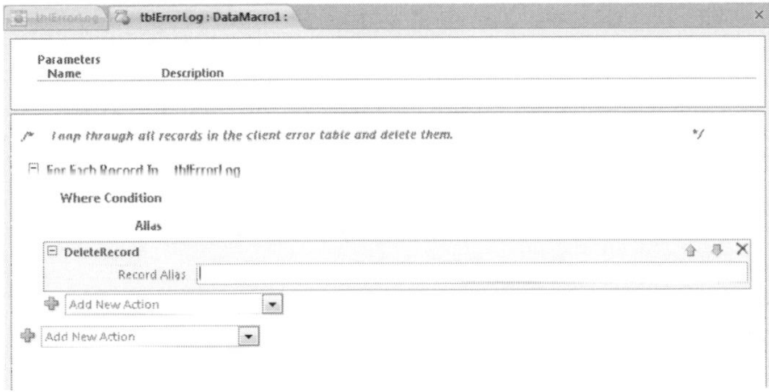

Figure 7-46 Add the DeleteRecord action inside the ForEachRecord data block.

The DeleteRecord action only has one argument—Alias—and it's an optional argument. We don't need to provide an alias for this example.

That's all the logic we need in this named data macro to delete all the records in the tblErrorLog table. When Access executes this named data macro, it comes into the ForEachRecord data block, finds the first record in the table if any exist, and then deletes the record. Access then repeats the loop by going to the next record in the table and deleting that record as well. Access continues this process until it cannot find any more records in the tblErrorLog table. If there were actions following the ForEachRecord loop, Access would execute those actions after it deleted the last record in the table.

Saving Named Data Macros

You've completed creating your first named data macro, but now you need to save it and give it a name. Unlike data macros attached to table events, named data macros require unique names. To save your new named data macro, click the Save button in the Close group on the Design contextual tab, or click the Save button on the Quick Access Toolbar. Access opens the Save As dialog box, as shown in Figure 7-47. Save the named data macro with the name ClearLogsTest.

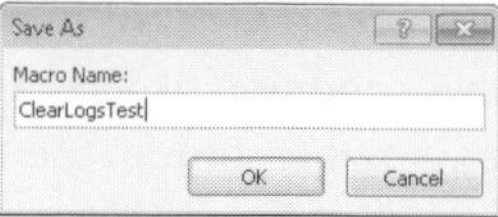

Figure 7-47 Provide a unique name for your new named data macro in the Save As dialog box.

Each named data macro attached to a table must have a unique name. You are allowed to have named data macros with the same if they are attached to different tables. If you attempt to save a named data macro with the same name as a named data macro attached to the same table, Access displays a warning message, as shown in Figure 7-48. If you click Yes, Access overwrites the existing named data macro with the new logic that you just defined.

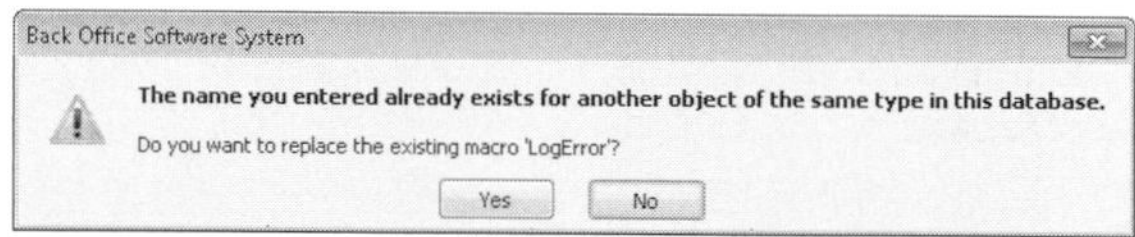

Figure 7-48 Access displays a warning message if you try to save a named data macro with the same name as an existing named data macro attached to the same table.

Calling Named Data Macros

We mentioned earlier that named data macros must be called for Access to execute them. If you want to test out a named data macro, you must therefore call a RunDataMacro action from a table event, a user interface macro, or from Visual Basic. In Chapter 21, you'll learn how to call named data macros from user interface macros, and in Chapter 25, "Automating Your Application with Visual Basic," (on the companion CD) you'll learn how to call named data macros from Visual Basic. For simplicity of this example, we'll create a data macro attached to a table event that will trigger the named data macro to execute.

Close the tblErrorLog table, if you still have it open, and then open the tblAppointments table in Datasheet view. Let's call the new named data macro you created to run whenever you insert a new record into the tblAppointments table. Click the Table contextual tab and then click the After Insert button in the After Events group to open the Logic Designer. To call the named data macro to run, you need to use the RunDataMacro action. By now, you should be very familiar with the different techniques for adding a new data action to the macro design surface. In this case, we'll do something different because we are calling a named data macro. In the Action Catalog, expand the In This Database node near the bottom of the screen. Next, expand the Tables node beneath In This Database, and then expand the tblErrorLog node to see the named data macros attached to this table, as shown in Figure 7-49.

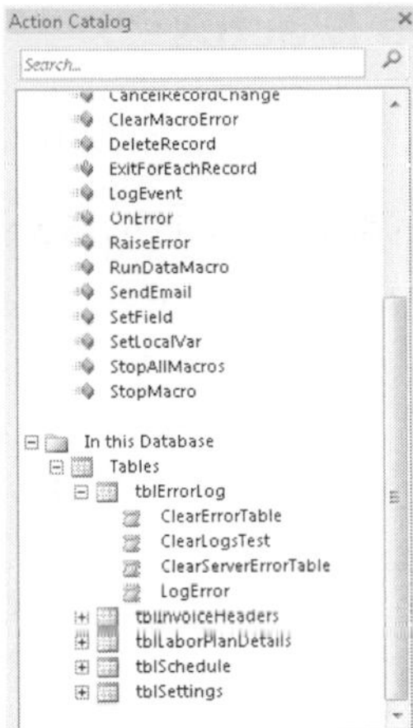

Figure 7-49 Expand the In This Database node in the Action Catalog to see a list of all the named data macros in the database.

Now, drag the ClearLogsTest named data macro that you created in the previous section onto the macro design surface. Access adds a new RunDataMacro data action to the macro design surface and also fills in the required Macro Name argument for you, as shown in Figure 7-50. The Macro Name argument requires the name of the table and the name of the named data macro separated by a period. Access also provides a drop-down list for this argument where you can select from a list of all the named data macros attached to the tables in your database.

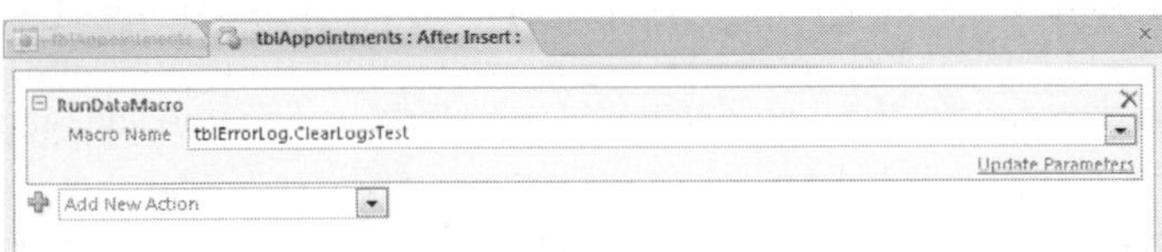

Figure 7-50 Access creates a new RunDataMacro action with the Macro Name argument filled in when you drag a named data macro on to the macro design surface.

To test out the named data macro, save the changes to this After Insert event and then create a new record in the tblAppointments table. After you insert a new record into the table, Access executes the RunDataMacro action and then deletes all the records in the tblErrorLog table. You can verify this by opening the tblErrorLog table and seeing that no records exist in the table.

Renaming and Deleting Named Data Macros

When you need to rename or delete named data macros, or even delete data macros attached to table events, Access provides a useful tool to assist you. Open the tblErrorLog table in Datasheet view, click the Table contextual tab, click the Named Macro button in the Named Macros group, and then click Rename/Delete Macro from the drop-down list, as shown in Figure 7-51.

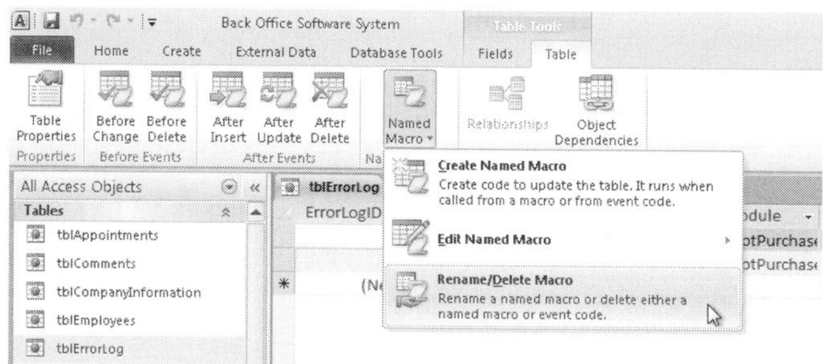

Figure 7-51 Click the Rename/Delete Macro option beneath Named Macro.

Access opens the Data Macro Manager, as shown in Figure 7-52. The Data Macro Manager displays a list of all the tables in your database that have data macros attached to table events, as well as all named data macros. You can expand the size of the Data Macro Manager by clicking the corner of the dialog box and dragging the window to a larger size. Beneath each table name, Access lists each table event or named data macro on a separate line in the Data Macro Manager. For table events, Access lists the name of the event, the words Event Data Macro, and a Delete link. For named data macros, Access lists the name of the named data macro, the words Named Data Macro, a Rename link, and a Delete link.

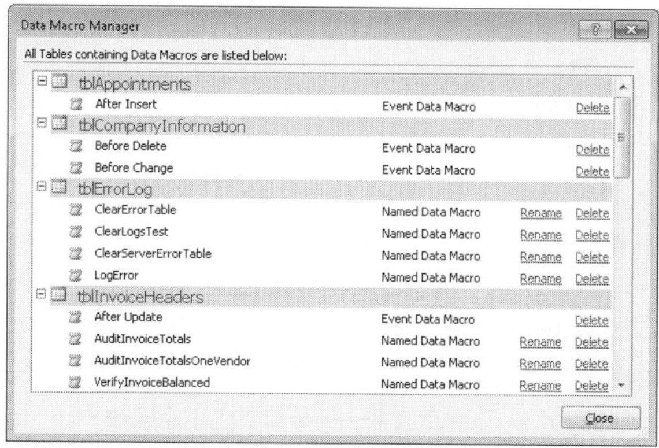

Figure 7-52 You can rename and delete data macros using the Data Macro Manager.

If you want to rename a named data macro, click the Rename link next to the named data macro that you want to rename. Access unlocks the name of the named data macro so you can change it, as shown in Figure 7-53. Access immediately saves the new name when you click away from the name box or click the Close button.

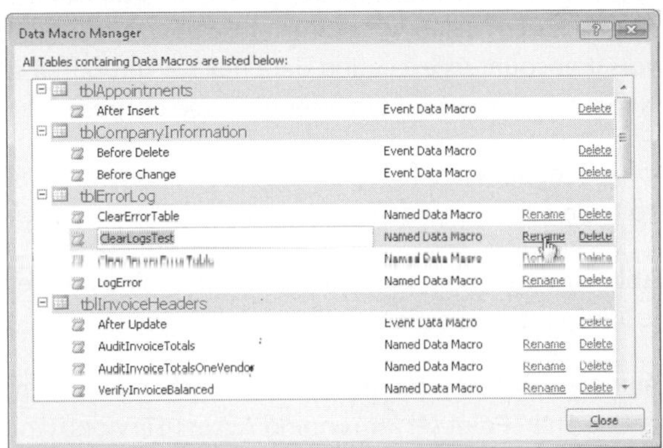

Figure 7-53 Click the Rename link to rename named data macros.

We don't need the named data macro we created in the previous section because it duplicates logic functionality we already have in the ClearErrorTable named data macro. To delete the test named data macro that you created previously, click the Delete link next to the ClearLogsTest named data macro. Access displays a confirmation message, as shown in Figure 7-54. If you are deleting a named data macro attached to a table that you currently have open, you also need to save the changes to the table after you close the Data Macro Manager. Click Yes to delete the ClearLogsTest named data macro.

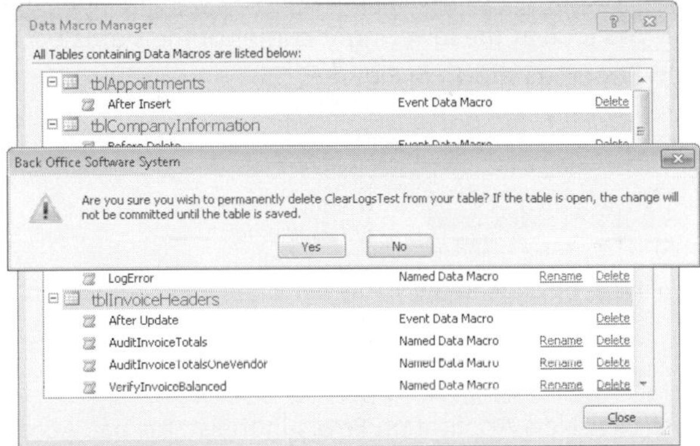

Figure 7-54 In the confirmation message, click Yes to delete the named data macro.

Analyzing Errors in the USysApplicationLog Table

So far in this chapter, all the data macros you've created and tested executed without problems. In a working application used by many users, however, it's quite possible that Access can and will encounter errors executing data macros. Access can also run into errors while you are in the development phase of creating, testing, and debugging your data macros. Access manages any errors it encounters executing data macros through a special system table called USysApplicationLog. This special table serves three purposes:

- Access uses it to log any data macro failures that it encounters while executing data macros attached to table events and named data macros.
- You can use the table for debugging purposes when designing and testing data macros by utilizing the LogEvent data action.
- Access uses this table to record any compilation errors when publishing or synchronizing web objects to a SharePoint server running Access Services. (You'll learn about publishing and synchronizing with Access Services in Chapter 22, "Using Web Applications in a Browser.")

In the previous section, you deleted the test named data macro called ClearLogsTest attached to the tblErrorLog table. In the After Insert event of the tblAppointments table, we still have a RunDataMacro action that calls the now deleted ClearLogsTest named data macro. If we add a new appointment record to the tblAppointments table, Access attempts to run a named data macro that no longer exists. Let's try this out and see how Access responds to this problem. Open the tblAppointments table in Datasheet view, create a new appointment record, and then save the record. You'll notice that Access does not display any error dialog boxes or messages to you, even though we know that it must have encountered a problem. Access does, however, provide you a small error indication message in the status bar. If you look at the lower-right corner of the status bar, you can see the words "New Application Errors," as shown in Figure 7-55.

Figure 7-55 Access displays a message in the status bar when it encounters an error while executing data macros.

If you hover your mouse over New Application Errors in the status bar, Access displays a tooltip explaining that there are new errors in the USysApplicationLog table. These words in the status bar also serve as an entry point to open this error table. Click New Application Errors, and Access opens the USysApplicationLog table in Datasheet view, as shown in Figure 7-56.

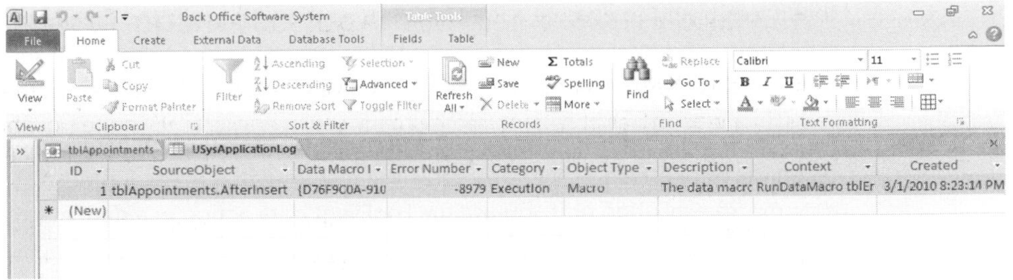

Figure 7-56 Click New Application Errors to open the USysApplicationLog table.

The USysApplicationLog table contains the following fields: SourceObject, Data Macro Instance ID, Error Number, Category, Object Type, Description, Context, and Created. You cannot see all the information in this table in Figure 7-56, so we've reproduced the information in Table 7-4.

Table 7-4 USysApplicationLog Table Results

Field Name	Data
SourceObject	tblAppointments.AfterInsert
Data Macro Instance ID	{D76F9C0A-910E-402D-B20E-7BC802F11274}
Error Number	-8979
Category	Execution
Object Type	Macro
Description	The data macro 'tblErrorLog.ClearLogsTest' could not be found.
Context	RunDataMacro tblErrorLog.ClearLogsTest
Created	3/1/2010 8:23:14 PM

The SourceObject field lists the name of the table and the specific event where Access encountered an error. In our example, you can see that Access logged an error for the AfterInsert event attached to the tblAppointments table. The Data Macro Instance ID is the unique ID that Access uses to track the execution of the data macro. The Error Number is the specific internal error number that Access uses to record errors while executing data macros. In the Category field, you can see Access lists this error as an Execution error. (In Chapter 22, you'll learn that Access also writes compilation errors to this USysAppicationLog table when you publish a web database to a SharePoint server running Access Services.) The Object Type field indicates the specific type of object where Access encountered an error; in our example, it was a macro. In the Description field, Access lists more specific information about the nature of the issue that it encountered. Access informs you that it could not find the ClearLogsTest data macro attached to the tblErrorLog table. Access lists the specific context where it hit an error in the Context field. Access gives you information that it was trying to execute a RunDataMacro action that calls the ClearLogsTest named data macro attached to the tblErrorLog table. The last field, Created, lists the date and time when Access hit the error.

By default, there is no USysApplicationLog table when you create a new client or web database. Access creates this error table the first time that it encounters errors during data macro execution or if you use the LogEvent data action in a data macro. (You'll see examples of the LogEvent data action later in this chapter.) If the USysApplicationLog table already exists in your database, Access appends new records to the table instead of creating an additional table. If you delete this table from the Navigation pane, Access recreates another table when it needs to log an error. You can also access the USysApplicationLog table at any time from the Backstage view. Click the File tab on the Backstage view, click Info, and then click the View Application Log Table button, as shown in Figure 7-57.

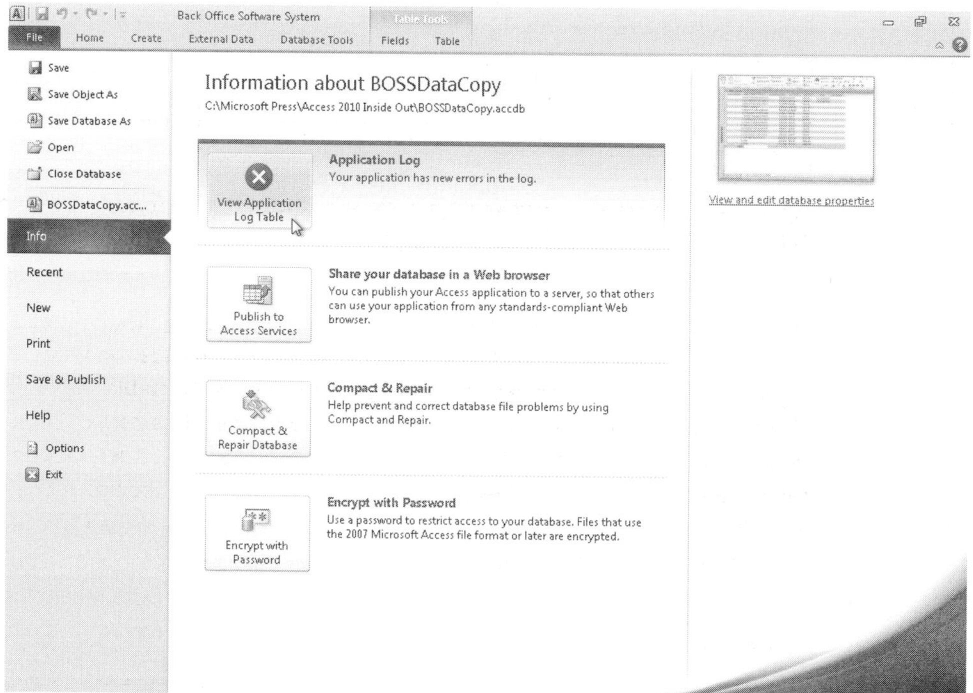

Figure 7-57 Click the View Application Log Table button on the Backstage view to open the USysApplicationLog table.

Access does not display the USysApplicationLog table in the Navigation pane by default because the table starts with the prefix USys. To see user-defined system tables—tables that start with the prefix USys—you need to change your navigation options to display system objects. To do this, right-click the menu bar at the top of the Navigation pane and then click Navigation Options on the shortcut menu. Access opens the Navigation Options dialog box, as shown in Figure 7-58.

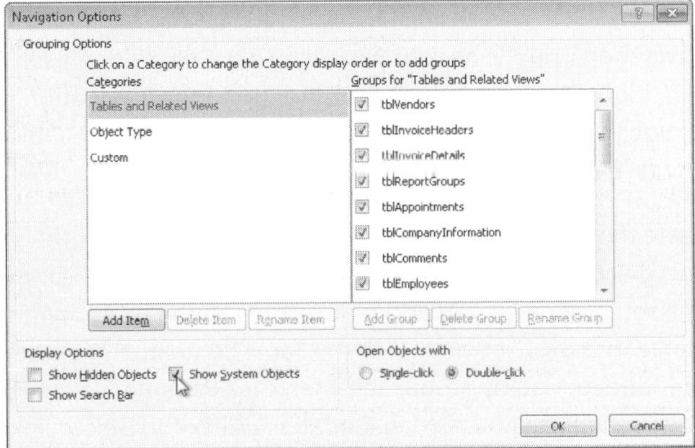

Figure 7-58 Select Show System Objects to see the USysApplicationLog table in the Navigation pane.

Under Display Options, select Show System Objects, and then click OK. You'll notice that Access now displays the USysApplicationLog table in the Navigation pane, as shown in Figure 7-59. You'll also notice that Access now displays another table with the USys prefix—USysRibbons—as well as several tables that start with the MSys prefix. The USysRibbons table holds the data needed to create custom ribbons for the Back Office Software System sample web database. (You'll learn all about creating custom ribbons in Chapter 26, "The Finishing Touches," on the companion CD.) Tables that start with the MSys prefix are system tables created by Access to control your database application.

CAUTION!

You should not attempt to modify any tables that start with the MSys prefix; you might cause irreparable damage to your database!

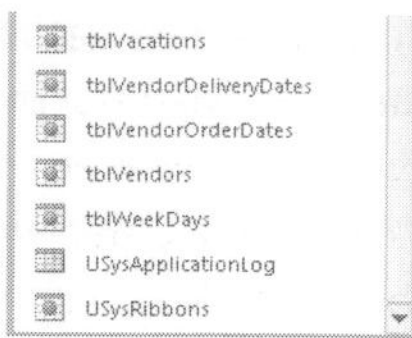

Figure 7-59 Access now displays the USysApplicationLog table in the Navigation pane.

Let's change the navigation options back to what they were so we don't see all the extra Access system tables. Right-click the menu bar at the top of the Navigation pane and then click Navigation Options on the shortcut menu. Clear the Show System Objects option on the Navigation Options dialog box and then click OK.

You should now delete the After Insert event that you created earlier for the tblAppointments table. Remember, we deleted the ClearLogsTest named data macro, which means Access will continue to hit errors whenever you add new records to the tblAppointments table. To do this, open any table in Datasheet view, click the Table contextual tab, click the Named Macro button in the Named Macros group, and then click Rename/Delete Macro from the drop-down list to open the Data Macro Manager again. Click the Delete link next to the After Insert event under the tblAppointments table and then close the dialog box.

INSIDE OUT **Access Logs Save Conflicts to USysApplicationLog Table**

When Access attempts to commit data using the SetField action inside an EditRecord block, it could encounter a save conflict because someone else is editing the data in the same record. If this happens, Access retries the SetField action up to five times. If Access fails to commit the requested changes on the fifth attempt, Access logs an entry into the USysApplicationLog table indicating that it encountered a save conflict and could not commit the data. If you have data macro logic attached to table events and named data macros in your application, we recommend that you periodically check the USysApplicationLog table for any types of errors, including save conflicts.

Using Parameters

In named data macros, you can define parameters to pass in information to the named data macro and use them in the data blocks and data actions. With parameters, you can pass in information to the named data macro from other data macros, forms, user interface macros, or Visual Basic. In the Back Office Software System sample web database, many of the named data macros attached to the web tables include parameters. Let's study an example that uses dates for parameters. Open the tblSchedule in Datasheet view. Next, click the Table contextual ribbon tab under Table Tools. Finally, click the Named Macro button in the Named Macros group, click Edit Named Macro in the drop-down list, and then click DeleteDateRangeRecords, as shown in Figure 7-60.

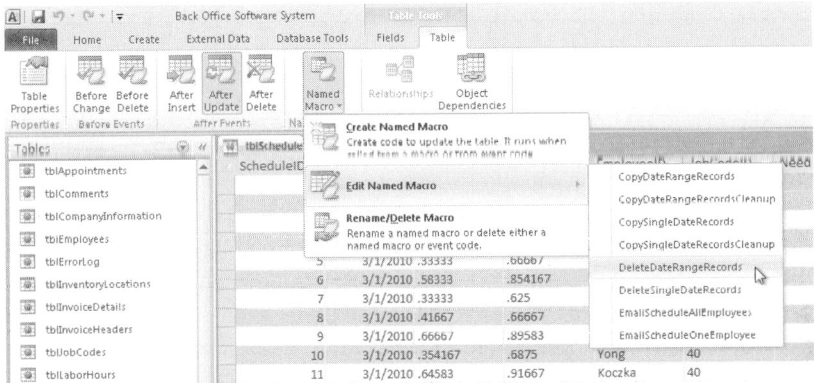

Figure 7-60 Click DeleteDateRangeReocrds to view the named data macro attached to the tblSchedule table.

Access opens the Logic Designer and displays the logic that we created for this named data macro, as shown in Figure 7-61.

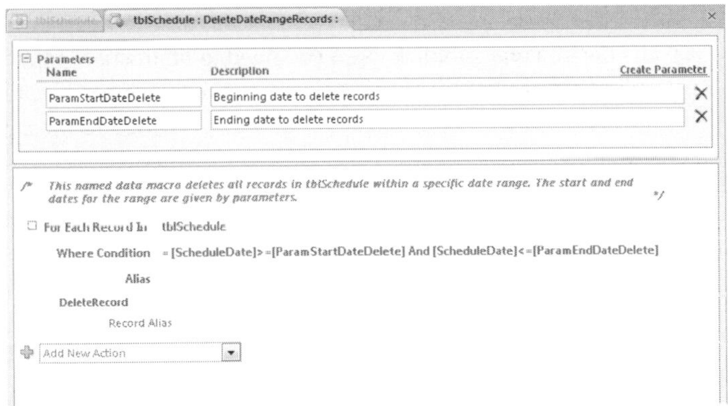

Figure 7-61 This named data macro includes two parameters.

The logic for the DeleteDateRangeRecords named data macro is as follows:

```
Parameter Name: ParamStartDateDelete
Parameter Description: Beginning date to delete records
Parameter Name: ParamEndDateDelete
Parameter Description: Ending date to delete records
Comment Block: This named data macro deletes all records in tblSchedule within a spe-
cific date range. The start and end dates for the range are given by parameters.
ForEachRecord In tblSchedule
 Where Condition = [ScheduleDate]>=[ParamStartDateDelete] And
                   [ScheduleDate]<=[ParamEndDateDelete]
 Alias
 DeleteRecord
    Record Alias
```

At the top of the macro design surface, you can see two parameters that we created. You must provide a name for each parameter that you create, up to 64 characters in length, but the description is optional. We recommend that you enter a description for each parameter that you create, for documentation purposes. To create a parameter for a named data macro, click the Create Parameter link in the upper-right corner of the Parameters block. Access adds an additional parameter line in the Parameters block. Figure 7-62 shows you an example of adding a new parameter to this named data macro. To remove a parameter, click the Delete button next to the parameter line.

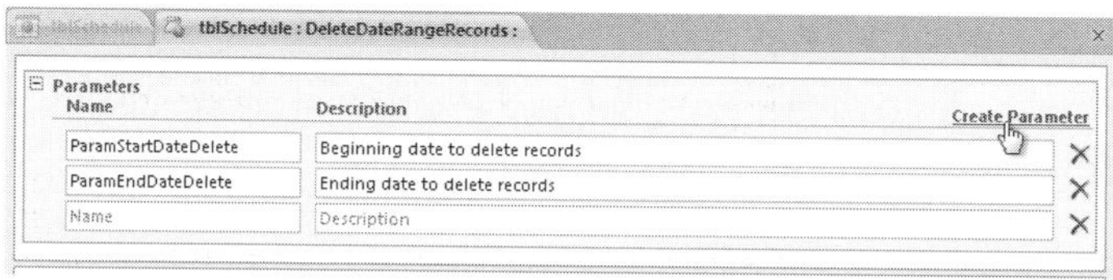

Figure 7-62 Click the Create Parameter link when you need to define new parameters for named data macros.

This named data macro deletes all records in the tblSchedule table, but only within a specific date range. The date range is determined by the two date parameters. In the Where condition argument for the ForEachRecord data block, we use these parameter values just like table fields by adding brackets around them. Our Where condition is as follows:

```
[ScheduleDate]>=[ParamStartDateDelete] And [ScheduleDate]<=[ParamEndDateDelete]
```

By using parameters, this named data macro can be very flexible because we are not hard-coding specific dates into the logic. We can use this named data macro at any time in the application by passing in any date range, and Access takes care of the work by deleting only the records in the tblSchedule table within that date range. In Chapter 21, you'll learn how to call named data macros from forms and pass in parameters from data in form controls.

Using Local Variables

You can use a local variable in data macros to store a value that can be used throughout the execution of the data macro. Local variables are very useful when you need Access to calculate values during the execution of the data macro or remember something for later use in the data macro. You can think of a local variable in a data macro as writing yourself a note to remember a number, a name, or an email address so that you can recall it at a later time in the data macro. All local variables have a unique name. To fetch, set, or examine a local variable, you reference it by its name. Local variables stay in memory until the data macro finishes executing, you assign it a new value, or until you clear the value.

Let's examine a named data macro that uses a local variable so you can understand how this works. Open the tblInvoiceHeaders table in Datasheet view. Next, click the Table contextual ribbon tab under Table Tools. Finally, click the Named Macro button in the Named Macros group, click Edit Named Macro in the drop-down list, and then click VerifyInvoiceBalanced. Access opens the Logic Designer and displays the logic that we created for this named data macro, as shown in Figure 7-63.

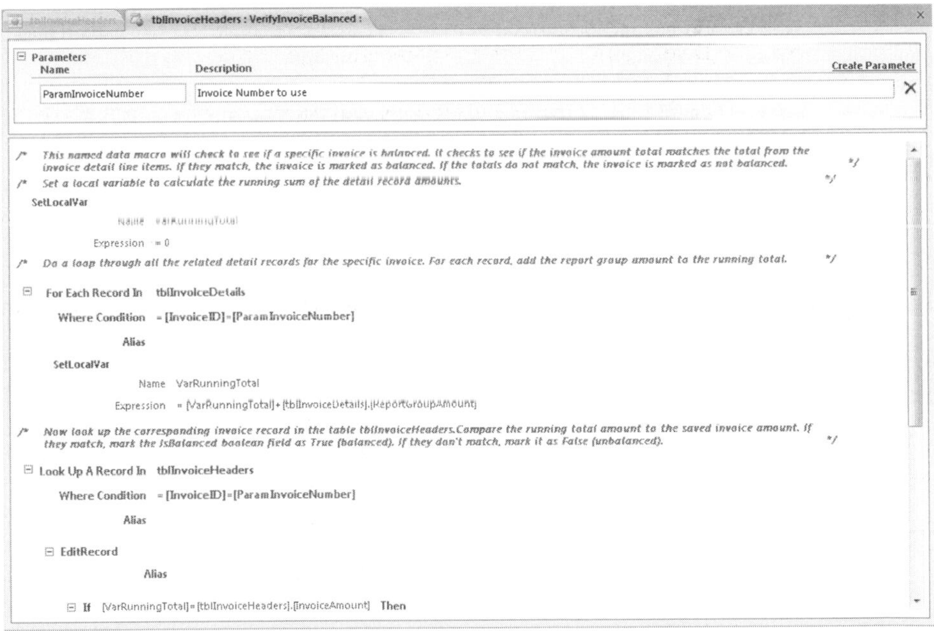

Figure 7-63 This named data macro uses a local variable to calculate a total of invoice detail items.

The logic for the VerifyInvoiceBalanced named data macro is as follows:

```
Parameter Name: ParamInvoiceNumber
Parameter Description: Invoice Number to use
Comment Block: This named data macro will check to see if a specific invoice is
balanced. It checks to see if the invoice amount total matches the total from the
invoice detail line items. If they match, the invoice is marked as balanced. If the
totals do not match, the invoice is marked as not balanced.
Comment Block: Set a local variable to calculate the running sum of the detail record
amounts.
SetLocalVar
 Name: VarRunningTotal
 Expression: 0
Comment Block: Do a loop through all the related detail records for the specific
invoice. For each record, add the report group amount to the running total.
ForEachRecord In tblInvoiceDetails
 Where Condition = [InvoiceID]=[ParamInvoiceNumber]
 Alias
 SetLocalVar
    Name: VarRunningTotal
    Expression: [VarRunningTotal]+[tblInvoiceDetails].[ReportGroupAmount]
Comment Block: Now, look up the corresponding invoice record in the table tblInvoice-
Headers.Compare the running total amount to the saved invoice amount. If they match,
mark the IsBalanced boolean field as True (balanced). If they don't match, mark it as
False (unbalanced).
LookupRecord In tblInvoiceHeaders
 Where Condition = [InvoiceID]=[ParamInvoiceNumber]
 Alias
 EditRecord
   Alias
   If [VarRunningTotal]=[tblInvoiceHeaders].[InvoiceAmount] Then
      Comment Block: Invoice is balanced.
      SetField
        Name: tblInvoiceHeaders.IsBalanced
        Value: True
   Else
      Comment Block: Invoice is not balanced.
      SetField
        Name: tblInvoiceHeaders.IsBalanced
        Value: False
   End If
 End EditRecord
```

At the beginning of this named data macro, we use the SetLocalVar action to define a new local variable. The SetLocalVar action takes two arguments:

- **Name** Required argument. The name of the local variable.
- **Expression** Required argument. The expression that Access uses to define the local variable.

We named our local variable VarRunningTotal and initially set it to a value of zero. Inside the ForEachRecord data block, Access loops through each record in the tblInvoiceDetails table where the InvoiceID equals the InvoiceID passed in as a parameter. Within the ForEachRecord data block, we use another SetLocalVar with the same name; however, we use the following expression in the Expression argument:

```
[VarRunningTotal]+[tblInvoiceDetails].[ReportGroupAmount]
```

With this expression, Access adds the existing current value of the local variable to the amount in the ReportGroupAmount field of the tblInvoiceDetails table. When Access finds the first record match, it adds 0 to the amount in the ReportGroupAmount field. On each subsequent loop through the ForEachRecord data block, Access keeps a running sum of the total amount of invoice line items. In the second half of the named data macro, we use the LookupRecord data block to look up the main parent invoice record stored in the tblInvoiceHeaders table with the given InvoiceID parameter. We then have an If condition block that compares the completed running sum total stored in our local variable with the InvoiceAmount field in the tblInvoiceHeaders table. If the amounts are equal, we know that the invoice is balanced with its child detail record amounts. Finally, if the invoice is balanced, we set the Boolean IsBalanced field to True, and if it is not balanced, we set the field to False. You'll find working with local variables can be very useful when defining complex business logic at the data layer.

INSIDE OUT **Committing Data in Nested Data Blocks**

If you are nesting the ForEachRecord or LookupRecord data block, you can only use the SetField data action to write data to the outermost block. You can read values from tables or queries within the nested blocks, but you can write data only to the outermost block.

Working with Return Variables

You can use a return variable in data macros to return data to the object that called the named data macro. In a sense, you can think of a return variable as the opposite of a parameter. You use parameters to *push* data into a named data macro, and you use return variables to *pull* data out of named data macros. Return variables are very useful when you need Access to read values from a table or query during the execution of the named data macro and perhaps perform different steps based on that value. Return variables can even be returned from the data layer up to the user interface level. All return variables have a unique name. To fetch, set, or examine a local variable, you reference it by its name. Return variables stay in memory until the data macro finishes executing, you assign it a new value, or until you clear the value. You can only set return variables in named data macros; however, you can retrieve them from After events, other named data macros, user interface macros, and Visual Basic.

Let's examine a named data macro that uses return variables so you can understand how this works. Open the tblSettings table in Datasheet view. Next, click the Table contextual ribbon tab under Table Tools. Finally, click the Named Macro button in the Named Macros group, click Edit Named Macro in the drop-down list, and then click GetCurrentValue. Access opens the Logic Designer and displays the logic that we created for this named data macro, as shown in Figure 7-64.

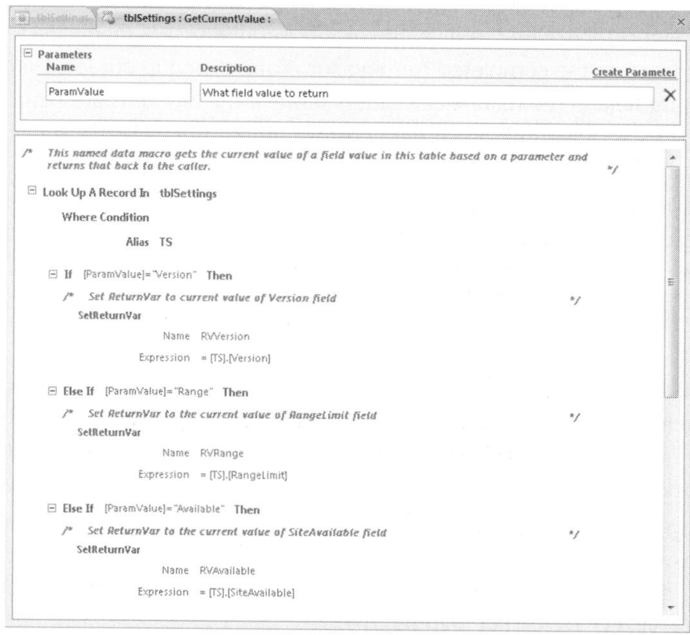

Figure 7-64 The GetCurrentValue named data macro uses return variables to return data to the caller.

The logic for the GetCurrentValue named data macro is as follows:

```
Parameter Name: ParamValue
Parameter Description: What field value to return
Comment Block: This named data macro gets the current value of a field value in this
table based on a parameter and returns that back to the caller.
LookupRecord In tblSettings
 Where Condition
 Alias: TS
 If [ParamValue]="Version" Then
    Comment Block: Set ReturnVar to current value of Version field
    SetReturnVar
      Name: RVVersion
      Expression: [TS].[Version]
 Else If [ParamValue]="Range" Then
    Comment Block: Set ReturnVar to the current value of RangeLimit field
    SetReturnVar
      Name: RVRange
      Expression: [TS].[RangeLimit]
 Else If [ParamValue]="Available" Then
    Comment Block: Set ReturnVar to the current value of SiteAvailable field
    SetReturnVar
      Name: RVAvailable
      Expression: [TS].[SiteAvailable]
 Else If [ParamValue]="LogEventEmail" Then
    Comment Block: Set ReturnVar to the current value of
                   LogEventsForMissingEmailAddress field
    SetReturnVar
      Name: RVLogEventEmail
      Expression: [TS].[LogEventsForMissingEmailAddress]
 Else If [ParamValue]="SendEmailOnError" Then
    Comment Block: Set ReturnVar to the current value of the
                    SendEmailForAppErrors field
    SetReturnVar
      Name: RVSendEmailOnError
      Expression: [TS].[SendEmailForAppErrors]
 Else If [ParamValue]="AdminEmail" Then
    Comment Block: Set ReturnVar to the current value of the AdminEmailAddress field
    SetReturnVar
      Name: RVAdminEmailAddress
      Expression: [TS].[AdminEmailAddress]
 Else If [ParamValue]="AllEmailInfoForErrors" Then
    Comment Block: For this parameter value, send back the settings for both the
                   SendEmailOnError and AdminEmailAddress fields so the
                   caller doesn't need to make two trips.
    SetReturnVar
      Name: RVSendEmailForError
      Expression: [TS].[SendEmailForAppErrors]
    SetReturnVar
      Name: RVAdminEmailForErrors
      Expression: [TS].[AdminEmailAddress]
 End If
```

The tblSettings table holds application-specific settings in several fields. By storing these settings in the table, we can then use data macros to retrieve these values at any time. The GetCurrentValue named data macro uses a large If block inside a LookupRecord data block. The If/ElseIf conditions check the value of the parameter ParamValue being passed in from the caller. We then use the SetReturnVar data action to define a new return variable. The SetReturnVar action takes two arguments:

- **Name** Required argument. The name of the return variable.
- **Expression** Required argument. The expression that Access uses to define the return variable.

We set a unique name for each return variable inside the various ElseIf condition blocks. For the Expression argument of each SetReturnVar action, we use an alias of the table name and read the data from a specific field. In the last ElseIf condition block, we return data from two fields with two different return variables to save the caller from having to make two RunDataMacro calls for related application settings. You could optionally create a named data macro that returns all data from the fields with return variables in one call, but we didn't want to be passing around data when it would not be needed. By itself, this named data macro does not do anything more than read values from the tblSettings table. However, the real power of the return variables is the ability of the object calling this named data macro to use these values.

To see how this data in return variables can be used, close the Logic Designer for this named data macro and then close the tblSettings table. Now, open the tblErrorLog table in Datasheet view. Next, click the Table contextual ribbon tab under Table Tools. Finally, click the Named Macro button in the Named Macros group, click Edit Named Macro in the drop-down list, and then click LogError. Access opens the Logic Designer and displays the logic that we created for this named data macro, as shown in Figure 7-65.

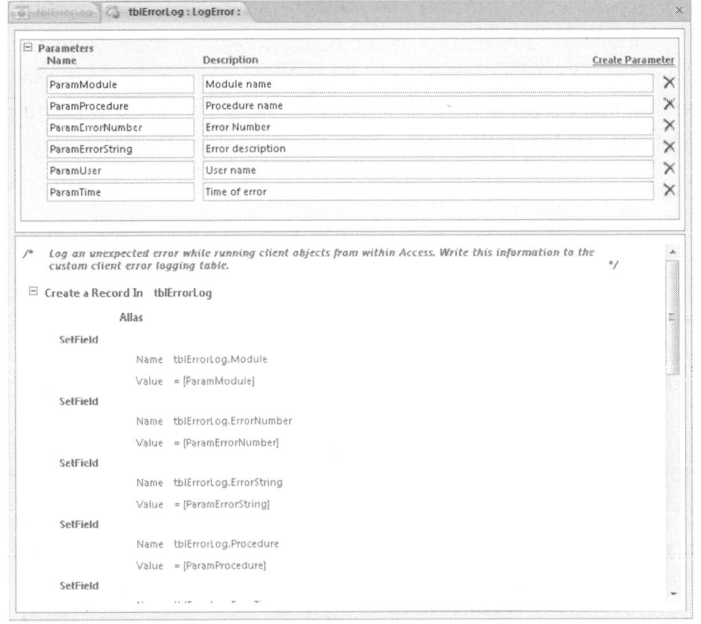

Figure 7-65 Open the LogError named data macro attached to the tblErrorLog table.

This named data macro is quite lengthy, so we'll break up our discussion of the logic behind this named data macro into two parts. The logic for the first part of the LogError named data macro is as follows:

```
Parameter Name: ParamModule
Parameter Description: Module Name
Parameter Name: ParamProcedure
Parameter Description: Procedure name
Parameter Name: ParamErrorNumber
Parameter Description: Error Number
Parameter Name: ParamErrorString
Parameter Description: Error description
Parameter Name: ParamUser
Parameter Description: User name
Parameter Name: ParamTime
Parameter Description: Time of error
Comment Block: Log an unexpected error while running client objects from within
Access. Write this information to the custom client error logging table.
CreateRecord In tblErrorLog
 Alias:
 SetField
   Name: tblErrorLog.Module
   Value: [ParamModule]
```

```
SetField
  Name: tblErrorLog.ErrorNumber
  Value: [ParamErrorNumber]
SetField
  Name: tblErrorLog.ErrorString
  Value: [ParamErrorString]
SetField
  Name: tblErrorLog.Procedure
  Value: [ParamProcedure]
SetField
  Name: tblErrorLog.ErrorTime
  Value: [ParamTime]
SetField
  Name: tblErrorLog.UserID
  Value: [ParamUser]
```

The LogError named data macro includes six parameters. We pass in all six of these values to record any unexpected application errors with the client objects. We then use the CreateRecord block to create a new record in the tblErrorLog table. Inside the CreateRecord block, we use the SetField action and pass in the data from the parameters into the appropriate fields.

In Figure 7-66, you can see the second half of the LogError named data macro. Note that in Figure 7-66, we collapsed the Parameters block so you can see the rest of the logic.

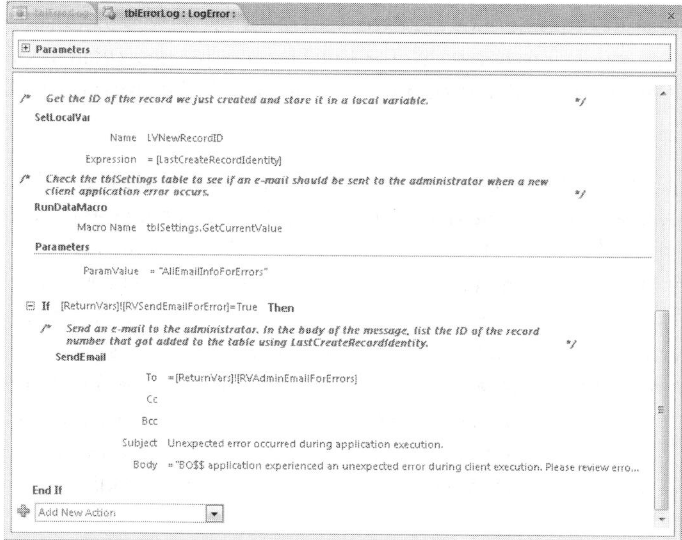

Figure 7-66 This is the second half of the LogError named data macro attached to the tblErrorLog table.

The logic for the second half of the LogError named data macro is as follows:

```
Comment Block: Get the ID of the record we just created and store it in a local
variable.
SetLocalVar
 Name: LVNewRecordID
 Expression: [LastCreateRecordIdentity]
Comment Block: Check the tblSettings table to see if an e-mail should be sent to the
administrator when a new client application error occurs.
RunDataMacro
 Macro Name: tblSettings.GetCurrentValue
 Parameters
   ParamValue: "AllEmailInfoForErrors"
If [ReturnVars]![RVSendEmailForError]=True Then
 Comment Block: Send an e-mail to the administrator. In the body of the message,
 list the ID of the record number that got added to the table using
 LastCreateRecordIdentity.
 SendEmail
   To: =[ReturnVars]![RVAdminEmailForErrors]
   CC:
   BCC:
   Subject: Unexpected error occurred during application execution.
   Body: ="BO$$ application experienced an unexpected error during client execution.
         Please review error logs for more information. The record ID of this new
         entry is " & [LVNewRecordID] & " in the client error log table."
```

After the CreateRecord block is complete, Access immediately commits that record to disk. We then use the SetLocalVar action to create a new local variable. For the expression argument, we use the LastCreateRecordIdentity property. The LastCreateRecordIdentity property returns the ID value of the last record that Access just committed to disk using the CreateRecord data block.

The next step we take is to use the RunDataMacro action. For the Macro Name argument of the RunDataMacro action, we use the GetCurrentValue named data macro attached to tblSettings, which you saw in the previous section. You'll notice in Figure 7-66 that Access displays a Parameters section beneath the Macro Name argument. When you add a named data macro that includes parameters to the macro design surface, Access shows those parameters to you by providing a text box to enter the parameters. In our example, we pass in the AllEmailInfoForErrors parameter to get both the values of the SendEmailForAppErrors Boolean field and the AdminEmailAddress text field from the tblSettings table. We then use an If block to test the value we got back from one of the return variables. To reference a return variable, add the [ReturnVars] qualifier in front. Our If condition expression is as follows:

```
[ReturnVars]![RVSendEmailOnError]
```

If the value is True, this means that we should send an email to the database administrator stating that Access encountered an error in the application. Inside the If block, we use the SendEmail action to send an email to the database administrator. For the To argument, we use an expression that uses the return variable of the email address from the RunDataMacro action so we know to whom to send the email. In the Body argument, we use an expression to display a custom message. Inside the expression, we concatenate our message with the local variable that contains the ID of the record that Access just committed to the tblErrorLog table.

As you can see, return variables are a very useful feature with data macros. When you use them in conjunction with parameters, you can create some very complex business logic at the data layer and even pass information back up to the user interface layer.

The Back Office Software System sample web database includes many named data macros attached to several web tables. Table 7-5 lists all the named data macros with a short description of their purpose. You can explore these samples for additional examples of how to design and use named data macros. In Chapter 21, you'll learn how to call some of these named data macros from user interface macros.

Table 7-5 Named Data Macros in BOSS Web Database

Table Name	Macro Name	Description
tblErrorLog	ClearErrorTable	Deletes all records from the tblErrorLog table.
	ClearServerErrorTable	Deletes all records from the USysApplicationLog table.
	LogError	Logs client application errors to tblErrorLog table.
tblInvoiceHeaders	AuditInvoiceTotals	Audits all invoices within a given date range.
	AuditInvoiceTotalsOneVendor	Audits all invoices within a given date range for a specific vendor.
	VerifyInvoiceBalanced	Checks to see if a specific invoice is balanced.
tblLaborPlanDetails	ApplyLaborPlanToSchedule	Loops through records in tblLaborPlanDetails and updates two fields in preparation for creating new records in tblSchedule.
	CleanupUpdatedRecords	Loops through records in tblLaborPlanDetails and clears two fields that were initially set with ApplyLaborPlanToSchedule named data macro.

Table Name	Macro Name	Description
	CopyDateRangeRecords	Loops through records in tblSchedule within a date range and updates two fields in preparation for creating additional new records in tblSchedule.
tblSchedule	CopyDateRangeRecordsCleanup	Loops through records in tblSchedule and clears two fields that were initially set with the CopyDateRangeRecords named data macro.
	CopySingleDateRecords	Loops through records in tblSchedule for a specific date and updates two fields in preparation for creating additional new records in tblSchedule.
	CopySingleDateRecordsCleanup	Loops through records in tblSchedule and clears two fields that were initially set with the CopySingleDateRecords named data macro.
	DeleteDateRangeRecords	Deletes all records in tblSchedule within a given date range.
	DeleteSingleDateRecords	Deletes all records in tblSchedule for a given date.
	EmailScheduleAllEmployees	Emails weekly schedule details to all employees.
	EmailScheduleOneEmployee	Emails weekly schedule details to a specific employee.
	EmailScheduleOneEmployee	Adjusts date values of sample data to work easily with data around the current time frame.
	AdjustSampleDate	Gets application settings data from the tblSettings table.

Debugging Data Macros

You're likely to encounter unexpected errors or unintended results when you're designing data macros attached to table events and complex named data macros attached to tables for the first time. You might even be wondering if Access is even executing your data macros at all if you see no visible results. In Chapter 24, you'll learn that you have several tools available in the Visual Basic Editor for debugging Visual Basic code. Data macros, unfortunately, do not have a rich set of tools available for debugging purposes. You cannot, for example, set breakpoints on data macro logic to halt execution. You also cannot single-step through the macro logic as you can with user interface macros.

The best tools you have for debugging data macro logic are the LogEvent data action and the USysApplicationLog table. You learned previously that Access logs any unexpected errors that it encounters during data macro execution to the USysApplicationLog table. You can write data to this table as well as use the LogEvent data action. The LogEvent data action takes only one required argument—Description.

Earlier in this chapter, you studied the data macro logic attached to the After Delete event of the tblTerminations table. When you delete a termination record, the After Delete logic looks up the employee's record in the tblEmployees table and sets the Active field back to True. In the LookupRecord data block, we used the Old property to refer to the EmployeeID that Access just finished deleting. Our data macro logic, again, is as follows:

```
LookupRecord In qryDMTermQuery
 Where Condition = [EmployeeID]=[Old].[EmployeeID]
 Alias
 EditRecord
    Alias
    Comment Block: Now set Active field to True
    SetField
       Name: [qryDMTermQuery].[Active]
       Value: True

 End EditRecord
```

What would happen, though, if you forgot to use the Old property in the Where condition argument and instead just referenced the value of the EmployeeID field from tblTerminations? Your expression would look like the following:

```
[EmployeeID]=[tblTerminations].[EmployeeID]
```

When Access evaluates this expression in the context of the After Delete event, the current value of EmployeeID in tblTerminations is Null because Access already deleted the record. When Access executes the LookupUpRecord data block, it tries to find an employee record in the saved query (the saved query is pulling the EmployeeID from the tblEmployees table) where the EmployeeID is Null. Access does not find such a record and therefore never executes the actions that are inside the LookupRecord block. As a result of not executing those actions, Access does not change the employee's Active field back to True. If you navigate to that employee's record, you can see no change to the Active field. Access is doing exactly what you told it to, but it might not be readily obvious what the problem is, or even if Access executed the data macro, because you're not seeing the results you want and Access is not displaying any errors.

To help debug and find the cause of the data macro logic not returning the results you want, you can take advantage of the LogEvent data action. For this specific example, the first thing that you should verify is whether Access is even running the data macro logic. (This is more important with named data macros rather than with Before and After events.)

You can test this by adding a LogEvent as the first action in the After Delete event. In Figure 7-67, you can see we added a LogEvent to the top of the macro design surface beneath the Comment blocks.

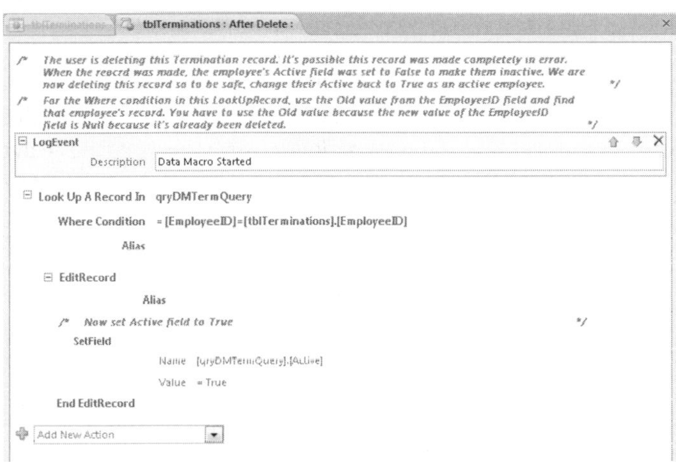

Figure 7-67 You can add LogEvent data actions to help debug your data macro logic.

For the Description argument of the LogEvent action, we used a simple message of "Data Macro Started." If you save your changes, create a new termination record, and then delete the termination record, Access creates a new record in the USysApplicationLog table, as shown in Figure 7-68. When you use a LogEvent data action, Access uses an Error Number of 1. In the Description field, you can see the custom message that we entered into the Description argument.

ID	SourceObject	Data Macro I	Error Numbe	Category	Object Type	Description	Context
1	tblTerminations.AfterDelete	{B78656D8-90F	1	User	Macro	Data Macro Started	
(New)							

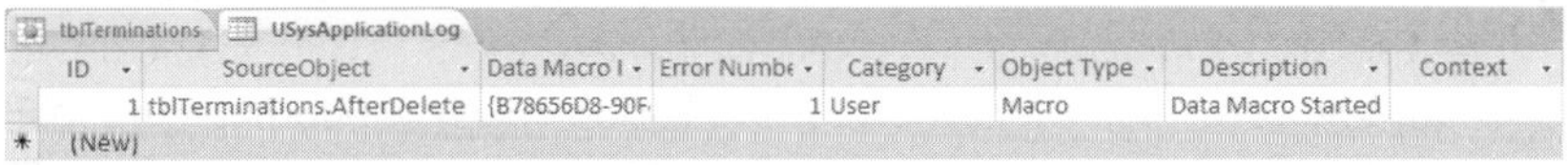

Figure 7-68 Access writes LogEvent information to the USysApplicationLog table.

At this point, you at least know Access is firing the After Delete event and starting your data macro logic. The next step in this example is to verify that Access is entering the LookupRecord data block and finding a record. We can test this by adding another LogEvent action as the first action inside the LookupRecord block. For the Description argument, we'll enter another simple message such as "Found Record," as shown in Figure 7-69.

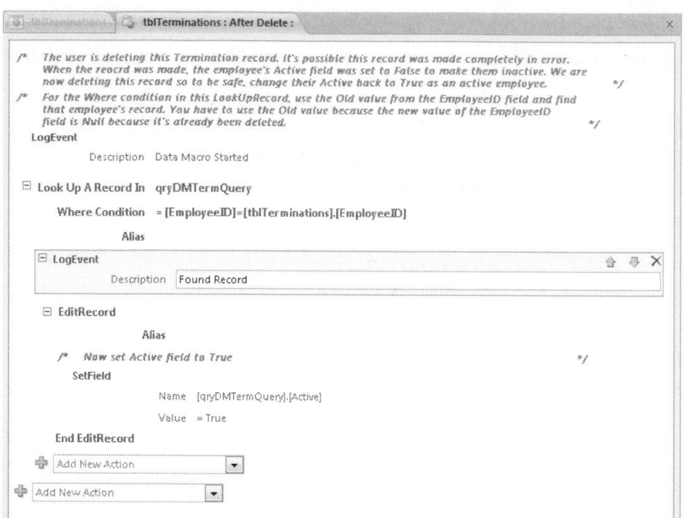

Figure 7-69 We can check to see if Access entered into the block when it executes our logic by adding a LogEvent inside the LookupRecord block.

If you save your new changes, create another new termination record, and then delete the termination record, you'll notice that Access creates another new record in the USysApplicationLog table for the first LogEvent, but not the second. This should give you an immediate clue that Access did not enter into the LookupRecord block based on the Where condition expression that you defined. By utilizing the LogEvent data action, you've narrowed down the cause of your issue considerably, and you can then focus your attention on why Access is not finding a record based on your Where condition argument.

The LogEvent action can also be especially helpful when checking the value of local variables and return variables. During the normal execution of data macros, you cannot see the current value of any local or return variables. When debugging data macro logic that involves local and return variables, it can very useful to know what the current value of those variables are at any given time, especially if they are being changed dynamically, for instance, inside a ForEachRecord loop. You can add LogEvent actions throughout your data macro logic and capture the current value of your variables by using expressions such as the following (with your variable names, of course):

```
=[LocalVariableName]
```

or

```
=[ReturnVars]![ReturnVariableName]
```

After Access finishes executing your data macro logic, you can examine the values of your local variables and return variables in the USysApplicationLog table at different points in time to help determine what Access is doing during the data macro execution. You can use this information to assist with debugging your logic. When you have everything working just the way you want, you can remove the LogEvent actions if you don't want to keep logging information to the USysApplicationLog table.

INSIDE OUT **Data Macro Error Differences with Published Applications**

When Access encounters an error during data macro execution, Access records the error number and error description in the USysApplicationLog table. The error numbers and error descriptions that you see in the USysApplicationLog table might differ if you are working in an unpublished web database versus a web database that you published to a SharePoint server. You should be aware of these differences when testing your data macro logic before and after publishing to a SharePoint server.

Understanding Recursion in Data Macros

When you're designing data macros, you have the potential to run into a recursion issue. Access runs into a recursion issue when it tries to execute the same data macro logic continually over and over in a repeated loop. For example, suppose that you created data macro logic attached to the After Update event of a table that changed data in the current record of the same table. Access makes the field changes and then commits the data. Access then fires the After Update again because data in the table changed. The After Update event fires again, changes the data, and the cycle begins again. Access is now in a perpetual loop executing the data macro in the After Update event. Access could also get into a loop, for example, when working with two tables that have After Update events that update each other, or even with complex named data macros that end up repeating themselves.

Data macros are limited to 10 levels of recursion, which means Access stops the data macro execution after 10 iterations through a recursion loop. Access does not display any messages in the user interface to indicate that it fell into a recursive loop, so you might not even be aware that anything is wrong. Access does, however, display the New Application Errors message in the status bar and logs an error into the USysApplicationLog table with the following error description:

```
A data macro resource limit was hit. This may be caused by a data macro recursively
calling itself. The Updated(<Field>) function may be used to detect which field in a
record has been updated to help prevent recursive calls.
```

In most cases, you can correct recursive calls by using the Updated function to determine which field or fields Access changed in the last record update. You can add conditional logic with If blocks to determine if a field was changed and perform different actions, or no actions, based on the evaluation of the condition. As you are designing and testing your data macro logic, it's a good idea to check the USysApplicationLog continually for any errors relating to recursion.

Sharing Data Macro Logic

The new Logic Designer in Access 2010 includes a very useful feature for sharing and reusing data macro logic. To illustrate this feature, open the tblTerminations table in Datasheet view in the Back Office Software System data copy sample web database (BOSSDataCopy.accdb). Next, click the Table contextual ribbon tab under Table Tools, and then click the After Insert button in the After Events group to open the Logic Designer. You've already explored the data macro logic attached to this table event earlier in this chapter. Press Ctrl+A to highlight all the logic on the macro design surface and then press Ctrl+C to copy all the logic to the Windows Clipboard. Now, open Notepad or a different text editor and then press Ctrl+V to paste all the logic into Notepad.

As you can see in Figure 7-70, Access copied the data macro logic from the Logic Designer as XML. You can send this XML to someone else, and that person can copy and paste the XML directly into a Logic Designer window for a data macro in his or her Access 2010 database. (We'll discuss XML in Chapter 23, "Using Business Connectivity Services.") This feature can be especially useful if you are trying to help someone else write or debug data macro logic, such as in an Access forum or newsgroup. You can create the logic for the person you're helping and explain how you structured the program flow constructs, data blocks, and data actions.

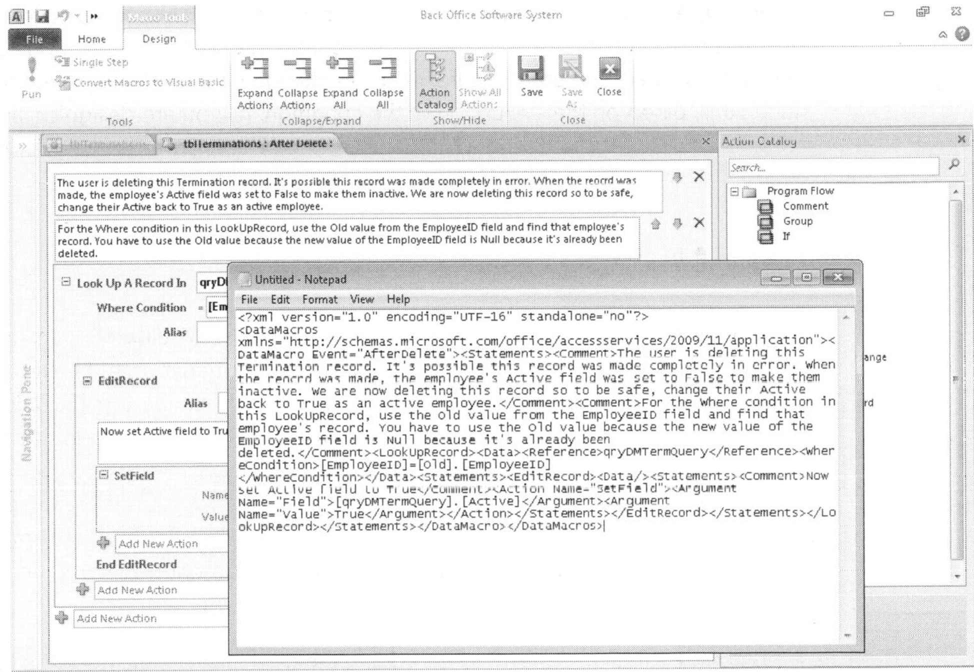

Figure 7-70 You can copy and paste data macro logic directly out of the Logic Designer.

You now have all the information that you need to modify and maintain your database table definitions. In Chapter 8, you'll explore importing data from other sources and linking to data in other files.

CHAPTER 8

Importing and Linking Data

You can certainly build all your tables, design queries, forms, and reports, and then enter from scratch all the data into your empty tables. However, in many cases, you'll have some of the data you need lying around in other files. For example, you might have a customer list in a spreadsheet or a text file, but your list of products might be in another non-Access database file. Microsoft Access 2010 provides tools to help you bring the data into your new application.

Although you can use Access 2010 as a self-contained database and application system, one of its primary strengths is that it allows you to work with many kinds of data in other databases, in spreadsheets, in text files, or in Microsoft SharePoint lists. In addition to using data in your local Access 2010 database, you can *import* (copy in) or *link* (connect to) data that's in text files, spreadsheets, other Access databases, dBASE, Microsoft SharePoint lists, and any other SQL database that supports the Open Database Connectivity (ODBC) software standard.

A Word About Open Database Connectivity (ODBC)

If you look under the hood of Access, you'll find that it uses a database language called SQL (Structured Query Language) to read, insert, update, and delete data. SQL grew out of a relational database research project conducted by IBM in the 1970s. It has been adopted as the official standard for relational databases by organizations such as the American National Standards Institute (ANSI) and the International Organization for Standardization (ISO). When you're viewing a query window in Design view, you can see the SQL statements that Access uses by first clicking the Design tab below Query Tools, clicking the arrow below the View button in the Results group, and then clicking the SQL View command.

Article 2, "Understanding SQL," on the companion CD, provides more details about how Access uses SQL. Appendix A, "Installing Your Software," provides details about installing and managing ODBC connections on your computer.

In an ideal world, any product that "speaks" SQL should be able to "talk" to any other product that understands SQL. You should be able to build an application that can work with the data in several relational database management systems (RDMSs) using the same database language. Although standards exist for SQL, most software companies have implemented variations on or extensions to the language to handle specific features of their products. Also, several products evolved before standards were well established, so the companies producing those products invented their own SQL syntaxes, which differ from the official standard. An SQL statement intended to be executed by Microsoft SQL Server might require modification before it can be executed by other databases that support SQL, such as DB2 or Oracle, and vice versa.

To solve this problem, a group of influential hardware and software companies—more than 30 of them, including Microsoft Corporation—formed the SQL Access Group. The group's goal was to define a common base SQL implementation that its members' products could all use to "talk" to one another. The companies jointly developed the *Common Language Interface (CLI)* for all the major variants of SQL, and they committed themselves to building CLI support into their products. About a dozen of these companies jointly demonstrated this capability in early 1992.

In the meantime, Microsoft formalized the CLI for workstations and announced that Microsoft products—especially those designed for the Microsoft Windows operating system—would use this interface to access SQL databases. Microsoft calls this formalized interface the *Open Database Connectivity (ODBC) standard*. In the spring of 1992, Microsoft announced that more than a dozen database and application software vendors had committed to providing ODBC support in their products by the end of 1992. With Access, Microsoft provides the basic ODBC Driver Manager and the driver to translate ODBC SQL to the SQL understood by SQL Server. Microsoft has also worked with several database vendors to develop drivers for other databases. You can see a diagram of the ODBC architecture in Figure 8-1.

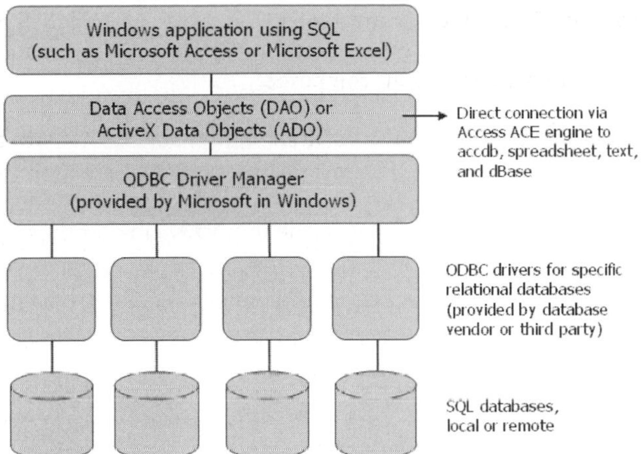

Figure 8-1 The Microsoft ODBC architecture allows any ODBC-enabled application to link to any SQL database for which you have a driver.

Access was one of Microsoft's first ODBC-compliant products, and the ODBC Driver Manager is a standard part of Microsoft's operating system. Microsoft has further refined this architecture with ActiveX Data Objects (ADO). ADO is a special library of objects that you can use to fetch and modify information about the database structure and fetch and update data from any database, including Access. You can also fetch data from ODBC databases using the standard Data Access Objects (DAO) library used to manipulate native Access tables. After you've added the drivers for the other SQL databases that you want to work with, you can use Access to build an application using data from any of these databases.

Note

You can use ADO as a "universal interface" to both databases that support ODBC as well as to those that do not. See Chapter 24, "Understanding Visual Basic Fundamentals," on the companion CD, for details about working with ADO using Microsoft Visual Basic.

Creating a Data Source to Link to an ODBC Database

Before you can connect to a database that requires ODBC, you must first create a data source—either a data source name (DSN) file or a data source entry in your Windows registry. A data source is simply a named set of ODBC driver parameters that provide the information the driver needs to dynamically link to the data. To create a new data source name file or registry entry, on the External Data tab in the Import & Link group, begin importing or linking a file by clicking the ODBC Database button. Access 2010 opens the Get External Data - ODBC Database dialog box. Select either the Import The Source Data Into A New Table In The Current Database option or the Link To The Data Source By Creating A Linked Table option, and then click OK. Access opens the Select Data Source dialog box where you can begin creating a new data source.

To start creating a new data source, you can click the New button on either the File Data Source or Machine Data Source tab on the Select Data Source dialog box. If you create a new file data source, Access 2010 stores a file with a .dsn file name extension in your default folder for data source name files. The resulting text file will contain a list of keyword assignment statements to set the values needed by the driver. (You can find an example of a data source name file at the end of this section.) If you create a new machine data source, Access stores the parameters in the Windows registry.

To create a new machine data source, click the Machine Data Source tab and click the New button. Access displays the Create New Data Source wizard, shown here.

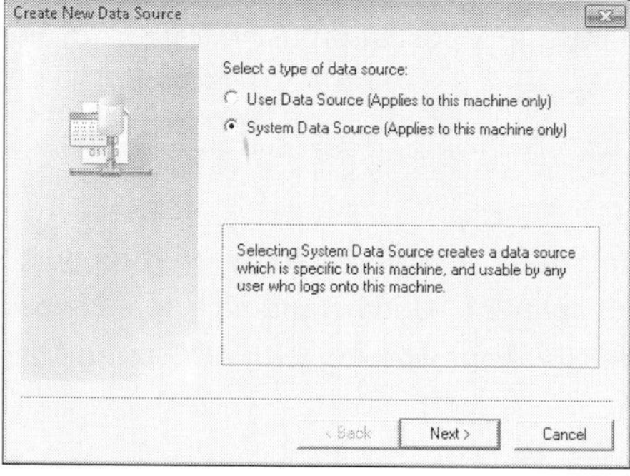

Note

If you receive an error message indicating that you are not logged on with sufficient administrative privileges when you click the New button on the Machine Data Source tab, you'll need to log onto your computer with an account that has administrative privileges to create a new machine data source.

To create a data source that applies to all users on your computer, select System Data Source (Applies To This Machine Only) and click Next. Access displays a list of the available ODBC drivers on your system. To create a data source for SQL Server, select SQL Server at the bottom of the list and click Next. Access confirms that you are ready to create a system data source for the driver you specified. Click Finish, and Access displays the Create A New Data Source To SQL Server wizard, shown here.

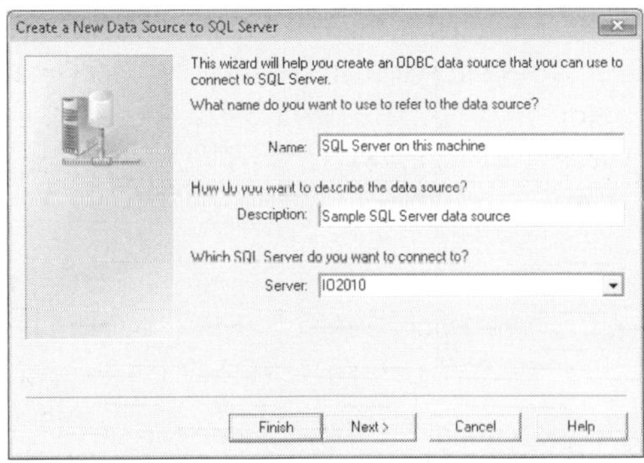

Enter a name and description for your data source. To connect to the server on your computer, enter your computer name in the Server box. If you are authorized to connect to other servers on your network, click the arrow in the Server box. When you do this, Access 2010 searches your network for other computers running SQL Server and places the names of all servers found in the list. Click Next to go to the next page, shown here.

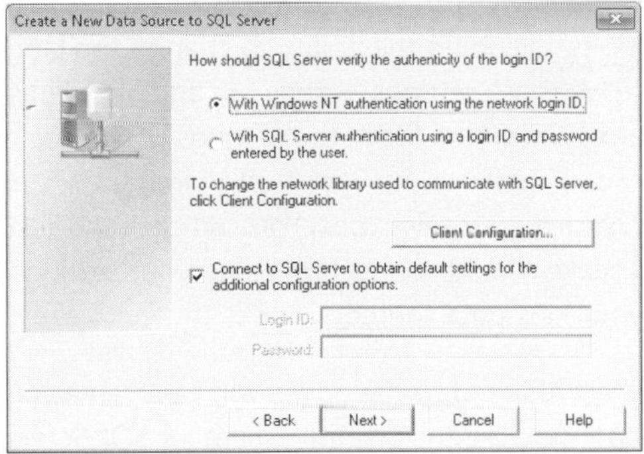

Depending on how SQL Server 2008 is configured, you might need to enter a login ID and password. By default, SQL Server 2008 uses your Windows logon information (your user name and password) to authenticate you. This means that you don't have to enter your user name and password a second time when you access the computer running SQL Server.

If, however, the server is configured to use SQL authentication, you must select With SQL Server Authentication Using A Login ID And Password Entered By The User, and enter your login ID and password. Click Next to see the page where you can specify the default database for this data source, as shown here.

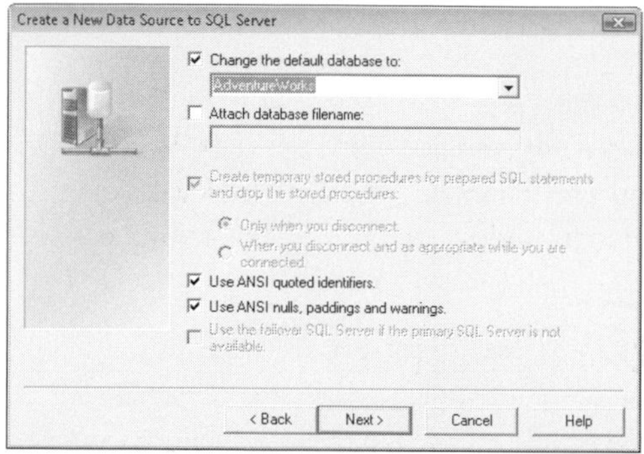

If you are authorized to connect to more than one database on the server and you want to connect to a database other than your default database, select the Change The Default Database To check box. Access logs on to the server and returns a list of available database names. (The preceding figure shows the sample AdventureWorks database that you can install with SQL Server 2008 selected.) If you don't specify a database name and if multiple databases exist on the server, you'll be connected to the default database for your login ID. (You don't need to worry about the other options displayed on this screen.) Select the database you want, and click Next.

The last page shows various options, including the ability to change the language of error messages or log data. You can leave these settings as they are and click Finish. Access displays a final confirmation dialog box with a list of the settings you chose. If you need to change anything, click Cancel and then use the Back button in the Create A New Data Source To SQL Server wizard to correct your selections. You can click the Test Data Source button to verify that Access can make a valid connection using your settings. If the test runs successfully, click OK to create your new data source.

If you're familiar with the parameters required by the driver, you can create your own data source name file. A data source name file like the one listed here for SQL Server begins with the [ODBC] section delimiter and then includes keyword assignment statements for each piece of information the ODBC service needs to correctly load the driver you want. (You can find this file, named SQLServerLocal.dsn, on the companion CD.) Note that you must supply your Windows user ID (your user name) and computer name for YOURID and YOURCOMPUTER, respectively, to connect to the server running on your computer. You can edit any data source name file using a text editor such as Notepad.

```
[ODBC]
DRIVER=SQL Server
UID=YOURID
DATABASE=AdventureWorks
WSID=YOURCOMPUTER
APP=Microsoft® Windows® Operating System
Trusted_Connection=Yes
SERVER=YOURCOMPUTER
Description=Sample DSN for SQL Server
```

The first time you create a data source name file, you'll probably want to use the Create New Data Source wizard, but after you understand the structure of a valid data source name file for a particular data source, it's easy to modify an existing file or create a new one.

Importing vs. Linking Database Files

You have the choice of importing or linking data from other databases, but how do you decide which type of access is best? Here are some guidelines.

You should consider importing another database file when any of the following is true:

- The file you need is relatively small and is not changed frequently by users of the other database application.
- You don't need to share the data you create with users of the other database application.
- You're replacing the old database application, and you no longer need the data in the old format.
- You need to load data (such as customers or products as we mentioned earlier) from another source to begin populating your Access tables.
- You need the best performance while working with the data from the other database (because Access performs best with a local copy of the data in its native format).

On the other hand, you should consider linking to another database file when any of the following is true:

- The file is larger than the maximum capacity of a local Access database (2 GB).
- The file is changed frequently by users of the other database application.
- You must share the data on a network with users of the other database application.

- You'll be distributing your application to several individual users, and you will need to make changes to the queries, forms, reports, and modules in the application without disturbing data already entered in the tables.

INSIDE OUT **Using Linked Tables in a Complex Application Is a Good Idea**

Even when we're building an application that we know will be run by only a single user, we usually create a separate .accdb file that contains all the tables and link those tables back into the .accdb file that contains all our queries, forms, reports, and code. If we've been careful creating our original table design, we rarely have to change it. But users are always thinking up some new feature that they would like to have. We can add a new form or report and send the user an update without having to disturb all the data they've already entered.

If you look closely at the tables in the Conrad Systems Contacts sample database (Contacts.accdb), you can see that most of the tables have a little arrow next to the table icon in the Navigation pane, like this:

This indicates that these tables are linked from another data source.

Note

The samples in this chapter use data you can find in files on the companion CD. You can import the data into or export the data from the Conrad Systems Contacts or Housing Reservations databases. You might want to work from a copy of these databases to follow along with the examples in this chapter. You can find the result of following many of these examples in the ImportLink.accdb sample database, which contains a Companies table that has columns using nearly every available data type in Access.

Importing Data and Databases

You can copy data from a number of different file formats to create an Access table. In addition to copying data from a number of popular database file formats, Access 2010 can also create a table from data in a spreadsheet or a text file. When you copy data from another database, Access uses information stored by the source database system to convert or name objects in the target Access table. You can import data not only from other Access databases but also from dBASE and—using ODBC—any SQL database that supports the ODBC standard.

INSIDE OUT **What Happened to Paradox and Lotus File Support?**

In Access 2010, Microsoft has deprecated support for importing or linking to Paradox and Lotus files.

Importing dBASE Files

On the companion CD, you'll find a dBASE 5 file named COMPANIE.dbf that you can use to follow along with the next procedure to import this file into the Conrad Systems Contacts sample database or into a new blank database. To import a dBASE file, do the following:

1. Open the Access database that will receive the dBASE file. If that database is already open, close all open objects so that you see only the Navigation pane.
2. On the External Data tab, in the Import & Link group, click the More command, and then click dBASE File, as shown here.

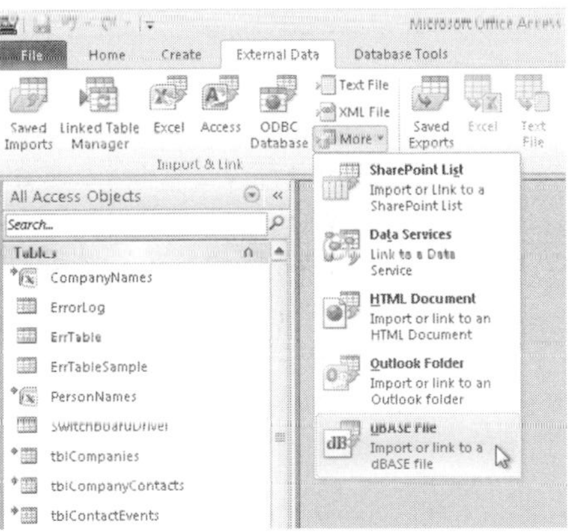

3. Access opens the Get External Data - dBASE File dialog box, shown here. Click Browse to browse for the dBASE file you need to import.

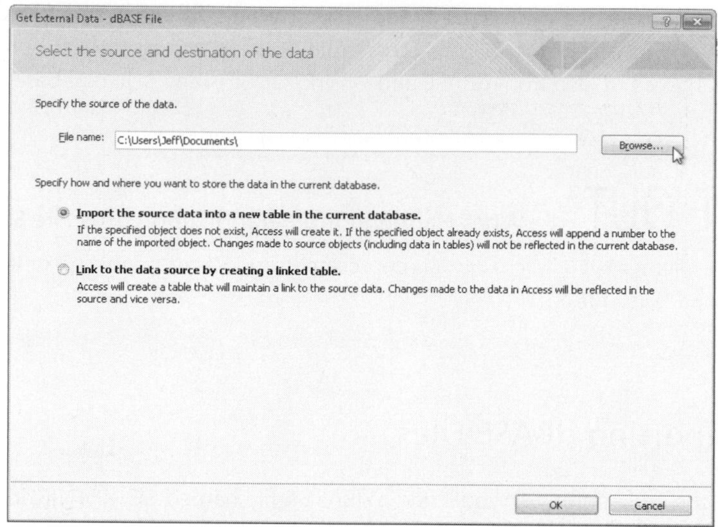

4. Access opens the File Open dialog box, shown next. Select dBASE III, dBASE IV, or dBASE 5, as appropriate, in the list to the right of the File Name box. (In Windows XP, this list is labeled Files Of Type and appears below the File Name box.) Select the source file folder, and then select or type the file name in the File Name box. If you're having difficulty finding the file you want, type a search string in the Search field.

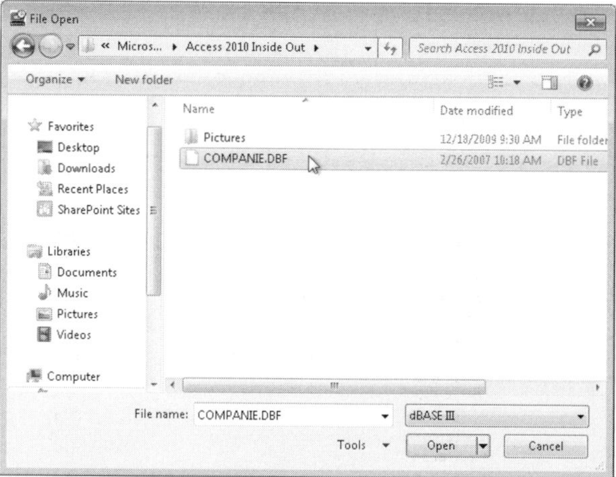

5. Click the Open button to return to the Get External Data - dBASE File dialog box with the file path to the dBASE file you need in the File Name box. Make sure the first option, Import The Source Data Into A New Table In The Current Database, is selected, and then click OK to import the dBASE file you selected. Access displays a message that informs you of the result of the import procedure, as shown here.

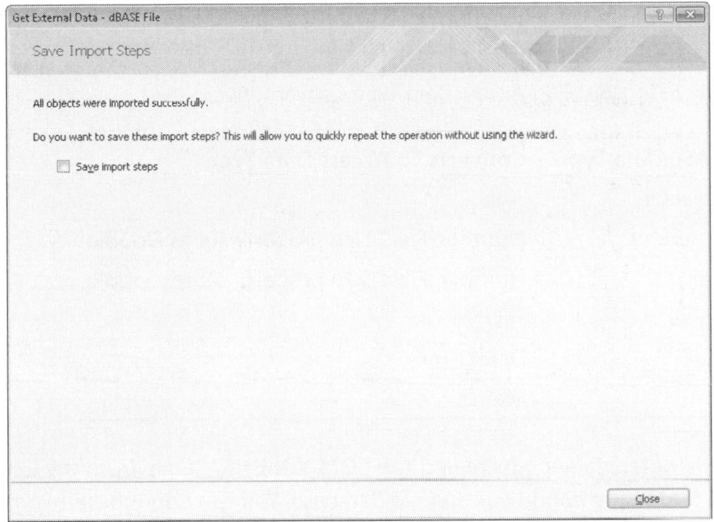

If the import procedure is successful, the new table will have the name of the dBASE file (without the file name extension). If Access finds a duplicate table name, it will generate a new name by adding a unique integer to the end of the name. For example, if you import a file named Company.dbf and you already have tables named Company and Company1, Access creates a table named Company2.

6. Click Close to dismiss the message that confirms the import procedure.

Open the table that Access creates from this dBASE format data and you'll see data for the sample companies, as shown in Figure 8-2.

COMPANIE

ID	COMPANYN	WEB	ADDRESS	CITY	COUNTY	STATE	ZIP	CREDITLIMI	DISCOU
1	Contoso, Ltd	Contoso, Ltd#h	7890 Lincoln A	Youngsville	Warren	PA	16371	100000	
2	Fourth Coffee	Fourth Coffee#	7890 3rd Street	Kalamazoo	Kalamazoo	MI	49004	85000	
3	Coho Vineyard	Coho Vineyard	6789 4th Street	Grosse Pointe	Wayne	MI	48236	90000	
4	Southridge Vid	Southridge Vid	1234 1st Avenu	Warriors Mark	Huntingdon	PA	16877	150000	
5	Consolidated M	Consolidated M	4567 Lincoln Dr	Yorktown	York	VA	23692	40000	
6	Baldwin Muse	Baldwin Muse	7890 Central D	Matoaka	Mercer	WV	24736	55000	
7	Fabrikam, Inc.	Fabrikam, Inc.#	4567 2nd Stree	Easton	Fresno	CA	93706	60000	
8	Alpine Ski Hou	Alpine Ski Hou	3456 3rd Boule	Pingree Grove	Kane	IL	60140	90000	
9	School of Fine	School of Fine	5678 3rd Avenu	Elias	Jackson	KY	40486	43000	
10	City Power & L	City Power & L	5678 Willow A	Conway	Franklin	MA	01341	80000	
11	Blue Yonder Ai	Blue Yonder Ai	5678 Central A	Riverside	Cass	ND	58078	70000	
12	Margie's Travel	Margie's Travel	4567 3rd Avenu	Grandy	Currituck	NC	27939	75000	
13	Lucerne Publis	Lucerne Publis	6789 1st Parkw	Irrigon	Morrow	OR	97844	90000	
14	Humongous In	Humongous In	6789 Willow Pa	Flushing	Queens	NY	11351	25000	
15	Viescas Consul	Viescas Consul	379 Amherst St	Nashua	Hillsborough	NH	030631226	30000	

Record: 1 of 15 No Filter Search

Figure 8-2 Access can import every data type supported in a dBASE file.

When you look at a table imported from dBASE in Design view, you'll find that Access has converted the data types, as shown in Table 8-1.

Table 8-1 dBASE-to-Access Data Type Conversions

DBASE Data Type	Converts To Access Data Type
Character	Text
Numeric	Number, Field Size property set to Double
Float	Number, Field Size property set to Double
Logical	Yes/No
Date	Date/Time
Memo	Memo

As we noted earlier, we created the COMPANIE dBASE file from the Companies table you can find in the ImportLink sample database. You can open these two tables side by side to see the differences. First, dBASE doesn't support field names longer than 10 characters. So CompanyName in the original file is shortened to COMPANYNAM, and LastOrderDate appears as LASTORDERD. Also, dBASE doesn't support the Hyperlink, Currency, or Decimal data type, so it stores Hyperlink data types as Memo, and Currency and Decimal data types as Number, Double.

Importing SQL Tables

To import a table from another database system that supports ODBC SQL (such as SQL Server or Oracle), you must first have the ODBC driver for that database installed on your computer. Your computer must also be linked to the network that connects to the computer running SQL Server from which you want to import data, and you must have an account on that server. Check with your system administrator for information about correctly connecting to the computer running SQL Server.

If you have SQL Server 2008 installed or have downloaded and installed SQL Server 2008 Express Edition, which you can download from *www.microsoft.com/express/sql/default.aspx*, you already have SQL Server at your disposal. One of the best ways to be sure SQL Server is running on your computer is to use the SQL Server Configuration Manager. You can start the Configuration Manager from the Windows Start menu in the Configuration Tools folder under Microsoft SQL Server 2008. You can also start the Configuration Manager by running C:\Windows\System32\SQLServerManager.msc. In the Configuration Manager, select SQL Server 2008 Services and be sure the SQL Server (MSSQLSERVER) service is marked as Running. If it is not running, right-click the service name and click Start on the shortcut menu.

To import data from a SQL table, do the following:

1. Open the Access database that will receive the SQL data. If that database is already open, close all open objects so that you see only the Navigation pane.
2. On the External Data tab, in the Import & Link group, click the ODBC Database button. Access opens the Get External Data - ODBC Database dialog box. Make sure the Import The Source Data Into A New Table In The Current Database option is selected and then click OK.
3. Access opens the Select Data Source dialog box, shown here, from which you can select the data source that maps to the computer running SQL Server that contains the table you want to import.

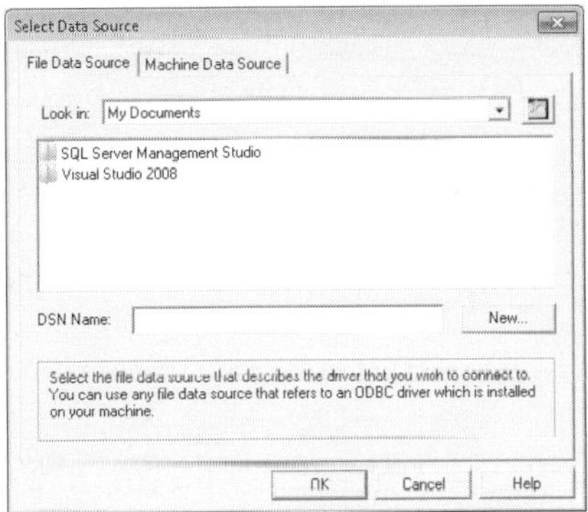

You can select a data source name (.dsn) file that you created previously, or click the Machine Data Source tab, as shown here, to see data sources that are already defined for your computer.

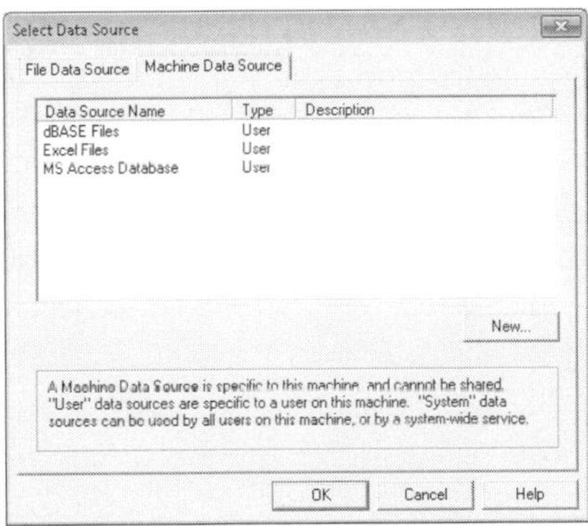

TROUBLESHOOTING

Access won't use ODBC for all file types.

Notice that the Machine Data Source tab lists installed sources for dBASE, Access, and Microsoft Excel. Access will not let you use ODBC for dBASE, Excel, and Access because it uses its own, more efficient, direct connection via its database engine.

If you don't see the data source you need, see "Creating a Data Source to Link to an ODBC Database," on page 448, for instructions. After you select a data source, click OK.

4. When Access connects to the server, you'll see the Import Objects dialog box, which lists the available tables on that server, as shown here.

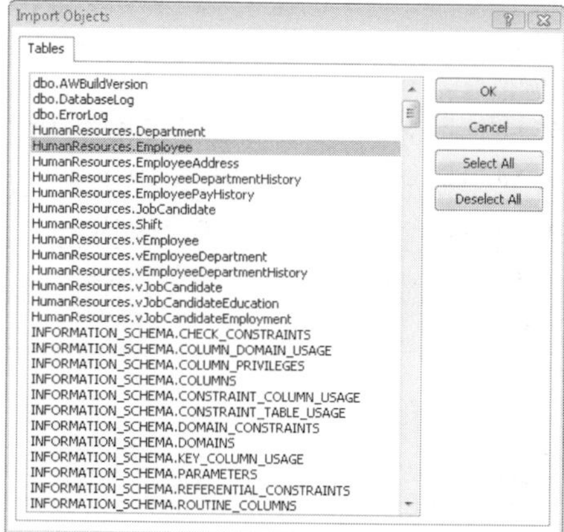

5. From the list of tables or list of files, select the ones you want to import. If you select a table name in error, you can click it again to deselect it or you can click the Deselect All button to start over. Click OK to import the SQL tables you selected.

6. If the import procedure is successful, the new table will have the name of the SQL table. If Access finds a duplicate table name, it will generate a new name by adding a unique integer to the end of the name, as explained earlier about dBASE files.

Note

You've no doubt noticed by now that the different databases use different style conventions (dbo.newstore, Newstore, NEWSTORE) for table names.

In general, Access converts SQL data types to Access data types, as shown in Table 8-2.

Table 8-2 SQL-to-Access Data Type Conversions

SQL Data Type	Converts To Access Data Type
CHAR[ACTER]	Text, or Memo if more than 255 characters in length
VARCHAR	Text, or Memo if more than 255 characters in length
TEXT	Memo
TINYINT	Number, Field Size property set to Byte
SMALLINT	Number, Field Size property set to Integer
INT	Number, Field Size property set to Long Integer
REAL	Number, Field Size property set to Double
FLOAT	Number, Field Size property set to Double
DOUBLE	Number, Field Size property set to Double
DATE	Date/Time
TIME	Date/Time
TIMESTAMP	Binary[1]
IMAGE	OLE Object

[1]The Access Database Engine (ACE) supports a Binary data type (raw hexadecimal), but the Access user interface does not. If you link to a table that has a data type that maps to Binary, you will be able to see the data type in the table definition, but you won't be able to successfully edit this data in a datasheet or form. You can manipulate Binary data in Visual Basic.

Importing Access Objects

If the database from which you want to import data is another Access database, you can import any of the six major types of Access objects: tables, queries, forms, reports, macros, or modules. To achieve the same result, you can also open the source database, select the object you want, click the Copy command in the Clipboard group on the Home tab of the ribbon, open the target database, and then click the Paste command in the Clipboard group on the Home tab. Using the Import command, however, allows you to copy several objects without having to switch back and forth between the two databases.

To import an object from another Access database, take the following steps:

1. Open the Access database that will receive the object. If that database is already open, close any open objects so that only the Navigation pane is showing.
2. On the External Data tab, in the Import & Link group, click the Access command. Access opens the Get External Data - Access Database dialog box, shown here.

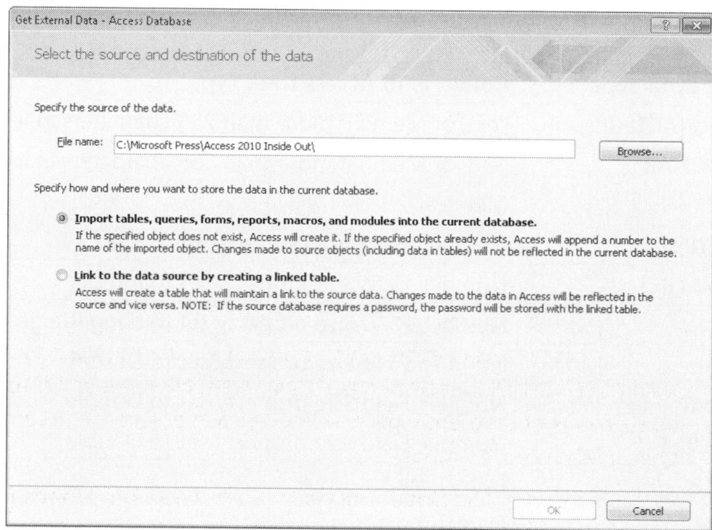

3. Click Browse to open the File Open dialog box, previously shown on page 454. Select the folder and the name of the .accdb, .mdb, .adp, .mda, .accda, .mde, .accde, or .ade file containing the object that you want to import, and then click Open.

Note

Access 2010 provides a database utility to create a compiled version of a .mdb or .accdb desktop application or .adp project file that contains no source code. The compiled versions have .mde, .accde and .ade extensions, respectively. You cannot import forms, reports, or modules from a .mde, .accde or .ade file. For details about creating a compiled version of your application, see Chapter 27, "Distributing Your Application," on the companion CD.

4. Click OK. Access opens the Import Objects dialog box, shown here, which provides tabs for each of the object types in the database you selected. First, click the tab for the object type, and then select the specific object you want to import.

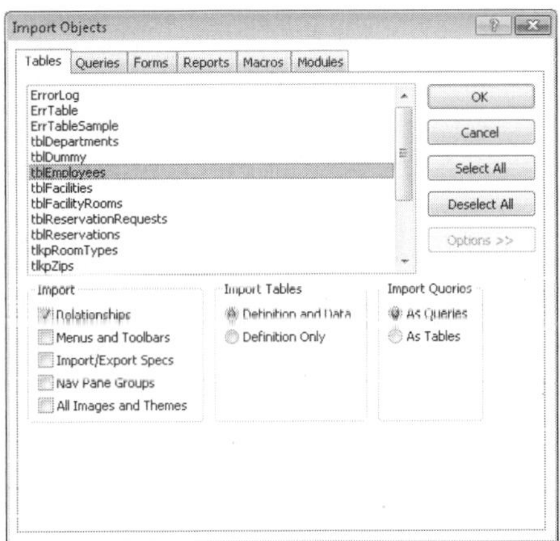

If you select an object in error, you can click the name again to deselect it. If you want to import all objects of a particular type, click Select All. You can import multiple objects of different types by clicking each object tab in turn and selecting the objects you want to import.

You can also click the Options button (which was clicked in the preceding illustration) to select additional options. If you import any tables from the source database, you can select the option to import the table relationships (if any) defined for those tables in the source database. If the object is a table, you can select the option to import the table structure (the table definition) only or to import the structure and the stored data. If your source database is an .mdb or .adp file created in a version of Access before 2007, you can select the Menus And Toolbars check box to import all the custom menus and toolbars from your source database. Be aware, however, that these items appear on a special Add-Ins tab on the ribbon, and some of the commands you designed in your custom menus and toolbars might not work in Access 2010. You can also select the Import/Export Specs check box. (See the sidebar "Defining an Import Specification," on page 480, for details.) If you select the Nav Pane Groups check box, Access imports any custom Navigation pane groups you have defined in the database. (See Chapter 2, "Exploring the Access 2010 Interface," for details about creating custom groups.) You can also choose to import a query object (the definition of the query) by selecting As Queries under Import Queries, or you can ask Access to run the query and import the data results into a table by selecting As Tables. (See Chapter 9, "Creating and Working with Simple Queries," for details about building and using queries.) Click OK to copy the objects you selected to the current database.

5. If the import procedure is successful, the new object will have the name of the object you selected. If Access finds a duplicate name, it will generate a new name by adding a unique integer to the end of the name, as explained previously. Because objects such as queries, forms, reports, macros, and modules might refer to each other or to tables you're importing, you should carefully check name references if Access has to rename an imported object.

Note

If the source Access database is a secured file created in a previous version of Access, you must have at least read permission for the database, read data permission for the tables, and read definition permission for all other objects to import objects. After you import the objects into your database, you will own the copies of those objects in the target database.

Importing Spreadsheet Data

Access 2010 also allows you to import data from spreadsheet files created by Excel version 5 and later. You can specify a portion of a spreadsheet or the entire spreadsheet file to import into a new table or to append to an existing table. If the first row of cells contains names suitable for field names in the resulting Access table, as shown in the Companies.xls spreadsheet in Figure 8-3, you can tell Access to use these names for your fields.

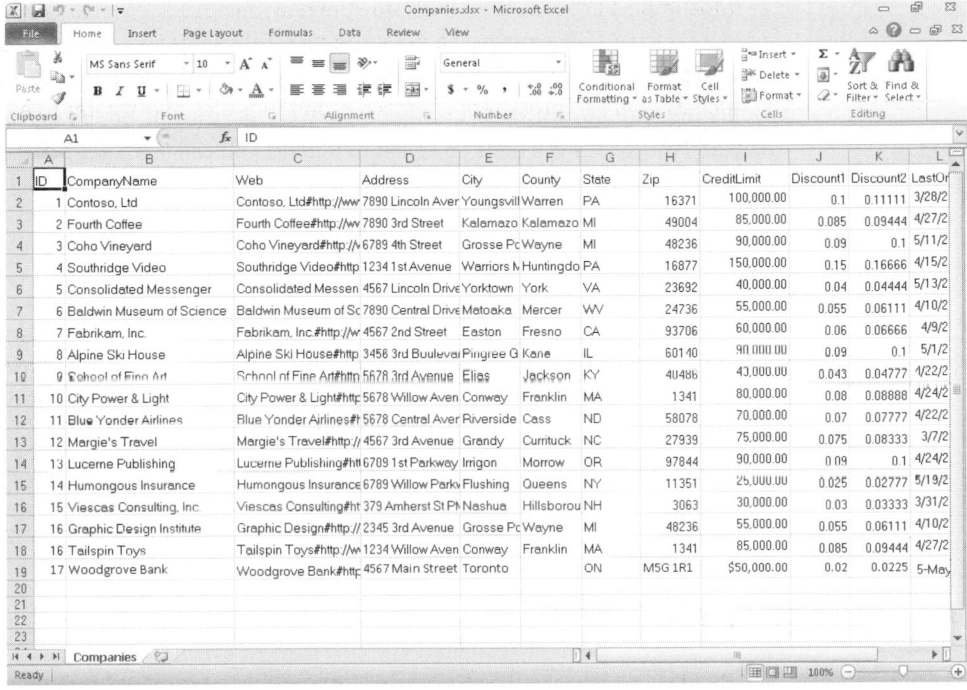

Figure 8-3 The data in the first row of this Excel spreadsheet can be used as field names when you import the spreadsheet into a new Access table.

Preparing a Spreadsheet

Access 2010 determines the data type for the fields in a new table based on the values it finds in the first few rows of data being imported (excluding the first row if that row contains field names). When you import a spreadsheet into a new table, Access stores alphanumeric data as the Text data type with an entry length of 255 characters, numeric data as the Number type with the Field Size property set to Double, numeric data with currency formatting as the Currency type, and any date or time data as the Date/Time type. If Access finds a mixture of data in any column in the first few rows, it imports that column as the Text data type.

Chapter 8

INSIDE OUT Importing to a Temporary Table First

If you want to append all or part of a spreadsheet to a target table, you should import or link the entire spreadsheet as a new table and then use an append query to edit the data and move it to the table you want to update. You can learn about append queries in Chapter 11, "Modifying Data with Action Queries."

If the first several rows are not representative of all the data in your spreadsheet (excluding a potential field names row), you might want to insert a single "dummy" row at the beginning of your spreadsheet with data values that establish the data type you want to use for each column. You can easily delete that row from the table after you import the spreadsheet. For example, if you scroll down in the Companies.xlsx sample spreadsheet shown in Figure 8-3, you'll find that the last entry is a Canadian address, as shown in Figure 8-4.

17	16	Graphic Design Institute	Graphic Design#http://	2345 3rd Avenue	Grosse Pc	Wayne	MI	48236
18	16	Tailspin Toys	Tailspin Toys#http://w	1234 Willow Aven	Conway	Franklin	MA	1341
19	17	Woodgrove Bank	Woodgrove Bank#http	4567 Main Street	Toronto		ON	M5G 1R1
20								

Figure 8-4 The Zip field entry contains data that can't be stored in numeric format.

Because Access sees only numbers in the first few rows of the Zip column, it will use a Number data type for the Zip field. However, the entry for the Canadian address has letters and spaces, which requires the field to be defined as text. As you'll see later, if you attempt to import this spreadsheet without fixing this problem, Access generates an error for each row that contains nonnumeric data. Access sets the contents of fields it cannot import to Null. You can solve this by inserting a dummy row at the top with the proper data types in each column, moving the row to the top, or fixing the one bad row after you import the file.

Importing a Spreadsheet

To import a spreadsheet into an Access database, do the following:

1. Open the Access database that will receive the spreadsheet. If that database is already open, close any open objects so that you see only the Navigation pane.

2. On the External Data tab, in the Import & Link group, click the Excel command to open the Get External Data - Excel Spreadsheet dialog box shown here. Note, if you do not have any tables in your database, you won't see the second option to append a copy of the records to one of the tables in your database.

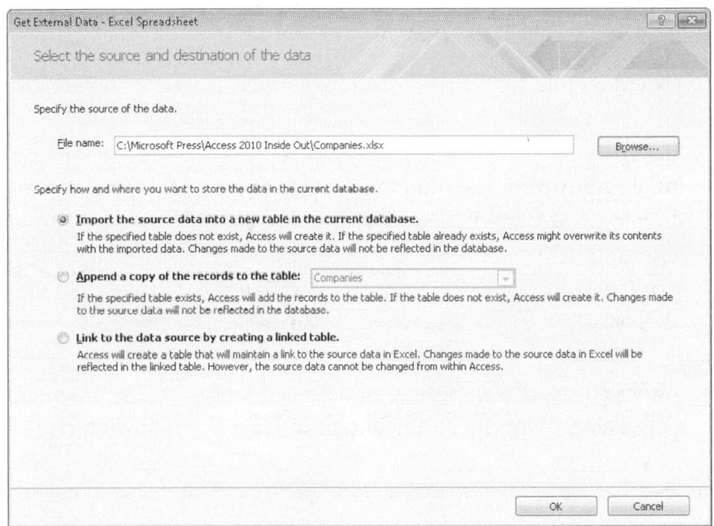

3. Click Browse to open the File Open dialog box shown previously on page 454. Select the folder and the name of the spreadsheet file that you want to import and click Open to return to the Get External Data - Excel Spreadsheet dialog box. If you want to follow along with this example, select the Companies.xlsx file from the companion CD.

4. Make sure the Import The Source Data Into A New Table In The Current Database option is selected and then click OK. If your spreadsheet is from Excel version 5.0 or later, it can contain multiple worksheets. If the spreadsheet contains multiple worksheets or any named ranges, Access shows you the first window of the Import Spreadsheet Wizard, as shown in the following illustration. (If you want to import a range that isn't yet defined, exit the wizard, open your spreadsheet to define a name for the range you want, save the spreadsheet, and then restart the import process in Access.) Select the worksheet or the named range that you want to import, and click Next to continue.

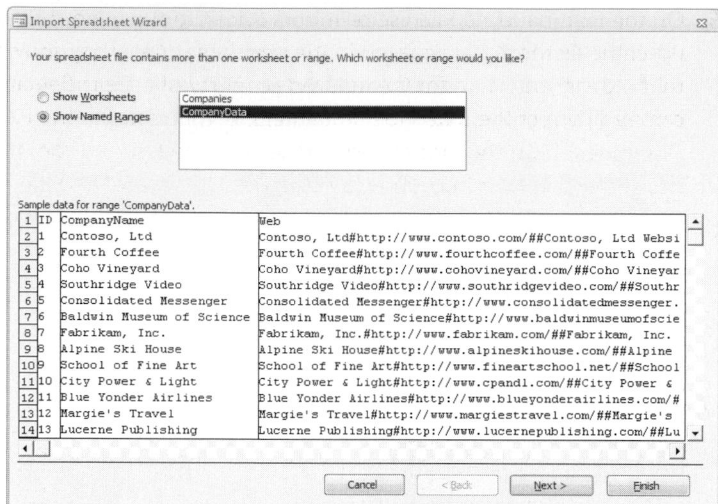

5. After you select a worksheet or a named range, or if your spreadsheet file contains only a single worksheet, the wizard displays the following page.

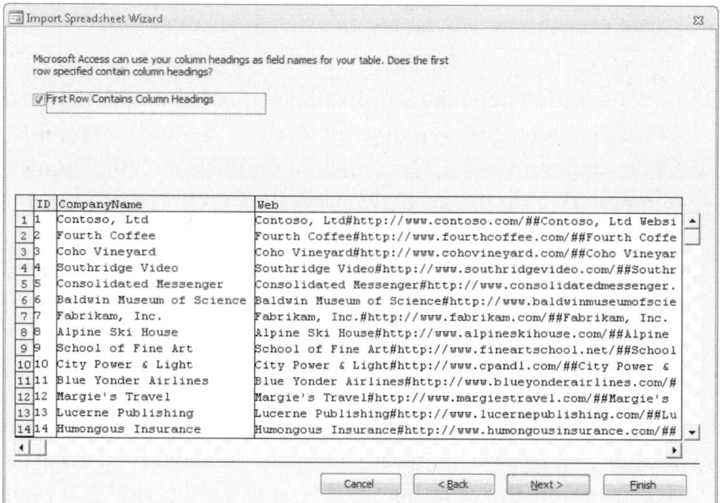

Select the First Row Contains Column Headings check box if you've placed names at the tops of the columns in your spreadsheet. Click Next to go to the next step.

6. On the next page, you can scroll left and right to the various fields and tell the wizard which fields should be indexed in the new table. Your indexing choices are identical to the ones you'll find for the Indexed property of a table field in Design view. You can also correct the data type of the field. In this case, for the ID field, select Yes (No Duplicates) from the Indexed list and select Long Integer from the Data Type list, as shown here, and for the Zip field, select Yes (Duplicates OK).

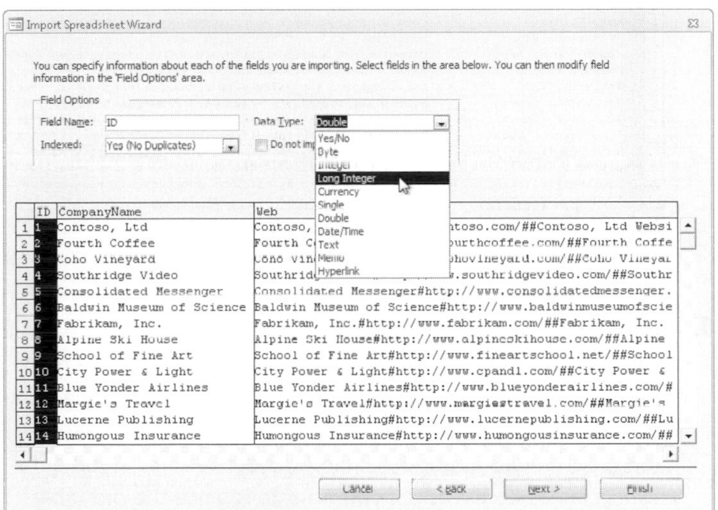

As you move from field to field, the Data Type box displays the data type that the wizard chooses for each field (based on the data it finds in the first few rows). If what you see here is incorrect, click the arrow and select the correct data type from the list. Access 2010 allows you to select the correct data type on this page of the Import Spreadsheet Wizard. You can also choose to eliminate certain columns that you don't want to appear in the final table. For example, it's quite common to have intervening blank columns to control spacing in a spreadsheet that you print. You can eliminate blank columns by scrolling to them and selecting the Do Not Import Field (Skip) check box. Click Next to go to the next step.

7. On the next page, you can designate a field as the primary key of the new table. If you want, you can tell the wizard to build an ID field for you that uses the AutoNumber data type. (It so happens that this sample spreadsheet already has a numeric ID field that we'll attempt to use as the primary key.) If multiple fields form a unique value for the primary key, you can tell the wizard not to create a primary key. Later, you can open the resulting table in Design view to set the primary key.

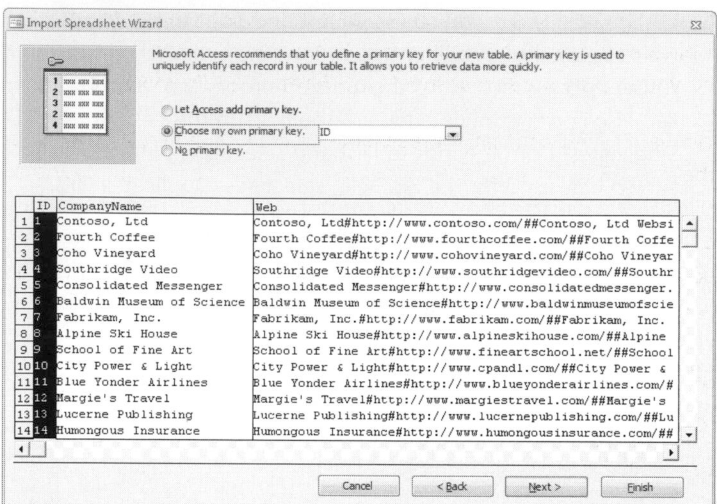

8. Click Next to go to the final page of the wizard, where you can change the name of your new table. (The Import Spreadsheet Wizard uses the name of the spreadsheet or the named range you chose in step 4.) You can also select the option to start the Table Analyzer Wizard to analyze your new table. See Chapter 4, "Designing Client Tables," for details about the Table Analyzer Wizard. If you enter the name of an existing table, Access asks if you want to replace the old table.

9. Click Finish on the last page to import your data. Access opens a dialog box that indicates the result of the import procedure. If the procedure is successful, the new table will have the name you entered in the last step. If you asked to create a new table and Access found errors, you will find a new table that has the name of the import table you specified with a $_ImportErrors suffix. If you asked to append the data to an existing table and Access found errors, you can choose to complete the import with errors or go back to the wizard to attempt to fix the problem (such as incorrectly defined columns). You might need to exit the wizard and correct data in the original spreadsheet file, as noted in the following section.

Fixing Errors

In "Preparing a Spreadsheet," on page 463, you learned that Access 2010 determines data types for the fields in a new table based on the values it finds in the first several rows being imported from a spreadsheet. Figures 8-3 and 8-4 show a spreadsheet whose first few rows would generate a wrong data type for the Zip column in a new Access table. The Number data type that Access would generate for that field, based on the first several entries, would not work for the last row, which contains character data. In addition, one of the rows has a duplicate value in the ID column. If you attempt to use this column as the primary key when you import the spreadsheet, you'll get an additional error.

If you were to import that spreadsheet, Access would first display an error message similar to the one shown in Figure 8-5. This indicates that the wizard found a problem with the column that you designated as the primary key. If you have duplicate values, the wizard will also inform you. When the wizard encounters any problems with the primary key column, it imports your data but does not define a primary key. This gives you a chance to correct the data in the table and then define the primary key yourself.

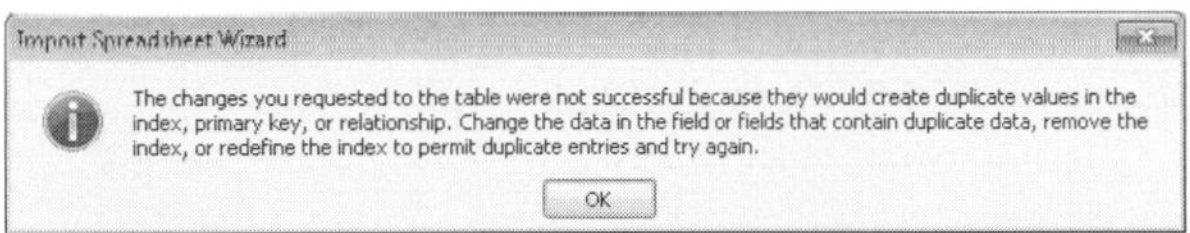

Figure 8-5 Access displays this error message when it encounters a problem with your primary key values.

In addition, if the wizard has any problems with data conversion, it displays a message similar to the one shown in Figure 8-6.

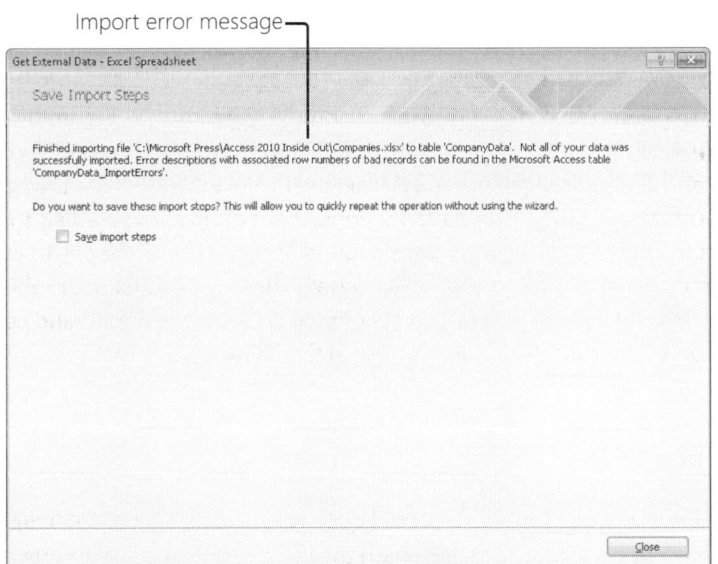

Figure 8-6 Access displays this message at the top of the Save Import Steps page of the Get External Data - Excel Spreadsheet dialog box if it encounters data conversion errors while importing a spreadsheet.

Note that if your import was successful, you might want to select the Save Import Steps check box before you click Close if you might run the exact same import again in the future. You can find all saved imports by clicking the Saved Imports button in the Import & Link group on the External Data tab.

When the Import Spreadsheet Wizard has problems with data conversion, it creates an import errors table in your database (with the name of the spreadsheet in the title) that contains a record for each error. Figure 8-7 shows the import errors table that Access creates when you import the spreadsheet shown in Figure 8-3. Notice that the table lists not only the type of error but also the field and row in the spreadsheet in which the error occurred. In this case, it lists the one row in the source spreadsheet that contains the Canadian postal code. The row number listed is the relative row number in the source spreadsheet, not the record number in the resulting table.

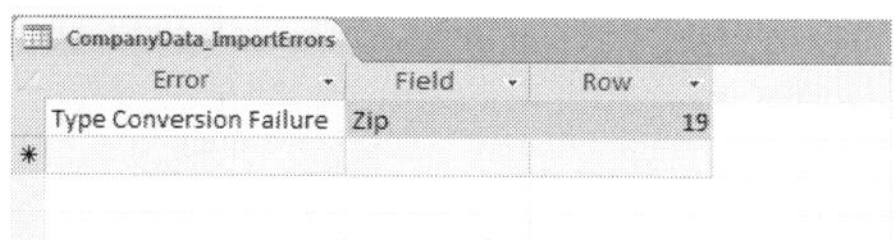
CompanyData_ImportErrors

Error	Field	Row
Type Conversion Failure	Zip	19

Figure 8-7 Here is the import errors table that results from importing the spreadsheet shown in Figure 8-3.

Figure 8-8 shows the table that results from importing the spreadsheet shown in Figure 8-3. You can find one row that has no entry in the Zip column. If you switch to Design view, you can see that the Import Spreadsheet Wizard selected the Number data type for the Zip field. If you want to be able to store values that include letters, the Zip field must be a text field. Notice that in Design view there is no primary key defined.

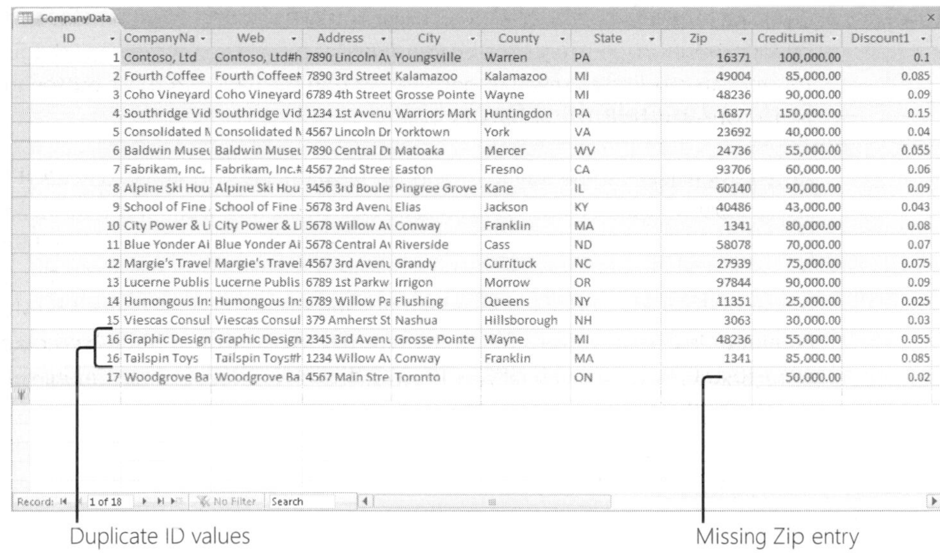

CompanyData

ID	CompanyNa	Web	Address	City	County	State	Zip	CreditLimit	Discount1
1	Contoso, Ltd	Contoso, Ltd#h	7890 Lincoln A\	Youngsville	Warren	PA	16371	100,000.00	0.1
2	Fourth Coffee	Fourth Coffee#	7890 3rd Street	Kalamazoo	Kalamazoo	MI	49004	85,000.00	0.085
3	Coho Vineyard	Coho Vineyard	6789 4th Street	Grosse Pointe	Wayne	MI	48236	90,000.00	0.09
4	Southridge Vid	Southridge Vid	1234 1st Avenu	Warriors Mark	Huntingdon	PA	16877	150,000.00	0.15
5	Consolidated M	Consolidated M	4567 Lincoln Dr	Yorktown	York	VA	23692	40,000.00	0.04
6	Baldwin Museu	Baldwin Museu	7890 Central Di	Matoaka	Mercer	WV	24736	55,000.00	0.055
7	Fabrikam, Inc.	Fabrikam, Inc.#	4567 2nd Stree	Easton	Fresno	CA	93706	60,000.00	0.06
8	Alpine Ski Hou	Alpine Ski Hou	3456 3rd Boule	Pingree Grove	Kane	IL	60140	90,000.00	0.09
9	School of Fine	School of Fine	5678 3rd Avenu	Elias	Jackson	KY	40486	43,000.00	0.043
10	City Power & Li	City Power & Li	5678 Willow Av	Conway	Franklin	MA	1341	80,000.00	0.08
11	Blue Yonder Ai	Blue Yonder Ai	5678 Central Av	Riverside	Cass	ND	58078	70,000.00	0.07
12	Margie's Travel	Margie's Travel	4567 3rd Avenu	Grandy	Currituck	NC	27939	75,000.00	0.075
13	Lucerne Publis	Lucerne Publis	6789 1st Parkw	Irrigon	Morrow	OR	97844	90,000.00	0.09
14	Humongous In	Humongous In	6789 Willow Pa	Flushing	Queens	NY	11351	25,000.00	0.025
15	Viescas Consul	Viescas Consul	379 Amherst St	Nashua	Hillsborough	NH	3063	30,000.00	0.03
16	Graphic Design	Graphic Design	2345 3rd Avenu	Grosse Pointe	Wayne	MI	48236	55,000.00	0.055
16	Tailspin Toys	Tailspin Toys#h	1234 Willow Av	Conway	Franklin	MA	1341	85,000.00	0.085
17	Woodgrove Ba	Woodgrove Ba	4567 Main Stre	Toronto		ON		50,000.00	0.02

Figure 8-8 After importing the spreadsheet shown in Figure 8-3, one row is missing a postal code entry, and there is a duplicate value in the ID column.

You can correct some of the errors in the table in Design view. For example, you can change the data type of the Zip field to Text (and perhaps change the name to PostalCode since it includes postal codes outside the United States), save the table, and then enter the missing value. For the row that has a duplicate ID (16), you can switch to Datasheet view and either delete one of the rows or supply a unique value. You can then set ID as the primary key in Design view.

Importing Text Files

You can import data from a text file into Access 2010 even though, unlike the data in a spreadsheet, the data in a text file isn't arranged in columns and rows in an orderly way. You make the data in a text file understandable to Access either by creating a *delimited text file*, in which special characters delimit the fields in each record, or by creating a *fixed-width text file*, in which each field occupies the same location in each record.

Preparing a Text File

You might be able to import some text files into Access 2010 without changing them, particularly if a text file was created by a program using standard field delimiters. However, in many cases, you'll have to modify the contents of the file, define the file for Access with an import specification, or do both before you can import it. See the sidebar "Defining an Import Specification," on page 480, for details.

Setting Up Delimited Data

Access 2010 needs some way to distinguish where fields start and end in each incoming text string. Access supports four standard separator characters: a comma, a tab, a semicolon, and a space. When you use a comma as the separator (a very common technique), the comma (or the carriage return at the end of the record) indicates the end of each field, and the next field begins with the first nonblank character. The commas are not part of the data. To include a comma within a text string as data, you must enclose all text strings within single or double quotation marks (the text qualifier). If any of your text strings contain double quotation marks, you must enclose the strings within single quotation marks, and vice versa. Access accepts only single or double quotation marks (but not both) as the text qualifier, so all embedded quotes in a file that you want to import into Access must be of the same type. In other words, you can't include a single quotation mark in one field and a double quotation mark in another field within the same file. Figure 8-9 shows a sample comma-separated and double-quote-qualified text file. You can find this file (CompaniesCSV.txt) on the companion CD.

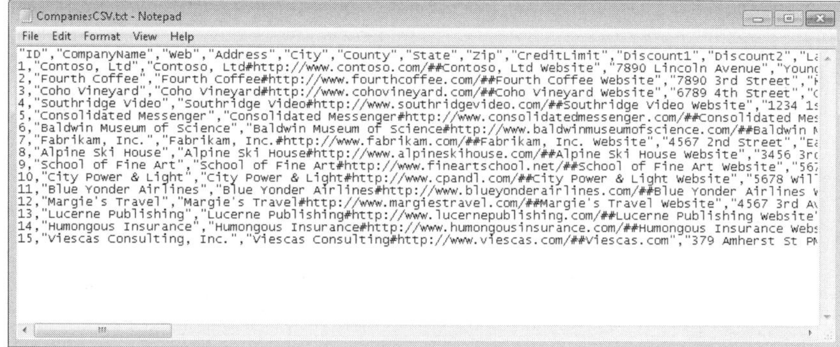

Figure 8-9 A comma-separated and double-quote-delimited text file uses commas between the field values and surrounds text values in double quotations marks.

Another common way to separate data is to use the tab character between fields. In fact, when you save a spreadsheet file as text in most spreadsheet programs, the program stores the columns with tab characters between them. Figure 8-10 shows one of the worksheets from the CompaniesTABxl.txt Excel spreadsheet saved as text in WordPad. (You can see the tab alignment marks that we placed on the ruler to line up the columns.) Notice that Excel added double quotation marks around several of the text fields—the company names that contain a comma. Because this file is tab-delimited, Access accepts the text fields without quotation marks. However, if all or part of your incoming data contains a text qualifier surrounding some of the fields, you should specify that qualifier when you import the data. If you do not do that, Access imports the qualifier characters as well.

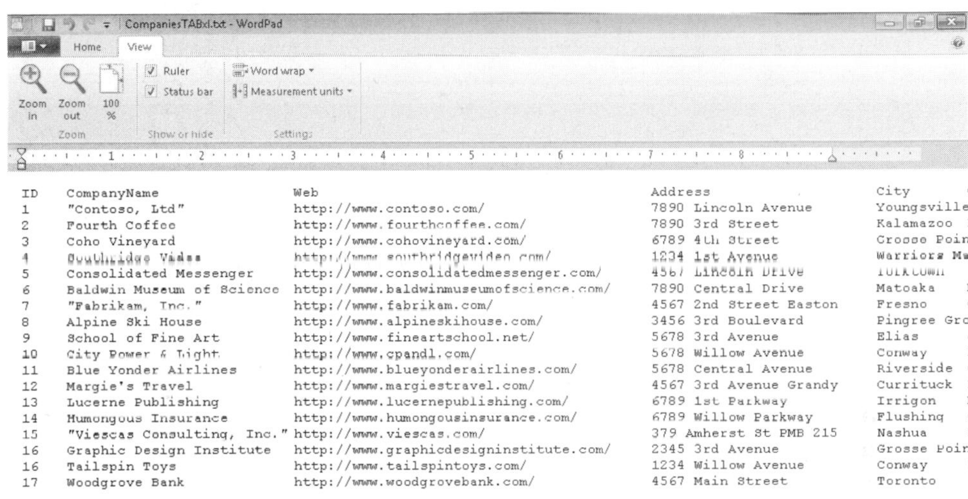

ID	CompanyName	Web	Address	City
1	"Contoso, Ltd"	http://www.contoso.com/	7890 Lincoln Avenue	Youngsville
2	Fourth Coffee	http://www.fourthcoffee.com/	7890 3rd Street	Kalamazoo
3	Coho Vineyard	http://www.cohovineyard.com/	6789 4th Street	Grosse Poin
4	Southridge Video	http://www.southridgevideo.com/	1234 1st Avenue	Warriors Ma
5	Consolidated Messenger	http://www.consolidatedmessenger.com/	4567 Lincoln Drive	Yorktown
6	Baldwin Museum of Science	http://www.baldwinmuseumofscience.com/	7890 Central Drive	Matoaka
7	"Fabrikam, Inc."	http://www.fabrikam.com/	4567 2nd Street Easton	Fresno
8	Alpine Ski House	http://www.alpineskihouse.com/	3456 3rd Boulevard	Pingree Gro
9	School of Fine Art	http://www.fineartschool.net/	5678 3rd Avenue	Elias
10	City Power & Light	http://www.cpandl.com/	5678 Willow Avenue	Conway
11	Blue Yonder Airlines	http://www.blueyonderairlines.com/	5678 Central Avenue	Riverside
12	Margie's Travel	http://www.margiestravel.com/	4567 3rd Avenue Grandy	Currituck
13	Lucerne Publishing	http://www.lucernepublishing.com/	6789 1st Parkway	Irrigon
14	Humongous Insurance	http://www.humongousinsurance.com/	6789 Willow Parkway	Flushing
15	"Viescas Consulting, Inc."	http://www.viescas.com/	379 Amherst St PMB 215	Nashua
16	Graphic Design Institute	http://www.graphicdesigninstitute.com/	2345 3rd Avenue	Grosse Poin
16	Tailspin Toys	http://www.tailspintoys.com/	1234 Willow Avenue	Conway
17	Woodgrove Bank	http://www.woodgrovebank.com/	4567 Main Street	Toronto

Figure 8-10 A tab-separated text file uses tab characters to separate the fields.

As with data type analysis, Access examines the first few rows of your file to determine the delimiter and the text qualifier. Notice in Figure 8-10 that tabs are clearly the delimiter, but two of the company name fields are qualified with double quotes. As you'll see later in this chapter, if you want to import a file that is delimited differently, you can specify different delimiters and separators in the Import Text Wizard. The important thing to remember is that your data should have a consistent data type in all the rows for each column, just as it should in spreadsheet files. If your text file is delimited, the delimiters must be consistent throughout the file.

Setting Up Fixed-Width Data

Access 2010 can also import text files when the fields appear in fixed locations in each record in the file. You might encounter this type of file if you download a print output file from a host computer. Figure 8-11 shows a sample fixed-width text file. Notice that each field begins in exactly the same location in all the records. (To see this sort of fixed spacing on your screen, you must display the file using a monospaced font such as Courier New.) Unlike delimited files, to prepare this type of file for importing, you must first remove any heading or summary lines from the file. The file must contain only records, with the data you want to import in fixed locations.

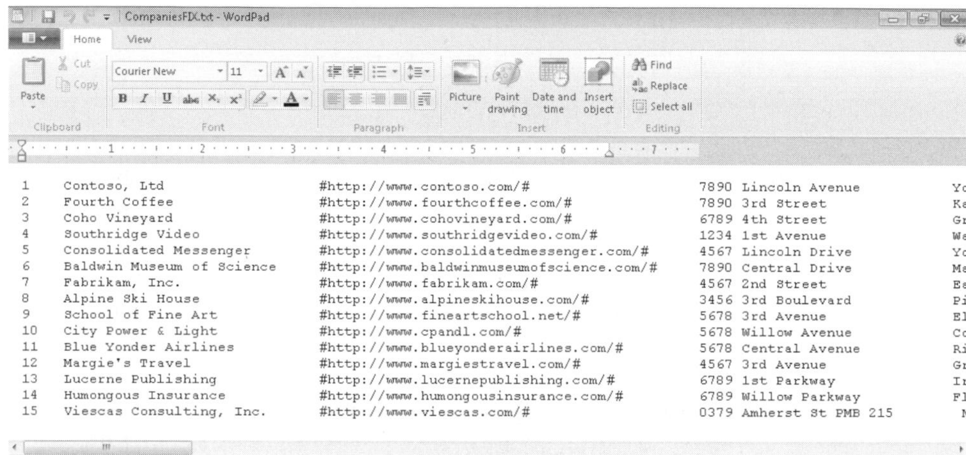

Figure 8-11 A fixed-width text file contains data in fixed-width columns.

Importing a Text File

Before you can import a text file, you'll probably need to prepare the data or define the file for Access 2010 with an import specification, or both, as discussed in "Preparing a Text File," on page 471. After you do that, you can import the text file into an Access database by doing the following:

1. Open the Access database that will receive the text data. If that database is already open, close any objects so that only the Navigation pane is visible.

2. On the External Data tab, in the Import & Link group, click the Text File command, as shown here.

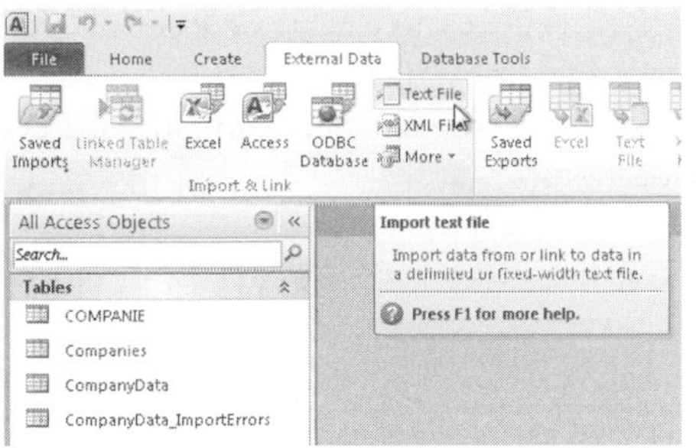

3. Access opens the Get External Data - Text File dialog box, shown next. Click Browse to open the File Open dialog box, shown previously on page 454. Select the folder and the name of the file you want to import. (For these examples, we used the CompaniesTAB.txt and CompaniesFIX.txt files on the companion CD.) Click the Open button in the File Open dialog box to return to the Get External Data - Text File dialog box.

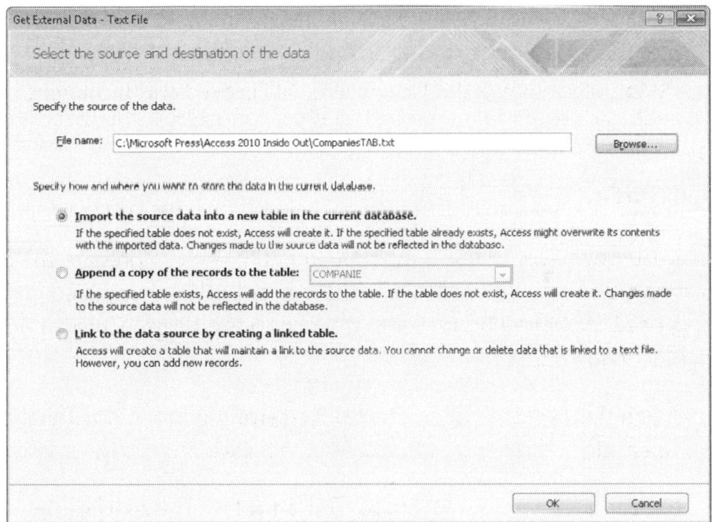

4. Make sure the Import The Source Data Into A New Table In The Current Database option is selected and then click OK. Access starts the Import Text Wizard and displays the first page of the wizard, as shown here.

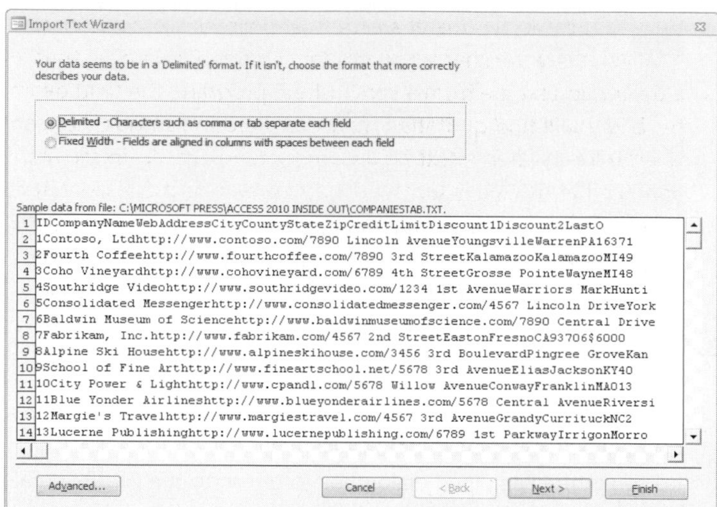

On this page, the wizard makes its best estimation about whether the data is delimited or fixed-width. It displays the first several rows of data, which you can examine to confirm the wizard's choice. If the wizard has made the wrong choice, your data is probably formatted incorrectly. You should exit the wizard and fix the source file as suggested in "Preparing a Text File," on page 471. If the wizard has made the correct choice, click Next to go to the next step.

5. If your file is delimited, the Import Text Wizard displays the following page.

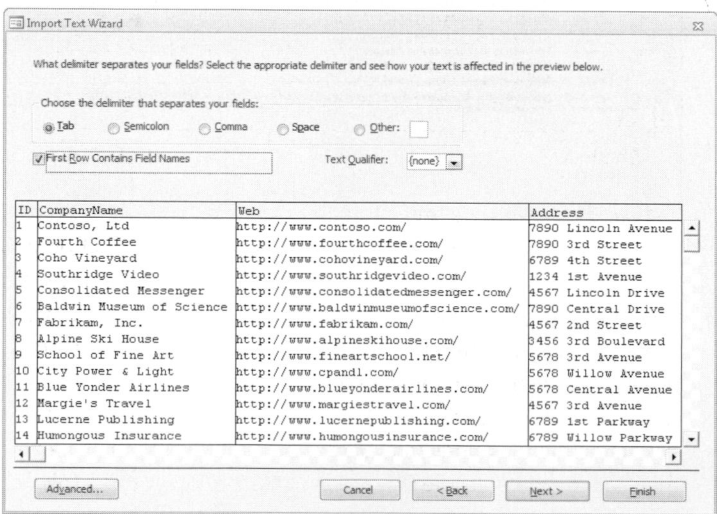

Here, you can verify the character that delimits the fields in your text file and the qualifier character that surrounds text strings. Remember that usually when you save a delimited text file from a spreadsheet program, the field delimiter is a tab character, and you'll find quotation marks only around strings that contain commas. If the wizard doesn't find a text field with quotation marks in the first few lines, it might assume that no text is surrounded by quotes, and therefore, it might set the Text Qualifier field to {none}. You might need to change the Text Qualifier field from {none} to " if this is the case. (You'll need to do this if you use the CompaniesTabxl.txt sample file.) Also be sure to select the First Row Contains Field Names check box if your file has column names in the first row. If you don't do that, the wizard assigns generic field names (Field1, Field2, and so on) and might misidentify the field data types.

If your file is in fixed-width format, the wizard displays this page. (We have scrolled to the right to show one of the problems.)

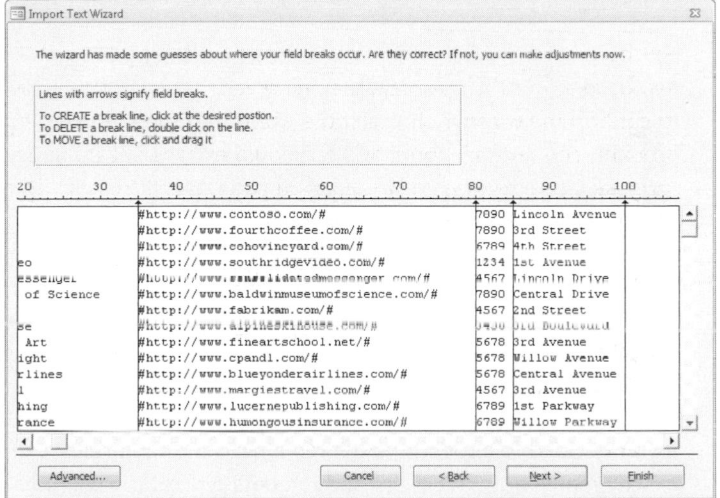

Instead of showing delimiting characters, the wizard offers a graphic representation of where it thinks each field begins. To change the definition of a field, you can drag any line to move it. You can also create an additional field by clicking at the position on the display where fields should be separated. If the wizard creates too many fields, you can double-click any extra delimiting lines to remove them. In the example shown in the preceding illustration (using the CompaniesFIX.txt file on the companion CD), the wizard assumes that the street number is separate from the rest of the address. It also assumes that the State and Zip fields are one field. Because many of the spaces in the sample Comments field line up, it splits this field into several fields.

You can double-click the line following the street number to remove it. You can click between the state and zip data to separate those into two fields. Finally, you can double-click all the extra lines the wizard inserted in Comments to turn that into one field. Click Next to go to the next step.

6. If you decided to create a new table in the Get External Data - Text File dialog box, the wizard displays the page shown here. Use this page to specify or confirm field names (you can change field names even if the first row in the text file contains names), select field data types, and set indexed properties. If you're working in a fixed-width text file, you should provide the field names; otherwise, Access names the fields Field1, Field2, and so on.

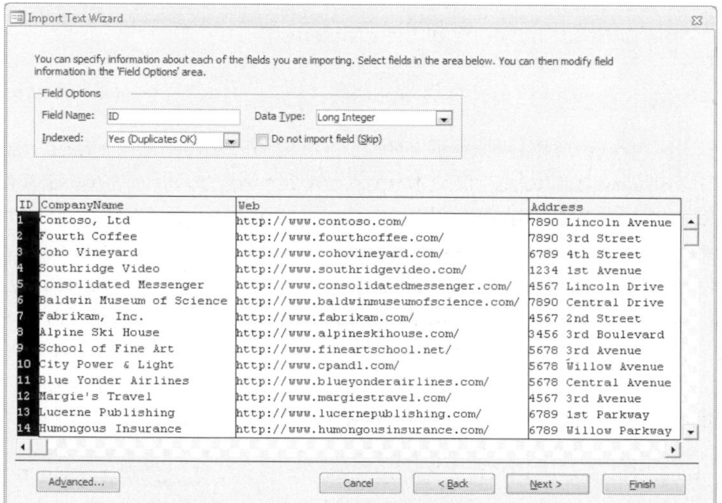

If you decided to append the data to an existing table, either the columns must exactly match both the count and the data type of the columns in the target table (left to right) or the file must be a delimited file with column names in the first row that match column names in the target table.

7. Click Next to go to the next page, where you can select a primary key, much as you did for spreadsheet files. Click Next when you are finished setting a primary key.

8. On the final page of the wizard, you confirm the name of the new table or the target table. You can also select the check box to start the Table Analyzer Wizard to analyze your new table. (See Chapter 4 for details about the Table Analyzer Wizard.) If you enter the name of an existing table, Access asks if you want to replace the old table.

Click Finish to import your data. Access displays a confirmation message at the top of the Get External Data - Text File dialog box to show you the result of the import procedure. If the wizard encounters an error that prevents any data from being imported, it creates an import errors table in your database (with the name of the text file in the title) that contains a record for each error. The final page of the wizard also includes a check box you can select to save the import steps you just completed.

Fixing Errors

While importing text files, you might encounter errors that are similar to those described in "Importing Spreadsheet Data," on page 462. For example, when you append a text file to an existing table, some rows might be rejected because of duplicate primary keys. Unless the primary key for your table is an AutoNumber field, the rows you append from the text file must contain primary key fields and the values in those fields must be unique.

For delimited text files, Access 2010 determines the data type (and delimiter and text qualifier) based on the fields in the first several records being imported. If a number appears in a field in the first several records but subsequent records contain text data, you must enclose that field in quotation marks in at least one of the first few rows so that Access will use the Text data type for that field. If a number first appears without decimal places, Access will use the Number data type with the Field Size property set to Long Integer. This setting will generate errors later if the numbers in other records contain decimal places. You can also explicitly tell Access the data type to use by defining a custom import specification. See the sidebar, "Defining an Import Specification," for details.

Access displays a message if it encounters any errors. As with errors that are generated when you import a spreadsheet, Access creates an import errors table. The table contains a record for each error. The import errors table lists not only the type of error but also the column and row in the text file in which the error occurred. The errors you can encounter with a text file are similar to those described earlier for a spreadsheet file.

You can correct some errors in the table in Design view. For example, you can change the data type of a field if the content of the field can be converted to the new data type. With other errors, you must either add missing data in Datasheet view or delete the imported records and import the table again after correcting the values in the text file that originally caused the errors.

Defining an Import Specification

If you are likely to import the same fixed-width file often (for example, a text file you receive from a mainframe once a month) or if you want to be able to use a macro or a Visual Basic procedure to automate importing a text file, you can use the Import Text Wizard to save an import specification for use by your automation procedures. To do so, begin by clicking Text File in the Import & Link group on the External Data tab. Next, select the file you want to import and click OK. Access now opens the Import Text Wizard, which you should use to examine your file, and verify that the wizard identifies the correct fields. At this point, click Advanced to see an Import Specification dialog box like the one shown here.

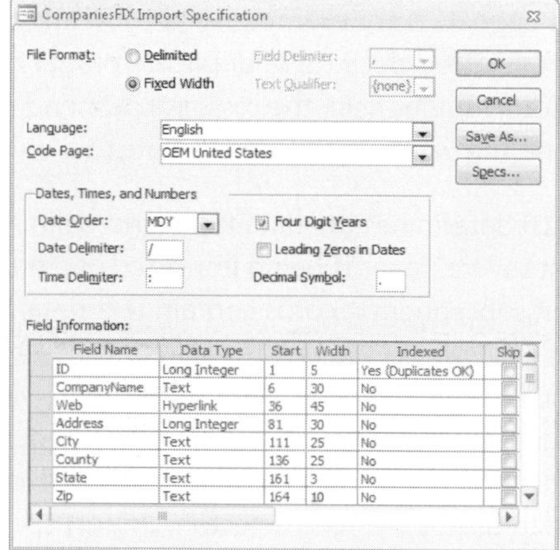

For fixed-width specifications, you can define the field names, data types, start column, width, indexed properties, and whether to skip a field. You can identify the language in the Language box and the character set in the Code Page box. You can also specify the way Access recognizes date and time values and numeric fractions. (For example, for a file coming from a non-U.S. computer, the Date Order might be DMY, and the Decimal Symbol might be a comma.) Click Save As to save your specification, and give it a name. You can also click Specs to load and edit other previously saved specifications. The loaded specification is the one Access uses to import the current file.

For details about modifying your table design, see Chapter 5, "Modifying Your Table Design." See Table 5-3 on page 262 for data conversion limitations.

Modifying Imported Tables

When you import data from an external source, Access 2010 often has to use default data types or lengths that can accommodate all the incoming data. You will then need to correct these default settings for your needs. For example, Access assigns a maximum length of 255 characters to text data imported from a spreadsheet or a text file. Even when the source of the data is another database, Access might choose numeric data types that can accept the data but that might not be correct. For example, numeric data in dBASE might be of the Integer type, but Access stores all numeric data from dBASE with a Field Size setting of Double.

Unless you're importing data from a SQL database that has a primary key defined, Access does not define a primary key in the new table so you must do that yourself. Also, if you did not include field names when importing a text or spreadsheet file, you'll probably want to enter meaningful names in the resulting table.

Linking Files

You can link tables from other Access databases—whether the other databases are local or on a network—and work with the data as if these tables were defined in your current Access database. If you want to work with data stored in another database format supported by Access (dBASE, or any SQL database that supports ODBC), you can link the data instead of importing it.

Note

Although you can import queries, forms, reports, macros, and modules from another Access database file, you cannot link these types of objects. Any object that Access needs to run (rather than simply be a container for data) must be in your local database.

In most cases, you can read data, insert new records, delete records, or change data just as if the linked file were an Access table in your database. You can also link text and spreadsheet format data so that you can process it with queries, forms, and reports in your Access database. You can only read the data in linked text and spreadsheet files.

This ability to link data is especially important when you need to access data on a host computer or share data from your application with many other users.

Note

Access 2010 supports linking to dBASE, and it allows full update if it can find the associated index files. If you need to work with later versions, you must install the Borland Database Engine (BDE).

Security Considerations

If you attempt to link a file or a table from a database system that is protected, Access 2010 asks you for a password. If the security information you supply is correct and Access successfully links the secured data, Access can store the security information with the linked table entry so that you do not have to enter this information each time you or your application opens the table. Access stores this information in the hidden Connect property of a linked table, so a knowledgeable person might be able to retrieve it by writing code to examine this property. Therefore, if you have linked sensitive information to your Access database and have supplied security information, you should consider encrypting your database. Consult Chapter 27 for information about encrypting your Access database.

If you are linking your database to SQL Server tables and are using Windows domain security, you can set options in SQL Server to accept the Windows domain user ID if the user logs on correctly to the network. Therefore, you won't need to store security information with the link. If your server contains particularly sensitive information, you can disable this option to guard against unauthorized access from logged on but unattended network workstations.

Performance Considerations

Access 2010 always performs best when working with its own files on your local computer. If you link tables or files from other databases on other computers, you might notice slower performance. In particular, you can expect slower performance if you connect over a network to a table or a file in another database, even if the remote table is an Access table. You won't see any performance difference if you link to Access tables in another .accdb file on your local computer.

When sharing data over a network, you should consider how you and other people can use the data in a way that maximizes performance. For example, instead of working directly with the tables, you should work with queries on the shared data whenever possible to limit the amount of data you need at any one time. When inserting new data in a shared table, you should use an Access form that is set only for data entry so that you don't have to access the entire table to add new data.

You can view and set options for multiple users sharing data by clicking the File tab on the Backstage view, clicking Options, and then clicking the Client Settings category in the Access Options dialog box, as shown in Figure 8-12. The original settings for these options are often appropriate when you share data over a network, so it's a good idea to consult your system administrator before making changes.

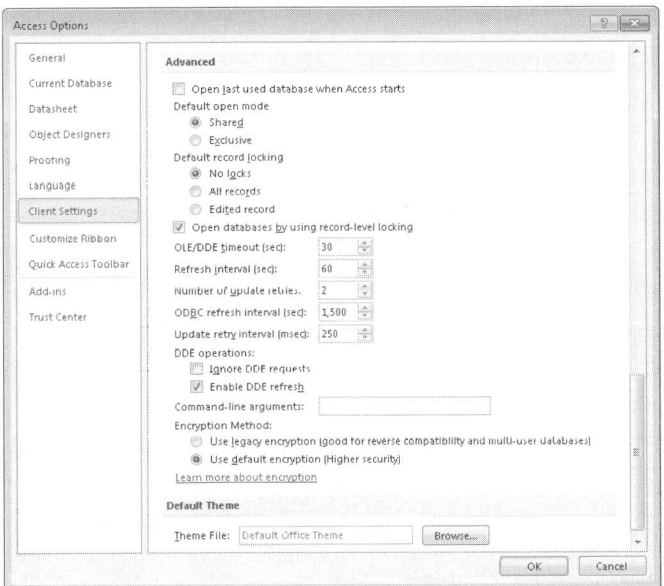

Figure 8-12 In the Advanced section of the Client Settings category in the Access Options dialog box, you can set options that affect the performance of linked tables.

One very important consideration is record locking. When Access 2010 needs to update data in a shared file, it must lock the data to ensure that no other computer is trying to write the same data at the same time. You should set options so that records are not locked if you are simply browsing through data. Even if your application frequently updates and inserts data, you should leave Default Record Locking set to No Locks. With this setting, Access 2010 locks individual records only for the short period of time that it is writing the row, so the chance of receiving an update error while two users are trying to update the same row at the exact same time is very small.

If you want to ensure that no one else can change a record that you have begun to update, you should set Default Record Locking to Edited Record. Note, however, that no other user will be able to edit a record that another has begun to change. If a user begins to type a change in a record and then goes to lunch, no one else will be able to change that record from another computer until that user either saves the row or clears the edit.

INSIDE OUT **Leave Default Record Locking Alone**

We never set either All Records or Edited Record as the default. Either one can cause extra overhead while updating data and can lock out other users unnecessarily. In the rare case that an update conflict occurs with No Locks, Access gives the second user the opportunity to refresh the data and reenter the blocked update. Also, you can set record locking individually in forms and reports. See Chapter 14, "Customizing a Form," and Chapter 18, "Advanced Report Design," for details.

You can set options to limit the number of times Access 2010 will retry an update to a locked record and how long it will wait between retries. You can also control how often Access reviews updates made by other users to shared data by setting the refresh interval. If this setting is very low, Access will waste time performing this task repeatedly.

Access 97 (version 8) and earlier locked an entire 2-KB page each time you updated, inserted, or deleted rows. This meant that only one user could update any of the rows stored physically within the page. The page size in Access 2000 increased to 4 KB, but Access 2000 (version 9) and later also support record-level locking that eliminates locking collisions when two users attempt to update different rows stored on the same data storage page. Unless you are designing an application that frequently needs to update hundreds of rows at a time (for example, with action queries), you should leave the Open Databases By Using Record-Level Locking check box selected.

Linking Access Tables

To link a table from another Access database to your database, do the following:

1. Open the Access database to which you want to link the table. If that database is already open, close any objects so that only the Navigation pane is visible.
2. On the External Data tab, in the Import & Link group, click the Access command, and then select Link To The Data Source By Creating A Linked Table in the Get External Data - Access Database dialog box shown here.

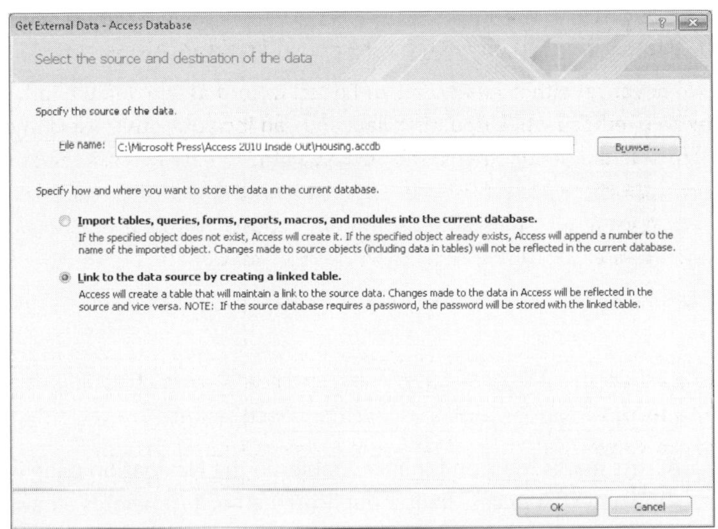

3. Click Browse to open the File Open dialog box shown earlier on page 454, which lists the types of databases you can link. Select the folder and the name of the .accdb, .mdb, .mda, .accda, .mde, or .accde file that contains the table to which you want to link. (You cannot link tables from an .adp or .ade file because those are actually tables in SQL Server—use an ODBC link to the server directly as explained in "Linking SQL Tables," on page 490.) If you're connecting over a network, select the logical drive that is assigned to the network server containing the database you want. If you want Access to automatically connect to the network server each time you open the table, type the full network location (also known as the UNC or Universal Naming Convention name) in the File Name box instead of selecting a logical drive. For example, on a Windows network you might enter a network location such as

   ```
   \\dbsvr\access\shared\northwind.accdb
   ```

   After you select the Access database file you want, click Open to return to the Get External Data - Access Database dialog box, and then click OK to see the tables in that database.

4. Access opens the Link Tables dialog box, shown next, which lists the tables available in the database you selected. Select one or more tables, and click OK to link the tables to the current database. If the link procedure is successful, the new table will have the name of the table you selected.

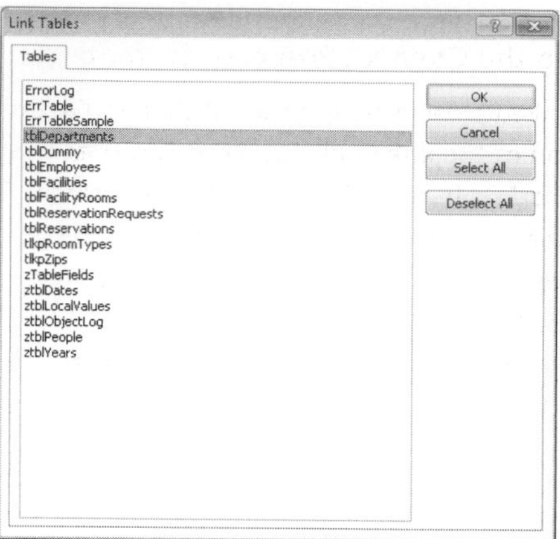

Access marks the icon for linked tables in the Navigation pane with an arrow, as shown next. If Access finds a duplicate name, it generates a new name by adding a unique integer to the end of the name as described earlier. Because objects such as forms, reports, macros, and modules might refer to the linked table by its original name, you should carefully check name references if Access has to rename a linked table.

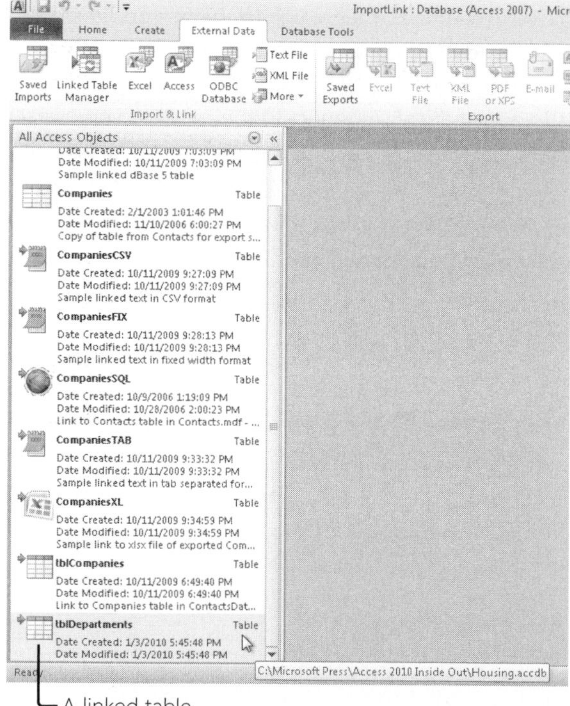

INSIDE OUT **Keeping the Connect Property Current**

One problem with using linked data in an application that you're going to distribute to someone else is the location of the linked files on your computer might not be exactly the same as it is on your user's computer. For example, the internal Connect property might point to D:\MyDatabases\MyData.accdb, but your user installs the application on the C drive. You might have noticed that a form always opens when you open the Conrad Systems Contacts sample database and that it takes a few seconds before it returns you to the Navigation pane. We wrote code behind this initial form that verifies the table links and fixes them. You can learn how we built this code in Chapter 27.

Linking dBASE Files

Linking files from a foreign database is almost as easy as linking an Access table. To link to a file from dBASE, do the following:

1. Open the Access database to which you want to link the file. If that database is already open, close any objects so that only the Navigation pane is visible.
2. On the External Data tab, in the Import & Link group, click the More command, and then click dBASE File. Select Link To The Data Source By Creating A Linked Table in the Get External Data - dBASE File dialog box, as shown here.

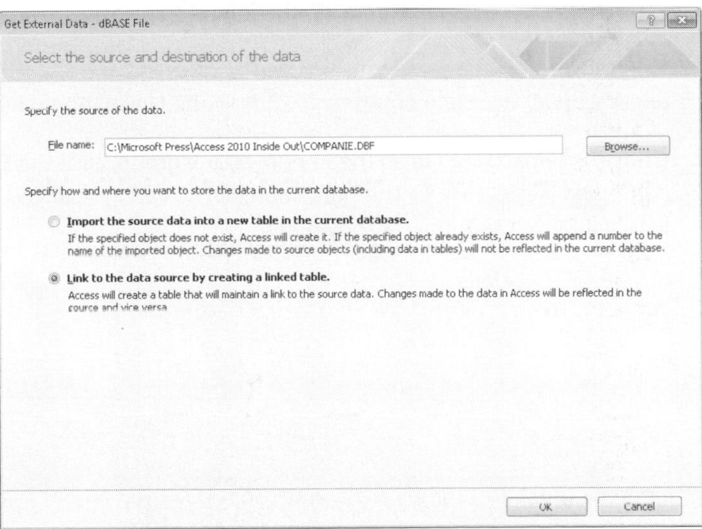

3. Click the Browse button to open the File Open dialog box shown earlier on page 454, which lists the types of dBASE files to which you can link. Select dBASE III, dBASE IV, or dBASE 5, as appropriate, in the list to the right of the File Name box, and then select the folder and the name of the file to which you want to link. If you're connecting over a network, select the logical drive that is assigned to the network server that contains the database you want. If you want Access to automatically connect to the network server each time you open the linked file, type the full network location in the File Name box instead of selecting a logical drive. For example, on a Windows network you might enter a network location such as

   ```
   \\dbsvr\dbase\shared\newstore.dbf
   ```

4. Click Open to return to the Get External Data - dBASE File dialog box, and then click OK to link to the selected dBASE file.
5. If the link procedure is successful, the new table will have the name of the file you selected (without the file name extension). If Access finds a duplicate name, it will generate a new name by adding a unique integer to the end of the name.

Linking Text and Spreadsheet Files

Linking a text file or an Excel spreadsheet file is almost identical to importing these types of files, as discussed earlier in this chapter. As noted, you can only read linked text and Excel spreadsheet files.

To link a spreadsheet file or a text file, do the following:

1. Open the Access database to which you want to link the file. If that database is already open, close any objects so that only the Navigation pane is visible.
2. On the External Data tab, in the Import & Link group, click the Excel or Text File command. Select Link To The Data Source By Creating A Linked Table in the Get External Data dialog box, as shown here.

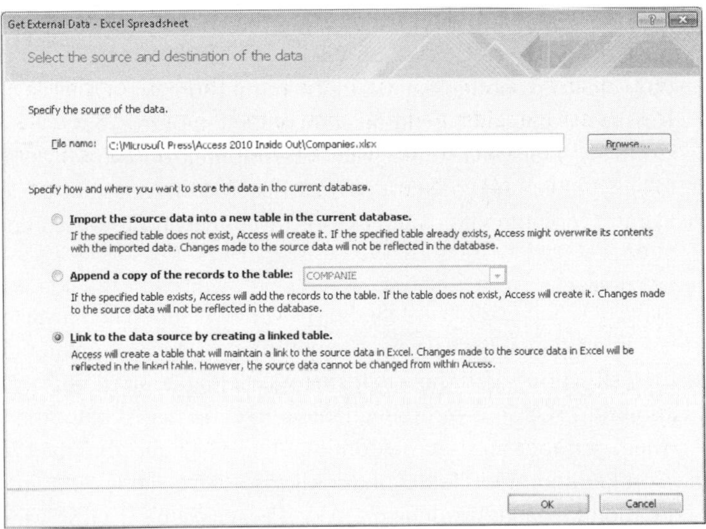

3. Click Browse to open the File Open dialog box shown earlier on page 454. Select the folder and the name of the file to which you want to link. If you're connecting over a network, select the logical drive that is assigned to the network server that contains the database you want. If you want Access to automatically connect to the network server each time you open the linked file, type the full network location in the File Name box instead of choosing a logical drive, path, and file name. For example, on a Windows network you might enter a network location such as

   ```
   \\filesvr\excel\shared\companies.xlsx
   ```

4. Click Open to return to the Get External Data dialog box, and then click OK to start the Link Spreadsheet Wizard or the Link Text Wizard.

5. Follow the steps in the wizard, which are identical to the steps for importing a spreadsheet or text file, as described earlier in this chapter.

CAUTION!

You can have the same problems with delimiters, text qualifiers, data types, and primary keys noted under importing. You might need to correct or reformat the data in your text or spreadsheet file to be able to successfully link to it. For example, if Access guesses the wrong data type for a column in an Excel file, you will see #Error in fields that have the incorrect data type.

Linking SQL Tables

To link a table from another database system that supports ODBC SQL, you must have the ODBC driver for that database installed on your computer. Your computer must also be linked to the network that connects to the computer running SQL Server from which you want to link a table, and you must have an account on that server. Check with your system administrator for information about correctly connecting to the computer running SQL Server.

If you have SQL Server 2008 installed or have downloaded and installed SQL Server 2008 Express Edition, you already have a server running SQL Server at your disposal. See Appendix A for instructions about how to install SQL Server 2008 Express Edition. One of the best ways to be sure SQL Server is running on your computer is to use the SQL Server Configuration Manager. You can start the Configuration Manager from the Windows Start menu in the Configuration Tools folder under Microsoft SQL Server 2008. You can also start the Configuration Manager by running C:\Windows\System32\SQLServerManager.msc. In the Configuration Manager, choose SQL Server 2008 Services and be sure the SQL Server (MSSQLSERVER) service is marked as Running. If it is not running, right-click the service name and click Start on the shortcut menu.

To link an SQL table, do the following:

1. Open the Access database to which you want to link the SQL table. If that database is already open, close all open objects so that you see only the Navigation pane.
2. On the External Data tab, in the Import & Link group, click the ODBC Database command. Access opens the Get External Data - ODBC Database dialog box. Make sure the Link To The Data Source By Creating A Linked Table option is selected and then click OK.
3. Access opens the Select Data Source dialog box, shown earlier on page 457, in which you can select the data source that maps to the computer running SQL Server containing the table you want to link. Select a data source, and click OK. If you don't see the data source you need, see "Creating a Data Source to Link to an ODBC Database," on page 448, for instructions. The ODBC driver displays the SQL Server Login dialog box for the SQL data source that you selected if the server is not set up to accept your Windows login.
4. When you are required to enter a login ID and password, and if you are authorized to connect to more than one database on the server and you want to connect to a database other than your default database, enter your login ID and password. Then click the Options button to open the lower part of the dialog box. When you click in

the Database box, Access logs on to the server and returns a list of available database names. Select the one you want, and click OK. If you don't specify a database name and if multiple databases exist on the server, Access will connect you to the default database for your login ID.

TROUBLESHOOTING

You can't connect to a specific database using trusted authentication because you use more than one data source.

When you connect to a server using trusted authentication (your Windows user ID), you automatically connect to the database specified in the data source. You might need to create more than one data source if you need to connect to more than one database on that server. See "Creating a Data Source to Link to an ODBC Database," on page 448, for details about defining ODBC data sources.

5. From the list of tables, select the ones you want to link. If you select a table name in error, you can click it again to deselect it, or you can click the Deselect All button to start over. Click OK to link to the tables you selected.

6. If the link procedure is successful, the new table will have the name of the SQL table (without the file name extension). If Access finds a duplicate name, it will generate a new name by adding a unique integer to the end of the name.

Modifying Linked Tables

You can make some changes to the definitions of linked tables to customize them for use in your Access 2010 environment. When you attempt to open the table in Design view, Access opens a dialog box to warn you that you cannot modify certain properties of a linked table. You can still click OK to open the linked table in Design view.

You can open a linked table in Design view to change the Format, Decimal Places, Caption, Description, and Input Mask property settings for any field. You can set these properties to customize the way you look at and update data in Access forms and reports. You can also give any linked table a new name for use within your Access database (although the table's original name remains unchanged in the source database) to help you better identify the table or to enable you to use the table with the queries, forms, and reports that you've already designed.

Changing a table's design in Access has no effect on the original table in its source database. However, if the design of the table in the source database changes, you must relink the table to Access. You must also unlink and relink any table if your user ID or your password changes.

Unlinking Linked Tables

It is easy to unlink tables that are linked to your Access database. In the Navigation pane, simply select the table you want to unlink and then press the Delete key or click the Delete command in the Records group on the Home tab on the ribbon. Access displays the confirmation message shown in Figure 8-13. Click Yes to unlink the table. Unlinking the table does not delete the table; it simply removes the link from your table list in the Navigation pane.

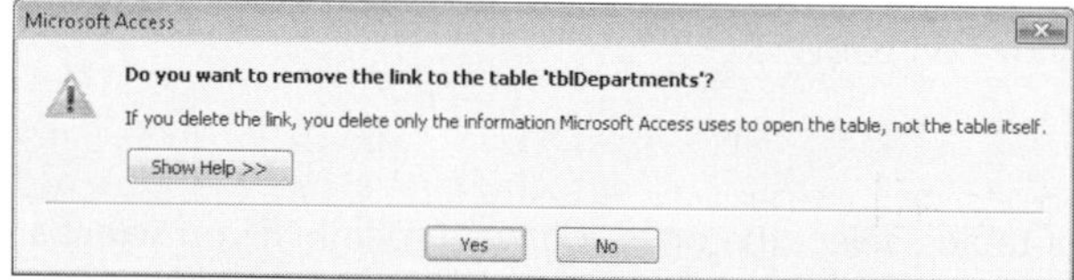

Figure 8-13 Access displays a message to confirm that you want to unlink a table.

> **Note**
>
> **If you click the Cut command in the Clipboard group on the Home tab of the ribbon to unlink a table, Access does not display the confirmation message shown in Figure 8-13.**

Using the Linked Table Manager

If you move some or all of your linked tables to a different location, you must either delete your linked tables and relink them or update the location information before you can open the tables. You can easily update the location information in the table links by using the Linked Table Manager. To use this handy utility, open the database that contains linked tables that you need to relink, and on the External Data tab, in the Import & Link group, click the Linked Table Manager command. The utility opens a dialog box that displays all the linked tables in your database, as shown in Figure 8-14. Simply select the check boxes for the ones that you think need to be verified and updated, and then click OK. If any linked table has been moved to a different location, the Linked Table Manager prompts you with a dialog box so that you can specify the new file location. You can also select the Always Prompt For New Location check box to verify the file location for all linked tables.

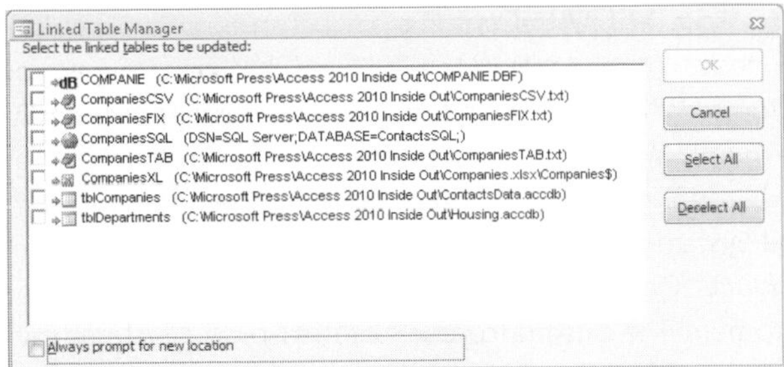

Figure 8-14 You can use the Linked Table Manager to correct links to files that have moved.

Now you have all the information you need to import and link data using Access 2010. For information on how to export data see Article 3, "Exporting Data," on the companion CD. For information on how to import or link to SharePoint lists, see the section, "Importing and Linking SharePoint Data," on page 531.

Collecting Data via Email

Access 2010 includes a feature that allows you to collect data through email and import it into your database. The data is collected through either HTML forms or rich Microsoft InfoPath 2010 forms. Access 2010 allows you to either update existing data in a table or add new records to a table. By integrating Access 2010 with email collection capabilities, you can have users update and add information to your database from different locations. This feature can be used, for example, in a club membership application that periodically needs to update its member records.

To use the email data collection capabilities in Access 2010, you must also have Microsoft Outlook 2007 or later installed to send the data entry forms and to process the data returned. If you are sending the data collection forms in HTML format, your recipients need only have an email client program that accepts HTML. If you want to send InfoPath 2010 collection forms, you also need to have InfoPath 2010 installed. The users receiving these forms must also have Outlook 2007 and InfoPath 2007 or later installed to fill out the forms and send them back.

> **Note**
>
> **To demonstrate the various capabilities of collecting data through email, we use the ContactsDataCopy.accdb and TasksEmailCollection.accdb sample databases on the companion CD. This TasksEmailCollection.accdb sample database is based on the Tasks database template with sample records added to the two tables.**

Collecting Data via HTML Forms

Open ContactsDataCopy.accdb from the folder where you installed your sample files. Click the Navigation Pane menu, click Object Type under Navigate To Category, and then click Tables under Filter By Group to display the list of tables in the database. For the continued success of the Conrad Systems business, its owners need to find new customers who want to purchase their products. One of the best ways to find leads to potential new customers is to ask existing customers. The existing contacts in the Conrad Systems Contacts database could provide names of people through their own personal network of friends who could, in turn, become new clients. By using the data collection feature in Access 2010, you could send an email form to all the existing contacts in the database, asking whether they know of anyone who might be interested in Conrad Systems products. To entice existing contacts to provide some names, you could offer an incentive of free support time.

You can update a single table using email data collection, or you can update multiple tables using a saved select query as the record source for the data entry form. You'll learn about creating queries using multiple tables in Chapter 10, "Building Complex Queries." For this example, let's create an email form to collect data to add a new record to the tblContacts table. Because we're going to send an email message to the contacts in the tblContacts table, you'll need to add your name and email address if you want to follow along in this section. Open the tblContacts table in Datasheet view, go to the new record at the end, add your name and valid email address, and save the record. Close the table when you're done. Next, right-click the tblContacts table in the Navigation pane and click Collect And Update Data Via E-Mail on the shortcut menu, as shown in Figure 8-15. Alternatively, you can select the table in the Navigation pane and click the Create E-Mail button in the Collect Data group on the External Data tab on the ribbon.

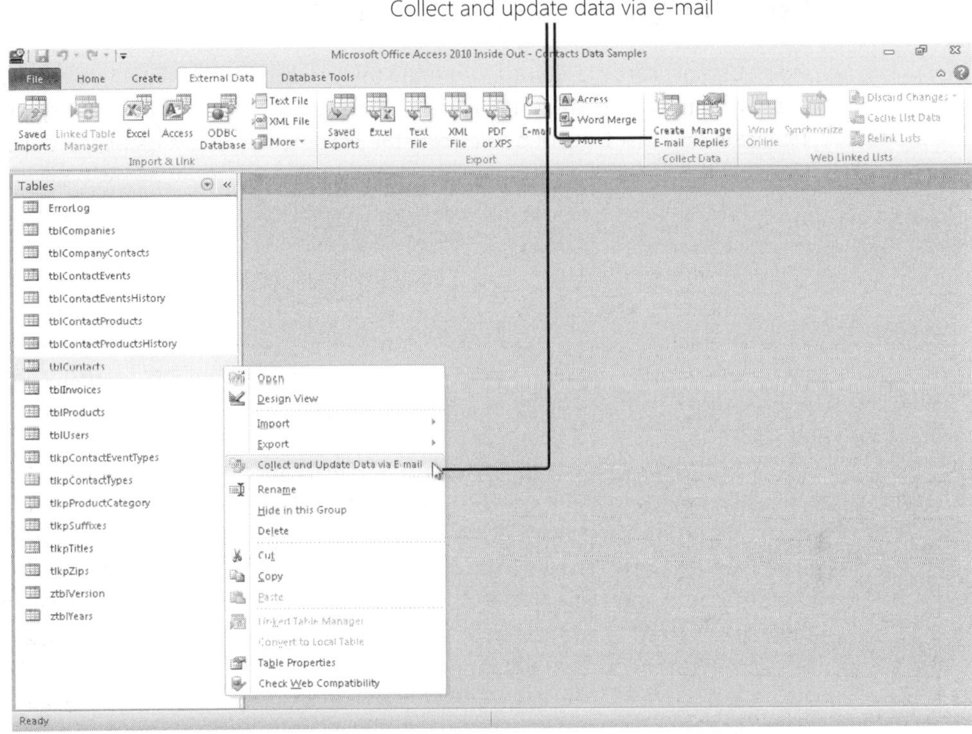

Figure 8-15 You can begin the process of collecting data via email by using the table's shortcut menu or the Create E-Mail button on the ribbon.

Access opens the first page of the email collection wizard, as shown in Figure 8-16. This first page is an introductory page, which outlines the steps you take to complete the process. For this example, you need to complete six major steps. (If you are adding records to a table with no records, Access displays five steps on this first page.) Click Next to proceed to the second page of the wizard.

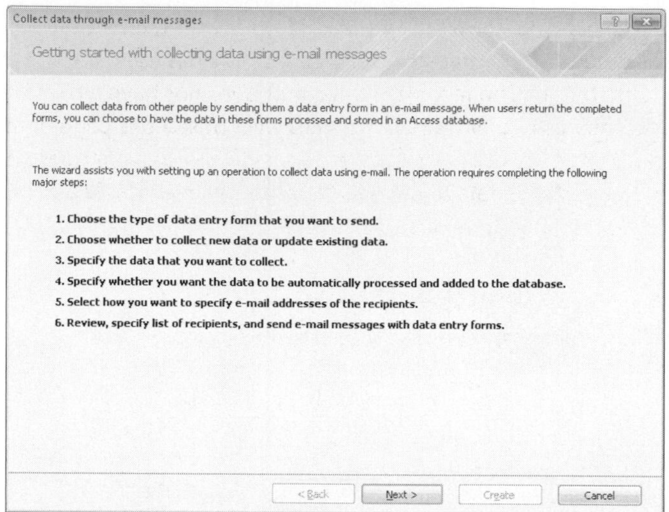

Figure 8-16 The first page of the email collection wizard is an introductory page.

The second page of the wizard, shown in Figure 8-17, asks you to choose between creating an HTML form or an InfoPath form for data entry. Remember that the people who receive the InfoPath form need to have InfoPath 2007 and Outlook 2007 or later installed on their computers to be able to read and fill out the data form. When you send an HTML form, the recipient needs only an email client that can handle messages in HTML. For this example, select HTML Form (the default) and click Next.

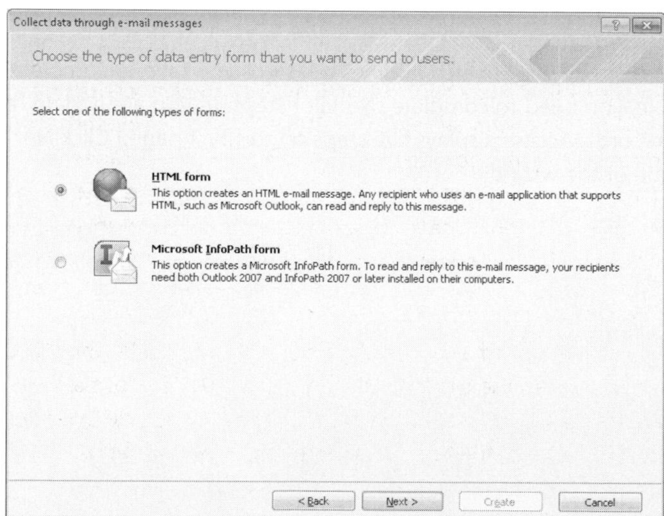

Figure 8-17 The second page of the wizard asks you to choose a type of form.

The next page of the wizard, shown in Figure 8-18, asks you to choose whether users receive a blank form or a form that includes data from within the database they will update. If you chose a table that has no records, a table that does not have a primary key defined, or a query that combines two or more tables, you will not see this page of the wizard. In those cases, Access assumes you only want to add new records, so it does not display this page. Note also that to send data to update, you must have available within one of your database tables the email address of the recipient.

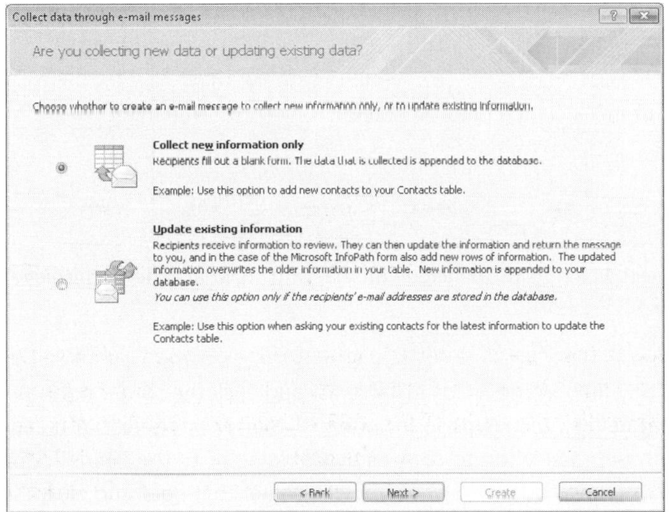

Figure 8-18 You can choose to collect new information or update existing records on this page of the wizard.

When you select the Collect New Information Only option after choosing to send an HTML message, the recipients can only send back a reply that inserts one record into your table. To insert multiple records, the recipients must send multiple messages. If you select Update Existing Information after choosing to send an HTML message, recipients can view and update all the records you send. The information the recipient returns in a reply will overwrite the existing rows. For this current example, select Collect New Information Only, and then click Next to continue.

On the next page of the wizard, shown in Figure 8-19, you decide which fields from the table or query to include in the email form. By default, Access automatically places any fields whose Required property is set to Yes in the Fields To Include In E-Mail Message list on the right. Access also puts the * symbol next to any required fields.

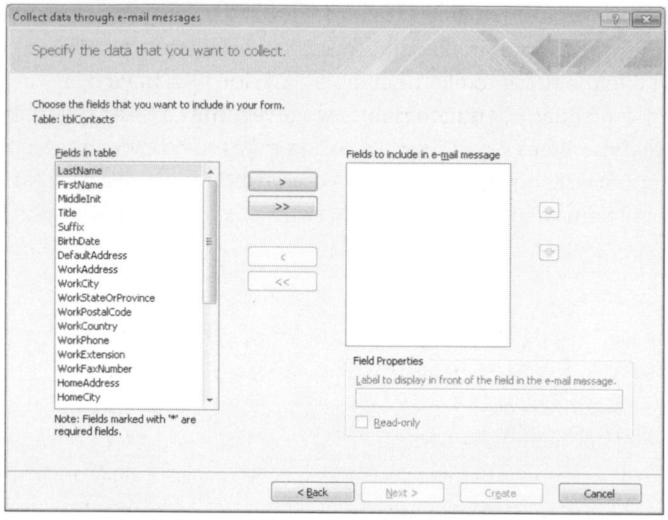

Figure 8-19 Select which fields to include on the form, in what order to display them, and what labels to display on the form.

You can select any field in the Fields In Table list and click the single right arrow (>) button to copy that field to the Fields To Include In E-Mail Message list. You can also click the double right arrow (>>) button to copy all available fields to the Fields To Include In E-Mail Message list. If you copy a field in error, you can select that field and click the single left arrow (<) button to remove it from the list. You can remove all fields and start over by clicking the double left arrow (<<) button.

INSIDE OUT Including the Primary Key in the Data Collection Process

Notice that Access did not include the primary key of the tblContacts table (the ContactID field) in the list of available fields. Whenever the primary key is the AutoNumber data type, you cannot include the field regardless of whether you are adding or updating records. If the primary key is not an AutoNumber data type, you should include it only when adding records. When updating records, Access includes the key value in the data it sends in the email form, but the user cannot see nor update it. The only case that requires the primary key field is when the key is not an AutoNumber and the user will be inserting records. When adding records to a table that has a primary key that is not an AutoNumber data type, the user must supply a key value that is unique to be able to add data to the table via email.

For this example, you want to include some of the fields in the tblContacts table, but not all of them. The existing Conrad Systems contacts might not know the information for every field, but they should be able to fill out at least the basic information for new contacts, such as last name, first name, and email address. Select the LastName field and then click the single right arrow (>) to move the field to the Fields To Include In E-Mail Message list. Now repeat this procedure and move the following fields to the Fields To Include In E-Mail Message list: FirstName, MiddleInit, Title, Suffix, WorkPhone, WorkExtension, MobilePhone, EmailName, and Website. These 10 fields should suffice for obtaining information on prospective leads.

After you move fields to the Fields To Include In E-Mail Message list, the up and down arrows to the right of this list become available along with the Field Properties section. You can click the up and down arrows to change the order of the fields you are including in the form. For this example, select the LastName field and click the down arrow twice to move it down two spots in the display order. (You could have moved the FirstName and MiddleInit fields before the LastName field, but we wanted you to see how to change the order of fields within the list.) Access fills in the field's Caption property (or the field name if the field does not have a caption) in the Label To Display In Front Of The Field In The E-Mail Message box under Field Properties. You can customize this label to display different text or leave it as is. (You're limited to using 64 characters for a custom label.) For this example, click the FirstName field and type **Enter the First Name of the new contact here . . .** as the label for the FirstName field, as shown in Figure 8-20.

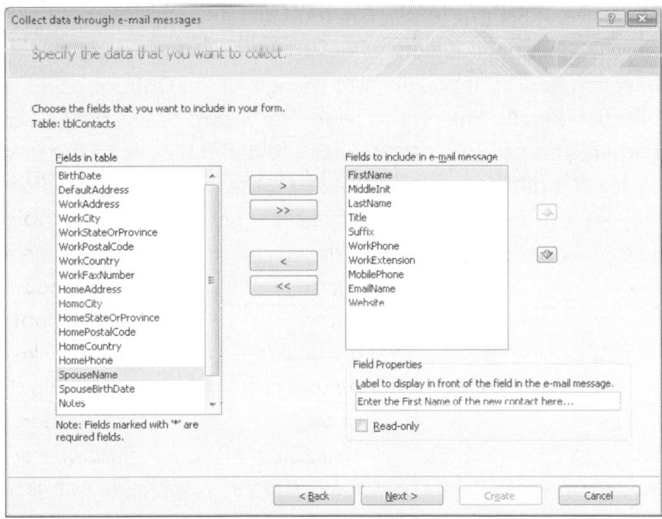

Figure 8-20 Change the display order by moving the LastName field down two positions and type a more descriptive label for the FirstName field.

If you do not want to allow the recipient to enter any information or change existing data in that field, you could select the Read-Only check box. (This option is more suited for updating data when you want to display data in a field from an existing record, but do not want the user to change it.) For this example, do not select this check box for any of the fields. If you like, you can experiment with entering captions for some of the other fields—we had you change one caption so that you can see the result in the email message. Click Next to continue to the next page.

TROUBLESHOOTING

Why can't I see all the fields from my table in the data collection process?

You might have noticed that not only the AutoNumber primary key ContactID field but also the ContactType and Photo fields from the tblContacts table are not shown as available fields. You cannot use AutoNumber, Attachment, OLE Object, Calculated, or Multi-Value Field Lookup data types in the data collection process. None of these data types are supported for email collection in Access 2010. You will have to add or update these fields manually, except for Calculated fields. Access automatically updates Calculated fields whenever any of the dependent fields are changed.

The next page of the wizard, shown in Figure 8-21, asks you to specify whether you want to manually process the replies as they arrive (the default) or let Outlook and Access automatically process the replies. By default, all replies are stored in an Outlook folder called Access Data Collection Replies. If you want to change where Outlook saves replies, click the Access Data Collection Replies link on this page. The wizard opens the Select Folder dialog box in Outlook where you can select the Outlook folder you want to use or create a new folder. After you select a different folder, the link on the wizard page changes to the name of this folder.

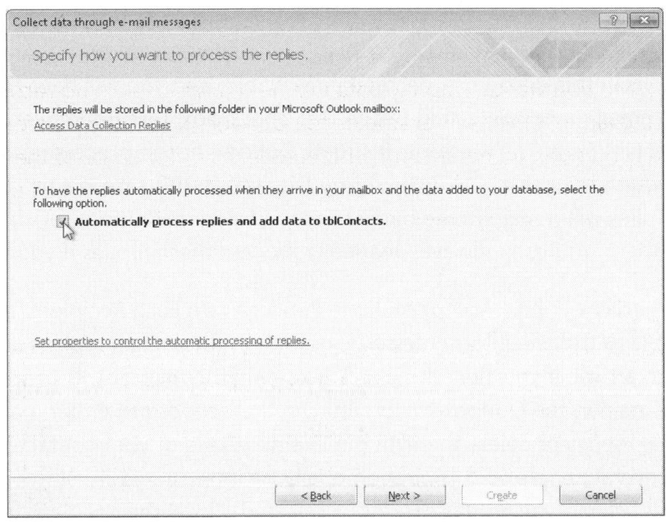

Figure 8-21 Choose whether to have the replies automatically processed or to manually process them yourself.

To have the replies automatically processed, select the Automatically Process Replies And Add Data To tblContacts check box (the default). For our example, make sure this option is selected. The Set Properties To Control The Automatic Processing Of Replies link allows you to customize various settings for automatic processing. Click this link to open the Collecting Data Using E-Mail Options dialog box, as shown in Figure 8-22.

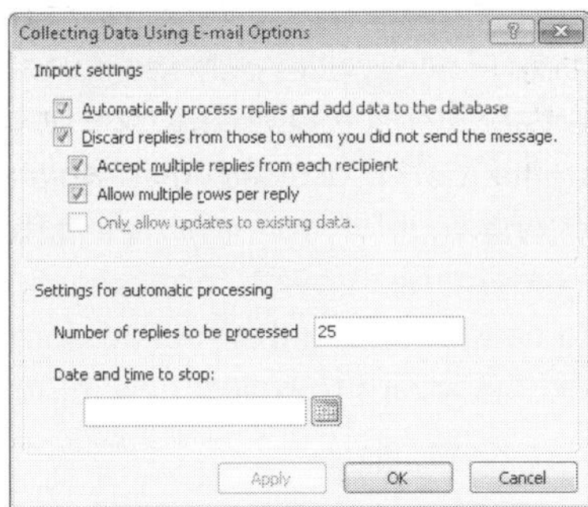

Figure 8-22 You can set options for processing email forms in the Collecting Data Using E-Mail Options dialog box.

The default settings for adding data are as shown in Figure 8-22. If you clear the Automatically Process Replies And Add Data To The Database check box under Import Settings, all the other options in this dialog box become unavailable, and you will have to manually process all the email replies. Selecting the second check box, Discard Replies From Those To Whom You Did Not Send The Message, instructs Outlook not to process replies from people to whom you did not send the email form. "Discard" in this case is a bit of a misnomer because the replies will remain in the data collection folder in Outlook—Outlook simply won't process them. You can, however, manually process these replies if you so choose.

Selecting the third check box, Accept Multiple Replies From Each Recipient, allows a recipient to reply to the email form message more than once. Each reply is automatically processed upon arrival. If you clear this check box, only the first reply is processed, but all other replies remain in the Outlook folder. You can then choose to either manually process these additional replies or delete them. In our example, one of your contacts might know the names of several people who could potentially be interested in buying products that Conrad Systems offers. Leaving this check box selected allows the recipient to provide more than one name to you.

Note

The Accept Multiple Replies From Each Recipient check box does not apply to multiple records within an InfoPath form. If a recipient adds more than one record to an InfoPath form, each record is processed because all the records are stored in one email message.

The fourth check box, Allow Multiple Rows Per Reply, applies only to InfoPath forms. If you select this check box, the recipient can insert additional rows in the form to create more records. Each record in the form is then automatically processed. The fifth check box, Only Allow Updates To Existing Data, also applies only to InfoPath forms. Select this check box to prevent a recipient from adding new records in the InfoPath form when updating data. If you clear this check box, the user can add new records in the InfoPath form as well as update existing data. Because we have asked the wizard to collect new information only, this option is unavailable.

Under Settings For Automatic Processing, you can specify the maximum number of replies to be automatically processed. The default for Number Of Replies To Be Processed is 25. You can enter any positive integer between 1 and 10 billion for this setting. If Outlook receives more replies than the number you entered, you can still process the remaining replies manually. If you want all replies to be automatically processed, enter a number larger than the number of replies you expect to receive.

Under Date And Time To Stop, you can define a date and time to have Outlook stop processing any further replies to this message. Any replies received after that time are stored in the Outlook folder, but are not automatically processed. You can, however, choose to manually process replies received after this date. Leave all the settings at their defaults for this example, click Cancel to close the dialog box, and then click Next to go to the next page of the wizard.

INSIDE OUT Why Set a Date to Stop Processing Replies?

This setting might be required in time-sensitive situations. For example, you might be conducting a survey that has to be completed before a certain date. To ensure that no records are updated or added after the cutoff date, you can designate a date and time to stop automatic processing in the Collecting Data Using E-Mail Options dialog box.

On the next page of the wizard, shown in Figure 8-23, you can choose whether to enter the email addresses using Outlook or have Access use email addresses that are stored in the database. If you choose Enter The E-Mail Addresses In Microsoft Outlook (the default), you can either manually type each recipient's address in the Outlook message or you can choose addresses from your Outlook address book. If you choose Use The E-Mail Addresses Stored In A Field In The Database, you can use addresses that are stored in the table you are adding or editing. You can also use email addresses stored in a field in a related table. For this example, you'll use the email addresses stored in the tblContacts table, so select Use The E-Mail Addresses Stored In A Field In The Database, and then click Next to continue.

Note

This page of the wizard appears only when you are adding new information. If you are updating records, you must have a field containing the email addresses in the table you are updating or in a related table being updated.

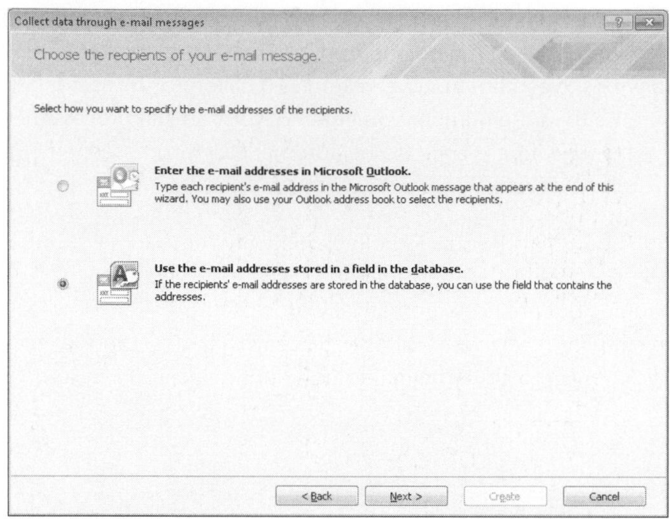

Figure 8-23 Access asks for the source of the email addresses on this page of the wizard.

Note

If you select the Enter The E-Mail Addresses In Microsoft Outlook option and click Next, the wizard allows you to customize the subject of the message and include an introductory message for your recipients. After Access creates the message, you can click the To button in the Outlook message to open your Outlook address book and select one or more recipients for this message or manually type an email address, and then click Send to send the message.

On the next page of the wizard, shown in Figure 8-24, you tell Access which field contains the recipients' email addresses. When you first see this page of the wizard, the default option is to select a field within the current table or query. If a field with email addresses exists in the table you are updating, click the arrow in the Select A Field box below The Current Table Or Query and select the field that contains the email addresses. In this example, Access correctly found the EmailName field and selected it for you.

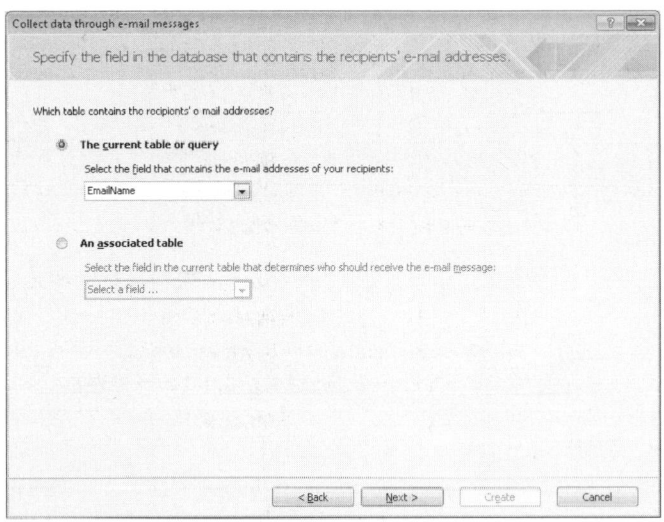

Figure 8-24 You can choose a field in the current table or query or in an associated table from which to obtain the email addresses.

You can also select the An Associated Table option to find the email addresses in an associated table (one that is defined as related to the target table in the Relationships window). After you select An Associated Table, Access enables the Select A Field box beneath this option. First specify the linking field from the current table or query, and then select the field containing the email addresses in the list of fields from the related table. In this sample database, there is a relationship defined between the ContactID field in the tblContacts table and the ContactID field in the tblCompanyContacts, tblContactEvents, and tblCompanies tables. Because ContactID is associated with more than one table, Access displays two lists, as shown in Figure 8-25. The first list displays the names of the associated tables. Choose the table you want, and then select the associated field from the second list, which displays the names of all the fields in the table you select from the first list. Note that if the field you choose under An Associated Table is associated with only one table, Access displays only one list with the names of the fields in the associated table. Because the tblContacts table already contains the email addresses you need, select The Current Table Or Query (if it isn't already), select the EmailName field from the list, and then click Next to continue.

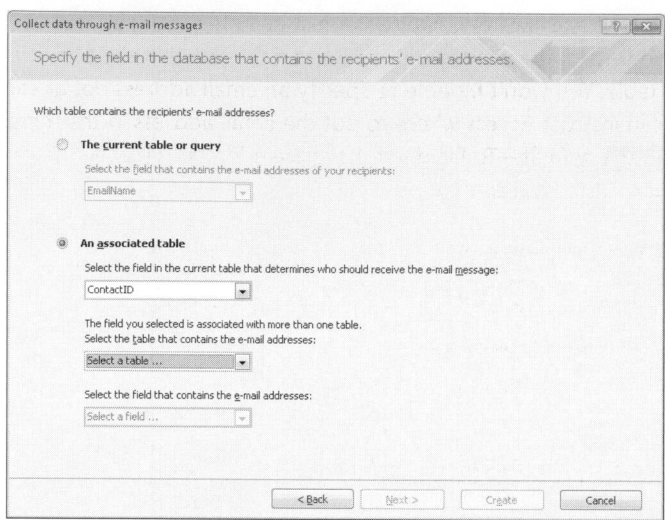

Figure 8-25 Select the associated table and field that contain the email addresses.

On the next page of the wizard, Customize The E-Mail Message, you can specify the Subject line of the email, write an introductory message, and choose in which Outlook message field the address will appear (To, Cc, or Bcc), as shown in Figure 8-26. We designed our introduction to explain to our customers what the purpose of our message is and to offer them an incentive to provide us with some new contact information. In the Subject box, type

Special offer for BO$$ customers!

In the Introduction box, type

We hope you're enjoying our BO$$ software and find it useful. Send us the contact information for any of your friends whom you think would benefit from our software, and we'll extend your support contract for one month for free for each contact who buys our product. Simply fill in the information below and send it back to us, and we'll do the rest!

To start, please make sure to click Reply first to fill out the form. Click Send when you are finished. To send information for more than one contact, click Reply again, fill out another form, and then click Send when you are finished.

Thank you for your business!

Conrad Systems Development.

If you were updating existing rows, Outlook must be able to validate the update by matching the email address of the sender with an email field stored in the table being updated or in a related table. You won't be able to specify an email address not already in the database, but you can instruct Access where to put the email address in the message being sent. Leave this set to the default—To Field—to have the address displayed in the To field in the Outlook message. Click Next to continue.

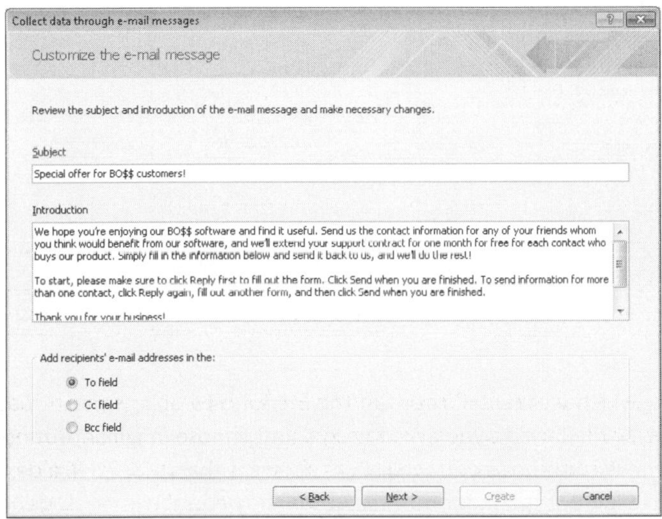

Figure 8-26 Enter a descriptive subject line and introduction on this page of the wizard and specify where to place the email address in the sent messages.

INSIDE OUT Instruct the Recipient to Click Reply

We recommend that in your introductory message for HTML and InfoPath forms, you always include text instructing the recipient to click Reply before starting. It's not always intuitive from a user's perspective that he or she first needs to click Reply to fill out the form. By including some additional instruction in the introduction, you can avoid potential misunderstandings and support calls.

The next page of the wizard, shown in Figure 8-27, informs you that Access has all the information it needs to create the email form and message. This page also provides information on how to view the status of email messages and how Outlook will process the replies if you chose to have them automatically processed. Click Next to go to the final page of the wizard.

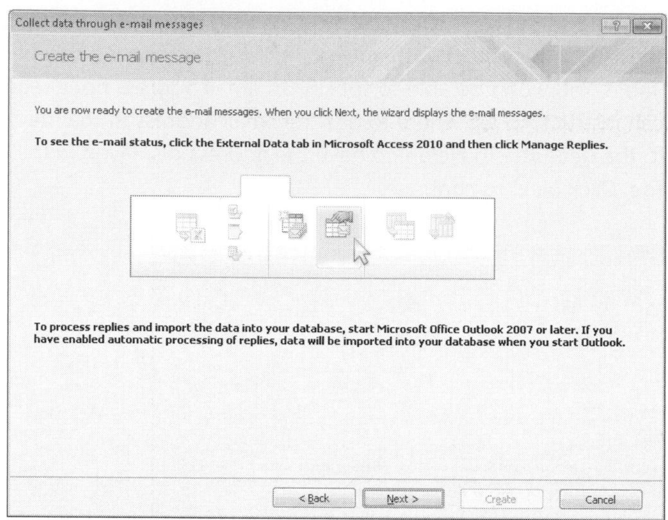

Figure 8-27 Access is now ready to create your email form.

You can choose which recipients to send the HTML form to on this page of the wizard, as shown in Figure 8-28. Because you asked Access to fetch the email addresses from a field in your table, the wizard shows you the list of addresses that it found. Each email address you're about to send out to ask for new records is shown in the list with a check box at its right. Above the list, on the right, is a Select All check box. If you select this check box, Access selects all the email addresses in the list. You can individually clear any check boxes next to the addresses to have Access not send the email form to that person. If you added your email address in the tblContacts table as instructed at the beginning of this section, select the check box for your email address and clear all the other check boxes. (Much as we like to hear from our readers, we really don't need an email message from you every time you follow this example!) Click Send to have Access create the form message and send it using Outlook. You won't be able to edit the messages further before Access sends them.

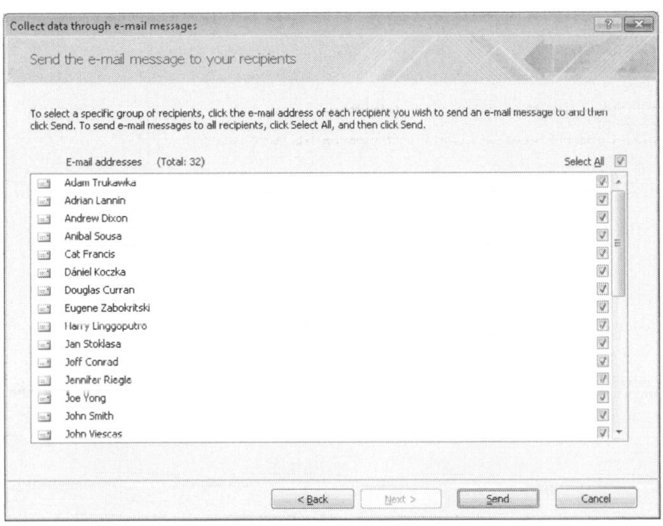

Figure 8-28 You can select the people to whom you want to send the message on the final page of the wizard.

If you chose to enter the email addresses instead of using addresses in the database, Access opens a new Outlook message with the information you provided in the wizard, as shown in Figure 8-29. (The message might not receive immediate focus, so look on your Windows taskbar for the message and maximize the window if necessary.) Figure 8-29 shows what your preview message looks like if you followed the previous instructions but chose to enter the email addresses instead of using addresses in the database. You can see the subject line you typed in the wizard and the custom introductory message at the top of the body section. Following the introduction, you can see Access has added some important information in a Note section. You can manually adjust the text in this part of the message body or leave it as is. (The warning about not altering the message applies to the recipient.) The rest of the message body has the 10 fields we selected to include in this form. In Figure 8-29, you can also see the custom label we used for the FirstName field. After previewing the message, you can click To to open your Outlook address book and select one or more recipients to send this message to or manually type an email address, and then click Send to send the message.

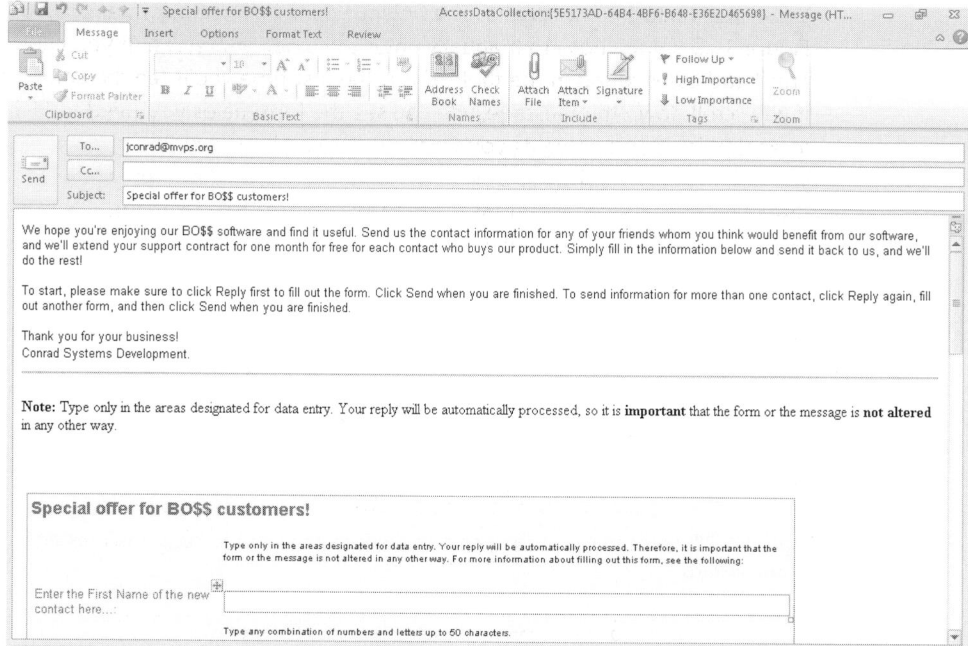

Figure 8-29 You can preview your message if you select to manually enter the email addresses.

Filling Out the HTML Form

When recipients receive the email message form, it appears in their Inbox with the subject line you specified in the wizard, as shown in Figure 8-30. If you sent this message to yourself to see how this process works, open the message now to see what it looks like.

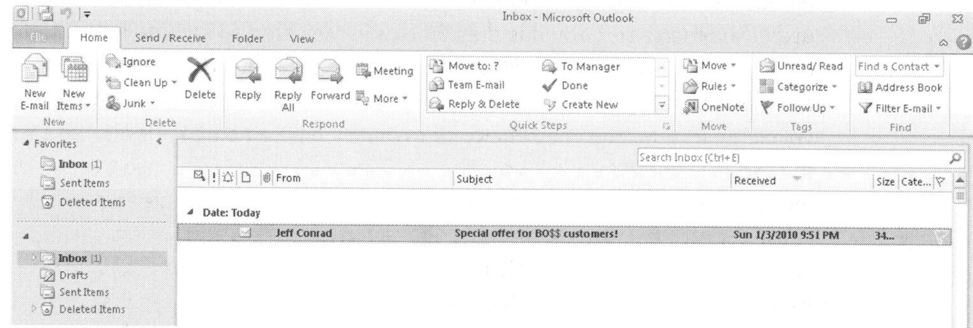

Figure 8-30 An email data collection form has arrived in the Inbox.

When you open the message as a recipient, you see all the information you previewed in Figure 8-29 if you chose to manually enter the email addresses. (If you chose to use the email addresses found in the table, this is the first time you'll see the completed message.) If you scroll down the message, you can see the form fields you need to fill in, but Outlook locks the fields and prevents you from filling them in. To be able to fill in the form fields, you need to click Reply first, as we discussed previously. Click Reply now and begin filling in the 10 fields, as shown in Figure 8-31. (We entered the information for a fictitious employee found in the Housing Reservations sample database.)

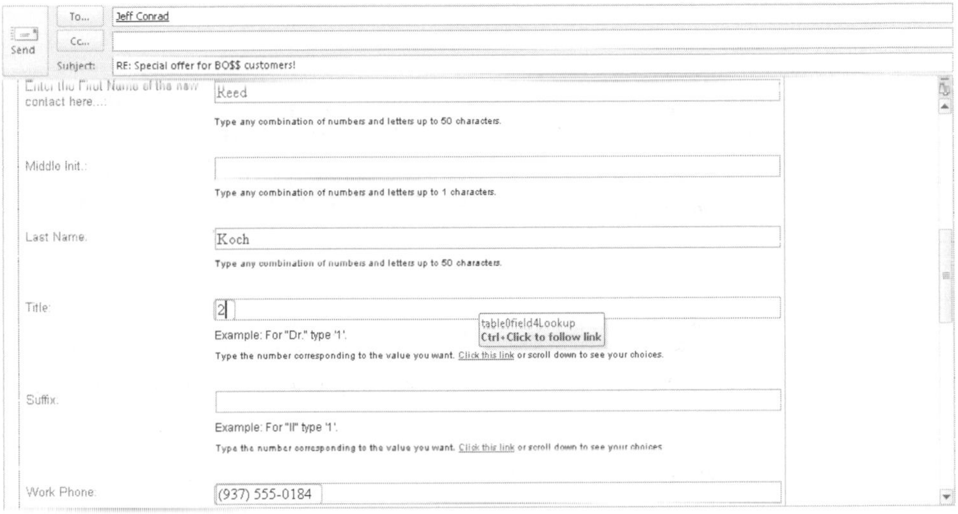

Figure 8-31 After clicking Reply, you can fill in the fields on the form.

In Figure 8-31, you'll notice additional instructions beneath each form field. The HTML form recognizes the data type and size of each table field and displays some helpful text for the user. The FirstName field's Field Size property is set to 50, so the HTML form instructs the user to enter any text up to 50 characters. For fields defined as a Hyperlink data type—such as the EmailName and Website fields—the HTML form instructs the user to enter a hyperlink address in this field. For fields defined as the Number data type, the user is prompted to enter a numeric value. If you look at Figure 8-31, you'll also see that the HTML form includes a link under both the Title and Suffix form fields. These fields are designed to require a specific set of values with a lookup combo box or list box. When Access builds your email message using HTML, it includes the lookup values at the bottom of the HTML form. Press and hold down the Ctrl key and click the link labeled Click This Link (a bookmark actually) beneath the Title field. Outlook moves you to the bottom of the HTML form, as shown in Figure 8-32. You can see the four title values and their numeric equivalents defined in the tlkpTitles table (Dr., Mr., Mrs., and Ms.) and the four suffix values defined in the tlkpSuffixes table (II, Jr., PhD, and Sr.). Find the values you need to enter for the two fields and then either scroll back up in the form or click the Title or Suffix link on the left to move back up in the form. At the bottom of the message, Outlook places a sentence instructing the user to click Send to submit the information. After you finish filling in the form, click Send to send the message back to yourself.

INSIDE OUT Formatting Rich Text Fields

You might see HTML tags in an HTML or InfoPath update data collection form for fields defined in your table as Memo data types with the Text Format property set to Rich Text. If you highlight all the text and HTML tags in the HTML form field, you'll see a mini-bar appear over the field with a group of controls to format the text. (You won't see this *mini-bar* on an InfoPath form.) These controls are similar to the controls in the Text Formatting group on the Home tab in Access 2010. If you change or remove any rich text formatting on the data collection form, Outlook exports the new formats into the Access field.

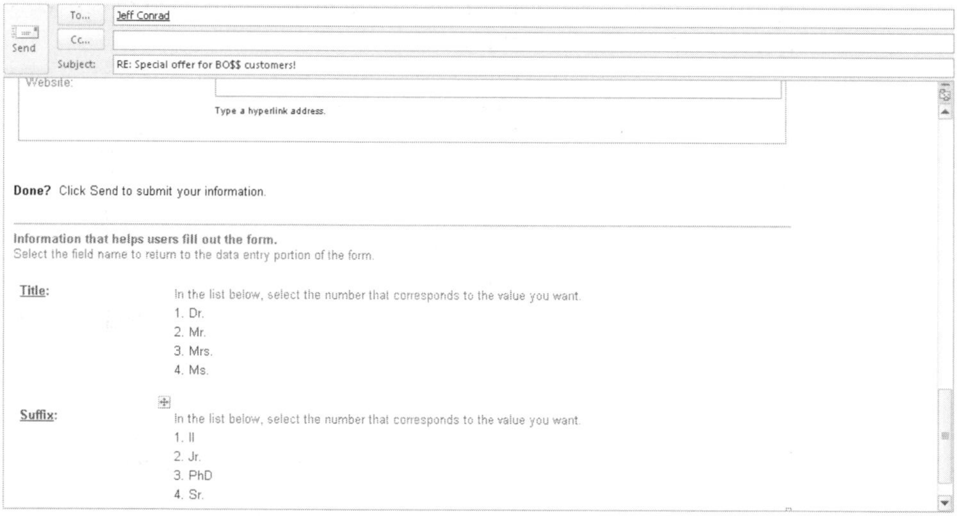

Send
To... Jeff Conrad
Cc...
Subject: RE: Special offer for BO$$ customers!
Website:
Type a hyperlink address.

Done? Click Send to submit your information.

Information that helps users fill out the form.
Select the field name to return to the data entry portion of the form.

Title: In the list below, select the number that corresponds to the value you want.
1. Dr.
2. Mr.
3. Mrs.
4. Ms.

Suffix: In the list below, select the number that corresponds to the value you want.
1. II
2. Jr.
3. PhD
4. Sr.

Figure 8-32 Access includes the lookup values at the bottom of the HTML form to help you enter the correct values in the form fields.

CAUTION!

Be careful when using fields defined as lookup values in a data collection form because Access needs to load all of these values into the HTML or InfoPath form. If your lookup table has hundreds or thousands of records, it will take Access a very long time to load all this information into the data collection form. In this example, we purposely omitted the WorkPostalCode and HomePostalCode fields because the related lookup table (tlkpZips) has more than 50,000 rows!

Having Outlook Automatically Process the Replies

After the message returns to you, Outlook places it in the folder you designated in the wizard. In our example, we left the designated folder set to the default—Access Data Collection Replies. In Figure 8-33, you can see that the message has arrived in the appropriate folder. You chose to have this message automatically processed, so Outlook immediately exported the new record to the tblContacts table. Notice, under the Data Collection Status column, that Outlook successfully exported the record to Access. You can open the message to see how the recipient filled in the form fields, but it's not necessary to open the reply to have Outlook export the data.

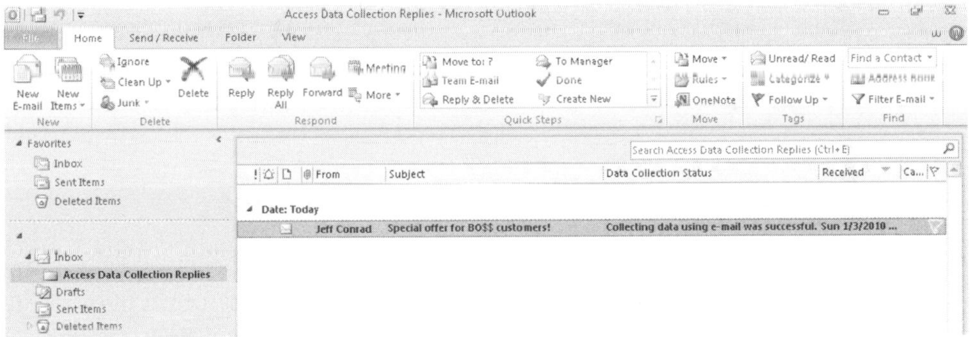

Figure 8-33 Access automatically processes the message when you receive it.

CAUTION!

If you're using an HTTP-based email system such as MSN or Hotmail, your new messages arrive in the inbox for your email account, not the primary Inbox in Outlook. You'll have to move the messages to your Outlook Inbox and process them manually by opening each message and clicking the Export To Access button on the message ribbon.

Minimize your Outlook program and then maximize the ContactsDataCopy.accdb database again (or open the database if you closed it) to see if the record has been added. Select the tblContacts table in the Navigation pane and then open it in Datasheet view. As you can see in Figure 8-34, a new record has been added to the table with the contact information you provided on the HTML form. Our client has helped add new information to the database without ever opening Access; in fact, the recipients do not even need to have Access installed for this process.

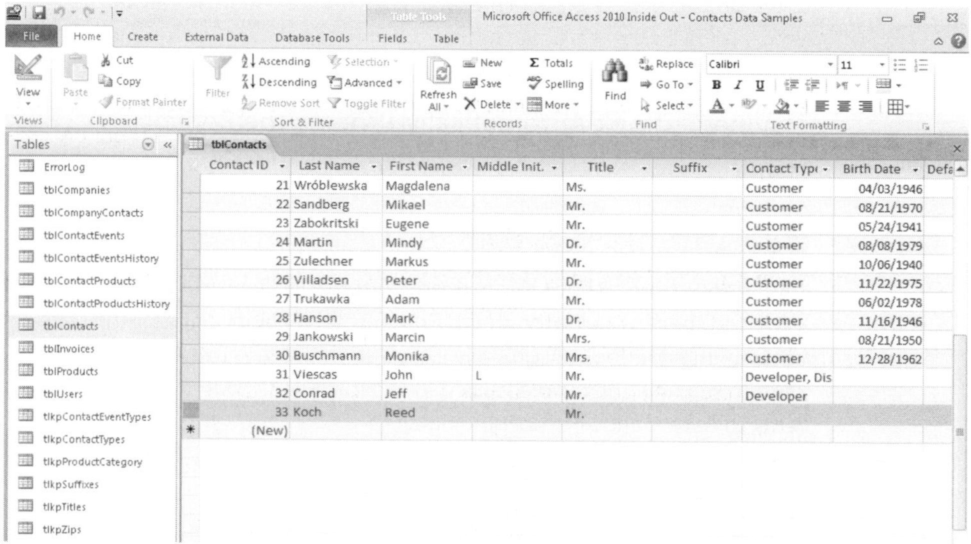

Figure 8-34 Our new contact information has now been added to the tblContacts table.

Collecting Data Using InfoPath Forms

Access 2010 also allows you to send InfoPath forms to email recipients to collect data. Unlike HTML forms, InfoPath forms provide richer tools, such as the ability to display drop-down lists. To be able to reply to messages sent with InfoPath forms, your recipients need to have Outlook 2007 and InfoPath 2007 or later installed on their computers. In addition to demonstrating collecting data through InfoPath forms, we'll choose different options in the wizard so that you can understand some of the other features available with using InfoPath.

Open the TasksEmailCollection.accdb from the folder where you installed your sample files. For this example, we'll update an existing record in the Tasks table and add a new record to the Tasks table. However, because updating data via email requires an email address in the database to validate your authority to perform the update, you'll need to add yourself and your email address if you want to follow along in this section. You'll also need to add a task assigned to you that you can update. Open the Contacts table in Datasheet view, go to the new record at the end, and add your name and valid email address and save the record. Open the Tasks table in Datasheet view, and add a new sample task assigned to yourself. Close both tables when you're done.

Close any open database objects, select the Tasks table in the Navigation pane, and on the External Data tab, in the Collect Data group, click the Create E-Mail button. Alternatively, you can right-click the table in the Navigation pane and click Collect And Update Data Via E-Mail on the shortcut menu. Access opens the first page of the email collection wizard, as shown in Figure 8-35. This first page is an introductory page, which outlines the steps you take to complete the process. For this example, you need to complete six major steps. Click Next to proceed to the second page of the wizard.

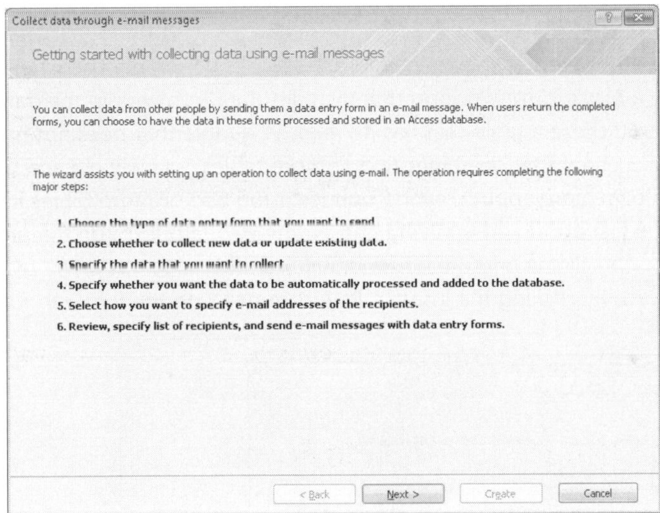

Figure 8-35 The first page of the wizard outlines the steps you take to collect data through email.

The second page of the wizard, shown in Figure 8-36, asks you to choose between creating an HTML form or an InfoPath form for data entry. Remember that the people who receive the InfoPath form need to have InfoPath 2007 and Outlook 2007 or later installed on their computers to be able to read and fill out the data form. For this example, select Microsoft InfoPath Form and click Next.

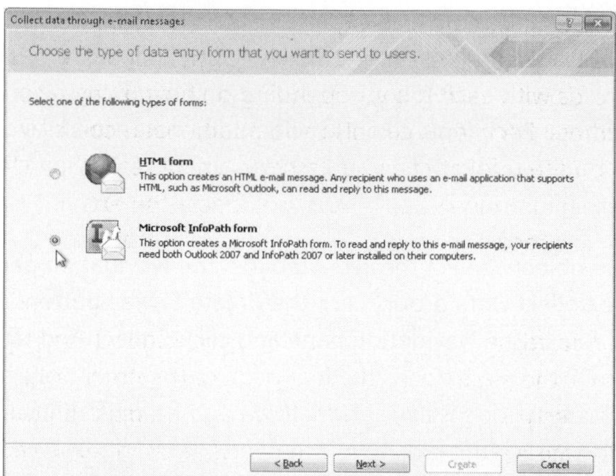

Figure 8-36 Select the second option to create an InfoPath form.

The next page of the wizard, shown in Figure 8-37, asks you to choose whether users should receive a blank form or a form that includes data from within the database they will update. If you chose a table that has no records, a table that does not have a primary key defined, or a query that combines two or more tables, you will not see this page of the wizard. (You'll learn more about creating queries using two or more tables in Chapter 10.) If you select the first option after having chosen the InfoPath form on the previous page, a recipient of your email can add one or more records with each reply. The recipients can add additional records by clicking the Insert A Row command on the InfoPath form.

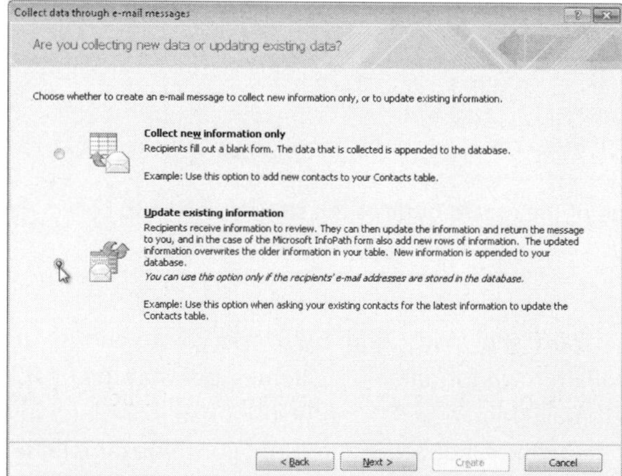

Figure 8-37 You can choose to collect new information or update existing records on this page of the wizard.

You can use the second option, Update Existing Information, only if email addresses are stored in a field in the table or a related table. With this option, email recipients can view or update one or more records with each reply, depending on how many records are associated with their email address. Recipients can also add additional records by clicking the Insert A Row command on the InfoPath form unless you disable this capability in an option presented later in the wizard. In this example, you will update the existing record in the Tasks table and create a new record, so select Update Existing Information and then click Next to proceed.

On the next page of the wizard, shown in Figure 8-38, you decide which fields from the table or query to include in the email form. By default, Access automatically places any fields whose Required property is set to Yes in the Fields To Include In E-Mail Message list on the right. Notice that Access places the Title and Status fields in the Fields To Include In E-Mail Message list because they are required fields. For this example, we want to use all the fields in the Tasks table, so click the double right arrow (>>) button to move the remaining six fields to the list on the right, as shown in Figure 8-38. If you don't want to include all fields and you move a field in error, you can select that field and move it back by clicking the left arrow (<) button. If you decide you want to start over, you can remove all fields (except the required fields) by clicking the double left arrow (<<) button.

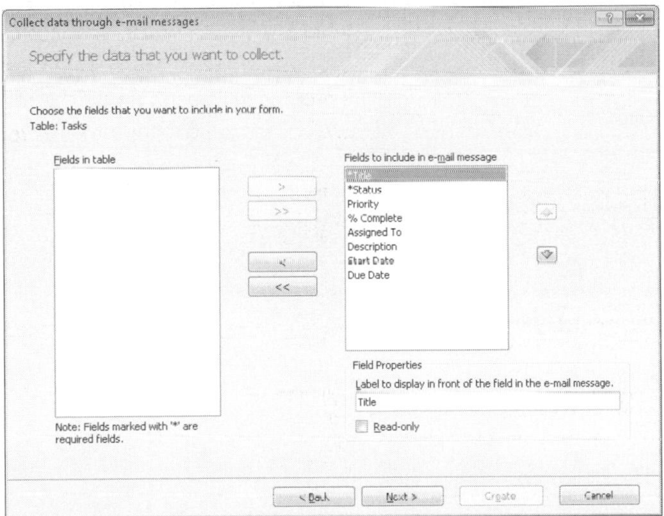

Figure 8-38 Move all the fields in the Tasks table to the Fields To Include In E-Mail Message list.

Notice that Access fills in the field's Caption property (or the field name if the field does not have a caption) in the Label To Display In Front Of The Field In The E-Mail Message box under Field Properties. You can customize this label to display different text or leave it as is. For this example, leave each of the label captions set to their defaults. The recipients will see the fields in the order that they appear in the list on the right. You can select any field in this list and move it up or down in the sequence by clicking the up and down arrows to the right of the list. The default sequence is fine for this example, so you don't need to move any fields. Also, leave the Read-Only check box cleared for all of the fields, and then click Next to continue to the next page.

The next page of the wizard, shown in Figure 8-39, asks you to specify how you want to manage the replies. By default, all replies are stored in an Outlook folder called Access Data Collection Replies. If you want to change where Outlook saves replies, click the Access Data Collection Replies link. The wizard opens the Select Folder dialog box in Outlook where you can select the Outlook folder you want to use or create a new folder. In this case, leave the default Access Data Collection Replies folder as the destination folder. In the HTML example earlier, you chose to have Outlook automatically process the replies. In this example, leave the Automatically Process Replies And Add Data To Tasks check box cleared so that you can see how to manually process the replies. The Only Allow Updates To Existing Data check box is available only when you are updating data and you have chosen to automatically process the replies. If you choose to automatically process the replies and then select this option, Access does not allow new records to be added to the table. This option appears dimmed in our example because we are going to manually process the replies. Remember also from the HTML example that when you ask Outlook to automatically process replies, you can click Set Properties To Control The Automatic Processing Of Replies. For details, refer to Figure 8-22 on page 501. Click Next to continue.

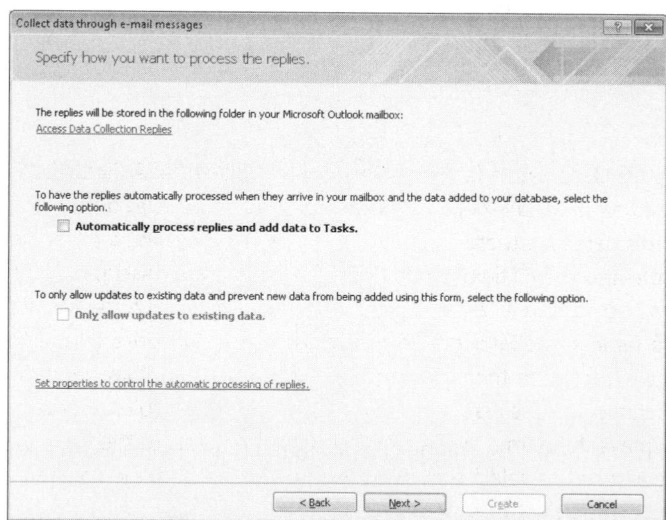

Figure 8-39 Leave these check boxes cleared to manually process the replies.

On the next page of the wizard, shown in Figure 8-40, you tell Access which field contains the recipients' email addresses. When you first see this page of the wizard, the default option is to select a field within the current table or query. If an email address exists in the table you are updating, click the arrow in the Select A Field box below The Current Table Or Query and select the field that contains the email addresses. However, in this case, no email addresses are stored in the Tasks table in this database; rather, they are stored in the E-mail Address field in the Contacts table, so select the An Associated Table option.

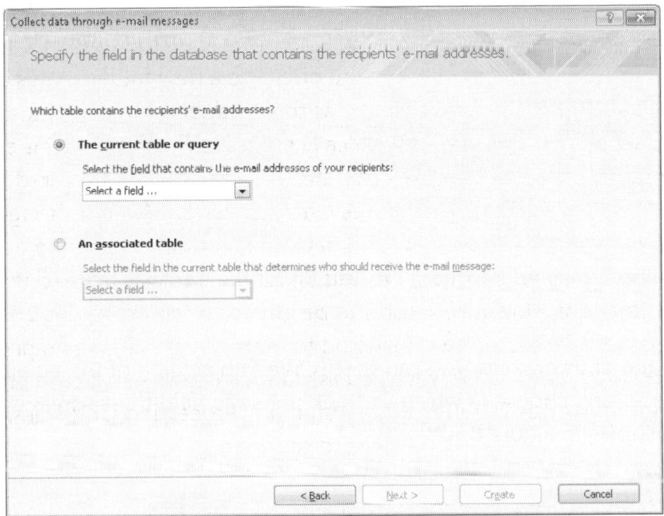

Figure 8-40 You can choose a field in the current table or query or in an associated table from which to obtain the email addresses.

After you select An Associated Table, Access enables the Select A Field box beneath this option. You need to select the field in the Tasks table that links to a related field in the Contacts table. In this database there is a relationship defined between the Assigned To field in the Tasks table and the ID field in the Contacts table. Select Assigned To in this box, and Access displays one additional option, as shown in Figure 8-41. Access displays all the fields in the Contacts Table in the Select A Field box. Select E-mail Address from the list of fields and then click Next to go to the next page of the wizard. Note that if the field you choose under An Associated Table is associated with more than one table, Access displays two lists. The first list displays the names of the associated tables. Choose the table you want, and then select the associated field from the second list, which displays the names of all the fields in the table you select from the first list.

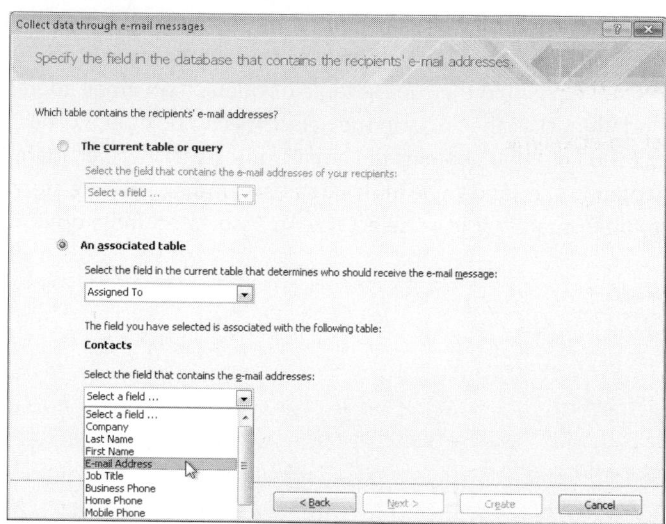

Figure 8-41 Select E-mail Address from the field list for the Contacts table.

On the next page of the wizard, you can specify the Subject line of the email, write an introductory message, and choose in which Outlook message field the address will appear (To, Cc, or Bcc), as shown in Figure 8-42.

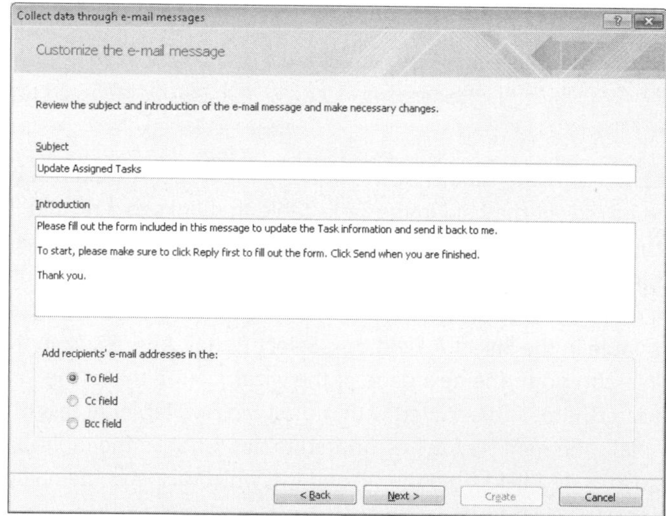

Figure 8-42 Enter a descriptive subject line and introduction on this page of the wizard and specify where to place the email address in the sent messages.

In the Subject box, type

Update Assigned Tasks

In the Introduction box, type

Please fill out the form included in this message to update the Task information and send it back to me.

To start, please make sure to click Reply first to fill out the form. Click Send when you are finished.

Thank you.

Because you chose to update data, three options appear at the bottom of this page, under Add Recipients' E-Mail Addresses In The. To be able to validate the updating of existing rows, Outlook must be able to match the email address of the sender with an email field stored in the table being updated or in a related table. You won't be able to specify an email address not already in the table, but you can tell Access where to put the email address in the message being sent. Leave this set to the default option—To Field—to have the address displayed in the To field in the Outlook message. Click Next to continue.

The next page of the wizard, shown in Figure 8-43, informs you that Access has all the information it needs to create the email form and message. You'll notice in Figure 8-43 that Access displays a warning message at the bottom of this page. You might see any one of three possible messages in this box:

- **"Note: These e-mail messages might contain data that is of a confidential or sensitive nature."** Access always displays this message when you update existing records because the recipients might see data currently in the table that is of a sensitive nature. You might consider removing from the email any fields with sensitive data if you are concerned that this could be a problem.

- **"You currently have an exclusive lock on the database; automatic processing will fail until the lock is released."** Outlook cannot process replies if you have the database open in exclusive mode. To process the replies, you need to close the database and then reopen it in shared mode. By default, Access should open all databases in shared mode unless you changed the setting in the Client Settings category of the Access Options dialog box. You can also open a database in exclusive or shared mode using the Open dialog box if you click the arrow on the Open button and then click the appropriate command (such as Open Exclusive).

- **"Some records do not contain a valid address in the specified e-mail address field. No data will be returned for these rows."** Before you get to this page of the wizard, Access runs a quick scan for any Null values in the email address field you designated on the previous page of the wizard. Access displays this warning message if it finds any Null values because it will not be able to send a message for all records that could be updated. You can either proceed with the data collection process with some being left out, or cancel the wizard and then add any missing email addresses to the table.

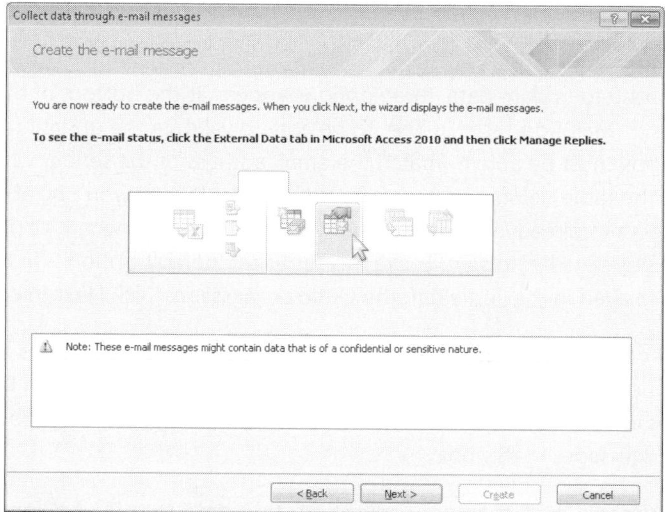

Figure 8-43 Access displays potential issues that might cause problems with the data collection process.

Click Next to go to the final page of the wizard. On this page, you can choose which recipients to send the InfoPath form to on the final page of the wizard, as shown in Figure 8-44. Each email address related to a record you're about to send out for update is shown in the list with a check box at its right. Above the list, to the right, is a Select All check box. If you select this check box, Access selects all the email addresses in the list. You can individually clear any check boxes next to the addresses to have Access not send the email form to that person.

When we ran our example, there was only one email address related to the one record in the Tasks table. If you added your email address in the Contacts table and a related record in the Tasks table as instructed at the beginning of this section, select your email address and clear the check box next to jconrad@proseware.com. Click Send to have Access create the form message and send it using Outlook.

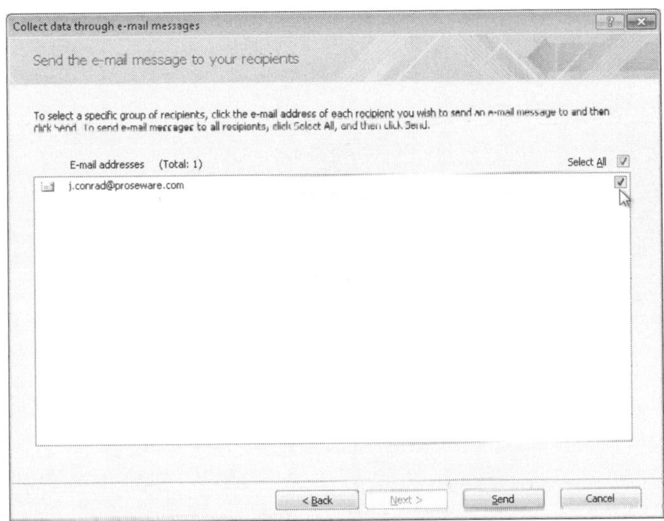

Figure 8-44 You can select the people to whom you want to send the message on the final page of the wizard.

Filling Out the InfoPath Form

When recipients receive an email form created using InfoPath, the message arrives in their Inboxes with an attachment. After opening the message and clicking Reply, a recipient can fill out the form and update the information. Unlike HTML forms, InfoPath allows you to send forms that are easier for the recipients to fill out. In Figure 8-45, you can see that the Status field is displayed as a combo box. The recipient must select from one of the five available Status options because this field is a lookup field in the Tasks table.

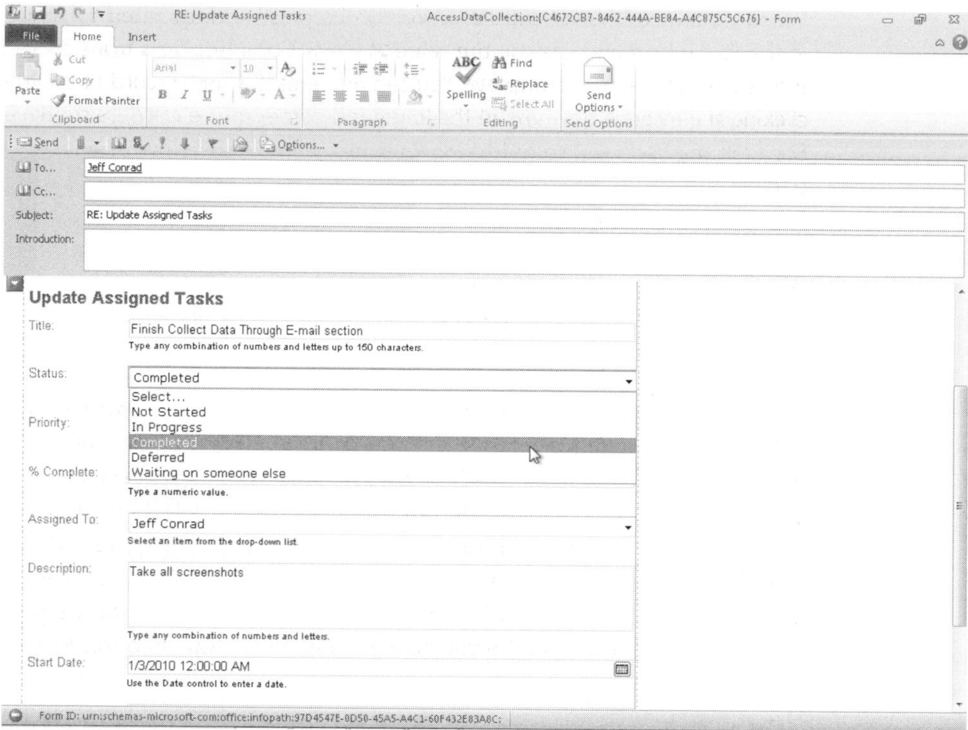

Figure 8-45 InfoPath forms allow you to use combo box controls for data entry.

With InfoPath forms, you can have more control over the data that comes back in the replies. You achieve this by designing fields in your tables that require a specific set of values with a lookup combo box or list box. When Access builds your email message using InfoPath, it includes the lookup values in the InfoPath form. If you were, for example, to send an HTML form with the same fields in the Tasks table, the recipients can see all the lookup values listed at the bottom of the form. However, they could still type any value into the Status box, including text that is not one of your five choices. Outlook will encounter errors processing the HTML reply if it tries to export that record into the Tasks table in Access because the Limit To List property of the Status field is set to True. In Figure 8-45, you also see a button next to any date field, which opens a calendar for you to select a date, just as you can from within Access. If you use InfoPath forms, you can reduce the number of problems with inaccurate data, and make it easier for users to fill out the form with the built-in InfoPath form controls.

For this example, change the status from In Progress to Completed by selecting Completed in the Status box, and change the value in the % Complete field from 25 to 100 to indicate the task is 100 percent complete. You can also create a new record in the InfoPath form by clicking the Insert A Row link in the lower-left corner of the form, as shown in Figure 8-46. For example, you might want to assign a new task to yourself or to another contact in the database.

Figure 8-46 Click Insert A Row on an InfoPath form to add additional records.

After you click the link, a new InfoPath form appears below the existing form with blank fields, as shown in Figure 8-47. You can now fill out the form fields for a new record. You'll notice the two required fields—Title and Status—have a red asterisk on the right to indicate to the recipient that those fields are required. You might also notice the InfoPath form recognizes the data type and size of each table field and displays some helpful text for the user. The Title field's Field Size property is set to 150, so InfoPath instructs the user to enter any text up to 150 characters. The % Complete field is a Number data type in the Tasks table, so InfoPath instructs the user to enter a numeric value into this field.

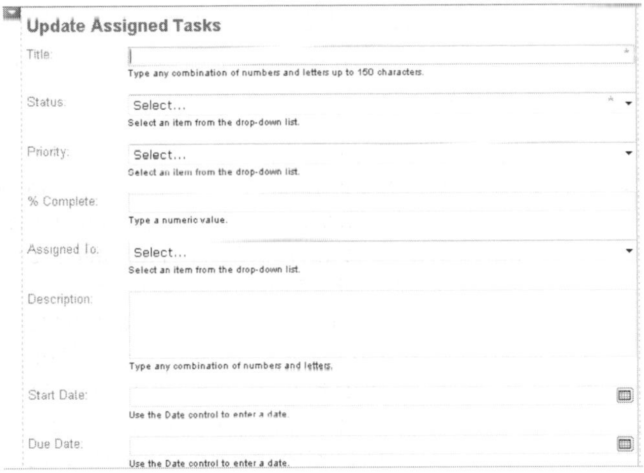

Figure 8-47 The recipient of the email can add new records in the InfoPath form if you selected this option in the wizard.

If you like, you can create a new record in this blank InfoPath form using the following information:

Title	**Review Chapter 8**
Status	Not Started
Priority	(1) High
% Complete	**0**
Assigned To	John Viescas
Description	**Please review all the changes to Chapter 8**
Start Date	Click the calendar control and click the current date
Due Date	Click the calendar control and select the date three days after the start date

Your completed record should be similar to Figure 8-48.

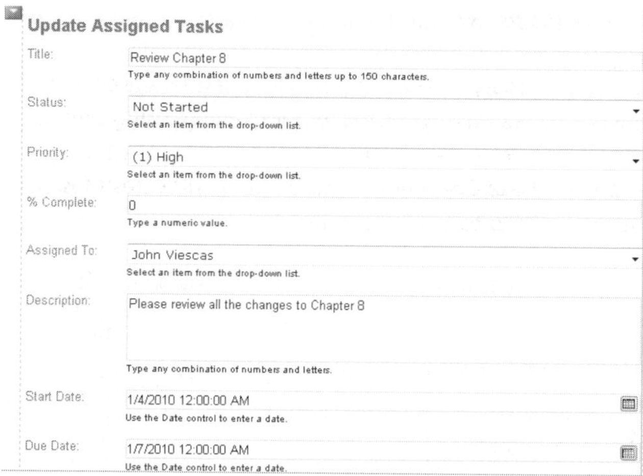

Figure 8-48 Fill out the blank form to add a new record to the Tasks table.

If you want to create more records, you can scroll down and click the Insert A Row link again to display an additional blank form. If you need to delete a record, click the arrow button in the upper-left corner of the InfoPath form and then click Remove on the menu that appears, as shown in Figure 8-49. You can also insert a new blank record above or below the current record by clicking the Insert Above or Insert Below options. You can click the Move Up option to move this record up in order in the InfoPath form.

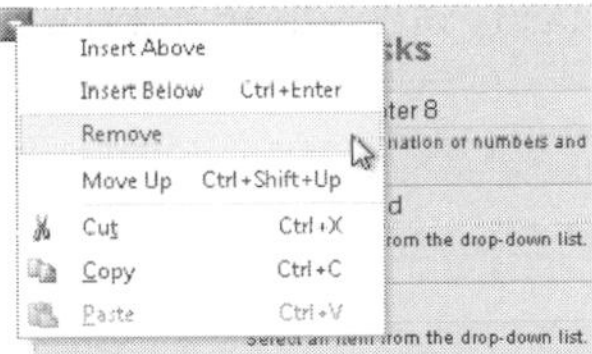

Figure 8-49 Click Remove to delete a record in the InfoPath form.

After you update the first record and add the new record on this InfoPath form, click Send on the Outlook Standard toolbar to send this message. Note, you can also modify the To, Cc, or Bcc addresses, change the subject, and enter explanatory text. Click Send now to send your updates.

Manually Processing the Replies

When you collect data via email, you can choose to have the replies automatically processed or to manually process them yourself. In our example using InfoPath forms, you chose to manually process the replies. In Figure 8-50, you can see the message is in the destination folder, but the Data Collection Status column indicates Message Unprocessed. No data has yet been exported to the Tasks table.

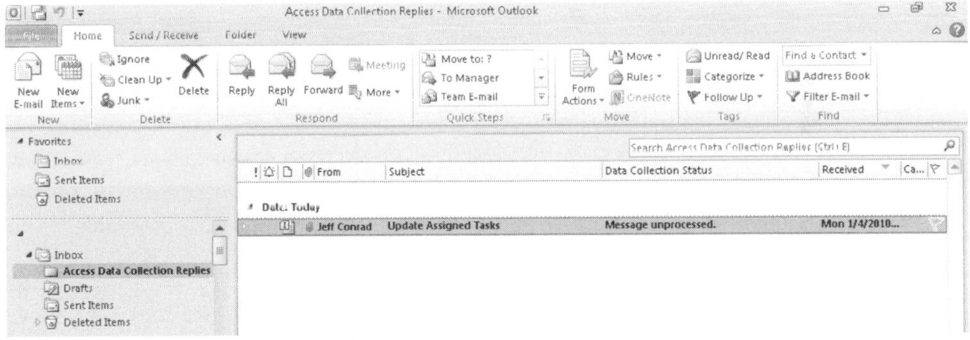

Figure 8-50 The Data Collection Status column in Outlook indicates that the message has not been processed.

To manually process this reply, right-click the message in Outlook 2010 and click Export Data To Microsoft Access on the shortcut menu, as shown in Figure 8-51.

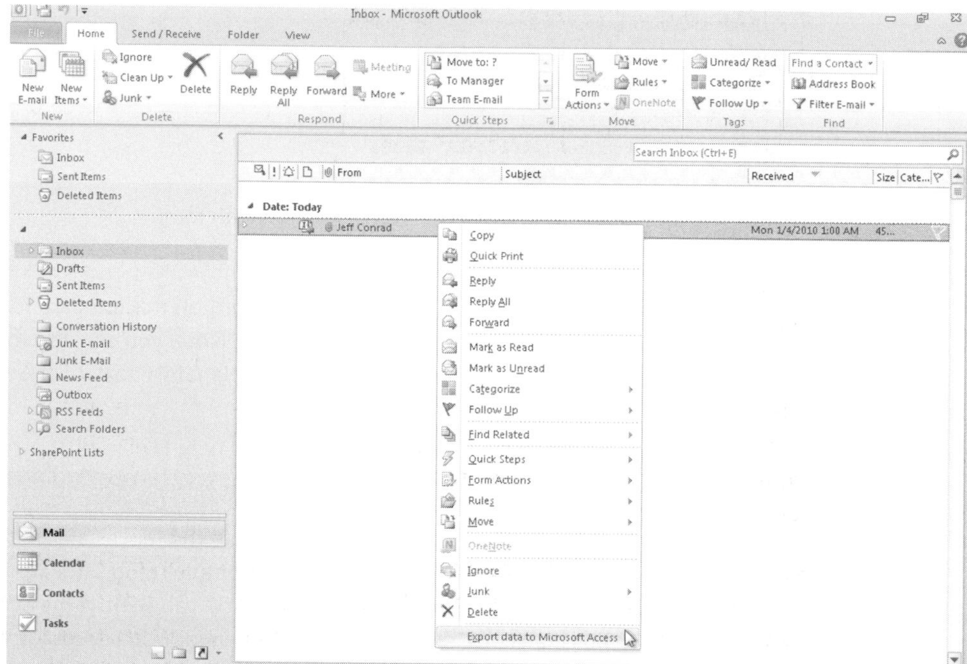

Figure 8-51 Use the message's context-sensitive menu within Outlook to export the data to Access.

Access opens the Export Data To Microsoft Access dialog box, as shown in Figure 8-52. You can see that the first record is the one with updates, and the second is the new record. You can use the horizontal scroll bar to scroll to the right to see what data will be added or changed in the various fields. If you find something inaccurate, perhaps an invalid Start Date or Due Date value, you can click Cancel to stop the export process. You can then send the message back to the recipient and ask for corrected data. See "Managing and Resending Data Collection Messages from Access," on page 529, for more information. All the data in this example should be fine, so click OK to have Outlook export the data to Access.

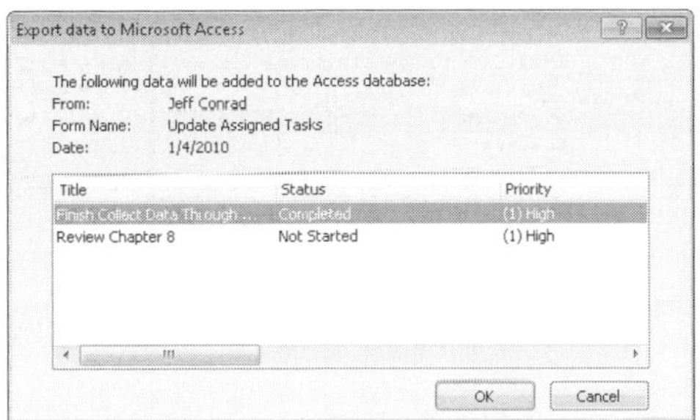

Figure 8-52 You can review the data to be exported to Access in this dialog box.

If the export process is successful, Outlook displays a confirmation dialog box. Click OK to close the dialog box. If Outlook encounters any errors in the export process, it displays a message indicating that it failed to export all or part of the data. In this case, you should resend the message and ask for corrected data.

Return to the TasksEmailCollection.accdb sample database and open the Tasks table in Datasheet view. In Figure 8-53, you can see the first record is updated with the correct data—the Status field is now changed from In Progress to Completed and the % Complete field is changed from 25 to 100 to indicate the task is 100 percent complete. You can also see that the new record concerning Chapter 8 has been added.

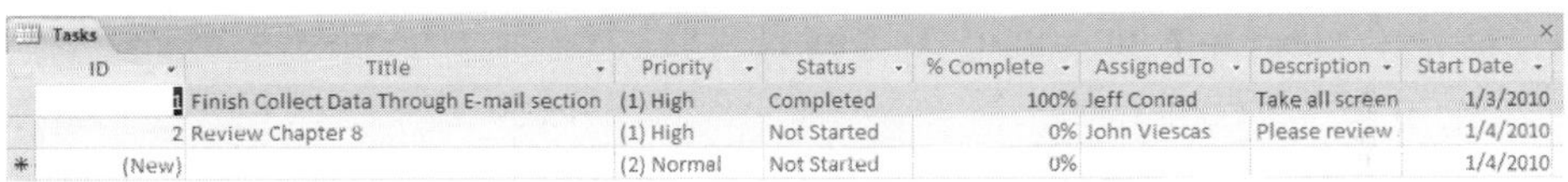

Tasks

ID	Title	Priority	Status	% Complete	Assigned To	Description	Start Date
1	Finish Collect Data Through E-mail section	(1) High	Completed	100%	Jeff Conrad	Take all screen	1/3/2010
2	Review Chapter 8	(1) High	Not Started	0%	John Viescas	Please review	1/4/2010
(New)		(2) Normal	Not Started	0%			1/4/2010

Figure 8-53 The updated and new data is now added to the Tasks table.

Managing and Resending Data Collection Messages from Access

You can review the status of sent data collection messages and resend messages by clicking the Manage Replies button in the Collect Data group on the External Data tab on the ribbon. Access opens the Manage Data Collection Messages dialog box, as shown in Figure 8-54. Under Select A Data Collection Message, you can see the example message we sent, which table or query the message was based on, the message type, and the destination Outlook folder. When you select a message in the list, the Message Details section in the bottom half of the dialog box displays the fields included in the message, the date and time the message was created and last sent, whether the reply was automatically or manually processed, and the date and time to stop automatic processing.

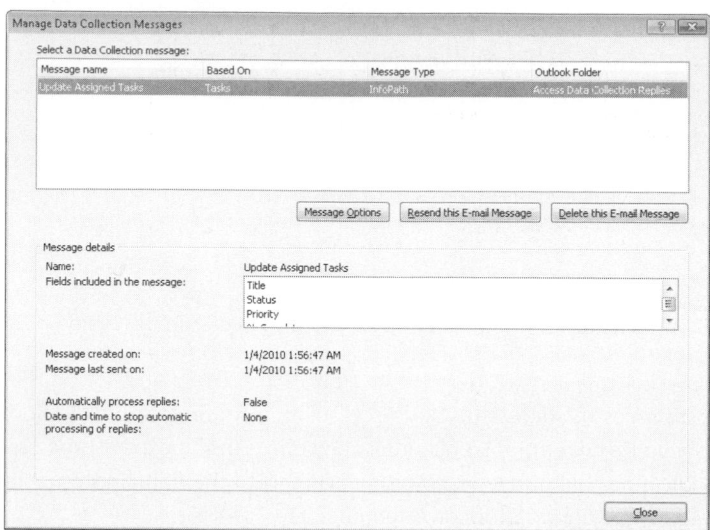

Figure 8-54 You can review the status of sent messages in the Manage Data Collection Messages dialog box.

To delete a message from this dialog box, select it and then click Delete This E-Mail Message. To review the message options, select the message and click Message Options. Access opens the Collecting Data Using E-Mail Options dialog box, previously shown in Figure 8-22 on page 501. Here, you can review and modify the settings for the message. For example, if you set the original message to automatically process replies, you can turn off automatic processing, change the number of messages to be processed, or change the automatic processing end date. You can also turn on automatic processing if it wasn't enabled in the original message. Note that any changes you make apply to new replies you receive.

If you want to send a message again—either because the recipient entered incorrect or incomplete data or you want the recipient to send new data—you can select the message and click the Resend This E-Mail Message button. You might also want to send the same message to additional people or resend it to someone who failed to receive the initial message. Note that you cannot go to Outlook and forward a data collection message; you must use the resend process. When you click the Resend This E-Mail Message button, Access restarts the Collecting Data Through E-Mail Messages wizard beginning with the page that asks you how you want to process replies, as shown in Figure 8-55. (This page is similar to Figure 8-39 on page 518.) You can adjust any settings—such as manual or automatic replies or where the email addresses come from—and customize the message details. You can click through the remaining steps of the wizard and then click Create or Send depending on what type of message (HTML or InfoPath) you are sending. Access creates a new message and sends it to the recipients using Outlook.

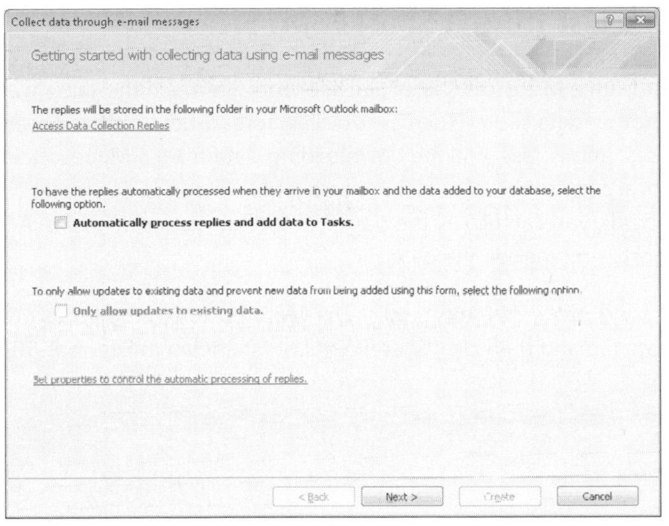

Figure 8-55 The resend process takes you back to the data collection wizard page.

INSIDE OUT Starting Over or Resending?

Note that the resend process starts beyond the point in the wizard where you select the format of the message (HTML or InfoPath), choose whether records will be added or updated, and specify the fields in the message. If you do not need to adjust the format of the message, the add or update option, or the fields used in the data collection message, you can simply resend a previous message. If, however, you need to choose different fields or a different table or query to update, you must create a new message.

Importing and Linking SharePoint Data

In Microsoft SharePoint terminology, a table is referred to as a *list* that stores information about a single subject. In a list you have *columns* (fields) that contain the different kinds of information about the subject. Similar to how you work in Access 2010, you can work with lists in different views for adding and editing records. In order to import or link to a list from a SharePoint site into an Access database, you need to have appropriate permissions to the SharePoint site. Contact your SharePoint administrator to give you permissions if you are having trouble accessing the SharePoint list.

Importing a List from a SharePoint Site

Importing a list from a Microsoft SharePoint site works in much the same way as importing a table from another data source such as text files, spreadsheets, other Access databases, or SQL databases. In this case, you are downloading data from a Microsoft SharePoint site and saving a local copy of the data in an Access table. After Access creates the table and imports the records, you can use all the powerful tools at your disposal in Access—queries, forms, and reports—to analyze the data.

To begin the import process in Access, click the More button in the Import & Link group on the External Data tab and then click SharePoint List, as shown in Figure 8-56.

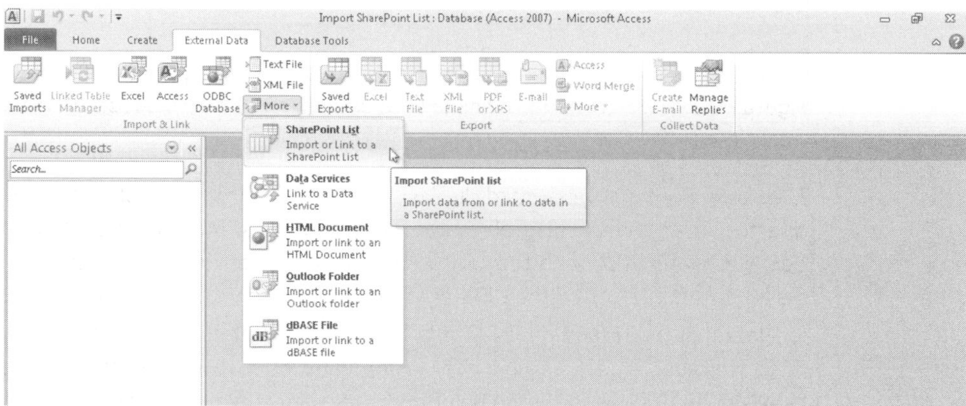

Figure 8-56 Click SharePoint List to start the import process.

Access opens the first page of the Get External Data – SharePoint Site wizard, as shown in Figure 8-57. You can use this wizard to either import or link to SharePoint Services lists. We'll discuss linking in the next section. Under Specify A SharePoint Site, enter a valid address to a SharePoint Services site or subdirectory. Any SharePoint Services sites that you have previously imported from, linked to, or exported to are displayed in a list box. If one of these sites is the location from which you want to import the table, you can click that address and Access fills in the address text box below the list with that link. Enter a valid SharePoint Services address in the text box, or select a previously visited SharePoint Services address from the list box. Select the first option, Import The Source Data Into A New Table In The Current Database, to import the list and records to a local table and then click Next.

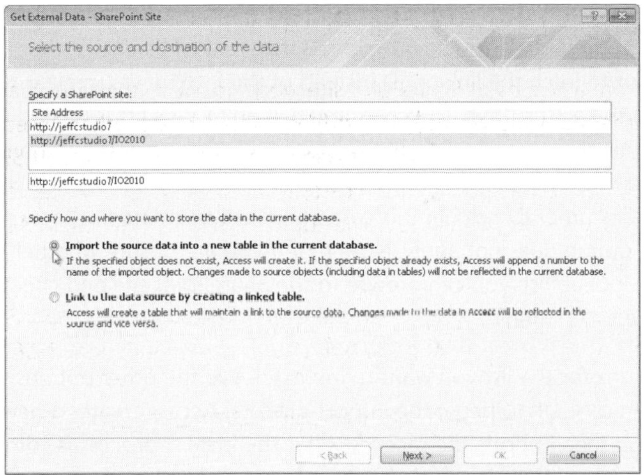

Figure 8-57 You can import or link to Windows SharePoint Services lists using this wizard.

The second page of the wizard displays all the lists found in the SharePoint Services site directory that you specified on the previous page, as shown in Figure 8-58. Select a check box in the Import column to specify which list to import to Access. The Type column displays icons representing the different types of lists. The Name column displays the names of the lists on the SharePoint site. The fourth column, Items To Import, shows a list of views. If the list has more than one view defined in SharePoint, you can select which specific view you want to import. The default view, All Contacts, is the only view defined in our example. The last column, Last Modified Date, displays the date the list was last modified.

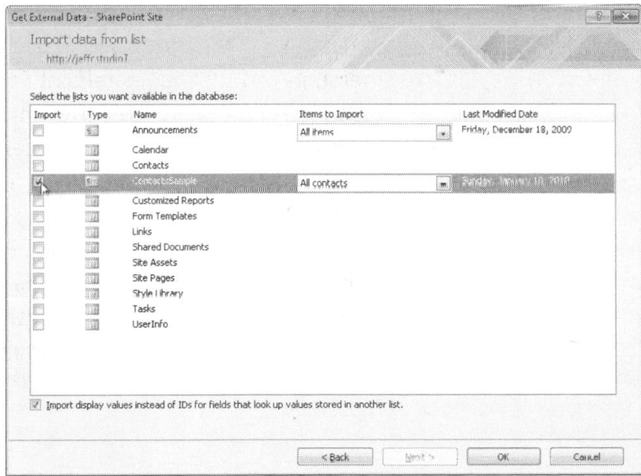

Figure 8-58 Select which lists to import to Access on the second page of the wizard.

Near the bottom of this page is an option to import the display values from any lookup fields instead of the actual lookup field ID. If you think a list has one or more related lookup lists, and you want to fetch the linking ID instead of the lookup value, clear this check box so that you fetch the actual ID value. For example, if an Orders list is related to a Customers list, clearing this check box fetches the Customer ID instead of the customer name that might be defined in a lookup. If you leave this item selected, you'll see the customer name imported in the Customer ID field. In this case, there are no related or lookup tables for Contacts, so this option does not apply. Note that if you are unsure whether a list has more than one related lookup list, you can browse to the SharePoint site and check the field properties for the list columns.

Select the check box for the list you want to import, leave the other options set to their defaults, and then click OK to begin the import process. Access creates a new local table in your database and then imports the records. After the import process is complete, Access displays the last page of the wizard, as shown in Figure 8-59. A message at the top of this page indicates whether the import process was a success or if any problems were encountered. The wizard also displays an option to save your import steps in case you want to perform the exact import procedure again in the future. You can execute saved imports by clicking the Saved Imports button in the Import & Link group of the External Data tab on the ribbon. Click Close to dismiss the wizard.

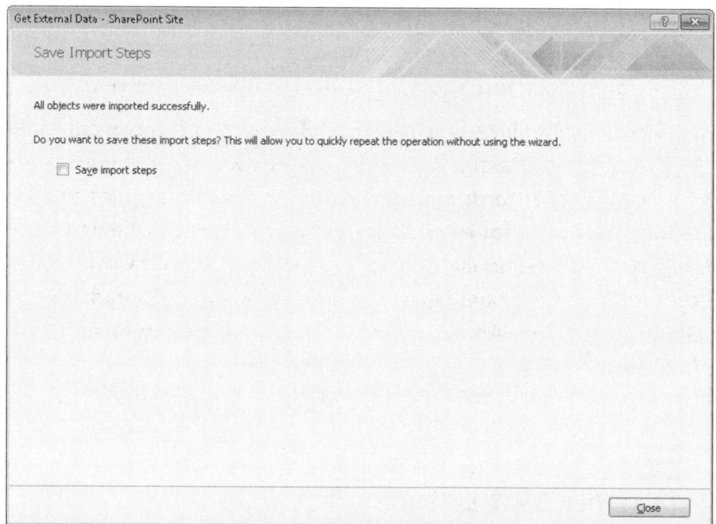

Figure 8-59 The last page of the wizard asks if you want to save the import steps.

Access now displays the new table you imported in the Navigation pane. In our import example, you can see the two records we imported from the SharePoint list displayed in Datasheet view, as shown in Figure 8-60. You can now analyze the data using queries and reports or build data entry forms for adding records to the table or editing them. Note, however, that you've made a copy of the data stored on the SharePoint site. Any changes you make to the local copy won't be reflected in the SharePoint site list. If you want to be able to update the data in the list directly from Access, continue to the next section.

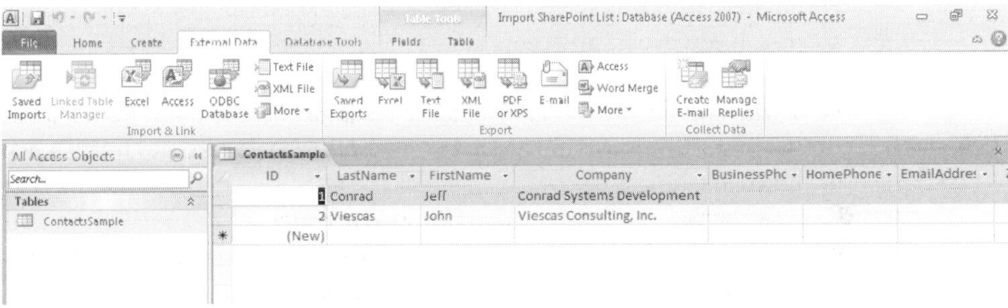

Figure 8-60 The list from the SharePoint site has now been imported as a local table into Access.

TROUBLESHOOTING

Why doesn't my imported SharePoint list include all the records?

You can create different views of a list in SharePoint sites. You can define filters, include only certain columns, and assign sort orders to a custom view. If your custom view restricts the number of records returned, Access follows those rules and imports only those specific records. So, for example, if you define a custom view that shows only contacts whose last name equals Conrad and then import that view into Access, the only records imported are ones where the last name equals Conrad. If you need to import all the records into Access, make sure you import a view that returns all the records in the list.

Linking a SharePoint List into Access

As you might recall from earlier in this chapter, we discussed the differences between deciding to import from and deciding to link to another data source. If you need to share your data with other users or if the data changes frequently, you should consider linking to instead of importing from another data source. You just imported a sample list from a SharePoint site to an Access database. If you add new records, edit existing records, or delete records in this table, these changes are not reflected in the list on the SharePoint site. This can be problematic if all users need to have the most up-to-date data available to them. You could make changes to your local table and then export the table to the SharePoint list, but what if another user had also made changes to the records in the list? You can see the dilemma this causes when trying to keep accurate data.

Fortunately, with Access, you can link to a SharePoint site just as you can to other data sources. If you export an Access table to SharePoint and then link it back, this allows both your desktop application users and authorized members of your SharePoint site team to work with and update the same data. To link to a SharePoint list from Access, click the More button in the Import & Link group on the External Data tab, and then click SharePoint List, as shown in Figure 8-61.

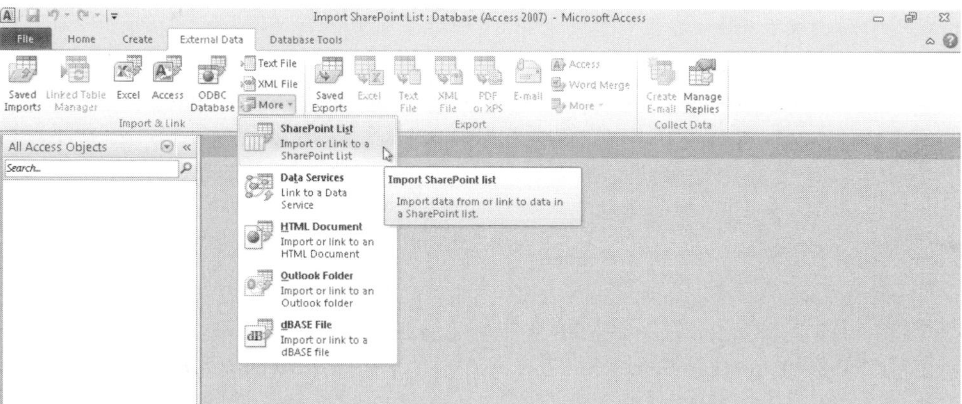

Figure 8-61 Click the SharePoint List button to start the Get External Data – SharePoint Site wizard.

Access opens the first page of the Get External Data – SharePoint Site wizard, shown in Figure 8-62. This particular wizard is the same one you used for importing lists from a SharePoint site in the previous section. Enter a valid SharePoint address in the address text box below the list of previously visited sites or select a previously visited SharePoint address from the list box. Select the second option, Link To The Data Source By Creating A Linked Table, to link to an existing list on a SharePoint site and then click Next.

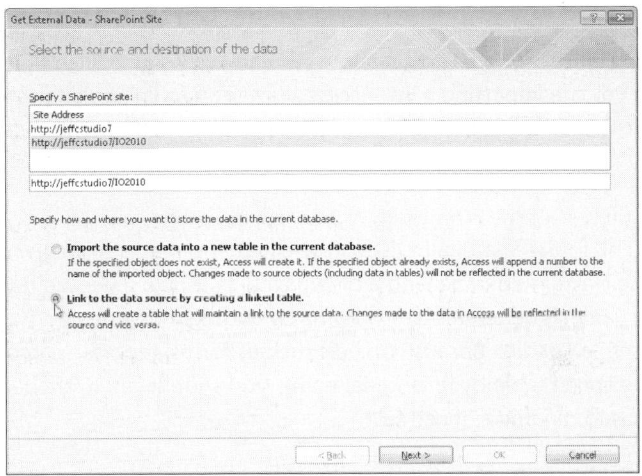

Figure 8-62 Select the link option on the first page of the wizard to link to a list.

The second page of the wizard displays all the lists found in the SharePoint site directory that you specified on the previous page, as shown in Figure 8-63. Select a check box in the Link column to specify which list you want to link to Access. The Type column displays icons representing the type of list. The Name column displays the names of the lists on the SharePoint site. The last column, Last Modified Date, displays the date the list was last modified. Select the Link check box next to the list you want to link to and then click OK to start the linking process.

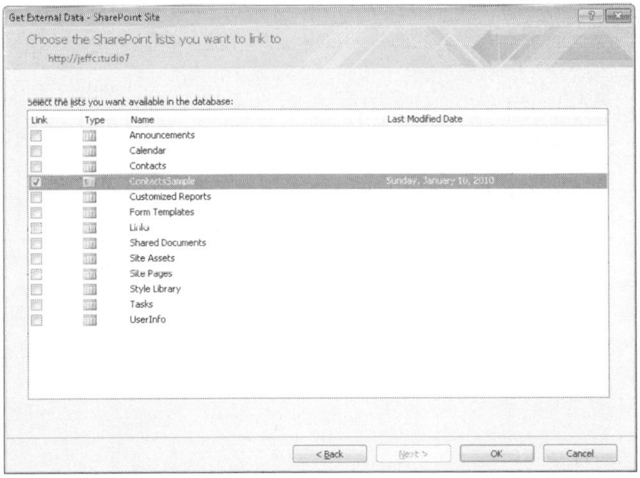

Figure 8-63 Select the list you want to link to on this wizard page.

Chapter 8

Note

You'll notice in Figure 8-63 that you cannot select any views on a SharePoint site as you can when you are importing a list. Access allows you to link only to the full list, as opposed to views created from lists.

Access creates a link to the SharePoint list you selected and marks the icon for linked SharePoint tables in the Navigation pane with a blue arrow, as shown in Figure 8-64. If Access finds a duplicate name, it generates a new name by adding a unique integer to the end of the name, as described earlier. Because objects such as forms, reports, macros, and modules might refer to the linked table by its original name, you should carefully check name references if Access has to rename a linked table.

On the status bar at the bottom of the Access window shown in Figure 8-64, you'll notice that Access displays Online With SharePoint. This message appears on the status bar whenever you have any active links to a SharePoint site.

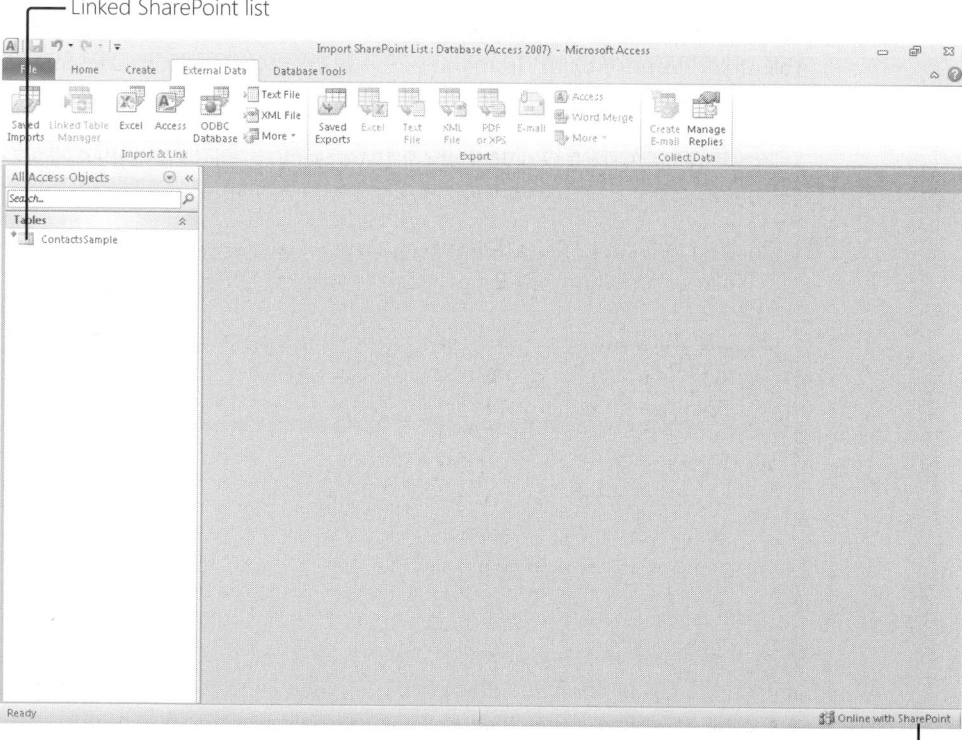

Figure 8-64 Access now has a link to the list we selected on the SharePoint site.

You can now use this list just like a local table in your application. You can create data entry forms in Access and use this linked list as a record source. If you add a new record to the linked table, the list on the SharePoint site is also updated. Note that using data from a SharePoint list as a linked table in Access requires a high-speed Internet connection or local area connection to your intranet server. Performance will be significantly slower over a dial-up connection.

Saving Import Procedures

As you've been working through the import examples in this chapter, you've no doubt realized that there can be quite a few steps involved in completing an import procedure. For a one-time operation, this might not seem like a time-consuming task. But, what if your import procedure steps are fairly complex and you need to perform the same import task on a regular basis? Access 2010 includes a feature that allows you to save your import procedures and run them again at a later time. If you're running the same import procedure on a regular basis, you can even set up a reminder task in Outlook 2010 from Access to remind you to perform the task.

To save an import procedure, you first need to create one. For this example, let's import the tblEmployees table object from the Housing Reservations database into a new empty database file. Take the following steps:

1. Create a new empty blank database and then close any open objects so that only the Navigation pane is showing.

2. On the External Data tab, in the Import & Link group, click the Access command. Access opens the Get External Data - Access Database dialog box.

3. Click Browse to open the File Open dialog box, previously shown on page 454. Select the folder where you installed the sample files, select the Housing.accdb file, click Open, and then Click OK.

4. Access opens the Import Objects dialog box, previously shown on page 461, which provides tabs for each of the object types in the database you selected. Click the Tables tab for the object type, select the tblEmployees table, and then click OK to import the table into your database.

After the import process is complete, Access displays the last page of the wizard, as shown in Figure 8-65. A message at the top of this page indicates whether the import process was a success or if any problems were encountered. The wizard also displays an option to save your import steps in case you want to perform the exact import procedure again in the future. Select the Save Import Steps check box and Access shows additional information on this dialog box.

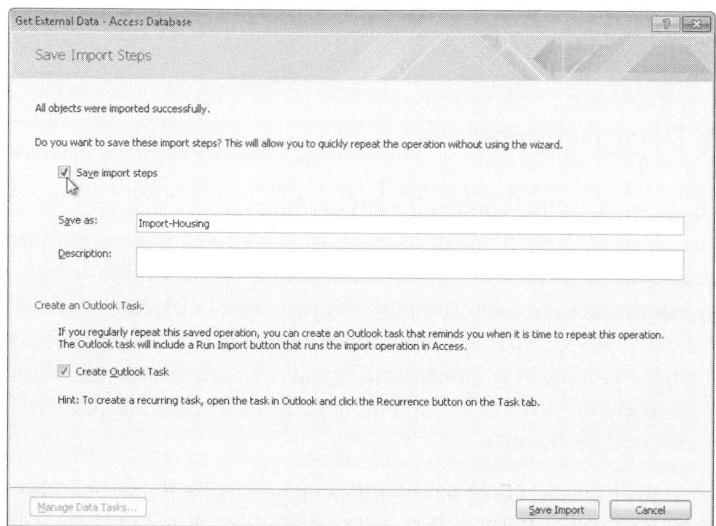

Figure 8-65 Select Save Import Steps to save the import procedure you just created.

In the Save As text box, you can define a name you want to use to identify this specific import procedure. By default, Access lists the word *Import*, followed by a hyphen, and then the name of the database file. In the Description text box, you can provide a brief description of the import procedure if you want. Providing a description can be very useful if, in the future, you or someone else need to understand more details about the import procedure. Select the Create Outlook Task check box, cleared by default, and Access creates a new Outlook task to remind you to run this import procedure. If you have already saved import procedures for this database, you can click the Manage Data Tasks button to open a dialog box listing all the previously saved imports. (We'll discuss that dialog box in just a moment.) Click Save Import to finish importing the tblEmployees table into your database and close the dialog box.

In Figure 8-66, you can see an example of the Outlook task that Access creates when you select the Create Outlook Task option, shown previously in Figure 8-65. You can click Recurrence if you want to set this task to be recurring and have Outlook remind you to run this import procedure. You can also click the Run Import button in the Microsoft Access group on the Task Ribbon to run the saved import procedure from within Outlook.

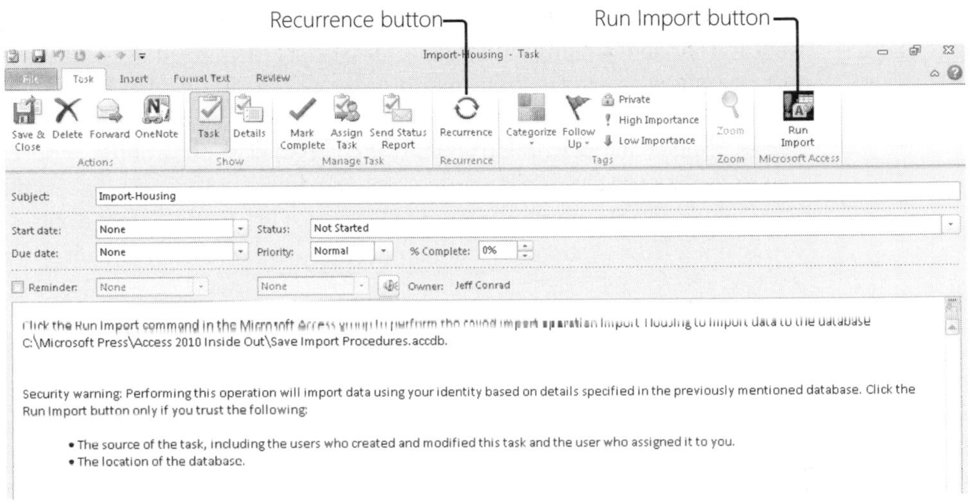

Figure 8-66 Click Run Import from within the Outlook task to run the saved import procedure.

To see a list of your saved import procedures in Access, click the Saved Imports button in the Import & Link group on the ribbon. Access opens the Manage Data Tasks dialog box, as shown in Figure 8-67. The Manage Data Tasks dialog box has two tabs—Saved Imports and Saved Exports—both of which function exactly the same. Access displays a list of import procedures on the Saved Imports tab and a list of export procedures on the Saved Exports tab in this database.

For information on how to export data, see Article 3 on the companion CD.

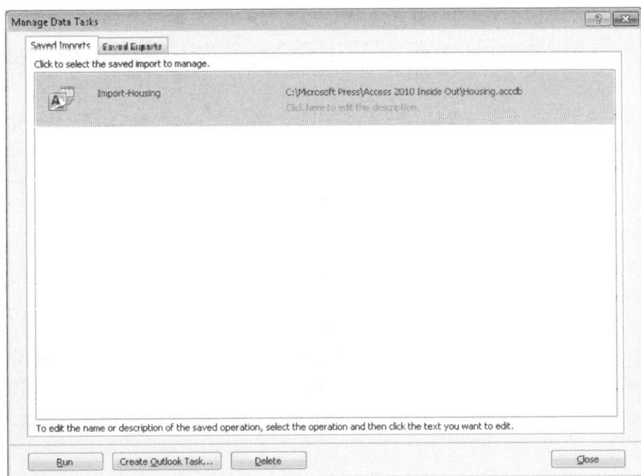

Figure 8-67 The Manage Data Tasks dialog box lists any saved import or procedures in your database.

In Figure 8-67, you can see the name of the import procedure you saved previously. If you want to change the name of this import procedure, click the name and Access displays a text box where you can edit the import name. Access displays the file path to the database you imported the tblEmployees table on the right side of the screen. Beneath the file path, Access displays any description you provided on the last page of the import wizard dialog box. If you did not define a description for your import procedure, Access displays Click Here To Edit The Description, under the file path. Click it and Access displays a text box for you to enter a description for your import procedure. You can also edit any existing text in this text box.

Click Run, and Access performs the highlighted import procedure. Click Create Outlook Task, and Access creates a new Outlook task for this import procedure. Click Delete, and Access deletes the highlighted import procedure. (Access prompts you for confirmation before deleting the import procedure.) Click Close to dismiss the Manage Data Tasks dialog box.

Note

You cannot edit the individual import steps you saved when you went through the import wizard steps. If you need to change one or more of the import procedure steps, perhaps to use a different file for import, you need to walk through the pages of the import wizard again and save your new import procedure.

Now that you know how to build tables, modify them, and import and link them, it's time to move on to more fun stuff—building queries on your tables—in the next chapter.

PART 3

Building Queries

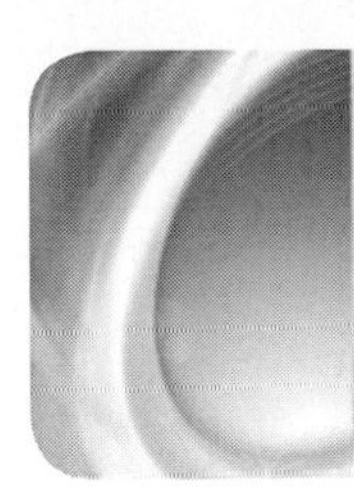

CHAPTER 9

Creating and Working with Simple Queries

In the last five chapters, you learned how to create tables, modify them, and link or import tables from other data sources. Although you can certainly build forms and reports that get their data directly from your tables, most of the time you will want to sort or filter your data or display data from more than one table. For these tasks, you need queries.

When you define and run a *select query*, which selects information from the tables and queries in your database, Microsoft Access 2010 creates a *recordset* of the selected data. In most cases, you can work with a recordset in the same way that you work with a table: you can browse through it, select information from it, print it, and even update the data in it. But unlike a real table, a recordset doesn't actually exist in your database. Access 2010 creates a recordset from the data in the source tables of your query at the time you run the query. *Action queries*—which insert, update, or delete data—will be covered in Chapter 11, "Modifying Data with Action Queries." In Chapter 10, "Building Complex Queries," you'll learn how to create queries in web databases. In this chapter, we'll start by discussing queries in client databases.

As you learn to design forms and reports later in this book, you'll find that queries are the best way to focus on the specific data you need for the task at hand. You'll also find that queries are useful for providing choices for combo and list boxes, which make entering data in your database much easier.

Note

The examples in this chapter are based on the tables and data from the Conrad Systems Contacts sample database (Contacts.accdb), a backup copy of the data for the Contacts sample database (ContactsDataCopy.accdb), the Housing Reservations database (Housing.accdb), and the backup copy of the data for the Housing Reservations sample database (HousingDataCopy.accdb) on the companion CD included with this book. The query results you see from the sample queries you build in this chapter might not exactly match what you see in this book if you have reloaded the sample data using zfrmLoadData in either application or have changed any of the data in the tables.

To begin your study of queries, open the Conrad Systems Contacts database (Contacts.accdb). Access 2010 provides two ways to begin creating a new query in a client database:

- Click the Query Wizard button in the Queries group on the Create tab on the ribbon. A dialog box appears that lets you select one of the four query wizards. (You'll learn about query wizards in Chapter 10.)
- Click the Query Design button in the Queries group on the Create tab on the ribbon to begin creating a new query using the query designer.

To open an existing query in Design view, make sure you have queries showing in the Navigation pane. To display all the queries in your database, click the bar at the top of the Navigation pane and click Object Type under Navigate To Category and then click Queries under Filter By Group. You can open the query you want in Design view by selecting the query in the Navigation pane and then pressing Ctrl+Enter. You can also right-click a query name in the Navigation pane and click Design View from the shortcut menu. Figure 9-1 shows the list of queries for the Conrad Systems Contacts database. Please note that the figure shows you only some of the queries in the database. Use the scroll bar in the Navigation pane to see the complete list of queries available in the Conrad Systems Contacts database.

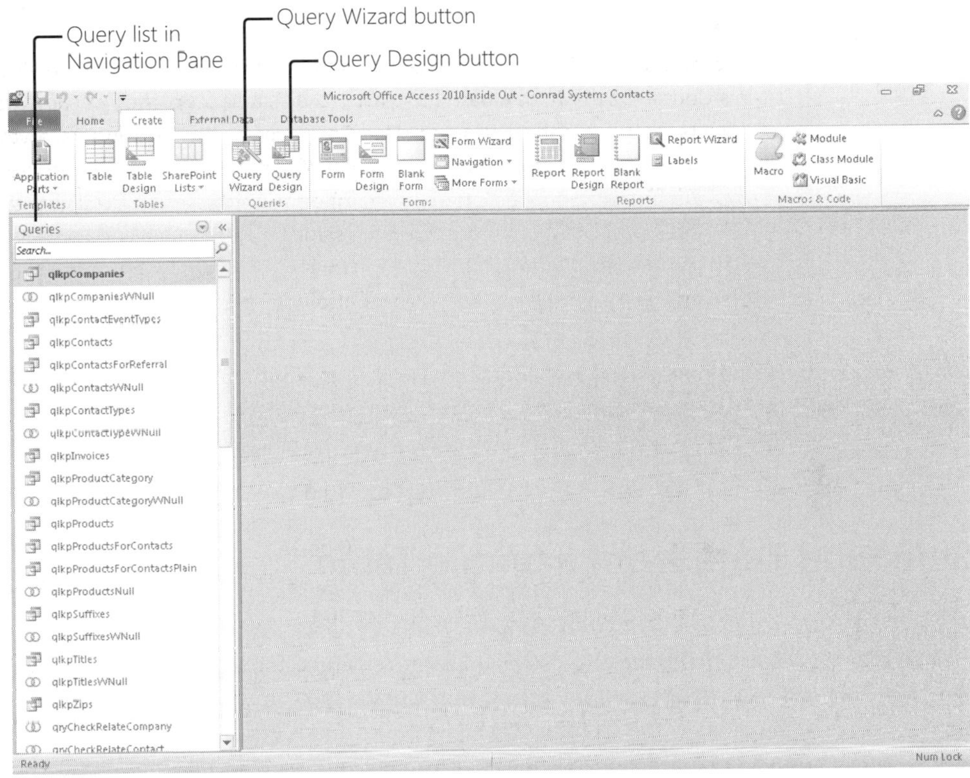

Figure 9-1 The Navigation pane has been filtered to show all the queries in the Conrad Systems Contacts database.

Figure 9-2 shows a query that has been opened in Design view. The upper part of the Query window contains field lists, and the lower part contains the design grid.

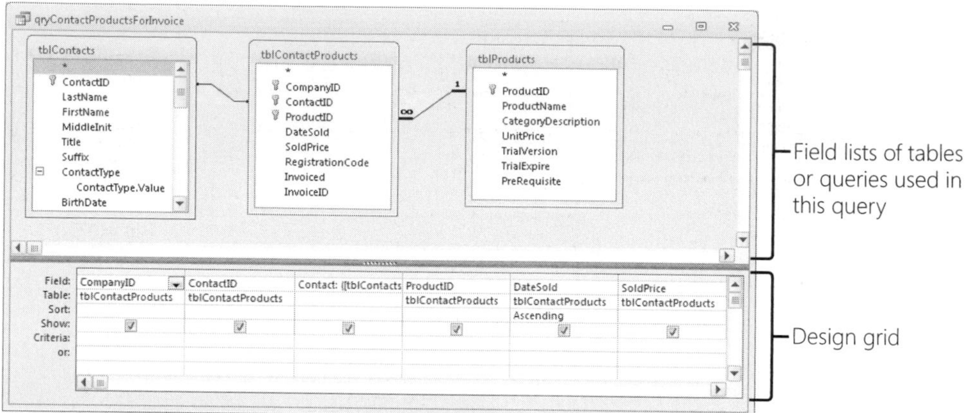

Figure 9-2 A query open in Design view shows the tables and field lists.

Selecting Data from a Single Table

One advantage of using queries is that they allow you to find data easily in multiple related tables. Queries are also useful, however, for sifting through the data in a single table. All the techniques you use for working with a single table apply equally to more complex multiple-table queries. This chapter covers the basics about building queries to select data from a single table. The next chapter shows you how to build more complex queries with multiple tables, totals, parameters, and more.

The easiest way to start building a query on a single table is to click the Query Design button in the Queries group on the Create tab (see Figure 9-1). Access 2010 displays the Show Table dialog box on top of the query design grid, as shown in Figure 9-3.

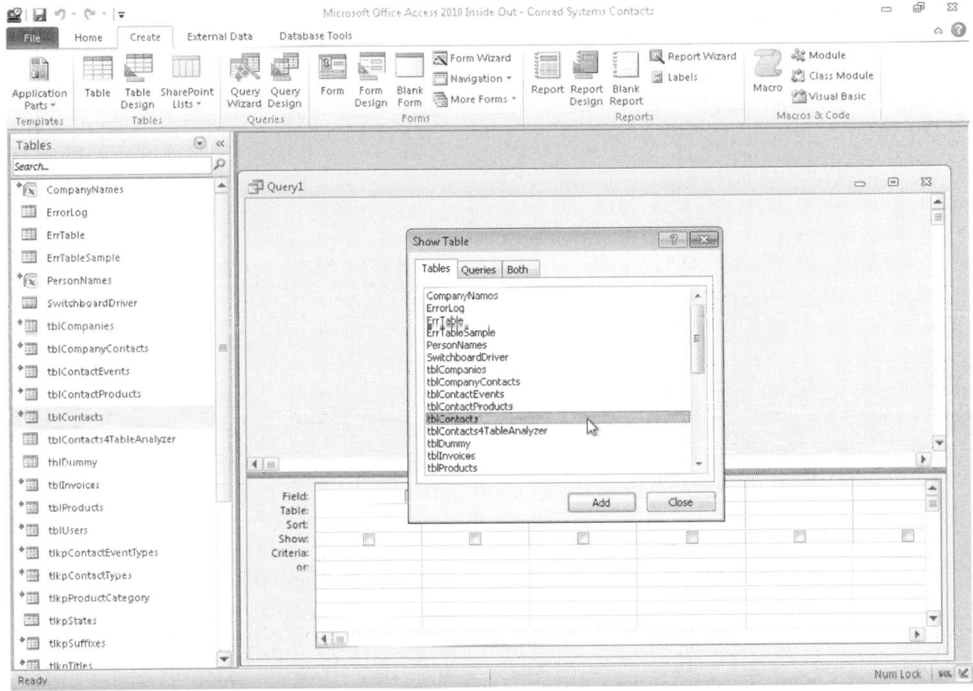

Figure 9-3 The Show Table dialog box allows you to select one or more tables or queries to build a new query.

Select tblContacts on the Tables tab of the Show Table dialog box and then click Add to place tblContacts in the upper part of the Query window. Click Close in the Show Table dialog box to view the window shown in Figure 9-4.

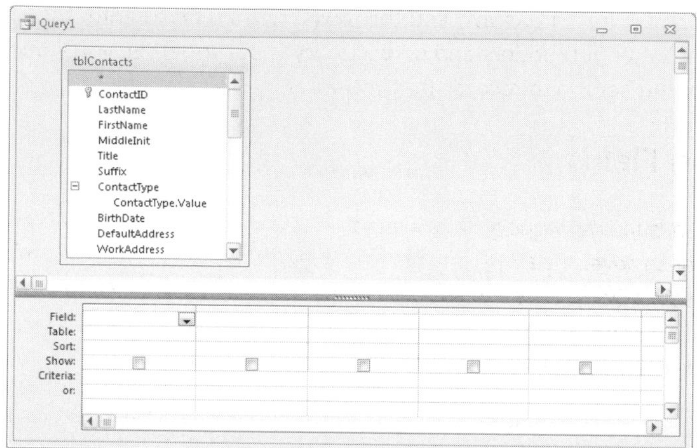

Figure 9-4 The Query window in Design view for a new query on tblContacts shows the table with its list of fields in the top part of the window.

As mentioned earlier, the Query window in Design view has two main parts. In the upper part, you find field lists with the fields for the tables or queries you chose for this query. The lower part of the window is the design grid, in which you do all the design work. Each column in the grid represents one field that you'll work with in this query. As you'll see later, a field can be a simple field from one of the tables or a calculated field based on several fields in the tables.

You use the first row of the design grid to select fields—the fields you want in the resulting recordset, the fields you want to sort by, and the fields you want to test for values. As you'll learn later, you can also generate custom field names (for display in the resulting recordset), and you can use complex expressions or calculations to generate a calculated field.

The second row shows you the name of the table from which you selected a field. If you don't see this row, you can display it by clicking Table Names in the Show/Hide group on the Design tab below Query Tools. This isn't too important when building a query on a single table, but you'll learn later that this row provides valuable information when building a query that fetches data from more than one table or query.

In the Sort row, you can specify whether Access 2010 should sort the selected or calculated field in ascending or descending order. In the Show row, you can use the check boxes to indicate the fields that will be included in the recordset. By default, Access 2010 includes all the fields you place in the design grid. Sometimes you'll want to include a field in the query to allow you to select the records you want (such as contacts born in a certain date range), but you won't need that field in the recordset. You can add that field to the design grid so that you can define criteria, but you should clear the Show check box beneath the field to exclude it from the recordset.

Finally, you can use the Criteria row and the row(s) labeled *Or* to enter the criteria you want to use as filters. After you understand how a query is put together, you'll find it easy to specify exactly the fields and records that you want.

Specifying Fields

The first step in building a query is to select the fields you want in the recordset. You can select the fields in several ways. Using the keyboard, you can tab to a column in the design grid and press Alt+Down Arrow to open the list of available fields. (To move to the design grid, press F6.) Use the Up Arrow and Down Arrow keys to highlight the field you want, and then press Enter to select the field.

Another way to select a field is to drag it from one of the field lists in the upper part of the window to one of the columns in the design grid. In Figure 9-5, the LastName field is being dragged to the design grid. When you drag a field, the mouse pointer turns into a small rectangle.

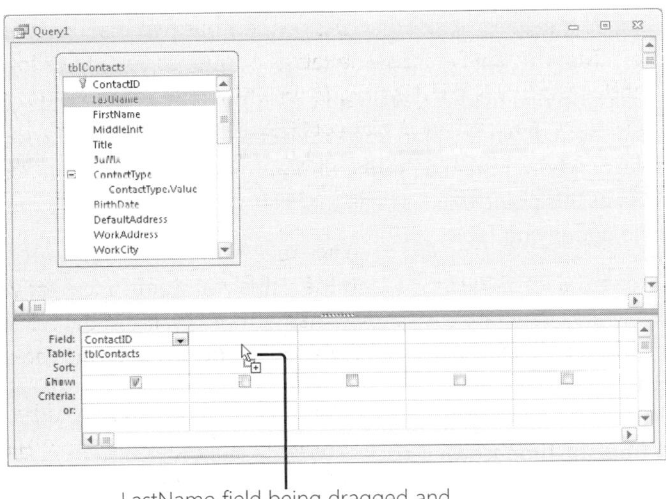

Figure 9-5 You can drag a field from the table field list to a column in the design grid.

At the top of each field list in the upper part of the Query window (and also next to the first entry in the Field drop-down list in the design grid) is an asterisk (*) symbol. This symbol is shorthand for selecting "all fields in the table or the query" with one entry on the Field line. When you want to include all the fields in a table or a query, you don't have to define each one individually in the design grid unless you also want to define some sorting or selection criteria for specific fields. You can simply add the asterisk to the design grid to include all the fields from a list. Note that you can add individual fields to the grid in addition to the asterisk to define criteria for those fields, but you should clear the Show check box for the individual fields so that they don't appear twice in the recordset.

INSIDE OUT Another Way to Select All Fields

Another easy way to select all the fields in a table is to double-click the title bar of the field list in the upper part of the Query window—this highlights all the fields. Then click any of the highlighted fields and drag them as a group to the Field row in the design grid. While you're dragging, the mouse pointer changes to a multiple rectangle icon, indicating that you're dragging multiple fields. When you release the mouse button, you'll see that Access 2010 has copied all the fields to the design grid for you.

For this exercise, select ContactID, LastName, FirstName, WorkStateOrProvince, and BirthDate from the tblContacts table in the Conrad Systems Contacts database. You can select the fields one at a time by dragging them to the design grid. You can also double-click each field name, and Access will move it to the design grid into the next available slot. Finally, you can click on one field you want and then hold down the Ctrl key as you click on additional fields or hold down the Shift key to select a group of contiguous fields. Grab the last field you select and drag them all to the design grid. If you switch the Query window to Datasheet view at this point, you'll see all the records, containing only the fields you selected from the underlying table.

INSIDE OUT A Quick Way to Clear the Design Grid

A quick way to clear all the fields from the design grid is to click the Advanced Filter Options button in the Sort & Filter group on the Home tab, and then click the Clear Grid option from the drop-down list.

Setting Field Properties

In general, a field that is output by a query inherits the properties defined for that field in the table. You can define a different Description property (the information that is displayed on the status bar when you select that field in a Query window in Datasheet view), Format property (how the data is displayed), Decimal Places property (for numeric data other than integers), Input Mask property, Caption property (the column heading), and Smart Tags property. We'll show you the details of how to use the Smart Tag property in Chapter 14, "Customizing a Form."

For details about field properties in client databases, see Chapter 4, "Designing Client Tables."

When you learn to define calculated fields later in this chapter, you'll see that it's a good idea to define the properties for these fields. If the field in the query is a foreign key linked to another table, you can also set the Lookup properties as described in Chapter 5, "Modifying Your Table Design." Access propagates Lookup properties that you have defined in your table fields; however, you can use the properties on the Lookup tab in the query's Property Sheet pane to override them.

Note

The Access 2010 query designer lets you define Lookup properties for any text or numeric field (other than AutoNumber). The field doesn't have to be a defined foreign key to another table. You might find this useful when you want the user to pick from a restricted value list—such as *M* or *F* for a Gender field.

To set the properties of a field, click any row of that field's column in the design grid, and then click the Property Sheet button in the Show/Hide group of the Design contextual tab to display the property sheet, shown in Figure 9-6. Even though the fields in your query inherit their properties from the underlying table, you won't see those properties displayed here. For example, the BirthDate field in tblContacts has both its Description and Caption set to Birth Date and a Format set to mm/dd/yyyy at the table level. If you click in the BirthDate field in your query and open the property sheet, however, you will see that none of the properties show values. You can use the property settings in the property sheet to override any inherited properties and to customize how a field looks when viewed *for this query*. Try entering new property settings for the BirthDate field, as shown in Figure 9-6.

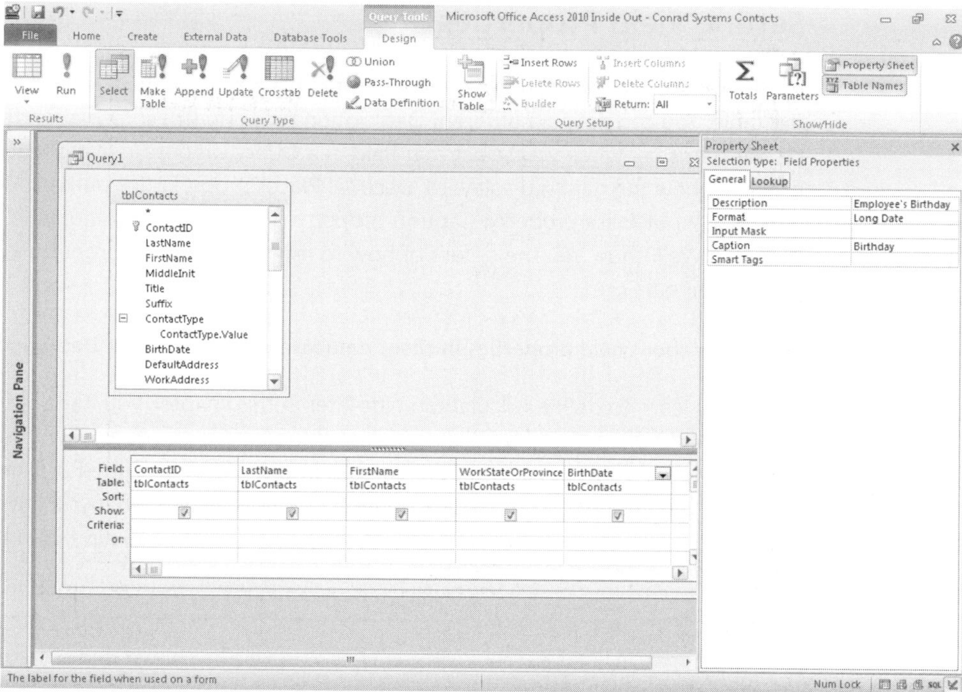

Figure 9-6 In the property sheet, you can set properties for the BirthDate field.

INSIDE OUT **Switching Views to Check Field Properties**

One of the quickest ways to see if a field in a query has the properties you want is to switch to Datasheet view. If the field isn't displayed the way you want, you can switch back to Design view and override the properties in the query.

If you make these changes and switch to Datasheet view (click the View button in the Results group and then click Datasheet), you'll see that the BirthDate column heading is now Birthday; that the date displays day name, month name, day number, and year; and that the text on the status bar matches the new description, as shown in Figure 9-7. When you first view the query results in Datasheet view, you'll see pound signs (#) in the BirthDate field because Access cannot display all the data in the allotted column width. To fix this issue, grab the right edge of the Birthday header with your mouse and drag it to the right to open the column so that you can see all the date values.

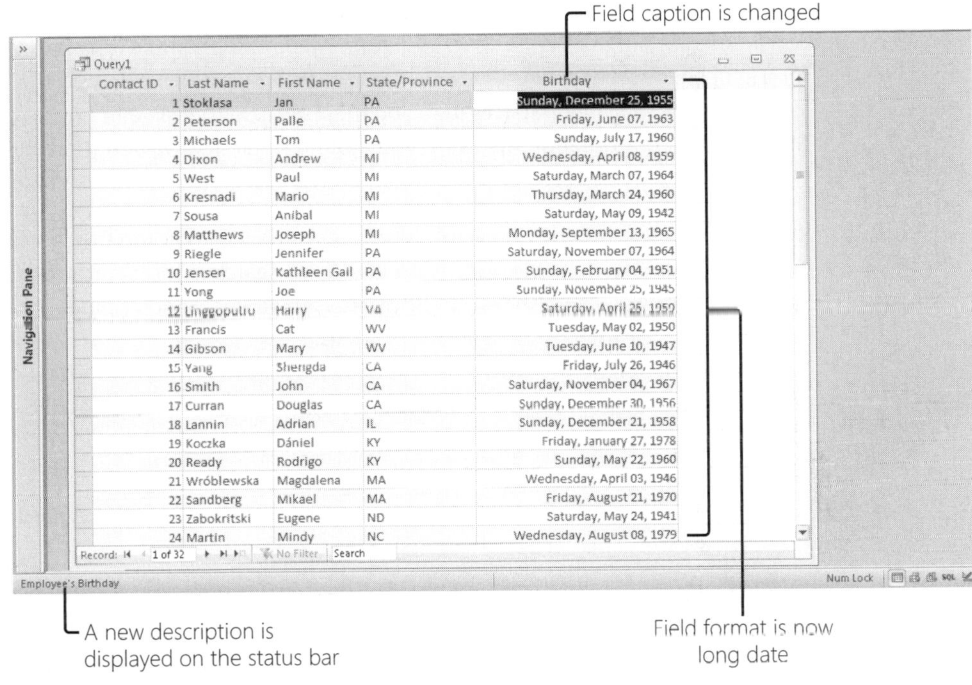

Figure 9-7 The BirthDate field is now displayed with new property settings.

Entering Selection Criteria

The next step is to further refine the records you want by specifying criteria on one or more fields. The example shown in Figure 9-8 selects contacts working in the state of California.

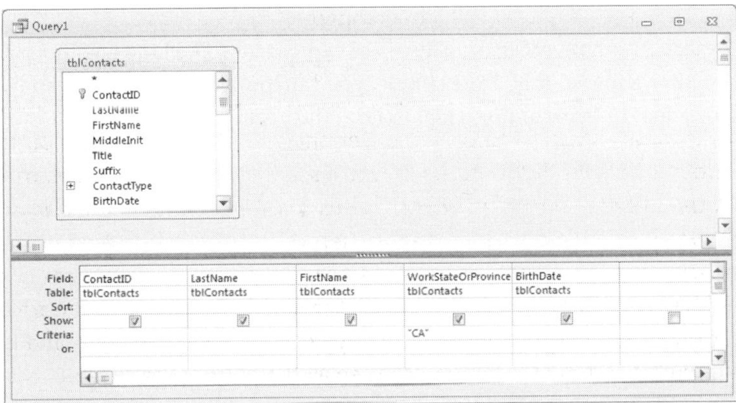

Figure 9-8 When you specify "CA" as the selection criterion in the design grid, Access returns only records with a WorkStateOrProvince value equal to California.

Entering selection criteria in a query is similar to entering a validation rule for a field, which you learned about in Chapter 4. To look for a single value, simply type it in the Criteria row for the field you want to test. If the field you're testing is a text field and the value you're looking for has any blank spaces in it, you must enclose the value in quotation marks. Note that Access adds quotation marks for you around single text values. (In Figure 9-8, we typed CA, but Access replaced what we typed with "CA" after we pressed Enter.)

If you want to test for any of several values, enter the values in the Criteria row, separated by the word *Or*. For example, specifying *CA Or NC* searches for records for California or North Carolina. You can also test for any of several values by entering each value in a separate Criteria or Or row for the field you want to test. For example, you can enter *CA* in the Criteria row, *NC* in the next row (the first Or row), and so on—but you have to be careful if you're also specifying criteria in other fields, as explained in "AND vs. OR," on page 557.

INSIDE OUT

Be Careful When Your Criterion Is Also a Keyword

You should be careful when entering criteria that might also be an Access 2010 keyword. In the examples shown here, we could have chosen to use criteria for the two-character abbreviation for the state of Oregon (OR)—but or, as you can see in the examples, is also a keyword. In many cases, Access is smart enough to figure out what you mean from the context. You can enter:

Or Or Ca

in the criteria under State, and Access assumes that the first *Or* is criteria (by placing quotation marks around the word for you) and the second *Or* is the Boolean operator keyword. If you want to be sure that Access interprets your criteria correctly, always place double quotation marks around criteria text. If you find that Access guessed wrong, you can always correct the entry before saving the query.

In the section "AND vs. OR," you'll see that you can also include a comparison operator in the Criteria row so that, for example, you can look for values less than (<), greater than or equal to (>=), or not equal to (<>) the value that you specify.

Working with Dates and Times in Criteria

Access 2010 stores dates and times as 8-byte decimal numbers. The value to the left of the decimal point represents the day (day zero is December 30, 1899), and the fractional part of the number stores the time as a fraction of a day, accurate to seconds. Fortunately, you don't have to worry about converting internal numbers to specify a test for a particular date value because Access 2010 handles date and time entries in several formats.

You must always surround date and time values with pound signs (#) to tell Access that you're entering a date or a time. To test for a specific date, use the date notation that is most comfortable for you. For example, *#April 15, 1962#*, *#4/15/62#*, and *#15-Apr-1962#* are all the same date if you chose English (United States) in the Regional And Language Options item in the Control Panel. Similarly, *#5:30 PM#* and *#17:30#* both specify 5:30 in the evening.

INSIDE OUT **Understanding Date/Time Criteria**

You must be careful when building criteria to test a range in a date/time field. Let's say you want to look at all records between two dates in the ContactEvents table, which has a date/time field—ContactDateTime—that holds the date and time of the contact. For all contact events in the month of January 2011, you might be tempted to put the following on the Criteria line under ContactDateTime.

```
>=#1/1/2011# AND <=#1/31/2011#
```

When you look at the results, you might wonder why no rows show up from January 31, 2011 even when you know that you made and recorded several calls on that day. The reason is simple. Remember, a date/time field contains an integer offset value for the date and a fraction for the time. Let's say you called someone at 9:55 A.M. on January 31, 2011. The internal value is actually 40,574.4132—January 31, 2011 is 40,574 days later than December 30, 1899 (the zero point), and .4132 is the fraction of a day that represents 9:55 A.M. When you say you want rows where ContactDateTime is less than or equal to January 31, 2011, you're comparing to the internal value 40,574—just the day value, which is midnight on that day. You won't find the 9:55 A.M. record because the value is greater than 40,574, or later in the day than midnight. To search successfully, you must enter

```
>=#1/1/2011# AND <#2/1/2011#
```

AND vs. OR

When you enter criteria for several fields, all the tests in a single Criteria row or Or row must be true for Access 2010 to include a record in the recordset. That is, Access 2010 performs a logical AND operation between multiple criteria in the same row. So if you enter *CA* in the Criteria row for StateOrProvince and *<#1 JAN 1972#* in the Criteria row for BirthDate, the record must be for the state of California *and* must be for someone born before 1972 to be selected. If you enter *CA Or NC* in the Criteria row for StateOrProvince and

>=#01/01/1946# AND <#1 JAN 1972# in the Criteria row for BirthDate, the record must be for the state of California or North Carolina, *and* the person must have been born between 1946 and 1971.

Figure 9-9 shows the result of applying a logical AND operator between any two tests. As you can see, both tests must be true for the result of the AND to be true and for the record to be selected.

AND	True	False
True	True (Selected)	False (Rejected)
False	False (Rejected)	False (Rejected)

Figure 9-9 When you specify the logical AND operator between two tests, the result is true only if both tests are true.

When you specify multiple criteria for a field and separate the criteria by a logical OR operator, only one of the criteria must be true for Access 2010 to select the record. You can specify several OR criteria for a field, either by entering them all in a single Criteria cell separated by the logical OR operator, as shown earlier, or by entering each subsequent criterion in a separate Or row. When you use multiple Or rows, if the criteria in any one of the *Or* rows is true, Access 2010 selects the record. Figure 9-10 shows the result of applying a logical OR operation between any two tests. As you can see, only one of the tests must be true for the result of the OR to be true and for Access 2010 to select the record.

OR	True	False
True	True (Selected)	True (Selected)
False	True (Selected)	False (Rejected)

Figure 9-10 When you specify the logical OR operator between two tests, the result is true if either or both of the tests is true.

INSIDE OUT Don't Get Confused by AND and OR

It's a common mistake to get *OR* and *AND* mixed up when typing compound criteria for a single field. You might think to yourself, "I want all the work contacts in the states of Washington *and* California," and then type WA AND CA in the Criteria row for the WorkStateOrProvince field. When you do this, you're asking Access to find rows where *(WorkStateOrProvince = "WA") AND (WorkStateOrProvince = "CA")*. Because a field in a record can't have more than one value at a time (can't contain both the values WA and CA in the same record), there won't be any records in the output. To look for all the rows for these two states, you need to ask Access to search for *(WorkStateOrProvince = "WA") OR (WorkStateOrProvince = "CA")*. In other words, type WA OR CA in the Criteria row under the WorkStateOrProvince field.

Let's look at a specific example. In Figure 9-11, you specify CA in the first Criteria row of the WorkStateOrProvince field and *>=#01/01/1946# AND <#1 JAN 1972#* in that same Criteria row for the BirthDate field. (By the way, when you type #1 JAN 1972# and press Enter, Access changes your entry to #1/1/1972#.) In the next row (the first Or row), you specify *NC* in the WorkStateOrProvince field. When you run this query, you get all the contacts from the state of California born between 1946 and 1971. You also get any records for the state of North Carolina regardless of the birth date.

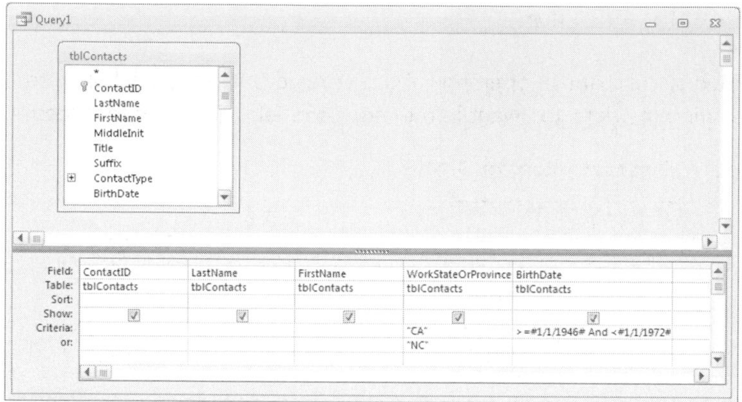

Figure 9-11 You can specify multiple AND and OR selection criteria in the design grid with additional OR lines.

In Figure 9-12, you can see the recordset (in Datasheet view) that results from running this query.

Query1

Contact ID	Last Name	First Name	State/Province	Birthday
15	Yang	Shengda	CA	Friday, July 26, 1946
16	Smith	John	CA	Saturday, November 04, 1967
17	Curran	Douglas	CA	Sunday, December 30, 1956
24	Martin	Mindy	NC	Wednesday, August 08, 1979
25	Zulechner	Markus	NC	Sunday, October 06, 1940
26	Villadsen	Peter	NC	Saturday, November 22, 1975
(New)				

Record: 1 of 6 No Filter Search

Figure 9-12 The recordset of the query shown in Figure 9-11 shows only the records that match your criteria.

If you also want to limit rows from contacts in North Carolina to those who were born between 1946 and 1971, you must specify *>=#01/01/1946# AND <#1/1/1972#* again under BirthDate in the second Or row—that is, on the same row that filters for NC under WorkStateOrProvince. Although this seems like extra work, this gives you complete flexibility to filter the data as you want. You could, for example, include people who were born before 1969 in California and people who were born after 1970 in North Carolina by placing a different criterion under BirthDate in the two rows that filter WorkStateOrProvince.

Between, In, and Like

In addition to comparison operators, Access provides three special operators that are useful for specifying the data you want in the recordset. Table 9-1 describes these operators.

Table 9-1 Criteria Operators for Queries

Predicate	Description
Between	Useful for specifying a range of values. The clause *Between 10 And 20* is the same as specifying *>=10 And <=20*.
In	Useful for specifying a list of values separated by commas, any one of which can match the field being searched. The clause In *("CA", "NC", "TN")* is the same as *"CA" Or "NC" Or "TN"*.
Like[1]	Useful for searching for patterns in text fields. You can include special characters and ranges of values in the Like comparison string to define the character pattern you want. Use a question mark (?) to indicate any single character in that position. Use an asterisk (*) to indicate zero or more characters in that position. The pound-sign character (#) specifies a single numeric digit in that position. Include a range in brackets ([ ]) to test for a particular range of characters in a position, and use an exclamation point (!) to indicate exceptions. The range *[0-9]* tests for numbers, *[a-z]* tests for letters, and *[!0-9]* tests for any characters except *0* through *9*. For example, the clause *Like"?[a-k]d[0-9]*"* tests for any single character in the first position, any character from *a* through *k* in the second position, the letter *d* in the third position, any character from *0* through *9* in the fourth position, and any number of characters after that.

[1] As you'll learn in Article 2, "Understanding SQL," the pattern characters supported by Microsoft SQL Server when you are working in an Access project file are different. The pattern characters discussed here work in desktop applications (.accdb and .accde files) only.

Suppose you want to find all contacts in the state of California or Pennsylvania who were born between 1955 and 1972 and whose first name begins with the letter J. Figure 9-13 shows how you would enter these criteria. Figure 9-14 shows the recordset of this query.

INSIDE OUT Choosing the Correct Date/Time Criteria

If you're really sharp, you're probably looking at Figure 9-13 and wondering why we chose Between *#1/1/1955# And #12/31/1972#* instead of >= *#1/1/1955# And < #1/1/1973#* to cover the case where the BirthDate field might also include a time. In this case, we know that the BirthDate field has an input mask that doesn't allow us to enter time values. So we know that using Between and the simple date values will work for this search.

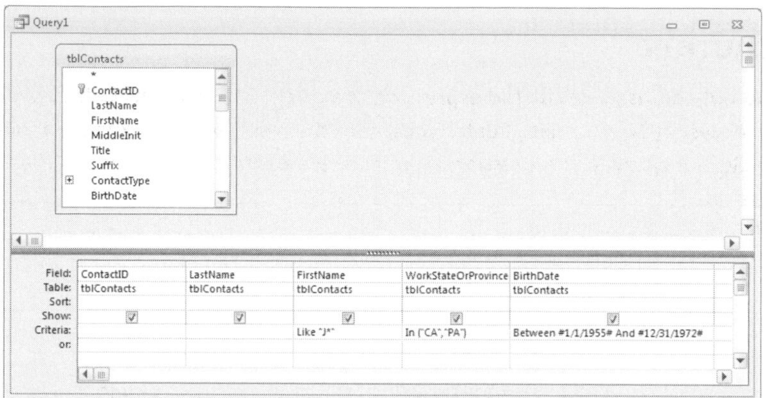

Figure 9-13 You can also restrict records by using Between, In, and Like, all in the same design grid.

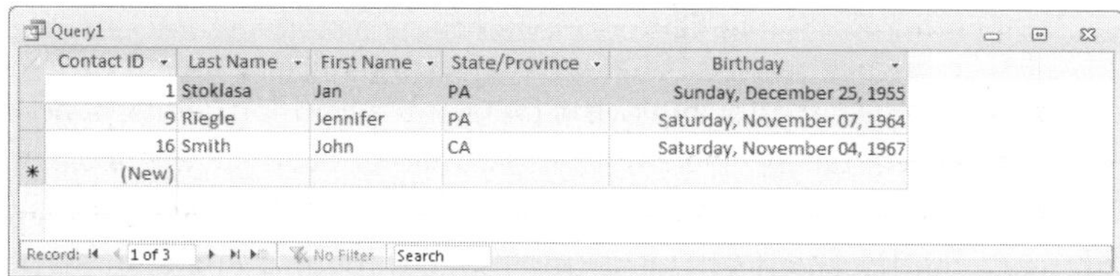

Figure 9-14 The recordset of the query shown in Figure 9-13 shows only the records that match your criteria.

For additional examples that use the Between, In, and Like comparison operators, see "Defining Simple Field Validation Rules," on page 201, and the "Predicate" sections in Article 2 on the companion CD.

Using Expressions

You can use an expression to combine fields or to calculate a new value from fields in your table and make that expression a new field in the recordset. You can use any of the many built-in functions that Access 2010 provides as part of your expression. You *concatenate*, or combine, text fields by stringing them end to end, or you use arithmetic operators on fields in the underlying table to calculate a value. Let's switch to the HousingDataCopy.accdb database to build some examples.

CAUTION

Do not confuse a calculated expression in a query with the new Calculated data type in Access 2010. Calculated data types store the result of their expression directly in the table, but calculated expressions in queries are calculated only when Access executes the query.

Creating Text Expressions

One common use of expressions is to create a new text (string) field by concatenating fields containing text, string constants, or numeric data. You create a string constant by enclosing the text in double or single quotation marks. Use the ampersand character (&) between fields or strings to indicate that you want to concatenate them. For example, you might want to create an output field that concatenates the LastName field, a comma, a blank space, and then the FirstName field.

Try creating a query on the tblEmployees table in the HousingDataCopy.accdb database that shows a field containing the employee last name, a comma and a blank, first name, a blank, and middle name. You can also create a single field containing the city, a comma and a blank space, the state or province followed by one blank space, and the postal code. Your expressions should look like this:

```
LastName & ", " & FirstName & " " & MiddleName

City & ", " & StateOrProvince & " " & PostalCode
```

You can see the Query window in Design view for this example in Figure 9-15. We clicked in the Field row of the second column and then pressed Shift+F2 to open the Zoom window, where it is easier to enter the expression. Note that you can click the Font button to select a larger font that's easier to read. After you choose a font, Access 2010 uses it whenever you open the Zoom window again.

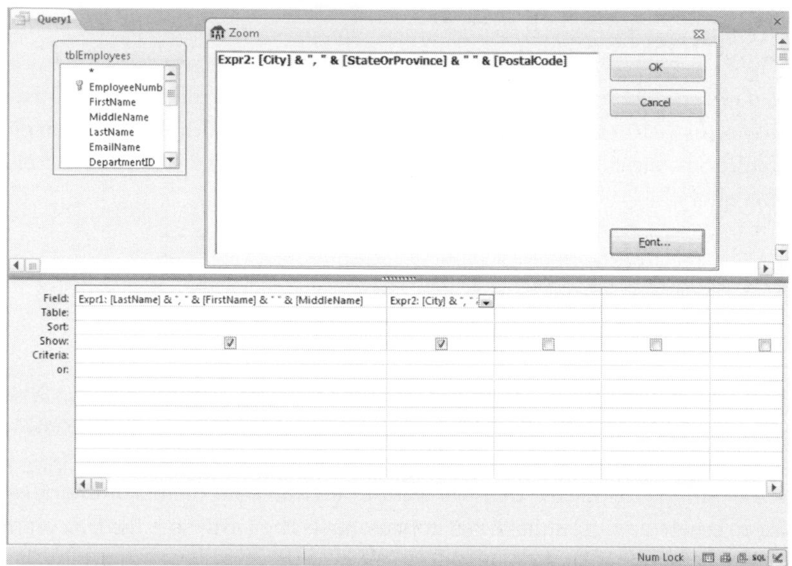

Figure 9-15 If you use the Zoom window to enter an expression, you can see more of the expression and select a different font.

> **Note**
>
> **Access 2010 requires that all fields on the Field row in a query have a name. For single fields, Access uses the name of the field. When you enter an expression, Access generates a field name in the form *ExprN:*. See "Specifying Field Names," on page 582, for details about changing the names of fields or expressions. Notice also that Access automatically adds brackets around field names in expressions. It does this so that the field names in the Structured Query Language (SQL) for the query are completely unambiguous. If this table had been designed with blanks in the field names, you would have to type the brackets yourself to ensure that the query designer interprets the names correctly.**

When you look at the query result in Datasheet view, you should see something like the one shown in Figure 9-16.

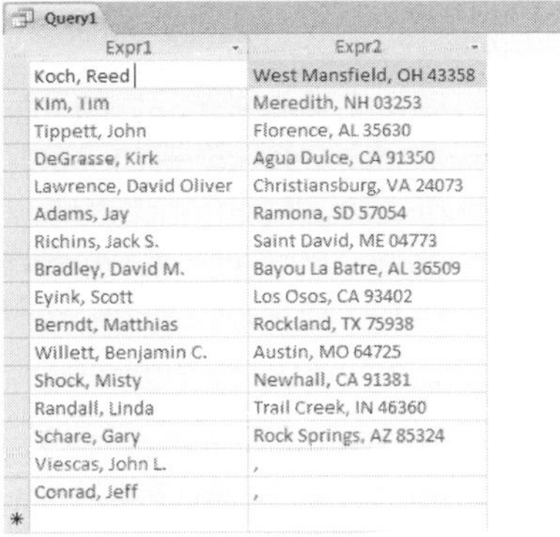

Query1

Expr1	Expr2
Koch, Reed	West Mansfield, OH 43358
Kim, Tim	Meredith, NH 03253
Tippett, John	Florence, AL 35630
DeGrasse, Kirk	Agua Dulce, CA 91350
Lawrence, David Oliver	Christiansburg, VA 24073
Adams, Jay	Ramona, SD 57054
Richins, Jack S.	Saint David, ME 04773
Bradley, David M.	Bayou La Batre, AL 36509
Eyink, Scott	Los Osos, CA 93402
Berndt, Matthias	Rockland, TX 75938
Willett, Benjamin C.	Austin, MO 64725
Shock, Misty	Newhall, CA 91381
Randall, Linda	Trail Creek, IN 46360
Schare, Gary	Rock Springs, AZ 85324
Viescas, John L.	,
Conrad, Jeff	,
*	

Figure 9-16 This query is a result using concatenated text fields.

Try typing within the Expr1 field in Datasheet view. Because this display is a result of an expression (concatenation of strings), Access 2010 won't let you update the data in this column.

INSIDE OUT Eliminating Extra Spaces When Concatenating Null Values

If you look very closely at Figure 9-16, you can see that we captured the image with the insertion point displayed at the end of the Expr1 calculated field on the first row. Do you notice that there's an extra space after the first name? This happened because that person has no middle name, so what we're seeing is the extra blank we inserted after the first name that is supposed to provide spacing between the first and middle name.

This isn't too much of a problem in this particular expression because you're not going to notice the extra blank displayed at the end of the name. But if you create the expression *First (blank) Middle (blank) Last* and if a record has no middle name, the extra blank will be noticeable.

When you use an ampersand, any Null field in the expression doesn't cause the entire expression to be Null. A little secret: You can also use the arithmetic plus sign (+) to concatenate strings. As you'll learn when you create arithmetic expressions, if a field in the expression is Null, the expression evaluates to Null. So, to solve the extra blank problem, you can create an expression to concatenate the parts of a name as follows:

```
FirstName & (" " + MiddleName) & " " & LastName
```

If MiddleName is a Null, the arithmetic expression inside the parentheses evaluates to Null, and the extra blank disappears!

Defining Arithmetic Expressions

In a reservations record (tblReservations in the Housing Reservations database), code in the form that confirms a reservation automatically calculates the correct TotalCharge value for the reservation before Access 2010 saves a changed row. If you strictly follow the rules for good relational table design (see Article 1, "Designing Your Database Application," on the companion CD), this isn't normally a good idea, but we designed it this way to demonstrate what you have to code to maintain the calculated value in your table. (Access 2010 won't automatically calculate the new value for you because we did not define this field using the new Calculated data type.) You can see how this code works in Chapter 25, "Automating Your Application with Visual Basic," on the companion CD. This technique also saves time later when calculating a total by month or total by facility in a report.

Table 9-2 shows the operators you can use in arithmetic expressions.

Table 9-2 Operators Used in Arithmetic Expressions

Operator	Description
+	Adds two numeric expressions.
–	Subtracts the second numeric expression from the first numeric expression.
*	Multiplies two numeric expressions.
/	Divides the first numeric expression by the second numeric expression.
\	Rounds both numeric expressions to integers and then divides the first integer by the second integer. The result is truncated to an integer.
^	Raises the first numeric expression to the power indicated by the second numeric expression.
Mod	Rounds both numeric expressions to integers, divides the first integer by the second integer, and returns only the remainder.

The expression to calculate the TotalCharge field is complex because it charges the lower weekly rate for portions of the stay that are full weeks and then adds the daily charge for extra days. Let's say you want to compare the straight daily rate with the discounted rate for longer stays. To begin, you need an expression that calculates the number of days. You can do this in a couple of different ways. First, you can use a handy built-in function called DateDiff to calculate the difference between two Date/Time values in seconds, minutes, hours, days, weeks, months, quarters, or years. In this case, you want the difference between the check-in date and the check-out date in days.

The syntax for calling DateDiff is as follows:

```
DateDiff(<interval>, <date1>, <date2>[, <firstdayofweek>])
```

The function calculates the difference between <*date1*> and <*date2*> using the interval you specify and returns a negative value if <*date1*> is greater than <*date2*>. You can supply a <*firstdayofweek*> value (the default is 1, Sunday) to affect how the function calculates the *"ww"* interval. Table 9-3 explains the values you can supply for *interval*.

Note

You can also use the settings you find in Table 9-3 for the *interval argument* in the DatePart function (which extracts part of a Date/Time value) and DateAdd function (which adds or subtracts a constant to a Date/Time value).

Table 9-3 Interval Settings for DateDiff Function

Setting	Description
"yyyy"	Calculates the difference in years. DateDiff subtracts the year portion of the first date from the year portion of the second date, so *DateDiff*`("yyyy", #31 DEC 2010#, #01 JAN 2011#)` returns 1.
"q"	Calculates the difference in quarters. If the two dates are in the same calendar quarter, the result is 0.
"m"	Calculates the difference in months. DateDiff subtracts the month portion of the first date from the month portion of the second date, so *DateDiff*`("m", #31 DEC 2010#, #01 JAN 2011#)` returns 1.
"y"	Calculates the difference in days. DateDiff handles this option the same as "d" below. (For other functions, this extracts the day of the year.)
"d"	Calculates the difference in days.
"w"	Calculates the difference in weeks based on the day of the week of <*date1*>. If, for example, the day of the week of the first date is a Tuesday, DateDiff counts the number of Tuesdays between the first date and the second date. For example, March 23, 2011 is a Wednesday, and March 28, 2011 is a Monday, so *DateDiff*`("w", #23 MAR 2011#, #28 MAR 2011#)` returns zero.
"ww"	Calculates the difference in weeks. When the first day of the week is Sunday (the default), DateDiff counts the number of Sundays greater than the first date and less than or equal to the second date. For example, March 23, 2011 is a Wednesday, and March 28, 2011 is a Monday, so *DateDiff*`("ww", #23 MAR 2011#, #28 MAR 2011#)` returns 1.
"h"	Calculates the difference in hours.
"n"	Calculates the difference in minutes.
"s"	Calculates the difference in seconds.

The second way to calculate the number of days is to simply subtract one date from the other. Remember that the integer portion of a date/time data type is number of days. If you're sure that the fields do not contain any time value, subtract the check-in date from the check-out date to find the number of days. Let's see how this works in the sample database.

Open the HousingDataCopy.accdb database if you have closed it and start a new query on tblReservations. Add EmployeeNumber, FacilityID, RoomNumber, CheckInDate, CheckOutDate, and TotalCharge to the query design grid. You need to enter your expression in a blank column on the Field row. You'll build your final expression in two parts so you can understand the logic involved. Using DateDiff, start the expression by entering:

```
DateDiff("d", [CheckInDate], [CheckOutDate])
```

To calculate the number of days by subtracting, the expression is:

```
[CheckOutDate] - [CheckInDate]
```

To calculate the amount owed at the daily rate, multiply either of the previous expressions by the DailyRate field. With DateDiff, the final expression is:

```
DateDiff("d", [CheckInDate], [CheckOutDate]) * [DailyRate]
```

If you want to use subtraction, you must enter:

```
([CheckOutDate] - [CheckInDate]) * [DailyRate]
```

You might be wondering why the second expression includes parentheses. When evaluating an arithmetic expression, Access evaluates certain operations before others, known as *operator precedence*. Table 9-4 shows you operator precedence for arithmetic operations. In an expression with no parentheses, Access performs the operations in the order listed in the table. When operations have the same precedence (for example, multiply and divide), Access performs the operations left to right.

Table 9-4 Arithmetic Operator Precedence

Access Evaluates Operators in the Following Order:	
1	Exponentiation (^)
2	Negation—a leading minus sign (–)
3	Multiplication and division (*, /)
4	Integer division (\)
5	Modulus (Mod)
6	Addition and subtraction (+, –)

Access evaluates expressions enclosed in parentheses first, starting with the innermost expressions. (You can enclose an expression in parentheses inside another expression in parentheses.) If you do not include the parentheses in the previous example, Access would first multiply CheckInDate times DailyRate (because multiplication and division occur before addition and subtraction) and then subtract that result from CheckOutDate. That not only gives you the wrong answer but also results in a #NUM! error because you cannot subtract a Double value (the result of multiplying a date/time times a currency) from a date/time value.

After you select the fields from the table and enter the expression to calculate the total based on the daily rate, your query design grid should look something like Figure 9-17.

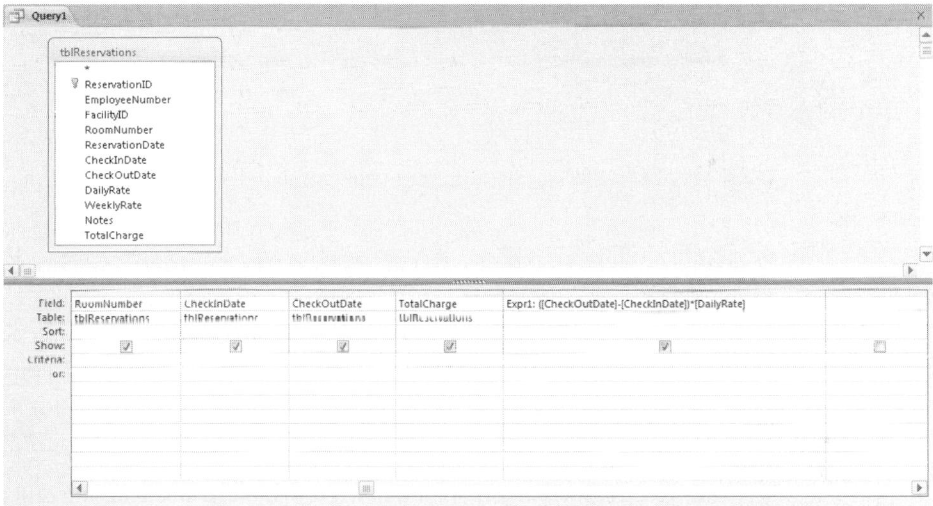

Figure 9-17 Use an expression to calculate the amount owed based on the daily rate.

When you switch to Datasheet view, you can see the calculated amount from your expression, as shown in Figure 9-18.

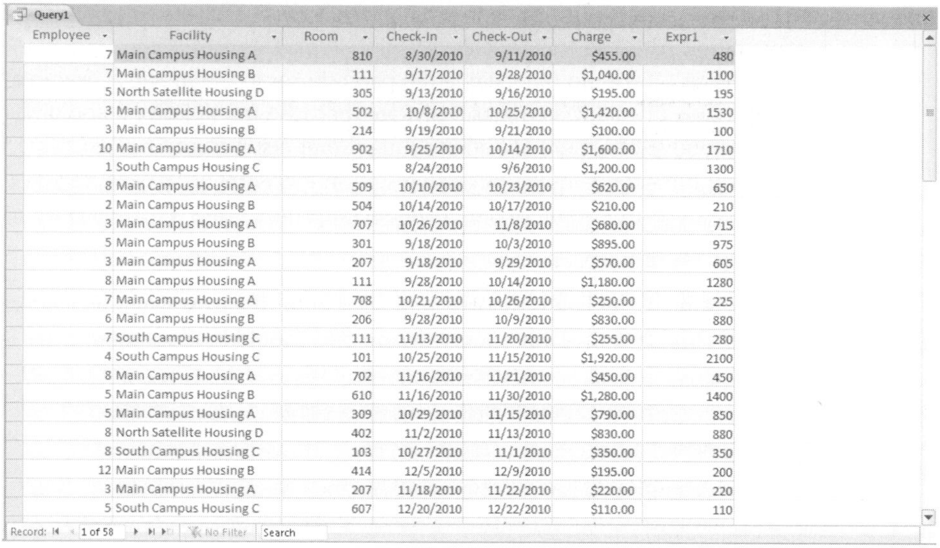

Query1

Employee	Facility	Room	Check-In	Check-Out	Charge	Expr1
7	Main Campus Housing A	810	8/30/2010	9/11/2010	$455.00	480
7	Main Campus Housing B	111	9/17/2010	9/28/2010	$1,040.00	1100
5	North Satellite Housing D	305	9/13/2010	9/16/2010	$195.00	195
3	Main Campus Housing A	502	10/8/2010	10/25/2010	$1,420.00	1530
3	Main Campus Housing B	214	9/19/2010	9/21/2010	$100.00	100
10	Main Campus Housing A	902	9/25/2010	10/14/2010	$1,600.00	1710
1	South Campus Housing C	501	8/24/2010	9/6/2010	$1,200.00	1300
8	Main Campus Housing A	509	10/10/2010	10/23/2010	$620.00	650
2	Main Campus Housing B	504	10/14/2010	10/17/2010	$210.00	210
3	Main Campus Housing A	707	10/26/2010	11/8/2010	$680.00	715
5	Main Campus Housing B	301	9/18/2010	10/3/2010	$895.00	975
3	Main Campus Housing A	207	9/18/2010	9/29/2010	$570.00	605
8	Main Campus Housing A	111	9/28/2010	10/14/2010	$1,180.00	1280
7	Main Campus Housing A	708	10/21/2010	10/26/2010	$250.00	225
6	Main Campus Housing B	206	9/28/2010	10/9/2010	$830.00	880
7	South Campus Housing C	111	11/13/2010	11/20/2010	$255.00	280
4	South Campus Housing C	101	10/25/2010	11/15/2010	$1,920.00	2100
8	Main Campus Housing A	702	11/16/2010	11/21/2010	$450.00	450
5	Main Campus Housing B	610	11/16/2010	11/30/2010	$1,280.00	1400
5	Main Campus Housing A	309	10/29/2010	11/15/2010	$790.00	850
8	North Satellite Housing D	402	11/2/2010	11/13/2010	$830.00	880
8	South Campus Housing C	103	10/27/2010	11/1/2010	$350.00	350
12	Main Campus Housing B	414	12/5/2010	12/9/2010	$195.00	200
3	Main Campus Housing A	207	11/18/2010	11/22/2010	$220.00	220
5	South Campus Housing C	607	12/20/2010	12/22/2010	$110.00	110

Record: 1 of 58 No Filter Search

Figure 9-18 Access displays the results of your calculated expression in the Datasheet view.

Note that not all the calculated amounts are larger than the amount already stored in the record. When the reservation is for six days or fewer, the daily rate applies, so your calculation should match the existing charge. You might want to display only the records where the new calculated amount is different than the amount already stored. For that, you can add another expression to calculate the difference and then select the row if the difference is not zero.

Switch back to Design view and enter a new expression to calculate the difference in an empty column. Your expression should look like this:

```
TotalCharge - (([CheckOutDate] - [CheckInDate]) * [DailyRate])
```

In the Criteria line under this new field, enter **<> 0**. Your query design should look like Figure 9-19, and the datasheet for the query now displays only the rows where the calculation result is different, as shown in Figure 9-20.

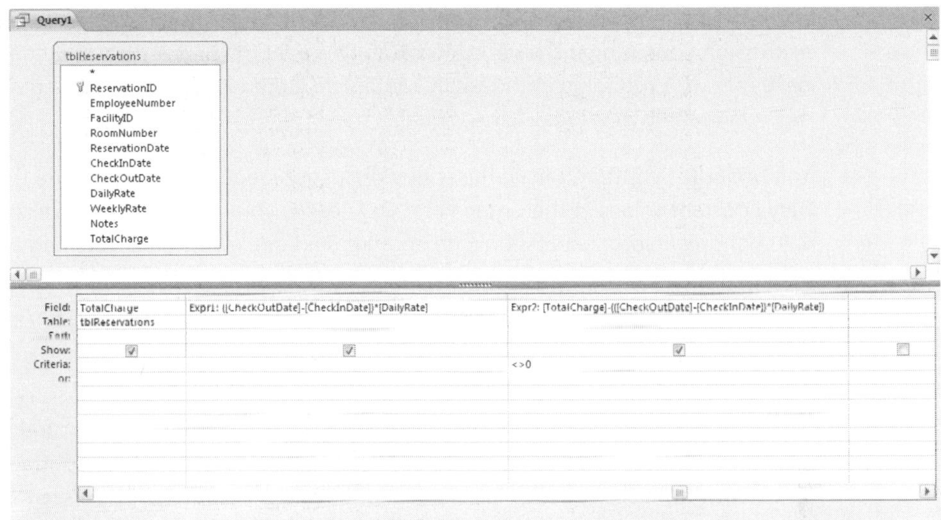

Figure 9-19 This expression and criterion finds the rows that are different.

Query1

Employee	Facility	Room	Check-In	Check-Out	Charge	Expr1	Expr2
7	Main Campus Housing A	810	8/30/2010	9/11/2010	$455.00	480	($25.00)
7	Main Campus Housing B	111	9/17/2010	9/28/2010	$1,040.00	1100	($60.00)
3	Main Campus Housing A	502	10/8/2010	10/25/2010	$1,420.00	1530	($110.00)
10	Main Campus Housing A	902	9/25/2010	10/14/2010	$1,600.00	1710	($110.00)
1	South Campus Housing C	501	8/24/2010	9/6/2010	$1,200.00	1300	($100.00)
8	Main Campus Housing A	509	10/10/2010	10/23/2010	$620.00	650	($30.00)
3	Main Campus Housing A	707	10/26/2010	11/8/2010	$680.00	715	($35.00)
5	Main Campus Housing B	301	9/18/2010	10/3/2010	$895.00	975	($80.00)
3	Main Campus Housing A	207	9/18/2010	9/29/2010	$570.00	605	($35.00)
8	Main Campus Housing A	111	9/28/2010	10/14/2010	$1,180.00	1280	($100.00)
7	Main Campus Housing A	708	10/21/2010	10/26/2010	$250.00	225	$25.00
6	Main Campus Housing B	206	9/28/2010	10/9/2010	$830.00	880	($50.00)
7	South Campus Housing C	111	11/13/2010	11/20/2010	$255.00	280	($25.00)
4	South Campus Housing C	101	10/25/2010	11/15/2010	$1,920.00	2100	($180.00)
5	Main Campus Housing B	610	11/16/2010	11/30/2010	$1,280.00	1400	($120.00)
5	Main Campus Housing A	309	10/29/2010	11/15/2010	$790.00	850	($60.00)
8	North Satellite Housing D	402	11/2/2010	11/13/2010	$830.00	880	($50.00)
12	Main Campus Housing B	414	12/5/2010	12/9/2010	$195.00	200	($5.00)
8	Main Campus Housing B	403	11/18/2010	12/2/2010	$1,150.00	1260	($110.00)
13	Main Campus Housing B	103	11/27/2010	12/11/2010	$1,150.00	1260	($110.00)
2	Main Campus Housing A	410	12/2/2010	12/21/2010	$750.00	760	($10.00)
3	North Satellite Housing D	203	12/30/2010	1/15/2011	$960.00	1040	($80.00)
4	Main Campus Housing B	402	12/20/2010	1/7/2011	$1,180.00	1260	($80.00)
7	Main Campus Housing A	404	1/6/2011	1/15/2011	$380.00	405	($25.00)
5	Main Campus Housing B	304	1/2/2011	1/20/2011	$1,180.00	1260	($80.00)

Record: 1 of 39 No Filter Search

Figure 9-20 The datasheet now shows only the rows where the calculation is different than the stored value.

Finding the rows that differ in this way has the added benefit of displaying the calculated difference. If you're interested only in finding the rows that differ but don't care about the amount of the difference, you don't need the second expression at all. You can find the rows you want by placing the expression <>*[TotalCharge]* in the Criteria line under the first expression you entered. This asks Access to compare the amount calculated at the straight daily rate with the value in the TotalCharge field stored in the record and display the row only when the two values are not equal.

You might have inferred from the earlier discussion about entering criteria that you can use only constant values in the Criteria and Or lines. As you can see, you can also compare the value of one field or expression with another field or expression containing a reference to a field.

INSIDE OUT Adding Parentheses to Expressions for Clarity

You might have noticed that we placed an extra set of parentheses around the original expression we built to calculate the amount at the daily rate before subtracting that amount from the stored value. If you study Table 9-4 carefully, you'll see that we really didn't have to do this because Access would perform the multiplication before doing the final subtract. However, we find it's a good practice to add parentheses to make the sequence of operations crystal clear—we don't always remember the order of precedence rules, and we don't want to have to go looking up the information in Help every time we build an expression. Adding the parentheses makes sure we get the results we want.

So far, you have built fairly simple expressions. When you want to create a more complex expression, sometimes the Expression Builder can be useful, as discussed in the next section.

Using the Expression Builder

For more complex expressions, Access 2010 provides a utility called the Expression Builder. In Chapter 6, "Designing Web Tables," you learned about the Expression Builder when you created Calculated data types and validation rules. You also learned how to use the new IntelliSense feature built into the Expression Builder in Access 2010. In this section, we'll show you additional ways the Expression Builder can help you construct expressions.

Let's say you want to double-check the total amount owed for a reservation in the sample database. You have to work with several fields to do this—CheckInDate, CheckOutDate, DailyRate, and WeeklyRate. You need to calculate the number of weeks to charge at the WeeklyRate and then charge the remaining days at the DailyRate. To see how the Expression Builder works, start a new query on the tblReservations table. Click in an empty field in the design grid, and then click the Builder button in the Query Setup group of the Design contextual tab. Access opens the Expression Builder dialog box, shown in Figure 9-21.

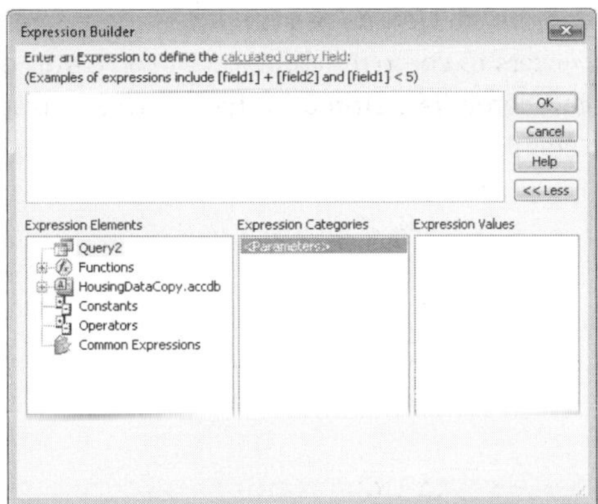

Figure 9-21 The Expression Builder dialog box helps you build simple and complex expressions.

In the upper part of the dialog box is a blank text box in which you can build an expression. You can type the expression yourself, but it's sometimes more accurate to find field names, operators, and function names in the three panes in the lower part of the dialog box.

In Access 2010, the Expression Builder shows the functions, constants, and operators applicable to the current context. For example, in Figure 9-21, Access shows you only the list of functions, constants, and operators you can use for expressions in a client query under the Expression Elements pane on the far left. Access also lists the name of your database file along with all the field names and objects contained within your database. The middle pane, Expression Categories, changes based on what you select in the Expression Elements pane. For example, if you click Operators under Expression Elements, the Expression Categories pane lists several group names of operators you can use in your expression. The right pane, Expression Values, shows you all possible values you can use based on the currently highlighted category selected in the middle pane. The expression you need to build, which we'll walk you through in detail in the next few pages, will ultimately look like this:

```
((DateDiff("d", [tblReservations]![CheckInDate], [tblReservations]![CheckOutDate]) \
7) * [WeeklyRate]) + ((DateDiff("d", [tblReservations]![CheckInDate], [tblReservation
s]![CheckOutDate]) Mod 7) * [DailyRate])
```

You can use the Expression Builder in a couple of different ways to help you correctly construct this expression. Start by double-clicking the Functions category in the left pane, then select Built-In Functions to see the list of function categories in the center pane and the list of functions within the selected category in the right pane. Select the Date/Time category in the center pane to narrow down the choices. Here, you can see the DateDiff function (which you used earlier) as well as several other built-in functions you can use. (You can find a list of the most useful functions and their descriptions in Article 4, "Visual Basic Function Reference," on the companion CD.)

Double-click the DateDiff function in the right pane to add it to the expression text box at the top of the Expression Builder. When you add a function to your expression in this way, the Expression Builder shows you the parameters required by the function. Access also displays the parameters of the function and additional information about the DateDiff function at the bottom of the dialog box. You can click any parameter to highlight it in the text box at the top of the Expression Builder and type a value or select a value from one of the lists in the bottom panes. Click <<interval>> and overwrite it with **"d"**. (See Table 9-3 for a list of all the possible interval settings.) You'll notice that Access displays a ScreenTip beneath the expression after you overwrite <<interval>>, as shown in Figure 9-22. Access highlights which parameter you are currently working on in the ScreenTip.

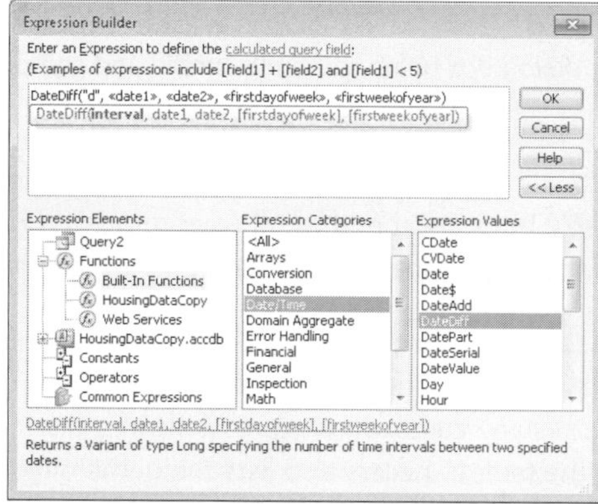

Figure 9-22 Access displays the parameters for the expression in a ScreenTip as you fill in the expression.

INSIDE OUT Moving the Expression Builder ScreenTip

If the ScreenTip beneath the expression obstructs your view, you can move it to a different location on the screen. When you place the mouse pointer over the ScreenTip, the pointer changes to a four-arrow cross-hair, and you can then drag the ScreenTip to a new location.

You need to insert the CheckInDate field from tblReservations for <<date1>> and the CheckOutDate field for <<date2>>. Click <<date1>> to highlight it and double-click HousingDataCopy in the left pane to open the list of objects in the database. Click the plus sign next to Tables to expand the list to show all the tables in this database. Scroll down until you find tblReservations and select it to see the list of field names in the second pane. Double-click CheckInDate. Then click <<date2>>, and double-click CheckOutDate. You don't need the <<firstweekday>> or <<firstweek>> parameters, so click them and press the Delete key to remove them. (You can also remove the extra commas, such as after the CheckOutDate field, if you like.) The Expression Builder should now look like Figure 9-23. Note that in Figure 9-23, we expanded the height of the Expression Builder dialog box so you can see more objects listed in the Expression Elements pane.

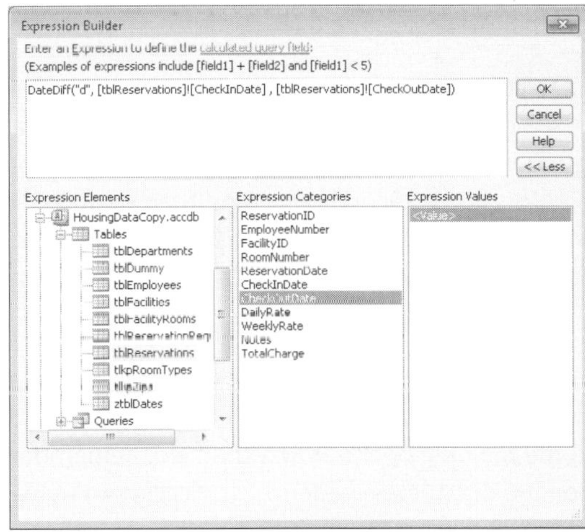

Figure 9-23 Create a calculation using table field names in the Expression Builder dialog box.

You'll notice that the Expression Builder pastes *[tblReservations]![CheckInDate]* into the expression area, not just *CheckInDate*. There are two good reasons for this. First, the Expression Builder doesn't know whether you might include other tables in this query and whether some of those tables might have field names that are identical to the ones you're selecting now. The way to avoid conflicts is to *fully qualify* the field names by preceding them with the table name. When working in queries, separate the table name from the field name with a period or an exclamation point. Second, you should enclose all names of objects in Access in brackets ([ ]). If you designed the name without any blank spaces, you can leave out the brackets, but it's always good practice to include them.

INSIDE OUT Understanding Name Separators in SQL

As you'll learn in Chapter 25, in most cases you should separate the name of an object from the name of an object within that object (for example, a field within a table) with an exclamation point. When you build an expression in the Expression Builder, you'll find that the Expression Builder separates names using exclamation points. However, as you'll learn in Article 2, the standard for the SQL database query language uses a period between the name of a table and the name of a field within the table. To be most compatible with the SQL standard when constructing a query expression, use a period between a table name and a field name. Access accepts either an exclamation point or a period in query design.

Next, you need to divide by 7 to calculate the number of weeks. You're not interested in any fractional part of a week, so you need to use the integer divide (\) operator. You can either type the operator, or scroll down in the leftmost pane, select Operators to open that list, select Arithmetic operators in the second pane, and then double-click the integer divide operator (\) in the rightmost list to add it to your expression. Make sure the insertion point in the expression box is positioned after the integer divide operator and then type the number 7.

The next operation you need is to multiply the expression you have thus far by the WeeklyRate field from tblReservations. If you like, you can add left and right parentheses around the expression before adding the multiply operator and the field. Remember from Table 9-4 that multiplication and division are of equal precedence, so Access evaluates the division before the multiplication (left to right) even if you don't add the parentheses. But, as we noted earlier, we like to make the precedence of operations crystal clear, so we recommend that you add the parentheses. Press the Home key to go to the beginning of the expression, add a left parenthesis, press the End key to go to the end, add a right parenthesis, double-click the multiply operator (*) in the rightmost list, and finally select the field WeeklyRate from the tblReservations field list.

Note

WeekyRate and DailyRate are currency fields. DateDiff returns an integer, and the result of an integer divide (\) or a modulus (Mod) operation is an integer. Whenever you ask Access to evaluate an arithmetic expression, it returns a result that has a data type sufficiently complex to contain the result. As you might expect, multiplying an integer (a simple data type) with a currency field (a more complex data type) returns a currency field.

You need to add this entire expression to the calculation for remaining days at the daily rate, so press Ctrl+Home again and add one more left parenthesis, press the Ctrl+End key, and add one more right parenthesis to complete this first part of the expression. Double-click the addition operator (+) in the rightmost list to add it to your expression. Rather than scan back and forth to add parentheses as we build the second part of the expression, add two more left parentheses to start building the calculation for extra days. You need to create another DateDiff expression, but this time we'll utilize the IntelliSense feature of the Expression Builder. Type the letter **d** and Access shows you a list of functions that all start with that letter, as shown in Figure 9-24.

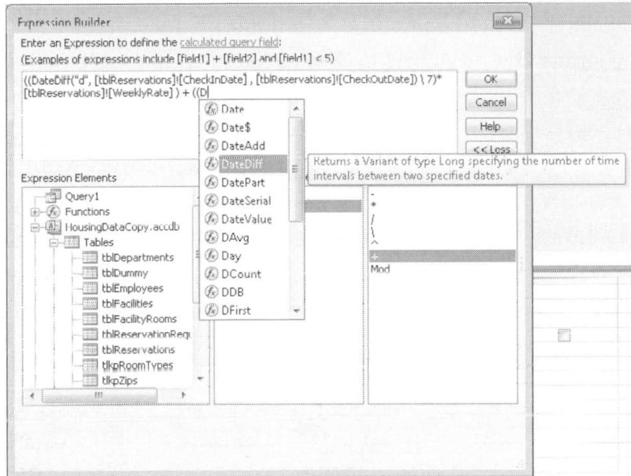

Figure 9-24 Access displays a list of functions when you begin to type an expression.

If you continue typing letters, Access reduces the list of functions to match the letters you are typing. If no functions or objects exist with the letters you type, Access dismisses the list. (You can also dismiss the list yourself by pressing Esc at any time.) Use the down arrow to highlight the DateDiff function and then press Enter or Tab. Access writes the rest of the letters for the DateDiff function for you, adds a left parenthesis, and displays the arguments for the DateDiff function in a screens tip, as shown in Figure 9-25. Note that in Figure 9-25, we clicked Less to collapse the bottom part of the Expression Builder dialog box to focus just on writing the expression. To expand the dialog box, click the button again, now labeled More, and Access shows you the three panes in the bottom part of the dialog box.

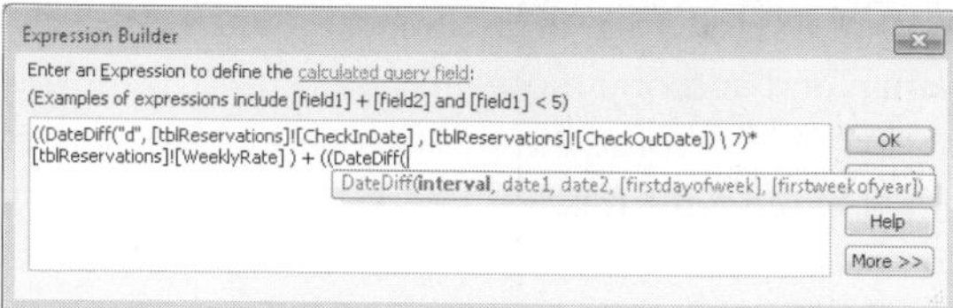

Figure 9-25 Access can finish typing your function name when you select it from the IntelliSense drop-down list of functions.

Type **"d"** for the first parameter of the DateDiff function followed by a comma. Next, you need to add the CheckInDate field again from the tblReservations table for the date1 parameter. Type the letters **tb** and Access displays a list of all the table names in this database. Use the down arrow to highlight tblReservations and press Enter or Tab to select it. To view a list of all the field names in the tblReservations table, you can either type a period (.) or exclamation point (!). Remember, as discussed earlier, that Access accepts either an exclamation point or a period in query design. Type a period and Access displays all the fields in the tblReservations table, as shown in Figure 9-26. You'll notice in Figure 9-26 that Access adds brackets around the table name.

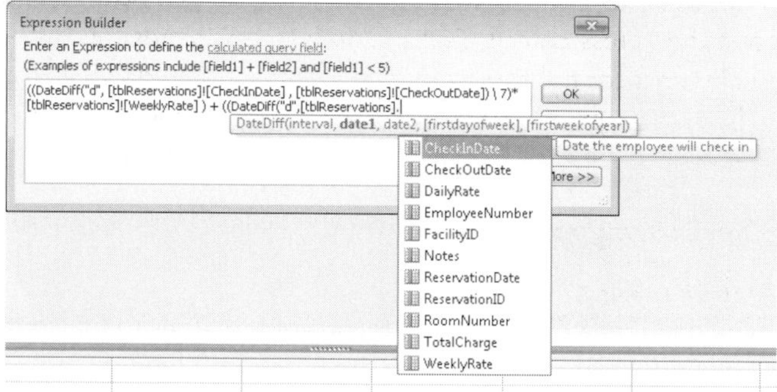

Figure 9-26 The IntelliSense feature in Access can display all the field names in your table.

Press Enter or Tab and Access adds the CheckInDate field to the expression because it is the first field in the drop-down list of field names. Type a comma to move to the second parameter, type **tb** again to bring up a list of the tables, use the down arrow to highlight the tblReservations table, and then press Enter or Tab to add the table name to the expression. Now, type a period to display a list of all the field names in the tblReservations table, use the down arrow to highlight the CheckOutDate field, and then press Enter or Tab to add the field to your expression. You don't need the last two parameters of the DateDiff function—firstweekday and firstweek—so end this part of the expression by typing a right parentheses. Your expression up to this point should look like Figure 9-27.

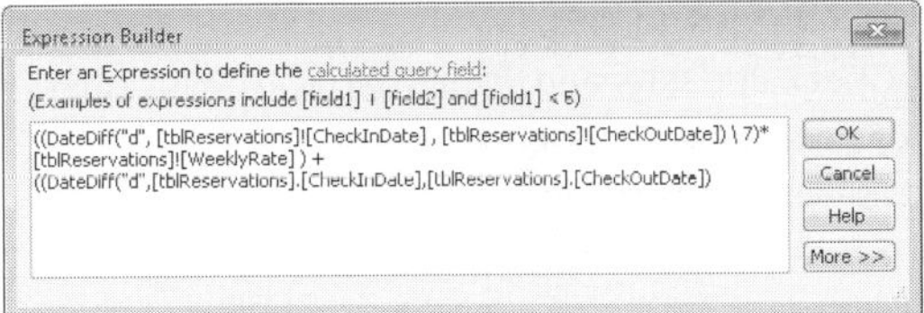

Figure 9-27 After you finish the second DateDiff function, your expression should match this figure.

Now, you need to know how many days beyond full weeks are in the reservation. You might be tempted to divide by 7 again and try to extract the remainder, but there's a handy operator that returns only the remainder of a division for you—Mod. Scroll down in the left pane and select Operators. In the middle pane, select Arithmetic to see only the arithmetic operators in the right pane. Double-click Mod to add it to your expression after the parentheses.

We're almost done. Type the number **7**, add a right parentheses to close the Mod calculation, and then double-click the multiply operator button in the right pane. The last step you need to take is to add the DailyRate field from the tblReservations table to complete the expression. Type **tb** to display the list of table names, use the down arrow to highlight tblReservations, and then press Enter or Tab to add it to the expression. Type a period to display a list of field names for the tblReservations table, use the down arrow to highlight the DailyRate field, and then press Enter or Tab. Type one last right parentheses to finish the expression. Verify that your completed expression exactly matches the one in Figure 9-28.

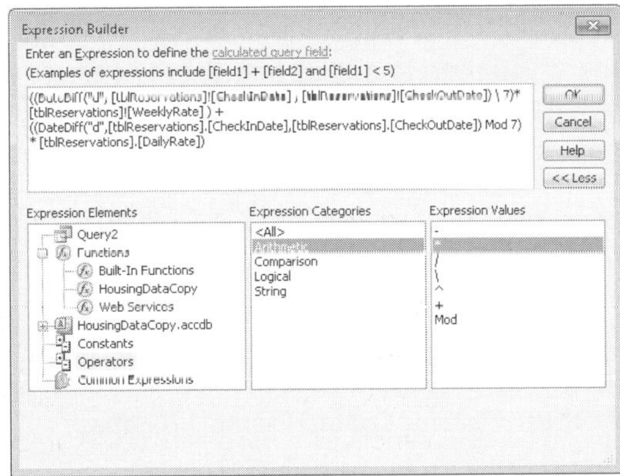

Figure 9-28 Your completed expression in the Expression Builder dialog box should match this figure.

Click OK to paste your result into the design grid. Go ahead and add ReservationID, FacilityID, RoomNumber, CheckInDate, CheckOutDate, and TotalCharge to your query grid. When you switch to Datasheet view, your result should look like Figure 9-29.

Query2

Expr1	Reservation ID	Facility	Room	Check-In	Check-Out	Charge
$455.00	1	Main Campus Housing A	810	8/30/2010	9/11/2010	$455.00
$1,040.00	2	Main Campus Housing B	111	9/17/2010	9/28/2010	$1,040.00
$195.00	3	North Satellite Housing D	305	9/13/2010	9/16/2010	$195.00
$1,420.00	4	Main Campus Housing A	502	10/8/2010	10/25/2010	$1,420.00
$100.00	5	Main Campus Housing B	214	9/19/2010	9/21/2010	$100.00
$1,600.00	6	Main Campus Housing A	902	9/25/2010	10/14/2010	$1,600.00
$1,240.00	7	South Campus Housing C	501	8/24/2010	9/6/2010	$1,200.00
$620.00	8	Main Campus Housing A	509	10/10/2010	10/23/2010	$620.00
$210.00	9	Main Campus Housing B	504	10/14/2010	10/17/2010	$210.00
$680.00	10	Main Campus Housing A	707	10/26/2010	11/8/2010	$680.00
$895.00	11	Main Campus Housing B	301	9/18/2010	10/3/2010	$895.00
$570.00	12	Main Campus Housing A	207	9/18/2010	9/29/2010	$570.00
$1,180.00	13	Main Campus Housing A	111	9/28/2010	10/14/2010	$1,180.00
$225.00	14	Main Campus Housing A	708	10/21/2010	10/26/2010	$250.00
$830.00	15	Main Campus Housing B	206	9/28/2010	10/9/2010	$830.00
$255.00	16	South Campus Housing C	111	11/13/2010	11/20/2010	$255.00
$1,920.00	17	South Campus Housing C	101	10/25/2010	11/15/2010	$1,920.00
$450.00	18	Main Campus Housing A	702	11/16/2010	11/21/2010	$450.00
$1,280.00	19	Main Campus Housing B	610	11/16/2010	11/30/2010	$1,280.00
$790.00	20	Main Campus Housing A	309	10/29/2010	11/15/2010	$790.00
$830.00	21	North Satellite Housing D	402	11/2/2010	11/13/2010	$830.00
$350.00	22	South Campus Housing C	103	10/27/2010	11/1/2010	$350.00
$200.00	23	Main Campus Housing B	414	12/5/2010	12/9/2010	$195.00
$220.00	24	Main Campus Housing A	207	11/18/2010	11/22/2010	$220.00
$110.00	25	South Campus Housing C	607	12/20/2010	12/22/2010	$110.00

Record: 7 of 58 No Filter Search

Figure 9-29 Switch to Datasheet view to see the result of your complex calculation expression.

Do you notice any stored values that don't match what you just calculated? (Hint: Look at the highlighted row.) If you haven't changed the sample data, you'll find several rows that we purposefully updated with invalid TotalCharge values. Here's a challenge: Go back to Design view and enter the criteria you need to display only the rows where your calculated charge doesn't match the TotalCharge stored in the table. You can find the solution saved as qxmplUnmatchedCharges in the HousingDataCopy.accdb sample database.

We used the DateDiff function to solve this problem, but Access 2010 has several other useful functions to help you deal with date and time values. For example, you might want to see only a part of the date or time value in your query. You might also want to use these functions to help you filter the results in your query. Table 9-5 explains each date and time function and includes filter examples that use the ContactDateTime field in the tblContactEvents table in the Conrad Systems Contacts sample database.

Table 9-5 Date and Time Functions

Function	Description	Example
Day(*date*)	Returns a value from 1 through 31 for the day of the month.	To select records with contact events that occurred after the 10th of any month, enter **Day([ContactDateTime])** in an empty column on the Field line and enter **>10** as the criterion for that field.
Month(*date*)	Returns a value from 1 through 12 for the month of the year.	To find all contact events that occurred in March (of any year), enter **Month([ContactDateTime])** in an empty column on the Field line and enter **3** as the criterion for that field.
Year(*date*)	Returns a value from 100 through 9999 for the year.	To find contact events that happened in 2011, enter **Year([ContactDateTime])** in an empty column on the Field line and enter **2011** as the criterion for that field.
Weekday(*date*)	As a default, returns a value from 1 (Sunday) through 7 (Saturday) for the day of the week.	To find contact events that occurred between Monday and Friday, enter **Weekday([ContactDateTime])** in an empty column on the Field line and enter **Between 2 And 6** as the criterion for that field.
Hour(*date*)	Returns a value from 0 through 23 for the hour of the day.	To find contact events that happened before noon, enter **Hour([ContactDateTime])** in an empty column on the Field line and enter **<12** as the criterion for that field.
DateAdd(*interval, amount, date*)	Adds an amount in the interval you specify to a date/time value.	To find contact events that occurred more than six months ago, enter **<DateAdd("m", –6, Date())** as the criterion under ContactDateTime. (See also the Date function below.)
DatePart(*interval, date*)	Returns a portion of the date or time, depending on the interval code you supply. Useful interval codes are "q" for quarter of the year (1 through 4) and "ww" for week of the year (1 through 53).	To find contact events in the second quarter, enter **DatePart("q", [ContactDateTime])** in an empty column on the Field line, and enter **2** as the criterion for that field.
Date()	Returns the current system date.	To select contact events that happened more than 30 days ago, enter **<(Date() – 30)** as the criterion under ContactDateTime.

For additional useful functions, see Article 4, "Visual Basic Function Reference," on the companion CD.

Specifying Field Names

Every field must have a name. By default, the name of a simple field in a query is the name of the field from the source table. However, when you create a new field using an expression, the expression doesn't have a name unless you or Access assigns one. You have seen that when you create an expression in the Field row of the design grid, Access adds a prefix such as *Expr1* followed by a colon—that is the name that Access is assigning to your expression. Remember, the column heading for the field is, by default, the field name unless you specify a different caption property setting. As you know, you can assign or change a caption for a field in a query by using the field's property sheet.

Understanding Field Names and Captions

In the world of tables and queries, every field—even calculated ones—must have a name. When you create a field in a table, you give it a name. When you use a table in a query and include a field from the table in the query output, the name of the field output by the query is the same as the field name in the table. If you create a calculated field in a query, you must assign a name to that field. If you don't, Access assigns an ugly *ExprN* name for you. But you can override this and assign your own field name to expressions. You can also override the default field name for a simple field with another name. When you use a query in another query or a form or report, or you open a query as a recordset in Microsoft Visual Basic, you use the field name to indicate which field you want to fetch from the query.

You can also define a Caption property for a field. When you do that, what you put in the caption becomes the external label for the field. You'll see the caption in column headings in Datasheet view. Later, when you begin to work with forms and reports, you'll find that the caption becomes the default label for the field. If you don't define a caption, Access shows you the field name instead.

You can change or assign field names that will appear in the recordset of a query. This feature is particularly useful when you've calculated a value in the query that you'll use in a form, a report, or another query. In the queries shown in Figures 9-15, 9-17, and 9-19, you calculated a value and Access assigned a temporary field name. You can replace this name with something more meaningful. For example, in the first query, you might want to use something like FullName and CityStateZip. In the second query, RecalculatedCharge might be appropriate. To change a name generated by Access, replace *ExprN* with the name you want in the Field row in the query design grid. To assign a new name to a field, place the insertion point at the beginning of the field specification and insert the new name followed by a colon. Figure 9-30 shows the first query with the field names changed.

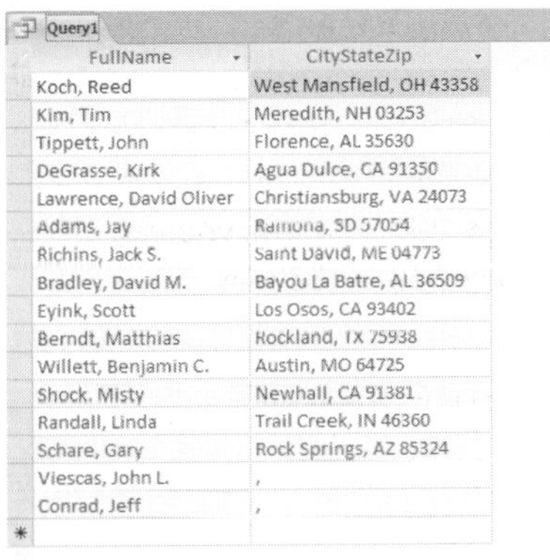

Query1

FullName	CityStateZip
Koch, Reed	West Mansfield, OH 43358
Kim, Tim	Meredith, NH 03253
Tippett, John	Florence, AL 35630
DeGrasse, Kirk	Agua Dulce, CA 91350
Lawrence, David Oliver	Christiansburg, VA 24073
Adams, Jay	Ramona, SD 57054
Richins, Jack S.	Saint David, ME 04773
Bradley, David M.	Bayou La Batre, AL 36509
Eyink, Scott	Los Osos, CA 93402
Berndt, Matthias	Rockland, TX 75938
Willett, Benjamin C.	Austin, MO 64725
Shock, Misty	Newhall, CA 91381
Randall, Linda	Trail Creek, IN 46360
Schare, Gary	Rock Springs, AZ 85324
Viescas, John L.	,
Conrad, Jeff	,
*	

Figure 9-30 You can change the Expr1 and Expr2 field names shown in Figure 9-16 to display more meaningful field names.

Note that we could have made the column headings you see even more readable by also assigning a caption to these fields via the field's property sheet. We might have chosen something like Person Name for the first field and City-State-Zip for the second field. Keep in mind that setting the caption does not change the actual name of the field when you use the query in a form, a report, or Visual Basic code.

Sorting Data

Normally, Access 2010 displays the rows in your recordset in the order in which they're retrieved from the database. You can add sorting information to determine the sequence of the data in a query. Click in the Sort row for the field you want to sort on, click the arrow in this row, and then select Ascending or Descending from the list. In the example shown in Figure 9-31, the query results are to be sorted in descending order based on the calculated NewTotalCharge field. (Note that we have given the calculated field a field name.) The recordset will list the most expensive reservations first. The resulting Datasheet view is shown in Figure 9-32. You can find this query saved as qryXmplChargeCalcSorted in the HousingDataCopy.accdb sample database.

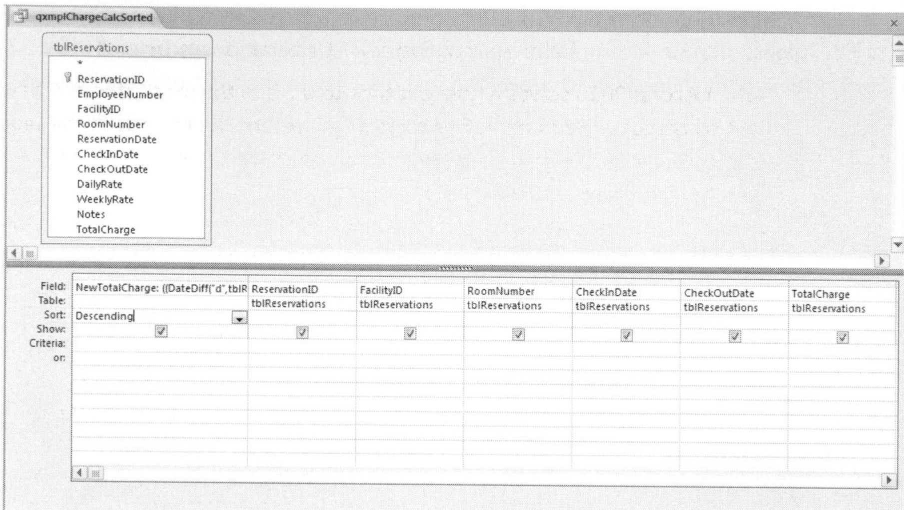

Figure 9-31 Access sorts the query on the NewTotalCharge field in descending order.

qxmplChargeCalcSorted

NewTotalCharge	Reservation	Facility	Room	Check-In	Check-Out	Charge
$1,920.00	17	South Campus Housing C	101	10/25/2010	11/15/2010	$1,920.00
$1,690.00	53	South Campus Housing C	106	2/14/2011	3/6/2011	$1,690.00
$1,600.00	6	Main Campus Housing A	902	9/25/2010	10/14/2010	$1,600.00
$1,420.00	4	Main Campus Housing A	502	10/8/2010	10/25/2010	$1,420.00
$1,380.00	41	South Campus Housing C	401	12/13/2010	12/28/2010	$1,380.00
$1,280.00	56	South Campus Housing C	109	2/3/2011	2/17/2011	$1,280.00
$1,280.00	19	Main Campus Housing B	610	11/16/2010	11/30/2010	$1,280.00
$1,240.00	7	South Campus Housing C	501	8/24/2010	9/6/2010	$1,200.00
$1,180.00	13	Main Campus Housing A	111	9/28/2010	10/14/2010	$1,180.00
$1,180.00	35	Main Campus Housing B	402	12/20/2010	1/7/2011	$1,180.00
$1,180.00	38	Main Campus Housing B	304	1/2/2011	1/20/2011	$1,180.00
$1,150.00	30	Main Campus Housing B	103	11/27/2010	12/11/2010	$1,150.00
$1,150.00	28	Main Campus Housing B	403	11/18/2010	12/2/2010	$1,150.00
$1,040.00	48	Main Campus Housing B	402	2/4/2011	2/20/2011	$1,040.00
$1,040.00	2	Main Campus Housing B	111	9/17/2010	9/28/2010	$1,040.00
$960.00	34	North Satellite Housing D	203	12/30/2010	1/15/2011	$960.00
$960.00	49	Main Campus Housing B	114	2/10/2011	3/3/2011	$960.00
$910.00	42	Main Campus Housing B	212	1/8/2011	1/20/2011	$910.00
$895.00	11	Main Campus Housing B	301	9/18/2010	10/3/2010	$895.00
$850.00	43	South Campus Housing C	208	1/25/2011	2/14/2011	$850.00
$830.00	21	North Satellite Housing D	402	11/2/2010	11/13/2010	$830.00
$830.00	15	Main Campus Housing B	206	9/28/2010	10/9/2010	$830.00
$790.00	20	Main Campus Housing A	309	10/29/2010	11/15/2010	$790.00
$730.00	44	Main Campus Housing B	102	1/15/2011	1/26/2011	$730.00
$710.00	32	Main Campus Housing A	410	12/2/2010	12/21/2010	$750.00

Record: 1 of 58 No Filter Search

Figure 9-32 Datasheet view shows the recordset of the query shown in Figure 9-31 sorted on the NewTotalCharge field.

INSIDE OUT Why Specifying Sort Criteria Is Important

When Access 2010 solves a query, it tries to do it in the most efficient way. When you first construct and run a query, Access might return the records in the sequence you expect (for example, in primary key sequence of the table). However, if you want to be sure Access always returns rows in this order, you must specify sort criteria. As you later add and remove rows in your table, Access might decide that fetching rows in a different sequence might be faster, which, in the absence of sorting criteria, might result in a different row sequence than you intended.

You can also sort on multiple fields. Access honors your sorting criteria from left to right in the design grid. If, for example, you want to sort by FacilityID ascending and then by NewTotalCharge descending, you should include the FacilityID field to the left of the NewTotalCharge field. If the additional field you want to sort is already in the design grid but in the wrong location, click the column selector box (the tinted box above the field row) to select the entire column and then click the selector box again and drag the field to its new location. If you want the field that is out of position to still appear where you originally placed it, add the field to the design grid again in the correct sorting sequence, clear the Show check box (you don't want two copies of the field displayed), and set the Sort specification. Figure 9-33 shows the query shown in Figure 9-31 modified to sort first by FacilityID and then by NewTotalCharge, but leave FacilityID displayed after ReservationID. We saved this query in the HousingDataCopy.accdb sample database as qxmplChargeCalcSortedTwo.

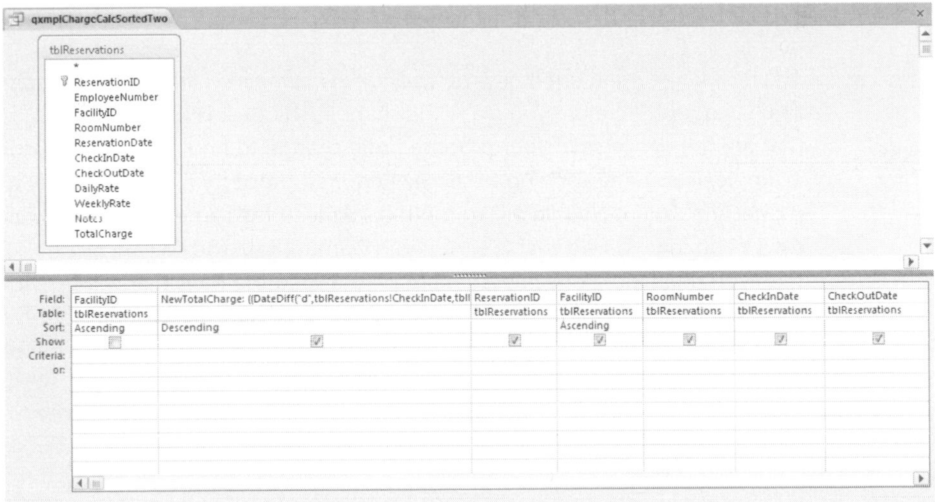

Figure 9-33 This example sorts on two fields while maintaining the original field sequence in the query output.

INSIDE OUT **A Reminder: Why Lookup Properties Can Be Confusing**

If you open the datasheet of qxmplChargeCalcSortedTwo and scroll down in the recordset, you'll find the Facility column sorted as Main Campus Housing A, Main Campus Housing B, South Campus Housing C, and North Satellite Housing D. Why does South appear before North if the values are supposed to be sorted in ascending order? Remember, in Chapter 5, that we warned you about Lookup properties confusing the display you see. The information you're seeing in the datasheet comes from the Lookup defined on the FacilityID column in tblReservations—you're seeing the related facility name from tblFacilities. However, the actual value of FacilityID is a number. You can click on the FacilityID column, open the field's property sheet, click the Lookup tab, and set the Display Control property to Text Box to see the actual number value. When you do this and look at the datasheet again, you'll see that the values are sorted correctly.

Testing Validation Rule Changes

You learned in Chapters 4 and 6 how to define both field and table validation rules. You also learned in Chapter 5 that you can change these rules even after you have data in your table. Access 2010 warns you if some of the data in your table doesn't satisfy the new rule, but it doesn't tell you which rows have problems.

Checking a New Field Validation Rule

The best way to find out if any rows will fail a new field validation rule is to write a query to test your data before you make the change. The trick is that you must specify criteria that are the converse of your proposed rule change to find the rows that don't match. For example, if you are planning to set the Required property to Yes or specify a Validation Rule property of Is Not Null on a field (both tests mean the same thing), you want to look for rows containing a field that Is Null. If you want to limit the daily price of a room to <= 90, then you must look for values that are > 90 to find the rows that will fail. Another way to think about asking for the converse of a validation rule is to put the word *Not* in front of the rule. If the new rule is going to be <= 90, then Not <= 90 will find the bad rows.

Let's see what we need to do to test a proposed validation rule change to tblFacilityRooms in the sample database. The daily room rate should not exceed $90, so the new rule in the DailyRate field will be <=90. (We're only *proposing* changing the validation rule at the table level, so don't change the rule.) To test for rooms that exceed this new limit, start a new query on tblFacilityRooms. Include the fields FacilityID, RoomNumber, RoomType, DailyRate, and WeeklyRate in the query's design grid. (You need at least FacilityID and RoomNumber—the primary key fields—to be able to identify which rows fail.) Under DailyRate, enter the converse of the new rule: either **>90** or **Not <=90**. Your query should look like Figure 9-34.

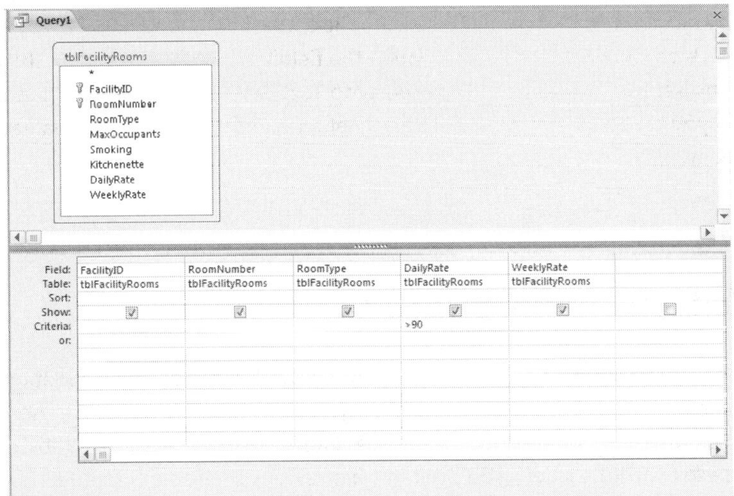

Figure 9-34 Create a new query to test a proposed new field validation rule.

If you run this query against the original data in the sample database, you'll find 26 rooms that are priced higher than the new proposed rule. As you'll learn in "Working in Query Datasheet View," on page 589, you can update these rows by typing a new value directly in the query datasheet.

Let's try something. Select one of the invalid values you found in the query datasheet and try to type the new maximum value of $90. If you try to save the row, you'll get an error message because there's a table validation rule that prevents you from setting a DailyRate value that when multiplied by 7 is more than the WeeklyRate value. It looks like you'll have to fix both values if you want to change your field validation rule.

Checking a New Table Validation Rule

Checking a proposed new field validation rule is simple. But what about making a change to a table validation rule? Typically, a table validation rule compares one field with another, so to check a new rule, you'll need more complex criteria in your query.

There's already a table validation rule in tblFacilityRooms in the HousingDataCopy.accdb sample database. The rule makes sure that the weekly rate is not more than seven times the daily rate—it wouldn't be much of a discount if it were! Suppose you now want to be sure that the weekly rate reflects a true discount from the daily rate. Your proposed new rule might make sure that the weekly rate is no more than six times the daily rate—if an employee stays a full week, the last night is essentially free. Your new rule might look like the following:

```
([DailyRate]*6)>=[WeeklyRate]
```

Therefore, you need to write a query that checks the current values in the WeeklyRate field to see if any will fail the new rule. Note that you could also create an expression to calculate DailyRate times 6 and compare that value with WeeklyRate. When the expression you want to test involves a calculation on one side of the comparison with a simple field value on the other side of the comparison, it's easier to compare the simple field with the expression. Remember, you need to create the converse of the expression to find rows that won't pass the new rule.

You can start with the query you built in the previous section or create a new query. You need at least the primary key fields from the table as well as the fields you need to perform the comparison. In this case, you need to compare the current value of WeeklyRate with the expression on DailyRate. Let's turn the expression around so that it's easier to see what you need to enter in the query grid. The expression looks like this:

```
[WeeklyRate]<=([DailyRate]*6)
```

To test the converse on the WeeklyRate field's Criteria row of your query, you need either

```
>([DailyRate]*6)
```

or

```
Not <=([DailyRate]*6)
```

Your test query should look like Figure 9-35.

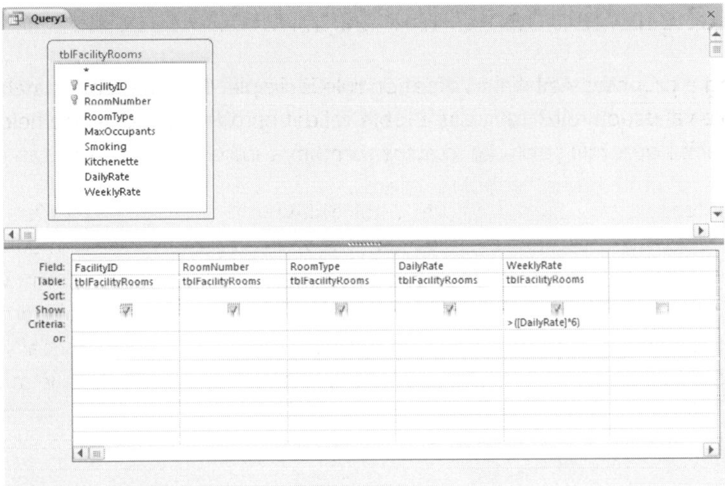

Figure 9-35 You can create a query to test a new table validation rule.

If you run this query, you'll find that nearly all the rows in the table fail the new test. When we loaded sample data into the table, we created weekly rates that are approximately 6.4 times the daily rate—so none of the rates pass the new test. In Chapter 11, you'll learn how to create an update query to fix both the daily and weekly rates to match the new rules discussed in this section.

Working in Query Datasheet View

When you're developing an application, you might need to work in table or query Datasheet view to help you load sample data or to solve problems in the queries, forms, and reports you're creating. You might also decide to create certain forms in your application that display information in Datasheet view. Also, the techniques for updating and manipulating data in forms are very similar to doing so in datasheets, so you need to understand how datasheets work to be able to explain to your users how to use your application. If you're using Access 2010 as a personal database to analyze information, you might frequently work with information in Datasheet view. In either case, you should understand how to work with data editing, and the best way to learn how is to understand viewing and editing data in Datasheet view.

Before you get started with the remaining examples in this chapter, open ContactsDataCopy.accdb from your sample files folder. In that database, you'll find a query named qryContactsDatasheet, which we'll use in the remainder of this chapter. We defined this query to select key fields from tblContacts and display a subdatasheet from tblContactEvents.

Moving Around and Using Keyboard Shortcuts

Open the qryContactsDatasheet query in the ContactsDataCopy.accdb database. You should see a result similar to Figure 9-36. Displaying different records or fields is simple. You can use the horizontal scroll bar to scroll through a table's fields, or you can use the vertical scroll bar to scroll through a table's records.

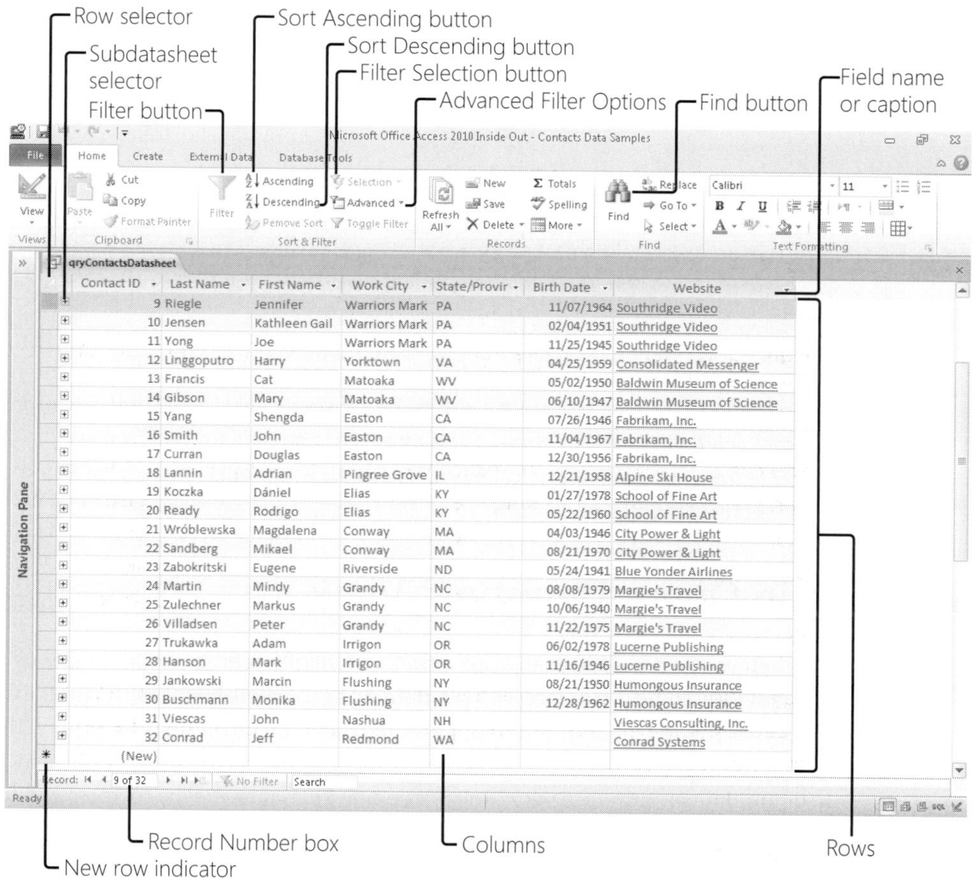

Figure 9-36 Open the Datasheet view of the qryContactsDatasheet query to begin learning about moving around and editing in a datasheet.

In the lower-left corner of the table in Datasheet view, you can see a set of navigation buttons and the Record Number box, as shown in Figure 9-37. The Record Number box shows the *relative record number* of the current record (meaning the number of the selected record in relation to the current set of records, also called a recordset). You might not see the current record in the window if you've scrolled the display. The number to the right of the new record button shows the total number of records in the current recordset. If you've applied a filter against the table (see "Searching for and Filtering Data," on page 611), this number might be less than the total number of records in the table or query.

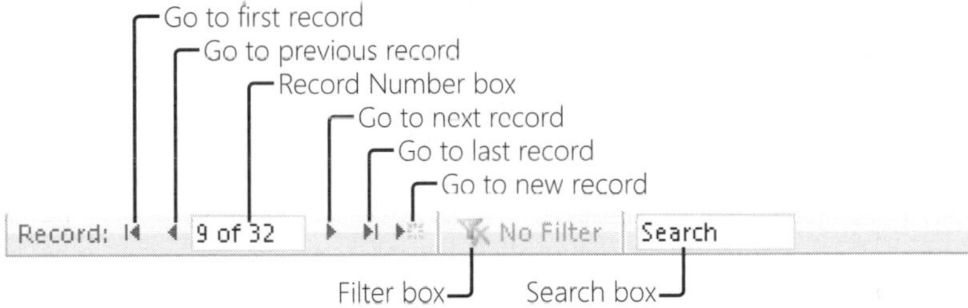

Figure 9-37 You can navigate through the datasheet records using the navigation buttons and Record Number box.

You can quickly move to the record you want by typing a value in the Record Number box and pressing Enter or by using the navigation buttons. You can also click the Go To command in the Find group on the Home tab on the ribbon to move to the first, last, next, or previous record, or to move to a new, empty record. You can make any record current by clicking anywhere in its row; the number in the Record Number box will change to indicate the row you've selected.

You might find it easier to use the keyboard rather than the mouse to move around in a datasheet, especially if you're typing new data. Table 9-6 lists the keyboard shortcuts for scrolling in a datasheet. Table 9-7 lists the keyboard shortcuts for selecting data in a datasheet.

Table 9-6 Keyboard Shortcuts for Scrolling in a Datasheet

Keys	Scrolling Action
Page Up	Up one page
Page Down	Down one page
Ctrl+Page Up	Left one page
Ctrl+Page Down	Right one page

Table 9-7 Keyboard Shortcuts for Selecting Data in a Datasheet

Keys	Selecting Action
Tab	Next field
Shift+Tab	Previous field
Home	First field, current record
End	Last field, current record
Up Arrow	Current field, previous record
Down Arrow	Current field, next record
Ctrl+Up Arrow	Current field, first record
Ctrl+Down Arrow	Current field, last record
Ctrl+Home	First field, first record
Ctrl+End	Last field, last record
Alt+F5	Record Number box
Ctrl+Spacebar	The current column
Shift+Spacebar	The current record
F2	When in a field, toggles between selecting all data in the field and single-character edit mode

Working with Subdatasheets

Access 2000 introduced a new feature that lets you display information from multiple related tables in a single datasheet. In the design we developed for the Conrad Systems Contacts sample database, contacts can have multiple contact events and contact products. In some cases, it might be useful to open a query on contacts and be able to see either related events or products in the same datasheet window.

You might have noticed the little plus-sign indicators in the datasheet for qryContactsDatasheet in Figure 9-36. Click the plus sign next to the second row to open the Contact Events Subdatasheet, as shown in Figure 9-38.

qryContactsDatasheet

	Contact ID	Last Name	First Name	Work City	State/Provir	Birth Date	Website
+	1	Stoklasa	Jan	Youngsville	PA	12/25/1955	Contoso, Ltd
−	2	Peterson	Palle	Youngsville	PA	06/07/1963	Contoso, Ltd

	Date / Time	Type	Notes	Follow up?	Follow-up D	Click to Add
	09/11/2010 17:23	1		☐		
	01/18/2011 15:06	1		☐		
*	01/16/2010 19:08			☐		

	Contact ID	Last Name	First Name	Work City	State/Provir	Birth Date	Website
+	3	Michaels	Tom	Youngsville	PA	07/17/1960	Contoso, Ltd
+	4	Dixon	Andrew	Kalamazoo	MI	04/08/1959	Fourth Coffee
+	5	West	Paul	Kalamazoo	MI	03/07/1964	Fourth Coffee
+	6	Kresnadi	Mario	Grosse Pointe	MI	03/24/1960	Coho Vineyard
+	7	Sousa	Anibal	Grosse Pointe	MI	05/09/1942	Coho Vineyard
+	8	Matthews	Joseph	Grosse Pointe	MI	09/13/1965	Coho Vineyard
+	9	Riegle	Jennifer	Warriors Mark	PA	11/07/1964	Southridge Video
+	10	Jensen	Kathleen Gail	Warriors Mark	PA	02/04/1951	Southridge Video
+	11	Yong	Joe	Warriors Mark	PA	11/25/1945	Southridge Video
+	12	Linggoputro	Harry	Yorktown	VA	04/25/1959	Consolidated Messenger
+	13	Francis	Cat	Matoaka	WV	05/02/1950	Baldwin Museum of Science
+	14	Gibson	Mary	Matoaka	WV	06/10/1947	Baldwin Museum of Science
+	15	Yang	Shengda	Easton	CA	07/26/1946	Fabrikam, Inc.
+	16	Smith	John	Easton	CA	11/04/1967	Fabrikam, Inc.
+	17	Curran	Douglas	Easton	CA	12/30/1956	Fabrikam, Inc.
+	18	Lannin	Adrian	Pingree Grove	IL	12/21/1958	Alpine Ski House
+	19	Koczka	Dániel	Elias	KY	01/27/1978	School of Fine Art
+	20	Ready	Rodrigo	Elias	KY	05/22/1960	School of Fine Art
+	21	Wróblewska	Magdalena	Conway	MA	04/03/1946	City Power & Light

Record: 1 of 2 | No Filter | Search

Figure 9-38 Click the plus sign to view the contact event details for the second contact in a subdatasheet.

A subdatasheet doesn't appear automatically in a query, even if you've defined subdatasheet properties for your table, as described in Chapter 4. We had to open the property sheet for the query in Design view and specify the subdatasheet you see. Figure 9-39 shows the properties we set. Note that you need to click the top part of the query design window around the tables to see the properties for the query in the Property Sheet window. You can find more details about setting these properties in Chapters 4 and 10.

Property Sheet

Selection type: Query Properties

General

Description	Sample query from Chapter 9
Default View	Datasheet
Output All Fields	No
Top Values	All
Unique Values	No
Unique Records	No
Source Database	(current)
Source Connect Str	
Record Locks	No Locks
Recordset Type	Dynaset
ODBC Timeout	60
Filter	
Order By	
Max Records	
Orientation	Left-to-Right
Subdatasheet Name	Table.tblContactEvents
Link Child Fields	ContactID
Link Master Fields	ContactID
Subdatasheet Height	0"
Subdatasheet Expanded	No
Filter On Load	No
Order By On Load	Yes

Figure 9-39 The property sheet for the qryContactsDatasheet query displays the subdatasheet properties.

You can click the plus sign (+) next to each order row to see the contact event detail information for that contact. If you want to expand or collapse all the subdatasheets, click More in the Records group on the Home tab, click Subdatasheet on the menu, and then click the option you want as shown in Figure 9-40.

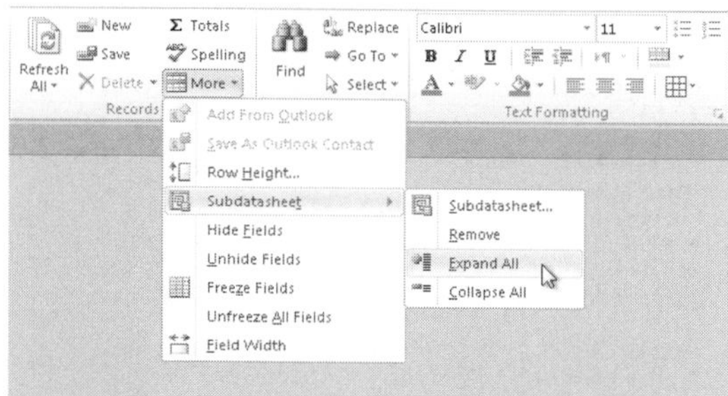

Figure 9-40 The Subdatasheet menu allows you to easily expand all subdatasheets, collapse all subdatasheets, or remove the currently displayed subdatasheet.

The information from the related tblContactEvents table is interesting, but what if you want to see the products the contact has purchased instead? To do this, while in Datasheet view, click More on the Home tab, click Subdatasheet on the menu, and then click Subdatasheet to see the dialog box shown in Figure 9-41.

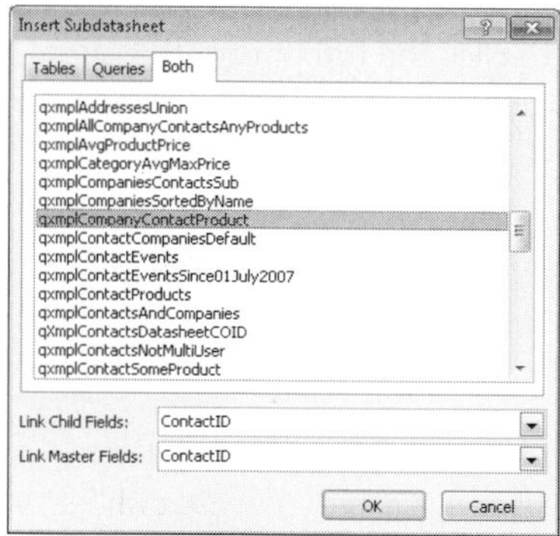

Figure 9-41 You can choose a different table to display other related information in a subdatasheet from the Insert Subdatasheet dialog box.

We built a query in the sample database that displays the related company and product information for a contact. Click the Queries tab or the Both tab and select qxmplCompany-ContactProduct to define the new subdatasheet. Click OK to close the Insert Subdatasheet dialog box.

When you return to the qryContactsDatasheet window, click More on the Home tab, click Subdatasheet on the menu, and click the Expand All option on the submenu. You will now see information about each product ordered, as shown in Figure 9-42. Note that you can also entirely remove a subdatasheet by clicking Remove on the menu, shown in Figure 9-40. Close the query when you are finished.

qryContactsDatasheet

Contact ID	Last Name	First Name	Work City	State/Provir	Birth Date	Website
1	Stoklasa	Jan	Youngsville	PA	12/25/1955	Contoso, Ltd

Company / Organization	FullName	Product Name	Product Typ	Date Sold	Price
Contoso, Ltd	Mrs. Jan Stoklasa	BO$$ Remote User	Remote User	12/4/2010	$99.00
Contoso, Ltd	Mrs. Jan Stoklasa	Upgrade to BO$$ Multi-Us	Multi-User	8/23/2010	$129.00
Contoso, Ltd	Mrs. Jan Stoklasa	BO$$ Single User Support,	Support	11/15/2010	$99.00
Contoso, Ltd	Mrs. Jan Stoklasa	BO$$ Multi-User Support,	Support	8/20/2010	$149.00
Contoso, Ltd	Mrs. Jan Stoklasa	CSD Tools Add-In	Single User	12/4/2010	$19.99
*					

Contact ID	Last Name	First Name	Work City	State/Provir	Birth Date	Website
2	Peterson	Palle	Youngsville	PA	06/07/1963	Contoso, Ltd

Company / Organization	FullName	Product Name	Product Typ	Date Sold	Price
*					

Contact ID	Last Name	First Name	Work City	State/Provir	Birth Date	Website
3	Michaels	Tom	Youngsville	PA	07/17/1960	Contoso, Ltd

Company / Organization	FullName	Product Name	Product Typ	Date Sold	Price
Contoso, Ltd	Mr. Tom Michaels	BO$$ Demo Edition, Multi	Multi-User	11/13/2010	$0.00
Contoso, Ltd	Mr. Tom Michaels	BO$$ Remote User	Remote User	12/3/2010	$99.00
Contoso, Ltd	Mr. Tom Michaels	CSD Tools Add-In	Single User	1/4/2011	$19.99
Contoso, Ltd	Mr. Tom Michaels	CSD Tools Add-In Demo E	Single User	8/31/2010	$0.00
*					

Contact ID	Last Name	First Name	Work City	State/Provir	Birth Date	Website
4	Dixon	Andrew	Kalamazoo	MI	04/08/1959	Fourth Coffee

Company / Organization	FullName	Product Name	Product Typ	Date Sold	Price
Fourth Coffee	Mr. Andrew Dixon	BO$$ Remote User	Remote User	8/12/2010	$99.00
Fourth Coffee	Mr. Andrew Dixon	Upgrade to BO$$ Multi-Us	Multi-User	12/25/2010	$129.00
Fourth Coffee	Mr. Andrew Dixon	BO$$ Multi-User Support,	Support	1/18/2011	$149.00
Fourth Coffee	Mr. Andrew Dixon	CSD Tools Add-In	Single User	9/20/2010	$19.99
*					

Record: 1 of 32 No Filter Search

Figure 9-42 You can review all product information for a contact from the subdatasheet by expanding it.

In the next section, you'll learn more about editing data in Datasheet view. You can use these editing techniques with the main datasheet as well as with any expanded subdatasheet.

CAUTION

When you close qryContactDatasheet after modifying the subdatasheet, as explained in this section, Access will prompt you to ask if you want to save your changes. You should click No to retain the original subdatasheet on tblContactEvents that we defined so that the remaining examples in this chapter make sense.

Changing Data

Not only can you view and format data in a datasheet, you can also insert new records, change data, and delete records.

Understanding Record Indicators

You might have noticed as you moved around in the datasheet that icons occasionally appeared on the row selector at the far left of each row. (See Figure 9-36.) These *record indicators* and their meanings follow. Note also that Access 2010 highlights the current row.

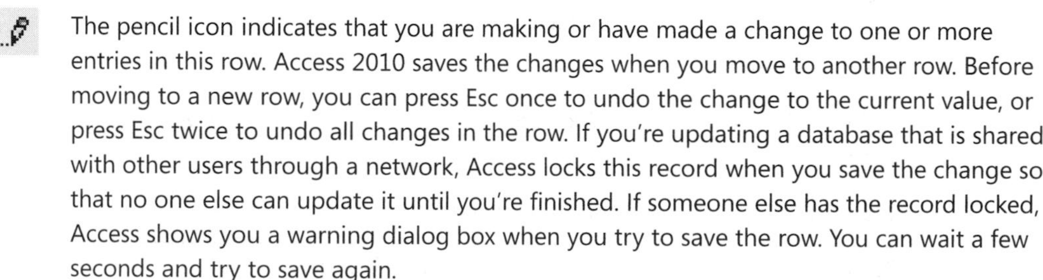

The pencil icon indicates that you are making or have made a change to one or more entries in this row. Access 2010 saves the changes when you move to another row. Before moving to a new row, you can press Esc once to undo the change to the current value, or press Esc twice to undo all changes in the row. If you're updating a database that is shared with other users through a network, Access locks this record when you save the change so that no one else can update it until you're finished. If someone else has the record locked, Access shows you a warning dialog box when you try to save the row. You can wait a few seconds and try to save again.

The asterisk icon indicates a blank row at the end of the table that you can use to create a new record.

Adding a New Record

As you build your application, you might find it useful to place some data in your tables so that you can test the forms and reports that you design. You might also find it faster sometimes to add data directly to your tables by using Datasheet view rather than by opening a form. If your table is empty when you open the table or a query on the table in Datasheet view, Access 2010 shows a single blank highlighted row with dimmed rows beneath. If you have data in your table, Access shows a blank row beneath the last record as well as dimmed rows below the blank row. You can jump to the blank row to begin adding a new record either by clicking the Go To command on the Home tab and then clicking New Record on the submenu, by clicking the New button in the Records group on the Home tab, or by pressing Ctrl+plus sign. Access places the insertion point in the first column when you start a new record. As soon as you begin typing, Access changes the record indicator to the pencil icon to show that updates are in progress. Press the Tab key to move to the next column.

If the data you enter in a column violates a field validation rule, Access 2010 notifies you as soon as you attempt to leave the column. You must provide a correct value before you can move to another column. Press Esc or click the Undo button on the Quick Access Toolbar to remove your changes in the current field.

Press Shift+Enter at any place in the record or press Tab in the last column in the record to commit your new record to the database. You can also click the Save command in the Records group on the Home tab. If the changes in your record violate the validation rule for the table, Access warns you when you try to save the record. You must correct the problem before you can save your changes. If you want to cancel the record, press Esc twice or click the Undo button on the Quick Access Toolbar until the button appears dimmed. (The first Undo removes the edit from the current field, and clicking Undo again removes any previous edit in other fields until you have removed them all.)

Access 2010 provides several keyboard shortcuts to assist you as you enter new data, as shown in Table 9-8.

Table 9-8 Keyboard Shortcuts for Entering Data in a Datasheet

Keys	Data Action
Ctrl+semicolon (;)	Enters the current date
Ctrl+colon (:)	Enters the current time
Ctrl+Alt+Spacebar	Enters the default value for the field
Ctrl+single quotation mark (') or Ctrl+double quotation mark (")	Enters the value from the same field in the previous record
Ctrl+Enter	Inserts a carriage return in a memo or text field
Ctrl+plus sign (+)	Moves to the new record row
Ctrl+minus sign (–)	Deletes the current record

INSIDE OUT Setting Keyboard Options

You can set options that affect how you move around in datasheets and forms. Click the File tab on the Backstage view, click Options, and click the Client Settings category to see the options shown here.

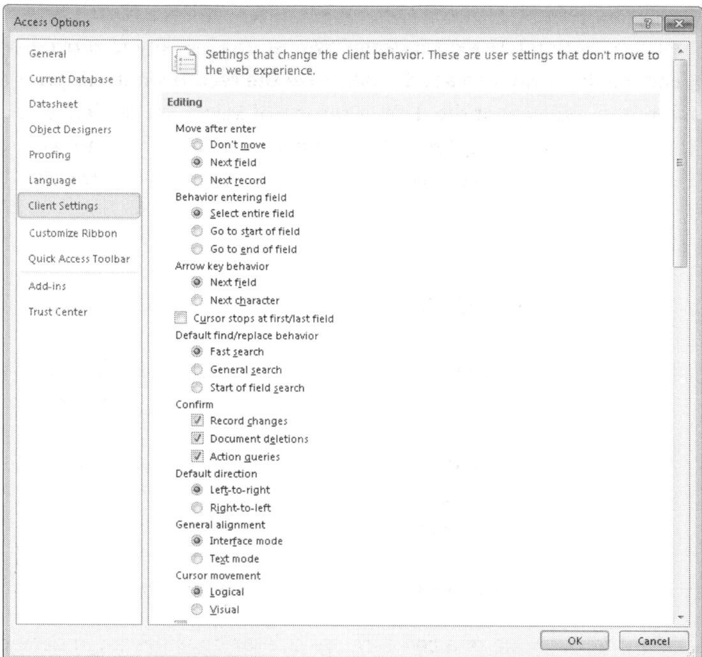

You can change the way the Enter key works by selecting an option under Move After Enter. Select Don't Move to stay in the current field when you press Enter. When you select Next Field (the default), pressing Enter moves you to the next field or the next row if you're on the last field. Select Next Record to save your changes and move to the next row when you press Enter.

You can change which part of the data of the field is selected when you move into a field by selecting an option under Behavior Entering Field. Choose Select Entire Field (the default), to highlight all data in the field. Select Go To Start Of Field to place an insertion point before the first character, and select Go To End Of Field to place the insertion point after the last character.

Under Arrow Key Behavior, select Next Field (the default) if you want to move from field to field when you press the Right Arrow or Left Arrow key. Select Next Character to change to the insertion point and move one character at a time when you press the Right Arrow or Left Arrow key. You can select the Cursor Stops At First/Last Field check box if you don't want pressing the arrow keys to move you off the current row.

We personally prefer to set the Move After Enter option to Don't Move and the Arrow Key Behavior option to Next Character. We use the Tab key to move from field to field, and we don't want to accidentally save the record when we press Enter. We leave Behavior Entering Field at the default setting of Select Entire Field so that the entire text is selected, but setting Arrow Key Behavior to Next Character allows us to press the arrow keys to shift to single-character edit mode and move in the field.

Selecting and Changing Data

When you have data in a table, you can easily change the data by editing it in Datasheet view. You must select data before you can change it, and you can do this in several ways.

- In the cell containing the data you want to change, click just to the left of the first character you want to change (or to the right of the last character), and then drag the insertion point to select all the characters you want to change.
- Double-click any word in a cell to select the entire word.
- Click at the left edge of a cell in the grid (that is, where the mouse pointer turns into a large white cross). Access selects the entire contents of the cell.

Any data you type replaces the old, selected data. In Figure 9-43, we have moved to the left edge of the First Name field, and Access has shown us the white cross mentioned in the last bullet. We can click to select the entire contents of the field. In Figure 9-44, we have changed the value to Mike but haven't yet saved the row. (You can see the pencil icon indicating that a change is pending.) Access also selects the entire entry if you tab to the cell in the datasheet grid (unless you have changed the keyboard options as noted earlier). If you want to change only part of the data (for example, to correct the spelling of a street name in an address field), you can shift to single-character mode by pressing F2 or by clicking the location at which you want to start your change. Use the Backspace key to erase characters to the left of the insertion point, and use the Delete key to remove characters to the right of the insertion point. Hold down the Shift key and press the Right Arrow or Left Arrow key to select multiple characters to replace. You can press F2 again to select the entire cell. A useful keyboard shortcut for changing data is to press Ctrl+Alt+Spacebar to restore the data in the current field to the default value specified in the table definition.

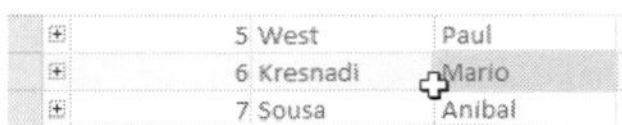

Figure 9-43 You can select the old data by clicking the left side of the column.

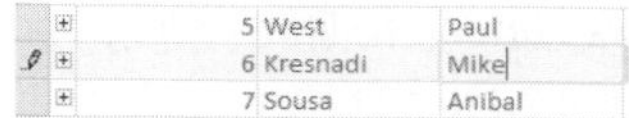

Figure 9-44 You can then replace the old data with new data by typing the new information.

Replacing Data

What if you need to make the same change in more than one record? Access 2010 provides a way to do this quickly and easily. Select any cell in the column whose values you want to change (the first row if you want to start at the beginning of the table), and then click the Replace command in the Find group on the Home tab or press Ctrl+F to see the dialog box shown in Figure 9-45. Suppose, for example, that you suspect that the city name *Easton* is misspelled as *Eaton* in multiple rows. (All the city names are spelled correctly in the sample table.) To fix this using Replace, select the Work City field in any row of qryContactsDatasheet, click the Replace command, type **Eaton** in the Find What text box, and then type **Easton** in the Replace With text box, as shown in Figure 9-45. Click Find Next to search for the next occurrence of the text you've typed in the Find What text box. Click Replace to change data selectively, or click Replace All to change all the entries that match the Find What text. Note that you can select options to look in all fields or only the current field; to select an entry only if the Find What text matches the entire entry in the field; to search All, Up, or Down; to exactly match the case for text searches (because searches in Access are normally case-insensitive); and to search based on the formatted contents (most useful when updating date/time fields).

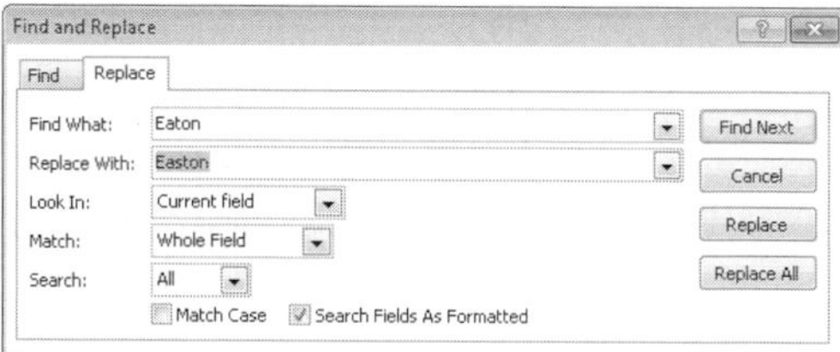

Figure 9-45 The Find And Replace dialog box allows you to quickly replace data in more than one record.

Copying and Pasting Data

You can copy or cut any selected data to the Clipboard and paste this data into another field or record. To copy data in a field, tab to the cell or click at the left edge of the cell in the datasheet grid to select the data within it. Click the Copy command in the Clipboard group on the Home tab or press Ctrl+C. To delete (cut) the data you have selected and place a copy on the Clipboard, click the Cut command in the Clipboard group on the Home tab or press Ctrl+X. To paste the data in another location, move the insertion point to the new location, select the data you want to replace, and click the Paste command in the Clipboard group on the Home tab, or press Ctrl+V. If the insertion point is at the paste location (you haven't selected any data in the field), Access inserts the Clipboard data.

INSIDE OUT Using the Office Clipboard

If you select and copy to the Clipboard several items of text data, Access 2010 shows you the Office Clipboard task pane. Unlike the Windows Clipboard, this facility allows you to copy several separate items and then select any one of them later to paste into other fields or documents. You might find this feature useful when you want to copy the contents of several fields from one record to another. You can, for example, copy a City field and then copy a State field while in one record and then later individually paste the values into another row. If you don't see the Office Clipboard, you can open it by clicking the Dialog Box Launcher button to the right of the word Clipboard in the Clipboard group of the Home tab. The Office Clipboard task pane will appear just to the left of the Navigation pane.

To select an entire record to be copied or cut, click the row selector at the far left of the row. You can drag through the row selectors or press Shift+Up Arrow or Shift+Down Arrow to extend the selection to multiple rows. To select all records in the datasheet, press Ctrl+A. Click the Copy command or press Ctrl+C to copy the contents of multiple rows to the Clipboard. You can also click the Cut command or press Ctrl+X to delete the rows and copy them to the Clipboard.

You can open another table or query and paste the copied rows into that datasheet, or you can use the Paste Append command on the submenu beneath the Paste command in the Clipboard group on the Home tab to paste the rows at the end of the same datasheet. When you paste rows into another table with the same field structure, the rows you're adding must satisfy the validation rules of the receiving table, and the primary key values (if any) must be unique. If any validation fails, Access shows you an error message and cancels the paste. You cannot paste copies of entire records into the same table if the table has a primary key other than the AutoNumber data type. (You'll get a duplicate primary key value error if you try to do this.) When the primary key is AutoNumber, Access generates new primary key values for you.

The Cut command is handy for moving those records that you don't want in an active table to a backup table. You can have both tables open (or queries on both tables open) in Datasheet view at the same time. Simply cut the rows you want to move, switch to the backup table window, and paste the cut rows by using the Paste Append command.

When you paste one row, Access inserts the data and leaves your insertion point on the new record but doesn't save it. You can always click Undo on the Quick Access Toolbar to avoid saving the single pasted record. When you paste multiple rows, Access must save them all as a group before allowing you to edit further. Access asks you to confirm the paste operation. (See Figure 9-46.) Click Yes to proceed, or click No if you decide to cancel the operation.

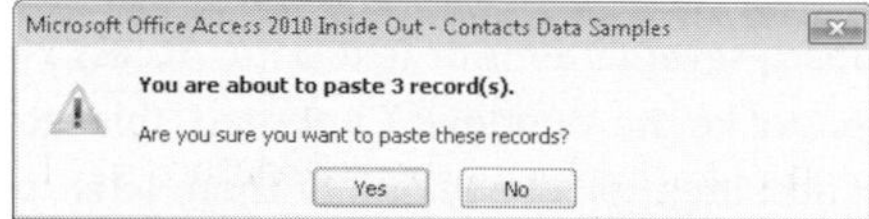

Figure 9-46 This message box asks whether you want to proceed with a paste operation.

> **Note**
>
> **You can't change the physical sequence of rows in a relational database by cutting rows from one location and pasting them in another location. Access always pastes new rows at the end of the current display. If you close the datasheet after pasting in new rows and then open it again, Access displays the rows in sequence by the primary key you defined. If you want to see rows in some other sequence, see "Sorting and Searching for Data," on page 607.**

Deleting Rows

To delete one or more rows, select the rows using the row selectors and then press the Delete key. For details about selecting multiple rows, see the previous discussion on copying and pasting data. You can also use Ctrl+minus sign to delete the current or selected row. When you delete rows, Access 2010 gives you a chance to change your mind if you made a mistake. (See Figure 9-47.) Click Yes in the message box to delete the rows, or click No to cancel the deletion. Because this database has referential integrity rules defined between tblContacts and several other tables, you won't be able to delete contact records using qryContactsDatasheet. (Access shows you an error message telling you that related rows exist in other tables.) You would have to remove all related records from tblContactEvents, tblContactProducts, and tblCompanyContacts first.

> **CAUTION!**
>
> **After you click Yes in the confirmation message box, you cannot restore the deleted rows. You have to reenter them or copy them from a backup if you want to restore that data.**

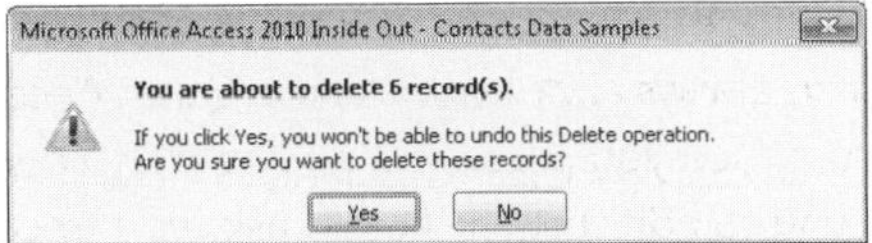

Figure 9-47 This message box appears when you delete rows.

Working with Hyperlinks

Access 97 (also known as version 8.0) introduced the Hyperlink data type. The Hyperlink data type lets you store a simple or complex link to a file or document outside your database. This link pointer can contain a Uniform Resource Locator (URL) that points to a location on the World Wide Web or on a local intranet. It can also use a Universal Naming Convention (UNC) file name to point to a file on a server on your local area network (LAN) or on your local computer drives. The link might point to a file that is a web page or in a format that is supported by an ActiveX application on your computer.

A Hyperlink data type is actually a memo field that can contain a virtually unlimited number of characters. The link itself can have up to four parts:

- An optional descriptor that Access displays in the field when you're not editing the link. The descriptor can start with any character other than a pound sign (#) and must have a pound sign as its ending delimiter. If you do not include the descriptor, you must start the link address with a pound sign.
- The link address expressed as either a URL (beginning with a recognized Internet protocol name such as *http:* or *ftp:*) or in UNC format (a file location expressed as *\\server\share\path\file name*). If you do not specify the optional descriptor field, Access displays the link address in the field. Terminate the link address with a pound sign (#).
- An optional subaddress that specifies a named location (such as a cell range in a Microsoft Excel spreadsheet or a bookmark in a Microsoft Word document) within the file. Separate the subaddress from the ScreenTip with a pound sign (#). If you entered no subaddress, you still must enter the pound sign delimiter if you want to define a ScreenTip.
- An optional ScreenTip that appears when you move your mouse pointer over the hyperlink.

For example, a hyperlink containing all four items might look like the following:

```
Viescas Download Page#http://www.viescas.com/Info/links.htm
#Downloads#Click to see the files you can download from Viescas.com
```

A hyperlink that contains a ScreenTip but no bookmark might look like this:

```
Viescas.com Books#http://www.viescas.com/Info/books.htm
##Click to see recommended books on Viescas.com
```

When you have a field defined using the Hyperlink data type, you work with it differently than with a standard text field. We included the Website field from tblContacts in the qryContactsDatasheet sample query (in ContactsDataCopy.accdb). Open the query and scroll to the right, if necessary, so that you can see the Website field, and place your mouse pointer over one of the fields that contains data, as shown in Figure 9-48.

qryContactsDatasheet

Last Name	First Name	Work City	State/Provir	Birth Date	Website
Martin	Mindy	Grandy	NC	08/08/1979	Margie's Travel
Zulechner	Markus	Grandy	NC	10/06/1940	Margie's Travel
Villadsen	Peter	Grandy	NC	11/22/1975	Margie's Travel
Trukawka	Adam	Irrigon	OR	06/02/1978	Lucerne Publishing
Hanson	Mark	Irrigon	OR	11/16/1946	Lucerne Publishing
Jankowski	Marcin	Flushing	NY	08/21/1950	Humongous Insurance
Buschmann	Monika	Flushing	NY	12/28/1962	Humongous Insurance
Viescas	John	Nashua	NH		Viescas Consulting, Inc.
Conrad	Jeff	Redmond	WA		Conrad Systems Development

Access Junkie Website

Figure 9-48 Place your mouse pointer over a hyperlink field in Datasheet view to show the hyperlink or the ScreenTip.

Activating a Hyperlink

Notice that the text in a hyperlink field is underlined and that the mouse pointer becomes a hand with a pointing finger when you move the pointer over the field. If you leave the pointer floating over the field for a moment, Access displays the ScreenTip. In the tblContacts table, the entries in the Website hyperlink field for some of the contacts contain pointers to Microsoft websites. When you click a link field, Access starts the application that supports the link and passes the link address and subaddress to the application. If the link starts with an Internet protocol, Access starts your web browser. In the case of the links in the tblContacts table, all are links to pages on the Microsoft website. If you click one of them, your browser should start and display the related web page, as shown in Figure 9-49.

Figure 9-49 Here is the result of clicking a website link in the tblContacts table.

Inserting a New Hyperlink

To insert a hyperlink in an empty hyperlink field, tab to the field or click in it with your mouse. If you're confident about the format of your link, you can type it, following the rules for the four parts noted earlier. If you're not sure, right-click inside the hyperlink field, select Hyperlink from the submenu that appears, and then select Edit Hyperlink from the second submenu to see the dialog box shown in Figure 9-50. This dialog box helps you correctly construct the four parts of the hyperlink.

The dialog box opens with Existing File Or Web Page selected in the Link To pane and Current Folder selected in the center pane, as shown in Figure 9-50. What you see in the list in the center pane depends on your current folder, the web pages you've visited recently, and the files you've opened recently. You'll see a Look In list where you can navigate to any drive or folder on your system. You can also click the Browse The Web button (the button with a globe and a spyglass) to open your web browser to find a website you want, or the Browse For File button (an open folder icon) to open the Link To File dialog box to find the file you want. Click Existing File Or Web Page and click the Recent Files option to see a list of files that you recently opened.

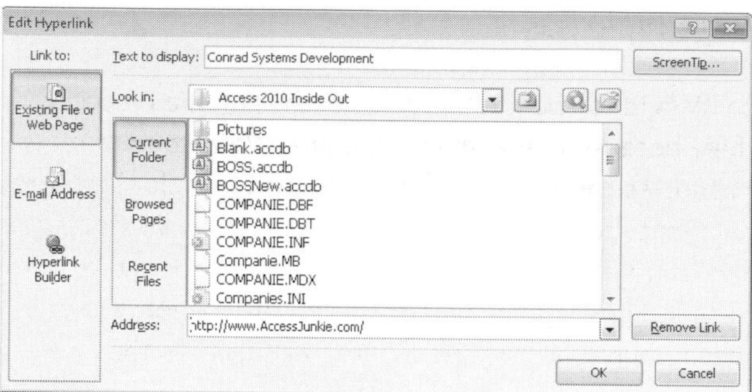

Figure 9-50 The dialog box used to insert a hyperlink shows you a list of files in the current folder.

We clicked the Browsed Pages option because we knew the hyperlink we wanted was a web page that we had recently visited. You can enter the descriptor in the Text To Display box at the top. We clicked ScreenTip to open the Set Hyperlink ScreenTip dialog box you see in Figure 9-51. You can type the document or website address directly into the Address box. (Yes, that's Jeff's real website address!)

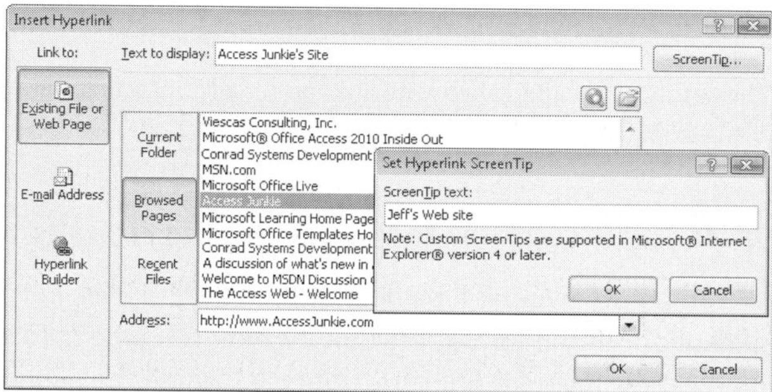

Figure 9-51 You can choose a website address from a list of recently visited websites.

The E-Mail Address button in the left pane lets you enter an email address or choose from a list of recently used addresses. This generates a *mailto:* hyperlink that will invoke your email program and start a new email to the address you enter. You can also specify a subject for the new email by adding a question mark after the email address and entering what you want to appear on the subject line.

The Hyperlink Builder button in the left pane helps you build a hyperlink that includes parameters. You'll learn more about using parameters in hyperlinks in Chapter 12, "Using Forms in an Access Application."

Click OK to save your link in the field in the datasheet.

Editing an Existing Hyperlink

Getting into a hyperlink field to change the value of the link is a bit tricky. You can't simply click in a hyperlink field because that activates the link. What you can do is click in the field before the hyperlink and use the Tab key to move to the link field. Then press F2 to shift to character edit mode to edit the text string that defines the link. Figure 9-52 shows you a hyperlink field after following this procedure. You can use the arrow keys to move around in the text string to change one or more parts. In many cases, you might want to add an optional descriptor at the beginning of the link text, as shown in the figure.

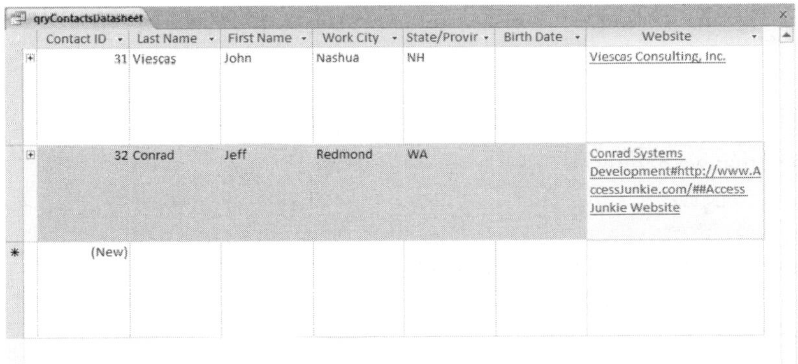

Figure 9-52 You can edit the text that defines a hyperlink directly in a datasheet.

The most comprehensive way to work with a hyperlink field is to right-click a link field to open a shortcut menu. Clicking Hyperlink on this menu displays a submenu with a number of options. You can edit the hyperlink (which opens the dialog box shown in Figure 9-50), open the link document, copy the link to the Clipboard, add the link to your list of favorites, change the text displayed in the field, or remove the hyperlink.

Sorting and Searching for Data

When you open a table in Datasheet view, Access 2010 displays the rows sorted in sequence by the primary key you defined for the table. If you didn't define a primary key, you'll see the rows in the sequence in which you entered them in the table. If you want to see the rows in a different sequence or search for specific data, Access provides you with tools to do that. When you open a query in Datasheet view (such as the qryContactDatasheet sample query we're using in this chapter), you'll see the rows in the order determined by sort specifications in the query. If you haven't specified sorting information, you'll see the data in the same sequence as you would if you opened the table or query in Datasheet view.

Sorting Data

Access 2010 provides several ways to sort data in Datasheet view. As you might have noticed, two handy ribbon commands allow you to quickly sort the rows in a query or table datasheet in ascending or descending order. To see how this works, open the qryContactsDatasheet query, click anywhere in the Birth Date column, and click the Descending command in the Sort & Filter group on the Home tab. Access sorts the display to show you the rows ordered alphabetically by Birth Date, as shown in Figure 9-53.

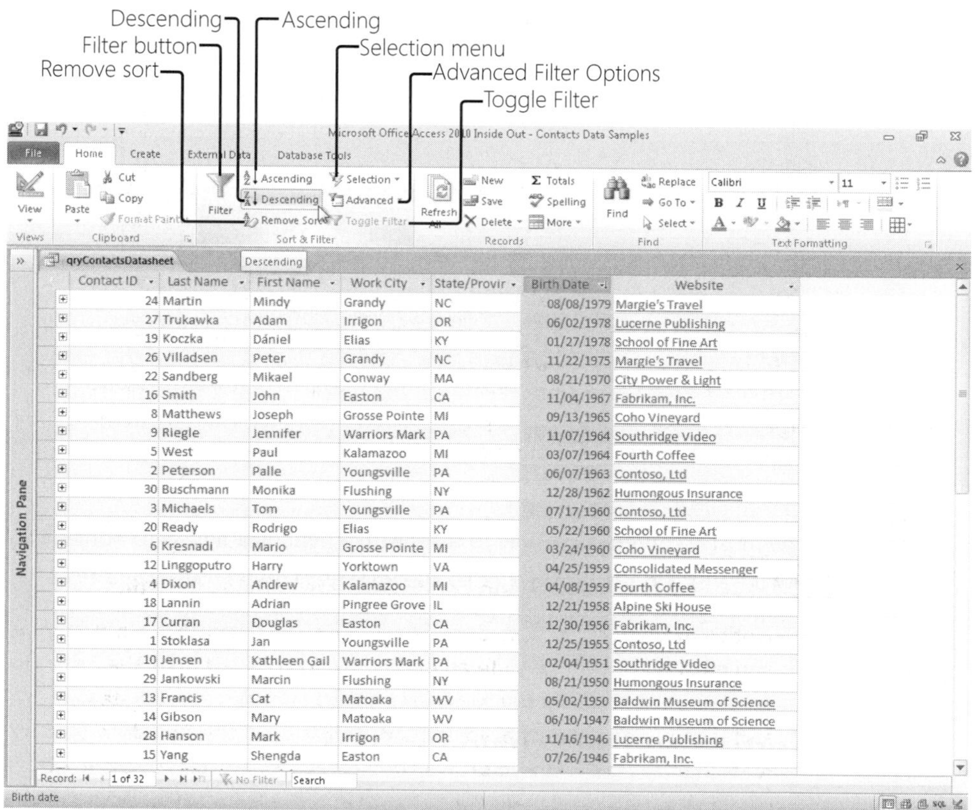

Figure 9-53 You can sort contacts by birth date by using the sort buttons on the ribbon.

You can click Ascending to sort the rows in ascending order or click Remove Sort to return to the original data sequence. But before you change the sort or clear the sort, suppose you want to see contacts sorted by state or province ascending and then by birth date descending. You already have the data sorted by birth date, so click anywhere in the State/Province column and click Ascending to see the result you want, as shown in Figure 9-54.

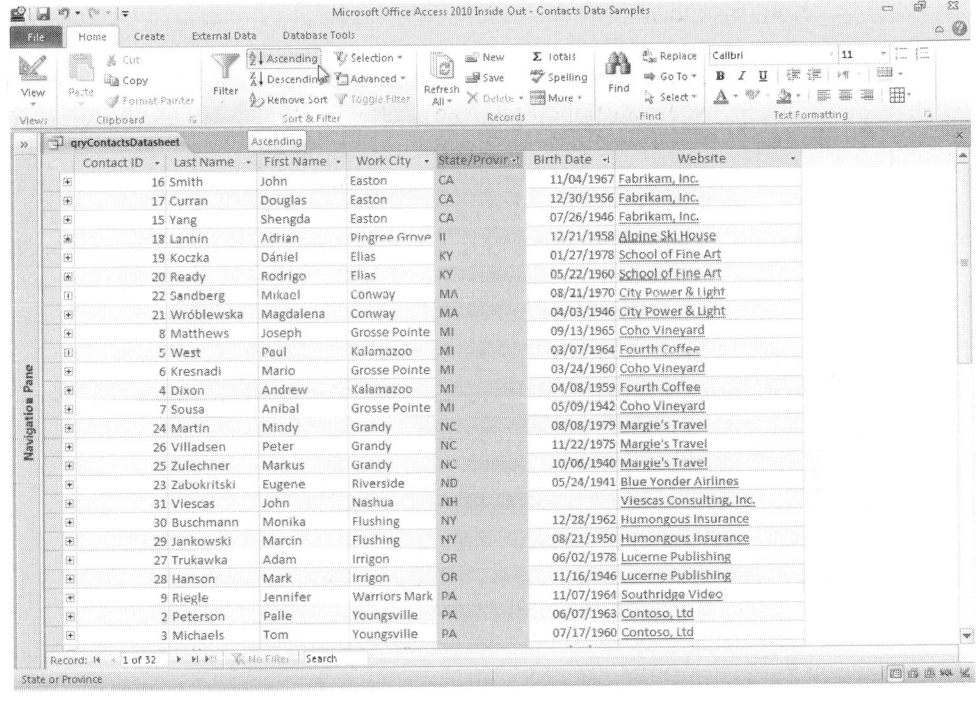

Figure 9-54 After applying the second sort, the records are now sorted by state or province ascending and then by birth date descending within state.

INSIDE OUT Applying Multiple Sorts in Reverse Order

Notice that to sort by state or province and then birth date within state or province, you must first sort birth date and then sort state or province. We think that's backwards, but that's the way it works. If you had applied a sort on state or province first and then sorted birth date, you would have seen all the records in date order, with any records having the same date subsequently sorted by state or province. If you want to sort on multiple fields, remember to apply the *innermost* sort first and then work your way outward.

Another way to sort more than one field is to use the Advanced Filter/Sort feature. Let's assume that you want to sort by State/Province, then by City within State/Province, and then by Last Name. Here's how to do it:

1. Click the Advanced button in the Sort & Filter group on the Home tab, and then click Advanced Filter/Sort on the submenu. You'll see the Advanced Filter Design window (shown in Figure 9-55) with a list of fields in the qryContactsDatasheet query shown in the top part of the window.

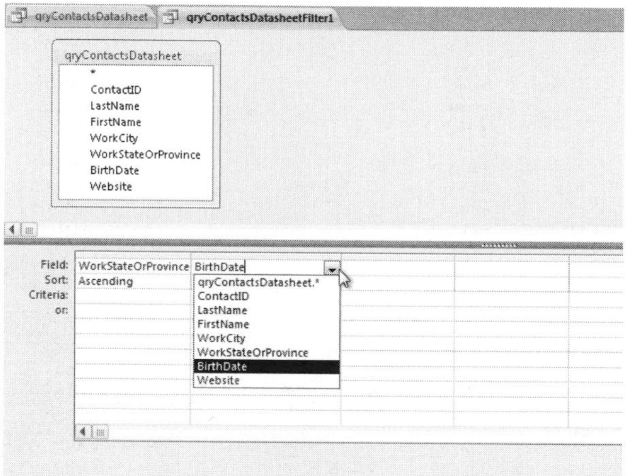

Figure 9-55 Select the fields you want to sort in the Advanced Filter Design window.

2. If you didn't click Remove Sort before opening this window, you should see the sorts you previously defined directly in Datasheet view on the WorkStateOrProvince and BirthDate fields. If so, click the bar above the BirthDate field to select it and then press the Delete key to remove the field.

3. Because you recently sorted by State/Province, the Advanced Filter Design window will show this field already added to the filter grid. If you skipped the sort step in Figure 9-53 or closed and reopened the datasheet without saving the sort, open the field list in the first column by clicking the arrow or by pressing Alt+Down Arrow on the keyboard. Select the WorkStateOrProvince field in the list. You can also place the WorkStateOrProvince field in the first column by finding WorkStateOrProvince in the list of fields in the top part of the window and dragging it into the Field row in the first column of the filter grid.

4. Click in the Sort row, immediately below the WorkStateOrProvince field, and select Ascending from the drop-down list.

5. Add the WorkCity and LastName fields to the next two columns, and select Ascending in the Sort row for both.

6. Click the Toggle Filter button in the Sort & Filter group of the Home tab on the ribbon to see the result shown in Figure 9-56.

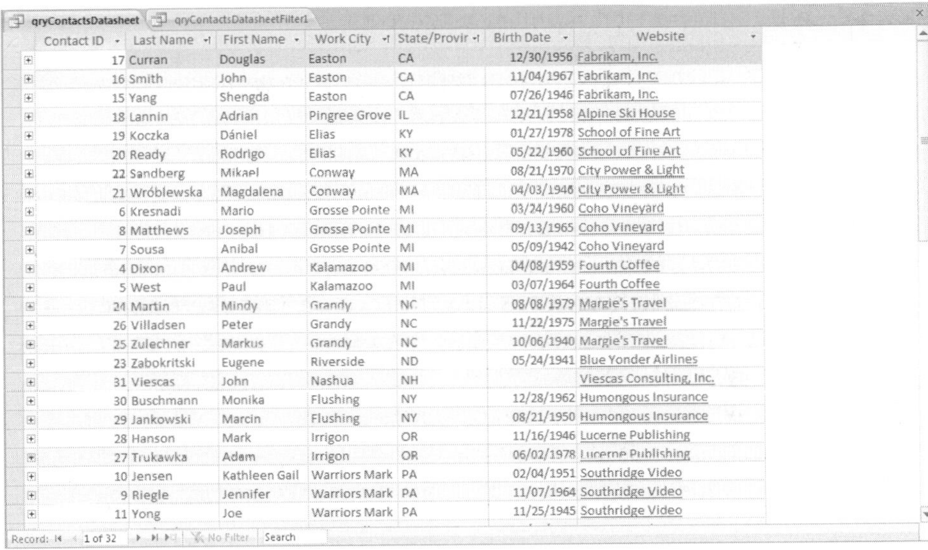

Contact ID	Last Name	First Name	Work City	State/Provir	Birth Date	Website
17	Curran	Douglas	Easton	CA	12/30/1956	Fabrikam, Inc.
16	Smith	John	Easton	CA	11/04/1967	Fabrikam, Inc.
15	Yang	Shengda	Easton	CA	07/26/1946	Fabrikam, Inc.
18	Lannin	Adrian	Pingree Grove	IL	12/21/1958	Alpine Ski House
19	Koczka	Dániel	Elias	KY	01/27/1978	School of Fine Art
20	Ready	Rodrigo	Elias	KY	05/22/1960	School of Fine Art
22	Sandberg	Mikael	Conway	MA	08/21/1970	City Power & Light
21	Wróblewska	Magdalena	Conway	MA	04/03/1946	City Power & Light
6	Kresnadi	Mario	Grosse Pointe	MI	03/24/1960	Coho Vineyard
8	Matthews	Joseph	Grosse Pointe	MI	09/13/1965	Coho Vineyard
7	Sousa	Anibal	Grosse Pointe	MI	05/09/1942	Coho Vineyard
4	Dixon	Andrew	Kalamazoo	MI	04/08/1959	Fourth Coffee
5	West	Paul	Kalamazoo	MI	03/07/1964	Fourth Coffee
24	Martin	Mindy	Grandy	NC	08/08/1979	Margie's Travel
26	Villadsen	Peter	Grandy	NC	11/22/1975	Margie's Travel
25	Zulechner	Markus	Grandy	NC	10/06/1940	Margie's Travel
23	Zabokritski	Eugene	Riverside	ND	05/24/1941	Blue Yonder Airlines
31	Viescas	John	Nashua	NH		Viescas Consulting, Inc.
30	Buschmann	Monika	Flushing	NY	12/28/1962	Humongous Insurance
29	Jankowski	Marcin	Flushing	NY	08/21/1950	Humongous Insurance
28	Hanson	Mark	Irrigon	OR	11/16/1946	Lucerne Publishing
27	Trukawka	Adam	Irrigon	OR	06/02/1978	Lucerne Publishing
10	Jensen	Kathleen Gail	Warriors Mark	PA	02/04/1951	Southridge Video
9	Riegle	Jennifer	Warriors Mark	PA	11/07/1964	Southridge Video
11	Yong	Joe	Warriors Mark	PA	11/25/1945	Southridge Video

Figure 9-56 After defining your sorts and clicking the Toggle Filter button, you can see the results of your sorting contact records by state or province, city, and then last name.

Note

If you compare Figure 9-54 with Figure 9-56, it looks like the records in Figure 9-54 were already sorted by city name within state. You might be tempted to leave out the sort on city in this exercise, but if you do that, you will not see the city names maintained in the same order. Remember, if you want data presented in a certain sequence, you must ask for it that way!

Close the qryContactsDatasheet window and click No when asked if you want to save design changes. We'll explore using the other options in the Sort & Filter group in the next sections.

Searching for and Filtering Data

If you want to look for data anywhere in your table, Access 2010 provides several powerful searching and filtering capabilities.

Using Find To begin this exercise, open the qryContactsDatasheet query in Datasheet view again. To perform a simple search on a single field, select that field, and then open the Find And Replace dialog box (shown in Figure 9-57) by clicking the Find command in the Find group on the Home tab or by pressing Ctrl+F.

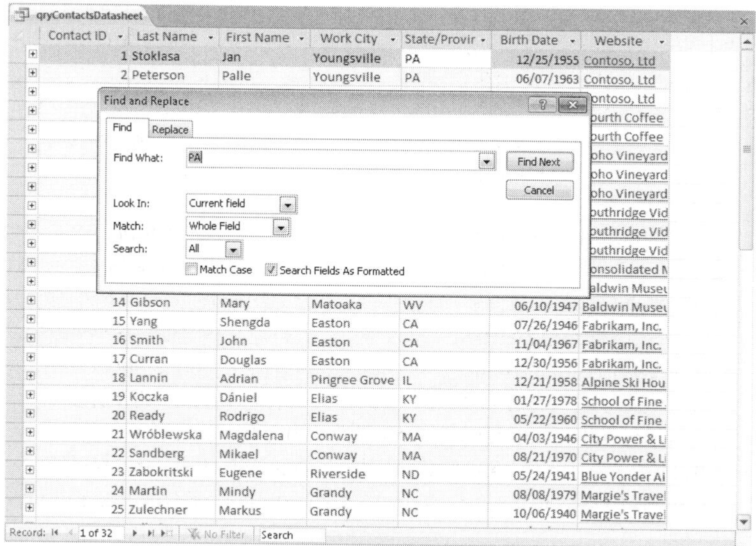

Figure 9-57 You can use the Find And Replace dialog box to search for data.

In the Find What text box, type the data that you want Access to find. You can include wildcard characters similar to those of the LIKE comparison operator. See "Defining Simple Field Validation Rules," on page 201, to perform a generic search. Use an asterisk (*) to indicate a string of unknown characters of any length (zero or more characters), and use a question mark (?) to indicate exactly one unknown character or a space. For example, **AB??DE** matches *Aberdeen* and *Tab idea* but not *Lab department*.

By default, Access searches the field that your insertion point was in before you opened the Find And Replace dialog box. To search the entire table, select Current Document from the Look In list. By default, Access searches all records from the top of the recordset unless you change the Search list to search down or up from the current record position. Select the Match Case check box if you want to find text that exactly matches the uppercase and lowercase letters you typed. By default, Access is case-insensitive unless you select this check box.

The Search Fields As Formatted check box appears dimmed unless you select a field that has a format or input mask applied. You can select this check box if you need to search the data as it is displayed rather than as it is stored by Access. Although searching this way is slower, you probably should select this check box if you are searching a date/time field. For example, if you're searching a date field for dates in January, you can specify **-Jan-** if the field is formatted as Medium Date and you select the Search Fields As Formatted check box. You might also want to select this check box when searching a Yes/No field for Yes because any value except 0 is a valid indicator of Yes.

Click Find Next to start searching from the current record. Each time you click Find Next again, Access moves to the next value it finds, and loops to the top of the recordset to continue the search if you started in the middle. After you establish search criteria and you close the Find And Replace dialog box, you can press Shift+F4 to execute the search from the current record without having to open the dialog box again.

Filtering by Selection If you want to see all the rows in your table that contain a value that matches one in a row in the datasheet grid, you can use the Selection command in the Sort & Filter group on the Home tab. Select a complete value in a field to see only rows that have data in that column that completely matches. Figure 9-58 shows the value *PA* selected in the State/Province column and the result after clicking the Selection button in the Sort & Filter group of the Home tab and clicking Equals "PA" on the submenu. If the filtering data you need is in several contiguous columns, click the first column, hold down the Shift key, and click the last column to select all the data; click Selection; and then click a filter option on the submenu to see only rows that match the data in all the columns you selected.

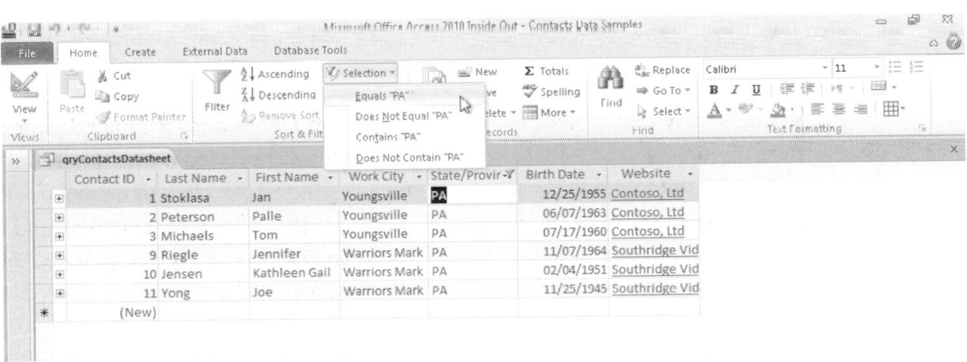

Figure 9-58 Here is the list of contacts in Pennsylvania, compiled using the Selection filter option.

Alternatively, if you want to see all the rows in your table that contain a part of a value that matches one in a row in the datasheet grid, you can select the characters that you want to match and use Selection. For example, to see all contacts that have the characters *ing* in their work city name, find a contact that has *ing* in the WorkCity field and select those characters. Click the Selection button in the Sort & Filter group of the Home tab, and then select Contains "ing" from the submenu. When the search is completed, you should see only the three contacts who work in the cities named P*ingree* Grove and Flush*ing*. To remove a filter, click the Toggle Filter button in the Sort & Filter group, or click Advanced in the Sort & Filter group and click Clear All Filters on the submenu.

> **Note**
>
> **You can open any subdatasheet defined for the query and apply a filter there. If you apply a filter to a subdatasheet, you will filter all the subdatasheets that are open.**

You can also add a filter to a filter. For example, if you want to see all contacts who live in Youngsville in Pennsylvania, find the value *PA* in the State/Province column, select it, click the Selection button in the Sort & Filter group of the Home tab, and then click Equals "PA" on the submenu. In the filtered list, find a row containing the word *Youngsville* in the Work City field, select the word, click Selection again, and click Equals "Youngsville" on the submenu. Access displays a small filter icon that looks like a funnel in the upper-right corner of each column that has a filter applied, as shown in Figure 9-59. If you rest your mouse on one of these column filter icons, Access displays a ScreenTip telling you what filter has been applied to that particular column. To remove all your filters, click Toggle Filter, or click Advanced in the Sort & Filter group of the Home tab and click Clear All Filters on the submenu.

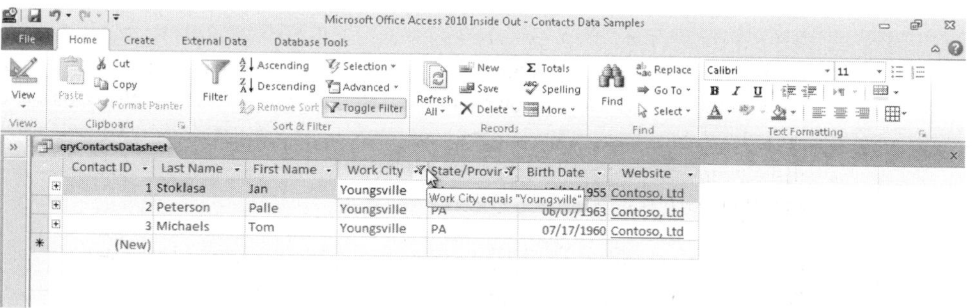

Figure 9-59 Access displays a ScreenTip on the filter icon in the column header to show you what filter is applied.

Using the Filter Window To further assist you with filtering rows, Access 2010 provides a Filter window with predefined filter selections for various data types. Suppose you want to quickly filter the rows for contacts who have birthdays in the month of December. Click inside the Birth Date column in any row and then click the Filter button in the Sort & Filter group of the Home tab, and Access opens the Filter window for this field, as shown in Figure 9-60.

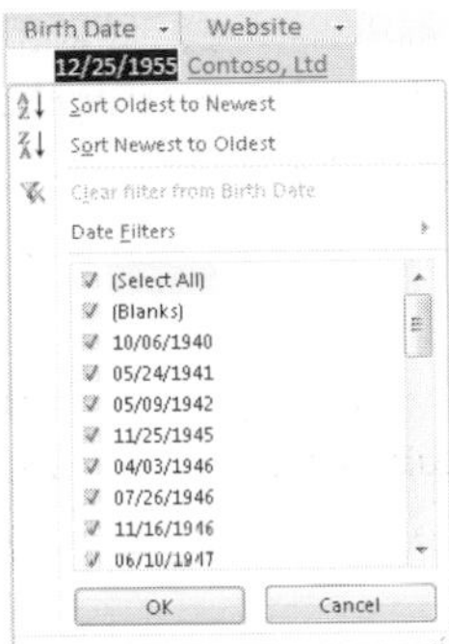

Figure 9-60 The Filter window for date/time fields displays filter criteria based on the dates entered in the field.

The Ascending and Descending buttons, discussed previously, are the first two options in the Filter window. (For a date/time field, Access shows you Sort Oldest To Newest and Sort Newest To Oldest. For a text field, Access shows you Sort A To Z and Sort Z To A, and for a numeric field, Access shows you Sort Smallest To Largest and Sort Largest To Smallest.) The third option, Clear Filter From Birth Date, removes all filters applied to the Birth Date field. The fourth option is Date Filters, which displays several submenus to the right that allow you to filter for specific date criteria. (For text fields, this option presents a list of text filters. For number fields, Access displays a list of the available numeric values.)

Beneath the Date Filters option is a list. The first two options in this list are the same for all data types. Select All selects all the options presented in the list. Blanks causes Access to search the field for any rows with no value entered—a Null value or an empty string. Beneath Select All and Blanks are every unique value entered into the Birth Date field for the current datasheet. If you select only one of these options, Access filters the rows that exactly match the value you choose.

In our example, to find all contacts who have a birthday in the month of December, click Date Filters, and a submenu appears to the right. Select All Dates In Period, and a second submenu appears to the right of the first, which allows you to filter the rows by an individual quarter or by a specific month. Click December and Access filters the rows to display only contacts who have birthdays in December, as shown in Figure 9-61.

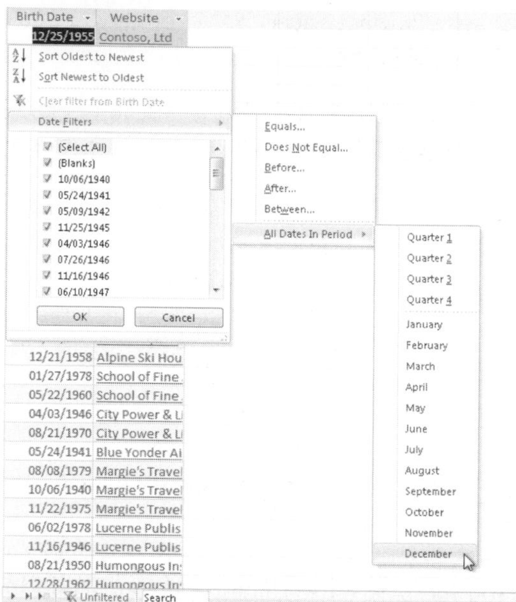

Figure 9-61 Date Filters presents built-in date filters for periods and months.

The result of this filter should return the four contacts who have birthdays in December, as shown in Figure 9-62. Click the Toggle Filter button in the Sort & Filter group of the Home tab to remove the filter.

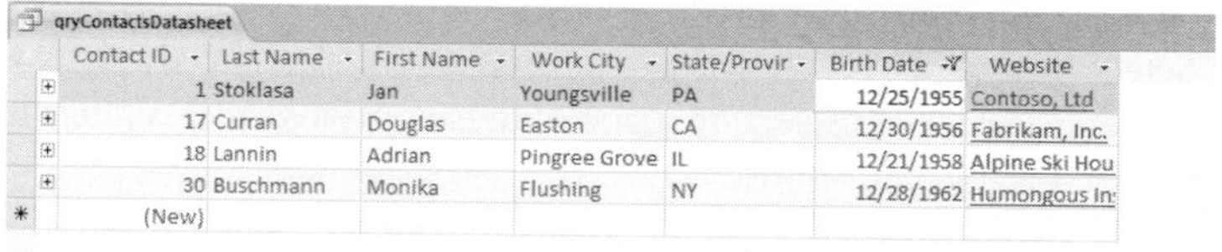

Contact ID	Last Name	First Name	Work City	State/Provir	Birth Date	Website
1	Stoklasa	Jan	Youngsville	PA	12/25/1955	Contoso, Ltd
17	Curran	Douglas	Easton	CA	12/30/1956	Fabrikam, Inc.
18	Lannin	Adrian	Pingree Grove	IL	12/21/1958	Alpine Ski Hou
30	Buschmann	Monika	Flushing	NY	12/28/1962	Humongous In
(New)						

Figure 9-62 Four contacts in the table have birthdays in the month of December.

Using Filter by Form Applying a filter using Selection is great for searching for rows that match *all* of several criteria (Last Name like "*son*" and State/Province equals "OR"), but what if you want to see rows that meet *any* of several criteria (Last Name like "*son" and

State/Province equals "OR" or State/Province equals "PA")? You can use Filter By Form to easily build the criteria for this type of search.

When you click the Advanced button in the Sort & Filter group of the Home tab and click Filter By Form on the submenu, Access 2010 shows you a Filter By Form example that looks like your datasheet but contains no data. If you have no filtering criteria previously defined, Access shows you the Look For tab and one Or tab at the bottom of the window. Move to each column in which you want to define criteria and either select a value from the drop-down list or type search criteria, as shown in Figure 9-63. Notice that each drop-down list shows you all the unique values available for each field, so it's easy to pick values to perform an exact comparison. You can also enter criteria, much the way that you did to create validation rules in Chapter 4. For example, you can enter *Like "*son*"* in the Last Name field to search for the letters son anywhere in the name. You can use criteria such as *>#01 JAN 1963#* in the Birth Date date/time field to find rows for contacts born after that date. You can enter multiple criteria on one line, but *all* the criteria you enter on a single line must be true for a particular row to be selected.

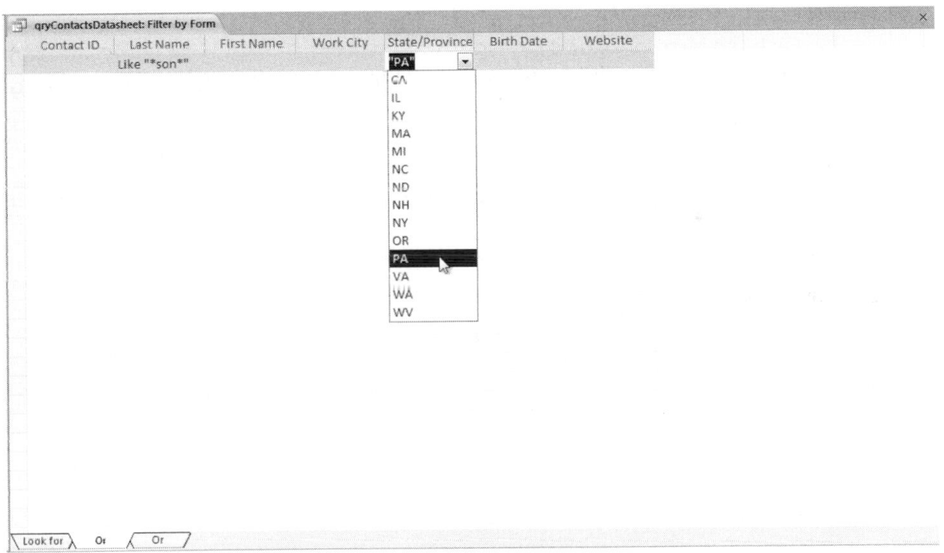

Figure 9-63 Use Filter By Form to search for one of several states.

INSIDE OUT Limiting the Returned Records

When your table or query returns tens of thousands of rows, fetching the values for each list in Filter By Form can take a long time. You can specify a limit by clicking the File tab on the Backstage view and clicking Options. Select the Current Database category in the Access Options dialog box, and then scroll down to Filter Lookup Options For <*name of your database*>. In the Don't Display Lists When More Than This Number Of Records Is Read option, you can specify a value for display lists to limit the number of discrete values returned. The default value is 1,000.

If you want to see rows that contain any of several values in a particular column (for example, rows from several states), enter the first value in the appropriate column, and then click the Or tab at the bottom of the window to enter an additional criterion. In this example, "OR" was entered in the State/Province column on the Look For tab and "PA" on the first Or tab; you can see "PA" being selected for the first Or tab in Figure 9-63.

Each tab also specifies Like "*son*" for the last name. (As you define additional criteria, Access makes additional Or tabs available at the bottom of the window.) Figure 9-64 shows the result of applying these criteria when you click the Toggle Filter button in the Sort & Filter group of the Home tab.

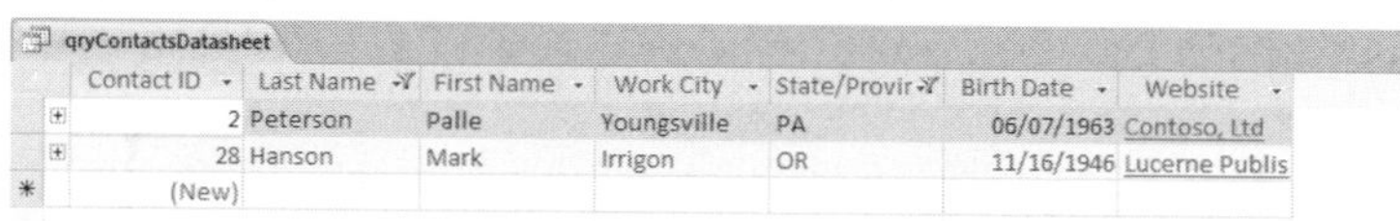

qryContactsDatasheet

	Contact ID	Last Name	First Name	Work City	State/Provir	Birth Date	Website
+	2	Peterson	Palle	Youngsville	PA	06/07/1963	Contoso, Ltd
+	28	Hanson	Mark	Irrigon	OR	11/16/1946	Lucerne Publis
*	(New)						

Figure 9-64 The contacts with names containing *son* in the states of OR and PA.

INSIDE OUT Saving and Reusing Your Filters

Access 2010 always remembers the last filtering and sorting criteria you defined for a datasheet. The next time you open the datasheet, click the Advanced button in the Sort & Filter group on the Home tab and click Filter By Form or Advanced to apply the last filter you created (so long as you replied Yes to the prompt to save formatting changes when you last closed the datasheet). If you want to save a particular filter/sort definition, click the Advanced button in the Sort & Filter group on the Home tab, click Save As Query on the submenu, and give your filter a name. The next time you open the table, return to the Advanced button and then click Load From Query on the submenu to find the filter you previously saved.

You can actually define very complex filtering criteria using expressions and the Or tabs in the Filter By Form window. If you look at the Filter By Form window, you can see that Access builds all your criteria in a design grid that looks similar to a Query window in Design view. In fact, filters and sorts use the query capabilities of Access to accomplish the result you want, so in Datasheet view, you can use all the same filtering capabilities you'll find for queries.

In Chapter 10, we'll explore creating more complex queries—including creating queries from multiple tables or queries, calculating totals, and designing PivotTable and PivotChart views. You'll also learn how to create queries that will publish to Access Services.

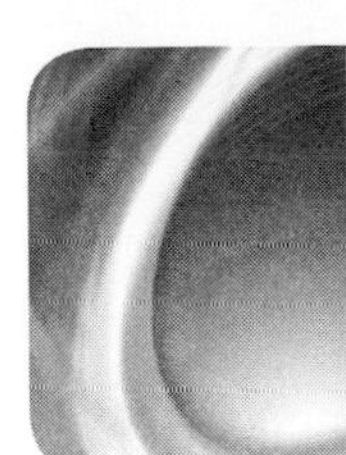

CHAPTER 10

Building Complex Queries

Creating queries on a single table, as you did in Chapter 9, "Creating and Working with Simple Queries," is a good way to get acquainted with the basic mechanics of the query designer. It's also useful to work with simple queries to understand how datasheets work.

However, for many tasks, you'll need to build a query on multiple tables or queries (yes, you can build a query on a query!), calculate totals, add parameters, customize query properties, or work in SQL view. In fact, there are some types of queries that you can build only in SQL view. This chapter shows you how.

CAUTION!

When you build an application, you should never allow users to view or edit data directly from table or query datasheets. Although, with Microsoft Access 2010, you can protect the integrity of your data with data macros to enforce more complex business rules, we still recommend you do all your data entry, editing, and reviewing through forms and reports. If you're working with a web database using Access Services, you cannot view query datasheets in the browser, but you can see the results of web queries in your forms and reports.

The purpose of this chapter is to teach you the concepts you must learn to build the queries you'll need for your forms and reports. You'll also learn how to create web queries for Access Services applications.

Selecting Data from Multiple Tables

At this point, you've been through all the variations on a single theme—queries on a single table. It's easy to build on this knowledge to retrieve related information from many tables and to place that information in a single view. You'll find this ability to select data from multiple tables very useful in designing forms and reports.

Note

The examples in this chapter are based on the tables and data in HousingDataCopy.accdb, ContactsDataCopy.accdb, and BOSSDataCopy.accdb on the companion CD included with this book. These databases are copies of the data from the Housing Reservations, Conrad Systems Contacts, and Back Office Software System sample applications, respectively, and they contain the sample queries used in this chapter. The query results you see from the sample queries you build in this chapter might not exactly match what you see in this book if you have changed the sample data in the files. Also, all the screen images in this chapter were taken on a Windows 7 system with the Access color scheme set to Silver. Your results might look different if you are using a different operating system or a different theme.

Creating Inner Joins

A *join* is the link you need to define between two related tables in a query so that the data you see makes sense. If you don't define the link, you'll see all rows from the first table combined with all rows from the second table (also called the *Cartesian product*). When you use an *inner join* (the default for joins in queries), you won't see rows from either table that don't have a matching row in the other table. This type of query is also called an *equi-join query*, meaning that you'll see rows only where there are *equal* values in *both* tables. For example, in a query that joins departments and employees, you won't see any departments that have no employees or any employees that aren't assigned to a department. To see how to build a query that returns all rows from one of the tables, including rows that have no match in the related table, see "Using Outer Joins," on page 634.

Correctly designing your tables requires you to split out (normalize) your data into separate tables to avoid redundant data and problems updating the data. (For details about designing your tables, see Article 1, "Designing Your Database Application," on the companion CD.) For many tasks, however, you need to work with the data from multiple tables. For example, in the Housing Reservations application, to work with employees and the departments to which they are assigned, you can't get all the information you need from just tblEmployees. Sure, you can see the employee's DepartmentID, but what about the department name and location? If you want to sort or filter employees by department name, you need both tblDepartments and tblEmployees.

In the previous chapter, we built several queries on tblReservations. Because we defined Lookup properties in that table, you can see the facility name in the reservation record, but as you discovered, that's really a numeric field. If you want to sort on the real name value or see other information about the facility, you must create a query that uses both tblFacilities and tblReservations.

Try the following example, in which you combine information about a reservation and about the facility in which the reservation was confirmed. Start by opening the HousingDataCopy.accdb database. Click the Query Design button in the Queries group on the Create tab. Access 2010 immediately opens the Show Table dialog box. In this dialog box, you select the tables and queries that you want in your new query. Select the tblFacilities and tblReservations tables (hold down the Ctrl key as you click each table name), click Add, and then close the dialog box.

TROUBLESHOOTING

How can I be sure I'm using the correct table in the query designer?

Whenever your query is based on more than one table, it's a good idea to select the Show Table Names option in the Query Design section of the Object Designers category of the Access Options dialog box. (Click the File tab on the Backstage view, click Options, and then click the Object Designers category in the left column. Below Query Design, make sure that the Show Table Names check box is selected.) Because you might have the same field name in more than one of the tables, showing table names in the design grid helps to ensure that your query refers to the field you intend it to.

Whenever you have relationships defined, the query designer automatically links (joins) multiple tables on the defined relationships. You might also want to verify the Enable AutoJoin check box is selected in the Object Designers category of the Access Options dialog box. When you enable this option (selected by default) and build a query on two tables that aren't directly related, the query designer attempts to link the two tables for you. The query designer looks at the primary key of each table. If it can find a field with the same name and data type in one of the other tables you added to the query designer, the query designer builds the link for you. Some advanced users might prefer to always create these links themselves.

The two tables, tblFacilities and tblReservations, aren't directly related to each other. If you look in the Relationships window (click Relationships on the Database Tools tab), you'll see a relationship defined between tblFacilities and tblFacilityRooms on the FacilityID field. There's also a relationship between tblFacilityRooms and tblReservations on the combination of the FacilityID and the RoomNumber fields. So, tblFacilities is related to tblReservations via the FacilityID field, but indirectly. In other words, the FacilityID field in tblReservations is a *foreign key* that points to the related row in tblFacilities. So, it's perfectly legitimate to build a query that links these two tables on the FacilityID field.

INSIDE OUT Query Joins Don't Always Need to Match Relationships

It's a good idea to define relationships between related tables to help ensure the integrity of your data. However, you don't need to define a relationship between the foreign key in a table and the matching primary key in every other related table at the query level. For example, if table A is related to table B, and table B is related to table C, you don't necessarily need a relationship defined between table A and table C even though table C might contain a foreign key field that relates it to table A. Even when you haven't explicitly defined a relationship between table A and table C, it is perfectly valid to join table A to table C in a query so long as there's a legitimate matching field in both tables.

The upper part of the Query window in Design view should look like that shown in Figure 10-1. Access 2010 first links multiple tables in a query based on the relationships you have defined. If no defined relationship exists, and you have Enable AutoJoin selected in the Object Designers category in the Access Options dialog box (this option is enabled by default), then Access attempts to match the primary key from one table with a field that has the same name and data type in the other table.

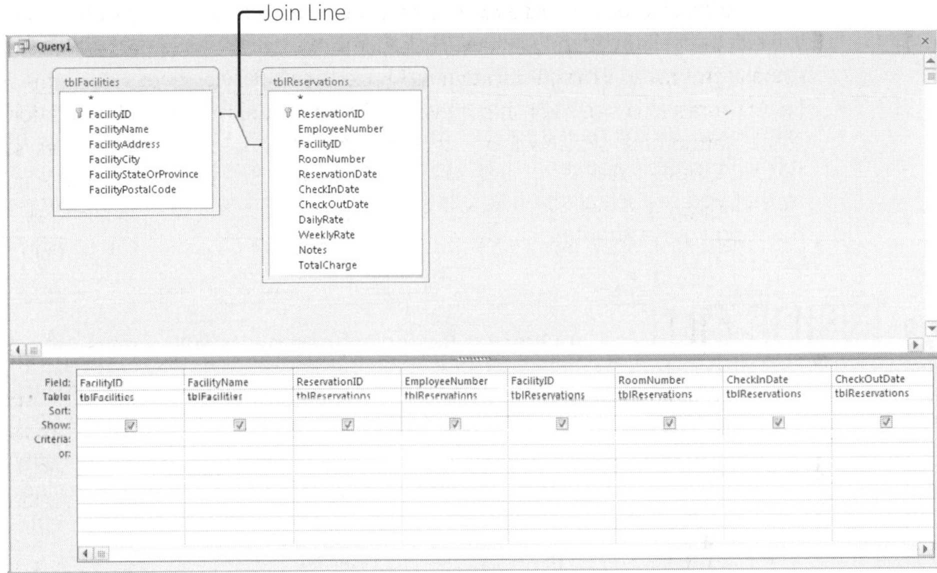

Figure 10-1 This query selects information from the tblFacilities and tblReservations tables.

Access shows the links between tables as a line drawn from the primary key in one table to its matching field in the other table. As already noted, no direct relationship exists between these two tables in this example. With Enable AutoJoin selected, however, Access sees that FacilityID field is the primary key in tblFacilities and finds a matching FacilityID field in tbl-Reservations. So, it should create a join line between the two tables on the FacilityID fields. If you don't see this line, you can click FacilityID in tblFacilities and drag it on FacilityID in tblReservations, just like you learned to do in "Defining Relationships," on page 215.

Note

If you haven't defined relationships, when you create a query that uses two tables that are related by more than one field (for example, tblFacilityRooms and tblReservations in this database), the Join Properties dialog lets you define only one of the links at a time. You must click New again to define the second part of the join. If you're using the drag method, you can do this with only one field at a time even though you can select multiple fields in either table window. We'll discuss the Join Properties dialog box in "Building a Simple Outer Join," on page 634.

In this example, you want to add to the query the FacilityID and FacilityName fields from the tblFacilities table and the ReservationID, EmployeeNumber, FacilityID, RoomNumber, CheckInDate, and CheckOutDate fields from the tblReservations table.

When you run the query, you see the recordset shown in Figure 10-2. The fields from the tblFacilities table appear first, left to right. We resized the columns displayed in Figure 10-2 so that you can see all the fields. You might need to scroll right in the datasheet to see them on your computer.

INSIDE OUT A Query Is Really Defined by Its SQL

The query designer converts everything you build in a query grid into Structured Query Language (SQL)—the lingua franca of database queries. Access 2010 actually stores only the SQL and rebuilds the query grid each time you open a query in Design view. Later in this chapter, we'll examine some of the actual syntax behind your queries, and you can study the full details of SQL in Article 2, "Understanding SQL," on the companion CD.

ID	Name	Reservation	Employee	Facility	Room	Check-In	Check-Out
1	Main Campus Housing A	1	7	Main Campus Housing A	810	8/30/2010	9/11/2010
1	Main Campus Housing A	4	3	Main Campus Housing A	502	10/8/2010	10/25/2010
1	Main Campus Housing A	6	10	Main Campus Housing A	902	9/25/2010	10/14/2010
1	Main Campus Housing A	8	8	Main Campus Housing A	509	10/10/2010	10/23/2010
1	Main Campus Housing A	10	3	Main Campus H Chicago	707	10/26/2010	11/8/2010
1	Main Campus Housing A	12	3	Main Campus H Chicago	207	9/18/2010	9/29/2010
1	Main Campus Housing A	13	8	North Satellite Chicago	111	9/28/2010	10/14/2010
1	Main Campus Housing A	14	7	South Campus Chicago	708	10/21/2010	10/26/2010
1	Main Campus Housing A	18	8		702	11/16/2010	11/21/2010
1	Main Campus Housing A	20	5	Main Campus Housing A	309	10/29/2010	11/15/2010
1	Main Campus Housing A	24	3	Main Campus Housing A	207	11/18/2010	11/22/2010
1	Main Campus Housing A	27	11	Main Campus Housing A	505	11/26/2010	11/27/2010
1	Main Campus Housing A	31	5	Main Campus Housing A	311	1/8/2011	1/10/2011
1	Main Campus Housing A	32	2	Main Campus Housing A	410	12/2/2010	12/21/2010
1	Main Campus Housing A	36	2	Main Campus Housing A	507	1/1/2011	1/7/2011
1	Main Campus Housing A	37	7	Main Campus Housing A	404	1/6/2011	1/15/2011
1	Main Campus Housing A	45	13	Main Campus Housing A	102	12/22/2010	12/27/2010
1	Main Campus Housing A	46	1	Main Campus Housing A	501	12/15/2010	12/25/2010
1	Main Campus Housing A	51	9	Main Campus Housing A	103	2/17/2011	3/2/2011
1	Main Campus Housing A	54	12	Main Campus Housing A	704	3/11/2011	3/22/2011
1	Main Campus Housing A	57	11	Main Campus Housing A	104	3/10/2011	3/18/2011
1	Main Campus Housing A	58	10	Main Campus Housing A	601	2/13/2011	2/17/2011
2	Main Campus Housing B	2	7	Main Campus Housing B	111	9/17/2010	9/28/2010
2	Main Campus Housing B	5	3	Main Campus Housing B	214	9/19/2010	9/21/2010
2	Main Campus Housing B	9	2	Main Campus Housing B	504	10/14/2010	10/17/2010

Figure 10-2 Here, you can see the recordset of the query shown in Figure 10-1. The facility information in the drop-down list comes from the Lookup properties defined in the tblReservations table.

Notice the facility name in the column for the FacilityID field from the tblReservations table. (The caption for the field is Facility.) If you check the definition of the FacilityID field in the tblReservations table, you'll see a Lookup combo box defined—the query has inherited those properties. Click in a field in the Facility column in this datasheet, and the combo box appears. If you choose a different Facility name from the list, you will change the FacilityID field for that reservation. But the room number already in the row might not exist in the new Facility, so you might get an error if you try to save the row. This is yet another example of a business rule that you will have to ensure is verified in a form that you create for users to edit this data.

If you choose a different Facility (the FacilityID field in tblReservations), you can see the ID and Name change on the left side of the datasheet. When you change the value in a foreign key field (in this case, the FacilityID field in tblReservations) in a table on the *many* side of a one-to-many query (there are many reservations for each facility), Access performs an *AutoLookup* to retrieve the related row from the one side (tblFacilities) to keep the data synchronized. You'll find this feature handy later when you build a form to display and edit information from a query like this.

Try changing the entry in the Facility column (remember, this is the FacilityID field from tblReservations; you see the name of the facility because we defined Lookup properties on this field) in the first row from Main Campus Housing A to South Campus Housing C. When you select the new value for the FacilityID field in tblReservations, you should see the ID field from tblFacilities change to 3 and the Name entry (the FacilityName field from tblFacilities) change from Main Campus Housing A to South Campus Housing C. Note that in this case you're changing only the linking FacilityID field in tblReservations, not the name of the facility in tblFacilities. Access is retrieving the row from tblFacilities that matches the changed FacilityID value in tblReservations to show you the correct name.

Note

If you change the facility in one of the rows in this query, Access won't let you save the row if the room number in the reservation doesn't exist in the new facility you chose. You can press Escape to back out of the changes to the query, in this case.

One interesting aspect of queries on multiple tables is that in many cases you can update the fields from either table in the query. See "Limitations on Using Select Queries to Update Data," on page 680, for a discussion of when joined queries are not updatable. For example, you can change the facility name in the tblFacilities table by changing the data in the Name column in this query's datasheet.

CAUTION!

In most cases, Access lets you edit fields from the table on the *one* side of the join (in this case, tblFacilities). Because the facility name comes from a table on the one side of a one-to-many relationship (one facility has many reservations, but each reservation is for only one facility), if you change the name of the facility in any row in this query, you change the name for all reservations for the same facility.

Although the dangers to doing this are apparent, this is actually one of the benefits of designing your tables properly. If the facility is renamed (perhaps it gets renamed in honor of a beloved ex-president of the company), you need to change the name in only one place. You don't have to find all existing reservations for the facility and update them all.

You might use a query like the one in Figure 10-1 as the basis for a report on reservations by facility. However, such a report would probably also need to include the employee name and department to be truly useful. Switch back to Design view, click the Show Table button in the Query Setup group of the Design contextual tab, and add tblEmployees and tblDepartments to the query. You can also drag any table or query from the Navigation pane to your query.

You'll run into a small problem when you add tblDepartments to your query: There are two relationships defined between tblDepartments and tblEmployees. First, each employee must have a valid department assigned, so there's a relationship on DepartmentID. Also, any manager for a department must be an employee of the department, and an employee can manage only one department, so there's a second relationship defined between EmployeeNumber in tblEmployees and ManagerNumber in tblDepartments.

The query designer doesn't know which relationship you want to use as a join in this query, so it includes them both in the query grid. If you leave both join lines in your query, you'll see only reservations for managers of departments because the join between EmployeeNumber in tblEmployees and ManagerNumber in tblDepartments forces the query to include only employees who are also managers. Click the join line between EmployeeNumber in tblEmployees and ManagerNumber in tblDepartments and press the Delete key to remove the join.

If you're going to use this query in a report, you probably don't need EmployeeNumber and FacilityID from tblReservations, so you can delete them. Next, click on RoomNumber in the design grid and click Insert Columns in the Query Setup group on the Design tab to give you a blank column to work with. You need the employee name for your report, but you most likely don't need the separate FirstName, MiddleName, and LastName fields. Use the blank column to create an expression as follows:

```
EmpName: tblEmployees.FirstName & " " & (tblEmployees.MiddleName + " ") & LastName
```

Note that you're using the little trick you learned in Chapter 9: using an arithmetic operation to eliminate the potential extra blank when an employee has no middle name. Drag the Department field from tblDepartments on top of RoomNumber in the design grid—this should place it between the EmpName field you just defined and RoomNumber. Your query grid should now look like Figure 10-3.

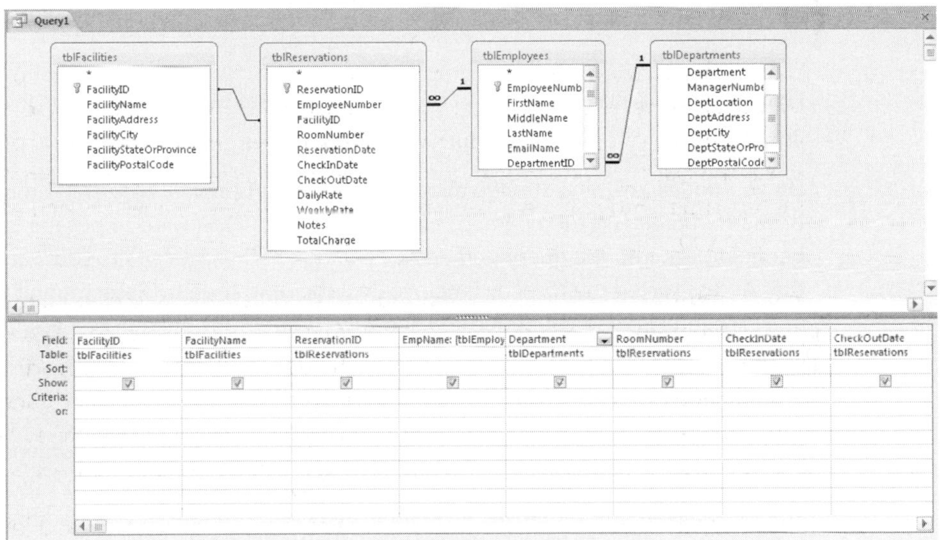

Figure 10-3 In this example, we are creating a complex query using four tables.

You can switch to Datasheet view to see the results of your work, as shown in Figure 10-4.

Query1

ID	Name	Reservation ID	EmpName	Department	Room	Check-In	Check-Out
3	South Campus Housing C	7	Reed Koch	Sales	501	8/24/2010	9/6/2010
1	Main Campus Housing A	46	Reed Koch	Sales	501	12/15/2010	12/25/2010
2	Main Campus Housing B	9	Tim Kim	Finance	504	10/14/2010	10/17/2010
2	Main Campus Housing B	29	Tim Kim	Finance	206	12/14/2010	12/19/2010
1	Main Campus Housing A	32	Tim Kim	Finance	410	12/2/2010	12/21/2010
1	Main Campus Housing A	36	Tim Kim	Finance	507	1/1/2011	1/7/2011
2	Main Campus Housing B	44	Tim Kim	Finance	102	1/15/2011	1/26/2011
1	Main Campus Housing A	4	John Tippett	Product Development	502	10/8/2010	10/25/2010
2	Main Campus Housing B	5	John Tippett	Product Development	214	9/19/2010	9/21/2010
1	Main Campus Housing A	10	John Tippett	Product Development	707	10/26/2010	11/8/2010
1	Main Campus Housing A	12	John Tippett	Product Development	207	9/18/2010	9/29/2010
1	Main Campus Housing A	24	John Tippett	Product Development	207	11/18/2010	11/22/2010
4	North Satellite Housing D	34	John Tippett	Product Development	203	12/30/2010	1/15/2011
3	South Campus Housing C	41	John Tippett	Product Development	401	12/13/2010	12/28/2010
2	Main Campus Housing B	55	John Tippett	Product Development	212	1/30/2011	2/5/2011
3	South Campus Housing C	17	Kirk DeGrasse	Sales	101	10/25/2010	11/15/2010
2	Main Campus Housing B	35	Kirk DeGrasse	Sales	402	12/20/2010	1/7/2011
2	Main Campus Housing B	47	Kirk DeGrasse	Sales	514	12/30/2010	12/31/2010
2	Main Campus Housing B	48	Kirk DeGrasse	Sales	402	2/4/2011	2/20/2011
2	Main Campus Housing B	49	Kirk DeGrasse	Sales	114	2/10/2011	3/3/2011
3	South Campus Housing C	53	Kirk DeGrasse	Sales	106	2/14/2011	3/6/2011
4	North Satellite Housing D	3	David Oliver Lawrence	Product Development	305	9/13/2010	9/16/2010
2	Main Campus Housing B	11	David Oliver Lawrence	Product Development	301	9/18/2010	10/3/2010
2	Main Campus Housing B	19	David Oliver Lawrence	Product Development	610	11/16/2010	11/30/2010
1	Main Campus Housing A	20	David Oliver Lawrence	Product Development	309	10/29/2010	11/15/2010

Record: 1 of 58 No Filter Search

Figure 10-4 In Datasheet view, you can see the recordset of the query shown in Figure 10-3.

Do you notice anything strange about the sequence of rows? Why aren't the rows sorted by facility name and then perhaps employee name? If you were to put the EmployeeNumber field back into the query grid and take a look at the data again, you would discover that Access sorted the rows by EmployeeNumber and then by ReservationID. Access looked at all the information you requested and then figured out the quickest way to give you the answer—probably by fetching rows from tblEmployee first (which are sorted on the primary key, EmployeeID) and then fetching the matching rows from tblReservations.

Remember from Chapter 9 that the only way you can guarantee the sequence of rows is to specify a sort on the fields you want. In this case, you might want to sort by facility name, employee last name, employee first name, and check-in date. You buried first name and last name in the EmpName expression, so you can't use that field to sort the data by last name. You can find the correct answer saved as qxmplSortReservations in the sample database. (Hint: You need to add tblEmployees.LastName and tblEmployees.FirstName to the grid to be able to specify the sort.)

Building a Query on a Query

When you're building a very complex query, sometimes it's easier to visualize the solution to the problem at hand by breaking it down into smaller pieces. In some cases, building a query on a query might be the only way to correctly solve the problem.

For this set of examples, let's switch to the data in the Conrad Systems Contacts database. Start Access 2010 and open ContactsDataCopy.accdb. Customers who purchase a Single User copy of the BO$$ software marketed by Conrad Systems can later decide to upgrade to the Multi-User edition for a reduced price. Assume you're a consultant hired by Conrad Systems, and the company has asked you to produce a list of all customers and their companies who purchased a Single User copy and then later purchased the upgrade.

To solve this, you might be tempted to start a new query on tblContacts and add the tblCompanies, tblContactProducts, and tblProducts tables. You would include the CompanyID and CompanyName fields from tblCompanies; the ContactID, FirstName, and LastName fields from tblContacts; and the ProductID and ProductName fields from tblProducts. Then you would place a criterion like *"BO$$ Single User" And "Upgrade to BO$$ Multi-User"* on the Criteria line under ProductName. However, any one row in your query will show information from only one contact and product, so one row can't contain both "BO$$ Single User" and "Upgrade to BO$$ Multi-User." (See the discussion in "AND vs. OR," on page 557.) Your query will return no rows.

Your next attempt might be to correct the criterion to *"BO$$ Single User" Or "Upgrade to BO$$ Multi-User"*. That will at least return some data, but you'll get an answer similar to Figure 10-5. (You can find this query saved as qxmplTwoProductsWrong in the sample database.)

qxmplTwoProductsWrong

Company / Org.	Company / Organization	Contact	First Name	Last Nam	Product	Product Name
1	Contoso, Ltd	1	Jan	Stoklasa	6	Upgrade to BO$$ Multi-User
2	Fourth Coffee	4	Andrew	Dixon	6	Upgrade to BO$$ Multi-User
3	Coho Vineyard	6	Mario	Kresnadi	3	BO$$ Single User
3	Coho Vineyard	7	Anibal	Sousa	6	Upgrade to BO$$ Multi-User
3	Coho Vineyard	8	Joseph	Matthews	3	BO$$ Single User
3	Coho Vineyard	8	Joseph	Matthews	6	Upgrade to BO$$ Multi-User
4	Southridge Video	10	Kathleen Gail	Jensen	6	Upgrade to BO$$ Multi-User
5	Consolidated Messenger	12	Harry	Linggoputro	3	BO$$ Single User
6	Baldwin Museum of Science	13	Cat	Francis	6	Upgrade to BO$$ Multi-User
7	Fabrikam, Inc.	16	John	Smith	3	BO$$ Single User
7	Fabrikam, Inc.	16	John	Smith	6	Upgrade to BO$$ Multi-User
9	School of Fine Art	19	Dániel	Koczka	3	BO$$ Single User
9	School of Fine Art	19	Dániel	Koczka	6	Upgrade to BO$$ Multi-User
12	Margie's Travel	24	Mindy	Martin	3	BO$$ Single User
12	Margie's Travel	25	Markus	Zulechner	3	BO$$ Single User
12	Margie's Travel	26	Peter	Villadsen	6	Upgrade to BO$$ Multi-User
13	Lucerne Publishing	28	Mark	Hanson	3	BO$$ Single User
13	Lucerne Publishing	28	Mark	Hanson	6	Upgrade to BO$$ Multi-User
14	Humongous Insurance	29	Marcin	Jankowski	6	Upgrade to BO$$ Multi-User
*					(New)	

Figure 10-5 This query is an attempt to find out which contacts have purchased both BO$$ Single User and the BO$$ Multi-User upgrade.

Because there aren't very many rows in this table, you can scan this 19-row result and see that the correct answer is four contacts—Joseph Matthews, John Smith, Daniel Koczka, and Mark Hanson. But if there were thousands of rows in the database, you wouldn't be able to easily find the contacts who purchased both products. And if you need to display the output in a report, you really need a single row for each contact that meets your criteria.

One way to solve this sort of problem is to build a query that finds everyone who owns BO$$ Single User and save it. Then, build another query that finds everyone who purchased the BO$$ Multi-User upgrade and save that. Finally, build a third query that joins the first two results to get your final answer. Remember that a simple join returns only the rows that match in both tables—or queries. So, someone who appears in both queries clearly owns both products! Here's how to build the solution:

1. Build the first query to find customers who own BO$$ Single User, as follows:

   a. Start a new query on tblContactProducts and add tblProducts to the query. You should see a join line between tblProducts and tblContactProducts on the ProductID field because there's a relationship defined.

   b. From tblContactProducts, include the CompanyID and the ContactID fields.

   c. Add ProductName from tblProducts, and enter **"BO$$ Single User"** on the Criteria line under this field. Save this query and name it qrySingle.

2. Build the second query to find customers who bought the upgrade, as follows:

   a. Start another query on tblContactProducts and add tblProducts to the query.

   b. From tblContactProducts, include the CompanyID and the ContactID fields.

   c. Add ProductName from tblProducts, and enter **"Upgrade to BO$$ Multi-User"** on the Criteria line under this field. Save this query and name it qryMultiUpgrade.

3. Build the final solution query, as follows:

   a. Start a new query on tblCompanies. Add your new qrySingle and qryMultiUpgrade queries.

   b. The query designer will link tblCompanies to both queries on CompanyID, but you don't need a link to both. Click on the join line between tblCompanies and qryMultiUpgrade and delete it.

c. You do need to link qrySingle and qryMultiUpgrade. Drag CompanyID from qrySingle to qryMultiUpgrade. Then, drag ContactID from qrySingle to qryMultiUpgrade. Because you are defining an inner join between the two queries, the query only fetches rows from the two queries where the CompanyID and ContactID match.

d. Add tblContacts to your query. Because there's a relationship defined between ContactID in tblContacts and ReferredBy in tblCompanies, the query designer adds this join line. You don't need this join (the query would return only contacts who have made referrals), so click the line and delete it. The query designer does correctly create a join line between tblContacts and qrySingle.

e. On the query design grid, include CompanyName from tblCompanies, and FirstName and LastName from tblContacts. Your result should look like Figure 10-6.

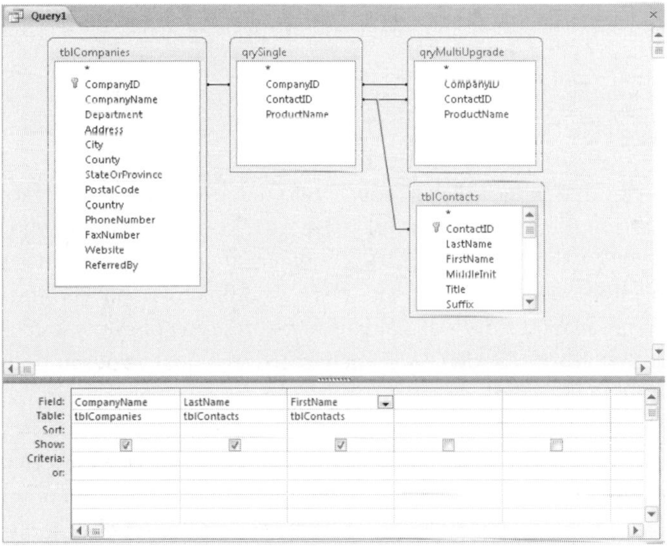

Figure 10-6 Here, you are solving the "contacts who own two products" problem the right way by building a query on queries.

Switch to Datasheet view, and, sure enough, the query gives you the right answer, as shown in Figure 10-7.

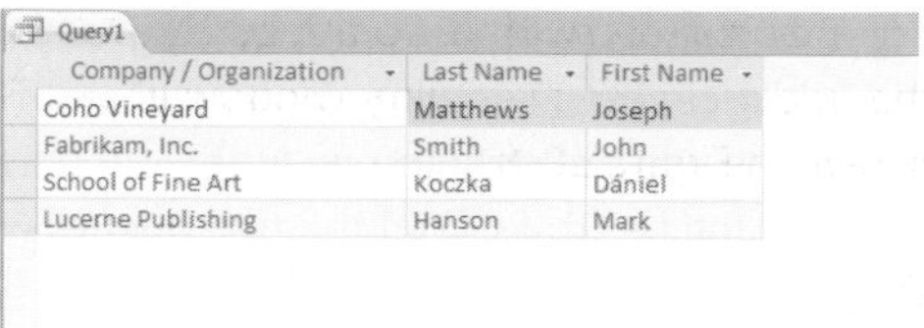
Query1

Company / Organization	Last Name	First Name
Coho Vineyard	Matthews	Joseph
Fabrikam, Inc.	Smith	John
School of Fine Art	Koczka	Dániel
Lucerne Publishing	Hanson	Mark

Figure 10-7 You can now correctly see the four contacts who purchased a BO$$ Single User edition and later upgraded.

This works because you're using the two queries to filter each other via the join. The qrySingle query finds contacts who own BO$$ Single User. The qryMultiUpgrade query finds contacts who bought the BO$$ Multi-User upgrade. The join lines between these two queries ask the final query to return rows only where the CompanyID and ContactID in the first two queries match, so you won't see rows from qrySingle that don't have a matching combination of CompanyID and ContactID in qryMultiUpgrade, and vice versa. (You can find this query saved as qxmplTwoProductsRight in the sample database.)

For more examples of building queries on queries, see Article 2, "Understanding SQL," on the companion CD.

Using Outer Joins

Most queries that you create to request information from multiple tables will show results on the basis of matching data in one or more tables. For example, the Query window in Datasheet view, shown in Figure 10-4, contains the names of facilities that have reservations in the tblReservations table—and it does not contain the names of facilities that don't have any reservations booked. As explained earlier, this type of query is called an equi-join query, meaning that you'll see rows only where there are equal values in both tables. But what if you want to display facilities that do not have any reservations in the database? Or, how do you find employees who have no reservations? You can get the information you need by creating a query that uses an outer join. An outer join lets you see all rows from one of the tables even if there's no matching row in the related table. When no matching row exists, Access returns the special Null value in the columns from the related table.

Building a Simple Outer Join

To create an outer join, you must modify the join properties. Let's see if we can find any employees who don't have any reservations booked. Start a new query on tblEmployees in the HousingDataCopy database. Add tblReservations to the query. Double-click the join line between the two tables in the upper part of the Query window in Design view to see the Join Properties dialog box, shown in Figure 10-8.

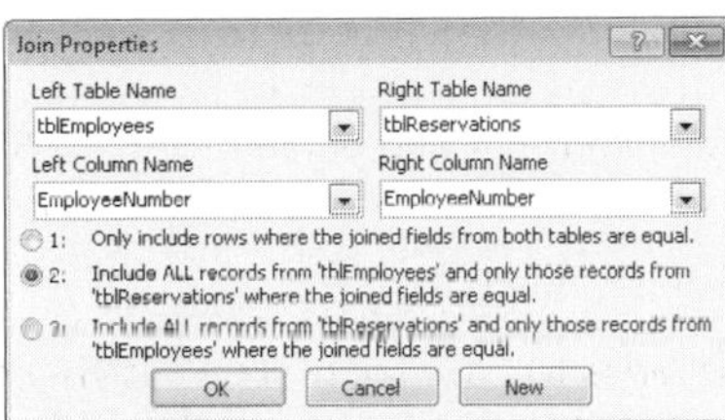

Figure 10-8 The Join Properties dialog box allows you to change the join properties for the query.

The default setting in the Join Properties dialog box is the first option—where the joined fields from both tables are equal. You can see that you have two additional options for this query: to see all employees and any reservations that match, or to see all reservations and any employees that match. If you entered your underlying data correctly, you shouldn't have reservations for employees who aren't defined in the database. If you asked Access to enforce referential integrity (discussed in Chapter 4, "Designing Client Tables") when you defined the relationship between the tblEmployees table and the tblReservations table, Access won't let you create any reservations for nonexistent employees.

Select the second option in the dialog box. (When the link between two tables involves more than one field in each table, you can click New to define the additional links.) Click OK. You should now see an arrow on the join line pointing from the tblEmployees field list to the tblReservations field list, indicating that you have asked for an outer join with all records from tblEmployees regardless of match, as shown in Figure 10-9. For employees who have no reservations, Access returns the special Null value in all the columns for tblReservations. So, you can find the employees that aren't planning to stay in any facility by including the Is Null test for any of the columns from tblReservations. When you run this query, you should find exactly two employees who have no reservations, as shown in Figure 10-10. The finished query is saved as qxmplEmployeesNoReservations in the HousingDataCopy.accdb database.

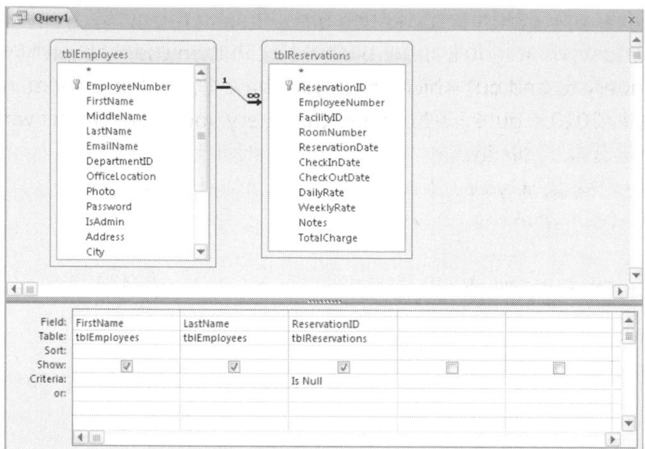

Figure 10-9 This query design finds employees who have no reservations.

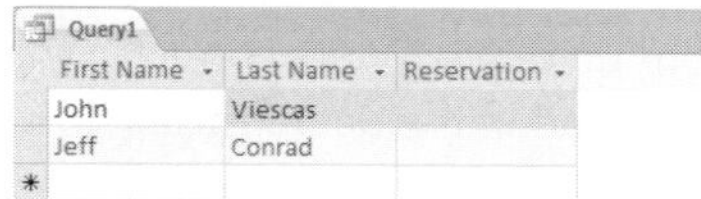

Query1

First Name	Last Name	Reservation
John	Viescas	
Jeff	Conrad	

Figure 10-10 This recordset shows the two employees who have no reservations.

Solving a Complex "Unmatched" Problem

As discussed earlier in this chapter, you know that to solve certain types of problems you must first build one query to define a subset of data from your tables and then use that query as input to another query to get the final answer. For example, suppose you want to find out which employees have no reservations in a certain time period. You might guess that an outer join from the tblEmployees table to the tblReservations table will do the trick. That would work fine if the tblReservations table contained reservations for only the time period in question. Remember, to find employees who haven't booked a room, you have to look for a special Null value in the columns from tblReservations. But to limit the data in tblReservations to a specific time period—let's say November and December 2010—you have to be able to test real values. In other words, you have a problem because a column from tblReservations can't be both Null and have a date value at the same time. (You can find an example of the wrong way to solve this problem saved as qxmplEmpNotBookedNovDecWRONG in the sample database.)

To solve this problem, you must first create a query that contains only the reservations for the months you want. As you'll see in a bit, you can then use that query with an outer join in another query to find out which employees haven't booked a room in November and December 2010. Figure 10-11 shows the query you need to start with, using tblReservations. This example includes the EmployeeNumber field as well as the FacilityID and RoomNumber fields, so you can use it to search for either employees or facilities or rooms that aren't booked in the target months.

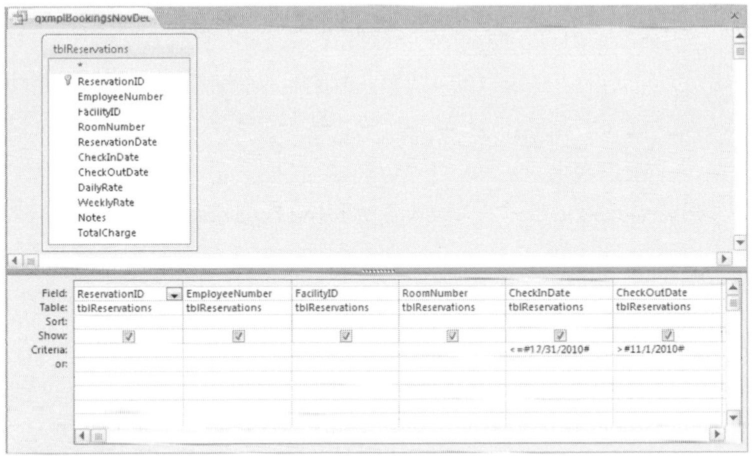

Figure 10-11 You can add a filter to your query to list reservation data for particular months.

Notice that if you truly want to see all reservations in these two months, you need to specify a criterion on both CheckInDate and CheckOutDate. Anyone who checked in on or before December 31, 2010—provided they didn't check out before November 1, 2010—is someone who stayed in a room between the dates of interest. You don't want anyone who checked out on November 1 (who stayed the night of October 31, but didn't stay over into November), which explains why the second criterion is >#11/1/2010# and not >=#11/1/2010#. This query is saved as qxmplBookingsNovDec in the HousingDataCopy.accdb database.

Finding Records Across Date Spans

You might be looking at the problem of finding any reservation that crosses into or is contained within a certain date span and scratching your head. You want any reservation that meets one of these criteria:

- **The reservation begins before the start of the date span but extends into the date span.**

- **The reservation is contained wholly within the date span.**
- **The reservation begins before the end of the date span but extends beyond the date span.**
- **The reservation starts before the beginning of the date span and ends after the end of the date span.**

You can see these four conditions in the following illustration:

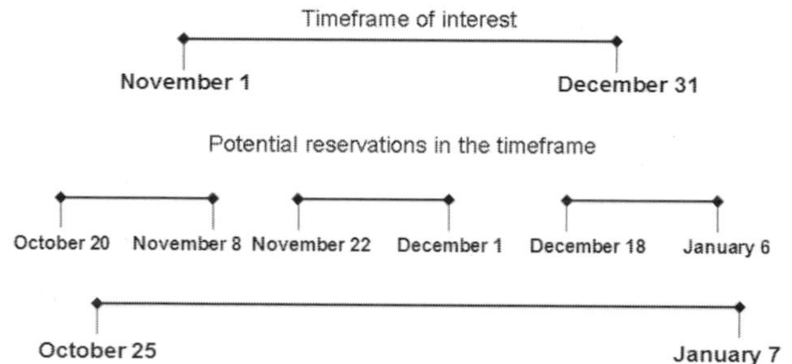

You might be tempted to include four separate criteria in your query, but that's not necessary. So long as a reservation begins before the end of the span and ends after the beginning of the span, you've got them all! Try the criteria shown in Figure 10-11 to see if that simple test doesn't find all the previous cases.

After you save the first query, click the Query Design button in the Queries group on the Create tab to start a new query. In the Show Table dialog box, add tblEmployees to the design grid by double-clicking tblEmployees. Click the Queries tab in the Show Table dialog box and then double-click qxmplBookingsNovDec to add it to the query grid. Click Close to close the Show Table dialog box. Access should automatically link tblEmployees to the query on matching EmployeeNumber fields. Double-click the join line to open the Join Properties dialog box, and select option 2 to see all rows from tblEmployees and any matching rows from the query. The join line's arrow should point from tblEmployees to the query, as shown in Figure 10-12.

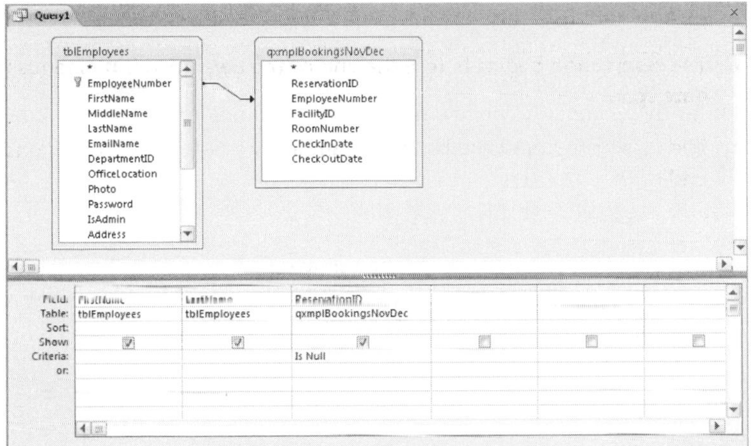

Figure 10-12 An outer join query searches for employees not booked in November and December 2010.

As you did in the previous outer join example, include some fields from the tblEmployees table and at least one field from the query that contains reservations only from November and December 2010. In the field from the query, add the special Is Null criterion. When you run this query (the results of which are shown in Figure 10-13), you should find six employees who haven't booked a room in November and December 2010—including the two employees that you found earlier who haven't booked any rooms at all. This query is saved as qxmplEmpNotBookedNovDec in the HousingDataCopy.accdb database.

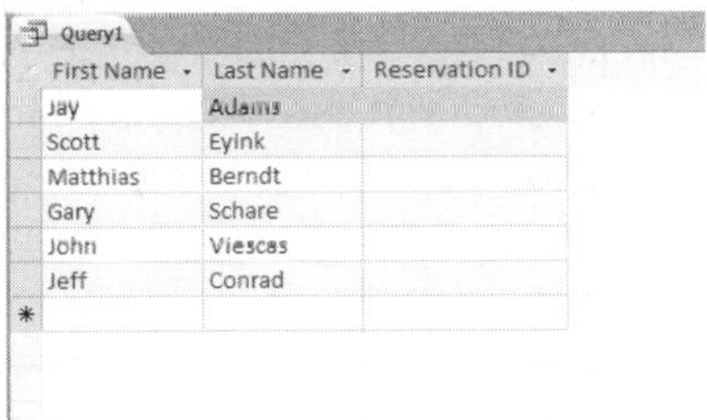

Query1

First Name	Last Name	Reservation ID
Jay	Adams	
Scott	Eyink	
Matthias	Berndt	
Gary	Schare	
John	Viescas	
Jeff	Conrad	

Figure 10-13 These employees have no bookings in November and December 2010.

Let's study another example. When you're looking at reservation requests, and each request indicates the particular type of room desired, it might be useful to know either which facilities have this type of room or which facilities do not. (Not all facilities have all the different types of rooms.) You can find a complete list of the room types in the tlkpRoomTypes table in the Housing Reservations application.

To find out which room types aren't in a facility, you might try an outer join from tlkpRoomTypes to tblFacilityRooms and look for Null again, but all you'd find is that all room types exist somewhere—you wouldn't know which room type was missing in what facility. In truth, you need to build a query first that limits room types to one facility. Your query should look something like Figure 10-14.

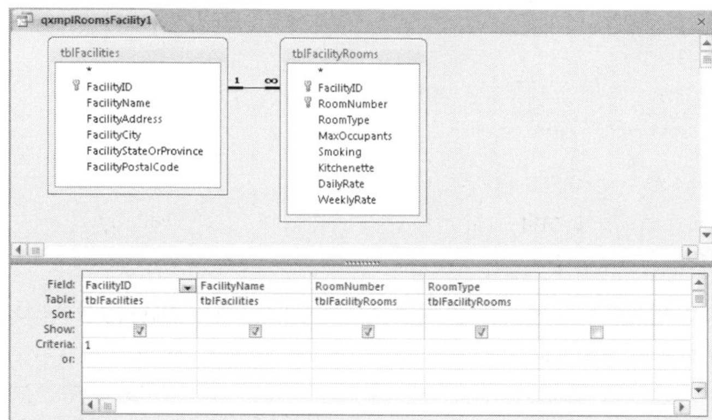

Figure 10-14 This query lists all the rooms and their room types in Facility 1.

Now you can build your outer join query to find out which room types aren't in the first housing facility. Start a new query by clicking the Query Design button in the Queries group on the Create tab. In the Show Table dialog box, add tlkpRoomTypes to the design grid by double-clicking tlkpRoomTypes. Click the Queries tab in the Show Table dialog box and then double-click the qxmplRoomsFacility1 query to add it to the query grid. Close the Show Table dialog box. Double-click the join line and ask for all rows from tlkpRoomTypes and any matching rows from the query. Add the RoomType field from tlkpRoomTypes and the field FacilityID from the query to the grid. Under FacilityID, place a criterion of Is Null. Your query should look like Figure 10-15.

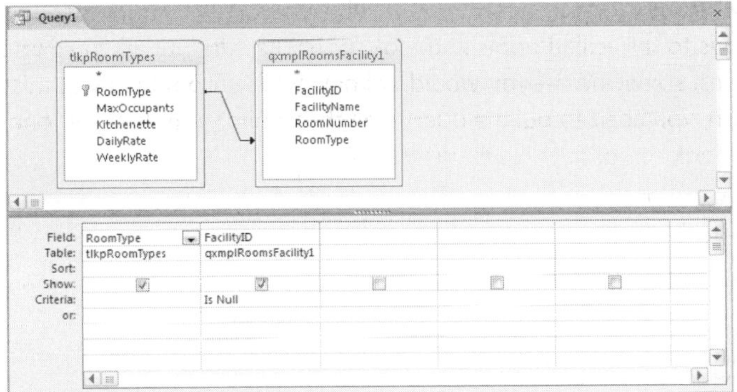

Figure 10-15 This query determines which room types are not in Facility 1.

If you run this query, you'll find that Facility 1 has no one-bedroom suites with a king-size bed, no one-bedroom suites with two queen-size beds, and no two-bedroom suites with a king-size bed, queen-size bed, and kitchenette. In the sample database, you'll find sample queries that return the room types for the other three facilities, so you can build queries like the one in Figure 10-15 to find out what room types are missing in those facilities.

Using a Query Wizard

Every time you have clicked the Query Wizard button in the Queries group on the Create tab, you have seen the interesting query wizard entries. You can use query wizards to help you build certain types of "tricky" queries such as crosstab queries (discussed later in this chapter) and queries to find duplicate or unmatched rows. For example, you could have used a query wizard to build the query shown in Figure 10-9 to locate employees who have no room reservations. Let's use a query wizard to build a query to perform a similar search in the ContactsDataCopy.accdb sample file to find contacts who don't own any products.

To try this, click the Query Wizard button in the Queries group on the Create tab. Select the Find Unmatched Query Wizard option in the New Query dialog box, as shown in Figure 10-16, and then click OK.

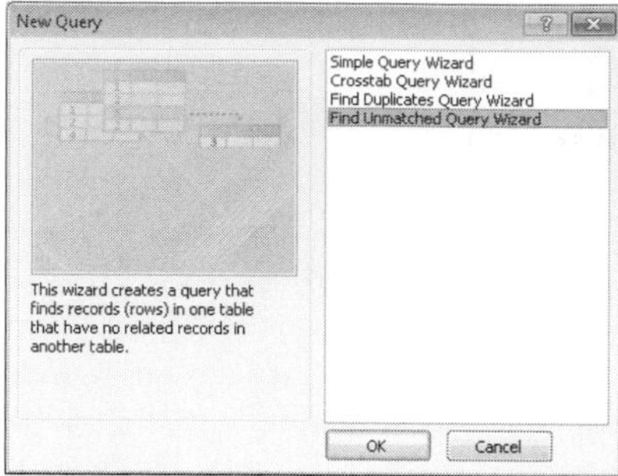

Figure 10-16 Select a query wizard in the New Query dialog box.

The wizard opens a page with a list of tables from which you can select the initial records, as shown in Figure 10-17. If you want to use an existing query instead of a table, select the Queries option. If you want to look at all queries and tables, select the Both option. In this case, you're looking for contacts who haven't purchased any products, so select the tblContacts table and then click Next.

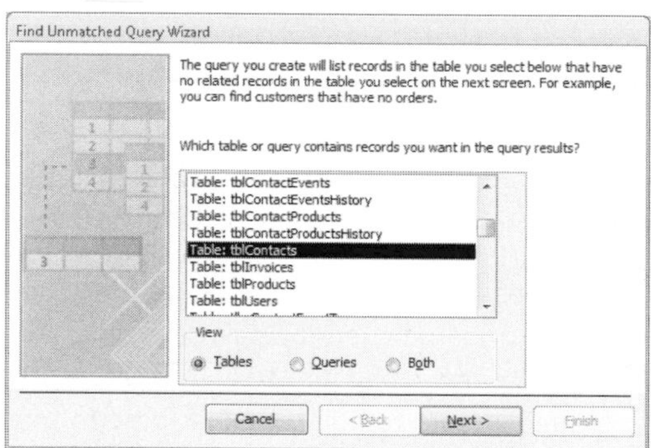

Figure 10-17 You can select tables or queries on the first page of the Find Unmatched Query Wizard.

On the next page, select the table that contains the related information you expect to be unmatched. You're looking for contacts who have purchased no products, so select the tblContactProducts table and then click Next to go to the next page, shown in Figure 10-18.

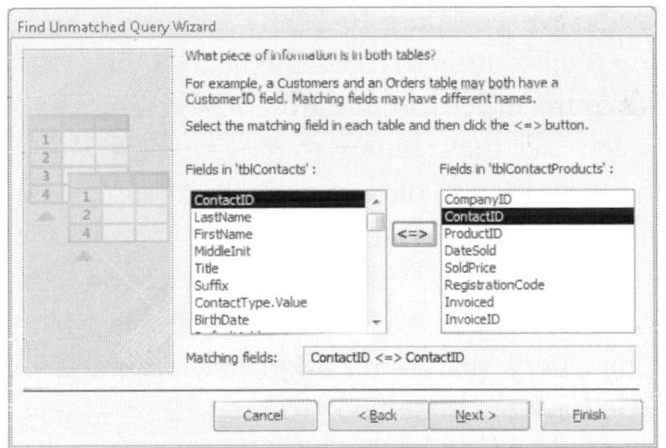

Figure 10-18 This page is where you define the unmatched link.

Next, the wizard needs to know the linking fields between the two tables. Because no direct relationship is defined between tblContacts and tblContactProducts, the wizard won't automatically choose the matching fields for you. Click the ContactID field in tblContacts and the ContactID field in tblContactProducts to select those two fields. Click the <=> button between the field lists to add those fields to the Matching fields box. Click Next to go to the page, shown in Figure 10-19.

Note

The Find Unmatched Query Wizard can work with only the tables that have no more than one field that links the two tables. If you need to "find unmatched" records between two tables that require a join on more than one field, you'll have to build the query yourself.

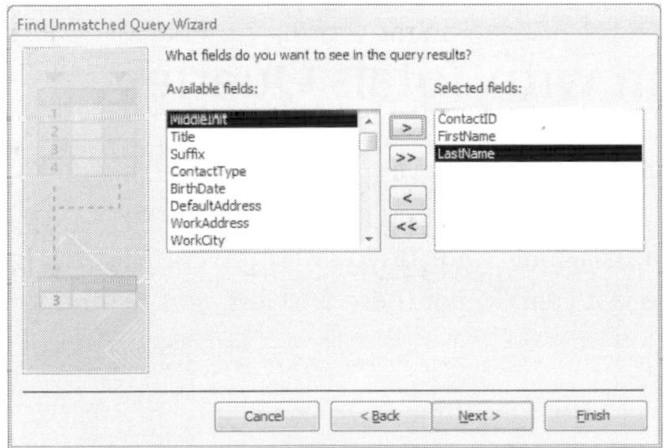

Figure 10-19 On this page, you select the fields to be displayed in a query.

Choose the fields you want to display (see Figure 10-19) by selecting a field in the Available Fields list and then clicking the > button to move the field to the Selected Fields list. The query will display the fields in the order you select them. If you choose a field in error, select it in the list on the right and click the < button to move it back. You can click the >> button to select all fields or the << button to remove all fields. When you're finished selecting fields, click Next. On the final page, you can specify a different name for your query. (The wizard generates a long and ugly name.) You can select an option to either view the results or modify the design. So that you can see the design first, select Modify The Design and then click Finish to open the Query window in Design view. Figure 10-20 shows the finished query to find contacts who have purchased no products.

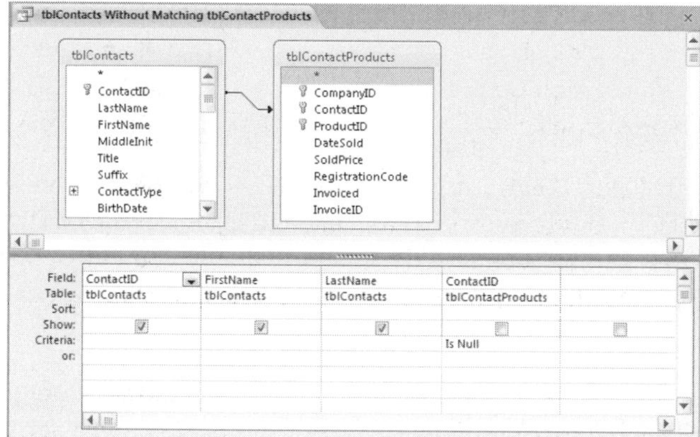

Figure 10-20 The query wizard has helped you build a query that finds contacts who have purchased no products.

If you run this query, you'll find three contacts who haven't bought anything. Perhaps you should schedule a call to these people to find out why!

Summarizing Information with Totals Queries

Sometimes you aren't interested in each and every row in your table—you'd rather see calculations across groups of data. For example, you might want the total product purchase amount for all companies in a particular state, or you might want to know the average of all sales for each month in the last year. To get these answers, you need a totals query.

Totals Within Groups

If you're the housing facilities manager, you might be interested in producing sales and usage numbers by facility or by date range. For this series of exercises, open HousingDataCopy.accdb and start a new query with tblFacilities and tblReservations in the query design grid. Include in the Field row the FacilityName field from tblFacilities and the CheckInDate and TotalCharge fields from tblReservations.

> **INSIDE OUT** **When Totals Queries Are Useful**
>
> **We might occasionally build totals queries to display high-level summaries in a report. More often, we create a regular query that fetches all the detail we need and then use the powerful summarization facilities in reports to calculate totals. You'll learn more about summarizing data in a report in Chapter 18, "Advanced Report Design."**
>
> **A totals query groups the fields you specify, and every output field must either be one of the grouping fields or the result of a calculation using one of the available aggregate functions. (See Table 10-1.) Because all fields are calculated, you cannot update any fields returned by a totals query. So, you're not likely to find totals queries useful in forms.**
>
> **This does not mean that learning about how to build totals queries is not useful. You need to understand the concepts of grouping and totaling to build reports. You will also find that constructing and opening a totals query in Visual Basic code is useful to perform complex validations.**

To turn this into a totals query, click the Totals button in the Show/Hide group of the Design contextual tab under Query Tools to open the Total row in the design grid, as shown in Figure 10-21. When you first click the Totals button in the Show/Hide group, Access displays Group By in the Total row for any fields you already have in the design grid. At this point, the records in each field are grouped but not totaled. If you were to run the query now, you'd get one row in the recordset for each set of unique values—but no totals. You must replace Group By with an *aggregate function* in the Total row.

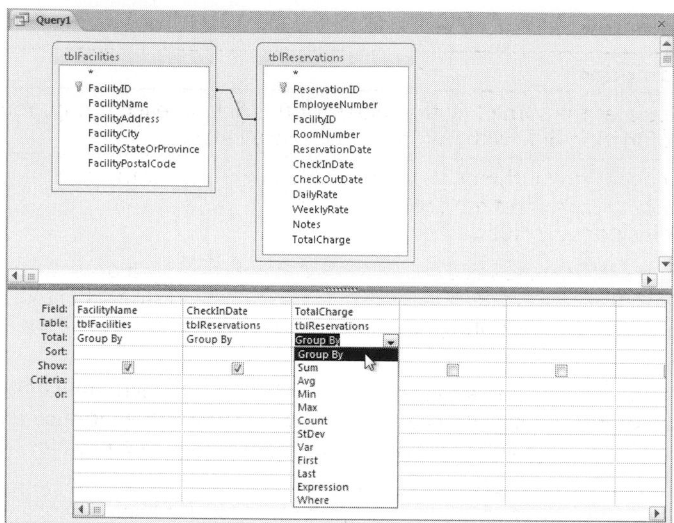

Figure 10-21 The Total row in the design grid allows you to define aggregate functions.

Access provides nine aggregate functions for your use. You can choose the one you want by typing its name in the Total row in the design grid or by clicking the small arrow and selecting it from the list. You can learn about the available functions in Table 10-1.

Let's experiment with the query you're currently working on to understand some of the available functions. First, you probably don't want to see information grouped by individual date. Data summarized over each month would be more informative, so create an expression to replace the CheckInDate field as follows:

```
CheckInMonth: Format([CheckInDate], "yyyy mm")
```

The Format function works similarly to the table field Format property you learned about in Chapter 4. The first parameter is the name of the field or the expression that you want to format, and the second parameter specifies how you want the data formatted. In this case, we're asking Format to return the four-digit year and two-digit month number.

For more information about Format settings, see "Setting Control Properties for Client Forms," on page 865.

Table 10-1 Total Functions

Function	Description
Sum	Calculates the sum of all the values for this field in each group. You can specify this function only with number or currency fields.
Avg	Calculates the arithmetic average of all the values for this field in each group. You can specify this function only with number or currency fields. Access does not include any Null values in the calculation.
Min	Returns the lowest value found in this field within each group. For numbers, Min returns the smallest value. For text, Min returns the lowest value in collating sequence ("dictionary"[1] order), without regard to case. Access ignores Null values.
Max	Returns the highest value found in this field within each group. For numbers, Max returns the largest value. For text, Max returns the highest value in collating sequence ("dictionary"[1] order), without regard to case. Access ignores Null values.
Count	Returns the count of the rows in which the specified field is not a Null value. You can also enter the special expression COUNT(*) in the Field row to count all rows in each group, regardless of the presence of Null values.
StDev	Calculates the statistical standard deviation of all the values for this field in each group. You can specify this function only with number or currency fields. If the group does not contain at least two rows, Access returns a Null value.
Var	Calculates the statistical variance of all the values for this field in each group. You can specify this function only with number or currency fields. If the group does not contain at least two rows, Access returns a Null value.
First	Returns the value for the field from the first row encountered in the group. Note that the first row might not be the one with the lowest value. It also might not be the row you think is "first" within the group. Because First depends on the actual physical sequence of stored data, it essentially returns an unpredictable value from within the group.
Last	Returns the value for the field from the last row encountered in the group. Note that the last row might not be the one with the highest value. It also might not be the row you think is "last" within the group. Because Last depends on the actual physical sequence of stored data, it essentially returns an unpredictable value from within the group.

[1]You can change the sort order for new databases you create by clicking the File tab on the Backstage view, clicking Options, and then using the New Database Sort Order list in the General category. The default value is General-Legacy, which sorts your data according to the language specified for your operating system.

Change the Total row under TotalCharge to Sum. Add the TotalCharge field from tblReservations three more times, and choose Avg, Min, and Max, respectively, under each. Finally, add the ReservationID field from tblReservations and choose Count in the Total row under that field. Your query design should now look like Figure 10-22.

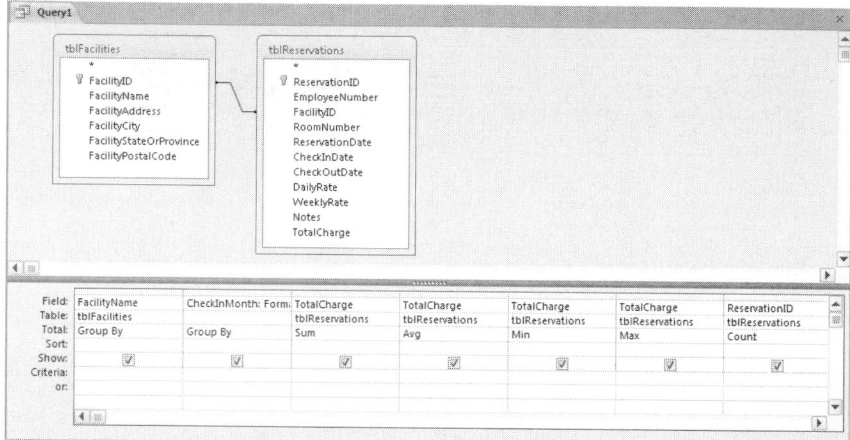

Figure 10-22 This query design explores many different aggregate functions.

Switch to Datasheet view to see the results, as shown in Figure 10-23. The sample data file has 306 available rooms in four different facilities. From the results of this query, you could conclude that this company has far more housing than it needs! Perhaps the most interesting row is the third row (the row that is highlighted in Figure 10-23). The five reservations for Housing A in October 2010 show how the various functions might help you analyze the data further.

TROUBLESHOOTING

I didn't specify sorting criteria, so why is my data sorted?

A totals query has to sort your data to be able to group it, so it returns the groups sorted left to right based on the sequence of your Group By fields. If you need to sort the grouping columns in some other way, change the sequence of the Group By fields. Note that you can also sort any of the totals fields.

Query1

Name	CheckInMon	SumOfTotalCharge	AvgOfTotalC	MinOfTotalC	MaxOfTotalC	CountOfRes
Main Campus Housing A	2010 08	$455.00	$455.00	$455.00	$455.00	1
Main Campus Housing A	2010 09	$3,350.00	$1,116.67	$570.00	$1,600.00	3
Main Campus Housing A	2010 10	$3,760.00	$752.00	$250.00	$1,420.00	5
Main Campus Housing A	2010 11	$725.00	$241.67	$55.00	$450.00	3
Main Campus Housing A	2010 12	$1,575.00	$525.00	$375.00	$750.00	3
Main Campus Housing A	2011 01	$870.00	$290.00	$160.00	$380.00	3
Main Campus Housing A	2011 02	$720.00	$360.00	$160.00	$560.00	2
Main Campus Housing A	2011 03	$805.00	$402.50	$335.00	$470.00	2
Main Campus Housing B	2010 09	$2,865.00	$716.25	$100.00	$1,040.00	4
Main Campus Housing B	2010 10	$210.00	$210.00	$210.00	$210.00	1
Main Campus Housing B	2010 11	$3,580.00	$1,193.33	$1,150.00	$1,280.00	3
Main Campus Housing B	2010 12	$2,005.00	$401.00	$50.00	$1,180.00	5
Main Campus Housing B	2011 01	$3,450.00	$690.00	$150.00	$1,180.00	5
Main Campus Housing B	2011 02	$2,000.00	$1,000.00	$960.00	$1,040.00	2
North Satellite Housing D	2010 09	$195.00	$195.00	$195.00	$195.00	1
North Satellite Housing D	2010 11	$830.00	$830.00	$830.00	$830.00	1
North Satellite Housing D	2010 12	$1,240.00	$620.00	$280.00	$960.00	2
North Satellite Housing D	2011 02	$680.00	$340.00	$200.00	$480.00	2
South Campus Housing C	2010 08	$1,200.00	$1,200.00	$1,200.00	$1,200.00	1
South Campus Housing C	2010 10	$2,270.00	$1,135.00	$350.00	$1,920.00	2
South Campus Housing C	2010 11	$255.00	$255.00	$255.00	$255.00	1
South Campus Housing C	2010 12	$1,490.00	$745.00	$110.00	$1,380.00	2
South Campus Housing C	2011 01	$1,265.00	$632.50	$415.00	$850.00	2
South Campus Housing C	2011 02	$2,970.00	$1,485.00	$1,280.00	$1,690.00	2

Record: 3 of 24 No Filter Search

Figure 10-23 Running the query in Figure 10-22 returns total revenue, average revenue, smallest revenue per reservation, largest revenue per reservation, and count of reservations by facility and month.

In the list for the Total row in the design grid, you'll also find an Expression setting. Select this when you want to create an expression in the Total row that uses one or more of the aggregate functions listed earlier. For example, you might want to calculate a value that reflects the range of reservation charges in the group, as in the following:

```
Max([TotalCharge]) - Min([TotalCharge])
```

As you can with any field, you can give your expression a custom name. Notice, in Figure 10-23, that Access has generated names such as SumOfTotalCharge or AvgOfTotalCharge. You can fix these by clicking in the field in the design grid and prefixing the field or expression with your own name followed by a colon. In Figure 10-24, we removed the separate Min and Max fields, added the expression to calculate the range between the smallest and largest charge, and inserted custom field names. You can see the result in Datasheet view in Figure 10-25.

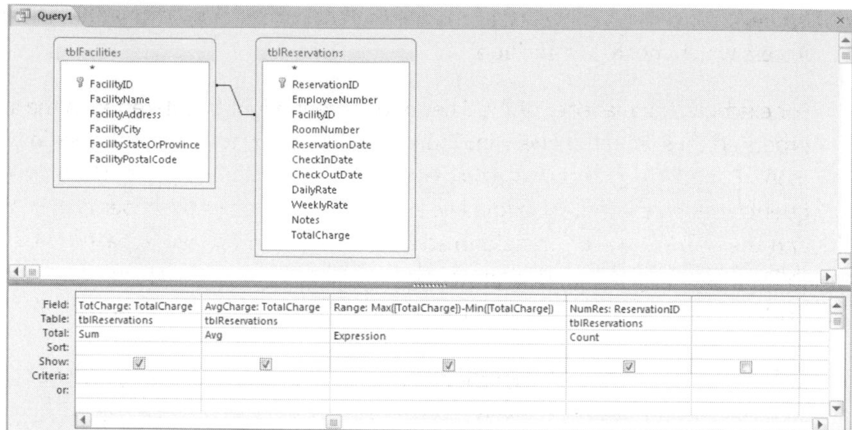

Figure 10-24 In this figure, we are adding an expression and defining custom field names in a totals query.

Query1

Name	CheckInMonth	TotCharge	AvgCharge	Range	NumRes
Main Campus Housing A	2010 08	$455.00	$455.00	$0.00	1
Main Campus Housing A	2010 09	$3,350.00	$1,116.67	$1,030.00	3
Main Campus Housing A	2010 10	$3,760.00	$752.00	$1,170.00	5
Main Campus Housing A	2010 11	$725.00	$241.67	$395.00	3
Main Campus Housing A	2010 12	$1,575.00	$525.00	$375.00	3
Main Campus Housing A	2011 01	$870.00	$290.00	$220.00	3
Main Campus Housing A	2011 02	$720.00	$360.00	$400.00	2
Main Campus Housing A	2011 03	$805.00	$402.50	$135.00	2
Main Campus Housing B	2010 09	$2,865.00	$716.25	$940.00	4
Main Campus Housing B	2010 10	$210.00	$210.00	$0.00	1
Main Campus Housing B	2010 11	$3,580.00	$1,193.33	$130.00	3
Main Campus Housing B	2010 12	$2,005.00	$401.00	$1,130.00	5
Main Campus Housing B	2011 01	$3,450.00	$690.00	$1,030.00	5
Main Campus Housing B	2011 02	$2,000.00	$1,000.00	$80.00	2
North Satellite Housing D	2010 09	$195.00	$195.00	$0.00	1
North Satellite Housing D	2010 11	$830.00	$830.00	$0.00	1
North Satellite Housing D	2010 12	$1,240.00	$620.00	$680.00	2
North Satellite Housing D	2011 02	$680.00	$340.00	$280.00	2
South Campus Housing C	2010 08	$1,200.00	$1,200.00	$0.00	1
South Campus Housing C	2010 10	$2,270.00	$1,135.00	$1,570.00	2
South Campus Housing C	2010 11	$255.00	$255.00	$0.00	1
South Campus Housing C	2010 12	$1,490.00	$745.00	$1,270.00	2
South Campus Housing C	2011 01	$1,265.00	$632.50	$435.00	2
South Campus Housing C	2011 02	$2,970.00	$1,485.00	$410.00	2

Record: 1 of 24 No Filter Search

Figure 10-25 This is the result in Datasheet view of the query shown in Figure 10-24.

Selecting Records to Form Groups

You might filter out some records before your totals query gathers the records into groups. To filter out certain records from the tables in your query, you can add to the design grid the field or fields you want to filter. Then create the filter by selecting the Where setting in the Total row (which will clear the field's Show check box), and entering criteria that tell Access which records to exclude.

For example, the manager of the Sales department might be interested in the statistics you've produced thus far in the query in Figure 10-24, but only for the employees in the Sales department. To find this information, you need to add tblEmployees and tblDepartments to your query (and remove the extra join line between the EmployeeNumber field in tblEmployees and the ManagerNumber field in tblDepartments). Add the Department field from tblDepartments to your design, change the Total line to Where, and add the criterion **"Sales"** on the Criteria line under this field. Your query should now look like Figure 10-26.

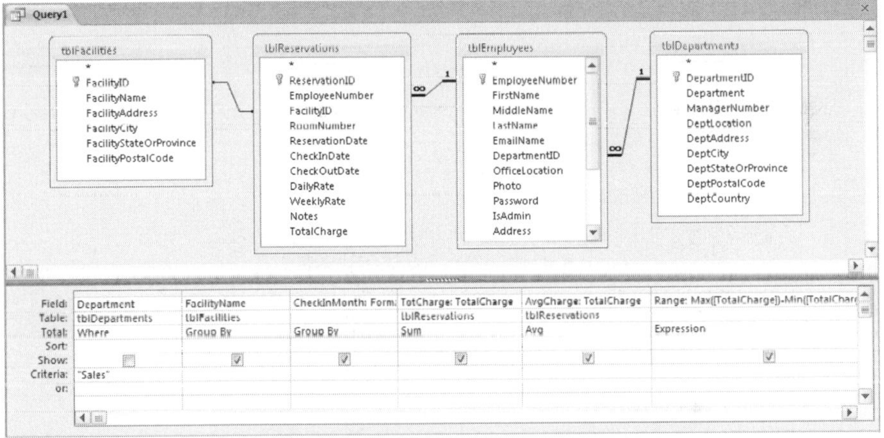

Figure 10-26 Use the Department field to select the rows that will be included in groups.

Now, when you run the query, you get totals only for the employees in the Sales department. The result is shown in Figure 10-27.

Query1

Name	CheckInMonth	TotCharge	AvgCharge	Range	NumRes
Main Campus Housing A	2010 12	$375.00	$375.00	$0.00	1
Main Campus Housing A	2011 02	$560.00	$560.00	$0.00	1
Main Campus Housing B	2010 12	$1,230.00	$615.00	$1,130.00	2
Main Campus Housing B	2011 02	$2,000.00	$1,000.00	$80.00	2
South Campus Housing C	2010 08	$1,200.00	$1,200.00	$0.00	1
South Campus Housing C	2010 10	$1,920.00	$1,920.00	$0.00	1
South Campus Housing C	2011 02	$1,690.00	$1,690.00	$0.00	1

Figure 10-27 This figure displays the recordset of the query shown in Figure 10-26.

Selecting Specific Groups

You can also filter groups of totals after the query has calculated the groups. To do this, enter criteria for any field that has a Group By setting, one of the aggregate functions, or an expression using the aggregate functions in its Total row. For example, you might want to know which facilities and months have more than $1,000 in total charges. To determine that, use the settings shown in Figure 10-26 and enter a Criteria setting of >1000 for the TotalCharge field, as shown in Figure 10-28. This query should return five rows in the sample database. You can find this query saved as qxmplSalesHousingGT1000 in the sample database.

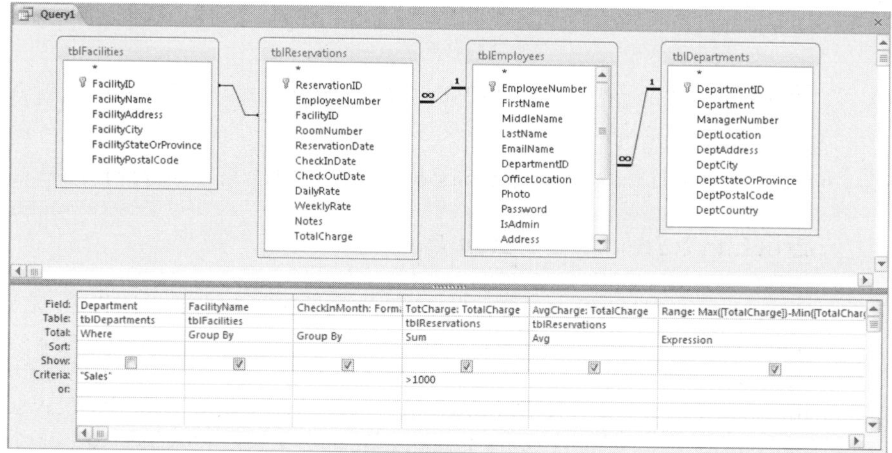

Figure 10-28 Enter a Criteria setting for the TotCharge field to limit the records to months with more than $1,000 in total charges.

Building Crosstab Queries

Access 2010 supports a special type of totals query called a *crosstab query* that allows you to see calculated values in a spreadsheet-like format. For example, you can use this type of query to see total revenue by month for each facility in the Housing Reservations application. If you were entering the data in a spreadsheet, the layout of the result you want might look like Figure 10-29.

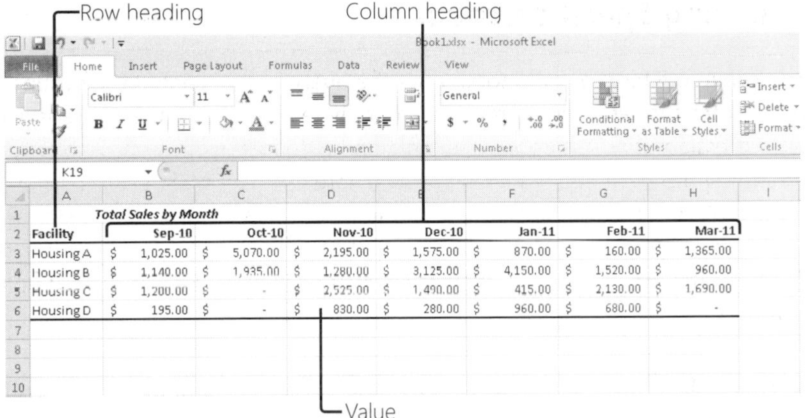

Figure 10-29 A spreadsheet mockup shows the result you want in your crosstab query.

We have pointed out the key components in the mockup that you'll design into your query.

Creating a Simple Crosstab Query

Open the HousingDataCopy.accdb database. To see revenue by facility, you'll need tblFacilities and tblReservations. Start a new query on tblFacilities and tblReservations. Add the FacilityName field from tblFacilties to the design grid. Revenue gets collected when the employee checks out, and you want to summarize by month. So, enter **RevMonth: Format(CheckOutDate, "yyyy mmm")** in the next empty field in the design grid. This expression returns the year as four digits and the month as a three-character abbreviation. Finally, add the TotalCharge field from tblReservations.

Click the Design contextual tab below Query Tools on the ribbon. Then, click the Crosstab command in the Query Type group. Access changes your query to a totals query and adds a Crosstab row to the design grid, as shown in Figure 10-30. Each field in a crosstab query can have one of four crosstab settings: Row Heading, Column Heading, Value (displayed in the crosstab grid), or Not Shown.

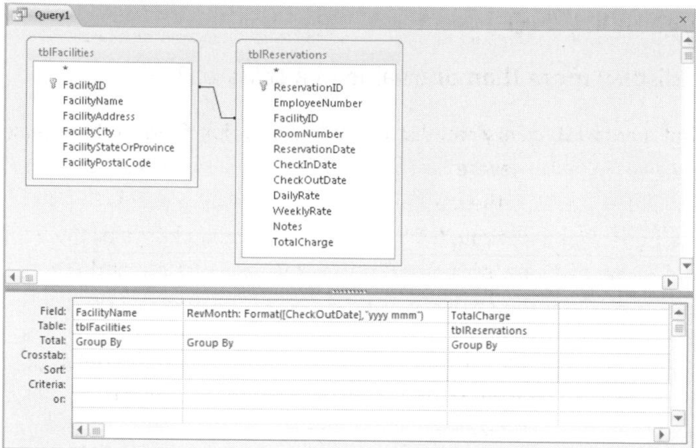

Figure 10-30 This is a crosstab query in Design view.

You must have at least one row heading in a crosstab query, and you can specify more than one field as a row heading. Each row heading must be a grouped value or expression, and the expression can include one or more of the aggregate functions—Count, Min, Max, Sum, and so on. The row heading fields form the columns on the left side of the crosstab. Think of the grouped values of the row heading fields as forming the horizontal "labels" of the rows. In this example, we'll be grouping by FacilityName. We'll later modify the basic query we're building here to add a second row heading using Sum—the total value of each facility's reservations.

You must also have one (and only one) field defined as a column heading, and this must also be a grouped or totaled value. These values form the headings of the columns across the crosstab datasheet. Think of a regular totals query where one of the columns "pivots," and the values in the rows become labels for additional columns in the output. These columns appear sorted in value sequence immediately following the columns you define as row headings. Because the values in the data you're selecting determine the column names when you run the query, you cannot always predict in advance the field names that the query will output.

Finally, you need one (and only one) field designated as the value. This field must be a totaled value or an expression that contains one of the aggregate functions. The value appears in the cells that are the intersections of each of the row heading values and each of the column heading values. In the following example, the facility names will appear down the left side, the year and month values will appear as column headings across the top, and the sum of the reservation charge for each group for each month will appear in the intersection.

TROUBLESHOOTING

How do I display more than one value in a crosstab?

The fact that a crosstab query can display only one value field in the intersection of row and column headings is a severe limitation. What if you want to display both the total reservation value as well as the count of reservations? One way is to build two separate crosstab queries—one that provides the sum of the total charge as the value field, and one that provides the count of reservations as the value field—and then join the two queries on the row heading columns. That's an inelegant way to do it.

Another solution is to create a simple query that includes all the detail you need and then switch to PivotTable view to build the data display you need. You'll learn about PivotTable and PivotChart views later in this chapter.

As in other types of totals queries, you can include other fields to filter values to obtain the result you want. For these fields, you should select the Where setting in the Total row and the Not Shown setting in the Crosstab row and then enter your criteria. You can also enter criteria for any column headings, and you can sort on any of the fields.

To finish the settings for the crosstab query that you started to build in Figure 10-30, under the FacilityName field in the Crosstab row, click the small arrow and select Row Heading from the list, select Column Heading under the RevMonth expression, and select Value under the TotalCharge field. Also change the Group By setting under the TotalCharge field to Sum.

Switch to Datasheet view to see the result of your query design, as shown in Figure 10-31.

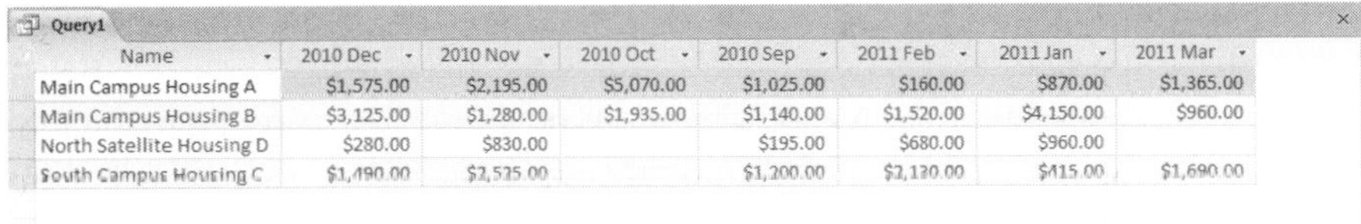

Query1

Name	2010 Dec	2010 Nov	2010 Oct	2010 Sep	2011 Feb	2011 Jan	2011 Mar
Main Campus Housing A	$1,575.00	$2,195.00	$5,070.00	$1,025.00	$160.00	$870.00	$1,365.00
Main Campus Housing B	$3,125.00	$1,280.00	$1,935.00	$1,140.00	$1,520.00	$4,150.00	$960.00
North Satellite Housing D	$280.00	$830.00		$195.00	$680.00	$960.00	
South Campus Housing C	$1,490.00	$2,535.00		$1,200.00	$2,130.00	$415.00	$1,690.00

Figure 10-31 This is the recordset of the crosstab query you're building.

Notice that although you didn't specify a sort sequence on the dates, Access sorted the dates left to right in ascending collating order anyway. Notice also that the month names appear in alphabetical order, not in the desired chronological order.

Access provides a solution for this: You can specifically define the order of column headings for any crosstab query by using the query's property sheet. Return to Design view and click in the upper part of the Query window, and then click the Property Sheet button in the Show/Hide group of the Design tab to see the property sheet, as shown in Figure 10-32. (You can verify that you are looking at the property sheet for the query by examining what you see after Selection Type at the top of the property sheet. For queries, you should see "Query Properties.")

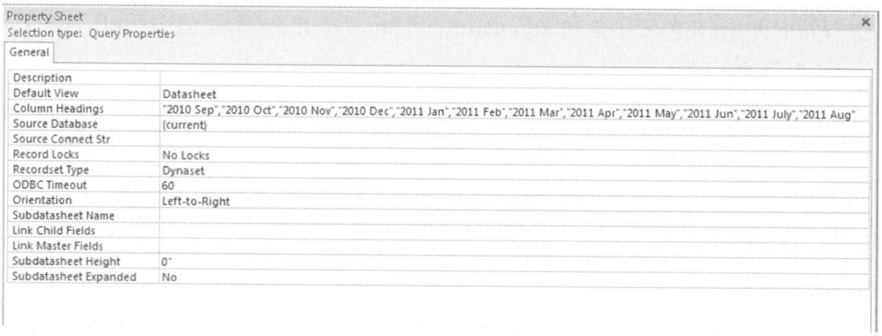

Property Sheet
Selection type: Query Properties
General

Description	
Default View	Datasheet
Column Headings	"2010 Sep","2010 Oct","2010 Nov","2010 Dec","2011 Jan","2011 Feb","2011 Mar","2011 Apr","2011 May","2011 Jun","2011 July","2011 Aug"
Source Database	(current)
Source Connect Str	
Record Locks	No Locks
Recordset Type	Dynaset
ODBC Timeout	60
Orientation	Left-to-Right
Subdatasheet Name	
Link Child Fields	
Link Master Fields	
Subdatasheet Height	0"
Subdatasheet Expanded	No

Figure 10-32 These entries in the property sheet fix the order of column headings for the query shown in Figure 10-31.

To control the order of columns displayed, enter the headings exactly as they are formatted and in the order you want them in the Column Headings row, separated by commas. In this case, you are entering text values, so you must also enclose each value in double quotes. Be sure to include all the column headings that match the result of the query. (Notice that we specified more months in 2011 even though the sample data covers only September 2010 to March 2011.) If you omit (or misspell) a column heading, Access won't show that column at all. When you run the query with formatted column headings, you see the recordset shown in Figure 10-33.

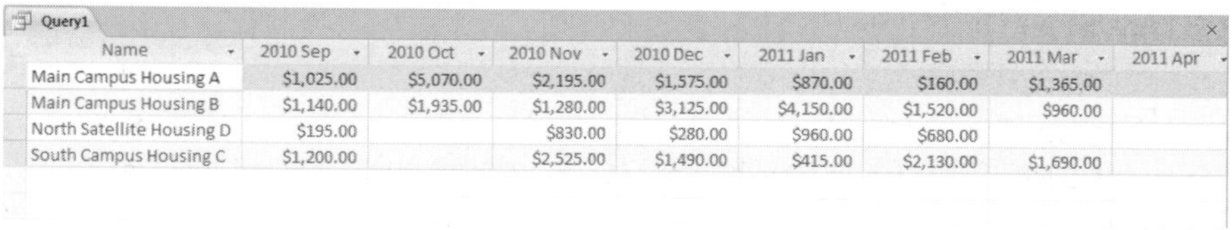

Query1

Name	2010 Sep	2010 Oct	2010 Nov	2010 Dec	2011 Jan	2011 Feb	2011 Mar	2011 Apr
Main Campus Housing A	$1,025.00	$5,070.00	$2,195.00	$1,575.00	$870.00	$160.00	$1,365.00	
Main Campus Housing B	$1,140.00	$1,935.00	$1,280.00	$3,125.00	$4,150.00	$1,520.00	$960.00	
North Satellite Housing D	$195.00		$830.00	$280.00	$960.00	$680.00		
South Campus Housing C	$1,200.00		$2,525.00	$1,490.00	$415.00	$2,130.00	$1,690.00	

Figure 10-33 This crosstab query recordset has custom headings and a custom column order, as defined in Figure 10-32.

CAUTION!

Specifying correct column headings can be difficult. You must run your query first to determine what headings you'll see. You might be able to define criteria in your query that guarantee the column headings—for example, you could filter the query to return rows only from a specific year. If you misspell a column heading in the query property sheet, the real danger is that Access gives you no warning that your query returns columns that aren't in your column heading specification. You'll see blanks in your misspelled columns, and you could mistakenly assume that no data exists for those columns.

Let's add a grand total for each row (the total per facility regardless of month) and do something about the blank cells. Wouldn't it be nice to see a zero in months when there were no reservations?

Switch back to Design view and add another TotalCharge field to the Field row. Give it a name of GrandTotal and choose Sum on the Total row and Row Heading on the Crosstab row.

Remember the little trick we used earlier to use a plus sign (+) arithmetic operator in a concatenation to remove extra blanks? In this case, we want to do exactly the reverse—wherever there are no values, the Sum returns a Null that we want to convert to a zero. Also, remember that when you concatenate two values with the ampersand (&) operator, that operator ignores Nulls. You can force a Null to a zero by concatenating a leading zero character. If the Sum is not Null, adding a zero in front of the value won't hurt it at all.

In the TotalCharge field you chose as the value field, change Sum to Expression and change the Field line to use this expression:

```
0 & Sum(TotalCharge)
```

Any concatenation returns a string value, so you'll need to convert the value back to a currency number for display. There's a handy "convert to currency" function (CCur) that will perform this conversion for you. Further modify the expression to read:

```
CCur(0 & Sum(TotalCharge))
```

Switch back to Datasheet view, and your query result should now look like Figure 10-34.

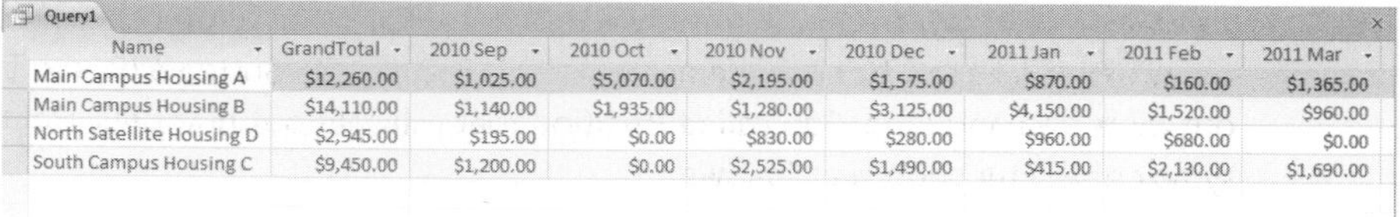

Query1

Name	GrandTotal	2010 Sep	2010 Oct	2010 Nov	2010 Dec	2011 Jan	2011 Feb	2011 Mar
Main Campus Housing A	$12,260.00	$1,025.00	$5,070.00	$2,195.00	$1,575.00	$870.00	$160.00	$1,365.00
Main Campus Housing B	$14,110.00	$1,140.00	$1,935.00	$1,280.00	$3,125.00	$4,150.00	$1,520.00	$960.00
North Satellite Housing D	$2,945.00	$195.00	$0.00	$830.00	$280.00	$960.00	$680.00	$0.00
South Campus Housing C	$9,450.00	$1,200.00	$0.00	$2,525.00	$1,490.00	$415.00	$2,130.00	$1,690.00

Figure 10-34 Your crosstab query now shows a grand total on each row as an additional row heading, and all empty cells are filled with zero values.

As with most tasks in Access, there's usually more than one way to solve a problem. You can also generate the missing zero values by using the Null-to-zero function (NZ) in your expression instead of using concatenation. Your expression could look like:

```
CCur(NZ(Sum(TotalCharge),0))
```

If you're not quite getting the result you expect, you can check what you have built against the qxmplRevenueByFacilityByMonthXtab sample query you'll find in the database.

Partitioning Data in a Crosstab Query

The total sales by month is interesting, but what can you do if you want to break the data down further? For example, you might want to know the value of sales across a range of room prices. This sort of information might be invaluable to the operator of a commercial hotel. What amount of revenue is the hotel receiving from various room prices?

You'll learn in Chapter 18 that you can ask the report writer to group data by data ranges. Well, you can also do this in a totals or crosstab query. Let's continue to work in the HousingDataCopy.accdb database to see how this works.

Start a new query with tblFacilities and tblReservations. Add the FacilityName field from tblFacilities, and create a CkOutMonth field by using the Format function to return a four-digit year and month abbreviation, as you did earlier. Add the TotalCharge field from tblReservations to the query grid twice. Click the Crosstab button in the Query Type group of the Design tab to convert your query to a crosstab query.

In the Crosstab row, select Row Heading under the FacilityName field, your CkOutMonth expression, and the first TotalCharge field. Change the name of this first TotalCharge field to GrandTotal and select Sum in the Group By row. For the second TotalCharge field, select Sum in the Group By row and Value in the Crosstab row.

You still don't have a Column Heading field or expression defined, but here's where the fun begins. In this query, your sales manager has asked you for a breakdown of amounts spent per month based on ranges of the DailyRate field. In this database, the lowest daily charge is $40 a day, and the highest is $100 a day. The manager has asked you to display ranges from $40 to $119 in increments of $20 ($40 to $59, $60 to $79, and so on). It turns out there's a handy function called Partition that will split out numbers like this for you. The syntax of the function is as follows:

Partition(<*number*>, <*start*>, <*stop*>, <*interval*>)

The *number* argument is the name of a numeric field or expression you want to split up into ranges. *Start* specifies the lowest value you want, *stop* specifies the highest value you want, and *interval* specifies the size of the ranges. The function evaluates each number it sees and returns a string containing the name of the range for that number. You can group on these named ranges to partition your data into groups for this crosstab query. So, the expression you need is as follows:

Partition(DailyRate, 40, 119, 20)

The function will return values "40: 59", "60: 79", "80: 99", and "100:119". Add that expression to your query grid and select Column Heading in the Crosstab row. Your query should now look like Figure 10-35.

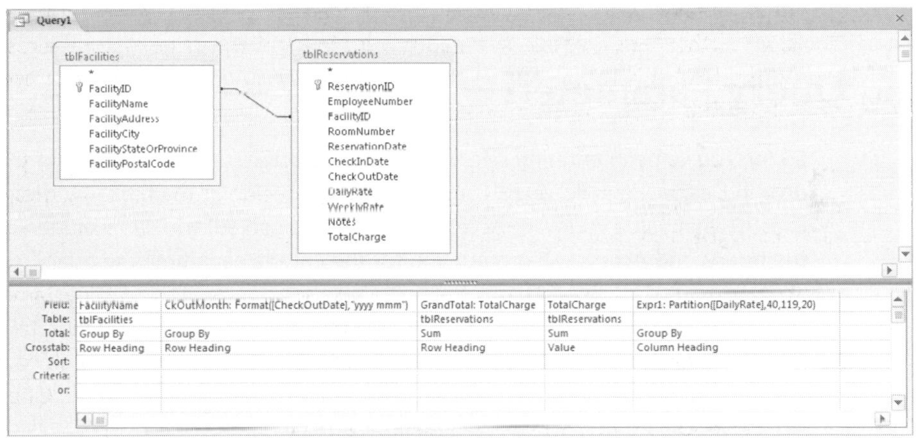

Figure 10-35 This crosstab query uses partitioned values.

Switch to Datasheet view to see the result that should satisfy your sales manager's request, shown in Figure 10-36. Note that we didn't use the trick discussed earlier to fill blank cells with zeros. In this case, the blank cells seem to visually point out the rate ranges that had no sales. You can find this query saved as qxmplRevenueByFacilityByRateRangeXtab in the sample database.

Query1

Name	CkOutMonth	GrandTotal	40: 59	60: 79	80: 99	100:119
Main Campus Housing A	2010 Dec	$1,575.00	$1,125.00		$450.00	
Main Campus Housing A	2010 Nov	$2,195.00	$1,745.00		$450.00	
Main Campus Housing A	2010 Oct	$5,070.00	$870.00		$4,200.00	
Main Campus Housing A	2010 Sep	$1,025.00	$1,025.00			
Main Campus Housing A	2011 Feb	$160.00	$160.00			
Main Campus Housing A	2011 Jan	$870.00	$710.00		$160.00	
Main Campus Housing A	2011 Mar	$1,365.00	$1,365.00			
Main Campus Housing B	2010 Dec	$3,125.00	$245.00		$2,880.00	
Main Campus Housing B	2010 Nov	$1,280.00				$1,280.00
Main Campus Housing B	2010 Oct	$1,935.00		$1,105.00	$830.00	
Main Campus Housing B	2010 Sep	$1,140.00	$100.00			$1,040.00
Main Campus Housing B	2011 Feb	$1,520.00		$1,040.00	$480.00	
Main Campus Housing B	2011 Jan	$4,150.00	$150.00	$3,090.00	$910.00	
Main Campus Housing B	2011 Mar	$960.00	$960.00			
North Satellite Housing D	2010 Dec	$280.00		$280.00		
North Satellite Housing D	2010 Nov	$830.00			$830.00	
North Satellite Housing D	2010 Sep	$195.00		$195.00		
North Satellite Housing D	2011 Feb	$680.00	$200.00	$480.00		
North Satellite Housing D	2011 Jan	$960.00		$960.00		
South Campus Housing C	2010 Dec	$1,490.00	$110.00			$1,380.00
South Campus Housing C	2010 Nov	$2,525.00	$255.00	$350.00		$1,920.00
South Campus Housing C	2010 Sep	$1,200.00				$1,200.00
South Campus Housing C	2011 Feb	$2,130.00	$850.00			$1,280.00
South Campus Housing C	2011 Jan	$415.00	$415.00			
South Campus Housing C	2011 Mar	$1,690.00			$1,690.00	

Record: 1 of 25 No Filter Search

Figure 10-36 Run the crosstab query shown in Figure 10-34 to see the result of partitioning sales totals on ranges of room rates.

Using Query Parameters

So far, you've been entering selection criteria directly in the design grid of the Query window in Design view. However, you don't have to decide at the time you design the query exactly what value you want Access to search for. Instead, you can include a parameter in the query, and Access will prompt you for the criteria each time the query runs.

To include a parameter, you enter a name or a phrase enclosed in brackets ([ ]) in the Criteria row instead of entering a value. What you enclose in brackets becomes the name by which Access knows your parameter. Access displays this name in a dialog box when you run the query, so you should enter a phrase that accurately describes what you want. You can enter several parameters in a single query, so each parameter name must be unique as well as informative. If you want a parameter value to also appear as output in the query, you can enter the parameter name in the Field row of an empty column.

Let's say you're the housing manager, and you want to find out who might be staying in any facility over the next several days or weeks. You don't want to have to build or modify a query each time you want to search the database for upcoming reservations. So, you ask your database developer to provide you with a way to dynamically enter the beginning and ending dates of interest.

Let's build a query to help out the housing manager. Start a new query with tblFacilities in the HousingDataCopy.accdb database. Add tblReservations and tblEmployees. From tblReservations, include the ReservationID, RoomNumber, CheckInDate, CheckOutDate, and TotalCharge fields. Insert the FacilityName field from tblFacilities between ReservationID and RoomNumber. Add an expression to display the employee name in a field inserted between ReservationID and FacilityName. Your expression might look like this:

```
EmpName: tblEmployees.LastName & ", " & tblEmployees.FirstName
```

Now comes the tricky part. You want the query to ask the housing manager for the range of dates of interest. Your query needs to find the reservation rows that show who is in which rooms between a pair of dates. If you remember from the previous example in this chapter where we were looking for employees occupying rooms in November or December, you want any rows where the check-in date is less than or equal to the end date of interest, and the check-out date is greater than the start date of interest. (If they check out on the beginning date of the range, they're not staying in the room that night.) So, you can create two parameters on the Criteria line to accomplish this. Under CheckInDate, enter: **<=[Enter End Date:]**, and under CheckOutDate, enter: **>[Enter Start Date:]**. Your query should look like Figure 10-37.

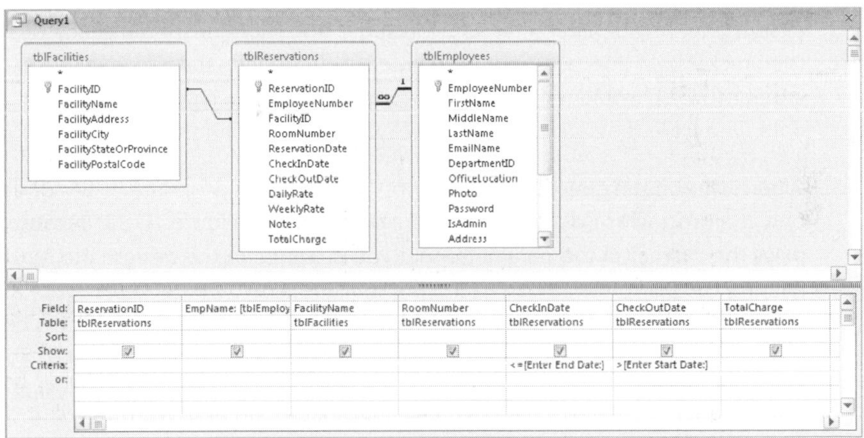

Figure 10-37 You can use query parameters to accept criteria for a range of reservation dates.

For each parameter in a query, you should tell Access what data type to expect. Access uses this information to validate the value entered. For example, if you define a parameter as a number, Access won't accept alphabetic characters in the parameter value. Likewise, if you define a parameter as a Date/Time data type, Access won't accept anything but a valid date or time value in the parameter prompt. (See Figure 10-39.) By default, Access assigns the

Text data type to query parameters. In general, you should always define the data type of your parameters, so click the Parameters command in the Show/Hide group of the Design tab. Access then displays the Query Parameters dialog box, as shown in Figure 10-38.

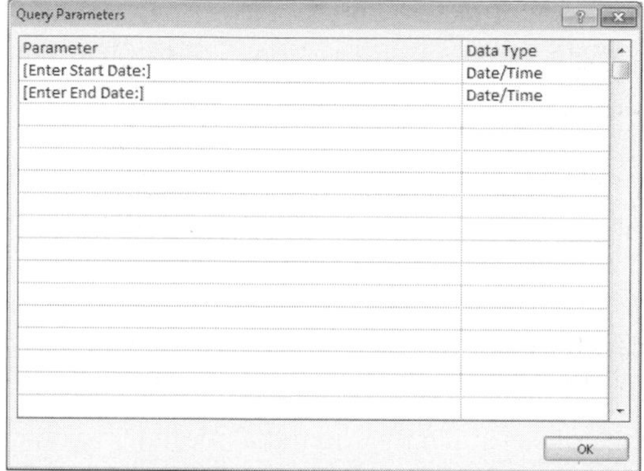

Figure 10-38 Use the Query Parameters dialog box to assign data types for query parameters.

In the Parameter column, enter each parameter name exactly as you entered it in the design grid. If your parameter name includes no spaces or special characters, you can omit the brackets. (In this case, your parameters include both spaces and the colon character—either of which would require the brackets.) In the Data Type column, select the appropriate data type from the drop-down list. Click OK when you finish defining all your parameters.

When you run the query, Access prompts you for an appropriate value for each parameter, one at a time, with a dialog box like the one shown in Figure 10-39. Because Access displays the "name" of the parameter that you provided in the design grid, you can see why naming the parameter with a useful phrase can help you enter the correct value later. If you enter a value that does not match the data type you specified, Access displays an error message and gives you a chance to try again. You can also click Cancel to abort running the query. If you click OK without typing a value, Access returns a Null value for the parameter to the query.

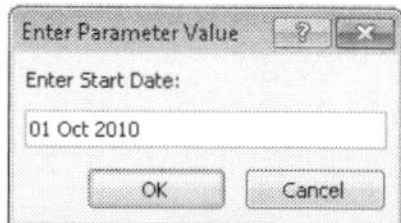

Figure 10-39 The Enter Parameter Value dialog box asks for the query parameter value.

Notice that Access accepts any value that it can recognize as a date/time, such as a long date or short date format. If you respond to the query parameter prompts with October 1, 2010, for the Start Date and October 12, 2010, for the End Date, you'll see a datasheet like Figure 10-40.

Query1

Reservation	EmpName	Name	Room	Check-In	Check-Out	Charge
4	Tippett, John	Main Campus Housing A	502	10/8/2010	10/25/2010	$1,420.00
6	Berndt, Matthias	Main Campus Housing A	902	9/25/2010	10/14/2010	$1,600.00
8	Bradley, David	Main Campus Housing A	509	10/10/2010	10/23/2010	$620.00
11	Lawrence, David Oliver	Main Campus Housing B	301	9/18/2010	10/3/2010	$895.00
13	Bradley, David	Main Campus Housing A	111	9/28/2010	10/14/2010	$1,180.00
15	Adams, Jay	Main Campus Housing B	206	9/28/2010	10/9/2010	$830.00
*						

Figure 10-40 This figure displays the recordset of the query shown in Figure 10-37 when you reply with October 1, 2010, and October 12, 2010, to the parameter prompts.

You can find this query saved in the sample database as qxmplReservationLookupParameter.

Customizing Query Properties

Access 2010 provides a number of properties associated with queries that you can use to control how a query runs. To open the property sheet for queries, click in the upper part of a Query window in Design view outside of the field lists and then click the Property Sheet button in the Show/Hide group of the Design contextual tab. Figure 10-41 shows the property sheet Access provides for select queries.

Property Sheet

Selection type: Query Properties

General

Description	
Default View	Datasheet
Output All Fields	No
Top Values	All
Unique Values	No
Unique Records	No
Source Database	(current)
Source Connect Str	
Record Locks	No Locks
Recordset Type	Dynaset
ODBC Timeout	60
Filter	
Order By	
Max Records	
Orientation	Left-to-Right
Subdatasheet Name	
Link Child Fields	
Link Master Fields	
Subdatasheet Height	0"
Subdatasheet Expanded	No
Filter On Load	No
Order By On Load	Yes

Figure 10-41 The property sheet for select queries lets you customize the way the query works.

Use the Description property to document what the query does. This description appears next to the query name when you view query objects in Details view in the Navigation pane. You can also right-click the query in the Navigation pane and open the Properties dialog box to enter this property without having to open the query in Design view.

The Default View property determines how the query opens when you open it from the Navigation pane. Datasheet view is the default, but you might want to change this setting to PivotTable or PivotChart if you have designed either of these views for the query. See "Creating PivotTables and PivotCharts from Queries," on page 681, for details.

Controlling Query Output

You normally select only specific fields that you want returned in the recordset when you run a select query. However, if you're designing the query to be used in a form and you want all fields from all tables used in the query available to the form, set the Output All Fields property to Yes. It's a good idea to keep the default setting of No and change this option only for specific queries.

INSIDE OUT **Don't Change the Default Setting for the Output All Fields Property**

You can change the default Output All Fields property for all queries in the Object Designers category of the Access Options dialog box, but we strongly recommend that you do not do this. Queries execute most efficiently when they return only the fields that you need. Also, when your query includes more than one table and a field exists more than once in different tables, an expression you use to reference the field will fail unless you qualify the field name with the table name. You might include the field only once on the design grid, but Output All Fields causes the query to include all copies of the field.

You can use the Top Values property to tell Access that you want to see the first *n* rows or the first *x* percent of the rows. If you enter an integer value, Access displays the number of rows specified. If you enter a decimal value between 0 and 1 or an integer less than 100 followed by a percent sign (%), Access displays that percentage of rows. For example, you might want to find the top 10 best-selling products or the top 20 percent of highest paid employees. Note that in most cases, you'll need to specify sorting criteria—perhaps by count of products sold descending or salary descending—to place the rows you want at the "top" of the recordset. You can then ask for the top 10 or top 20 percent to get the answers you want.

When working in a query datasheet, you can define and apply filters and specify sorting just as you can in a table datasheet. Access stores this filtering and sorting criteria in the query's Filter and Order By properties. When you design a query, you can use the Filter and Order By properties to predefine filtering and sorting criteria. When you open the query and click Toggle Filter in the Sort & Filter group on the Home tab, Access applies the filter and/or sorts the data using these saved properties. If you change the filter or sorting criteria while in Datasheet view and then save the change, Access updates these properties.

You can also affect whether the fields returned by the query can be updated by changing the Recordset Type property. The default setting, Dynaset, allows you to update any fields on the *many* side of a join. It also lets you change values on the one side of a join if you have defined a relationship between the tables and enabled Cascade Update Related Fields in the Edit Relationships dialog box. If you choose Dynaset (Inconsistent Updates), you can update any field that isn't a result of a calculation, but you might update data that you didn't intend to be updatable. If you want the query to be read-only (no fields can be updated), choose theone Snapshot setting.

CAUTION!

You should rarely, if at all, choose the Dynaset (Inconsistent Updates) setting for Recordset Type. This setting makes fields updatable in queries that might not otherwise allow updating. Although Access still enforces referential integrity rules, you can make changes to tables independently from each other, so you might end up reassigning relationships unintentionally. You can read about the details of when fields are updatable in a query later in this chapter in "Limitations on Using Select Queries to Update Data," on page 680.

Working with Unique Records and Values

When you run a query, Access often returns what appear to be duplicate rows in the recordset. The default in Access 2010 is to return all records. You can also ask Access to return only unique records. (This was the default for all versions of Access prior to version 8, also called Access 97.) Unique records mean that the identifier for each row (the primary key of the table in a single-table query or the concatenated primary keys in a multiple-table query) is unique. If you ask for unique records, Access returns only rows with identifiers that are different from each other. If you want to see all possible data (including duplicate rows), set both the Unique Values property and the Unique Records property to No. (You cannot set both Unique Records and Unique Values to Yes. You can set them both to No.)

To understand how the Unique Values and Unique Records settings work, open the ContactsDataCopy.accdb database and create a query that includes both the tblContacts table and the tblContactEvents table. Let's say you want to find out from which cities you've received a contact over a particular period of time. Include the WorkCity and WorkStateOrProvince fields from tblContacts. Include the ContactDateTime field from tblContactEvents, but clear the Show check box. Figure 10-42 shows a sample query with a date criterion that will show contact cities between June 2010 and September 2010. (Remember, ContactDateTime includes a time value, so you need to enter a criterion one day beyond the date range you want.) You can find this query saved as qxmplNoUnique in the sample database.

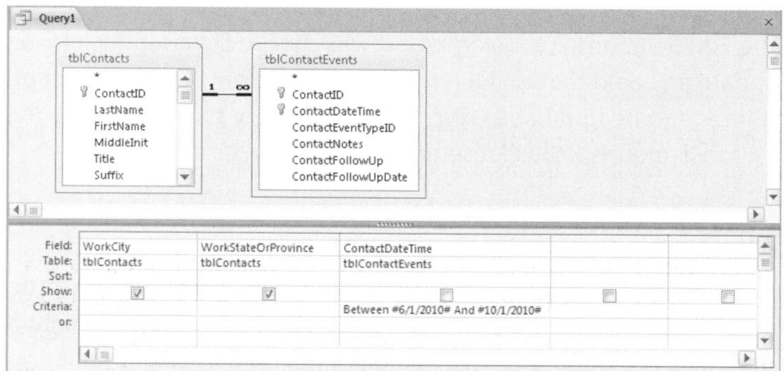

Figure 10-42 You can build a query that demonstrates setting both Unique Values and Unique Records to No when you're using two tables.

If you switch to Datasheet view, as shown in Figure 10-43, you can see that the query returns 46 rows—each row from tblContacts appears once for each related contact event that has a contact date between the specified days. Some of these rows come from the same person, and some come from different people in the same city. The bottom line is there are 46 rows in tblContactEvents within the specified date range.

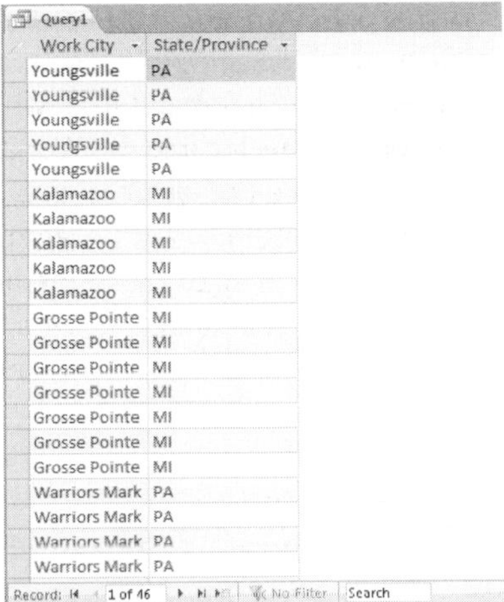
Query1

Work City	State/Province
Youngsville	PA
Youngsville	PA
Youngsville	PA
Youngsville	PA
Youngsville	PA
Kalamazoo	MI
Kalamazoo	MI
Kalamazoo	MI
Kalamazoo	MI
Kalamazoo	MI
Grosse Pointe	MI
Grosse Pointe	MI
Grosse Pointe	MI
Grosse Pointe	MI
Grosse Pointe	MI
Grosse Pointe	MI
Grosse Pointe	MI
Warriors Mark	PA
Warriors Mark	PA
Warriors Mark	PA
Warriors Mark	PA

Record: 1 of 46 No Filter Search

Figure 10-43 Run your sample query to see the result of retrieving all rows across a join even though the output columns are from only one of the tables.

If you're interested only in one row per contact (per person) from tblContacts, regardless of the number of contact events, you can set the Unique Records property to Yes. The result is shown in Figure 10-44 (saved as qxmplUniqueRecords). This tells us that there were 23 different people who had a contact event within the date range. Again, some of these rows come from different people in the same city, which is why you see the same city listed more than once. The recordset now returns *unique records* from tblContacts (the only table providing output fields in this query).

Note

Setting Unique Records to Yes has no effect unless you include more than one table in your query and you include fields from the table on the one side of a one-to-many relationship. You might have this situation when you are interested in data from one table but you want to filter it based on data in a related table without displaying the fields from the related table.

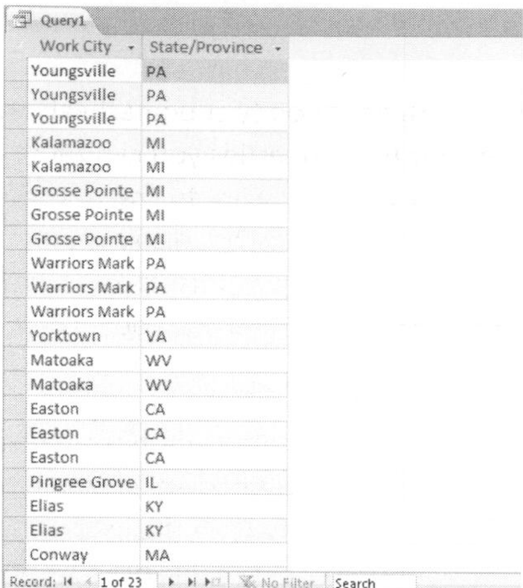

Query1

Work City	State/Province
Youngsville	PA
Youngsville	PA
Youngsville	PA
Kalamazoo	MI
Kalamazoo	MI
Grosse Pointe	MI
Grosse Pointe	MI
Grosse Pointe	MI
Warriors Mark	PA
Warriors Mark	PA
Warriors Mark	PA
Yorktown	VA
Matoaka	WV
Matoaka	WV
Easton	CA
Easton	CA
Easton	CA
Pingree Grove	IL
Elias	KY
Elias	KY
Conway	MA

Record: 1 of 23 No Filter Search

Figure 10-44 Even though your query uses two tables, when you set the Unique Records property to Yes, your query returns records that are unique in the one table that provides output columns.

Finally, if you're interested in only which cities you received a contact from in the specified date range, and you want to see each city name only once, then set Unique Values to Yes. (Access automatically resets Unique Records to No.) The result is 12 records, as shown in Figure 10-45 (saved as qxmplUniqueValues).

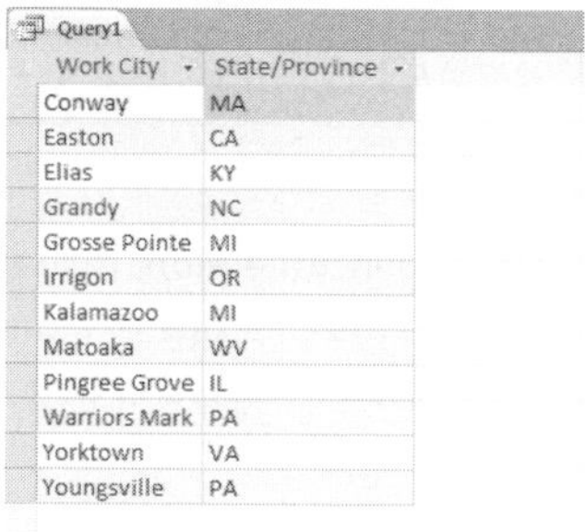

Query1

Work City	State/Province
Conway	MA
Easton	CA
Elias	KY
Grandy	NC
Grosse Pointe	MI
Irrigon	OR
Kalamazoo	MI
Matoaka	WV
Pingree Grove	IL
Warriors Mark	PA
Yorktown	VA
Youngsville	PA

Figure 10-45 When you set the Unique Values property to Yes, Access removes all duplicate records.

When you ask for unique values, you're asking Access to calculate and remove duplicate values. As with any calculated value in a query, fields in a unique values query can't be updated.

Defining a Subdatasheet

In Chapter 9, we showed you how to work with and modify subdatasheets from query Datasheet view. Now, let's take a closer look at the properties you can set in a query to predefine a subdatasheet within the query. Let's say you want to create a query to show company information and make a subdatasheet available that displays information about the primary contact for the company. You can use the qryContactsDatasheet query in ContactsDataCopy.accdb that you studied in Chapter 9, but first you'll need to modify that query for this exercise.

In the ContactsDataCopy.accdb database, open qryContactsDatasheet in Design view. To link this query to another that displays company information, you'll need the CompanyID field. Click the Show Table button in the Query Setup group of the Design contextual tab, and add the tblCompanyContacts table to the query. Click Close to close the Show Table dialog box. You should see a join line linking ContactID in the two tables. Add the CompanyID and DefaultForContact fields from tblCompanyContacts to the first two columns in the design grid. It makes sense to list only the default company for each contact, so add a criterion of True on the Criteria line under the DefaultForContact field. You should clear the Show check box because you don't really need to see this field in the output. Your query should now look like Figure 10-46. Click the File tab on the Backstage view, click Save Object As, and save the query as qryContactsDatasheetCOID. You can also find this query saved in the sample database as qryXmplContactsDatasheetCOID.

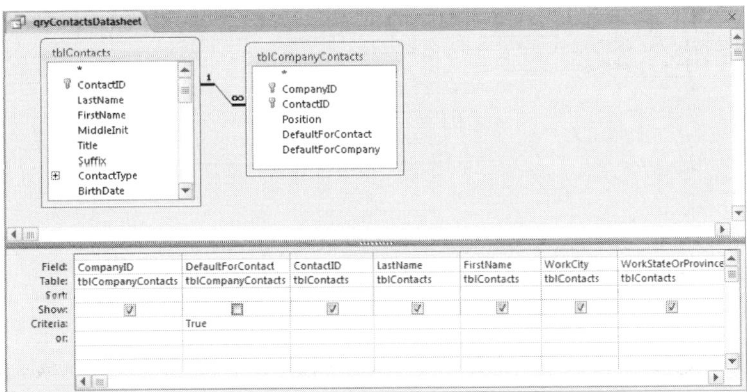

Figure 10-46 To modify a query to use it as a subdatasheet that displays contacts, include the appropriate linking field.

You need the CompanyID field to provide a link to the outer datasheet that you will build shortly, but you don't necessarily need to see it in your datasheet. Switch to Datasheet view, click in the Company/Org column (this is the CompanyID field), click the More command in the Records group on the Home tab, and select Hide Fields from the list to hide the field. Note that this affects the display only. CompanyID is still a field in the query. (Alternatively, you could clear the Show check box in the design grid.) Close the query and click Yes when Access asks you if you want to save your layout changes.

Now you're ready to build the query in which you'll use the query you just modified as a subdatasheet. Start a new query, add the tblCompanies table to the design grid, and close the Show Tables dialog box. Include the CompanyID, CompanyName, City, and StateOrProvince fields from tblCompanies. Click in the blank space in the top part of the Query window, and click the Property Sheet button in the Show/Hide group on the Design tab to open the property sheet for the query. Click in the Subdatasheet Name property and then click the small arrow to open a list of all tables and queries saved in your database. Scroll down and choose the query that you just saved—qryContactsDatasheetCOID—and select it, as shown in Figure 10-47. (You might have to widen the property sheet to see the complete names of queries.)

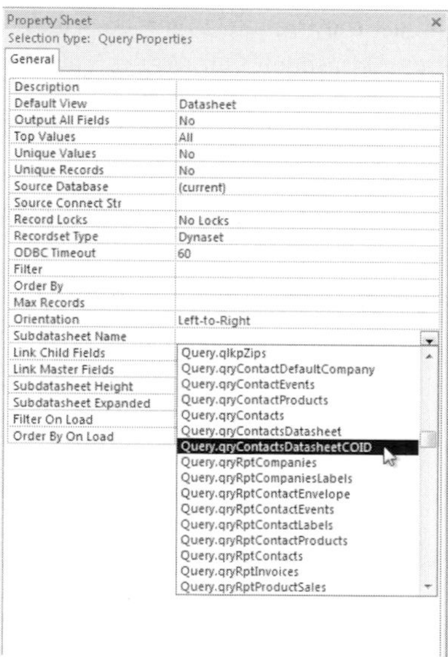

Figure 10-47 Select the qryContactsDatasheetCOID query to provide the subdatasheet for this query.

You need to tell your query which field links the query you're creating to the query in the subdatasheet. In Link Child Fields, type the name of the field in the subdatasheet query you just selected that matches a field in the query you're designing—in this case, CompanyID. Note that when you're linking to another table or query that requires more than one field to define the relationship, you enter the field names separated by semicolons. In Link Master Fields, enter the name of the field in the query you're creating that should match the value in the field in Link Child Fields—CompanyID again. (You'll see these same properties again when inserting a subform in a form in Chapter 15, "Advanced Form Design.")

Two additional properties apply to subdatasheets—Subdatasheet Height and Subdatasheet Expanded. If you leave Subdatasheet Height at its default setting of 0, the subdatasheet area expands to show all available rows when you open it. You can limit the maximum height by entering a setting in inches (centimeters on a computer with regional settings set to the metric system). If the height you specify isn't large enough to show all rows, you'll see a scroll bar to move through the rows in the subdatasheet. If you set Subdatasheet Expanded to Yes, the subdatasheet for every row opens expanded when you open the query or switch to Datasheet view. Just for fun, change this setting to Yes.

INSIDE OUT Cycling Through Property Box Values

When a property box has a list of values from which you can select, you can cycle through the values by double-clicking in the property value box instead of clicking the small arrow to the right of the property box.

Switch to Datasheet view, and your result should look like Figure 10-48.

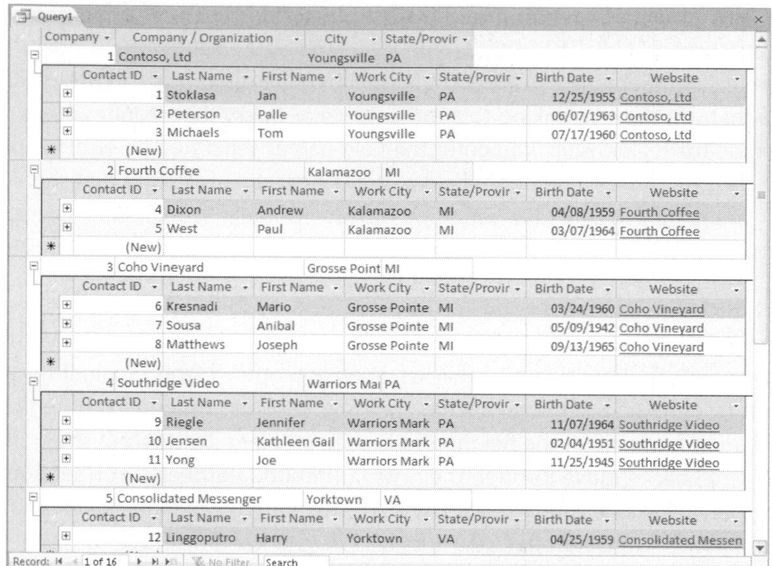

Figure 10-48 This query shows company information with its contact subdatasheet information expanded.

Do you notice that there are little plus signs on the rows in the subdatasheet? Remember that qryContactsDatasheet, from which you built the new qryContactsDatasheetCOID query, also has a subdatasheet defined. If you click one of the plus signs in the subdatasheet, you'll see the related contact event subdatasheet information from qryContactsDatasheet, as shown in Figure 10-49. You can actually nest subdatasheets like this up to seven levels.

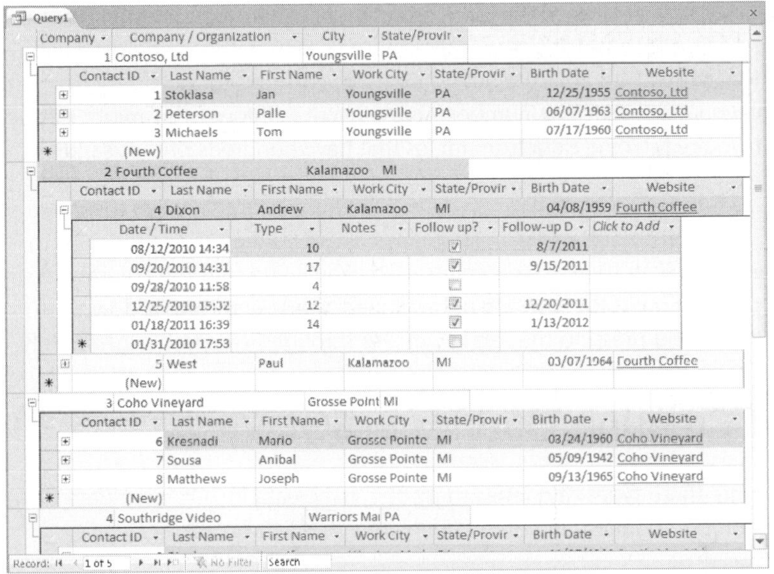

Figure 10-49 You can expand the subdatasheet of the subdatasheet to see contact event information.

You can find this query saved as qxmplCompaniesContactsSub in the sample database.

Other Query Properties

Use the Record Locks property to control the level of editing integrity for a query that is designed to access data shared across a network. The default is No Locks—not to lock any records when the user opens the query. With this setting, Access applies a lock temporarily only when it needs to write a row back to the source table. Select the Edited Record setting to lock a row as soon as a user begins entering changes in that row. The most restrictive setting, All Records, locks every record retrieved by the query so long as the user has the query open. Use this setting only when the query must perform multiple updates to a table and no other users should access any data in the table until the query is finished.

Four of the remaining properties—Source Database, Source Connect Str, ODBC Timeout, and Max Records—apply to dynamically linked tables. You can, for example, run a query against tables in another Access database by entering the full path and file name of that database in Source Database. Access dynamically links to the database when you run the query. Use Source Connect Str when you are dynamically linking to an ODBC or non-Access database that requires connection information. ODBC Timeout specifies how long Access will wait (in seconds) for a response from the ODBC database before failing with an error. Use Max Records to limit the number of rows returned to this query from a database server. When you don't specify a number, Access fetches all rows. This might not be desirable when you're fetching data from tables that have hundreds of thousands of rows.

The last property, Orientation, specifies whether you want to see the columns in Left-to-Right or Right-to-Left order. In languages where reading proceeds right to left, this setting is handy. You can try it out on your system. You'll find that the columns show up right to left, the caption of the query is right-aligned, the selector bar is down the right side of the datasheet, and pressing the Tab key moves through fields from right to left.

Editing and Creating Queries in SQL View

There are three types of queries that you must create in SQL view: data definition queries, pass-through queries, and union queries.

In a desktop application, Access supports a limited subset of the ANSI-standard SQL language for data definition. You can execute basic CREATE TABLE and ALTER TABLE commands in a data definition query, but you cannot define any Access-specific properties such as the Input Mask or Validation Rule property. The syntax is so limited that we don't cover it in Article 2.

When you're using linked tables to a server database system, such as Microsoft SQL Server or Oracle, you might need to execute a query on the server that takes advantage of the native SQL supported by the server. You can do most of your work in queries you build in the Access query designer, but the SQL that the query designer builds is only a subset of what your server probably supports. When you need to send a command to your database server in its native syntax, use a pass-through query. If all your data is stored in SQL Server, you should consider building an Access project that links directly to the server data. For more information on Access Data Projects, see *Microsoft Office Access 2007 Inside Out* (Microsoft Press, 2007).

So, that leaves us with union queries that you might want to build in SQL view. When you create a query that fetches data from multiple tables, you see the related fields side by side in the resulting datasheet. Sometimes it's useful to fetch similar data from several tables and literally stack the rows from different tables on top of one another. Think of pulling the pages containing your favorite recipes out of two different cookbooks and piling them on top of one another to make a new book. For that, you need a union query, and you must build it in SQL view.

SQL—The Basic Clauses

One way to begin learning SQL (and we strongly recommend that you do) is to look at any query you've built in the query designer in SQL view. You can see the SQL view of any query you've built by opening it in Design view and then clicking the small arrow below the View button in the Views group on the Home tab and selecting SQL View. queYou also find the View button in the Results group on the Design contextual tab below Query Tools. You can learn all the details in Article 2, but a quick overview of the main clauses will help you begin to understand what you see in SQL view.

SQL Clause	Usage
SELECT	This clause lists the fields and expressions that your query returns. It is equivalent to the Field row in the query designer. In a totals query, aggregate functions within the SELECT clause, such as Min or Sum, come from specifications in the Total line.
FROM	This clause specifies the tables or queries from which your query fetches data and includes JOIN clauses to define how to link your tables or queries. It is equivalent to the graphical display of table or query field lists and join lines in the top of the query designer.
WHERE	This clause specifies how to filter the rows returned by evaluating the FROM clause. It is equivalent to the Criteria and Or lines in the query designer
GROUP BY	This clause lists the grouping field for a totals query. Access builds this clause from the fields indicated with Group By in the Total line of the query designer.
HAVING	This clause specifies filtering in a totals query on calculated values. This clause comes from the Criteria and Or lines under fields with one of the aggregate functions specified in the Total line.

Let's say you need to build a mailing list in the Conrad Systems Contacts application. You want to send a brochure to each primary contact for a company at the company's main mailing address. You also want to include any other contacts who are not the primary contact for a company but send the mailing to their home address. It sounds easy enough to pull the primary contact mailing address from tblCompanies and the address for everyone else from tblContacts. But how do you get all this information in one set of data to make it easy to print your mailing labels in one pass?

First, build a query to get the information you need for each company's primary contact. In the ContactsDataCopy.accdb database, start a new query with tblCompanies. Add tblCompanyContacts and tblContacts and remove the extra join line between the ContactID field in tblContacts and the ReferredBy field in tblCompanies. In the first column on the Field line, enter:

```
EmpName: (tblContacts.Title + " ") & tblContacts.FirstName & " " &
(tblContacts.MiddleInit + ". ") & tblContacts.LastName & (" " + tblContacts.Suffix)
```

Add the CompanyName and Address fields from tblCompanies. In the fourth column on the Field line, enter:

```
CSZ: tblCompanies.City & ", " & tblCompanies.StateOrProvince & " " &
tblCompanies.PostalCode
```

Add the DefaultForCompany field from tblCompanyContacts, clear its Show check box, and enter True on the Criteria line. If you switch to Datasheet view, your result should look like Figure 10-50.

Query1

EmpName	Company / Organization	Billing Address	CSZ
Mrs. Jan Stoklasa	Contoso, Ltd	7890 Lincoln Avenue	Youngsville, PA 16371
Mr. Andrew Dixon	Fourth Coffee	7890 3rd Street	Kalamazoo, MI 49004
Mr. Mario Kresnadi	Coho Vineyard	6789 4th Street	Grosse Pointe, MI 48236
Dr. Jennifer Riegle	Southridge Video	1234 1st Avenue	Warriors Mark, PA 16877
Mr. Harry Linggoputro	Consolidated Messenger	4567 Lincoln Drive	Yorktown, VA 23692
Mrs. Cat Francis	Baldwin Museum of Science	7890 Central Drive	Matoaka, WV 24736
Mrs. Shengda Yang	Fabrikam, Inc.	4567 2nd Street	Easton, CA 93706
Ms. Adrian Lannin	Alpine Ski House	3456 3rd Boulevard	Pingree Grove, IL 60140
Mr. Dániel Koczka	School of Fine Art	5678 3rd Avenue	Elias, KY 40486
Ms. Magdalena Wróblewska	City Power & Light	5678 Willow Avenue	Conway, MA 01341
Mr. Eugene Zabokritski	Blue Yonder Airlines	5678 Central Avenue	Riverside, ND 58078
Dr. Mindy Martin	Margie's Travel	4567 3rd Avenue	Grandy, NC 27939
Mr. Adam Trukawka	Lucerne Publishing	6789 1st Parkway	Irrigon, OR 97844
Mrs. Marcin Jankowski	Humongous Insurance	6789 Willow Parkway	Flushing, NY 11351
*			

Figure 10-50 You can switch to Datasheet view to verify that you have correctly built the first part of a union query to display names and addresses.

OK, that's the first part. You do not have to save this query—leave it open in Design view. Start another query with tblContacts and add tblCompanyContacts. Create an EmpName field exactly as you did in the first query. In the second column, enter:

```
CompanyName: ""
```

Say what? Well, one of the requirements to build a union query is that the two recordsets must both have the exact same number of columns and the exact same data types in the relative columns. A mailing label sent to a home address doesn't have a company name, but you need this field to line up with the ones you created in the first query. In Chapter 17, "Constructing a Report," you'll see how the Mailing Label Wizard eliminates the blank row that would otherwise be created by including this field.

Add the HomeAddress field from tblContacts in the third column and create this expression in the fourth column on the Field line:

```
CSZ: tblContacts.HomeCity & ", " & tblContacts.HomeStateOrProvince & " " &
tblContacts.HomePostalCode
```

Finally, include the DefaultForCompany field from tblCompanyContacts and clear the Show check box, but this time set a criterion of False. The Datasheet view of this query should look like Figure 10-51.

Query1 | Query2

EmpName	CompanyName	Home Address	CSZ
Dr. Palle Peterson		1234 Central Parkway	Emlenton, PA 16373
Mr. Tom Michaels		7890 Lincoln Boulevard	Kennerdell, PA 16374
Mr. Paul West		3456 Main Boulevard	Kalamazoo, MI 49004
Dr. Anibal Sousa		4567 Main Street	Grosse Pointe Shores, MI 48236
Mr. Joseph Matthews		5678 2nd Avenue	Detroit, MI 48231
Ms. Kathleen Gail Jensen		1234 4th Boulevard	Warriors Mark, PA 16877
Mr. Joe Yong		5678 Main Boulevard	Shawville, PA 16873
Ms. Mary E. Gibson		5678 Central Drive	Kellysville, WV 24732
Mr. John Smith		4567 Main Avenue	Fresno, CA 93707
Mr. Douglas Curran		2345 Willow Drive	Easton, CA 93706
Mr. Rodrigo Ready		2345 Church Avenue	Stanford, KY 40484
Mr. Mikael Sandberg		4567 3rd Parkway	Colrain, MA 01340
Mr. Markus Zulechner		1234 Lincoln Boulevard	Harrellsville, NC 27942
Dr. Peter Villadsen		6789 3rd Drive	Frisco, NC 27936
Dr. Mark Hanson		6789 1st Avenue	Imbler, OR 97841
Mrs. Monika Buschmann		4567 1st Avenue	Flushing, NY 11355
Mr. John L. Viescas			,
Mr. Jeff Conrad			Redmond, WA 98052
*			

Figure 10-51 The second part of a union query to display names and addresses displays the home addresses for persons who are not the primary contact for each company.

Again, you don't have to save this query. Now, you're ready to assemble your union query. Click the Query Design button in the Queries group on the Create tab. You'll see a blank third query window with the Show Table dialog box opened in front. Click Close to dismiss the dialog box. When Access sees that you haven't chosen any tables or queries, it makes SQL the default option on the View button at the left end of the ribbon. (This means that if you simply click above the View button, which now displays *SQL*, you open the SQL view for the query.) Click the SQL button in the Views group on the Home tab or the Results group of the Design contextual tab to switch to SQL view for this empty query. You should see a blank window with *SELECT;* displayed in the upper-left corner.

Go back to your first query, click the small arrow below the View button on the Home tab, and then click SQL View (or you can follow the same steps using the Results group on the Design contextual tab below Query Tools). You should see a window like Figure 10-52.

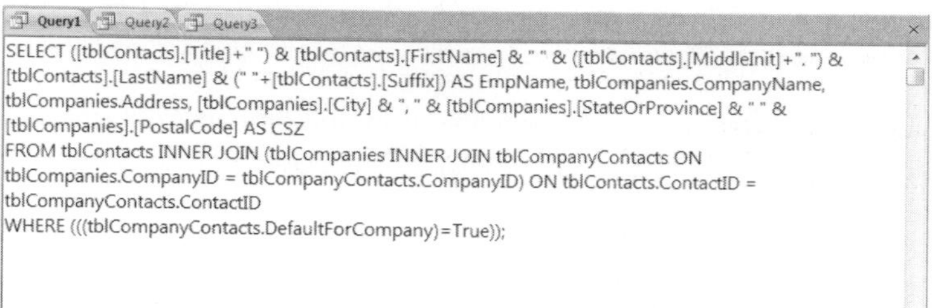

Figure 10-52 You're going to copy the first part of your union query from the first query's SQL view.

INSIDE OUT Changing Font Size for the Query Window

By default, Access sets the font size for text in the Query window to 8. To make Figures 10-52 and 10-53 more readable in the printed book, we temporarily changed our font size to 12 for the Query window. Click the File tab on the Backstage view, click Options, click the Object Designers category, and then select a font size in the Query Design Font Size text box in the Query Design section. Click OK to save this change.

Select all the text you see in this window and copy it to the Clipboard. Switch to the third empty query, and replace *SELECT;* with the text you copied. Remove the ending semicolon, place the insertion point at the end of the text, press Enter, type the word **UNION**, and press Enter again.

Go to your second query, switch to SQL view, select all the text, and copy it to the Clipboard. Go back to the third query and paste this text at the end. Your new union query should look like Figure 10-53.

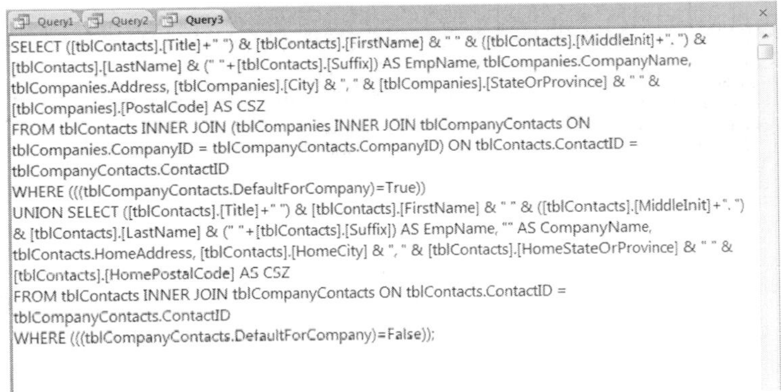

```
SELECT ([tblContacts].[Title]+" ") & [tblContacts].[FirstName] & " " & ([tblContacts].[MiddleInit]+". ") &
[tblContacts].[LastName] & (" "+[tblContacts].[Suffix]) AS EmpName, tblCompanies.CompanyName,
tblCompanies.Address, [tblCompanies].[City] & ", " & [tblCompanies].[StateOrProvince] & " " &
[tblCompanies].[PostalCode] AS CSZ
FROM tblContacts INNER JOIN (tblCompanies INNER JOIN tblCompanyContacts ON
tblCompanies.CompanyID = tblCompanyContacts.CompanyID) ON tblContacts.ContactID =
tblCompanyContacts.ContactID
WHERE (((tblCompanyContacts.DefaultForCompany)=True))
UNION SELECT ([tblContacts].[Title]+" ") & [tblContacts].[FirstName] & " " & ([tblContacts].[MiddleInit]+". ")
& [tblContacts].[LastName] & (" "+[tblContacts].[Suffix]) AS EmpName, "" AS CompanyName,
tblContacts.HomeAddress, [tblContacts].[HomeCity] & ", " & [tblContacts].[HomeStateOrProvince] & " " &
[tblContacts].[HomePostalCode] AS CSZ
FROM tblContacts INNER JOIN tblCompanyContacts ON tblContacts.ContactID =
tblCompanyContacts.ContactID
WHERE (((tblCompanyContacts.DefaultForCompany)=False));
```

Figure 10-53 You can assemble a union query by copying and pasting the SQL from two other queries.

Switch to Datasheet view to see the final result, as shown in Figure 10-54.

EmpName	CompanyName	Address	CSZ
Dr. Anibal Sousa		4567 Main Street	Grosse Pointe Shores, MI 48236
Dr. Jennifer Riegle	Southridge Video	1234 1st Avenue	Warriors Mark, PA 16877
Dr. Mark Hanson		6789 1st Avenue	Imbler, OR 97841
Dr. Mindy Martin	Margie's Travel	4567 3rd Avenue	Grandy, NC 27939
Dr. Palle Peterson		1234 Central Parkway	Emlenton, PA 16373
Dr. Peter Villadsen		6789 3rd Drive	Frisco, NC 27936
Mr. Adam Trukawka	Lucerne Publishing	6789 1st Parkway	Irrigon, OR 97844
Mr. Andrew Dixon	Fourth Coffee	7890 3rd Street	Kalamazoo, MI 49004
Mr. Dániel Koczka	School of Fine Art	5678 3rd Avenue	Elias, KY 40486
Mr. Douglas Curran		2345 Willow Drive	Easton, CA 93706
Mr. Eugene Zabokritski	Blue Yonder Airlines	5678 Central Avenue	Riverside, ND 58070
Mr. Harry Linggoputro	Consolidated Messenger	4567 Lincoln Drive	Yorktown, VA 23692
Mr. Jeff Conrad			Redmond, WA 98052
Mr. Joe Yong		5678 Main Boulevard	Shawville, PA 16873
Mr. John L. Viescas			,
Mr. John Smith		4567 Main Avenue	Fresno, CA 93707
Mr. Joseph Matthews		5678 2nd Avenue	Detroit, MI 48231
Mr. Mario Kresnadi	Coho Vineyard	6789 4th Street	Grosse Pointe, MI 48236
Mr. Markus Zulechner		1234 Lincoln Boulevard	Harrellsville, NC 27942
Mr. Mikael Sandberg		4567 3rd Parkway	Colrain, MA 01340
Mr. Paul West		3456 Main Boulevard	Kalamazoo, MI 49004
Mr. Rodrigo Ready		2345 Church Avenue	Stanford, KY 40484

Record: 1 of 32 No Filter Search

Figure 10-54 The union query displays the company address for all primary contacts and the home address for all other contacts.

You should save this query, but you can close and not save the first two queries that you used to build this. You can find this query saved as qxmplAddressesUnion in the sample database. If you want to learn more about SQL, see Article 2.

Limitations on Using Select Queries to Update Data

The recordset that Access creates when you run a query looks and acts pretty much like a real table containing data. In fact, in most cases, you can insert rows, delete rows, and update the information in a recordset, and Access will make the necessary changes to the underlying table or tables for you.

In some cases, however, Access won't be able to figure out what needs to be changed. Consider, for example, a calculated field named Total that is the result of multiplying two fields named Quantity and Price. If you try to increase the amount in a Total field, Access can't know whether you mean to update the Quantity field or the Price field. On the other hand, you can change either the Price field or the Quantity field and then immediately see the change reflected in the calculated Total field.

In addition, Access won't accept any change that might potentially affect many rows in the underlying table. For that reason, you can't change any of the data in a totals query or in a crosstab query. A Group By field is the result of gathering together one or more rows with the same value. Likewise, a Sum is most likely the result of adding values from potentially many rows. A Min or Max value might occur in more than one row.

When working with a recordset that is the result of a join, you can update all fields from the *many* side of a join but only the non-key fields on the one side, unless you have specified Cascade Update Related Fields in the relationship. Also, you cannot set or change any field that has the AutoNumber data type. For example, you can't change the ContactID field values in the tblContacts table in the Conrad Systems Contacts sample application.

The ability to update fields on the *one* side of a query can produce unwanted results if you aren't careful. For example, you could intend to assign a contact to a different company. If you change the company name, you'll change that name for all contacts related to the current CompanyID. What you should do instead is change the CompanyID field in the tblCompanyContacts table, not the company name in the tblCompanies table. You'll learn techniques in Chapter 15 to prevent inadvertent updating of fields in queries.

When you set Unique Values to Yes in the query's property sheet, Access eliminates duplicate rows. The values returned might occur in multiple rows, so Access won't know which one you mean to update. And finally, when Access combines rows from different tables in a union query, the individual rows lose their underlying table identity. Access cannot know which table you mean to update when you try to change a row in a union query, so it disallows all updates.

Query Fields That Cannot Be Updated

The following types of query fields cannot be updated:

- Any field that is the result of a calculation
- Any field in a totals or crosstab query
- Any field in a query that includes a totals or crosstab query as one of the row sources
- A primary key participating in a relationship, unless Cascade Update Related Fields is specified
- AutoNumber fields
- Calculated data types
- Any field in a unique values query or a unique records query
- Any field in a union query

Creating PivotTables and PivotCharts from Queries

Access 2002 (in Office XP) introduced two very useful new features for tables, queries, and forms—PivotTables and PivotCharts. These are additional views of a table, query, or form that you can design to provide analytical views of your data. These views are built into the objects; they're not implemented via a separate ActiveX control as was the old and venerable Microsoft Graph feature.

You learned in this chapter that you can build a crosstab query to *pivot* the values in a column to form dynamic column headings. However, crosstab queries have a major drawback—you can include only one calculated value in the intersection of your row headings and single column heading. PivotTables in Access are very similar to the PivotTable facility in Microsoft Excel. You can categorize rows by several values, just as you can in a crosstab query, but you can also include multiple column categories and multiple raw or calculated values in each intersection of rows and column. As its name implies, you can also pivot the table to swap row headings with column headings.

A PivotChart is a graphical view of the data that you included in your PivotTable. You can build a PivotChart without first defining the PivotTable, and vice versa. When you design a PivotChart, you're also designing or modifying the related PivotTable to provide the data you need for your chart. When you modify a PivotTable, you'll also change (or destroy) the related PivotChart you have already designed.

As you explore the possibilities with PivotTables and PivotCharts, you'll find powerful capabilities to analyze your data in more detail. Unlike a crosstab query that's built on summarized data, you can begin with a table or query that contains very detailed information. The more detail you have to begin with, the more you can do with your PivotTable and PivotChart.

CAUTION !

You might be tempted to design a very detailed query that returns thousands of rows for your user to work with. However, the filtering capabilities inside a PivotTable aren't nearly as efficient as defining a filter in your query to begin with. If you're loading hundreds of thousands of rows over a network, your PivotTable or PivotChart might be very, very slow. You should provide enough detail to get the job done, but no more. You should limit the fields in your query to those focused on the task at hand and include filters in your underlying query to return only the subset of the data that's needed.

Building a Query for a PivotTable

Although you can build a PivotTable directly on a table in your database, you most likely will need a query to provide the level of detail you want to pivot. Let's build a query in the HousingDataCopy.accdb database that provides some interesting detail.

Start a new query with tblFacilities and add tblReservations, tblEmployees, and tblDepartments. (Be sure to remove the extra relationship between the EmployeeNumber field in tblEmployees and the ManagerNumber field in tblDepartments.) Create an expression to display the employee name in the first field as follows:

```
EmpName: tblEmployees.LastName & ", " & tblEmployees.FirstName & (" " +
tblEmployees.MiddleName)
```

In the query grid, include the Department field from tblDepartments, the ReservationID field from tblReservations (we're going to use this field later to count the number of reservation days), the FacilityName field from tblFacilities, and the RoomNumber field from tblReservations. Add an expression in the next field to calculate the actual charge per day. You could use the DailyRate field from tblReservations, but that's not an accurate reflection of how much the room costs per day when the employee stays a week or more. Your expression should look like this:

```
DailyCharge: CCur(Round(tblReservations.TotalCharge / (tblReservations.CheckOutDate -
tblReservations.CheckInDate), 2))
```

Remember that you can calculate the number of days by subtracting the CheckInDate field from the CheckOutDate field. Divide the TotalCharge field by the number of days to obtain the actual daily rate. This division might result in a value that has more than two decimal places, so asking the Round function to round to two decimal places (the 2 parameter at the end) takes care of that. Finally, the expression uses the CCur (Convert to Currency) function to make sure the query returns a currency value.

Now comes the fun part. Each row in tblReservations represents a stay of one or more days. In this example, we ultimately want to be able to count individual days to find out the length of stay within any month. To do that, we need to "explode" each single row in tblReservations into a row per day for the duration of the reservation. In this sample database, you'll find what we call a "driver" table—ztblDates—which is full of dates to accomplish this feat. The table contains date values, one per day, for dates from January 1, 1992, to December 31, 2035. We created this table to "drive" the complete list of dates we need (at least, complete enough for our purposes) against the rows in tblReservations in order to provide the explosion.

Include this table in your query and notice that there's no join line to any of the tables. When you add a table with no join defined to another table or set of records, the query returns the Cartesian product of the two sets of records—every row in the first table or set of records is matched with every row in the second table or set of records. For example, if there are 90 rows in one set and 12 rows in the second set, the query returns 1080 rows (90 times 12). In this case, each reservation will now be matched with each of the separate date values in ztblDates.

As we mentioned earlier, you should try to limit the output of a query that you'll use to build a PivotTable to only the rows you need to solve the problem. Let's say the facilities manager is interested in data for October, November, and December of 2010. Add the DateValue field from ztblDates and enter **Between #10/1/2010# And #12/31/2010#** under this field on the Criteria line. You have now limited the explosion of rows to dates in the months of interest.

The final step is to further limit the rows created based on the CheckInDate and CheckOutDate fields in tblReservations. Any reservation that crosses the time span of interest is going to be for a few days or a few weeks. Add the CheckInDate and CheckOutDate fields from tblReservations and clear the Show check box under both. On the Criteria row under CheckInDate, enter **<=ztblDates.DateValue**. Under CheckOutDate, enter **>ztblDates.DateValue**.

This forces the query to keep any rows where the DateValue field from ztblDates is within the time span of each reservation row. Voilà! You now have one row per date for each reservation. Your query should now look like Figure 10-55.

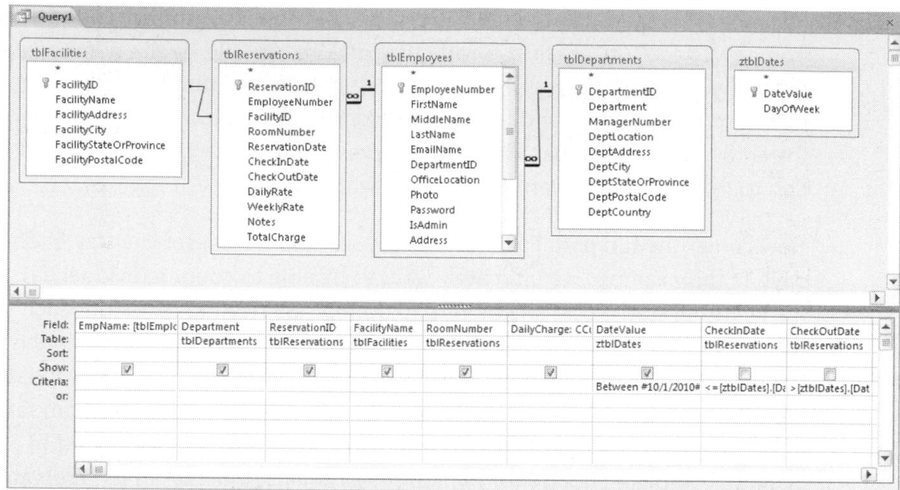

Figure 10-55 This complex query generates the data you need for a PivotTable.

To better understand how this query expands each reservation into one row per day, look at Table 10-2. The table represents expanded rows after applying the final two criteria on CheckInDate and CheckOutDate.

Table 10-2 How ztblDates Expands Reservation Rows

ReservationID	CheckIndate	CheckoutDate	DateValue
14	October 21, 2010	October 26, 2010	October 21, 2010
14	October 21, 2010	October 26, 2010	October 22, 2010
14	October 21, 2010	October 26, 2010	October 23, 2010
14	October 21, 2010	October 26, 2010	October 24, 2010
14	October 21, 2010	October 26, 2010	October 25, 2010

The result is that the query selects only the rows from ztblDates that are within the date range of the individual reservation. Because there's one (and only one) row for every date of interest coming from ztblDates, you end up with one row per day that's within the span of days in each reservation. Figure 10-56 shows you the Datasheet view of your query. You can find this query saved as qxmplReservationsByDay in the sample database.

Query1

EmpName	Department	Reservation	Name	Room	DailyCharge	DateValue
Lawrence, David Oliver	Product Development	11	Main Campus Housing B	301	$59.67	01-Oct-10
Adams, Jay	Housing Administration	15	Main Campus Housing B	206	$75.45	01-Oct-10
Bradley, David M.	Product Development	13	Main Campus Housing A	111	$73.75	01-Oct-10
Berndt, Matthias	Finance	6	Main Campus Housing A	902	$84.21	01-Oct-10
Lawrence, David Oliver	Product Development	11	Main Campus Housing B	301	$59.67	02-Oct-10
Adams, Jay	Housing Administration	15	Main Campus Housing B	206	$75.45	02-Oct-10
Bradley, David M.	Product Development	13	Main Campus Housing A	111	$73.75	02-Oct-10
Berndt, Matthias	Finance	6	Main Campus Housing A	902	$84.21	02-Oct-10
Adams, Jay	Housing Administration	15	Main Campus Housing B	206	$75.45	03-Oct-10
Bradley, David M.	Product Development	13	Main Campus Housing A	111	$73.75	03-Oct-10
Berndt, Matthias	Finance	6	Main Campus Housing A	902	$84.21	03-Oct-10
Adams, Jay	Housing Administration	15	Main Campus Housing B	206	$75.45	04-Oct-10
Bradley, David M.	Product Development	13	Main Campus Housing A	111	$73.75	04-Oct-10
Berndt, Matthias	Finance	6	Main Campus Housing A	902	$84.21	04-Oct-10
Adams, Jay	Housing Administration	15	Main Campus Housing B	206	$75.45	05-Oct-10
Bradley, David M.	Product Development	13	Main Campus Housing A	111	$73.75	05-Oct-10
Berndt, Matthias	Finance	6	Main Campus Housing A	902	$84.21	05-Oct-10
Adams, Jay	Housing Administration	15	Main Campus Housing B	206	$75.45	06-Oct-10
Bradley, David M.	Product Development	13	Main Campus Housing A	111	$73.75	06-Oct-10
Berndt, Matthias	Finance	6	Main Campus Housing A	902	$84.21	06-Oct-10
Adams, Jay	Housing Administration	15	Main Campus Housing B	206	$75.45	07-Oct-10
Bradley, David M.	Product Development	13	Main Campus Housing A	111	$73.75	07-Oct-10

Record: 1 of 281 No Filter Search

Figure 10-56 The reservations for October, November, and December are expanded into one row per day.

Designing a PivotTable

Now that you have the data you need, you're ready to start building a PivotTable. From Design or Datasheet view, switch to PivotTable view by clicking the small arrow below the View button and then clicking PivotTable View from the list. (You can find the View button on both the Home tab and the Design contextual tab.) You should see a blank PivotTable design area, as shown in Figure 10-57. If you don't see the field list, as shown in Figure 10-57, click the Field List command in the Show/Hide group of the Design contextual tab below PivotTable Tools.

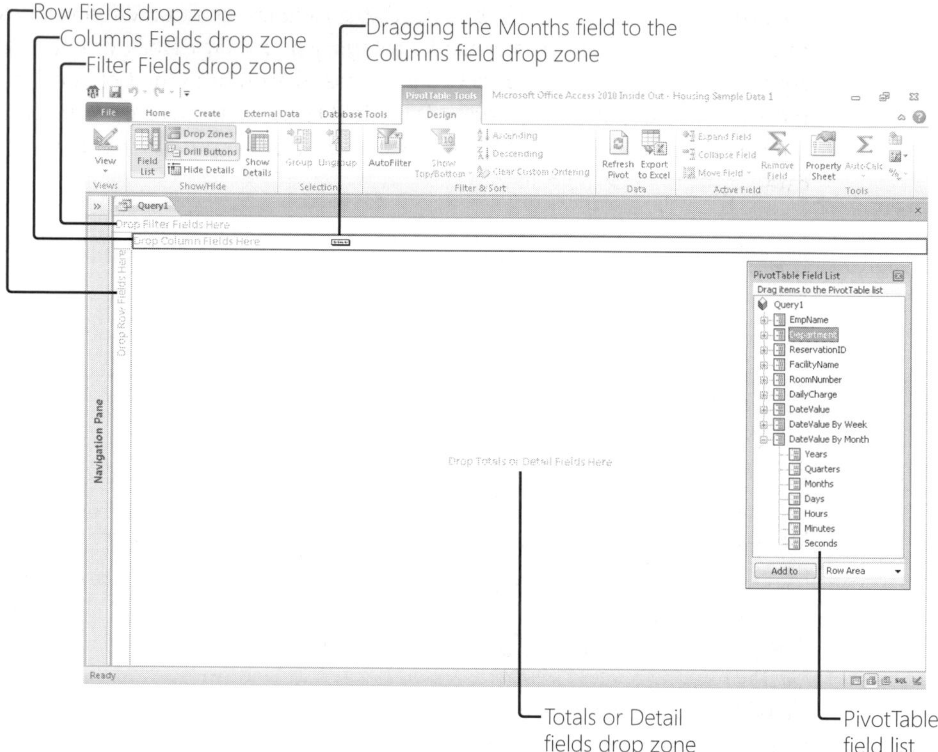

Figure 10-57 You can design PivotTables using the PivotTable design window.

In general, you should use as columns those fields that have the fewest values. If you place too many values across your PivotTable, you'll find that you must scroll left a long way to see all the details. In this case, we're interested in statistics by month, and we know there are only three months of data in the underlying recordset. You'll still be able to show the details by day, if you like, because the recordset includes information by date—you can expand any Months field to show all the days in the month. We might want to see the data organized by department and facility. It might also be interesting to provide an easy way to filter on employee name, but we don't need the data from that field displayed in the table.

Expand the DateValue By Month list and drag Months to the Column Fields drop zone. Drag the Department field and the FacilityName field to the Row Fields drop zone. Drag the EmpName field to the Filter Fields drop zone. Finally, drag the ReservationID and DailyCharge fields on the Totals or Detail Fields drop zone. Notice that fields you choose are now highlighted in bold in the PivotTable Field List window. Within the PivotTable, you can click any plus sign (+) to expand a category or display details, or any minus sign (–) to contract a category or hide details. If you expand Months in the Column Fields drop zone, the PivotTable automatically adds a Days field to the Columns area. You can also expand the categories in the PivotTable Field List window by clicking on the plus sign next to each category. Your PivotTable should look like Figure 10-58.

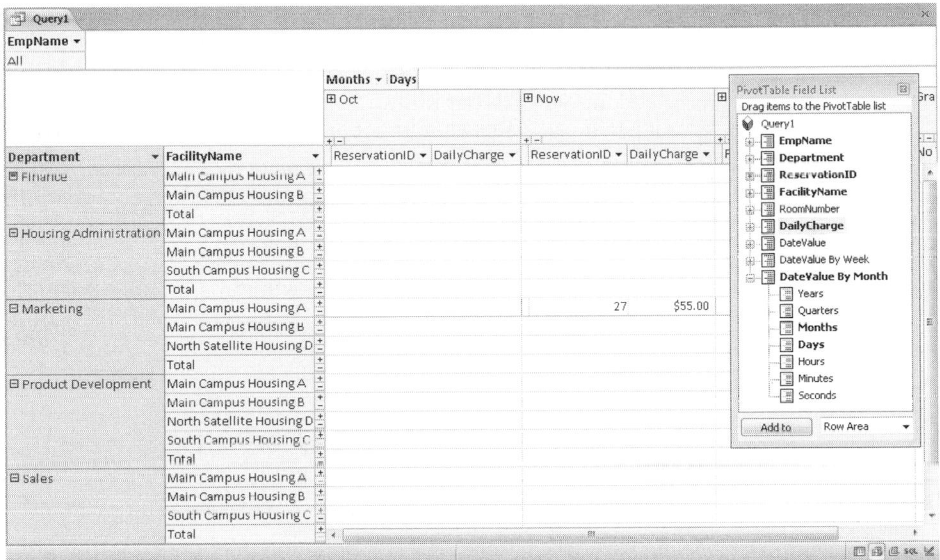

Figure 10-58 This PivotTable shows fields added to all drop zones.

Now would be a good time to take a quick look at the buttons available on the Design contextual tab below PivotTable Tools, which you saw previously in Figure 10-57. Table 10-3 shows you the details.

Table 10-3 PivotTable Tools on the Ribbon

Button	Usage
AutoFilter	When highlighted, indicates automatic filtering is active for the PivotTable. You can click this button to remove all filters. If you define a filter, this button becomes highlighted again.
Show Top/Bottom	You can select a column or row field and then click this button to define a filter to display only the first or last number or percentage of rows. This feature works similarly to the Top Values property of a query.

Button	Usage
AutoCalc	You can select a column, row, or detail/total field and then click this button to insert an aggregate function. The available list of functions includes those you can use in totals queries except for First and Last. (See Table 10-1 on page 647.) The functions available in AutoCalc are appropriate to the field data type and location on the grid. (For example, you can't use a Sum function in a text field.)
Subtotal	You can click a column or row field and then click this button to insert a subtotal based on the values in that field. You must define an AutoCalc field before you add a subtotal.
Formulas	You can click this button to insert an expression in the detail/total area that calculates an additional value based on the fields in the recordset.
Show As	After you insert AutoCalc total fields, you can click in a field and then click this button to convert the value to a percentage of the row, column, or grand totals.
Collapse Field	Click a row or column field and then click this button to collapse all subcategories for the field and show summaries only.
Expand Field	Performs the opposite of Collapse Field.
Hide Details	Hides the details for the selected row or column and shows only totals.
Show Details	Performs the opposite of Hide Details.
Refresh Pivot	Refetches the underlying data. You might need to do this if others are sharing the data and updating it.
Export to Excel	Exports your PivotTable in Extensible Markup Language (XML) format to a Hypertext Markup Language (HTML; .htm , .html) file and opens it in Excel.
Field List	Opens or closes the PivotTable field list.
Property Sheet	Opens or closes the Properties window.

You're going to need some total calculations for your PivotTable. Click the Reservation ID column heading, click AutoCalc to display the list of available functions, and click Count. Click the DailyCharge column heading, click AutoCalc, and click Sum. Click the DailyCharge column heading again, and then click Hide Details to show only totals. Your PivotTable should now look like Figure 10-59. (We closed the PivotTable Field List window to show you more of the PivotTable.)

Query1

EmpName: All

Months / Days: Oct

Department	FacilityName	01-Oct Count of ReservationID	01-Oct Sum of DailyCharge	02-Oct Count of ReservationID	02-Oct Sum of DailyCharge	03-Oct Count of Reservat
Finance	Main Campus Housing A	1	$84.21	1	$84.21	
	Main Campus Housing B					
	Total	1	$84.21	1	$84.21	
Housing Administration	Main Campus Housing A					
	Main Campus Housing B	1	$75.45	1	$75.45	
	South Campus Housing C					
	Total	1	$75.45	1	$75.45	
Marketing	Main Campus Housing A					
	Main Campus Housing B					
	North Satellite Housing D					
	Total					
Product Development	Main Campus Housing A	1	$73.75	1	$73.75	
	Main Campus Housing B	1	$59.67	1	$59.67	
	North Satellite Housing D					
	South Campus Housing C					
	Total	2	$133.42	2	$133.42	
Sales	Main Campus Housing A					
	Main Campus Housing B					
	South Campus Housing C					
	Total					

Figure 10-59 The PivotTable now shows two totals calculations, and we are hiding all the details.

There are literally hundreds of properties you can set in a PivotTable. Let's change the captions of the two totals fields to something more meaningful. Click the Count Of ReservationID field and then click the Property Sheet button in the Tools group of the Design contextual tab below PivotTable Tools to open the Properties dialog box, as shown in Figure 10-60.

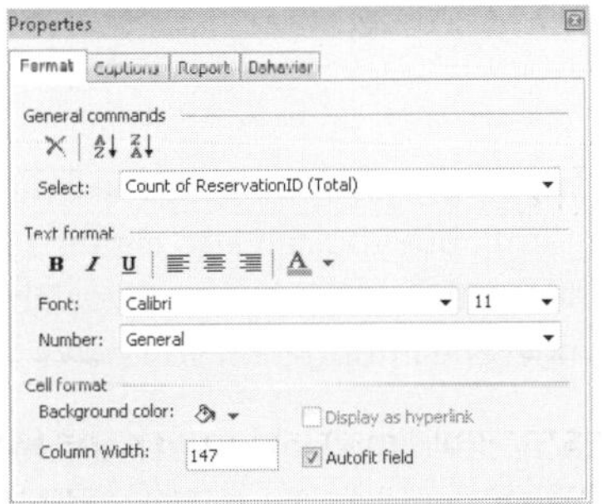

Figure 10-60 You can change a field's caption in the Properties window for a field in a PivotTable.

As you can see, you can modify the text format on the first tab. You can also click the arrow to the right of Select to choose any other element you have defined thus far. The Properties window changes depending on the type of element you choose. Click the Captions tab and change the caption to Room Days. Go back to the Format tab, select Sum Of Daily Charge (Total) from the Select list, click the Captions tab again, and change the caption to Revenue.

You can spend a couple of days playing around in this PivotTable to see what else you can do. One last thing we might want to do before turning this into a PivotChart is to actually pivot the table. You do that by grabbing the fields in the column area and moving them to the row area and vice versa. We decided we'd rather see details about departments first and then facility usage within department, so we placed Department to the left of FacilityName when we moved the fields. You can see the final result in Figure 10-61.

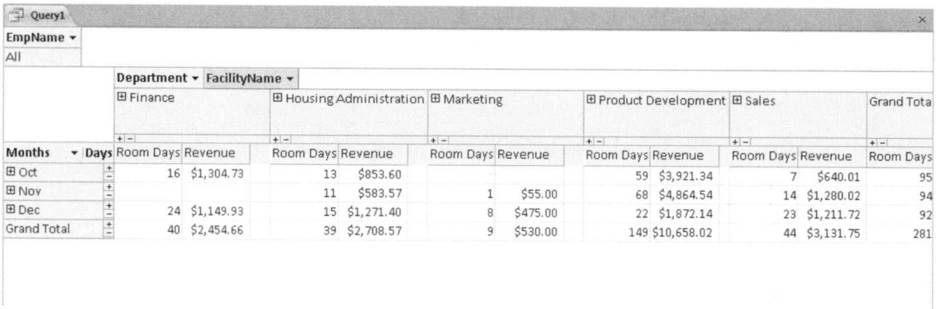

Query1

EmpName
All

Department FacilityName

Months	Days	Finance Room Days	Finance Revenue	Housing Administration Room Days	Housing Administration Revenue	Marketing Room Days	Marketing Revenue	Product Development Room Days	Product Development Revenue	Sales Room Days	Sales Revenue	Grand Tota Room Days
Oct		16	$1,304.73	13	$853.60			59	$3,921.34	7	$640.01	95
Nov				11	$583.57	1	$55.00	68	$4,864.54	14	$1,280.02	94
Dec		24	$1,149.93	15	$1,271.40	8	$475.00	22	$1,872.14	23	$1,211.72	92
Grand Total		40	$2,454.66	39	$2,708.57	9	$530.00	149	$10,658.02	44	$3,131.75	281

Figure 10-61 You can look at the data in a PivotTable another way by "pivoting" the rows and columns and displaying only totals.

If you switch to Design view, you can open the property sheet for the query and set the Default View property to PivotTable. We saved this query as qxmplReservationsByDayPT in the sample database. You should save this query under a new name so that you can start fresh building a PivotChart in the next section.

Designing a PivotChart

Designing a PivotChart is almost as easy as building a PivotTable. You will most likely use PivotCharts in reports (as an embedded subform), but you can also create a PivotChart view of a table, query, or form. As mentioned earlier in the discussion on PivotTables, you most often need to start with a query to pull together the information you need.

To start building a new PivotChart from scratch, open the qxmplReservationsByDay sample query again and switch to PivotChart view. You can see the PivotChart design window in Figure 10-62. (If necessary, click Field List in the Show/Hide group on the Design contextual tab to display the Chart Field List window.)

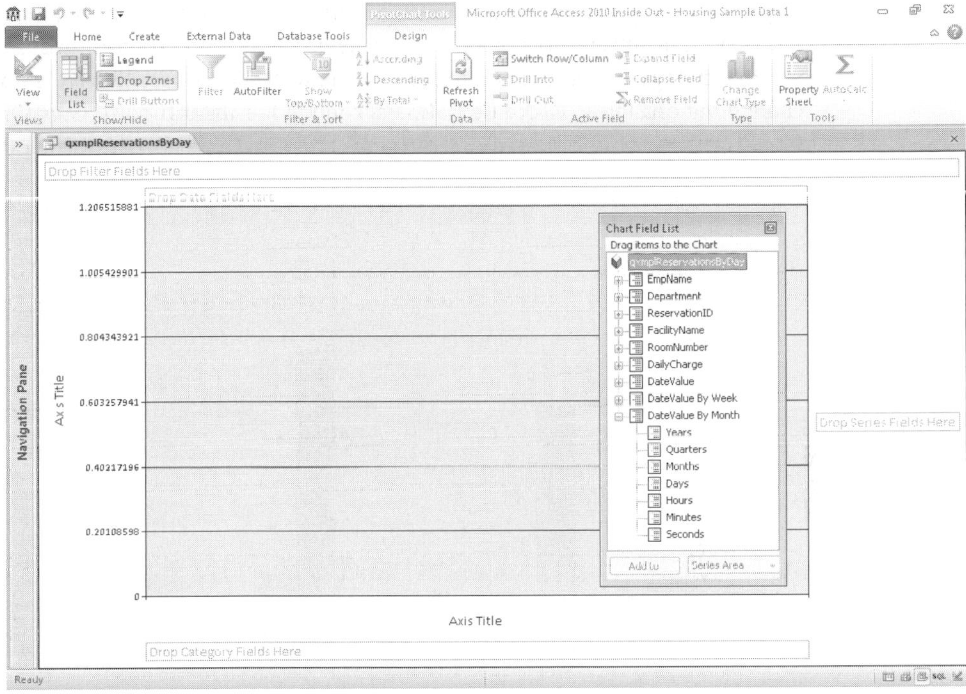

Figure 10-62 We are beginning to design a PivotChart on a query.

Notice that the filter area is still near the upper-left corner of the window. However, the area for data fields is now along the top of the gray chart drawing area in the center. Drop fields that you want to use for data points along the bottom axis in the bottom-left corner. Drop fields that you want to use for the vertical axis in the right center area. To begin designing your PivotChart, expand DateValue By Month in the field list and drag Months onto the Category Fields drop zone. Next, drag Department onto the Series Fields drop zone on the right.

INSIDE OUT Switching into PivotChart View

You can switch directly into PivotChart view from the Design view or Datasheet View of any query. If you haven't previously defined the PivotTable, you can still create your chart by dragging and dropping fields from the field list. Keep in mind that any change you make in PivotChart view also changes what you see in PivotTable view. If you want to keep separate PivotTable and PivotChart views, you should save two versions of your query.

We don't have anything charted yet, so drag the DailyCharge field from the field list to the Data Fields drop zone along the top of the chart. Notice that the chart assumes we want to Sum the field. If you had added the ReservationID field, you would have to click the Sum Of ReservationID field, click AutoCalc, and change the calculation to Count. Your PivotChart should now look like Figure 10-63.

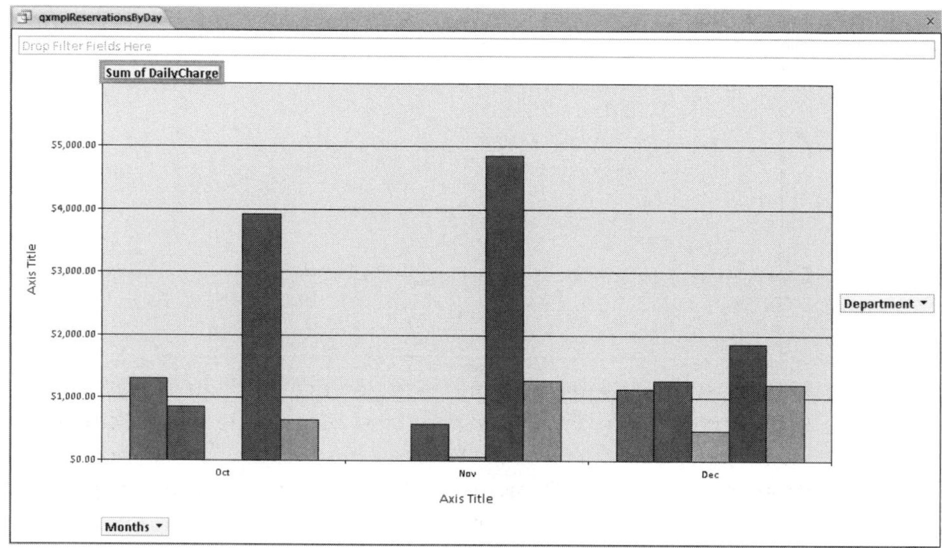

Figure 10-63 You can create totals and display them using a PivotChart.

This doesn't look all that informative yet, but we're starting to make some progress. It would be nice to add a title, a *legend* (a description of each of the colored bars), and a vertical axis with some values. You might also want to display the actual value of each bar at the top of it. Let's get started.

First, open the Properties window by clicking the Property Sheet button in the Tools group of the Design tab and select Chart Workspace from the Select list on the General tab, as shown in Figure 10-64. (Notice as you go through this exercise that the tabs available in the Properties window change as you select different objects on your PivotChart.)

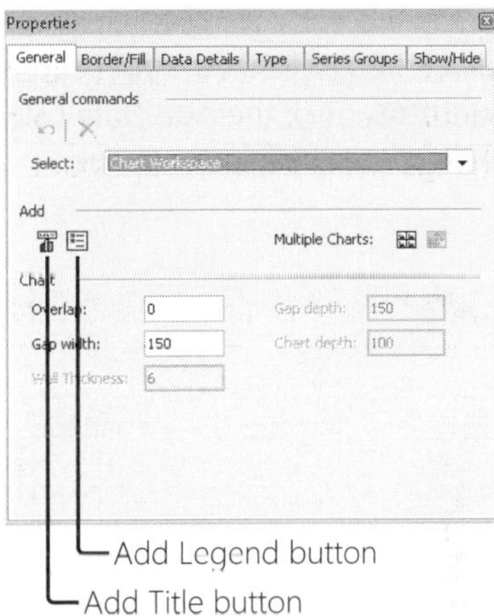

Figure 10-64 In the Properties window, you can add a title and legend to the PivotChart workspace.

Click the Title and Legend buttons on the left under Add to create these elements on your PivotChart. Click the Chart Workspace title you just added (or select Title from the Select list on the General tab), click the Format tab, and change the caption to something like Revenue by Month and Department. Notice that you can also change the font, font size, font color, and position of the title on this tab.

Go back to the General tab and select Chart Workspace again. Click the Series Groups tab to see the settings in Figure 10-65. On this tab, you can select one or more items in the Series Groups box and create a separate set of plot bars by placing them in their own group. For each group, you can also add an axis and specify its location. Access already created an axis on the left side of the chart for us, but if you want to add one yourself, click group 1 in the Groups box under Add Axis, select Left in the Axis Position list, and click Add to create the axis.

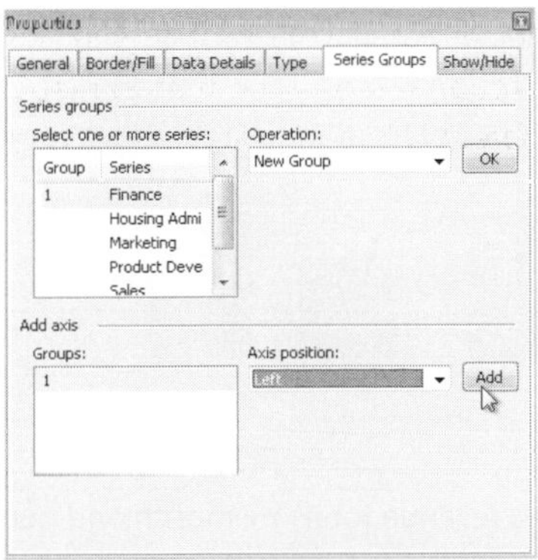

Figure 10-65 On the Series Groups tab, you can add an axis to your PivotChart.

Finally, go back to the General tab and select the five values in the Select list for the Department field one at a time, beginning with Finance. You'll see Add Data Label, Add Trendline, and Add Errorbar buttons, as shown in Figure 10-66. Click the Add Data Label button for each department name to add the total value at the top of each column.

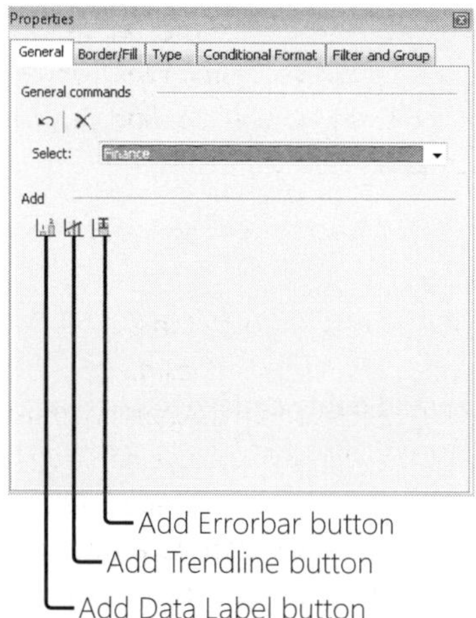

Figure 10-66 Use the Add Label button to display labels on data points on your PivotChart.

Your PivotChart should now look like Figure 10-67.

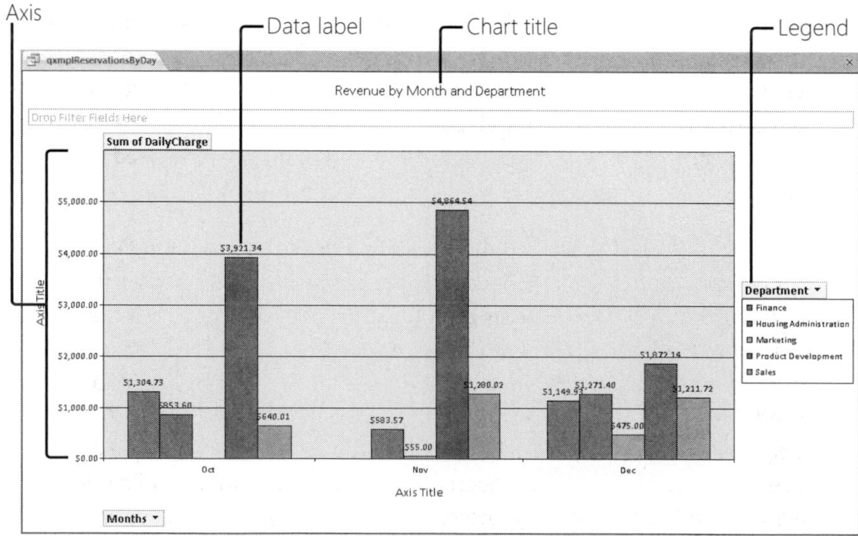

Figure 10-67 The completed PivotChart shows revenue totals by month and department.

INSIDE OUT **Manipulating the Caption of a Data Field in a PivotChart**

If you think about it, you went to some trouble to assign a different caption to Sum of DailyCharge when you built the sample PivotTable. There's actually no way to correct the caption of a data field in PivotChart view. We recommend that you save what you've done so far, and then switch to PivotTable view, hide the details, and change the caption for Sum of DailyCharge to Revenue, as you did earlier. When you switch back to PivotChart view, you'll find the new caption displayed. You can find this chart saved as qxmplReservationsByDayPC in the sample database.

If you want to see what your PivotChart might look like plotted in a different way, you can click the Change Chart Type button in the Type group of the Design contextual tab below PivotChart Tools to open the Properties window with the PivotChart workspace selected and the focus on the Type tab. The chart we've been building thus far is a simple column chart, but you can choose from Bar, Line, Smooth Line, Pie, Scatter, and several other chart type options. Be aware that changing the chart type often throws away some detail settings, so you might have to tweak properties again to get exactly what you want.

Creating Queries for the Web

When you're designing a web database that will be published to a Microsoft SharePoint server running Access Services, you must create all queries that you want to run on the server from scratch. Access 2010 is the first version of Access to include the new features of web support with Access Services running on top of SharePoint server, which means web queries are a completely new object type in Access databases. You cannot convert client queries used in existing databases into web queries and make them run on the server. You can, however, still run your saved client queries in a published application from Access client.

Throughout this chapter and the previous chapter, you've been learning how to create simple queries using one table and complex queries joining more than one table. The process of creating a web query is essentially the same as creating a client query, which means you don't have to learn a new design process when creating web queries. To create a web query, you must be working in a web database. If you started with a blank web database or used one of the installed web templates that ship with Access 2010, you can immediately begin to create web queries for your web tables. If you are using a client database, however, you cannot create web queries in that database until you first publish the database to a SharePoint server running Access Services. After you publish your client database to the server, your local client tables become web tables and your database is now a web database. You'll learn about the publishing process to SharePoint server in Chapter 22, "Using Web Applications in a Browser."

To illustrate the process of creating web queries, open the Back Office Software System data copy (BOSSDataCopy.accdb). Note that when you open the database, you see a copyright notice for a few seconds and then Access closes the notice. After the database opens, click the Navigation Pane menu, click Object Type under Navigate To Category, and then click Queries under Filter By Group to see the list of available queries, as shown in Figure 10-68. Note that Figure 10-68 shows only a few of the saved query objects in this database.

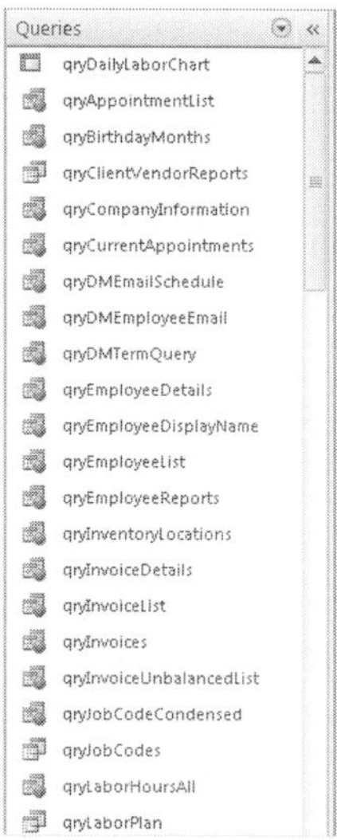

Figure 10-68 The Back Office Software Systems database includes client and web queries.

In Figure 10-68, you can see most of the query icons in the Navigation pane have a globe icon, but some do not. Any query in a web database that has a globe icon is a web query and all others are client queries. You can see in Figure 10-58 that the first query, qryDailyLaborChart, is a client query and the second query, qryAppointmentList, is a web query. A web database that includes both client and web objects is also referred to as a *hybrid* application.

In a web database, the commands in the various groups on the Create tab on the ribbon are organized so the web objects are listed on the left side of each group and the corresponding client objects are listed on the right side of the group. For example, to create a new web query in a web database, you can click the Query button in the Queries group on the Create tab, as shown in Figure 10-69. Notice that the Query button has a globe icon on it to indicate that this command creates a web object. If you click the Client Queries button in the Queries group, Access displays two options for client queries—Query Wizard and Query Design. The Client Queries button is your entry point for creating client queries in web databases.

> **Note**
>
> **You cannot use the Query Wizard when creating web queries; you must create all your web queries manually within the Query window.**

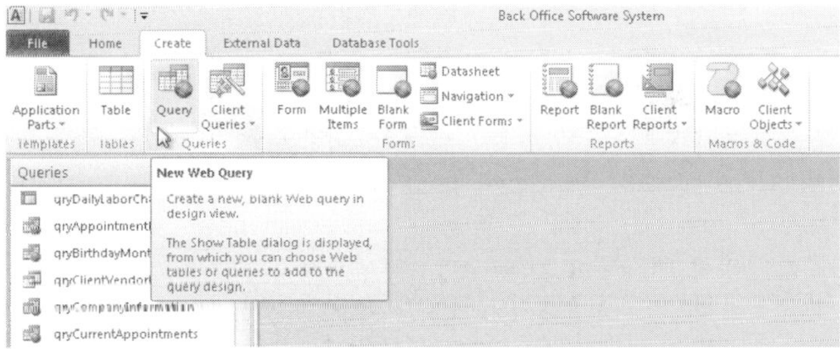

Figure 10-69 Click the Query button in the Queries group to create a new web query.

When you click the Query button in the Queries group in a web database, Access opens the familiar Query Design window that you have been working with throughout this chapter and the previous chapter. The process of creating a web query is essentially the same as a client query—you select the tables or queries you want to use in the Show Table dialog box, adjust any join lines between the tables or queries, select the fields you want to return, and optionally define parameters, calculated fields, sorting, and criteria. When you open the Show Table dialog box and click the Queries tab, Access shows you only a list of the web queries in the web database. You cannot use a client query as a source for a web query, nor can you use a linked table to other data sources besides the published web tables. In Figure 10-70, you can see the query design window for a new web query after we selected the tblAppointments web table in the Show Table dialog box.

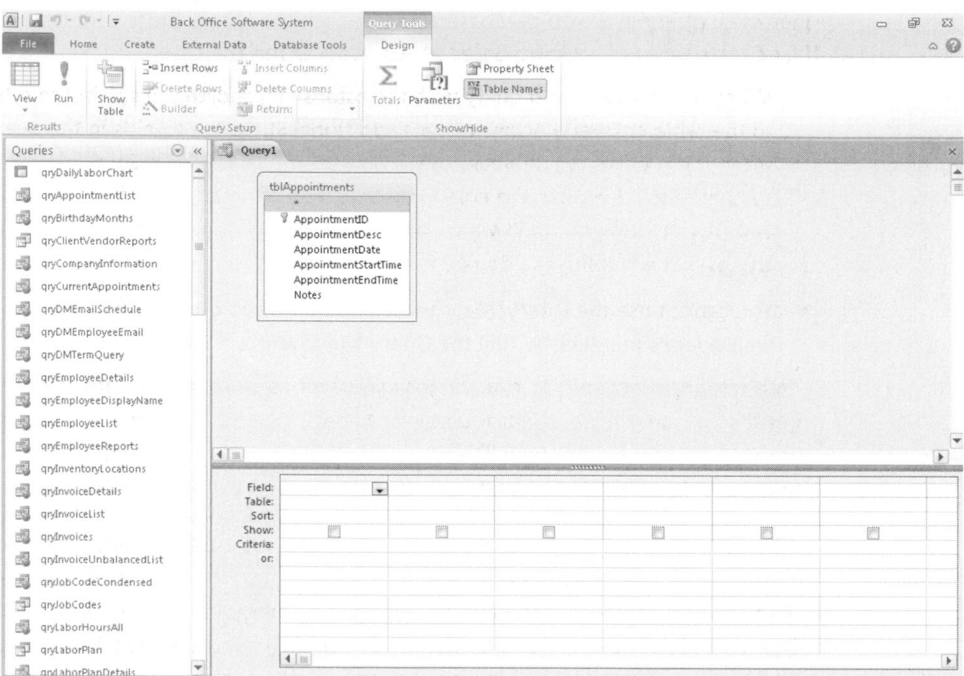

Figure 10-70 The query design window for web queries is the same as it is for client queries.

Web queries are much more limited in their capabilities compared to their client query counterparts. You can create inner and outer joins with web queries, but you cannot create Cartesian product web queries—queries with no join lines between the web tables. You also cannot create union, data definition, pass-through, or action web queries and you cannot use subdatasheets in web queries. You'll learn all about client action queries in Chapter 11, "Modifying Data with Action Queries." PivotTables and PivotCharts views are not supported in web queries. You also cannot use the DISTINCT keyword with web queries. Essentially, you can only create select queries for use on the web. When you're designing web queries, Access also disables the ability to open the web query in SQL view so you must do all your design work within the Query window.

INSIDE OUT Using Select * for Web Queries

When you create a web query with the asterisk (*) shorthand symbol to select all fields in the table or query, Access returns additional SharePoint fields in the query results after you publish the database to the SharePoint server. Each SharePoint list includes system fields showing who created or modified a record and when it was created and last modified. If you don't want these extra SharePoint fields showing up in your web queries after publishing, do not use the shorthand asterisk symbol for the field output.

Web queries do not support any aggregate functions, so you cannot create any totals queries that will run on the web. You can still create client queries with aggregate functions or use the summarization facilities in web reports to calculate totals. You can also use data macros to calculate aggregates at the table level if you need this functionality.

Web queries support less functions in expressions than client queries. You can find a list of the supported functions and their descriptions you can use in web queries in Article 4, "Function Reference," on the companion CD. When you're designing any expressions in the Query window, Access provides IntelliSense options for the supported web functions. If you try to use an unsupported function in a web query, Access prompts you that the expression is not supported on the web. You cannot save your changes to the web query design until you remove the unsupported function.

INSIDE OUT Sorting on a Calculated Field

When you create a calculated expression in a web query, Access disables the sort options for that field because you cannot sort on a calculated field on the web. You can, however, work around this limitation by creating a second query and using the base query with the calculated field as its source. When you place the calculated field from the base query onto the bottom half of the Query window, Access allows you to sort on the calculated field in this second query.

When you're designing parameters for web queries, you must use explicit parameters; web queries do not support implicit parameters. For example, you cannot have a web query prompt you for an implicit parameter when executing the web query on the web or use a form control reference, such as the following, in a Criteria line:

[Forms]![NameOfForm]![NameOfFormControl]

Parameter values must be *pushed* into the query when executing on the web; they cannot directly *pull* values during execution. You can push parameter values into a web query through data macros or user interface macros. You'll learn how to push parameter values from web forms into web queries through user interface macros in Chapter 21, "Automating a Web Application Using Macros." The one exception to this rule is with combo box row sources. You can use an implicit parameter in the Criteria of a field for a combo box row source. You can use this, for example, for a *cascading* combo box where the values of one combo box depend on the values displayed in another combo box on a form. You'll learn how to build combo boxes in Chapter 13, "Building a Form."

Access Services has several configurable server settings concerning web queries that you should be aware of when designing queries that will run on the web. Table 10-4 summarizes these server settings with a description of each setting as well as the default values. You should carefully design your web queries to stay under the default settings because you might not have appropriate permissions to change these settings on the server. If you need to increase the default values, you'll need to talk with your SharePoint server administrator.

Table 10-4 Server Settings for Web Queries

Setting	Description	Default Value	Range
Maximum Columns Per Query	The maximum number of columns that can be referenced in a query. Note that some columns may automatically be referenced by the query engine and will be included in this limit.	40	1 to 255
Maximum Rows Per Query	The maximum number of rows that a list used in a query can have, or that the output of the query can have.	25,000	1 to 200,000
Maximum Sources Per Query	The maximum number of lists that may be used as input to one query.	12	1 to 20
Maximum Calculated Columns Per Query	The maximum number of inline calculated columns that can be included in a query, either in the query itself or in any sub-query on which it is based. Calculated columns in the underlying Microsoft SharePoint Foundation list are not included.	10	0 to 32
Maximum Order By Clauses Per Query	The maximum number of Order By clauses in the query.	4	0 to 8

Setting	Description	Default Value	Range
Allow Outer Joins	Allows left and right outer joins in a query. Inner joins are always allowed.	True	True or False
Allow Non Remoteable Queries	Allow queries that cannot be remoted to the database tier to run.	True	True or False
Maximum Records Per Table	The maximum number of records that a table can contain in an application.	500,000	-1 (indicates no limit), any positive integer

Now that you understand the fundamentals of building complex select queries, working with PivotTables and PivotCharts, and designing web queries with Access, you're ready to move on to updating sets of data with client action queries in Chapter 11.

CHAPTER 11

Modifying Data with Action Queries

In Chapter 9, "Creating and Working with Simple Queries," you learned how to insert, update, and delete single rows of data within a datasheet. In Chapter 10, "Building Complex Queries," you discovered that you can use queries to select the data you want—even from multiple tables. You also learned under what conditions you cannot update a field in a query. Now, you can take the concept of queries one step further and use action queries to change, insert, create, or delete sets of data in your database quickly.

The four types of queries you'll study in this chapter are

- **Update query** Allows you to update the fields in one or more rows.
- **Make-table query** Allows you to create a new table by selecting rows from one or more existing tables.
- **Append query** Allows you to copy rows from one or more tables into another table.
- **Delete query** Allows you to remove one or more rows from a table.

Note

The examples in this chapter are based on the tables and data in HousingDataCopy.accdb and ContactsDataCopy.accdb on the companion CD included with this book. These databases are copies of the data from the Housing Reservations and Conrad Systems Contacts sample applications, respectively, and they contain the sample queries used in this chapter. The query results you see from the sample queries that you build in this chapter might not exactly match what you see in this book if you have changed the sample data in the files.

Updating Groups of Rows

It's easy enough to use a table or a query in Datasheet view to find a single record in your database and change one value. But what if you want to make the same change to many records? Changing each record one at a time could be very tedious.

Remember that in Chapter 9, you learned how to construct queries to test proposed new validation rules. In the HousingDataCopy.accdb database, there's a table-level validation rule defined in tblFacilityRooms that doesn't let you enter a WeeklyRate value that is greater than seven times the DailyRate value. If you want to change this rule to ensure that the WeeklyRate value is no more than six times the DailyRate value (thereby ensuring that the weekly rate is a true discount), you must first update the values in the table to comply with the new rule.

You could open tblFacilityRooms in Datasheet view and go through the individual rows one by one to set all the WeeklyRate values by hand. But why not let Microsoft Access 2010 do the work for you with a single query?

Testing with a Select Query

Before you create and run a query to update many records in your database, it's a good idea to first create a select query using criteria that select the records you want to update. You'll see in the next section that it's easy to convert this select query to an update query or other type of action query after you're sure that Access will process the right records.

You could certainly update all the rows in tblFacilityRooms, but what about rows where the WeeklyRate value is already less than or equal to six times the DailyRate value? You don't want to update rows that already meet the proposed validation rule change—you might actually increase the WeeklyRate value in those rows. For example, a room might exist that has a DailyRate value of $50 and a WeeklyRate value of $275. If you blanket update all rows to set the WeeklyRate field to six times the DailyRate field, you'll change the WeeklyRate value in this row to $300. So, you should first build a query on tblFacilityRooms to find only those rows that need to be changed.

Open HousingDataCopy.accdb and start a new query on tblFacilityRooms. Include the FacilityID, RoomNumber, DailyRate, and WeeklyRate fields. Enter the criterion **>[DailyRate]*6** under the WeeklyRate field. Your query should look like Figure 11-1.

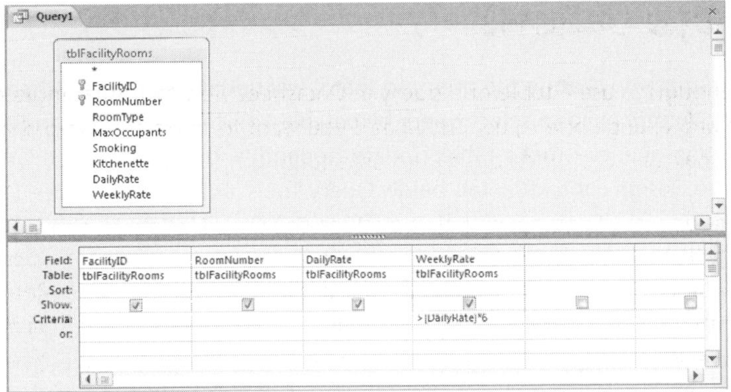

Figure 11-1 This select query finds weekly rates that will fail the new table validation rule.

When you run the query, you'll see 276 records that you want to change, as shown in Figure 11-2. (There are 306 records in the table.)

Facility	Room No.	Daily	Weekly
1	101	$10.00	$255.00
1	102	$90.00	$575.00
1	103	$45.00	$290.00
1	104	$45.00	$290.00
1	105	$55.00	$350.00
1	106	$90.00	$575.00
1	107	$55.00	$350.00
1	108	$45.00	$290.00
1	109	$50.00	$320.00
1	110	$40.00	$255.00
1	111	$80.00	$510.00
1	201	$40.00	$255.00
1	202	$90.00	$575.00
1	203	$45.00	$290.00
1	204	$45.00	$290.00
1	205	$55.00	$350.00
1	206	$90.00	$575.00
1	207	$55.00	$350.00
1	208	$45.00	$290.00
1	209	$50.00	$320.00
1	210	$40.00	$255.00
1	211	$80.00	$510.00

Record: 1 of 276 No Filter Search

Figure 11-2 This is the recordset of the select query shown in Figure 11-1.

Converting a Select Query to an Update Query

Now you're ready to change the query so that it will update the table. When you first create a query, Access builds a select query by default. You can find commands for the four types of action queries—make-table, update, append, and delete—in the Query Type group of the Design contextual tab below Query Tools, as shown in Figure 11-3. (Switch back to Design view if you haven't already done so.) Click Update to convert the select query to an update query.

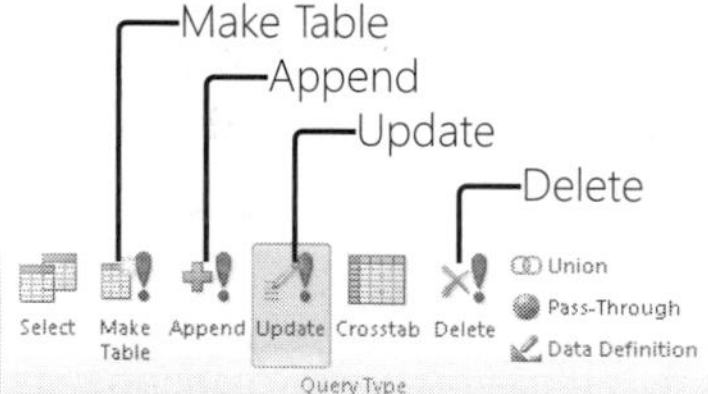

Figure 11-3 The Query Type group on the Design contextual tab below Query Tools contains commands for the four types of action queries.

When you convert a select query to an update query, Access highlights the Update button in the Query Type group when the query is in Design view and adds a row labeled Update To to the design grid, as shown in Figure 11-4. You use this row to specify how you want your data changed for those rows that meet the query's criteria. In this case, you want to change the WeeklyRate value to **[DailyRate]*6** for all rows where the rate is currently too high.

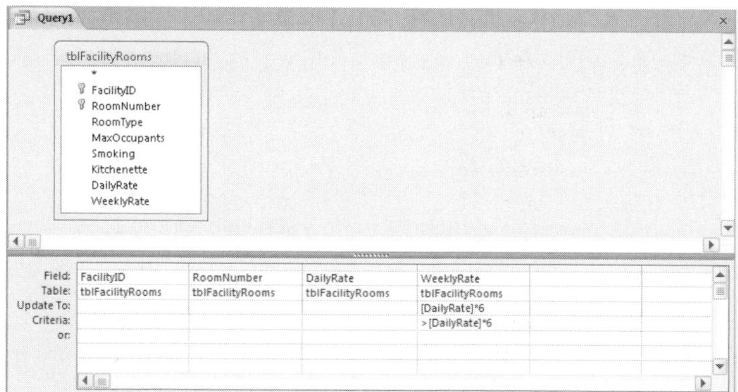

Figure 11-4 An update query shows an Update To row in the design grid.

INSIDE OUT **What Can I Put in Update To?**

You can enter any valid expression in the Update To row. You can include in the expression one or more of the fields from the source tables in the query. For example, if you want to raise the DailyRate value for a certain type of room by 10 percent, rounded to the nearest dollar (zero decimal places), you can include the DailyRate field in the design grid and enter:

Round(CCur([DailyRate] * 1.1), 0)

in the Update To row. Note that this formula uses the Round and CCur built-in functions discussed in Chapter 10 to round the result to the nearest dollar.

Running an Update Query

If you want to be completely safe, you should make a backup copy of your table before you run an update query. To do that, go to the Navigation pane, select the table that you're about to update, and click the Copy command in the Clipboard group on the Home tab on the ribbon. Then, click the Paste command in the same Clipboard group and give the copy of your table a different name when Access prompts you with a dialog box. (Be sure you select the default Structure And Data option.) Now you're ready to run the update query.

To run the query, click the Run command in the Results group on the Design tab below Query Tools. Access first scans your table to determine how many rows will change based on your selection criteria. It then displays a confirmation dialog box like the one shown in Figure 11-5.

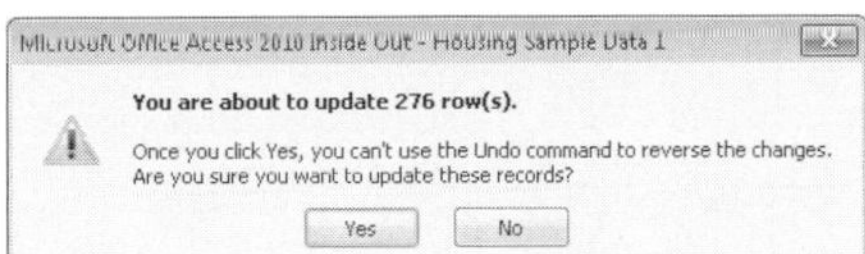

Figure 11-5 This dialog box reports the number of rows that will be changed by an update query.

You already know that you need to update 276 records, so you can perform the update by clicking Yes in the dialog box. (If the number of rows indicated in the dialog box is not what you expected, or if you're not sure that Access will update the right records or fields, click No to stop the query without updating.) After the update query runs, you can look at the table or create a new select query to confirm that Access made the changes that you wanted. Figure 11-6 shows the result—no weekly rate is greater than six times the daily rate.

Query1 | tblFacilityRooms

Facility	Room No.	Type	Max Occ.	Smoking	Kitchenette	Daily	Weekly
1	101	Studio - Queen Sofa	2	☐	☐	$40.00	$240.00
1	102	2BR Suite - 1 King, 2 Queen beds	6	☐	☐	$90.00	$540.00
1	103	Studio - Queen Sofa, Kitchenette	2	☐	☑	$45.00	$270.00
1	104	Studio - Queen Sofa, Kitchenette	2	☐	☑	$45.00	$270.00
1	105	Room - King bed	2	☐	☐	$55.00	$330.00
1	106	2BR Suite - 1 King, 2 Queen beds	6	☐	☐	$90.00	$540.00
1	107	Room - King bed	2	☐	☐	$55.00	$330.00
1	108	Studio - Queen Sofa, Kitchenette	2	☐	☑	$45.00	$270.00
1	109	Room - 2 Queen beds	4	☐	☐	$50.00	$300.00
1	110	Studio - Queen Sofa	2	☐	☐	$40.00	$240.00
1	111	1BR Suite - 1 King Bed, Kitchenette	2	☐	☑	$80.00	$480.00
1	201	Studio - Queen Sofa	2	☐	☐	$40.00	$240.00
1	202	2BR Suite - 1 King, 2 Queen beds	6	☐	☐	$90.00	$540.00
1	203	Studio - Queen Sofa, Kitchenette	2	☐	☑	$45.00	$270.00
1	204	Studio - Queen Sofa, Kitchenette	2	☐	☑	$45.00	$270.00
1	205	Room - King bed	2	☐	☐	$55.00	$330.00
1	206	2BR Suite - 1 King, 2 Queen beds	6	☐	☐	$90.00	$540.00
1	207	Room - King bed	2	☐	☐	$55.00	$330.00
1	208	Studio - Queen Sofa, Kitchenette	2	☐	☑	$45.00	$270.00
1	209	Room - 2 Queen beds	4	☐	☐	$50.00	$300.00
1	210	Studio - Queen Sofa	2	☐	☐	$40.00	$240.00
1	211	1BR Suite - 1 King Bed, Kitchenette	2	☐	☑	$80.00	$480.00
1	301	Studio - Queen Sofa	2	☑	☐	$40.00	$240.00
1	302	2BR Suite - 1 King, 2 Queen beds	6	☑	☐	$90.00	$540.00
1	303	Studio - Queen Sofa, Kitchenette	2	☑	☑	$45.00	$270.00

Record: 1 of 306 No Filter Search

Figure 11-6 You can now see the updated data in the tblFacilityRooms table.

If you think that you might want to perform this update again, you can save the query and give it a name. This sample query is saved in the sample database as qxmplUpdateWeekly. In the Navigation pane, Access distinguishes action queries from select queries by displaying a special icon, followed by an exclamation point, before action query names. For example, Access displays a pencil and an exclamation point next to the new update query that you just created. You'll see later that make-table queries have a small datasheet with a starburst in one corner, append queries have a green cross, and delete queries have a red X. Note that if you open an action query from the Navigation pane, you'll execute it. If you want to see the datasheet of the action query, open it in Design view first, and then switch to Datasheet view.

Note

It's a good idea to include identifying fields (such as FacilityID and RoomNumber, in the preceding example) when you build a test select query that you plan to convert to an action query. However, Access discards any fields for which you have not specified criteria or that you do not want to update when you save your final action query. This is why you won't see anything but the WeeklyRate field in qxmplUpdateWeekly.

To run an action query again, right-click the query name in the Navigation pane and click Open on the shortcut menu that appears. When you run an action query from the Navigation pane, Access displays a confirmation dialog box similar to the one shown in Figure 11-7. Click Yes to complete the action query. If you want to disable this extra confirmation step (but we don't recommend that you do so), click the File tab on the Backstage view, click Options, and in the Client Settings category of the Access Options dialog box, clear the Action Queries check box under Confirm in the Editing section.

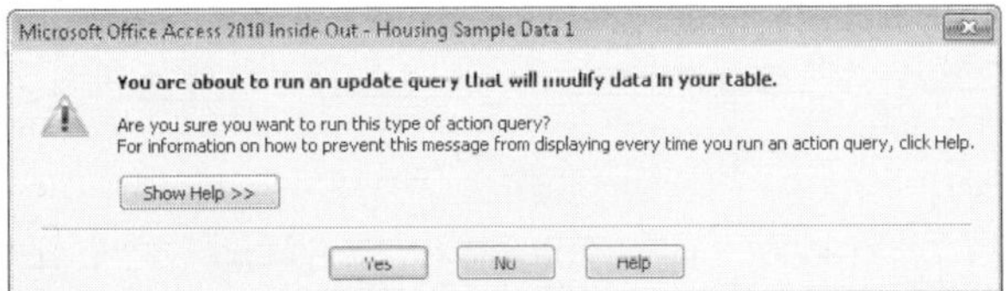

Figure 11-7 This dialog box asks you to confirm an action query.

Updating Multiple Fields

When you create an update query, you aren't limited to changing a single field at a time. You can ask Access to update any or all of the fields in the record by including them in the design grid and then specifying an update formula.

Before Access updates a record in the underlying table or query, it makes a copy of the original record. Access applies the formulas that you specify using the values in the original record and places the result in the updated copy. It then updates your database by writing the updated copy to your table. Because updates are made to the copy before updating the table, you can, for example, swap the values in a field named A and a field named B by specifying an Update To setting of [B] for the A field and an Update To setting of [A] for the B field. If Access were making changes directly to the original record, you'd need to use a third field to swap values because the first assignment of B to A would destroy the original value of A.

If you remember from Chapter 9, we also discussed the possibility of reducing the highest daily rate charged for a room to $90. If you do that, you must also update the WeeklyRate value to make sure that it doesn't exceed six times the new daily rate. First, build a query to find all rows that have a value in the DailyRate field that exceeds the new maximum. As before, start a query on tblFacilityRooms and include the FacilityID, RoomNumber, DailyRate, and WeeklyRate fields. Place the criterion **>90** under the DailyRate field. Your query should look like Figure 11-8. If you run this query, you'll find 26 rows that meet this criterion in the sample database.

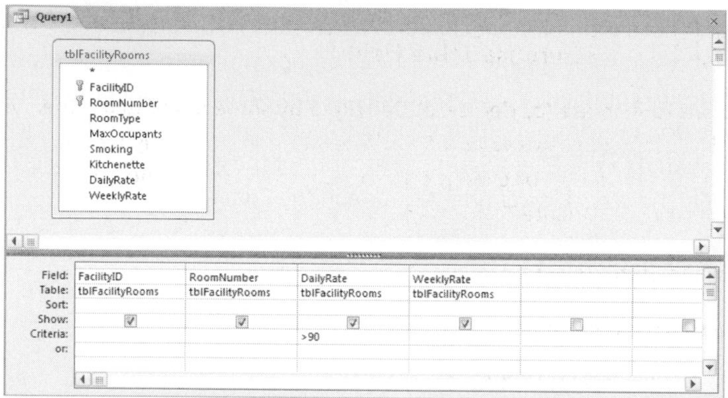

Figure 11-8 This query finds daily rates greater than $90.

Now comes the tricky part. Change your query to an update query and enter **90** on the Update To row under DailyRate. You might be tempted to set Update To under WeeklyRate to **[DailyRate]*6** again, but you would be wrong. The reference to [DailyRate] gets you the *original* value of that field in each row—*before* it gets updated to the value 90. You know you're going to set DailyRate in rows that qualify to 90, so enter the constant **540** or the expression **(90 * 6)** in the Update To line under WeeklyRate. Your update query should now look like Figure 11-9.

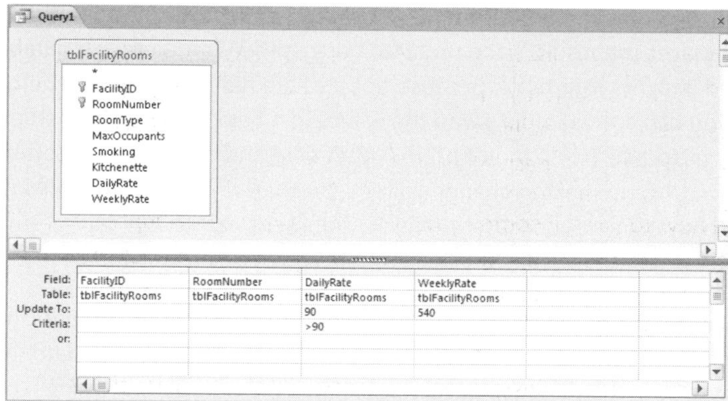

Figure 11-9 This query finds daily rates greater than $90.

INSIDE OUT Performing Multiple Updates with Expressions That Reference Table Fields

If you want to increase (or decrease) DailyRate by some percentage, then you should repeat the calculation for the new DailyRate value and multiply by 6 to calculate the new WeeklyRate value. For example, if you want to increase the rate by 10 percent, your expression in Update To for DailyRate is

CCur(Round([DailyRate] * 1.1, 0))

Then your expression under WeeklyRate should be

CCur(Round([DailyRate] * 1.1), 0)) * 6

Remember, DailyRate in any expression references the *old* value in the row before it is updated.

You can find this query saved as qxmplUpdateDailyWeekly in the sample database.

Creating an Update Query Using Multiple Tables or Queries

The target of an update query should generally be one table, but you might need to update a table based on criteria you apply to a related query or table. Consider the tblContacts table in the Conrad Systems Contacts sample application. The table contains an Inactive field that you can set to Yes to remove that contact from most displays without removing the row from the database. Although you can edit each contact individually and choose to mark them inactive, you occasionally might want to run an update query that automatically sets this flag when the contact hasn't had any activity for a long time.

You studied how to solve a complex unmatched problem in Chapter 10. You need to apply a similar concept to this problem—find the contacts who have activity since a certain date of interest and then use an outer join to identify those who have no activity so that you can mark them inactive.

The sample database contains contact events from July 29, 2010, through January 24, 2011. If you were using this data actively, you would be entering new contact events every day, but this sample data is static. Let's assume that today is July 1, 2011, and you want to flag any contact who hasn't had any event in the last six months.

First, you need to find out who hasn't contacted you since January 1, 2011. Start by opening the ContactsDataCopy.accdb sample database. Start a query with tblContactEvents and include the ContactID and ContactDateTime fields in the query grid. Under ContactDateTime, enter a criterion of **>=#1/1/2011#**. Your query should look like Figure 11-10.

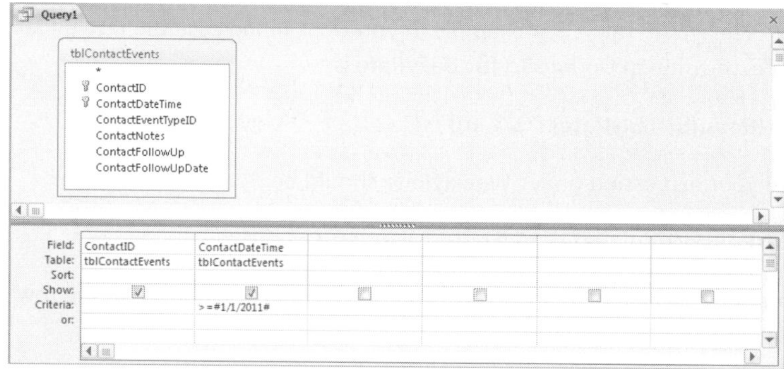

Figure 11-10 This query finds contact events since January 1, 2011.

If you run this query, you'll find 22 rows for 15 different contacts. Save this query as qryContactsSinceJanuary2011. (You can also find the query saved as qxmplContact-EventsSince01January2011 in the sample database.)

Next, you want to find who has not contacted you in this time frame. Start a new query with tblContacts and add the query that you just built. You should see a join line linking the ContactID field in tblContacts and the ContactID field in your query. Remember from Chapter 10 that you need an outer join from the table to the query to fetch all rows from tblContacts and any matching rows from the query. Double-click the join line to open the Join Properties dialog box and choose the option to include all rows from tblContacts and any matching rows from qryContactsSinceJanuary2011. You should now have an arrow pointing from the table to the query.

Include in the query grid the ContactID, FirstName, LastName, and Inactive fields from tblContacts and the ContactID field from the query. You want contacts who aren't in the list of "recent" contact events, so add the Is Null test on the Criteria line under ContactID from the query. Your query should now look like Figure 11-11.

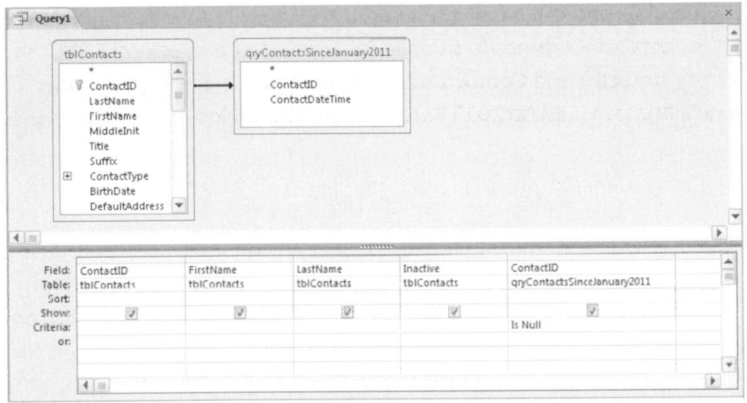

Figure 11-11 This query finds contacts with no contact events since January 1, 2011.

If you run this query, you'll find out that there are no contact events after the specified date for 17 of the 32 contacts. Remember, this is only an example.

Now you have the contacts that you want to set as inactive. In Design view, turn the query into an update query. Under the Inactive field, set Update To to True. You can now run this query to verify that it does mark the 17 contacts as inactive. You can find this query saved as qxmplUpdateInactive in the sample database.

INSIDE OUT Making Update Queries Generic With Parameters

In Chapter 9, you learned how to create a date/time comparison expression using the DateDiff function. In Chapter 10, you learned how to define parameters in your queries. In the example to update inactive status, you entered a specific comparison date in the select query you built. If you really want to save and run a query like this periodically, the select query shouldn't use a static value that you would have to change each time you wanted to perform this update. Using DateDiff, you can define a comparison with an offset relative to the current date. With a parameter, you can create a dynamic prompt for the date you want at the time that you run the query.

You might also want to write a converse query that clears the Inactive field for contacts who *do* have recent contact events.

Creating a New Table with a Make-Table Query

Sometimes you might want to save as a new table the data that you extract with a select query. If you find that you keep executing the same query over and over against data that isn't changing, it can be faster to access the data from a table rather than from the query, particularly if the query must join several tables.

In Chapter 10, you created a very complex query using a Cartesian product to drive your PivotTable and PivotChart. At the end of each month or quarter, you might want to use a query like this to create a series of reports. When you have tens of thousands of reservations in your database, this complex query might take a long time to run for each report. You will save a lot of time if you first save the result of the complex query as a temporary table and then run your reports from that table. Also, after reservations are completed for a prior period of time, they're not likely to change, so permanently saving the data selected by a query as a table could be useful for gathering summary information that you intend to keep long after you delete the detailed data on which the query is based.

Creating a Make-Table Query

In the Housing Reservations application, assume that at the end of each quarter you want to create and save a table that captures reservations detail for the quarter by facility, department, and employee. Open the HousingDataCopy.accdb sample database to follow along with the examples in this section. You might recall from the exercises in building the complex query to provide data for a PivotTable that you need to include tblDepartments, tblFacilities, tblEmployees, and tblReservations. You might also want to include a second copy of tblEmployees to capture the department manager and a copy of tblFacilityRooms to capture the room types. You're essentially unnormalizing the data to create a single archive table that you can also use in reports.

As with most action queries, it's a good idea to start with a select query to verify that you're working with the correct data. Start a new query with tblFacilities, and add tblFacilityRooms, tblReservations, tblEmployees, and tblDepartments. Click the relationship line that the query draws between FacilityID in tblFacilities and FacilityID in tblReservations and press the Delete key to remove this extra join line. Be sure to also remove the extra relationship between the EmployeeNumber field in tblEmployees and the ManagerNumber field in tblDepartments. Add tblEmployees one more time—we plan to use the first instance of tblEmployees to get employees who have reservations, and the second instance to get the managers for the departments. Access names this second table tblEmployees_1 to avoid a duplicate name. Create a join line from EmployeeNumber in tblEmployees_1 to ManagerNumber in tblDepartments.

To avoid confusion with the two copies of tblEmployees, select tblEmployees_1 and click the Property Sheet button on the Design tab below Query Tools to open the property sheet shown in Figure 11-12. You can actually assign an alias name to any field list (table or query) in your query. In this case, change the name of the second copy of tblEmployees to Managers.

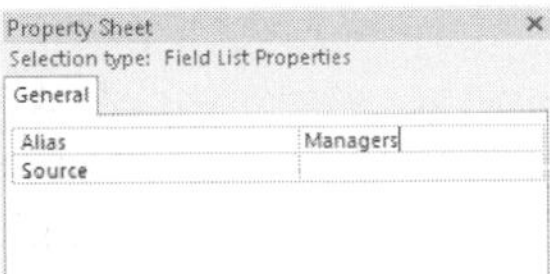

Figure 11-12 You can use the property sheet to assign an alias name to a field list in a query.

Now, you're ready to begin defining fields. Create an expression to display the employee name in the first field:

EmpName: tblEmployees.LastName & "," & tblEmployees.FirstName & (" " + tblEmployees.MiddleName)

In the query grid, include the Department field from tblDepartments, and then add the manager name in the next column with an expression:

MgrName: Managers.LastName & "," & Managers.FirstName & (" " + Managers.MiddleName)

Notice that you're using the new alias name of the second copy of tblEmployees. On the next Field line, add the ReservationID field from tblReservations, the FacilityName field from tblFacilities, the RoomNumber field from tblReservations, and the RoomType field from tblFacilityRooms. Add an expression in the next field to calculate the actual charge per day. Remember, you could use the DailyRate field from tblReservations, but that's not an accurate reflection of how much the room costs per day when the employee stays a week or more. Your expression should look like this:

```
DailyCharge: CCur(Round(tblReservations.TotalCharge / (tblReservations.CheckOutDate -
tblReservations.CheckInDate), 2))
```

Your query design should now look something like Figure 11-13.

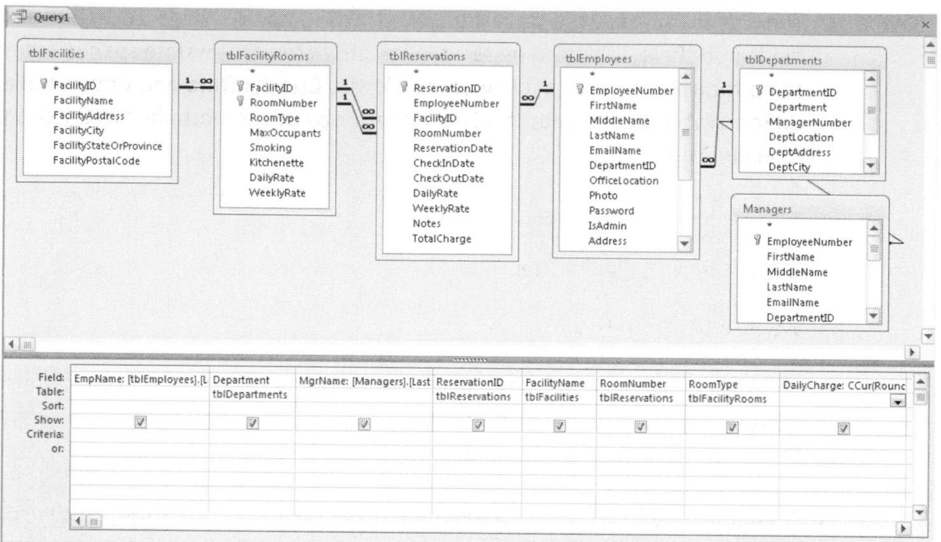

Figure 11-13 You can design a complex query to gather together many details about reservations.

Each row in tblReservations represents a stay of one or more days, but any report that you create later might need to work with detail by individual day. To do that, you need to "explode" each single row in tblReservations into a row per day for the duration of the reservation. Recall from Chapter 10 that you'll find a "driver" table—ztblDates—full of dates to accomplish this task. The table contains date values, one per day, for dates from January 1, 1992, to December 31, 2035.

Include this table in your query and notice that there's no join line from it to any of the tables. When you add a table with no join defined to another table or set of records, the query returns the Cartesian product of the two sets of records—every row in the first table or set of records is matched with every row in the second table or set of records. In this case, each reservation will now be matched with each of the separate date values in ztblDates.

When you run this query later to create your working statistics table, you're not going to want to have to open up the query each time in Design view to filter the dates. A couple of parameters would be a good idea here. Add the DateValue field from ztblDates and enter **Between [Start Date] And [End Date]** under this field on the Criteria line. Click the Parameters button in the Show/Hide group of the Design contextual tab, enter both parameters ([Start Date] and [End Date]), and set the data type to Date/Time. You have now provided a way to limit the "explosion" of rows to the dates of interest.

The final step is to further limit the rows created based on the CheckInDate and CheckOutDate fields in tblReservations. Any reservation that crosses the time span of interest is going to be for a few days or a few weeks. Add the CheckInDate and CheckOutDate fields from tblReservations, and clear the Show check box under both. In the Criteria row under CheckInDate, enter

<=ztblDates.DateValue

Under CheckOutDate, enter

>ztblDates.DateValue

This forces the query to keep any rows where the DateValue from ztblDates is within the time span of each reservation row. You now have one row per date for each reservation. Your query should now look like Figure 11-14.

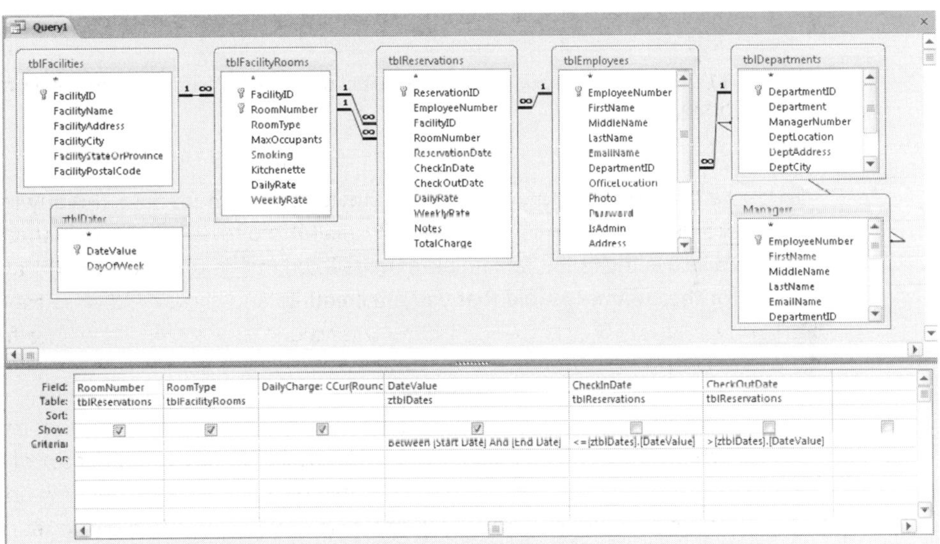

Figure 11-14 Build a complex parameter query to expand reservation details over a specified time span.

Switch to Datasheet view to verify that you'll get the rows you want. The sample data contains reservations from August 24, 2010, through March 11, 2011. To get data for the fourth quarter of 2010, you can reply to the two parameter prompts with October 1, 2010, and December 31, 2010. Your result should look like Figure 11-15.

Query1

EmpName	Department	MgrName	Reservation	Name	Room	Type	DailyCharge	DateValue
Adams, Jay	Housing Admir	Richins, Jack S.	15	Main Campus H	206	1BR Suite - 1 King Bed, Kitch	$75.45	01-Oct-10
Adams, Jay	Housing Admir	Richins, Jack S.	15	Main Campus H	206	1BR Suite - 1 King Bed, Kitch	$75.45	02-Oct-10
Adams, Jay	Housing Admir	Richins, Jack S.	15	Main Campus H	206	1BR Suite - 1 King Bed, Kitch	$75.45	03-Oct-10
Adams, Jay	Housing Admir	Richins, Jack S.	15	Main Campus H	206	1BR Suite - 1 King Bed, Kitch	$75.45	04-Oct-10
Adams, Jay	Housing Admir	Richins, Jack S.	15	Main Campus H	206	1BR Suite - 1 King Bed, Kitch	$75.45	05-Oct-10
Adams, Jay	Housing Admir	Richins, Jack S.	15	Main Campus H	206	1BR Suite - 1 King Bed, Kitch	$75.45	06-Oct-10
Adams, Jay	Housing Admir	Richins, Jack S.	15	Main Campus H	206	1BR Suite - 1 King Bed, Kitch	$75.45	07-Oct-10
Adams, Jay	Housing Admir	Richins, Jack S.	15	Main Campus H	206	1BR Suite - 1 King Bed, Kitch	$75.45	08-Oct-10
Richins, Jack S.	Housing Admir	Richins, Jack S.	14	Main Campus H	708	Studio - Queen Sofa, Kitche	$50.00	21-Oct-10
Richins, Jack S.	Housing Admir	Richins, Jack S.	14	Main Campus H	708	Studio - Queen Sofa, Kitche	$50.00	22-Oct-10
Richins, Jack S.	Housing Admir	Richins, Jack S.	14	Main Campus H	708	Studio - Queen Sofa, Kitche	$50.00	23-Oct-10
Richins, Jack S.	Housing Admir	Richins, Jack S.	14	Main Campus H	708	Studio - Queen Sofa, Kitche	$50.00	24-Oct-10
Richins, Jack S.	Housing Admir	Richins, Jack S.	14	Main Campus H	708	Studio - Queen Sofa, Kitche	$50.00	25-Oct-10
Richins, Jack S.	Housing Admir	Richins, Jack S.	16	South Campus	111	Studio - Queen Sofa	$36.43	13-Nov-10
Richins, Jack S.	Housing Admir	Richins, Jack S.	16	South Campus	111	Studio - Queen Sofa	$36.43	14-Nov-10
Richins, Jack S.	Housing Admir	Richins, Jack S.	16	South Campus	111	Studio - Queen Sofa	$36.43	15-Nov-10
Richins, Jack S.	Housing Admir	Richins, Jack S.	16	South Campus	111	Studio - Queen Sofa	$36.43	16-Nov-10
Richins, Jack S.	Housing Admir	Richins, Jack S.	16	South Campus	111	Studio - Queen Sofa	$36.43	17-Nov-10
Richins, Jack S.	Housing Admir	Richins, Jack S.	16	South Campus	111	Studio - Queen Sofa	$36.43	18-Nov-10
Richins, Jack S.	Housing Admir	Richins, Jack S.	16	South Campus	111	Studio - Queen Sofa	$36.43	19-Nov-10
Randall, Linda	Housing Admir	Richins, Jack S.	30	Main Campus H	103	2BR Suite - 1 King, 2 Queen I	$82.14	27-Nov-10
Randall, Linda	Housing Admir	Richins, Jack S.	30	Main Campus H	103	2BR Suite - 1 King, 2 Queen I	$82.14	28-Nov-10
Randall, Linda	Housing Admir	Richins, Jack S.	30	Main Campus H	103	2BR Suite - 1 King, 2 Queen I	$82.14	29-Nov-10
Randall, Linda	Housing Admir	Richins, Jack S.	30	Main Campus H	103	2BR Suite - 1 King, 2 Queen I	$82.14	30-Nov-10
Randall, Linda	Housing Admir	Richins, Jack S.	30	Main Campus H	103	2BR Suite - 1 King, 2 Queen I	$82.14	01-Dec-10

Record: 1 of 281 No Filter Search

Figure 11-15 This is the recordset of the select query shown in Figure 11-14, for the fourth quarter of 2010.

To convert this select query to a make-table query, switch back to Design view and click the Make Table command in the Query Type group of the Design tab below Query Tools. Access displays the Make Table dialog box, shown in Figure 11-16. Type in an appropriate name for the summary table that you are creating, and click OK to close the dialog box.

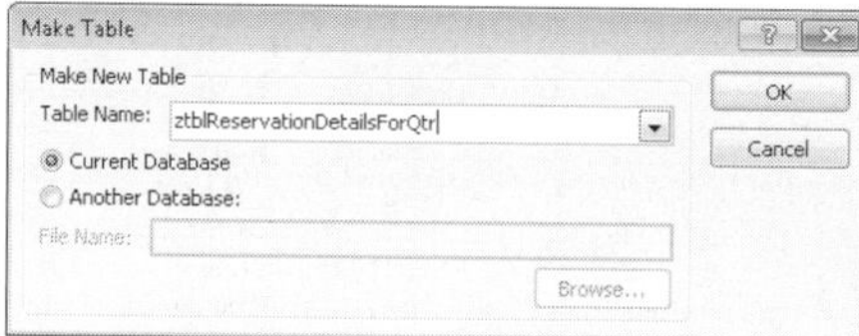

Figure 11-16 In the Make Table dialog box, type a name for your summary table.

At any time, you can change the name of the table that your query creates. Click the Property Sheet button in the Show/Hide group of the Design tab below Query Tools whenever the query is in Design view and change the Destination Table property. In this case, we entered a working table name. (We tend to prefix our working tables with the letter *z* to put them at the bottom of the table list.) After you run this query for a particular quarter, you're probably going to rename the table to indicate the actual quarter's worth of data that the table contains. You can find this make-table query saved in the sample database as qxmplReservationDetailsMakeTable.

Running a Make-Table Query

After you set up a make-table query, you can run it by clicking the Run command in the Results group on the Design tab below Query Tools. After you respond to the date parameter prompts, Access selects the records that it will place in the new table and displays a confirmation dialog box, as shown in Figure 11-17, that informs you how many rows you'll be inserting into the new table.

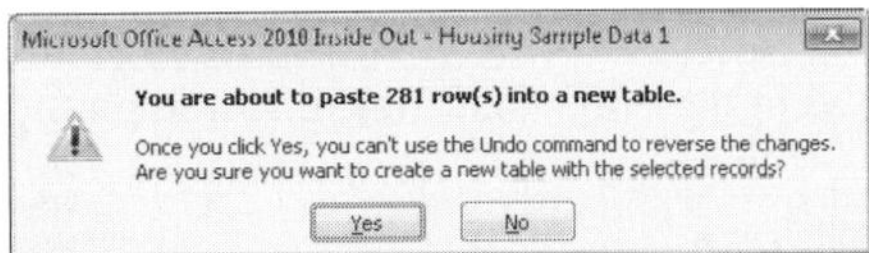

Figure 11-17 This dialog box asks you to confirm the preliminary results of a make-table query.

Click Yes to create your new table and insert the rows. Click the menu at the top of the Navigation pane, click Object Type under Navigate To Category, and click Tables under Filter By Group to bring up the table list, which should now include the name of your new table. Open the table in Datasheet view to verify the information, as shown in Figure 11-18.

ztblReservationDetailsForQtr

EmpName	Department	MgrName	Reservation	FacilityName	RoomNumb	RoomType	DailyCharge	DateValue
Adams, Jay	Housing Administr	Richins, Jack S.	15	Main Campus Housi	206	1BR Suite - 1 King E	$75.45	10/1/2010
Adams, Jay	Housing Administr	Richins, Jack S.	15	Main Campus Housi	206	1BR Suite - 1 King E	$75.45	10/2/2010
Adams, Jay	Housing Administr	Richins, Jack S.	15	Main Campus Housi	206	1BR Suite - 1 King E	$75.45	10/3/2010
Adams, Jay	Housing Administr	Richins, Jack S.	15	Main Campus Housi	206	1BR Suite - 1 King E	$75.45	10/4/2010
Adams, Jay	Housing Administr	Richins, Jack S.	15	Main Campus Housi	206	1BR Suite - 1 King E	$75.45	10/5/2010
Adams, Jay	Housing Administr	Richins, Jack S.	15	Main Campus Housi	206	1BR Suite - 1 King E	$75.45	10/6/2010
Adams, Jay	Housing Administr	Richins, Jack S.	15	Main Campus Housi	206	1BR Suite - 1 King E	$75.45	10/7/2010
Adams, Jay	Housing Administr	Richins, Jack S.	15	Main Campus Housi	206	1BR Suite - 1 King E	$75.45	10/8/2010
Richins, Jack S.	Housing Administr	Richins, Jack S.	14	Main Campus Housi	708	Studio - Queen Sol	$50.00	10/21/2010
Richins, Jack S.	Housing Administr	Richins, Jack S.	14	Main Campus Housi	708	Studio - Queen Sol	$50.00	10/22/2010
Richins, Jack S.	Housing Administr	Richins, Jack S.	14	Main Campus Housi	708	Studio - Queen Sol	$50.00	10/23/2010
Richins, Jack S.	Housing Administr	Richins, Jack S.	14	Main Campus Housi	708	Studio - Queen Sol	$50.00	10/24/2010
Richins, Jack S.	Housing Administr	Richins, Jack S.	14	Main Campus Housi	708	Studio - Queen Sol	$50.00	10/25/2010
Richins, Jack S.	Housing Administr	Richins, Jack S.	16	South Campus Hous	111	Studio - Queen Sol	$36.43	11/13/2010
Richins, Jack S.	Housing Administr	Richins, Jack S.	16	South Campus Hous	111	Studio - Queen Sol	$36.43	11/14/2010
Richins, Jack S.	Housing Administr	Richins, Jack S.	16	South Campus Hous	111	Studio - Queen Sol	$36.43	11/15/2010
Richins, Jack S.	Housing Administr	Richins, Jack S.	16	South Campus Hous	111	Studio - Queen Sol	$36.43	11/16/2010
Richins, Jack S.	Housing Administr	Richins, Jack S.	16	South Campus Hous	111	Studio - Queen Sol	$36.43	11/17/2010
Richins, Jack S.	Housing Administr	Richins, Jack S.	16	South Campus Hous	111	Studio - Queen Sol	$36.43	11/18/2010
Richins, Jack S.	Housing Administr	Richins, Jack S.	16	South Campus Hous	111	Studio - Queen Sol	$36.43	11/19/2010
Randall, Linda	Housing Administr	Richins, Jack S.	30	Main Campus Housi	103	2BR Suite - 1 King,	$82.14	11/27/2010
Randall, Linda	Housing Administr	Richins, Jack S.	30	Main Campus Housi	103	2BR Suite - 1 King,	$82.14	11/28/2010
Randall, Linda	Housing Administr	Richins, Jack S.	30	Main Campus Housi	103	2BR Suite - 1 King,	$82.14	11/29/2010
Randall, Linda	Housing Administr	Richins, Jack S.	30	Main Campus Housi	103	2BR Suite - 1 King,	$82.14	11/30/2010
Randall, Linda	Housing Administr	Richins, Jack S.	30	Main Campus Housi	103	2BR Suite - 1 King,	$82.14	12/1/2010

Record: 1 of 281 No Filter Search

Figure 11-18 The new table is the result of running the qxmplReservationDetailsMakeTable query.

INSIDE OUT Make-Table Query Limitations

One of the shortcomings of a make-table query is it propagates only the field name and data type to the resulting table. Running the query does not set other property settings such as Caption or Decimal Places in the target table. This is why you see only field names instead of the original captions in Datasheet view. Notice also that the sequence of rows in the new table (Figure 11-18) might not match the sequence of rows that you saw when you looked at the Datasheet view of your make-table query (Figure 11-15). Because the data in a table created with a make-table query has no primary key, Access returns the rows in the order that they're stored physically in the database.

You might want to switch to Design view, as shown in Figure 11-19, to correct field names or to define formatting information. As you can see, Access copies only basic field attributes when creating a new table.

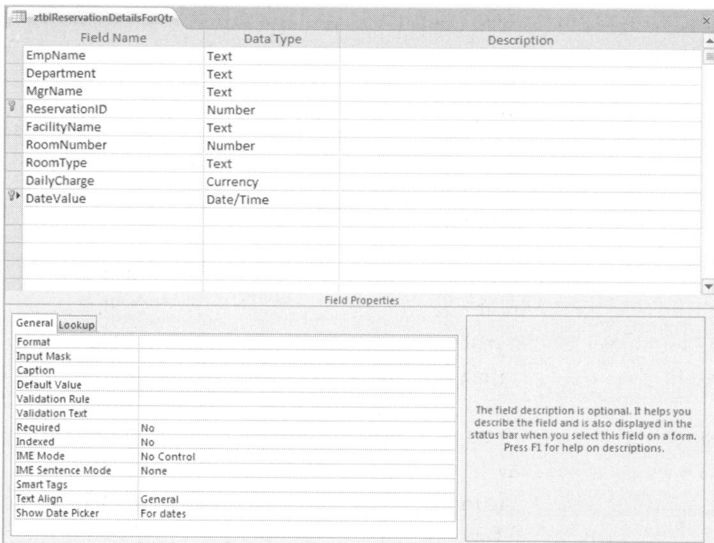

Figure 11-19 In Design view, you can modify the design of the table created by the qxmplReservationDetailsMakeTable make-table query.

At a minimum, you should define a primary key that contains the DateValue and ReservationID fields. You might also want to define default formats for the date/time fields. If you're planning to create reports on this data that sort or group by department or facility, you should add indexes to those fields.

Inserting Data from Another Table

Using an append query, you can copy a selected set of information from one or more tables and insert it into another table. You can also use an append query to bring data from another source into your database—for example, a list of names and addresses purchased from a mailing list company—and then edit the data and insert it into an existing table. (You learned how to import data from external sources in Chapter 8, "Importing and Linking Data.")

An append query, like a make-table query, provides a way to collect calculated totals or unnormalized rows from several tables. The difference is that a make-table query always creates a new table from the data you select, but an append query copies the data into an existing table that might or might not contain data. You must always modify the design of the table that a make-table query creates (if only to add efficient search indexes) to make it work optimally. Because the target table must already exist for an append query, you can explicitly define needed field properties and indexes (including a primary key) in advance. However, it's easier to run into errors because you're trying to insert data that's already there (based on the primary key you defined), because the data you're adding doesn't match the data type you defined in the table, or because the new data fails one or more validation rules.

See the section "Troubleshooting Action Queries," on page 730, for a specific discussion of potential errors.

Creating an Append Query

In the previous example, you saw how to take one of the complex queries that you learned about in Chapter 10 and turn it into a make-table query. In truth, if you plan to collect such data over several months or years, you should probably design a table to hold the results and use append queries to insert new historical data periodically.

Another good use of append queries is to copy old transaction data to an archive table—either in the current database or another database. For example, after several months or years, the contact events table in the Conrad Systems Contacts application might contain thousands of rows. You might want to keep all events, but copying them to an archive table and deleting them from the main table can improve application performance. (You'll learn about delete queries later in this chapter.)

Let's build an append query to select old contact events and copy them to an archive table. Open the ContactsDataCopy.accdb database to follow along in this exercise. You'll find an empty tblContactEventsHistory table defined in this database.

Start a new query with tblContactEvents. Because the ContactEventTypeID field is a "lookup" to tlkpContactEventTypes, it would be a good idea to preserve the original description of the event rather than the code number. If you kept the original ContactEventTypeID numbers, any changes you make in the future to the related ContactEventTypeDescription information will also change the meaning in the archived records. So, add the tlkpContactEventTypes table so that you can store the current description rather than the ID in the history table. You should see a join line linking the ContactEventTypeID fields in the two tables.

Add the ContactID and ContactDateTime fields from tblContactEvents to the query grid. Include in the grid the ContactEventTypeDescription field from tlkpContactEventTypes. Finally, add to the query design grid the ContactNotes field from tblContactEvents. Because you are saving events in a history table, you don't need the ContactFollowUp and ContactFollowUpDate fields from tblContactEvents.

You want to be able to filter the records on the date and time of the event. Each time you run this query, you probably don't want to archive any recent events, so you need to create a prompt to select events that are a specified number of months old. A couple of handy date/time functions are available for you to do this: DateSerial and DateAdd. DateSerial returns a date value from a year, month, and day input. You can use it to calculate the first date of the current month like this:

DateSerial(Year(Date()), Month(Date()), 1)

Remember from Table 9-5 on page 581 that the Date function returns today's date, the Year function returns the four-digit year value from a date value, and the Month function returns the month number from a date value. Supplying the value **1** for the day number gets you the date of the first day of the current month.

INSIDE OUT Using Other Date Expressions

You can usually think of more than one way to calculate a date value that you want. To calculate the date of the first day of the current month, you could also write the expression

(Date() – Day(Date()) + 1)

This subtracts the day number of the current date from the current date—resulting in the last day of the previous month—and adds one. For example, August 17, 2010, minus 17 yields July 31, 2010, plus one yields August 1, 2010.

DateAdd adds or subtracts seconds, minutes, hours, days, months, or years from a date value. You specify the interval you want by choosing a value from Table 9-3 on page 567—in this case, you want m to indicate that you want to add or subtract months. Finally, you can include a parameter so that you can specify the number of months you want to subtract. So, under the ContactDateTime field, include the criterion

<DateAdd("m", –[MonthsAgo], DateSerial(Year(Date()),Month(Date()),1))

Click the Parameters button in the Show/Hide group of the Design tab below Query Tools and define the MonthsAgo parameter as Integer. The DateAdd function will return the date that is the number of specified months in the past from the first date of the current month. For example, if today is February 17, 2011, when you respond **6** to MonthsAgo, the expression returns August 1, 2010 (six months prior to February 1). Making sure that the value in ContactDateTime is less than this value ensures that you archive only contacts that are at least six months old. Your query up to this point should look like Figure 11-20.

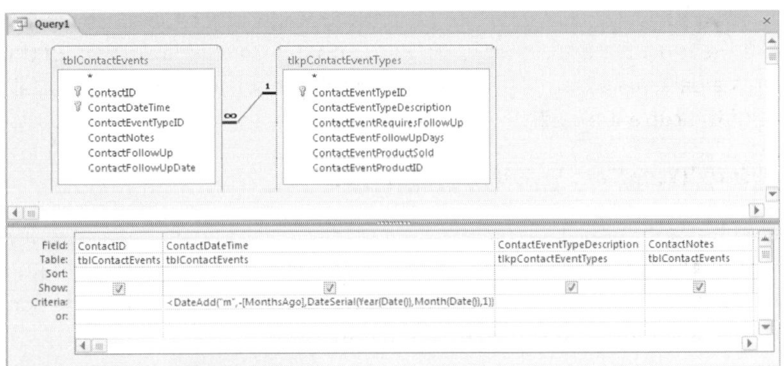

Figure 11-20 This query finds old contact events to archive.

The sample database contains contact events from July 29, 2010, through January 24, 2011. If you want to experiment with this query, you need to take into account the current date on your computer. For example, if you're running this query in July of 2011, you must specify a MonthsAgo value of no more than 12 to see any records. Likewise, specifying a MonthsAgo value of less than 6 shows you all the records. (Note that if the current date on your computer is in July 2010, enter **–1** to see records, and if your current date is in August 2010, enter **0** to see records.)

Now, it's time to turn this into an append query. Click the Append button in the Query Type group of the Design tab below Query Tools. You'll see the dialog box shown in Figure 11-21, asking you where you want the selected rows inserted (appended).

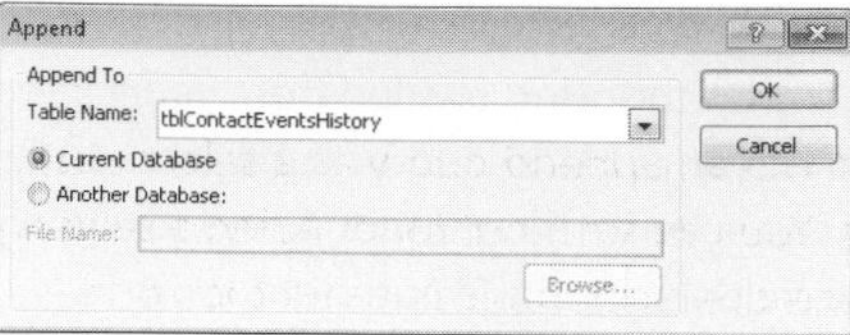

Figure 11-21 After you click the Append button on the ribbon, specify the target table of an append query.

Notice that the default is to append the data into a table in the current database. You can select the Another Database option and either type the path and name of the target database or click Browse to find the file you want. This feature could be particularly handy if you want to archive the records to another file. In this case, click the arrow to the right of Table Name, select tblContactEventsHistory in the current database, and click OK. Your query design now looks like Figure 11-22.

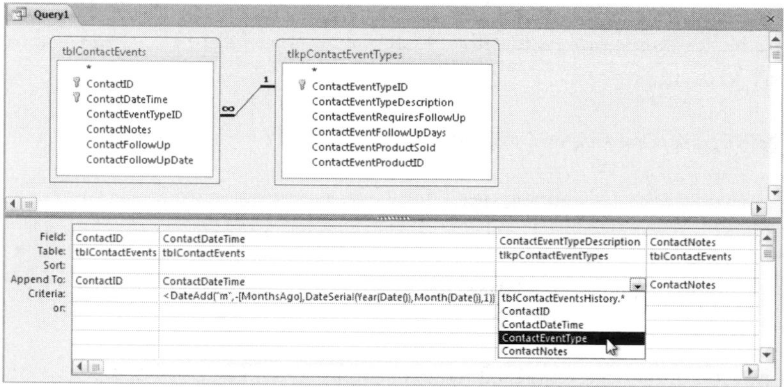

Figure 11-22 In the Append To row, you can specify the target fields in an append query.

Notice that Access added an Append To line and automatically filled in the matching field names from the target table. Remember, you want to append the ContactEventTypeDescription field from tlkpContactEventTypes to the ContactEventType field in the history table, so select that field from the list on the Append To line under ContactEventTypeDescription.

You're now ready to run this query in the next section. You can find the query saved as qxmplArchiveContactEvents in the sample database. You'll also find a companion qxmplArchiveContactProducts query.

Running an Append Query

As with other action queries, you can run an append query as a select query first to be sure that you'll be copying the right rows. You can start out by building a select query, running it, and then converting it to an append query, or you can build the append query directly and then switch to Datasheet view from Design view to examine the data that the query will add. Although you can find and delete rows that you append in error, you can save time if you make a backup of the target table first.

After you confirm that the query will append the right rows, you can either run it directly from Design view or save it and run it from the Navigation pane. When you run the qxmplArchiveContactEvents query and respond to the MonthsAgo prompt so that Access archives events earlier than September 1, 2010, Access should tell you that 23 rows will be appended, as shown in Figure 11-23. (For example, if the current date on your computer is any day in November 2010, enter **2** in response to the prompt for the MonthsAgo value.) If you want to append the rows to the tblContactEventsHistory table, click Yes in the confirmation dialog box. Note that after you click Yes, the only way to undo these changes is to go to the target table and either select and delete the rows manually or build a delete query to do it.

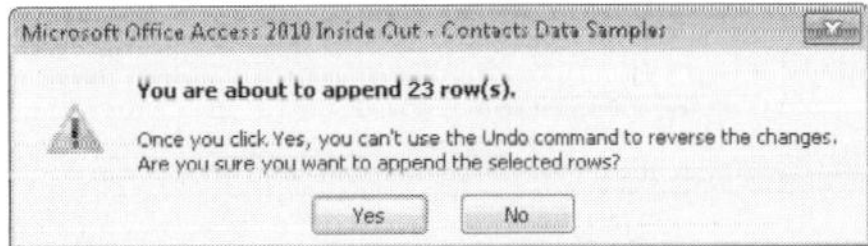

Figure 11-23 This dialog box asks you to confirm the appending of rows.

Go ahead and append these 23 rows. In the section "Troubleshooting Action Queries," on page 730, we'll take a look at what happens if you try to run this query again.

Deleting Groups of Rows

You're not likely to keep all the data in your database forever. You'll probably summarize some of your detailed information as time goes by and then delete the data that you no longer need. You can remove sets of records from your database using a delete query.

Testing with a Select Query

After you have copied all the old contact event and contact product data to the archive tables, you might want to remove this information from the active tables. This is clearly the kind of query that you will want to save so that you can use it again and again. You can design the query to calculate automatically which records to delete based on the current system date and a month parameter, as you did in the append queries.

As with an update query, it's a good idea to test which rows will be affected by a delete query by first building a select query to isolate these records. Start a new query with tblContactEvents in the ContactsDataCopy.accdb database and include the asterisk (*) field in the query grid. A delete query acts on entire rows, so including the "all fields" indicator will ultimately tell the delete query from which table the rows should be deleted. Add the ContactDateTime field to the design grid, and clear the Show check box. This time, let's use a specific date value to choose rows to delete. In the Criteria line under the ContactDateTime field, enter

<[Oldest Date to Keep:]

Click the Parameters button in the Show/Hide group of the Design tab, and define your parameter as a Date/Time data type. Your query should look like Figure 11-24.

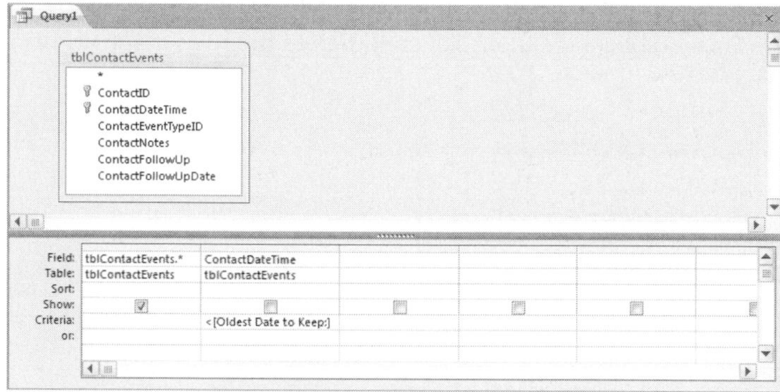

Figure 11-24 This query uses a date parameter to select old contact events.

When you switch to Datasheet view for this query, Access prompts you for a date parameter, as shown in Figure 11-25. In the Enter Parameter Value dialog box, enter **9/1/2010** to see all the old contact events from September 1, 2010, or earlier. The result is shown in Figure 11-26.

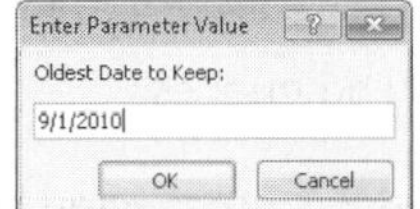

Figure 11-25 Enter the query date parameter when Access prompts you.

Query1

ContactID	Date / Time	Type	Notes	Follow up?	Follow-up Date
1	08/20/2010 15:57	14		☑	8/15/2011
1	08/23/2010 14:28	12		☑	8/18/2011
3	08/31/2010 10:00	16		☑	9/30/2010
4	08/12/2010 14:34	10		☑	8/7/2011
5	07/29/2010 11:44	17		☑	7/24/2011
5	08/10/2010 14:57	9		☑	8/5/2011
6	07/31/2010 16:24	8		☑	8/30/2010
6	08/13/2010 10:47	5		☐	
6	08/13/2010 13:32	1		☐	
7	08/18/2010 11:58	5		☐	
10	08/22/2010 13:03	12		☑	8/17/2011
14	08/29/2010 12:50	5		☐	
16	07/30/2010 8:41	12		☑	7/25/2011
16	08/03/2010 16:35	13		☑	7/29/2011
16	08/20/2010 17:06	7		☑	8/15/2011
17	07/30/2010 12:47	5		☐	
17	08/15/2010 8:43	4		☐	
18	08/24/2010 12:11	13		☑	8/19/2011
20	08/21/2010 8:02	11		☐	
21	08/26/2010 14:30	1		☐	
26	08/07/2010 17:08	2		☐	
26	08/23/2010 14:32	10		☑	8/18/2011
28	07/29/2010 15:20	13		☑	7/24/2011

Record: 1 of 23 No Filter Search

Figure 11-26 When you run the select query, you can verify the rows to delete.

INSIDE OUT Using Different Date Formats

Access 2010 recognizes several different formats for date parameters. For example, for the first day of September in 2010, you can enter any of the following:

```
9/1/2010        September 1, 2010        1 SEP 2010
```

The append query that you saw earlier that copied these rows to an archive table copied 23 rows, which matches what you see here. After you verify that this is what you want, go back to Design view and change the query to a delete query by clicking the Delete command in the Query Type group of the Design tab below Query Tools. Your query should look like Figure 11-27. *Do not run this query!* We'll explain why in the next section.

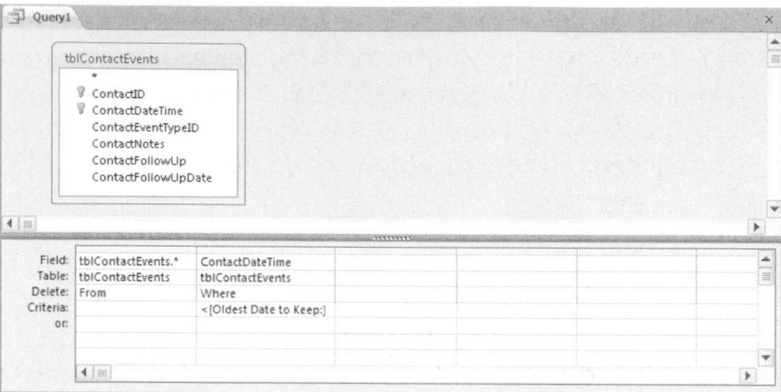

Figure 11-27 Click the Delete button in the Query Type group on the ribbon to convert your query to a delete query.

Notice that the query has a new Delete line. In any delete query, you should select From under the "choose all fields" (*) field for the one table from which you want to delete rows. All other fields should indicate Where and have one criterion or more on the Criteria and Or lines.

Using a Delete Query

Because you won't be able to retrieve any deleted rows, it's a good idea to first make a backup copy of your table, especially if this is the first time that you've run this delete query. Use the procedure described earlier in the section "Running an Update Query," on page 707, to make a copy of your table.

As you just learned, you can create a delete query from a select query by clicking the Delete command on the Design tab below Query Tools when your query is in Design view. You must be sure that at least one table includes the "all the rows" indicator (*) and has From specified on the Delete line. Simply click Run in the Results group on the Design tab to delete the rows you specified. Because you included a parameter in this query, you'll need to respond to the Enter Parameter Value dialog box (shown in Figure 11-25) again. Access selects the rows to be deleted and displays the confirmation dialog box shown in Figure 11-28.

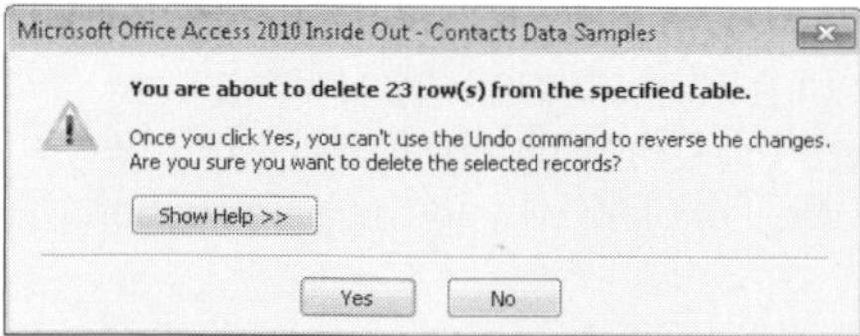

Figure 11-28 This dialog box asks you to confirm the deletion of rows.

Are you *really*, *really* sure you want to delete these rows? Are you sure these rows are safely tucked away in the archive table? If so, click Yes to proceed with the deletion. Click No if you're unsure about the rows that Access will delete. (We recommend that you click No for now and read on!) You can find this query saved as qxmplDeleteOldContactEventsUnsafe in the sample database. (Does the query name give you a clue?)

Deleting Inactive Data

You now know how to copy old contact event and contact product data to an archive table, and how to delete the old contact events from the main table. In some applications, you might want to delete more than just the event records. For example, in an order entry database, you might want to archive and delete the records of old customers who haven't given you any business in more than two years.

In the Conrad Systems Contacts application, you can mark old contacts as inactive so that they disappear from the primary forms you use to edit the data. In the section "Updating Groups of Rows," on page 704, we showed you how to identify contacts who haven't had any activity in a specified period of time and set the Inactive field so that they don't show up anymore. Because of this feature, archiving and deleting old contacts isn't an issue.

However, you might still want to delete old contact events and contact products that you have archived. We just showed you how to create a delete query to remove rows, but there's a safer way to do it if you have copied the rows elsewhere. Go back to the query you have been building and add tblContactEventsHistory. Create a join line between the ContactID field in tblContactEvents and the ContactID field in tblContactEventsHistory. Create another join line between the ContactDateTime field in tblContactEvents and the same field in tblContactEventsHistory. Your query should now look like Figure 11-29.

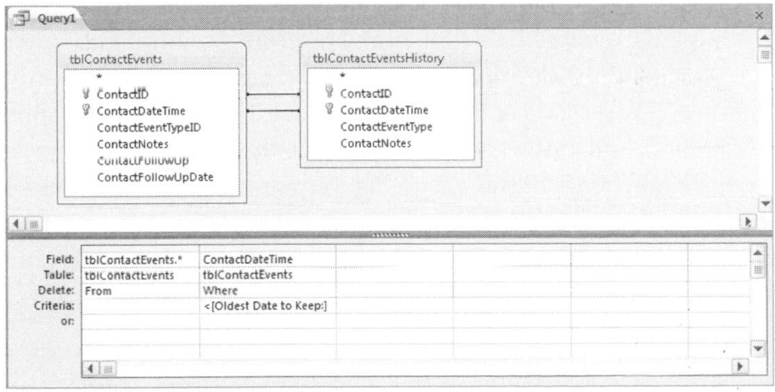

Figure 11-29 This query allows you to delete archived rows safely.

Remember that the default for a join is to include rows only where the values in both tables match. Now, your Delete query won't return any rows from tblContactEvents (where you're performing the delete) unless the row already exists in tblContactEventHistory. Run this query now and reply with any date you like. The query won't delete rows from tblContactEvents unless a copy is safely saved in the archive table. You can find this query saved as qxmplDeleteOldContactEventsSafe in the sample database. There's also a companion query, qxmplDeleteOldContactProductsSafe, to deal with contact products.

Troubleshooting Action Queries

Access 2010 analyzes your action query request and the data that you are about to change before it commits changes to your database. When it identifies errors, Access always gives you an opportunity to cancel the operation.

Solving Common Action Query Errors and Problems

Access identifies (traps) four types of errors during the execution of an action query.

- **Duplicate primary keys** This type of error occurs if you attempt to append a record to a table or update a record in a table, which would result in a duplicate primary key or a duplicate of a unique index key value. Access will not update or append any rows that would create duplicates. For example, if the primary key of a contact event archive table is ContactID and ContactDateTime, Access won't append a record that contains a ContactID and ContactDateTime value already in the table. Before attempting to append such rows, you might have to modify your append query not to select the duplicate rows.

- **Data conversion errors** This type of error occurs if you attempt to append data to an existing table and the data type of the receiving field does not match that of the sending field (and the data in the sending field cannot be converted to the appropriate data type). For example, this error will occur if you attempt to append a text field to an integer field and the text field contains either alphabetic characters or a number string that is too large for the integer field. You might also encounter a conversion error in an update query if you use a formula that attempts a calculation on a field that contains characters. For information on data conversions and potential limitations, see Table 5-3 on page 262.

- **Locked records** This type of error can occur when you run a delete query or an update query on a table that you share with other users on a network. Access cannot update records that are in the process of being updated by some other user. You might want to wait and try again later when no one else is using the affected records to be sure that your update or deletion occurs. Even if you're not sharing the data on a network, you can encounter this error if you have a form or another query open on the data you're updating and have started to change some of the data.
- **Validation rule violations** If any of the rows being inserted or any of the rows being updated violates either a field validation rule or the table validation rule, Access notifies you of an error and does not insert or update any of the rows that fail the validation test. When you have a referential integrity rule defined, you cannot update or delete a row in a way that would violate the rule.

Another problem that can occur—although it isn't an error—is that Access truncates data that is being appended to text or memo fields if the data does not fit. Access does not warn you when this happens. You must be sure (especially with append queries) that you have made the receiving text and memo fields large enough to store the incoming data.

Looking at an Error Example

Earlier in this chapter, you learned how to create an append query to copy old contact events to an archive table. What do you suppose would happen if you copied rows through December 31, 2010, forgot to delete them from the main table, and then later asked to copy rows through April 30, 2011? If you try this starting with an empty archive table in the ContactsDataCopy.accdb database, run qxmplArchiveContactEvents once, and then run it again with the same or later cutoff month, you'll get an error dialog box similar to the one shown in Figure 11-30.

Figure 11-30 This dialog box alerts you to action query errors.

The dialog box in Figure 11-30 declares that 23 records won't be inserted because of duplicate primary key values. Access didn't find any data conversion errors, locking problems, or validation rule errors. Note that if some fields have data conversion problems, Access might still append the row but leave the field set to Null. When you see this dialog box, you can click Yes to proceed with the changes that Access can make without errors. You might find it difficult later, however, to track down all the records that were not updated successfully. Click No to cancel the append query.

To solve this problem, you can change the "select" part of the query to choose only the rows that haven't already been inserted into the target table. Remember from Chapter 10 the technique that you used to find "unmatched" rows. You'll apply that same technique to solve this problem.

Open the query that you built in the previous section (or qxmplArchiveContactEvents) in Design view. Add tblContactEventsHistory (the target table) to your query. Create join lines from the ContactID field in tblContactEvents to the same field in tblContactEventHistory. Do the same with ContactDateTime. Double-click each join line to open the Join Properties dialog box and choose the option to include all rows from tblContactEvents and the matching rows from tblContactEventsHistory. You must do this for each join line so that you end up with both lines pointing to tblContactEventsHistory. Include the ContactID field from tblContactEventsHistory in the design grid, clear the Append To box underneath it (you don't want to try to insert ContactID twice), and place the criterion Is Null on the Criteria line. Your query should now look like Figure 11-31.

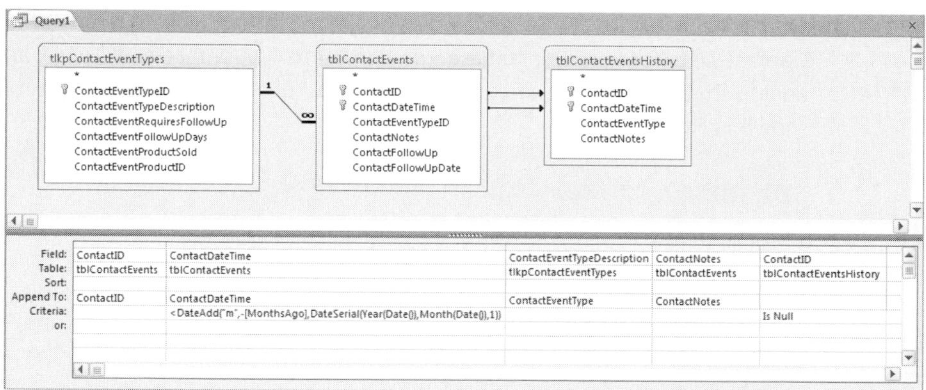

Figure 11-31 You can design an append query to avoid duplicate row errors.

The result is that this query will select rows from tblContactEvents only if they don't already exist in the archive table. You can now run this query as many times as you like. If all the rows you choose already exist, the query simply inserts no additional rows. You can find this query saved as qxmplArchiveContactEventsNoDuplicates in the sample database. There's also a companion query, qxmplArchiveContactProductsNoDuplicates, to handle the archiving of contact product records.

At this point, you should have a reasonable understanding of how action queries can work for you. You can find some more examples of action queries in Article 2, "Understanding SQL," on the companion CD. Now, it's time to go on to building the user interface for your application with forms and reports.

PART 4

Creating Forms

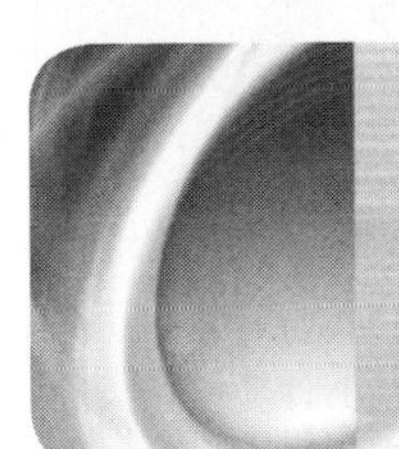

CHAPTER 12

Using Forms in an Access Application

If you've worked through this book to this point, you should understand all the mechanics of designing and building databases (and connecting to external ones), entering and viewing data in tables, and building queries. An understanding of tables and queries is important before you jump into forms because most of the forms you design will be bound to an underlying table or a query.

This chapter focuses on the external aspects of forms—why forms are useful, what they look like, and how to use them. You'll look at examples of forms from the Conrad Systems Contacts sample client database and the Back Office Software System sample web database. In Chapters 13, 14, and 15, you'll learn how to design, build, and customize your own forms by learning to build some of the forms you see in the Conrad Systems Contacts, Housing Reservations, and Back Office Software System databases.

Uses of Forms

Forms are the primary interface between users and your Microsoft Access 2010 application. You can design forms for many different purposes:

- **Displaying and editing data** This is the most common use of forms. Forms provide a way to customize the presentation of the data in your database. You can also use forms to change or delete data in your database or add data to it. You can set options in a form to make all or part of your data read-only, to fill in related information from other tables automatically, to calculate the values to be displayed, or to show or hide data on the basis of either the values of other data in the record or the options selected by the user of the form.
- **Controlling application flow** You can design forms that work with macros or with Microsoft Visual Basic procedures to automate the display of certain data or the sequence of certain actions. You can create special controls on your form, called command buttons, which run a macro or a Visual Basic procedure when you click them.

With macros and Visual Basic procedures, you can open other forms, run queries, run named data macros, restrict the data that is displayed, execute a ribbon command, set values in records and forms, display customized ribbons, print reports, and perform a host of other actions. You can also design a form so that macros or Visual Basic procedures run when specific events occur—for example, when someone opens the form, tabs to a specific control, clicks an option on the form, or changes data in the form. See Part 6, "Automating an Application Using Macros," and Part 8, "Automating an Access Application Using Visual Basic" for details about using macros and Visual Basic with forms to automate your application.

- **Accepting input** You can design forms that are used only for entering new data in your database or for providing data values to help automate your application.
- **Displaying messages** Forms can provide information about how to use your application or about upcoming actions. Access 2010 also provides a MessageBox macro action and a MsgBox Visual Basic function that you can use to display information, warnings, or error messages. See Chapter 25, "Automating Your Application with Visual Basic," for more detail.
- **Printing information** Although you should design and use reports to print most information, you can also print the information displayed in a form. Because you can specify one set of options when Access displays a form and another set of options when Access prints a form, a form can serve a dual role. For example, you might design a form with two sets of display headers and footers, one set for entering an order and another set for printing a customer invoice from the order.

A Tour of Forms

The Conrad Systems Contacts sample client database and Back Office Software System sample web database are full of interesting examples of forms. The rest of this chapter takes you on a tour of some of the major features of those forms and shows you some of the basic techniques for editing data in a form. In the next chapter, you'll learn how to design and build forms for these databases.

Begin by opening the Conrad Systems Contacts database (Contacts.accdb) and set the Navigation pane to display only the forms. To do so, click the Navigation Pane menu, click Object Type under Navigate To Category, and then click Forms under Filter By Group to see the list of available forms. Note that when you open the database, you see a copyright notice, followed by a message telling you which form to open to start the application.

Headers, Detail Sections, and Footers

You'll normally place the information that you want to display from the underlying table or query in the detail section in the center of the Form window. You can add a header at the top of the window or a footer at the bottom of the window to display information or controls that don't need to change as you move through the records.

An interesting form in the Conrad Systems Contacts database that includes both a header and a footer is frmContactSummary. The application uses this form to display the summary results of a contact search whenever the search finds more than five matching contacts. You can also open this form directly from the Navigation pane—if you do so, it will show you all the contacts in the database. Find the frmContactSummary form in the forms list in the Navigation pane, right-click the form name, and then click the Open command on the shortcut menu to see a window similar to the one shown in Figure 12-1.

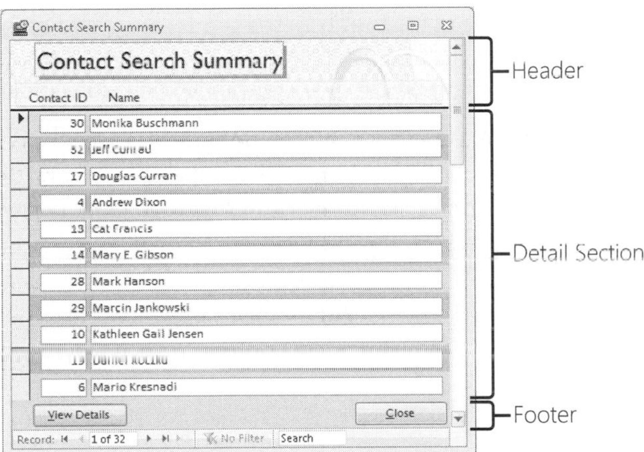

Figure 12-1 The frmContactSummary form has a header, a detail section, and a footer.

The area at the top of the window containing the title *Contact Search Summary* is the header for the form. The header also includes the column names. The area at the bottom of the window is the footer for the form. You can click View Details to see all details for the currently selected contact (the contact with the arrow on the row selector), or you can click Close to close the form. In the lower-left corner of the form is the Record Number box that you saw in tables and queries in Datasheet view. Click the arrow button immediately to the right of the record number to move the row selector arrow to the next contact record in the detail section of the form; notice that the header and footer don't change when you do this. If you move down several records, you can see the records scroll up in the detail section of the form.

If you click the View Details button in the footer, this form closes and the frmContacts form opens, showing details of the contact record that you selected before you clicked the button. The way the form is designed, the View Details button opens the frmContacts form using a filter to show you the currently selected contact. If you decide that you don't want to see details, you can click the Close button in the form footer to dismiss the form.

Multiple-Page Forms

When you have a lot of information from each record to display in a form, you can design a *multiple-page form*. Open the frmContactsPages form in the Conrad Systems Contacts database to see an example. When you open the form, you'll see the first page of contact data for the first contact. You can use the Record Number box and the buttons in the lower-left corner of the form to move through the records, viewing the first page of information for each contact. Figure 12-2 shows the first page of the second contact record—the records are sorted by last name. (For those of you who want to visit Jeff's website, that's his real website address in the form!) To see the second page of information for any contact, press the Page Down key. Figure 12-3 shows the second page of Jeff's contact record. (Notice that this form has a header but no footer.) As you view different pages of a multiple-page form, the header at the top of the form (with the form title and some command buttons) doesn't change.

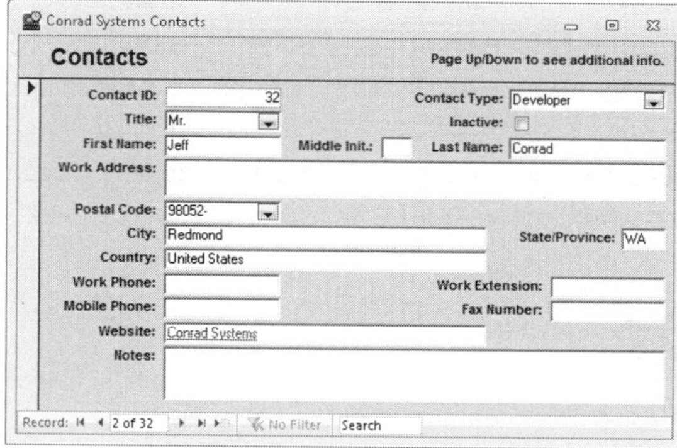

Figure 12-2 This is the first page of a record in the multiple-page frmContactsPages form.

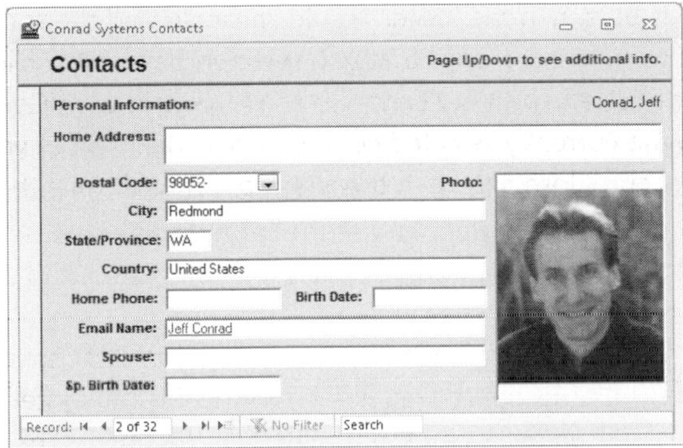

Figure 12-3 Here is the second page of the same record in the frmContactsPages form.

Continuous Forms

You can create another type of form that is useful for browsing through and editing a list of records when each record has only a few data fields. This type of form is called a *continuous form*. Rather than showing you only a single record at a time, a continuous form displays formatted records one after the other, in the manner of a datasheet.

The frmContactSummary form, shown earlier in Figure 12-1, is a simple continuous form. The frmLkpContactEventTypes form, shown in Figure 12-4, is also a continuous form. You can use the vertical scroll bar to move through the record display, or you can click the buttons in the lower-left corner of the form to move from record to record. Also, you can click New Record to move to the blank row below the last record. The application uses this form to let you view and edit the different types of contact events that you might want to log.

Conrad Systems - Contact Event Types

Close | Cancel | Save | Add New

ID	Description	Requires Follow-up?	Follow-up Days	Product Sold?	Product	
1	Phone call - received	☐	0	☐		Delete
2	Phone call - made	☐	0	☐		Delete
3	Email - received	☐	0	☐		Delete
4	Email - sent	☐	0	☐		Delete
5	Brochure mailed	☐	0	☐		Delete
6	Sample disk mailed, Single	☑	30	☑	BO$$ Demo Edition, Single User	Delete
7	Sold Single User	☑	360	☑	BO$$ Single User	Delete
8	Sample disk mailed, Multi	☑	30	☑	BO$$ Demo Edition, Multi-User	Delete
9	Sold Multi-User	☑	360	☑	BO$$ Multi-User	Delete
10	Sold Remote User	☑	360	☑	BO$$ Remote User	Delete

Record: 1 of 17 No Filter Search

Figure 12-4 The frmLkpContactEventTypes form in the Conrad Systems Contacts database is a continuous form.

Split Forms

A type of form view called *Split Form* allows you to simultaneously display a record in a regular form view and see a list of records in Datasheet view. Open the frmProducts form in the Conrad Systems Contacts database to see an example, as shown in Figure 12-5. When you open the form, you'll see that the upper half of the form displays the details about one specific product and the lower half of the form displays the complete list of 11 products offered by Conrad Systems.

You can use the Record Number box and the buttons in the lower-left corner of the form to move through the records. Click Next Record and notice that the record you are currently viewing in the top half becomes the highlighted record in the bottom half of the form. Depending on the settings in the form's design, you can edit the information about any specific product in either the top or the bottom half of the form.

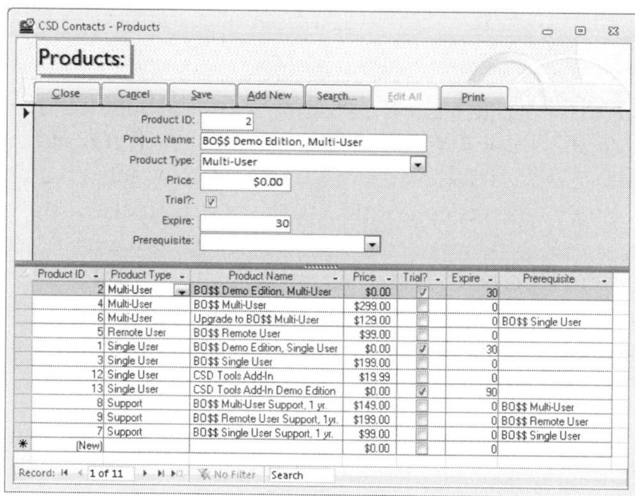

Product ID	Product Type	Product Name	Price	Trial?	Expire	Prerequisite
2	Multi-User	BO$$ Demo Edition, Multi-User	$0.00	✓	30	
4	Multi-User	BO$$ Multi-User	$299.00		0	
6	Multi-User	Upgrade to BO$$ Multi-User	$129.00		0	BO$$ Single User
5	Remote User	BO$$ Remote User	$99.00		0	
1	Single User	BO$$ Demo Edition, Single User	$0.00	✓	30	
3	Single User	BO$$ Single User	$199.00		0	
12	Single User	CSD Tools Add-In	$19.99		0	
13	Single User	CSD Tools Add-In Demo Edition	$0.00	✓	90	
8	Support	BO$$ Multi-User Support, 1 yr.	$149.00		0	BO$$ Multi-User
9	Support	BO$$ Remote User Support, 1yr.	$199.00		0	BO$$ Remote User
7	Support	BO$$ Single User Support, 1 yr.	$99.00		0	BO$$ Single User
(New)			$0.00		0	

Figure 12-5 The frmProducts form in the Conrad Systems Contacts database is a split form.

Subforms

A *subform* is a good way to show related data from the *many* side of a one-to-many relationship. For example, the frmCompanies form, shown in Figure 12-6, has a subform to display the related contacts. Although this form looks much like a single display panel, it has a subform (which looks more like a datasheet than a form) embedded in the main form. The main part of the frmCompanies form displays information from the tblCompanies table, while the subform in the lower part of the window shows information from the tblCompanyContacts table about the contacts related to the current company.

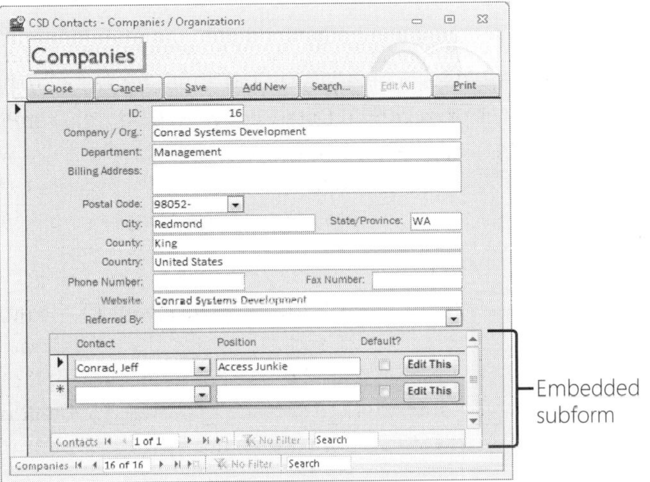

Figure 12-6 The frmCompanies form has an embedded subform that shows the related contacts.

This form looks quite complicated, but it really isn't difficult to build. Because the Conrad Systems Contacts database is well designed, it doesn't take much effort to build the queries that allow the form to display information from three different tables. Most of the work of creating the form goes into selecting and placing the controls that display the data. To link a subform to a main form, you have to set only two properties that tell Access which linking fields to use. (These are actually the same Link Master Fields and Link Child Fields properties that you learned about in Chapter 10, "Building Complex Queries," when you defined a subdatasheet for a query.) In Chapter 15, "Advanced Form Design," you'll build a subform and link it to a form.

Pop-Up Forms

Sometimes it's useful to provide information in a window that stays on top regardless of where you move the focus in your application. You've probably noticed that the default behavior for windows in Microsoft Windows is for the active window to move to the front and for all other windows to move behind the active one. One exception in Access is the property sheet for any object in Design view. If you grab the property sheet and undock it, it stays floating on top so that you can access its settings regardless of what you are doing behind it. This sort of floating window is called a *pop-up window*.

You can create forms in Access that open in pop-up windows (called pop-up forms in Access). If you open any form in the Conrad Systems Contacts application and then click the About command on the custom ribbon, this opens the frmAbout form shown in Figure 12-7, which is designed as a pop-up form. See Chapter 26, "The Finishing Touches," for more details about how to create custom ribbons for forms. If you still have frmCompanies open, you can click the About command on the ribbon; or you can switch to the Navigation pane and open the frmAbout form directly to see how it behaves. Notice that if you click in the open form or the window behind it, the frmAbout form stays on top. Click the Close button on the pop-up form to close it.

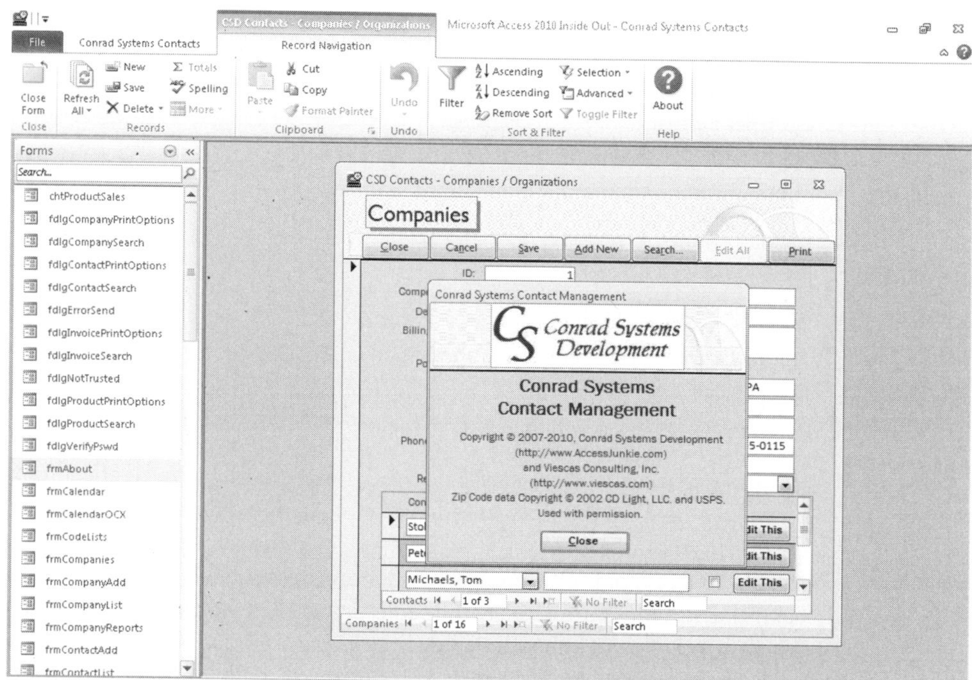

Figure 12-7 The frmAbout pop-up form "floats" on top of frmCompanies, which has the focus.

Modal Forms

As you add functionality to your application, you'll encounter situations in which you need to obtain some input from the user or convey some important information to the user before Access can proceed. Access 2010 provides a special type of form, called a *modal form*, which requires a response before the user can continue working in the application. The fdlgContactSearch dialog box in the Conrad Systems Contacts database, shown in Figure 12-8, is a modal form. This dialog box normally opens when you click the Contacts button on the main switchboard form and then click the Search button on the resulting Select Contacts (frmContactList) form. This dialog box also opens if you first open the frmContactsPlain form and then click Search. You can open the form on which the dialog box is based directly from the Navigation pane. You'll notice that so long as this dialog box is open, you can't select any other window or ribbon command in the application.

To proceed, you must either enter some search criteria and click Search or click Cancel to dismiss the form.

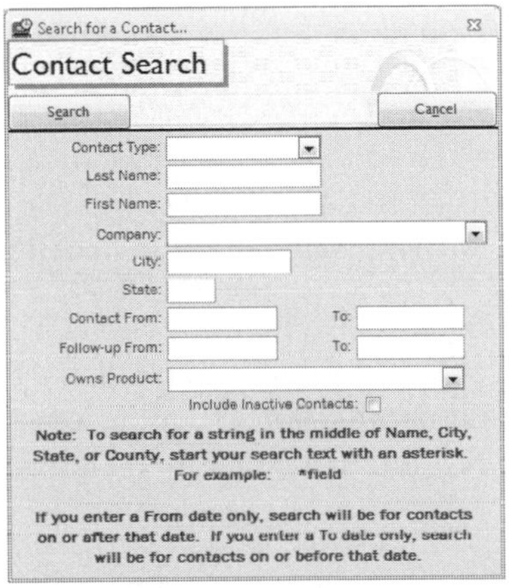

Figure 12-8 The fdlgContactSearch form in the Conrad Systems Contacts database is a modal form that opens as a Windows dialog box.

INSIDE OUT **Using Name Prefixes to Organize Your Objects**

Have you noticed the different prefixes on the form names that we designed in the Conrad Systems Contacts application? We like to create a prefix that helps us know more about the type of form when we look at the form list in the Navigation pane. For example, we prefix the names of forms that are designed to open in PivotChart view with *cht*. We prefix dialog forms with *fdlg*, normal edit forms with *frm*, forms designed to edit lookup tables with *frmLkp*, and subforms with *fsub*. You may want to adopt a similar naming convention to help you keep your list of forms organized.

Special Controls

The information in a form is contained in *controls*. The most common control you'll use on a form is a simple text box. A *text box* can display data from an underlying table or query, or it can display the result of an expression calculated in the control. You've probably noticed that many controls allow you to choose from among several values or to see additional content. You can also use controls to trigger a macro or a Visual Basic procedure. These controls are discussed in the next five sections.

Option Buttons, Check Boxes, Toggle Buttons, and Option Groups

Whenever the data you're displaying can have only two or three valid values, you can use *option buttons*, *check boxes*, or *toggle buttons* to see or set the value you want in the field. For example, when there are two values, as in the case of a simple Yes/No field, you can use a check box to graphically display the value in the field. A check box that's selected means the value is Yes, and a check box that's cleared means the value is No. The Inactive control on the frmContactsPages form (see Figure 12-2) and the Default? control in the subform of frmCompanies (see Figure 12-6) are good examples of the use of a check box.

Stand-alone option buttons and toggle buttons work in the same way as a check box. When the value of an option button is Yes or True, the option button has a black dot in it. When the value of an option button is No or False, the option button appears empty. Likewise, a toggle button appears pressed in when True and not pressed in when False.

To provide a graphical choice among more than two values, you can place option buttons, check boxes, or toggle buttons in an *option group*. When grouped this way, each control in the group should have a unique integer value. When the control appears selected, the value of the option group is the value of the control. Because an option group can have only one value, when you select a control within the group, all other controls in the group appear unselected because their values no longer match the value of the option group.

For example, open frmProducts (this form displays the different products available), and click Print to see the fdlgProductPrintOptions form (shown in Figure 12-9) that lists the various contact reporting options. (You cannot open fdlgProductPrintOptions directly from the Navigation pane—it has Visual Basic code that runs when the form opens to verify that the companion frmProducts form is already open. If not, the code tells Access not to allow the form to open.) If you open this form and click the available option buttons, you can see that when you click one button, the previously selected one clears. When you click one of the sales report buttons on this form, the form reveals additional date range options for your sales report.

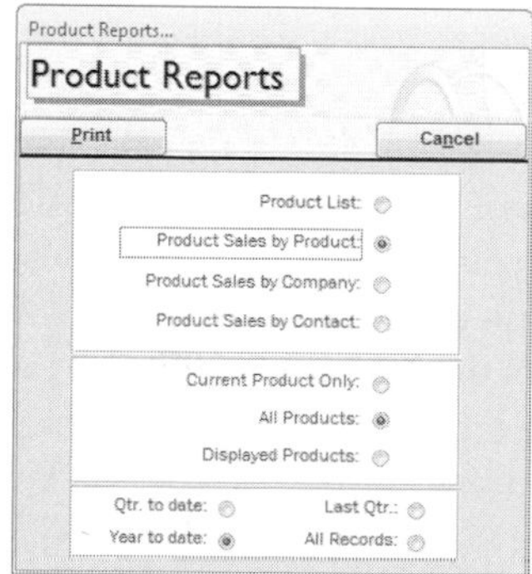

Figure 12-9 You can see option groups on the fdlgProductPrintOptions form.

List Boxes and Combo Boxes

When you want to display a list of data values in an open list, a *list box* is a good choice. When you view objects in Windows Explorer, the list of file names and properties in the pane on the right side when you're in Details view is a list box.

A list box can show a list of values you entered when you designed the control, a list of values returned by a Structured Query Language (SQL) statement, the values of one or more fields in a table or in a query, or a list of field names from a table or a query. When you select a value from the list, you set the value of the control. You can use a list box on a form that edits data to display the value of one of the fields. When you choose a new value in the list box, you update the underlying field.

You can also define a list box in which you can select multiple values. When you do this, however, the list box cannot update an underlying field. This type of list box is useful to allow a user to choose multiple items or options that your application code will use to perform some action. As we discussed in "Working with Multi-Value Lookup Fields," on page 280, Multi-Value Lookup Fields, when bound to a combo box, do provide a list box that allows you to select and save multiple values back to the table.

In the example shown in Figure 12-10 (the frmContactList form), the list box allows multiple selections and includes the set of names from the tblContacts table. This list box lets you select one or more entries by holding down the Shift key to select a contiguous range or by holding down the Ctrl key to select several noncontiguous entries. When you click Edit, a Visual Basic procedure evaluates your choices and opens the frmContacts form (see Figure 12-2) to display the selected contacts.

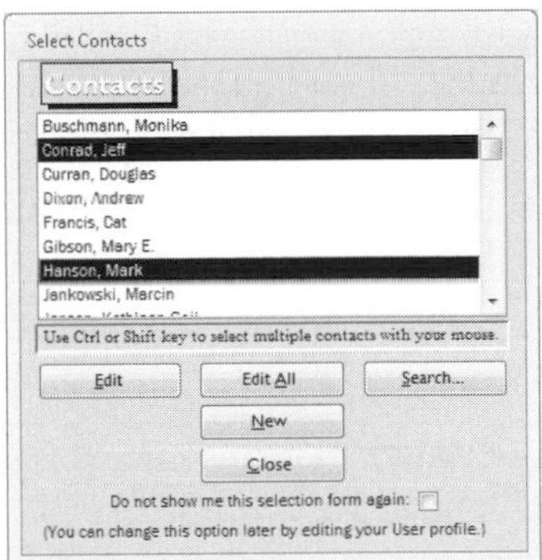

Figure 12-10 A list box on the frmContactList form allows you to choose multiple contacts to edit.

A list box like this one can use data from more than one field. In fact, the query behind this list box returns both the ContactID field (the primary key) from tblContacts and the expression that you see containing last name, first name, and middle initial. The list box hides the ContactID, but Visual Basic code behind the form uses that hidden value to quickly find the contacts you want.

Combo boxes are similar to list boxes. The primary difference is that a *combo box* has both a text box *and* a drop-down list. One major advantage of a combo box is that it requires space on the form only for one of the values in the underlying list. However, you can choose only one value in a combo box.

The PostalCode field in the frmCompanies form (see Figure 12-6) is set using a combo box, as shown in Figure 12-11. The combo box uses four fields from the underlying query—the Zipcode, City, State, and County fields from the lookup query qlkpZips. When you select a postal code, the combo box sets the PostalCode field in the underlying record—a very useful feature. Visual Basic code attached to this control also automatically copies the related City, County, and State data from the selected row in the combo box to the fields on the form for you. So long as you know the postal code, you don't have to enter the other related information. You'll find a similar combo box used in the application wherever you need to enter a postal code on a form.

Figure 12-11 When you click the arrow on a combo box, you can see a list of options.

> **Note**
>
> **In most cases, you will choose settings that disallow choosing a value that's not in the list in your combo boxes that update fields. You can also write Visual Basic code to examine a new value that a user tries to enter and determine whether it should appear in the list. You can learn about how to create code to deal with "not in list" values in Chapter 25.**

In Chapter 5, "Modifying Your Table Design," you learned about Multi-Value Lookup Fields. When you define a field as a Multi-Value Lookup Field, Access 2010 provides a special control in the Datasheet view of the table and on a form similar to a combo box to display the valid list of values. When you click the arrow, you'll see a list box with a check box next to each of the available value choices. Selecting the check box next to one or more of the values stores the selected values in the field.

The ContactType field in the frmContactsPlain form is a Multi-Value Lookup Field. Open this form and you can see a Contact Type field with an arrow on its right side. Clicking the arrow opens the list of available choices for Contact Type, as shown in Figure 12-12. You can see that John Viescas is designated as both a Developer and a Distributor. You can have Access store multiple values for this single record by selecting the check box next to an available contact type.

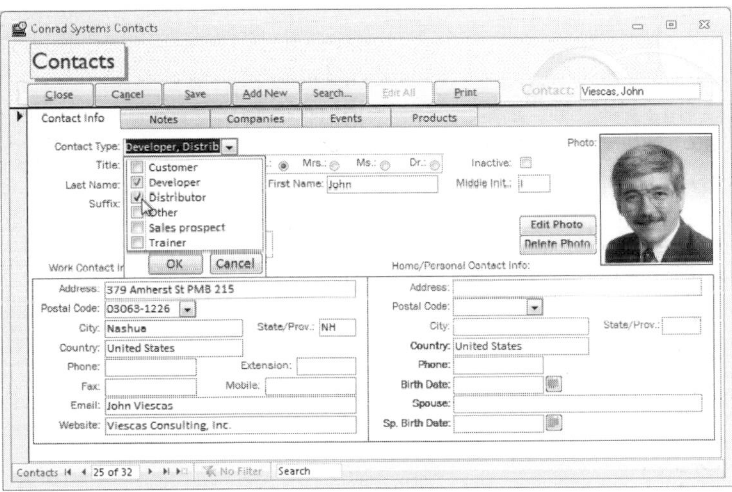

Figure 12-12 The Contact Type field on the frmContactsPlain form is a Multi-Value Lookup Field control.

Tab Controls

Earlier in this chapter, you saw that one way to deal with the need to display lots of information on one form is to use a multiple-page form (frmContactsPages, shown in Figures 12-2 and 12-3). Another way to organize the information on a single form is to use the *tab control* to provide what look like multiple folder tabs that reveal different information depending on the tab chosen—much like the main ribbon in Access 2010 provides Home, Create, External Data, and Database Tools tabs. In the Conrad Systems Contacts database, a contact has basic contact information and notes, as well as related companies, contact events, and products. Open the frmContacts form to see how the tab control displays only one of these types of information at a time, as shown in Figure 12-13.

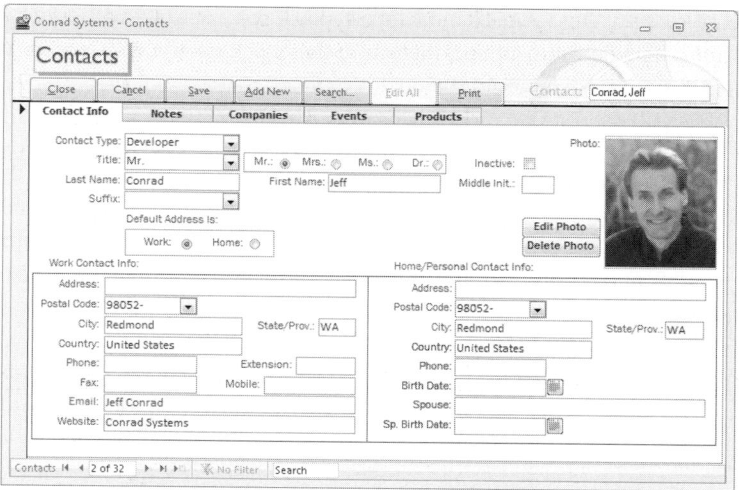

Figure 12-13 When you first open the frmContacts form, you see information on the Contact Info tab.

You can click the Companies tab (as shown in Figure 12-14) or any of the other tabs to see additional information. Note that there's no programming required to implement tab selection and data display. See Chapter 15 for details about how to use the tab control.

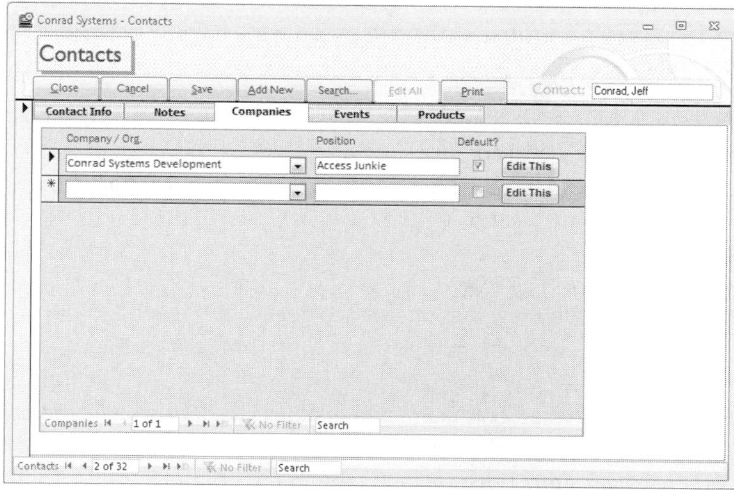

Figure 12-14 When you click another tab in a complex form, you can see different data.

Attachment Controls

In Chapter 4, "Designing Client Tables," you learned about the Attachment data type to store complex data. Access 2010 includes a type of control, called an *attachment control*, to add and delete data from this data type. If you still have the frmContactsPlain form open, click the Contact Info tab to see the contact's picture displayed on the right side of the form. The picture is stored in an attachment field in the contact's record. On the frmContactsPlain form, you can use the attachment control to add and delete the contact's picture. When you right-click the attachment control, Access shows a shortcut menu with Forward, Back, and Manage Attachments commands, as shown in Figure 12-15.

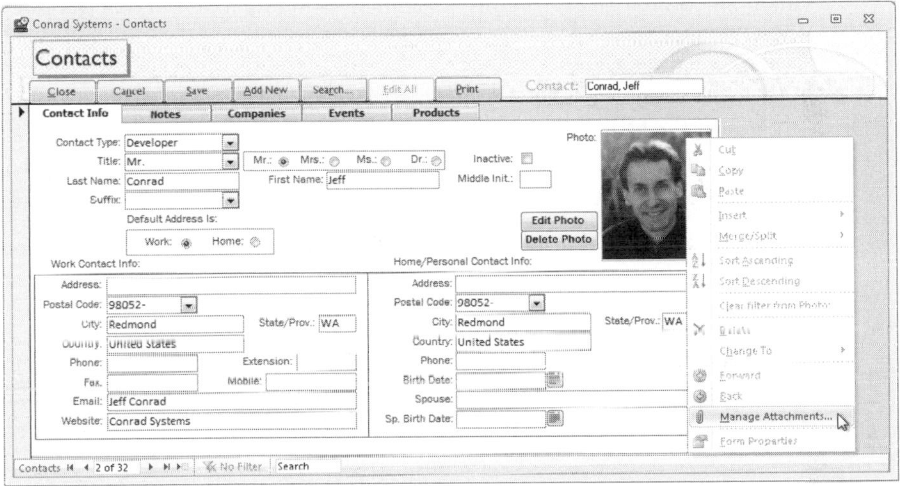

Figure 12-15 Right-click an attachment control to see a shortcut menu with a Manage Attachments command.

The Forward and Back commands are unavailable because there is only one attachment assigned to the attachment field in this record. Select Manage Attachments, and Access displays the Attachments dialog box, as shown in Figure 12-16.

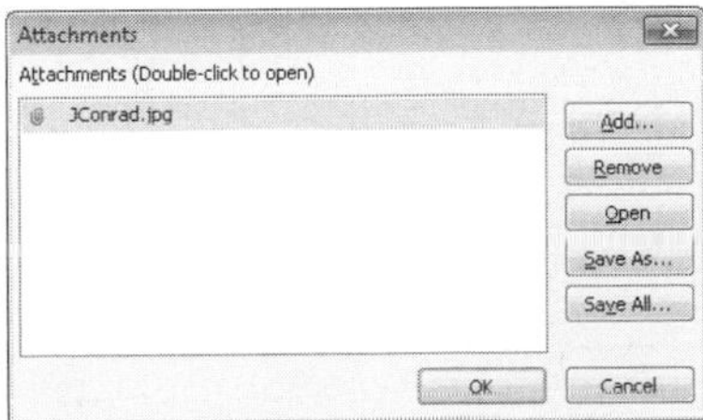

Figure 12-16 You can add and delete different data files bound to an Attachment data type using the Attachments dialog box.

The left side of the Attachments dialog box lists all the files stored in the attachment field in the current record. The Add button opens the standard Windows Choose File dialog box, where you can browse to another file to attach to this field. The Remove button deletes the attachment selected on the left side from the attachment field in the current record.

The Open button opens the selected attachment using the application that's defined in the Windows registry as the default application for this type of data. (On a computer running Windows 7, the .jpg file opens in the Windows Photo Viewer program unless you have installed another program to view and edit pictures.) The Save As button opens the Save Attachment dialog box where you can save the selected attachment to a folder. The Save All button functions the same as Save As except that you can save all the attachments (if there are more than one) in this attachment field to a folder in one step.

Use the record navigation buttons to move to Jeff's record, click Add to open the Choose File dialog box, browse to the Documents subfolder where you installed the sample files, and select the Microsoft Word document for Jeff called JeffConrad.docx. After you select the file, click Open to add the file to the attachment field in the current record. You can see the additional file listed in the Attachments dialog box, as shown in Figure 12-17.

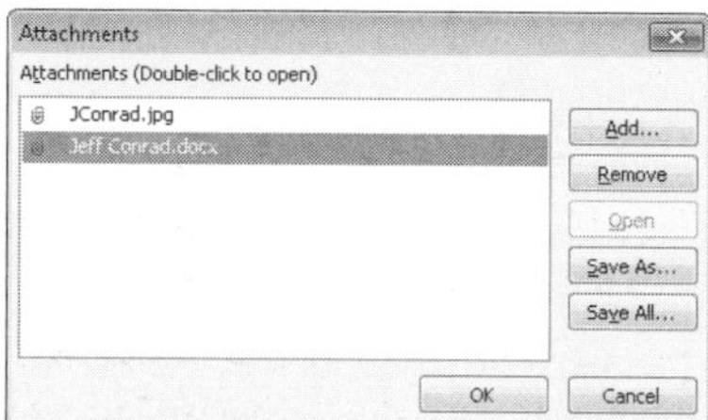

Figure 12-17 Jeff's document has now been added to the attachment field in the current record.

Click OK in the Attachments dialog box to return to the frmContactsPlain form and notice that you still see only one picture displayed for this record. Right-click the attachment control again. You can now use the Forward and Back commands on the shortcut menu to view the two different files saved in the attachment field in the current record, as shown in Figure 12-18.

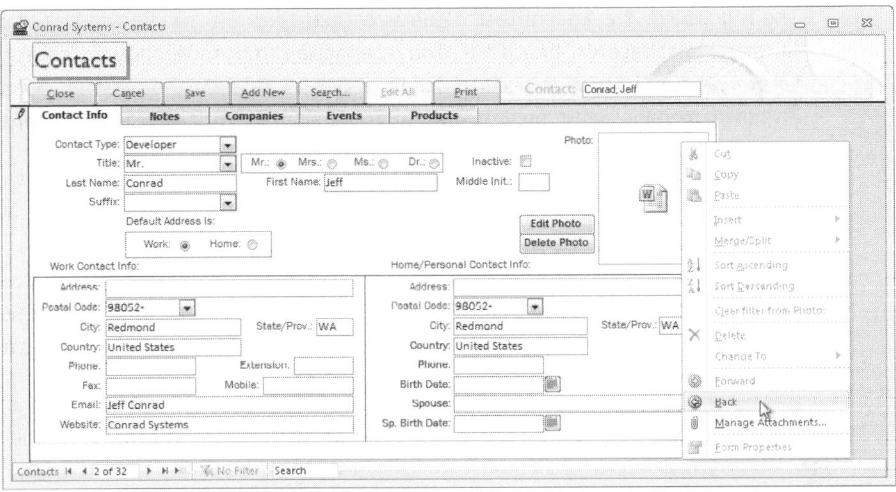

Figure 12-18 When you store multiple files in an attachment field, you can use the Forward and Back commands on the shortcut menu to view the files.

ActiveX Objects

To demonstrate an ActiveX object, close the Contacts.accdb database and then open the Contacts2Upsize.accdb database. Open the frmContactsPlain form in this database from the Navigation pane to see a form that is nearly identical to frmContactsPlain in the Contacts.accdb database. Unlike the contact picture you saw earlier on the frmContactsPlain form in the Contacts.accdb database, this picture is stored in a field in the tblContacts table using Microsoft ActiveX technology.

Note

The Contacts2Upsize.accdb database is a version of the Conrad Systems Contacts application that has been modified to upsize the data to Microsoft SQL Server and the application code to an Access project file (.adp). Because SQL Server cannot store the data in attachment fields, we changed the Photo field in the tblContacts table from the Attachment data type to the OLE Object data type. Also, we changed the control on the forms displaying the Photo field from an attachment control to a bound object frame control.

The logo in the top part of the main switchboard form (frmMain) in the Conrad Systems Contacts database, on the other hand, is a picture that Access has stored as part of the form. The control that you use to display a picture or any other ActiveX object is called an *object frame*. A *bound object frame* control is used to display an ActiveX object that is stored in a field in a table—such as the picture on frmContactsPages or frmContactsPlain in this database. When you edit the object in a bound object frame, you're updating a field in the table. Use an *unbound object frame* or an *image* control to display an object that is not stored in a table. Access stores the object with the form definition, and you cannot edit it in Form view.

When you include a bound object frame control on a form and bind the control to an OLE object field in the database, you can edit that object by selecting it and then right-clicking the picture to open the shortcut menu. On the Bitmap Image object submenu, select Edit, as shown in Figure 12-19.

Note

If you use an unbound object frame or image control on a form, you can edit the contents of the control only when you have the form in Design view.

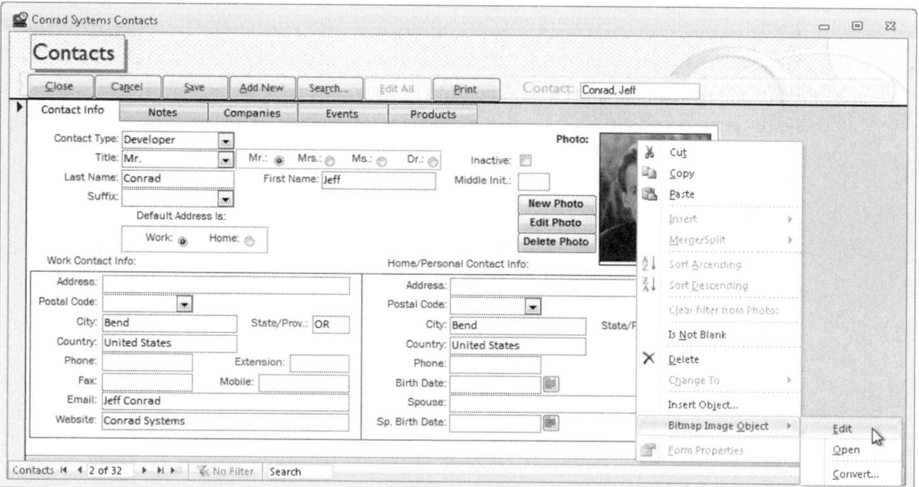

Figure 12-19 You can select a picture and then edit it by selecting Bitmap Image Object on the shortcut menu and then selecting Edit on the submenu.

Note

The Contacts2Upsize application also provides handy New Photo, Edit Photo, and Delete Photo buttons on the frmContactsPlain form. When the form loads, it examines your Windows registry and determines the default program on your computer to edit Bitmap (.bmp) or Joint Photographic Experts Group (JPEG; .jpg) files. When you click the New Photo or Edit Photo button, Visual Basic code behind the form starts that program for you. You don't have to worry about navigating the complex shortcut menu.

If the object is a picture, a graph, or a spreadsheet, you can see the object in the object frame control and you can activate its application by double-clicking the object. If the object is a sound file, you can hear it by double-clicking the object frame control.

Figure 12-19 shows one of the photographs stored in the tblContacts table that is bound in an object frame control on the frmContactsPlain form. When you double-click the picture—or select the picture, right-click, select Bitmap Image Object from the shortcut menu, and then select Edit from the submenu—Access starts the default application on your computer to edit bitmaps. On most computers, this is the Microsoft Paint application. In Windows, Paint is an ActiveX application that can "activate in place," as shown in Figure 12-20. You can update the picture by using any of the commands on the Home or View tab of the Paint program. You can paste in a different picture by copying a picture to the Clipboard and clicking the Paste command in the Clipboard group. After you make your changes, simply click in another area on the Access form to deactivate Paint and store the result of your edits in the object frame control. If you save the record, Access saves the changed data in your OLE object field.

Note

If you have registered an application other than Paint to handle bitmap objects, that application will be activated when you select Edit from the submenu.

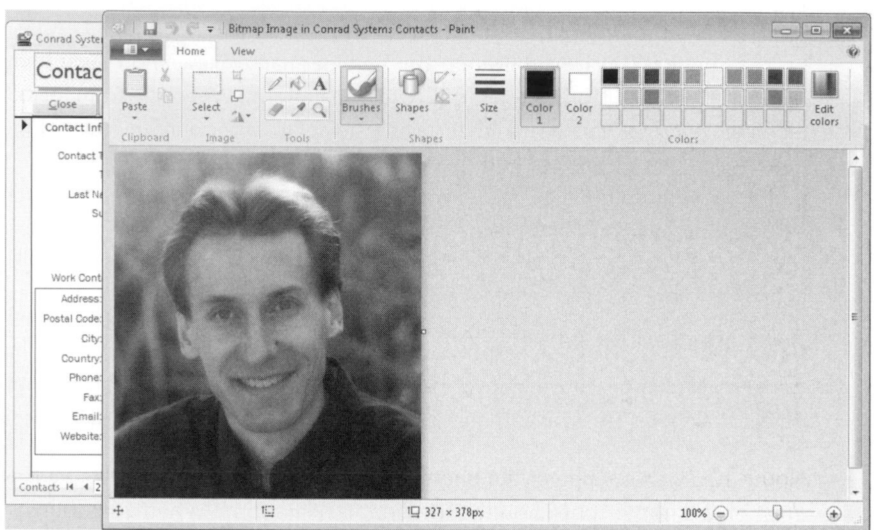

Figure 12-20 The Photo OLE object field from Figure 12-19 is being edited "in place" with its host application.

Command Buttons

Another useful control is the command button, which you can use to link many forms to create a complete database application. Close the Contacts2Upsize.accdb database and return to the Contacts.accdb database. In the Conrad Systems Contacts database, for example, most of the forms are linked to the main switchboard form (frmMain), shown in Figure 12-21, in which the user can click command buttons to start various functions in the application. The advantage of command buttons is really quite simple—they offer an easy way to trigger a macro or a Visual Basic procedure. The procedure might do nothing more than open another form, print a report, or run an action query to update many records in your database. As you'll see when you get to the end of this book, you can build a fairly complex application using forms, reports, macros, and some simple Visual Basic procedures.

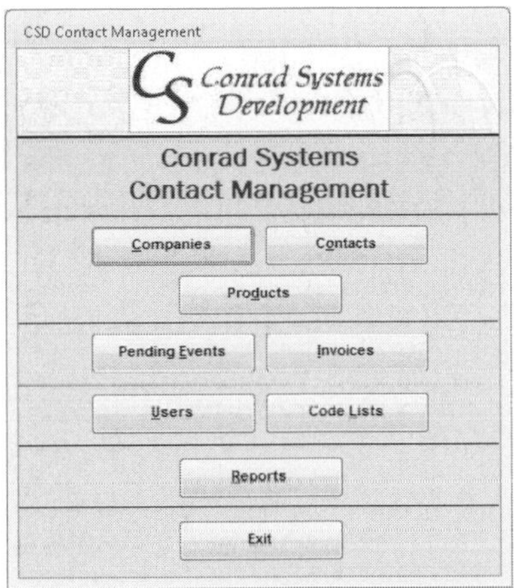

Figure 12-21 The command buttons on the frmMain switchboard form take the user to various parts of the application.

Navigational Control

You've seen examples previously in this chapter of how to display lots of information on one form using multiple-page forms and tab controls. Access 2010 includes a new type of control, called a *navigational control*, to provide an easy way to navigate to different forms and reports in your database. A navigational control provides an interface similar to what you see on websites. To demonstrate a navigation control, close the Contacts.accdb database and then open the BOSS.accdb database. When the database first opens, you'll see a splash form showing copyright information. After a few seconds, the splash form closes and you'll see the main form in the application—frmMainMenu, as shown in Figure 12-22.

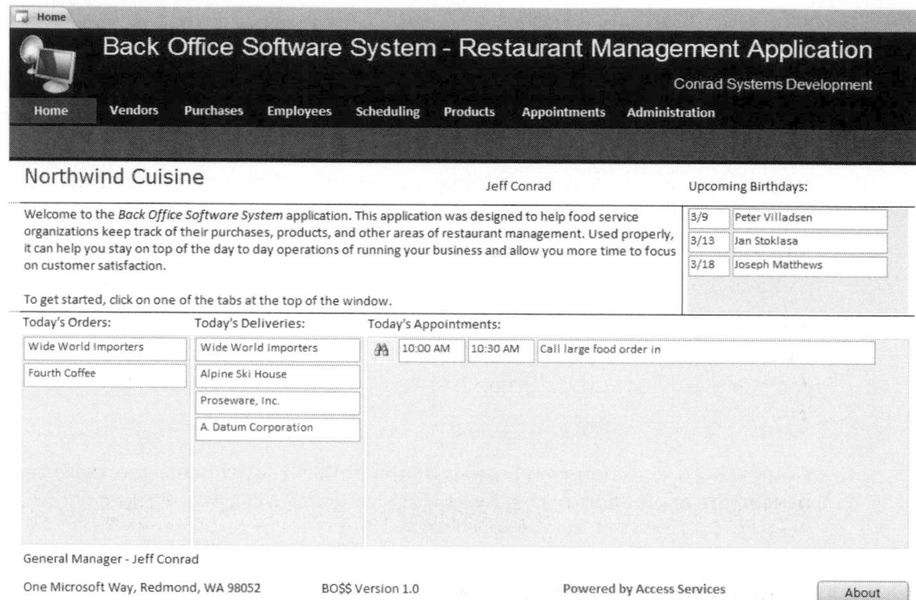

Figure 12-22 The navigational control provides a easy way to navigate through different forms and reports in your database.

At first glance of the frmMainMenu form, you might be thinking this is actually a completely new form type. It might look that way; however, frmMainMenu is essentially just an unbound form—a form not bound to any table or query—with a navigational control on it. The navigation control is a unique control that uses command button and subform functionality together. When you click the different navigational buttons across the top of frmMainMenu, Access unloads and loads a new form or report into the sub-form control beneath the buttons. When frmMainMenu first loads, Access displays the frmHome form in the subform container beneath the navigation buttons. When you click on the other navigational buttons across the top of the form, you'll see different forms and reports displayed in the subform container. You can have second-level navigation buttons that hide and show based on their top-level parent navigation button. Click any navigation button besides Home and you'll notice that Access displays additional navigational buttons just below the top-level navigational buttons. You can also create a navigational control that displays buttons on the left or on the right side of the form, much like navigational elements you see on popular websites. By using a navigation control, you can have an easy method for users of your database to access any areas of your application. You'll learn more about designing forms with navigation controls in Chapter 15.

Web Browser Control

Access 2010 includes another new control called the *web browser control*, which you can use on your database forms. A web browser control displays the content of other web pages directly inside a form. You can use a web browser control to display, for example, a map of an address stored in a table, a video posted on a website, or the content of a Microsoft Office web application hosted on a server running Microsoft SharePoint. To demonstrate a web browser control, click the Employees navigation button on the frmMainMenu in the BOSS.accdb database, previously shown in Figure 12-22. Access displays a list of the employees in this database. Click the Edit button next to Jeff Conrad's name, and Access opens the frmEmployeeDetails form for Jeff's record. Click the Map tab at the top of the form and Access displays a map from the Bing search engine of Jeff's address, as shown in Figure 12-23.

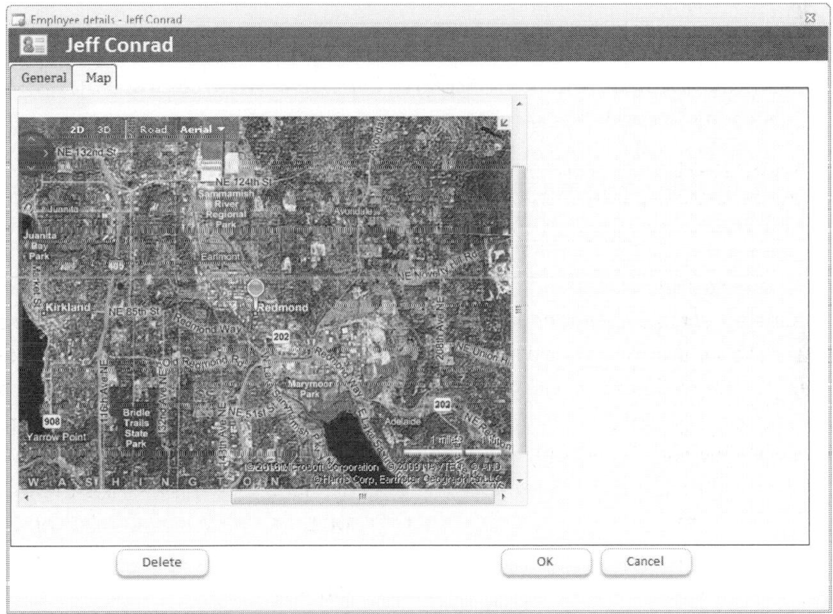

Figure 12-23 The frmEmployeeDetails form displays a map of the employee's address inside the form.

The web browser control on frmEmployeeDetails is bound to a calculated field in the tblEmployees table. The calculated field concatenates the address, city, state, and ZIP code data for each employee, along with a Uniform Resource Locator (URL) to the Bing Maps website. When the form opens, the web browser control makes a call to the Bing Maps site with the completed URL of the employee's address and displays the web page on the frmEmployeeDetails form. If you navigate to a different employee's record, you'll see the web browser control change to display the address of the employee you just navigated to. You can also bind the web browser control to a specific URL, such as Jeff's website at *http://www.AccessJunkie.com*. Whenever a form opens that includes a web browser control to that URL, Access displays the main home page of Jeff's site directly in your Access form. You'll learn more about designing forms with web browser controls in Chapter 15.

TROUBLESHOOTING

Why doesn't my web browser control display anything?

To view the website content displayed in a web browser control in Access, the database must be "trusted." For security reasons, Access needs to know it's OK to make a request to an external website or to an internal website on your local intranet. The simplest way to trust this database is to click the Enable Content button on the Message Bar. You can also go to the Trust Center and mark the folder containing this database as Trusted. Click the File tab on the Backstage view and then click Options. In the left column, choose Trust Center and then click Trust Center Settings. In the Trust Center dialog box, select Trusted Locations in the left column and then click Add New Location. Add the folder containing your database to the Trusted Locations list.

PivotTables and PivotCharts

In Chapter 10, you learned how to create the PivotTable or PivotChart view of a query. You can also build a form that is connected to a table or query and switch to either PivotTable or PivotChart view to define a custom view of the underlying data. To demonstrate this functionality, close the BOSS.accdb web database and then open the Contacts.accdb database again. Look at the ptContactProducts form in the Contacts database, shown in Figure 12-24. This form is designed to open only in PivotTable view or Design view. Note that even though the query on which this form is based is updateable, you cannot update any of the field values via the PivotTable.

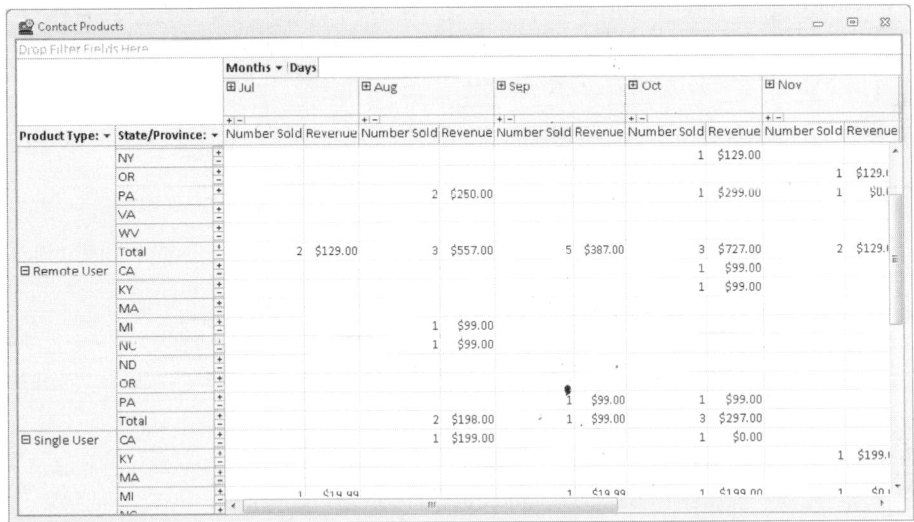

Product Type:	State/Province:	Jul Number Sold	Jul Revenue	Aug Number Sold	Aug Revenue	Sep Number Sold	Sep Revenue	Oct Number Sold	Oct Revenue	Nov Number Sold	Nov Revenue
	NY							1	$129.00		
	OR									1	$129.
	PA			2	$250.00			1	$299.00	1	$0.
	VA										
	WV										
	Total	2	$129.00	3	$557.00	5	$387.00	3	$727.00	2	$129.
⊟ Remote User	CA							1	$99.00		
	KY							1	$99.00		
	MA										
	MI			1	$99.00						
	NC			1	$99.00						
	ND										
	OR										
	PA					1	$99.00	1	$99.00		
	Total			2	$198.00	1	$99.00	3	$297.00		
⊟ Single User	CA			1	$199.00			1	$0.00		
	KY									1	$199.
	MA										
	MI	1	$19.99			1	$19.99	1	$199.00	1	$0.

Figure 12-24 The ptContactProducts form is designed to open in PivotTable view.

PivotCharts can be useful in an application to provide a related graphical representation of data displayed on a form. In the Conrad Systems Contacts sample database, you can find the chtProductSales form that charts sales by product and by month. This form is embedded in a report that displays product details (rptProductSalesByProductWChart) and in a sample form that lets you edit product information while viewing the related past sales data as a chart (frmProductsWithSales). You can see frmProductsWithSales in Figure 12-25.

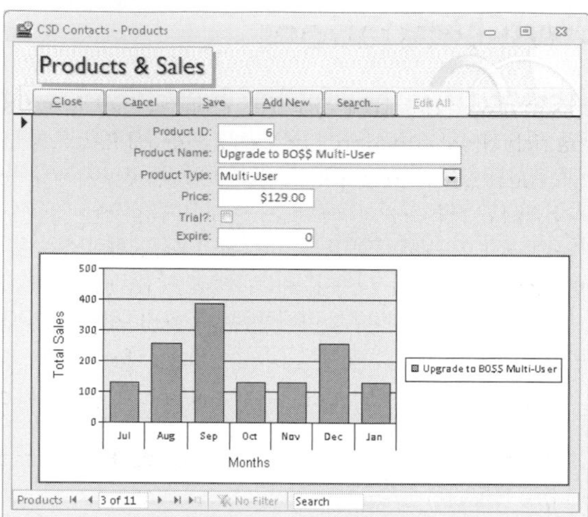

Figure 12-25 This form to edit product data also has an embedded subform in PivotChart view to show related sales information.

Designing a form as a PivotTable or PivotChart has three distinct advantages over performing these functions in queries:

1. You can restrict the views of the form to display the PivotTable, the PivotChart, or both. You can set a default view for a query, but you cannot prevent the user from switching to Datasheet or Design view.

2. You can embed a form designed as a PivotTable or PivotChart in another form or in a report to display related information. You cannot embed a query in a form or report.

3. You can write Visual Basic code behind the form to dynamically modify the PivotTable or PivotChart. You can also restrict the changes a user can make to the table or chart. You cannot write code behind a query.

You'll learn more about designing forms as PivotTables or PivotCharts in Chapter 15.

Understanding Web Form Limitations

When you're creating forms in a web database, you can create client forms and web forms. Client forms support all the rich client functionality such as Visual Basic code, client macro actions, and different form types. Web forms, forms that will display in a web browser, are limited in their functionality and complexity. There are only three form types you can use for web forms—single record forms, continuous forms, and datasheet forms. You can still create split forms, multiple-page forms, PivotTables, and PivotCharts in a web database; however, they will not run in a web browser. Client forms can still run in Access client in a published Access Services application, but if you want to display forms in a web browser for your published application, you'll need to create new web forms in your web database.

Web forms also support fewer types of controls than client forms. For example, web forms do not support option groups, toggle buttons, page breaks, charts, line controls, and rectangle controls. Web forms also do not support Visual Basic code, but you can use web macros to automate your web forms. In the next three chapters, you'll learn not only how to create client forms in client databases, but also web forms in web databases. You'll see examples of the three form types you can create for web forms and learn how to add web-supported controls to your web forms.

Moving Around on Forms and Working with Data

The rest of this chapter shows you how to move around on and work with data in the various types of forms discussed earlier in the chapter.

Viewing Data

Moving around on a form is similar to moving around in a datasheet, but there are a few subtle differences between forms and datasheets (usually having to do with how a form was designed) that determine how a form works with data. You can use the frmContactsPlain form in the Conrad Systems Contacts database (which is a copy of frmContacts without custom ribbons) to explore the ways in which forms work.

First, if necessary, open the Conrad Systems Contacts database. Next, click the Navigation Pane menu, click Object Type under Navigate To Category, and then click Forms under Filter By Group. Select the frmContactsPlain form, right-click the form name, and click the Open command on the shortcut menu to see the form shown in Figure 12-26.

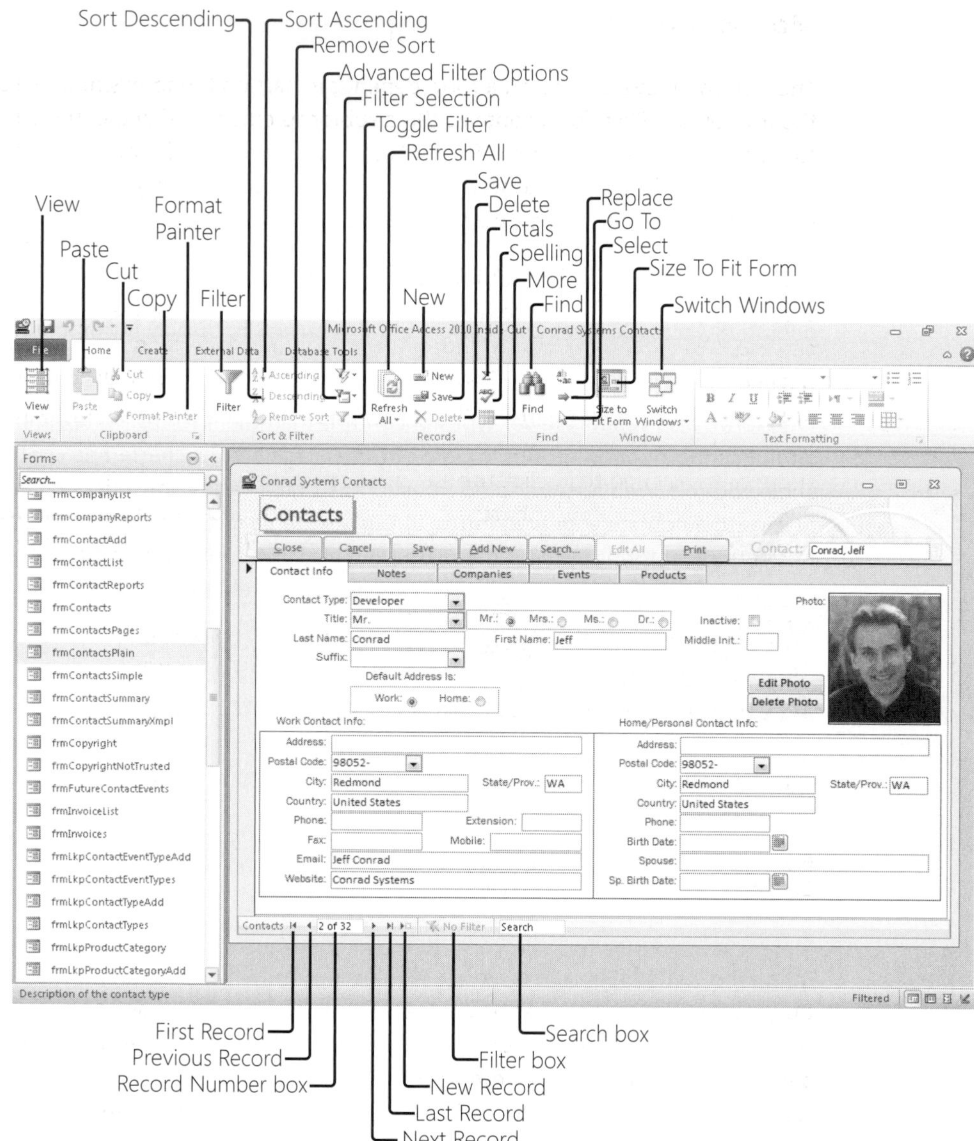

Figure 12-26 You can use the frmContactsPlain form in the Conrad Systems Contacts database to explore moving around on a form.

Moving Around

The way you move around on a form depends in part on the form's design. For example, the frmContactsPlain form contains three subforms embedded within the tab control—one for contact companies, another for contact events, and a third for contact products. The two boxes you see on the Contact Info tab aren't subforms—they're rectangle controls that we added to enhance the grouping of the main detail fields.

The fsubContactEventsPlain subform on the Events tab is a continuous form. You move around on it in ways similar to how you move around in a datasheet. On this subform, you can use the vertical scroll bar to move the display up or down. You can toggle the subform between two different views—Form view (its current state) and Datasheet view. If you want to see the Datasheet view of the fsubContactEventsPlain subform, right-click in any of the fields on the subform (to ensure that the focus is on the subform), click Subform on the shortcut menu, and then click the Datasheet command. (Notice that the PivotTable and PivotChart options on the shortcut menu appear dimmed—we have disallowed those views in the design of this subform.) The fsubContactEvents subform will now look like Figure 12-27.

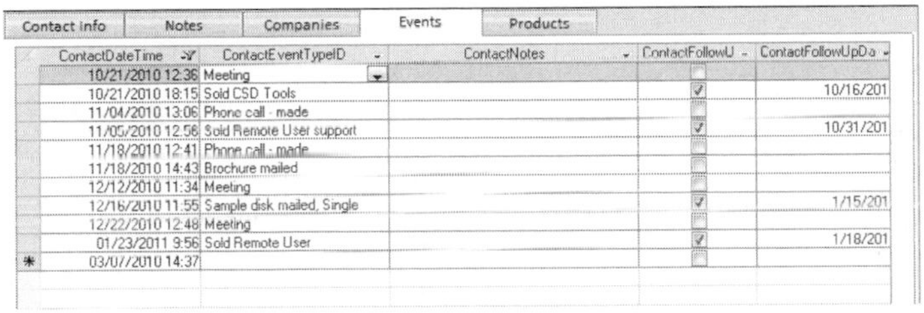

Figure 12-27 You can display the fsubContactEventsPlain subform in Datasheet view on the Events tab of the frmContactsPlain form.

In the frmContactsPlain form, you view different contact records by using the navigation buttons and Record Number box at the bottom of the form. To see the next contact, use the main form's navigation buttons. To see different companies, events, or products for a particular contact, use the vertical scroll bar within the subform or the navigation buttons within the subform window. Note that you can also design a subform without its own Record Number box and navigation buttons. You might want to do this if you think the set of navigation buttons will be confusing to your users.

You can also click the Go To command in the Find group on the Home tab on the ribbon to move to the first, last, next, or previous record in the main form or in the subform. You can select any field in the form by clicking anywhere in that field. To use the Go To command, you must first move to the form or the subform containing those records you want to view.

Keyboard Shortcuts

If you're typing new data, you might find it easier to use the keyboard rather than the mouse to move around on a form. Some of the keyboard shortcuts you can use with forms are listed in Table 12-1 (for moving around in fields and records) and in Table 12-2 (for actions in a list box or in a combo box). Note that a form that edits data can be in one of two modes: Edit mode or Navigation mode. You're in *Edit mode* on a form when you can see a flashing insertion point in the current field. To enter *Navigation mode*, tab to the next field or press the F2 key to select the current field. As you can see in the following tables, some keyboard shortcuts work differently depending on the mode. Other keyboard shortcuts work in only one mode or the other.

Table 12-1 Keyboard Shortcuts for Fields and Records

Key(s)	Movement in Fields and Records
Tab	Moves to the next field.
Shift+Tab	Moves to the previous field.
Home	In Navigation mode, moves to the first field of the current record. In Edit mode, moves to the beginning of the current field.
End	In Navigation mode, moves to the last field of the current record. In Edit mode, moves to the end of the current field.
Ctrl+Page Up	Moves to the current field of the previous record.
Ctrl+Page Down	Moves to the current field of the next record.
Ctrl+Up Arrow	In Navigation mode, moves to the current field of the first record. In Edit mode, moves to the beginning of the current field.
Ctrl+Down Arrow	In Navigation mode, moves to the current field of the last record. In Edit mode, moves to the end of the current field.
Ctrl+Home	In Navigation mode, moves to the first field of the first record. In Edit mode, moves to the beginning of the current field.
Ctrl+End	In Navigation mode, moves to the last field of the last record. In Edit mode, moves to the end of the current field.
Ctrl+Tab	If in a subform, moves to the next field in the main form. If the subform is the last field in the tab sequence in the main form, moves to the first field in the next main record. If the focus is on a field on a tab, moves the focus to the first field in the tab order on the next tab. If the focus is on a subform within a tab, moves the focus to the tab. If the subform within the tab is the last control on the form, moves the focus to the tab on the next record. If the focus is on a tab (not a field within the tab), cycles forward through the tabs.

Key(s)	Movement in Fields and Records
Ctrl+Shift+Tab	If in a subform, moves to the previous field in the main form. If the subform is the first field in tab sequence in the main form, moves to the last field in the next main record. If the focus is on a field on a tab, moves the focus to the first field in the tab order on the previous tab. If the focus is on a subform within a tab, moves the focus to the tab. If the subform within the tab is the first control on the form, moves the focus to the tab on the previous record. If the focus is on a tab (not a field within the tab), cycles backward through the tabs.
Ctrl+Shift+Home	In Navigation mode, moves to the first field in the record. When in Navigation mode in a field on a tab, moves the focus to the tab. When the focus is on a tab (not a field within the tab), moves to the first tab on the tab control. In Edit mode, selects all characters from the current insertion point to the beginning of the field.
Ctrl+Shift+End	In Navigation mode, moves to the last field in the record. When in Navigation mode in a field on a tab, moves the focus to the tab. When the focus is on a tab (not a field within the tab), moves to the last tab on the tab control. In Edit mode, selects all characters from the current insertion point to the end of the field.
Alt+F5	Moves to the Record Number box.
Enter	Depends on your settings for the Move After Enter option in the Editing section of the Advanced category in the Access Options dialog box.
Shift+Enter	Saves the current record.

Table 12-2 Keyboard Shortcuts for a List Box or a Combo Box

Key(s)	Action in a List Box or a Combo Box
F4 or Alt+Down Arrow	Opens or closes a combo box or a drop-down list box.
Down Arrow	Moves down one line in a list box or in a combo box when the list is open.
Up Arrow	Moves up one line in a list box or in a combo box when the list is open.
Page Down	Moves down to next group of lines.
Page Up	Moves up to next group of lines.
Tab	Exits the box and moves to the next field.

Adding Records and Changing Data

You'll probably design most forms so that you can insert new records, change field values, or delete records in Form view or in Datasheet view. The following sections explain procedures for adding new records and changing data.

Adding a New Record

The procedure for entering a new record varies depending on the design of the form. With a form that's been designed for data entry only, you open the form and enter data in the (usually empty) data fields. Sometimes forms of this type open with default values in the fields or with data entered by a macro or Visual Basic procedure. In the Conrad Systems Contacts application, frmCompanyAdd and frmContactAdd are two examples of forms that open in Data Entry mode. You can see frmContactAdd in Figure 12-28.

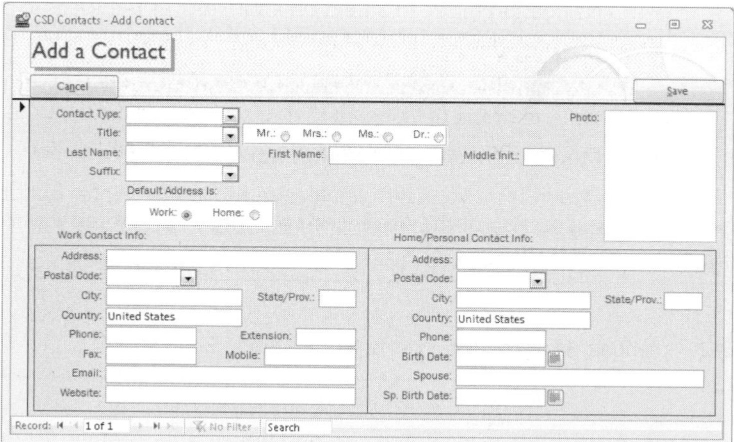

Figure 12-28 The frmContactAdd form opens in Data Entry mode.

When you're editing company information in frmCompanies and need to enter a new contact that doesn't exist, the application opens this form to allow you to fill in the required information for the new contact. After you save the record, the new contact becomes available to assign to the company displayed in frmCompanies.

You'll normally create a form that allows you to display and edit data and also add new records. The frmContactsPlain form is this type of form. On this form, you can go to a new record in several ways. Open the frmContactsPlain form and try the following:

- Click the Last Record button on the navigation bar at the bottom of the Form window, and then click Next Record.
- Click the New Record button on the navigation bar at the bottom of the form.
- Click Go To in the Find group on the Home tab, and then click New on the submenu.
- Click the New button in the Records group on the Home tab.
- Press Ctrl+Plus Sign.
- Click the Add New command button in the header area of the form. (This last method puts the form into Data Entry mode, something you cannot do from any standard command on the ribbon.)

The first five methods take you to the empty record at the end of the recordset being edited by this form. This is similar to going to the blank row at the end of a table or query datasheet to begin entering data for a new row. The last method shifts the form into Data Entry mode, as shown in Figure 12-29. Notice that there now appears to be only one record—the new record you're about to enter—and that record displays the default value specified for Country even though you haven't started to enter any data yet.

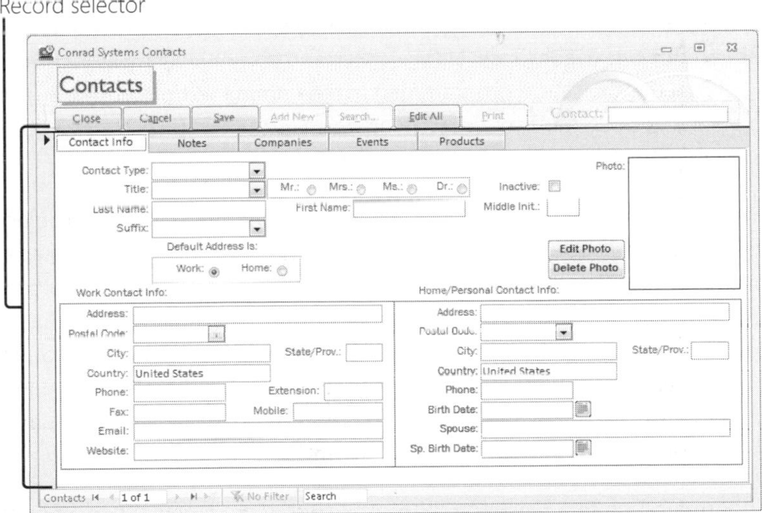

Figure 12-29 When you click the Add New command button in the header of the frmContactsPlain form, Access displays the form in Data Entry mode.

Access places the insertion point in the first field when you start a new record. As soon as you begin typing, Access changes the indicator on the record selector (if your form shows the record selector) to a pencil icon to indicate that updates are in progress. Press Tab to move to the next field.

> **Note**
>
> **The frmContactsPlain form provides an Edit All button on the form to return to normal data display if you clicked the Add New button to enter Data Entry mode.**

If you violate a field's validation rule, Access notifies you as soon as you attempt to leave the field. You must provide a correct value before you can move to another field. Press Shift+Enter in any field in the record or press Tab in the last field in the record to save your new record in the table. If the data you enter violates a table validation rule, Access displays an error message and does not save the record. If you want to cancel a new record, press Escape twice. (There's also a Cancel button on frmContactsPlain that clears your edits and closes the form.)

If you're adding a new record in a form that has an Attachment or OLE Object data type, you'll encounter a special situation. When you tab to the Photo attachment control, you'll notice that you can't type anything in it. This is because the field in the underlying table is an Attachment data type, and this control is an attachment. In fact, when the focus is in this control and you happen to type one of the keyboard navigation letters on one of the command buttons (C for Close, N for Cancel, and so on), you'll "click" that command button and execute the action programmed in the command button. You'll notice this same problem if you open the frmContactsPlain form in the Contacts2Upsize.accdb database and tab into the Photo bound object frame control.

To enter data in this type of field in a new record, you must create the object in another application before you can store the data in Access. To insert a file in an attachment field, follow the instructions given earlier to right-click the attachment control and click Manage Attachments on the shortcut menu. Click Add in the Attachments dialog box, shown in Figure 12-17 on page 752, to open the Choose File dialog box, where you can select the file that you want to store in the attachment field.

If you want to see how to work with an OLE Object field, you'll have to close the Contacts.accdb database and reopen the Contacts2Upsize.accdb database. Open the frmContactsPlain form and go to a new record. To create and store a new file in a bound object frame, right-click the bound object frame control and click the Insert Object command on the shortcut menu. Access displays the Microsoft Access dialog box, shown in Figure 12-30. To create a new object, select the object type you want (in this case, Bitmap Image), and click OK. Access starts the application that's defined in the Windows registry as the default application for this type of data (for bitmaps, usually the Paint application).

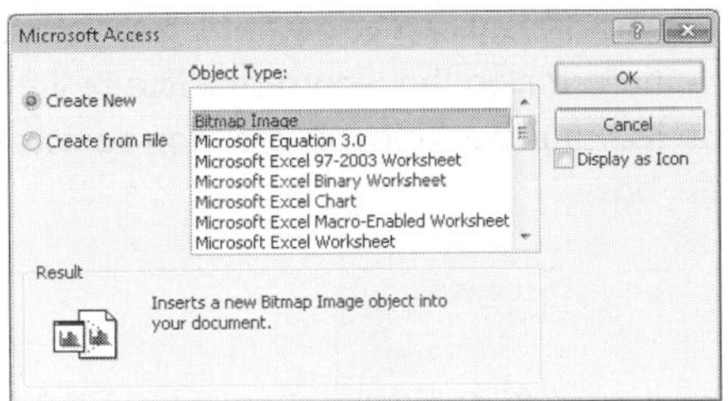

Figure 12-30 The Microsoft Access dialog box allows you to enter data into an OLE object field.

If you have an appropriate file available to copy into the OLE object field in Access, select the Create From File option in the Microsoft Access dialog box. Access replaces the Object Type list with a File box where you can enter the path name and file name, as shown in Figure 12-31. You can click Browse to open the Browse dialog box, which lets you search for the file you want. After you select a file, you can select the Link check box to create an active link between the copy of the object in Access and the actual file. If you do so, whenever you change the file, the linked object in Access will also change. Select the Display As Icon check box to display the application icon instead of the picture in the bound object frame. Your picture will still be stored or linked in your table even when you choose to display the icon.

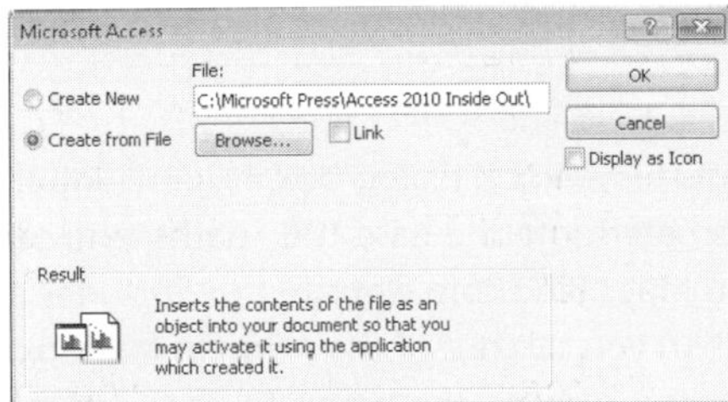

Figure 12-31 You can insert an object from a file using the Create From File option in the Microsoft Access dialog box.

If you opened the Contacts2Upsize.accdb database to experiment with editing in a bound object frame, close it and reopen the Contacts.accdb database.

The frmContactsPlain form also includes two text boxes that let you specify the email address or the website address of the contact. To add or edit a hyperlink, you can tab to the hyperlink field (remember that if the link field contains a valid link, clicking in it activates the link!), right-click the link field, click Hyperlink on the shortcut menu, and then click Edit Hyperlink on the submenu. Access displays the dialog box, shown in Figure 12-32, which lets you edit or define the link.

You can enter the descriptor in the Text To Display box at the top. We clicked the ScreenTip button to open the Set Hyperlink ScreenTip dialog box you see in Figure 12-32. The ScreenTip appears when you rest your mouse pointer on the hyperlink. You can type the document address directly into the Address box.

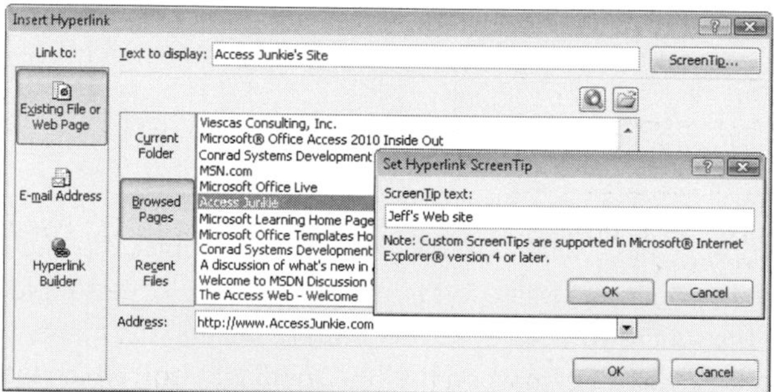

Figure 12-32 The Insert Hyperlink dialog box shows a link to the AccessJunkie.com website.

The second option on the left in the Insert Hyperlink dialog box, E-Mail Address, lets you enter an email address or choose from a list of recently used addresses. This generates a Mailto: hyperlink that will invoke your email program and start a new email message to the address you specify here. You can also optionally enter Subject text for the new email, which adds a question mark after the email address followed by the subject in the stored hyperlink.

The third option on the left in the Insert Hyperlink dialog box, Hyperlink Builder, helps break down a URL that includes parameters into the base URL, paths, and parameters. In Figure 12-33, we copied a URL to the Maps.Bing.com website that includes address information into the Address text box. When you tab out of the Address text box, Access breaks down the various parts of the URL. Access displays the base URL in the Base URL text box, any paths in the Paths list box, and any parameters in the Parameters list box. In Figure 12-33, you can see Access displays the name and value of each parameter in the Parameters list box. You can type in a new value in the list box and Access saves the information into the completed URL. This feature is especially helpful when building complex URLs that include different parameters.

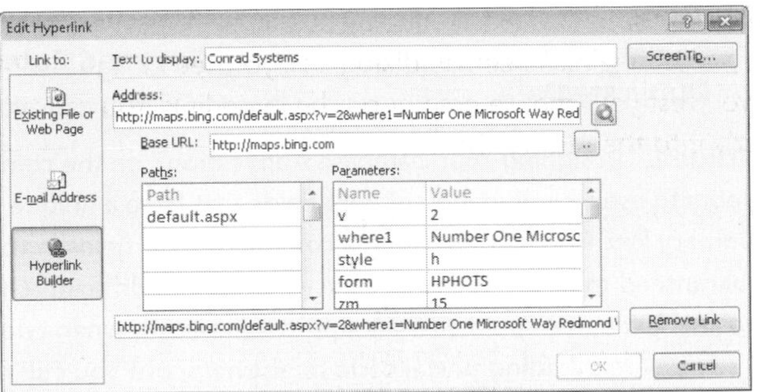

Figure 12-33 Access can break down a URL into its various parts using the Hyperlink Builder on the Edit Hyperlink dialog box.

Click OK to save your link. See "Working with Hyperlinks," on page 603, for more details and cautions about hyperlinks.

Try adding a new record by using the frmContactsPlain form. Open the form, click the Go To command in the Find group on the Home tab, and click New on the submenu. You should see a screen similar to the one shown earlier in Figure 12-29. Make any selection you like from the Contact Type drop-down list. Because this field is a Multi-Value Lookup Field, you can select more than one contact type. Click the OK button at the bottom of the list when you have finished selecting one or more contact types. You must enter at least a last name (the only required field in tblContacts). Tab to the Photo field and follow the procedure discussed previously in the "Attachment Controls" section to add a new picture attachment to this record. You can find several appropriately sized bitmap pictures of contacts in the Pictures subfolder on the companion CD.

INSIDE OUT Dealing with AutoNumber Primary Keys and Potentially Duplicate Data

As discussed in Article 1, "Designing Your Database Application," on the companion CD, it's usually preferable to use a combination of data fields that have a unique value in each row to create a primary key. However, choosing a combination of fields in tblContacts that would be guaranteed to be unique in all rows could prove difficult. The combination of first name and last name could easily result in a duplicate when two different people have the same name. Adding postal code might help, but you still might run into two people named *John Smith* who live in the same area.

The simple solution for tables in an Access 2010 desktop database is to use an AutoNumber field as the primary key. In fact, in the Conrad Systems Contacts database, tblCompanies, tblContacts, tblInvoices, and tblProducts all use an AutoNumber field for the primary key. This guarantees that all rows will have a unique primary key, but it doesn't guard against duplicate records—entering the same person twice.

To avoid potential duplicates, you should consider writing Visual Basic code or creating a data macro in the Before Change table event to check a new row just before Access saves it. We included some simple Visual Basic code to perform a Soundex check on the last name in both frmContacts and frmContactsPlain. (Soundex is an algorithm created by the United States National Archive and Records Administration to generate a code from a name to identify names that sound alike.) If you try to add a person in a new row with the last name *Camred*, you'll see a warning about a potential duplicate (*Conrad*, for example) and a list of all similar names. The warning allows you to cancel saving the new row. You can learn how this code works in Chapter 25.

One last point about using AutoNumber: As soon as you begin to enter new data in a table that has an AutoNumber field, Access assigns a new number to that field. If you decide to cancel the new record before saving it, Access won't reuse this AutoNumber value. Access does this to ensure that multiple users sharing a database don't get the same value for a new table row. So, if you want primary key numbers to remain consecutive, you should not use AutoNumber.

To begin adding some events for your new contact, click the Events tab to reveal the appropriate subform. Note that when you click in the subform, Access saves the contact data you entered in the main form. Access does this to ensure that it can create a link between the new record in the main form and any record you might create in the subform. (The new contact ID has to be saved in the main form before you can create related contact category records in a subform.)

Select an event type, as shown in Figure 12-34, or type a new one. As soon as you select an event type, Access automatically fills in the Date/Time field with the current date and time on your computer. You can correct this value or click the small calendar button to open a calendar form to set a new date and time graphically. Select an event type, as shown in Figure 12-34, or type a new one. If you enter an event type that isn't already defined, code behind the form prompts you to ask whether you want to add a new event type. If you click Yes, you'll see a dialog form open to allow you to enter the details for your new event type.

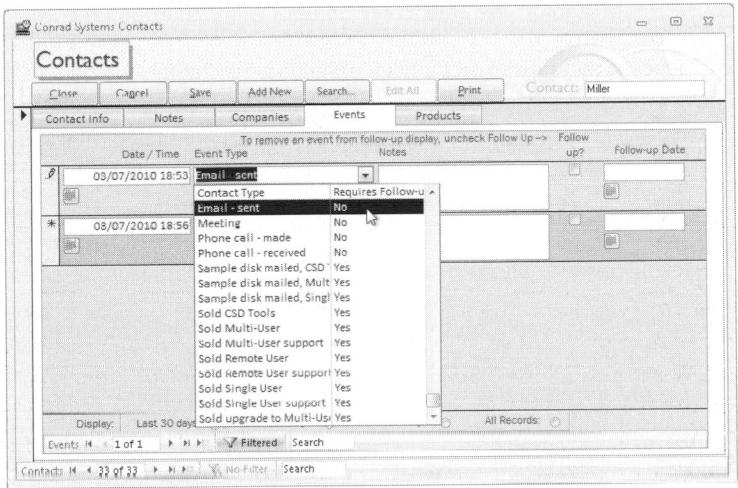

Figure 12-34 You can add a new contact event record on the Events tab in the frmContactsPlain form.

When you press Tab in the last field or press Shift+Enter in any field, Access adds the new event for you. Access also inserts the information required to link the record in the main form and the new record in the subform. Access fetches the ContactID from the record in the outer form and creates the new record in the tblContactEvents table with the related ContactID value. You can't see or edit the ContactID field on either the outer form or the subform. You don't need to see it in the outer form because ContactID in tblContacts is an AutoNumber field. Because Access automatically copies the value for you for new rows in the subform, you don't need to see it there, either.

You can define very functional forms using combo boxes, tab controls, and subforms. To really make your application user-friendly, you need to further automate your forms with macros or Visual Basic. For details about how many of the forms in the sample databases are automated with Visual Basic, see Chapter 25.

Changing and Deleting Data

If your form permits updates, you can easily change or delete existing data in the underlying table or query. If you design the form to be used in Datasheet view, you can use the techniques from Chapter 9, "Creating and Working with Simple Queries," to work with your data.

In Form view, your data might appear in one of several formats. If you design the form as a single form, you can see the data for only one record at a time. If you design the form as a continuous form, you might be able to see data for more than one record at a time.

As with datasheets, you must select a field in the form to change the data in the field. To select a field, either tab to the field or click in the field with the mouse. (Remember, if the field contains a hyperlink, clicking in it will activate the link. To edit a hyperlink, either tab to the field or right-click the field to open the shortcut menu, from which you can click commands to edit the hyperlink.) After you select a field, you can change the data in it by using the same techniques you used for working with data in a datasheet. You can type over individual characters, replace a sequence of characters, or copy and paste data from one field to another.

You might find that you can't tab to or select some fields in a form. When you design a form, you can set the properties of the controls on the form so that a user can't select the control. These properties prevent users from changing fields that you don't want updated, such as calculated values or fields from the one side of a query. You can also set the tab order to control the sequence of field selection when you use Tab or Shift+Tab to move around on the form. See Chapter 14, "Customizing a Form," for details.

Deleting a record in a single form or in a continuous form is different from deleting a record in a datasheet. First, you must select the record as you would select a record in a datasheet. If the form is designed with record selectors, simply click the record selector to select the record. If the form does not have record selectors, click the Select command in the Find group on the Home tab, and then click Select on the menu. To delete a selected record, press the Delete key or click the arrow next to the Delete command in the Records group on the Home tab, and then click Delete Record. You can also click the Delete Record command on this same menu to delete the current record without first having to select it.

When a record you're trying to delete contains related records in other tables, you will see an error message unless the relationship defined between the tables tells access to cascade delete the related fields and records. See Chapter 4 for details about defining relationships between tables. In frmContacts and frmContactsPlain in the Conrad Systems Contacts application, Visual Basic code behind the forms checks to see if dependent rows exist in other tables. This code issues a custom error message, shown in Figure 12-35, that gives you specific information about the problem. (The standard Access error message is not very user-friendly.) Rather than automatically delete dependent records (you might have asked to delete the contact record in error), the application requires you to specifically go to the tabs that show the related records and delete all these records first. You can see how this code works in Chapter 26.

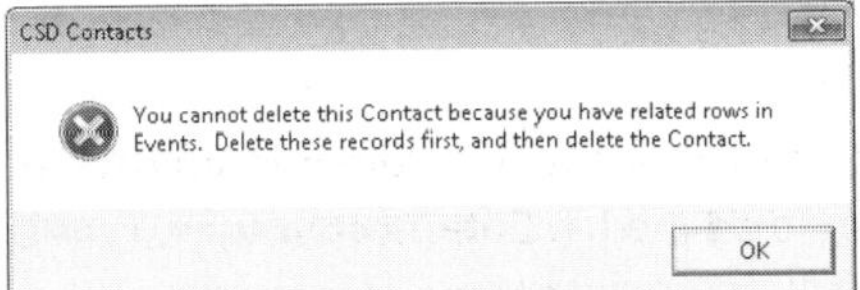

Figure 12-35 The Conrad Systems Contacts application shows you a custom error message when you attempt to delete a contact that has dependent records in other tables.

Searching for and Sorting Data

When you use forms to display and edit your data, you can search for data or sort it in a new order in much the same way that you search for and sort data in datasheets. (See Chapter 9.) The following sections show you how to use some of the form filter features to search for data in a form or use the quick sort commands to reorder your data.

Performing a Simple Search

You can use the Find feature of Access 2010 in a form exactly as you would in a datasheet. Open the frmContactsPlain form if you closed it, select the field you want to search, and then click the Find command in the Find group on the Home tab to open the Find And Replace dialog box, as shown in Figure 12-36. You can enter search criteria exactly as you would for a datasheet. Note that in a form, you can also perform a search on any control that you can select, including controls that display calculated values.

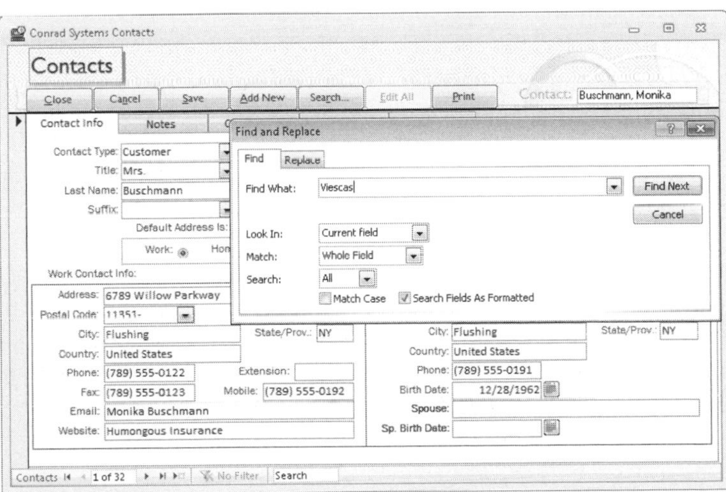

Figure 12-36 You can use the Find And Replace dialog box to search your records for specific information.

In Figure 12-36, we clicked inside the Last Name field and then opened the Find And Replace dialog box. By default, the Look In list in the Find And Replace dialog box remembers what you selected the last time you used Find. If you select Current Document from the Look In list, Access will search through all the fields in this form for your criterion. Type the word **Viescas** in the Find What box, and make sure you select Current Field from the Look In list to search through only the Last Name field.

In the Match list, you can ask Access to search Any Part Of Field, Whole Field, or Start Of Field. When you select Any Part Of Field, Access looks for the characters you type in the Find What box anywhere within the field or fields you specified to search. If you select Whole Field, what you type in the Find What box must exactly match the contents of the field. When you select Start Of Field, the characters you type in the Find What box must be at the beginning of the field, but any or no characters can appear in the field after that.

By default, Access searches all records from the beginning of the recordset (the first record displayed in the form) unless you select either Up or Down in the Search list to search up or down from the current record position. Select the Match Case check box if you want to find text that exactly matches the uppercase and lowercase letters you typed. By default, Access is case-insensitive unless you select this check box.

You can select the Search Fields As Formatted check box if you need to search the data as it is displayed rather than as it is stored by Access. Although searching this way is slower, you should select this check box if you are searching a Date/Time field. You should also probably select this check box when searching any field that has a format or input mask applied—such as the postal code and phone number fields in this sample form. For example, if you're searching a date field for dates in January, you can specify ***-Jan-*** if the field is formatted as Medium Date and you select the Search Fields As Formatted check box. You might also want to select this check box when searching a Yes/No field for Yes because any value except 0 is a valid indicator of Yes. Clear this check box to improve performance when searching a simple text or numeric field.

After selecting the options you want, click Find Next. Access proceeds to search through the last names in the form's recordset for the value *Viescas*, and it finds John's record. Click Find Next to continue searching from the current record. Each time you click Find Next again, Access moves to the next value it finds. When Access can find no additional records (either by searching up to the first record when you select Up in the Search list or by searching to the last record when you select Down or All), it opens a message box to inform you that it has completed the search. Click OK to dismiss the message box and return to the Find And Replace dialog box. Click Cancel to close the dialog box.

After you've established search criteria in the Find And Replace dialog box, you can press Shift+F4 to execute the search from the current record without having to open the dialog box again.

Using the Search Box

Access 2010 includes a Search box on the record navigation bar at the bottom of the form window, as shown in Figure 12-37. The Search box functions similarly to the Find And Replace dialog box discussed previously. Unlike the Find And Replace dialog box, the Search box does not give you any choices as to what fields to search in, what part of a string to match, or whether to match the string case. When you type something in the Search box, Access immediately begins to search through all fields in the form for the sequence of characters you enter. The characters you type can appear anywhere in the field, and Access performs the match "as formatted." For example, if you type **/196** in the Search box, you're likely to find the first person whose birthday is in the 1960s.

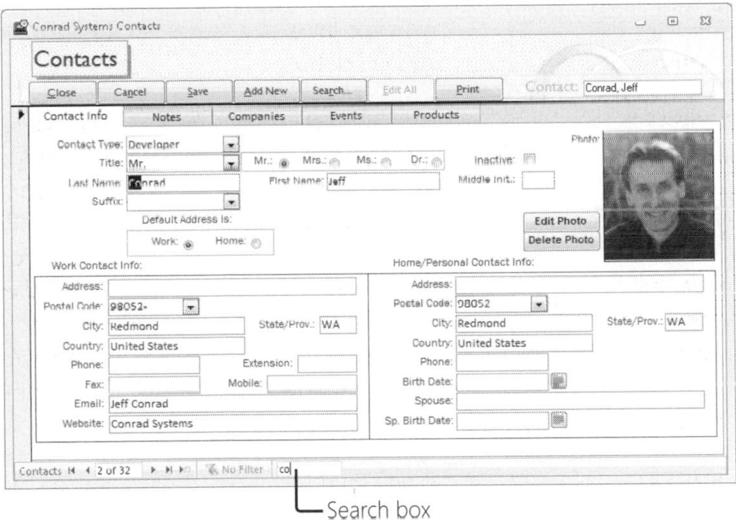

Figure 12-37 You can also use the Search box to search through your form records.

Move to the first record in the frmContactsPlain form and type the letter **c** in the Search box. Notice that Access stays on the first record and highlights the letter C of the word Customer in the Contact Type field. Now type the letter **o** after the letter c and observe that Access moves the focus to the Last Name field on the second record and highlights the letters Co in the name Conrad, as shown previously in Figure 12-37. To clear your search criteria, highlight all the text in the Search box and press Delete or use the Backspace key to remove the text.

Performing a Quick Sort on a Form Field

As you can with a datasheet, you can select just about any control that contains data from the underlying recordset and click the Ascending or Descending button in the Sort & Filter group on the Home tab to reorder the records you see, based on the selected field. If you want to perform a quick sort, open the frmContactsPlain form, click in the Postal Code field in the form under Work Contact Info, and then click the Descending button in the Sort & Filter group on the Home tab. The contact with the highest postal code is displayed first.

Adding a Filter to a Form

One of the most powerful features of Access 2010 is its ability to further restrict or sort the information displayed in the form without your having to create a new query. This restriction is accomplished with a filter that you define while you're using the form. When you apply the filter, you see only the data that matches the criteria you entered.

As with datasheets, you can define a filter using Filter By Selection, Filter By Form, or the Advanced Filter definition facility. Open the frmProducts form, click the Advanced button in the Sort & Filter group on the Record Navigation tab, and click Filter By Form on the menu. (This form uses a custom ribbon so you'll find the Sort & Filter group on the custom Record Navigation Ribbon tab.) Access adds features to the form to let you enter filter criteria, as shown in Figure 12-38. In this example, we're looking for all products where the product type is Single-User and the Trial field is True. You'll see that you can click the arrow to the right of each field to display a list that contains all the values for that field currently in the database. If your database contains many thousands of rows, Access might not show the list if the field has more than several hundred unique values—it would take an unacceptably long time to retrieve the entire list. When the list is too long, Access gives you simple Is Null and Is Not Null choices instead. You can also type your own criteria into a field.

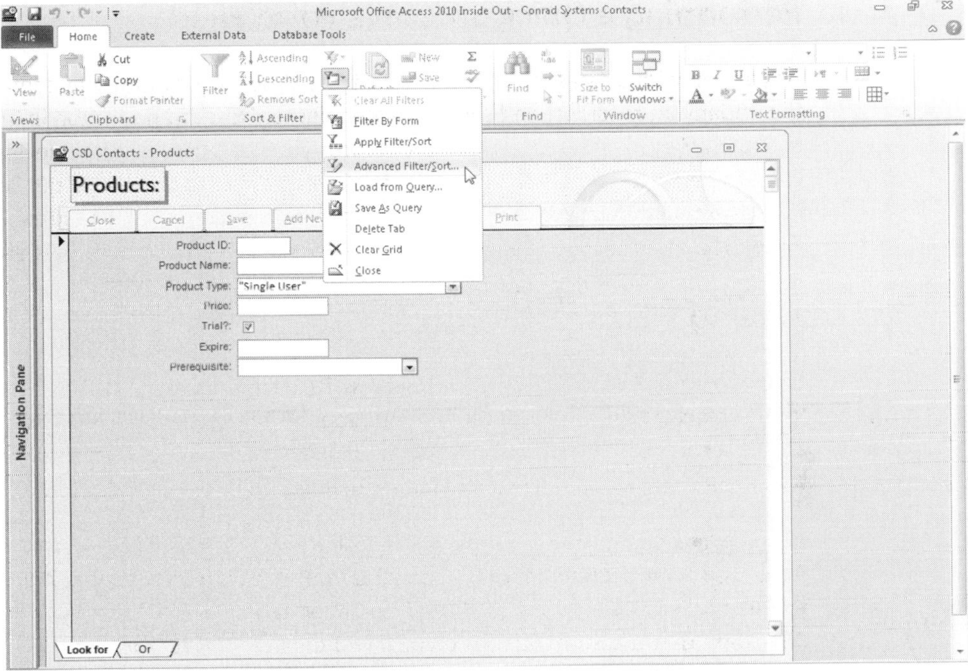

Figure 12-38 Enter filter criteria for the frmProducts form in the Filter By Form window.

As you can with datasheets, you can enter one set of criteria and then click an Or tab at the bottom of the blank form to enter additional criteria. If you don't like some of the criteria you've entered, click the Advanced button in the Sort & Filter group of the Home tab, and then click Clear Grid to start over. Click the Toggle Filter button in the Sort & Filter group to filter your records. Click the Clear All Filters command on this menu to exit the Filter By Form window without applying the new filter. Note that if you specify criteria on a subform, Access applies the filter only for records related to the record currently displayed on the main form.

To turn off the filter, click the Toggle Filter button in the Sort & Filter group on the Home tab. To see the filter definition, click the Advanced button in the Sort & Filter group and then click Advanced Filter/Sort on the submenu. After you apply the filter, shown in Figure 12-38, and do an ascending quick sort on the ProductName field, the Advanced Filter/Sort window should look something like Figure 12-39.

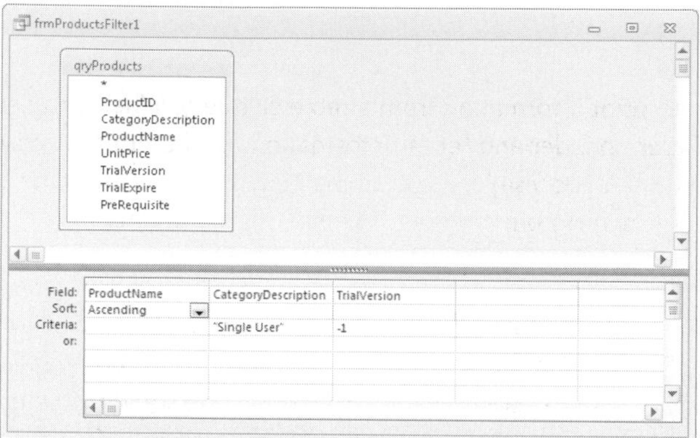

Figure 12-39 In the Advanced Filter/Sort window for the frmProducts form, you can see criteria previously entered using the Filter By Form command.

Note

If you use the Sort Ascending or Sort Descending button, you'll discover that this "quick sort" uses the form's filter definition to create the sorting criteria. For example, if you do a quick sort to arrange products in descending order by product name, you'll find the ProductName field in the form filter with the Sort row set to Descending when you click Advanced Filter/Sort on the Advanced submenu in the Sort & Filter group on the Home tab.

If you often use the same filter with your form, you can save the filter as a query and give it a name. Open the Advanced Filter/Sort window and create the filter. Click the Advanced command in the Sort & Filter group on the Home tab, click the Save As Query command, and then type a name for the query when Access prompts you.

You can load an existing query definition to use as a filter. Click Advanced in the Sort & Filter group on the Home tab and click Load From Query when you're in the Filter By Form window. Access presents a list of valid select queries (those that are based on the same table or tables as the form you're using).

Printing Forms

You can use a form to print information from a table or query. When you design the form, you can specify different header and footer information for the printed version. You can also specify which controls are visible. For example, you might define some gridlines that are visible on the printed form but are not displayed on the screen.

An interesting form to print in the Conrad Systems Contacts database is the frmContactSummaryXmpl form. Open the form, click the File tab on the Backstage view, click Print, and then click Print Preview. On the Print Preview tab, click Zoom and scroll to the top of the first page. You should see a screen that looks like the one shown in Figure 12-40. Notice that the form footer that you saw earlier in Figure 12-1 (on page 739) does not appear in the printed version. In fact, this form has one set of headers and footers designed for printing and another set for viewing the form on the screen.

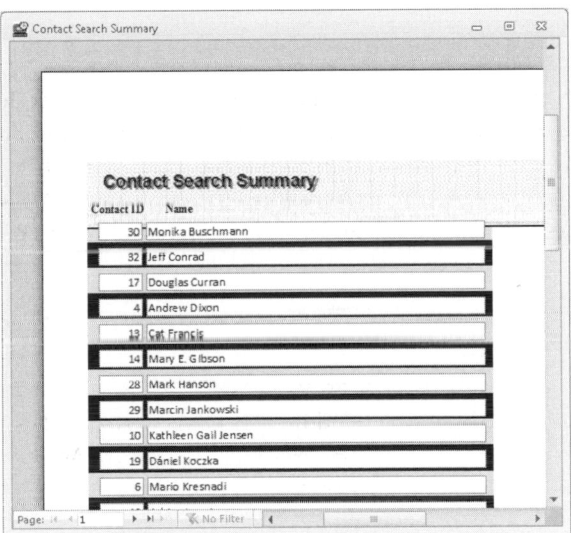

Figure 12-40 When you view the frmContactSummaryXmpl form in Print Preview, you see a different set of headers and footers.

You can use the scroll bars to move around on the page. Use the Page Number box in the lower-left corner of the Print Preview window in the same way that you use the Record Number box on a form or in a datasheet—type a page number into the Number box and then press Enter. Click Zoom again to see the entire page on the screen.

Click the Margins command in the Page Size group on the Print Preview tab to set top, bottom, left, and right margins. Click the Page Setup button in the same Page Layout group to set additional options. Access displays the Page Setup dialog box, in which you can customize the way the form prints. Click the Page tab in the Page Setup dialog box (shown in Figure 12-41) to select Portrait or Landscape orientation, the paper size and source, and the printer. Access will store these specifications with the definition of your form.

Figure 12-41 The Page tab of the Page Setup dialog box for forms includes several page options.

Click the Columns tab of the Page Setup dialog box to see additional options, as shown in Figure 12-42. We'll explore the Columns options in detail in Chapter 16, "Using Reports."

Figure 12-42 The Columns tab of the Page Setup dialog box for forms lets you define grid and column settings.

You should now have a good understanding of how forms work and of many design elements that you can include when you build forms. Now, on to the fun part—building your first form—in the next chapter.

CHAPTER 13

Building a Form

From the perspective of daily use, forms are the most important objects you'll build in your Microsoft Access 2010 application because they're what users see and work with every time they run the application. This chapter shows you how to design and build forms in an Access 2010 client database. You'll learn how to work with a Form window in Design view to build a basic form based on a single table, and you'll learn how to use the Form Wizard to simplify the form-creation process. You'll also learn how to use some of the special form controls to simplify data entry on your forms. The last section of this chapter shows you how to use Application Part Forms to get a jumpstart on creating forms.

Note

The examples in this chapter are based on the forms, the tables, and the data in ContactsDataCopy.accdb on the companion CD included with this book. The results you see from the samples in this chapter might not exactly match what you see in this book if you have changed the sample data in the file. Also, all the screen images in this chapter were taken on a Windows 7 system with the Access color scheme set to Silver, and Use Windows-Themed Controls On Forms has been turned on in the sample databases. Your results might look different if you are using a different operating system or a different theme.

Forms and Object-Oriented Programming

Access was not designed to be a full object-oriented programming environment, yet it has many characteristics found in object-oriented application development systems. Before you dive into building forms, it's useful to examine how Access implements objects and actions, particularly if you come from the world of procedural application development.

In classic procedural application development, the data you need for the application is distinct from the programs you write to work with the data and from the results produced by your programs. Each program works with the data independently and generally has little structural connection with other programs in the system. For example, an order entry program accepts input from a clerk and then writes the order to data files. Later, a billing program processes the orders and prints invoices. Another characteristic of procedural systems is that events must occur in a specific order and cannot be executed out of sequence. A procedural system has difficulty looking up supplier or price information while in the middle of processing an order.

In an object-oriented system, however, an object is defined as a subject that has properties, and you can invoke certain actions, or *methods*, to be performed on that subject. Objects can contain other objects. When an object incorporates another object, it inherits the attributes and properties of the other object and expands on the object's definition. In Access, queries define actions on tables, and the queries then become new logical tables known as *recordsets*. That is, a query doesn't actually contain any data, but you can work with the data fetched by the query as though it were a table. You can base a query on another query with the same effect. Queries inherit the integrity and formatting rules defined for the tables. Forms further define actions on tables or queries, and the fields you include in forms initially inherit the underlying properties, such as formatting and validation rules, of the fields in the source tables or queries. You can define different formatting or more restrictive rules, but you cannot override the rules defined for the tables.

Within an Access database, you can interrelate application objects and data. For example, you can set startup properties that prepare your application to run. As part of the application startup, you will usually open a switchboard or navigation form. The switchboard form might act on some of the data in the database, or it might offer controls that open other forms, print reports, or close the application.

For more information about startup properties, see Chapter 26, "The Finishing Touches," on the companion CD.

Figure 13-1 shows the conceptual architecture of an Access form. In addition to operating on tables or queries in a database, forms can contain other forms, called *subforms*. These subforms can, in turn, define actions on other tables, queries, or forms. Events that occur in forms and subforms (such as changing the value of a field or moving to a new record) can trigger macro actions or Microsoft Visual Basic procedures. As you'll learn when you read about advanced form design, macro actions and Visual Basic procedures can be triggered in many ways. The most obvious way to trigger an action is by clicking a command button on a form. But you can also define macros or Visual Basic procedures that execute when an event occurs, such as clicking in a field, changing the data in a field, pressing a key, adding or deleting a row, or simply moving to a new row in the underlying table or query.

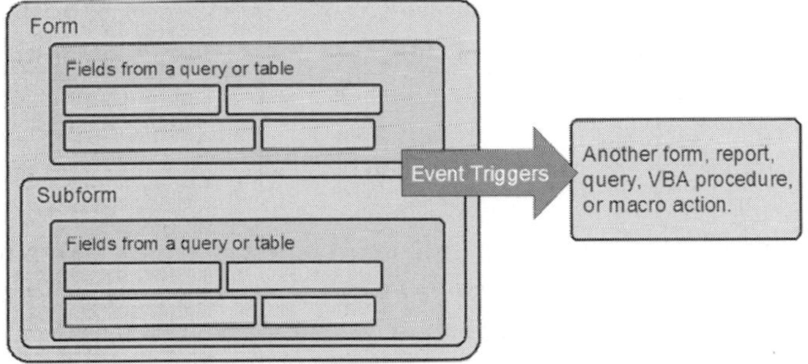

Figure 13-1 An Access form can contain other objects, including other forms, and you can set some of its properties to define procedures that respond to events.

In Chapter 25, "Automating Your Application with Visual Basic," on the companion CD, you'll learn how several of the more complex forms in the Conrad Systems Contacts and Housing Reservations sample databases are automated with Visual Basic. Figure 13-2 shows a few of the automated processes for the frmContacts form in the Conrad Systems Contacts database. For example, printing the contact currently displayed in the form is triggered by using a command button.

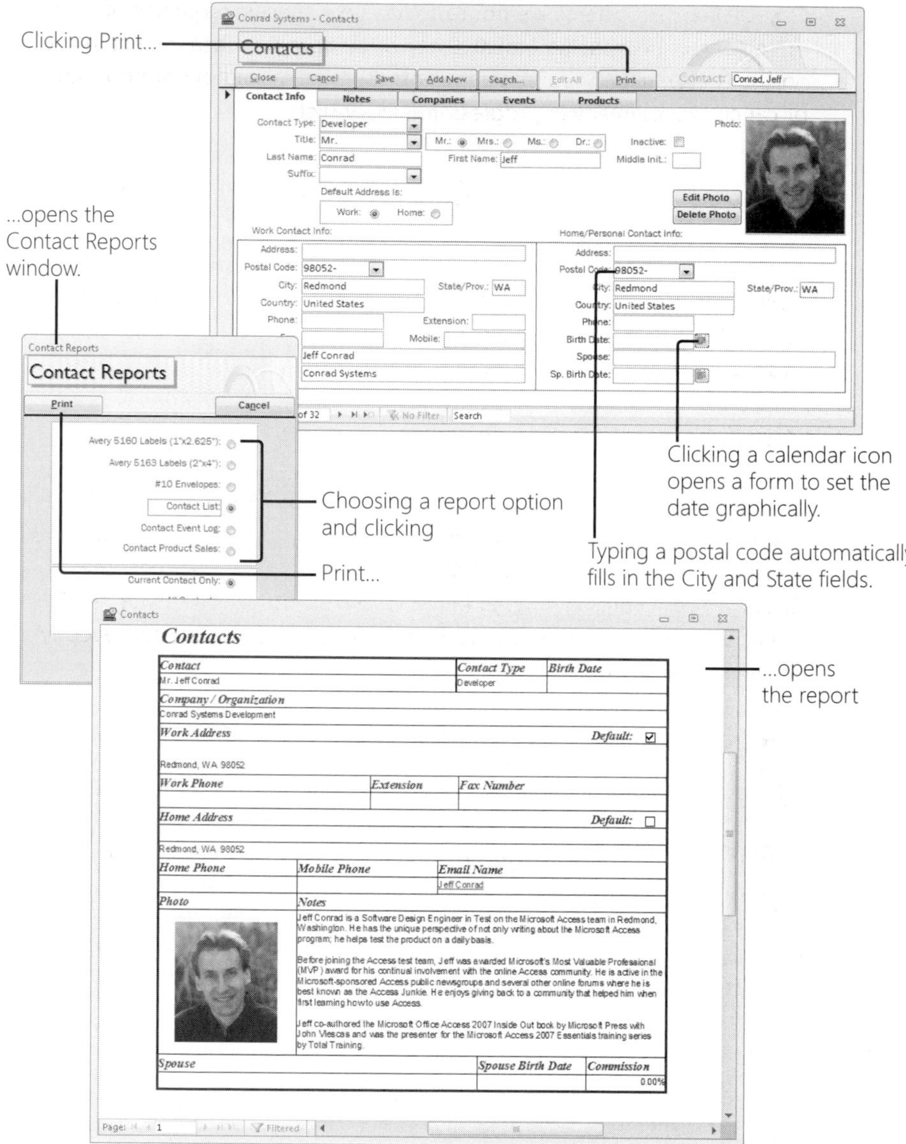
Clicking Print...
...opens the Contact Reports window.
Choosing a report option and clicking
Print...
...opens the report
Clicking a calendar icon opens a form to set the date graphically.
Typing a postal code automatically fills in the City and State fields.

Figure 13-2 Some of the automated processes for the frmContacts form include opening a dialog box to choose a contacts report or automatically filling in city and state when you enter a postal code.

In addition to automating print options, code behind the frmContacts form automatically fills in city and state when you enter a postal code and provides a graphical way to choose a date if you click the button next to a date. On the Events tab, when you enter a sale of a product to the contact, code automatically generates a product record.

Object-oriented systems are not restricted to a specific sequence of events. So, a user entering a contact event in Access 2010 can open up a new form object in the Navigation pane and start a search in a companies or products form window without having to first finalize or cancel work already in progress in frmContacts.

Starting from Scratch—A Simple Input Form

To start, you'll create a simple form that accepts and displays data in the tblCompanies table in the Conrad Systems Contacts database. Later, you'll create a form for the tblProducts table in this same database by using the Form Wizard. To follow along in this section, open the ContactsDataCopy.accdb database.

Building a New Form with Design Tools

To begin building a new form that allows you to display and edit data from a table, you need to start with a blank form window. You'll build this first form without the aid of the Form Wizard so that you'll understand the variety of components that go into form design. Click the Blank Form command in the Forms group on the Create tab. By default, Access opens a blank Form window in Layout view with the field list displayed on the right, as shown in Figure 13-3.

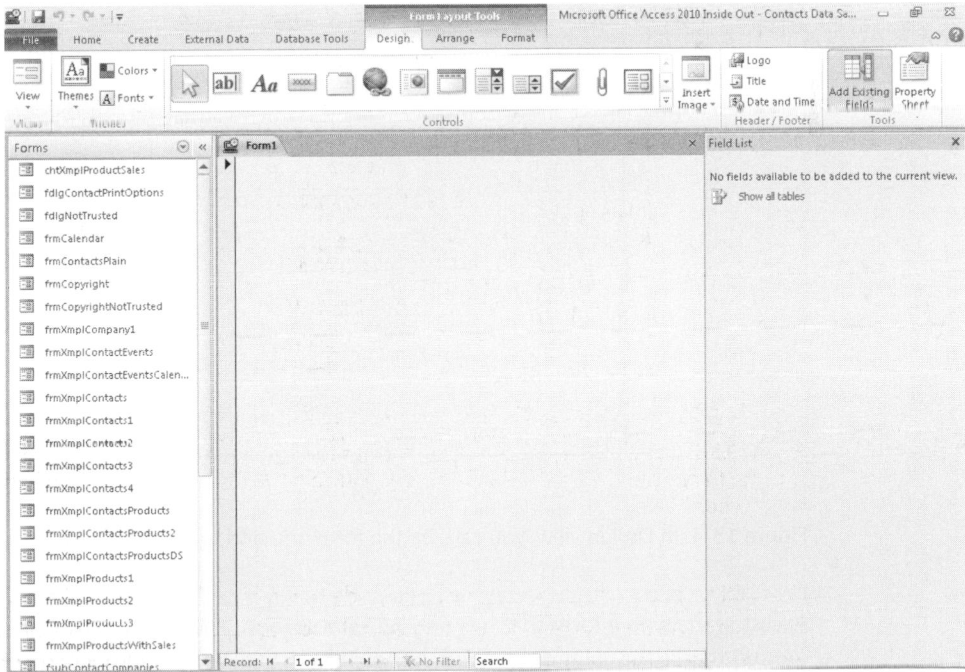

Figure 13-3 When you click the Blank Form command on the ribbon, Access opens a new Form window in Layout view.

Access does not know at this point from which tables or queries you want to display and edit data. If you click the Show All Tables hyperlink, Access displays a list of each local or linked table, as shown in Figure 13-4. If you click the plus symbol next to the name of a table, Access expands the list and displays the name of every field in that table. You can click a field name in the field list and drag it onto your form. If you click the Edit Table hyperlink on the right side of the field list, Access opens that specific table in Design view.

When you ask Access to create a new blank form, it initially displays the form in Layout view. We'll discuss Layout view in more detail in Chapter 14, "Customizing a Form"; for now, we'll focus on Design view. To switch to Design view, click the arrow under the View button in the Views group and click Design View. Access switches the Form window to Design view and provides several design tools on the Design contextual tab under Form Design Tools on the ribbon, as shown in Figure 13-4.

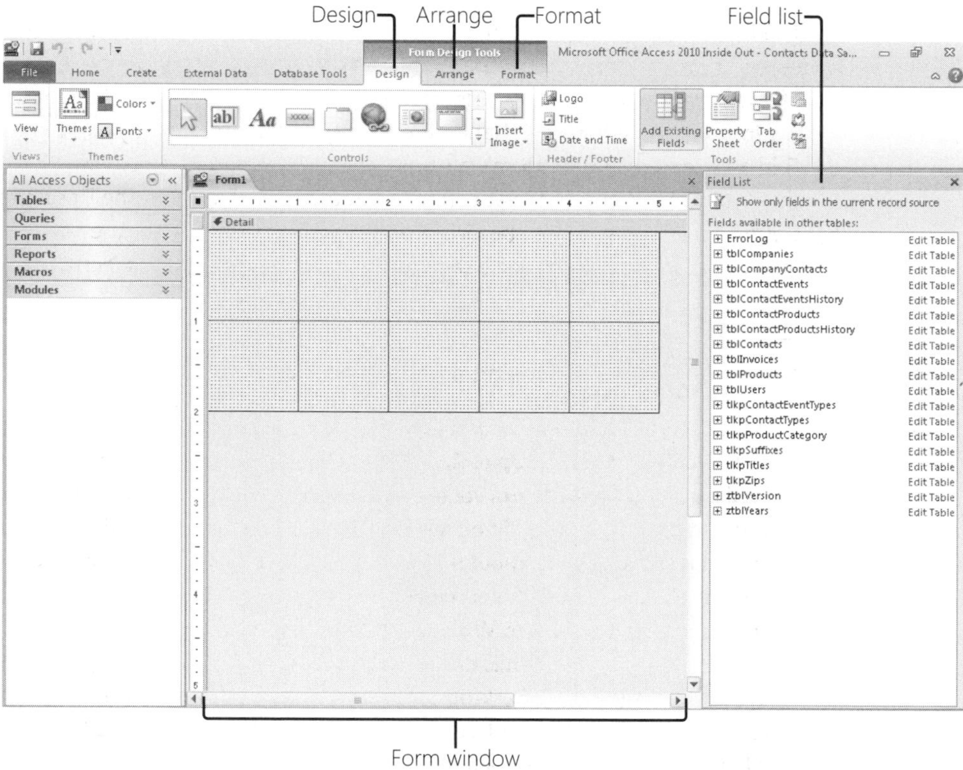

Figure 13-4 In Design view, you can use the form grid and tools to create your form elements.

Access starts with a form that has only a *Detail* section. The section has a grid on a background that is the color defined for 3-D objects in the Windows Appearance Settings dialog box—usually a light gray or beige. You can click the edge of the Detail section and then drag the edge to make the section larger or smaller. (To see more of the grid, you might also want to collapse the Navigation pane on the left.) You can remove the grid dots from the Detail section by clicking the Grid command under the Size/Space drop-down list in the Sizing & Ordering group on the Arrange tab under Form Design Tools. If you want to add a Header section or a Footer section to the form, right-click the Detail section of the form and then click the Form Header/Footer command from the shortcut menu that appears.

Note

To set the color for 3-D objects, right-click the desktop and then click Personalize. Click the Windows Color link at the bottom of the Personalization dialog box to open the Window Color and Appearance dialog box. In the Item list, click 3D Objects. Use the Color 1 list to set the color you want to use for 3-D objects.

The Detail section starts out at 5 inches (12.7 centimeters) wide by 2 inches (5.08 centimeters) high. The measurement gradations on the rulers are relative to the size and resolution of your screen. By default, Access sets the grid at 24 dots per inch horizontally and 24 dots per inch vertically. You can change the density of the grid dots by altering the Grid X and Grid Y properties on the form's property sheet. To replace the field list with the property sheet, click the Property Sheet command in the Tools group on the Design tab under Form Design Tools. You can find the Grid X and Grid Y properties near the bottom of the list on the Format tab of the property sheet when you have the Form selected.

INSIDE OUT Choosing a Form Width and Height

Although you can design a form that is up to 22 inches (55.87 centimeters) wide, and each form section can also be up to 22 inches high (a total of 66 inches if you include all three sections), you should design your forms to fit on your users' screens. We tend to design all our forms to comfortably fit on the lowest common screen resolution—1024×768. A form to fit this size should be about 9.75 inches (24.8 centimeters) wide, and the sum of the heights of the sections should be about 5.6 inches (14.2 centimeters) to allow space for the ribbon, status bar, and Windows taskbar. If your user has set a higher screen resolution, and your application is designed using overlapping windows, extra space will be available on the Access desktop to work with multiple form windows at a time. If you are using tabbed documents, extra space appears to the right and bottom of the form when the user opens it on a higher-resolution screen.

You can find a handy form, zsfrm1024x768, in several of the sample databases. When you're working in a higher resolution, you can open this form and overlay it on the form you're designing. If your form fits behind the sample form, your form should be displayed properly at the lowest common resolution.

The Grid X and Grid Y property settings determine the intervals per unit of measurement in the grid. You can enter a number from 1 (coarsest) through 64 (finest). You set the unit of measure (U.S. or metric) by default when you select a country on the Location tab in the Regional And Language Options dialog box. (You open this dialog box by first clicking Clock, Language, And Region in Control Panel and then clicking Regional And Language.)

For example, if your unit of measurement is inches and you specify a Grid X setting of 10, Access divides the grid horizontally into 0.1-inch increments. When your measurement is in inches and you set the Grid X and Grid Y values to 24 or less, Access displays the grid dots on the grid. In centimeters, you can see the grid dots when you specify a setting of 9 or less. If you set a finer grid for either Grid X or Grid Y, Access won't display the grid dots but you can still use the grid to line up controls. Access always displays grid lines at 1-inch intervals (U.S.) or 1-centimeter intervals (metric), even when you set fine Grid X or Grid Y values.

Some Key Form Design Terms

As you begin to work in form design, you need to understand a few commonly used terms.

A form that displays data from your tables must have a record source. A record source can be the name of a table, the name of a query, or a Structured Query Language (SQL) statement.

When a control can display information (text boxes, option groups, toggle buttons, option buttons, check boxes, combo boxes, list boxes, bound object frames, and many ActiveX controls), its *control source* defines the name of the field from the record source or the expression that provides the data to display. A control that has an expression as its control source is not updateable.

When a form has a record source, it is *bound* to the records in that record source—the form displays records from the record source and can potentially update the fields in the records. When a control is on a bound form and its control source is the name of a field in the record source, the control is *bound* to the field—the control displays (and perhaps allows you to edit) the data from the bound field in the current row of the record source. A control cannot be bound unless the form is also bound.

A form that has no record source is *unbound*. A control that has no control source is *unbound*.

Before proceeding further, you need to specify a record source for your new form. Although you can drag fields from the field list and Access will figure out the appropriate record source for you, you have more control if you select a record source first. To display the form's properties in the property sheet, click anywhere outside the Detail section of the form, click the small square box in the upper-left corner of the Form window, or select Form from the Selection Type combo box on the property sheet. Now, click the All tab in the property sheet, click the arrow to the right of the Record Source property, and select the tblCompanies table from the list, as shown in Figure 13-5.

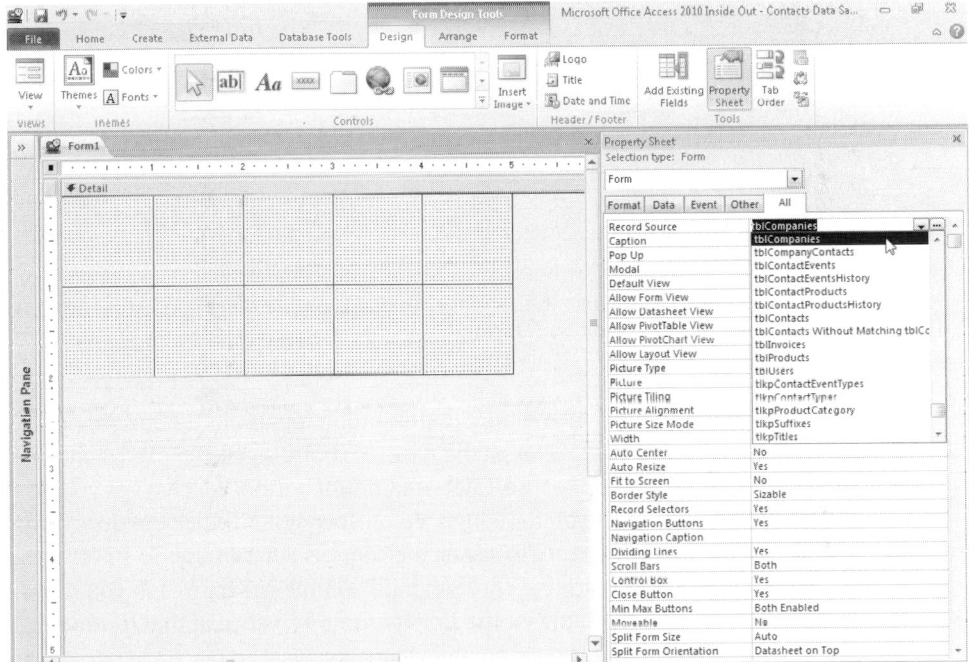

Figure 13-5 Select a record source to specify which table or query to use for the data on your form.

The following sections describe some of the tools you can use to design a form.

The Form Design Tools Contextual Ribbon Tabs

As you learned in Chapter 2, "Exploring the Access 2010 Interface," and Chapter 3, "Access 2010 Overview," the ribbon provides contextual tabs when Access displays objects in various views. When a form is in Design view, three contextual tabs appear—Design, Arrange, and Format under Form Design Tools. These contextual tabs, shown in Figure 13-6, are the "command center" of form design. These tabs provide all the essential tools and commands you need to design and modify your forms.

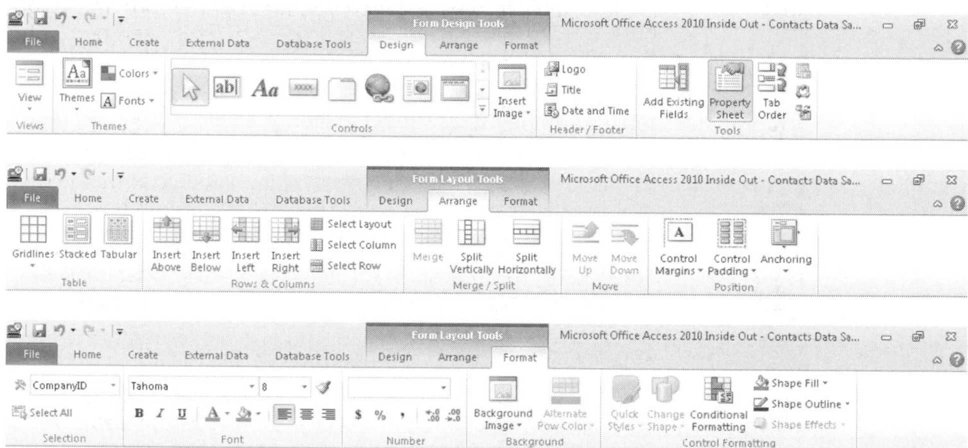

Figure 13-6 You can use the various commands on the three contextual tabs under Form Design Tools to create and edit your forms.

At the heart of these tabs is the Controls group found on the Design tab. This group contains a gallery of buttons for all the types of controls you can use when you design a client form. It also contains the Insert ActiveX Control button, which gives you access to all the ActiveX controls that you have installed on your system. Click the down arrow on the right side of the controls gallery to see all the controls you can use. To select a particular control to place on a form, click the control's button in the gallery. When you move the mouse pointer over the form, the mouse pointer turns into an icon that represents the control you selected. Position the mouse pointer where you want to place the control, and click the left mouse button to place the control on the form. If you want to size the control as you place it, drag the mouse pointer to make the control the size you want. (You can also size a control after you place it by dragging the sizing handles at its sides or corners.)

The buttons in the Controls group are described in Table 13-1, listed from left to right and top to bottom.

Table 13-1 Controls Group Buttons

Button	Description
	Select. Click this button to select, size, move, and edit existing controls. This is the default command when you first open a form in Design view. This button becomes selected again after you have used one of the control commands to place a new control on your form.
ab|	**Text Box.** Click this button to create text box controls for displaying text, numbers, dates, times, and memo fields. You can bind a text box to one of the fields in an underlying table or query. If you let a text box that is bound to a field be updated, you can change the value in the field in the underlying table or query by entering a new value in the text box. You can also use a text box to display calculated values.
Aa	**Label.** Click this button to create label controls that contain fixed text. By default, controls that can display data have a label control automatically attached. You can use this command to create stand-alone labels for headings and for instructions on your form.
XXXX	**Button.** Click this button to create a command button control that can activate a macro or a Visual Basic procedure. You can also specify a hyperlink address that Access opens when a user clicks the button.
	Tab Control. Click this button to create a series of tab pages on your form. Each page can contain a number of other controls to display information. The tab control works much like many of the option dialog boxes or property sheet windows in Access—when a user clicks a different tab, Access displays the controls contained on that tab. See Chapter 15, "Advanced Form Design," for details about using the Tab Control button.
	Insert Hyperlink. Click this button to add a hyperlink in a label control to your form design grid. This hyperlink can contain a Uniform Resource Locator (URL) that points to a location on the Internet, on a local intranet, or on a local drive. It can also use a Universal Naming Convention (UNC) file name to point to a file on a server on your local area network (LAN) or on your local computer drives. The link might point to a file that is a web page or even another object in your current database. Clicking this button opens the Insert Hyperlink dialog box discussed previously in "Working with Hyperlinks," on page 603.
	Web Browser Control. Click this button to add a web browser control to your form design grid. A web browser control displays the content of web pages directly inside a form. You can use a web browser control to display, for example, a map of an address stored in a table. You can bind the web browser control to a field in your form's record source by using the Control Source property of the control. Note that you cannot have a bound web browser control in the Detail section of a continuous form.
	Navigational Control. Click this button to add a navigational control to your form design grid. You can use a navigational control to provide an easy way to navigate to different forms and reports in your database. A navigational control provides an interface similar to what you see on websites with buttons and tabs to navigate a website. Note that you cannot have a navigational control in the Detail section of a continuous form.

Button	Description
	Option Group. Click this button to create option group controls that contain one or more toggle buttons, option buttons, or check boxes. (See the descriptions of these controls later in this table.) You can assign a separate numeric value to each button or check box that you include in the group. When you have more than one button or check box in a group, you can select only one button or check box at a time, and the value assigned to that button or check box becomes the value for the option group. If you have incorrectly assigned the same value to more than one button or check box, all buttons or check boxes that have the same value appear highlighted when you click any of them. You can select one of the buttons or check boxes in the group as the default value for the group. If you bind the option group to a field in the underlying query or table, you can set a new value in the field by selecting a button or a check box in the group.
	Insert Or Remove Page Break. Click this button to add a page break between the pages of a multiple-page form. (We think this tool is misnamed. To remove a page break, you must select the page break control and press the Delete key.)
	Combo Box. Click this button to create a combo box control that contains a list of potential values for the control and an editable text box. To create the list, you can enter values for the Row Source property of the combo box. You can also specify a table or a query as the source of the values in the list. Access displays the currently selected value in the text box. When you click the arrow to the right of the combo box, Access displays the values in the list. Select a new value in the list to reset the value in the control. If you bind the combo box to a field in the underlying table or query, you can change the value in the field by selecting a new value in the list. If you bind the combo box to a multi-value field, Access displays the list with check boxes to allow the user to select multiple values. You can bind multiple columns to the list, and you can hide one or more of the columns in the list by setting a column's width to 0. You can bind the actual value in the control to such a hidden column. When a multiple-column list is closed, Access displays the value in the first column whose width is greater than 0. Access displays all nonzero-width columns when you open the list.
	**Insert Chart.** Click this button to add a chart on your form grid. Clicking this button and then placing the control on your form starts the Chart Wizard, which walks you through the steps necessary to create a new chart.
	**Line.** Click this button to add lines to a form to enhance its appearance.

Button	Description
	**Toggle Button.** Click this button to create a toggle button control that holds an on/off, a true/false, or a yes/no value. When you click a toggle button, its value becomes –1 (to represent on, true, or yes), and the button appears pressed in. Click the button again, and its value becomes 0 (to represent off, false, or no) and the button returns to normal. You can include a toggle button in an option group and assign the button a unique numeric value. If you create a group with multiple controls, selecting a new toggle button clears any previously selected toggle button, option button, or check box in that group (unless other buttons or check boxes in the group also have the same value). If you bind the toggle button to a field in the underlying table or query, you can toggle the field's value by clicking the toggle button.
	**List Box.** Click this button to create a list box control that contains a list of potential values for the control. To create the list, you can enter the values in the Row Source property of the list box. You can also specify a table or a query as the source of the values in the list. List boxes are always open, and Access highlights the currently selected value in the list box. You select a new value in the list to reset the value in the control. If you bind the list box to a field in the underlying table or query, you can change the value in the field by selecting a new value in the list. If you bind the list box to a multi-value field, Access displays the list with check boxes to allow the user to select multiple values. You can bind multiple columns to the list, and you can hide one or more of the columns in the list by setting a column's width to 0. You can bind the actual value in the control to such a hidden column. Access displays all nonzero-width columns that fit within the defined width of the control. If the list box control is unbound, you can allow the user to select multiple values in the list (also called a multiple-selection list box).
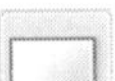	**Rectangle.** Click this button to add filled or empty rectangles to a form to enhance its appearance.
	**Check Box.** Click this button to create a check box control that holds an on/off, a true/false, or a yes/no value. When you select a check box, its value becomes –1 (to represent on, true, or yes), and a check mark appears in the box. Select the check box again, and its value becomes 0 (to represent off, false, or no), and the check mark disappears from the box. You can include a check box in an option group and assign the check box a unique numeric value. If you create a group with multiple controls, selecting a new check box clears any previously selected toggle button, option button, or check box in that group (unless other buttons or check boxes in the group also have the same value). If you bind the check box to a field in the underlying table or query, you can toggle the field's value by clicking the check box.
	**Unbound Object Frame.** Click this button to add an object from another application that supports object linking and embedding (OLE). The object becomes part of your form, not part of the data from the underlying table or query. You can add pictures, sounds, charts, or slides to enhance your form. When the object is a chart, you can specify a query as the source of data for the chart, and you can link the chart display to the current record in the form by one or more field values.

Button	Description
	**Attachment.** Click this button to insert an attachment control on the form design grid. You can bind this control to an attachment field in the underlying data. You can use this control, for example, to display a picture or to attach other files. In Form view, this control presents the Manage Attachments dialog box, where you can attach, delete, and view multiple attachment files stored in the underlying field.
	**Option Button.** Click this button to create an option button control (sometimes called a radio button control) that holds an on/off, a true/false, or a yes/no value. When you select an option button, its value becomes –1 (to represent on, true, or yes), and a filled circle appears in the center of the button. Select the button again, and its value becomes 0 (to represent off, false, or no), and the filled circle disappears. You can include an option button in an option group and assign the button a unique numeric value. If you create a group with multiple controls, selecting a new option button clears any previously selected toggle button, option button, or check box in that group (unless other buttons or check boxes in the group also have the same value). If you bind the option button to a field in the underlying table or query, you can toggle the field's value by clicking the option button.
	**Subform/Subreport.** Click this button to embed another form or report in the current form. You can use the subform or subreport to show data from a table or a query that is related to the data in the main form. Access maintains the link between the main form and the subform or subreport for you.
	**Bound Object Frame.** Click this button to display and edit an OLE object field from the underlying data. Access can display most pictures and graphs directly on a form. For other objects, Access displays the icon for the application in which the object was created. For example, if the object is a sound object created in Windows Sound Recorder, you'll see a speaker icon on your form.
	**Image.** Click this button to place a static picture on your form. You cannot edit the picture on the form, but Access stores it in a format that is very efficient for application speed and size. If you want to use a picture as the entire background of your form, you can set the form's Picture property.
	Set Control Defaults. Click this button if you want to change the default property settings for all new controls of a particular type. Select a control of that type, set the control's properties to the desired default values, and then click the Set Control Defaults command. The settings of the currently selected control become the default settings for any subsequent definitions of that type of control on your form.
	Use Control Wizards. Click this button to activate a control wizard. Click the button again to deactivate the wizards. When this button appears pressed in, a control wizard helps you enter control properties whenever you create a new option group, combo box, list box, or command button. The Combo Box and List Box Wizards also offer you an option to create Visual Basic code to move to a new record based on a selection the user makes in the combo or list box. The Command Button Wizard offers to generate an embedded macro code that performs various automated actions when the user clicks the button.

Button	Description
	Insert ActiveX Control. Click this button to open a dialog box showing all the ActiveX controls you have installed on your system. You can select one of the controls and then click OK to add the control to the form design grid. Not all ActiveX controls work with Access.
Insert Image	**Insert Image.** Click this button to drop down a gallery of any shared images in your database. When you click a shared image in the gallery, Access places the image on the form grid wherever you click. You can also click the Browse button at the bottom of the gallery to browse for a graphic file on your computer. If you browse for a new graphic file, Access adds that new image to the gallery. You can use shared images on both client and web forms and reports. You'll learn more about using shared images in Chapter 14.

To the right of the Controls group, you'll see a group called Header/Footer with three buttons that you can use to add controls to the header and footer section of your form. Top to bottom the buttons in the Header/Footer group are described in Table 13-2.

Table 13-2 Header/Footer Group Buttons

Button	Description
Logo	**Logo.** Click this button to insert into a form a picture to be used as a logo displayed in an image control. (See the description of the image control in Table 13-1.) When you click Logo, Access opens the Insert Picture dialog box, where you can select the graphic or picture that you want to use as a logo. By default, Access places the logo in the form's Header section. If you have not revealed the form header and footer, the command adds those sections to your form before inserting the logo in the Header section.
Title	**Title.** Click this button to insert a new label control in a form's Header section to be used as a title for the form. If you have not revealed the form header and footer, the command adds those sections to your form before inserting the label control in the Header section.
Date and Time	**Date & Time.** Click this button to open the Date And Time dialog box, where you can choose to insert the date, the time, or both the date and time displayed in text box controls in the form's Header section. You can choose different formats for both the date and time. If you have not revealed the form header and footer, the command adds those sections to your form before inserting the text box controls in the Header section.

For more information about using controls on forms, see Chapters 14 and 15.

INSIDE OUT **Locking a Control Button**

When you click a button that is a form control, your mouse pointer reverts to the Select button after you place the selected control on your form. If you plan to create several controls using the same tool—for example, a series of check boxes in an option group—right-click the button for that control in the Controls group and select Drop Multiple Controls to "lock" it. You can unlock it by clicking any other button (including the Select button).

The Field List

Use the field list in conjunction with the Controls group to place bound controls (controls linked to fields in a table or a query) on your form. You can open the field list by clicking the Add Existing Fields button in the Tools group on the Design tab. If the form is bound to a table or query, Access displays the name of the underlying table or query along with all the fields available, as shown in Figure 13-7. Any tables that have relationships to the underlying table defined are displayed under Fields Available In Related Tables. The last section of the field list, Fields Available In Other Tables, lists the tables and fields from all other tables in this database. Click the Show Only Fields In The Current Record Source link to remove the bottom two sections of the field list. You can undock the field list by clicking the title bar and dragging it away from the right edge of the Form window. After you undock the field list, you can drag the edges of the window to resize it so that you can see any long field names. You can drag the title bar to move the window out of the way. When the list of available field names is too long to fit in the current size of the window, use the vertical scroll bar to move through the list.

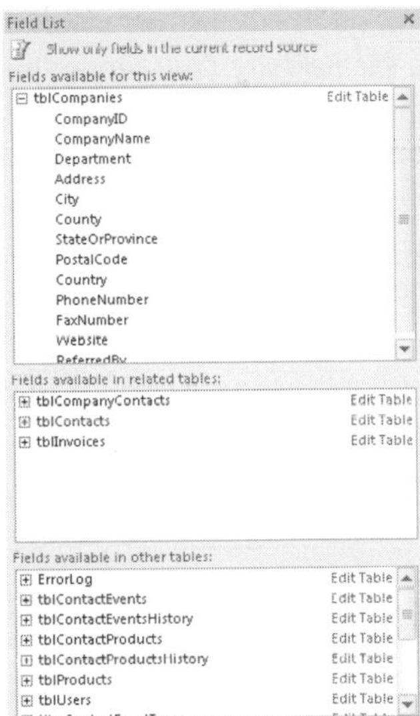

Figure 13-7 The field list shows the names of the fields in the bound table or query, any related tables, and fields from all other tables in the current database.

To use the field list to place a bound control on a form, first click the button for the type of control you want in the Controls group. Then, drag the field you want from the field list and place it into position on the form. If you click the button for a control that's inappropriate for the data type of the field, Access selects the default control for the data type. For example, if you click anything but the Attachment button when placing an attachment field on a form, Access creates an attachment control for you anyway. If you try to drag any field after clicking the button for the subform/subreport, unbound object frame, line, rectangle, or page break control, Access creates a text box control or bound object frame control, as appropriate, instead. If you drag a field from the field list without clicking a control, Access uses either the display control you defined for the field in the table definition or a control appropriate for the field data type.

The Property Sheet

The form, each section of the form (header, detail, footer), and each control on the form have a list of properties associated with them, and you set these properties using a property sheet. Each control on a form, each section on a form, and the form itself are all objects. The kinds of properties you can specify vary depending on the object. To open the property sheet for an object, select the object and then click the Property Sheet button in the Tools group on the Design tab. Access opens a window, similar to the one shown in Figure 13-8 on the right side of the Form window, replacing the field list. (You cannot have both the property sheet and the field list open at the same time.) If you have previously undocked either the field list or property sheet, the property sheet appears in the undocked window. If the property sheet is already open, you can view the properties specific to an object by clicking the object. You can also click the arrow under Selection Type and then select the object name from the list at the top of the property sheet.

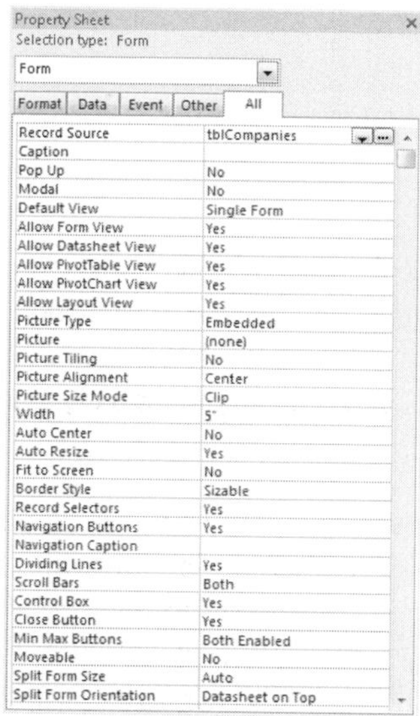

Figure 13-8 You can view the properties of form controls and sections using the property sheet.

You can drag the title bar to move the property sheet around on your screen. You can also drag the edges of the window to resize it so that you can see more of the property settings. Because a form has more than 100 properties that you can set and because many controls have more than 70 properties, Access provides tabs at the top of the property sheet so that you can choose to display all properties (the default) or to display only format properties, data properties, event properties, or other properties. A form property sheet displaying only the data properties is shown in Figure 13-9.

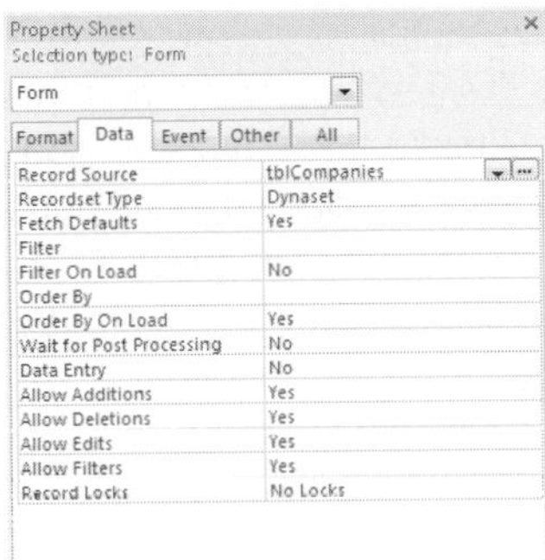

Figure 13-9 If you click the Data tab on the form property sheet, Access displays only the data properties.

When you click in a property box that provides a list of valid values, a small arrow appears on the right side of the property box. Click this arrow to see a list of the values for the property. For properties that can have a very long value setting, you can click the property and then press Shift+F2 to open the Zoom dialog box. The Zoom dialog box provides an expanded text box for entering or viewing a value.

In many cases, a window, dialog box, or wizard is available to help you create property settings for properties that can accept a complex expression, a query definition, or code (a macro or a Visual Basic procedure) to respond to an event. When such help is available for a property setting, Access displays a small button with an ellipsis next to the property box when you select the property; this is the Build button. If you click the Build button, Access responds with the appropriate window, dialog box, or wizard.

For example, suppose that you want to see the companies displayed in this form in ascending order by company name. The easiest way to accomplish this is to create a query that includes the fields from tblCompanies sorted on the CompanyName field, and then specify that query as the *Record Source* property for the form. To start, display the property sheet for the form, click the Data tab to display the form's data properties, click in the Record Source property box, and then click the Build button next to Record Source to start the Query Builder. Access asks whether you want to build a new query based on the table that is currently the source for this form. If you click Yes, Access opens a new Query window in Design view with the tblCompanies field list displayed in the upper part of the window and the property sheet open either in an undocked window or to the right, as shown in Figure 13-10.

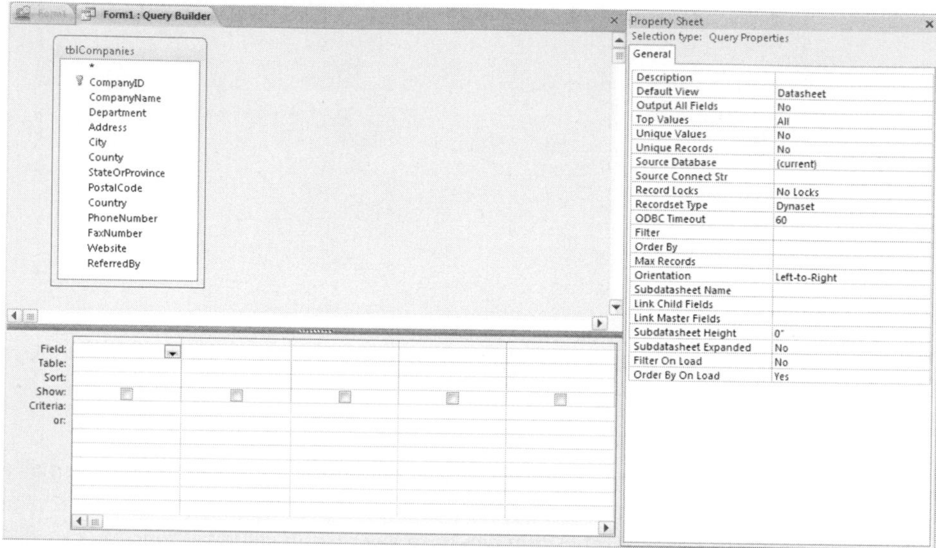

Figure 13-10 You can use the Query Builder to create a query for the form's Record Source property.

> **Note**
>
> **After you open the property sheet in table, query, form, or report Design view, the window will be open for all objects in Design view until you close it. Likewise, if you close the property sheet in Design view, the window will be closed for all other objects in Design view until you reopen it.**

You'll need all the fields in the tblCompanies table for this form, so select them and drag them to the design grid. For the CompanyName field, specify Ascending as the sorting order. Close the property sheet for now by clicking the Close button on its title bar. Your Query Builder window should look like the window shown in Figure 13-11.

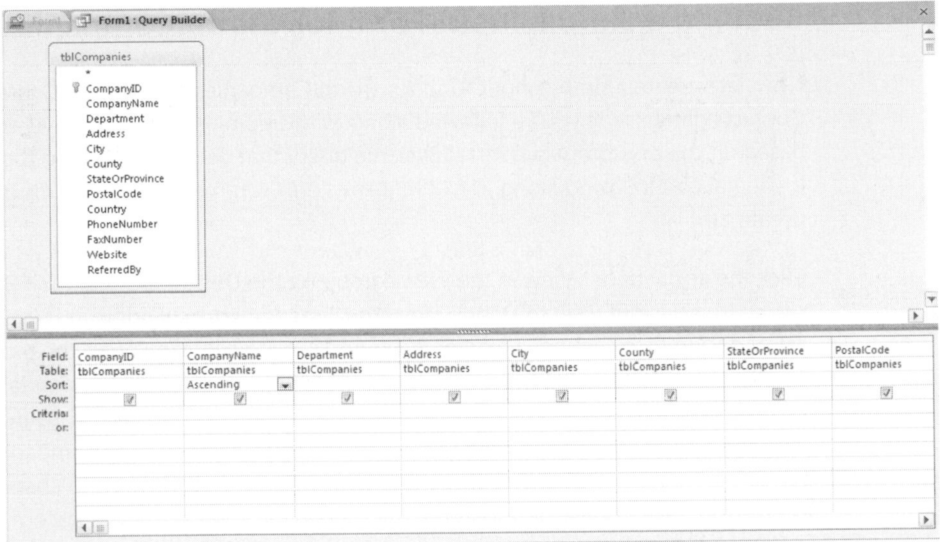

Figure 13-11 Select all the fields from the table to include them in the query for the Record Source property of the form.

INSIDE OUT Selecting All the Fields

To easily select all the fields from a field list displayed in the upper part of the Query window, double-click the title bar of the field list. Access highlights all the fields for you. Then simply click any of them and drag the fields as a group to the design grid.

If you close the Query Builder window at this point, Access asks whether you want to update the property. If you click Yes, Access stores the SQL text for the query in the Record Source property box. A better approach is to save the query and give it a name, such as **qryCompaniesSortedByName**. Do that now by clicking the Save As command in the Close group on the Design contextual tab under Query Tools, entering qryCompaniesSortedByName in the Save As dialog box, and then clicking OK. Now, when you close the query, Access asks whether you want to save the query and update the property. Click Yes, and Access places the name of the query (rather than the SQL text) in the property sheet.

Building a Simple Input Form for the tblCompanies Table

Now, let's create a simple input form for the tblCompanies table in the Conrad Systems Contacts database. If you've followed along to this point, you should have a blank form based on the qryCompaniesSortedByName query that you created using the Query Builder. If you haven't followed along, click the Blank Form command in the Forms group on the Create tab.

Click the arrow under View in the Views group on the Design tab and click Design View to switch from Layout view to Design view. You'll see the Form window in Design view and a set of design tools, as shown earlier in Figure 13-4. If necessary, open the property sheet by clicking the Property Sheet command in the Tools group of the Design tab under Form Design Tools. By default, this new form is unbound, so click the Record Source property, click the arrow that appears next to the property box, and select tblCompanies from the list. Now, the form is bound to the tblCompanies table, but we want to change the record source to a saved query based on the tblCompanies table. Select the Record Source property again, click the Build button, and follow the procedures discussed in the previous sections, whose results are shown in Figures 13-10 and 13-11; this will create the query you need and make it the source for the form.

In the blank form that now has the qryCompaniesSortedByName query as its record source, drag the bottom of the Detail section downward to make some room to work. All the fields in tblCompanies are defined to be displayed with a text box, so you don't need to click a button in the Controls group. If you'd like to practice, though, right-click the Text Box button in the Controls group and then click Drop Multiple Controls before dragging fields from the field list. If the field list is not displayed, click the Add Existing Fields button in the Tools group of the Design tab. You can drag fields (for this exercise, all except the ReferredBy field) one at a time to the Detail section of the form, or you can click the first field (CompanyID), hold down the Shift key, and click the last field (Website) to select them all. After you drag the fields, your form should now look something like the one shown in Figure 13-12. If you right-clicked Text Box and selected the Drop Multiple Controls option to select it for multiple operations, click Select to unlock the selection.

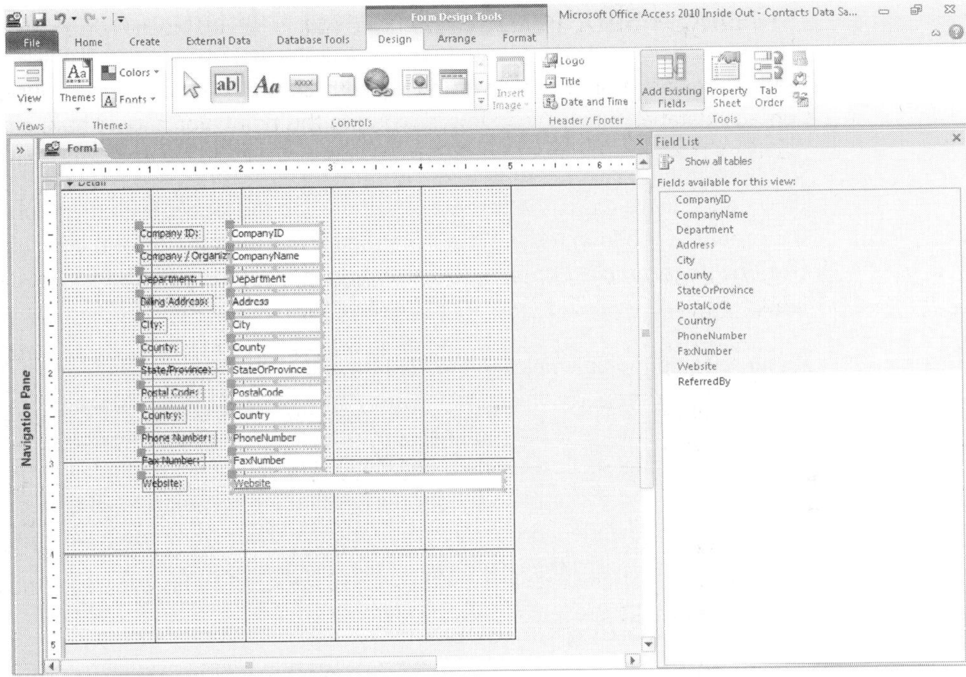

Figure 13-12 You can drag the fields from the qryCompaniesSortedByName field list to place these text box controls on the form design grid.

INSIDE OUT Using the Shift or the Ctrl Key to Select Multiple Fields

A quick way to place several successive fields on a form is to click the first field you want in the field list, scroll down until you see the last field you want, and then hold down the Shift key while you click the last field. This procedure selects all the fields between the first and last fields you clicked. Holding down the Ctrl key and clicking several noncontiguous fields works, too. If you include a field in error, hold down the Ctrl key and click the selected field that you don't want. Click any of the selected fields and drag the fields as a group to the Detail section of the form. This has the added benefit of lining up all the controls into a vertical column.

When you position the field icon that you've dragged from the field list, the upper-left corner of the new text box will be at the position of the mouse pointer when you release the mouse button. Note that the default text box control has a label control automatically attached to display the bound field's Caption property (or the field name if the field does not have a caption), positioned 1 inch to the left of the text box. Also, in Design view, the label control displays its Caption property, and the text box control displays its Control Source property (the name of the field to which it is bound).

You should drop each text box about 1.25 inches (3 centimeters) from the left edge of the Detail section to leave room to the left of the text box for Access to place the control labels. If you don't leave room, the text boxes will overlap the labels. Even if you do leave room, if a caption is too long to fit in the 1-inch space between the default label and the default text box (for example, Company/Organization in Figure 13-12), the text box will overlap the label.

If you selected multiple fields in the field list and added them all with one drag action, when you click Property Sheet immediately after adding the fields, the property sheet indicates that you have selected multiple controls. (In this example, we dragged all the selected fields to the Detail section at one time.) Whenever you select multiple controls on a form in Design view, Access displays the properties that are common to all the controls you selected. If you change a property in the property sheet while you have multiple controls selected, Access makes the change to all the selected controls.

Moving and Sizing Controls

By default, Access creates text boxes that are 1 inch wide (except for Hyperlink and Memo fields). For some of the fields, 1 inch is larger than necessary to display the field value—especially if you are using the default 11-point font size. For other fields, the text box isn't large enough. You probably also want to adjust the location of some of the controls.

To change a control's size or location, you usually have to select the control first. Be sure that you have clicked the Select button in the Controls group on the Design tab. Click the control you want to resize or move, and moving and sizing handles appear around the control. The handles are small boxes that appear at each corner of the control—except at the upper-left corner, where the larger handle indicates that you cannot use it for sizing. In Figure 13-12, handles appear around all the text boxes because they are all selected. To select just one control, click anywhere in the design area where there is no control; this changes the selection to the Detail section. Then, click the control you want. If the control is wide enough or high enough, Access provides additional handles at the midpoints of the edges of the control.

To change the size of a control, you can use the sizing handles on the edges, in either of the lower corners, or in the upper-right corner of the control. When you place the mouse pointer over one of these sizing handles, the pointer turns into a double arrow, as shown in Figure 13-13. With the double-arrow pointer, drag the handle to resize the control. You can practice on the form by shortening the CompanyID text box so that it's 0.5 inch long.

You need to stretch the company name, department, and address fields until they are each about 1.75 inches long. You might also want to reduce the state or province field to display two characters and decrease the website field to 1.75 inches.

Figure 13-13 You can drag a corner handle of a selected control to change the control's width or height or both.

To move a control that is not currently selected, click the control and drag it to a new location. After you click a control, you can move it by placing your mouse pointer anywhere between the handles along the edge of the control. When you do this, the mouse pointer turns into a pointer with a four-arrow crosshair, as shown in Figure 13-14, and you can then drag the control to a new location. Access displays an outline of the control as you move the control to help you position it correctly. When a control has an attached label, moving either the control or the label in this way moves both of them.

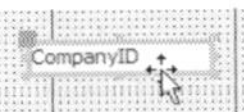

Figure 13-14 You can drag the edge of a selected control to move the control.

You can position a control and its attached label independently by dragging the larger handle in the upper-left corner of the control or label. When you position the mouse pointer over this handle, the pointer again turns into a pointer with a four-arrow crosshair, as shown in Figure 13-15. Drag the control to a new location relative to its label.

Figure 13-15 You can drag the large handle of a selected control to move the control independently of its label.

You can delete a label from a control by selecting the label and pressing the Delete key. If you want to create a label that is independent of a control, you can click Label. If you inadvertently delete a label from a control and you've made other changes so that you can no longer undo the deletion, you can attach a new label by doing the following:

1. Click the Label button in the Controls group on the Design tab to create a new, unattached label.
2. Select the label, and then click the Cut command in the Clipboard group on the Home tab to move the label to the Clipboard.

3. Select the control to which you want to attach the label, and then click the Paste command in the Clipboard group.

The Font Group

The Font group on the Format tab under Form Design Tools, shown in Figure 13-16, provides a quick and easy way to alter the appearance of a control by allowing you to click buttons rather than set properties. Select the object you want to format and then click the appropriate button in the Font group. The Font group is also handy for setting background colors for sections of the form. Table 13-3 describes each of the buttons in this group.

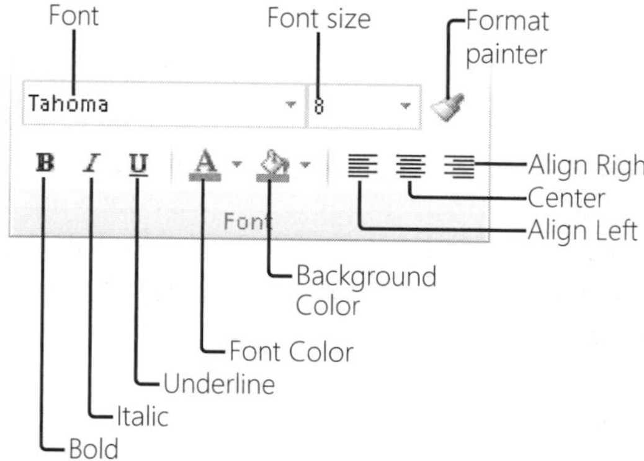

Figure 13-16 The Font group provides you with tools to change the appearance of form controls.

Table 13-3 Font Group Buttons

Button	Description
Font	Use to set the font for labels, text boxes, command buttons, toggle buttons, combo boxes, and list boxes.
Bold	Click to set font style to bold. Click again to remove bold.
Italic	Click to set font style to italic. Click again to remove italic.
Underline	Click to underline text. Click again to remove underline.
Font Color	Use to set the font color of the control.
Background Color	Use to set the background color of the control or form area. You can also set the background color to transparent.
Font Size	Use to set font size.
Format Painter	Use to copy formatting from one control to another control.

Button	Description
Align Left	Click to left-align text.
Center	Click to center text.
Align Right	Click to right-align text.

INSIDE OUT **Using the Alignment Buttons**

You can click only one of the alignment buttons—Align Left, Align Right, or Center—at a time. If you do not click a button, alignment is set to General—text data aligns left and numeric data aligns right. You can also set the Text Align property in the property sheet.

Depending on the object you select, some of the Font group options might not be available. For example, you can't set text color on an attachment or a bound object frame control. If you have the property sheet open and you scroll through it so that you can see the properties the Font group sets, you can watch the settings in the property sheet change as you click different options in the Font group.

The Control Formatting Group

You can find a special set of commands in the Control Formatting group on the Format tab, below Form Design Tools, to further customize the look of the controls on your form, as shown in Figure 13-17. Table 13-4 explains each of these buttons.

Figure 13-17 You can use commands in the Control Formatting group of the Format tab to customize the borders, colors, shapes, and styles of your controls.

Table 13-4 Control Formatting Group Buttons

Button	Description
Quick Styles	Use this command to select a predefined set of colors, styles, and shapes for the selected control. When you click this button, Access displays a gallery of 42 Quick Style colors, styles, and shapes. You can use these Quick Style options with command buttons, toggle buttons, and navigation buttons.

Button	Description
Change Shape	Use this command to change the shape of the selected control. When you click this button, Access displays a gallery of eight shapes. You can use these shape options with command buttons, toggle buttons, navigation buttons, and tab controls.
Conditional Formatting	Use to define dynamic modification of the formatting of text boxes and combo boxes by testing the value in the control, by comparing values in one or more fields, or when the control has the focus.
Shape Fill	Use to set the background color of the selected control. Under this gallery, you'll see color options for the control and options for Gradient. You can choose between a gallery of 13 gradients or select No Gradient (the default).
Shape Outline	Use this command to set the color, width, and line style for the outline of the selected control. Under this gallery, you'll see color options for the control, and options for Line Thickness and Line Type. You can also set the border color to a specific color or make it transparent. For Line Thickness, you can set the border width from hairline to 6 points wide. For Line Type, you can make the border transparent or specify a border that is a solid line, dashes, short dashes, dots, sparse dots, dash dot, or dash dot dot.
Shape Effects	Use this command to apply visual effects to the selected control. Under this gallery, you'll see options for Shadow, Glow, Soft Edges, and Bevel. Access displays many options under each category to further customize the effect of the selected control. You can use these Shape Effect options with command buttons, toggle buttons, and navigation buttons.

Depending on the object you select, some of the Control Formatting group options might not be available. For example, you can't apply a Quick Style to a text box, and you can't apply Conditional Formatting to a command button. If you have the property sheet open and you scroll through it so that you can see the properties these commands set, you can watch the settings in the property sheet change as you click different options in the group.

INSIDE OUT

Finding the Special Effect Options

If you're looking for the Special Effect options for controls from previous versions of Access, they are no longer on the ribbon. If you want to use one of the six special effect options—Flat, Raised, Sunken, Etched, Shadowed, or Chiseled—you can right-click a selected control on the design grid, click Special Effects from the shortcut menu, and then click one of the six options. You can also set these properties manually on the property sheet.

Setting Text Box Properties

The next thing you might want to do is change some of the text box properties. Figure 13-18 shows some of the properties for the CompanyID text box control. Because the CompanyID field in the tblCompanies table is an AutoNumber field, which a user cannot change, you should change the properties of this control to prevent it from being selected on the form. Access provides two properties that you can set to control what the user can do. The *Enabled* property determines whether the control can receive the focus (the user can click in or tab to the control). The *Locked* property determines whether the user can enter data in the control. The defaults are Enabled Yes and Locked No.

You can set the Enabled property of the control to No so that the user cannot click in or tab to the control. When you do this, Access prohibits access to the field but causes the control and its label to appear dimmed because the control is not locked. (When Access sees that a control is disabled but is still potentially updateable, despite being bound to an AutoNumber, it causes the control to appear dimmed.) Set Enabled to No and Locked to Yes so that the control cannot have the focus but the control appears normal.

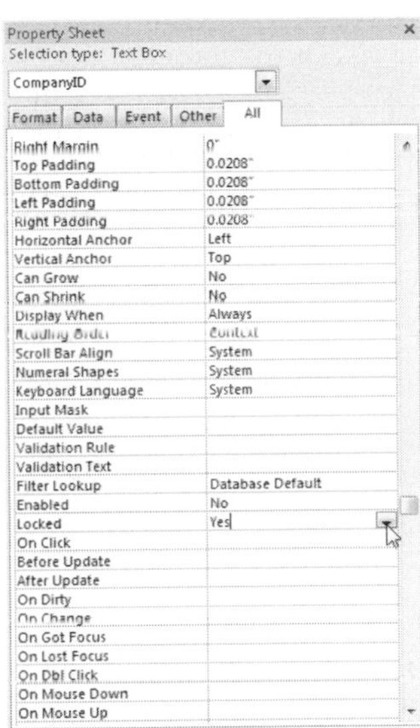

Figure 13-18 You can set the Enabled and Locked properties of the CompanyID text box control so that users cannot click into that control.

If you specify a Format, Decimal Places, or Input Mask property setting when you define a field in a table, Access copies these settings to any text box that you bind to the field. Any data you enter using the form must conform to the field validation rule defined in the table; however, you can define a more restrictive rule for this form. Any new row inherits default values from the table unless you provide a different default value in the property sheet. The Status Bar Text property derives its value from the Description property setting you entered for the field in the table. You can learn more about control properties in Chapter 14, "Customizing a Form."

Setting Label Properties

You can also set separate properties for the labels attached to controls. Click the label for CompanyID to see the property sheet, shown in Figure 13-19. Access copies the Caption property from the field in the underlying table to the Caption property in the associated control label. The default settings for the text box control on a form specify that all text boxes have labels and that the caption should have a trailing colon. When you added the CompanyID text box to the form, Access used the caption from the field's definition in the tblCompanies table (Company ID instead of the field name CompanyID), and added the trailing colon. Also, all controls on a form must have a name, so Access generated a name (Label0) that is the control type followed by an integer.

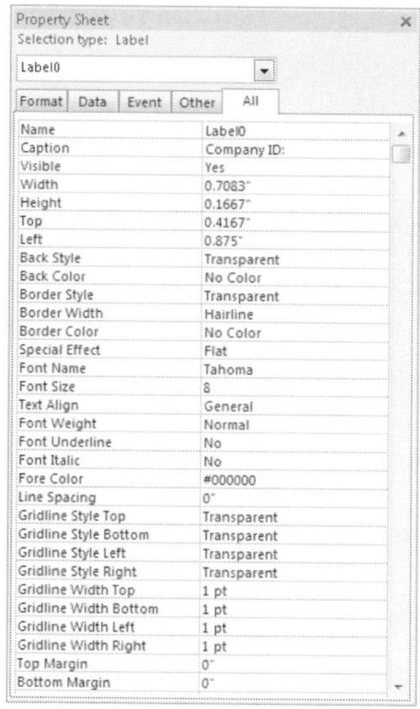

Figure 13-19 This is the property sheet for the CompanyID label control.

You also can correct the caption from inside a label by selecting the label, moving the mouse pointer inside the label until the pointer changes into an I-beam shape, and then clicking to set the insertion point inside the label text. You can delete unwanted characters, and you can type new characters. When you finish correcting a label caption, Access automatically adjusts the size of the control smaller or larger to adequately display the new name. You can change settings using the property sheet to adjust the size of a label, or you can also select the control and drag the control's handles to override the automatic resizing and manually adjust the size and alignment of the control.

Setting Form Properties

You can display the form's properties in the property sheet, as shown in Figure 13-20, by clicking anywhere outside the Detail section of the form, by clicking the small square box in the upper-left corner of the Form window, or by selecting Form from the Selection Type combo box on the property sheet. On the Format tab in Figure 13-20, we set the caption to Companies / Organizations. This value will appear on the Form window's title bar in Form view or Datasheet view.

Figure 13-20 You can use the Caption property on the Format tab of the property sheet for the form to define a title for the form.

Toward the bottom of the list of properties on the Format tab are the Grid X and Grid Y properties that control the density of dots on the grid, as discussed earlier in this chapter. The defaults are 24 dots per inch across (Grid X) and 24 dots per inch down (Grid Y), if your measurements are in U.S. units. For metric measurements, the defaults are 5 dots per centimeter in both directions. Access also draws a shaded line on the grid every inch or centimeter to help you line up controls. If you decide to turn on the Snap To Grid command, under the Size/Space button in the Sizing & Ordering group of the Arrange tab, to help you line up controls on your form, you might want to change the density of the grid dots to give you greater control over where you place objects on the form.

Note

You won't see the grid dots if you set either the Grid X or Grid Y property to more than 24 in U.S. measurements or more than 9 in metric measurements.

You can set the properties beginning with On Current on the Event tab of the property sheet to run macros or Visual Basic procedures. The events associated with these properties can trigger macro actions.

Customizing Colors and Checking Your Design Results

Let's explore some of the interesting effects you can design using colors. To make the fields on the form stand out, you can click in the Detail section and then set the background to dark gray using the Background button in the Font group of the Format tab. To make the labels stand out against this dark background, drag the mouse pointer around all the label controls or click the horizontal ruler directly above all the label controls, and then set the Background color to white. If you haven't already moved and resized the labels, you can select all the labels and then widen them all to the left by clicking the left edge sizing handle of any of the labels and dragging left. This pulls the long Company / Organization caption over so that it doesn't overlap the CompanyName field. If you also want to make the Detail section fit snugly around the controls on your form, drag the edges of the Detail section inward.

INSIDE OUT **Using the Ruler to Select All Controls**

To select all controls in a vertical area, click the horizontal ruler above the area containing the controls you want to select. Likewise, to select all controls in a horizontal area, click the vertical ruler.

When you finish working on this form in Design view, it might look something like the one shown in Figure 13-21.

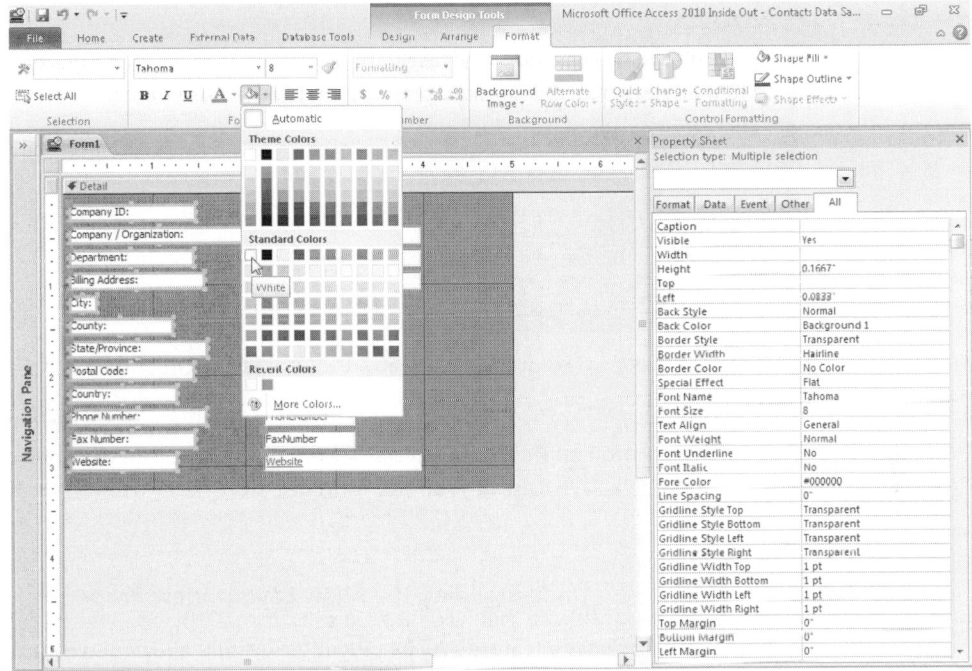

Figure 13-21 You can add contrast to the Companies/Organizations form by using the Background Color button.

Click the arrow below the View button in the Views group on the ribbon and click Form View to see your form. It will look similar to the form shown in Figure 13-22. (You can find this form saved as frmXmplCompany1 in the sample database.) Note that the labels are all different sizes and the contrast might be too distracting. You could further refine the look of this form by making all the labels the same size and perhaps aligning the captions to the right. You could also make the label background transparent or the same color as the Detail section and change the font color to white. You'll learn more about customizing your form design in Chapter 14.

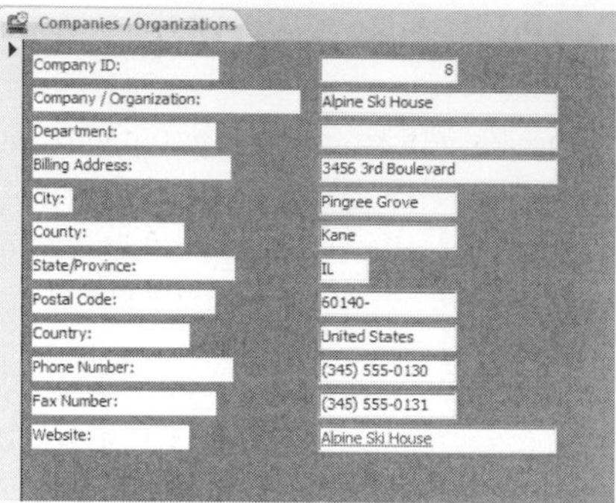

Figure 13-22 Switch to Form view to see how the Companies/Organizations form looks so far.

Click the Save button on the Quick Access Toolbar or click the File tab on the Backstage view and then click Save to save your new form design.

INSIDE OUT Understanding the Allow Layout View Property

Access 2010 includes a feature—Allow Layout view—that allows you to further modify the design of your forms, even in a finished application. All new forms in Access have the Allow Layout property set to Yes by default. This lets any user open the form in Layout view to make design changes. You should be sure to set this property to No in all forms in a client database before distributing a finished application to users. If you don't do this, users can make design changes to your forms, which is probably not a good idea in a production application.

Note that this property was called Allow Design Changes in Access 2003. Setting this property to Yes in Access 2003 allowed the user to open the property sheet while in Form view and make changes to the form design by changing property settings. But Layout view in Access 2007 and 2010 is much more powerful, because the user can not only change properties but also move and add controls. We will discuss Layout view in more detail in the next chapter when we discuss creating web forms.

Working with Quick Create and the Form Wizard

Now that you understand the basic mechanics of form design, you could continue to build all your forms from scratch in Design view. However, even the most experienced developers take advantage of the many wizards built into Access 2010 to get a jump-start on design tasks. This section shows you how to use Quick Create form commands and the Form Wizard to quickly build a custom form.

Creating a Form with the Quick Create Commands

Access 2010 includes Quick Create commands so that you can create new forms with one click on a ribbon command. As you'll learn in this section, you can build forms designed in a variety of different views, so you can pick the style you need for the data-editing task at hand. You just walked through creating a form from scratch, so you should recall how much time it took to place all the fields on the form design grid, resize and move some of the controls, and change some of the form properties. The Quick Create commands can do a lot of the heavy work in designing a base form, which you can then modify to meet your specific needs.

Suppose you want to create a data entry form for the tblProducts table in the Conrad Systems Contacts database. Begin by opening the ContactsDataCopy.accdb database and click the top of the Navigation pane to open the Navigation Pane menu. Click Object Type under Navigate To Category and Tables under Filter By Group to display a list of only the tables in this database. Select the tblProducts table in the Navigation pane and then click the Form command in the Forms group on the Create tab. Access immediately creates a new single form based on the tblProducts table, including a control for every field in that table, and displays it in Layout view, as shown in Figure 13-23.

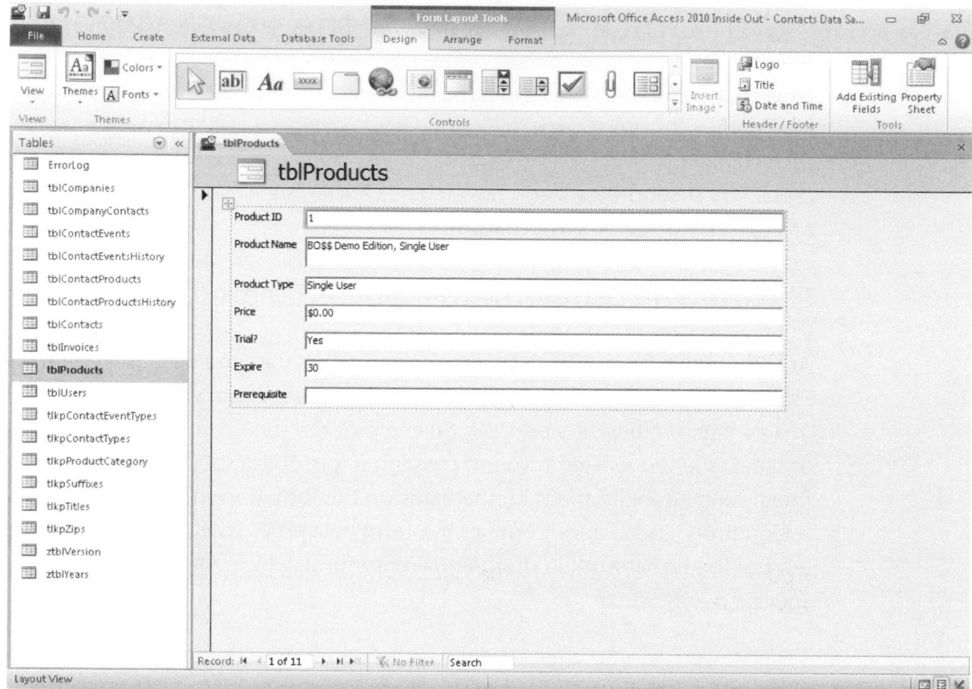

Figure 13-23 Access can save you time by creating a single form using all the fields in the selected table.

As you can see, Access creates this form very quickly, and it looks professional. Switch to Design view for this form by clicking the arrow below the View button in the Views group on the Home tab and clicking Design View. Notice how Access creates a text box on the form for each field in the tblProducts table and an associated label for each text box with a caption, and then aligns all the controls. Access also creates a bitmap picture logo and a label for the form's title in the Header section.

This form could still use some modification, such as entering a different form title and resizing some controls, but overall Access has completed a lot of the hard work of creating the form. Close this form and do not save it.

Select the tblProducts table again in the Navigation pane, click the More Forms command in the Forms group on the Create tab, and then click Split Form from the drop-down list of form types. Access immediately creates a new split form containing every field in the tblProducts table and displays it in Layout view, as shown in Figure 13-24.

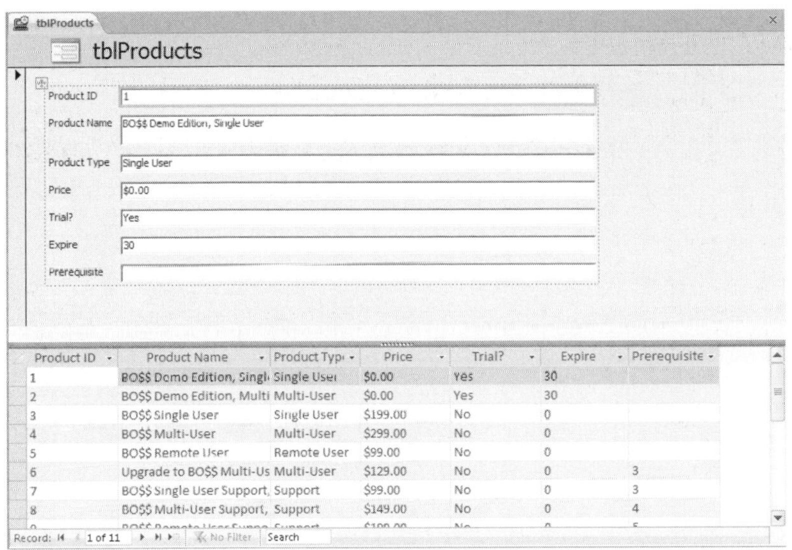

Figure 13-24 When you click the Split Form command, Access creates a new split form based on your table.

Here again, Access creates controls and associated labels for all the fields in the tblProducts table. Switch to Design view by clicking the arrow in the Views group and clicking Design View. The form's Default View property is set to Split Form, and the Split Form Orientation property is set to Datasheet On Bottom. The top of the Form window displays the fields from the tblProducts table in Single Form view, and the bottom of the form displays all the records from the tblProducts table in Datasheet view. Close this form now and do not save it when prompted.

Select the tblProducts table again in the Navigation pane, click the More Forms command in the Forms group on the Create tab, and then click Multiple Items from the drop-down list of form types. Access immediately creates a new continuous form based on all the fields in the tblProducts table and displays it in Layout view, as shown in Figure 13-25.

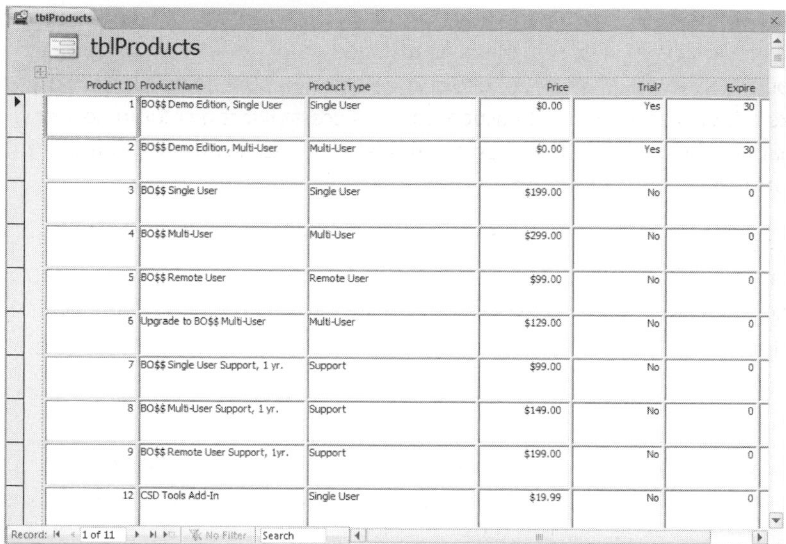

Figure 13-25 Use the Multiple Items command to create a continuous form.

In this continuous form, Access creates controls for all the fields in the tblProducts table horizontally across the Form window. Switch to Design view by clicking the arrow in the Views group and clicking Design View. The form's properties have been set to display the products in Continuous Form view, which means you can view more one than record at a time. Notice that Access places the associated label for each control in the form's Header section. Close this form now and do not save it when prompted.

Select the tblProducts table again in the Navigation pane, click the More Forms command in the Forms group on the Create tab, and then click the Datasheet command. Access immediately creates a new form in Datasheet view using all the fields in the tblProducts table and displays it, as shown in Figure 13-26.

tblProducts

Product ID	Product Name	Product Type	Price	Trial?	Expire	Prerequisite
1	BO$$ Demo Edition, Single	Single User	$0.00	Yes	30	
2	BO$$ Demo Edition, Multi-l	Multi-User	$0.00	Yes	30	
3	BO$$ Single User	Single User	$199.00	No	0	
4	BO$$ Multi-User	Multi-User	$299.00	No	0	
5	BO$$ Remote User	Remote User	$99.00	No	0	
6	Upgrade to BO$$ Multi-Use	Multi-User	$129.00	No	0	3
7	BO$$ Single User Support,	Support	$99.00	No	0	3
8	BO$$ Multi-User Support, 1	Support	$149.00	No	0	4
9	BO$$ Remote User Suppor	Support	$199.00	No	0	5
12	CSD Tools Add-In	Single User	$19.99	No	0	
13	CSD Tools Add-In Demo Ec	Single User	$0.00	Yes	90	
* (New)			$0.00	No	0	

Figure 13-26 This datasheet form was created using the Datasheet command on the More Forms menu.

Switch to Design view by clicking the arrow in the Views group and clicking Design View. The form's properties have been set to display the products in Datasheet view, which means you can view more than one record at a time, and all the records are stacked close together like a table datasheet. In datasheet forms, Access places a column header with the name that normally appears for an associated label for each control. Close this form now and do not save it when prompted.

Access 2010 also has Quick Create commands for PivotChart and PivotTable views in the Forms group. You can use these commands to get a jump-start on creating PivotChart and PivotTable forms. You'll learn more about creating and using PivotChart forms in Chapter 15.

Note

When you use a Quick Create command to create a form, Access applies a control layout so that all the controls will move and resize together. We'll discuss control layouts in more detail in Chapter 14.

Creating the Basic Products Form with the Form Wizard

The Quick Create form commands are easy to use, but you have no flexibility with how Access initially creates the form. The Form Wizard is another tool you can use to quickly create forms in your database. Begin by opening the ContactsDataCopy.accdb database, and click the top of the Navigation pane to display the Navigation Pane menu. Select Object Type under Navigate To Category and Tables under Filter By Group to display a list of only the tables in this database. Select the tblProducts table in the Navigation pane and then click the Form Wizard command in the Forms group on the Create tab. Access opens the first page of the Form Wizard, as shown in Figure 13-27.

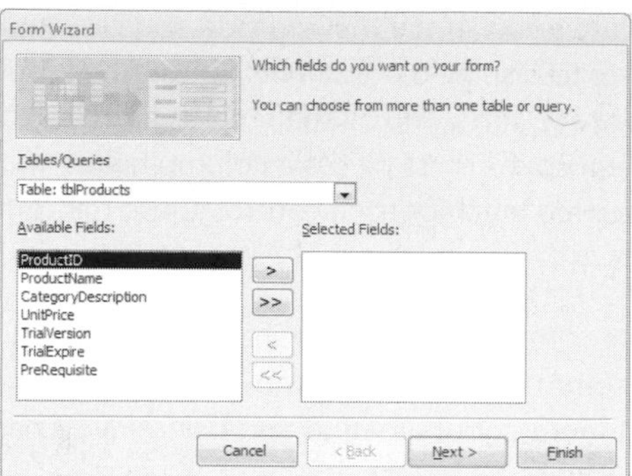

Figure 13-27 The first page of the Form Wizard displays fields you can select to include in your form.

You can select any field in the Available Fields list and click the single right arrow (>) button to copy that field to the Selected Fields list. You can also click the double right arrow (>>) button to copy all available fields to the Selected Fields list. If you copy a field in error, you can select the field in the Selected Fields list and click the single left arrow (<) button to remove the field from the list. You can remove all fields and start over by clicking the double left arrow (<<) button. For this example, click the double right arrow button to use all the fields in the tblProducts table in the new form.

As you'll learn in Chapter 15, you can select fields from one table or query and then change the data source name in the Tables/Queries combo box to select a different but related table or query. If you have defined the relationships between tables in your database, the Form Wizard can determine how the data from multiple sources is related and can offer to build either a simple form to display all the data or a more complex one that shows some of the data in the main part of the form with related data displayed in an embedded subform. You'll use this technique to build a more complex form in Chapter 15.

At any time, you can click Finish to go directly to the last step of the wizard. You can also click Cancel at any time to stop creating the form.

After you select all the fields from the tblProducts table, click Next. On the next page, the wizard gives you choices for the layout of your form. You can choose to display the controls on your form in columns, arrange the controls across the form in a tabular format (this creates a continuous form), create a form that opens in Datasheet view, or place the fields in a block "justified" view. For this example, select Columnar, and then click Next.

On the final page of the Form Wizard, shown in Figure 13-28, Access asks for a title for your form. Type an appropriate title, such as **Products**. The wizard places this title in the Caption property of the form and also saves the form with this name. (If you already have a form named Products, Access appends a number to the end of the name to create a unique name.)

Select the Open The Form To View Or Enter Information option, and then click Finish to go directly to Form view. Alternatively, you can select the Modify The Form's Design option, and then click Finish to open the new form in Design view. The finished form is shown in Form view in Figure 13-29. Notice that the Form Wizard created labels sized alike with no ending colons on the captions.

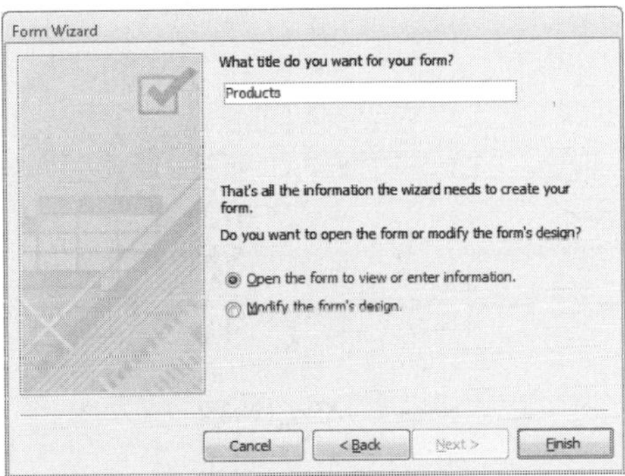

Figure 13-28 You can type a name for your form on the final page of the Form Wizard.

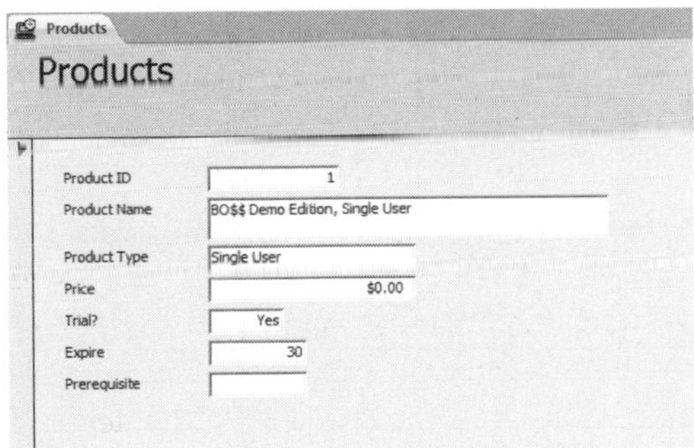

Figure 13-29 The Form Wizard creates a form in a columnar format that is similar to the form produced with the Quick Create commands.

If you're curious to see the tabular format, you can start a new form on the tblProducts table and use the Form Wizard again. Select all the fields on the first page of the Form Wizard, select Tabular for the layout, and then click Next to go to the final page of the wizard. For a title, type **Products - Tabular**, and open the new form in Form view. It should look something like the form shown in Figure 13-30. Close this form when you finish looking at it.

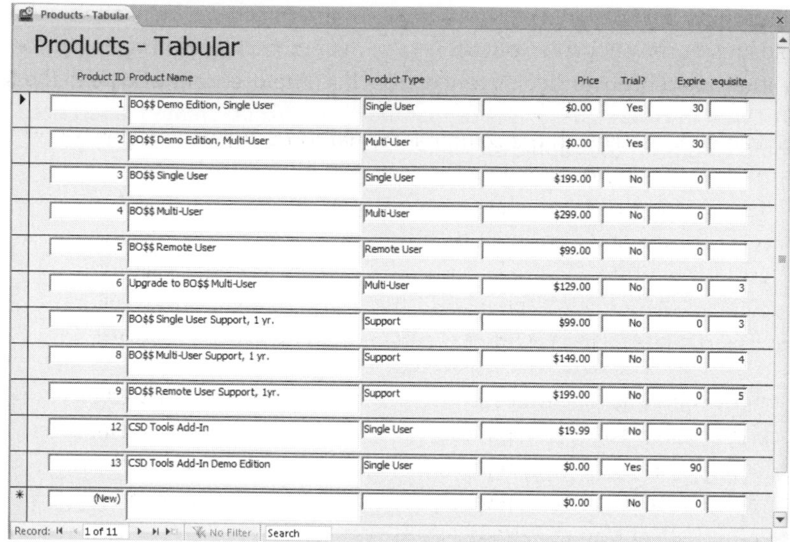

Figure 13-30 This Products form, created by the Form Wizard, is in a tabular format.

You can also investigate what a justified form looks like by going through the exercise again and selecting Justified for the layout on the second page in the Form Wizard. If you name the form **Products – Justified**, your result should look something like the one shown in Figure 13-31. Close this form when you finish looking at it.

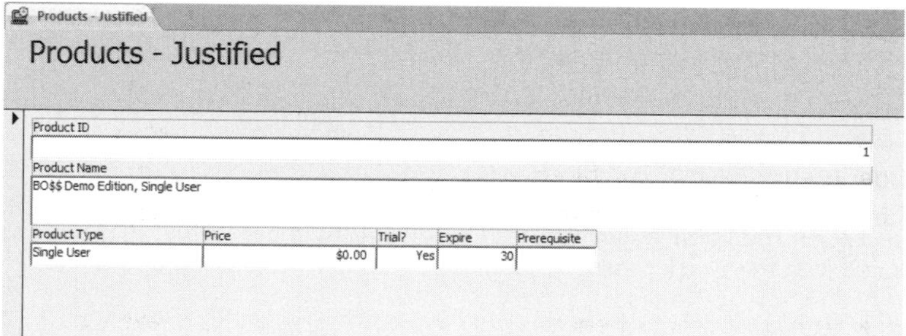

Figure 13-31 This is the Products form in a justified format.

Modifying the Products Form

The Form Wizard took care of some of the work, but there's still a lot you can do to improve the appearance and usability of this form. And even though the Form Wizard adjusted the display control widths, they're still not perfect. Most of the text boxes are larger than they need to be. The Form Wizard created a two-line text box for the product name when one should suffice. We personally prefer to see field labels right-aligned and bold so that they're easier to read. Finally, the ProductID field is an AutoNumber data type, so you should probably lock it and disable it so the user cannot type in the field.

You can either start with the columnar format form, shown in Figure 13-29, or start a new form. (We decided to modify the form from Figure 13-29 for the following examples.) Open the form in Design view. To help align controls, click outside the Detail section so that the form is selected, and make sure that the Grid X and Grid Y properties on the form's property sheet are set to 24. (Leave the settings at Grid X = 5 and Grid Y = 5 if you're working in metric measurements.) Be sure the Show Grid command is selected under the Size/Space command in the Sizing & Ordering group on the Arrange contextual tab.

Begin by selecting the ProductID text box and change the Enabled property to No and the Locked property to Yes, as you learned to do earlier. The ProductName text box needs to be about 3 inches wide. You can set a specific width by clicking the control, opening the property sheet, clicking the Format tab, and typing **3"** in the Width property (the fifth property down the list). The Form Wizard created a text box that is two lines high for ProductName, but it doesn't need to be bigger than one line. Select the control, and then grab the bottom sizing box in the middle of the control and drag it up to make the control smaller. Click the Size/Space command in the Sizing & Ordering group on the Arrange tab and then click the To Fit command to resize the control to display one line. Click the Format tab in the property sheet and change the Scroll Bars property to None—the Form Wizard specified a vertical scroll bar in the two-line control that it designed. It doesn't make sense to show a scroll bar in a one-line control that is already wide enough to display all the data.

Now that you've made the ProductName text box smaller, you have extra space between it and the CategoryDescription text box. Select the CategoryDescription, UnitPrice, TrialVersion, TrialExpire, and PreRequisite text boxes and move them up close to the ProductName text box. Unless you turned off Snap To Grid under the Size/Space command in the Sizing & Ordering group on the Arrange tab, it should be easy to line up the controls in their new positions. As you move these four controls, their associated labels will stay aligned with the text boxes.

The five text box controls beneath the ProductName text box have varying column widths. Let's make them all the same width for clarity. Select each of these text box controls one at a time while holding down the Ctrl key to select them all as a group. Now type **1"** in the Width property on the property sheet to change the width of all these text boxes at the same time.

Next, fix all the labels. Click in the horizontal ruler above the column of labels to select them all. (Access selects the Products label in the form header during this procedure as well, so hold down the Shift key and click the label in the form header to clear it.) Click the Align Right and Bold buttons in the Font group on the Format contextual tab to change the appearance of the labels. Click the Products label in the form header and then click the Italic button in the Font group to add emphasis. Finally, click the To Fit command under the Size/Space command in the Sizing & Ordering group on the Arrange tab to make the Product label shrink in size around the text. After you move all the controls up closer to the form header and left side of the form grid and shrink the bottom margin of the form, it should now look similar to the one shown in Figure 13-32.

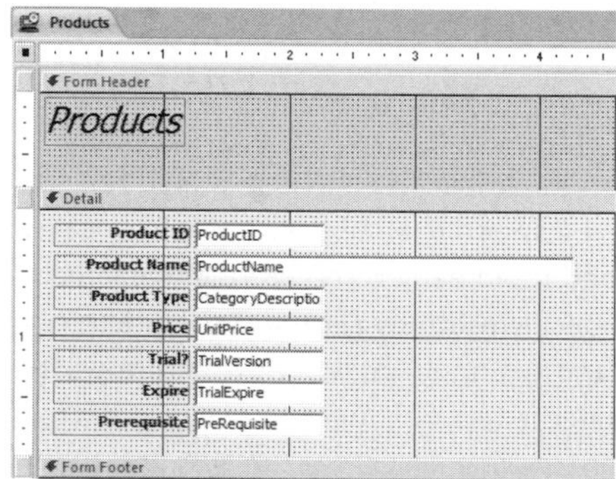

Figure 13-32 You can now see the modified Products form in Design view with the changes you applied.

Finally, switch to Form view and your form should look something like the one shown in Figure 13-33. The form now looks a bit more customized—and somewhat more like the frmProducts form in the Conrad Systems Contacts application. You can find this form saved as frmXmplProducts1 in the sample database.

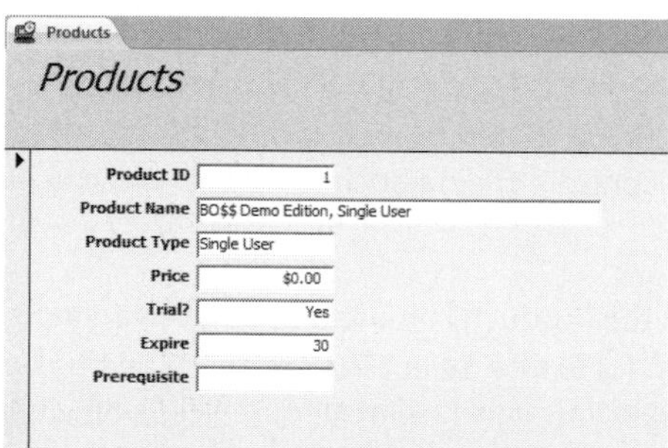

Figure 13-33 When you switch to Form view, you can see how the modified Products form looks at this point.

Simplifying Data Input with a Form

One drawback to working with a relational database is that often you have to deal with information stored in multiple tables. That's not a problem if you're using a query to link data, but working with multiple tables can be confusing if you're entering new data. Access 2010 provides some great ways to show information from related tables, thus making data input much simpler.

Taking Advantage of Combo Boxes and List Boxes

In Chapter 12, "Using Forms in an Access Application," you saw how you can use a combo box or a list box to present a list of potential values for a control. To create the list, you can type the values in the Row Source property box of the control. You can also specify a table or a query as the source of the values in the list. Access 2010 displays the currently selected value in the text box portion of the combo box or as a highlighted selection in the list.

The CategoryDescription field in the tblProducts table is a simple Text data type. To help ensure data consistency, there's a separate lookup table that contains a list of predefined product types. There's also a referential-integrity rule that keeps you from entering anything other than a predefined type in the CategoryDescription field. However, you can type anything you like in the CategoryDescription text box (labeled *Product Type*) that the Form Wizard designed. Go ahead and type any random string of characters in the text box and then try to save the record. You should see an unfriendly message about "related record is required in 'tlkpProductCategory'."

You can help avoid this problem by providing a combo box to edit and display the CategoryDescription field instead. The combo box can display the list of valid values from tlkpProductCategory lookup table to make it easy for your user to choose a valid value. The combo box can also limit what the user enters to only values in the list. In Chapter 25, you'll learn how to write Visual Basic code to detect when a user tries to enter something that's not in the list so that you can provide your own, more user-friendly, message.

To see how a combo box works, you can replace the CategoryDescription text box control with a combo box on the Products form. In Design view, select the CategoryDescription text box control and then press the Delete key to remove the text box control from the form (this also removes the related label control). Be sure the Use Control Wizards button is selected in the Controls group on the Design tab. Display the field list by clicking the Add Existing Fields button in the Tools group on the same Design tab. Next, click the Combo Box button in the Controls group and drag the CategoryDescription field from the field list to the form. The new control appears on the form, and Access starts the Combo Box Wizard, as shown in Figure 13-34, to help you out.

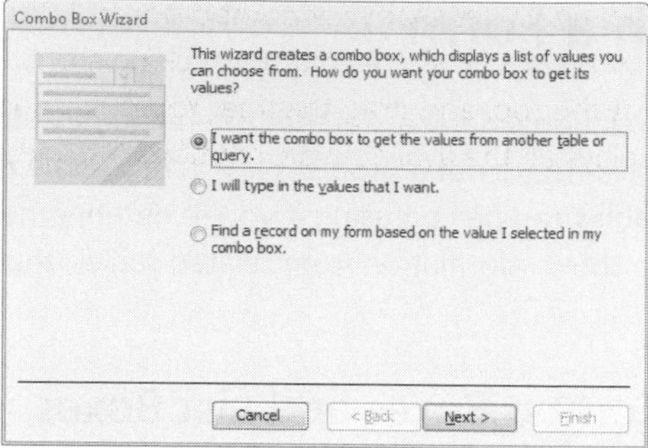

Figure 13-34 After you drop the CategoryDescription field onto the form grid, Access opens the first page of the Combo Box Wizard.

> **INSIDE OUT** **Manually Changing a Text Box to a Combo Box**
>
> **You can change a text box to a combo box by right-clicking the text box control, clicking Change To on the shortcut menu, and then clicking Combo Box on the submenu. However, after you change a text box to a combo box in this way, you have to set the properties for the display list yourself.**

Follow this procedure to build your combo box:

1. You want the combo box to display values from the tlkpProductCategory lookup table, so select the I Want The Combo Box To Get The Values From Another Table Or Query option, and then click Next to go to the next page.

2. On the second page, the wizard displays a list of available tables in the database. Note that the wizard also provides an option to view queries or both tables and queries. Scroll down the list and click Table: tlkpProductCategory to select that table, and click Next to go to the next page.

3. On the third page, the wizard shows you the single field in the table, CategoryDescription. Select that field and click the right arrow (>) to move it to the Selected Fields list. Click Next to go on.

4. The fourth page allows you to select up to four fields to sort either Ascending or Descending. Click the arrow to the right of the first field and then select the CategoryDescription field. The button next to the first box indicates *Ascending*, and you want to leave it that way. If you click the button, it changes to *Descending*, which is not what you want. (You can click the button again to set it back.) Click Next to go to the next page.

5. The wizard shows you the lookup values that your combo box will display as an embedded datasheet, as shown here. To size a column, click on the dividing line at the right edge of a column at the top, and drag the line. You can adjust the size of the column to be sure it displays all the available descriptions properly. Click Next to go on.

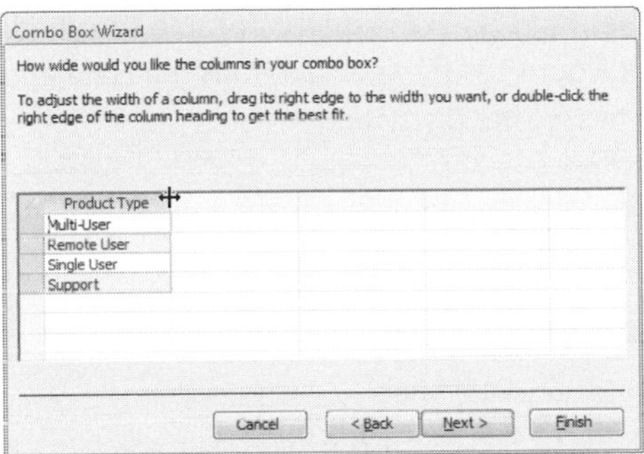

6. On the next page, the wizard asks whether you want to store the value from the combo box in a field from the table or query that you're updating with this form or simply save the value selected in an unbound control "for later use." You'll see in Parts 6 and 9 of this book that unbound controls are useful for storing calculated values or for providing a way for the user to enter parameter data for use by your macros or Visual Basic procedures. In this case, you want to update the CategoryDescription field, so be sure to select the Store That Value In This Field option and verify that CategoryDescription is selected in the list. Click Next to go to the last page of the wizard.

7. On the final page, shown here, the wizard suggests a caption that you probably want to correct. In this case, enter **Product Type** in the box. Click Finish, and you're all done.

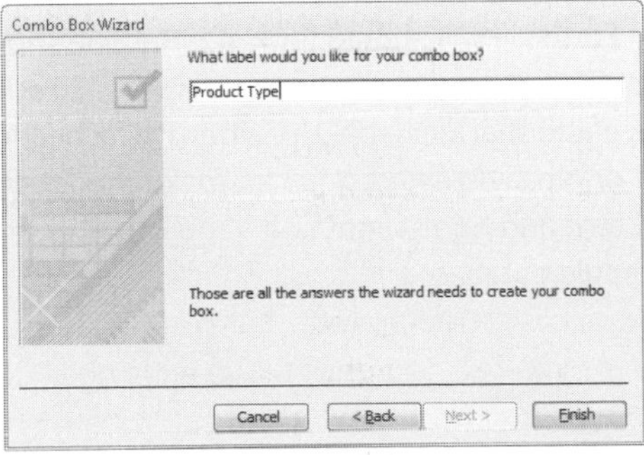

If you have the property sheet open, you can study the properties set by the Combo Box Wizard, as shown in Figure 13-35. The Control Source property shows that the combo box is bound to the CategoryDescription field. The Row Source Type property indicates that the data filling the combo box comes from the table or query entered in the Row Source property box. Notice that the wizard generated an SQL statement in the Row Source property box. You can also specify a value list as the Row Source property, or you can ask Access to create a list from the names of fields in the query or table specified in the Row Source property. Please note that in Figure 13-35, we show both the Data and the Format tabs so that you can see the properties we are discussing.

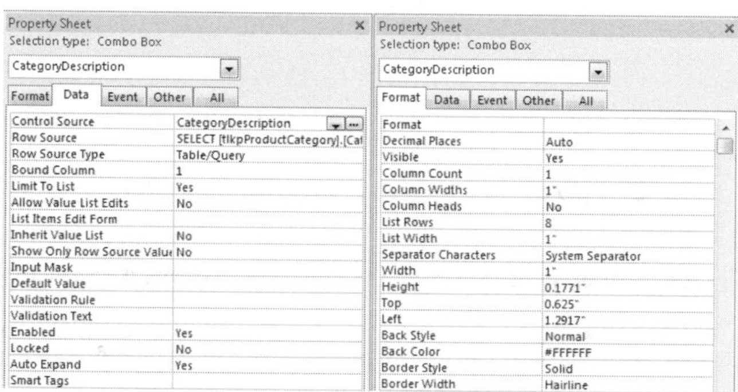

Figure 13-35 The Combo Box Wizard set these properties for the CategoryDescription field.

The Column Count property is set to 1 to indicate that one column should be created from the list. You have the option of asking Access to display column headings when the combo box is open, but you don't need that for this example, so leave the Column Heads property set to No. The wizard sets the Column Widths property based on the width you set in step 5. The next property on the Data tab, Bound Column, indicates that the first column (the only column in this case) is the one that sets the value of the combo box and therefore the value of the bound field in the table.

When you open the form in Form view, it should look like the one shown in Figure 13-36. You can see that the CategoryDescription combo box now shows the list of valid values from the lookup table. Notice also that the label the wizard attached looks more like the labels that the Form Wizard originally created. You can make this label look like the others by changing it to a bold font and right-aligning it. (You can find this form saved as frmXmplProducts2 in the sample database.)

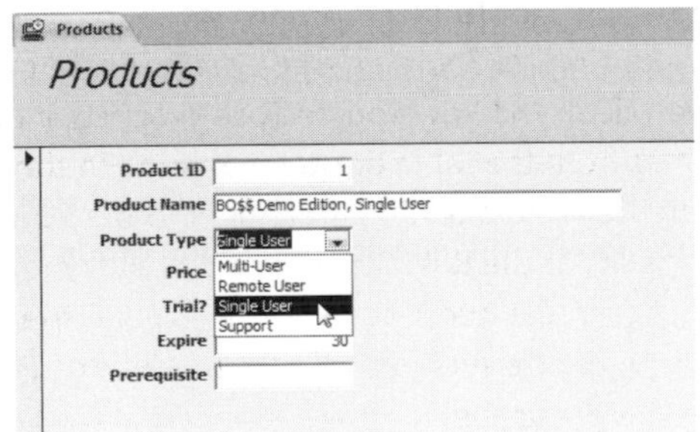

Figure 13-36 A combo box for the CategoryDescription field makes it much easier for the user to select a correct value.

> **INSIDE OUT** **Having Access Select Closest Matches While Typing**
>
> If you want Access to select the closest matching entry when you type a few leading characters in a combo box, set the control's Auto Expand property to Yes.

Using Toggle Buttons, Check Boxes, and Option Buttons

If your table contains a field that has a yes/no, a true/false, or an on/off value, you can choose from three types of controls that graphically display and set the status of this type of field: toggle buttons, check boxes, and option buttons.

> **INSIDE OUT** **Choosing Toggle Buttons and Check Boxes and Option Buttons—How to Decide?**
>
> Although you can certainly use any of these three controls to display an underlying Yes/No data type, you should try to use these controls in your application similarly to the way Windows uses them. Your users might be confused if you try to use them in a different way. Here are some good principles to follow:
>
> - Use a toggle button to display an option value. A toggle button works best to display an option that is on or off.
> - Use a check box to display all simple yes/no or true/false values.

- **Use an option button when the user needs to make a choice from several options. You should not use an option button to display simple yes/no or true/false values.**

We personally never use a toggle button or an option button except inside an option group control. You can learn more about working with the option group control in Chapter 15.

The tblProducts table has a TrialVersion field that indicates whether the particular product is a free trial edition that expires in a specific number of days. As you can see in the original text box control created by the Form Wizard (see Figure 13-29), the word *Yes* or *No* appears, depending on the value in the underlying field. This field might be more appealing and understandable if it were displayed in a check box control.

To change the TrialVersion control on the Products form, first delete the TrialVersion text box control. Display the field list by clicking the Add Existing Fields button in the Tools group. Next, click the Check Box button in the Controls group, and then drag the TrialVersion field from the field list into the open space you left on the form. Your form in Design view should now look like the one shown in Figure 13-37. Notice that the default check box also includes a label, but the label is positioned to the right of the control and does not include a colon. If you want to move the label, select it, and then use the large handle, shown earlier in Figure 13-15, to move the label to the left of the check box. You should also change the font to bold to match the other labels.

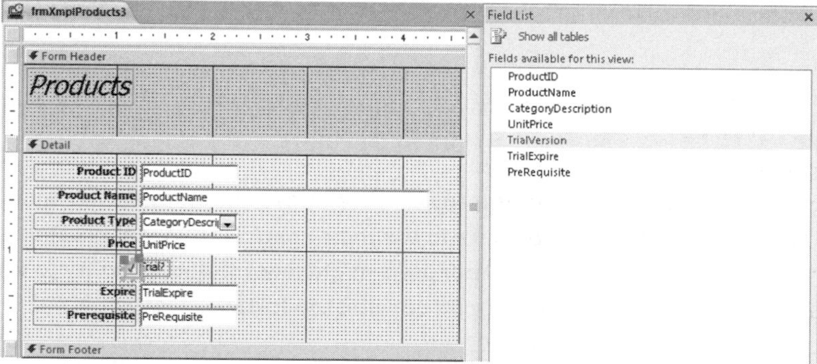

Figure 13-37 The Products form now contains a check box control to display the TrialVersion field.

After making final adjustments to the TrialVersion label, click the arrow under the Views button and click Form View to see the result. Your form should look like the one shown in Figure 13-38. This design sample is saved as frmXmplProducts3 in the sample database.

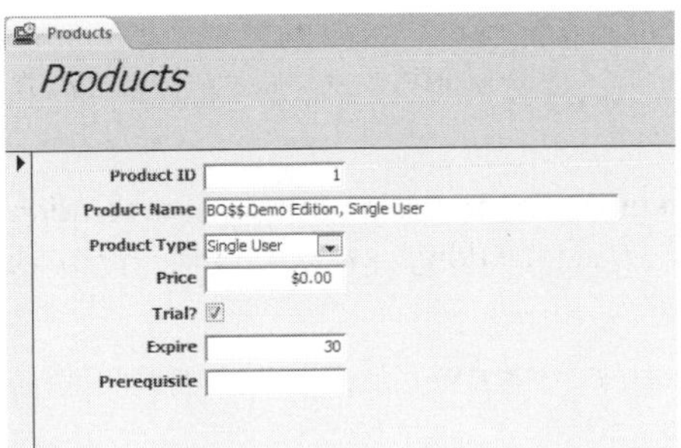

Figure 13-38 Your Products form now has both a combo box control and a check box control to simplify data entry.

Working with Application Part Forms

In Chapter 4, "Designing Client Tables," you learned about a new feature in Access 2010 called Application Parts. You learned that Application Parts allow you to easily add new tables to your database. In addition to just adding tables, you can also add new forms into your database using Application Part Forms.

Earlier in this chapter, you learned that you can use the Quick Create options and the Form Wizard to quickly create forms that are bound to a table or query. When you use Application Part Forms, Access creates unbound forms. You can bind these unbound forms to a record source and then use the field list to create controls bound to the fields in the record source of the form.

You might be asking yourself why you would use an Application Part Form instead of a Quick Create option or the Form Wizard. There are a couple of reasons why you might want to use an Application Part Form instead of other options. First, most Application Part Forms include command buttons complete with embedded macros to perform actions such as saving a record or closing a form. You won't have to create these objects for your form manually because Access does the work for you. Second, not every form you create for your database needs to be a bound form. For example, you might want to create a form that only displays information to a user or prompts the user for confirmation of an application action. The frmCopyright form in the Contacts Data Copy is a good example of an unbound form that displays information to the user.

To create an Application Part Form, click the Application Parts button in the Templates group on the Create tab. Access displays the Application Parts gallery, as shown in Figure 13-39. Beneath Blank Forms, you'll see buttons for the 10 Application Part Forms included with Access 2010. If you hover your mouse over one of the buttons, Access displays a tooltip indicating the purpose of the Application Part Form.

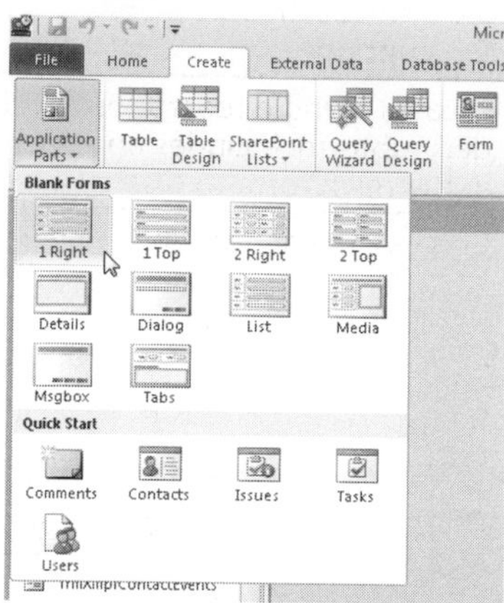

Figure 13-39 Access includes 10 Application Part Forms you can use to get a jump start on creating forms.

Left to right, top to bottom, the Application Part Form buttons in the gallery are described in Table 13-5. The form name that Access creates when you click one of these buttons is in the Form Name column.

Table 13-5 Application Part Forms

Button	Form Name	Description
1 Right	SingleOneColumnRightLabels	Creates a single record form with placeholders for one column of data. Includes four labels on the left side and two command buttons for saving the record and saving and closing the form.
1 Top	SingleOneColumnTopLabels	Creates a single record form with placeholders for one column of data. Includes four labels positioned above each field placeholder and two command buttons for saving the record and saving and closing the form.
2 Right	SingleTwoColumnRightLabels	Creates a single record form with placeholders for two columns of data. Includes eight labels on the left side of each field placeholder and two command buttons for saving the record and saving and closing the form.
2 Top	SingleTwoColumnTopLabels	Creates a single record form with placeholders for two columns of data. Includes eight labels positioned above each field placeholder and two command buttons for saving the record and saving and closing the form.

Button	Form Name	Description
Details	Details	Creates a single record form with an embedded subform. Includes an attachment control in the main form to display a picture.
Dialog	Dialog	Creates a small form with two command buttons for saving and one for saving and closing the form. Use this form for a confirmation dialog box.
List	List	Creates a continuous form with a command button in the form header section to create a new record. Includes two command buttons in the detail section—Edit and Delete.
Media	Media	Creates a single record form ideal for displaying details about a specific record. Includes large placeholders for displaying media content, perhaps by placing a web browser control in the placeholder that points to a URL with media content.
Msgbox	MessgeBox	Creates a small form with three command buttons—Yes, No, and Cancel. Use this form for a confirmation dialog box.
Tabs	SingleTwoColumnTabsTopLabels	Creates a single record form with placeholders for four fields of data. Includes a com mand button for saving the record and a tab control at the bottom of the form to display additional data and subforms.

Click the first button in the gallery, 1 Right, to create a new Application Part Form. Note that if you have any objects open, Access prompts you to close any open objects before proceeding. Unlike the Quick Create commands, Access does not immediately open the form for you in Layout view after it creates the form; in fact, Access does not even open the form at all in any view. When you click the 1 Right button, Access creates a form called SingleOneColumnRightLabels. Find this form in the Navigation pane and then open it. You'll notice that Access creates a form with a title label, two command buttons, and four placeholder labels for fields, as shown in Figure 13-40. The label captions have generic text that you can easily change to suit your individual needs.

Note

If you already have a form name in your database with the same name as the Application Part Form that Access creates, Access appends a number to the end of the form name so it will not conflict with your existing form.

Figure 13-40 Application Part Forms include different control types and placeholder labels.

INSIDE OUT Creating Web-Compatible Application Part Forms

When you create a form using the Application Part Form options in a client database, Access creates client forms. If you are using a web database, Access creates web forms when you click any of the Application Part Form buttons.

Now, switch to Design view for the new SingleOneColumnRightLabels form. If you try to resize any of the controls on the form, you'll notice that Access resizes or moves other controls as well. When you create an Application Part Form, Access applies a control layout so that all the controls will move and resize together. You can tell whether Access has applied a control layout to the controls by the small box with a crosshair inside just to the left of and slightly above the title label, as shown in Figure 13-41. We'll discuss control layouts in more detail in Chapter 14.

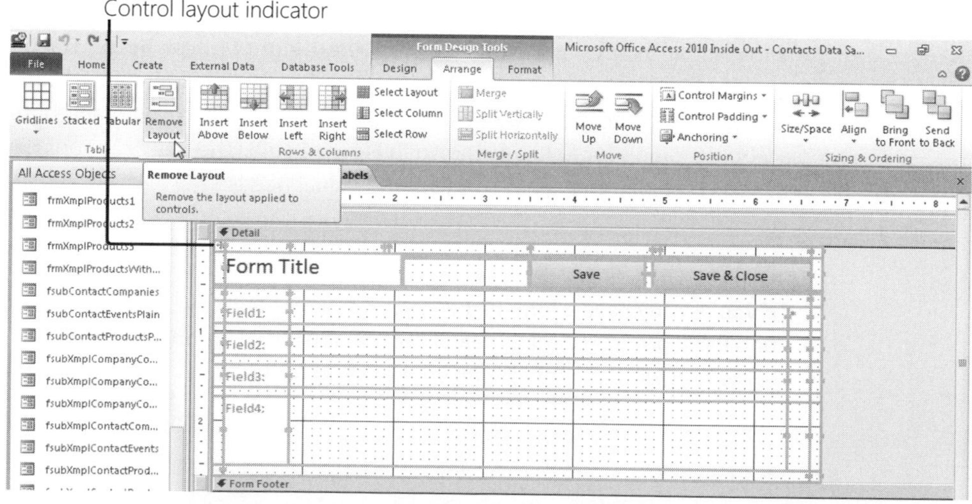

Figure 13-41 Access applied a control layout to the form controls in the Application Part Form.

To make individual size adjustments to the form controls, you need to highlight all the controls and turn off this control layout. Start by clicking the horizontal ruler just above the left edge of the label controls, and then drag in the ruler toward the right until the selection indicator touches all the controls. (If you can't see the rulers, be sure that you have clicked the Ruler button under the Size/Shape command in the Sizing & Ordering group on the Arrange tab.) Release the mouse button to select all the controls on the form grid, and then click the Remove Layout button in the Table group on the Arrange tab, as shown in Figure 13-41. Now that you have removed any control layouts, you can make individual size adjustments to the form controls. As you can see, Application Part Forms are very useful in creating forms for specific application needs in your database.

By now, you should be getting a feel for the process of building forms. In Chapter 14, you'll learn how to customize the appearance of your forms and how to create web forms in web databases.

CHAPTER 14

Customizing a Form

In Chapter 13, "Building a Form," you created a client form from scratch based on the tblCompanies table in the ContactsDataCopy.accdb sample database. You also had a chance to build a simple form on tblProducts using a wizard and to make some modifications in Design view. These forms are functional, but they're not yet professional grade. In this chapter, you'll learn how to customize your forms in both Design view and the Layout view to make them more attractive and useful. You'll also learn how to create web forms in web databases.

Note

The examples in this chapter are based on the forms, queries, tables, and data in the HousingDataCopy.accdb, BOSSDataCopy2, and ContactsMapCopy.accdb databases on the companion CD included with this book. The results you see from the samples in this chapter might not exactly match what you see in this book if you have changed the sample data in the file. Also, all the screen images in this chapter were taken on a Windows 7 system with the Access color scheme set to Silver. Your results might look different if you are using a different operating system or a different theme.

Aligning and Sizing Controls in Design View

To learn how to customize a form, open the HousingDataCopy.accdb sample client database. You need a form to edit and display employee data, and the easiest way to get started is to create a blank form based on the tblEmployees table. On the Create tab, in the Forms group, click the Blank Form button. A blank form grid appears in Layout view with the field list showing on the right side of the screen. Switch to Design view by clicking the small arrow below the View button in the Views group on either the Home tab or the Design contextual tab under Form Layout Tools. Right now the form is *unbound*—meaning there is no Record Source—so you need to bind this form to the tblEmployees table. Click the Property Sheet button in the Tools group on the Design tab under Form Design Tools. Find the Record Source property on the All or Data tab of the Property Sheet window for the form, and select tblEmployees from the list of table and query names to bind this form to the tblEmployees table.

Drag down the bottom margin of the Detail area to give yourself some room to work. Click the Arrange contextual tab under Form Design Tools, click the Size/Space command in the Sizing & Ordering group and make sure Snap To Grid is not selected. (We're asking you to do this on purpose so you can learn ways to line up and evenly space controls.) Open the field list by clicking the Add Existing Fields button in the Tools group on the Design tab. If the field list displays other tables in the bottom half of the field list, click the Show Only Fields In The Current Record Source link at the top of the Field List window to show only the fields in the tblEmployees table. Drag each field from the field list into a vertical column on your form about 1.5 inches from the left edge, beginning with the EmployeeNumber field and ending with the BirthDate field. Your starting point should look something like Figure 14-1. (If you don't want to do the work yourself to get to this point, you can find this form saved as frmXmplEmployee1 in the sample database.)

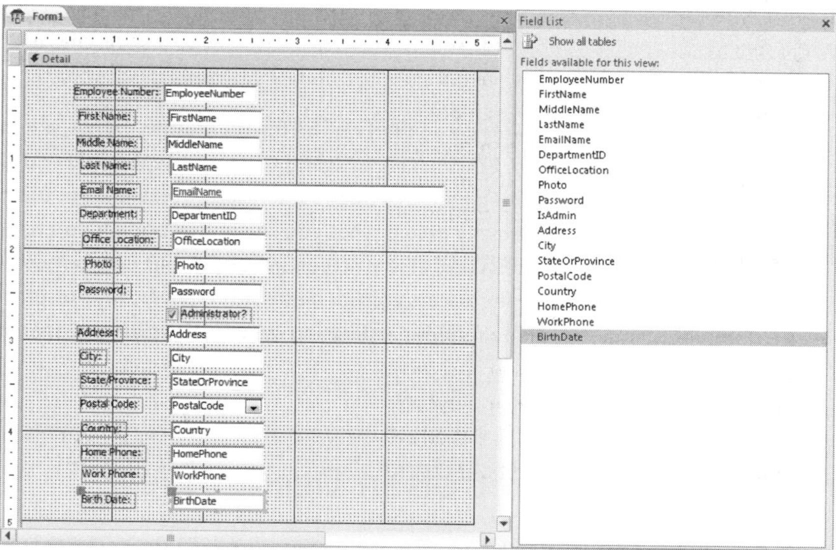

Figure 14-1 Start to build a form in Design view to display and edit employee data.

Note

The HousingDataCopy.accdb sample database has a special template form called Normal that has its default control properties set to preserve the sunken and etched special effects. This ensures that you'll see the default sunken text boxes when you follow the exercises in this chapter, even when you're using a computer running Windows Vista or Windows 7 with themed controls enabled. You'll learn more about creating template forms later in this chapter.

If you threw the form together quickly to help you enter some data (as you did in Chapter 13 to create a simple Companies input form in the ContactsDataCopy.accdb database), it probably doesn't matter if the form doesn't look perfect. But all the text boxes except EmailName are the same size, which means some are too large and some are too small to display the data. The long EmailName control looks completely out of place compared to the other controls. Also, the labels are different sizes and not right-aligned. Finally, all the text boxes and labels are out of alignment. If you're designing the form to be used continuously in an application, it's worth the extra effort to fine-tune the design so that it will look professional and be easy to use.

Note

Even if you follow along precisely with the steps described in this chapter, your results might vary slightly. All the alignment commands are sensitive to your current screen resolution. When your screen driver is set to a high resolution (for example, 1280 × 1024), the distance between grid points is logically smaller than it is when the screen driver is set to a low resolution (such as 800 × 600). You should design your forms at the same resolution as the computers that will run your application.

To examine the alignment and relative size of controls on your form, you can open the property sheet in Design view and click various controls. For example, Figure 14-2 shows the property sheets for the EmployeeNumber and the FirstName text box controls. You can see by looking at the values for the Left property (the distance from the left edge of the form) that the EmployeeNumber control is a bit closer to the left margin than the FirstName control.

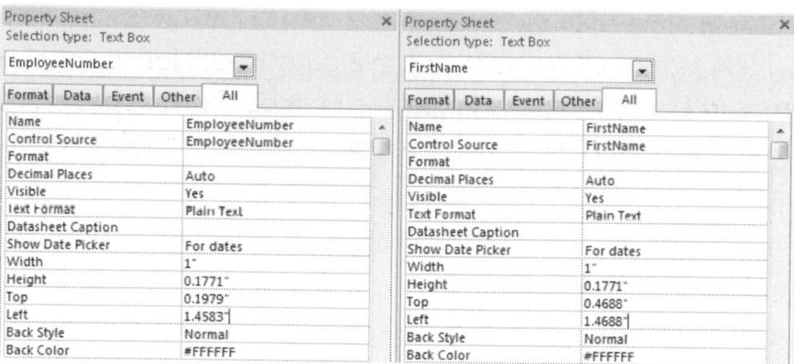

Figure 14-2 You can see on the Property Sheet windows for the EmployeeNumber and FirstName text box controls that the two controls are not aligned vertically.

You could move around the form and adjust controls so that they fit your data. You could painstakingly enter values for each control's Left property to get all controls in a column to line up exactly and then set the Top property (defining the distance from the top of the Detail section) for controls that you want to appear in a row. You could also adjust the values for the Width and Height properties so that controls and labels are the same width and height where appropriate. Fortunately, there are easier ways to make all these adjustments.

Sizing Controls to Fit Content

One adjustment you might want to make on this employees form is to bold the font for all the labels. Remember from Chapter 13 that you can click the horizontal ruler at the top of the design area to select all controls in a column, so do this to select all the label controls on the left. You can then hold down the Shift key and click the Administrator? label that's not in the column to include it in your selection. Click the Bold button in the Font group on the Format tab to change the font in all selected controls.

INSIDE OUT Setting Selection Options

If you think you'll select multiple controls often, you might want to experiment with an option setting that governs how you can select controls with your mouse pointer. Click the File tab on the Backstage view, click Options, and then click the Object Designers category in the Access Options dialog box. Under Form/Report Design View, when you select the Partially Enclosed option, the selection box you draw with your mouse needs to touch only part of a control to select it. If you select the Fully Enclosed option, the selection box must contain the entire control for the control to be selected. Fully Enclosed is most useful for complex forms with many controls that are close to each other so that you don't have to worry about inadvertently selecting controls that you touch but don't fully enclose with the selection box.

However, now that you have changed the font, the label controls are no longer large enough to display all the characters, as shown in Figure 14-3. Notice, for example, that the last two letters and the colon in the Employee Number label appear clipped off. Also, although all the text boxes and the combo box appear high enough to adequately display the data in the default Tahoma 8-point font, they're actually too small.

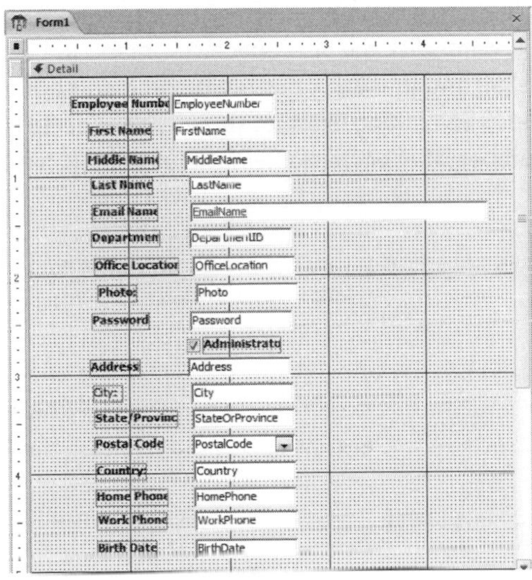

Figure 14-3 With the bold font, the label controls are no longer large enough to fit the caption text.

Microsoft Access 2010 has a command called Size To Fit that sizes label controls to fit the width of the caption text in the label. This command also ensures that text boxes and combo boxes are tall enough to display your data using the font size you've selected. You can, if you like, select all the controls so that you can resize them all at once. You can click the Select All button in the Selection group on the Format tab to highlight all the controls on your form. To select a specific group of controls, click the first one and then hold down the Shift key as you click each additional control that you want to select. You can also drag the mouse pointer across the form—so long as you don't start dragging while you are on a control—and the mouse pointer will delineate a selection box. (If you start by clicking a control and then attempt to delineate other controls by dragging, you'll move only the control.) Any controls that are inside the selection box when you release the mouse button will be selected. You can also select all controls in a vertical or a horizontal band by making the rulers visible (click the Size/Space command in the Sizing & Ordering group on the Arrange tab and then click Ruler) and then dragging the mouse along the top or side ruler.

> **INSIDE OUT** **Sizing Individual Controls**
>
> **You can "size to fit" any individual control or label by clicking the control to select it and then double-clicking any of its sizing handles.**

After you select the controls you want, click the Size/Space command in the Sizing & Ordering group on the Arrange tab and then click the To Fit command beneath Size. The Detail section should now look something like that shown in Figure 14-4. (You cannot see the entire Employee Number label because the right end of it is hidden under the EmployeeNumber text box.)

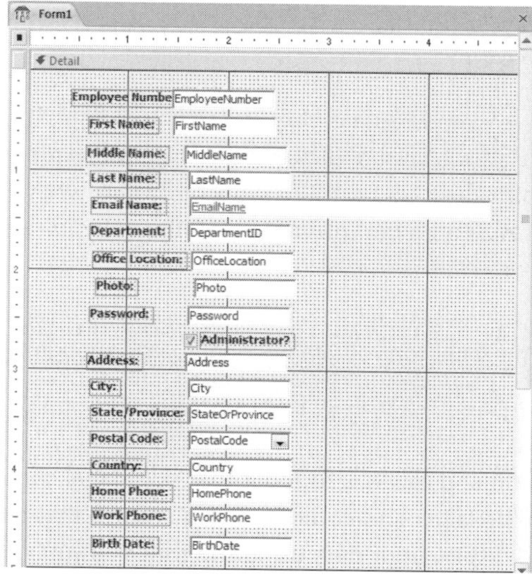

Figure 14-4 After clicking the Size To Fit command, you can see all the text in the labels.

> **INSIDE OUT** **Limitations in Using the Size To Fit Command**
>
> **The Size To Fit command works very well to set the height of labels, text boxes, and combo boxes based on the font you have chosen. It also does a reasonable job setting the width of labels based not only on the font but also on the characters you have specified in the Caption property. However, it's not perfect, so you should be aware of the following:**

- **When a label contains a long caption and has a large font that is bold or italic or both, the result of the Size To Fit command is often not wide enough. You will have to adjust the width manually.**
- **The Size To Fit command does not adjust the width of a text box or combo box because it cannot predict in advance how many characters might need to be displayed from the Control Source property. You must specifically set the width based on the data you expect the control to display.**
- **The Size To Fit command does not work for list boxes. When you switch to Form view and your list box Row Source contains enough rows to fill the list box, you might find that you see only part of a row at the bottom. (You'll see only the top part of the characters.) You must switch back and forth between Design view and Form view, adjusting the height of the control manually so that it displays complete rows. If you use Layout view for this example, you can see the data while you adjust the size of the list box.**

Switch to Form view, and scroll through several of the records to get an idea of which controls aren't wide enough to display the data from the table and which ones could be narrower. You could painstakingly resize each control to exactly fit what you see in the sample data, but this is a bad idea for two reasons:

- The data is a sample of only 16 records, so new data you enter later might be much longer in some fields. You should size the fields that aren't long enough to be 25 percent to 50 percent wider than what you think you need right now.
- A form that has a hodgepodge of a dozen or more different control widths won't make for a very visually pleasing design. You should pick two or three standard widths to use, even if some of the controls end up being wider than necessary.

You can logically group the text box controls and the combo box control in this form into three separate lengths, as follows:

- **Short** EmployeeNumber, DepartmentID, and StateOrProvince
- **Medium** FirstName, MiddleName, LastName, Password, PostalCode, HomePhone, WorkPhone, and BirthDate
- **Long** EmailName, OfficeLocation, Photo, Address, City, and Country

> **Note**
>
> **The Photo field in tblEmployees is a text field containing the name of the picture file. In Chapter 25, "Automating Your Application with Visual Basic," you'll learn how to load the file into an image control using Microsoft Visual Basic code to display the picture. Also, although you can resize the check box control, the size of the graphic image inside the control doesn't change.**

You can make the necessary adjustments by leaving the medium-length fields as they are and adjusting the fields in the other two groups. Switch back to Design view now so that you can begin resizing the controls. First, select the EmployeeNumber control and then hold down the Shift key while you select the DepartmentID and StateOrProvince controls. Next, click the sizing box in the middle of the right edge of one of the controls, and drag the right edge to the left until all three controls are about half their original sizes. Now, click the EmailName control, and resize this control to about half of its original width. Next, click the Office Location control and hold down the Shift key while you select the Photo, Address, City, and Country controls. Click the sizing box in the middle of the right edge of one of these controls, and drag the edge right until all three controls are about 50 percent bigger than their original sizes. Your layout should now look something like Figure 14-5.

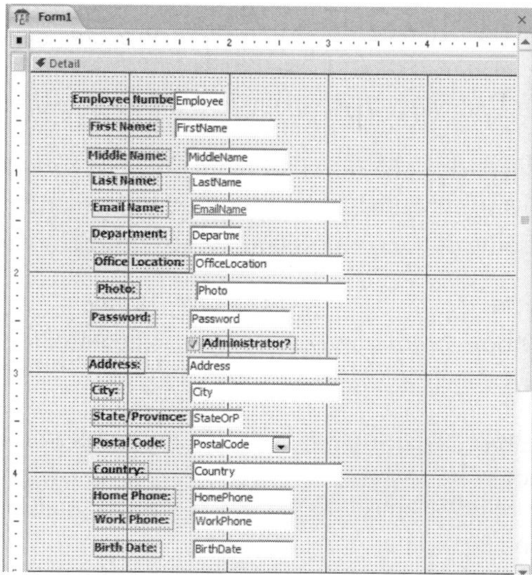

Figure 14-5 The form for employee data has controls sized to better fit the data.

Before you go on, you might want to save the form and name it frmEmployees. You can find the form at this stage saved as frmXmplEmployee2 in the sample database.

Adjusting the Layout of Controls

Setting up two columns to edit the data from the tblEmployees table is probably a good idea to better use the screen space that is wider than it is tall. By doing these adjustments yourself, you can choose which fields go in which column. For example, you might want to place the work-related fields (EmailName, Department, WorkPhone, OfficeLocation, Password, and IsAdmin) in one column, and place the personal fields (Address, City, StateOrProvince, PostalCode, Country, HomePhone, BirthDate, and Photo) in another.

To adjust your sample employees form in this way, follow these steps:

1. Stretch the Detail area to about 6 inches wide to give yourself some room to work.
2. Select as a group the Address, City, StateOrProvince, PostalCode, Country, and HomePhone controls, and move them into a new column on the right. You're going to end up with two fewer controls in the right column than in the left, so line up the Address control opposite the MiddleName control.
3. Grab the Photo control, and move it under HomePhone opposite Password.
4. Select the WorkPhone control, and move it into the space vacated by Photo.
5. Move the BirthDate control under Photo and across from IsAdmin (the Administrator check box).
6. Grab the lower edge of the Detail section and shrink the section so that it's now wider than it is high.
7. Select the Employee Number label, grab the positioning handle in the upper-left corner, and move the label to the left, out from under the EmployeeNumber text box.

When you're done, you should have a form design that looks something like the one shown in Figure 14-6. Now, you're ready to fine-tune your form using alignment and control-size adjustments.

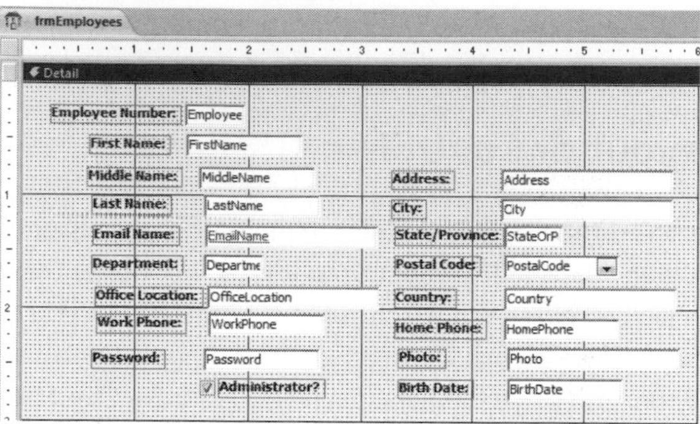

Figure 14-6 The employees form has the controls arranged into columns that make sense.

"Snapping" Controls to the Grid

It's a good idea to design your form so that all the controls are spaced evenly down the form and all controls in a column line up. One way that you might find convenient to do this is to take advantage of the grid. If you enable Snap To Grid in the Size/Space command in the Sizing & Ordering group on the Arrange tab, when you move any control, its upper-left corner "snaps" to the nearest grid point. You can use this feature to help you line up controls both horizontally and vertically.

You can adjust the density of the grid by changing the Grid X and Grid Y properties in the property sheet of the form. Be sure that the property sheet is open (Alt+Enter for a shortcut), and then select Form in the Selection Type list near the top of the Property Sheet window. For this example, set the Grid X and Grid Y properties to 16—0.0625 inch between grid points. (If you're using metric, select a Grid X and Grid Y setting of 6.) This works well for the default 8-point Tahoma font because the "sized to fit" text boxes will be 0.17 inch high. You can place these text boxes every 0.25 inch (four grid points) down the form, which leaves adequate space between the controls. This reduced density also makes it easier to see the grid points so that you can move controls close to the point you want. You could set Grid X and Grid Y to 4, but that reduces flexibility for placing your controls.

The fastest way to snap all controls to the grid is to click Select All in the Selection group on the Format tab, click Align in the Sizing & Ordering group on the Arrange tab, and then click To Grid. The result might look something like that shown in Figure 14-7.

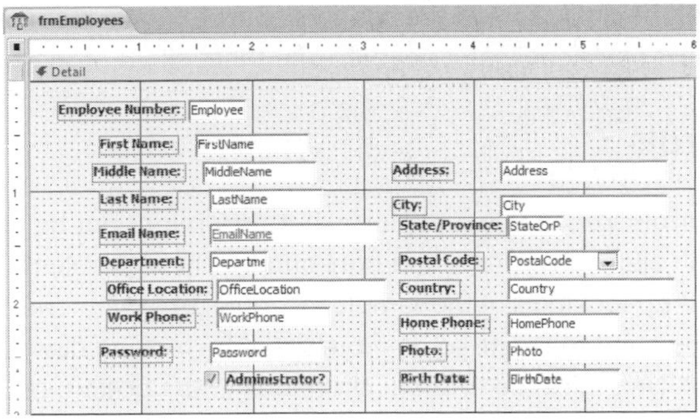

Figure 14-7 This is how your employees form should look after you "snap" the controls to the grid.

INSIDE OUT What's the Difference Between Snap To Grid and To Grid?

When you enable Snap To Grid, under Size/Space, Access aligns the upper-left corner of a control to the grid when you move the control. When you select a control and click To Grid, under Align in the Sizing & Ordering group, Access immediately moves that control's upper-left corner to the nearest grid point. The difference is with Snap To Grid, you're moving the control, and with To Grid, Access moves the control for you.

If you want to position each control individually, enable Snap To Grid by making sure it is selected under the Size/Space command in the Sizing & Ordering group on the Arrange tab. (The button appears highlighted and raised when it is active.) Click each text box, combo box, or check box control, and drag it vertically to positions every 0.25 inch (every fourth grid point) down the grid. When you release the mouse button, you'll see the upper-left corner of the control "snap" to the nearest grid point. As you saw in Chapter 13, when you select and move a control that has an attached label, Access 2010 moves the control and its label as a unit. If you previously moved a label up or down independent of its attached control by using the positioning handle in the upper-left corner, you might need to select either the control or its label and use the positioning handle again to realign each label and associated control.

Note

For a simple form with a few controls, Snap To Grid works well to help you line up controls. For more complex forms, using the commands under the Align command in the Sizing & Ordering group produces a better result. Read the next section to learn about these commands.

Snapping to the grid can help you spread the controls apart to make them easier to work with. You'll see in the next few steps that it's easy to line them all up properly.

Lining Up Controls

You now have your controls spaced down the form, but they might not be equally spaced, and they probably aren't aligned vertically and horizontally. These problems are easy to fix. First, if your form ended up looking like the sample in Figure 14-7 with one or more pairs of controls touching, you need to create some more space by moving down the bottom controls in each column. First, click the IsAdmin check box at the bottom of the first column to select it, and press the down arrow once for each pair of touching controls. Do the same, if necessary, to the BirthDate control at the bottom of the second column. (We needed to move the control down one row of dots in our sample.) Next, select all the text box controls and the check box control in the first column. You can do this by clicking the first text box control (not its associated label) and then holding down the Shift key as you click each of the remaining controls in the column. Alternatively, you can click the ruler above the controls. On the Arrange tab, in the Sizing & Ordering group, click the Size/Space command and then click Equal Vertical. Finally, choose all the text box controls and the combo box control in the second column, and click Equal Vertical again.

Now you're ready to line up the labels. To get started, select all the labels in the left column except the label for the IsAdmin check box. (You can do this the same way you selected all the data-bound controls in a column.) When you have selected them, your form should look something like the one shown in Figure 14-8. Notice that Access also shows large positioning handles in the upper-left corners of all the related controls but no sizing handles.

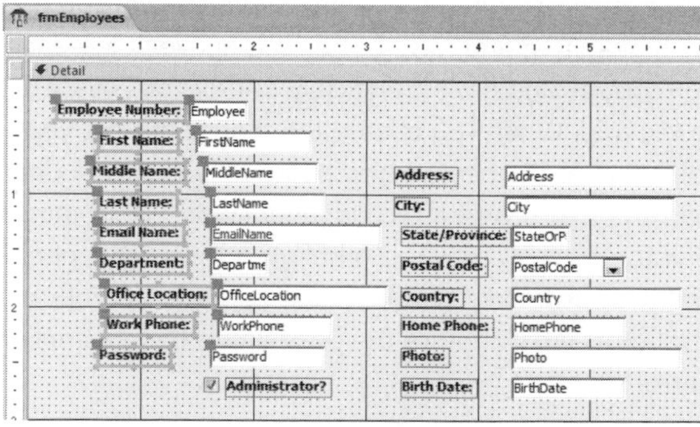

Figure 14-8 The employees form has a column of labels selected.

The labels will look best if their right edges align. You have two choices at this point. If you turn off the Snap To Grid command, you can have Access align all the labels with the label whose right edge is farthest to the right, even if that edge is between dots on the grid. If you leave Snap To Grid on, you can have Access align the labels with the label farthest to the right and then snap the entire group to the nearest grid point.

Note

For this example, we left Snap To Grid turned on, but you can try it both ways to see which gives you the best result. Try it with Snap To Grid on, and then click the Undo button on the Quick Access Toolbar and try it with Snap To Grid turned off.

INSIDE OUT Resizing Controls with Arrow Keys

If you want to resize a control or group of controls, you can hold down the Shift key while the controls are selected, and then press the arrow keys to adjust their height and width. For example, if you press the up arrow key, Access decreases the height of the control and if you press the down arrow key, Access increases the height of the control. Press the right arrow key to increase the width of the control and press the left arrow key to decrease the width of the control.

When you're ready to align the selected labels on your form, on the Arrange tab, in the Sizing & Ordering group, click the Align command and then click Right. While you're at it, click the Align Text Right button in the Font group on the Format tab to align the captions to the right edges of all the label controls. Click outside the design area to select the form, which will cancel the selection of the labels. Your form should look similar to the one shown in Figure 14-9.

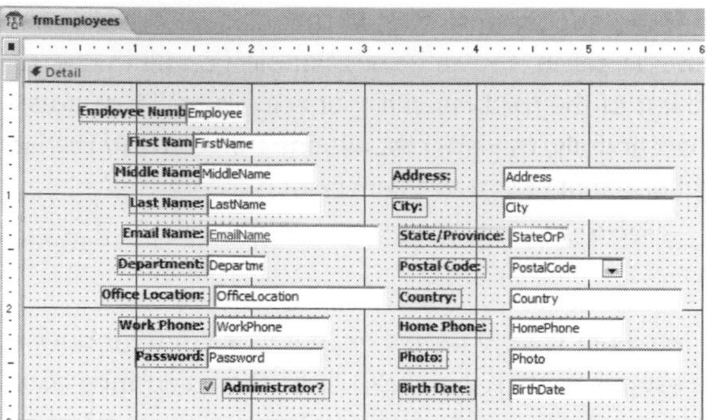

Figure 14-9 The labels from Figure 14-8 are right-aligned.

To further improve the alignment of the controls on the employees form (assuming your form now looks like Figure 14-9), do the following:

1. The EmployeeNumber text box is a bit too far to the left. Click the control to select it, then click the positioning handle in the upper-left corner, and finally drag the control to the right. If you still have Snap To Grid turned on, it should line up with the FirstName control.

2. Select the EmployeeNumber, FirstName, MiddleName, LastName, EmailName, DepartmentID, OfficeLocation, WorkPhone, Password, and IsAdmin controls. Click the Align command in the Sizing & Ordering group on the Arrange tab and then click Left.

3. Select the labels in the right column and right-align them. Click the Align Text Right button in the Font group on the Format tab to align the captions to the right edge of the label controls.

4. In our sample, the labels in the left and right columns end up a bit too close to the related data controls. Fixing this is a bit tricky. Select the longest label (Employee Number for the left column and State/Province for the right column), grab its positioning handle in the upper-left corner, and drag it left three rows of dots. Grab the sizing handle in the middle of the right edge, and expand the label size until it snaps to one row of dots away from the EmployeeNumber text box. Now, select all the labels again, align them left, and then align them right. Note that by first setting the right edge of the longest label and then aligning all the labels first to the left, the longest label is now assured to protrude farthest to the right. Thus, when the labels are all aligned right again, they line up with the new right offset of the longest label. Repeat the process using the State/Province label for the columns on the right.

5. We like all our labels to appear to the left of the related control, so click the Administrator? label to select it, grab its positioning handle in the upper-left corner, and drag it to the left of the IsAdmin check box. If you still have Snap To Grid turned on and you do this carefully, the label should line up vertically with the other labels in the column and horizontally with the check box. While you're at it, click the Align Text Right button in the Font group on the Format tab. If you like, click the Administrator? label, and add a colon to the end of the text.

6. Close up the bottom of the Detail area a bit so that you have the same amount of space below the bottom control as you do above the top control.

After you complete these steps, your form should look something like the one shown in Figure 14-10.

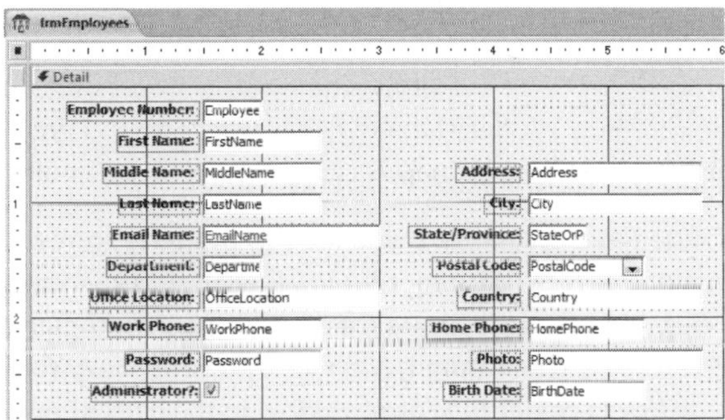

Figure 14-10 The controls and labels are aligned horizontally and vertically.

INSIDE OUT Moving Controls in a Horizontal or Vertical Plane

If you want to move one or more controls only horizontally or only vertically, hold down the Shift key as you select the control (or the last control in a group) that you want to move, and then drag either horizontally or vertically. When Access detects movement either horizontally or vertically, it "locks" the movement and won't let the objects stray in the other axis. If you inadvertently start to drag horizontally when you mean to move vertically (or vice versa), click Undo and try again. Moving controls in this way is especially useful when you have Snap To Grid turned off.

If you switch to Form view, you can see the result of your work, as shown in Figure 14-11. Click the Save button on the Quick Access Toolbar to save this form. You can also find this form saved as frmXmplEmployee3 in the sample database.

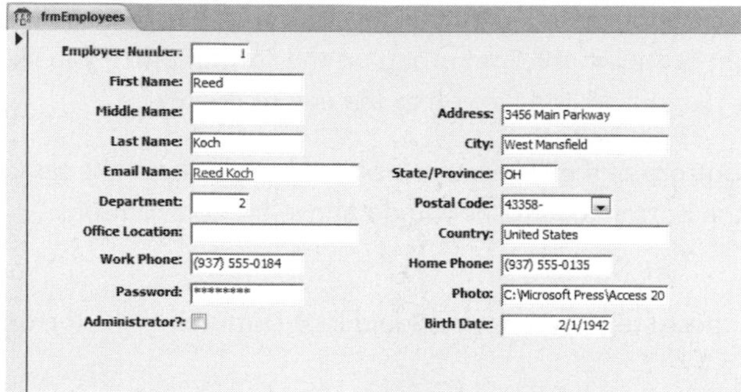

Figure 14-11 This is your employees form with controls aligned and sized.

> **INSIDE OUT** **Using the Auto Resize Property**
>
> **Client forms have an Auto Resize property. If you set this property to Yes and you are using multiple-document interface (MDI) mode with overlapping windows, Access sizes the Form window to exactly fit the form. Note that Access won't automatically resize a form, in this case, if you've switched from Design view to Form view. You can set the Auto Center property to Yes to center the Form window in the current Access workspace if you are using overlapping windows.**

Enhancing the Look of a Form

The employees form you've built thus far in Design view looks fairly plain. The form uses default fonts and a background color that's inherited from the color you have defined in Windows for three-dimensional (3-D) objects (sometimes called the Button Face color). In this section, you'll learn about additional enhancements you can make to your form's design. Open your frmEmployees form you've been building in Design view, if you closed it, to continue with the next examples.

Lines and Rectangles

Access comes with two drawing tools, the Line tool and the Rectangle tool, that you can use to enhance the appearance of your forms. You can add lines to separate parts of your form visually. Rectangles are useful for surrounding and setting off a group of controls on a form.

On your employees form, it might be helpful to add a line to separate the primary information about the employee in the first column from personal information in the second column. To make sufficient room for the line, you should move the controls in the first column to the left. The easiest way to do this is to switch to Design view, select all the affected controls and labels, and then move them as a group. Start by clicking the top ruler just above the right edge of the controls, and then drag inside the ruler toward the left until the selection indicator touches all the controls in the left column. (If you can't see the rulers, be sure that the Ruler button is selected under the Size/Space command in the Sizing & Ordering group on the Arrange tab.) Release the mouse button, and all the controls and labels in the left column will be selected. To be sure you move all these controls as a group, click the Group button under the Size/Space command in the Sizing & Ordering group on the Arrange tab. (When you select a control that is grouped, Access highlights all the other controls in the group to indicate they are grouped controls.) Rest the mouse pointer anywhere on the grouped controls so that the pointer changes to a pointer with a crosshairs shape (see Figure 14-12), and slide the entire group left a bit.

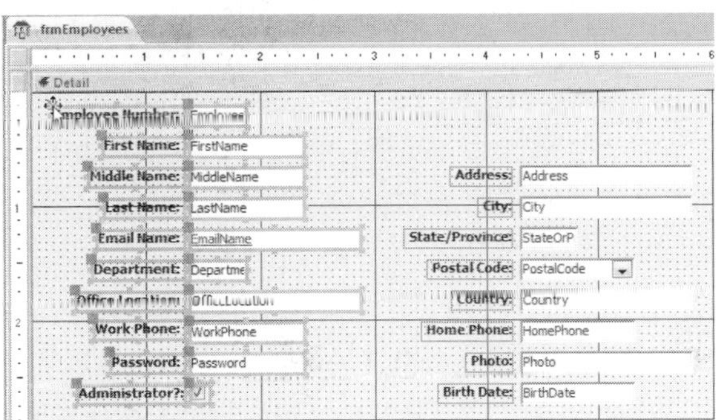

Figure 14-12 You can group a set of controls and then move them together.

Next, on the Design tab, in the Controls group, click Line. To draw your line, click near the top of the form between the two columns, about two grid rows below the top edge, and drag toward the form's bottom edge. If the line isn't exactly vertical, you can drag the bottom end left or right to adjust it. You can also set its Width property to 0 in the property sheet to make it perfectly vertical. (As you might imagine, setting the Height property to 0 makes the line horizontal.) Use the Line Thickness options under the Shape Outline command in the Control Formatting group on the Format tab to make the line a little thicker if you want. (Alternatively, change the Border Width property in the property sheet.) Click the button, and choose the thickness you want. Your form should now look similar to the one shown in Figure 14-13.

INSIDE OUT Ensuring Your Lines Are Straight

When drawing a line on your form, you can make your line exactly horizontal or exactly vertical if you hold down the Shift key as you click and draw the line.

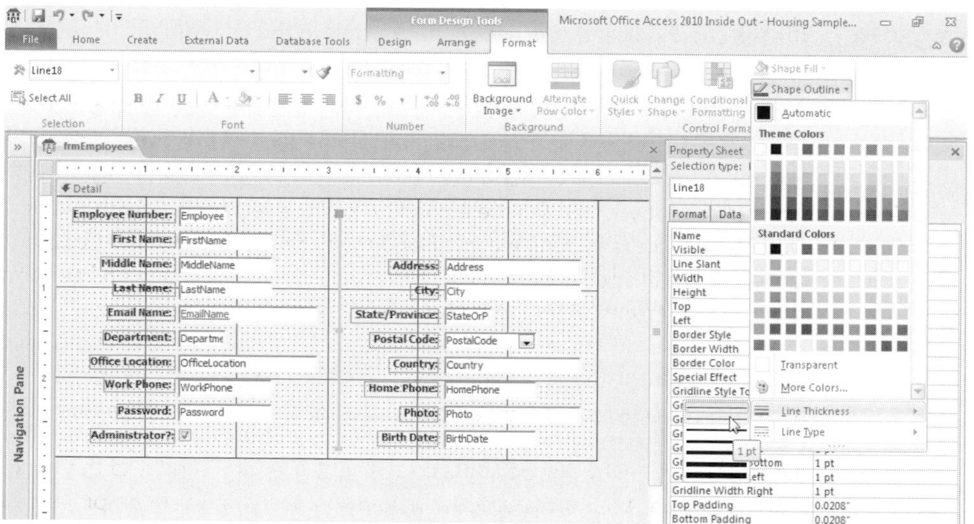

Figure 14-13 Use the Line tool to draw a line on a form; use the Border Thickness button to adjust the line width.

You can add emphasis to the form by drawing a rectangle around all the controls. To do this, you might first need to move all the controls down and to the right a bit and make the Detail section slightly wider and taller. First, expand your form by about 0.5 inch across and down. Click the Select All button in the Selection group on the Format tab, and then drag all the controls so that you have about 0.25 inch of space around all the edges. (This might seem like too much space, but we'll use the extra space to have some fun later.) Select the Rectangle tool in the Controls group, click where you want to place one corner of the rectangle, and drag to the intended location of the opposite corner. When you draw a rectangle around all the controls, your form will look similar to the one shown in Figure 14-14.

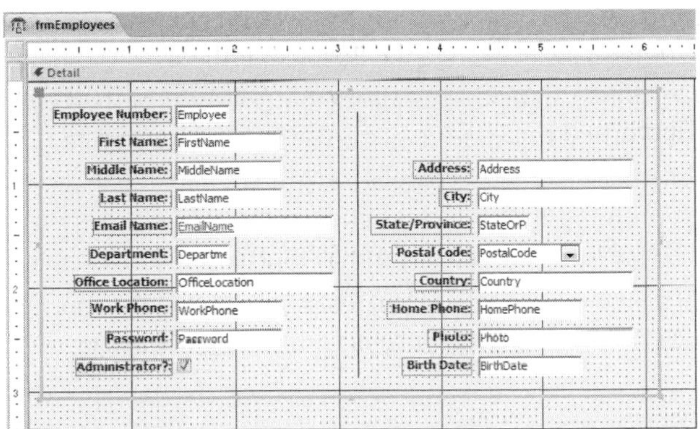

Figure 14-14 Use the Rectangle tool to place a rectangle with a default etched look on the employees form.

Note that the rectangle control actually covers and is on top of all the other controls. However, because the default rectangle is transparent with an etched special effect, you can see the other controls through the rectangle. (You might need to click the form or another control so that you can see the etched look of the rectangle.) If you prefer a solid rectangle, you can select the rectangle control and then use the Background Color button in the Font group or the Shape Fill button in the Control Formatting group on the Format tab to select the color you want. (A light gray will work best.) When you add a solid control like this after you've created other controls, the solid control will cover the previous controls. You can select the control and click Send To Back in the Sizing & Ordering group on the Arrange tab to reveal the covered controls and keep the solid control in the background.

Go ahead and make the rectangle a solid light gray and send it to the back. Now, switch to Form view, and see how your form looks up to this point. Your employees form should look similar to the one shown in Figure 14-15.

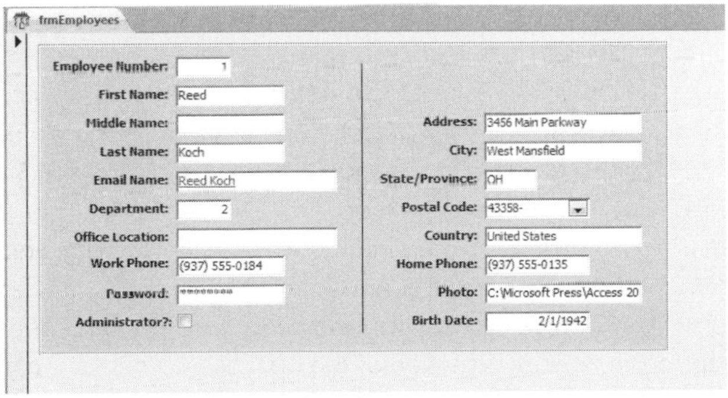

Figure 14-15 The employees form in Form view has a line and a solid rectangle added.

Colors and Special Effects

You can also use color and special effects to highlight objects on your form. For example, you can make all the controls appear to "float" on a raised surface on the form. To do so, switch to Design view and select the rectangle you just created. Right-click the rectangle control, click the arrow on the Special Effect option in the shortcut menu, and then click Raised to change the rectangle from Etched to Raised. (You could also make this change on the control's property sheet.) Your form in Form view will look similar to the one shown in Figure 14-16.

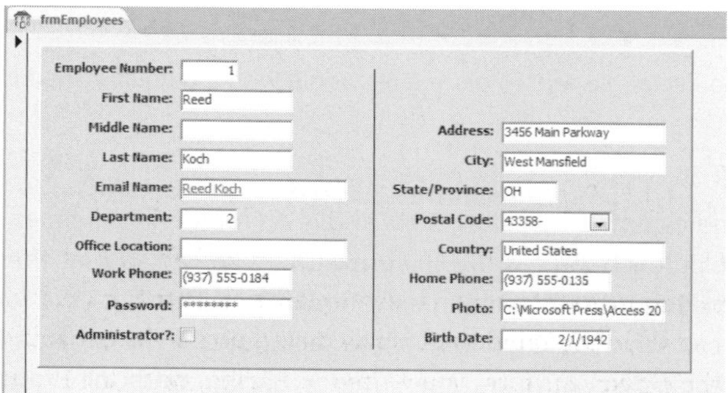

Figure 14-16 The rectangle behind the controls appears raised above the surface of the form background.

Next, switch to Design view if you changed to Form view, select the Rectangle tool again, and set Background Color to dark gray using the Background Color button in the Font group. Draw a second rectangle so that it forms a border about halfway between the edge of the first rectangle and the edge of the grid. Click Send To Back in the Sizing & Ordering group on the Arrange tab to send this latest rectangle to the background. On the property sheet, set the second rectangle's Special Effect property to Sunken. Switch to Form view to see the result. The first gray rectangle now appears to float on the form, surrounded by a "moat" of dark gray, as shown in Figure 14-17. You can find this form saved as frmXmplEmployee4 in the sample database.

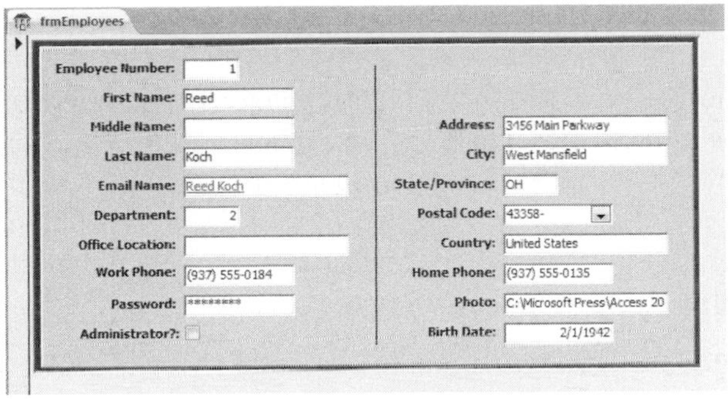

Figure 14-17 The first light gray rectangle appears to float on the form using special effects.

INSIDE OUT Using System Colors and the Color Palette

Although you can certainly pick from a broad palette of colors for any design object, you might want to design your forms so that they always inherit colors from the options the user has set in the Windows Display dialog box. In fact, if you select the Detail section of the employees form you've been building, open the Property Sheet window, and find the Back Color property, then you'll find the property set to System Button Face. This special option tells Access to use the color set in Windows for button faces and other 3-D objects. In any color property, Access lists 31 system color names that you can use to set colors in your forms and controls to match those set in Windows objects. All these color names begin with the word *System*.

You can also see in the Back Color property (or, for that matter, any color property) a list of 20 additional options. These include Alternate Row, Background Form, Background Light Header, Background Dark Header, Borders/Gridlines, Text Black, Text Description, Text Light, Text Dark, Highlight, and Access Theme 1, Access Theme 2, and so on, up to Access Theme 10. These are shades of the color scheme you chose in Access Options—shades of blue for the Blue or Silver theme, and shades of gray and black for the Black theme, and with a shade of orange in all themes for Highlight. If you click the Build button on the Back Color property line or click the arrow next to the Font Color or Background Color commands in the Font group on the Design tab or the Shape Fill and Shape Outline commands in the Control Formatting group, Access opens a color palette where you can see the color defined for each of these options, as shown here:

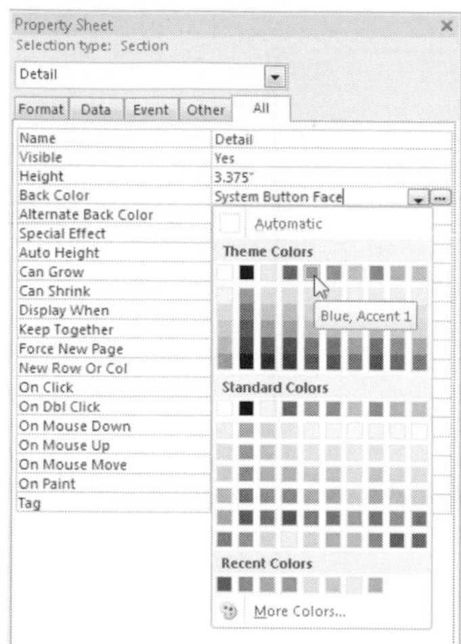

If you select any of the colors under Theme Colors, Access enters the name of the theme or color option on the property line. If you click one of the colors under Standard Colors, Access sets a hexadecimal value in the property that represents the red, green, and blue (RGB) color value—#000000 for Black, #FF0000 for Red, #00FF00 for Green, #0000FF for Blue, and #FFFFFF for White, for example. See Article 5, "Color Names and Codes," on the companion CD, for a list of common color hexadecimal equivalents.

Under Recent Colors on the color palette, Access displays up to 10 recently used colors. Click one of these to enter the code or name for that color in the color property. If you want to create your own custom color, you can click More Colors to open the Colors dialog box. In the Colors dialog box, you can choose from a wider selection of colors on the Standard tab or define a custom color on the Custom tab by adjusting individual RGB values or selecting the color you want from a color rainbow palette.

Fonts

Another way you can enhance the appearance of your forms is by varying the fonts and font sizes you use. When you select any control that can display text or data, Access makes font, font size, and font attribute controls available in the Font group on the Format tab so that you can easily change how the text in that control looks. Click the arrow next to the Font Name combo box to open a list of all the available fonts, as shown in Figure 14-18. Select the font you want for the control.

Figure 14-18 This is a partial list of fonts available to you in the Font Name combo box.

> **Note**
>
> **The font list shows all fonts currently installed on your computer. Use the Fonts folder in the Control Panel to add or remove fonts. A double-T icon next to the font name in the list indicates a TrueType font that is suitable for both screen display and printing. A printer icon next to the font name indicates a font designed for your printer but that might not look exactly the same when displayed on your screen. A font with no icon indicates a font designed for your screen; a screen font might look different when you print it.**

If you want to add some variety, you can use bold or italic type in a few key places. In this case, select all the labels on the form, and select a serif font such as Times New Roman.

You can add a label to the header of the form to display a title, such as Employees. You can either do this manually or use a button on the ribbon designed specifically for this task. If you'd like Access to do most of the work, click the Title button in the Header/Footer group on the Design tab. Access opens the Header and Footer section, places a new label in the Header section, and sets the caption to the name of your form. Double-click the new label to select the existing text, type **Employees** in the label, and press Enter. Access also creates an empty cell to the left of the label. You can select the empty cell and then press Delete to remove it because we do not need it for our example form.

To do this same task manually, you need to first open the header and footer of the form by right-clicking the Detail section and then clicking the Form Header/Footer button on the shortcut menu. Grab the bottom edge of the footer and close it up so that it has zero height. Expand the header to give yourself some room to work. Choose the Label tool in the Controls group on the Design tab, draw a label about 1.5 inches wide and 0.5 inches high, type the word **Employees** in the label, and press Enter.

Set the label in the header to the Tahoma font (a sans serif font), bold, italic, and 18 points in size. Double-click one of the sizing boxes to size the control to fit, and drag the right edge to the left to reduce the label size so it fits just around the letters. If you created the label manually, you might need to expand the label width to the right if all the letters don't show in the label. You can see a portion of this work underway in Figure 14-19.

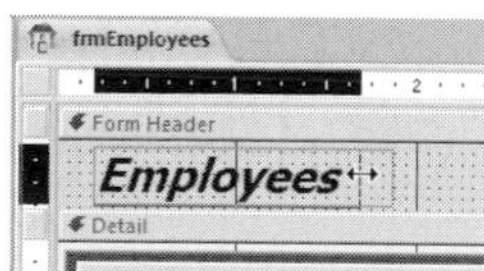

Figure 14-19 Adjust the size of the label to fit the form header title.

When you finish, the form should look similar to the one shown in Figure 14-20. (You can find this form saved in the sample database as frmXmplEmployee5.)

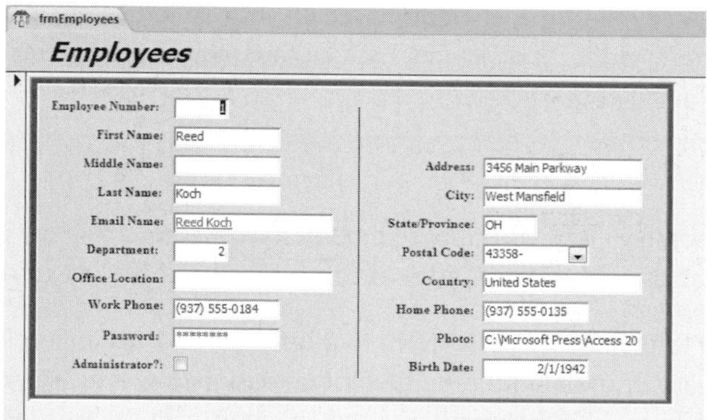

Figure 14-20 The employees form now has a title and some different fonts for variety.

INSIDE OUT **More Is Not Always Better When It Comes to Fonts**

A form with too many fonts or font sizes will look busy and jumbled. In general, you should use only two or three fonts per form. Use one font and font size for most bound data displayed in controls. Make label text bold or colored for emphasis. Select a second font for controls in the headers and perhaps a third (at most) for information in the footers.

Setting Control Properties for Client Forms

Access 2010 gives you many properties for each control to allow you to customize the way your client form works. These properties affect formatting, the presence or absence of scroll bars, the enabling or locking of records, the tab order, and more.

Formatting Properties

In the property sheet for each text box, combo box, and list box are three properties that you can set to determine how Access displays the data in the form. These properties are Format, Decimal Places, and Input Mask, as shown in Figure 14-21. (The Input Mask property is listed farther down the list on the All tab of the property sheet and isn't shown in Figure 14-21.)

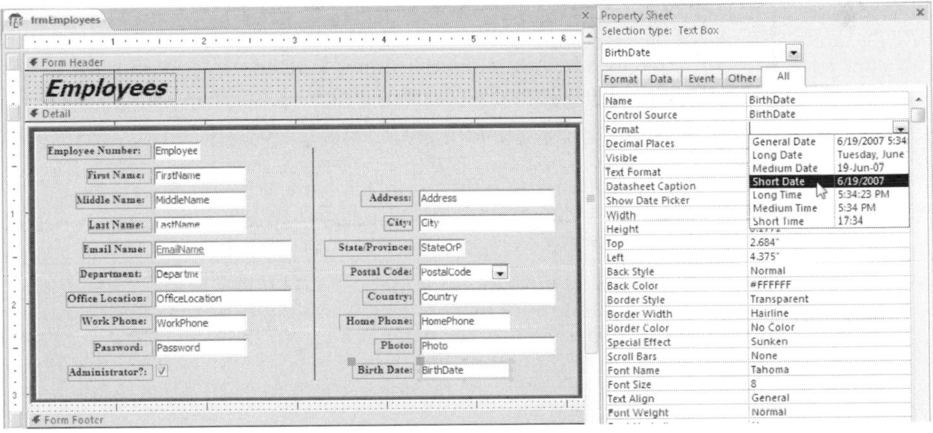

Figure 14-21 You can select a format from the list of format settings for the BirthDate control, which uses the Date/Time data type.

INSIDE OUT **Always Use Four-Digit Year Values**

We recommended earlier that you change the date display in the Regional And Language Options section of the Control Panel to display a four-digit year. Although Access adjusts the century digits automatically when you enter two-digit years, you will avoid confusion about the actual value stored after the year 1999 if you always display the full year. All samples you see in this book using the Short Date format show four-digit years because we changed the settings on our computers. If your computer is set to display a two-digit year, you will see a different result everywhere we used the Short Date format.

For details on the Input Mask property, see Chapter 4, "Designing Client Tables." For details on dynamically changing format properties (also called *conditional formatting*) based on the value currently displayed, see Chapter 15, "Advanced Form Design."

Access copies these properties from the definition of the fields in the underlying table. If you haven't specified a Format property in the field definition, Access sets a default Format property for the control, depending on the data type of the field bound to the control. In the control's property sheet, you can customize the appearance of the data on your form by selecting a format setting from the Format property's list or by entering a custom set of formatting characters. The following sections present the format settings and formatting characters available for each data type.

Specifying a Format for Numbers and Currency

If you don't specify a Format property setting for a control that displays a number or a currency value, Access displays numbers in the General Number format and currency in the Currency format. You can choose from seven Format property settings, as shown in Table 14-1.

Table 14-1 Format Property Settings for Number and Currency Data Types

Format	Description
General Number	Displays numbers as entered, with up to 11 significant digits. If a number contains more than 11 significant digits or the control you are using to display the value is not wide enough to show all digits, Access first rounds the displayed number and then uses scientific (exponential) notation for very large or very small numbers (more than 10 digits to the right or to the left of the decimal point).

Format	Description
Currency	Displays numeric data according to the Currency setting in the Regional And Language Options section of the Control Panel. In the English (U.S.) layout, Access uses a leading dollar sign, maintains two decimal places (rounded), and encloses negative numbers in parentheses.
Euro	Displays numeric data according to your Currency setting in the Control Panel but always uses a leading euro symbol.
Fixed	Displays numbers without thousands separators and with two decimal places. The number displayed is rounded if the underlying value contains more than two decimal places.
Standard	Displays numbers with thousands separators and with two decimal places. The number displayed is rounded if the underlying value contains more than two decimal places.
Percent	Multiplies the value by 100, displays two decimal places, and adds a trailing percent sign. The number displayed is rounded if the underlying value contains more than four decimal places.
Scientific	Displays numbers in scientific (exponential) notation.

You can also create a custom format. You can specify a different display format for Access to use (depending on whether the numeric value is positive, negative, 0, or Null) by providing up to four format specifications in the Format property. You must separate the specifications by semicolons. When you enter two specifications, Access uses the first for all nonnegative numbers and the second for negative numbers. When you provide three specifications, Access uses the third specification to display numbers with a value of 0. Use the fourth specification to indicate how you want Null values handled.

To create a custom number format, use the formatting characters shown in Table 14-2. Notice that you can include text strings in the format and specify a color to use.

Table 14-2 Formatting Characters for Number and Currency Data Types

Character	Usage
Decimal separator	Use to indicate where you want Access to place the decimal point. Use the decimal separator defined in the Regional And Language Options section of the Control Panel. In the English (U.S.) layout, the separator is a period (.).
Thousands separator	Use to indicate placement of the thousands separator character that is defined in the Regional And Language Options section of the Control Panel. In the English (U.S.) layout, the separator is a comma (,). When the position immediately to the left of the separator is # and no digit exists in that position, the thousands separator also does not display.
0	Use this placeholder character to indicate digit display. If no digit exists in the number in this position, Access displays 0.

Character	Usage
#	Use this placeholder character to indicate digit display. If no digit exists in the number in this position, Access displays a blank space.
– + $ ( ) or a blank space	Use these characters anywhere you want in your format string.
"text"	Use double quotation marks to embed any text you want displayed.
\	Use to always display the character immediately following (the same as including a single character in double quotation marks).
!	Use to force left-alignment. You cannot use any other *digit* place-holder characters (0 or #) when you force left-alignment; however, you can use character placeholders, as shown in Table 14-3 on page 870.
*	Use to designate the immediately following character as the fill character. Access usually displays formatted numeric data right-aligned and filled with blank spaces to the left. You can embed the fill character anywhere in your format string. For example, you can specify a format string for a Currency value as follows: $#,##0*^.00 Using the above format, the value $1,234.57 appears as follows: $1,234^^^^^^^^^^.57 Access generates fill characters so that the displayed text completely fills the display area.
%	Place as the last character in your format string to multiply the value by 100 and include a trailing percent sign.
E– or e–	Use to generate scientific (exponential) notation and to display a minus sign preceding negative exponents. It must be used with other characters, as in 0.00E–00.
E+ or e+	Use to generate scientific (exponential) notation and to display a minus sign preceding negative exponents and a plus sign preceding positive exponents. It must be used with other characters, as in 0.00E+00.
[color]	Use brackets to display the text in the color specified. Valid color names are Black, Blue, Green, Cyan, Red, Magenta, Yellow, and White. A color name must be used with other characters, as in 0.00[Red].

INSIDE OUT

Don't Get Fooled by the Format Property

Keep in mind that what you specify in Format and Decimal Places properties affects only what you see on your screen—these settings do not modify the actual data in the underlying table in any way. For example, if you specify a format that displays two decimal places but the underlying data type contains additional precision (such as a Currency data type that always contains four decimal places), you'll see a rounded value. If you later sum the values, the total might not agree with the sum of the displayed values. Likewise, if you specify a format that displays only the date portion of a Date/Time data type, you won't see any time portion unless you click the control.

For example, to display a number with two decimal places and comma separators when positive, enclosed in parentheses and shown in red when negative, *Zero* when 0, and *Not Entered* when Null, you would specify the following:

```
#,##0.00;(#,##0.00)[Red];"Zero";"Not Entered"
```

To format a U.S. phone number and area code from a numeric field, you would specify the following:

```
(000) 000-0000
```

Specifying a Format for Text

If you don't specify a Format property setting for a control that displays a text value, Access left-aligns the data in the control. You can specify a custom format with one entry or with two entries separated by semicolons. If you include a second format specification, Access uses that specification to show empty values (a zero-length string). If you want to test for Null, you must use the Immediate If (IIf) and IsNull built-in functions. See the "Showing the Null Value in Text Fields" sidebar, on page 871, for details.

By default, Access fills text placeholder characters (@ and &) using characters from the underlying data from right to left. If a text field contains more characters than the number of placeholder characters you provide, Access first uses up the placeholder characters and then displays the remaining characters as though you had specified the @ placeholder character in that position. Table 14-3 lists the formatting characters that are applicable to the Text data type.

Table 14-3 Formatting Characters for the Text Data Type

Character	Usage
@	Use this placeholder character to display any available character in this position. If all available characters in the underlying text have been placed, any extra @ placeholder characters generate blanks. For example, if the text is *abc* and the format is @@@@@, the resulting display is left-aligned and has two blank spaces on the left preceding the characters.
&	Use to display any available character in this position. If all available characters in the underlying text have been placed, any extra & placeholder characters display nothing. For example, if the text is *abc* and the format is &&&&&, the resulting display shows only the three characters left-aligned.
<	Use to display all characters in lowercase. This character must appear at the beginning of the format string and can be preceded only by the *!* specification.
>	Use to display all characters in uppercase. This character must appear at the beginning of the format string and can be preceded only by the *!* specification.
– + $ ( ) or a blank space	Use these characters anywhere you want in your format string.
"text"	Use double quotation marks to embed any text you want displayed.
\	Use to always display the character immediately following (the same as including a single character in double quotation marks).
!	Use to force placeholders to fill left to right instead of right to left. If you use this specification, it must be the first character in the format string.
*	Use to designate the immediately following character as the fill character. Access usually displays formatted text data left-aligned and filled with blank spaces to the right. You can embed the fill character anywhere in your format string. For example, you can specify a format string as follows: >@@*!@@@@@ Using the above format, the value *abcdef* appears as follows: A!!!!!!!!!!!!!!!BCDEF (And the above string has a leading blank.) If you force the pattern to be filled from the left by adding a leading exclamation point, the data appears as follows: AB!!!!!!!!!!!!!!CDEF (And the above string has a trailing blank.) Access generates fill characters so that the displayed text completely fills the display area.

Character	Usage
[color]	Use brackets to display the text in the color specified. Valid color names are Black, Blue, Green, Cyan, Red, Magenta, Yellow, and White. A color name must be used with other characters, as in >[Red]. (Keep in mind that in the absence of placeholder characters, Access places the characters as though you had specified @ in all positions.)

For example, if you want to display a six-character part number with a hyphen between the second character and the third character, filled from the left, specify the following:

```
!@@-@@@@
```

To format a check amount string in the form of *Fourteen Dollars and 59 Cents* so that Access displays an asterisk (*) to fill any available space between the word *and* and the cents amount, specify the following:

```
**@@@@@@@@
```

Using this format in a text box wide enough to display 62 characters, Access displays *Fourteen Dollars and 59 Cents* as

```
Fourteen Dollars and *********************************59 Cents
```

and *One Thousand Two Hundred Dollars and 00 Cents* as

```
One Thousand Two Hundred Dollars and *****************00 Cents
```

INSIDE OUT Showing the Null Value in Text Fields

As you might have noticed, there is no third optional format specification you can supply for a Null value in a text field as there is with Number, Currency, and Date/Time data types. If the field is Null, Access displays it as though it is empty. If the field can contain an empty string or a Null, you can distinguish it visibly by using the second optional format specification. Assuming your text field is five characters long, your Format specification could look like

```
@@@@@;"<empty string>"
```

If the field has a value, Access displays the value. If the field is an empty string, you will see *<empty string>* in the text box until you click it. If the field is Null, the text box will

An alternative is to use the IIf and IsNull built-in functions in the Control Source property of the text box. Your control source could look like

```
=IIf(IsNull([FieldToDisplay]), "*Null Value*",[FieldToDisplay])
```

If you do this, however, you won't be able to update the field because the source will be an expression.

Specifying a Format for Date/Time

If you don't specify a Format property setting for a control that displays a date/time value, Access displays the date/time in the General Date format. You can also select one of the six other Format property settings shown in Table 14-4.

You can also specify a custom format with one entry or with two entries separated by semicolons. If you include a second format specification, Access uses that specification to show Null values. Table 14-5 lists the formatting characters that are applicable to the Date/Time data type.

For example, to display a date as full month name, day, and year (say, *May 29, 2011*) with a color of cyan, you would specify the following:

```
mmmm dd, yyyy[Cyan]
```

Table 14-4 Format Property Settings for the Date/Time Data Type

Format	Description
General Date	Displays the date as numbers separated by the date separator character. Displays the time as hours, minutes, and seconds separated by the time separator character and followed by an AM/PM indicator. If the value has no time component, Access displays the date only. If the value has no date component, Access displays the time only. Example: 3/17/2011 06:17:55 PM.
Long Date	Displays the date according to the Long Date setting in the Regional And Language Options section of the Control Panel. Example: Thursday, March 17, 2011.
Medium Date	Displays the date as dd-mmm-yyyy. Example: 17-Mar-2011.
Short Date	Displays the date according to the Short Date setting in the Regional And Language Options section of the Control Panel. Example: 3/17/2011. To avoid confusion for dates in the twenty-first century, we strongly recommend you take advantage of the Use Four-Digit Year formatting options. Click the File tab on the Backstage view, click Options, click the Client Settings category, and then set these options in the General section.

Format	Description
Long Time	Displays the time according to the Time setting in the Regional And Language Options section of the Control Panel. Example: 6:17:12 PM.
Medium Time	Displays the time as hours and minutes separated by the time separator character and followed by an AM/PM indicator. Example: 06:17 PM.
Short Time	Displays the time as hours and minutes separated by the time separator character, using a 24-hour clock. Example: 18:17.

Table 14-5 Formatting Characters for the Date/Time Data Type

Character	Usage
Time separator	Use to show Access where to separate hours, minutes, and seconds. Use the time separator defined in the Regional And Language Options section of the Control Panel. In the English (U.S.) layout, the separator is a colon (:).
Date separator	Use to show Access where to separate days, months, and years. Use the date separator defined in the Regional And Language Options section of the Control Panel. In the English (U.S.) layout, the separator is a slash (/).
c	Use to display the General Date format.
d	Use to display the day of the month as one or two digits, as needed.
dd	Use to display the day of the month as two digits.
ddd	Use to display the day of the week as a three-letter abbreviation. Example: Saturday = Sat.
dddd	Use to display the day of the week fully spelled out.
ddddd	Use to display the Short Date format.
dddddd	Use to display the Long Date format.
w	Use to display a number for the day of the week. Example: Sunday = 1.
m	Use to display the month as a one-digit or two-digit number, as needed.
mm	Use to display the month as a two-digit number.
mmm	Use to display the name of the month as a three-letter abbreviation. Example: March = Mar.
mmmm	Use to display the name of the month fully spelled out.
q	Use to display the calendar quarter number (1–4).
y	Use to display the day of the year (1–366).
yy	Use to display the last two digits of the year.
yyyy	Use to display the full year value (within the range 0100–9999).

Character	Usage
h	Use to display the hour as one or two digits, as needed.
hh	Use to display the hour as two digits.
n	Use to display the minutes as one or two digits, as needed.
nn	Use to display the minutes as two digits.
s	Use to display the seconds as one or two digits, as needed.
ss	Use to display the seconds as two digits.
ttttt	Use to display the Long Time format.
AM/PM	Use to display 12-hour clock values with trailing AM or PM, as appropriate.
A/P or a/p	Use to display 12-hour clock values with trailing A or P, or a or p, as appropriate.
AMPM	Use to display 12-hour clock values using morning/afternoon indicators as specified in the Regional And Language Options section of the Control Panel.
– + $ ( ) or a blank space	Use these characters anywhere you want in your format string.
"text"	Use double quotation marks to embed any text you want displayed.
\	Use to always display the character immediately following (the same as including a single character in double quotation marks).
*	Use to designate the immediately following character as the fill character. Access usually displays formatted date/time data right-aligned and filled with blank spaces to the left. You can embed the fill character anywhere in your format string. For example, you can specify a format string as follows: mm/yyyy ** hh:nn Using the above format, the value March 17, 2011 06:17:55 PM appears as follows: 03/2011 ************** 18:17 Access generates fill characters so that the displayed text completely fills the display area.
[color]	Use brackets to display the text in the color specified. Valid color names are Black, Blue, Green, Cyan, Red, Magenta, Yellow, and White. A color name must be used with other characters, as in ddddd[Red].

Specifying a Format for Yes/No Fields

You can choose from among three standard formats—Yes/No, True/False, or On/Off—to display Yes/No data type values, as shown in Table 14-6. The Yes/No format is the default. As you saw earlier, it's often more useful to display Yes/No values using a check box or a button rather than a text box.

Table 14-6 Format Property Settings for the Yes/No Data Type

Format	Description
Yes/No (the default)	Displays 0 as No and any nonzero value as Yes.
True/False	Displays 0 as False and any nonzero value as True.
On/Off	Displays 0 as Off and any nonzero value as On.

You can also specify your own custom word or phrase for Yes and No values. Keep in mind that a Yes/No data type is actually a number internally. (–1 is Yes, and 0 is No.) So, you can specify a format string containing three parts separated by semicolons just as you can for a number. Leave the first part empty (a Yes/No value is never a positive number) by starting with a semicolon, specify a string enclosed in double quotation marks (and with an optional color modifier) followed by a semicolon in the second part for the negative Yes values, and specify another string (also with an optional color modifier) in the third part for the zero No values.

To display *Invoice Sent* in red for Yes and *Not Invoiced* in blue for No, you would specify the following:

```
;"Invoice Sent"[Red];"Not Invoiced"[Blue]
```

How Format and Input Mask Work Together

If you specify both an Input Mask setting (see Chapter 4 for more about this) and a Format property setting, Access uses the Input Mask setting to display data when you move the focus to the control and uses the Format setting when the control does not have the focus. If you don't include a Format setting but do include an Input Mask setting, Access formats the data using the Input Mask setting. Be careful not to define a Format setting that conflicts with the Input Mask. For example, if you define an Input Mask setting for a phone number that looks like

```
!\(###") "000\-0000;0;_
```

(which stores the parentheses and hyphen with the data) and a Format setting that looks like

```
(&&&) @@@-@@@@
```

your data will display as

```
(206() 5) 55-1212
```

Adding a Scroll Bar

When you have a field that can contain a long data string (for example, the Notes field in the tbReservationRequests table), it's a good idea to provide a scroll bar in the control to make it easy to scan through all the data. This scroll bar appears whenever you select the control. If you don't add a scroll bar, you must use the arrow keys to move up and down through the data.

To add a scroll bar, first open the form in Design view. Select the control, and open its property sheet. Then set the Scroll Bars property to Vertical. For example, if you open the frmXmplReservationRequests form in Form view and tab to (or click) the Notes text box, the vertical scroll bar appears, as shown in Figure 14-22.

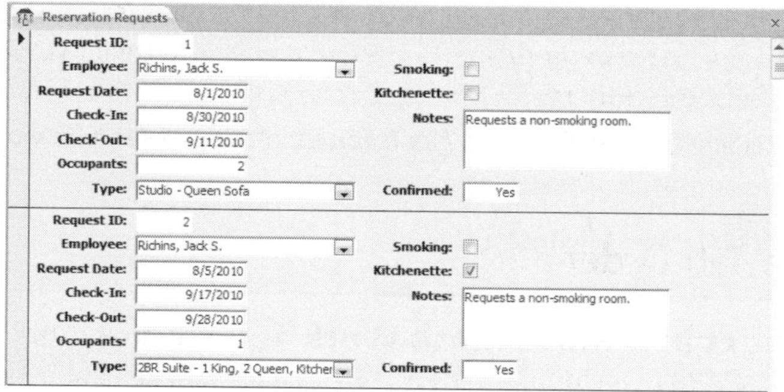

Figure 14-22 When you click into the Notes text box, Access displays a scroll bar.

Enabling and Locking Controls

You might not want users of your form to select or update certain controls. You can set these conditions with the control's Enabled and Locked properties. For example, if you use a control to display an AutoNumber field, you can be certain that Access will provide the field's value. So, it's a good idea to set the control's Enabled property to No (so that the user can't select it) and the control's Locked property to Yes (so that the user can't update it). Table 14-7 shows the effects of the Enabled and Locked property settings. Note, however, that if you want the user to be able to use the Access built-in Find facility to search for a particular AutoNumber value, you should leave Enabled set to Yes to allow the user to select the field and find values in it.

Table 14-7 Settings for the Enabled and Locked Properties

Enabled	Locked	Description
Yes	Yes	Control can have the focus. Data is displayed normally and can be copied or searched but not changed.
No	No	Control cannot have the focus. Control and data appear dimmed.
Yes	No	Control can have the focus. Data is displayed normally and can be copied and changed.
No	Yes	Control cannot have the focus. Data is displayed normally but can't be copied or changed.

In some cases, you might want to allow a control to be selected with the mouse but to be skipped over as the user tabs through the controls on the form. You can set the control's Tab Stop property to No while leaving its Enabled property set to Yes. This might be useful for controls for which you also set the Locked property to Yes. Setting the Tab Stop property to No keeps the user from tabbing into the control, but the user can still select the control with the mouse to use the Find command or to copy the data in the control to the Clipboard.

Setting the Tab Order

As you design a client form, Access sets the tab order for the controls in the order in which you place the controls on the form. When you move a control to a new location, Access doesn't automatically change the tab order. Also, when you delete a control and replace it with another, Access places the new control at the end of the tab order. If you want to change the tab order that Access created, you can set a different tab order.

You probably should do this with your sample employees form because you moved controls around after you initially placed them on the form. (If you want to test the existing order, try tabbing through the controls in one record in frmXmplEmployee5—you should see the cursor jump from OfficeLocation in the first column to Photo in the second column and then back to Password in the first column.) Open your form in Design view, select the Detail area (or any control in the Detail area), and then click the Tab Order button in the Tools group on the Design tab to open the Tab Order dialog box, as shown in Figure 14-23.

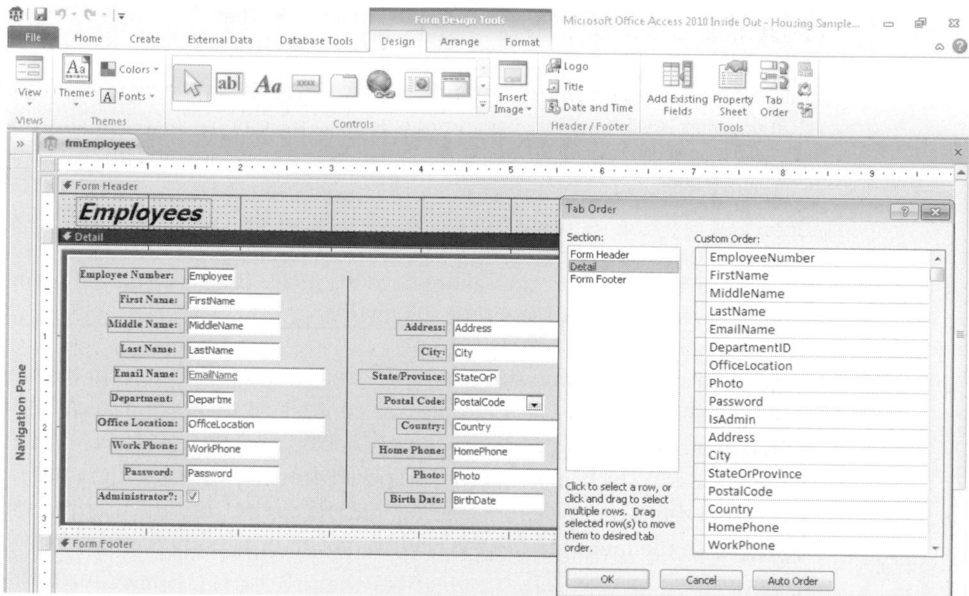

Figure 14-23 You can change the tab order on the form by using the Tab Order dialog box.

You can click Auto Order to reorder the controls so that the tab order corresponds to the arrangement of the controls on the form, from left to right and from top to bottom—but that's probably not what you want in this case. Because this form has two columns, you might want to rearrange the tab order to first move down one column all the way and then move down the other one. You can make custom adjustments to the list by clicking the row selector for a control to highlight it and then clicking the row selector again and dragging the control to its new location in the list. As you can see, the Photo and WorkPhone controls don't appear where they should in the Custom Order list. Click Photo and drag it down after HomePhone. Click WorkPhone, and drag it up to follow OfficeLocation. Click OK to save your changes to the Custom Order list.

You can also change an individual control's place in the tab order by setting the control's Tab Index property. The Tab Index property of the first control on the form is 0, the second is 1, and so on. If you use this method to assign a new Tab Index setting to a control and some other control already has that Tab Index setting, Access resequences the Tab Index settings for controls appearing in the order after the one you changed. The result is the same as if you had dragged the control to that relative position (as indicated by the new Tab Index setting) in the Tab Order dialog box. (We find it easier to use the Tab Order dialog box.)

Adding a Smart Tag

Microsoft introduced *smart tags* in Microsoft Office XP. Smart tags are little applications that you can hook into your documents to recognize items such as names, addresses, or stock symbols and provide options, or actions, for recognized fields. For example, you might have an address smart tag in a Microsoft Word document that provides an option to open a map to the location. In a Microsoft Excel spreadsheet, you might define a smart tag for a stock symbol column to go look up the latest price on the Web.

If you have Microsoft Visual Studio, you can actually build your own smart tag applications with Visual Basic. You can download the Smart Tag Software Development Kit (SDK) by going to *www.microsoft.com/downloads/* and performing a search on the keywords *smart tag*. Most Word and Excel smart tag applications have two parts: a recognizer and a set of actions. When a smart tag is active in Word or Excel, the recognizer code runs as you type data and decides whether what you typed is something for which the smart tag has an action. If the smart tag recognizes the text, it passes available actions back to the application, and you see a Smart Tag option available that you can click to invoke one of the actions.

Access 2010 supports smart tags, but in a slightly different way than Word or Excel. You can define a smart tag for labels, text boxes, combo boxes, and list boxes. For text boxes, combo boxes, and list boxes, the smart tag uses the current value of the control as specified in the Control Source property. For labels, the smart tag uses the contents of the Caption property. Because data in Access not only has a specific data type but also a specific meaning, the recognizer code in a smart tag does not come into play. Access assumes that you know that the data in the label, text box, combo box, or list box is something the smart tag understands. So, you can use smart tags in Access that have only actions defined.

Office 2010 installs a few smart tags that you can use in Access 2010:

- **Date** A smart tag that uses a date/time value to schedule a meeting or show your Microsoft Outlook calendar on that date.
- **Telephone Number** A smart tag that accepts a phone number and opens the matching contact from your contacts list.
- **Financial Symbol** A smart tag that can accept a NYSE or NASDAQ stock symbol and display the latest quote, company report, or news from the MSN Money Central website.

- **Instant Messaging Contacts** A smart tag that can accept a person name (first name and last name) or email address and opens the matching contact card from your instant messaging program.
- **Person Name** A smart tag that can accept a person name (first name and last name) or email address and send an email, schedule a meeting, open the matching contact from your contacts list, or add the name to your contacts list.

CAUTION!

If you assign a smart tag to a control containing data that the smart tag cannot handle, the smart tag won't work, and it might generate an error.

In your employees form, the EmailName is a hyperlink field that opens a new message to the email address when you click it. However, you might also want to use the Person Name smart tag to provide additional options. To add this smart tag, open your form in Design view, click the EmailName text box, open the Property Sheet window, click the Data tab, and scroll down to the last property on the list—Smart Tags. Click the property, and then click Build to open the Smart Tags dialog box, as shown in Figure 14-24.

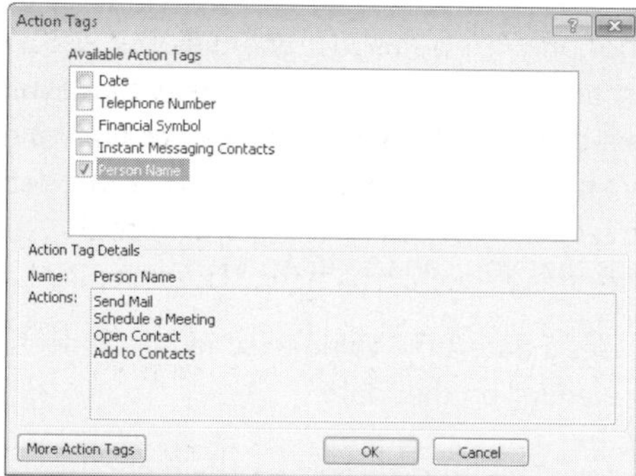

Figure 14-24 You can define smart tags for your controls using the Smart Tags dialog box.

Select the Person Name check box, and click OK to set the property. Note that you can also click More Action Tags to go to the Microsoft website to download and install additional smart tags.

After defining a smart tag, switch to Form view. Controls that have a smart tag defined display a small triangle in the lower-right corner. Rest your mouse pointer on the triangle or tab into the control, and you'll see the smart tag information box appear. Click the down arrow next to the box to see the action choices, as shown in Figure 14-25. Click the action you want to activate that action.

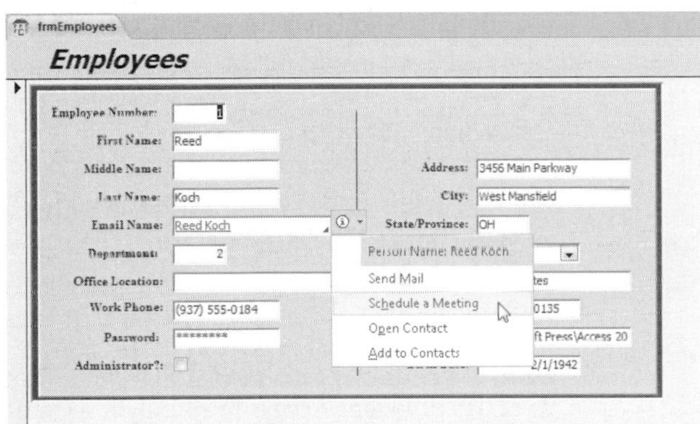

Figure 14-25 You can select a smart tag action from the menu that appears.

Understanding Other Control Properties for Client Forms

As you've already discovered, many of the properties for controls that can be bound to fields from your client form's record source are exactly the same as those you can set in table Design view on the General or Lookup tab. (See Chapter 4 for more details.) If you do not specify a different setting in the control, the client form uses the properties you defined for the field in your table. In some cases, a particular field property setting migrates to a different property in the bound control on your client form. For example, the Description property of a field becomes the Status Bar Text property of the bound control. The Caption property of a field moves to the Caption property of a bound control's associated label.

Table 14-8 describes control settings on client forms not yet discussed and explains their usage. The table lists the properties in the sequence you will find them on the All tab in the Property Sheet window.

Table 14-8 Other Control Properties

Property	Description
Visible	Specify Yes (the default) to make the control visible in Form view. Specify No to hide the control. You will find this property useful when you begin to automate your application and write code to display or hide controls depending on the contents of other fields. See Chapter 25 for details.
Text Format	For controls that can display or be bound to text, you can specify whether the data is stored as plain text or rich text. When you set this property to Rich Text, the data can appear with embedded formatting such as *italics* or **bold**.
Datasheet Caption	You can assign a caption for this control that will display when the form is in Datasheet view. The caption appears as a column header.
Show Date Picker	You can specify For Dates (the default) to instruct Access to display a Date Picker button to the right of the control when the control is bound to a date/time field. Select Never if you do not want Access to display the Date Picker control.
Width, Height, Top, Left	These properties specify the location and size of the control. Access automatically adjusts these settings when you move a control to a new location or adjust its size. You can enter specific values if you want a control to be placed in a particular location or have a specific size.
Back Style	Choose Normal (the default) to be able to specify a color for the background of the control. Choose Transparent to allow the color of any control or section behind the control to show through.
Back Color, Border Style, Border Width, Border Color, Special Effect, Font Name, Font Size, Font Weight, Font Underline, Font Italic, Fore Color	Access automatically sets these properties when you choose a setting on one of the available buttons in the Font group on the Format contextual tab under Form Tools. You can enter a specific setting in these properties rather than choose an option on the ribbon. For the color options, you can click the Build button next to the property to select a custom color from the palette of available colors on your machine.
Text Align	The default setting is General, which left-aligns text and right-aligns numbers. You also can choose Left, Center, and Right options (also available on the Font group of the Format tab) to align the text to the left, in the center, or to the right, respectively. The final option, Distribute, spreads the characters evenly across the available display space in the control.
Line Spacing	You can specify a different line spacing for the text displayed. The default is 0, which spaces the lines based on the font type and size.

Property	Description
Is Hyperlink	Fields that are the Hyperlink data type are always displayed as a hyperlink. You can change this setting to Yes to treat non-Hyperlink data type fields as hyperlinks. The default is No.
Display As Hyperlink	Choose If Hyperlink (the default) to instruct Access to display the data as a hyperlink only if the underlying data type is Hyperlink. Choose Always to display the data as a hyperlink even if the data type is not Hyperlink. Choose Screen Only to display the control as a hyperlink only when in Form view.
Hyperlink Target	If you have at least one web browser control on the form, you can designate in which web browser control Access opens the hyperlink. If you leave this setting at nothing (blank), Access opens your default web browser in a new window when you click the hyperlink.
Gridline Style Top, Gridline Style Bottom, Gridline Style Left, Gridline Style Right	These properties control the style of the gridlines around the control. Transparent (the default) specifies that no gridlines appear. You can choose between Solid, Dashes, Short Dashes, Dots, Sparse Dots, Dash Dot, and Dash Dot Dot. You can also use the Style button in the Gridlines group on the Design tab to set these properties. Note that in a client form, the control must be in a Control layout to see any of these effects when viewing the form in Form view.
Gridline Color	Specify a color to use if you have set gridlines to a value other than Transparent. You can click the Build button next to the property to select a custom color from the palette of available colors on your machine. The default color is black (#000000). Note that in a client form, the control must be in a Control layout to see this property on the Property Sheet window.
Gridline Width Top, Gridline Width Bottom, Gridline Width Left, Gridline Width Right	These properties control the thickness of the gridlines around controls if you have specified a Control Style setting other than Transparent. You can choose from Hairline, 1 pt (the default), 2 pt, 3 pt, 4 pt, 5 pt, and 6 pt. You can also use the Width button in the Gridlines group on the Design tab to set these properties. Note that in a client form, the control must be in a Control layout to see any of these effects when viewing the form in Form view.
Top Margin, Bottom Margin, Left Margin, Right Margin	In a text box control, you can specify alternative margins for the text displayed. The default for all these properties is 0, which provides no additional margin space. You can also use the Control Margins button in the Position group on the Arrange tab to adjust these settings to four options—None, Narrow, Medium, or Wide.
Top Padding, Bottom Padding, Left Padding, Right Padding	These properties control the amount of space between the control and any gridlines. You can set an amount in inches different from the default of 0.0208 inches.

Property	Description
Horizontal Anchor	This specifies how the control is anchored horizontally when it is in a Control layout. You can choose Left (the default) to place the control on the left side, Right to place the control on the right side, or Both to stretch the control equally across the Control layout. You can also use the Anchoring button in the Position group on the Arrange tab to set this property.
Vertical Anchor	This specifies how the control is anchored vertically when it is in a Control layout. You can choose Top (the default) to place the control at the top, Bottom to place the control at the bottom, or Both to stretch the control equally across the Control layout from top to bottom. You can also use the Anchoring button in the Position group on the Arrange tab to set this property.
Can Grow, Can Shrink	These properties apply to controls on a Report or in Print Preview. See Chapter 18, "Advanced Report Design," for details.
Display When	Choose Always (the default) to display this control in Form view, in Print Preview, and when you print the form. Choose Print Only to display the control only when you view the form in Print Preview or when you print the form. Choose Screen Only to display the control only when in Form view.
Reading Order	Choose Context (the default) to set the order the characters are displayed based on the first character entered. When the first character is from a character set that is normally read right to left (such as Arabic), the characters appear right to left. Choose Left-To-Right or Right-To-Left to override the reading order.
Scroll Bar Align	Choose System (the default) to align scroll bars based on the form's Orientation property setting. See the section "Understanding Other Client Form Properties," on page 892, for details. Choose Right or Left to override the form setting.
Numeral Shapes	On an Arabic or Hindi system, you can choose settings to alter the way numbers are displayed. The default setting is System, which displays numbers based on your system settings.
Keyboard Language	System (the default setting) assumes the keyboard being used is the default for your system. You can also choose from any available installed keyboard.
Filter Lookup	Choose Database Default (the default setting) to honor the options you set in the Client Settings category in the Access Options dialog box. Choose Never to disable the lookup of values in Filter By Form. Choose Always to enable the lookup of values in Filter By Form regardless of your Access Options settings.

Property	Description
On Click through On Undo	You can set these properties to run a macro, a function, or an event procedure when the specific event described by the property occurs for this control. See Part 6, "Automating an Application Using Macros," for details.
Enter Key Behavior	Default (the default setting) specifies that pressing the Enter key in this control performs the action described in the Move After Enter setting on the Client Settings category in the Access Options dialog box. The New Line In Field setting specifies that pressing Enter creates a new line in the underlying text. This setting is useful for large text or memo fields, especially when the control is more than one line high and has a vertical scroll bar defined.
ControlTip Text	You can enter a custom message that appears as a control tip when you rest your mouse pointer on the control for a few seconds. You might find this especially useful for command buttons to further describe the action that occurs when the user clicks the button.
Shortcut Menu Bar	You can design a custom shortcut menu for your forms and reports, and you enter the name of your custom menu in this property. This property exists for backward compatibility with Access 2003 and earlier.
Help Context ID	You can create a custom Help file for your application and identify specific topics with a context ID. If you want a particular topic to appear when a user presses F1 when the focus is in this control, enter the ID of the topic in this property.
Auto Tab	Choose Yes to cause an automatic tab to the next field when the user enters a number of characters equal to the field length. The default is No.
Vertical	You can design a control that displays text to run vertically down the form (narrow width and tall height). When you do that, you can set Vertical to Yes to turn the text display 90 degrees clockwise. The default is No.
Allow AutoCorrect	Specify Yes (the default) to enable autocorrection as you type text, similar to the AutoCorrect feature in Word. You can customize AutoCorrect options by clicking the AutoCorrect Options button in the Proofing category in the Access Options dialog box. Specify No to turn off this feature.
IME Hold, IME Mode, IME Sentence Mode	These properties determine how Kanji characters are processed on a Japanese language system.
Tag	You can use this property to store additional descriptive information about the control. You can write Visual Basic code to examine and set this property or take a specific action based on the property setting. The user cannot see the contents of the Tag property.

Be Careful When Setting Control Validation Rules

Two properties that deserve special mention are Validation Rule and Validation Text. As you know, you can specify these properties for most fields in your table. When you build a form that is bound to data from your table, the validation rules in the table always apply. However, you can also specify a validation rule for many bound controls on your form. You might want to do this if, on this particular form, you want a more restrictive rule to apply.

However, you can get in trouble if you specify a rule that conflicts with the rule in the underlying table. For example, in the HousingDataCopy.accdb sample database, you can find a validation rule on the BirthDate field in the tblEmployees table that disallows entering a birth date for someone who is younger than 18 years old. The validation rule is as follows:

```
<=(Date()-(365*18))
```

What do you suppose happens if you subsequently enter a Validation Rule property for the BirthDate text box control on your form that requires the person to be 18 or younger? You can try it by opening your employees form in Design view, clicking the BirthDate text box, and entering the following in the Validation Rule property in the property sheet:

```
>(Date()-(365*18))
```

So that you can determine which validation rule is preventing you from changing the data, set the Validation Text property to something like "Violating the control validation rule." Now, switch to Form view and try to type a value that you know violates the table rule, such as 1/1/2010. When you try to tab out of the field, you should see the message from the table: "You cannot enter an employee who is younger than 18 years old." Now, try to enter a date for an older person, such as 1/1/1969, and press Tab to move out of the control. You should see the validation text that you just entered for the control. The bottom line is you have set up the rules so that no value is valid when you try to edit with this form. (You'll have to press Esc to clear your edit to be able to close the form.)

Setting Client Form Properties

In addition to the controls on a client form, the client form itself has a number of properties that you can use to control its appearance and how it works.

Allowing Different Views

When you build a client form from scratch (such as the employees form you've been working on in this chapter), the Default View property of the form is Single Form. This is the view you'll see first when you open the form. With the Single Form setting, you can see only one record at a time, and you have to use the Record Number box, the Previous Record and Next Record arrow buttons to the left and right of the Record Number Box, or the Go To command in the Find group on the Home tab to move to another record. If you set the Default View property of the form to Continuous Forms, you can see multiple records on a short form, and you can use the scroll bar on the right side of the form to scroll through the records. If you set the Default View property of the form to Split Form, you can see your employee records in Datasheet view at the top of the form window. At the bottom of the form window, you can see one record at a time displayed in the form controls you've been designing. Because one record's data in the tblEmployees table fills your employees form, the Single Form setting is probably the best choice.

Another set of properties lets you control whether a user can change to Form view, Datasheet view, PivotTable view, PivotChart view, or Layout view. These properties are Allow Form View, Allow Datasheet View, Allow PivotTable View, Allow PivotChart View, and Allow Layout View. The default setting for all these properties is No except Form View and Layout View, meaning that a user cannot use the View button on the ribbon to switch to Datasheet, PivotTable, or PivotChart views. (Users also cannot switch to these views if they right-click the form tab when their Document Windows Options setting is set to Tabbed Documents.) If you're designing a form to be used in an application, you will usually want to eliminate some of the views. For your employees form, set all but the Allow Form View property to No; if you click the arrow in the Views group, the Layout View option should not appear.

INSIDE OUT

Keeping Users Out of Design and Layout Views

You can make it more difficult to enter Design and Layout views by designing a custom ribbon for all your forms. See Chapter 26, "The Finishing Touches," on the companion CD for details. You can completely prevent a user from opening a form in Design view or switching to Design view only if you give your users an execute-only copy of your application (see Chapter 27, "Distributing Your Application," on the companion CD). You can prevent users from opening a form in Layout view or switching to Layout view by clearing the Enable Layout View check box in the Current Database category in the Access Options dialog box. This setting affects all forms *and* reports in your database.

Setting Navigation Options

Because the employees form you've been designing displays one record at a time, it is not useful to display the row selector on the left side of the form. You've also designed the form to show all the data in a single window, so a scroll bar along the right side of the window isn't necessary. You also don't need a horizontal scroll bar. You probably should keep the Record Number Box at the bottom of the form, however. To make these changes, set the form's Record Selectors property on the property sheet to No, the Scroll Bars property to Neither, and the Navigation Buttons property to Yes. Your form should look something like the one shown in Figure 14-26.

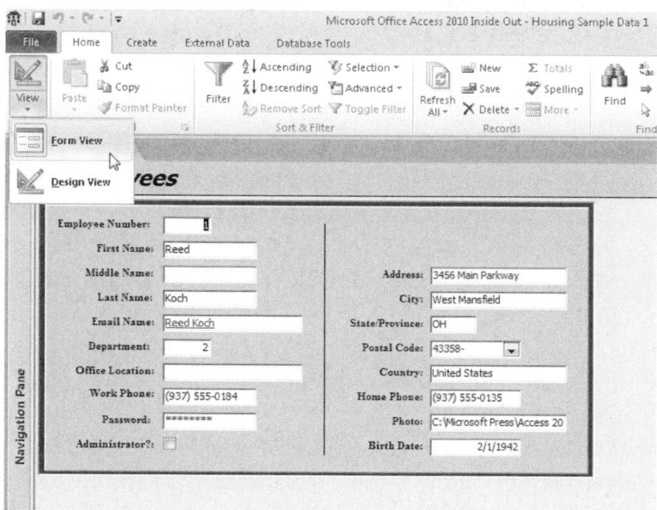

Figure 14-26 The employees form now has views restricted and does not have a record selector or scroll bars.

Defining a Pop-Up and/or Modal Form

You might occasionally want to design a form that stays on top of all other forms even when it doesn't have the focus. Notice that the undocked property sheet and field list in Design view both have this characteristic. These are called *pop-up forms*. You can make your employees form a pop-up form by setting the form's Pop Up property to Yes. Figure 14-27 shows the employees form as a pop-up form on top of the Navigation pane, which has the focus. Note that the form can "float" on top of other forms or windows, and it can also be moved on top of the ribbon. A form that isn't a pop-up form cannot leave the Access work-space below the ribbon. You might also notice that when you change the employees form's Pop Up property to Yes, the form no longer has the tab across the top. Even though the

Document Windows Options setting is still set to Tabbed Documents for this database, this form now looks like we are using the Overlapping Windows setting.

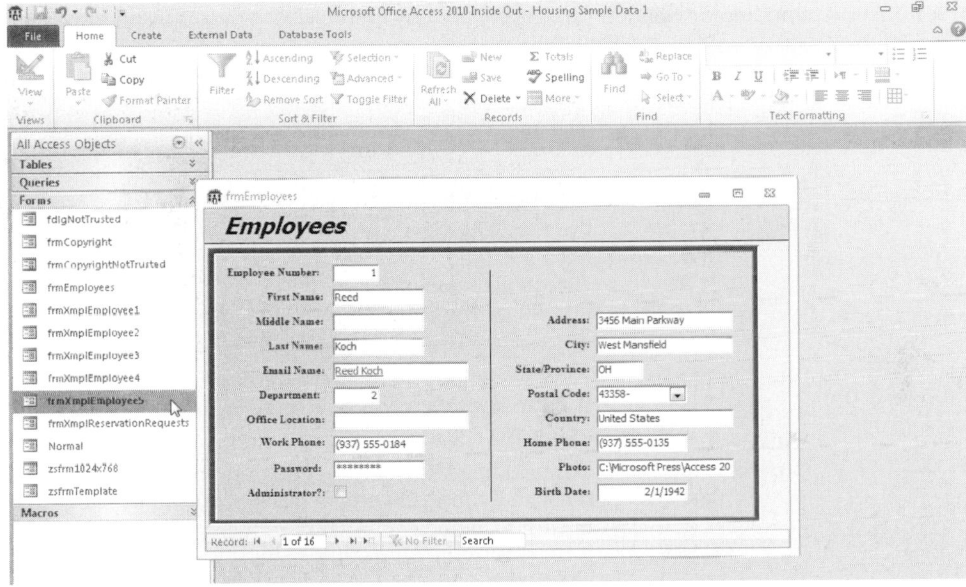

Figure 14-27 The employees form as a pop up form floats on top of the Navigation pane and the ribbon

CAUTION!

If you play with the frmXmplEmployee5 form to do this, be sure to set the form's Pop Up property back to No or don't save your design changes when you close the form.

As you'll learn in Part 6, "Automating an Application Using Macros," and Part 8, "Automating an Access Application Using Visual Basic," it's sometimes useful to create forms that ask the user for information that's needed to perform the next task. Forms have a Modal property that you can set to Yes to "lock" the user into the form when it's open. The user must make a choice in the form or close the form to go on to other tasks. When a modal form is open, you can switch to another application, but you can't select any other form or ribbon button in Access until you dismiss the modal form. You've probably noticed that most dialog boxes, such as the various wizards in Access, are modal forms. Modal isn't a good choice for your employees form, but you'll use the Modal property later to help control application flow.

Controlling Edits, Deletions, Additions, and Filtering

You can set several properties on client forms to control whether data in the form can be updated or whether data in the underlying tables can change. You can also prevent or allow user-applied filters on the form. These properties and their settings are shown in Table 14-9.

Table 14-9 Client Form Properties for Controlling Editing and Filtering

Property	Description
Filter	Contains the latest criteria applied as a filter on this form. Forms also have a FilterOn property that you can't see in the Form window in Design view. When FilterOn is True, the data displayed in the form is filtered by the criteria string found in the Filter property. On a new form, the Filter property is empty.
Filter On Load	You can define criteria in the Filter property and then set Filter On Load to Yes to apply the filter when the form opens. The default setting is No.
Order By	Contains the latest sorting criteria applied to this form. Forms also have an OrderByOn property that you can't see in the Form window in Design view. When OrderByOn is True, the data displayed in the form is sorted by the criteria string found in the Order By property. On a new form, the Order By property is empty.
Order By On Load	You can define sorting criteria in the Order By property and then set Order By On Load to Yes to apply the sort when the form opens. The default setting is Yes.
Data Entry	Determines whether the form opens a blank record in which you can insert new data. Access won't retrieve rows from the form's recordset. The valid settings are Yes and No, and the default setting is No. Setting Data Entry to Yes is effective only when Allow Additions is set to Yes.
Allow Additions	Determines whether a user can add records using this form. The valid settings are Yes and No. The default setting is Yes.
Allow Deletions	Determines whether a user can delete records in this form. The valid settings are Yes and No. The default setting is Yes.
Allow Edits	Determines whether a user can change control values in this form. The valid settings are Yes and No. The default setting is Yes. Note that when you set Allow Edits to No, you cannot change the value of any control on the form, including unbound controls.
Allow Filters	Determines whether a user can see selected records by applying filtering and sorting criteria and whether the user can see all records by clicking the Toggle Filter command in the Sort & Filter group. If you set the Data Entry property to Yes and set the Allow Filters property to No, the user can only enter new data and cannot change the form to view other existing records. The valid settings for the Allow Filters property are Yes and No. The default setting is Yes.

Defining Window Controls

In some cases, you might want to prevent the user from opening the client form's control menu (clicking the control menu in the upper-left corner of a window displays a shortcut menu containing the Restore, Move, Size, Minimize, Maximize, Close, and Next commands) or from using the Minimize and Maximize buttons. (This applies only if you have your Document Windows Options setting set to Overlapping Windows. If you have Tabbed Documents selected, you see only a Close button on the right side.) If you want to perform special processing before a form closes (such as clearing the application status before your main switchboard closes), you might want to provide a command button to do the processing and then close the form with a Visual Basic command. (See Part 9 for details about writing a command to close a form.) You can set the form's Control Box property to No to remove the control menu button from the form window and the Close button from the upper-right corner. This also removes the Minimize and Maximize buttons.

You can set the form's Close Button property to No to remove the Close button but leave the control menu button (with Close disabled on the Control menu). You can set the form's Min Max Buttons property to Both Enabled, None, Min Enabled, or Max Enabled. If you disable the Minimize or Maximize button, the related command on the form's Control menu becomes disabled.

CAUTION!

If you are using overlapping windows, you can set a form's Control Box property to No to remove all control features from the form's title bar. This means that both the control menu button (which contains the Close command) and the form's Close button (at the right end of the title bar) will not appear. If you also set the form's Modal property to Yes, you should always provide an alternative way to close a modal form, such as a command button that executes a macro or Visual Basic command to close the form. Otherwise, the only way to close the form is to use the Windows Ctrl+F4 key combination. See Part 6 and Part 9 for details about writing a command to close a form.

Setting the Border Style

In most cases, you'll want to create forms with a regular border—one that allows you to size the window and move it around if you have the Document Windows Options setting set to Overlapping Windows. Client forms have a Border Style property that lets you define the look of the border and whether the window can be sized or moved. The Border Style property settings are shown in Table 14-10.

Table 14-10 Settings for the Border Style Property

Setting	Description
None	The form has no borders, control menu button, title bar, Close button, or Minimize and Maximize buttons. You cannot resize or move the form when it is open. You can select the form and press Ctrl+F4 to close it unless the form's Pop Up property is set to Yes. You should write Visual Basic code or create a macro to provide an alternative way to close this type of form.
Thin	The form has a thin border, signifying that the form cannot be resized.
Sizable	This is the default setting. The form can be resized.
Dialog	If the Pop Up property is set to Yes, the form's border is a thick line (like that of a true Windows dialog box), signifying that the form cannot be resized. If the Pop Up property is set to No, the Dialog setting is the same as the Thin setting.

Understanding Other Client Form Properties

Table 14-11 describes client form settings not yet discussed and explains their usage. The table lists the properties in the sequence you will find them on the All tab in the property sheet.

Table 14-11 Other Client Form Properties

Property	Description
Picture Type	Choose Embedded (the default) to store a copy of the picture in your form design. Use Linked to save space in your database, but the form must then always load the picture from the specified Picture path when it opens; and if you move the picture to a different location, it might not display. Use Shared to use a shared image stored in the database. When an image is shared, you can use the image in other forms and reports. You can reference the shared image name on the Picture property. You'll learn about shared images at the end of this chapter.
Picture	Enter the path name and file name of a graphic file to use as the background of the form. You can click the Build button next to the property to locate the picture you want. You might find this useful to display an image such as a company logo on the background of your forms. If you have any shared images stored in the database, Access displays a list of the image names in a drop-down list.
Picture Tiling	The default setting, No, places one copy of the picture on the form. Choose Yes if you want multiple copies "tiled" on the form. When you choose Yes, you must set Picture Alignment to Clip or Zoom, and the picture should be smaller than the form design or form window. Setting Picture Tiling to Yes is useful if your picture is a small pattern bitmap.

Property	Description
Picture Alignment	This property applies only when Picture Size Mode is Clip or Zoom. The default setting, Center, centers the picture in the form window area. Form Center centers the picture in the form design area. You can also specify that the picture align in the Top Left, Top Right, Bottom Left, or Bottom Right of the form.
Picture Size Mode	Clip (the default) specifies that the picture appears in its original resolution. If the form is larger than the picture, the picture will not cover the entire form area. If the form is smaller than the picture, you'll see only part of the picture. Use Stretch to stretch the picture to the dimensions of the form, but the picture might appear distorted. Use Zoom to stretch the picture to the dimensions of the form without distorting it; but if the aspect ratio of the picture does not match the display space of the form, the picture won't cover the entire form background.
Width	Specifies the width of the form in inches or centimeters. Access automatically updates this property when you drag the right edge of the design area wider or narrower in Design view or Layout view. You cannot set this property to nothing (blank).
Auto Center	Choose No (the default) to open the form on the screen wherever it was placed when you last saved its definition from Design view, Layout view, or Form view. Choose Yes to automatically center the form in the Access workspace when you open it. This applies only if you are using an MDI.
Auto Resize	The default Yes setting automatically resizes the form window to its design height and width when you open the form. Choose No if you want to set a specific window size. This applies only if you are using an MDI.
Fit To Screen	The default setting, No, tells Access not to reduce the width of the form if the form window size is reduced. Choose Yes if you want Access to automatically reduce the width of the form to fit within the available screen space. This applies only if you are using an MDI.
Navigation Caption	You can use this property to set a descriptive text to be used to the left of the form's navigation buttons. If left blank, Access uses the word Record.
Dividing Lines	When you design your form with a Header or Footer section, Yes (the default) specifies that you will see a horizontal line separating each section. No removes the line(s).
Moveable	The default setting, No, locks the form on the screen where you last saved it. Set this property to Yes to allow the user to move the form in the Access window if using an MDI.
Split Form Size	You can use this setting to adjust the size of the form and datasheet if the form is displayed in Split Form view. If you use a larger setting here, Access displays more of the form and less of the datasheet. The default setting, Auto, tells Access to reset the form and datasheet size.

Property	Description
Split Form Orientation	The default setting, Datasheet On Top, displays the datasheet portion of a form in Split Form view at the top of the form window. You can also choose to display the datasheet potion in different positions using the other three options—Datasheet On Bottom, Datasheet On Left, or Datasheet On Right.
Split Form Splitter Bar	The default setting, Yes, displays a separator bar between the form and datasheet potions of a form in Split Form view. Choose No to hide the separator bar. When the splitter bar is hidden, the user cannot change the size of the two portions.
Split Form Datasheet	The default setting, Allow Edits, allows you to make changes to the data in the datasheet potion of a form in Split Form view. Choose Read Only to disallow any edits of the data in the datasheet portion.
Split Form Printing	The default setting, Form Only, specifies that Access prints only the form portion of a form in Split Form view if the user decides to print the form. Choose Datasheet Only to have Access print only the contents of the datasheet portion.
Save Splitter Bar Position	The default setting, Yes, specifies that Access attempts to save the splitter bar position when you close a form in Split Form view. You can move the splitter bar to display more or less of either the form or datasheet portion of the form, but you cannot do this when the Split Form Splitter Bar property is set to No. If this property is set to Yes when you close the form, Access prompts you to save the changes to the form. If you choose No, Access does not save the new location. Set this property to No to discard any changes to the splitter bar location upon closing the form.
Subdatasheet Expanded and Subdatasheet Height	These properties are identical to those that you can define for tables and queries. Your form must be in Datasheet view and must have a subform that is also in Datasheet view. See Chapter 15 for details.
Layout for Print	The default setting, No, indicates that printer fonts installed on your machine will not be available in any font property settings, but screen fonts and TrueType fonts will be available. Choosing Yes disables screen fonts but makes printer fonts and TrueType fonts available.
Orientation	The default in most versions of Access 2010 is Left-To-Right. In versions that support a language that is normally read right to left, the default is Right-To-Left. When you use Right-To-Left, captions appear right-justified, the order of characters in controls is right to left, and the tab sequence proceeds right to left.

Property	Description
Recordset Type	The default setting, Dynaset, specifies that all controls bound to fields in the record source will be updatable as long as the underlying field would also be updatable. If your form is bound to a query, see "Limitations on Using Select Queries to Update Data," on page 680. Dynaset (Inconsistent Updates) specifies that all fields (other than fields resulting from expressions or AutoNumber fields) can be updated, even if the update would break a link between related tables. (We do not recommend this option because it can allow a user to attempt to make a change that would violate integrity rules.) Snapshot specifies that the data is read-only and cannot be updated.
Fetch Defaults	Choose Yes (the default) to have the form fetch the default values from the field definitions when you move to a new row. Set this property to No to use only the Default Value settings you have specified for controls.
Wait for Post Processing	The default setting, No, specifies that Access does not need to wait for data macros called from the form to finish processing before returning control back to you. If you call a long-running named data macro from a form (or fire a table event that performs a lot of processing) with this setting at No, you can immediately perform additional actions. Choosing Yes tells Access to wait for the data macro to finish processing before returning control to you. Access displays a message indicating that you must wait for post processing to finish.
On Current through Before Screen Tip	You can set these properties to run a macro, a function, or an event procedure when the specific event described by the property occurs for this form. See Parts 6 and 8 for details.
Cycle	Use the default setting, All Records, to tab to the next record when you press the Tab key in the last control in the tab order. Choose Current Record to disallow tabbing from one record to another. Choose Current Page on a multipage form to disallow tabbing onto the next or previous page—you must use Page Up or Page Down to move between pages. When you set Current Record or Current Page, you must use the navigation buttons or ribbon commands to move to other records.
Record Locks	No Locks (the default) specifies that Access will not lock any edited row until it needs to write the row back to the table. This is the most efficient choice for most applications. Edited Record specifies that Access apply a lock to the row the instant you begin typing in the record. This can lock out other users in a shared environment. All Records (not recommended) locks every record in the record source as soon as you open the form.
Ribbon Name	You can design a custom ribbon to display for your forms and reports, and you can enter the name of your custom ribbon in this property. See Chapter 26 for more details.

Property	Description
Toolbar, Menu Bar, and Shortcut Menu Bar	Using Access 2000, 2002, or 2003 in an MDB format database, you can design a custom menu bar, toolbar, and shortcut menu for your forms and reports, and you enter the name of your custom menus or toolbars in these properties. These properties are supported in Access 2010 for backward compatibility with earlier versions.
Shortcut Menu	The default setting, Yes, indicates shortcut menus will be available for the form and all controls on the form. Choose No to disable shortcut menus.
Help File	When you create a custom help file for your application, enter the path and file name in this property.
Help Context ID	You can create a custom Help file for your application and identify specific topics with a context ID. If you want a particular topic to appear when a user presses F1 when using this form, enter the ID of the topic in this property. If the focus is in a control that also has a Help Context ID defined, the topic for that control is displayed.
Has Module	If you create Visual Basic event procedures for this form, Access automatically sets this property to Yes. If you change this property from Yes to No, Access warns you that doing so will delete all your code and gives you a chance to cancel the change. See Part 8 for details.
Use Default Paper Size	The default setting, No, specifies that Access use the paper size specified when the form or report was designed when printing the form or report. Choose Yes to use the default paper size of the current printer when printing the form or report.
Fast Laser Printing	The default setting, Yes, specifies that Access will use laser printer line fonts to draw lines and rectangles if you print the form on a printer that supports this option. Choose No to send all lines to your printer as graphics.
Tag	You can use this property to store additional descriptive information about the form. You can write Visual Basic code to examine and set this property or take a specific action based on the property setting. The user cannot see the contents of the Tag property.
Palette Source	Enter the name of a graphic file or Windows palette file that provides a color palette to display this form. You might need to set this property if you have also set the Picture property so that the colors of the background picture display properly. The default setting, (Default), uses your current Windows palette.
Key Preview	You can use this property to specify whether the form-level keyboard event procedures are invoked before a control's keyboard event procedures. The default setting, No, specifies that only the active control receives keyboard events. When you choose Yes, the form receives keyboard events first, and then the active control receives keyboard events next.

Setting Client Form and Control Defaults

When you're building an application, you should establish a standard design for all your client forms and the controls on your forms.

Changing Control Defaults

You can use the Set Control Defaults button in the Controls group on the Design tab to change the defaults for the various controls on your form. If you want to change the default property settings for all new controls of a particular type, select a control of that type, set the control's properties to the desired default values, and then click the Set Control Defaults button in the Controls group on the Design tab. The settings of the currently selected control will become the default settings for any subsequent definitions of that type of control on your form.

For example, you might want all new labels to show blue text on a white background. To make this change, place a label on your form, and set the label's Fore Color property to blue and its Back Color property to white using the Font Color and Background Color buttons in the Font group on the Format tab. Click the Set Control Defaults button in the Controls group on the Design tab while this label is selected. Any new labels you place on the form will have the new default settings.

INSIDE OUT **What Happened to the AutoFormats?**

In Access 2010, the AutoFormats for forms and reports are no longer on the default ribbon. You can still use the AutoFormats, but you'll need to create an entry point for yourself by adding the command to the Quick Access Toolbar or to a custom ribbon group. On the Quick Access Toolbar or Customize Ribbon category of the Access Options dialog box, select Commands Not In The Ribbon from the Choose Commands From list. You can click the AutoFormat option on the left side and then click Add to add the command to the Quick Access Toolbar or custom ribbon group. Click OK to save your changes. You can then use the 25 AutoFormat options for your client forms and reports.

Defining a Template Form

You can also create a special form to define new default properties for all your controls. To do this, open a new blank form and place on it one of each type of control for which you want to define default properties. Modify the properties of the controls to your liking, use these controls to reset the control defaults for the form (by clicking the Set Control Defaults button in the Controls group on the Design tab for each control), and save the form with the name *Normal*. The Normal form becomes the *form template* for the current database. Any new control you place on any new form created after you define your form template (except forms for which you've already changed the default for one or more controls) will use the default property settings you defined for that control type on the Normal form. Note that defining a form template does not affect any existing forms. Also, you can revert to the standard settings by deleting the form Normal from your database.

To define a name other than Normal for your default form and report templates, click the File tab on the Backstage view, click Options, and then click the Object Designers category. Enter the new name in the Form Template text box in the Form/Report Design View section. Then save your template under the new name you specified in the Object Designers category. Note that this new setting becomes the default for all databases on your machine, but if Access doesn't find a form in your database with the name you specified, it uses the standard default settings instead.

If you want to see how this works in the HousingDataCopy.accdb sample database, click the File tab on the Backstage view, click Options, and then click the Object Designers category. In the Form/Report Design View section, enter **zsfrmTemplate** in the Form Template box, and click OK. Next, click the Blank Form button in the Forms group on the Create tab to create a blank form. Your new form should have a header and footer and a custom background. Try dropping a few controls onto the form. Figure 14-28 shows you our template in Design view. Note that your new form not only inherits control properties but also inherits the height and width of each of the sections from the template.

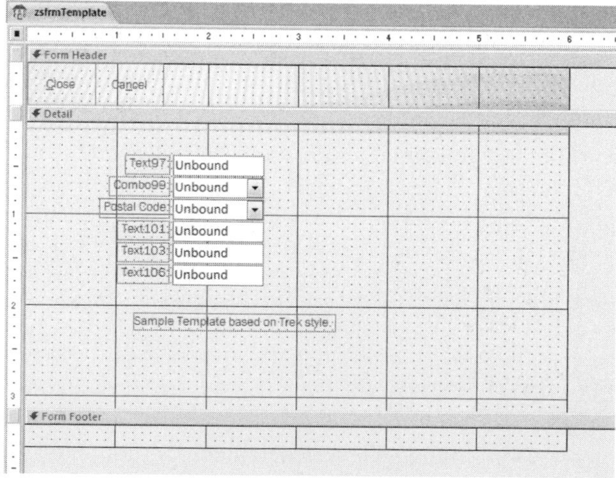

Figure 14-28 This is the zsfrmTemplate sample template form in the HousingDataCopy.accdb sample client database.

CAUTION!

Be sure to change your default template name back to Normal before going any further. This setting affects all your databases but won't hurt anything unless you happen to have a form named zsfrmTemplate in some of your databases.

Working with Web Forms in Layout View

Up to this point, you've been building a client form in Design view to add and edit records in the tblEmployees table with the Housing Data Copy client database. You've seen how to start with a blank client form and add fields to the form grid, position the controls into a two-column layout, and then align the controls both horizontally and vertically. You can create the same type of employee client form working exclusively in Layout view. When you work in Layout view, you are able to see live data from the form's record source while working with the controls. When you create and edit web forms in a web database, however, your only design surface is Layout view; you cannot open a web form in Design view to make edits to the controls and web form.

In this section, you'll follow a similar procedure as you did previously in this chapter with a client form to build a new web form, except this time, you'll use Layout view. The procedures we show you in the following sections—namely, working with web forms in Layout view—can be applied to client forms as well, if you want to experiment with using Layout view on client forms.

To learn how to create and customize a web form, open the BOSSDataCopy2.accdb sample web database. After Access closes the information form displayed on startup, click the Create tab to see the commands listed in the Forms group for web databases, as shown in Figure 14-29.

Figure 14-29 The Forms group on the Create tab in web databases includes commands to create new web forms and client forms.

Here are the options you can use in the Forms group on the Create tab in web databases:

- **Form** Quick Create command to create a new single record web form based on the highlighted table or web query in the Navigation pane. Access creates a control for every field in that table or web query and displays it in Layout view. In the single record web form, Access creates controls for all the fields in columns on the Form window.
- **Multiple Items** Quick Create command to create a new continuous web form based on the highlighted table or web query in the Navigation pane. Access creates a control for every field in that table or web query and displays it in Layout view. In a continuous web form, Access creates controls for all the fields horizontally across the Form window.
- **Blank Form** Access creates a new, blank web form and displays it in Layout view. Use this button when you want to start creating a web form from scratch.
- **Datasheet** Quick Create command to create a new datasheet web form based on the highlighted table or web query in the Navigation pane. Access creates a control for every field in that table or web query and displays it in Layout view.
- **Navigation** A drop-down list of six options to create a new, blank web form with a Navigational Control. You'll learn how to work with Navigational Controls in Chapter 15.
- **Client Forms** A drop-down list of 11 options to create client forms in a web database. The client form options are the same ones you've studied previously in this chapter and in Chapter 13. You can create all client form types in a web database and they will function when you open them in an Access client. However, client forms will not open in a web browser.

Starting from Scratch—A Simple Input Web Form

You need a web form to edit and display product data, and the easiest way to get started is to create a blank web form based on the tblProducts table. Click the Blank Form button in the Forms group on the Create tab. A blank form grid appears in Layout view with the Field List window showing on the right side of the screen, as shown in Figure 14-30.

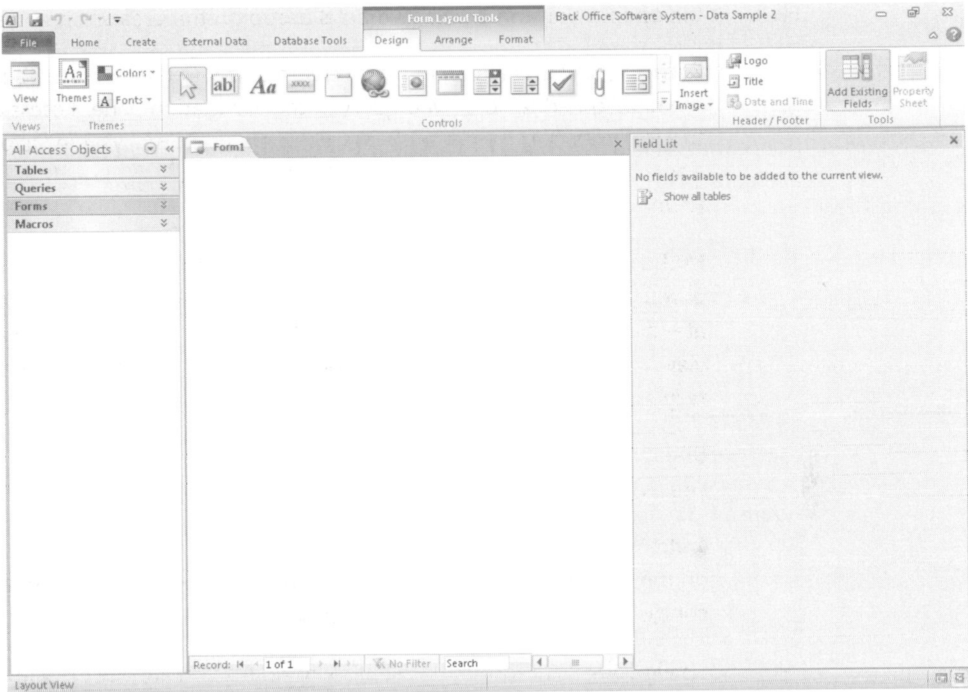

Figure 14-30 When you click the Blank Form command on the ribbon, Access opens a new Form window in Layout view.

The web form does not yet have a record source, so you need to bind this web form to the tblProducts table. Click the Property Sheet button in the Tools group on the Design tab under Form Layout Tools. Find the Record Source property on either the All or Data tab in the Property Sheet window for the form, and select tblProducts from the list of table and web query names to bind this form to the tblProducts table. Note that when you are working with web forms, Access does not list any client queries in the drop-down list of table and query names on the Record Source property. You cannot bind a web form to client queries, only tables, web queries, and web-compatible SQL statements.

Understanding Control Layouts and Control Anchoring

Now that you have the web form bound to the tblProducts table, you can begin to add the fields to the form grid, as you did previously in Design view, but this time using Layout view. Open the field list by clicking the Add Existing Fields button in the Tools group on the Design tab. If the field list displays other tables in the bottom half of the field list, click the Show Only Fields In The Current Record Source link at the top of the Field List window to show only the fields in the tblProducts table.

Earlier in this chapter, you were able to drag a control from the field list and place it on any part of the form grid in Design view. Let's perform the same step now in Layout view with this web form. Drag the ProductID field from the field list onto the form grid. (It doesn't matter on which part of the grid you place the field.) After you release the mouse, you'll notice that Access places the control near the upper-left corner of the form grid, as shown in Figure 14-31. Notice also that you can see actual data from the table in the text box.

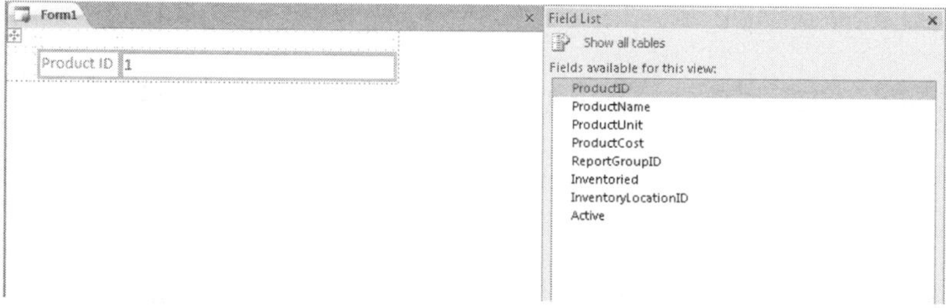

Figure 14-31 Access positions the ProductID control in the upper-left corner no matter where you drop it on the form grid.

Access applied a control layout to the grid and *anchored* the ProductID control in the upper-left corner. Access positioned the Product ID label about 0.25 inches from the top of the form and a third of an inch from the left side of the form. All controls on web forms must be in a control layout to be web-compatible. When Access anchors a control in a control layout for web forms, Access resizes or moves the control if you resize or move the section in which the control resides. In addition to anchoring controls to the default top left, you can choose to stretch the controls across the top, down the left side, and down and across the section. On the Arrange tab, in the Position group, click Anchoring to see the four possible anchoring configurations web forms, as shown in Figure 14-32.

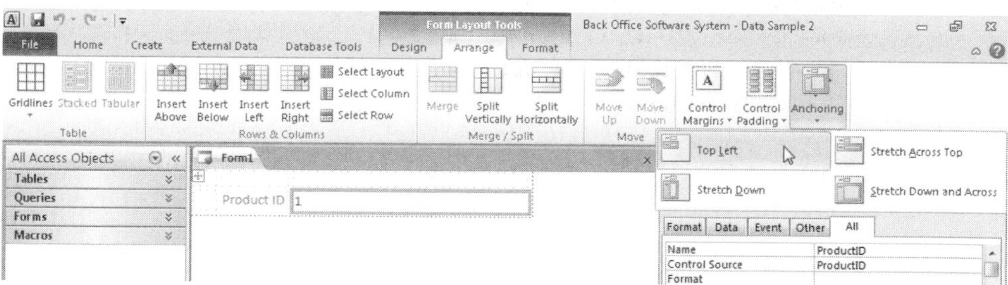

Figure 14-32 Use the anchoring options to select different anchoring positions for your controls.

To see how another anchoring option appears on the form grid, select the ProductID field, if it isn't already selected, and then click Stretch Across Top in the anchoring gallery. You'll notice that Access increases the width of the ProductID field so that it extends closer to the right edge of the form. If you close the Field List window, you can see that Access again increases the width of the control. Switch to Form view now by clicking the arrow in the Views group on the Home or Design tab and selecting Form View in the list of available views. Access displays the ProductID field nearly across the entire top of the form grid, as shown in Figure 14-33. In most cases, a control this wide is not very practical for a simple text field. Return to Layout view, select the ProductID control, click the Anchoring button in the Position group on the Arrange tab, and change the anchor option back to Top Left.

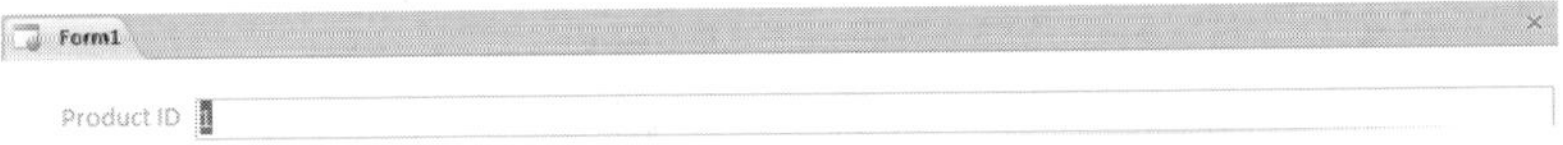

Figure 14-33 The Stretch Across Top anchoring option produces a very wide control.

If you like, you can try some of the other options. Stretch Down expands the control to fill the vertical space on the form. (If you have more than one control stacked in the layout, Access expands them all equally to fill the space.) Stretch Down And Across expands the control to fill the entire space.

Lining Up Controls

Now that you have the ProductID field on the grid, let's add the next field, ProductName, below ProductID. Click the ProductName field in the field list, drag it onto the form, and place it just below the ProductID text box, as shown in Figure 14-34. When you have it correctly positioned, Access displays a horizontal I-bar below the ProductID text box. Access displays this I-bar as a visual cue to indicate where it will drop the new control. If, for example, you want to place the new field to the right of the ProductID text box, position the mouse to the right of that control and you'll see a vertical I-bar to the right of the ProductID text box.

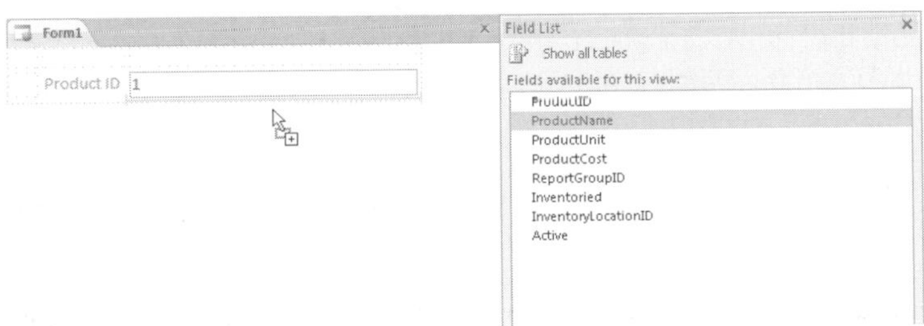

Figure 14-34 Drag the ProductName field below the ProductID field.

After you release the mouse, Access places the ProductName field directly below the ProductID label and text box controls, as shown in Figure 14-35. Now that you have two controls on the grid, you can really begin to see the advantages of control layouts in web forms. Unlike the Design view exercise you performed at the beginning of this chapter with a client form, Access creates a label and field control that exactly matches the dimensions of the first label and field control when you use a control layout in a web form. Access positions the new controls directly beneath the ProductID controls and aligns them vertically.

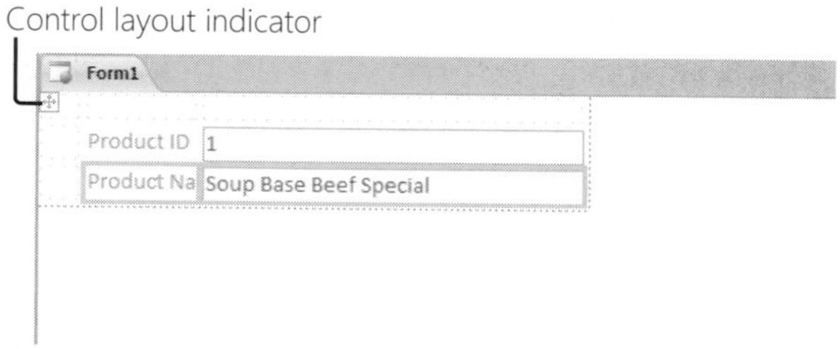

Control layout indicator

Form1

Product ID	1
Product Na	Soup Base Beef Special

Figure 14-35 Access sizes all the same types of controls to the same height and width when you use a control layout in web forms.

Control layouts help you align and position controls on forms and reports. It might be easier to think of a control layout as being similar to a table in Word or a spreadsheet in Excel. When you widen or narrow one control in a column, you change the width of any other controls in that column that are part of that control layout. Likewise, when you increase or decrease the height of a control, you're changing the height of all the controls in that row.

When you design web forms in web databases in Layout view, Access puts all controls into a control layout to be compatible with the web. In web forms, you have no control over how Access creates the control layouts. When you are creating client forms, however, you have additional flexibility when working with control layouts. Access 2010 has two kinds of control layouts for client forms—*stacked* and *tabular*. In a stacked control layout, Access stacks bound controls for different fields in a column and places all the labels down the left side. In client forms, you can have multiple sets of stacked controls within a section. Any controls (including associated labels) in a stacked layout must all be in one section. In the web form you've built thus far, Access placed the product number and product name controls in a stacked layout in the Detail section. You can tell these controls are in a control layout by noticing the small box with crosshairs just to the left of and slightly above the Employee Number label, previously shown in Figure 14-35.

In a tabular control layout, Access places bound controls horizontally with labels along the top as column headings—much like rows on a spreadsheet. A tabular control layout can include controls in different sections of a form—for example, the labels can appear in a

Header section and the data controls in the Detail section of the form. If you use the Quick Create Multiple Items button for client or web forms, Access creates a tabular control layout for the fields in the form's record source.

Moving Controls Within a Control Layout

Let's add the remaining fields onto the form grid now. Click the ProductUnit field in the field list, hold down the Shift key, and then click the Active field to highlight the remaining six fields. Drag all the controls as a group onto the form grid and place them just below the ProductName text box. After you put the fields on the grid, your form should now look like Figure 14-36.

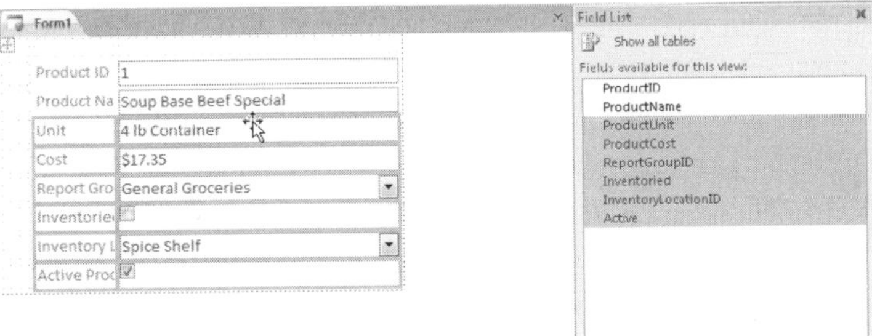

Figure 14-36 You can quickly move a group of fields from the field list into a control layout in Layout view.

When you work with a control layout in Layout view for web forms, you can save time positioning, moving, and resizing controls. As you can see in Figure 14-36, Access sizes all the labels and text box controls to the same dimensions. When you did this same exercise in Design view at the beginning of the chapter, you needed to perform extra steps to make all the labels the same size, change the widths of the labels to accommodate the caption text, and line up the controls both horizontally and vertically. You also had to swap positions for the IsAdmin check box and label. In the Layout view for web forms, though, Access correctly places the label to the left of the check box, which makes this part of the form creation process much easier and faster.

When you have controls in a control layout in web forms and move them around in Layout view, Access automatically snaps them into proper horizontal and vertical alignment. To see this feature, let's move half of these controls into a second column as you did for the employee client form earlier in this chapter. Click the Report Group label control and drop it to the right of the ProductID text box control. When you have it correctly positioned, Access displays a vertical I-bar to the right of the ProductID control, as shown in Figure 14-37.

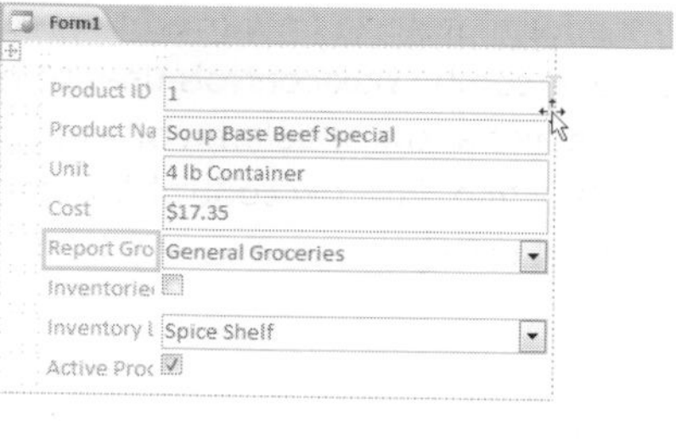

Figure 14-37 Drag the Report Group label to the right of the ProductID text box control.

After you release the mouse, Access moves the Report Group label control to the right of the ProductID text box control, as shown in Figure 14-38. Access also lines up all the controls both horizontally and vertically in the form grid. When you're working with web forms that use control layouts, you can easily move and swap control positions without having to line up the controls.

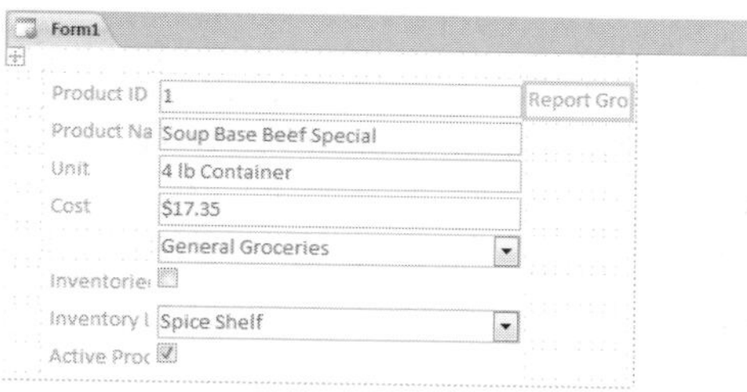

Figure 14-38 In a control layout, Access repositions controls when you move them around the form grid.

You'll notice in Figure 14-38 that there appear to be extra cells in the control layout above and to the left of the fields in the first column. There are also extra cells beneath the Report Group label control. These extra cells are called *empty cells*. These empty cells fill the remaining horizontal and vertical positions of the control layout grid. If you think of the control layout as a table or grid, each cell of the table is either empty or contains a single control. In web forms, you cannot have overlapping controls; each cell can contain only one control. When you moved the Report Group label to its new position, the old position is now an empty cell.

Using the technique you just learned, reposition the ReportGroupID combo box control to the right of the Report Group label control. After you reposition the control, your form should now look like Figure 14-39. You'll notice that Access removed the entire row of empty cells where the Report Group label and combo box controls used to be. After you move a control or set of controls, Access removes a row or column of empty cells by default if there are no longer any individual controls within that row control. You can add back in a row or column of empty cells if you still want extra space between your controls. (We'll show you how to do that in just a minute.)

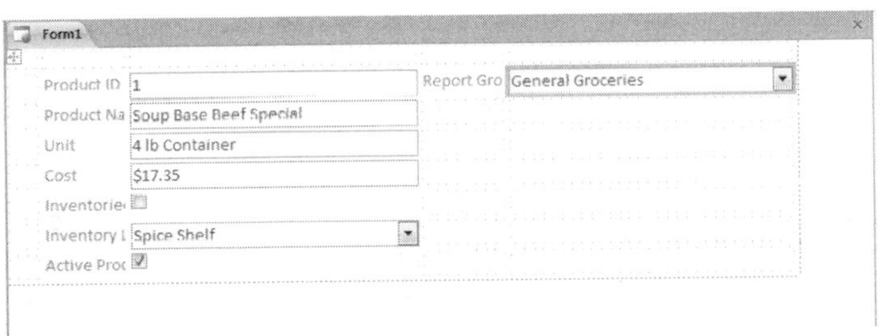

Figure 14-39 Move the ReportGroupID combo box to the right of the Report Group label control.

When you moved the controls for the report group, you put them into positions where no empty cells existed. We now want to move additional controls from the column on the left to the column on the right. To do this, we can drop controls directly into empty cells. Click the Inventoried label control and place it into the empty cell beneath the Report Group label. When you have it correctly positioned, Access highlights the empty cell beneath the Report Group label, as shown in Figure 14-40.

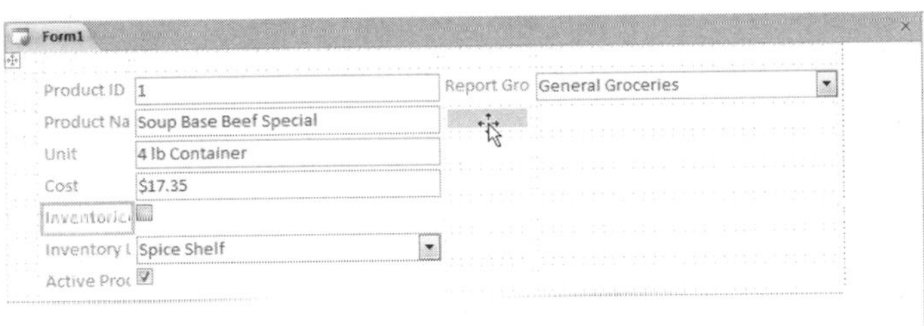

Figure 14-40 Move the Inventoried label control into the empty cell beneath the Report Group label control.

After you release the mouse, Access moves the Inventoried label control into the empty cell beneath the Report Group label control, as shown in Figure 14-41.

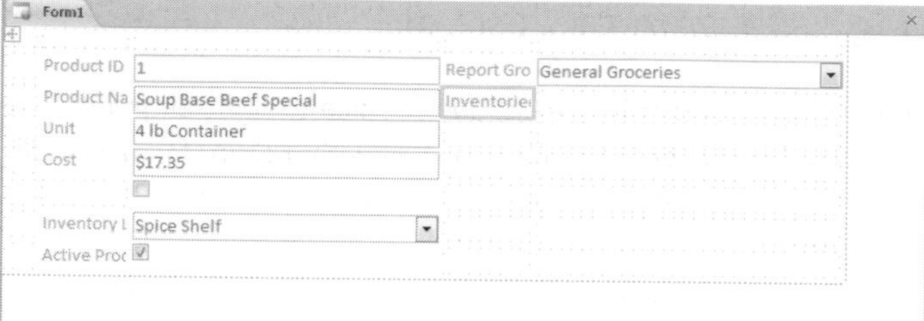

Figure 14-41 Access places the Inventoried label into the unoccupied empty cell.

INSIDE OUT Using the Keyboard to Move Controls

You can move a control into another cell by pressing the Alt key and then use the arrow keys to move the control up, down, left, or right in the layout. Note that if another control already occupies the cell you are trying to move into, Access moves the control past that existing control and into the next available empty cell in the direction of the arrow you pressed. If you are at the last cell in a row or column, Access creates a new row or column and moves the control into a cell in the new row or column. You need to be aware, though, that the new column or row remains even if you move the control back to its original location.

Using the techniques you've just learned, reposition the remaining fields below the ProductCost controls over to the second column. After you reposition all the controls, your form should now look like Figure 14-42. You repositioned and aligned the controls in a matter of seconds, whereas this same procedure in Design view for client forms could take much longer.

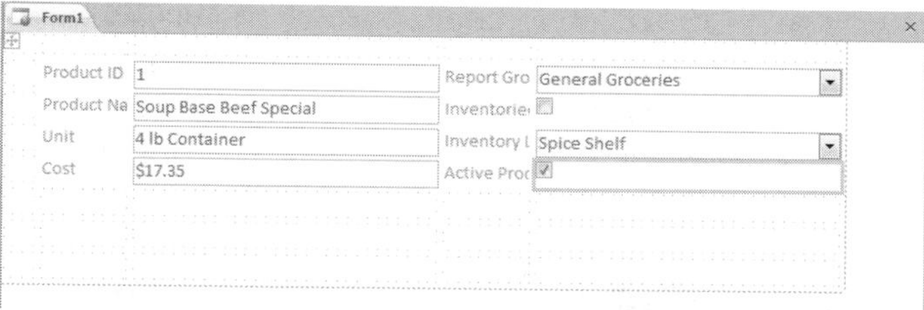

Figure 14-42 This is how your web form should look after repositioning the remaining controls.

Click the Save button on the Quick Access Toolbar to save this form and name it frmProducts. You can also find this form saved as frmXmplProducts1 in the sample database.

Formatting a Column of Controls

As you might recall from earlier in the chapter, we like to right-align our labels and bold the font. When you did this procedure in Design view with a client form, you clicked the horizontal ruler at the top of the design area to select all controls in a column. In Layout view, however, you cannot display the horizontal ruler. To select all the label controls in a column, select the Product ID label and then click the Select Column command in the Rows & Columns group on the Arrange tab, as shown in Figure 14-43. Access highlights all the labels in the columns as well as all the empty cells. Now, click the Bold button in the Font group on the Format tab to change the font in all the label controls to bold. Next, click the Align Text Right button in the Font group to right-align all the text in the labels. Finally, click the Font Color button in the Font group and change the font to black. (The default font color Access uses is a lighter shade of black.)

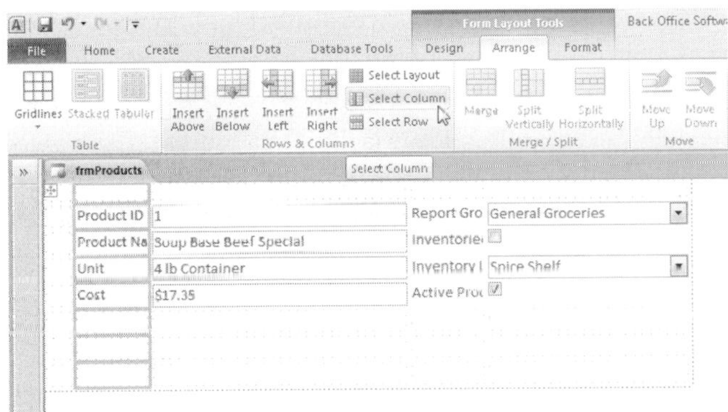

Figure 14-43 Select all the labels by resting your mouse pointer on the top edge of the Product ID label.

You'll notice that when you change the font to bold, Access increases the width of all the label controls and the empty cells in that column to make sure all the text still fits within the labels. Access then pushes all the text controls to the right to accommodate the wider labels. Repeat the same steps you just performed for the second column of label controls. Switch to Form view to view the results of your change. Your form should now look like Figure 14-44.

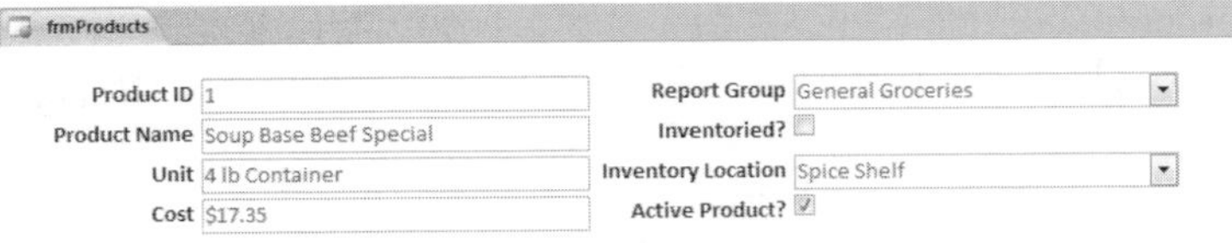

Figure 14-44 All your label controls should now be bold, right-aligned, and with a black font color.

INSIDE OUT **Selecting All Controls in a Column by Hovering over the Top of a Control**

You can also select all the controls in a column by selecting a control and then resting your mouse pointer on the top edge of the control until it changes to a down arrow. When you see the down arrow, click once; Access highlights all the controls and empty cells in that column.

Resizing Controls

Now that you have all the labels formatted just the way you want, you should adjust the width of the text box controls. Remember that earlier in the chapter, we discussed having three different widths for the various text box controls. Right now, all the text box controls are 2.5 inches wide, which is much larger than they need to be. Let's start by resizing all the text box controls to the longest length we want to have, 1.5 inches, and then we'll move the controls into two columns. Click the sizing box in the middle of the right edge of the ProductID text box, and drag the right edge to the left until the control is about 2 inches wide. As you drag the control to the left, you'll immediately notice that Access resizes every other text box in that column as well, as shown in Figure 14-45.

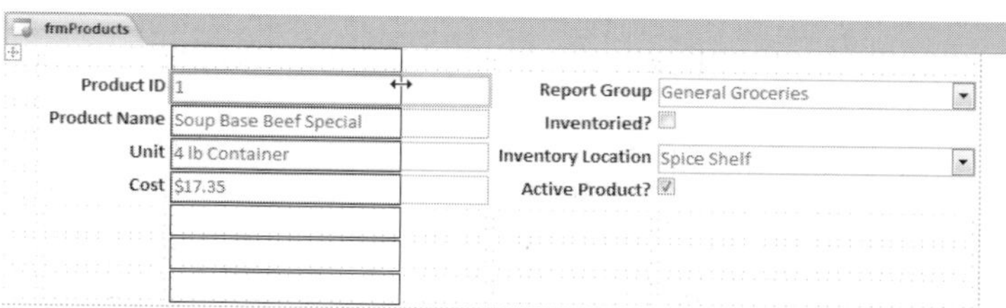

Figure 14-45 When you resize one control in a control layout for web forms, all other controls in the same column also resize.

Now, you can see one of the great advantages *and* disadvantages of using a control layout. If you need to resize all the controls in the same column on a form grid to the same width or height, using a control layout makes this process very simple. However, it is impossible to make *individual* sizing changes to some of the controls inside a control layout. To resize individual controls, you must either split the cells of the control layout grid or remove the control layout applied to the controls. But keep in mind that you can remove a control layout only for client forms. To make individual sizing changes to some of the controls on a web form, you must split the cells. We'll show you how to do that in just a moment.

After you reduced the size of the text box controls in the first column, Access moved the remaining controls and empty cells to the right of those controls, farther to the left side of the form window. Reduce the width of the second column of text boxes now by clicking the sizing box in the middle of the right edge of the ReportGroupID combo box, and drag the right edge to the left until the control is about 2 inches wide.

INSIDE OUT **Using the Property Sheet to Help Resize Controls**

In Layout view, you cannot display the horizontal ruler across the top of the form grid. When you want to resize a control to a *specific* height or width in this view, it can be difficult trying to guess exactly the right size when you drag the edges of the control. To make this process easier, first display the Property Sheet window by clicking the Property Sheet button in the Tools group on the Design tab. Click either the Format or All tab to display the Height and Width property settings, and then type the new height or width directly on the property sheet to resize the control. You can also click a control and then begin dragging the control edges. After you make an adjustment to the control's height or width, release the mouse and Access adjusts these properties on the property sheet. You'll immediately be able to gauge whether you need to make further adjustments.

Removing a Control Layout for Client Forms

To remove a control layout for client forms, you first need to select all the controls that you want removed from the control layout. If you want all the controls removed from the control layout, you can select them all by clicking the Select All button in the Selection group on the Format tab. Now that all the form controls are selected, on the Arrange tab, in the Table group, click Remove Layout. In Figure 14-46, you can see an example of this procedure, where we opened the frmAboutStartup client form in the sample database in Design view, selected all the controls, and then clicked Remove Layout.

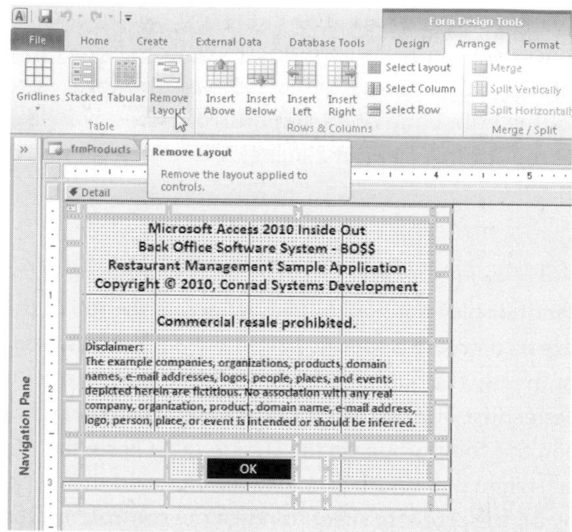

Figure 14-46 Click Remove Layout to remove control layouts applied to client form controls.

Now that you've removed the control layout for a client form, you can move and resize any controls independently. Remember, the above procedure only applies to client forms that have control layouts. You cannot remove control layouts on a web form.

Splitting and Merging Cells

To have different sizes for the controls in your products web form, you need to split the cells of the controls. The ProductID and Cost fields don't need to be as wide as the other controls in the first column. To split the ProductID text box control, select the control and then click the Split Horizontal command in the Merge/Split group on the Arrange tab, as shown in Figure 14-47. Access creates a new column in the structure of the control layout. You'll notice that the other cells in the same column remain the same size. The other columns now span the two underlying columns that Access created from the split operation.

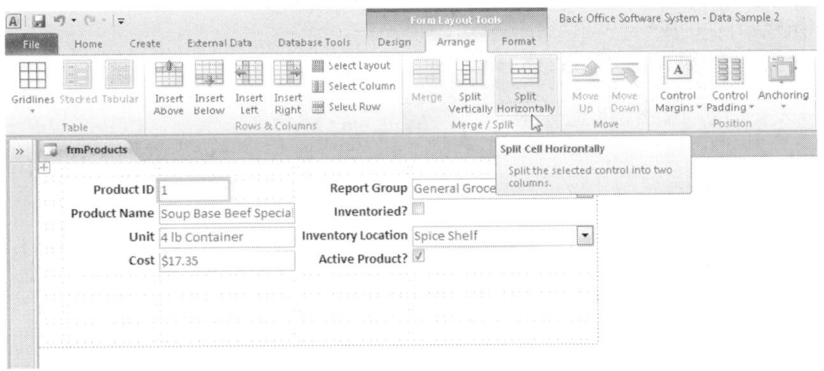

Figure 14-47 Click the Split Horizontal command to split a cell into two cells in the same row.

Select the Cost field and then click the Split Horizontal command again to split this field into two separate cells. The ProductID and Cost fields are now the same column width. By splitting cells, you can achieve the goal of having different sizes for different columns. Access also provides the ability to split cells vertically with the Split Vertically command in the Merge/Split group on the Arrange tab. When you split a cell vertically, Access creates a new row in the structure of the control layout. If there are other cells on the same row as the one that you are wanting to split, they remain the same size as they were.

If you want to make a control wider or taller without adjusting the size of any other columns or rows, you can merge the control with adjacent empty cells. For example, if you want to make the ProductID control wider again, select the ProductID control, hold the Ctrl key, click the empty cell to the right of the ProductID control, and then click the Merge command in the Merge/Split group on the Arrange tab, as shown in Figure 14-48. Access merges the ProductID control with the empty cell to make the width the same as the ProductName and Unit controls again. (Note: split the ProductID control back into two cells after doing this procedure or press the Undo button on the Quick Access Toolbar to undo this change before proceeding further.)

> ## Note
> **You can merge empty cells together, or you can merge a cell that contains a control with other empty cells. However, Access does not allow you to merge cells that contain more than one control. Each cell can contain only one control so you cannot perform a merge cell operation that would combine two controls into the same cell.**

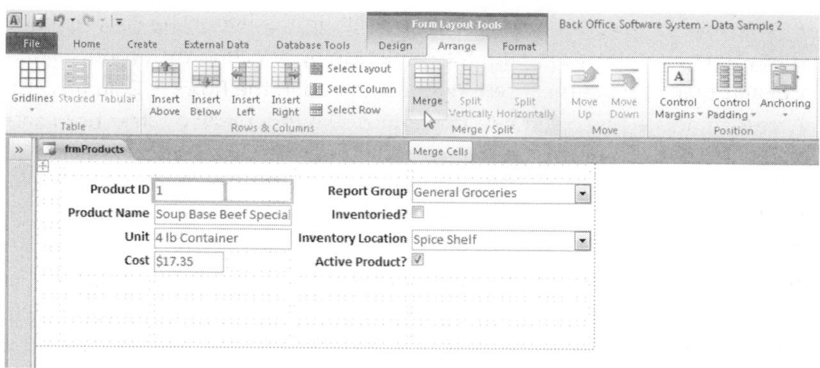

Figure 14-48 Click the Merge command to merge multiple cells together.

As you split cells vertically and horizontally, your control layout becomes more complex. If you find that the individual cells are becoming too small to easily manage, you might want to adjust the row heights and column widths first before doing additional splitting and merging of cells.

Inserting Rows and Columns

On your products form, it might be helpful to add a little more separation between the first column of text boxes and the second column of labels. You could extend the width of the second column of labels to the right line to make this separation because the labels are aligned to the right, but we'll add in an extra column of empty cells to the control layout instead. To create an extra column of empty cells to the left of the second column of labels, select the Report Group label, and then click the Insert Left command in the Rows & Columns group on the Arrange tab, as shown in Figure 14-49.

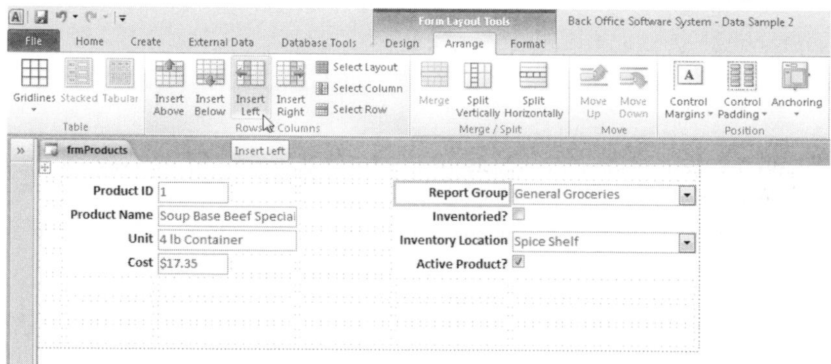

Figure 14-49 Click the Insert Left command to create a new column in the control layout to the left of the Report group label.

Access creates another column of empty cells to the left of the Report Group label. Note that you could also accomplish the same task by selecting the ProductName text box control and then clicking the Insert Right command in the Rows & Columns group. In that case, Access creates a new column to the right of the ProductName text box control.

If you need to insert new rows into your control layout, Access provides two commands in the Rows & Columns group for this task—Insert Above and Insert Below. When you click the Insert Above command, Access creates a new row above the selected control or empty cell. Click Insert Below and Access creates a new row beneath the selected control or empty cell. If you want to delete a row or column, select an empty cell and then press Delete. Note that Access deletes the entire row or column only if no controls exists within the highlighted row or column.

The new column Access just created is 1 inch wide and is a little more space than we need. Click the sizing box in the middle of the right edge of one of the empty cells in the new column, and drag the right edge to the left until the control is about a half inch wide. As you drag the empty cell to the left, Access resizes every other text box in that new column as well.

Let's make one last column width adjustment before we move on to the next section. If you move through some of the product records in Layout view using the record selector buttons at the bottom of the form window, you'll notice that the ProductName text box is actually a bit too small to fit many of the product names. Select the ProductName text box and expand the width to the right till the control is about 2 inches wide again. If you switch to Form view, you can see the result of your work so far, as shown in Figure 14-50. Click the Save button on the Quick Access Toolbar to save this form. You can also find this form saved as frmXmplProducts2 in the sample web database.

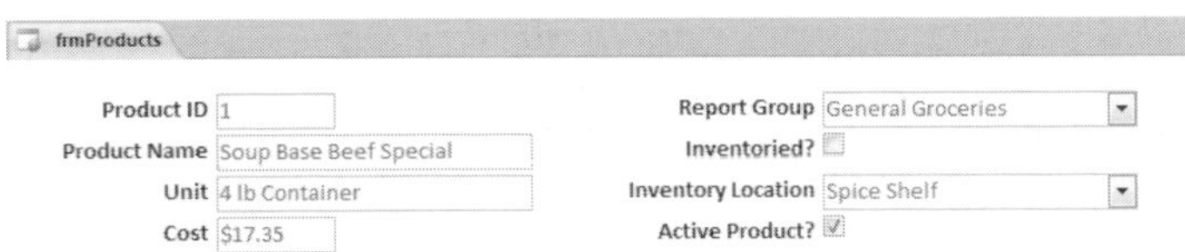

Figure 14-50 This is your products form with controls split and an extra column to create separation between the two columns of data.

> **INSIDE OUT** **Allow Space on the Right Edge of Web Forms for Certain Controls**
>
> On web forms, if you place a hyperlink, date/time, or attachment field on the far-right side of the form, you might not see the picker buttons (Insert Hyperlink, Date Picker, and Insert Attachment) to add or edit that data when you open the web form in Dialog mode in your web browser. The problem is that if you place those controls to the far-right edge of the form, the picker buttons will either be cut off or not shown at all if the web form is open in Dialog mode. If you need those controls on the far-right side of the web form, make sure to add some extra space (an empty cell works best) to the right of the controls to allow space to see the picker buttons in your web browser.

Using Web-Compatible Controls

Web forms do not support as many control types as their client form counterparts support. If you click the down arrow on the right side of the Controls group on the Design tab, you'll notice the list of controls is much smaller than for client forms, as shown in Figure 14-51.

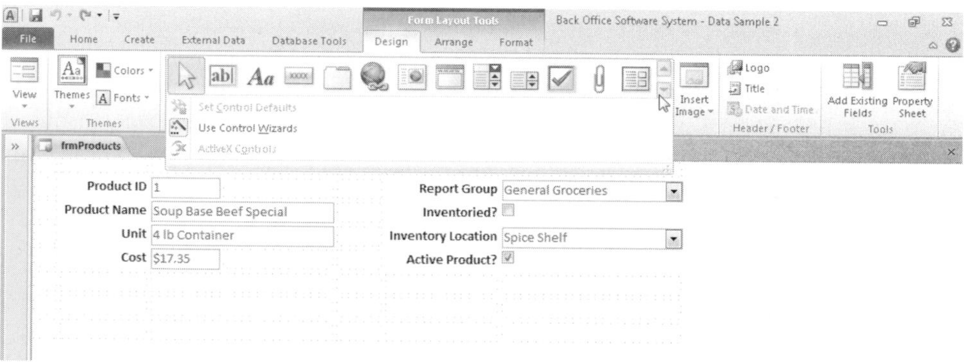

Figure 14-51 Web forms support less control types than client forms.

You'll notice in Figure 14-51 that Set Control Defaults and ActiveX Controls are dimmed. You cannot use the Set Control Defaults option on web forms as you can for client forms. Web forms also do not support any ActiveX controls. In Figure 14-51, you'll notice that Use Control Wizards is not dimmed, which implies you can use control wizards when dropping controls onto web forms. On client forms, control wizards are available for many control types such as command buttons, combo boxes, list boxes, and web browser controls. On web forms, however, the web browser control is the only control type that uses a control wizard. You'll learn more about the web browser control in the next chapter.

INSIDE OUT **Combo Boxes Display Only 500 Records on Web Forms**

Combo boxes on web forms displayed in a web browser support displaying only 500 records in Access Services. If you have more than 500 records in the record source of the combo box, Access Services displays text at the bottom of the drop-down list saying there are more items; however, there is no method to actually display more than the first 500 records in a combo box on a web form displayed in the browser. You'll need to keep this limit in mind when creating combo boxes on web forms. You should consider restricting the number of records returned in the record source through WHERE clauses.

The control types you can use on web forms are as follows:

- Text Box
- Label
- Command Button
- Tab Control
- Hyperlink
- Web Browser Control
- Navigation Control
- Combo Box
- List Box
- Check Box
- Attachment
- Subform/Subreport

Refer to Table 13-1 on page 795 for a detailed description of each control type and its usage. To place a control onto the web form, click the control in the Control group and then position your mouse over the form grid. If you want to place the control inside an empty cell, hover your mouse over the empty cell until the Access highlights the cell, and then click again to place the control. If you want to position the new control above, below, to the left, or to the right of an existing control or cell, position your mouse on the edge of the existing control or cell until Access display a horizontal or vertical I-bar and click. Access creates a new row or column and then places the new control inside the cell.

INSIDE OUT **Typing into Empty Cells to Create Label Controls**

When you're working in Layout view with control layouts, you can easily add a new label control to the form grid by typing directly into an empty cell. After you finish typing and press Enter, Access creates a new label control in the empty cell.

Adding Gridlines to Web Forms

Earlier in this chapter, you placed a rectangle control around the outside of your controls on the employee client form you created in Design view. Web forms do not support rectangle controls, but you can simulate the same behavior using gridlines. To add a gridline across the top of the controls on your products web form, select the Product ID label control, hold down the Shift key, and then click the ReportGroupID combo box control to select all the controls and empty cells between those two controls. Now, click the Gridlines button in the Tables group on the Arrange tab, and then click Top on the drop-down list of gridline options, as shown in Figure 14-52. Access adds a gridline to the top of each control and empty cell you selected.

In the drop-down list of gridline options, you can select options to add gridlines to both the vertical and horizontal sides of a control (all four sides), the horizontal sides of a control (top and bottom), the vertical sides of a control (left and right), the top side of a control, the bottom side of a control, and to no sides of a control (to remove any existing gridlines). You can also adjust the color, width, and border style of the gridlines by clicking the options beneath the None option on the Gridlines drop-down list.

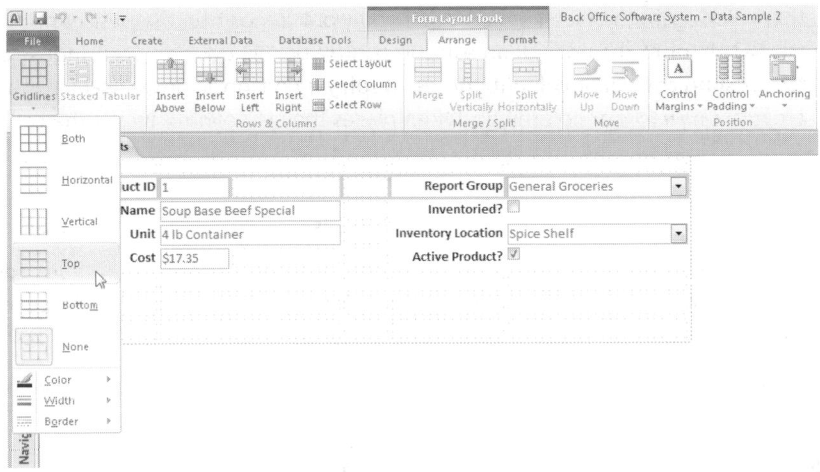

Figure 14-52 Click Top to add gridlines across the top of the selected controls.

To add gridlines across the bottom of the controls, click the Cost label control, hold down the Shift key, and then click the Active check box control to select all the controls and empty cells between those two controls. Now, click the Gridlines button in the Tables group on the Arrange tab, and then click Bottom on the drop-down list of gridline options. Access adds a gridline to the bottom of each control and empty cell you selected.

INSIDE OUT Using the Shortcut Menu for Quick Access to Formatting Options

You can find the gridline options on the shortcut menu that Access displays when you right-click a control on the form grid. You'll also find many other formatting options such as splitting cells, merging cells, inserting rows and columns, deleting rows and columns, and anchoring options.

You now have gridlines across the top and bottom of your controls. Next, we want to add gridlines to the left side of the label controls in the first column. The drop-down list of gridline options under the Gridlines command in the Tables group does not contain an option for just the left or right side of controls. To add gridlines just to these sides, we'll need to use the Property Sheet window. Click the Product ID label control, hold down the Shift key, and then click the Cost label to select all four of the label controls on the left side of the web form. Next, click the Property Sheet button in the Tools group on the Design tab to open the Property Sheet window. Finally, on the All or Format tab of the Property Sheet window, select the Solid option on the Gridline Style Left property, as shown in Figure 14-53. Access adds a gridline to the left side of the selected label controls.

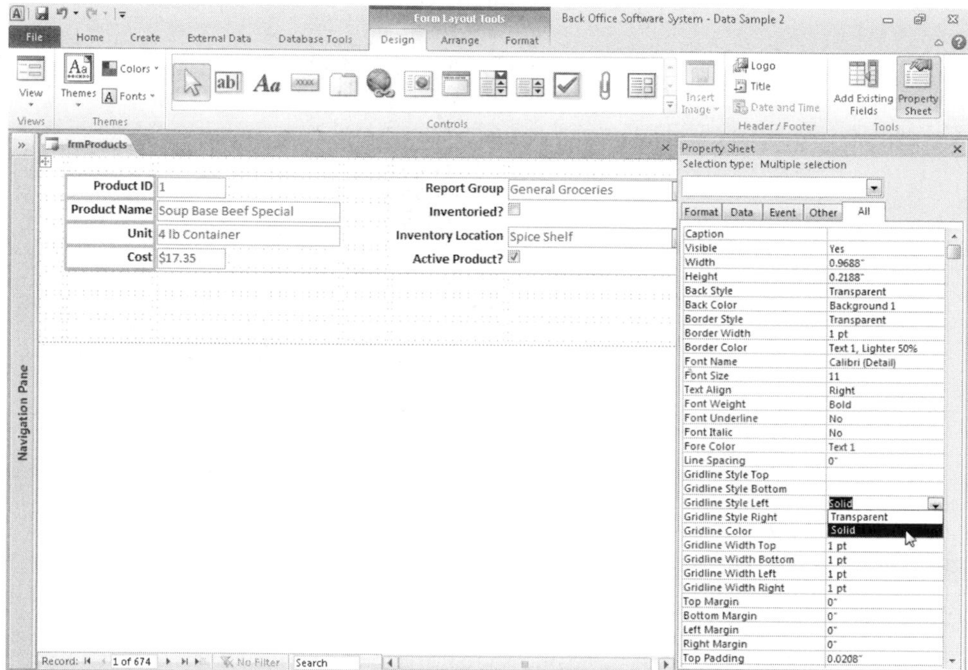

Figure 14-53 Select Solid on the Gridline Style Left property to add a gridline to the left side of the selected controls.

The last step we need to do to complete our gridlines is to add gridlines to the right side of the controls on the far-right side of the web form. Click the ReportGroupID combo box control, hold down the Shift key, and then click the Active check box control to select all the controls between those two controls. Now, select the Solid option on the Gridline Style Right property on the Property Sheet window. If you switch to Form view, you can see the result of your work, as shown in Figure 14-54.

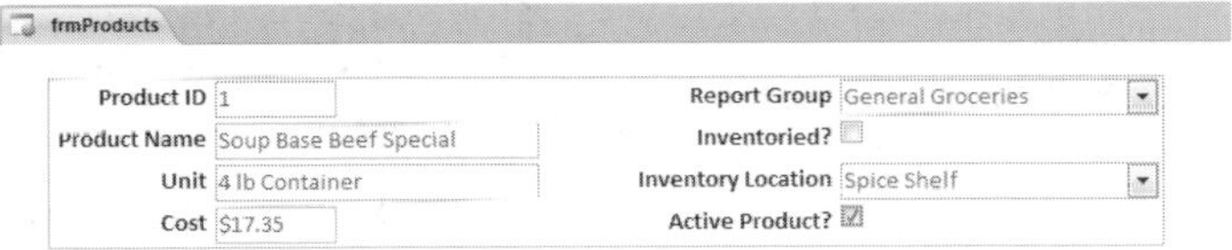

Figure 14-54 You can simulate the look of rectangle controls by adding gridlines to your web form.

Adding Some Space with Control Padding

All your controls from both sides of the web form are aligned vertically, but they seem to be too close together. Earlier in this chapter, you adjusted the space between the controls by using the grid properties and snapping the controls to the grid using Design view for a client form. You can also adjust the spacing between the controls by using the *control padding* commands. Control padding adjusts the amount of space between the controls on the form.

Access 2010 has four settings for control padding—None, Narrow (the default), Medium, and Wide. Let's change the control padding around all the controls from Narrow to Medium. Select all the controls on the grid by clicking the Select Layout button in the Rows & Columns group on the Arrange tab. Access highlights all the controls and empty cells in the control layout for the web form. Now, click Control Padding in the Position group on the Arrange tab, and then click Medium, as shown in Figure 14-55.

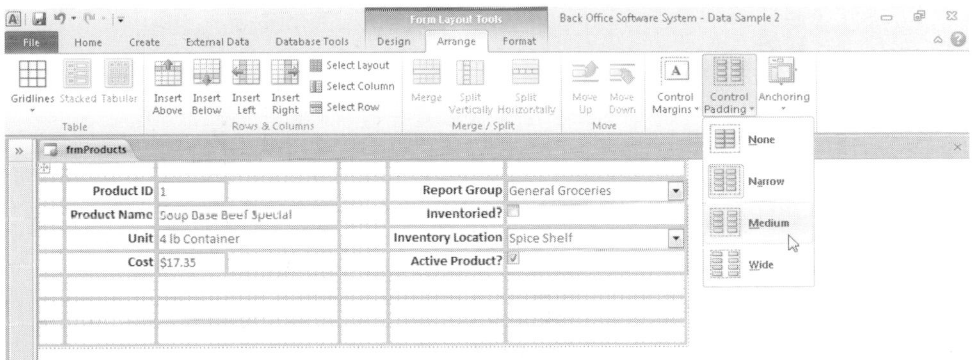

Figure 14-55 Change the control padding from Narrow to Medium to increase the space between the controls.

After you click Medium, Access increases the padding around all the controls so that they are spaced farther apart, as shown in Figure 14-56.

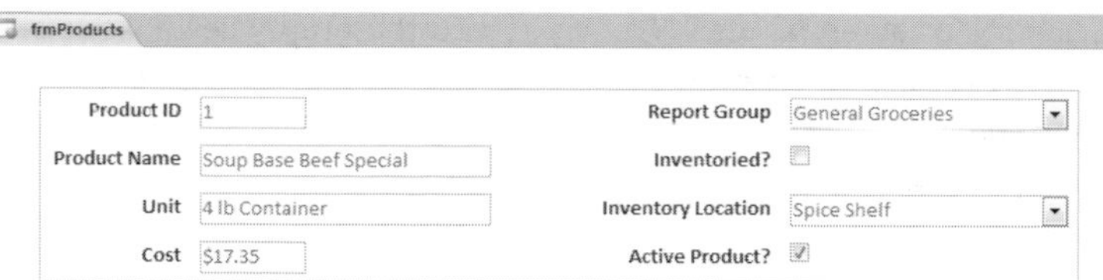

Figure 14-56 You now have more space between the controls after increasing the control padding.

Creating a Title

We should probably now add a label control to the Header section of the web form to display a title. When you performed this procedure on the employee client form in Design view earlier in this chapter, you first opened the Header/Footer section of the form grid. In Layout view for web forms, there is no option to open the Header/Footer section. If you use one of the Quick Create web form options—Form and Multiple Items—Access creates a label control in the Header section for you. When you start from scratch to create a web form using the Blank Form web option, Access does not open the Header/Footer section. To open the Header/Footer section on a blank web form in Layout view, you need to click the Title button in the Header/Footer group on the Design tab, as shown in Figure 14-57.

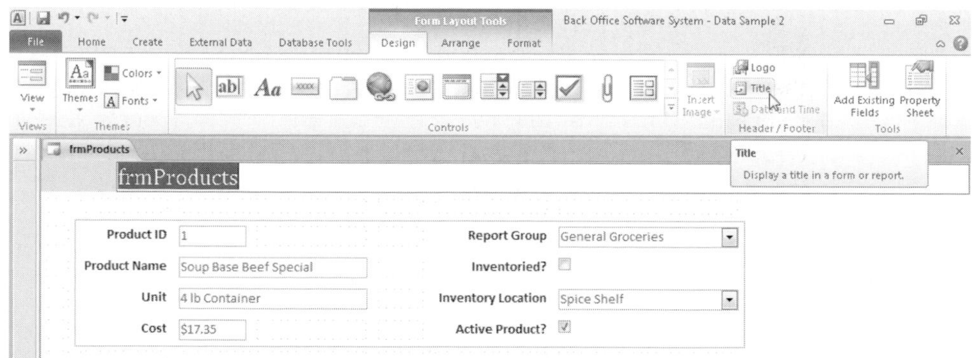

Figure 14-57 Click Title to open the Header section of the web form and add a label to the header.

Access opens the Header section of the web form, creates a new label control, and makes the caption of the label the same as the form name. Access creates this new label control in a control layout that spans the Header section of the web form. To the left of the label control, Access creates an empty cell. We don't need this empty cell for our purpose, so select it and then press Delete to remove it from the form grid. Next, click inside the label control and change the caption to Products. One final step we should make to the web form is to remove the three empty rows of empty cells at the bottom of the form grid. Select a cell in each of three rows while holding down the Shift key and then press Delete to remove these extra rows. If you switch to Form view, you can see the completed products web form, as shown in Figure 14-58. Click the Save button on the Quick Access Toolbar to save this form. You can also find this form saved as frmXmplProducts3 in the sample web database.

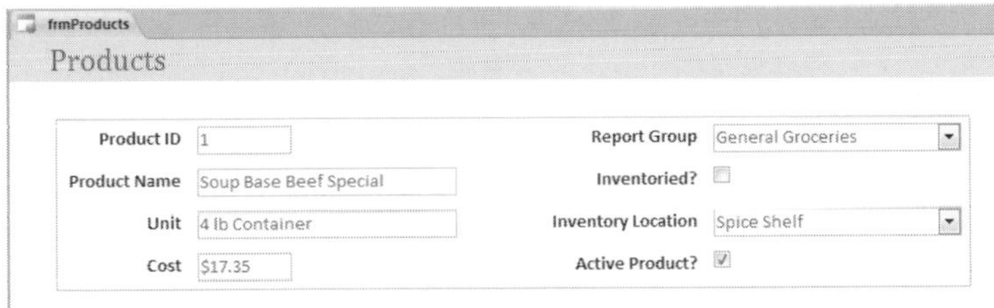

Figure 14-58 You now have a good, basic products web form created in Layout view.

Moving Controls to Different Sections on Web Forms

When you are working with control layouts, you cannot drag a control from one section to another, such as dragging a control from the Detail section into the Header section. When you need to move an existing control from one section of the form to another, you can use the Move Up and Move Down buttons in the Move group on the Arrange tab. For example, if you wanted to move the Active check box control in the products web form you've been creating down into the Footer section of the form, you can select the control and then click the Move Down button in the Move group, as shown in Figure 14-59.

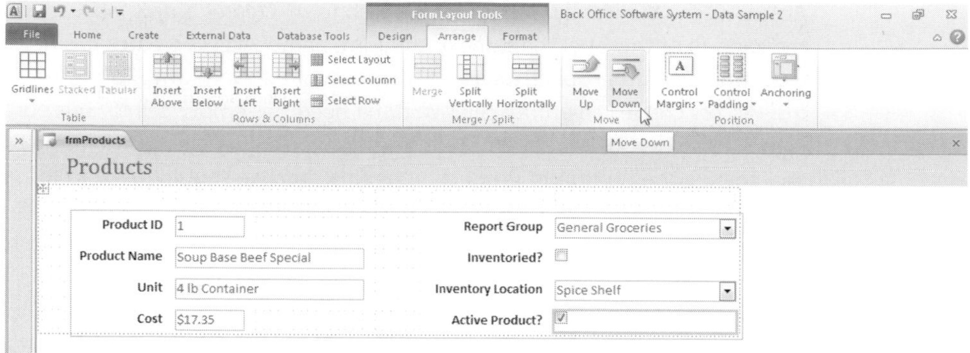

Figure 14-59 Use the Move Up and Move Down buttons to move controls into different form sections.

Access moves the Active check box control down into the Footer section of the form, as shown in Figure 14-60. When you use the Move Up or Move Down command, Access moves the control one place up or down in the control layout. If you are at the bottom of the control layout and click Move Down, Access moves that control down into the Footer section. Similarly, if you are at the top of the control layout and click Move Up, Access moves that control up into the Header section. If you are not at the top or bottom of a control layout, Access moves the control one row up or down in the control layout. If another control occupies the space you are trying to move into, Access creates a new row above or below the occupied control and places the control into the new row. For example, if you select the ReportGroupID combo box control and click Move Down, Access creates a new row below the Inventoried check box control and moves the ReportGroupID control into the unoccupied cell in the new row beneath the Inventoried control. If you are at the very top of a control layout in the Header section, Access dims the Move Up command because it cannot move anything higher up. Similarly, Access dims the Move Down command if you are at the very bottom of the control layout in the Footer section.

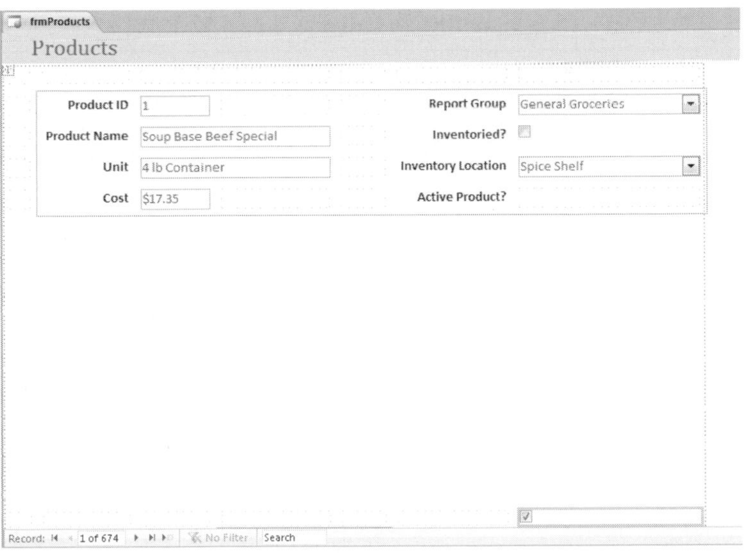

Figure 14-60 Access moves the control into the Footer section after you click Move Down.

If you moved any controls on your products web form, undo the changes by clicking the Undo button on the Quick Access Toolbar.

Setting Control Properties for Web Forms

Web forms support less format property settings for the different data types than client forms support. You also cannot specify any custom formats for the data types on web forms as you can for client forms; you must select a format option from the available list on the Property Sheet window. For text and Yes/No data types on web forms, there are no formatting options available. You can choose from six Format property settings for number and currency fields, as shown in Table 14-12.

Table 14-12 Format Property Settings for Number and Currency Data Types on Web Forms

Format	Description
General Number	Displays numbers as entered with up to 11 significant digits. If a number contains more than 11 significant digits or the control you are using to display the value is not wide enough to show all digits, Access first rounds the displayed number and then uses scientific (exponential) notation for very large or very small numbers (more than 10 digits to the right or to the left of the decimal point).

Format	Description
Currency	Displays numeric data according to the Currency setting in the Regional And Language Options section of the Control Panel. In the U.S. layout, Access uses a leading dollar sign, maintains two decimal places (rounded), and encloses negative numbers in parentheses.
Euro	Displays numeric data according to your Currency setting in the Control Panel, but always uses a leading euro symbol.
Fixed	Displays numbers without thousands separators and with two decimal places. The number displayed is rounded if the underlying value contains more than two decimal places.
Standard	Displays numbers with thousands separators and with two decimal places. The number displayed is rounded if the underlying value contains more than two decimal places.
Percent	Multiplies the value by 100, displays two decimal places, and adds a trailing percent sign. The number displayed is rounded if the underlying value contains more than four decimal places.

You can choose from five Format property settings for date/time fields, as shown in Table 14-13.

Table 14-13 Format Property Settings for the Date/Time Data Type on Web Forms

Format	Description
General Date	Displays the date as numbers separated by the date separator character. Displays the time as hours, minutes, and seconds separated by the time separator character and followed by an AM/PM indicator. If the value has no time component, Access displays the date only. If the value has no date component, Access displays the time only. Example: 3/17/2011 06:17:55 PM.
Long Date	Displays the date according to the Long Date setting in the Regional And Language Options section of the Control Panel. Example: Thursday, March 17, 2011.
Short Date	Displays the date according to the Short Date setting in the Regional And Language Options section of the Control Panel. Example: 3/17/2011. To avoid confusion for dates in the twenty-first century, we strongly recommend you take advantage of the Use Four-Digit Year formatting options. Click the File tab on the Backstage view, click Options, click the Client Settings category, and then set these options in the General section.
Long Time	Displays the time according to the Time setting in the Regional And Language Options section of the Control Panel. Example: 6:17:12 PM.
Medium Time	Displays the time as hours and minutes separated by the time separator character and followed by an AM/PM indicator. Example: 06:17 PM.

Setting Web Form Properties

Web forms support fewer form properties than client forms, and some of the web form properties apply only when viewing the form in an Access client. Table 14-14 lists all the supported web form properties and information on the server behavior. (See Tables 14-9 and 14-11 for detailed descriptions of the form properties.)

Table 14-14 Web Form Properties

Property	Server Functionality
Record Source	This property is honored on the server.
Caption	This property is honored on the server.
Width	The server displays the form in the size you designed it in Access. Remember though that if some of the controls on your form have their control anchoring set to stretch, the form might stretch to fill the available window space in your web browser.
Record Selectors	This property is ignored on the server. Record selectors do not show up on web forms displayed in a web browser, but you will see these on the web form if you open it in Access client.
Navigation Buttons	This property is honored on the server. Select Yes to display navigation buttons for your web form. Select No to not display navigation buttons.
Scroll Bars	This property is honored on the server, but you might see your web browser display scroll bars if it thinks you might need them, even if you selected not to show scroll bars for the form itself. For example, if the form is larger than the current browser screen window, your browser might display scroll bars that might make it seem that the server is ignoring your settings if you turned them off. In datasheets and top-level forms, the server shows scroll bars as necessary.
Orientation	This property is honored on the server. The server adjusts the position of the carets and drop-down lists on combo boxes based on this property setting.
Recordset Type	This property is ignored on the server. Access uses this property if you open the web form in Access client.
Filter	This property is ignored on the server because you cannot toggle the filter on the server and the server does not support the Filter On Load property for web forms.
Order By	This property is ignored on the server because you cannot toggle the Order By on the server and the server does not support the Order By On Load property for web forms.
Wait For Post Processing	This property is honored on the server.
Data Entry	This property is honored on the server.

Property	Server Functionality
Allow Additions	This property is honored on the server.
Allow Deletions	This property is honored on the server.
Allow Edits	This property is honored on the server.
On Current and On Load	These are the only two supported web form events. You can set these two properties to run a macro when the specific event described by the property occurs for this web form. See Part 4 for details.
Tag	This property is ignored on the server.

Using Themes

In Access 2007, Microsoft introduced AutoFormats, which made it easy to change the look and feel of a form or report to a predesigned set of fonts, colors, and backgrounds. When you applied an AutoFormat to a form or report in Access 2007, however, the changes applied only to that specific object. If you wanted to apply the same AutoFormat to all forms and reports, you needed to open each form and report separately and apply the AutoFormat to each individually. If you decided to change to a different AutoFormat at a later time, you needed to open each individual form and report and apply a new AutoFormat. Performing this task manually in a database with many objects could be very time-consuming. One other drawback with AutoFormats is that you cannot customize the colors and fonts.

Access 2010 introduces a new feature called *themes* to quickly change the colors and fonts used by your forms and reports. For those of you familiar with Access 2007, you might be a little confused by the terminology, because there were Access Theme Colors in the color picker dialog box in Access 2007. The Access Theme Colors were designed to make it easy to create an Access 2007 database that blended well with the Windows operating system or with other Office applications. In Access 2010, the color picker dialog box for properties that support color displays Theme Colors, as shown in Figure 14-61.

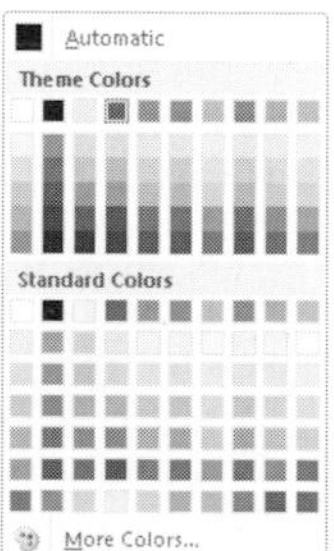

Figure 14-61 Access displays Theme Color options on the color picker dialog box.

When you select colors from the Theme Colors section of the color picker dialog box, Access enters the name of the theme color on several properties on the Property Sheet window. You can think of the theme as a collection of fonts and colors. Access uses the theme color to control what color to display for the form or report element. Access provides 12 theme colors—Background 1, Text 1, Background 2, Text 2, Accent 1 through Accent 6, Hyperlink, and Followed Hyperlink. In Figure 14-61, you'll notice that each color has lighter tints and darker shades of the base theme color. The different tints and shades are represented as a percentage lighter or darker than the base color. Access lists five color variations in each column for the base theme color. If you hover your mouse over any of these colors, Access displays a tooltip of the theme color name and any percentage lighter or darker.

To demonstrate the value of using themes in your Access databases, open the Contacts Map Copy sample web database (ContactsMapCopy.accdb) found on the companion CD. (Note that although we'll only show an example of using themes here with a web database, you can use this feature with client databases as well.) When the web database opens, Access displays the startup form called Home. This small contacts web database has four web forms and two web reports to add, edit, and display contact information. All the forms and reports in this web database were created using the Office theme, which uses various shades of blue for color and the Calibri (Detail) font. Switch to Layout view for the Home form and then click the Themes command in the Themes group on the Design tab. Access displays the Themes gallery, as shown in Figure 14-62.

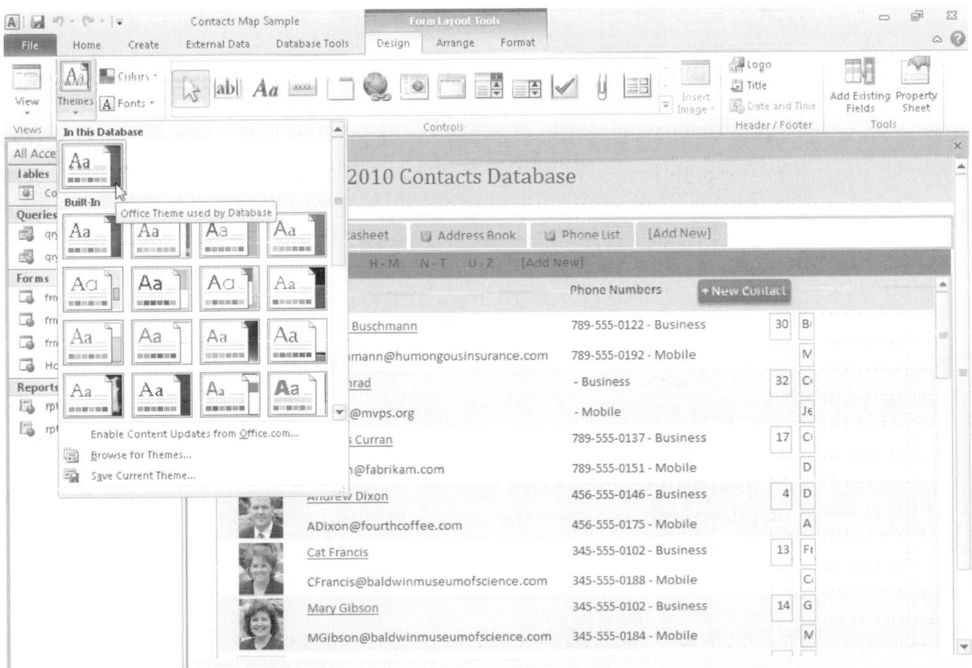

Figure 14-62 Access 2010 includes 40 built-in themes you can use in your databases.

Under the category In This Database, Access lists any themes that are currently saved with the database application. Access highlights the theme currently in use by the object you have open. Under the category Built-In, Access lists 40 built-in themes for Access 2010. You can choose from any of these themes to quickly apply a standardized look for your entire application or a specific form or report. The 40 themes you see in the gallery are also shared by the other Office 2010 applications so your Access application can easily have the same theme style as your Excel spreadsheets, Word documents, or your Microsoft PowerPoint presentations.

At the bottom of the Themes gallery, you'll see three options—Enable Content Updates From Office.Com, Browse For Themes, and Save Current Theme. When you click the Enable Content Updates From Office.Com option, Access automatically updates the Themes gallery options when new content becomes available. Updating the content occurs only if you have an active Internet connection established. Click the Browse For Themes option to browse for other theme files on your computer or on your local intranet if you are on a corporate domain. Theme files have a .thmx file extension. Click Save Current Theme to save a copy of the current theme to your computer.

Note

You won't see the Enable Content Updates From Office.Com option on the Themes gallery if you have already selected the Connect To Office.Com For Updated Content When I'm Connected To The Internet option in the Privacy Options category of the Access Options dialog box.

As you hover your mouse over any of the 40 built-in themes, Access shows you the theme's name and gives you an instant preview, called Live Preview, of what your changes will look like by changing the fonts and colors on the form or report you have open. Let's try one of these other themes so you can see how easy it is to change the entire look and feel of your application. Click the Black Tie theme button to change the theme for the database. Access changes the theme and you'll immediately see the difference with new fonts and colors being used on the form, as shown in Figure 14-63.

INSIDE OUT Disabling Live Preview

If you want to disable Live Preview, click the File tab on the Backstage view, click Options, and then clear the Enable Live Preview option on the General category of the Access Options dialog box. When you clear this option, you will no longer see the instant previewing of theme colors and fonts when you hover over the theme styles in the Themes gallery.

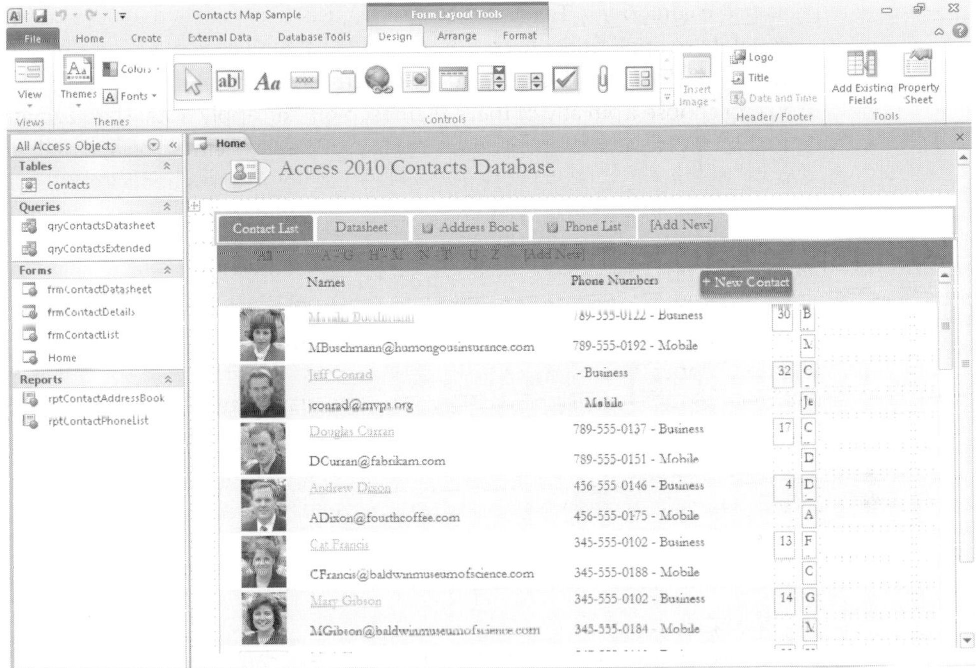

Figure 14-63 When you click a theme button, Access changes the fonts and colors of your form to match the theme styles.

The shades of blue color found on many areas of the form are now replaced with shades of gray. The font for the controls has also been changed from Cambria and Calibri to Garamond. If you close the form now, you'll notice Access does not prompt you to save any changes to your form. If you open any of the other three forms or the two reports in this web database, you'll notice that Access applies the new theme to all these objects as well. If you open the web table or the two web queries in Datasheet view, you can even see that Access applied the new fonts and colors there, too. With one click, you've changed the entire look of the application. You can easily try different themes and see how they look without a lot of work manually making adjustments to all the objects in your database.

Changing the theme of all the objects in the database at one time is a big time saver, but what if you wanted to have a specific form or report be unique, with its own theme? Access also allows you to apply a different theme to a specific form or report. Open the frmContactsList form in Layout view, click the Design tab, click the Themes button in the Themes group, and then right-click the Office theme gallery button under Built-In, as shown in Figure 14-64.

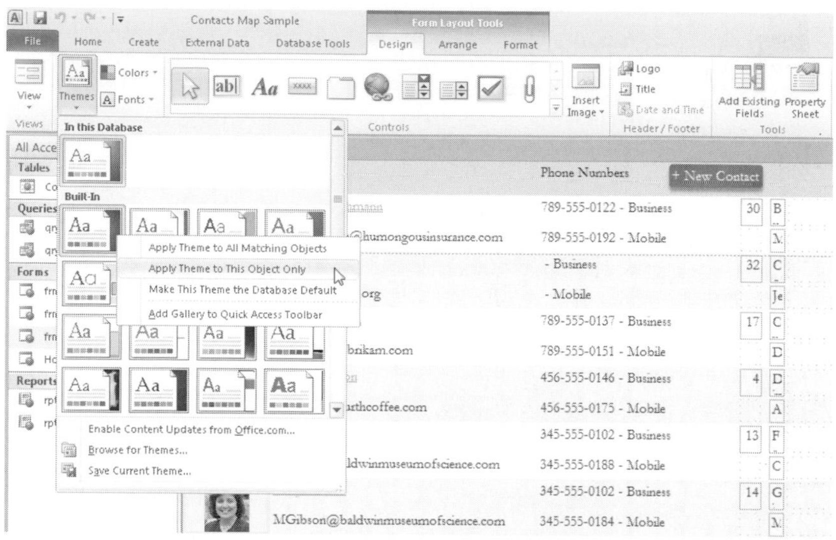

Figure 14-64 You can apply a theme to a specific object in your database.

Access displays a shortcut menu of options. If you click Apply Them To All Matching Objects, Access applies the selected theme to any other objects in the database that also have the same theme applied. For example, if two forms in your database use the Apex theme and you click this option to apply a new theme to matching objects, Access changes the theme for the current form as well as the other form that also uses the Apex theme. If you click Apply Theme To This Object Only, Access applies the selected theme only to the object that currently has focus. Click Make This Theme The Database Default to make the selected theme the default for any new objects you create in the database. Click the last option, Add Gallery To Quick Access Toolbar, to create a command in the Quick Access Toolbar that opens up the Themes gallery.

For our example, click Apply Theme To This Object Only, as shown previously in Figure 14-64. Access changes the theme for the frmContactsList form back to the Office theme color of blue. If you open the other forms or reports in this database, you'll notice that the other objects still have the Black Tie theme applied. If you drop down the themes gallery again, you'll notice Access now displays two themes under In This Database, as shown in Figure 14-65. If you hover your mouse over the Office Theme option, Access displays the specific name of the form that uses the theme in a tooltip. If you assign this theme to more than one object, Access displays the names of all the objects in the tooltip.

Figure 14-65 Access displays the name of objects using a specific theme in a tooltip.

In addition to using one of the built-in themes for Access, you can customize your own theme fonts and colors. Click the Colors command in the Themes group and Access displays the different colors used in the built-in themes, as shown in Figure 14-66. If you right-click one of the color options, Access displays three options—Apply Color Scheme To All Matching Objects, Apply Color Scheme To This Object Only, and Add Gallery To Quick Access Toolbar. These options have similar functionality as the options you saw previously when right-clicking a theme.

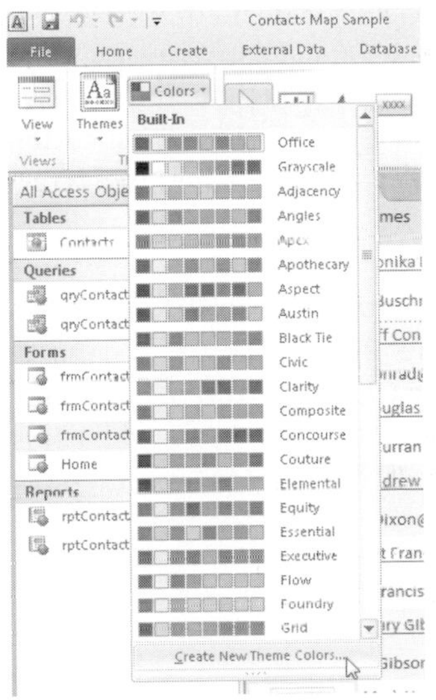

Figure 14-66 Click Create New Theme Colors to create your own colors for a new theme.

At the bottom of the Colors gallery, Access displays an option called Create New Theme Colors. Click this option, and Access opens the Create New Theme Colors dialog box, as shown in Figure 14-67. Under Theme Colors, Access lists the 12 colors you can modify for themes. You can click the down arrow next to the color button to choose a color from the color picker, or create a custom color. Under Sample, Access displays a preview of what your color choices will look like on a form or report. In the Name text box, you can enter a name for your new custom theme colors. Click Reset to reset all the theme colors to their defaults.

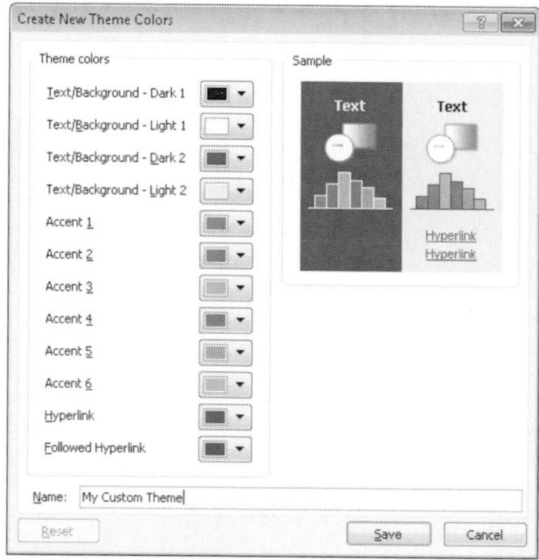

Figure 14-67 You can create your own custom theme colors to use with your database objects.

When you save new custom theme colors, Access displays those theme colors under a new category called Custom in the Colors gallery, as shown in Figure 14-68. You can apply your custom theme colors to any forms and reports in the database you are working on. You'll also see your new custom theme colors option displayed in the Colors gallery for any databases you work with on your computer. By default, Access stores your custom theme colors in the following folder (note that your file path might be different based on your operating system installation path):

C:\Users\<*UserName*>\AppData\Roaming\Microsoft\Templates\Document Themes\Theme Colors

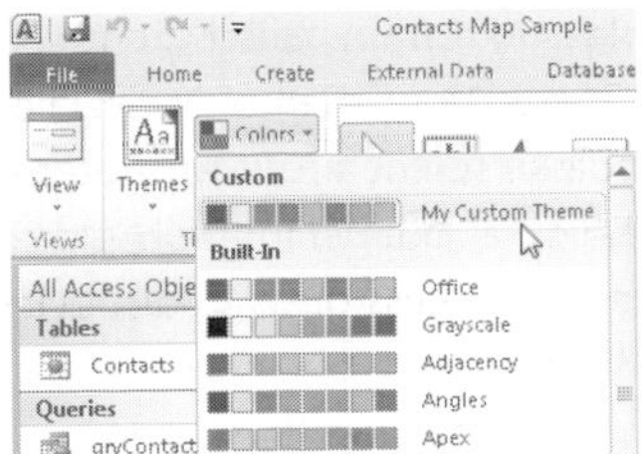

Figure 14-68 Access displays custom theme colors in the Colors gallery.

You can also create your own custom font choices for a theme. Click the Fonts button in the Themes group, and Access displays the different fonts used in the built-in themes, as shown in Figure 14-69. If you right-click one of the font options, Access displays three options—Apply Font Scheme To All Matching Objects, Apply Font Scheme To This Object Only, and Add Gallery To Quick Access Toolbar. These options have similar functionality as the options you saw previously when right-clicking a color theme.

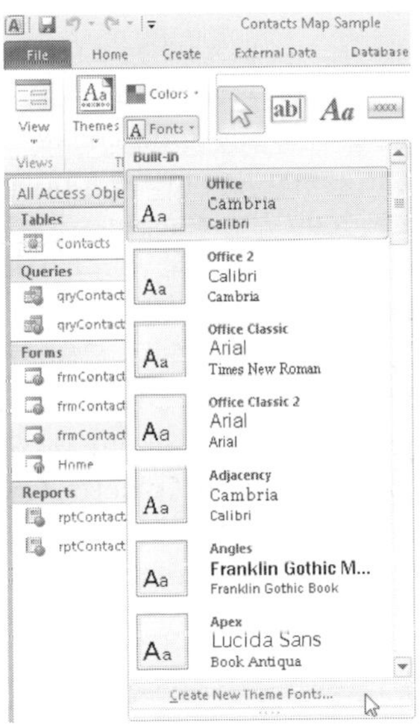

Figure 14-69 Click Create New Theme Fonts to create your own fonts for a new theme.

At the bottom of the Fonts gallery, Access displays an option called Create New Theme Fonts. Click this option, and Access opens the Create New Theme Fonts dialog box, as shown in Figure 14-70. Under Heading Font, you can select a font for Access to use in places where headings are needed, for example, in a title label in the Header section for a form or report. Under Body Font, you can select a font for Access to use in most controls found in the Detail section of forms and reports. Under Sample, Access displays a preview of what your font choices will look like on a form or report. In the Name text box, you can enter a name for your new custom theme fonts.

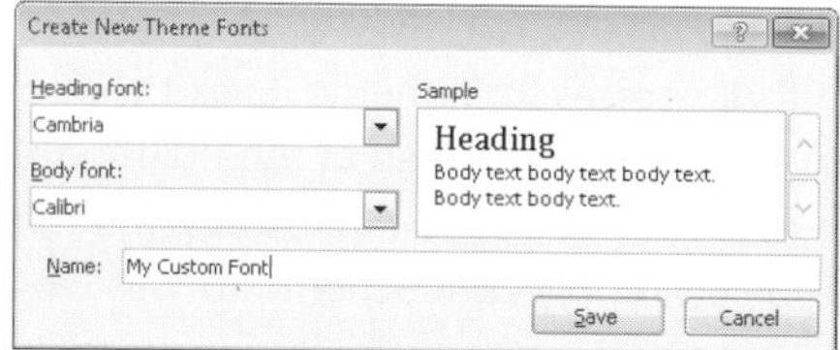

Figure 14-70 You can create your own custom theme fonts to use with your database objects.

When you save new custom theme fonts, Access displays those theme fonts under a new category called Custom in the Fonts gallery, as shown in Figure 14-68. As with custom theme colors, you can apply your custom theme fonts to any forms and reports in the database you are working on. You'll also see your new custom theme font option displayed in the Fonts gallery for any databases you work with on your computer. By default, Access stores your custom theme fonts in the following folder (note that your file path might be different based on your operating system installation path):

C:\Users\<*UserName*>\AppData\Roaming\Microsoft\Templates\Document Themes\Theme Fonts

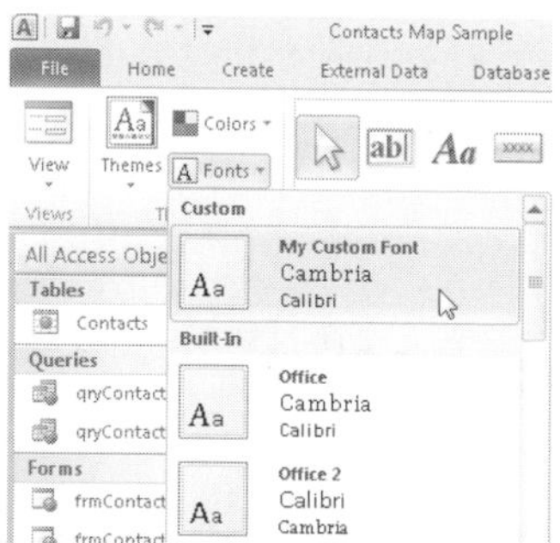

Figure 14-71 Access displays custom theme fonts in the Fonts gallery.

You can also save an entire custom theme by clicking the Theme command in the Themes group, and then clicking the Save Current Theme option, shown previously in Figure 14-64. By default, Access stores custom themes in the following folder (note that your file path might be different based on your operating system installation path):

C:\Users\<*UserName*>\AppData\Roaming\Microsoft\Templates\Document Themes

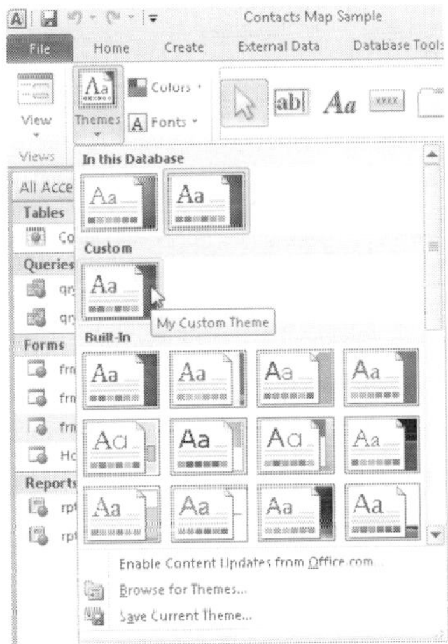

Figure 14-72 Access displays any custom themes stored on your computer under the Custom category in the Themes gallery.

If you want to delete a custom theme from the Themes gallery, you can right-click the custom theme and click Delete. Access prompts you for confirmation before deleting the custom theme file. Be aware, however, that Access permanently deletes the custom theme file from your hard drive. You cannot undo this action nor recover the file from the computer's Recycle Bin. Before moving on to the next section, change the theme back to Office for the Contacts Map Copy sample web database.

INSIDE OUT Use Standard Colors If You Don't Want Themes to Change Your Colors

If you don't want an element of your form or report, such as a command button or text box, to change color when you change a theme, assign a specific standard color to that element on the Property Sheet window instead of using a Theme color. When you change themes, Access keeps the standard color for the element instead of adjusting the color to the new theme.

Working with Shared Resources

Access 2010 includes a new feature called Shared Resources, which allows you to easily share images across multiple forms and reports. In previous versions of Access, when you wanted to display an image on a form or report, you embedded the image into the form or report design. In this case, Access saved the actual image with the form or report definition. You could also link to a graphic file stored on your computer or within a table to display on a form or report. Both of these methods of using images in your applications have drawbacks. When you wanted to reuse an image on multiple forms and reports, perhaps as a form or report background, you had to embed the image individually on each object. When you used this technique, however, your database size could increase dramatically because Access needed to save a copy of that image with each object. If you wanted to change the image used on all the objects, you had to manually delete each image and resave the new image into the object design. If you linked to images on your computer, the images would not show up in your objects if the file locations changed. Access developers also sometimes use subforms that display only a single image to reuse images across different objects; however, this technique does not work when you want to use an image on a command button or for a form or report background.

Shared Resources in Access 2010 helps you manage any images you use in your client or web databases by providing a simple way to share images across multiple forms and reports. When you use a shared image, Access stores the image file once in a system table. You can then reference that image on any form or report in your database without having to store multiple copies and unnecessarily increase the size of your database file.

You can use the Shared Resources feature in both client and web databases. In client forms and reports, you can easily convert existing embedded images into shared images. In web databases, all images used on web forms and web reports must be shared images; you cannot embed images into the web form or web report design as you can for client objects. For web forms and web reports displayed in a web browser, it makes sense to store an image once and reuse it in other places to decrease the amount of time it takes for web pages to load. The Shared Resources feature was built around this concept to make it easier for you to reuse images across forms and reports and increase the responsiveness of loading web forms and web reports in a web browser.

If you've closed the Contacts Map Copy sample web database, reopen the database and then open the Home form in Layout view. This web database includes several shared images used on the web forms and reports. Select the image control in the upper-left corner of the Home form and then click the Insert Image command on the far-right side of the Controls group on the Design tab to display the Image Gallery, as shown in Figure 14-73. Access displays all shared images in the current database in the Image Gallery.

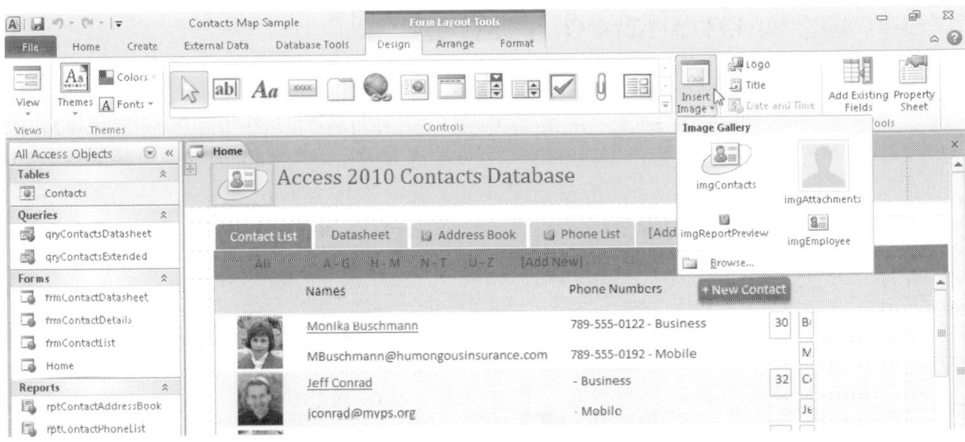

Figure 14-73 Access displays all shared images in the Image Gallery.

The Image Gallery serves multiple purposes for managing your shared images. You can place a new shared image into an empty cell on a form or report, change an existing image control to use a different shared image, browse your computer for new images to add to your database, and rename, update, or delete existing shared images. Access enables the Insert Image button in the Controls group whenever you are on an empty cell or a control with a Picture property in the form or report grid. If you are on an empty cell and click an image in the Image Gallery, Access creates an Image control in the empty cell and places the image into the image control.

As you can see in Figure 14-73, this web database includes four shared images. The image control on the Home form is currently using the shared image called imgContacts. Let's change this image control's properties to point to a different shared image. Click the shared image in the Image Gallery called imgEmployee. Access changes the image control and displays the imgEmployee shared image, as shown in Figure 14-74.

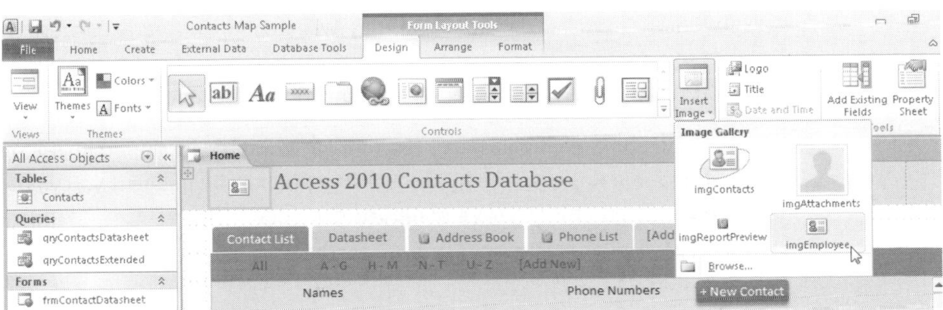

Figure 14-74 You can change an image control to use a different shared image by clicking a different shared image in the Image Gallery.

You can also change the shared image used by an image control through the Property Sheet window. Select the image control on the Home form and then click the Property Sheet button in the Tools group on the Design tab. On the Format or All tab, click the down arrow on the Picture property. Access displays a list of the four shared images stored in the database, as shown in Figure 14-75. When you click an image in the Image Gallery in Layout or Design view, Access changes this Picture property.

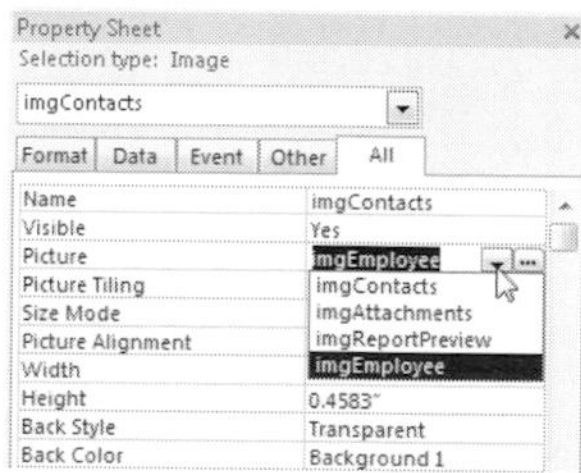

Figure 14-75 Click the Picture property to display a list of the shared images in the database.

INSIDE OUT Converting Embedded or Linked Images to Shared Images

If you have embedded or linked images in your forms and reports from existing databases, you can easily convert them to shared images through the Property Sheet window. Open the form or report in Design view or Layout view, select the image control (or select the Form or Report if you are using an embedded or linked image for the background), and then open the Property Sheet window. Click the down arrow on the Picture Type property and then click Shared, as shown here:

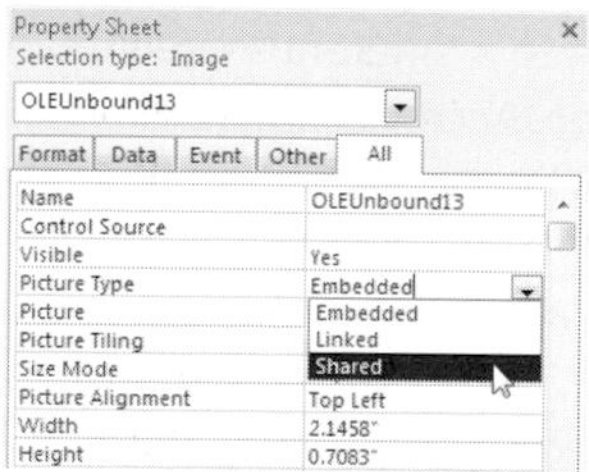

Access converts the embedded or linked image into a new shared image. You can now view the shared image in the Image Gallery, rename the image if you want, and use the shared image on other forms and reports.

If you want to use a different image for a form or report that is currently not in the database, you can click the Browse button on the bottom of the Image Gallery, shown previously in Figure 14-74. When you click Browse, Access opens the Insert Picture dialog box, as shown in Figure 14-76. You can browse the folders on your computer for a new image to add to your database. Note that by default, Access limits the image files shown in the Insert Picture dialog box to files with extensions of .jpg, .jpeg, .jpe, .gif, and .png. To view additional file extensions, select All Files from the Web-Ready Image Files drop-down list.

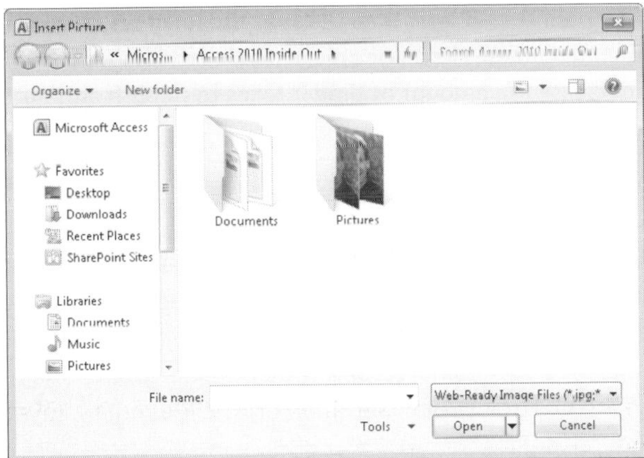

Figure 14-76 You can browse for images to use in your database from the Insert Picture dialog box.

When you select a new image to add to your database and click OK, Access inserts the new image into the system table, changes the Picture property of the selected control to use the new image, and adds the image to the Image Gallery. If you selected an empty cell on the form or report grid before clicking Browse, you can then add an image control to the grid. Access sets the Picture property to the name of the shared image and sets the Picture Type property to Shared for the image control. You can now use this new image for other controls on the current form or in other forms and reports. You can also browse for new images to add to your database by clicking the Builder button on the Picture property for a selected image. Access opens the Insert Picture dialog box from this entry point as well.

> **INSIDE OUT** **Convert All Embedded Images in Client Objects to Shared Images in Web Databases**
>
> If you are using a web database that includes client forms and reports, we recommend you change all embedded images on client forms and reports to shared images. When you publish a web database to a server running Microsoft SharePoint and Access Services, Access converts embedded images to text in client objects before sending to the server. Publishing and syncing client objects with embedded objects this way can significantly increase the publish and sync time because the image is converted to text. If you convert all embedded images in client objects to shared images in web databases, you'll significantly decrease the amount of time it takes to publish and sync changes for your web database.

When you add images to your database, Access by default uses the file name to display in the Image gallery. You can rename the image through the Image Gallery after Access adds the new image into the database. Previously, you changed the image control on the Home form to use the imgEmployee shared image. Select that image control again, click the Insert Image button in the Controls group, and then right-click imgEmployee in the Image Gallery, as shown in Figure 14-77.

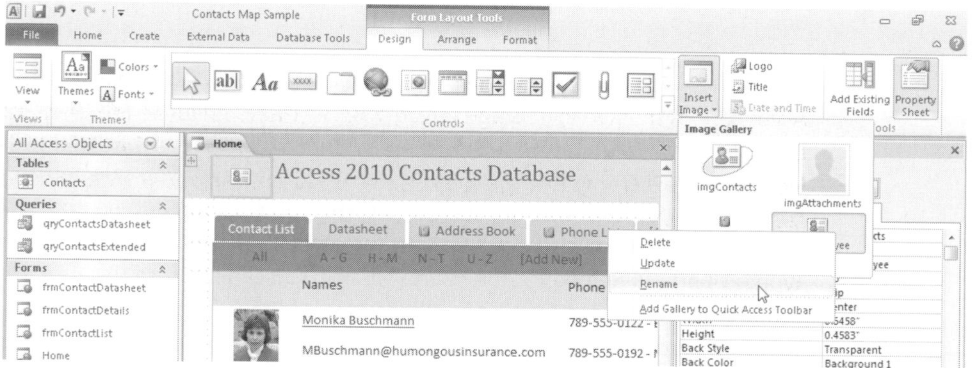

Figure 14-77 Right-click an image in the Image Gallery to rename it.

Access displays a shortcut menu of options for the selected shared image. If you click Delete, Access deletes the shared image from your database. Any image controls on any forms or reports that use that shared image will now display nothing because Access deleted the image. If you click Update on the shortcut menu, Access opens the Insert Picture dialog box so you can browse for a different image to use in place of the existing stored shared image. The update option is very useful, for example, when you want to replace an existing logo used on your forms and reports with an updated logo. If you click Rename on the shortcut menu, you can rename the stored shared image. (We'll do that in just a moment.) Click the last option in the shortcut menu—Add Gallery To Quick Access Toolbar—to add the Image Gallery to the Quick Access Toolbar.

CAUTION!

If you click Delete on the shortcut menu for the Image Gallery, as shown previously in Figure 14-77, Access does not prompt you for confirmation before deleting the image. Access permanently deletes the image from your database file, and there is no way to undo this action.

INSIDE OUT Using Shared Images as Backgrounds for Client Forms or Reports

You can use a shared image as the background for a client form or report. Click the Background Image button in the Background group on the Format tab and then select a shared image from the image gallery. You can also click Browse on the Image Gallery to browse for a new image to use for your form or report background.

Click Rename on the shortcut menu now so you can change the name of the shared image. Access opens the Rename Image dialog box, as shown in Figure 14-78. Access displays the existing the name of the shared image next to Old Name. Type **imgNewEmployee** in the New Name text box to change the name of this stored shared image, and then click OK to save your changes.

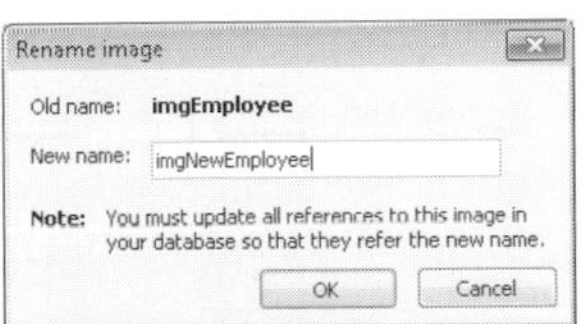

Figure 14-78 You can type a new name for shared images in the Rename Image dialog box.

When you rename a shared image, Access only renames the shared image in the system table. Access does not change the Picture property for the selected control (or form and report if you are using a shared image for the background) to use the new name. If you save, close, and then reopen the Home form now, you'll see nothing in the image control because Access still uses the old name of the shared image in the Picture property. If you rename a shared image, you'll need to change the Picture property for each control on your forms and reports to use the new shared image name. You can either select the new name in the drop-down list of shared images on the Picture property, or select the control and then click the new shared image name in the Image Gallery to change the property.

INSIDE OUT Importing Shared Images

When you import a form or report into an Access 2010 database that utilizes shared images from a different database, Access also imports any shared images used by the form or report. If an existing shared image in the database performing the import has the same name as a shared image being imported, Access appends a number followed by an underscore to the start of the shared image name. For example, if you have an image called Employee in one database and import a form or report from another database that also has a shared image with that name, Access names the imported shared image as 1_Employee. The imported forms and reports will have their image controls referencing the Employee image in the destination database.

Now you should be comfortable with designing both basic client and web forms and adding special touches to make your forms more attractive and usable. In Chapter 15, you'll learn advanced client and web form design techniques: using multiple-table queries in forms, building forms within forms, and working with Navigational Controls, Web Browser Controls, PivotTables, and PivotCharts.

CHAPTER 15

Advanced Form Design

In the previous two chapters, you learned how to design and build client and web forms that work with data from a single table, and you saw how to display data from another table by using a combo box or a list box. You also learned various techniques to enhance the appearance of your forms, and you explored control and form properties you can set to specify how a form looks and works.

In this chapter, you'll learn how to design client and web forms that consolidate information from multiple tables. You'll find out how to

- Create a form based on a query that joins multiple tables
- Embed a subform in a main form so that you can work with related data from two tables or queries at the same time
- Use an option group to display and edit information
- Define conditional formatting of a control based on the data values in the form
- Use the tab control to handle multiple subforms within one area on a form
- Create a form that spreads many data fields across multiple pages
- Design a client form in PivotTable or PivotChart view and embed a linked PivotChart form in another form
- Use a Navigation Control to easily allow navigation between other forms and reports
- Use a Web Browser Control to display a web page on a form

Note

The examples in this chapter are based on the tables and data in HousingDataCopy.accdb, ContactsDataCopy.accdb, and ContactsNavigation.accdb on the companion CD included with this book. These databases are copies of the data from the Housing Reservations, Conrad Systems Contacts, and Contacts Map application samples, respectively, and they contain the sample queries and forms used in this chapter. The results you see from the samples you build in this chapter might not exactly match what you see in this book if you have changed the sample data in the files. Also, all the screen images in this chapter were taken on a Windows 7 operating system with the Access color scheme set to Silver. Your results might look different if you are using a different operating system or a different theme.

Basing a Form on a Multiple-Table Query

When you bring together data from multiple tables using select queries, the result of that query is called a *recordset*. A recordset contains all the information you need, but it's in the unadorned Datasheet view format. Forms enable you to present this data in a more attractive and meaningful way. In the same way that you can update data with queries, you can also update data using a form that is based on a query.

Creating a Many-to-One Form

It's easy to design a form that allows you to view and update the data from a single table. Although you can include selected fields from related tables using a list box or a combo box, what if you want to see more information from the related tables? The best way to do this is to design a query based on two (or more) related tables and use that query as the basis of your form.

When you create a query with two or more tables, you're usually working with one-to-many relationships among the tables. As you learned earlier, Microsoft Access 2010 lets you update any data in the table that is on the *many* side of the relationship and any nonkey fields on the *one* side of the relationship. This means that when you base a form on a query, you can update all the fields in the form that come from the *many* table and most of the fields from the *one* side. Because the primary purpose of the form is to search and update records on the *many* side of the relationship while reviewing information on the *one* side, this is called a *many-to-one* form.

In Chapter 10, "Building Complex Queries," you learned how to build a multiple-table query that displays information from several tables in the HousingDataCopy.accdb sample database. Later, you explored the fundamentals of form construction by creating simple forms to display company and product data in the ContactsDataCopy.accdb sample database.

In Chapter 14, "Customizing a Form," you built and enhanced a simple client form to display employee information from the housing database. (See Figure 14-20 on page 864.) You could have used a combo box to display a department name instead of a number in your employees form. But what if you want to see the additional details about the department when you view an employee record? To do this, you need to base your employee form on a query that joins multiple tables.

Designing a Many-to-One Query

To build the query you need, follow these steps:

1. Open the HousingDataCopy.accdb sample database, and on the Create tab, in the Queries group, click the Query Design button to open a new Query window in Design view.

2. Add the tblDepartments table and two copies of the tblEmployees table using the Show Table dialog box. (You need the second copy to fetch the department manager name.) Close the Show Table dialog box after you add the tables to the query window.

3. Remove the extra relationship line between EmployeeNumber in the first copy of tblEmployees and ManagerNumber in the tblDepartments table.

4. Right-click the second copy of tblEmployees (the title bar of the field list displays *tblEmployees_1*), and click Properties on the shortcut menu, or click the Property Sheet button in the Show/Hide group on the Design tab. In the Property Sheet window, give the field list an alias name of Managers to make the purpose of this field list clear, and then close the Property Sheet window.

5. Click the EmployeeNumber field in the Managers field list, and drag it to ManagerNumber in the tblDepartments field list. This link establishes who the department manager is.

6. Drag the special "all fields" indicator (*) from the tblEmployees field list to the design grid.

7. Create an expression, **Manager: Managers.LastName & ", " & Managers. FirstName**, in the next empty column in the design grid to display the department manager name.

8. From the tblDepartments table, drag DeptLocation, DeptAddress, DeptCity, DeptStateOrProvince, DeptPostalCode, and DeptCountry to the query design grid. Do not include the DepartmentID field from tblDepartments; you want to be able to update the DepartmentID field, but only in the tblEmployees table. If you include the DepartmentID field from the tblDepartments table, it might confuse you later as you design the form. You'll use a combo box on DepartmentID on the form to display the department name. Save your query as qryEmployeesDepartmentManager, and close the query.

You can find a query already built for this purpose (named qryXmplEmployeesDepartment-Manager) in the sample database, as shown in Figure 15-1.

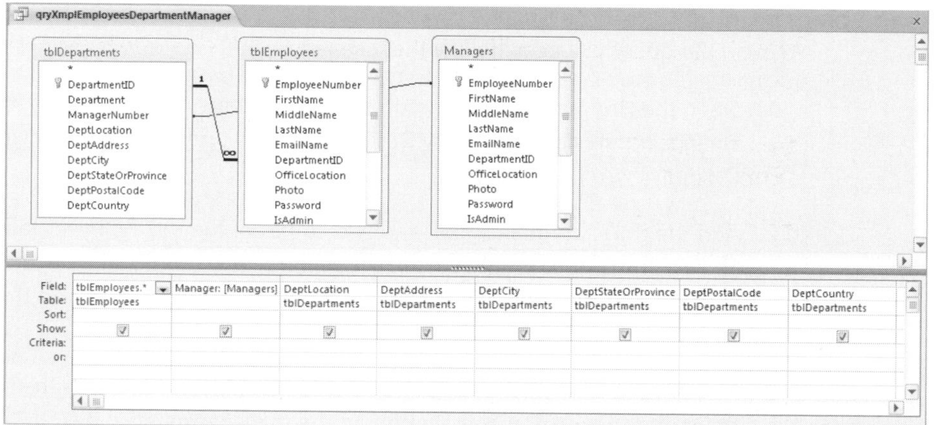

Figure 15-1 The qryXmplEmployeesDepartmentManager query serves as the record source for your form.

Designing a Many-to-One Form

Now that you have the query you need, find the query definition in the Navigation pane and create a new form based on the query. You can use the Form Wizard to quickly build a starting point for your form. Select the query in the Navigation pane, click the Create tab, and in the Forms group, click Form Wizard to get started.

You want to include all the fields from the query in this form, so click the double right arrow to move all the fields from the Available Fields list to the Selected Fields list. Click Next to go to the second page of the wizard. Select a columnar layout on the next page, as shown in Figure 15-2. Click Next to continue to the last page of the wizard.

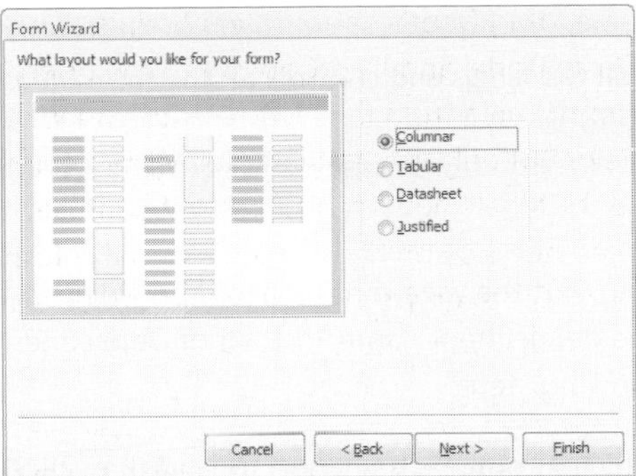

Figure 15-2 Select Columnar layout on the second page of the Form Wizard.

Give your form a title of Employees on the last page, and click Finish. When the wizard finishes, you should see a form similar to that shown in Figure 15-3.

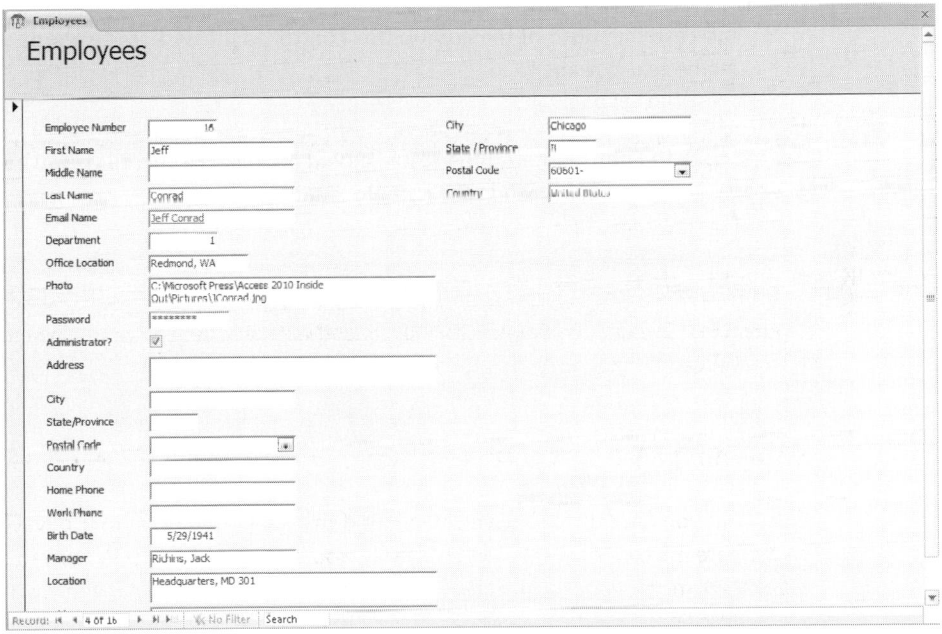

Figure 15-3 The Employees form is a many-to-one form to display data from multiple tables.

> **Note**
>
> **In Figure 15-3, you cannot see all the labels and controls on the form unless you use the scroll bar to scroll down the form.**

This form could use some polishing, but the wizard has placed the fields you chose on the form for you. To be able to see the department name, instead of Department ID, switch to Design view, and perform the following steps:

1. Right-click the DepartmentID text box, click Change To, and then click Combo Box. This converts the text box to a combo box.
2. Open the property sheet, and set Row Source to tblDepartments, Column Count to 2 (the first two fields of tblDepartments are DepartmentID and Department), and ColumnWidths to **0";1.5"** to hide the DepartmentID and display the department name.
3. Increase the width of the combo box control so it matches the width of the Email Name text box above it.

Switch back to Form view, and the result should look like Figure 15-4. You can find this form saved as frmXmplEmployee6 in the sample database.

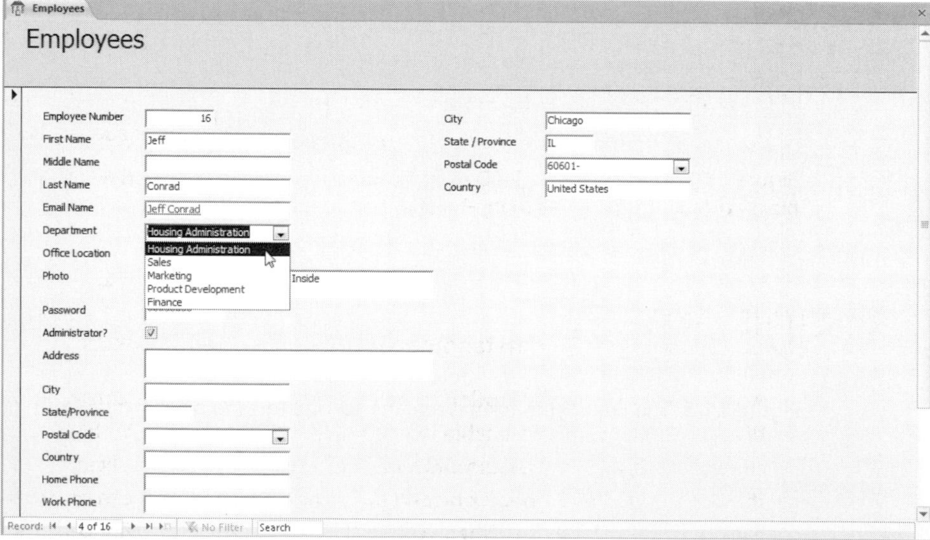

Figure 15-4 The DepartmentID control displays the related department name after you changed it to a combo box.

Try changing the department on any record to something else and watch what happens. You should see the corresponding manager name and department location information pop into view, as shown in Figure 15-5. Because you haven't set the Locked property for any of the fields, you can also update the location information for the displayed department. However, if you do this, the new location information appears for all employees assigned to that department.

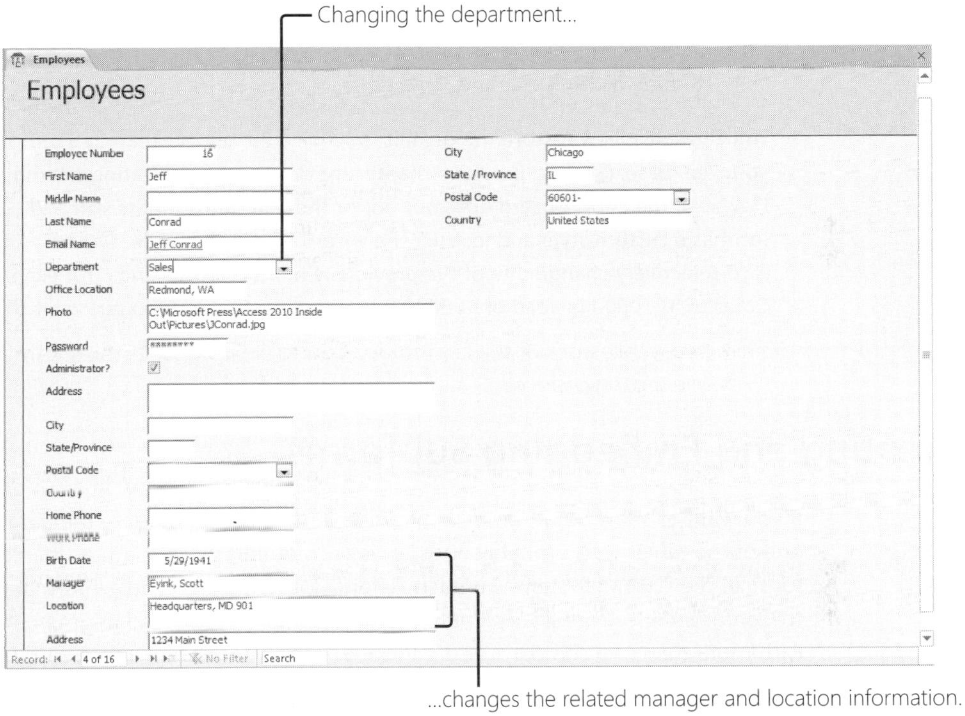

Changing the department...

...changes the related manager and location information.

Figure 15-5 If you change the Department field for the employee, new related information displays automatically on this many-to-one form.

INSIDE OUT Understanding Windows-Themed Controls

Access 2010 provides an option to help your forms look more consistent with Windows Vista and Windows 7. To enable this feature, click the File tab on the Backstage view, click Options, and in the Current Database category, under Application Options, select the Use Windows-Themed Controls On Forms check box. You can set this option for each individual database. When you do this, Access uses the Windows Vista or Windows 7 theme for your command buttons. It also applies the Windows theme for label,

text box, option group, option button, check box, combo box, list box, image, unbound object frame, bound object frame, subform, and rectangle controls. All these controls appear flat when all the following conditions are true:

- Special Effect is Sunken or Etched, or Special Effect is Flat and Border Style is not Transparent.
- Border Style is Solid, or Border Style is Transparent and Special Effect is not Flat.
- Border Color is #000000.
- Border Width is Hairline, 1, or 2.

You can selectively restore the default look for controls by creating a template form in your database. (See the previous chapter for details about creating a template form.) However, the Form Wizard does not honor these settings unless you add your template form as a custom style and instruct the wizard to use that style. The only other solution is to selectively change one of the previously mentioned settings (for example, set Back Color to #010000 instead of #000000) for controls that you do not want themed.

Creating and Embedding Subforms

If you want to show data from several tables and be able to update the data in more than one of the tables, you probably need to use something more complex than a standard form. In the Conrad Systems Contacts database, the main contacts information is in the tblContacts table. Contacts can have multiple contact events and might be associated with more than one company or organization. The information about companies is in the tblCompanies table.

Because any one contact might belong to several companies or organizations and each company probably has many contacts, the tblContacts table is related to the tblCompanies table in a many-to-many relationship. (See Chapter 4, "Designing Client Tables," for a review of relationship types.) The tblCompanyContacts table provides the link between companies and contacts.

Similarly, a particular contact within a company might own one or more products, and a product should be owned by multiple contacts. Because any one contact might have purchased many different products and any one product might be owned by multiple contacts, the tblCompanyContacts table is related to the tblProducts table in a many-to-many relationship. The tblContactProducts table establishes the necessary link between the contacts and the products owned. Figure 15-6 shows the relationships.

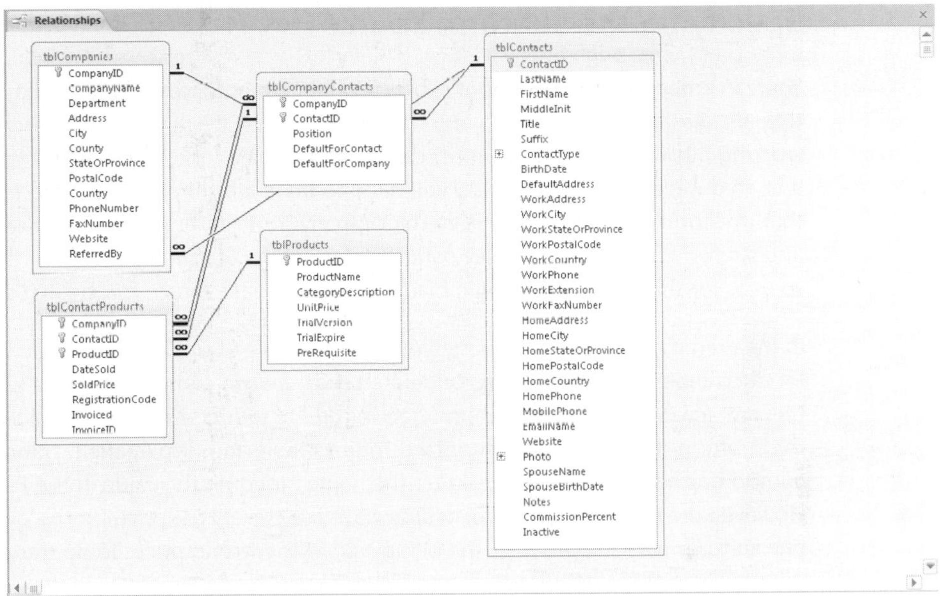

Figure 15-6 The Relationships window in the Conrad Systems Contacts application shows the relationships between companies, contacts, and products.

When you are viewing information about a particular contact, you also might want to see and edit the related company information and the product detail information. You could create a complex query that brings together the desired information from all five tables and use a single form to display the data, similar to the many-to-one employees form you built in the previous section. However, the focus would be on the contact products (the lowest table in the one-to-many relationship chain), so you would be able to see in a single form row only one product per row. You could design a form that has its Default View property set to Continuous Forms, but you would see the information from tblContacts and tblCompanyContacts repeated over and over.

Subforms can help solve this problem. You can create a main form that displays the contact's information and embed in it a subform that displays all the related rows from tblCompanyContacts. To see the related product information, you could then build a subform within the form that displays the tblCompanyContacts data to show the product information from tblContactProducts.

Specifying the Subform Source

You can embed up to 10 levels of subforms within another form (a form that has a subform that also has a subform, and so on). It's best to start by designing the innermost form and working outward because you must design and save an inner form before you can embed it in an outer one. In this exercise, you need to build a form on tblContactProducts, embed that in a form that shows data from tblCompanyContacts, and then finally embed that form and subform in a form to display contact information. But first, you must create the record sources for these subforms. Begin by designing the data source for the first subform.

In the example described previously, you want to create or update rows in the tblContact-Products table to create, modify, or delete links between company contact records in the tblCompanyContacts table and products in the tblProducts table. You could certainly base the subform directly on the tblContactProducts table and display the product name via a combo box on the form that looks up the name based on the value in the ProductID field. However, the user might find it useful to have the current list price for the product displayed to be sure the product isn't being sold at the wrong price. To do that, you need a query linking tblContactProducts and tblProducts.

Begin by opening the ContactsDataCopy.accdb sample database, and then start a new query in Design view. In the Show Table dialog box, add the field lists for the tblContactProducts and tblProducts tables to the Query window, and then click Close. You want to be able to update all the fields in the tblContactProducts table, so copy them to the design grid. You can do so by using the all fields indicator (*). Add the ProductName, CategoryDescription, UnitPrice, and TrialVersion fields from the tblProducts table.

Your query should look similar to the one shown in Figure 15-7. (This query is saved as qxmplContactProducts in the sample database.) Notice that the tblProducts table has a one-to-many relationship with the tblContactProducts table. This means that you can update any field in the tblContactProducts table (including all three primary key fields, so long as you don't create a duplicate row) because the tblContactProducts table is on the *many* side of the relationship. Save and close the query so that you can use it as you design the subform. You can save your query as qryContactProductsSub, as shown in Figure 15-7, or use the sample query.

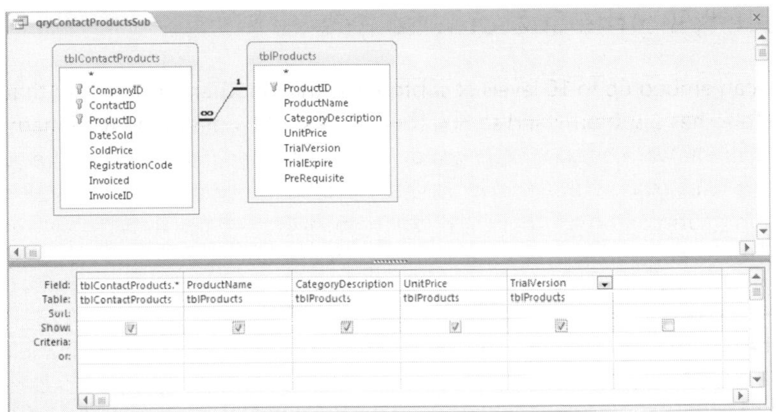

Figure 15-7 You can use this query to update the tblContactProducts table from a subform while displaying related information from the tblProducts table.

Next, you need a query for the form to display the information from tblCompanyContacts. You'll embed a subform to display contact products in this form and ultimately embed this form in the outermost form to display contact data. Again, although you could use the tblCompanyContacts table as the record source for this form, you might want to display additional information, such as company name and department name, from the related tblCompanies table. You also want to restrict the rows displayed to the one row for each contact that defines the default company for the contact.

Start a new query on the tblCompanyContacts table. Add the tblCompanies table to the design grid. You should see a link between the two tables on the CompanyID field in each. Close the Show Table dialog box after you add the two tables. In the design grid, include the CompanyID, ContactID, Position, and DefaultForContact fields from tblCompanyContacts. Under the DefaultForContact field, enter a criterion of True to restrict the output to the records that define the default company for each contact. Add the CompanyName and Department fields from the tblCompanies table.

Your query should look like the one shown in Figure 15-8. (This query is saved as qxmplContactCompaniesDefault in the sample database.) Notice that the tblCompanies table has a one-to-many relationship with the tblCompanyContacts table. This means that you can update any field in the tblCompanyContacts table (including the primary key fields, so long as you don't create a duplicate row) because the tblCompanyContacts table is on the *many* side of the relationship. Save the query so that you can use it as you design your form. You can save your query as qryContactCompaniesDefault, as shown in Figure 15-8, or use the sample query.

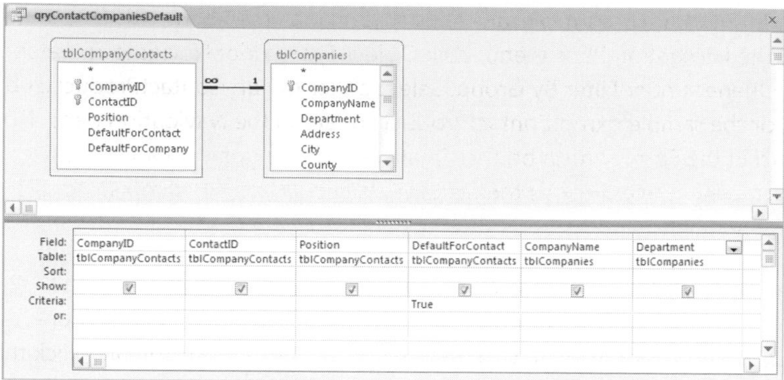

Figure 15-8 You can use this query to update the tblCompanyContacts table from a subform while displaying related information from the tblCompanies table.

You're now ready to start building the forms and subforms.

Designing the Innermost Subform

For the innermost subform, you'll end up displaying the single ProductID field bound to a combo box that shows the product name. After you choose a ProductID, you want to show the user the product category, name, and list price—but in controls that can't be updated. (You don't want a user to be able to accidentally change product names and list prices via this form!) Of course, you need the DateSold and SoldPrice fields from tblContactProducts so that you can update these fields.

For this purpose, you could use a form in either Datasheet or Continuous Forms view. It's simple to build a subform designed to be used in Datasheet view because you need to include only the fields you want to display in the Detail section of the form, without any regard to alignment or placement. Access takes care of ordering, sizing, and providing column headers in the datasheet. However, we like to use Continuous Forms view because that view lets you control the size of the columns—in Datasheet view, a user can resize the columns, including shrinking a column so that it's no longer visible. Furthermore, if the subform is in Single Form view or Continuous Form view, the Size To Fit command will make the subform control on the outer form the right size. If the subform is in Datasheet view, however, the Size To Fit command will size the control to the size of the subform in Form view, not to an even number of datasheet rows wide or high. Also, the user is free to resize the row height and column width in Datasheet view, so how you size the subform control in Design view is only a guess.

It turns out that the Form Wizard does a good job assembling this first subform for you. Click the Navigation Pane menu, click Object Type under Navigate To Category, and then click Queries under Filter By Group. Select either the qryContactProductsSub query you built or the sample qxmplContactProducts query in the Navigation pane. Now, click Form Wizard in the Forms group on the Create tab. You're going to ask the wizard to create a tabular form, which displays the fields you select in the order you select them in Continuous Forms view.

You don't need the CompanyID and ContactID fields—as you'll learn later, the form in which you'll embed this subform will supply these values via special properties you'll set in the subform control. First, click the ProductID field to select it, and click the single right arrow to move it to the Selected Fields list. Choose the additional fields you need in this order: CategoryDescription, ProductName, UnitPrice, DateSold, and SoldPrice. (If we had planned ahead, we could have placed the fields in this sequence in the query we're using as the record source.) Click Next to go to the next page in the wizard, as shown in Figure 15-9.

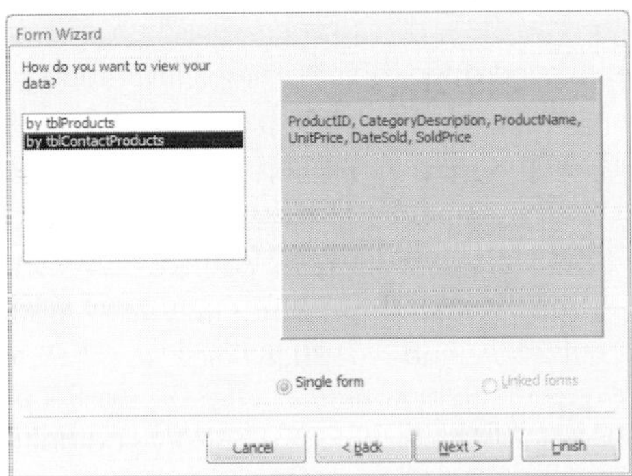

Figure 15-9 When you use the Form Wizard to build a form on a query using two tables, the wizard offers data layout choices.

Although you won't take advantage of the wizard features shown on this page this time, it's interesting to note the options if you click the By tblProducts option. The wizard offers to build a form on tblProducts and a subform on tblContactProducts or to build two separate forms that are linked with a command button. In this case, you want to build a single continuous form, so click By tblContactProducts, and then click Next to go to the next page. Choose the Tabular layout on this page and then click Next. On the final page, give your new form a name such as fsubContactProducts, select the Modify The Form's Design option, and click Finish. Your result should look like Figure 15-10.

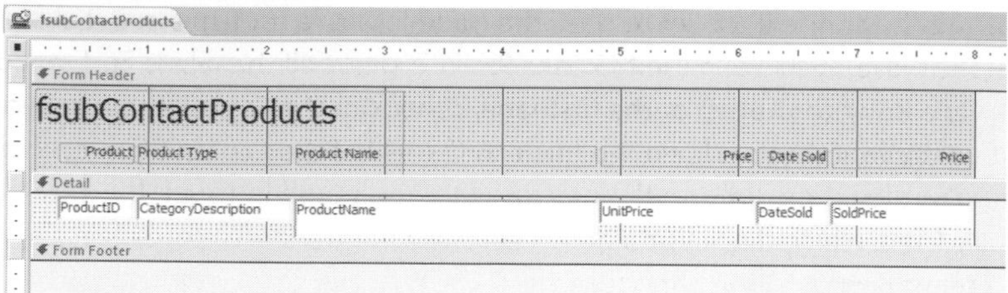

Figure 15-10 The Form Wizard created a continuous form to edit contact product information.

You could probably use this form as is, but we'll clean it up using the techniques in Design view and Layout view that you learned in previous chapters. Perform the following steps to perfect the design:

1. Switch to Design view if you are currently not in that view, and then open the Property Sheet window. In the Selection Type combo box at the top of the Property Sheet window, select Form to view the form's properties. When you started the Form Wizard, you first highlighted a saved query object in the Navigation pane and then selected six fields to display in the form on the first page of the wizard. If you look at the Record Source property of the form in the Property Sheet window, the Form Wizard created a Structured Query Language (SQL) statement that contains only the six fields and embedded the SQL statement into the form's Record Source property. Although we want to display only these six fields on the form, we still need the other fields in the underlying query to establish linking fields later in this chapter. Click the drop-down list of saved table and query objects on the Record Source property and select either the qryContactProductsSub query you built or the sample qxmplContactProducts query.

2. Delete the title label that Access created in the Form Header section on the form design grid. Because you've deleted the title, you can now move all the labels closer to the top of the form. Click in the Ruler to the left of the first label, Product, to highlight all the label controls in the Header section. Now, drag the labels up near the top of the form. Drag the bottom of the Form Header section up close to the label controls to get rid of the extra spacing in this section that we no longer need.

3. Select all the labels, and click the Bold button in the Font group on the Format tab to make the captions more readable. You'll notice that Access adjusts the width of all the controls to make room for the larger text.

4. All the controls are set to the Tahoma font with a font size of 8. Let's change the font of these controls to use MS Sans Serif. To select all the labels and text boxes, click in the Ruler to the left of the first label control in the Form Header section, and then drag your mouse down the Ruler to the left of the first text box control in the form Detail section. Release the mouse and Access highlights all the label and text box controls in both sections. Now, select the MS Sans Serif font from the Font list in the Font group on the Format tab.

5. You can move the labels and text boxes a little closer to the left edge of the form. Click in the Ruler to the left of the first label control in the Form Header section, and then drag your mouse down the Ruler to the left of the first text box control in the form Detail section. Release the mouse and Access highlights all the label and text box controls in both sections. Use your left arrow key to move all the controls closer to the left side of the form grid.

6. You can reduce the width of the CategoryDescription controls (the Product Type column). Click in the Ruler above the Product Type label to highlight the label and text box, and drag the right edge of the controls closer to the left edge of the form until they are about 1 inch in width. (You can switch the form into Layout view and then scroll through the records to make sure you've allowed adequate space in the CategoryDescription.) You now have extra space to the right of the CategoryDescription controls that you don't need. Click in the Ruler above the Product Name label and then drag your mouse to the right until you highlight the remaining controls. Now, use your left arrow key to move the controls closer to the CategoryDescription controls to close this gap.

7. The ProductName text box control does not need to be quite so wide. Click in the Ruler above the Product Name label to highlight the label and text box, and drag the right edge of the controls closer to the left edge of the form. Make sure you can still see all the data in this control by scrolling through a few of the records in Layout view. Switch back to Design view when you are finished. The Form Wizard initially created this text box to be two lines high, but this is unnecessary now. Click the ProductName text box, move your mouse pointer to the bottom edge of the control until it becomes a double-sided arrow, and then drag the bottom edge up closer until the control is only one line high. Access changes the height of the text box control, but now you have a gap below the controls. (We'll fix this in a minute.) To make sure you've sized the text box exactly one line high, you can double-click the edge of the text box or click the To Fit command under the Size/Space command in the Sizing & Ordering group on the Arrange tab. Now, move the UnitPrice, DateSold, and SoldPrice controls farther to the left so they are next to the ProductName controls again.

8. The two price text box controls are wider than necessary, so you should reduce the width of these controls as well. Click in the Ruler above the UnitPrice label (the first Price label), hold down the Shift key and then click in the Ruler above the SoldPrice label (the second Price label) to select these four controls, and reduce their width by dragging the right edge of either control closer to the left side of the form. Notice that Access resizes the text box controls for you. The DateSold control is currently too narrow to display the dates, so click in the Ruler above these controls, move your mouse pointer to the left edge of the control until it becomes a double-sided arrow, and then drag the left edge to expand the width until it is next to the UnitPrice control.

9. Click anywhere in the Detail section away from any controls to be sure no controls are selected. Right-click the ProductID text box control, click Change To on the menu, and then click Combo Box to convert the text box to a combo box. Open the Property Sheet window, and set Row Source to tblProducts, Column Count to **2**, Column Widths to **0.25"; 1.5"**, and List Width to **2"**. (In metric, the measurements would be about 0.635 cm, 3.81 cm, and 5.079 cm, respectively.)

10. You need to lock the three fields from tblProducts so that they cannot be updated via this form. Click the CategoryDescription text box control, and hold down the Shift key while you click the ProductName text box control and the UnitPrice text box control to add them to the selection. In the Property Sheet window, set Locked to Yes.

11. Because Access originally made the ProductName text box control a two-line control, it will display a vertical scroll bar when you switch to Form view. You sized the control in Layout view to be wide enough to display all product names, so you don't need the scroll bar. Click the ProductName text box, go to the Property Sheet window, and set the Scroll Bars property to None to ensure that this control does not display a scroll bar.

12. Open the form footer by dragging down its bottom edge. Click the Text Box tool in the Controls group on the Design tab, and drop a text box in the Footer section under the SoldPrice text box control. Make your new control the same size as the SoldPrice control, and line them up using the Align Left or Align Right button under the Align command in the Sizing & Ordering group on the Arrange tab, which you learned about in the previous chapter. Click the attached label, set its font to Bold, and in the Property Sheet window, type **Total:** in the Caption property. Now, move the label closer to the new text box. Click the new text box, and in the Property Sheet window, set Control Source to **=Sum([SoldPrice])**, Format to Currency, Enabled to No, and Locked to Yes. Finally, select both the new label and text box controls, and change the font to MS Sans Serif.

All you have left to do is to shrink the bottom of the Detail section to eliminate the extra space below the row of controls, reduce the width of the form, select the form, set the form's Scroll Bars property in the Property Sheet window to Vertical Only (your design should horizontally fit all the fields within the subform control on the main form so that the user won't need to scroll left and right), and set the Navigation Buttons property to No. (You can use the vertical scroll bar to move through the multiple rows.)

Because you didn't choose all the fields from the query, the wizard tried to help you out by creating an SQL statement to fetch only the fields you used on the form. You'll need all the fields for the subform filtering to work correctly. So, delete the SQL statement from the form's Record Source property, and set the property back to the name of your query (qryContactProductsSub). The result of your work should look something like Figure 15-11.

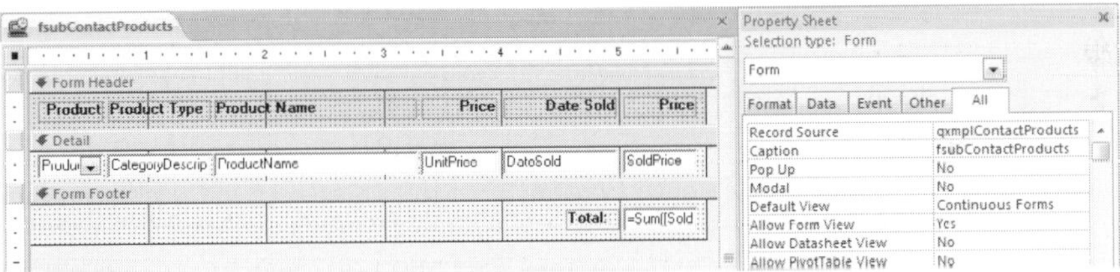

Figure 15-11 Here is your subform to edit contact products in Design view.

You can switch to the subform's Form view to check your work. You can see the Continuous Forms view in Figure 15-12. Because this form isn't linked in as a subform yet (which will limit the display to the current order), the totals displayed in the form footer are the totals for all orders. You can find this form saved as fsubXmplContactProducts in the sample database.

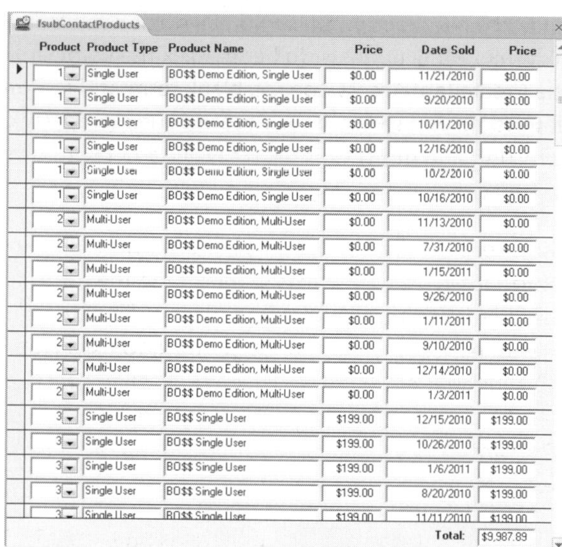

fsubContactProducts

Product	Product Type	Product Name	Price	Date Sold	Price
1	Single User	BO$$ Demo Edition, Single User	$0.00	11/21/2010	$0.00
1	Single User	BO$$ Demo Edition, Single User	$0.00	9/20/2010	$0.00
1	Single User	BO$$ Demo Edition, Single User	$0.00	10/11/2010	$0.00
1	Single User	BO$$ Demo Edition, Single User	$0.00	12/16/2010	$0.00
1	Single User	BO$$ Demo Edition, Single User	$0.00	10/2/2010	$0.00
1	Single User	BO$$ Demo Edition, Single User	$0.00	10/16/2010	$0.00
2	Multi-User	BO$$ Demo Edition, Multi-User	$0.00	11/13/2010	$0.00
2	Multi-User	BO$$ Demo Edition, Multi-User	$0.00	7/31/2010	$0.00
2	Multi-User	BO$$ Demo Edition, Multi-User	$0.00	1/15/2011	$0.00
2	Multi-User	BO$$ Demo Edition, Multi-User	$0.00	9/26/2010	$0.00
2	Multi-User	BO$$ Demo Edition, Multi-User	$0.00	1/11/2011	$0.00
2	Multi-User	BO$$ Demo Edition, Multi-User	$0.00	9/10/2010	$0.00
2	Multi-User	BO$$ Demo Edition, Multi-User	$0.00	12/14/2010	$0.00
2	Multi-User	BO$$ Demo Edition, Multi-User	$0.00	1/3/2011	$0.00
3	Single User	BO$$ Single User	$199.00	12/15/2010	$199.00
3	Single User	BO$$ Single User	$199.00	10/26/2010	$199.00
3	Single User	BO$$ Single User	$199.00	1/6/2011	$199.00
3	Single User	BO$$ Single User	$199.00	8/20/2010	$199.00
3	Single User	BO$$ Single User	$199.00	11/11/2010	$199.00
				Total:	$9,987.89

Figure 15-12 This is your contact products subform displayed in Continuous Forms view.

INSIDE OUT Using a Subform in Datasheet View

If you'll be using a subform in Datasheet view when it's embedded in another form, you have to switch to Datasheet view to adjust how the datasheet looks and then save the subform from Datasheet view to preserve the look you want. You must also use the Datasheet view of the form to make adjustments to fonts and row height. The font in Datasheet view is independent of any font defined for the controls in Form view.

Also, if you build a tabular form, such as the one shown in Figure 15-12, and then decide to use it as a subform in Datasheet view, you will see the field names as the column headings rather than the captions. In Datasheet view, columns display the defined caption for the field only when the bound control has an attached label. In a tabular form, the labels are detached from their respective controls and displayed in a separate section of the form design.

Designing the First Level Subform

You can now move on to the form to display the company contact information and act as a link between contacts and contact products. The purpose of the final form will be to view contacts and edit their contact products, so you don't need to have anything fancy in the middle or allow any updates. To begin, click the Form Design button in the Forms group on the Create tab. Access opens a blank form grid in Design view. Open the Property Sheet window, and select in the Record Source property either the query you built earlier (qryContactCompaniesDefault) or the sample query we provided (qxmplContactCompaniesDefault).

To make this form easy to build, set some control defaults first. Click the Label button in the Controls group on the Design tab, and click the Bold button in the Font group on the Format tab to give all your labels a default bold font. Click the Text Box button in the Controls group on the Design tab, and then, in the Property Sheet window, change the Special Effect property to Flat, the Label Align property to Right, and the Label X property (the offset of the label to the right) to **–.05"**. (For metric, set the Label X property to **–.15 cm**.) Note that when you click the Text Box button in the Controls group, the top of the Property Sheet window shows Default Text Box.

Open the Field List window by clicking the Add Existing Fields button in the Tools group on the Design tab, and then click the Show Only Fields In The Current Record Source link (if necessary). Click the CompanyID field to select it, and hold down the Ctrl key while you click the CompanyName and Department fields to add them to the selection. Drag these fields together onto your form about 2 inches from the left edge and near the top of the Detail design area. Drag the Position field onto the form directly below Department. If you have Snap To Grid turned on, it should be easy to line up the controls. Otherwise, select all the text box controls and use the Align buttons in the Sizing & Ordering group on the Arrange tab to line them up. Set the Locked property of all text box controls to Yes. Select the label control attached to the CompanyID text box, and change the caption from Company/Org.: to **Company ID:**. At this stage, your design should look like Figure 15-13.

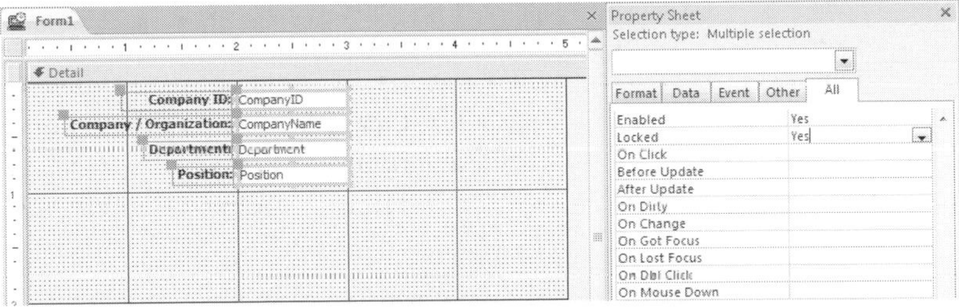

Figure 15-13 Your form to display company contact information is now beginning to take shape.

Embedding a Subform

You can use a couple of techniques to embed a subform in your outer form. First, you can cancel the selection of the Control Wizards button in the toolbox, select the Subform/Subreport tool in the Controls group, and then click the upper-left corner of the outer form's empty area and drag the mouse pointer to create a subform control. (If you leave the Control Wizards button selected, Access starts a wizard to help you build the subform when you place a subform control on your outer form. Because you already built the subform, you don't need the wizard's help.) After you have the subform control in place, set its Source Object property to point to the subform you built (or use the sample fsubXmplContactProducts).

A better way to embed the subform is to expand the Navigation pane, find the form you want to embed as a subform, and then drag it from the Navigation pane and place it on your form. To do this, expand the Navigation pane if you collapsed it, open the Navigation Pane menu, click Object Type under Navigate To Category, and then click Forms under Filter By Group to display the list of forms in the database. Click the subform you built in the previous section (or the fsubXmplContactProducts form that we supplied), and drag it onto your form at the left edge below the Position label and text box. Figure 15-14 shows this action in progress.

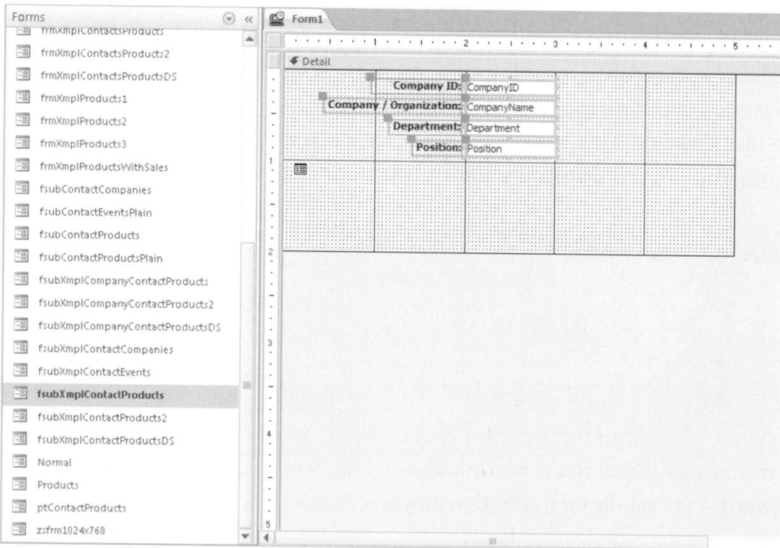

Figure 15-14 You can drag one form from the Navigation pane to the Design view of another form to create a subform.

Adding a subform in this way has the advantages that your new subform control will be sized correctly horizontally, will have a height to display at least one row, and will have some of its other properties automatically set. If the form you are designing has a table as its record source and Access can find related fields of the same name in the record source of the subform you're adding, then Access automatically defines the link properties as well. You'll have to set these properties yourself later in this exercise.

You don't need the label that Access added to your subform control, so you can select it and delete it. Click the subform control to select it (if you click more than once, you'll select an object on the form inside the subform control), drag the sizing handle in the middle of the bottom of the control so that it is about 2 inches high, and then click the To Fit button under the Size/Space command in the Sizing & Ordering group on the Arrange tab to correctly size the control to display multiple rows. Move up the bottom of the Detail section of the outer form if necessary so that there's only a small margin below the bottom of the resized subform control. Your form should look something like Figure 15-15.

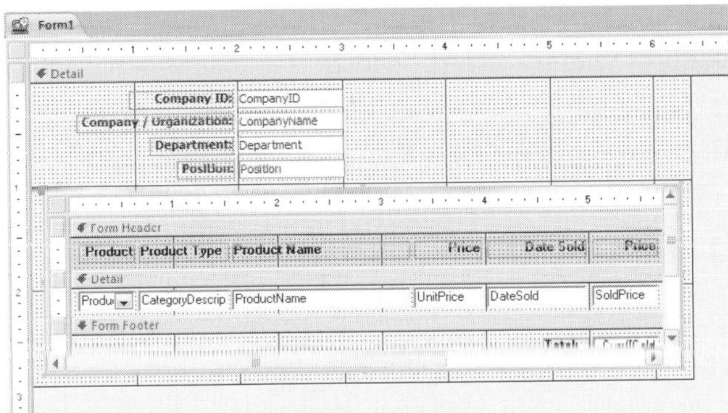

Figure 15-15 The contact products subform, embedded in your form, displays the products owned by a company contact.

INSIDE OUT Sizing a Subform Control

Sizing a subform that you display in Form view is quite simple. You might need to do this if you create the subform control directly on the form. Select the subform control, and then click To Fit under the Size/Space command in the Sizing & Ordering group von the Arrange tab. In this case, you're using a subform in Continuous Forms view, so Access will size the subform control to the correct width and to the nearest vertical height to fully display rows in the Detail section. Note that if your subform default view is Datasheet view, using the Size To Fit button won't work unless the form's Design view is exactly the same size as the datasheet. You have to switch in and out of Form view and manually adjust the size of the subform control.

You must set a couple of key properties to finish this work. If you remember from Figure 15-6, the tblCompanyContacts table is related to the tblContactProducts table on both the CompanyID and the ContactID fields. When you view records in an outer form and you want Access to filter the rows in the subform to show only related information, you must make sure that Access knows the field(s) that link the two sets of data. With the subform control selected, open the Property Sheet window and set the Link Child Fields and Link Master Fields properties, as shown in Figure 15-16.

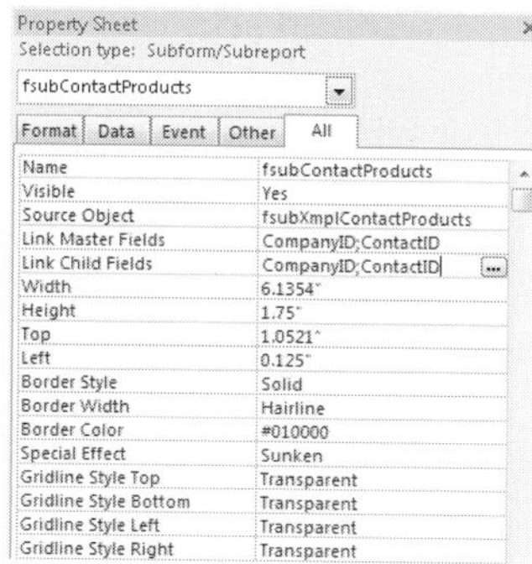

Figure 15-16 Set the link field properties of the subform control to tell Access how the data in the outer form is related to the data in the inner form.

The Link Child Fields property refers to the "child" form—the one in the subform. You must enter the names of the fields in the record source of the form inside the subform that should be filtered based on what row you have displayed in the outer form, separated by semicolons. Likewise, the Link Master Fields property should contain the name(s) of the related field(s) on the outer form. In most cases, both properties will contain only one field name, but the names might not be the same. In this case, you know it takes two fields to correctly relate the rows. Switch to Form view, and your form should look like Figure 15-17. As you move from record to record in the outer form, Access uses the values it finds in the field(s) defined in Link Master Fields as a filter against the fields in the subform defined in Link Child Fields.

INSIDE OUT

Use the Build Button to Set Master/Child Links

If you don't want to type in the link field properties, you can also click the Build button on either the Link Master Fields or Link Child Fields property line to open the Subform Linker Dialog box shown here.

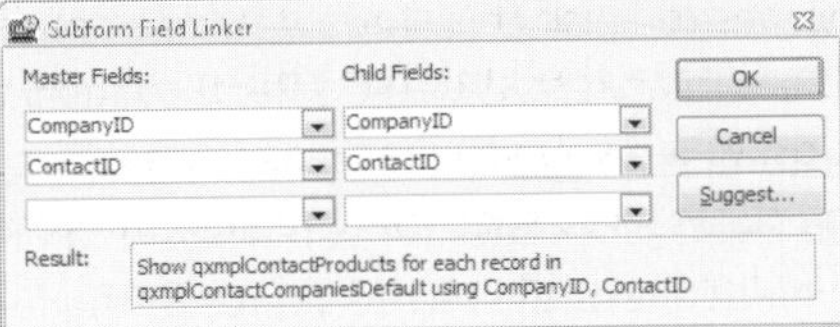

You can select the Master and Child fields from the respective combo boxes in the dialog box. When you click the drop-down lists, Access also displays the data type of each field next to the field name. Click Suggest and Access provides suggested link properties for the two forms.

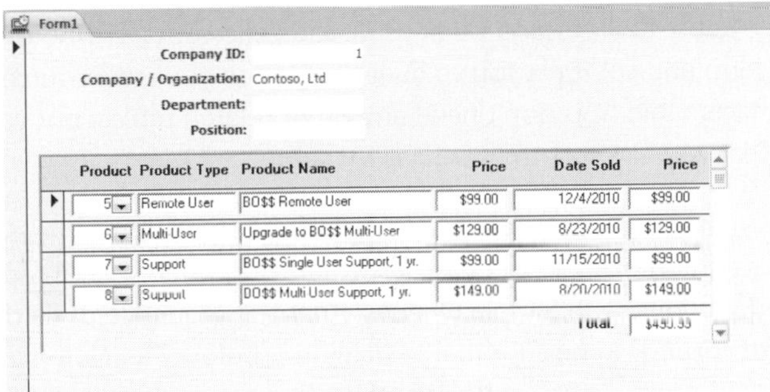

Figure 15-17 You now have a form to display company contact information with a subform that displays the related products owned.

We don't know which contact owns these products because we haven't built the final outer form yet to display contact information. You should return to Design view and make some adjustments to the length of the CompanyName, Department, and Position text boxes. You should also set the form's Scroll Bars property to Neither and the Record Selectors property to No. You really don't want users adding and deleting records in this outer form, so set Allow Additions and Allow Deletions to No. Save your form as fsubCompanyContactProducts. (Note that if you made any changes to the form inside the subform control, Access will ask you whether you want to save that form, too.) You can also find this form saved as fsubXmplCompanyContactProducts in the sample database.

INSIDE OUT **Access Might Create the Link for You**

If the record source of the outer form is a single table, Access automatically sets the Link Master Fields and Link Child Fields properties for you when it can find a related field in the table or query that you define as the record source of the form within the subform control. It does this when you either drag the subform to the main form or set the Source Object property of the subform control.

Specifying the Main Form Source

Now, it's time to create the main form. You need a table or a query as the source of the form. You want to be able to view (and perhaps update) the contacts who own the products shown in the form and subform you've built thus far, so your row source should include the tblContacts table. You don't need any other related tables, but you might want to use a query so that you can sort the contacts by name.

Start a new query on the tblContacts table, and include all the fields in the design grid. Add criteria to sort in ascending order under LastName and FirstName. (You'll recall from Chapter 9, "Creating and Working with Simple Queries," that the sequence of fields in the design grid is important for sorting, so be sure that LastName is before FirstName in the query design grid.) Save your query as qryContactsSorted. Your query should look something like that shown in Figure 15-18. You can find this query saved as qxmplContactsSorted in the sample database.

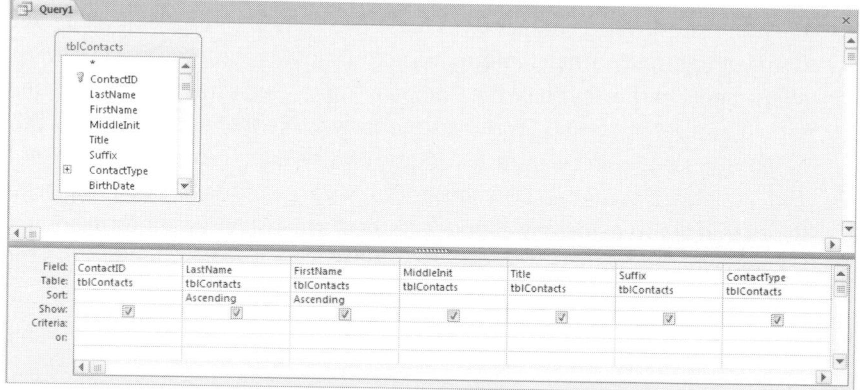

Figure 15-18 This query sorts the contact records to be used in a form.

Creating the Main Form

Building the form for the tblContacts table is fairly straightforward. In fact, you can use the Form Wizard to build the basic columnar format form from the query you just created. We recommend that you build this form from scratch, as you did to build the form for company contacts, because there are only a few fields you need to include, and you want to place them differently than the wizard would. To begin, click the Form Design button in the Forms group on the Create tab. Access opens a blank form grid in Design view. Open the Property Sheet window, and select in the Record Source property either the query you just built (qryContactsSorted) or the sample query we provided (qxmplContactsSorted).

As you did with the company contacts form, set some control defaults first. Click the Label button in the Controls group on the Design tab, and click the Bold button in the Font group to give all your labels a default bold font. Click Text Box, and change Label Align to Right and Label X (the offset of the label to the right) to **–0.05"**. (Use –0.15 cm for metric.) If you have Use Windows-Themed Controls On Forms enabled, also make sure that Border color is set to #010000 and Special Effect is set to Sunken. Click Combo Box, and make the same adjustments to the default Label Align, Label X, Border Color, and Special Effects properties.

Disable Use Control Wizards in the Controls group on the Design tab, open the Field List window, click the ContactType field, and with the combo box control still selected, drag the field about 1 inch from the left margin near the top of the design area. Add the Title, LastName, and Suffix fields, one at a time, in a column under ContactType. In a row aligned with the LastName text box, drag the FirstName field to about 3 inches out and the MiddleInit field to about 5 inches out. (Access expands the width of the design area when you do this.) You can shrink the MiddleInit text box to about a half-inch wide. Click the ContactType control, and in the Property Sheet window, change the Column Widths property to **1.25";0"**. By default, Access set this control to display two columns, but you need to display only the first column. Now, change the List Width property to **1.5"** to shorten the column display when you open the list in Form view, and change the Column Heads property to No.

The sample design shown in Figure 15-19 has a space at the bottom of the Detail section where you can place the subform to display company contact and product data. You can find this main form saved as frmXmplContacts1 in the sample database.

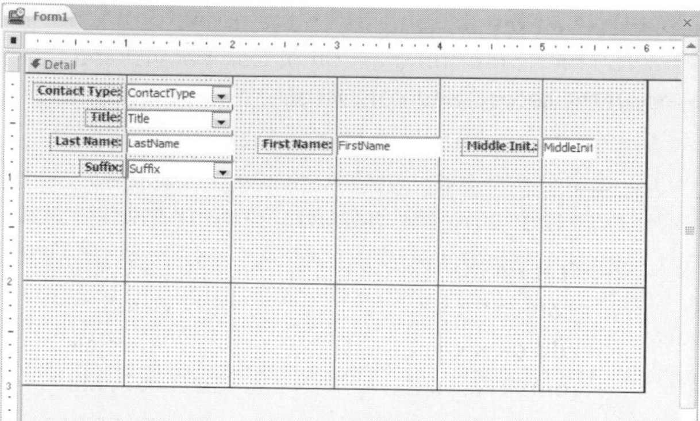

Figure 15-19 This is the start of your main form with space for a subform.

Now, you're ready to add the subform. This time, click the Subform/Subreport button in the Controls group on the Design tab (make sure the Control Wizards button is still turned off), and draw the control starting near the left edge under the Suffix combo box and extending to fill the blank area. Select the label control that came with the subform, and delete it. Select the subform control, open the Property Sheet window, and select the fsubCompanyContactProducts form you created earlier (or our sample fsubXmplCompanyContactProducts form) from the list in the Source Object property. Enter **ContactID** in the Link Child Fields and Link Master Fields properties. Finally, double-click one of the subform control sizing handles, or click the Size To Fit button under the Size/Space command in the Sizing & Ordering group on the Arrange tab to properly size the subform control. Your result should look something like Figure 15-20. Save your form as frmContactsProducts. You can find this form saved as frmXmplContactsProducts in the sample database.

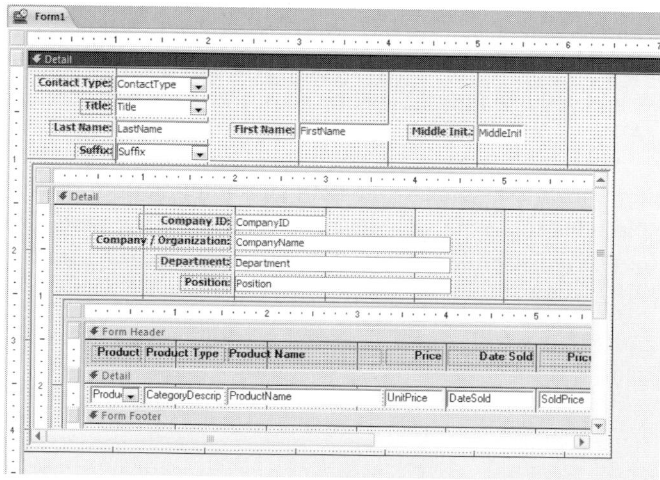

Figure 15-20 The new subform is embedded in the form to edit contacts.

In this case, the ContactID field from tblContacts on the outer form is the link to the related rows on the subform. If you recall, the combination of CompanyID and ContactID forms the link between the forms on the second and third level.

INSIDE OUT Editing the Form Inside a Subform Control

Access 2000 introduced a feature that allows you to directly edit your subform after you have defined it as the source for your subform control. As you can see in Figure 15-20, the design of the fsubCompanyContactProducts form is visible in the subform control on the outermost form. Likewise, the design of the fsubContactProducts form is visible inside that. You can click any control in the inner forms and change its size or adjust its properties using the property sheet or the contextual ribbon tabs under Form Design Tools and Form Layout Tools. You might need to temporarily expand the size of the subform control to work with the inner form easily. However, you cannot click the File tab on the Backstage view and then click Save As to save your changes to a different form definition. If you want to edit the form inside a subform control in its own window, right-click the subform control, and then click Subform In New Window.

Switch to Form View to see the completed form, as shown in Figure 15-21. Because you properly set the linking field information for the subform controls, you can see the companies for each contact and the products for each company and contact in the subforms as you move from one contact to another. Note that the inner set of navigation buttons is for the first subform. Use the scroll bar in the innermost subform to move through the product detail records. Also, because you locked the controls in the first subform (the company contact information), you cannot edit the controls you see there.

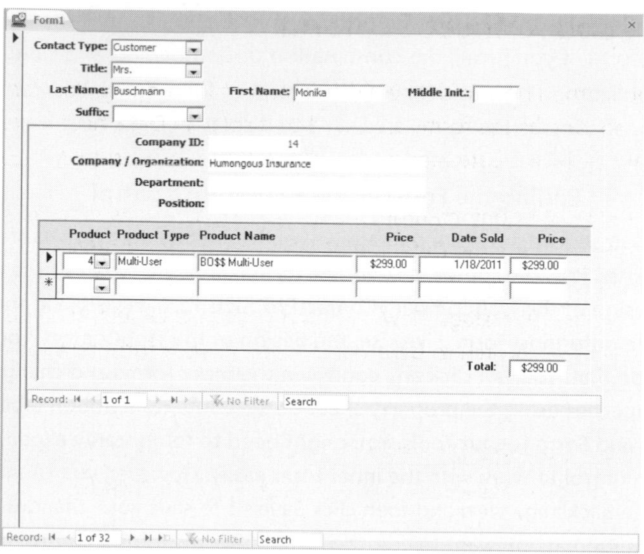

Figure 15-21 You now have a form to edit contacts in a main form and products owned by the contact in subforms.

Note

If you look at the frmContacts form in the Conrad Systems Contacts application, you'll see a products subform on the Products tab that has no intervening company contacts subform. This form has some Microsoft Visual Basic procedures that automatically supply the default company ID for the contact and disallow adding a product if the contact doesn't have a default company defined. You can see how this code works in Chapter 25, "Automating Your Application with Visual Basic," on the companion CD.

INSIDE OUT Using Subreports in Forms

Access 2010 now includes the ability to embed reports directly into forms as subreports. The procedures and usage for subreports are the same as the ones for subforms that you just learned about. You can set the Source Object property to the name of a report and you can optionally set the Link Child Fields and Link Master Fields properties to have the subreport display matching values as you tab through the records in the main form.

Creating a Subdatasheet Subform

In Chapter 9, you learned how to define a subdatasheet for a query. You can do the same thing with forms so long as the forms are saved to display in Datasheet view. The best way to see how this works is to create modified versions of the three forms you just built.

Start by opening your fsubContactProducts form (or the sample fsubXmplContactProducts form) in Design view. Change the Default View property of the form to Datasheet, change the Allow Datasheet View property to Yes, and save the form as fsubContactProductsDS. (Click the File tab on the Backstage view and then click Save Object As. Type the new object name, and then click OK.) Switch to Datasheet view, and your form now looks like Figure 15-22.

fsubContactProducts

CategoryDescription	ProductName	UnitPrice	DateSol	SoldPrice	ProductID
Single User	BO$$ Demo Edition, Single User	$0.00	#########	$0.00	1
Single User	BO$$ Demo Edition, Single User	$0.00	9/20/2010	$0.00	1
Single User	BO$$ Demo Edition, Single User	$0.00	#########	$0.00	1
Single User	BO$$ Demo Edition, Single User	$0.00	#########	$0.00	1
Single User	BO$$ Demo Edition, Single User	$0.00	10/2/2010	$0.00	1
Single User	BO$$ Demo Edition, Single User	$0.00	#########	$0.00	1
Multi-User	BO$$ Demo Edition, Multi-User	$0.00	#########	$0.00	2
Multi-User	BO$$ Demo Edition, Multi-User	$0.00	7/31/2010	$0.00	2
Multi-User	BO$$ Demo Edition, Multi-User	$0.00	1/15/2011	$0.00	2
Multi-User	BO$$ Demo Edition, Multi-User	$0.00	9/26/2010	$0.00	2
Multi-User	BO$$ Demo Edition, Multi-User	$0.00	1/11/2011	$0.00	2
Multi-User	BO$$ Demo Edition, Multi-User	$0.00	9/10/2010	$0.00	2
Multi-User	BO$$ Demo Edition, Multi-User	$0.00	#########	$0.00	2
Multi-User	BO$$ Demo Edition, Multi-User	$0.00	1/3/2011	$0.00	2
Single User	BO$$ Single User	$199.00	#########	$199.00	3
Single User	BO$$ Single User	$199.00	#########	$199.00	3
Single User	BO$$ Single User	$199.00	1/6/2011	$199.00	3
Single User	BO$$ Single User	$199.00	8/20/2010	$199.00	3
Single User	BO$$ Single User	$199.00	#########	$199.00	3
Single User	BO$$ Single User	$199.00	#########	$199.00	3
Single User	BO$$ Single User	$199.00	#########	$199.00	3
Single User	BO$$ Single User	$199.00	10/3/2010	$199.00	3
Multi-User	BO$$ Multi-User	$299.00	8/10/2010	$299.00	4
Multi-User	BO$$ Multi-User	$299.00	#########	$299.00	4
Multi-User	BO$$ Multi-User	$299.00	1/18/2011	$299.00	4
Multi-User	BO$$ Multi-User	$299.00	#########	$299.00	4
Multi-User	BO$$ Multi-User	$299.00	12/7/2010	$299.00	4
Multi-User	BO$$ Multi-User	$299.00	1/18/2011	$299.00	4
Remote User	BO$$ Remote User	$99.00	12/4/2010	$99.00	5

Figure 15-22 The contact products subform was changed to display in Datasheet view.

Notice that several of the columns are much wider than they need to be and the DateSold column is too narrow. If you scroll down to the bottom, you don't see the subtotal that's in the form footer anymore. Also, because the labels for these fields are in the form header (see Figure 15-11) and are not attached to their respective controls, you see the actual field names instead of the field captions. Let's not worry about the captions for now, but you should adjust the column widths to be more reasonable. You can do that by double-clicking the dividing line to the right of each column heading. This auto-sizes the columns to the widest data (or column caption) displayed. If the data you see isn't representative of the widest data you might store, you need to adjust the width by hand. You must save the form again to preserve this sizing, so click the Save button on the Quick Access Toolbar, and then close the form. You can find this form saved as fsubXmplContactProductsDS in the sample database.

Next, open your fsubCompanyContactProducts form (or the fsubXmplCompanyContact-Products sample form) in Design view. Change the Default View of the form to Datasheet. Click the subform control to select it, and change the Source Object property to point to the new datasheet subform you just saved—fsubContactProductsDS. Save the form as fsubCompanyContactProductsDS.

If you like, you can select the form again and change the Subdatasheet Height and Sub-datasheet Expanded properties. Because both this form and the embedded subform are set to be displayed in Datasheet view, you can set these properties exactly as you would for a table or query. You can specify a specific height in inches that you want to reserve for the subdatasheet (the subform inside this form). If you leave the default value of 0", the subdatasheet opens to display all available rows when you click the plus sign on any row to expand the subdatasheet for that row. You can also change Subdatasheet Expanded to Yes to always expand all subdatasheets within the subform when you open the form (as though you clicked the plus sign on all displayed rows). For now, leave these properties as is.

Switch to Datasheet view, and your form should look like Figure 15-23.

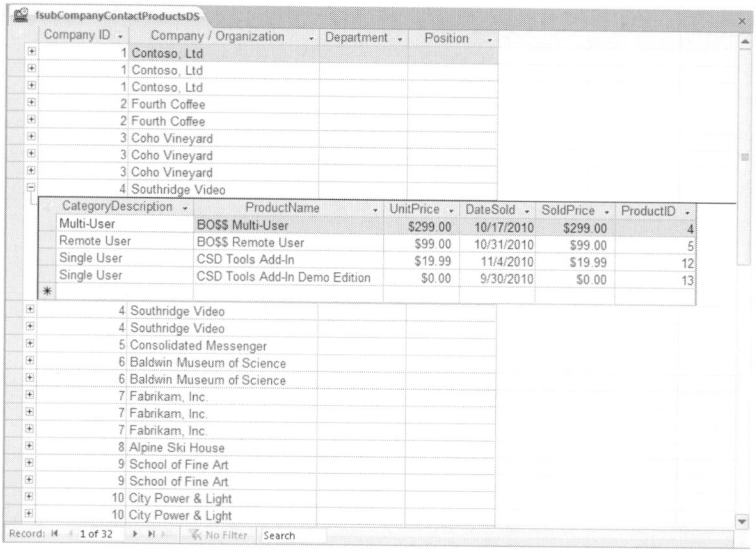

Figure 15-23 Your form now displays company contact information in Datasheet view with a subdatasheet to display products.

Because the controls on this form have attached labels (see Figure 15-15), the captions from those labels display as the column headings. Notice that the subdatasheet form has its columns sized as you saved them when you designed the subform. You can resize the columns in either display and save the form to save the new column width settings. Keep in mind that your user is also free to resize the column widths. However, because these are forms, you have more control over what the user can do than you have in a query. Try to type something in the Company / Organization or Department column. Because the controls in the underlying form are locked, you won't be able to update this information. Close this form now, and save it if you are prompted.

To finish putting this all together, you can now edit your frmContactsProducts form (or the frmXmplContactsProducts sample form) to use these new datasheet subforms. Open your form in Design view, click the subform control to select it, and change its Source Object property to fsubCompanyContactProductsDS. You also need to make the subform control about 7.75 inches wide because the subform in Datasheet view won't fit in the current window. However, you can also shorten the height of the subform control to about 1.5 inches.

Save your modified form as frmContactsProductsDS, and switch to Form view. Your form should now look like Figure 15-24.

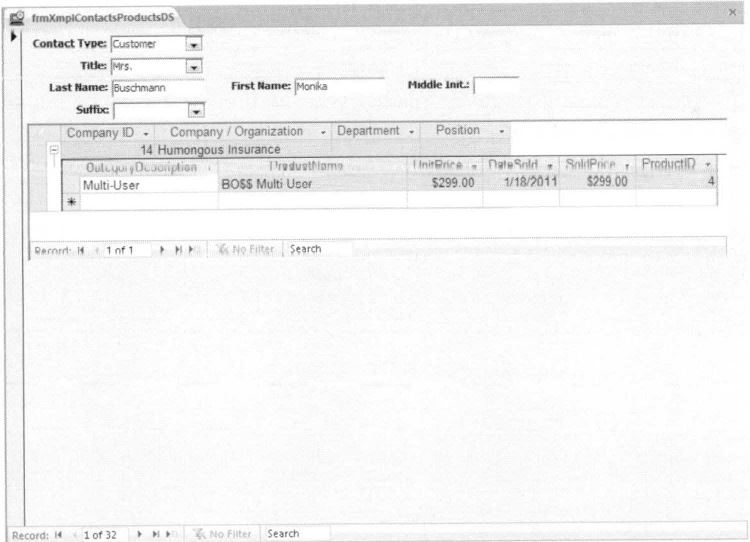

Figure 15-24 Your modified form now allows you to edit contacts in a main form and products owned by the contact in subforms displayed in Datasheet view.

Remember that one of the shortcomings of designing your form this way is you have to make a "best guess" at the size of the subform window, and your users can modify the width of the columns in both datasheets as they wish. We personally don't like this design very much, but you might find it useful to conserve vertical space in a subform design when displaying complex data levels. You can find this form saved as frmXmplContactsProductsDS in the sample database.

Displaying Values in an Option Group

Whenever you have a field that contains an integer code value, you need to provide some way for the user to set the value based on what your application knows the code means, not the number. You could certainly use a combo box or a list box to supply a descriptive list. However, when the number of different values is small, an option group might be the ideal solution.

In the Conrad Systems Contacts application, the tblContacts table contains both a home and a work address. The DefaultAddress field contains an integer code value that is used by some reports to generate a mailing address. When DefaultAddress is 1, the application uses the work address, and when DefaultAddress is 2, the home address is the default. However, a user isn't likely to always remember that 1 means work and 2 means home. You should provide a way to make these values obvious.

In the ContactsDataCopy.accdb sample file, you can find a form called frmXmplContacts that has the basic contact information and the two sets of addresses already laid out. Figure 15-25 shows you that form in Form view.

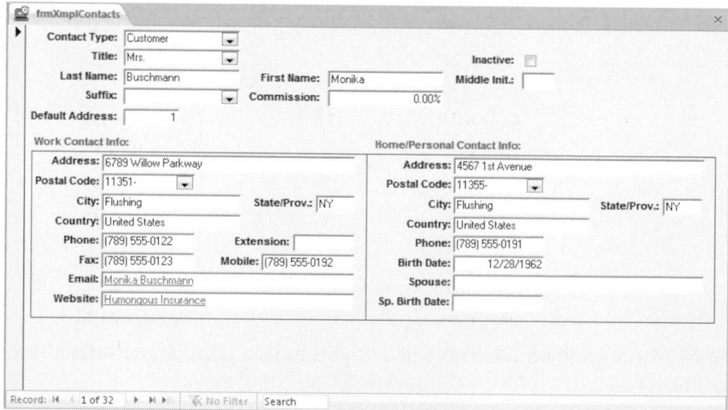

Figure 15-25 You can use this form to edit contact name and address information.

You can see that the Default Address field could be confusing on this form. To fix this, switch to Design view, and delete the DefaultAddress text box control. Click the Option Group button in the Controls group on the Design tab to select it, and then open the field list and drag the Default Address field to the form under the Suffix combo box control. (We set the defaults for the option group control on this form so that it should fit nicely under the Suffix control and be wide enough to add some buttons.)

Next, right-click the Option Button command in the Controls group on the Design tab and click Drop Multiple Controls to allow you to define multiple buttons without having to go back to the Controls group to click the button again. When you move your mouse pointer inside the option group control, you'll see the control becomes highlighted, indicating you're placing the button inside the control. Drag one toward the left end of the control (the label will appear to the right of the button) and a second one to the middle. Figure 15-26 shows what the form looks like as you add the second button.

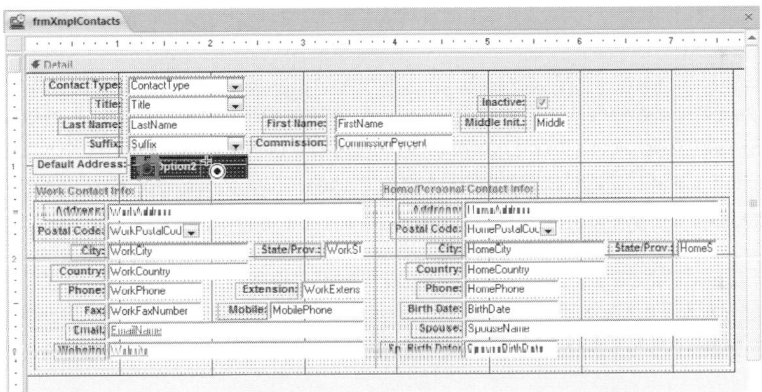

Figure 15-26 Add two option button controls inside an option group control.

Click the Select button in the Controls group on the Design tab to turn off the Option Button tool. Click the first button, and open the Property Sheet window. Near the top of the list on the All tab, you can see that Access has set the Option Value property of this button to 1. If you click the other button, you'll find that its Option Value property is 2. Because the option group control is bound to the DefaultValue field, the first button will be highlighted when you're on a record that has a value of 1 (work address) in this field, and the second button will be highlighted when the value is 2. If you click a different button when editing a record, Access changes the value of the underlying field to the value of the button.

You can actually assign any integer value you like to each option button in a group, but Access has set these just fine for this field. Note that if you assign the same value to more than one button, they'll all appear selected when you're on a record that has that value.

To make the purpose of these buttons perfectly clear, you need to fix the attached labels. Click the label for the first button, and change the Caption property from Option2 to **Work**. Set the Caption property for the label attached to the second button to **Home**. Switch to Form view to see the results, as shown in Figure 15-27. Save this form as frmContacts2. You can also find this form saved as frmXmplContacts2 in the sample database.

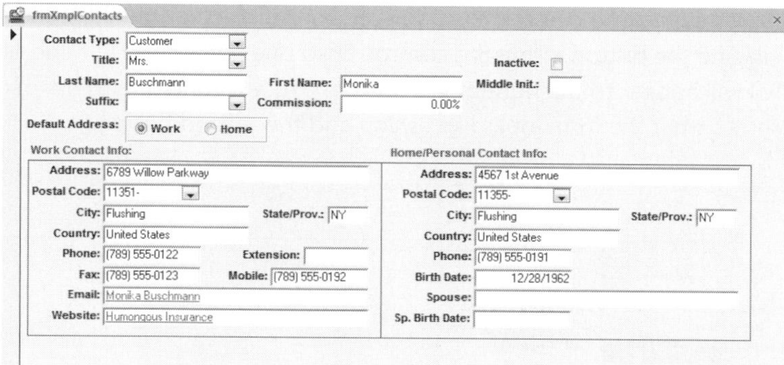

Figure 15-27 You can use an option group to set the default address for the contacts.

Using Conditional Formatting in Client Forms

Access includes a feature that allows you to define dynamic modification of the formatting of text boxes and combo boxes on client forms. (Web forms do not support conditional formatting.) You can define an expression that tests the value in the text box or combo box or any other field available in the form. If the expression is true, Access will modify the Bold, Italic, Underline, Back Color, Fore Color, and Enabled properties for you based on the custom settings you associate with the expression.

This feature can be particularly useful for controlling field display in a subform in Continuous Forms view. For example, you might want to highlight the ProductName field in the innermost subform shown in Figure 15-21 when the product is a trial version; or you might want to change the font of the address fields in the form shown in Figure 15-27 depending on the value of the DefaultAddress field.

For the first example, you can use the fsubCompanyContactProducts subform that you built earlier (or the *fsubXmplCompanyContactProducts* sample form you'll find in the sample database). To define conditional formatting, first open the form you need to modify in

Design view. Click the subform control, and then click the ProductName field within the subform to select it. On the Format tab, in the Control Formatting group, click the Conditional Formatting button to see the Conditional Formatting Rules Manager dialog box, as shown in Figure 15-28. In the Show Formatting Rules For combo box, Access displays a list of all names of controls that support conditional formatting. You can create, edit, and delete conditional formatting rules for the controls on your form by selecting the control name from this combo box, without having to close the dialog box to select a different control. In previous versions of Access, you were limited to three conditional formatting rules for each control. In Access 2010, you can now have up to 50 conditional formatting rules for each control.

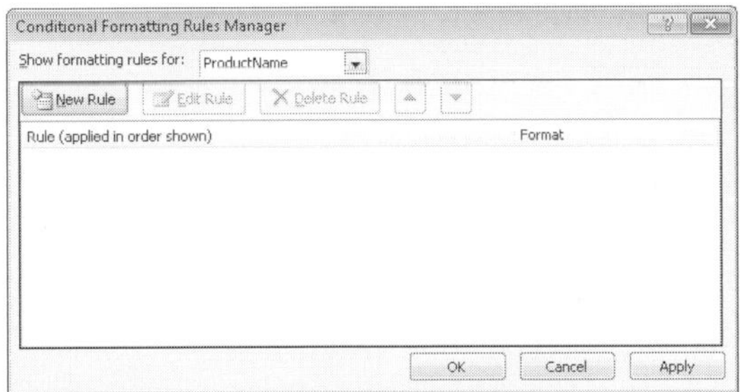

Figure 15-28 You can create, edit, and delete conditional formatting for controls using the Conditional Formatting Rules Manager dialog box.

To begin creating a new conditional formatting rule for the ProductName text box, select ProductName in the Show Formatting Rules For combo box (it should already be selected), and then click the New Rule button to open the New Formatting Rule dialog box, as shown in Figure 15-29. In Select A Rule Type, you can choose to create a conditional formatting rule that checks other values in the current record or use an expression. You can also choose to compare the value of this control with values in the same control for other records (we'll do the second option in just a moment). For this ProductName control rule, select Check Value In The Current Record Or Use An Expression. Access displays a single blank condition rule under the Select A Rule Type list box. In the leftmost list, you can choose Field Value Is to test for a value in the field, Expression Is to create a logical expression that can test other fields on the form or compare another field with this one, and Field Has Focus to define settings that the control will inherit when the user clicks in the control.

When you choose Field Value Is, the dialog box displays a second list with logical comparison options such as Less Than, Equal To, or Greater Than. Choose the logical comparison you want, and then enter the value or values to compare the field with in the text boxes on the right.

In this case, you want to set the format of ProductName based on the value of the TrialVersion field. So, choose Expression Is, and in the expression box, enter the following:

```
[TrialVersion]=True
```

If you need assistance creating your expression, you can click the Builder button to the right of the expression text box to open the Expression Builder. Set the formatting properties you want the control to have if the test is true by using the buttons to the right. You can use the Bold, Italic, Underline, Background Color, Font Color, and Enabled buttons to modify the default. In this case, set the Background Color to a bright yellow, as shown in Figure 15-29, and click OK to save the new rule.

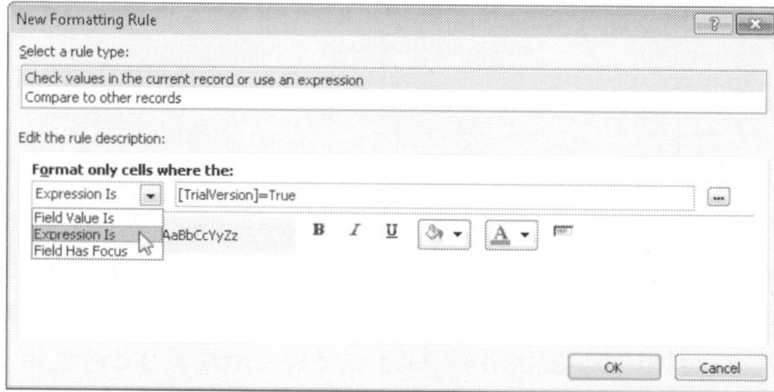

Figure 15-29 Define conditional formatting for the ProductName field using the New Formatting Rule dialog box.

You should now be back in the Conditional Formatting Rules Manager dialog box. Click Apply to save the rule changes you've created so far. Select UnitPrice in the Show Formatting Rules For combo box to define a new conditional formatting rule for the UnitPrice control. Note that if you did not click Apply before choosing a new control, Access prompts you that you will lose the rule changes if you don't apply the changes. You can choose to continue and discard your changes, continue but have Access apply the changes first, or cancel and stay in the current control. Click New Rule to open the New Formatting Rule dialog box again.

Access 2010 includes a new feature for conditional formatting called *data bars*. In the previous example, you created a conditional formatting rule that compares values only within the current record. Data bars allow you to compare values in the same control to other records. Data bars give a visual indication of how the value in this control compares to values in other records by displaying a colored bar inside the control. Access fills a proportional amount of the background color from the left side to indicate what percentage the current value has compared to the other records. For example, if the value in the current record is the highest value in all records, Access fills the entire control from left to right with a background color to indicate that it has the maximum value. (If you're using a right-to-left form orientation, Access fills the control from right to left.) Select the option Compare To Other Records under the Select A Rule Type to display the data bar rules description, as shown in Figure 15-30.

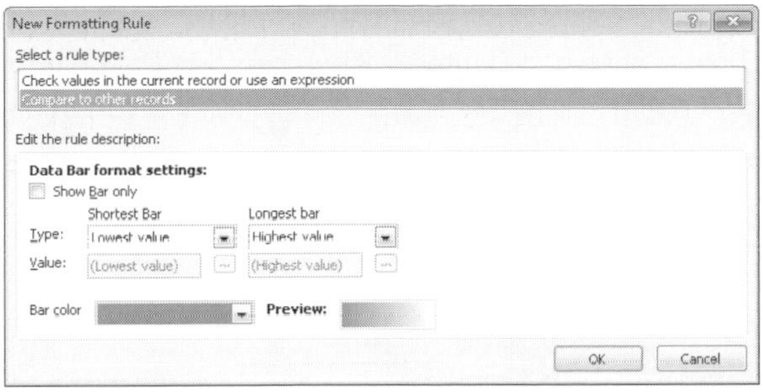

Figure 15-30 Define data bar rules to compare values across other records.

If you leave the Show Bar Only option cleared, Access displays the value of the control and fills the background color of the control. Select this option if you want Access only to fill the background color, not show control values. Under Shortest Bar and Longest Bar, Access displays two options—Type and Value. In the Type combo box, you can select to use Lowest Value (or Highest Value under Longest Bar), Number, or Percent. If you use the default, Lowest Value or Highest Value, Access uses the lowest and highest values it finds in the control for all records returned by the form's record source. If you select Number or Percent, Access enables the Value text box controls. In the Value text boxes, you can specify a specific value or percent for Access to use when it compares the control values for each record. On the right side of the Value text boxes, you can click the Builder button to open the Expression Builder if you want assistance building an expression to be used for the Value text boxes. For our example, leave the options here set on their defaults.

INSIDE OUT Opening Conditional Formatting Rules in Previous Versions of Access

If you open a form that includes the new data bar conditional formatting in previous versions of Access, you will not see the data bars in your form controls. Previous versions of Access do not know how to interpret these types of conditional formatting rules across other records, so they ignore these rules. If you define more than three conditional formatting rules on a form in Access 2010 and open that form in previous versions of Access, you will see only the first three rules applied. Previous versions of Access can understand only three conditional formatting rules, so that is all you will see displayed.

You can click the down arrow on the Bar Color combo box to select a background color to use for the data bar. Access displays a preview of your color choice to the right of the Preview label. In this example, click the down arrow next to Bar Color and set the bar color to a lighter blue than the default dark blue, as shown previously in Figure 15-30. Click OK to save your changes. Access displays your new data bar rule in the Conditional Formatting Rules Manager dialog box, as shown in Figure 15-31. Access lists Data Bar for each conditional formatting rule you define as a data bar. Access displays the conditional expression in this space if you define a rule that uses an expression.

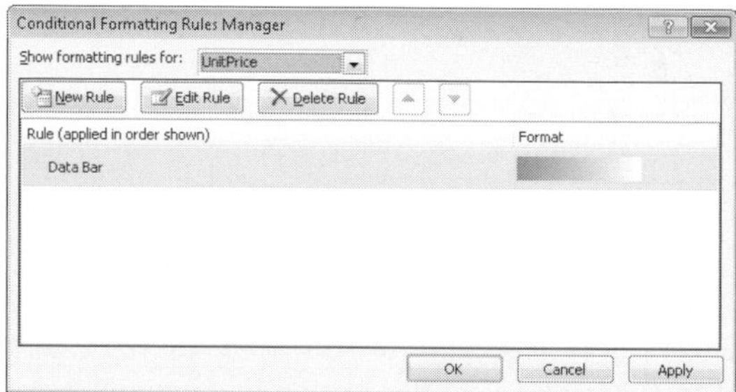

Figure 15-31 Access displays any saved rules for your controls in the Conditional Formatting Rules Manager dialog box.

If you need to edit your saved conditional rule, highlight the rule in the bottom half of the dialog box and then click Edit Rule. Access opens the New Formatting Rule dialog box again, where you can adjust your rule settings. If you want to delete an existing rule, highlight the rule and then click Delete Rule. If you have more than one conditional formatting rule for a control, you can use the Move Up and Move Down buttons to the right of the Delete Rule button to change the order in which Access evaluates your rules. Select a rule and then click Move Up to move the rule up one position in the sequence. Similarly, highlight a rule and click Move Down to move the rule down one position in the sequence. Click OK to save your changes for these two controls.

INSIDE OUT Using Multiple Data Bar Rules on the Same Control

You can define more than one data bar rule for a specific control. When you view the form in Form view, Access displays the colors you define in equal proportions across the height of the control.

Switch to Form view to see the result, as shown in Figure 15-32, and move to the third company record. You can find the sample saved as fsubXmplCompanyContactProducts2 and the inner subform saved as fsubXmplContactProducts2.

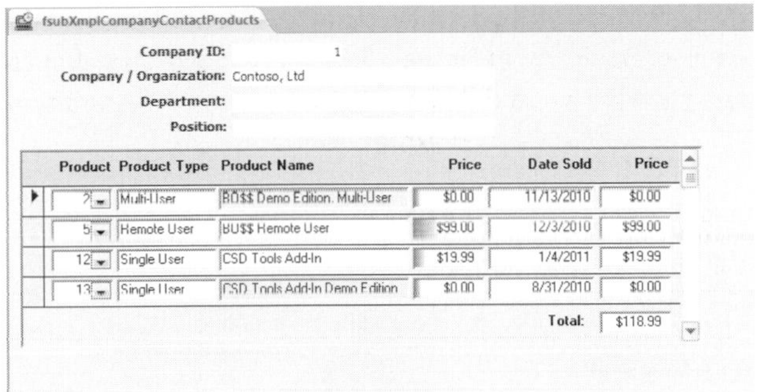

Figure 15-32 You can now see the effect of defining conditional formatting for the ProductName and UnitPrice fields.

INSIDE OUT Using Field and Data Bar Rules on the Same Control

Access allows you to create conditional formatting rules that compare values in the same record and values across other records (data bars) for the same control. You need to be aware that if you have the data bar rule first, Access ignores any formatting rules after the data bar rule that compares values in the same record. To work around this issue, move any data bar rules to the bottom of the sequence order.

You can make a similar change to frmContacts2, which you saved earlier, or you can use the sample frmXmplContacts2 form. Open that form in Design view, click the WorkAddress text box control to select it, and hold down the Shift key as you click the WorkPostalCode, WorkCity, and WorkStateOrProvince controls to add them to the selection. (Yes, you can set conditional formatting for multiple controls at one time.) Click the Conditional Formatting button in the Control Formatting group on the Format tab to see the Conditional Formatting Rules Manager dialog box.

In the Show Formatting Rules For combo box, Access displays Multiple to indicate you have selected multiple controls to apply conditional formatting rules. Click New Rule to begin defining a new rule for these four controls. Select Check Values In The Current Record Or Use An Expression under Select A Rule Type. Next, choose Expression Is in the leftmost list, and enter **[DefaultAddress]=1** in the Condition field to test whether the default is the work address. Underline and set the Background Color to yellow to highlight the text, as shown in Figure 15-33, and click OK to close the dialog box and set the conditional formatting for the controls you selected. Now, click OK on the Conditional Formatting Rules Manager dialog box to save your changes and close the dialog box.

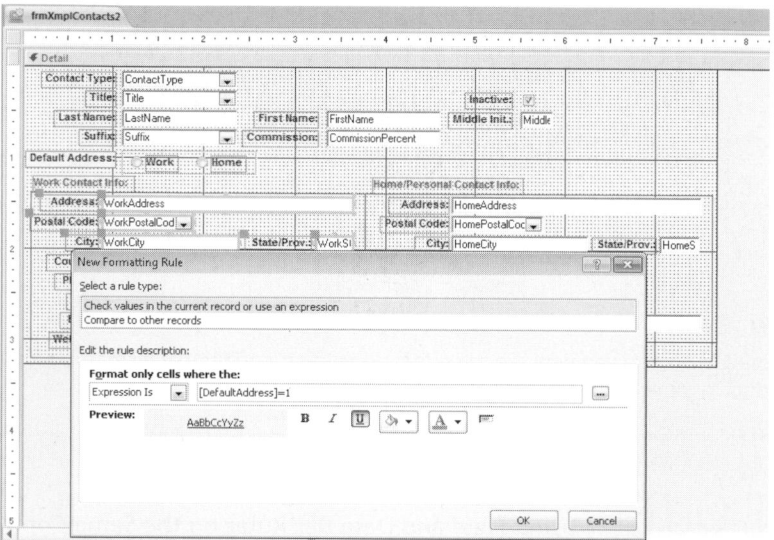

Figure 15-33 You can also define conditional formatting for a group of controls.

Click the HomeAddress text box, and hold down the Shift key as you click HomePostalCode, HomeCity, and HomeStateOrProvince to add them to the selection. Click the Conditional Formatting button in the Control Formatting group again, click New Rule, and then select Check Values In The Current Record Or Use An Expression to begin defining a new rule for these controls. Choose Expression Is in the leftmost list, enter **[DefaultAddress]=2** in the condition field, and underline and set the Background Color to yellow to highlight the text. Click OK to save the change to this rule on the New Formatting Rule dialog box, click OK on the Conditional Formatting Rules Manager dialog box, and then save your form as frmContacts3. Switch to Form view to see the result, as shown in Figure 15-34. All the records in the database have the work address as the default, so try changing the Default Address in one of the records to Home, and you should see the highlight move to the home address fields. You can also find this form saved as frmXmplContacts3 in the sample database.

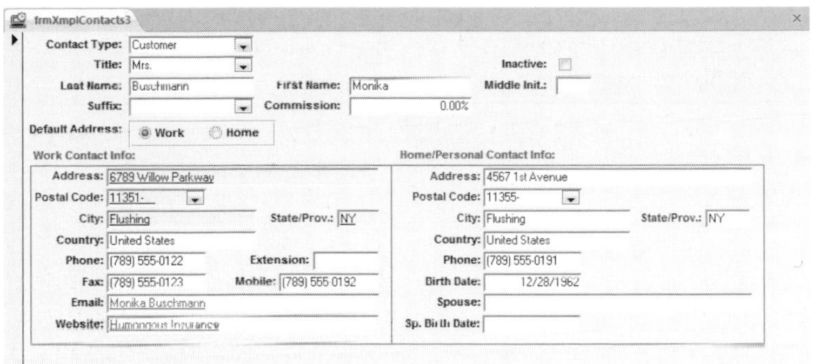

Figure 15-34 The default address fields are highlighted and underlined in the contacts form based on the value of the DefaultAddress field.

To define additional tests, click the New Rule button in the bottom half of the Conditional Formatting Rules Manager dialog box. For example, you might want to set the background of product name to one color if it's a trial version and use another color for products priced greater than $200.

Working with the Tab Control

As you have just seen, a subform is an excellent way to create a form that lets you edit information from the *one* side of a relationship in the main form (contacts) while editing or viewing data from the *many* side of a relationship (contact events or contact products) in the subform window. Building a subform is very simple for a single one-to-many relationship. But what can you do when you have either multiple relationships or lots of data you need to deal with on a form, and including all this information makes your form too large to fit on your screen? Access provides a tab control that lets you place multiple controls on individual tabs within a form. The controls on a tab can be as complex as subforms (in the case of the Conrad Systems Contacts database, to display related companies, events, and products) or as simple as text boxes (which can display the potentially lengthy information in the Notes field). You can see the frmContactsPlain form (the simple copy of the form that doesn't have all the advanced features of the production form) with the tab that shows contact events selected in Figure 15-35. You can select the other available tabs to see the detail information for the contact—the companies associated with the contacts (in a subform on that tab)—and the products the contact has purchased (in another subform).

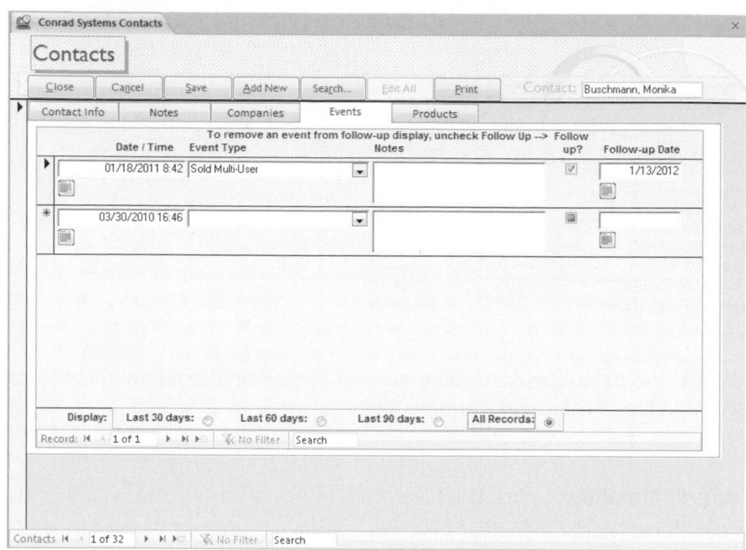

Figure 15-35 The tab control allows you to place multiple subforms and controls on a tab page, such as this tab, to edit contact events.

Working with the tab control is quite simple. If you like, you can start with a simple columnar form built by the Form Wizard. Use qxmplContactsSorted as the record source, and include the ContactType, Title, LastName, FirstName, MiddleInit, and Suffix fields. Switch to Design view, and create some space at the bottom of the form to add your tab control. You can also start with frmXmplContacts1, which you can find in the ContactsDataCopy.accdb sample database. To build a control that lets you alternately see company, contact event, or liner notes information for the current contact, perform the following steps:

1. On the Design tab, in the Controls group, click Tab Control, and drag an area on the form starting on the left side just under the Suffix combo box control and approximately 6.25 inches wide and 2 inches high. Access shows you a basic tab control with two tabs defined. Open the Property Sheet window, and set the Tab Fixed Width property to **1"** so that all the tabs will be the same size and wide enough to add captions later.

2. While the tab control has the focus, click the Insert Page button in the Controls group on the Design tab, as shown here. Access will add a third tab to the control.

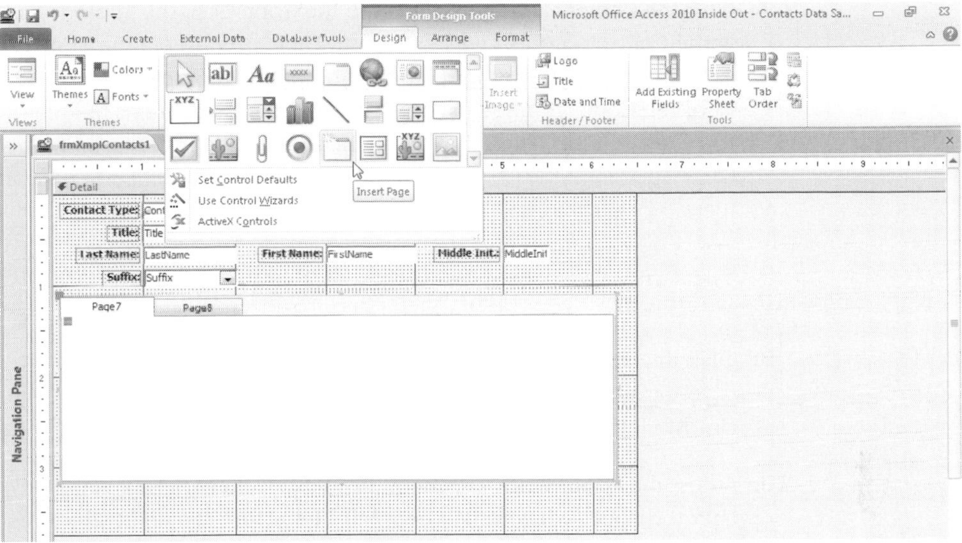

3. Access always inserts new tabs at the end of the tab sequence. If you want to place the new tab in the middle of the tab order, you can select the tab and set its Page Index property. The Page Index of the first tab is 0, the second is 1, and so on. Another way to set the tab sequence is to right-click the control and then click Page Order to see the dialog box shown next. Select a tab, and move it up or down to get the sequence you want.

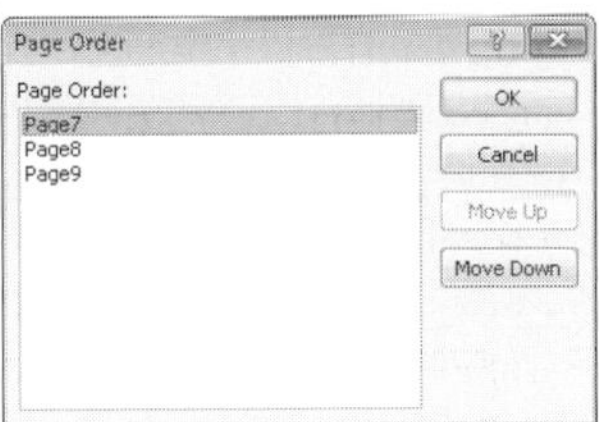

4. Click the first tab, open the Property Sheet window (if it's not already open), and set the Caption property to Companies.

5. Click the second tab, and set the Caption property to Events.

6. Click the third tab, and set the Caption property to Notes.

7. Click the Companies tab to bring it to the front. Click the Subform/Subreport button in the Controls group, and set the Auto Label property in the Property Sheet window to No. Add a subform control to the Companies tab, set its Source Object property to fsubXmplContactCompanies (the sample database contains built-in subforms to make this exercise easy), and set the Link Child Fields and Link Master Fields properties to ContactID. You can also drag the subform from the Navigation pane and place it on the tab if you like.

8. Click the Events tab, and add the fsubXmplContactEvents form to that tab as a subform. Be sure to set the link properties of the subform control to ContactID.

9. Click the Notes tab to bring it to the front. Open the field list, drag the Notes field onto this tab, and remove the attached label. Expand the Notes text box control to almost fill the tab.

10. Adjust the positioning and size of the controls on each tab. Place each control very near the upper-left corner of each tab. The actual Top and Left settings will vary depending on where you placed the tab control. (These settings are relative to the Detail section of the form, not the tab control.) You can place one where you want it and then copy the Top and Left settings to the other two controls so that they exactly line up. It's important you do this so that the controls don't appear to jump around on the tab control as you move from tab to tab. Select each control, and then click the To Fit button under the Size/Space command in the Sizing & Ordering group on the Arrange tab.

Save the changes to your form as frmContacts4. Your result up to this point should look something like Figure 15-36. You can find this form saved as frmXmplContacts4 in the sample database. Note that clicking each tab in Design view reveals the controls you stored on that tab.

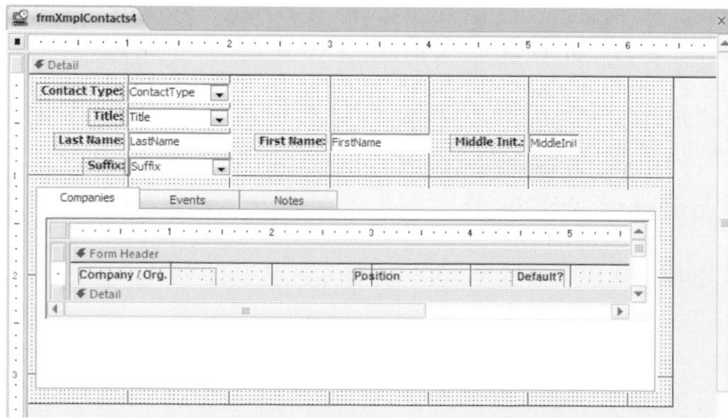

Figure 15-36 Your tab control in Design view shows three tabs with various controls.

Access 2010 includes several new formatting features you can use to customize the look and feel of your tab control. Select the tab control and then click the Change Shape button in the Control Formatting group on the Format tab. Access displays a gallery of eight shape styles you can use to change the shape of your tabs, as shown in Figure 15-37. The default shape for tabs is Rectangle, but let's select a different tab style for our form. Click the shape called Round Same Side Corner Rectangle to give your tabs a more rounded edge instead of the default sharp edges.

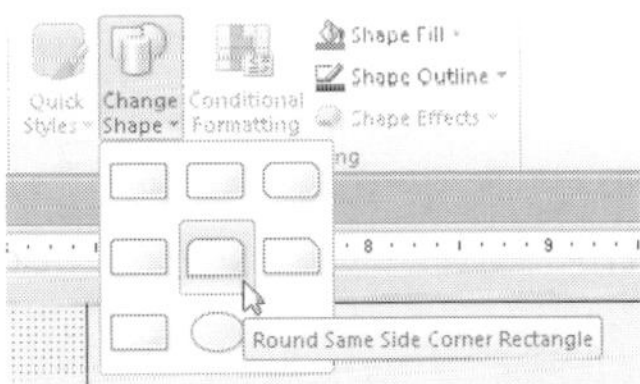

Figure 15-37 You can choose from a gallery of eight shape styles for tabs.

Now that you've applied a new shape style, Access changes the Use Theme property of the tab control to Yes because you are using one of the new theme styles in Access 2010. You cannot see the caption on the first tab because Access changes the Hover Fore Color and Pressed Fore Color properties to white, which blends in with the background. Open the Property Sheet window, select the tab control, and change these two properties so we can see the caption clearly. On the Hover Fore Color property, select the Dark Blue standard color option (you can enter **#2F3699** directly into the property if you want). The Hover Fore Color property lists the color used for the tab captions when you hover over the tab. Move down to the Pressed Fore Color property and select the Black standard color from the color picker. The Pressed Fore Color property lists the color used for the tab captions when you click a tab.

You can further customize the tab control by providing some color and gradients to the tabs. Select the tab control, click the Shape Fill command in the Control Formatting group on the Arrange tab, and then click Dark Blue 2 in the Standard Colors section of the color picker to fill the tabs with a blue color. Click the Shape Fill command again and then click Gradient. Access displays a gallery of 13 gradient variations, as shown in Figure 15-38. The default option, No Gradient, tells Access not to use any fill color gradients for the control. Click the Linear Right gradient variation to show a transition of darker to lighter color from right to left of the blue fill color you chose earlier.

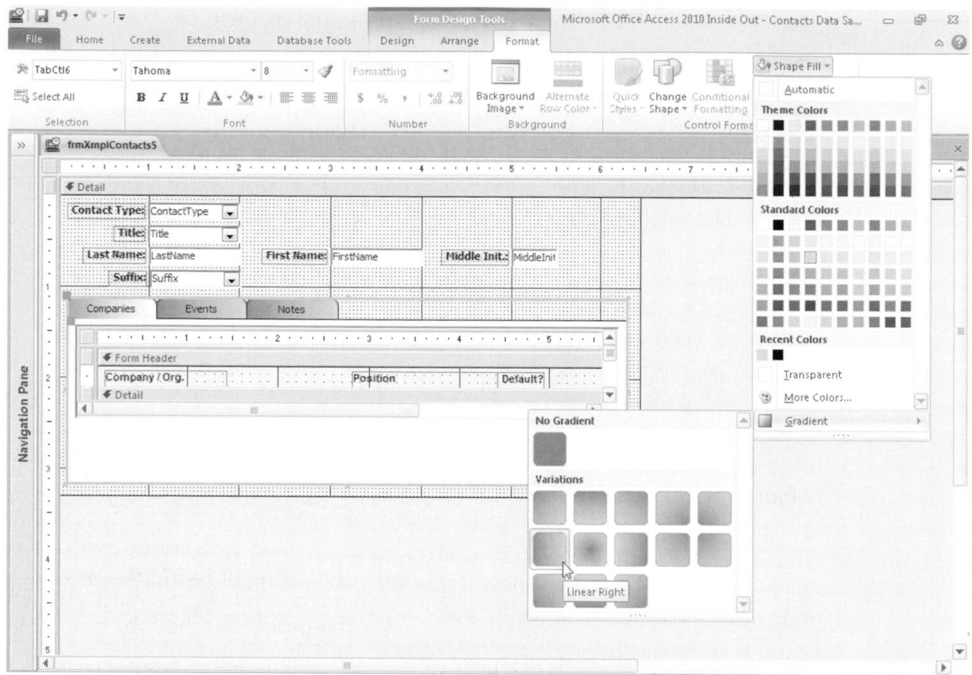

Figure 15-38 You can select different gradient variations to use with the fill color of the tabs on tab controls.

Save the changes to your form as frmContacts5. Switch to Form view to see the results of your changes, as shown in Figure 15-39. Click the tabs for the tab control and observe how Access changes the fore color of the captions as you hover over and click the tabs. You can find this form saved as frmXmplContacts5 in the sample database.

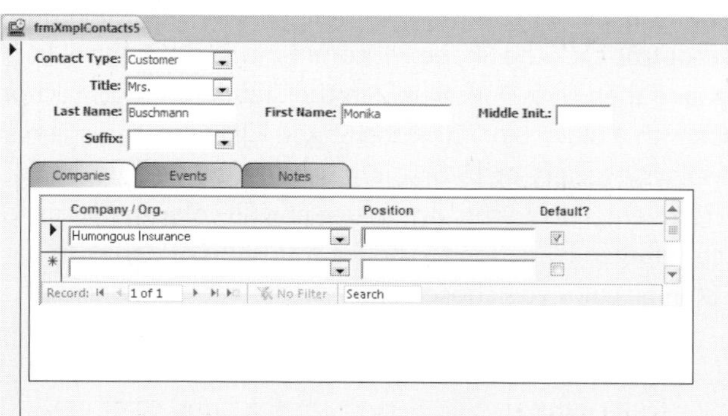

Figure 15-39 Your completed tab control in Form view should now look like this.

Table 15-1 lists other useful tab control property settings.

Table 15-1 Useful Tab Control Formatting Properties

Property	Settings	Usage
Multi Row	No (default)	If the control has more tabs than will fit on a single row, the control displays horizontal scroll arrows in the upper-right corner of the tab control to move through all the tabs.
	Yes	If the control has more tabs than will fit in a single row, the control displays multiple rows of tabs.
Style	Tabs (default)	The control displays tabs to select the various pages.
	Buttons	The control displays buttons (which look like command buttons but work like the buttons in an option group) to select the various pages.
	None	The control displays neither tabs nor buttons. Different pages can be displayed from a Visual Basic procedure or a macro by setting relative tab numbers in the tab control's Value property.
Tab Fixed Height	0 (default)	The tab height is based on the font properties of the tab control or the size of the bitmap you define as a picture to be displayed on the tab.
	[size in inches]	The tab height is fixed at the value entered.
Tab Fixed Width	0 (default)	The tab width is based on the font properties of the tab control and on the number of characters in the caption or the size of the picture on the tab.
	[size in inches]	The tab width is fixed at the value entered.
Back Style	Normal (default)	The control's back style is solid.
	Transparent	The control's background is transparent. If you have controls or a background image behind the tab control, those elements can be seen through the tab control.
Use Theme	Yes (default)	The control uses the new control theme styles such as gradients, shape fill, and shape styles.
	No	The control does not use any new control theme styles. Note that applying a Shape Style, Shape Fill, or Shape Outline to the control changes this property to Yes.
Back Color	[color values]	Sets the background color of the control.

Property	Settings	Usage
Border Style	Solid (default)	Sets the line style for the outline of the control. You can make the border transparent or specify a border that is a solid line, dashes, short dashes, dots, sparse dots, dash dot, or dash dot dot.
Border Color	[color values]	Sets the border color of the control.
Hover Color	[color values]	Sets the interior color of the tab when you hover the mouse over the tab.
Pressed Color	[color values]	Sets the interior color of the tab when you click the tab.
Hover Fore Color	[color values]	Sets the font color of the tab caption when you hover the mouse over the tab.
Pressed Fore Color	[color values]	Sets the font color of the tab caption when you click the tab.
Fore Color	[color values]	Sets the default font color of the tab captions.

TROUBLESHOOTING

Why can't I see multiple rows of tabs in my tab control?

If you are using a tab control with the Multi Row property set to Yes and the Use Theme property set to Yes, Access does not display the tab pages on multiple rows. To see multiple rows on your tab control, you must set the Multi Row property to Yes and the Use Theme property to No. Note that when you set the Use Theme property to No, you cannot use any of the new theme styles, such as gradients, shape fills, and shape styles, for the tab control.

Creating Multiple-Page Client Forms

As you've seen, Access 2010 makes it easy to display a lot of related information about one subject in a single form, either by using a query as the source of the form or by displaying the related information in a subform. As described in the previous section, if you have too much information to fit in a single, screen-sized form, you can use the tab control. Another way to handle the problem is to split the form into multiple pages.

In Chapter 2, "Exploring the Access 2010 Interface," you learned about the Document Window Options settings in the Access Options dialog box. In previous versions of Access, all objects opened in their own windows where you could edit, view, or print them. This multiple-document interface (MDI) made multiple-page forms a good method of displaying a lot of information on one form. The ContactsDataCopy.accdb sample database you have been using uses the single-document interface, which shows all open objects in a series of tabs along the top of the object window to the right of the Navigation pane. Unless you know in advance the height of the Access workspace, it's difficult to design a multiple-page form that works smoothly in the single document interface. To see how a multiple-page form works in the MDI, you should close the ContactsDataCopy.accdb database and open the Contacts.accdb database that uses the MDI.

You can create a form that's up to 22 logical inches high. If you're working on a basic 1024-by-768-pixel screen, you cannot see more than about 5.6 logical inches vertically at one time (if the ribbon is displayed). If the information you need to make available in the form won't fit in that height, you can split the form into multiple pages by using a page break control. When you view the form, you can use the Page Up and Page Down keys to move easily through the pages.

> **Note**
>
> **Access Services does not support page breaks so you can create only multiple-page client forms. You cannot add a page break control to a web form.**

Creating a smoothly working multiple-page form takes some planning. First, you should plan to make all pages the same height. If the pages aren't all the same size, you'll get choppy movement using the Page Up and Page Down keys. Second, you should design the form so that the page break control is in a horizontal area by itself. If the page break control overlaps other controls, your data might be displayed across the page boundary. You also need to be aware that when you set the form's Auto Resize property to Yes, Access sizes the form to the tallest page.

The frmXmplContactsPagesChap15 form in the Contacts.accdb database is a good example of a multiple-page form. If you open the form in Design view, open the Property Sheet window and select the Detail section of the form, you can see that the height of this area is exactly 5.8 inches. If you click the page break control, shown at the left edge of the Detail section in Figure 15-40, you'll find that it's set at 2.9 inches from the top of the page. Because this is exactly half the height of the Detail section, the page break control splits the section into two equally sized pages.

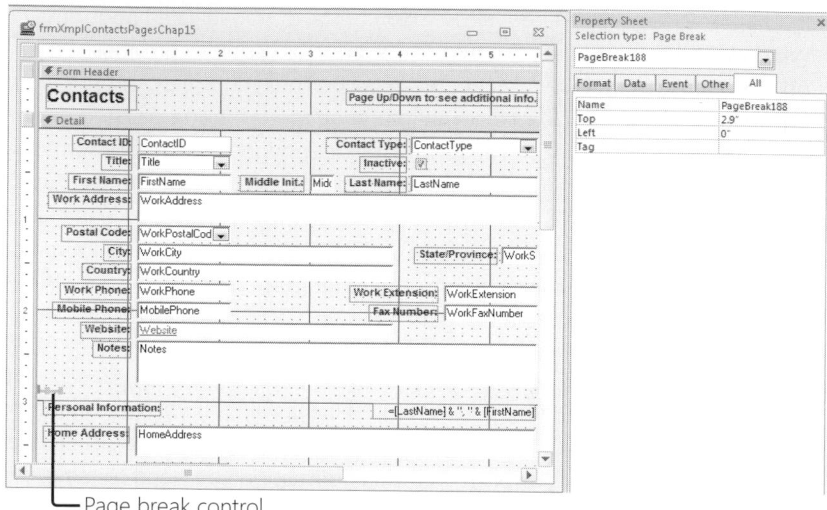

Figure 15-40 The frmXmplContactsPages form includes a page break control that splits the Detail section exactly in half.

When you look at this form in Form view, as shown in Figures 15-41 and 15-42, and use the Page Up and Page Down keys, you'll see that the form moves smoothly from page to page. If you switched from Design view to Form view, you must first click the Size To Fit Form button in the Window group on the Home tab to see the form page up and down correctly. When you open this form from the Navigation pane, it sizes correctly because the form has its Auto Resize property set to Yes.

If you're in a control on the second page of the form and you press Page Down again, you'll move smoothly to the second page of the next record. Note that certain key information (such as the contact name) is duplicated on the second page so that it's always clear which record you're editing. If you look at the second page of the form in Design view, you'll find a locked text box control at the top of the second page that displays the contact name again.

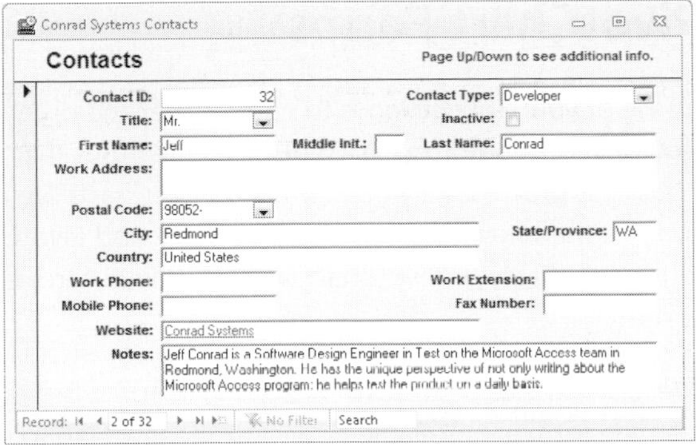

Figure 15-41 This is the first page of the frmXmplContactsPages form.

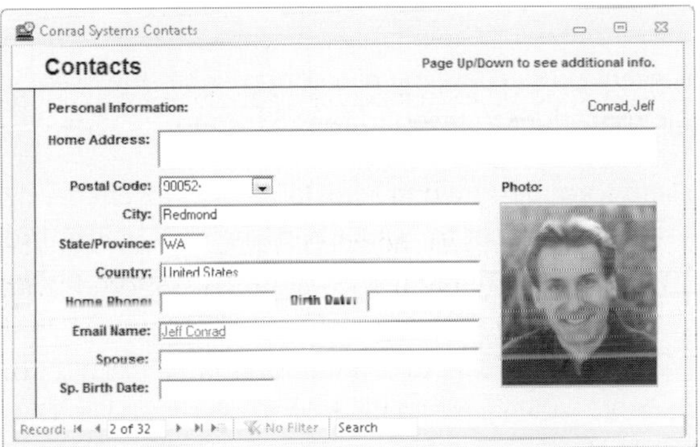

Figure 15-42 When you press Page Down, you can see the second page of the frmXmplContactsPages form.

A key form property that makes multiple-page forms work is the Cycle property. On this sample form, the Cycle property is set to Current Page. As you learned in Table 14-11 on page 892, other options are All Records (the default) and Current Record. If you don't set the Cycle property to Current Page, you must place the first and last controls on a page that can receive the focus exactly on the page boundary. If you don't do this, you'll find that the form scrolls partially down into the subsequent page as you tab from the last control on one page to the first control on the next page. Because it's not likely that you'll design your form with controls exactly aligned on the page boundary, you must use some special techniques to properly align form pages if you want to allow tabbing between pages or records. See "Controlling Tabbing on a Multiple-Page Form," in Chapter 25 for details. You can now close the Contacts.accdb database.

Working with Client PivotChart Forms

Even when the main purpose of your application is to enter, store, and organize data to support an active business function, you probably want to add features that allow management to analyze the business processes. PivotTables and PivotCharts are ideal for this purpose. In Chapter 10, you learned how to create the PivotTable and PivotChart views of a client query. Designing the PivotTable or PivotChart view of a client form is the same, but with some interesting twists:

- You can use any query or table as the record source of the form, but only fields bound to controls on the form are available to design the PivotTable or PivotChart.
- You can set form properties to control what users can modify in the PivotTable or PivotChart view, including locking the form so they can't modify what you designed at all.
- Because a form has event properties, you can control what the user can modify by writing a Visual Basic procedure to respond to the event.
- You can embed a client form designed in PivotTable or PivotChart view as the subform of another client form and set the Link Child and Link Master properties to filter the table or chart to display information relevant to the record on the outer form.

> **Note**
> **Access Services does not support PivotChart or PivotTable forms, so you can only create client PivotChart and PivotTable forms.**

Building a Client PivotChart Form

In the Housing Reservations application, you might want to track room revenue by month or quarter. In the Conrad Systems Contacts application, charting product sales or the number of contact events by week or month might be critical for judging how effectively the business is running.

In most cases, you should start by designing a query that fetches the fields you want to display in your PivotTable or PivotChart. In the Conrad Systems Contacts application, you might want to display product sales data by product or by company.

The ContactsDataCopy.accdb sample file has a query that gathers this information, qryXmplProductSalesForChart, as shown in Figure 15-43.

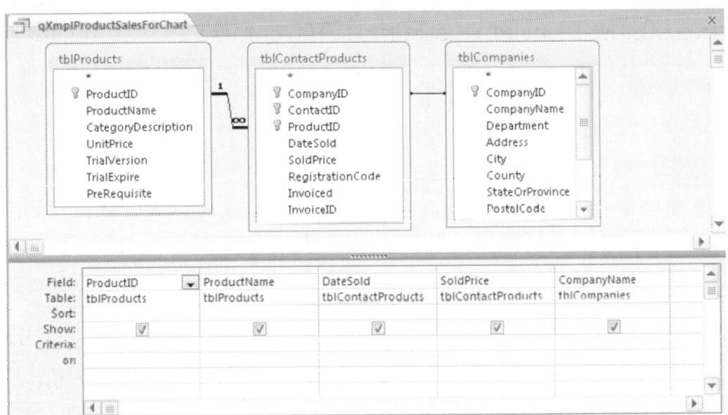

Figure 15-43 This sample query selects product sales data by product or by company.

Open the ContactsDataCopy.accdb sample database, select the qryXmplProductSalesForChart query in the Navigation pane, click the More Forms button in the Forms group on the Create tab, and then click PivotChart. Now, you can begin to design a chart to show sales by product by month in PivotChart view. From the chart's field list (click the Field List button in the Show/Hide group on the Design tab if you don't see this window), drag Product Name onto the Drop Series Fields Here area. Drag SoldPrice onto the Drop Data Fields Here area—the chart automatically calculates a sum for you. Open the Date Sold By Month list, drag Months onto the Drop Category Fields Here area, and then close the field list.

Click the Axis title on the left, and then click the Property Sheet button in the Tools group. Click the Format tab, and enter **Total Sales** in the Caption box. Click the General tab, and select Category Axis 1 Title in the Select list. Click the Format tab again, and change the Caption to **Months**. Return to the General tab, and select Chart Workspace in the Select list. Click the Add Legend button in the Add area to create a legend on the right side of the chart. Click the Show/Hide tab, clear all the check boxes in the Let Users View section, and clear the Field Buttons / Drop Zones and Field List check boxes to remove them from the chart. Your chart should now look like Figure 15-44.

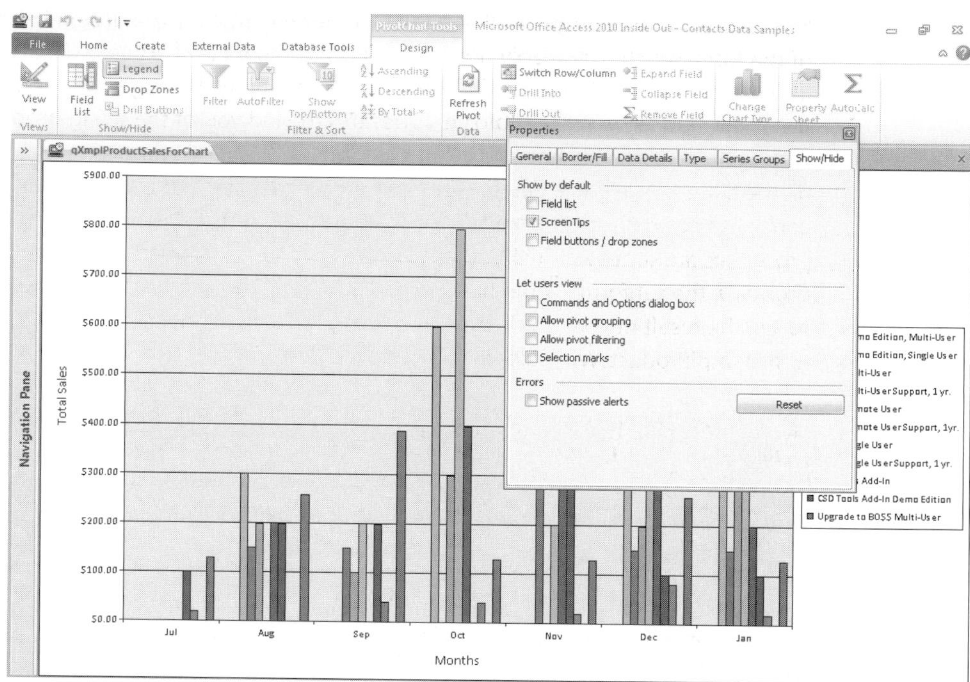

Figure 15-44 The chart you're building displays product sales by product and month.

Switch to Design view, and set Allow Edits, Allow Deletions, and Allow Additions all to No. Finally, change the Shortcut Menu property to No to keep the user from getting into the chart property settings that way. (You can see how much more control you have over what the user can do in a form.) Save the form as chtProductSalesByProduct. You can also find this form saved as chtXmplProductSales in the sample database.

Embedding a Linked PivotChart

To demonstrate how you can link the chart you just built into a form that displays product information, you can start with frmXmplProducts3, discussed in Chapter 13, "Building a Form." Open that form in Design view. Widen the design area to about 7.5 inches and expand the Detail section's height to about 4.25 inches to give you a space to place the chart. Drag the form you just created from the Navigation pane onto the blank area of the form, and select and delete the attached label.

Notice that Access automatically sizes the subform control to the design height and width of the form, which is probably not big enough to show the chart very well. Access doesn't look at the chart design to determine what height and width might work well to display the PivotChart view of the subform. (Does this remind you of the sizing problems you had with a subform in Datasheet view?) Stretch the width and height of the subform control to fill the blank space you created. Open the Property Sheet window, and with the subform control selected, set the Locked property to Yes. Verify that the Link Child and Link Master properties are set to ProductID. (Because the outer form is based on a table, dragging and dropping the subform should have set these properties automatically.) Switch to Form view to see the result of your work, as shown in Figure 15-45. You can also find this form saved as frmXmplProductsWithSales in the sample database.

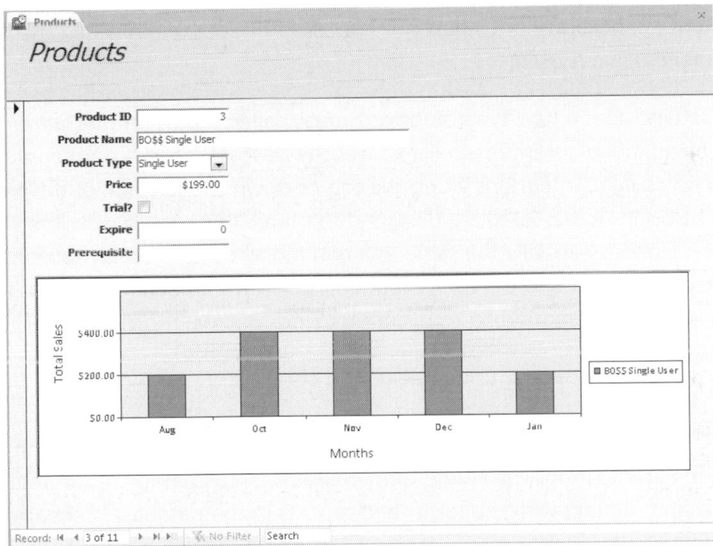

Figure 15-45 This form displays product information with a sales chart in a subform.

> **Note**
>
> **You might be wondering why the scale on the left in Figure 15-45 doesn't seem to match what you designed in Figure 15-44. The PivotChart view adjusts its horizontal and vertical scales to match the size of the display window. If you had designed the subform control taller, you might have seen the scale match.**

Working with Navigation Controls

When you build an Access application to be used by others, it's generally good practice to display to users only the parts of the database that they need to complete the major tasks in your application. Your main form that users interact with should be an intuitive interface that helps guide your users to the forms and reports they need to use in the database. The Switchboard Manager, included in Access for many releases, helps build a form that allows users to navigate to the various parts of an Access database. While the Switchboard Manager functions, at least on a simple level, to navigate to parts of an application such as opening forms and reports, it lacks the ability to do additional customization. In a large application with many objects, you have to navigate many levels deep into sublevels of the switchboard form to get to different areas. The Switchboard Manager might work for some Access client applications, but when you look at interfaces for websites, the switchboard model is generally not used.

Access 2010 includes a new type of form control, called a *navigation control*, to help you design a navigational interface similar to websites. Most websites on the Internet display tabbed style *navigation buttons* along the top or down the left side of the web page. Navigation controls in Access 2010 are designed to mimic this type of web interface. A navigation button works essentially the same as a command button. When you click a navigation button, Access responds to the click event and performs an action. (You'll learn all about events in Part 6, "Automating an Application Using Macros.")

To demonstrate creating and using navigation controls in your Access databases, open the Contacts Navigation sample web database (ContactsNavigation.accdb) found on the companion CD. When the web database opens, Access displays the startup form called Home, as shown in Figure 15-46. The Home form contains a navigation control that allows you to easily view and interact with the forms and reports in the database. Beneath the label title in the form's Header section, you'll see four buttons displayed horizontally across the top—Contact List, Datasheet, Address Book, and Phone List. If you click these buttons, Access changes the form or report displayed in the bottom portion of the navigation control. Underneath the Contact List button, you'll see another set of five buttons—All, A–G, H–M, N–T, and U–Z. If you click these buttons, Access displays the frmContactList form, but filtered to show only contact last names within a range of letters. You'll notice if you click any other top-level button besides the one labeled Contact List, you don't see the second level of buttons.

> **Note**
>
> A form with a navigation control is sometimes referred to as a navigation *form* because you can use the form as your main form to navigate to different parts of your application. You need to remember, though, that a navigation control is not a new form type, it is a control *on* a form.

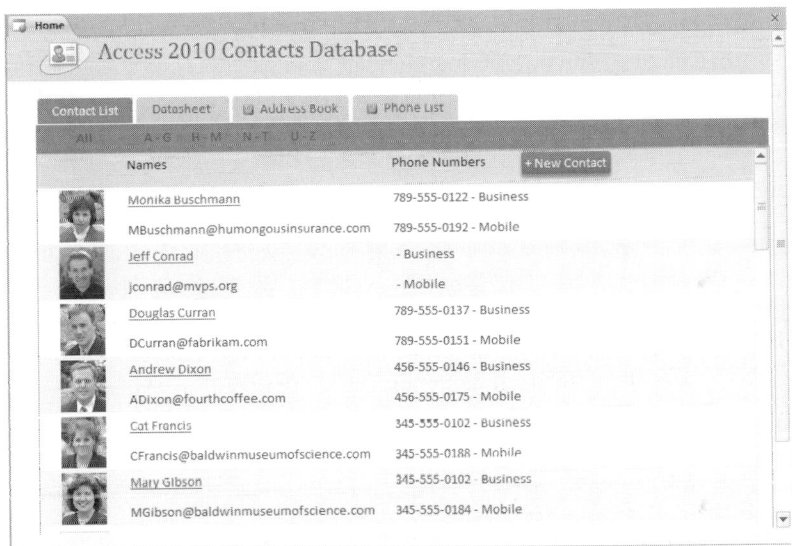

Figure 15-46 The navigation control on the Home form allows you to navigate to the forms and reports in the database.

Close the Home form now, and let's create a new form with a navigation control just like this Home form. In the Forms group on the Create tab, click Navigation. Access displays a drop-down list of six types of navigation controls, as shown in Figure 15-47. Here are the navigation control options in detail:

- **Horizontal Tabs** Create a navigation control with a single row of navigation buttons horizontally across the top of the control.
- **Vertical Tabs, Left** Create a navigation control with a single column of navigation buttons down the left side of the control.
- **Vertical Tabs, Right** Create a navigation control with a single column of navigation buttons down the right side of the control.

- **Horizontal Tabs, 2 Levels** Create a navigation control with two rows of navigation buttons horizontally across the top of the control. The second level of navigation buttons changes based on the navigation button selected in the top-level row.
- **Horizontal Tabs And Vertical Tabs, Left** Create a navigation control with a single row of navigation buttons horizontally across the top and a single column of navigation buttons down the left side of the control. The navigation buttons on the left side can change based on the navigation button selected in the top-level row.
- **Horizontal Tabs And Vertical Tabs, Right** Create a navigation control with a single row of navigation buttons horizontally across the top and a single column of navigation buttons down the right side of the control. The navigation buttons on the right side can change based on the navigation button selected in the top-level row.

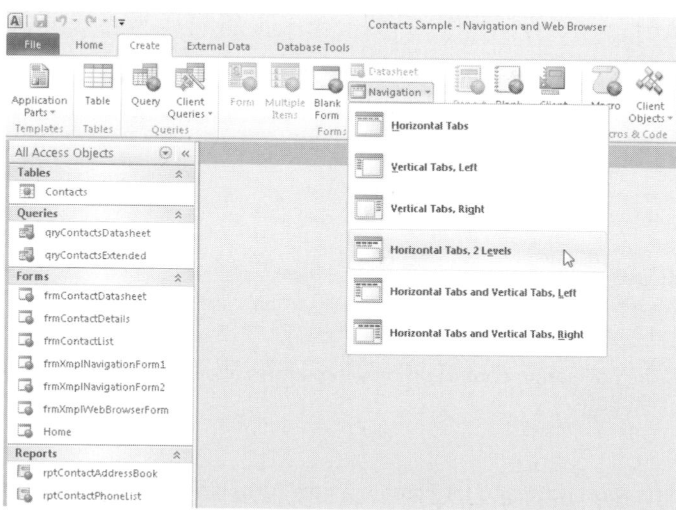

Figure 15-47 You can choose from a gallery of six types of navigation controls.

Click Horizontal Tabs, 2 Levels from the drop-down list of navigation control options to begin creating your form. Access creates a new blank, unbound form with your navigation control and opens the form in Layout view, as shown in Figure 15-48.

> **Note**
>
> Although we'll only be showing you an example of using navigation controls on a web form in a web database, you can also create navigation controls on client forms, too. If you are in a client database, you create a new form with a navigation control by clicking the Navigation button in the Forms group on the Create tab. You can also click the Navigation Control button in the Controls group on the Design tab to drop a navigation control onto an existing form.

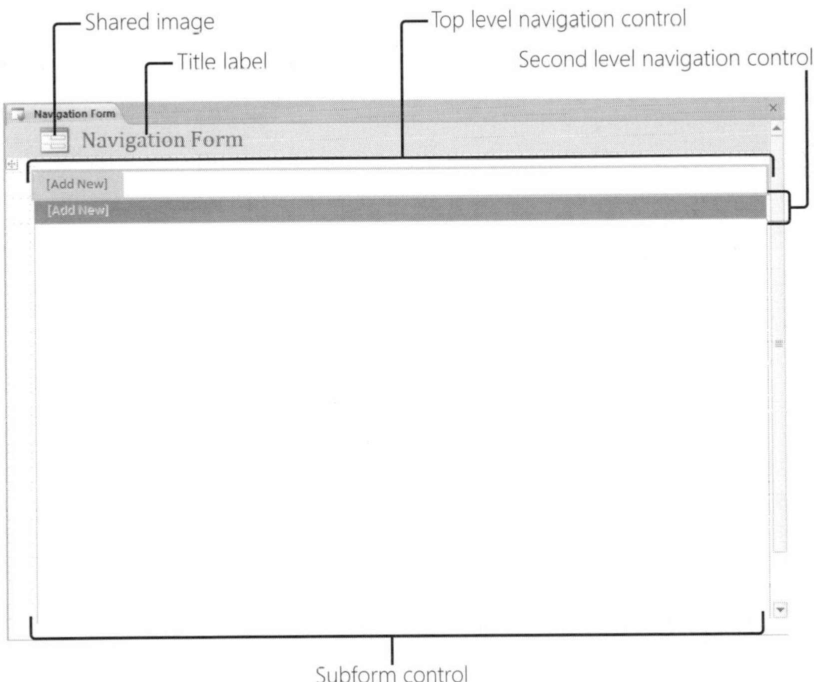

Figure 15-48 You now have a new blank form with a two-level navigation control.

A navigation control is a unique control in Access because it is actually a collection of controls interlinked together. At the top of the control, Access creates the top-level navigation control—the container for the main level of navigation buttons. Below the top-level navigation control, you'll see the second-level navigation control—the container for the child level of navigation buttons. Beneath the second-level navigation control, you'll see a large subform container. (By default, Access makes the subform container a large size, but you can resize the container to a smaller size if you want.) All these controls work together and depend on one another. It might be confusing to see in the Property Sheet window that these controls are all independent controls with their own properties; however, you cannot have a navigation control without a subform container. Access needs the subform container to display forms and reports.

In each of the navigation controls, you'll see an [Add New] navigation button. The [Add New] navigation button performs a special function to assist you with creating additional new navigation buttons in your navigation controls. You cannot delete the [Add New] navigation button from your navigation control, but Access does not display this button when you open the form in Form view.

The first form we'd like to display in the navigation control is the form called frmContactList. The frmContactList form is a continuous form that lists a few details about each contact in the database. To create a new navigation button that displays the frmContactList form in the subform container, click inside the top-level [Add New] navigation button and then type the name of the form frmContactList, as shown in Figure 15-49.

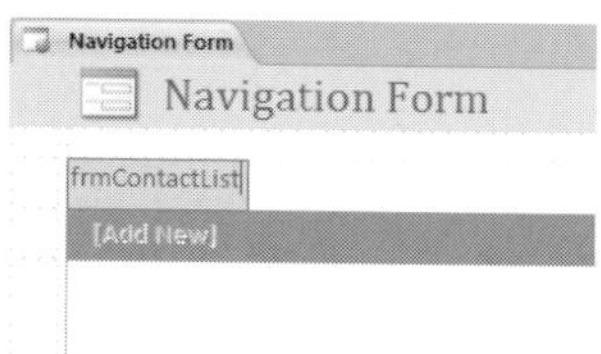

Figure 15-49 Type a form or report name in the [Add New] navigation button to create a new navigation button.

After you type the form name, press Enter and Access creates a new navigation button to the left of the [Add New] navigation button. Access also now displays the frmContactList form in the subform container, as shown in Figure 15-50.

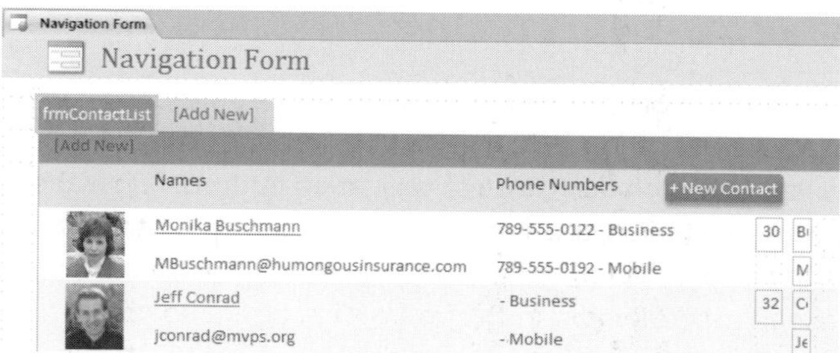

Figure 15-50 Access now displays your form in the subform container.

Open the Property Sheet window and let's take a look at the properties for a navigation button. A navigation button has properties that most other controls have as well, such as properties for the control name, caption, font size, font style, gridlines, color options, etc. Two properties, however, are unique to navigation buttons—Navigation Target Name and Navigation Where Clause, as shown in Figure 15-51. In the Navigation Target Name property, Access provides a drop-down list of all the form and report names in your database. This property tells Access which form or report to display when you click the navigation button. When you typed the form name into the [Add New] navigation button, Access filled in this property for you. You can use the Navigation Where Clause property to provide an optional WHERE clause to filter the results of the selected form or report in the Navigation Target Name property. (We'll show you how to do that later in this section.) By default, Access set the Caption property for the navigation button the same as the name of the form. Click in the Caption property, and change the caption to **Contact List**.

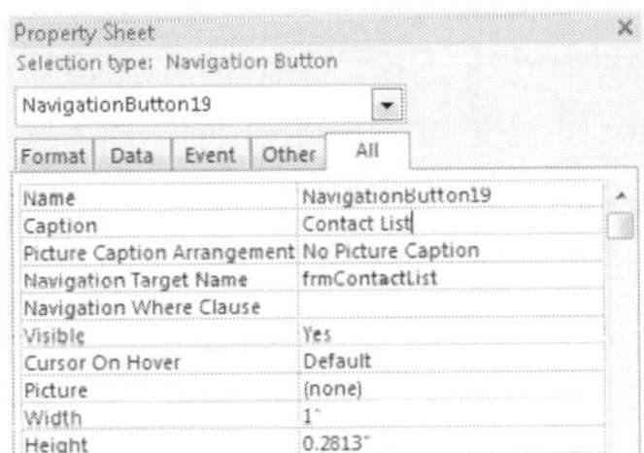

Figure 15-51 Change the Caption property of the navigation button you just created.

> **Note**
>
> **If you are using a web form in a web database, Access filters the drop-down list of form and report names in the Navigation Target Name property to display only web forms and web reports. If you are using a client form, Access displays both web and client forms and reports in your database in the drop-down list for the Navigation Target Name property.**

You can continue to add more navigation buttons to the top-level navigation control by typing in the other form and report names in the [Add New] navigation button; however, there is a much easier way to add additional navigation buttons. Close the Property Sheet window, if you still have it open, and make sure you've expanded the Navigation pane to see the database objects. Select the frmContactDatasheet from in the Navigation pane and then drag the form to the right of the Contact List navigation button you just created. When you have it positioned just right, Access displays a vertical I-bar to the right of the Contact List navigation button, as shown in Figure 15-52.

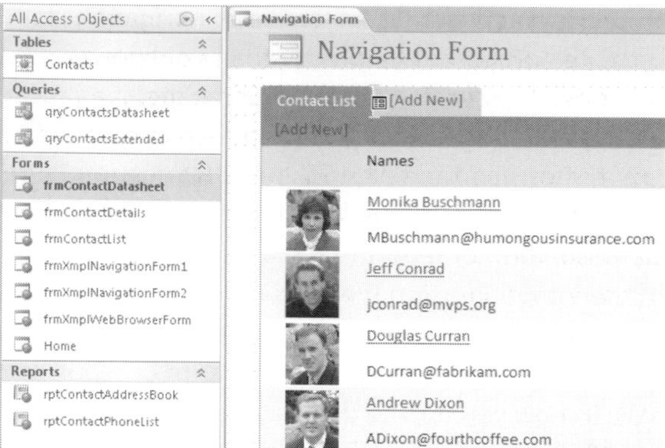

Figure 15-52 Drag the frmContactDatasheet form into the navigation control.

Release the mouse and Access creates another navigation button and displays the frmContactDatasheet in the subform container, as shown in Figure 15-53. As you can see, the drag procedure within Layout view is a very fast and easy way to build your navigation buttons. Note that this drag procedure works only in Layout view.

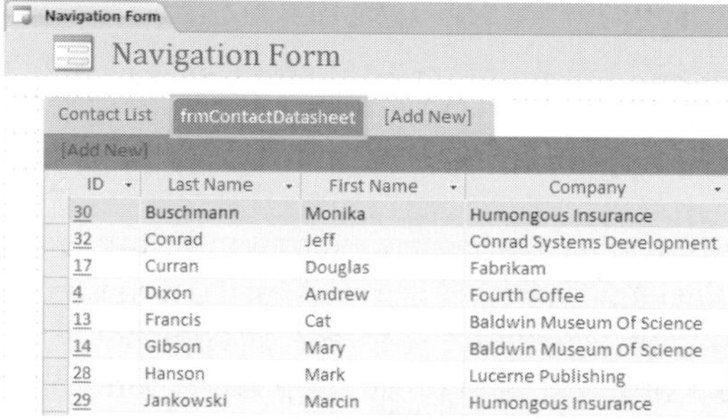

Figure 15-53 Access creates a new navigation button by dragging a form or report from the Navigation pane to the navigation control.

TROUBLESHOOTING

Why can't I drag my form or report to the navigation control in Layout view?

If you are using a web form with a navigation control, you cannot drag client forms and client reports to the navigation control. Web forms cannot be bound to or include any client elements. If you try to drag a client form or report into a navigation control on a web form, Access prevents you from completing the procedure. You can, however, drag web forms and web reports into a navigation control on a client form.

Now that you've added navigation buttons to the top-level navigation control for two of the database forms, let's create navigation buttons for the two reports in this database. Select the rptContactAddressBook report in the Navigation pane, drag the report to the right of the frmContactDatasheet navigation button, and then release the mouse. Access creates another navigation button and then displays the report in the subform container. Repeat this procedure one more time by dragging and dropping the rptContactPhoneList report to the right of the rptContactAddressBook navigation button. Open the Property Sheet window and change the captions for the three navigation buttons you just created to **Datasheet**, **Address Book**, and **Phone List**, respectively. Switch to Form view to view your results. Your form up to this point should look like Figure 15-54.

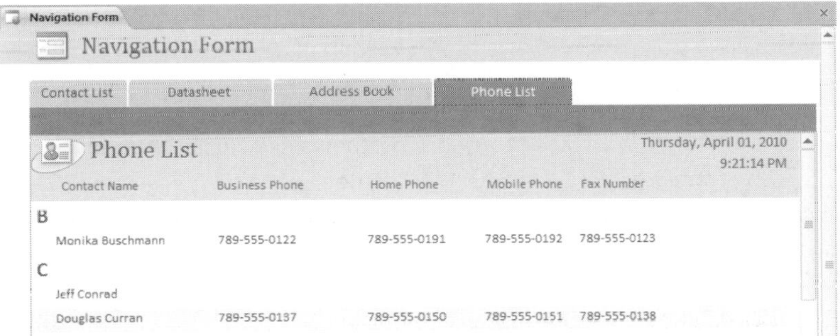

Figure 15-54 You've now created four navigation buttons that swap out different forms and reports in the subform container.

Click the navigation buttons and notice how Access swaps out the two forms and two reports in the subform container. You'll also notice that Access changes the back color and fore color of the selected navigation button to match the background color of the second-level navigation to give a clear visual indication which navigation button you selected. Access does this by utilizing the Back Color, Hover Color, Pressed Color, Hover Fore Color, Pressed Fore Color, and Fore Color properties of the navigation button.

Let's add a little extra customization to the two report navigation buttons by adding images. Open the Property Sheet window, select the Address Book navigation button, and on the Picture property, select the rptReportPreview shared image from the drop-down list. Access replaces the caption displayed on the navigation button with the shared image of a report icon. We want to include both the caption and the image, so change the Picture Caption Arrangement property from No Picture Caption to General. Access now displays the shared image and the caption on the navigation button. When you select General setting, Access uses the General alignment setting to display the image and text. You can also choose to display the image above, to the right, at the bottom, or to the left of the text. The navigation button is a little wider than it needs to be, so decrease the button's width by dragging the right edge of the control to the left until it's just wide enough to display both the shared image and the caption. Repeat these same steps for the Phone List navigation button—change the Picture property to use the same shared image, change the Picture Caption Arrangement property to General, and then resize the control. While you still have the form open in Layout view, reduce the width of the Datasheet navigation button, too. Your form, displayed in Form view and shown in Figure 15-55, is beginning to take shape. Click the Save button on the Quick Access Toolbar and name your form NavigationForm to save your changes. You can find this form saved as frmXmplNavigationForm1 in the sample database.

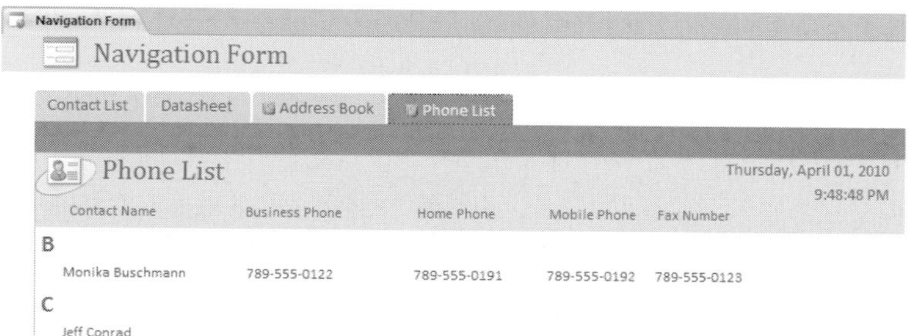

Figure 15-55 Your completed top-level navigation buttons should look like this.

When you click the Contact List navigation button, Access displays the entire list of contacts in the frmContactList form. Our sample database includes only 32 records, so it's not too difficult to scroll down the list of contacts. If you have a much larger list of contacts, however, it might be easier to filter the form to display fewer records at a time. We can achieve this functionality by reusing the same form on different navigation buttons, but filtering the form using the Navigation Where Clause property. Instead of displaying extra navigation buttons on the first-level navigation control, it would be more intuitive to display these extra filter buttons in the second-level navigation control beneath the Contact List navigation button.

Switch back to Layout view and then click the Contact List navigation button. Select the frmContactList form in the Navigation pane and then drag the form to the left of the [Add New] navigation button on the second-level navigation control. Access creates a new navigation button on the second-level navigation control that opens this form. Select the frmContactList form in the Navigation pane again and then drag the form to the right of the navigation button you just created on the second-level navigation control. Repeat these steps three more times using the same form until you have a total of five navigation buttons on the second-level navigation control, as shown in Figure 15-56.

Figure 15-56 Add five navigation buttons to the second-level navigation control using the frmContactList form.

When a user clicks the Contact List navigation button in the top-level navigation control, we want to display the entire list of contacts. To make it clear to users that they are looking at the entire list of contacts, we can make the first button in the second-level navigation control unfiltered and change the caption to **All**. Essentially, the first button in both the first- and second-level navigation controls do exactly the same thing, but we can repeat the functionality so when the user navigates to the other navigation buttons on the second level, they'll always have a way to view all the records without having to leave the second-level navigation control.

Open the Property Sheet window, select the first navigation button in the second-level navigation control, change the Caption property to **All**, and resize the navigation button to be 1 inch wide to match the top-level Contact List navigation button. Select the second button navigation button on the second level and change its Caption property to **A–G** to indicate that clicking this navigation button filters the form to show only contacts with last names that start with the letters A through G. In the Navigation Where Clause property, enter the expression **[Last Name]>="A" And [Last Name]< "H"** to limit the records to this range of letters, as shown in Figure 15-57. Note that in the Navigation Where Clause, you do not need to start the expression with an equals sign (=). Reduce the width of this navigation button to one-half of an inch.

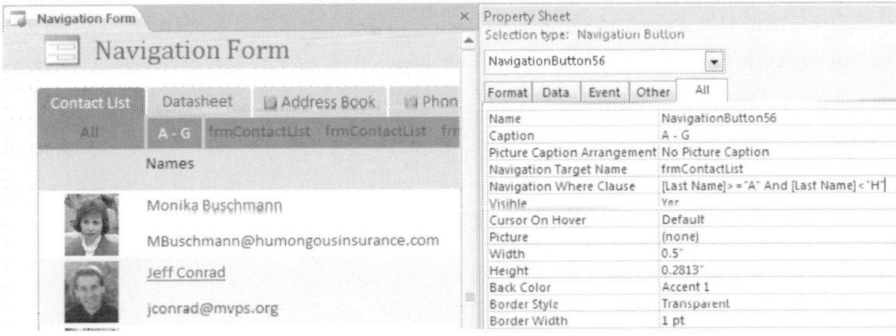

Figure 15-57 Change the Navigation Where Clause property to filter the records in the frmContactList form.

Using the example you just learned, make the following changes to the remaining three navigation buttons in the second-level navigation control:

1. For the third button, change the Caption property to **H–M**, reduce the width to one-half of an inch, and enter the expression **[Last Name]>="H" And [Last Name]<"N"** in the Navigation Where Clause property.

2. For the fourth button, change the Caption property to **N–T**, reduce the width to one-half of an inch, and enter the expression **[Last Name]>="N" And [Last Name]<"U"** in the Navigation Where Clause property.

3. For the fifth button, change the Caption property to **U–Z**, reduce the width to one-half of an inch, and enter the expression **[Last Name]>="U"** in the Navigation Where Clause property.

Save your changes to the form, and then switch to Form view to see your completed changes, as shown in Figure 15-58. When you click the first-level Contact List navigation button, you can see all the navigation buttons in the second-level navigation control. When you click the Datasheet, Address Book, or Phone List navigation buttons, you do not see the second-level navigation buttons. When you click the second-level navigation buttons below Contact List, Access filters the records to show only the contacts with last names that start with the letters specified. The second-level navigation buttons are referred to as *children* of the first-level navigation buttons. If you want to add child navigation buttons below a parent navigation button, you need to select the parent navigation button in Layout view, and then drag forms and reports into the child-level navigation control (or use the [Add New] button to do so). You can find this form saved as frmXmplNavigationForm2 in the sample database.

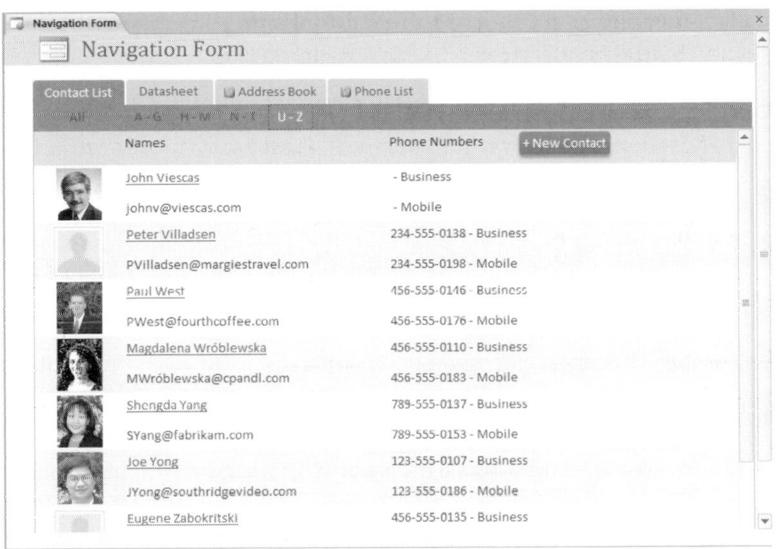

Figure 15-58 Your second-level navigation buttons filter the frmContactList form.

If you'd like, you can experiment with applying different formatting options to the navigation buttons. Access 2010 includes several new formatting options you can apply to buttons—the new navigation buttons as well as the standard Access command buttons. Switch back to Layout view for your form, select one of your navigation buttons, and then click the Quick Styles button in the Control Formatting group on the Format tab. Access displays a gallery of 42 Quick Styles that you can apply to your button, as shown in Figure 15-59. You can click any of these Quick Styles, and Access changes the colors and styles of your navigation button. By using a Quick Style, you can quickly adjust several color properties of your buttons for a modern look compared to previous versions of Access. When you click a Quick Style, Access changes the Back Color, Border Color, and Fore Color properties to Quick Style to indicate it is using Quick Style formatting properties.

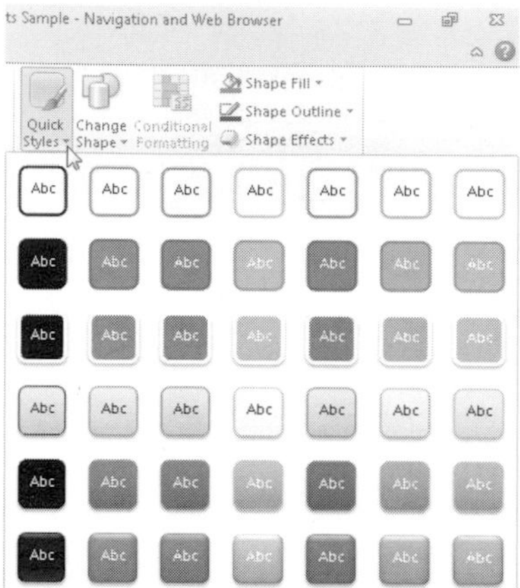

Figure 15-59 You can choose from a gallery of 42 Quick Styles to apply to buttons.

In addition to the Quick Styles, you can choose many other formatting options for buttons under the Shape Effects command. Select a navigation button in one of the navigation controls and then click the Shape Effects command in the Control Formatting group on the Format tab. Access displays a drop-down gallery with four main options—Shadow, Glow, Soft Edges, and Bevel—as shown in Figure 15-60. When you click any of these main options, Access displays additional galleries in a submenu gallery. You can choose many different formatting options from these submenu galleries. For example, you can add different shadow styles to your buttons to give them a three-dimensional look. You can also apply different glow color variations, different levels of soft edging around the borders, and even different styles of beveled edging to your buttons. You can click any of these options and see how they change the appearance of your buttons. If you don't like an option, you can always undo your last action or click a different formatting option. With all the many new formatting style options for buttons in Access 2010, you might have a hard time trying to decide which options to use!

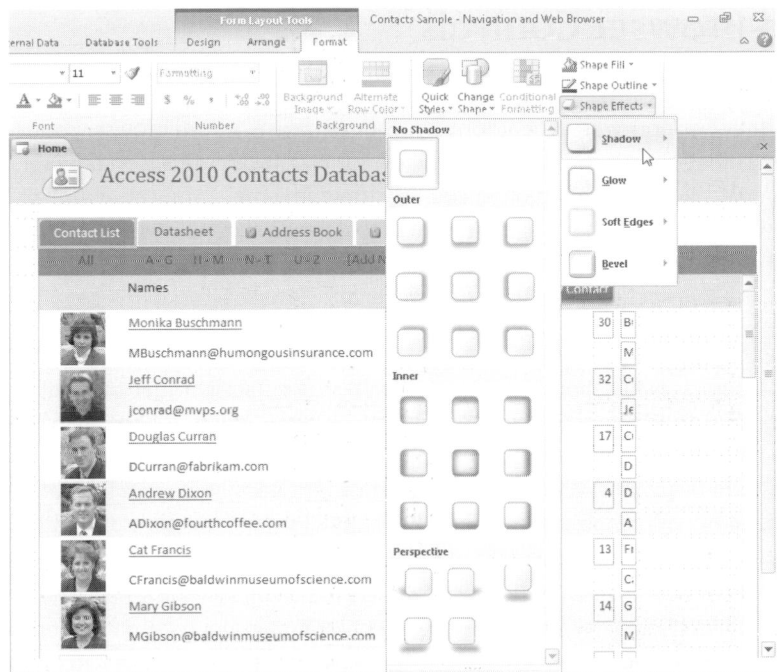

Figure 15-60 You can choose many shadow, glow, soft edge, and bevel formatting options for buttons in the Shape Effects gallery.

INSIDE OUT

Opening a Form with a Navigation Control in Access 2007

If you try and open a database that contains a client form with a navigation control in Access 2007, Access displays a compatibility warning message in the Business Bar. The warning says that the database uses some features that are incompatible with that version of Access. If you try to open that form in Access 2007 in any view, Access displays an error message indicating it cannot read the data in the form. You cannot edit or work with navigation controls in Access 2007.

Using Web Browser Controls

Access 2010 includes a new control type, called a *web browser control*, which you can use on both web forms and client forms in your database. A web browser control displays the content of web pages directly inside a form. You can use a web browser control, for example, to display a map of an address stored in a table. You can optionally bind the web browser control to a field in your form's record source by using the Control Source property of the control. You can also use a web browser control to display a static web page, such as a link to a specific website (for example, *http://www.AccessJunkie.com*), or you can use a web browser control to display a video hosted on a web page.

The Contacts Navigation sample web database (ContactsNavigation.accdb) you've been working with in the last section includes a web browser control on one of the forms. Open this database (if you've closed it) and then open the frmContactDetails form in Layout view. This form displays all the detail information about each contact in the database on the General tab of the tab control. Click the Map tab on the tab control, and Access displays a map of the contact's address using Bing Maps, as shown in Figure 15-61. If you navigate to different records using the navigational buttons at the bottom of the form, you can see the map change to display the current contact's address.

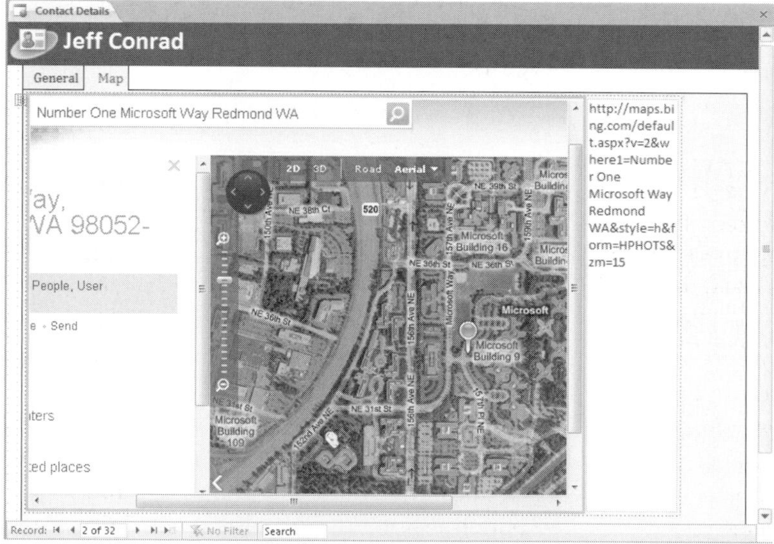

Figure 15-61 The web browser control displays a map of the contact's address using Bing Maps.

If you look to the right of the web browser control, you'll see a text box control that displays a Uniform Resource Locator (URL) to the Bing Maps website. This text box is bound to a field in the Contacts table called MapAddress. The MapAddress field is a Calculated data type that concatenates the URL to the Bing Maps base website along with the Address, City, and StateProvince fields from the contact's record. The completed URL is what you see displayed in the text box control on the form. (You can open the Contacts table in Datasheet view and examine the expression we used by selecting the MapAddress field, and then clicking the Modify Expression button in the Properties group on the Fields tab.) The web browser control is also bound to the MapAddress field. When you navigate to a different record, Access fetches the data from the MapAddress field, sends a request to that completed URL, and then displays the result in the web browser control.

Note

To view a website in a web browser control in Access, you must enable the content of the database. The simplest way to trust this database is to click the Enable Content button on the Message Bar. You can also go to the Trust Center and mark the folder containing this database as Trusted. Click the File tab on the Backstage view and then click Options. In the left column, choose Trust Center and then click Trust Center Settings. In the Trust Center dialog box, select Trusted Locations in the left column and then click Add New Location. Add the folder containing this sample database to the Trusted Locations list. For more information on enabling content in a database, see "Understanding Content Security," on page 47.

Let's create a new form with a web browser control so you can see how to work with this new control. First, close any objects you have open in the database. Next, open the Contacts table in Datasheet view and tab into the MapAddress field for one of the records in this table. Finally, click the Copy command in the Clipboard group on the Home tab to copy one of these address URLs to the Clipboard. (We'll use this URL as an example in just a moment.) Close the Contacts table and then click the Blank Form command in the Forms group on the Create tab to create a new blank web form in Layout view. Make sure you have Control Wizards enabled in the Controls group on the Design tab, select the Web Browser Control button in the Controls group, and then click in the form grid. Access adds a new web browser control to the form grid and then opens the Insert Hyperlink dialog box with the Hyperlink Builder button selected, as shown in Figure 15-62.

TROUBLESHOOTING

Why can't I see web browser control listed in the Controls group?

If you are working with a continuous form in Design or Layout view, Access does not display the Web Browser Control button in the Controls group on the Design tab. Web browser controls are not supported in the Detail section of continuous client or web forms, so Access does not display that control in the Controls group. If you want to display a web browser control in the form Header section of a continuous form, change the Default View property of the client form to Single Form, drop the web browser control in the form's Header section, and then change the Default View property back to Continuous Form. If you have a web browser control in the Detail section of a client datasheet form, Access does not display the web browser control when you view the form in Datasheet view.

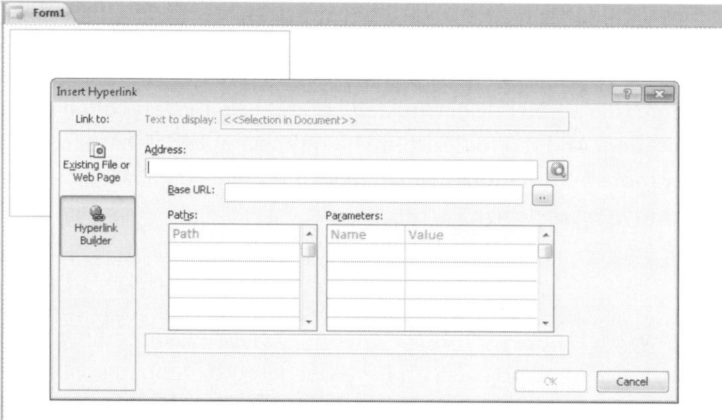

Figure 15-62 Access opens the Insert Hyperlink dialog box when you place a web browser control onto the form grid.

You used the Insert Hyperlink dialog box before when you studied how to insert and edit hyperlinks in Chapter 12, "Using Forms in an Access Application." You can use the Hyperlink Builder button in this dialog box to help break down a URL that includes parameters into the base URL, paths, and parameters. You'll notice the Text To Display box at the top is disabled when you build a hyperlink for a web browser control. There is really no need to have a text to display information for a web browser control when Access displays the contents of the web page inside the form. In the Address field, you can type in a website address.

You should still have the URL of one of the contact addresses in your Clipboard, so press Ctrl+V to paste that address into the Address field on the Insert Hyperlink dialog box. (The Insert Hyperlink dialog box is a pop-up form, so you cannot click the Paste command on the ribbon to perform this operation.)

When you tab out of the Address text box, Access breaks down the various parts of the URL, as shown in Figure 15-63. Access displays the base URL in the Base URL text box, any paths in the Paths list box, and any parameters in the Parameters list box. In Figure 15-63, you can also see that Access displays the name and value of each parameter in the Parameters list box. You can type a new value in the list box and Access saves the information into the completed URL. This feature is especially helpful when building complex URLs that include different parameters. (If you like, try entering your address information into the Value field next to Where1 under Parameters.) You can also click the button to the right of the Base URL text box to open the Expression Builder if you'd like to build an expression.

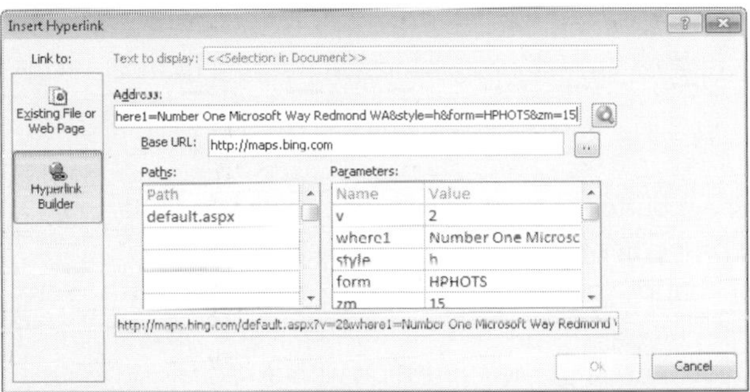

Figure 15-63 Access can break down a URL into its various parts using the Hyperlink Builder on the Insert Hyperlink dialog box.

Click OK to save your changes in the Insert Hyperlink dialog box and then resize the web browser control so it is bigger than the default size Access created. You should now see the web browser control pointing to the Bing Maps website, with a map displaying the address you provided, as shown in Figure 15-64. Note that if the address is invalid one, you'll see a generic page for the Bing Maps map control. Click the Save button on the Quick Access Toolbar and name your form WebBrowserForm. You can find this form saved as frmXmplWebBrowserForm in the sample database.

Figure 15-64 Access displays the web page content of the Bing Maps site in the web browser control.

Click the Property Sheet button in the Tools group on the Design tab, and let's take a quick look at some of the properties for the web browser control. In the Control Source property for the web browser control, you can see that Access saves the URL you provided on the Insert Hyperlink dialog box, as shown in Figure 15-65. If you are typing a URL directly into the Control Source, you must start the expression with an equals sign (=) and enclose the URL in quotation marks.

You can also bind a web browser control to a field in the form's record source by selecting a field from the drop-down list on the Control Source property. (You can look at the Control Source property of the web browser control on the frmContactDetails in this database for an example of this.) Note that the form must be bound to bind the web browser control to a field.

You can choose to turn off displaying scroll bars for the web browser control by changing the Scroll Bars Visible property from Auto to No. In client forms, you can also set the Scroll Bar Top and Scroll Bar Left properties of the web browser control to automatically scroll the web content to a specific area of a web page. The Scroll Bar Top and Scroll Bar Left properties of web browser controls on client forms take values in pixels to scroll the window down or to the right. By default, these properties are set at 0 pixels.

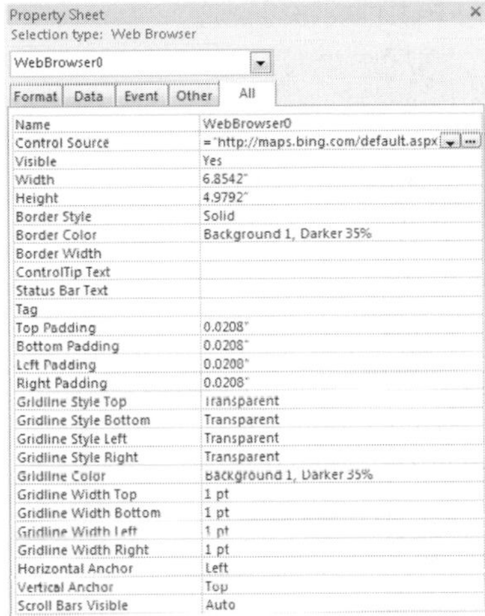

Figure 15-65 You can set the Control Source property of web browser controls to a URL or bind it to a field in the form's record source.

INSIDE OUT Review the Web Browser Controls in the Web Templates

You can see another use for web browser controls by opening any of the five sample web templates that come with Access 2010. If you look at the Getting Started tab of any of the sample web templates, you'll see that the forms use a web browser control to point to a video stored on a web page that displays help content on how to use the templates.

This is the last chapter about designing forms for desktop applications and web applications. You'll learn some additional design techniques that you can automate with macros in Part 6 and with Visual Basic code in Chapter 25.

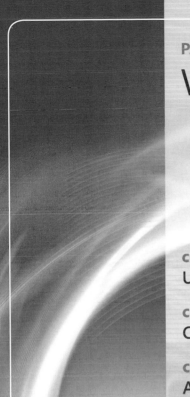

PART 5

Working with Reports

CHAPTER 16

Using Reports

You can certainly format and print tables and queries in Datasheet view, and that technique is useful for producing printed copies of simple lists of information. Although you primarily use forms to view and modify data, you can also use forms to print data—including data from several tables. However, because the primary function of forms is to allow you to view single records or small groups of related records displayed on the screen in an attractive way, forms aren't the best way to print and summarize large sets of data in your database.

This chapter explains why and when you should use a report instead of another method of printing data, and it describes the features that reports offer. The examples in this chapter are based on the Conrad Systems Contacts and Housing Reservations sample databases. After you learn what you can do with reports, you'll look at the process of building both client and web reports in the next two chapters.

Note

The examples in this chapter are based on the reports, tables, and data in ContactsDataCopy.accdb and Housing.accdb on the companion CD included with this book. You can find similar reports in the Conrad Systems Contacts sample application, but all the reports in that sample file have custom ribbons defined, so you won't see the main ribbon tabs when you open those reports. The results you see from the samples in this chapter might not exactly match what you see in this book if you have changed the sample data in the files. Also, all the screen images in this chapter were taken on a Windows 7 system with the Access color scheme set to Silver. Your results might look different if you are using a different operating system or a different theme.

Uses of Reports

Reports are the best way to create a printed copy of information that is extracted or calculated from data in your database. Reports have two principal advantages over other methods of printing data:

- Reports can compare, summarize, subtotal, and total large sets of data.
- Reports can be created to produce attractive invoices, purchase orders, mailing labels, presentation materials, and other output you might need to efficiently conduct business.

Reports are designed to group data, to present each grouping separately, and to perform calculations. They work as follows:

- You can define up to 10 grouping criteria to separate the levels of detail.
- You can define separate headers and footers for each group.
- You can perform complex calculations not only within a group or a set of rows, but also across groups.
- In addition to page headers and footers, you can define a header and a footer for the entire report.
- You can have your reports respond to events such as opening forms so that you can view detailed information.
- You can filter the report to show specific records before printing.

As with forms, you can embed pictures or charts in any section of a report. You can also embed subreports or subforms within report sections.

A Tour of Reports

You can explore reports in Microsoft Access 2010 by examining the features of the sample reports in the ContactsDataCopy.accdb sample database. A good place to start is the rptContactProducts report. Open the database, and go to the Navigation pane. Click the Navigation Pane menu, click Object Type under Navigate To Category, and then click Reports under Filter By Group to display a list of reports available in the database. Scroll down the list of reports in the Navigation pane until you see the rptContactProducts report, as shown in Figure 16-1. Double-click the report name (or right-click it and click the Open command on the shortcut menu) to see the report in Print Preview—a view of how the report will look when it's printed.

> ## Note
> **All the reports in the sample databases are set to print to the system default printer. The default printer on your system is probably not the same printer that we used as a default when we designed the report. Some of the sample reports are designed with margins other than the default of 1 inch on all sides. If your default printer cannot print as close to the edge of the paper as the report is designed, Access 2010 will adjust the margins to the minimums for your printer. This means that some reports might not appear exactly as you see them in this book, and some data might appear on different pages.**

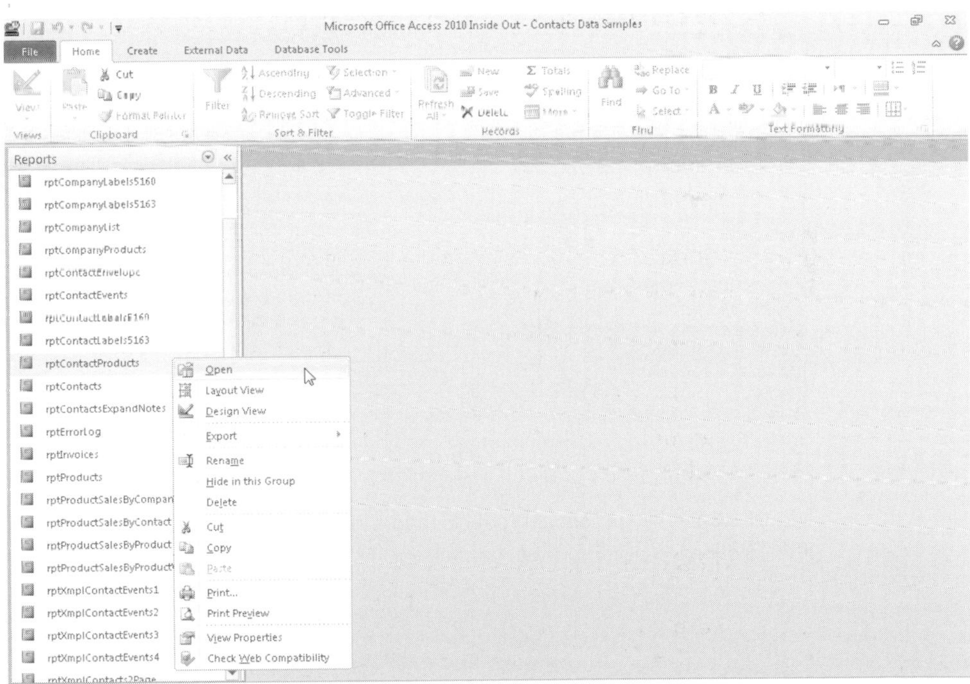

Figure 16-1 You can use the object shortcut menu to open a report from the Navigation pane.

Print Preview—A First Look

The rptContactProducts report is based on the qryRptContactProducts query, which brings together information from the tblContacts, tblProducts, and tblContactProducts tables. When the report opens in Print Preview, you'll see a view of the report in the Contact Products window, as shown in Figure 16-2. When you open the report from the Navigation pane, the report shows information for all contact product sales.

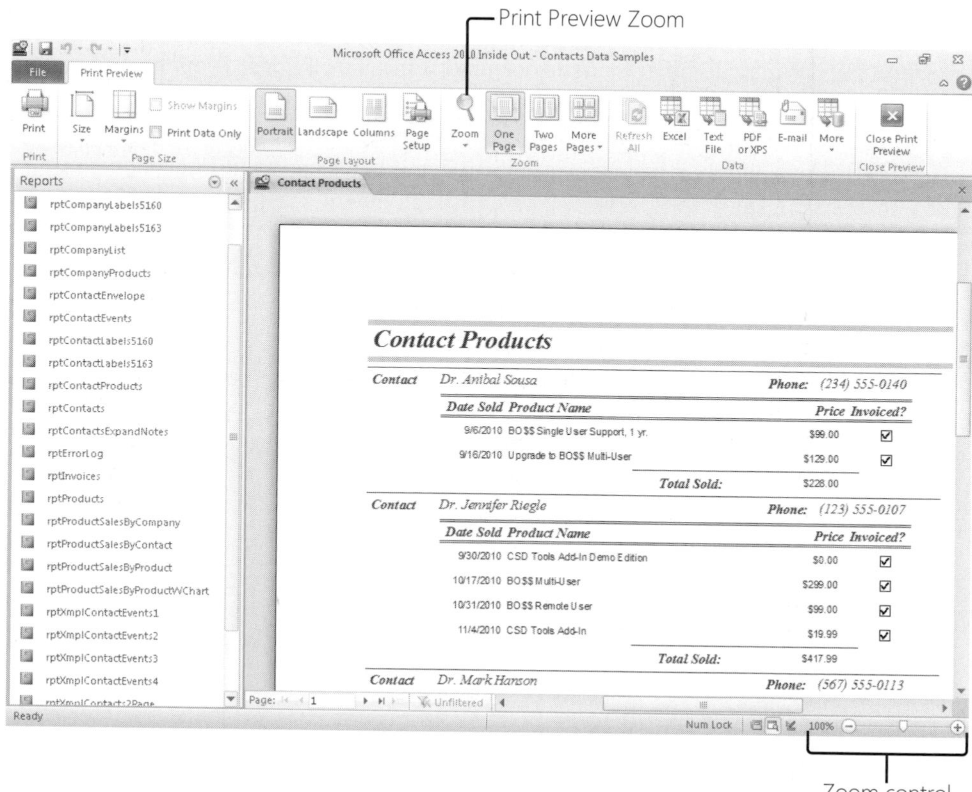

Figure 16-2 The rptContactProducts report in Print Preview shows sales data gathered from several tables.

Checking Out Reports in the Sample Application

You can see all the reports described in this chapter in the Conrad Systems Contacts application. Start the application by opening the database (Contacts.accdb), opening frmSplash, and then signing on as either Jeff or John—you don't need a password. To see the final version of the Contact Products report, for example, click the Products button on the main switchboard form, and then click the Print button on the CSD Contacts - Products form to open the Product Reports dialog box. Select Product Sales By Contact. Also select the Current Product Only and All Records options, and then click Print. You'll see the report in Print Preview for the product that was displayed on the Products form. You can also explore the reports by clicking the Reports button on the main switchboard. All reports in the application have custom ribbons that prevent you from switching to Design view when running the application. When you're finished looking at the reports in Contacts.accdb, be sure to go back to the ContactsDataCopy.accdb file to follow the remaining examples in this chapter.

You can expand the window in Print Preview by collapsing the Navigation pane to see more of the rptContactProducts report horizontally. Use the vertical and horizontal scroll bars to position the report so that you can see most of the upper half of the first page. If you are using a smaller Super Video Graphics Array (SVGA) screen (800 × 600 pixels), click the arrow below the Zoom button in the Zoom group on the ribbon and select 75% to see more of the report. If your screen resolution is 1024 × 768 or higher, you should be able to easily view the report at 100%. You can also use the Zoom control in the lower-right corner of your window to adjust the zoom level.

To view other pages of the report, use the navigation bar in the lower–left corner of the window, as shown here.

The four buttons, from left to right, are the First Page button, Previous Page button, Next Page button, and Last Page button. The Page Number box is in the middle. To move forward one page at a time, click Next Page. You can also click the Page Number box (or press Alt+F5 to select it), change the number, and press Enter to move to the exact page you want. Press Esc to exit the Page Number box. As you might guess, the Previous Page button moves you back one page, and the two outer buttons move you to the first or the last page of the report. You can also move to the top of the page by pressing Ctrl+Up Arrow, move to the bottom of the page by pressing Ctrl+Down Arrow, move to the left edge of the page by pressing Home or Ctrl+Left Arrow, and move to the right edge of the page by pressing End or Ctrl+Right Arrow. Pressing Ctrl+Home moves you to the upper-left corner of the page, and pressing Ctrl+End moves you to the lower-right corner of the page.

Headers, Detail Sections, Footers, and Groups

Although the rptContactProducts report looks simple at first glance, it actually contains a lot of information. Figure 16-3 shows you the report again with the various sections of the report marked. You can see a page header that appears at the top of every page. As you'll see later when you learn to design reports, you can also define a header for the entire report and choose whether to print this report header on a page by itself or with the first page header.

The data in this report is grouped by contact name, and the detail lines are sorted within contact name by date sold. You can print a heading for each group in your report, and this report has a heading for each contact. This report could easily be modified, for example, to display the product category in a header line (to group the products by category), followed by the related detail lines.

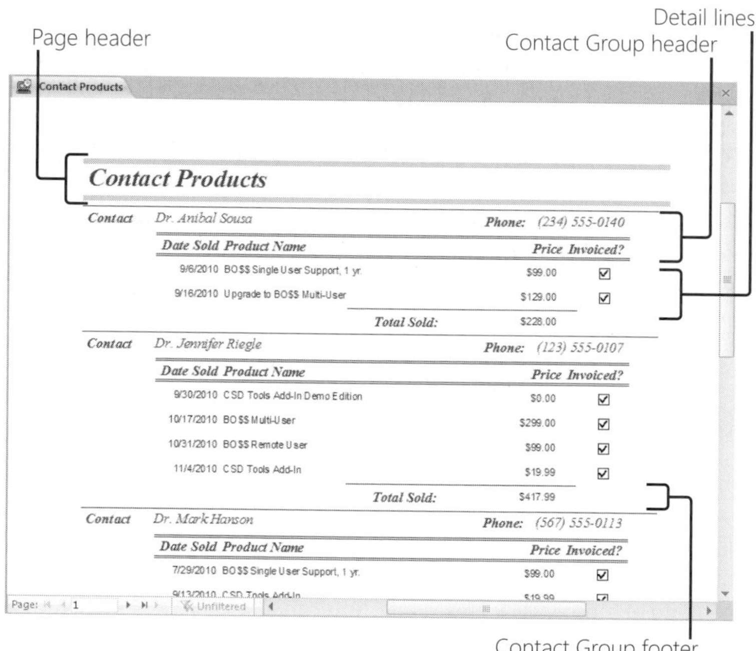

Figure 16-3 The rptContactProducts report has a subtotal for each contact.

Next, Access prints the detail information, one line for each row in the recordset formed by the query. In the Detail section of a report, you can add unbound controls to calculate a result using any of the columns in the record source.

Below the detail product lines for each contact, you can see the group footer for the contact. You could also calculate percentages for a detail record or for a group by including a control that provides a summary in the group footer (total for the group) or report footer (total for the report). To calculate the percentage, you would create an additional control that divides the detail or group value by the total value in an outer group or in the report footer. Access can do this because its report writer can look at the detail data twice—once to calculate any group or grand totals and a second time to calculate expressions that refer to those totals. If you scroll down to the bottom of the page, you'll see a page number, which is in the page footer.

Note

If you're working with a report that has many pages, it might take a long time to move to the first or last page or to move back one page. You can press Esc to cancel your movement request. Access 2010 then closes the report.

A slightly more complex report is rptProductSalesByProduct. Open that report, and go to the last page. At the end of this report, as shown in Figure 16-4, you can see the quantity and sales totals for the last product in the report, for the last category in the report, and for all sales in the database (Grand Total). There are two products in the Single User category, but the first is a demonstration edition that has a price of zero, so the total sales amount of the category matches the total sales amount of the second product. The grand total is in the report footer.

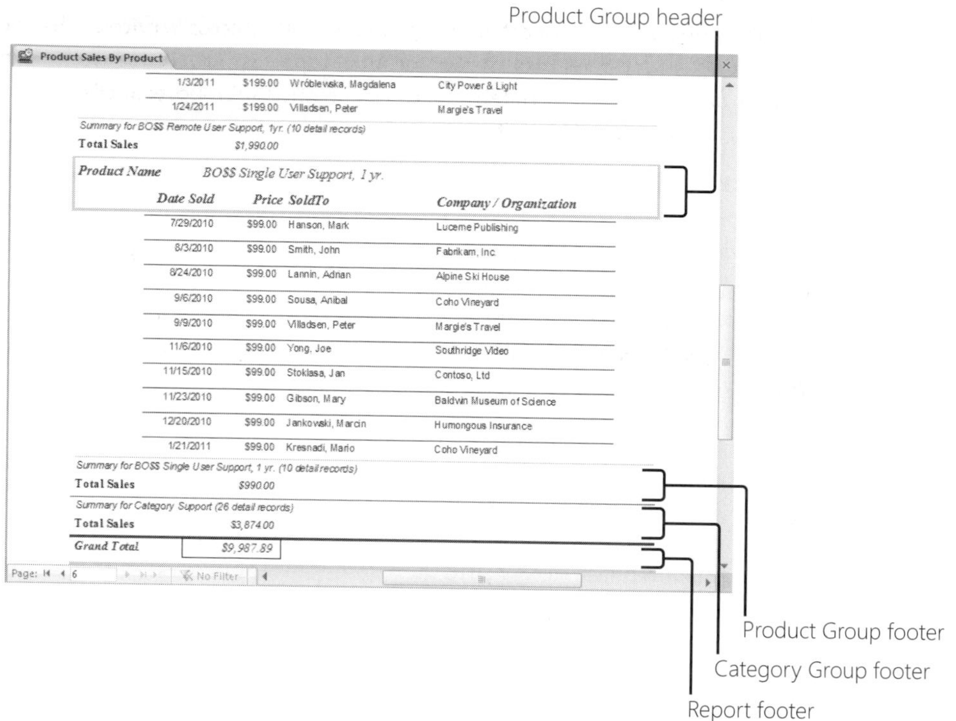

Figure 16-4 The rptProductSalesByProduct report's grand total calculation is in the report footer.

Subreports

Just as you can embed subforms within forms, you can embed subreports (or subforms) within reports. Subreports are particularly useful for showing related details or totals for the records that make up the source rows of your report. In the Conrad Systems Contacts database, you can bring together information about contacts and products—either contacts and the products they own or products and the contacts who own them. You can place detailed data about contacts and products in a subreport and then embed that subreport in the Detail section of a report that displays company data—much as you did for the fsubContactProducts form exercise in Chapter 15, "Advanced Form Design."

> **Note**
>
> **Subreports are not supported on web reports with Access Services. When you are working with web reports, the Subform/Subreport control is not available in the Controls group on the Design tab. You can still embed subreports in client reports in web databases and use them within Access.**

You can see an example of this use of a subreport in the rptCompanyProducts report and in the rsubCompanyProducts subreport in the Conrad Systems Contacts database. In the Navigation pane, right-click the rsubCompanyProducts subreport, and then click Design View on the shortcut menu to open the subreport in Design view, as shown in Figure 16-5. The Report window in Design view is shown in Figure 16-6.

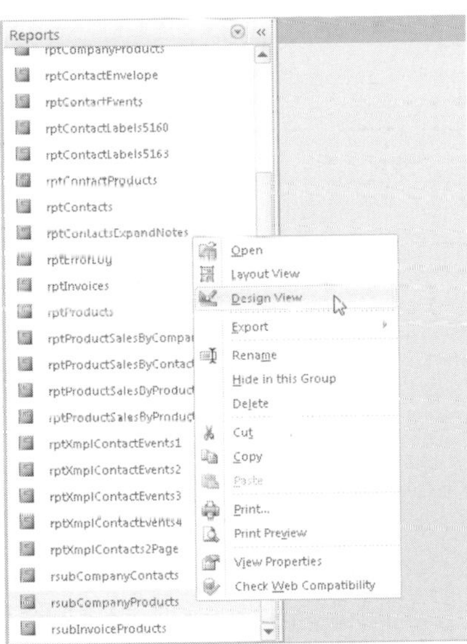

Figure 16-5 Select Design View from the shortcut menu to open rsubCompanyProducts in Design view.

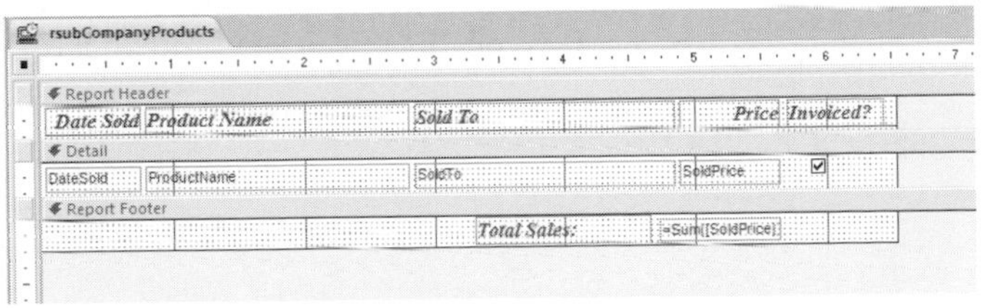

Figure 16-6 This is the Report window for the rsubCompanyProducts report in Design view.

You can see that this report looks very much like the continuous form that you designed earlier to be a subform. If you look at the Record Source property for the subreport, you'll find that it uses the qryRsubCompanyProducts query, which isn't at all simple. The query brings together information from the tblProducts, tblContactProducts, tblContacts, and tblCompanyContacts tables. This subreport doesn't display any company information at all. Switch to Print Preview by clicking the arrow in the Views group on the ribbon and clicking Print Preview in the list of available views. You'll see a list of various products and the contacts who own them, in date sold order, as shown in Figure 16-7.

rsubCompanyProducts

Date Sold	Product Name	Sold To	Price	Invoiced?
07/29/2010	BO$$ Single User Support, 1 yr.	Dr. Mark Hanson	$99.00	☑
07/29/2010	CSD Tools Add-In	Mr. Paul West	$19.99	☑
07/30/2010	Upgrade to BO$$ Multi-User	Mr. John Smith	$129.00	☑
07/31/2010	BO$$ Demo Edition, Multi-User	Mr. Mario Kresnadi	$0.00	☑
08/03/2010	BO$$ Single User Support, 1 yr.	Mr. John Smith	$99.00	☑
08/10/2010	BO$$ Multi-User	Mr. Paul West	$299.00	☑
08/12/2010	BO$$ Remote User	Mr. Andrew Dixon	$99.00	☑
08/20/2010	BO$$ Multi-User Support, 1 yr.	Mrs. Jan Stoklasa	$149.00	☑
08/20/2010	BO$$ Single User	Mr. John Smith	$199.00	☑
08/22/2010	Upgrade to BO$$ Multi-User	Ms. Kathleen Gail Jensen	$129.00	☑
08/23/2010	BO$$ Remote User	Dr. Peter Villadsen	$99.00	☑
08/23/2010	Upgrade to BO$$ Multi-User	Mrs. Jan Stoklasa	$129.00	☑
08/24/2010	BO$$ Single User Support, 1 yr.	Ms. Adrian Lannin	$99.00	☑
08/31/2010	CSD Tools Add-In Demo Edition	Mr. Tom Michaels	$0.00	☑
09/01/2010	BO$$ Multi-User Support, 1 yr.	Mrs. Cat Francis	$149.00	☑
09/05/2010	BO$$ Remote User	Mr. Joe Yong	$99.00	☑
09/06/2010	BO$$ Single User Support, 1 yr.	Dr. Anibal Sousa	$99.00	☑
09/09/2010	BO$$ Single User Support, 1 yr.	Dr. Peter Villadsen	$99.00	☑
09/09/2010	Upgrade to BO$$ Multi-User	Mr. Joseph Matthews	$129.00	☑

Page: 1 No Filter

Figure 16-7 Switch to Print Preview for the rsubCompanyProducts report to see a complex list of a sales history.

Close the subreport and open the rptCompanyProducts report in Print Preview, as shown in Figure 16-8. As you move from company to company, notice that the data displayed in the subreport changes to match the company currently displayed. The data from the rsubCompanyProducts report now makes sense within the context of a particular company. Access links the data from each subreport in this example using the Link Master Fields and Link Child Fields properties of the subreport (which are set to the linking CompanyID field)—just as with the subforms you created in Chapter 15.

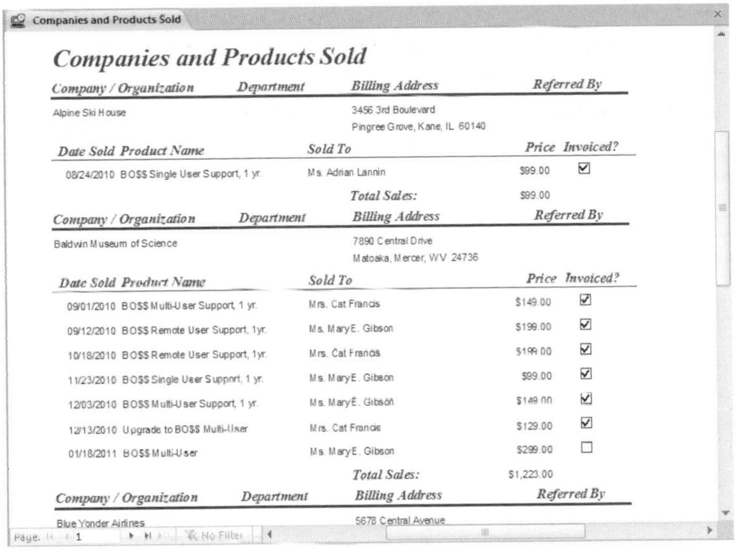

Companies and Products Sold

Companies and Products Sold

Company / Organization	Department	Billing Address	Referred By
Alpine Ski House		3456 3rd Boulevard Pingree Grove, Kane, IL 60140	

Date Sold	Product Name	Sold To	Price	Invoiced?
08/24/2010	BOSS Single User Support, 1 yr.	Ms. Adrian Lannin	$99.00	☑
		Total Sales:	$99.00	

Company / Organization	Department	Billing Address	Referred By
Baldwin Museum of Science		7890 Central Drive Matoaka, Mercer, WV 24736	

Date Sold	Product Name	Sold To	Price	Invoiced?
09/01/2010	BOSS Multi-User Support, 1 yr.	Mrs. Cat Francis	$149.00	☑
09/12/2010	BOSS Remote User Support, 1yr.	Ms. Mary E. Gibson	$199.00	☑
10/18/2010	BOSS Remote User Support, 1yr.	Mrs. Cat Francis	$199.00	☑
11/23/2010	BOSS Single User Support, 1 yr.	Ms. Mary E. Gibson	$99.00	☑
12/03/2010	BOSS Multi-User Support, 1 yr.	Ms. Mary E. Gibson	$149.00	☑
12/13/2010	Upgrade to BOSS Multi-User	Mrs. Cat Francis	$129.00	☑
01/18/2011	BOSS Multi-User	Ms. Mary E. Gibson	$299.00	☐
		Total Sales:	$1,223.00	

Company / Organization	Department	Billing Address	Referred By
Blue Yonder Airlines		5678 Central Avenue	

Page: 1 No Filter

Figure 16-8 The rptCompanyProducts report has an embedded subreport to display each company's purchase history.

As you'll see in the next section, when we examine some features of the rptInvoices report, that report also uses subreports to link information from three related tables to each row displayed from the tblInvoices table.

Objects in Reports

As with forms, you can embed objects in reports. The objects embedded in or linked to reports are usually pictures or charts. You can embed a picture or a chart as an unbound object in the report itself, you can link a picture or a chart as an object bound to data in your database, or you can use a shared image.

The rptInvoices report in the Conrad Systems Contacts database has an image object. When you open the rptInvoices report in Print Preview, you can see the Conrad Systems logo (a stylized font graphic) embedded in the report title as an unbound bitmap image object, as shown in Figure 16-9. This object is actually a part of the report design.

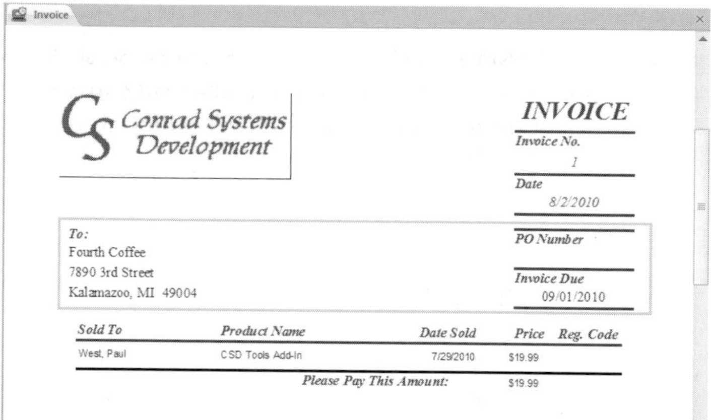

Figure 16-9 The rptInvoices report has an unbound bitmap image object (the Conrad Systems logo) embedded in the report header.

To see an example of how an object prints when it's stored in a table, open rptContacts, as shown in Figure 16-10. This picture is a bitmap image object stored in an attachment field in the tblContacts table—a picture of the contact.

Figure 16-10 The Photo field in the rptContacts report is a bitmap image object stored in an attachment field.

> **Note**
>
> You might notice that the Notes field in Figure 16-10 doesn't show all the text for some of the records. There's a special version of this report called rptContactsExpandNotes that fixes this problem with Microsoft Visual Basic code. See Chapter 25, "Automating Your Application with Visual Basic," for details.

Report View—A First Look

As you learned in Chapter 3, "Access 2010 Overview," Access 2010 includes a view for reports called Report view. Unlike Print Preview, which presents static data, you can use Report view to interact with data in the report. You can explore reports that take advantage of this view in the Housing.accdb sample database. A good place to start is the rptEmployeesPlain report. Open the database, and go to the Navigation pane. Click the Navigation Pane menu, click Object Type under Navigate To Category, and then click Reports under Filter By Group to display a list of reports available in the database. Scroll down the list of reports until you see the rptEmployeesPlain report, as shown in Figure 16-11. Right-click the report and click Open to see the report in Report view.

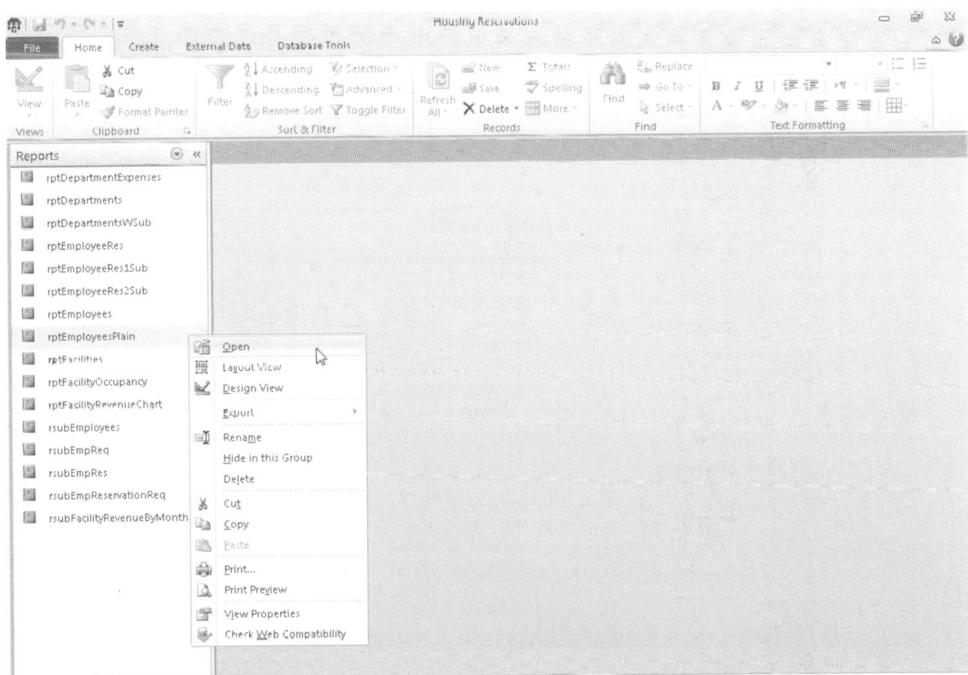

Figure 16-11 When you click Open on the shortcut menu for the rptEmployeesPlain report, Access opens it in Report view.

INSIDE OUT Understanding the Open Command for Reports

You might be wondering why clicking the Open command for the rptEmployeesPlain report opens it in Report view, but the same command opens the rptContactProducts report (discussed earlier in the chapter) in Print Preview. Access 2010 includes a report property called Default View. You can define whether a report opens in Report view or Print Preview by using this property. The default setting when you create a new report is Report view. For the rptEmployeesPlain report, we left this property set to Report view, so when you double-click the report in the Navigation pane or click the Open command on the object shortcut menu, Access opens the report in Report view. We will discuss this property further in Chapter 18, "Advanced Report Design."

The rptEmployeesPlain report is based on the qryRptEmployees query, which brings together information from the tblEmployees and tblDepartments tables. When the report opens in Report view, you'll see the data from these tables in the Housing database formatted in the report, as shown in Figure 14-12.

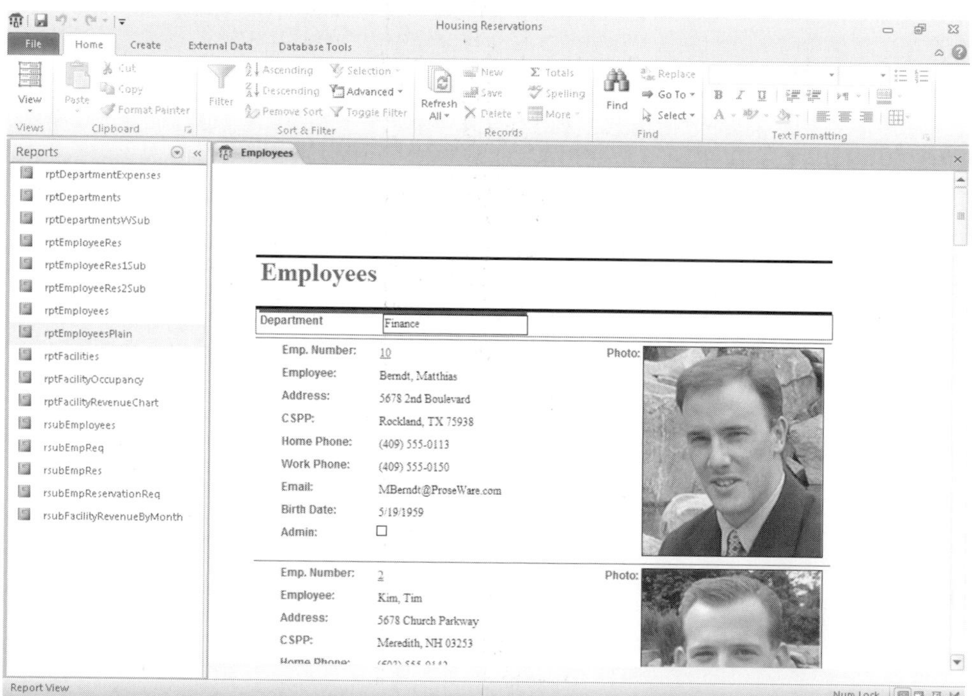

Figure 16-12 The rptEmployeesPlain is set to open in Report view.

If you look closely at Figure 16-12, you will no doubt notice that there is no Page Number box in the lower-left corner of the window. You can also see that the Print Preview contextual ribbon tab is not available. Access displays the four main ribbon tabs in Report view so that you can use filters to interact and display specific records and then print only this smaller group of records. If you were to print this report right now, all 16 employee records would be sent to your printer. Suppose, though, that you want to print only the records of employees who are in the Finance department. You could create a separate report that would show only the employees in the Finance department, but from within Report view, you can ask Access to filter the records to display only the employee records you need. With the rptEmployeesPlain open in Report view, right-click in the Department field for the first record and click Equals "Finance" on the shortcut menu, as shown in Figure 16-13.

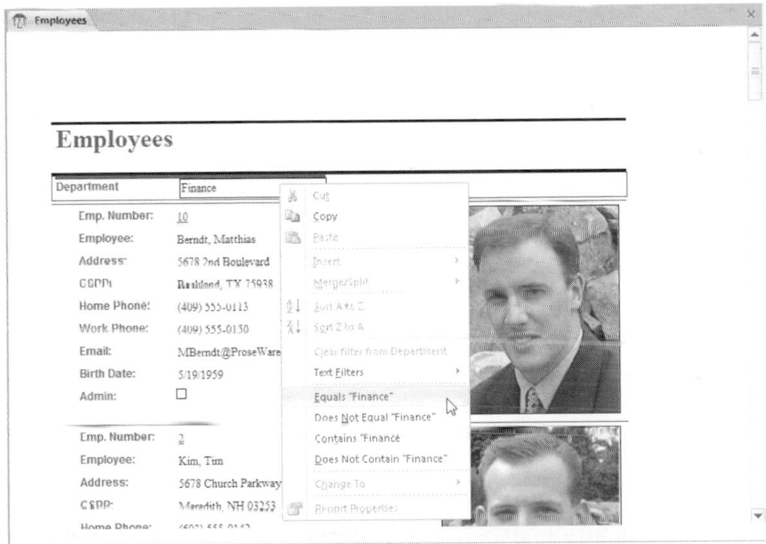

Figure 16-13 In Report view, you can filter the records to show just the ones you want to print.

After you click the Equals "Finance" command, Access filters all the records in the report record source to obtain the three employees in the Finance department, as shown in Figure 16-14. If you print the report at this point, Access prints only a one-page report with the three records.

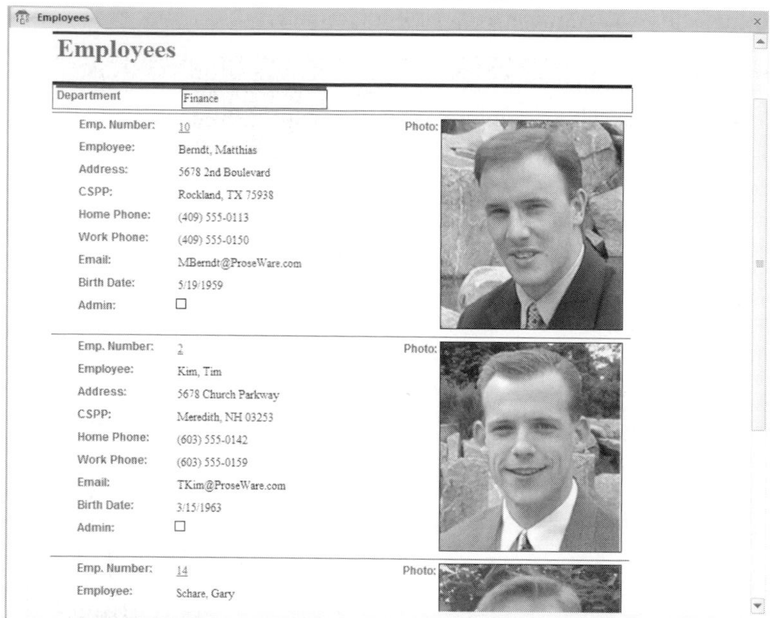

Figure 16-14 After you apply the filter shown in Figure 16-13, Access shows only the three employees in the Finance department.

By using Report view, you can create a single report that returns all records and then use the filtering capabilities of Access to show subsets of the data. To remove the filter applied to this report, click the Toggle Filter button in the Sort & Filter group on the Home tab, and Access again displays all 16 employee records. Report view gives you as many of the filtering and sorting capabilities as you have in forms, but in an object that's designed to be printed rather than to edit data.

In Report view, you can also define controls that respond to events, similar to what you can do with forms. We defined a Click event for the employee number text box and styled it as a hyperlink to provide a visual cue to the user. In Figure 16-15, you can see that the Employee Number field looks like a hyperlink with the data in blue and underlined. Clicking the Employee Number field opens the frmEmployeesPlain form as a dialog box displaying all information for that specific employee so that you can make any necessary changes. After closing the form and returning to the report, click the Refresh All command in the Records group on the Home tab to see any changes you made to the data using the form reflected in the report.

Figure 16-15 You can use Report view to respond to control events such as opening data entry forms.

Printing Reports

Earlier in this chapter, you learned the basics of viewing a report in Print Preview and in Report view. Here are a few more tips and details about setting up reports for printing.

Print Setup

Before you print a report, you might first want to check its appearance and then change the printer setup. Open the ContactsDataCopy database, right-click the rptContacts report (which you looked at earlier) in the Navigation pane, and click the Print Preview command on the shortcut menu to see the report. After Access shows you the report, click the arrow under the Zoom button in the Zoom group on the Print Preview contextual tab, and then size the window to see the full-page view by clicking Fit To Window. Click the Two Pages button in the same group to see two pages side by side, as shown in Figure 16-16.

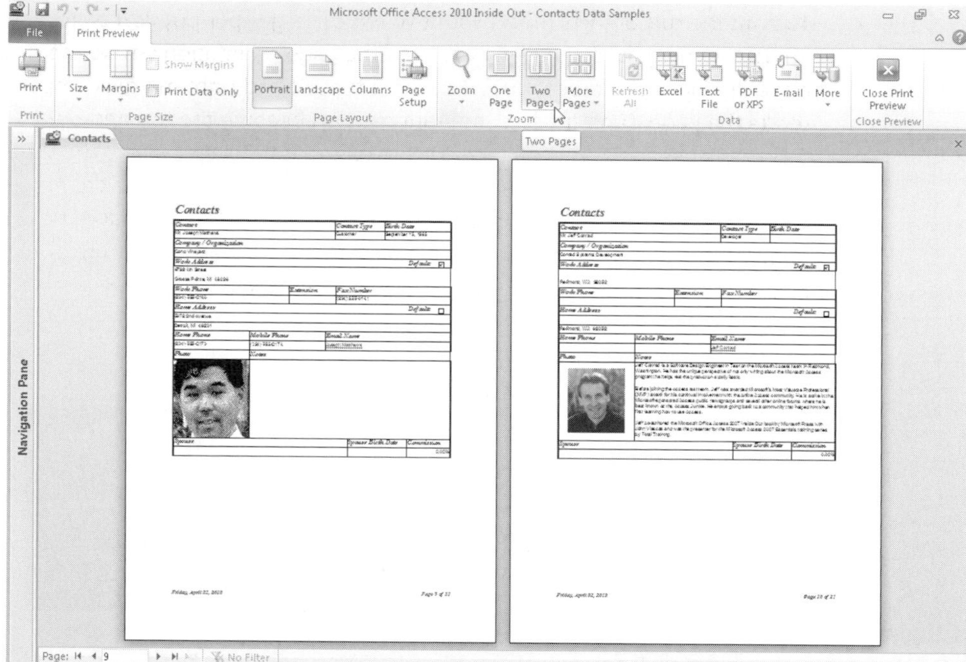

Figure 16-16 Click the Two Pages button on the ribbon to display a two-page view of the rptContacts report in Print Preview.

This report is narrow enough to print two contacts side by side in landscape orientation on 14-inch-long paper. To print it that way, you need to modify some parameters in the Page Setup dialog box.

Open the Page Setup dialog box by clicking the Page Setup button in the Page Layout group. Access displays a dialog box similar to the one shown in Figure 16-17.

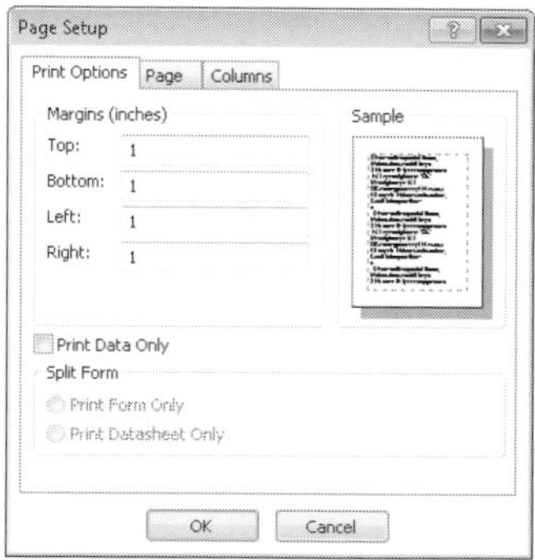

Figure 16-17 You can open the Page Setup dialog box from the Print Preview tab.

To print the rptContacts report with two logical pages per physical page, you first need to adjust the margins. You haven't changed the page orientation yet, so the settings that are currently the top and bottom will become the left and right margins, respectively, after you rotate the page. (And the left and right margins become the top and bottom, respectively.) The pages need to print very close to the edges of the paper, so set the top margin (this becomes the left margin in landscape orientation) to 0.25 inch, set the bottom margin to about 0.5 inch, and set the left and right margins to 0.5 inch. Effectively, the left margin will be the smallest after you change the orientation. Click the Page tab to display the next set of available properties, as shown in Figure 16-18.

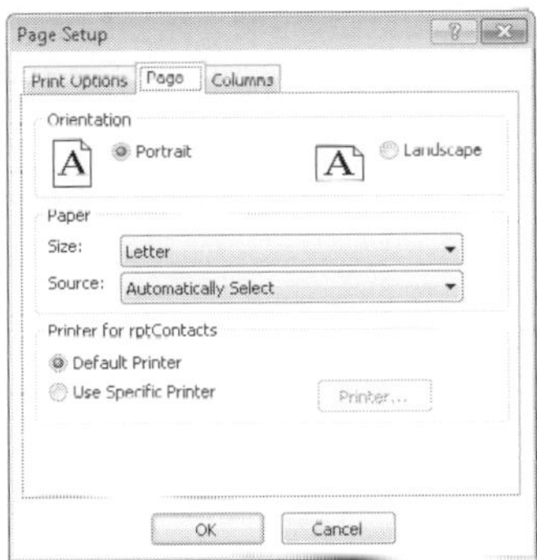

Figure 16-18 You can set page orientation options on the Page tab of the Page Setup dialog box.

On the Page tab, you can select the orientation of the printed page—Portrait to print vertically down the length of the page, or Landscape to print horizontally across the width of the page. Because we're trying to print two pages across a single sheet of paper, select the Landscape option. The report is also about 6½ inches wide, so you'll need wider paper to fit two logical pages to a printed page. Select Legal (8½-by-14-inch) paper from the Size list under Paper.

In general, it's best to leave the printer set to the default printer that you specified in your Windows settings. If you move your application to a computer that's attached to a different type of printer, you won't have to change the settings. You can print any report that you design in Access on any printer supported by Windows with good results.

However, if you've designed your report to print on a specific printer, you can save those settings by using the Page Setup dialog box. To do this, select the Use Specific Printer option on the Page tab and then click Printer to open a dialog box in which you can select any printer installed on your system. (The Printer button is available only if you have more than one printer installed on your computer.) Click the Properties button to adjust settings for that printer in its Properties dialog box, shown in Figure 16-19. The Properties dialog box you see might look different, depending on the capabilities of the printer you selected and how Windows supports that printer.

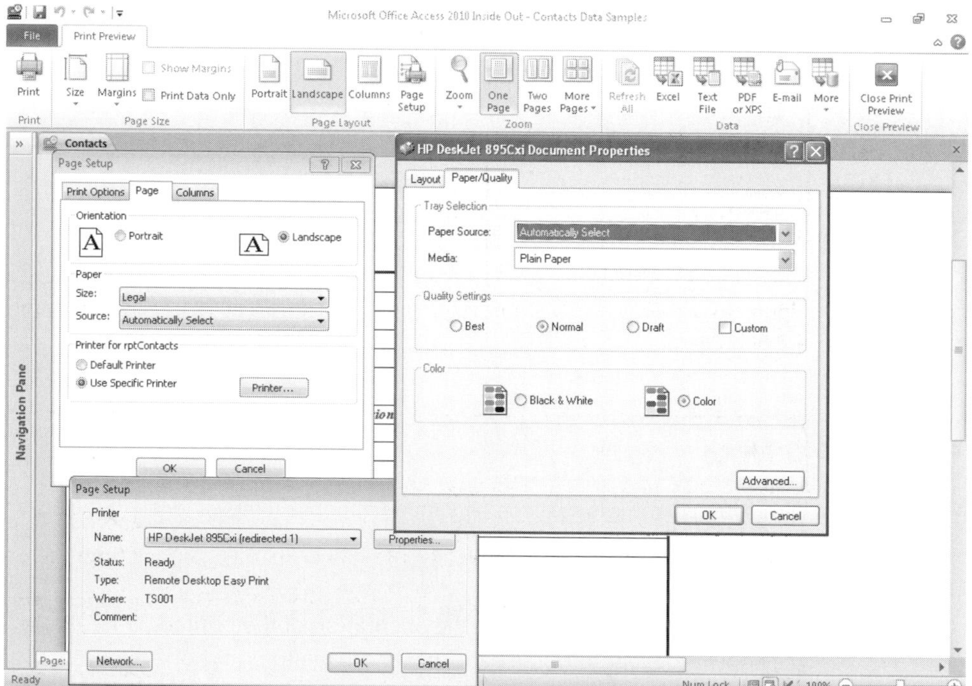

Figure 16-19 You can define properties for a specific printer to be used with your report.

After you finish selecting options on the Page tab, click the Columns tab, as shown in Figure 16-20, to set up a multiple-column report. In this case, you want to print two "columns" of information. After you set the Number Of Columns property to a value greater than 1 (in this case, 2), you can set spacing between rows and spacing between columns. By default, Access selects the Same As Detail check box and displays the design Width and Height measurements of your report. You can also clear the Same As Detail check box and set a custom width and height that are larger or smaller than the underlying report design size.

Note that if you specify a smaller size, Access crops the report. When you have detail data that fits in more than one column or row, you can also tell Access whether you want the detail printed down and then across the page or vice versa.

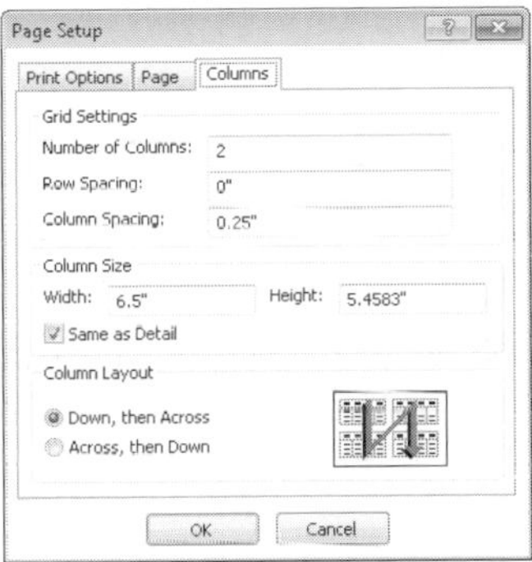

Figure 16-20 You can set report column properties on the Columns tab of the Page Setup dialog box.

> **Note**
>
> **If you created the report or have permission to modify the design of the report, you can change the page layout settings and save them with the report. The next time you print or view the report, Access will use the last page layout settings you specified.**

After you enter the appropriate settings in the Page Setup dialog box, click OK, and your report in Print Preview should look like the one shown in Figure 16-21. You can find this modified version of the Contacts report saved in the sample database as rptXmplContacts2Page.

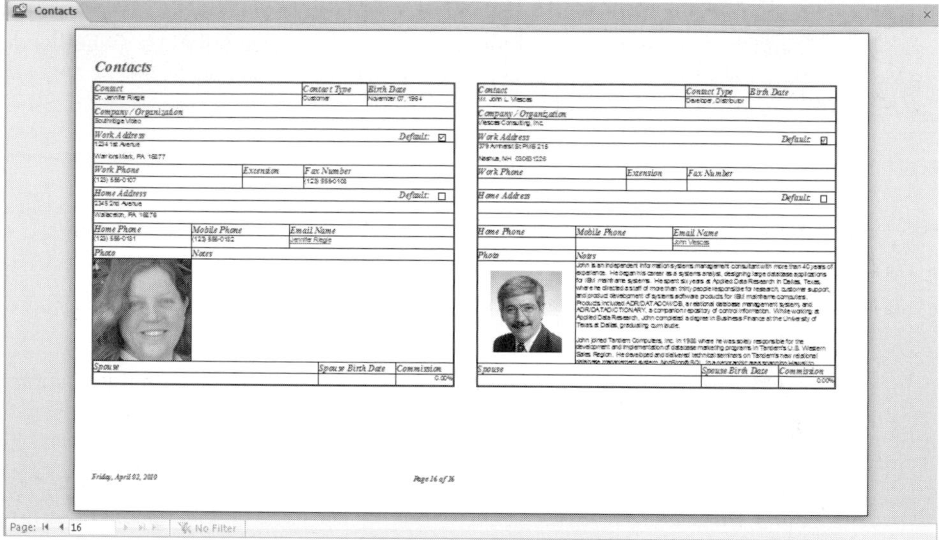

Figure 16-21 Print Preview now displays the rptContacts report in landscape orientation and in two columns.

The most common use for setting multiple columns is to print mailing labels. You can find four example reports in the sample database that do this: rptCompanyLabels5160 and rptContactLabels5160, which print company and contact labels two across in Avery 5160 format; and rptCompanyLabels5163 and rptContactLabels5163, which print company and contact labels three across in Avery 5163 format.

That covers the fundamentals of reports and how to view them and set them up for printing. The next two chapters will show you how to design and build client and web reports for your application.

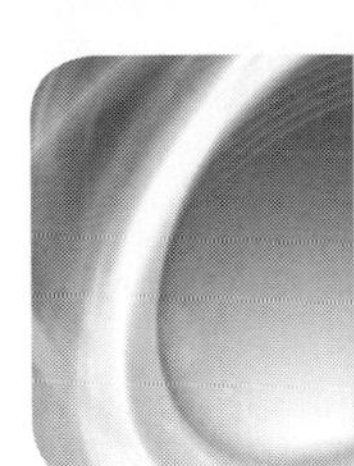

CHAPTER 17

Constructing a Report

Constructing a report is very similar to building a form. In this chapter, you'll apply many of the techniques that you used when working with client and web forms, and you'll learn about some of the unique features of reports. After a quick tour of the report design facilities, you'll build a simple report for the Conrad Systems Contacts client database, and then you'll use the Report Wizard to create the same report. You'll see how to use the quick create Report command to create a report with one mouse click. Finally, you'll learn how to create and modify web reports using Layout view in web databases.

Note

The examples in this chapter are based on the reports, tables, and data in the ContactsDataCopy.accdb and BOSSDataCopy2.accdb sample databases on the companion CD included with this book. You can find similar reports in the Conrad Systems Contacts and Back Office Software System sample client and web applications, but all the reports in those sample files have custom ribbons defined, so you won't see the four main ribbon tabs when you open those reports. The results you see from the samples in this chapter might not exactly match what you see in this book if you have changed the sample data in the files. Also, all the screen images in this chapter were taken on a Windows 7 system with the Access color scheme set to Silver. Your results might look different if you are using a different operating system or a different theme.

Starting from Scratch—A Simple Report

In a contact tracking application, the user is going to want to look at recent events and perhaps work through a list of events that require follow-ups. Although the user could search for events in a form, the application should also provide a report that lists events by contact and shows the phone numbers the user needs. This report can be filtered by the application to print out only recent and upcoming events.

Most reports gather information from several tables, so you'll usually design a query that brings together data from related tables as the basis for the report. In this section, you'll build a relatively simple report to list contact events as you tour the report design facilities. The report you'll build uses the tblContacts, tblContactEvents, and tlkpContactEventTypes tables in the ContactsDataCopy.accdb sample database. The report groups contact event data by contact, prints a single line for each contact event, and calculates the number of contact events and the number of follow-ups for each contact.

Building the Report Query

To construct the underlying query for the report, you need to start with the tblContactEvents table. Click the Query Design button in the Queries group on the Create tab. In the Show Table dialog box, select the tblContactEvents table, click the Add button to add it to the query design grid, and then add the tblContacts and the tlkpContactEventTypes tables as well. Click the Close button in the Show Table dialog box to dismiss it. You should see join lines between tblContacts and tblContactEvents on ContactID, and between tlkpContactEventTypes and tblContactEvents on ContactEventTypeID.

From the tblContacts table, add ContactID to the query design grid. The report needs to show the contact name, but it would be better to show the information concatenated in one field rather than separate title, first name, middle name, last name, and suffix fields. In the next column, enter this expression on the Field line:

```
Contact: ([tblContacts].[Title]+" ") & [tblContacts].[FirstName] & " " &
([tblContacts].[MiddleInit]+". ") & [tblContacts].[LastName] &
(", "+[tblContacts].[Suffix])
```

Notice that the expression uses the plus sign concatenation operator to eliminate extra blanks when one of the fields contains a Null value—a technique you learned in Chapter 9, "Creating and Working with Simple Queries."

The query also needs to include the contact's phone number, but the tblContacts table includes both a work and a home phone number. You can create an expression to examine the DefaultAddress field to decide which one to display. Microsoft Access 2010 provides a handy function, Choose, which accepts an integer value in its first argument and then uses that value to choose one of the other arguments. For example, if the first argument is 1, the function returns the second argument; if the first argument is 2, the function returns the third argument, and so on. The DefaultAddress field contains a 1 to indicate work address and a 2 to indicate home address. In the third field cell on the query design grid, enter the following:

```
Phone: Choose([tblContacts].[DefaultAddress], [tblContacts].[WorkPhone],
[tblContacts].[HomePhone])
```

To complete your query, include the ContactDateTime field from the tblContactEvents table and the ContactEventTypeDescription field from the tlkpContactEventTypes table. (ContactEventTypeID in tblContactEvents is a meaningless number.) Then include the ContactNotes, ContactFollowUp, and ContactFollowUpDate fields from the tblContactEvents table. Figure 17-1 shows the query you need for this first report. Click the Save button on the Quick Access Toolbar to save your new query. (You can find this query saved as qryRptContactEvents in the sample database.)

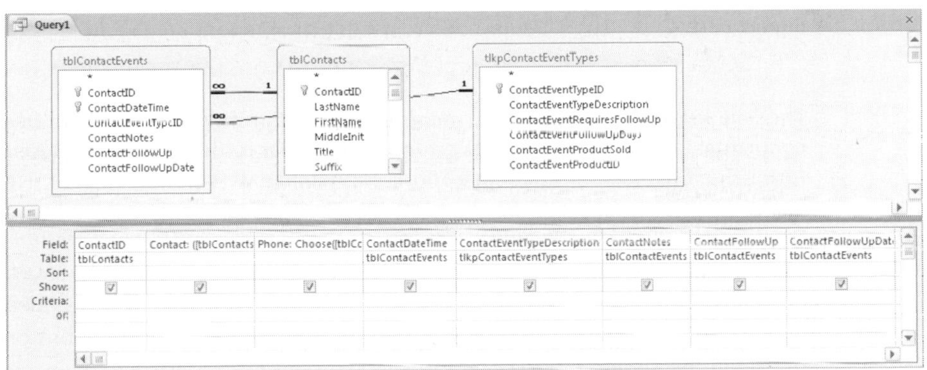

Figure 17-1 This query selects contact and contact event data for your report.

Note that although you're designing a report that will summarize the data, you are not building a totals query. If you used a totals query as the record source for the report, you would see only the summary in the report. One of the great advantages of reports is that you can see the detail information and also ask the report to produce summaries. In addition, you don't need to specify any sorting criteria here—you'll do that later in the report's Group, Sort, And Total pane.

Designing the Report

Now, you're ready to start designing the report. Click the Report Design button in the Reports group on the Create tab to tell Access 2010 that you want to begin creating a report in Design view, as shown in Figure 17-2.

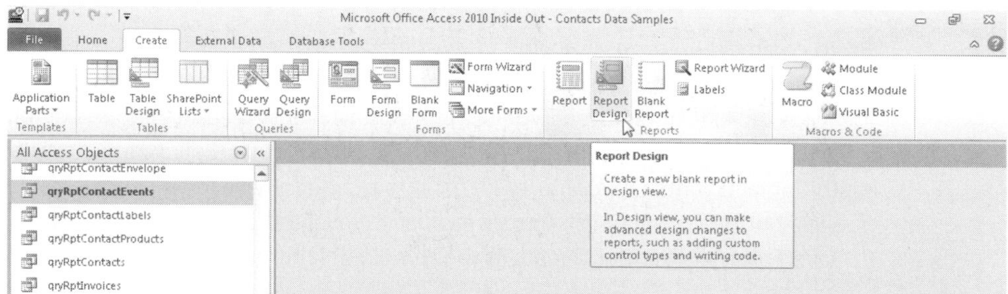

Figure 17-2 Click Report Design to start creating your report.

The field list, the property sheet, and the Font and Controls groups on the Design and Format contextual tabs under Report Design Tools are similar to the features you used in building forms. See Chapter 13, "Building a Form," for detailed descriptions of their uses.

Access 2010 opens a new Report window in Design view, as shown in Figure 17-3. You can see the Report Design Tools collection of ribbon tabs at the top of the Access window. The Report window is in the middle of the screen, and the property sheet is open to assist you in building your report. (If necessary, you can click the Property Sheet button in the Tools group on the Design tab to open this window.) To begin constructing your report, you need to tell Access to use the qryRptContactEvents query as its record source. In the property sheet, select qryRptContactEvents (or the name of the query you just created) in the Record Source property, as shown in Figure 17-3.

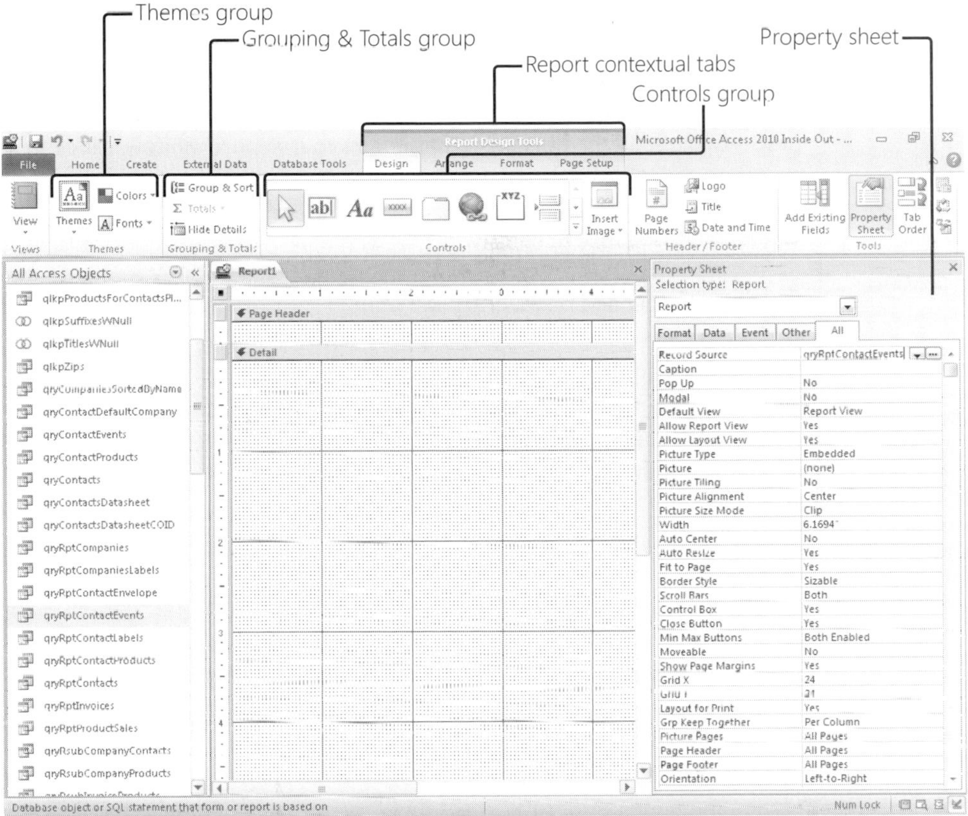

Figure 17-3 When you open a new Report window in Design view, Access displays all the tools you need to create the report.

The blank report has Page Header and Page Footer sections and a Detail section between them, which is 5.25 inches (13.333 cm) high and 6.1694 inches (15.668 cm) wide. The rulers along the top and left edges of the Report window help you plan space on the printed page. If you want standard 1-inch side margins, the body of the report can be up to 6½ inches wide on an 8½-by-11-inch page. The available vertical space depends on how you design your headers and footers and how you define the top and bottom margins. As with forms, you can drag the edge of any report section to make the section larger or smaller. Note that the width of all sections is the same, so if you change the width of one section, Access 2010 changes the width of all other sections to match.

Within each section, you see a grid that has 24 dots per inch horizontally and 24 dots per inch vertically, with a solid gray line displayed at 1-inch intervals. If you're working in centimeters, Access 2010 divides the grid into 5 dots per centimeter both vertically and horizontally. You can change these settings using the Grid X and Grid Y properties in the report's property sheet. (If the dots are not visible in your Report window, click the Grid command under the Size/Space in the Sizing & Ordering group on the Arrange contextual tab; if the Grid command is already selected and you still can't see the dots, try resetting the Grid X and Grid Y properties to lower numbers in the property sheet.)

The page header and page footer will print in your report at the top and bottom of each page. You can right-click anywhere on the report grid design surface and then click the Page Header/Footer button from the shortcut menu to add or remove the page header and page footer. You can also add a report header that prints once at the beginning of the report and a report footer that prints once at the end of the report. To add these sections to a report, right-click anywhere on the report grid design surface and then click the Report Header/Footer button from the shortcut menu. You'll learn how to add group headers and group footers in the next section.

Grouping, Sorting, and Totaling Information

A key way in which reports differ from forms is that in reports, you can group information for display using the Group, Sort, And Total pane. Click the Group & Sort button in the Grouping & Totals group on the Design tab (shown in Figure 17-3) to open the Group, Sort, And Total pane beneath the report design grid, as shown in Figure 17-4. (We collapsed the Navigation pane in Figure 17-4.) In this pane, you can define up to 10 fields or expressions that you will use to form groups in the report. The first item in the list determines the main group, and subsequent items define groups within groups. (You saw the nesting of groups in the previous chapter in the rptProductSalesByProduct report; each product category had a main group, and within that main group was a subgroup for each product.) Because we have not yet defined any grouping or sorting in this report, the Group, Sort, And Total pane opens to a blank pane that allows you to click either Add A Group or Add A Sort.

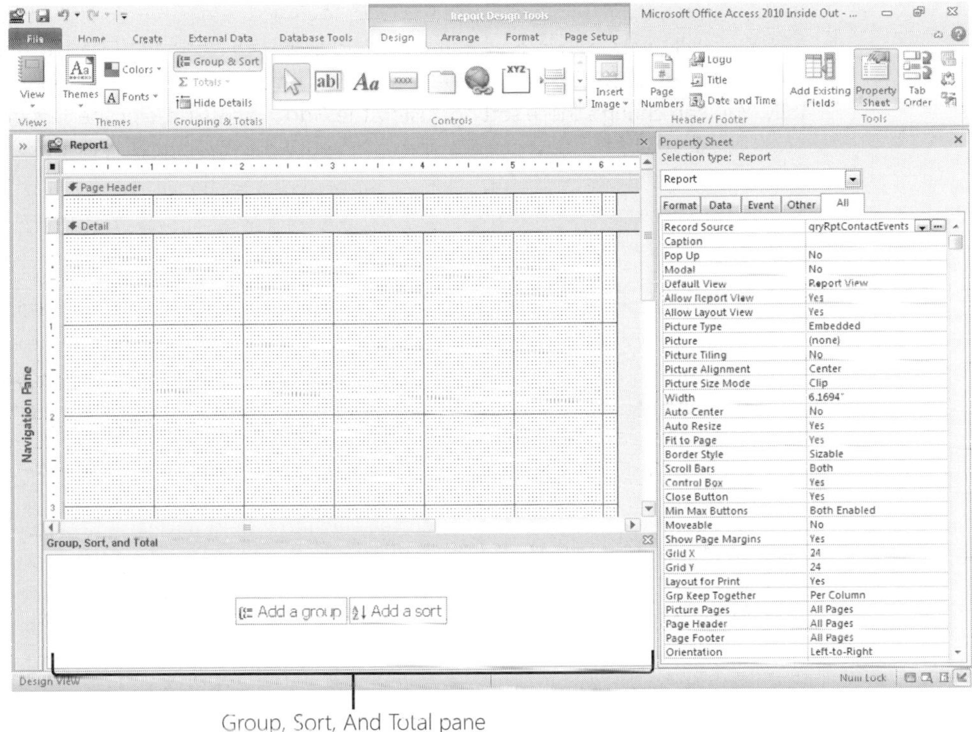

Figure 17-4 You can create groups and specify their sort order in the Group, Sort, And Total pane.

In the simple report you're creating for contact events, you need to group data by contact ID so that you can total the number of contact events as well as contact events that require follow-up for each contact. Click the Add A Group button in the Group, Sort, And Total pane. Access 2010 creates a new grouping specification and opens a list that contains all fields in the report's record source next to the Group On option, as shown in Figure 17-5. (We collapsed the Navigation pane and closed the property sheet in Figure 17-5 so that you can see more of the Group, Sort, And Total pane.)

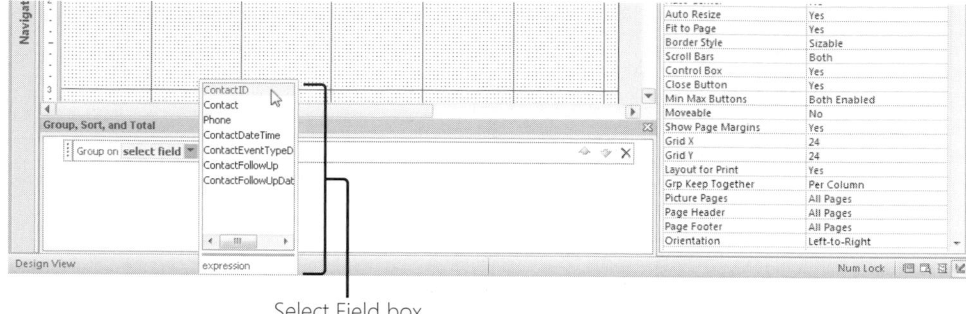

Figure 17-5 After you click Add A Group in the Group, Sort, And Total pane, Access creates a new grouping specification and opens a field list to let you select the field that defines the group.

If you click away from the field list before selecting a field to define the group, Access 2010 closes the field list. Click the arrow on the Select Field box (or press Alt+down arrow while the focus is on the Select Field box) to open the list of fields from the underlying query or table. Select the ContactID field to place it in the Select Field box. You can also use the Select Field box to enter an expression based on any field in the underlying table or query. Open the field list again and click the Expression option below the list of fields, and Access opens the Expression Builder to help you create the expression. You let Access know you're entering an expression by first typing an equals sign (=) followed by your expression. We discussed the Expression Builder in Chapter 9.

Note

When you define a grouping specification in a report, the report engine actually builds a totals query behind the scenes to perform the grouping. As you learned in Chapter 10, "Building Complex Queries," you cannot use Group By in a totals query on memo, OLE object, hyperlink, or attachment fields. For this reason, you cannot use Memo, OLE Object, Hyperlink, or Attachment data types in the Group, Sort, And Total pane.

After you select ContactID in the Select Field box, Access 2010 adds a new ContactID group header to the report grid beneath the Page Header group level, as shown in Figure 17-6. By default, Access sets the height of this new group level to ¼ inch. Access also displays the Add A Group and Add A Sort buttons beneath the first grouping specification so you can create additional grouping or sorting levels. To the right of the Group On ContactID in the Group, Sort, And Total pane, Access now adds two new options—From Smallest To Largest and More.

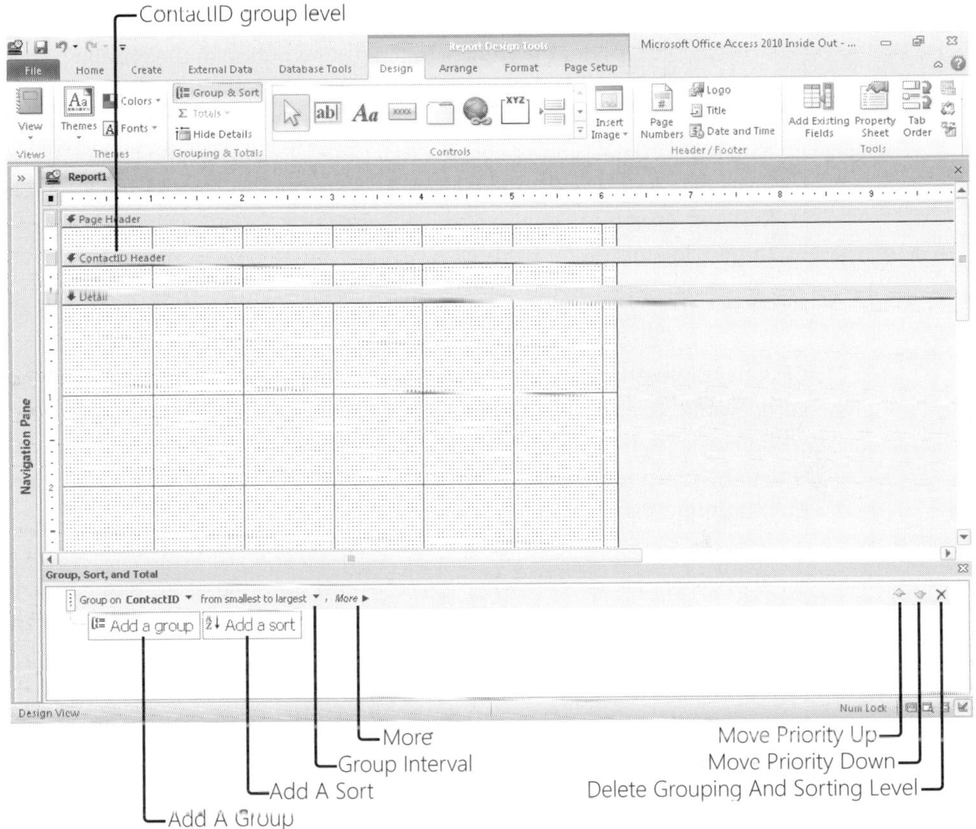

Figure 17-6 After you add a group in the Group, Sort, And Total pane, Access creates a new group level on the grid.

By default, Access 2010 sorts each field or expression in ascending order. You can change the sort order by selecting From Largest To Smallest from the list that appears when you click the arrow to the right of the second option (From Smallest To Largest, in this example). In this case, you want to include the ContactID field so that you can form a group for each contact. Leave the sort order on From Smallest To Largest so that the report will sort the rows in ascending numerical order by the ContactID field. If you wanted to see the contacts in alphabetical order by last name, you would need to include the LastName field in your query (even if you didn't display it on the report), and group and sort on the LastName field. You could use the Contact expression that you included in the query, but then the report would sort the rows by title and first name.

Note

Access 2010 changes the choices in the second option in the grouping specification depending on the data type of the field or expression you specified in Group On. When the data type is Text, you'll see With A On Top and With Z On Top options. When the data type is Date/Time, you'll see From Oldest To Newest and From Newest To Oldest. If the data type is Yes/No, you'll see From Selected To Cleared and From Cleared To Selected. As you saw in our example, Access uses From Smallest To Largest and From Largest To Smallest for fields with a Numeric data type.

Click the More option in the ContactID grouping specification to see all the grouping and sorting options, as shown in Figure 17-7. Access now displays a total of eight grouping and sorting options. If you look at Figure 17-7, you can see that Access creates a sentence structure to help you understand how this grouping level will take shape. If you want to collapse the list of options, click Less at the end of the list.

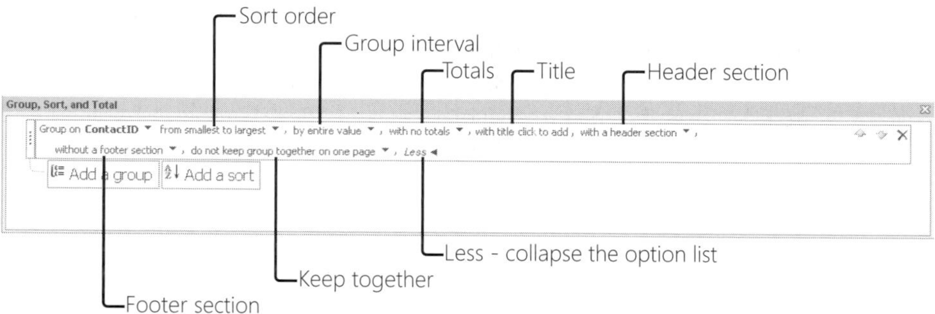

Figure 17-7 Click More to expand the list of grouping and sorting options.

The third option in the grouping specification (By Entire Value, in our example) is called the group interval, which tells Access how to group the records. Click the arrow to the right of this option for a grouping based on the ContactID field, as shown in Figure 17-8. For AutoNumber, Number, and Currency data types, Access displays the following grouping options—By Entire Value, By 5s, By 10s, By 100s, By 1000s, and Custom, which lets you set your own interval. For Text data types, you can set the group interval to By Entire Value, By First Character, By First Two Characters, or Custom, which lets you set your own interval. For Date/Time data types, you can set the group interval to By Entire Value, By Day, By Week, By Month, By Quarter, By Year, or Custom, which lets you set your own interval. Leave the group interval set to By Entire Value for the ContactID group level.

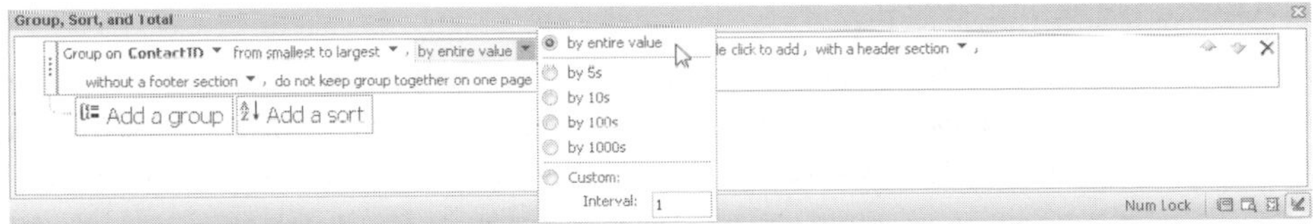

Figure 17-8 The group interval displays different options based on the field's data type.

You use the fourth option in the grouping specification (which currently displays With No Totals in our example) to configure Access to list totals for a single field or for multiple fields. Click the arrow to the right of this option for a grouping based on the ContactID field, as shown in Figure 17-9. Select the field on which you want Access to calculate and display totals from the Total On list. In the Type box, you can choose from several types of calculations based on the data type of the field you chose in the Total On box. Beneath the Type box are four check boxes for additional totaling options. Select the Show Grand Total check box to add a grand total for this field in the report's Footer section. Select the Show Group Subtotal As % Of Grand Total check box if you want Access to calculate the percentage of the grand total for each group and place that percentage in the group header or footer. Select the Show Subtotal In Group Header check box to place the total and optional percentage in the group's Header section and the Show Subtotal In Group Footer check box to place the total and optional percentage in the group's Footer section. Leave the option for the Totals list set at With No Totals for the ContactID group level.

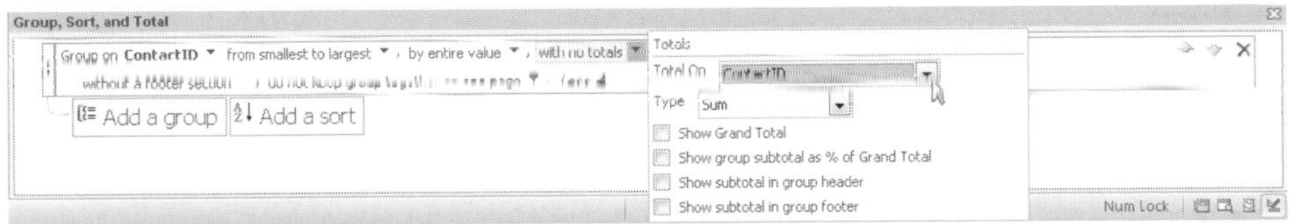

Figure 17-9 You can ask Access to calculate and display totals in the Totals list.

You use the fifth option in the grouping specification to define a title. You can choose to create a title that appears in a label control in the Header section of the group. To create a title, click the blue Click To Add text. Access opens the Zoom dialog box, shown in Figure 17-10, where you can enter a title. You can click Font to define the font, font style, size, and color of the title letters. After you enter a title, click OK, and Access creates a new label control in the Group Header section on the report grid. For the grouping based on the ContactID field, click Cancel to not enter a title at this time.

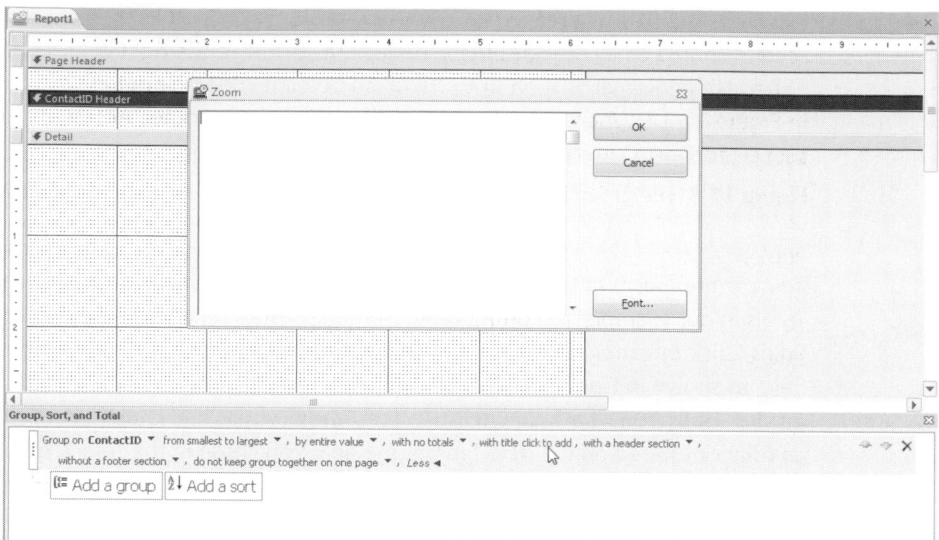

Figure 17-10 Access displays the Zoom dialog box when you want to add a title to a group header.

You use the sixth option in the grouping specification to display a Header section for the specific group. Click the arrow to the right of this option and you can select either With A Header Section (the default selection) or Without A Header Section, as shown in Figure 17-11. When you select the option to include a header, Access creates the Header section for the group for you. Conversely, Access removes the group header, and all controls in it, if you select the second option. If you have defined controls in the Header section when you choose Without A Header, Access displays a confirmation dialog box explaining that you're deleting both the header and all its controls, and asks you to confirm the deletion. For the ContactID field in our example, leave the option set to the default—With A Header Section.

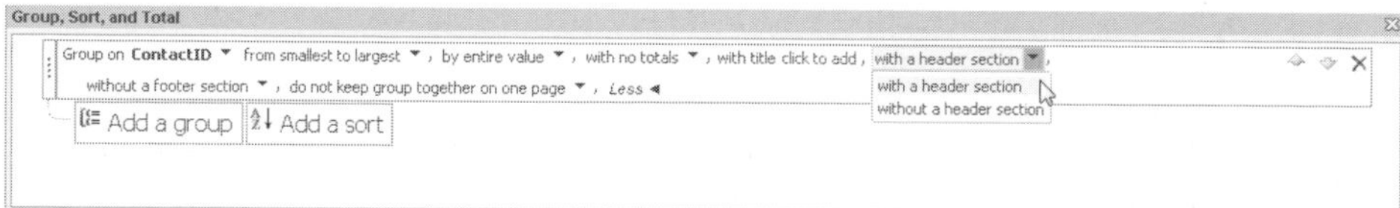

Figure 17-11 You can choose to have Access create a group header for you.

Similar to the Header section option, you can use the seventh option to display a Footer section for the grouping specification. Click the arrow to the right of this option and select either With A Footer Section or Without A Footer Section (the default selection), as shown in Figure 17-12. When you select the option to include a footer, Access creates the Footer section for you. Conversely, Access removes the group Footer, and all controls in it, if you select the second option. If you have defined controls in the footer section when you choose Without A Footer Section, Access displays a confirmation dialog box explaining that you're deleting both the footer and all its controls, and asks you to confirm the deletion. For the ContactID field, you will need a place to put two calculated total fields (the count of contact events and the count of follow-ups). Click the arrow to the right of this option and select With A Footer Section.

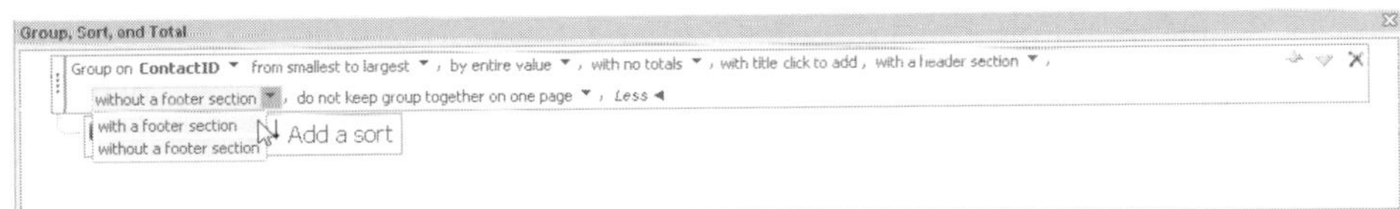

Figure 17-12 Select the With A Footer Section option to include a Footer section for the ContactID group on the report.

You use the last option in the grouping specification, as shown in Figure 17-13, to control how Access will lay out the report when you print it. Click the arrow to the right of this option, and you have three choices—Do Not Keep Group Together On One Page (the default), Keep Whole Group Together On One Page, and Keep Header And First Record Together On One Page.

The Do Not Keep Group Together On One Page option allows a section to flow across page boundaries. The Keep Whole Group Together On One Page option attempts to keep all lines within a section together on a page. If an entire group won't fit on the current page (and the current page isn't blank), Access moves to the top of the next page before starting to print the group, but the group still might overflow the end of the new page.

If you select Keep Header And First Record Together On One Page, Access does not print the header for the group at the bottom of the page if it cannot also print at least one detail record. For the ContactID field, leave the option set to the default—Do Not Keep Group Together On One Page. You'll learn more about how to use the group on, group interval, and keep together settings in the next chapter.

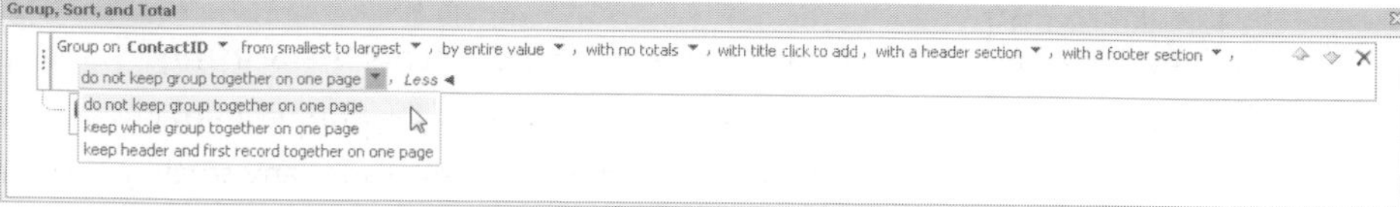

Figure 17-13 You can choose among several options to control how the report will look when printed.

It would also be nice to see the contact events in descending date order for each contact (most recent or newest events first). To add the ContactDateTime field below ContactID, click Add A Sort, and Access creates a new sort specification. Select ContactDateTime in the Select Field box and change the sort order to From Newest To Oldest. Click More to display the rest of the options available to you for the sort specification. Leave the group interval set to By Entire Value, and leave the Totals option set to the default With No Totals. Do not add a title for this field and make sure not to include a group header or group footer. (If you add a header or footer, Access changes your specification from a sorting specification to a grouping specification.) Finally, keep the last option set to Do Not Keep Group Together On One Page. Your completed sorting specification for the ContactDateTime field should look like Figure 17-14.

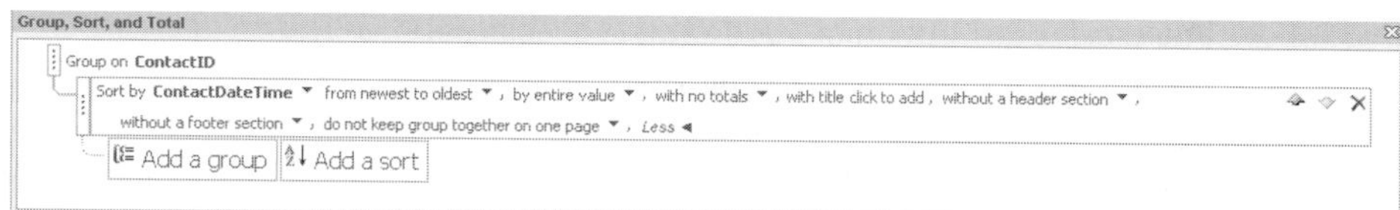

Figure 17-14 Access will now sort the contact event records for your report in descending order.

You can change the priority of two or more grouping or sorting specifications by using the arrows on the right side of the Group, Sort, And Total pane. If you need to move a group up one level, select that group and then click the up arrow one time. Similarly, if you need to move a group down one level, select that group and then click the down arrow one time. Access repositions any group headers and footers for you during this process. To delete a group level, select it and then click Delete (the X) to the right of the up and down arrows. Close the Group, Sort, And Total pane now by clicking the Close button on its title bar or by clicking the Group & Sort button in the Grouping & Totals group on the Design tab.

INSIDE OUT **Understanding Who Controls the Sorting**

You can specify sorting criteria in the query for a report, but after you set any criteria in the Group, Sort, And Total pane, the report overrides any sorting in the query. The best way to ensure that your report data sorts in the order you want is to always specify sorting criteria in the Group, Sort, And Total pane and not in the underlying query.

Completing the Report

Now, you're ready to finish building a report based on the tblContactEvents table. Take the following steps to construct a report similar to the one shown in Figure 17-15. (You can find this report saved as rptXmplContactEvents1 in the sample database.)

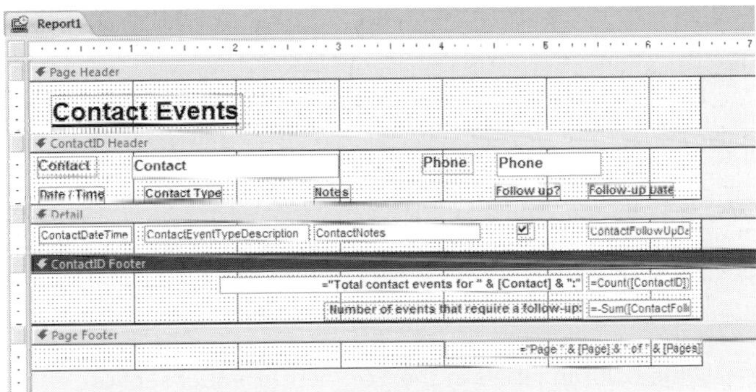

Figure 17-15 This is the completed Contact Events report that you will create in Design view.

1. Click the Title button in the Header/Footer group on the Design tab to place a new label control in the Report Header section. By default, Access enters the name of the report (in this case Report1) into the label. Click inside this label and highlight or delete the existing characters, type **Contact Events**, and press Enter to change the label's caption. Access placed this title in a new section it created—the Report Header. Any control placed in the Report Header section gets printed only on the first page of the report. We want to see this label on every page, so select the label control and then click the Move Down button in the Move group on the Arrange tab. Access moves the label control down into the Page Header section. (Note that

Access created this new label in a control layout which means you can't drag the label control down into a different section of the report.) Now, remove the Report Header section by right-clicking anywhere on the report grid design surface and then clicking the Report Header/Footer button on the shortcut menu. Access created an empty cell to the left of the label control which we don't need. Select the empty cell and then press Delete to remove it. Select the label control and use the commands in the Font group on the ribbon to change the font to Arial and the font color to Black. Next, click the Bold and Underline buttons in the Font group, and then click the To Fit command under the Size/Space command in the Sizing & Ordering group on the Arrange tab to size the control to accommodate the new font adjustments.

2. Click the Add Existing Fields button in the Tools group on the Design tab to show the field list. If you see Fields Available In Related Tables and Fields Available In Other Tables, click Show Only Fields In The Current Record Source at the top of the field list to reduce the number of fields and tables you see. Drag the Contact field from the field list and drop it into the ContactID Header section. Use Arial 10-point bold for the label control and the text box control and set the font color to Black for both controls. Select the text box control and make it about 2 inches wide so that there's room to display all the characters in the contact name. Also drag and drop the Phone field into the header, and set the resulting text box control and the label control to Arial 10-point bold and the font color to Black. Size all these controls to fit and line them up near the top of the section. Select the Phone text box control and set the Input Mask property to **\(999") "000\-0000** to display the data formatted as a phone number.

3. You'll need some column labels in the ContactID Header section. The easiest way to create them is to set up the text box control so that it has an attached label with no colon, set the defaults for the label control to the font you want, drag the fields you need to the Detail section, and then cut the label controls from their respective text box controls and paste them into the header.

   First, widen the design area of the report to about 6.5 inches and increase the height of the ContactID Header section to about 0.5 inch to give yourself some room to work. Next, to set the default properties for the text box and label controls, make sure the property sheet is open (click the Property Sheet button in the Tools group on the Design tab). Click the Text Box button in the Controls group on the Design tab. Select the All tab in the property sheet, scroll down, and check that the Auto Label property is set to Yes and that the Add Colon property is set to No. Also, set the Font Name property to Arial, the Font Size property to 8, and the Fore Color to Black (#000000). Click the Label button in the Controls group, and set its font to Arial 8-point bold, underlined, and black. (You set the font to bold by modifying the Font Weight property.) Click the Add Existing Fields button in the Tools group to hide the property sheet and open the field list. Now, drag the ContactDateTime, ContactEventTypeDescription, ContactNotes,

ContactFollowUp, and ContactFollowUpDate fields from the field list and drop them into the Detail section one at a time.

Select the label for ContactDateTime, and then choose the Cut command in the Clipboard group on the Home tab (or press Ctrl+X) to separate the label from the control and move it to the Clipboard. Click the ContactID Header bar, and then click the Paste command in the Clipboard group (or press Ctrl+V) to paste the label in the upper-left corner of the ContactID Header section. Notice that you can now move the label independently in the ContactID Header section. (If you move the label before you separate it from its control, the control moves with it.) Separate the labels from the ContactEventTypeDescription, ContactNotes, ContactFollowUp, and ContactFollowUpDate controls one at a time, and move them to the ContactID Header section of the report.

> **Note**
>
> **As you paste each label, you'll see warning smart tags appear that notify you that the labels aren't associated with any control. This is useful to know when you create labels in the Detail section. But in this case, this is what you want, so click the smart tag and select the Ignore Error option to turn off the warning for each label.**

4. Line up the column labels in the ContactID Header section, placing the Date / Time label near the left margin, the Contact Type label about 1.1 inches from the left margin, the Notes label about 2.75 inches from the left margin, the Follow Up? label about 4.5 inches from the left margin, and the Follow-up Date label about 5.4 inches from the left margin. You can set these distances in the Left property of each label's property sheet. Line up the tops of the labels by dragging a selection box around all five labels using the Select button in the Controls group on the Design tab and then clicking the Top command under the Align command in the Sizing & Ordering group on the Arrange tab.

5. You can enhance the appearance of the report by placing a line control across the bottom of the ContactID Header section. Click the Line button in the Controls group, and place a line in the ContactID Header section. To position this control at the bottom of the section, you need to find out the section's height. Click the ContactID Header bar to select the section, open the property sheet, and find the Height property. Next, select the line control, and set the following properties: Left 0, Width 6.5, and Height 0. Set the Top property equal to the Height of the section. (It's difficult to see this line in Figure 17-15, because it is hidden against the bottom of the section. You'll see it when you switch to Print Preview.)

6. You can make the text box control for ContactDateTime smaller (about 0.9 inch), and you need to make the ContactEventTypeDescription text box control about 1.6 inches wide. Set the Text Align property for the ContactDateTime and ContactFollowUpDate text box controls to Left. Access sized the text box for the ContactNotes field too wide because ContactNotes is a Memo data type. Select the ContactNotes and ContactEventTypeDescription text box controls together, click the Size/Space command in the Sizing & Ordering group on the Arrange tab, and then click the To Narrowest button to make the ContactNotes text box the same width as the ContactEventTypeDescription text box.

7. Align the text box controls for ContactDateTime, ContactEventTypeDescription, ContactNotes, ContactFollowUp, and ContactFollowUpDate under their respective labels. You can align each one by placing each text box control to the right of the left edge of its label, selecting them both (hold down the Shift key while selecting each one), and then left aligning them by clicking the Align command in the Sizing & Ordering group on the Arrange tab, and then clicking the Left button. Align the ContactFollowUp check box control visually under the center of its label. Select all the controls in the Detail section and top align them by clicking the Top button under the Align command in the same group.

8. The height of the Detail section determines the spacing between lines in the report. You don't need much space between report lines, so make the Detail section smaller, until it's only slightly higher than the row of controls for displaying your data. (About 0.3 inch should suffice.)

9. Expand the height of the ContactID Footer section and then add a text box in this section under the ContactFollowUpDate text box control and delete its attached label. To calculate the number of events, click the text box control, and in the Control Source property in the property sheet, enter

   =Count([ContactID])

   It's a good idea to repeat the grouping information in the footer in case the detail lines span a page boundary. One way to do that is to add an expression in a text box. Add a second text box to the left of the first one (also delete its label) and stretch it to about 3.5 inches wide. Click the leftmost text box control to select it, and in the Control Source property in the property sheet, type

   ="Total contact events for " & [Contact] & ":"

   Change the text box alignment to Right and change its font to Bold.

10. Add a third text box control in the ContactID Footer section under the first one. In the Control Source property in the property sheet, enter

    = –Sum([ContactFollowUp])

Keep in mind that a True value in a yes/no field is the value –1. So, summing the values and then displaying the negative should give you a count of the contact events that require a follow-up. Click the attached label control and change the Caption Property in the property sheet to

Number of events that require a follow-up:

Change Font Underline to No, right align the label, and size it to fit.

11. Add a line to the bottom of the ContactID Footer section to separate the end of the information about one contact from the next one. You can click the heading bar of the ContactID Footer to select the section and then look in the property sheet to find out the section's height, which should be about 0.5 inch. Select the line again, and in the property sheet, set Left to 0, Top to the height of the section, Width to 6.5, Height to 0, and Border Width (the thickness of the line) to 2 pt.

12. Click the Page Numbers button in the Header/Footer group on the Design tab to open the Page Numbers dialog box shown here.

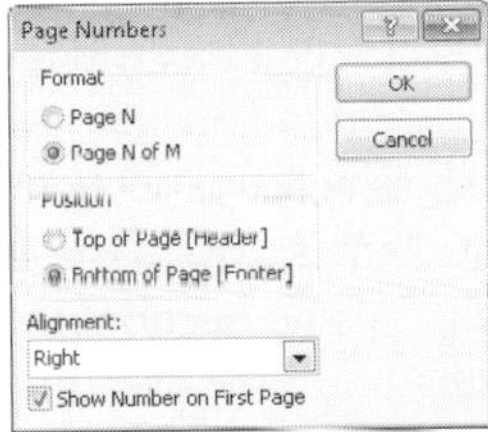

You want to display the current page number and the total number of pages on each page, so select the Page N Of M option under Format. The Page N option displays only the current page number. Next, to display these page numbers at the bottom of the report, select Bottom Of Page [Footer] under Position. The Top Of Page [Header] option places the control in the Page Header section of the report. In the Alignment list, select Right to display the page numbers on the right side of the page. The Left alignment option places the control that displays the page numbers on the left side of the report design grid, and the Center alignment option places the control in the center. The Inside alignment option places one control on the left side and one control on the right side of the report design grid. Access sets the Control Source property of these controls so that page numbers appear in the inside margin of pages in a bound book—odd page numbers appear on the left and even page numbers appear on the right. The Outside alignment option works just the opposite of Inside—even page numbers appear on the left and odd page numbers appear on the right.

Select the Show Number On First Page check box at the bottom of the dialog box to display the page numbers on all pages, including the first page. If you clear this check box, Access creates a control that will not show the page number on the first page. Click OK in the Page Numbers dialog box, and Access creates a new control in the Page Footer section.

13. Click the new text box control that you just created in the page footer, and look at the Control Source property in the property sheet. Access created the expression **="Page " & [Page] & " of " & [Pages]** in the Control Source property of the text box. [Page] is a report property that displays the current page number. [Pages] is a report property that displays the total number of pages in the report. Change the Text Align property to Right for this new control.

14. By default, Access added borders around nearly all the label and text box controls you added. You don't need the borders around these controls, so let's remove them. Hold down the Shift key and then select each label and text box one by one in the ContactID Header section, the Detail section, and the ContactID Footer section. (You do not need to select the label in the Page Header section nor the two line controls.) Now, set the Border Style property on the Property Sheet window to Transparent to change all the controls at once. Finally, Access added an alternating back color to the ContactID Header and Footer section and the Detail section. When the Alternate Back Color property for a section is set to a color, Access alternates between showing that color and white when it formats each successive section. To remove the color, select the ContactID Header section, click the bottom half of the Alternate Row Color button in the Background group on the Format tab to open the Color Picker dialog box, and then click No Color. Repeat this step for the Detail and ContactID Footer sections.

After you finish, click the arrow below the View button in the Views group on the ribbon and click Print Preview to see the result, shown in Figure 17-16. Notice, in this figure, that the detail lines are sorted in descending order by contact date/time. You'll recall from Figure 17-14 that the grouping and sorting specifications include a request to sort within a group on ContactDateTime.

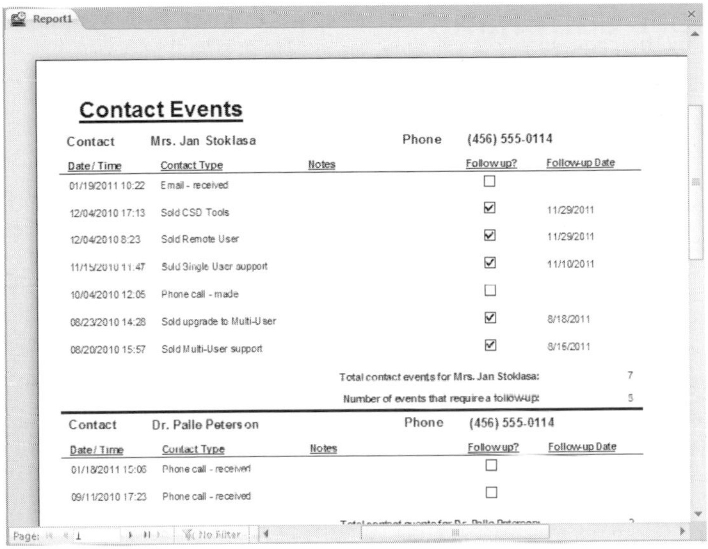

Figure 17-16 This is how your completed Contact Events report looks in Print Preview.

Now that you've seen how to create a report from scratch, you should have a good understanding of how to work with the individual design elements. In the next sections, we'll show you how to get a jump-start on your report design using the quick create Report command and the Report Wizard. You'll probably find that using one of these features is a good way to get a report started, and then you can use what you've learned thus far to fully customize your reports.

INSIDE OUT Summing Yes/No Fields on Web Reports

In this section, we showed you how to write an expression in the Control Source property of a text box to display a sum of True values in a Yes/No field in a group Footer section. We had you enter the following expression into the Control Source property: = –Sum([ContactFollowUp])

If you use this same expression on a web report, the expression evaluates to an error when you view the report in a web browser. On the server, you cannot use arithmetic expressions with values in a Yes/No field. If you are creating a web report and need to sum the True values in a Yes/No field, you should use the Immediate If function to evaluate the Yes/No field and then use 0 or 1 based on the field value for your Sum expression. Using the field name in the previous example, the following expression would correctly count the number of True values in the ContactFollowUp field on a web report and display them in a web browser: =Sum(IIf([ContactFollowUp]<>False,1,0))

Using the Report Command

Access 2010 includes a quick create Report command that makes it easy for you to quickly create quality reports. Similar to the quick create form commands, the Report command is a one-step process—you're not presented with any options or dialog boxes; Access simply creates a generic report with one click. You can use either a table or query as the base for the report. We'll create two quick reports to illustrate this process using the ContactsDataCopy.accdb sample database.

Open ContactsDataCopy.accdb, click the Navigation Pane menu, click Object Type under Navigate To Category, and then click Queries under Filter By Group to display a list of queries available in this database. The qryContacts query includes all the fields from the tblContacts table and sorts them by last name and then first name. Let's create a nice report of your contacts using this query. Scroll down to this query in the Navigation pane, select it, and then click the Report command in the Reports group on the Create tab, as shown in Figure 17-17.

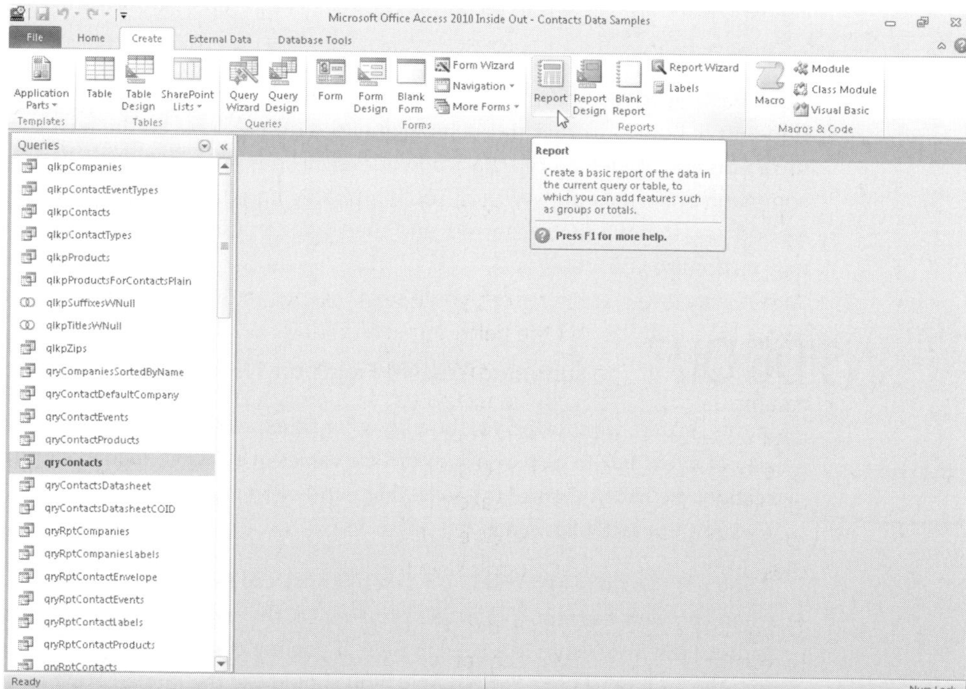

Figure 17-17 Click the Report command to let Access build a report using the qryContacts query.

After just a second or two, Access 2010 creates an entire report with all the fields in the query, complete with a logo, a title, the current date and time, a colored line beneath the column labels, and even a page count at the bottom of the pages, as shown in Figure 17-18. (You can best see the page count in Print Preview view.) Access opens the report in Layout view so that you can begin the process of making modifications.

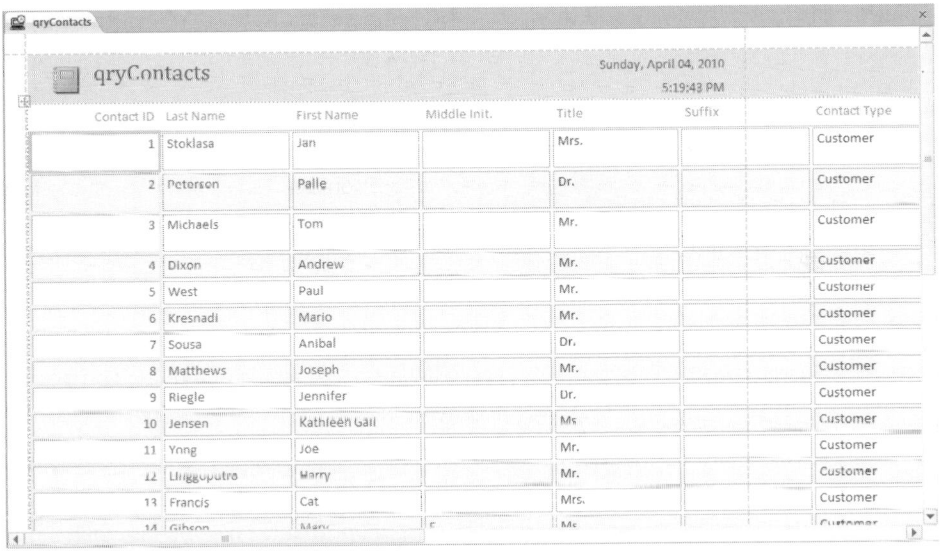

Figure 17-18 With one click, Access creates an entire formatted report for your convenience.

If you look closely at the report, you'll see that there are significant problems with this layout. Access spread all the fields out in a tabular control layout. If you switch to Print Preview, you can see that this report would not be easy to read because the data in many columns wraps to multiple lines, and you have to scan across three pages to find all the data for each contact. If the number of contact records were even larger, the report would be extremely hard to follow. Access did much of the hard work for you in creating the report, but you still need to make many modifications in either Layout view or Design view to make the report readable. (We'll discuss Layout view in more detail later in this chapter.) Close this report now, and don't save it when prompted.

The qlkpProducts query includes all the fields from the tblProducts table and sorts them by product name. Select this query in the Navigation pane, and then click the Report command in the Reports group on the Create tab. Access 2010 creates another report very similar to the first one, as shown in Figure 17-19.

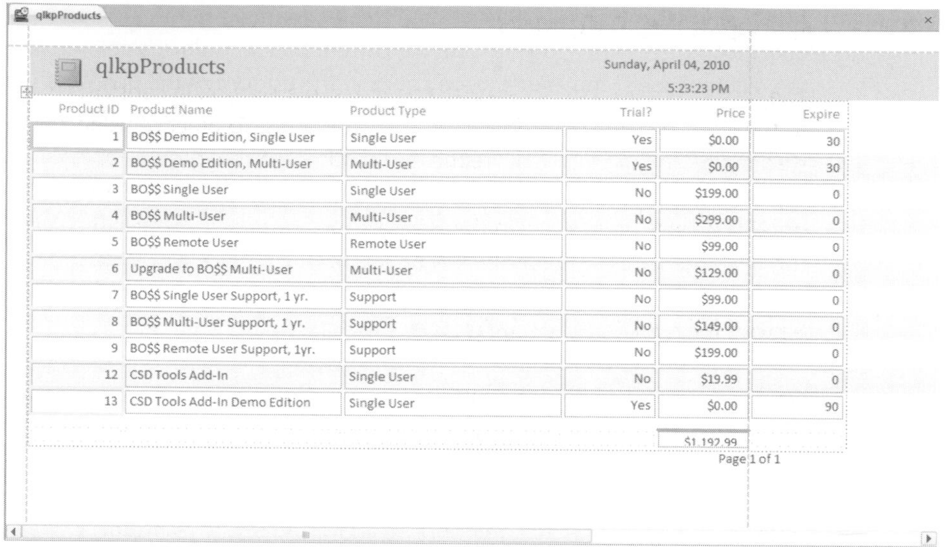

qlkpProducts

Sunday, April 04, 2010
5:23:23 PM

Product ID	Product Name	Product Type	Trial?	Price	Expire
1	BO$$ Demo Edition, Single User	Single User	Yes	$0.00	30
2	BO$$ Demo Edition, Multi-User	Multi-User	Yes	$0.00	30
3	BO$$ Single User	Single User	No	$199.00	0
4	BO$$ Multi-User	Multi-User	No	$299.00	0
5	BO$$ Remote User	Remote User	No	$99.00	0
6	Upgrade to BO$$ Multi-User	Multi-User	No	$129.00	0
7	BO$$ Single User Support, 1 yr.	Support	No	$99.00	0
8	BO$$ Multi-User Support, 1 yr.	Support	No	$149.00	0
9	BO$$ Remote User Support, 1yr.	Support	No	$199.00	0
12	CSD Tools Add-In	Single User	No	$19.99	0
13	CSD Tools Add-In Demo Edition	Single User	Yes	$0.00	90
				$1,192.99	

Page 1 of 1

Figure 17-19 This report is easier to understand than the one created on a more complex query.

This query has only six fields, so Access was able to do a better job of laying out the fields horizontally. However, the Expire field spills over onto a second page. Using the techniques you learned earlier in this chapter, it would probably take you less than a minute to resize some of the controls to fit everything onto one page and change the title. The rest of the report looks very usable as is. As you can see, the Report command can save you time compared to starting a report from scratch. Close the report, and don't save it when prompted.

INSIDE OUT When to Use the Report Command

The Report command's strength is speed, not finesse. As the previous two examples demonstrate, this report option is not suited for all occasions. For complex queries or tables with quite a few fields, it might take you longer to clean up a report created with this one-click approach compared to starting from scratch. Although the Report command does create a simple total for the Price field, it does not create any groups or sorts, so you would have to manually add these. We find that the Report command is best suited for simple tables or queries that do not require a lot of complex report analysis.

Using the Report Wizard

The Report Wizard that Access 2010 provides to assist you in constructing reports is similar to the Form Wizard you used earlier to create forms. To practice using the Report Wizard, we'll build the Contact Events report again. Click the Navigation Pane menu, click Object Type under Navigate To Category, and then click Queries under Filter By Group. Select the qryRptContactEvents query in the Navigation pane, and then click the Report Wizard button in the Reports group on the Create tab to open the Report Wizard.

Specifying Report Wizard Options

On the first page of the Report Wizard, shown in Figure 17-20, select the fields you want in your report. (If you have a table or query selected in the Navigation pane and then click Report Wizard, Access automatically uses that object as the record source for the report.) You can select all available fields in the order in which they appear in the underlying query or table by clicking the double right arrow (>>) button. If you want to select only some of the fields, or if you want to specify the order in which the fields appear in the report, select one field at a time in the Available Fields list and click the single right arrow (>) button to move the field to the Selected Fields list. If you make a mistake, you can select the field in the Selected Fields list and then click the single left arrow (<) button to move the field to the Available Fields list. Click the double left arrow (<<) button to remove all selected fields from the list on the right and start over.

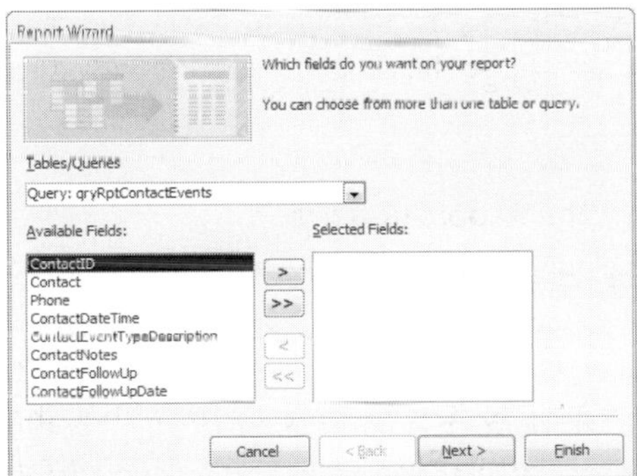

Figure 17-20 Select fields to include in the report on the first page of the Report Wizard.

To create the Contact Events report, you should select all the fields. Then click Next to go to the next page.

INSIDE OUT Selecting Fields from More Than One Table and/or Query

You can also select fields from one table or query and then change the table or query selection in the Tables/Queries list. The Report Wizard uses the relationships you defined in your database to build a new query that correctly links the tables or queries you specify. If the wizard can't determine the links between the data you select, it warns you and won't let you proceed unless you include data only from related tables.

The wizard examines your data and tries to determine whether there are any natural groups in the data. Because this query includes information from the tblContacts table that has a one-to-many relationship to information from the tblContactEvents table, the wizard assumes that you might want to group the information by contacts (the ContactID, Contact, and Phone fields), as shown in Figure 17-21. If you don't want any report groups or you want to set the grouping criteria yourself, select By tblContactEvents. In this case, the Report Wizard has guessed correctly, so click Next to go to the next step.

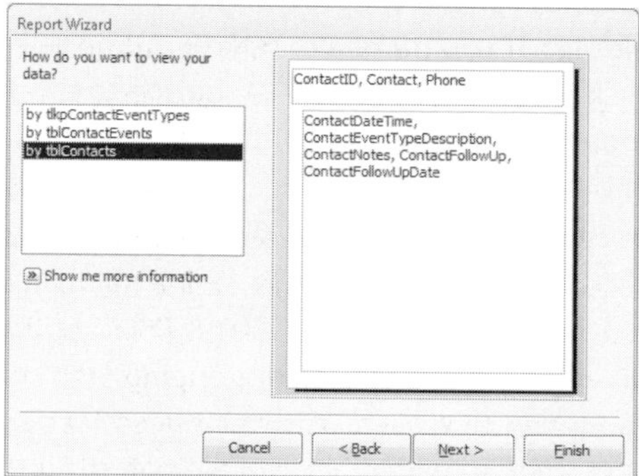

Figure 17-21 Make sure to verify the primary grouping criteria on the second page of the Report Wizard.

On the next page (shown in the background in Figure 17-22), the Report Wizard shows you the grouping already selected for ContactID and asks whether you want to add any grouping levels below that. (If you chose to set the criteria yourself by choosing By tblContactEvents on the previous page, you will see a similar window with no first group selected.) You can select up to four grouping levels. The wizard doesn't allow you to enter an expression as a grouping value—something you can do when you build a report from scratch. If you want to use an expression as a grouping value in a report that you create with the Report Wizard, you have to include that expression in the underlying query. For this report, you could also group within each contact by the ContactDateTime field, so select that field and click the single right arrow to temporarily add it as a grouping level.

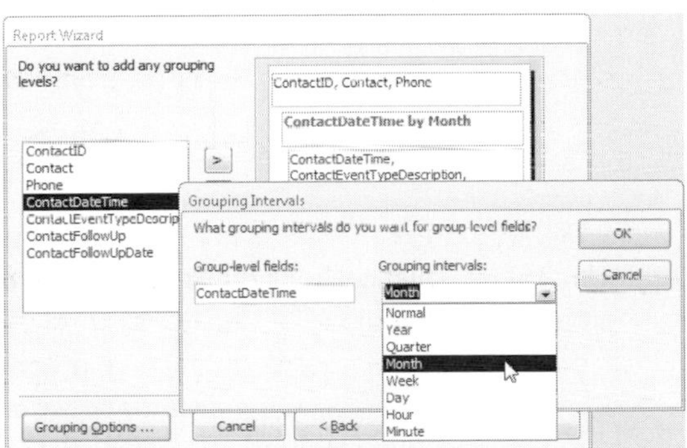

Figure 17-22 You can set grouping intervals on the grouping fields in the Report Wizard.

When you add grouping levels, the Report Wizard makes the Grouping Options button available for those levels. You can select the ContactDateTime By Month grouping level on the right side of this page and then click this button to see the Grouping Intervals dialog box, shown in Figure 17-22. For a text field, you can group by the entire field or by one to five of the leading characters in the field. For a date/time field, you can group by individual values or by year, quarter, month, week, day, hour, or minute. For a numeric field, you can group by individual values or in increments of 10, 50, 100, 500, 1,000, 5,000, or 10,000. As you can see, the Report Wizard has automatically assumed grouping by month when you added the ContactDateTime field as a grouping level. You don't need that grouping level in this sample, so cancel the Grouping Intervals dialog box, select ContactDateTime By Month on the right side of the page, and click the single left arrow to remove it. Then click Next.

On the next page, shown in Figure 17-23, the Report Wizard asks you to specify any additional sorting criteria for the rows in the Detail section. (Access will sort the report at this point by the grouping level fields you specified on the previous page.) You can select up to four fields from your table or query by which to sort the data. By default, the sort order is ascending. Click the button to the right of the field selection list box to switch the order to descending. You can't enter expressions as you can in the Group, Sort, And Total pane. In this report, click the arrow to the right of the first box and select the ContactDateTime field. Click the button to the right once to switch it to Descending, as shown in the figure.

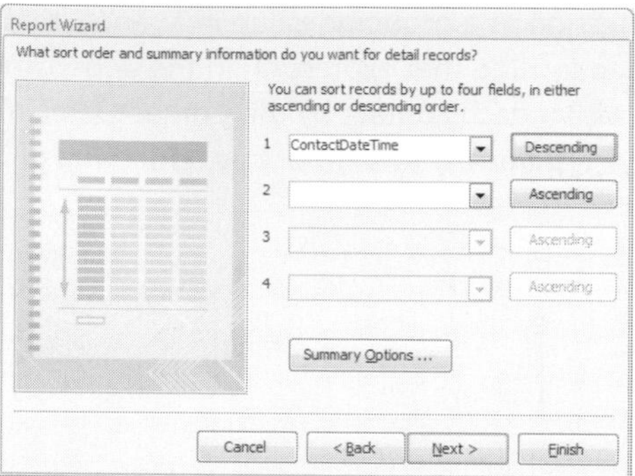

Figure 17-23 Select ContactDateTime on the fourth page of the Report Wizard to sort on that field.

Click Summary Options to open the dialog box shown in Figure 17-24. Here you can ask the Report Wizard to display summary values in the group footers for any numeric fields the wizard finds in the Detail section. In this case, the Report Wizard sees that the ContactFollowUp field is the only one in the Detail section that is a number (a Yes/No data type). As you'll see later in this chapter, the Report Wizard automatically generates a count of the rows, which explains why Count isn't offered as an option.

Select the Sum check box for this field. (You can add the minus sign after the wizard is done to get the correct count.) Note that you also have choices to calculate the average (Avg) of values over the group or to display the smallest (Min) or largest (Max) value. You can select multiple check boxes. You can also indicate that you don't want to see any detail lines by selecting the Summary Only option. (Sometimes you're interested in only the totals for the groups in a report, not all the detail.) If you select the Calculate Percent Of Total For Sums check box, the Report Wizard will also display, for any field for which you have selected the Sum check box, an additional field that shows what percent of the grand total this sum represents. When you have the settings the way you want them, click OK to close the dialog box. Click Next in the Report Wizard to go on.

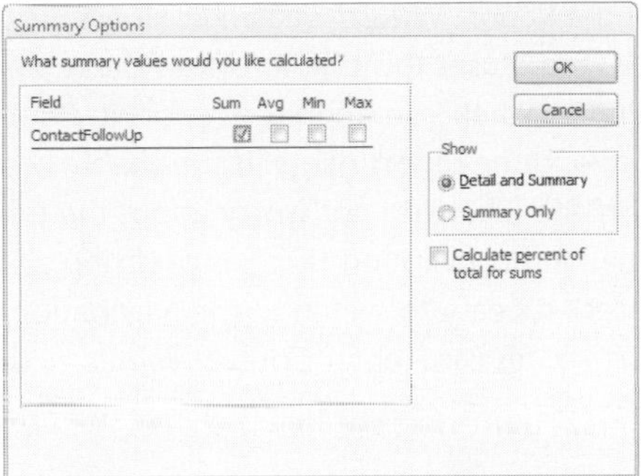

Figure 17-24 Click the Summary Options button on the fourth page of the Report Wizard to select additional summary options.

On the next page, shown in Figure 17-25, you can select a layout style and a page orientation for your report. When you select a layout option, the Report Wizard displays a preview on the left side of the page. In this case, the Outline layout option in Portrait orientation will come closest to the hand-built report you created earlier in this chapter. You should also select the check box for adjusting the field widths so that all the fields fit on one page (selected by default).

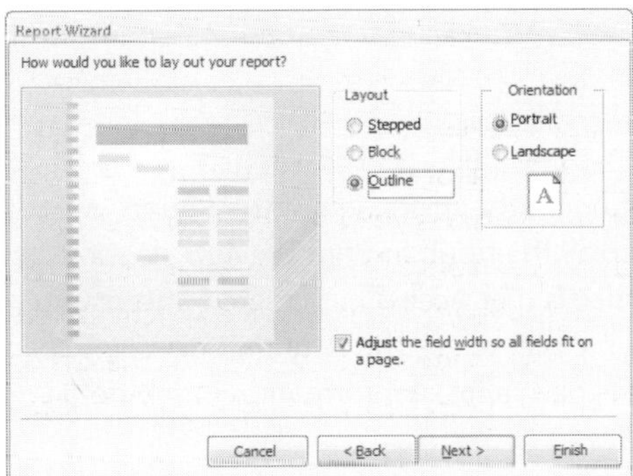

Figure 17-25 Choose a layout style and page orientation on this page of the Report Wizard.

Click Next to go to the final page of the Report Wizard, shown in Figure 17-26. Here, you can type a report title. Note that the wizard uses this title to create the report caption that is displayed in the title bar of the window when you open the report in Print Preview, the label that serves as the report header, and the report name. It's probably best to enter a title that's appropriate for the caption and label and not worry about the title being a suitable report name. If you're using a naming convention (such as prefixing all reports with *rpt* as we've done in the sample databases), it's easy to switch to the Navigation pane after the wizard is done to rename your report. In this case, enter Contact Events as the title.

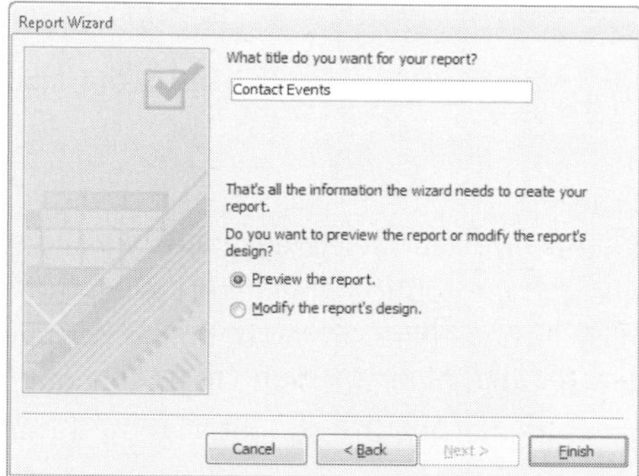

Figure 17-26 You can specify a report title on the last page of the Report Wizard.

Viewing the Result

Select the Preview The Report option on the final page of the Report Wizard, and then click Finish to create the report and display the result in Print Preview, as shown in Figure 17-27. One of the first things you will notice is that Access has created alternating background colors for the detail lines to make it easier to see the data that goes with each record. This feature can be very useful if reports have a lot of information in the detail records and if the lines are packed close together.

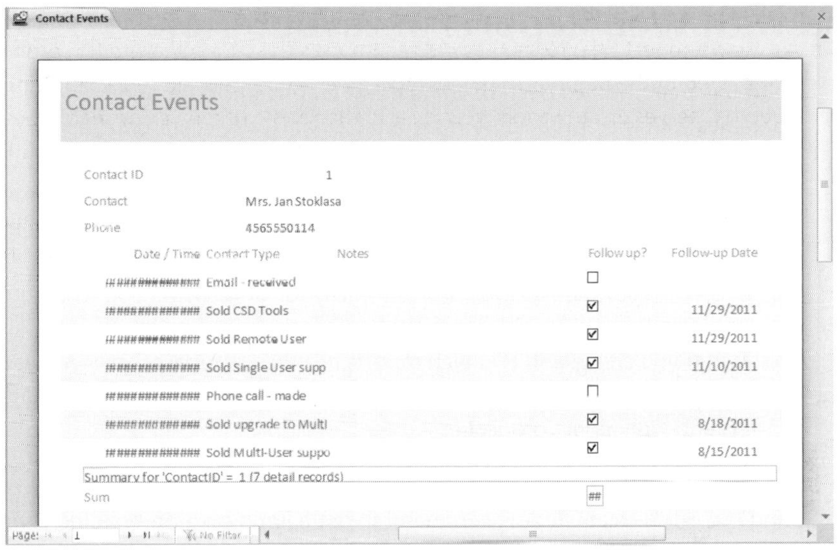

Figure 17-27 This is the first page of the Contact Events report created using the Report Wizard.

It's easy to use Design view or Layout view to modify minor items (such as adjusting the width and alignment of the ContactDateTime and ContactEventDescription fields and resizing the labels) to obtain a result nearly identical to the report you constructed earlier. You can see in Figure 17-27 that the ContactDateTime field displays # symbols for all the records. Access displays # symbols for date/time and numeric fields when it cannot display all the data in the control, but only when you select the Check For Truncated Number Fields check box under Application Options in the Current Database category of the Access Options dialog box. You need to fix the expression in the text box that calculates the Sum of the ContactFollowUp field and change the format to display the number. (The Report Wizard set the format to Yes/No.) You should also change the Sum label associated with this calculation. You can find the Report Wizard's report at this point saved as rptXmplContactEvents2 in the sample database. As you might imagine, the Report Wizard can help you to get a head start on more complex report designs.

Working with Web Reports in Layout View

Up to this point, you've been building client reports in Design view to view the data in several tables with the Conrad Systems Contacts Data Copy client database. You've seen how to start with a blank client report and add fields to the report grid, add grouping and sorting orders to the data, align and position the controls, and add controls to the report grid to count and sum the data. You've also learned how to use the Report command and the Report Wizard to get a jump start on creating new client reports. You can create the same type of client reports working exclusively in Layout view. When you work in Layout view, you are able to see live data from the report's record source while working with the controls. When you create and edit web reports in a web database, however, your only design surface is Layout view; you cannot open a web report in Design view to make edits to the controls and web report properties.

In this section, you'll follow similar procedures as you did previously in this chapter with using the quick create Report command to get a jump start on building a web report. You'll also build a new web report from scratch as you did previously with a client report, except this time, you'll use Layout view. The procedures we show you in the following sections—namely, working with web reports in Layout view—can be applied to client reports as well if you want to experiment with using Layout view on client reports.

To learn how to create and customize web reports in Layout view, open the BOSSData-Copy2.accdb sample web database. After Access closes the information form displayed on startup, click the Create tab to see the commands listed in the Reports group for web databases, as shown in Figure 17-28.

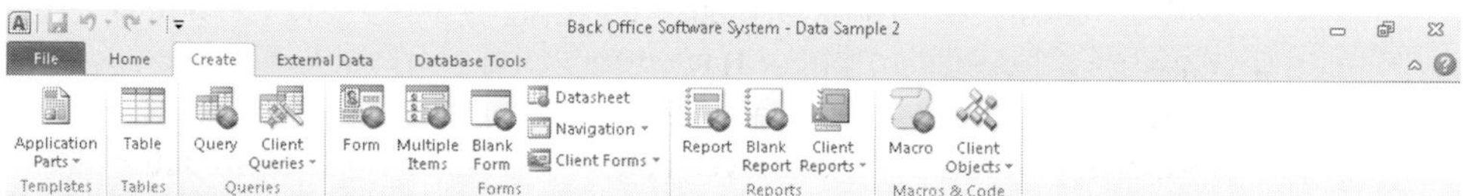

Figure 17-28 The Reports group on the Create tab in web databases includes commands to create new web reports and client reports.

Here are the three options you can use in the Reports group on the Create tab in web databases:

- **Report** Quick create command to create a web report based on the highlighted table or web query in the Navigation pane. Access creates a control for every field in that table or web query and displays it in Layout view. Access creates controls for all the fields in a tabular control layout on the Report window.

- **Blank Report** Access creates a new, blank web report and displays it in Layout view. Use this button when you want to start creating a web report from scratch.
- **Client Reports** Drop-down list of five options to create client reports in a web database. In this drop-down list, you can use the Report command to quickly create a client report, start a new blank client report in Design view, start a new blank client report in Layout view, start the client Report Wizard, or start the Label Wizard to create a client report to print labels. You can create client reports in a web database, and they will function when you open them in Access client. However, client reports will not open in a web browser when you publish your web database to a server running Microsoft SharePoint and Access Services.

> **Note**
>
> **You cannot use the Report Wizard or Label Wizard to create web reports in web databases. You can use only the Report web command to get a jump start on creating web reports, or you can start from scratch.**

Modifying a Report Command-Created Web Report in Layout View

Previously, you used the quick create Report command to create a client report for contacts and products. You can also use the quick create Report command to build a web report in web databases. Click the Navigation Pane menu in the BOSSDataCopy2 sample web database, click Object Type under Navigate To Category, and then click Queries under Filter By Group to display a list of queries available in this web database. The qryrptPermitDates web query includes the employee names and permit expiration date fields from the tblEmployees web table. Let's create a nice web report showing the permit expiration dates of the employees using this web query. We'll use the Report command here to save us some time creating this web report. Scroll down to the qryrptPermitDates query in the Navigation pane, select it, and then click the Report command in the Reports group on the Create tab, as shown in Figure 17-29. Notice that the Report command includes a globe icon to indicate that Access creates a web report when you click this command.

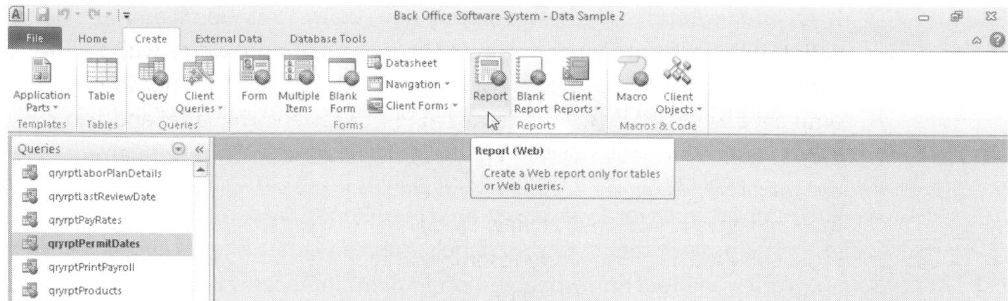

Figure 17-29 Click the Report command to let Access build a web report using the qryrptPermitDates web query.

After just a second or two, Access 2010 creates an entire web report with all the fields in the query, complete with a shared image logo, a title, the current date and time, a colored line beneath the column labels, and even a page count at the bottom of the pages, as shown in Figure 17-30. Access opens the report in Layout view so that you can begin the process of making modifications.

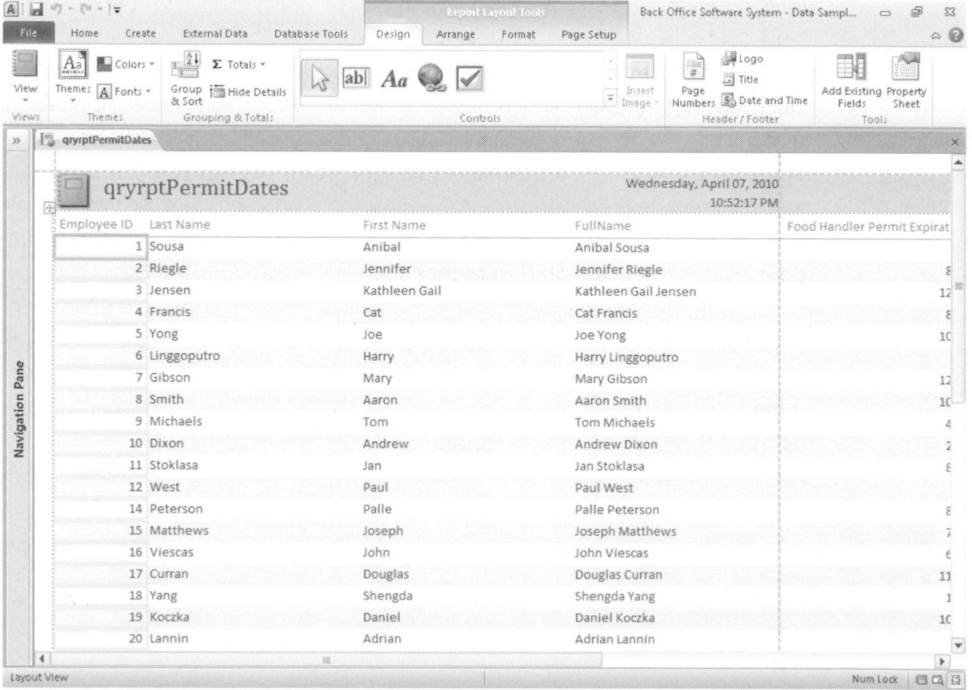

Figure 17-30 With one click, Access creates an entire formatted web report for your convenience.

If you look closely at the web report, you'll see that Access gives you a good starting point with the Report command; however, there are a few problems with this layout. Access spread all the fields out across two pages, which makes it harder to read the data for each employee when you view the report in Print Preview. The label and text box controls are much wider than they need to be, and the report caption is the name of the report. Access did much of the hard work for you in creating the web report, but you still need to make a few modifications in Layout view to make the web report readable. Now, let's clean up this report so that it more closely resembles the rptPermitExpDates report found in the Back Office Software System database.

Across the top of the application window, Access 2010 shows the Report Layout Tools collection of four contextual tabs—Design, Arrange, Format, and Page Setup—on the ribbon, shown previously in Figure 17-30. The report design grid in Layout view looks less like a grid than a sheet of paper. You'll also notice that there are no page breaks in Layout view, and by default, Access displays dashed lines along the edges of the report to denote the print margins.

You first need to make several of the fields narrower to fit all the controls onto a single page. In Layout view, you can see live data, so making column adjustments like this is easy. Click the Last Name label, move your mouse pointer to the right edge of the highlighted control until it becomes a double-sided arrow, and then drag the control to the left until the control is about 1 inch in width, as shown in Figure 17-31. You should still be able to clearly see all the records in the LastName field. You'll notice that Access adjusts the width of the LastName text box while you are adjusting the width for the Last Name label control. Both of these controls are in a tabular control layout, which means that whenever you adjust the width of any control in this column, Access adjusts the width of all controls in that column. Note that you can also change the Width property on the Property Sheet window for the LastName field to reduce the width of the control.

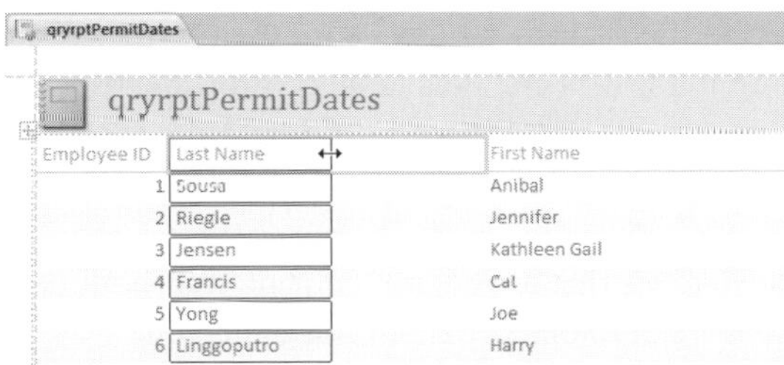

Figure 17-31 Drag the Last Name label control to the left to resize the entire column.

The First Name label and text box control also can be narrower that the current width. Click the First Name label (or FirstName text box), move your mouse pointer to the right edge of the highlighted control until it becomes a double-sided arrow, and then drag the control to the left until the width is about 1.1 inches. If you make the control too narrow, you'll notice that Access appears to increase the height of the Detail section for some of the records. In Figure 17-32, you can see that the controls for the third record appear to be taller. The reason some of the controls appear taller is that Access set the Can Grow property of the text box control to Yes. When the Can Grow property for a report control is set to Yes, Access expands the section to accommodate controls that might grow because they display long memo fields or long text strings. The Can Grow property is not available in page headers and footers. (Note that Access does not display the Can Grow property on web report property sheets for the individual sections because Access sets this property to Yes automatically for all sections except the page headers and footers.) For now, make sure you do not make your First Name controls so narrow that the controls expand in height.

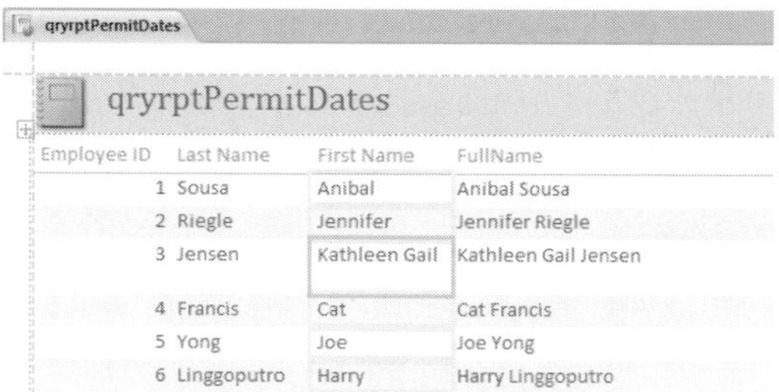

Figure 17-32 If a control has its Can Grow property set to Yes and you make the control too narrow to display the data, Access expands the height of the control.

The label for the FullName field needs to be changed. Click into the FullName label control, delete the existing text, and type **Employee Name**. The controls for both the FoodHandler-PermitExp and LiquorPermitExp are also too wide because their respective label controls display a lot of text. Click into the first permit date label control, delete the existing text, and type **Food Handler** to change the label caption. Click into the second permit label control and change the caption text to **Liquor Permit**. Now that you've changed the label captions for both of these fields, reduce the width of both of these controls until they are both about 1 inch wide. You'll notice that as you are reducing the width of these controls, you can almost fit all the controls onto one page, but not quite yet.

Now that you have a more manageable width for your fields, you need to move several of these fields into different positions and hide fields that don't need to be visible. (The rptPermitExpDates report in the Back Office Software System database displays only three fields and hides the remaining fields in the report's record source.) We don't need the EmployeeID, LastName, and FirstName fields to be in the first position on this report, nor do we really need these fields to be visible. (You can see both the employee's first and last names in the FullName calculated field.) You can reposition each of these fields and their label controls one at a time, but it will be much quicker to move them all as a group. Click the EmployeeID label control, hold down the Shift key, and then click the EmployeeID text box control to select both controls. Continue holding down the Shift key, and click the Last Name label control, the LastName text box, the First Name label control, and then the FirstName text box to select all six controls. Note that you can also select these six controls by holding down the Shift key, clicking each label, and then clicking the Select Column button in the Rows & Columns group on the Arrange tab. Click any of these six controls and drop them to the right of the LiquorPermitExp text box control. When you have them correctly positioned, Access displays a vertical I-bar to the right of the LiquorPermitExp control, as shown in Figure 14-33.

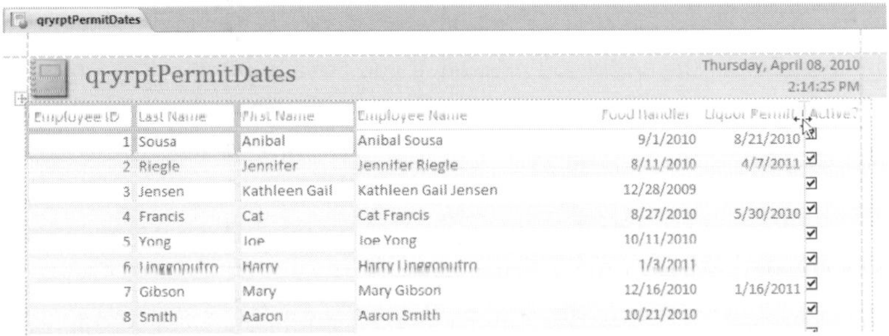

Figure 17-33 Move the first three fields to the right of the LiquorPermitExp field.

After you release the mouse, Access moves all three label and text box controls to the right of the LiquorPermitExp text box control, as shown in Figure 17-34. You'll notice that Access moves the FullName, FoodHandlerPermitExp, and LiquorPermitExp controls to the left edge of the report grid. Access also lines up all the controls both horizontally and vertically in the report grid. When you're working with web reports that use control layouts, you can easily move and swap control positions without having to line up the controls.

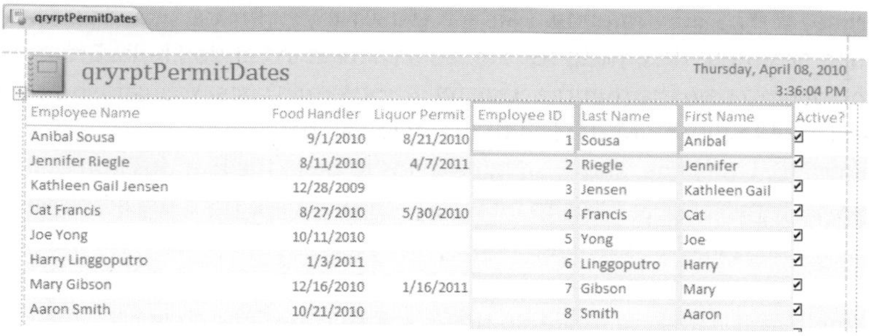

qryrptPermitDates

qryrptPermitDates — Thursday, April 08, 2010 3:36:04 PM

Employee Name	Food Handler	Liquor Permit	Employee ID	Last Name	First Name	Active?
Anibal Sousa	9/1/2010	8/21/2010	1	Sousa	Anibal	☑
Jennifer Riegle	8/11/2010	4/7/2011	2	Riegle	Jennifer	☑
Kathleen Gail Jensen	12/28/2009		3	Jensen	Kathleen Gail	☑
Cat Francis	8/27/2010	5/30/2010	4	Francis	Cat	☑
Joe Yong	10/11/2010		5	Yong	Joe	☑
Harry Linggoputro	1/3/2011		6	Linggoputro	Harry	☑
Mary Gibson	12/16/2010	1/16/2011	7	Gibson	Mary	☑
Aaron Smith	10/21/2010		8	Smith	Aaron	☑

Figure 17-34 Access repositions and aligns all the controls when you move controls in a control layout.

INSIDE OUT Using the Keyboard to Move Controls

You can also move a control, or a group of controls, by pressing the Alt key and then using the arrow keys to move the controls up, down, left, or right in the layout. Note that if another control already occupies the cell you are trying to move into, Access moves the control past that existing control and into the next available empty cell in the direction of the arrow you pressed. If you are at the last cell in a row or column, Access creates a new row or column and moves the control into a cell in the new row or column. You need to be aware, though, that the new column or row remains, even if you move the control back to its original location.

If you look closely at Figure 17-34, you can see that the Active field still extends past the print margin. Without even having to switch to Print Preview, you know you have to make further field size adjustments to keep the data from spanning across pages. Click the Full-Name field and reduce the width of this control until the Active field no longer extends past the print margin. You don't need to see the EmployeeID, LastName, FirstName, and Active fields when you print this report, but you should leave them on the report grid in case you want to open the web report to show specific records using a macro. (We'll discuss automating a web database with macros in Chapter 21, "Automating a Web Application Using Macros.") Hold down the Shift key, select the EmployeeID, LastName, FirstName, and Active label and text box controls, open the Property Sheet window, and then change the Visible property from Yes to No.

After you finish, click the arrow below the View button in the Views group on the Design tab and click Print Preview to see the result, shown in Figure 17-35. Before you go on, you might want to save the report and name it rptPermitDates. You can find this web report saved as rptXmplPermitDates1 in the sample database.

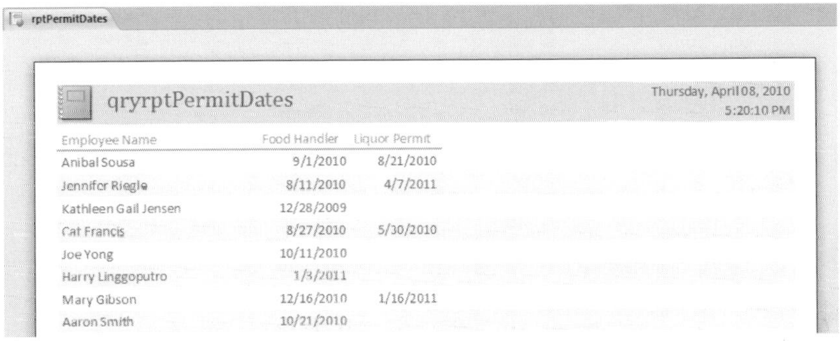

Figure 17-35 Your modified report now displays only three fields.

Completing the Web Report

Your modified report, started by using the quick create web Report command, is looking better, but you still need to make a few more adjustments to polish up the design. The Report command did not add any grouping or sorting to this report, which means the employee names are ordered by the EmployeeID field. You need to define sort orders on this report to display the records in alphabetical order by their names. Switch back to Layout view and then click the Group & Sort button in the Grouping & Totals group on the Design tab to open the Group, Sort, And Total pane. Click Add A Sort and then select the LastName field from the Select Field box to creates a new sort specification. Verify that the sort order for the LastName field sort specification is set to With A On Top. Click Add A Sort again and then select FirstName from the Select Field box to create a second sort specification. Access now sorts the records based on the LastName field and then on the FirstName field, as shown in Figure 17-36. Close the Group, Sort, And Total pane after you define these sort specifications.

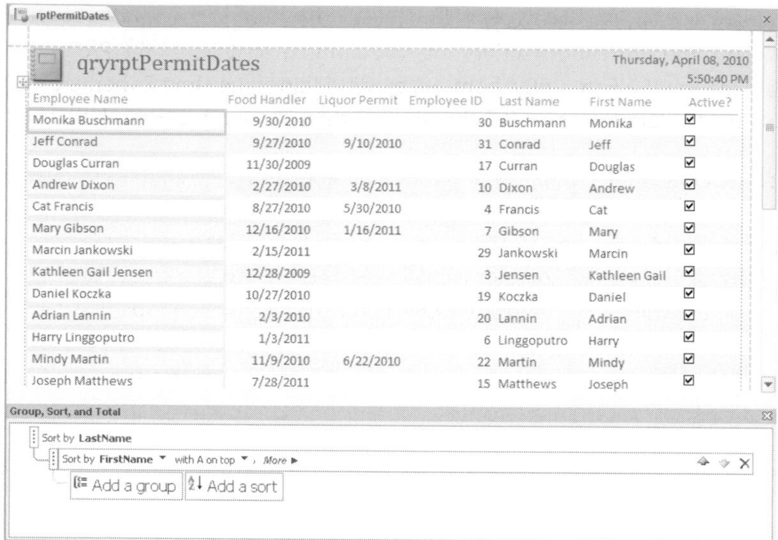

Figure 17-36 Create new sort specifications based on the LastName and FirstName fields.

The Report command created a label control in the Report Header section with a caption of the name of the query used for the report's record source. This caption is not very descriptive, so let's change it to something more meaningful. Click inside the label caption at the top of the report grid, delete the existing text, and then type Permit Expiration Dates for the new caption. The Report command also added a shared image—a report graphic—to the Report Header section. You don't need the graphic for this report, so select it and then press Delete to remove it from the report grid. You'll notice when you remove the shared image graphic, Access moves the title label caption to the left side of the report grid, but none of the fields or labels beneath the Header section change positions. The reason for this is that all the controls in the report header are in a separate control layout from the field and label controls.

Perform the following steps to adjust some of the formatting options on the report:

1. By default, the Report command applied a background color to the Report Header section. Let's remove that color for this employee permit report. Open the Property Sheet window, select ReportHeader from the Selection Type combo box, and then change the Back Color property to **Background 1**. Access changes the Report Header section to blend in with the rest of the report grid—in this case, the section is colored white.

2. Hold down the Shift key and then click the label control and two text box controls in the Report Header section to select all three controls. In the Property Sheet window, change the Fore Color from the existing light blue (Text 2 theme color) to a dark green standard color (**#325438**), and then change the Font Weight to Bold.

3. Hold down the Shift key and then click the Employee Name, Food handler, and Liquor Permit label controls. Change the Fore Color of these labels to also use the dark green standard color—**#325438**. While you still have all three of these controls selected, change the Gridline Color property to also use the same dark green color—**#325438**. (The Gridline Style Bottom property for these controls is Solid, which means Access draws a gridline on the bottom of these controls to simulate the look of a line control.) Select the FullName, FoodHandlerPermitExp, and LiquorPermitExp fields and change the Fore Color of these controls to the standard black color—**#000000**.

4. The Report command created alternating background colors for the detail records in this report. The color is a light shade of gray, so let's change that color to a light shade of green to provide more contrast. In the Property Sheet window, select Detail from the Selection Type combo box. Change the Alternate Back Color property to **#DDEBDF**. (When you select the Detail section, you can also adjust the alternating background colors by clicking the Alternate Row Color command in the Background group on the Format tab.)

5. Scroll down to the bottom of the report, and then select the control that shows the total number of records for this report—the AccessTotalsEmployeeID control in the Property Sheet window for our example report. Move this control to the far-left empty cell on the report grid in the same row. (This control is currently under the EmployeeID field.) Change the Control Source expression of this control to **="Number of employees: " & Count(*)**, change the Fore Color to **#325438**, and left-align the control.

6. In the Property Sheet window, select Report in the Selection Type combo box, and type **Permit Expiration Dates** for the Caption property.

Click the Save button on the Quick Access Toolbar to save the changes you made to this web report. Switch to Print Preview to see how your completed web report will look on paper, as shown in Figure 17-37. This web report now looks much closer to the rptPermitExpDates web report in the Back Office Software System web database. You can find this web report saved as rptXmplPermitDates2 in the sample database. By using the web Report command to do all the heavy lifting and Layout view to make some quick changes, you can create a professional-looking web report in a very short time.

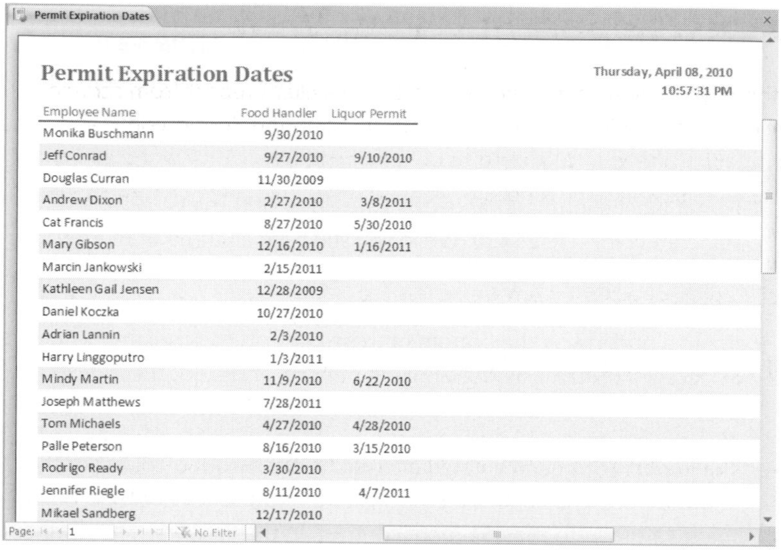

Permit Expiration Dates

Permit Expiration Dates

Thursday, April 08, 2010
10:57:31 PM

Employee Name	Food Handler	Liquor Permit
Monika Buschmann	9/30/2010	
Jeff Conrad	9/27/2010	9/10/2010
Douglas Curran	11/30/2009	
Andrew Dixon	2/27/2010	3/8/2011
Cat Francis	8/27/2010	5/30/2010
Mary Gibson	12/16/2010	1/16/2011
Marcin Jankowski	2/15/2011	
Kathleen Gail Jensen	12/28/2009	
Daniel Koczka	10/27/2010	
Adrian Lannin	2/3/2010	
Harry Linggoputro	1/3/2011	
Mindy Martin	11/9/2010	6/22/2010
Joseph Matthews	7/28/2011	
Tom Michaels	4/27/2010	4/28/2010
Palle Peterson	8/16/2010	3/15/2010
Rodrigo Ready	3/30/2010	
Jennifer Riegle	8/11/2010	4/7/2011
Mikael Sandberg	12/17/2010	

Page: 1 No Filter

Figure 17-37 Your completed web report now includes all the changes you made in Layout view.

TROUBLESHOOTING

Why do I see only the ID values of my lookup fields in a web report?

As you learned in Chapter 5, "Modifying Your Table Design," and Chapter 6, "Designing Web Tables," lookup fields can display one value but store a different value. When you build relationships in web tables, you must define lookup fields. If you want, for example, to store an employee's ID field in a related child table, such as a scheduling table, you create a lookup field in the scheduling table for the employee's ID from the employee parent table. You can optionally have a display column that displays the employee's name when you define the lookup field. You have to remember, however, that even though you might see the employee's name in the lookup field drop-down list, Access stores the ID of the employee in the related table. If you use the Report quick create command to build a report off the related table, you'll see the control on the web report display the ID value instead of the display value (the employee name). To see the display value on the report, you must base your report's record source on a query that joins the two tables. You can then reference the correct display value from the parent table on your report control.

Building a Web Report in Layout View

In this chapter, you've learned how to create a client report from scratch in Design view, quickly build simple client and web reports using the Report command, create a client report using the Report Wizard to get a jump start on your work, and use Layout view to modify an existing web report. Now, it's time to learn how to create web reports completely from scratch in Layout view without the assistance of the Report command. In this section, you'll create a new web report from scratch that lists the vendor address information in the Back Office Software System web database.

Starting with a Blank Web Report

If you want to follow along in this section, open the BOSSDataCopy2.accdb web database. Click the Blank Report button in the Reports group on the Create tab. Access 2010 opens a new blank web report in Layout view with the field list displayed on the right, as shown in Figure 17-38.

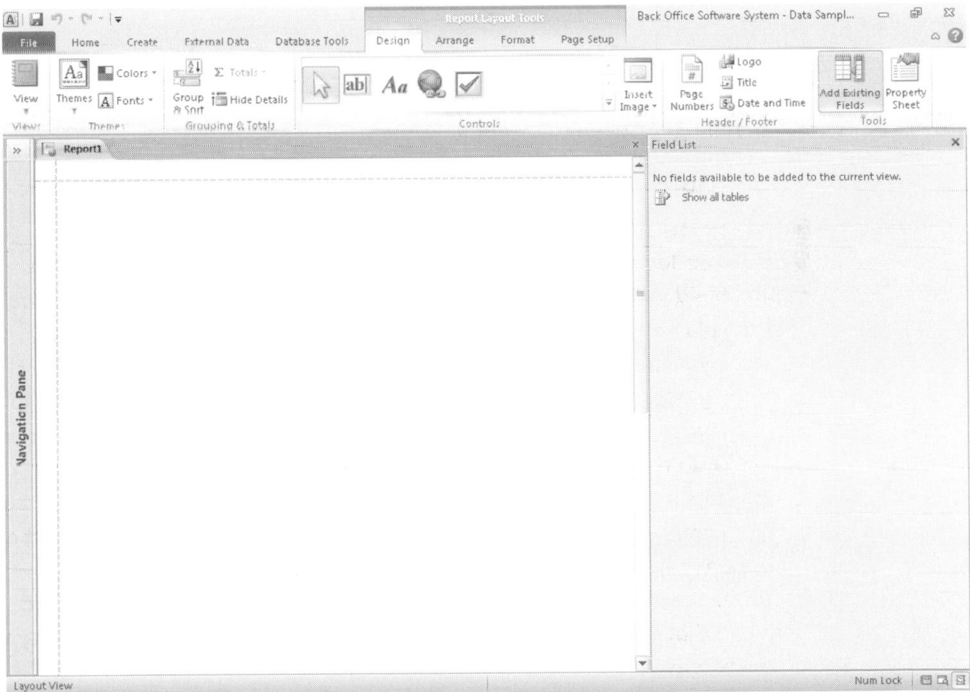

Figure 17-38 Access always opens web reports in Layout view when you click Blank Web Report.

The web report does not yet have a record source, so no fields are displayed in the field list. You can click Show All Tables in the field list to display a list of all tables in this web database, but you want to use the saved qryrptXmplWebAddressBook web query that contains all the fields you need from the tblVendors table. Click the Property Sheet button in the Tools group on the Design tab, click the All tab, and then select the qryrptXmplWebAddressBook web query for the Record Source property. Switch back to the field list by clicking the Add Existing Fields button in the Tools group on the Design tab to show only the eight fields in the web query, as shown in Figure 17-39.

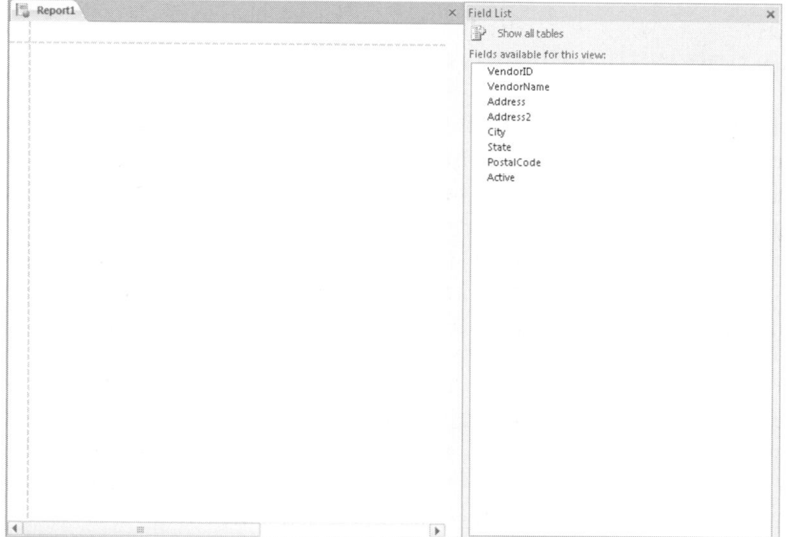

Figure 17-39 Assign the qryrptXmplWebAddressBook web query as the new web report's record source.

You should start this new report by entering a title, so click the Title button in the Header/Footer group on the Design tab. Access places a label control near the upper-left corner of the report and enters the name of the report as Report1. Click inside this label, highlight the existing characters, and change the text to **Vendor Address Book**. Press Enter to save the new title in the control. Select the empty cell to the left of the title label and press Delete to remove it from the report grid.

Note

In web reports, you are not allowed to have any spaces in control names. Whenever you place a new control on the report grid, Access always gives the control a default name with no spaces. If you place a field from the Field list that includes a space in the name on the report grid, Access adds an underscore (_) in place of every space in the control name.

Adding Grouping and Sorting

For this vendor web report, it would be useful to group the vendors by the first letter of the vendor name. You can accomplish this task by grouping on an expression instead of using a field name. Before you create the grouping specification, let's first add the VendorName field to the report grid so you can see the effect on the record display of adding this grouping level. Click the VendorName field in the Field list, drag the field onto any part of the report grid below the title label, and release the mouse. Access creates a new Vendor Name label below the title and a VendorName text box control below the Vendor Name label. You'll notice Access displays the vendor names in order of their VendorID field.

Click the Group & Sort button in the Grouping & Totals group on the Design tab to open the Group, Sort, And Total pane. Click Add A Group and then click Expression at the bottom of the Select Field box. Access opens the Expression Builder, where you can build an expression you want to use for the grouping level. Enter the expression **Left([VendorName],1)** in the Expression Builder and then click OK. This expression uses the Left function to determine the first letter of the vendor name. Access now displays the first letter once for every group of corresponding vendor records in the tblVendors table in a new control and pushes the VendorName field far to the right, as shown in Figure 17-40. If you click this new control and open the Property Sheet window, you'll see that Access names this new control AccessIntervalControl and uses the expression you defined in the Expression Builder for the Control Source property. You'll also notice that Access groups the vendor records by the first letter of their name.

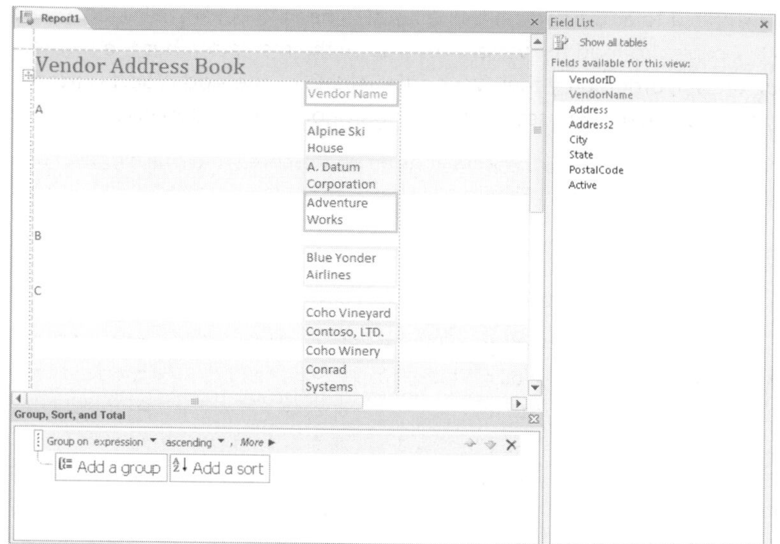

Figure 17-40 After you add your expression as a group level, Access adds a new control to display the first letter of the vendor names to the report grid.

Access made the width of the new grouping expression text box much wider than it needs to be, which means the VendorName field is now too far to the right. Click the AccessIntervalControl text box, move your mouse pointer to the right edge of the highlighted control until it becomes a double-sided arrow, and then drag the control to the left until the control is about one quarter of an inch in width. After you reduce the width of this control, Access moves the VendorName field back towards the left side of the report layout.

In Layout view, it's hard to see where the different report sections begin and end. When you create the expression group level, Access creates a header for this group, but because you see live data in Layout view, the actual design layout can sometimes be hard to visualize. Right now, it almost looks like the expression control is in the report's Detail section. Although you can't confirm this by switching to Design view with web reports, Access created a new grouping level for this expression and inserted the AccessIntervalControl text box into that Group Header section. In the grouping specification on the Group, Sort, And Total pane, verify that the following options are set for the specification you just created:

```
Group On Expression, Ascending, By Entire Value, With No Totals, With Title Click To
Add, With A Header Section, Without A Footer Section
```

You also need to add a sort on the VendorName field because if you look closely at Figure 17-40, Access grouped the vendor records by the first letter, but the records inside each group are still ordered by their VendorID field. Click the Add A Sort button in the Group, Sort, And Total pane and set the following options for VendorName:

```
Sort By VendorName, With A On Top, By Entire Value, With No Totals, With Title Click
To Add, Without A Header Section, Without A Footer Section
```

INSIDE OUT Save a Step by Choosing Add A Group Instead of Add A Sort

When you click Add A Group and use a field name for your grouping specification, Access automatically builds a Group Header section and adds the field to the report layout. If you instead first create a sorting specification by clicking Add A Sort on the same field, Access won't add the field to the report layout. If you change a grouping specification to Without A Header Section, Access moves the field into the Detail section for you. This saves time having to find the field in the field list and add it yourself. In the example we just showed you, we used an expression as a grouping specification, but keep this tip in mind when you create a grouping level using a field name.

Now that you have all your grouping and sorting set up, you need to add the remaining fields onto the report. Close the Group, Sort, And Total pane so you can see more of your report layout. If necessary, click the Add Existing Fields button in the Tools group on the Design tab to open the field list again. Click the Vendor Name label control on the report grid before continuing with the next step. Double-click the Address field in the field list and Access places a new label control and text box control on the report grid, as shown in Figure 17-41.

Figure 17-41 Double-click the Address field in the Field List to add it to the report grid.

Access places the Address label the right of the Vendor Name label. Access also places the Address field to the right of the VendorName field. We had you first select the Vendor Name label before double-clicking the Address field in the Field list because Access can potentially place your new controls on the grid in many different sections based on what control you currently have selected in the report layout. Here are the locations where Access places the new Address controls based on your starting focus point:

- If you select the title label control, Access places both Address controls beneath the title label in the Report Header section.
- If you select the empty cell to the left of the Vendor Name label, Access places both Address controls in the Page Header section.
- If you select the Expression group control, Access places the Address label in the Page Header section and the Address field in the Detail section, but both controls are to the left of the Vendor Name controls.
- If you select the empty cell to the right of the expression group control, Access places both Address controls in the Group Header section.
- If you select the empty cell to the left of the VendorName field, Access places both Address controls into the Detail section and pushes all other controls farther to the right.
- If you select the VendorName field, Access places both Address controls into the Detail section, but both controls are beneath the VendorName field.

As you can see, the locations and sections of where Access places your new controls can vary widely based on your starting position. Here again, it can be hard to tell in what sections of the report Access places these new controls when you're viewing the web report in Layout view.

INSIDE OUT

Add Color to Report Sections in Layout View to View Their Positions

If you find it difficult not seeing where each report or group section begins and ends while viewing reports in Layout view, we find it helpful to temporarily apply a background color to the different sections. By adding different background colors to the sections of the report, you'll have an easier time understanding where Access lays out the controls in Layout view when you're creating and moving controls. You can remove the temporary background colors from the sections after you complete your report design changes.

Now that you have the VendorName and Address fields in place, you should add the remaining fields to the report grid. (Skip the Address2 field for the moment.) Placing controls onto the web report grid when you have multiple report sections can be a little tricky, as you've just seen. If you find it a little too difficult using the double-click procedure to add fields to the report grid from the Field list, you can use the drag procedure instead. Click the City field in the Field list, drag it onto the report, and place it to the right of the Address text box. When you have it positioned correctly, Access displays an I-bar to the right of the Address text box control, as shown in Figure 17-42. Access places the City label in the Page Header section, the City field in the Detail section, and lines up the controls to match the VendorName and Address fields.

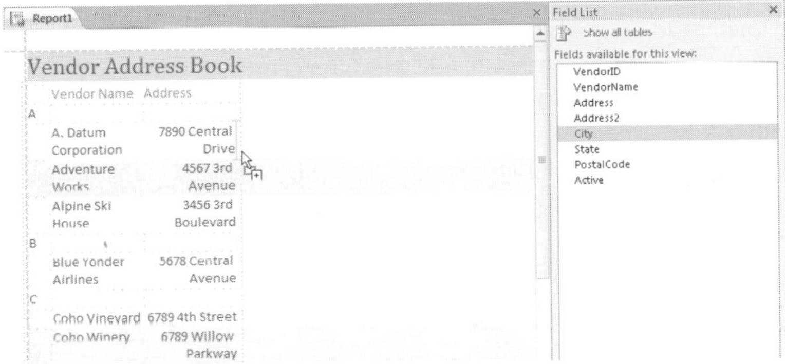

Figure 17-42 Drag the City field to the right of the Address field.

In Figure 17-43, you can see where Access places the City controls after you complete the drag procedure. You might find using the drag procedure for adding fields to the report grid in Layout view easier than using the double-click technique that we first showed you.

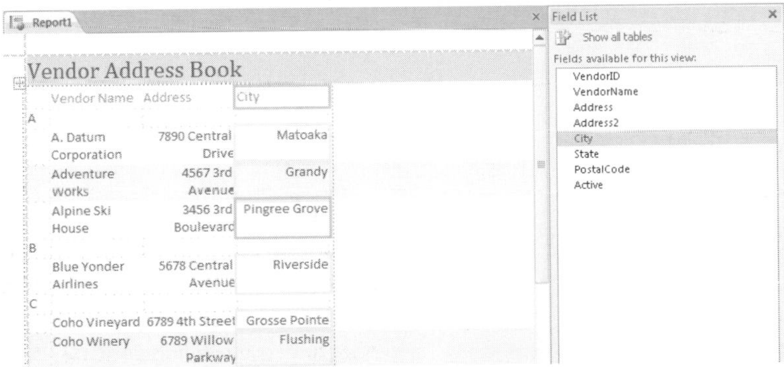

Figure 17-43 Access lines up the City controls with the Vendor Name and Address controls.

Using the technique you just learned, drag the fields from the Field list to the report grid to the right of the City field in the following order: State, PostalCode, Active, and VendorID. (Make sure you skip the Address2 field.) After completing these changes, you can close the Property Sheet window to see more of the report layout. After you finish, click the arrow below the View button in the Views group on the Design tab and click Print Preview to see the result, shown in Figure 17-44. Before you go on, you might want to save the report and name it rptVendorAddressBook. You can find this web report at this stage saved as rptXmplVendorAddressBook1 in the sample database.

INSIDE OUT Splitting and Merging Cells

In Chapter 14, "Customizing a Form," you learned how to split cells vertically, split cells horizontally, and merge cells in web form control layouts. You can also use these options in web reports as well to further customize the size of your web report controls with one exception—you cannot split cells vertically in web reports. You'll notice, in web reports, that Access dims the Split Vertically command in the Merge/Split group on the Arrange tab and on the shortcut menu when you right-click a control on the web report layout.

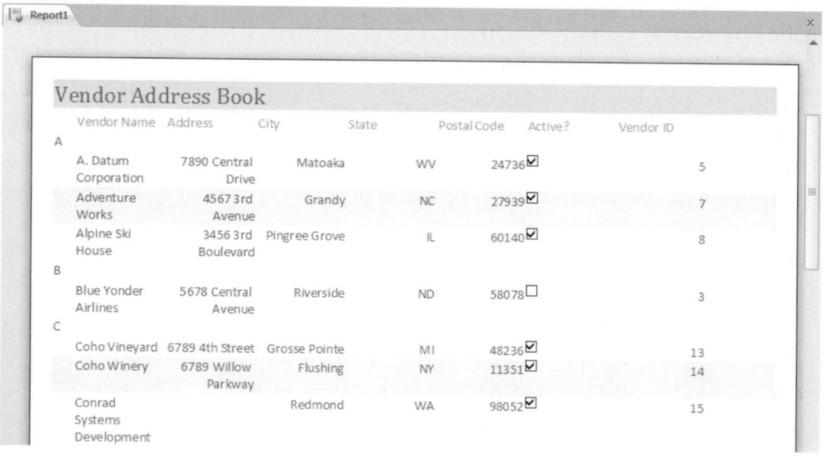

Report1

Vendor Address Book

	Vendor Name	Address	City	State	Postal Code	Active?	Vendor ID
A							
	A. Datum Corporation	7890 Central Drive	Matoaka	WV	24736	☑	5
	Adventure Works	4567 3rd Avenue	Grandy	NC	27939	☑	7
	Alpine Ski House	3456 3rd Boulevard	Pingree Grove	IL	60140	☑	8
B							
	Blue Yonder Airlines	5678 Central Avenue	Riverside	ND	58078	☐	3
C							
	Coho Vineyard	6789 4th Street	Grosse Pointe	MI	48236	☑	13
	Coho Winery	6789 Willow Parkway	Flushing	NY	11351	☑	14
	Conrad Systems Development		Redmond	WA	98052	☑	15

Figure 17-44 You should now have seven fields displayed on your web report.

INSIDE OUT **Moving Controls to Different Sections**

If you need to move controls between different sections on a web report, you can also use the Move Up and Move Down commands in the Move group on the Arrange tab.

Working with Control Layouts

When you're designing a web report in Layout view, Access 2010 automatically places any controls that you add to the report inside a *control layout*. As you learned in Chapter 14, control layouts help you to align and position controls on reports and forms. You can think of a control layout as being similar to a table in Microsoft Word or a spreadsheet in Microsoft Excel. When you widen or narrow one control in a column, you change the width of any other controls in that column that are part of that control layout. Likewise, when you increase or decrease the height of a control, you're changing the height of all the controls on that row.

When you are designing client reports, using control layouts is optional; however, all controls in web reports must exist inside control layouts to be web-compatible. There are two kinds of control layouts in Access 2010—*stacked* and *tabular*. In a stacked control layout, Access "stacks" bound controls for different fields in a column and places all the labels down the left side. In client reports, you can have multiple sets of stacked controls within a section, but not in web reports. Any controls (including associated labels) in a stacked layout must all be in one section. In the web report you've built thus far, Access has placed the title label and the two empty cells controls to the right of the label in a stacked layout. When you manually drag fields from the Field list in a blank web report, Access creates stacked layouts.

In a tabular control layout, Access places bound controls horizontally with labels along the top as column headings—much like rows on a spreadsheet. A tabular control layout can include controls in different sections of a report—for example, the labels can appear in a Header section and the data controls in the Detail section. In client reports, you can convert the stacked layout for fields in the Detail section into a tabular layout, but in web reports, you have no control over changing layout styles. When you have a web report in Layout view, you'll notice that both the Stacked and Tabular control layout buttons in the Table group on the Arrange tab are dimmed. In the web report you've built thus far, Access has placed the field labels, the expression group text box, and the field text boxes in a tabular layout across the Page Header, the Group Header, and the Detail sections.

When you are working with control layouts, you have to be careful when resizing controls because each change you make usually results in changing other controls. Before you begin resizing controls in the web report you've been building, let's change the print margins. Switch back to Layout view and then click the Page Setup button in the Page Layout group on the Page Setup tab. Change the Top, Bottom, Left, and Right margins all to **0.5**. Now that you've settled on the print margins, you can begin the process of resizing the controls in the control layouts and see if your controls cross over the print margins.

The text box controls for the VendorName, Address, and City fields are not wide enough at this point, and the State, PostalCode, Active, and VendorID fields are too wide. You can see that the VendorName and Address fields are not wide enough because these fields won't allow the data to fit on one line for all records. Access expands the height on those records that have more characters. Start by clicking the VendorName field text box, move your mouse to the right edge until it becomes a double-sided arrow, and then click and drag the edge of the field to the right until the control is about 1.75 inches in width. You'll notice that when you resize the VendorName text box in the Detail section, Access also resizes the other controls in the same column—the Vendor Name label in the Page Header section and the expression group control in the Group Header section. All these controls across the three sections are interconnected through the control layout. You can see the advantage of resizing controls when using control layouts; however, you have also have to be careful that you might resize controls in other sections.

> **Note**
>
> **You can also resize controls in Layout view by opening the Property Sheet window and manually typing in new values for the Width and Height properties.**

Select the Address field now and resize this control to about 2.5 inches in width. You need this control to be wider than all the other controls because you'll use it to display not only the Address field data, but also the Address2 field data. While you still have the Address field selected, open the Property Sheet window, and then change the Control Source for this field to the expression **=[Address] & " " & [Address2]**. This expression concatenates both address fields into one control on the report. After you change the Control Source for this field, you'll notice Access now displays a #Type! error in the field on the report grid, as shown in Figure 17-45. Access displays this error because it cannot figure out what data to display in the control. The Control Source uses the Address field in the report's record source as part of the expression; however, the name of this text box control is also Address.

Access is confused at this point because it thinks you want to use the contents of this control in the expression. In essence, you've created a circular reference error. To correct this problem, change the Name property to something other than Address; for example, change it to **txtAddress**. After you change the Name property, Access displays the data in the control again. While you still have the Property Sheet open, left-align the data in the txtAddress control.

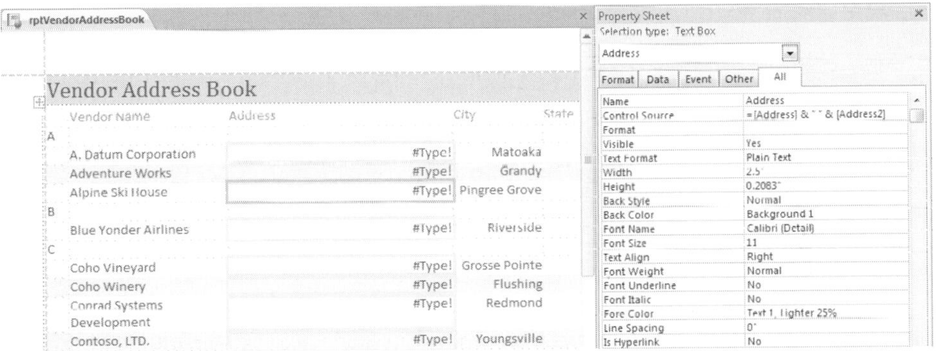

Figure 17-45 Access displays an error in the address control when it can't resolve the Control Source expression.

The City field needs to be only a little wider than it currently is, so expand the width of this field to about 1.2 inches. If you scroll to the right of the report layout, you'll see that Access pushed the PostalCode, Active, and VendorID controls past the print margin after you've expanded the width of the first three controls because all the controls are in a common control layout. You need to reduce the width of the remaining fields to fit everything back onto one page again. Start by clicking the State field text box, move your mouse to the right edge until it becomes a double-sided arrow, and then click and drag the edge of the field to the left until it is just wide enough to still display the text in the State label control. To make additional room for the remaining controls, change the caption of the Postal Code label control to **Zip** and reduce the width of the control to about 0.6 inches. We'll be hiding the Active and VendorID fields, so we don't need the labels for these two controls. Select the Active? and Vendor ID labels and press Delete to remove them from the control layouts. Now that you've removed the labels, reduce the width of both the Active and VendorID fields until all the controls fit inside the print margins. Finally, set the Visible property to No for both the Active and VendorID fields on the Property Sheet window.

After you finish, click the arrow below the View button in the Views group on the Design tab and click Print Preview to see the result, shown in Figure 17-46. You can find the web report at this stage saved as rptXmplVendorAddressBook2 in the sample database.

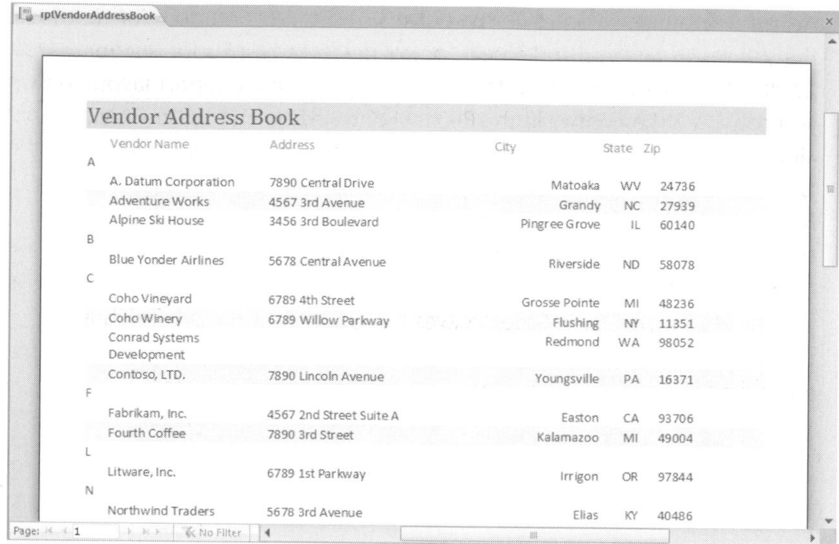

Figure 17-46 Your report should now look something like this after resizing the controls.

Adding Totals to Records

All your fields are in place, so now you can add a control for counting the number of vendors. Switch back to Layout view, select either the VendorName text box control or the Vendor Name label, click the Totals command in the Grouping & Totals group on the Design tab, and then click Count Records from the drop-down list, as shown in Figure 17-47.

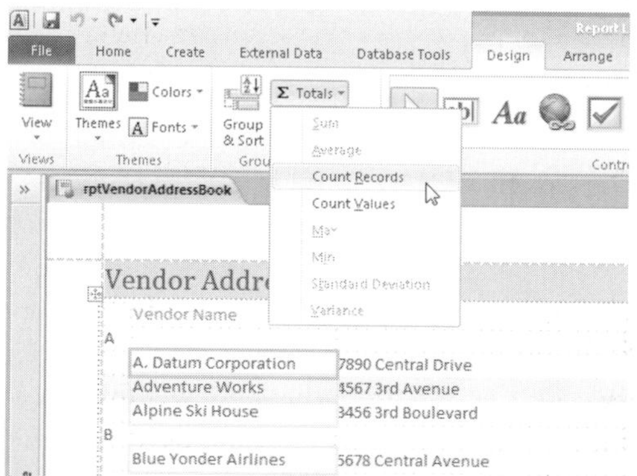

Figure 17-47 Click the Count Records command to create controls to total the number of vendor records.

Access places a new control in the expression Group Footer section, in the same column as the VendorName field, and a new control in the Report Footer section, as shown in Figure 17-48. Note that we scrolled down to the bottom of the report layout in Figure 17-48 so you could see the control in the Report Footer section. (The Count Values option, shown in Figure 17-47, would also create the same controls and show the same results for text fields. Use Count Values when you need Access to count the individual values of number or currency fields.) You don't need the extra control counting the number of vendors for each letter, so select that new control and press Delete to remove it from the report layout. (The control showing a number less than 16 is the one you want to remove.) After you remove the control, you'll notice Access leaves the empty cell behind, which is now creating extra unneeded space between each group. Select the empty cell and press Delete to remove the empty cell and collapse the extra space separating the groups.

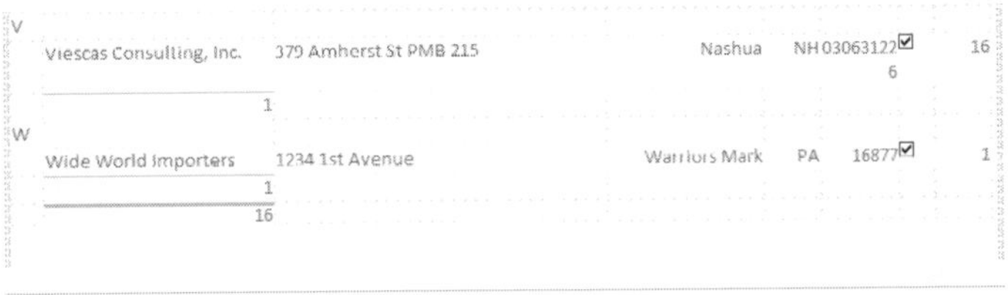

V
Viescas Consulting, Inc. 379 Amherst St PMB 215 Nashua NH 03063122 16
6
1
W
Wide World Importers 1234 1st Avenue Warriors Mark PA 16877 1
1
16

Figure 17-48 Access creates an expression to count the number of vendors for each letter and another to count the total number of vendors in the report.

Select the total number of records control in the Report Footer section now and then open the Property Sheet window. Access set the Control Source for this control to =Count(*). This expression totals the number of vendor records for the entire report. (If you chose the Count Values option, Access sets the Control Source to =Count([VendorName]) for this control.) Tab into or click in the Control Source property and change the expression to **="Number of vendors: " & Count(*)** to display a descriptive message explaining what the number represents. You'll notice that Access now aligns the text in this control to the left because you've included a string concatenation in the expression.

INSIDE OUT

Use a Filtered Web Query When Designing Web Reports to Reduce Scrolling

When you work in Layout view with web reports, you'll probably find yourself scrolling up and down the report layout quite often to see controls in different sections. To help reduce the amount of scrolling, you can use the Property Sheet window to select the control you want to work with or you can temporarily base the web report on a web query that limits the number of records returned. When you have fewer records to look at, you'll have to scroll less in the report layout to see controls in the different sections.

When the report is printed, it would be nice to have a page number at the bottom of the page. Click the Page Numbers button in the Header/Footer group on the Design tab to open the Page Numbers dialog box, discussed in "Completing the Report," on page 1059. Select the following options in the Page Numbers dialog box—Page N Of M, Bottom Of Page [Footer], Alignment set to Center, and Show Number On First Page. Click OK to close the Page Numbers dialog box. Access places a new control in the Page Footer section that spans the width of the entire report.

> **Note**
>
> **You won't immediately see a difference in the report in Layout view after you add a page count to a report that spans multiple pages. If you scroll to the bottom of the report, you'll see the control says Page 1 Of 1 even if you know the report spans more than one page. In Layout view, Access does not count the number of pages because it is not actually formatting the pages for printing. If you switch to Print Preview, you can see the correct page numbers displayed on each page.**

Using Gridlines

Your web report is functional right now, but with a little formatting, you can make it look more professional and easier to read. Web reports do not support Line controls; however, you can simulate the look of lines by adding gridlines to web reports. Switch back to Layout view for your report, select any of the label controls for the fields in the Page Header section, and then click the Select Row button in the Rows & Columns group on the Arrange tab to select the entire row of controls. Now, click the Gridlines command in the Table group on the Arrange tab and click Horizontal from the drop-down list of options, as shown in Figure 17-49.

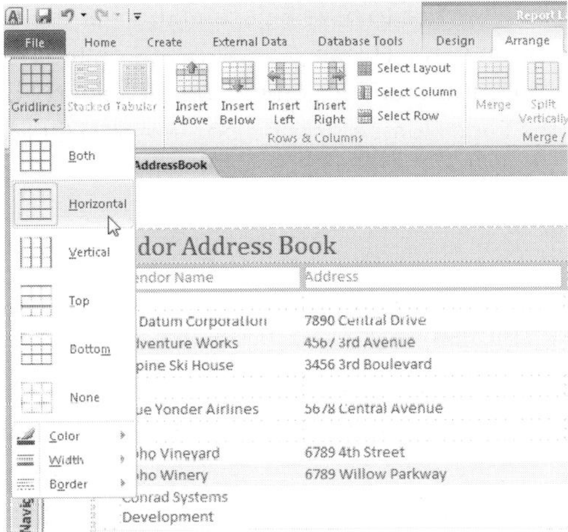

Figure 17-49 Click Horizontal to add gridlines to the top and bottom of your controls.

Access adds gridlines to the top and bottom of each label control and empty cell in the row of controls displayed in the Page Header section. Click the Gridlines command again, click Color (near the bottom of the drop-down list of options), and click the color called Dark Blue, Text 2. Access now changes the color of all those gridlines to a dark blue.

> **Note**
>
> **Access does not always display the gridlines around your controls when you view the report in Layout view. We recommend you periodically switch to Print Preview or Report View when you're creating or editing gridlines to make sure you are getting the look you want with your gridlines.**

Scroll down to the bottom of the report and select the control displaying the total number of vendor records—the control named AccessTotalsVendorName1 in the Property Sheet window. Click the Select Row button in the Rows & Columns group on the Arrange tab to select the entire row of controls. Now, click the Gridlines command in the Table group on the Arrange tab and click Top from the drop-down list of options. Access creates a gridline across the top of all these controls. Next, click the Gridlines command again, click Color, and then click the same color as you did previously—Dark Blue, Text 2. Finally, click the Gridlines command one last time, click Width, and then click 1 Pt from the gridline width options. Save your report and then switch to Print Preview to see how your report will print on paper with these changes, as shown in Figure 17-50.

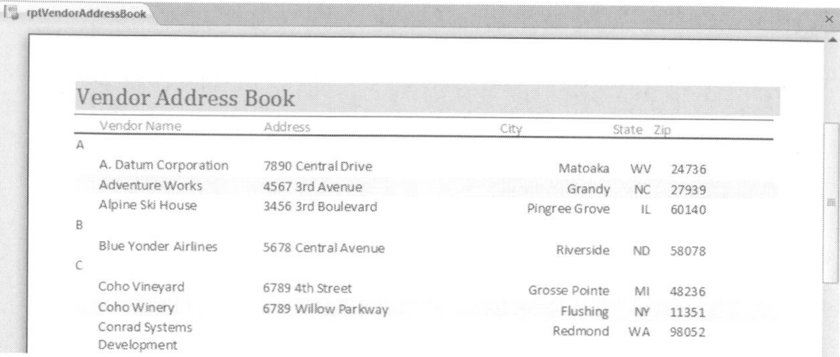

Figure 17-50 Use gridlines to create a visual separation between web report elements.

> **Note**
>
> **In a previous section, we had you delete the Active and Vendor ID label controls from the Page Header section instead of just hiding the controls. We instructed you to do this because if you set their Visible property to No, you would not see any gridlines around those two controls when you view the report in Print Preview or Report view. Your gridlines across the top would stop after the Zip label control. By removing those controls, you can set gridlines around the empty cells that occupy those spaces.**

Adding the Final Formatting Touches

Now that you've completed adding gridlines to your web report, let's add a few finishing formatting touches to the web report. When the web report is printed, it would be nice to have the date and time the report was printed at the top of the page. Switch back to Layout view and then click the Date And Time button in the Header/Footer group on the Design tab to open the Date And Time dialog box. Select the Include Date and Include Time options in the Date And Time dialog box, and leave the default formatting options. Click OK to close the Date And Time dialog box. Access places two new controls to the right of the title label caption in the Report Header section, as shown in Figure 17-51. You'll notice that Access reduces the width of the title label control to keep the new date and time controls from spanning over the page margin.

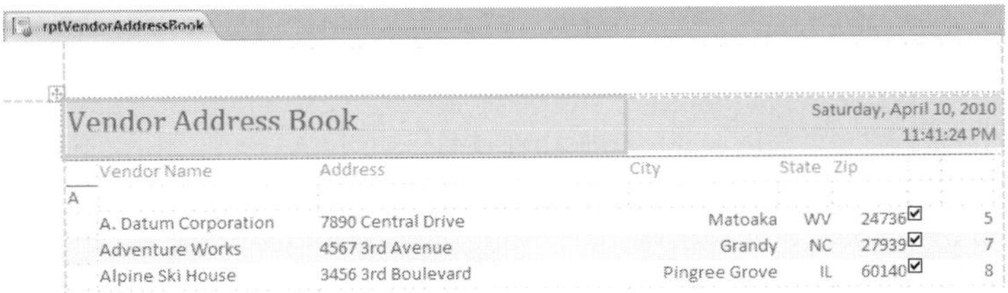

Figure 17-51 Access creates new date and time controls in the Report Header section when you use the Date And Time dialog box.

It would be nice to have the title caption centered in the report and the date and time controls on separate sides. You can make these changes easily by adding another row to the Report Header section. Select the title label caption and then click Insert Above in the Rows & Columns group on the Arrange tab. Access inserts a new row above the title label caption control. Click the new date control that Access created in the previous step, and drag the control into the new empty cell in the upper-left corner of the report layout. Left-align the text in this control after you finish moving the control. Now, click the time control and drag this control to the new empty cell in the upper-right corner of the report layout. Click the title label control, hold down the Shift key, and click the two empty cells where the date and time controls used to be. Click the Merge button in the Merge/Split group on the Arrange tab to merge all these controls into one large control that spans the entire width of the report. Center-align the text in the title label control by clicking the Center button in the Font group on the Format tab. Your Report Header section should now look like Figure 17-52.

Figure 17-52 Your report should now match this figure after moving the controls in the Report Header section.

Perform the following steps to adjust some of the formatting options on your web report:

1. By default, Access applied a background color to the Report Header section when you clicked the Title command. Let's remove that color for this web report. Open the Property Sheet window, select ReportHeader from the Selection Type combo box, and then change the Back Color property to **Background 1**. Access changes the Report Header section to blend in with the rest of the report grid—in this case, the section is colored white.

2. Click the date control text box in the upper-left corner of the report layout, hold down the Shift key, and then click the time text box control. On the Property Sheet window, change the Font Size to **9** to reduce the font size of these two controls.

3. Change the Fore Color of all the field label controls in the Page Header section to **Text 2**.

4. By default, Access created alternating background colors for the detail records in this web report, which we don't need. In the Property Sheet window, select Detail from the Selection Type combo box, click the drop-down list of color choices on the Alternate Back Color property, and then select **No Color**.

5. Select the expression group control that shows the first letter of the vendor names for this report—the AccessIntervalControl control in the Property Sheet window. Change the Fore Color to **Text 2**, set the Font Size to **16**, and the Font Weight to **Bold**.

6. Click the VendorName text box control, hold down the Shift key, and then select each of the field controls except the Active field. In the Property Sheet window, change the Fore Color to **Text 1** and the Font Size to **9**.

7. Select the City, State, and PostalCode fields, and then left-align these controls.

8. Scroll down to the bottom of the report and then select the control that shows the total number of records for this report—the AccessTotalsVendorName1 control, in the Property Sheet window. Change the Fore Color to **Text 1**, and left-align the control.

9. In the Property Sheet window, select Report in the Selection Type combo box, and type **Vendor Address Book** for the Caption property.

Click the Save button on the Quick Access Toolbar to save the changes you made to this web report. Switch to Print Preview to see how your completed web report looks on paper, as shown in Figure 17-53. This web report now looks very close to the rptWebVendorAddressBook web report in the Back Office Software System web database. You can find this web report saved as rptXmplVendorAddressBook3 in the sample database. As you can see, Layout view allows you to quickly create a professional-looking web report in Access 2010.

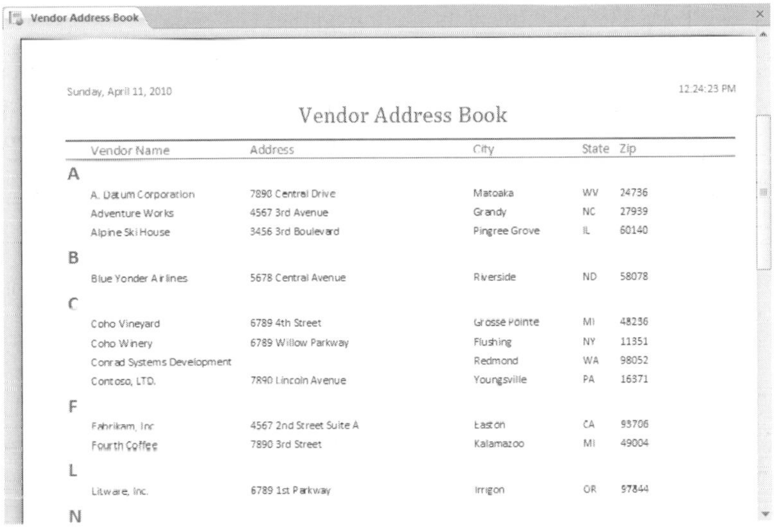

Vendor Address Book

Sunday, April 11, 2010 12:24:23 PM

Vendor Address Book

	Vendor Name	Address	City	State	Zip
A					
	A. Datum Corporation	7890 Central Drive	Matoaka	WV	24736
	Adventure Works	4567 3rd Avenue	Grandy	NC	27939
	Alpine Ski House	3456 3rd Boulevard	Pingree Grove	IL	60140
B					
	Blue Yonder Airlines	5678 Central Avenue	Riverside	ND	58078
C					
	Coho Vineyard	6789 4th Street	Grosse Pointe	MI	48236
	Coho Winery	6789 Willow Parkway	Flushing	NY	11351
	Conrad Systems Development		Redmond	WA	98052
	Contoso, LTD.	7890 Lincoln Avenue	Youngsville	PA	16371
F					
	Fabrikam, Inc	4567 2nd Street Suite A	Easton	CA	93706
	Fourth Coffee	7890 3rd Street	Kalamazoo	MI	49004
L					
	Litware, Inc.	6789 1st Parkway	Irrigon	OR	97844
N					

Figure 17-53 This is how your completed Vendor Address Book web report looks in Print Preview.

Understanding Web Report Limitations

Web reports are more limited than client reports. In addition to being limited to designing web reports in Layout view only, here are several more important limitations you should be aware of concerning web reports that we have not mentioned in preceding discussions:

- Web reports do not support embedded subforms or subreports.
- No report or control events are supported in web reports. (You'll learn all about events beginning in Part 6, "Automating an Application Using Macros.")
- You can use only text box, label, hyperlink, check box, and image controls in web reports.

- Web reports do not support setting report background images.
- Web reports do not support control padding.
- You cannot overlap controls in web reports as you can with client reports. All controls in web reports must be in control layouts, which means no controls can overlap.
- Web reports do support conditional formatting rules; however, you cannot use the new Data Bars conditional formatting options with them.

You should now feel comfortable with constructing client and web reports. In this chapter, you've seen that Access 2010 presents many tools and views to assist you in creating professional and functional reports. In most cases, you'll find that using a combination of these tools—Design view, Layout view, the Report command, and the Report Wizard—is the best way to create reports. In Chapter 18, "Advanced Report Design," you'll learn how to build more complex client reports that contain subreports and calculated values.

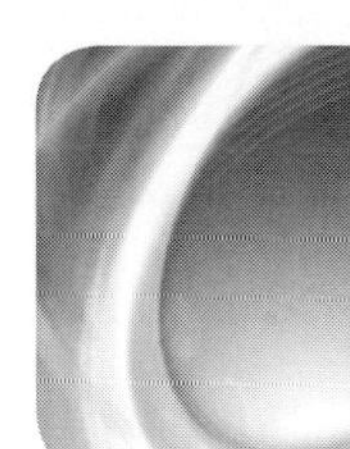

CHAPTER 18

Advanced Report Design

In Chapter 17, "Constructing a Report," you learned how to create a relatively simple client report with a single subtotal level. You also saw how the Report Wizard can help you construct a new client report. This chapter shows you how to do the following:

- Design a client report with multiple subtotal groups
- Add complex calculations to a client report
- Embed a report within another client report
- Create a client report with an embedded PivotChart form

To learn how to work with these features, you'll create a Facility Occupancy By Date client report for the Housing Reservations database. In a second example, you'll learn how to use the results from two queries in an embedded subreport and an embedded PivotChart to produce a client report that summarizes and graphs revenue by facility and month.

Note

The examples in this chapter are based on the reports, queries, tables, and data in HousingDataCopy2.accdb on the companion CD included with this book. You can find similar reports in the Housing Reservations sample application, but all the reports in that sample file have custom ribbons defined, so you won't see the four main ribbon tabs—Home, Create, External Data, and Database Tools—when you open those reports. The results you see from the samples in this chapter might not exactly match what you see in this book if you have changed the sample data in the files. Also, all the screen images in this chapter were taken on a Windows 7 system with the Access color scheme set to Silver. Your results might look different if you are using a different operating system or a different theme.

Building a Query for a Complex Report

To explore some of the advanced features you can include in a client report, let's build a report in the Housing database that displays room occupancy information by facility, date, room, and employee. As noted in Chapter 17, reports tend to bring together information from many tables, so you are likely to begin constructing a report by designing a query to retrieve the data you need for the report. For this example, you need information from the tblFacilities, tblReservations, and tblEmployees tables in the HousingDataCopy2.accdb database. Open a new Query window in Design view by clicking the Query Design button in the Queries group on the Create tab, and add these tables to the query window.

The tblReservations table contains one row per reservation, and the reservation could span many days. If you want to report on occupancy by day, you must use the special trick you learned in Chapter 10, "Building Complex Queries": Include a table containing all the dates you want, and add special criteria to expand each row in tblReservations into one row per day. The sample database contains a handy table, ztblDates, which has rows containing all the dates from January 1, 1992, to December 31, 2035, so add that table to your query. Close the Show Table dialog box. Next, add the fields listed in Table 18-1 to the design grid. (You can find this query saved as qryXmplRptReservationsByDay in the sample database.)

Table 18-1 Fields in the qryXmplRptReservationsByDay Query

Field/Expression	Source Table	Criterion
EmpName: tblEmployees.LastName & ", " & tblEmployees.FirstName & (" "+tblEmployees.MiddleName)		
ReservationID	tblReservations	
FacilityName	tblFacilities	
RoomNumber	tblReservations	
DateValue	ztblDates	Between #10/1/2010# And #12/31/2010#
CheckInDate	tblReservations	<= [ztblDates].[DateValue]
CheckOutDate	tblReservations	>[ztblDates].[DateValue]
TotalCharge	tblReservations	

Your Query window should look similar to the one shown in Figure 18-1.

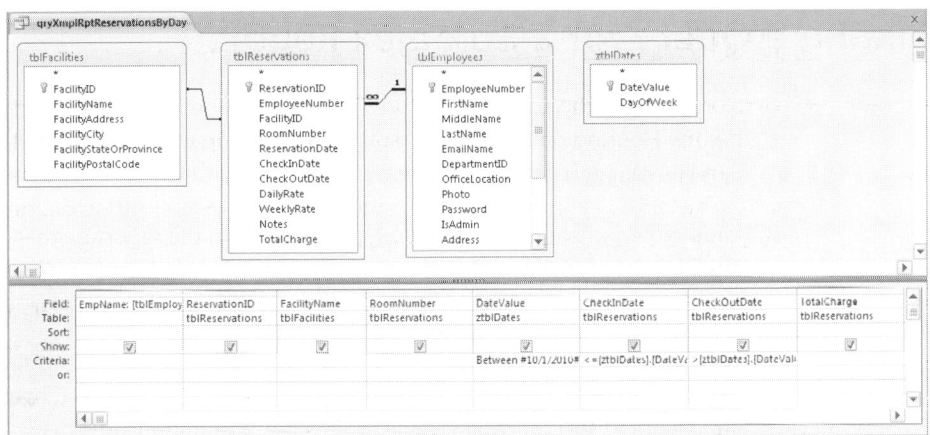

Figure 18-1 The qryXmplRptReservationsByDay query for the Facility Occupancy By Date report returns one row per day in each reservation.

You might be wondering why the query has a criterion to limit the range of dates returned from the ztblDates table. The sample database contains reservations from August 14, 2010, through April 4, 2011 (340 records). Although you could certainly create a report that includes all reservations, a user is typically going to want to look at records only for a specific date span. (For example, the housekeeping department might be interested in seeing this report only for the next few days or week.) Also, because the ztblDates table contains more than 16,000 rows, this query could take up to a minute to run—or more, on a slow computer—unless you filter the rows. In Chapter 25, "Automating Your Application with Visual Basic," on the companion CD, you'll learn how to provide the user with a custom date range dialog box to limit the records. For this example, the query includes a filter to limit the rows to the fourth quarter of 2010.

You can either save your query as qryMyRptReservationsByDay and select it in the Navigation pane, or select the qryXmplRptReservationsByDay query in the Navigation pane to follow along in the next section.

Creating the Basic Facility Occupancy By Date Report

For many reports, building the source query is the most difficult step. Once you have the data you need and understand the grouping options and properties you can set, building the report is easy. We actually like to use the Report Wizard to get a jump start on laying out our client reports. The wizard works especially well when the record source contains 10 or fewer fields.

To start designing the Facility Occupancy By Date report, select the query in the Navigation pane, and click the Report Wizard button in the Reports group on the Create tab. Build the basic report by taking the following steps:

1. On the first page of the wizard, choose the FacilityName, DateValue, RoomNumber, and EmpName fields, and click Next.

2. On the second page, the wizard suggests grouping the report by the RoomNumber field. However, you need to define custom grouping and sorting later, so click the left arrow to undo that selection and then click Next.

3. On the next page, the wizard offers to sort the information for you. You can ask the wizard to establish some of the grouping and sorting settings you need by asking for an ascending sort on FacilityName, DateValue, and RoomNumber. Click Next.

4. Because you didn't ask the wizard to create any groups, the wizard suggests a tabular layout, and this is just fine. Be sure that Orientation is set to Portrait and the Adjust The Field Width So All Fields Fit On A Page check box is selected. Click Next.

5. On the final page of the wizard, enter **Facility Occupancy By Date – 4th Quarter 2010** as the report title, select the Modify The Report's Design option, and click Finish to create your report.

The report the wizard built should look like that shown in Figure 18-2.

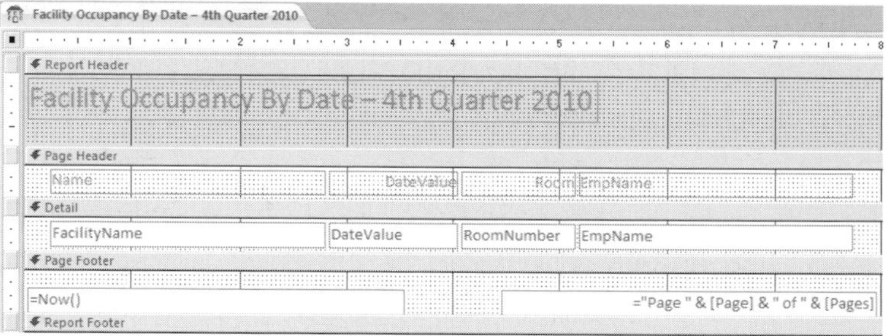

Figure 18-2 This is the initial Facility Occupancy By Date report created by the Report Wizard.

The wizard always places the report title label in the Report Header section, but that appears only once on the first page of the report. Especially when the report is likely to contain many pages, we like to see the report title repeated at the top of each page so that the subject of the report is clear throughout. You can move the report title from the Report Header section to the Page Header section. To do this, follow these steps:

1. Expand the bottom of the Page Header section about 0.7 inch.
2. Click in the ruler to the left of the four label controls in the page header to select all these label controls. Use the down arrow key to move the four label controls down to the bottom of the expanded Page Header section.
3. Click the label control in the Report Header section, and drag it down into the space you created in the Page Header section. You might want to select the column heading labels again and use the up arrow key to close any gap below the bottom of the report title label control. Also, move the bottom of the Page Header section up so that there's only a small space between the line and the bottom of the section.
4. Close up the bottom of the Report Header section so that it has zero height.

While you're refining the look of the report, click the DateValue label control and change its Caption to **Date**. Also, click the EmpName label control and change its caption to Employee. (You can change captions directly in a label control by selecting the control, clicking inside it with your mouse, and then typing the new caption.) Select all the controls in the Page Footer section and delete them. You'll learn later how to create controls to display the current date and time and page numbers.

Your report should now look like Figure 18-3. Click the Save button on the Quick Access Toolbar to preserve your work to this point.

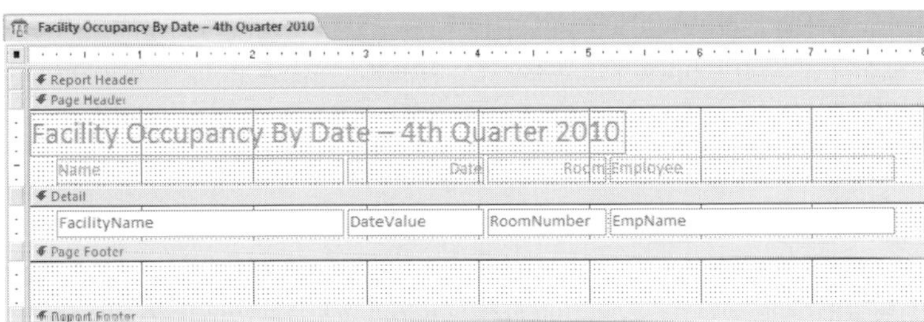

Figure 18-3 Your Facility Occupancy By Date report should look like this, after adjusting what the wizard built.

Defining the Grouping and Sorting Criteria

The next thing you need to do is define the grouping and sorting criteria for the report. Click the Group & Sort button in the Grouping & Totals group on the Design tab to open the Group, Sort, And Total pane. This report should display the daily reservation data from the query in the Detail section, with summaries of reservations by room number, by date, and by facility. Note that in the Group, Sort, And Total pane, you specify grouping values from the outermost to the innermost (like specifying a sorting criteria left to right). So, select the FacilityName sorting specification in the first line of the Group, Sort, And Total pane, click More to expand the options, click the arrow on the Without A Footer box, and then click With A Footer Section. Notice that when you add a group header or group footer for any field or expression in the Group, Sort, And Total pane, Access 2010 adds an appropriate section to your report. Access also changes this specification from Sort By to Group On. You want to make sure that a group header doesn't get "orphaned" at the bottom of a page, so click the arrow on the option that says Do Not Keep Group Together On One Page and click Keep Header And First Record Together On One Page. Note that you can also ask Access to attempt to keep all the detail for this level of grouping on one page by clicking the Keep Whole Group Together On One Page option. When you do this, Access will produce a new page if all the detail for the next group won't fit on the current page. As you'll see later, the report sections also have properties that you can set to force a new page with the start of each group.

The DateValue field from the query returns the date each room is occupied across a reservation span. When housing managers review reservations for more than one month, they might want to see subtotals by month. You can create a group on month by clicking the DateValue sorting specification, clicking More to expand the options, clicking the arrow on the group on property box (where it says By Entire Value), and clicking By Month. See the sidebar "Understanding Grouping Options," on page 1113, for details about other options you can set. Also, click the arrow on the group footer property (where it says Without A Footer Section), and click With A Footer Section to create a space to place monthly totals on your report. (Notice that Access changes this specification from Sort By to Group On.) Click the arrow on the option that says Do Not Keep Group Together On One Page, and click Keep Header And First Record Together On One Page, as you did for the FacilityName grouping specification.

You can include the DateValue field in the Group, Sort, And Total pane again, but set the group interval to Each Value to create a subtotal by day. Click Add A Group to create a blank specification row for a second DateValue. Click DateValue in the Select Field box, click More to see all the options, click the arrow on the group interval box (where it says By Quarter), and then click By Entire Value. Next, click Without A Header Section in the header section box, and click With A Footer Section in the footer section box. Finally, click Keep Whole Group Together On One Page for the last option so that a set of rows for a particular day doesn't split across a page boundary. You need to move this new grouping specification up one level in the grouping and sorting order, so click the Move Up arrow to move this second DateValue group specification above the RoomNumber sort specification. Remember that there's no sorting specification in the query you built or in the sample qryXmplRptReservationsByDay query. There wouldn't be any point in defining a sort in the query because reports ignore any sorting specification from the query when you define any criteria in the Group, Sort, And Total pane. Your result should look something like that shown in Figure 18-4. (Note that we clicked the first DateValue grouping specification so that you can see the group property settings for that field.)

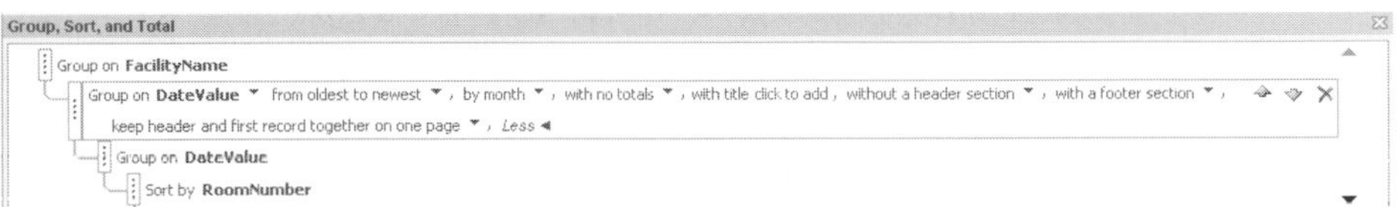

Figure 18-4 Set your grouping and sorting criteria for the Facility Occupancy By Date report in the Group, Sort, And Total pane.

Your report design should now look like Figure 18-5.

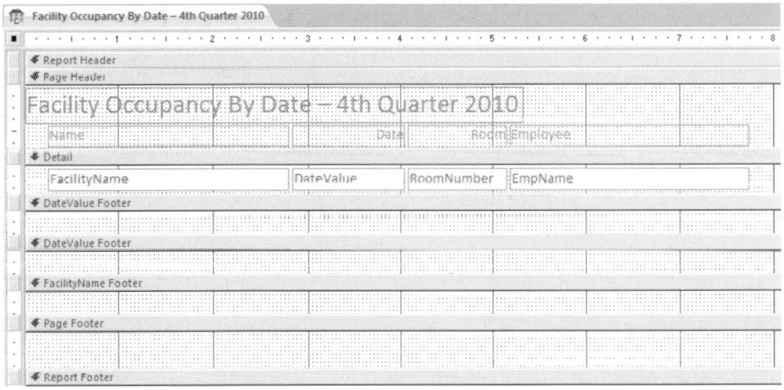

Figure 18-5 The Facility Occupancy By Date report has new Footer sections after you define the grouping and sorting criteria.

Click Save again to preserve your work to this point. You can find this stage of the report design saved as rptXmplFacilityDateOccupancyStep1 in the sample database.

Understanding Grouping Options

For each field or expression in the upper part of the Group, Sort, And Total pane, you can set group on and group interval properties. Normally, you'll want to start a new grouping of data whenever the value of your field or expression changes. You can, however, specify that a new grouping starts whenever a field or an expression changes from one range of values to another. The type of range you can specify varies depending on the data type of the field or the expression.

For text grouping fields, you can tell Access to start a new group based on a change in value of one or more leading characters in the string. For example, you can create a new group based on a change in the first letter of the field (rather than on a change anywhere in the field) to create one group per letter of the alphabet—a group of items beginning with A, a group of items beginning with B, and so on. To group on such a prefix, use the Custom interval and enter in the Characters box the number of leading characters that differentiates each group.

For numbers, you can enter a setting for the group interval property that clusters multiple values within a range. In the interval list, you can choose from By 5s, By 10s, By 100s, or By 1000s. Access calculates ranges from 0. For example, if you specify By 10s as the interval value, values ranging from –20 to 29 would be grouped from –20 through –11, –10 through –1, 0 through 9, 10 through 19, 20 through 29. You can also specify a Custom interval value.

For date/time fields, you can set the group interval property to calendar or time subdivisions and multiples of those subdivisions, such as By Year, By Quarter, By Month, By Week, or By Day. Use the Custom setting for the group interval property if you want to group on Hours or Minutes or a multiple of the subdivision—for example, select Custom in the group interval property, enter 2 in the By box, and select Years from the interval combo box if you want groupings for every two years.

When you create groupings in which the group interval property is set to something other than Each Value, Access sorts only the grouping value, not the individual values within each group. If you want Access to sort the detail items within the group, you must include a separate sort specification for those items. For example, if you group on the first letter of a LastName field and also want the names within each group sorted, you must select LastName in the field box in the Group, Sort, And Total pane, select With A Header Section (and possibly With A Footer Section), set the sort order to With A On Top, and set the group interval to By First Character. You must then enter LastName again as an additional sorting specification, set the sort order to With A On Top, and set the group interval to By Entire Value.

Setting Section and Report Properties

You've probably noticed that Access 2010 has a property sheet for each section in the Report window in Design view. You can set section properties not only to control how the section looks but also to control whether Access should attempt to keep a group together or start a new page before or after the group. There's also a property sheet for the report as a whole. You don't need to change any of these properties at this point, but the following sections explain the available property settings.

Section Properties for Reports

When you click in the blank area of any Group section or Detail section of a report and then click the Property Sheet button in the Tools group on the Design tab, Access displays a property sheet, such as the one shown in Figure 18-6.

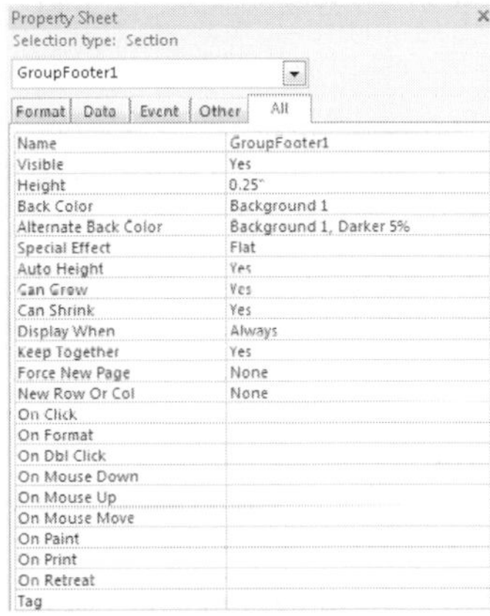

Figure 18-6 This is a property sheet for a client report section.

The available properties and their uses are described in Table 18-2. Under the Web Support column, you can see information concerning whether the property is listed on a web report's Property Sheet window and whether the server uses the property when it renders the report in a web browser. (If the property is available for a web report in the Property Sheet window, Access uses the property when you open the report in Access client, but the server might ignore the property.)

Table 18-2 Properties for a Report Section

Property	Description	Web Support
Name	Access automatically generates a unique section name for you.	Available on web reports and used on the server.
Visible	Set this property to Yes to make the section visible, or to No to make the section invisible. You can set this property from a macro or from a Microsoft Visual Basic procedure while Access formats and prints your report. You can make sections disappear depending on data values in the report.	Available on web reports and used on the server.

Property	Description	Web Support
Height	This property defines the height of the section. You normally change this property by dragging the bottom edge of the section. If you want a specific height, you can enter it here, and Access changes the display to match so long as all controls fit within the defined height. If you attempt to set the height smaller than will accommodate the controls in the section, Access sets the height to the minimum that can contain the controls.	Not available for web reports. Access adjusts the height of a section based on the height of the controls within the section.
Back Color	The default back color of a section is the color option for white, Background 1. You can also choose a custom color value by clicking in the property and then clicking the Build button (marked with ...) next to the property box to open the Color setting dialog box. You can also choose colors by clicking the Background Color button in the Font group on the Format tab.	Available on web reports and used on the server.
Alternate Back Color	The default alternate back color of a section is Background 1, Darker 5%. With this setting, Access applies the defined back color to all rows of data in that section. If you use the Report Wizard to create your report, Access sets an alternating back color in the Detail section of your report. If you want to display a different back color on alternating rows of data in a section, click the Build button (marked with ...) next to the property box to open the Color setting dialog box. You can also choose alternating colors by clicking the Alternate Row Color button in the Background group on the Format tab. When you define an Alternate Back Color, Access applies the Back Color to the first, third, fifth, and so on rows, and it applies the Alternate Back Color to the second, fourth, sixth, and so on, rows. You can also choose to set the option to No Color to have Access not apply an alternating color to the section. The Alternate Back Color property is not available in page headers and footers.	Available on web reports, but only for the Detail section. The server uses this property.
Special Effect	The default setting is a flat effect. You can also set a raised or sunken effect for a section by clicking this effect from the drop-down list for the property.	Not available for web reports.
Auto Height	The default setting, Yes, causes the section's height to adjust automatically when you resize controls resized in Layout view. If you shrink the height of controls in Layout view, for example, Access shrinks the height of the section as well. If no controls exist in a section, Access reduces the section height to 0 inches. Change this property to No to not allow Access to automatically resize the section when controls are resized.	Not available for web reports.

Property	Description	Web Support
Can Grow	Setting this property to Yes allows the section to expand to accommodate controls that might expand because they display memo fields or long text strings. You can design a control to display only one line of text, but you should allow the control to expand to display more lines of text as needed. If you set the Can Grow property for any control in the section to Yes, Access automatically sets the Can Grow property of the section to Yes. This property is not available in page headers and footers.	Not listed on the web report's property sheet, but Access sets this property to Yes automatically for all sections. The server uses this property.
Can Shrink	This property is similar to Can Grow. You can set it to Yes to allow the section to become smaller if controls in the section become smaller to enclose less text. Unlike Can Grow, setting the Can Shrink property for any control in the section to Yes does not automatically set Can Shrink for the section to Yes. The default setting is No. This property is not available in page headers and footers.	Not listed on the web report's property sheet, but Access sets this property to Yes automatically for all sections (excluding page headers and footers). The server uses this property.
Display When	The default setting, Always, displays this section in Report view, Layout view, Print Preview, and when you print the report. Choose Print Only to display the section only when you view the report in Print Preview or you print the report. Choose Screen Only to display the section only when in Report view and Layout view.	Not available for web reports.
Keep Together	Set this property to No to allow a section to flow across page boundaries. The default Yes setting tells Access to attempt to keep all lines within a section together on a page. (You can tell Access to attempt to keep detail lines together with group headers and footers by setting the Keep Together property in a Group, Sort, And Total specification to either Keep Whole Group Together On One Page or to Keep Header And First Record Together On One Page.) This property is not available in page headers and footers.	This property is available on web reports, but the server ignores these settings.
Repeat Section	Set this property to Yes to force the section to appear again at the top of the next page or column if the information in the Detail section overflows onto the next page. The default No setting tells Access not to display the section again on the next page or column if the information in the Detail section overflows onto the next page. This property applies only to group header sections. When you print a report that contains a subreport, the subreport's RepeatSection property determines whether the subreport group headers are displayed again across additional pages or columns.	This property is available on web reports, but the server ignores this property.

Property	Description	Web Support
Force New Page	Set this property to Before Section to force the section to print at the top of a new page. Set this property to After Section to force the next section to print at the top of a new page. You can also set this property to Before & After to force the section to print on a page by itself. The default setting is None. This property is not available in page headers and footers.	Available on web reports and used on the server.
New Row Or Col	When you use the Page Setup dialog box to format your report with more than one column (vertical) or more than one row (horizontal) of sections, you can set this property to Before Section, After Section, or Before & After to produce the section again at the top, bottom, or both top and bottom of a new column or row. This property is useful for forcing headers to print at the top of each column in a multiple-column report. The default setting is None. This property is not available in page headers and footers.	Not available for web reports.
On Click	Enter the name of a macro or a Visual Basic procedure that you want Access to execute when a user clicks inside this section in Report view. See Part 6, "Automating an Application Using Macros," for details.	Server reports do not support events.
On Format	Enter the name of a macro or a Visual Basic procedure that you want Access to execute when it begins formatting this section. See Part 6 for details.	Server reports do not support events.
On Dbl click	Enter the name of a macro or a Visual Basic procedure that you want Access to execute when a user double-clicks inside this section in Report view. See Part 6 for details.	Server reports do not support events.
On Mouse Down	Enter the name of a macro or a Visual Basic procedure that you want Access to execute when a user clicks the mouse button while the mouse pointer rests on this section in Report view. See Part 6 for details.	Server reports do not support events.
On Mouse Up	Enter the name of a macro or a Visual Basic procedure that you want Access to execute when a user releases a mouse button while the mouse pointer rests on this section in Report view. See Part 6 for details.	Server reports do not support events.
On Mouse Move	Enter the name of a macro or a Visual Basic procedure that you want Access to execute when a user rests their mouse pointer on this section in Report view. See Part 6 for details.	Server reports do not support events.
On Paint	Enter the name of a macro or a Visual Basic procedure that you want Access to execute when this section is redrawn in Print Preview or Report view. See Part 6 for details.	Server reports do not support events.
On Print	Enter the name of a macro or a Visual Basic procedure that you want Access to execute when it begins printing this section or when it displays the section in Print Preview. See Part 6 for details.	Server reports do not support events.

Property	Description	Web Support
On Retreat	Enter the name of a macro or a Visual Basic procedure that you want Access to execute when it has to back up over a section after it finds that the section won't fit on the current page and you've set the Keep Together property to Yes. This event happens after On Format but before On Print, so you can use it to undo settings you might have changed in your On Format routine. Access calls On Format again when it formats the section on a new page. See Part 6 for details. This property is not available in page headers and footers.	Server reports do not support events.
Tag	Use this property to store additional identifying information about the section. You can use this property in macros and in Visual Basic procedures to temporarily store information that you want to pass to another routine.	This property is available on web reports, but the server ignores this property.

Report Properties

If you select the Report option from the Selection Type list in the Property Sheet window (or click in the Report window beyond the right edge of the Detail section and then click the Property Sheet button in the Tools group on the Design tab), Access displays the report's properties in the property sheet, as shown in Figure 18-7.

Figure 18-7 The property sheet for a client report displays many properties that you can customize for the report object.

Some of the available properties and their uses are described in Table 18-3. Under the Web Support column, you can see information concerning whether the property is listed on a web report Property Sheet window and whether the server uses the property when it renders the report in a web browser. (If the property is available in the Property Sheet window for a web report, Access uses the property when you open the report in Access client, but the server might ignore the property.)

Table 18-3 Properties for a Report

Property	Description	Web Support
Record Source	This property displays the name of the table or query that provides the data for your report. You can also enter a valid Structured Query Language (SQL) statement for the record source.	Available on web reports and used on the server.
Caption	Use this property to set the text that appears in the title bar when you open the report in Report view, Layout view, and Print Preview. If you don't specify a caption, Access displays Report: and the name of the report in the window title bar if you are using a multiple-document interface (MDI) or on the report's tab if you are using single-document interface (SDI).	Available on web reports and used on the server.
Pop Up	Set this property to Yes to make the report window in Report view and Print Preview open as a pop-up. A pop-up window stays visible on top of other windows even when another window has the focus. The default setting is No. If you're using an SDI, Access does not display a tab for this report but instead shows the report as a pop-up window.	Not available for web reports.
Modal	Set this property to Yes to disallow clicking any other window or clicking the ribbon when the report window is open in Report view or Print Preview. The default setting is No.	Not available for web reports.
Default View	Use this property to tell Access in which view to first open the report. The default setting, Report view, tells Access to open the report in Report view when you double-click the report in the Navigation pane or click Open on the report's shortcut menu. Select Print Preview to have Access open the report in Print Preview when opened from the Navigation pane or from the Open command on the report's shortcut menu. If you set the Default View property to Report View and set the Allow Report View property to No, Access removes the Report View option from the Views group and opens the report in Print Preview.	This property is available on web reports, but the server ignores this property.

Property	Description	Web Support
Allow Report View	The default setting, Yes, specifies that you can open this report in Report view and you can switch to Report view from other views. If you change the setting to No, Access removes Report View as an option in the Views group on the ribbon.	Not available on the Property Sheet window for web reports, but Access sets this property to Yes automatically for all web reports.
Allow Layout View	The default setting, Yes, specifies that you can open this report in Layout view and you can switch to Layout view from other views. If you change the setting to No, Access removes Layout View as an option in the Views group on the ribbon.	Not available in the Property Sheet window for web reports, but Access sets this property to Yes automatically for all web reports.
Picture Type, Picture	To use a bitmap as the background of a report, you enter the full path name and file name in the Picture property. If you set the Picture Type property to Embedded, Access copies the bitmap specified to the Report object. If you set the Picture Type property to Linked, Access uses the path name stored in the Picture property to load the bitmap each time you open the report. If you set the Picture Type property to Shared, Access stores a copy of the image in a system table. You can then reference or reuse the shared image in other forms or reports by selecting the name of the shared image from the Picture property and setting the Picture Type to Shared. The default setting for Picture is (none), and the default setting for Picture Type is Embedded.	Not available for web reports.
Picture Tiling	When you set the Picture Size Mode property to Clip or Zoom and your picture is smaller than the page size, you can set the Picture Tiling property to Yes so that Access will place multiple copies of the picture across and/or down the page. The default setting is No.	Not available for web reports.
Picture Alignment	When you set the Picture Size Mode property to Clip or Zoom, you can use Picture Alignment to place the picture in the center of the page or in one of the corners. The default setting is Center.	Not available for web reports.

Property	Description	Web Support
Picture Size Mode	When your background picture is not the same size as your page, you can set the Picture Size Mode property so that Access adjusts the size. The Clip setting displays the picture in its original size, and if the page is smaller than the picture, Access clips the sides and top and bottom edges of the picture as necessary. The Zoom setting maintains the aspect ratio and shrinks or enlarges the picture to fit the page. If your picture doesn't have the same horizontal-to-vertical dimensions (aspect ratio) as your page, Access centers the image and shows some blank space at the sides or top and bottom of the page. The Stretch, Stretch Horizontal, and Stretch Vertical settings expand the picture to fit the page size and will distort the image if the aspect ratio of the picture does not match the aspect ratio of the page. The default setting is Clip.	Not available for web reports.
Width	Access sets this property when you increase the width of the report in the design grid. If you want a specific width, you can enter it here, and Access changes the display to match so long as all controls fit within the defined width. If you attempt to set the width smaller than will accommodate the controls in any section, Access sets the width to the minimum that can contain the controls.	Available on web reports and used on the server.
Fit To Page	Use this property to make Access expand the width of the report to fit a page while you are working in Layout view. The default setting, Yes, tells Access to automatically expand the width of the report to fit within the page margins. When you specify No, Access does not automatically expand the width and honors any width you specify for the report.	This property is available on web reports, but the server ignores this property.
Auto Center	This setting affects the positioning of the Report window when you open the report in Report view or Print Preview using an MDI. This property has no effect when you are using the SDI unless you have also set the Pop Up or Modal property to Yes. The default setting No leaves the upper-left corner in the same location as you last saved the report window from Design view. When you specify Yes, the report window opens centered in the Access workspace to the right of the Navigation pane or opens centered in the Access window if you set either Pop Up or Modal to Yes. If you collapse the Navigation pane after you open the report, Access moves the report to the left but does not center it again in the object workspace.	Not available for web reports.

Property	Description	Web Support
Auto Resize	This setting affects the size of the report window when you open the report in Print Preview. The default setting, Yes, asks Access to zoom the report to show the first entire page and size the window to fit within the Access workspace on your screen when you're using an MDI. When you're using an SDI, the report opens in a window sized to approximately 80 percent of the height available in the Access workspace, with a width relative to the layout of the page (portrait or landscape) and the report sized to display the entire first page. Unless you have a very high-resolution monitor, most portrait layout reports will be unreadable with this setting. When you specify No, the report opens at 100 percent resolution. When you're using an SDI, Access sizes the window the same as you last saved the report window from Design view or Layout view. We recommend you change this setting to No for most reports.	This property is available on web reports, but the server ignores this property.
Border Style	The default setting, Sizable, allows you to resize the Report window in Report view or Print Preview when you use an MDI or you have set the Pop Up or Modal property to Yes. This property has no effect when you use an SDI and both Pop Up and Modal are set to No. When you choose None, the report's Report view and Print Preview windows have no borders, control menu, title bar, Close button, or Minimize and Maximize buttons. You cannot resize or move the report when it is open. You can select the report and press Ctrl+F4 to close it unless the report's Pop Up property is set to Yes. You should write Visual Basic code to provide an alternative way to close this type of report. When you choose Thin, the report window in Report view or Print Preview has a thin border, signifying that the report cannot be resized. When you choose Dialog and the Pop Up property is set to Yes, the border of the Report window in Report view or Print Preview is a thick line (like that of a true Windows dialog box), signifying that you can resize the report. If the Pop Up property is set to No, the Dialog setting is the same as the Thin setting.	Not available for web reports.
Scroll Bars	Use this property to tell Access to display scroll bars for a report displayed in Report view or Layout view. The default setting, Both, causes Access to display both a horizontal and vertical scroll bar if needed to display the entire report. If you choose Neither, Access does not display either scroll bar, even if one is needed. You will not be able to scroll to see the rest of the report. Choose Horizontal Only to display only a horizontal scroll bar, or choose Vertical Only to display only a vertical scroll bar.	Not available for web reports.

Property	Description	Web Support
Control Box	You can set the Control Box property to No to remove the control menu and the Close, Minimize, and Maximize buttons from the report window in Report view or Print Preview when you're using an MDI. The default setting is Yes. You must use Ctrl+F4 to close the window when this property is set to No. This property has no effect when you're using the SDI.	Not available for web reports.
Close Button	You can set the Close Button property to No to remove the Close button from the report window in Report view or Print Preview. When you're using an MDI or you have set the Pop Up or Modal property to Yes, the control menu is still available unless you have also set the Control Box property to No, but the Close command is disabled on the menu. The default setting is Yes.	Not available for web reports.
Min Max Buttons	You can set the Min Max Buttons property to Both Enabled, None, Min Enabled, or Max Enabled when you are using an MDI or you have set the Pop Up or Modal property to Yes. If you disable a Minimize or Maximize button, the related command on the control menu becomes dimmed when the report window is in Report view or Print Preview. The default setting is Both Enabled.	Not available for web reports.
Moveable	The default setting, Yes, allows you to move the Report window in Report view or Print Preview when you're using an MDI or the Pop Up or Modal property is set to Yes. Set this property to No to lock the form on the screen where you last saved it.	Not available for web reports.
Show Page Margins	The default setting, Yes, displays print margins for your report when you open it in Layout view. The print margins are determined by your printer settings. You can use this setting in Layout view to make sure no controls extend past the print margins. Set this property to No to not display print margins.	This property is available on web reports, but the server ignores this property.
Grid X, Grid Y	Specify the number of horizontal (X) or vertical (Y) divisions per inch or per centimeter for the dots in the grid. When you use inches (when Measurement is set to U.S. in the Regional And Language Options item of the Control Panel), you can see the dots whenever you specify a value of 24 or less for both X and Y. When you use centimeters (when Measurement is set to Metric), you can see the dots when you specify values of 9 or less. The default setting is 24 for inches and 10 for metric.	These properties are available on web reports, but the server ignores these properties.
Layout For Print	When you set this property to Yes, you can select from among the TrueType and printer fonts installed on your computer. When you set this property to No, only TrueType and screen fonts are available. The default setting is Yes.	Not available for web reports.

Property	Description	Web Support
Grp Keep Together	Set this property to Per Page if you want Access to honor the Group, Sort, And Total keep together setting by page. Set it to Per Column (the default) for a multiple-column report if you want Access to attempt to keep a group together within a column. This property has no effect in a typical report with a single column.	Not available for web reports.
Picture Pages	You can set this property to show the picture on all pages, the first page, or no pages. The default setting is All Pages.	Not available for web reports.
Page Header	This property controls whether the page header appears on all pages. You might choose not to print the page header on the first page if the report contains a report header. Valid settings are All Pages (the default), Not With Rpt Hdr, Not With Rpt Ftr, and Not With Rpt Hdr/Ftr.	Not available for web reports.
Page Footer	This property controls whether the page footer appears on all pages. You might choose not to print the page footer on the last page if the report contains a report footer. Valid settings are All Pages (the default), Not With Rpt Hdr, Not With Rpt Ftr, and Not With Rpt Hdr/Ftr.	Not available for web reports.
Orientation	The default in most versions of Access 2010 is Left-to-Right. In versions that support a language that is normally read right to left, the default is Right-to-Left. When you use Right-to-Left, captions appear right-justified, and the order of characters in controls is right to left.	This property is available on web reports, but the server ignores this property.
Filter	This property shows any filter applied by a macro or Visual Basic procedure the last time the report was opened. You can also define a specific Filter setting that you want to save with the report definition. You can define a filter for a report, as you can with a form, using ribbon commands when the report is in Report view. To activate the Filter in code, set the report's FilterOn property (not displayed in the Property Sheet window) to True.	This property is available on web reports, but the server ignores this property.
Filter On Load	Set this property to Yes if you want Access to apply the filter defined for the report automatically each time the report opens. Note that you can set the Filter and FilterOn properties from a macro or a Visual Basic procedure. The default setting is No.	Not available for web reports.
Order By	This property shows any ordering criteria applied by a macro or a Visual Basic procedure the last time the report was opened. You can also define a specific Order By setting that you want to save with the report definition. You can activate the ordering criteria in code by setting the OrderByOn property (not displayed in the Property Sheet window) to True.	Not available for web reports.

Property	Description	Web Support
Order By On Load	Set this property to Yes if you want the Order By property defined for the report to be applied automatically each time the report opens. Note that you can set the OrderBy and OrderByOn properties from a macro or a Visual Basic procedure. Remember that Order By and Order By On Load have no effect if you have specified any settings in the Group, Sort, And Total pane. The default setting is No.	Not available for web reports.
Allow Filters	Use this property to determine whether a user can see selected records in Report view by applying filtering and sorting criteria using the commands in the Sort & Filter group on the Home tab or by applying the shortcut menu filtering options. If you set the Allow Filters property to No, the user cannot change the report to view other existing records, and Access dims all commands in the Sort & Filter group. The valid settings for the Allow Filters property are Yes and No. The default setting is Yes.	Not available for web reports.
On Current Through On Page	You can set these properties to run a macro, a function, or an event procedure when the specific event described by the property occurs for this report. See Part 6 for details.	Server reports do not support any events.
Timer Interval	When you create a macro or Visual Basic procedure to run in the On Timer event, you can use this property to specify the interval, in milliseconds, Access executes the On Timer event. The default setting, 0, tells Access not to execute the On Timer event. If, for example, you want to run your macro or Visual Basic procedure in the On Timer event every second, change this property to 1000.	Not available for web reports.
Date Grouping	Use this property to determine how Access groups date and time values that you've specified in the Group, Sort, And Total pane. You can set this property to US Defaults or Use System Settings (the default). For US Defaults, the first day of the week is Sunday, and the first week of the year starts on January 1. If you specify Use System Settings, the first day of the week and first week of the year are determined by the Regional And Language Options item in the Control Panel.	Not available for web reports.
Cycle	Use the default setting, All Records, to tab to the next record when you press the Tab key in the last control in the tab order. This setting applies when you display the report in Layout view or Report view. Choose Current Record to disallow tabbing from one record to another. Choose Current Page to disallow tabbing onto the next or previous record—you must use Page Up or Page Down to move between the records. When you set Current Record or Current Page, you must use the navigation buttons or ribbon commands to move to other records.	Not available for web reports.

Property	Description	Web Support
Record Locks	Set this property to All Records if the data for your report is on a network shared by others and you want to be sure that no one can update the records in the report until Access creates every page in the report. You should not set this property to All Records for a report that you plan to view in Layout view, Report view, or Print Preview because you'll lock out other users for the entire time that you're viewing the report on your screen. The default setting is No Locks.	Not available for web reports.
Ribbon Name	Enter the name of a custom ribbon. Access displays the ribbon when you open the report in Report view or Print Preview. See Chapter 26, "The Finishing Touches," on the companion CD, for details.	This property is available on web reports, but the server ignores this property.
Toolbar	Enter the name of a custom toolbar. Access displays the toolbar when you open the report in Report view or Print Preview. You can use this setting only if your database is in the .mdb file format and you defined custom menu bars in the database using a version of Access before Access 2007.	Not available for web reports.
Menu Bar	Enter the name of a custom menu bar. Access displays the menu bar when you open the report in Report view or Print Preview. You can use this setting only if your database is in the .mdb file format and you defined custom menu bars in the database using a prior version of Access before Access 2007.	Not available for web reports.
Shortcut Menu Bar	Enter the name of a custom shortcut menu. Access displays the shortcut menu when you open the report in Report view or Print Preview and right-click in the Report window. You must create custom shortcut menu bars by using Visual Basic code or by using the design facilities in a version of Access before Access 2007.	Not available for web reports.
Help File, Help Context Id	You can set the Help File property to specify the location of a Help file in any format supported by Windows and the Microsoft Office 2010 system, including the Hypertext Markup Language (HTML) help format. Use the Help Context Id property to point to a specific help topic within the file.	Not available for web reports.
Has Module	This property indicates whether the report has associated Visual Basic procedures. Access automatically changes this setting to Yes when you define any Visual Basic event procedures for the report. **Caution:** If you change this property to No when the report has procedures, Access warns you that this action will delete your code.	Not available for web reports.

Property	Description	Web Support
Use Default Paper Size	The default setting, No, tells Access not to use the default paper size of your default printer when printing the report. Instead, Access honors the section size properties you defined. Change this setting to Yes to have Access use the default printer settings.	Not available for web reports.
Fast Laser Printing	Some laser printers support the drawing of lines (such as the edges of rectangles, the line control, or the edges of text boxes) with rules. If you set the Fast Laser Printing property to Yes, Access sends rule commands instead of graphics to your printer to print rules. Rules print faster than graphics. The default setting is Yes.	Not available for web reports.
Tag	Use this property to store additional identifying information about the report. You can use this property in macros and in Visual Basic procedures to temporarily store information that you want to pass to another routine.	This property is available on web reports, but the server ignores this property.
Palette Source	With this property, if you have a color printer, you can specify a device-independent bitmap (.dib) file, a Windows Palette (.pal) file, a Windows icon (.ico) file, or a Windows bitmap (.bmp) file to provide a palette of colors different from those in the Access default palette. You might need to set this property if you have also set the Picture property so that the colors of the background picture display properly. The default setting, (Default), uses your current Windows palette.	Not available for web reports.
Key Preview	This property determines whether the report-level keyboard event procedures (KeyUp, KeyDown, and KeyPress) are invoked before a control's keyboard event procedures. The default setting, No, tells Access that only the active control can receive keyboard events when the report is displayed in Layout view or Report view. Choose Yes to have the report receive keyboard events before the active control receives keyboard events when the report is displayed in Layout view or Report view.	Not available for web reports.

Using Calculated Values

Much of the power of Access 2010 reports comes from their ability to perform both simple and complex calculations on the data from the underlying tables or queries. Access also provides dozens of built-in functions that you can use to work with your data or to add information to a report. The following sections provide examples of the types of calculations you can perform.

Adding the Print Date and Page Numbers

One of the pieces of information you might frequently add to a report is the date on which you prepared the report. You'll probably also want to add page numbers. Access provides two built-in functions that you can use to add the current date and time to your report. The Date function returns the current system date as a date/time value with no time component. The Now function returns the current system date and time as a date/time value.

> **Note**
>
> **When you create a report using the Report Wizard, it adds a similar control to the Page Footer section, and it uses the Now function that returns the date and the time. However, the wizard sets the Format property to Long Date, which displays only the date portion.**

To add the current date to your report, create an unbound text box control (delete the label) in the Page Footer section, and set its Control Source property to **=Date()**. Then, in the Format property box, specify Long Date. While you still have the Property Sheet window open, set the Text Align property to **Left** and the Border Style to **Transparent** for this control. You can see an example of using the Date function in Figure 18-8. The result in Print Preview is shown in Figure 18-9. Note that Access honors the Long Date settings from your computer's Control Panel settings. If your Control Panel settings, for example, do not include the day part, your results will differ from what is shown in Figure 18-9.

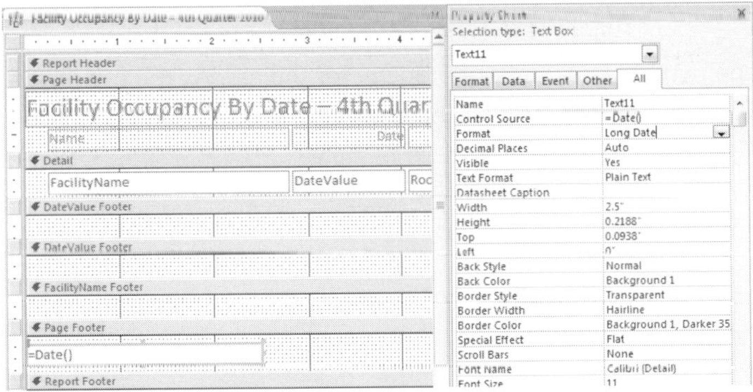

Figure 18-8 Use the Date function in an unbound control to add the date to a report.

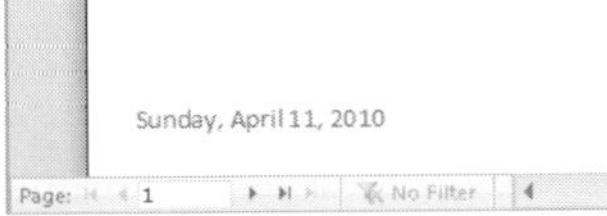

Figure 18-9 You can now see the current date displayed in the report in Print Preview.

In the Header/Footer group on the Design tab, Access 2010 includes a button that helps you create this type of control on your report. Switch back to Design view, click the Date & Time button in the Header/Footer group, and Access opens the Date And Time dialog box, shown in Figure 18-10. You can choose to insert the date, the time, or both the date and time displayed in a text box control into the report's Report Header section. You can choose different formats for both. Access displays a sample of what the control will display at the bottom of the dialog box. However, the tool does not offer you any choices of where it will place the control—Access always places this control in the Report Header section on the right side. You could create the control using this feature (selecting only the Include Date check box and the Long Date format), drag it to the Page Footer on the left, set the alignment to Left, and shrink the Report Header back to zero height, but we think it's just as easy to create the control yourself. Click Cancel to close the dialog box because you've already added a control to the report to display the date.

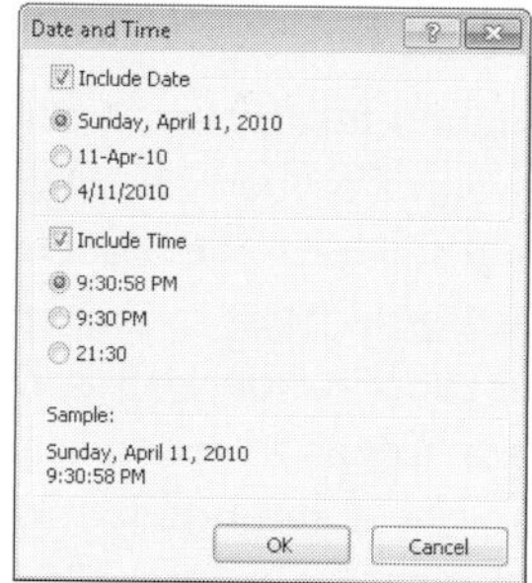

Figure 18-10 Use the Date And Time dialog box to assist you in building a report date control.

To add a page number, use the Page property for the report. You can't see this property in any of the property sheets because it is maintained by Access. Access also provides the Pages property, which contains a count of the total number of pages in the report. To add the current page number to a report (in this example, in the Page Footer section), create an unbound text box control (delete the label), set its Control Source property to **="Page" & [Page] & " of " & [Pages]** as shown in Figure 18-11, set the Text Align property to **Right**, and set the Border Style to **Transparent**.

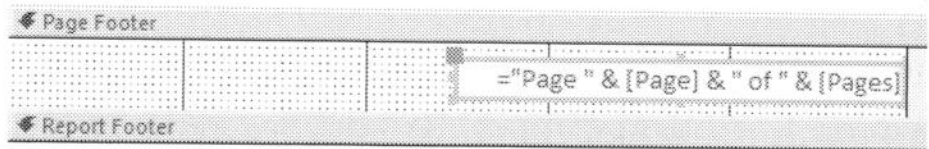

Figure 18-11 Use the Page and Pages properties to add page numbers to a report.

In the Header/Footer group on the Design tab, Access 2010 includes a button that helps you create this type of control on your report. Click the Page Numbers button in the Header/Footer group, and Access opens the Page Numbers dialog box, shown in Figure 18-12. (Remember, we discussed this command in Chapter 17.) You can choose to insert the page number or the page number and count of pages. Access also offers an option to display the page text box control in the report's Page Header or Page Footer section. In the Alignment drop-down list, you can choose where to have Access place the control—Left, Center, Right, Inside, or Outside. Note that Access adds two controls for the Inside and Outside options and includes a logical expression in the control source to display each text box on alternate pages. When you choose Inside, even page numbers appear on the right and odd page numbers appear on the left. When you choose Outside, even page numbers appear on the left, and odd numbers appear on the right. Select the Show Number On First Page check box at the bottom of the dialog box to display the page numbers on all pages, including the first page. If you clear this check box, Access creates a control that will not show the page number on the first page. You can try this feature using the settings in Figure 18-12 to compare the result with the text box you created previously, or you can click Cancel to close the dialog box.

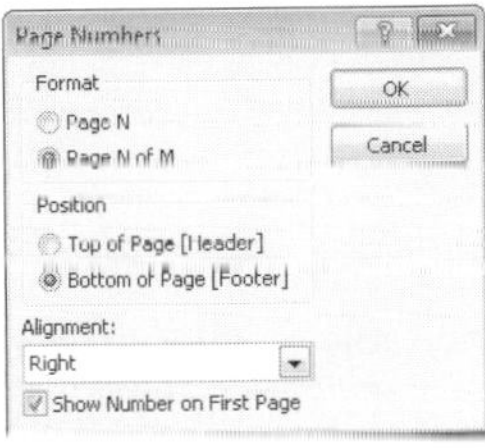

Figure 18-12 Use the Page Numbers dialog box to assist you in building a page number control.

INSIDE OUT You Can Change the Value of the Page Property in Code

You can reset the value of the Page property in a macro or a Visual Basic procedure that you activate from an appropriate report property. For example, if you're printing several multiple-page invoices for different customers in one pass, you might want to reset the page number to 1 when you start to format the page for a different customer. You can include a Group Header section for each customer and then use a macro or a Visual Basic procedure to set the Page property to 1 each time Access formats that section (indicating that you're on the first page of a new customer invoice).

Performing Calculations

Another task you might perform frequently is calculating extended values from detail values in your tables. If you understand the principles of good table design (see Article 1, "Designing Your Database Application," on the companion CD), you know that it's usually redundant and wasteful of storage space to define a field in your tables that you can calculate from other fields. The only situations in which this is acceptable are when saving the calculated value will greatly improve performance in parts of your application (perhaps in a web database), and when you have collected static historical data in a table designed specifically to support reporting.

Performing a Calculation on a Detail Line

You can use arithmetic operators to create complex calculations in the Control Source property of any control that can display data. You can also use any of the many built-in functions or any of the functions you define yourself in a module. If you want, you can use the Expression Builder that you learned about in Chapter 9, "Creating and Working with Simple Queries," to build the expression for any control. You let Access know that you are using an expression in a Control Source property by starting the expression with an equals sign (=).

> **Note**
>
> **To use a field in a calculation, that field must be in the table or query specified in the Record Source property of the report.**

One calculated value that housing management might find useful is the daily revenue for each room. You could have calculated that value in the query that is the record source of the report, but you can also calculate it as an expression in a text box in the Detail section of the report. To add the expression you need to the Facility Occupancy By Date report that you have been creating, follow these steps:

1. Before you add your new control to the Detail section, you should first reduce the widths of the controls because the Report Wizard made most of the controls a bit too wide. Click the FacilityName control, hold down the Shift key, click the label control for FacilityName (currently labeled Name), and drag the left edge of one of these controls toward the left side of the report to make them flush with the left side. Next, drag their right edge toward the left edge of the report to reduce the width of the controls until they are about 2 inches in width. (You can check this in the Property Sheet window if you want.) When the Report Wizard created this report, it did not

place all the controls in the Detail section into a tabular control layout, so when you resize the FacilityName control, Access does not adjust the other controls as well. You'll need to manually move the other fields and their labels farther to the left when you reduce the width of the controls. Go ahead and change the caption for the facility name label as well from Name to Facility by clicking the label and typing **Facility**.

2. Reduce the width of the DateValue controls to 0.9 inches, the RoomNumber controls to 0.8 inches, and the EmpName controls to 1.6 inches. Make sure to move these controls to the left after you reduce their width, so there are no large gaps between the different controls.

3. On the Design tab, in the Controls group, click the Text Box button, and place a text box in the Detail section to the right of the EmpName text box. Select the attached label, and delete it.

4. In the Control Source property of the new text box, enter

   ```
   =CCur(Round([TotalCharge]/([CheckOutDate]-[CheckInDate]),2))
   ```

   Because you included the TotalCharge, CheckInDate, and CheckOutDate fields in the query, you can reference them in your expression. This expression calculates the daily revenue by dividing the total charge for the reservation by the number of days. Set the Format property of the text box to Currency, the Border Style to Transparent, and set the Width property to 0.85 inches. Move this text box close to the EmpName text box, and line up the tops of the two text boxes. Also, make sure the height of both text boxes is the same by selecting them both and then clicking the Size To Tallest button under the Size/Space command in the Sizing & Ordering group on the Arrange tab.

5. Click the Line button in the Controls group on the Design tab, and place a horizontal line in the Page Header section below the labels. Move the line to the left edge of the report, and set its Width property to 6.4 inches so that it stretches over all the controls in the Detail section, including your new text box. Make sure the height of the control is 0 inches. Click the Shape Outline button in the Control Formatting group on the Format tab, click Line Thickness, and then click 2 pt for the thickness. (You can also set this directly on the Property Sheet window using the Border Width property.)

6. Click the Label tool in the Controls group on the Design tab, and draw a label control next to the Employee label in the page header. Type **Charge** in the label, and press Enter. (If you don't type anything, the label disappears when you click away from it.)

7. Make the new label the same height as the other labels in the page header, and give it the same width as the text box below it (0.85 inches). Align the left edge of the label with the left edge of the text box, and align the top of the label with the top of the other labels in the section.

Your report in Design view should now look like Figure 18-13.

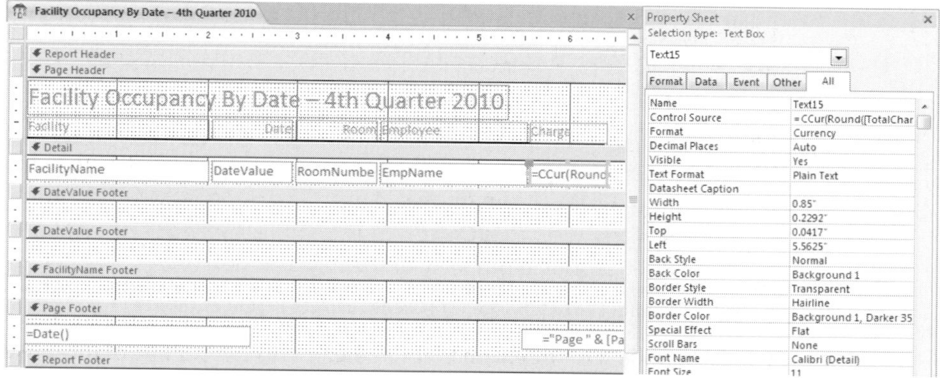

Figure 18-13 Add an expression to the Detail section to calculate daily revenue.

Figure 18-14 shows the result in Print Preview. (Note that the Report Wizard applied an alternating color for the Detail section.) You can see that Access has performed the required calculations for each day of each reservation.

Facility Occupancy By Date – 4th Quarter 2010

Facility	Date	Room	Employee	Charge
Main Campus Housing A	01-Oct-10	410	Sazanovich, Vadim	$36.43
Main Campus Housing A	01-Oct-10	507	Cheng, Yao-Qiang	$50.00
Main Campus Housing A	01-Oct-10	507	Fort, Garth	$50.33
Main Campus Housing A	02-Oct-10	209	Sanchez, Ken	$45.71
Main Campus Housing A	02-Oct-10	410	Sazanovich, Vadim	$36.43
Main Campus Housing A	02-Oct-10	507	Fort, Garth	$50.33
Main Campus Housing A	02-Oct-10	507	Cheng, Yao-Qiang	$50.00
Main Campus Housing A	02-Oct-10	802	Sneath, Timothy	$84.50
Main Campus Housing A	03-Oct-10	209	Sanchez, Ken	$45.71
Main Campus Housing A	03-Oct-10	507	Fort, Garth	$50.33
Main Campus Housing A	03-Oct-10	507	Cheng, Yao-Qiang	$50.00
Main Campus Housing A	03-Oct-10	802	Sneath, Timothy	$84.50
Main Campus Housing A	03-Oct-10	811	Steiner, Alan	$73.33

Page: 1 No Filter

Figure 18-14 The calculated detail line values within a group now appear in Print Preview.

INSIDE OUT **Avoiding #Error or #Type! in a Calculated Control**

Instead of starting with an unbound text box to perform a calculation, you might decide to drag one of the fields that you'll use in the calculation from the field list onto your report. When you do that, Access gives the text box the same name as the field. If you modify the control source to an expression that uses the field, you'll see #Error or #Type! in the text box when you view or print the report.

When you enter a name in an expression, Access first searches for another control that has that name. If it doesn't find the control, then it looks in the field list. So, if the name of the control is TotalCharge and you include an expression that uses [TotalCharge], the expression is referring to itself! Access can't figure out how to display the value of the TotalCharge text box, so it displays #Error or #Type! instead. If you decide to drag a field that you'll change to an expression, be sure to change the Name property of the control (for example, txtTotalCharge) before you enter the expression.

Of course, you'll also see #Error if your expression refers to a function that doesn't exist or provides invalid parameters to a function. However, using the name of the control itself inside the expression that is the control source is one of the most common sources of #Error or #Type!.

Adding Values Across a Group

Another task commonly performed in reports is adding values across a group. In Chapter 17, you saw a simple example of this in a client report that used the built-in Sum function. In the Facility Occupancy By Date report, you have three levels of grouping: one by facility, another by month, and another by date. When you specified grouping and sorting criteria earlier in this chapter, you asked Access to provide group footers. This gives you sections in your report in which you can add unbound controls that use any of the aggregate functions (Sum, Min, Max, Avg, Count, First, Last, StDev, or Var) in expressions to display a calculated value for all the rows in that group. In this example, you can create unbound controls in the FacilityName footer and both DateValue footers to hold the totals by facility, by month, and by date, for the daily charge for each room, as shown in Figure 18-15. In the Control Source property of each, enter

```
=Sum(CCur(Round([TotalCharge]/([CheckOutDate]-[CheckInDate]),2)))
```

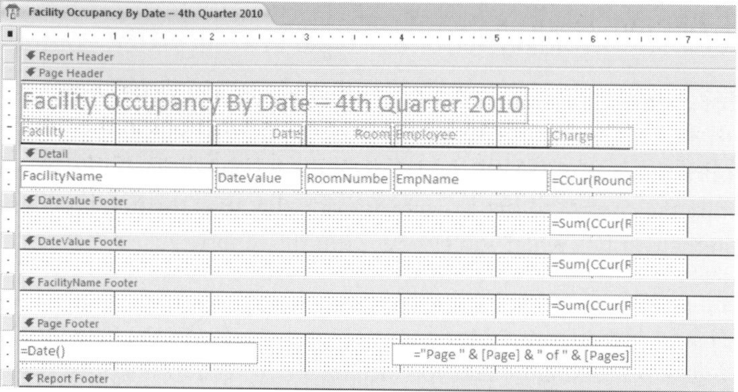

Figure 18-15 Add summaries by facility, by month, and by date to the three footer sections.

Set the Format property to Currency and the Border Style to Transparent for each of the three new controls. Notice, in this case, that you must repeat the original expression inside the aggregate function rather than attempt to sum the control you placed in the Detail section. (See the Inside Out, "How to Calculate Totals on Expressions," for an explanation.)

You should also add a line control at the top of each Footer section to provide a visual clue that the values that follow are totals. In this example, we placed lines approximately 5.5 inches in from the left and made them about 1 inch long, but they're difficult to see in Design view because they're right up against the top of the section. Also, move the page number control so the right edge lines up with these new calculated controls, and reduce the width of the design grid to 7 inches.

Access added an alternating row color to each of the group footers when you defined your grouping specifications. Remove these alternating colors before going any further by selecting each Group Footer section and changing the Alternate Back Color property to **No Color** in the Property Sheet window.

INSIDE OUT How to Calculate Totals on Expressions

An important point to remember about using an aggregate expression in a group section is that the expression cannot refer to any calculated controls in the Detail section. As you'll learn later, you can reference an outer control from an inner one (for example, a total calculation in a group from inside the Detail section), but not vice versa. So, you cannot create a calculated field in the Detail section, for example, that multiplies two numbers and then reference that control in the summary expression. You can, however, repeat the calculation expression in the summary. If a detail control named Total has an expression such as =[Quantity] * [Price], you must use an expression such as =Sum([Quantity] * [Price]) in your grouping section, not =Sum([Total]).

Creating a Grand Total

Use the Report Footer section to create grand totals for any values across the entire set of records in a report. You can use any of the aggregate functions in the report footer just as you did in the two grouping section footers. Expand the Report Footer section to about 0.32 inch to give yourself some room. Add a new text box control to the Report Footer section and set the Control Source property to the same expression used in the three footer controls. Set Format to Currency, Border Style to Transparent, and change the width of the text box to 1 inch to allow extra room for a larger number total. Align the right edge of the text box to the other three calculated controls. Click inside the label for this new text box, type **Grand Total:**, and align the text to the right. Finally, bold the text in the label and move the label so that its right edge is next to the left side of the text box. Figure 18-16 shows you this Sum function used in the new control in the report footer to produce a total for all records in the report.

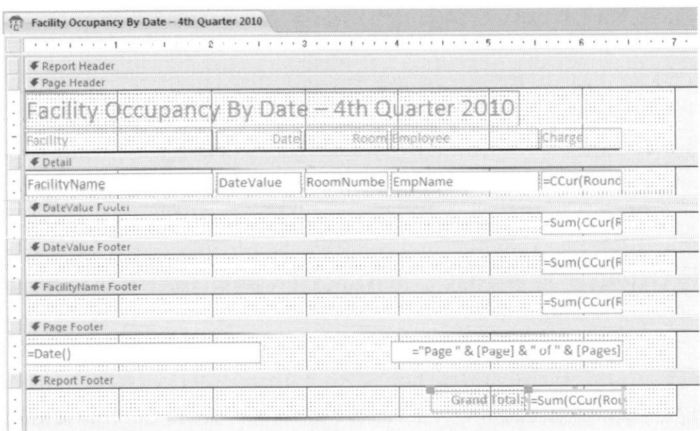

Figure 18-16 Use the Report Footer section to create a grand total control for all records.

If you switch to Print Preview, go to the last page in the report, and scroll down, you should see a result similar to that shown in Figure 18-17. (You should set the name of this grand total field to **txtSumGrand** so that you can use it to calculate percentages later.) You can find this stage of the report design saved as rptXmplFacilityDateOccupancyStep2 in the sample database.

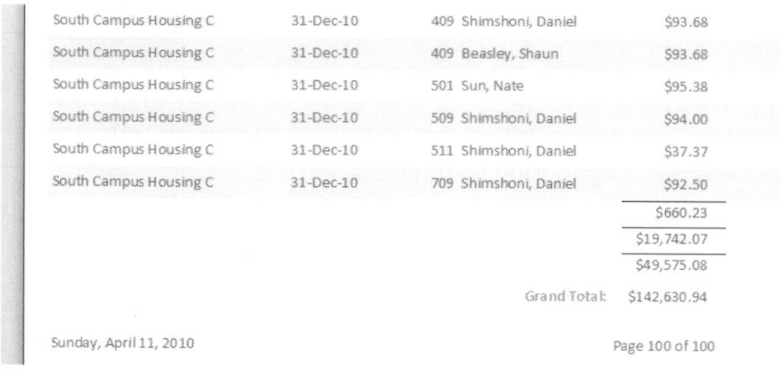

South Campus Housing C	31-Dec-10	409 Shimshoni, Daniel	$93.68
South Campus Housing C	31-Dec-10	409 Beasley, Shaun	$93.68
South Campus Housing C	31-Dec-10	501 Sun, Nate	$95.38
South Campus Housing C	31-Dec-10	509 Shimshoni, Daniel	$94.00
South Campus Housing C	31-Dec-10	511 Shimshoni, Daniel	$37.37
South Campus Housing C	31-Dec-10	709 Shimshoni, Daniel	$92.50
			$660.23
			$19,742.07
			$49,575.08
		Grand Total:	$142,630.94
Sunday, April 11, 2010			Page 100 of 100

Figure 18-17 You can see the various totals displayed in the report in Print Preview.

> **Note**
>
> **If you want to create percentage calculations for any of the groups over the grand total, you must create the control for the grand total in the report footer so that you can reference the total in percentage calculation expressions. See "Calculating Percentages," on page 1141. If you don't want the total to print, set the control's Visible property to No.**

Hiding Redundant Values and Concatenating Text Strings

You probably noticed in several of the preceding examples that the FacilityName and DateValue fields print for every detail line. When a particular detail line displays or prints values that match the previous line, the report looks less readable and less professional. You can control this by using the Hide Duplicates text box property (which is available only in reports). Switch to the Design view of this report and set the Hide Duplicates property to Yes for the FacilityName text box and the DateValue text box in the Detail section. The report will now print the facility name and the date only once per group or page, as shown in Figure 18-18. (The figure shows information from the last page of the report.) When Access moves to a new grouping level or page, it prints the facility name even if it matches the previous value displayed.

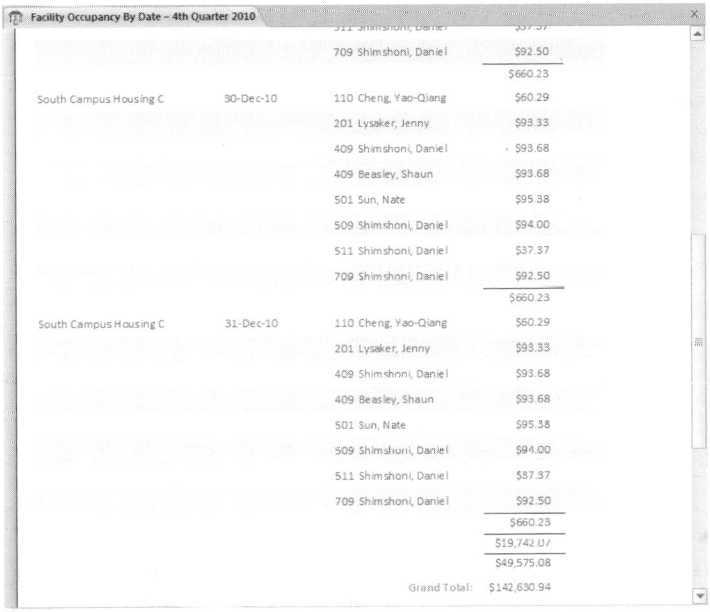

Facility Occupancy By Date - 4th Quarter 2010

		709 Shimshoni, Daniel	$92.50
			$660.23
South Campus Housing C	30-Dec-10	110 Cheng, Yao-Qiang	$60.29
		201 Lysaker, Jenny	$93.33
		409 Shimshoni, Daniel	$93.68
		409 Beasley, Shaun	$93.68
		501 Sun, Nate	$95.38
		509 Shimshoni, Daniel	$94.00
		511 Shimshoni, Daniel	$37.37
		709 Shimshoni, Daniel	$92.50
			$660.23
South Campus Housing C	31-Dec-10	110 Cheng, Yao-Qiang	$60.29
		201 Lysaker, Jenny	$93.33
		409 Shimshoni, Daniel	$93.68
		409 Beasley, Shaun	$93.68
		501 Sun, Nate	$95.38
		509 Shimshoni, Daniel	$94.00
		511 Shimshoni, Daniel	$37.37
		709 Shimshoni, Daniel	$92.50
			$660.23
			$19,742.07
			$49,575.08
		Grand Total:	$142,630.94

Figure 18-18 Set the Hide Duplicates property to Yes to eliminate redundant values in each group.

Notice that when the report gets to the end of data for a month or a facility, it's not clear what the total lines mean. For example, on the last page of the report, shown in Figure 18-18, $660.23 is clearly the total for the last date, but it's not obvious that $19,742.07 is the total for the month of December for the facility or that $49,575.08 is the total revenue for the facility. You can use string concatenation to display data that looks like a label but that also includes information from the record source. Sometimes it's useful to combine descriptive text with a value from a text field in the underlying query or table or to combine multiple text fields in one control. In Figure 18-19, you can see a descriptive label (created by a single text box control) on one of the subtotal lines. (In Figure 18-19, we dragged the Property Sheet window below the new text box so that you could see the Control Source property.)

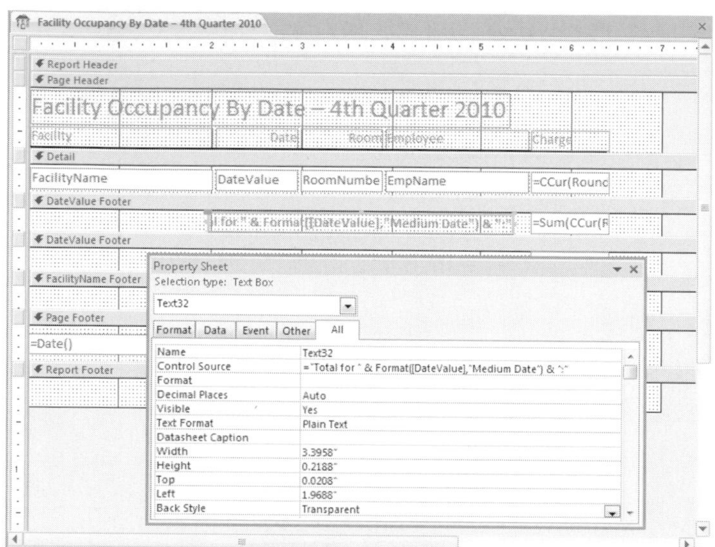

Figure 18-19 A text constant and a string derived from a field in the record source are concatenated as a "label" in a text box.

This "label" concatenates the words *Total* for with an expression that uses the Format function—applied here to the DateValue field to get the date in medium date format—and an ending string containing a colon. You can use the same technique in the group footer to create a "label" that reads *Total for facility* followed by the facility name and a trailing colon. You could certainly define a label followed by a text box followed by another label to create the same display. The advantage of using a single control is that you don't have to worry about lining up three controls or setting the font characteristics. In fact, because the string in the middle, containing the facility name, could vary significantly in length, you cannot create three separate controls that correctly line up all possible values end to end. Set the Text Alignment property of these controls to Right so that they line up correctly next to the summary controls, and match the formatting of the grand total label in the Report Footer section by selecting the grand total label, double-clicking the Format Painter button in the Font group on the Format tab to lock it, and then clicking the three text boxes. Click Format Painter again to unlock it when you're done.

When you look at the report in Print Preview, as shown in Figure 18-20, you can see that the duplicate values for the facility name and for the date have been eliminated. You can also see the nice result from using a concatenated string in a text box to generate labels for the total lines.

Facility Occupancy By Date – 4th Quarter 2010

		201 Lysaker, Jenny	$93.33
		409 Shimshoni, Daniel	$93.68
		409 Beasley, Shaun	$93.68
		501 Sun, Nate	$95.38
		509 Shimshoni, Daniel	$94.00
		511 Shimshoni, Daniel	$37.37
		709 Shimshoni, Daniel	$92.50
		Total for 30-Dec-10:	$660.23
South Campus Housing C	31-Dec-10	110 Cheng, Yao-Qiang	$60.29
		201 Lysaker, Jenny	$93.33
		409 Shimshoni, Daniel	$93.68
		409 Beasley, Shaun	$93.68
		501 Sun, Nate	$95.38
		509 Shimshoni, Daniel	$94.00
		511 Shimshoni, Daniel	$37.37
		709 Shimshoni, Daniel	$92.50
		Total for 31-Dec-10:	$660.23
		Total for December 2010:	$19,742.07
		Total for facility South Campus Housing C:	$49,575.08
		Grand Total:	$142,630.94

Figure 18-20 The total lines now have descriptive captions using data from the record source.

Calculating Percentages

In any report that groups and summarizes data, you might want to determine what percentage of an outer group total or the grand total is represented in a particular sum. You can do this in a report because Access makes two passes through the data. On the first pass, it calculates simple expressions in detail lines, sums across groups, sums across the entire report, and calculates the length of the report. On the second pass, it resolves any expressions that reference totals that were calculated in the first pass. Consequently, you can create an expression in a detail or group summary section that divides by a sum in an outer group or the grand total to calculate percentages.

Figure 18-21 shows an example of a percentage calculation in the FacilityName Footer section. (We dragged the Property Sheet window below the control so that you could see the Control Source property.) The expression divides the sum of the calculated charge for this facility by the value in a field called txtSumGrand—the name of the grand total control in the report footer. (Remember, when you created the grand total earlier, we instructed you to give it this name.)

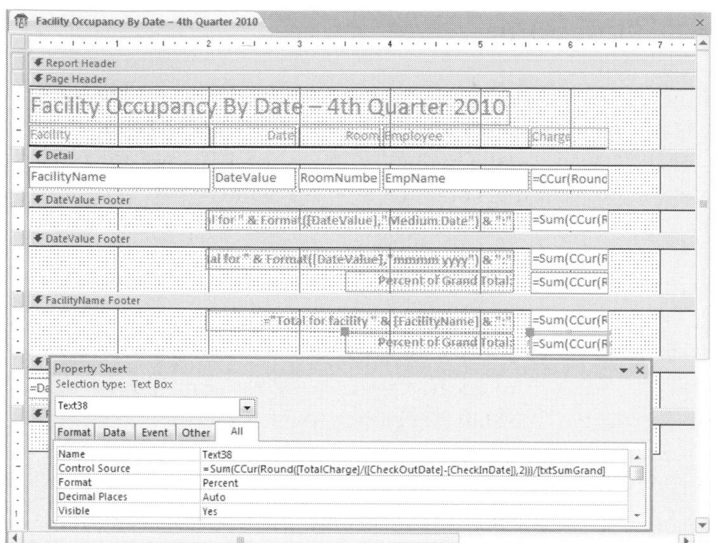

Figure 18-21 You can add a calculation in the group footer for a percentage of a grand total.

Set the Format property of the text box to Percent and switch to Print Preview. Scroll down to find a total by month or by facility, and you'll also see the percent of the grand total, as shown in Figure 18-22. You can find this stage of the report design saved as rptXmplFacilityDateOccupancyStep3 in the sample database.

Facility Occupancy By Date – 4th Quarter 2010

Facility Occupancy By Date – 4th Quarter 2010

Facility	Date	Room	Employee	Charge
Main Campus Housing A	31-Dec-10	203	Sanchez, Ken	$42.73
		203	Moseley, Julia	$41.88
		210	Wycoff, Pieter	$37.06
		411	Fort, Garth	$72.86
		810	Steiner, Alan	$36.43
		906	Mohamed, Shammi	$83.89
		909	Schmidt, Steve	$46.84
			Total for 31-Dec-10:	$361.69
			Total for December 2010:	$7,384.07
			Percent of Grand Total:	5.18%
			Total for facility Main Campus Housing A:	$28,515.10
			Percent of Grand Total:	19.99%

Figure 18-22 At the end of the report, you can see percentage calculations for two groups in Print Preview.

Using Running Sum

In addition to producing totals for any group you define, Access lets you create running totals within the Detail section or any group header or footer. For any text box that displays a numeric value, you can set the Running Sum property to produce a total that is reset at the start of each group or that continues totaling through the entire report. Let's further refine rptXmplFacilityDateOccupancyStep3 to see how this works.

Before you can add any controls horizontally, you need to adjust the sizes of some of the controls to provide more horizontal space within the design width of the report. Select the Room label control, hold down the Shift key, select the RoomNumber text box, and change the width for both controls to 0.5 inch in the Property Sheet window. Click the Employee label control, hold down the Shift key, select the EmpName text box, and set the width to 1.3 inches for both of these controls. Move the EmpName controls to the left so that they remain close to the Room controls. (The Left property for these controls should be about 3.52 inches now.) Select both the Charge label control and the calculated text box control below it, and slide them both to the left about 0.7 inches. (The Left property for these controls should be about 4.85 inches now.) Click the line control in the page header that runs beneath all the labels, and set its width to 6.6 inches. Select all the controls in both DateValue footers, the FacilityName footer, and the report footer, and slide them to the left so that they now line up with the new position of the charge calculation text box in the Detail section.

Now, you have some horizontal room to add another label control and companion text box control. Start by selecting the Charge label control, copy it to the Clipboard, and paste it back into the page header. Move it just to the right of the existing Charge label control, and line it up vertically with all the other labels. Now, change its caption to **Cum. Charge**, and set its width to 0.85 inch.

> **INSIDE OUT** **Select the Section Before Pasting**
>
> **If you select the Page Header section before you perform the paste, Access places the control in the upper-left corner of the section and doesn't change the size of the section. If you leave the original control selected when you perform the paste, Access places the new copy below the original and expands the section, which you might not want it to do.**

Likewise, select the text box control below the original Charge label control, copy it to the Clipboard, and paste it back into the Detail section. Move it to the right of the existing charge calculation text box, and line it up horizontally with all the other text boxes. Line up the new text box control with the label control above it, and set its width to 0.95 inch to allow room for larger numbers. Finally, select the new text box control, and set its Running Sum property in the Property Sheet window to Over Group. Your report should now look like Figure 18-23.

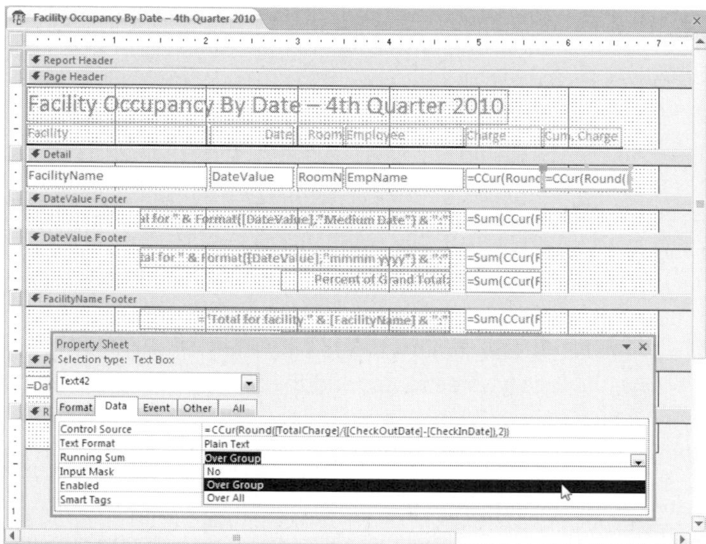

Figure 18-23 For the Running Sum property of the new calculated text box, select Over Group to add a running sum calculation on the charge.

No, this isn't a second copy of the charge calculation. As you'll see when you look at the report in Print Preview, this produces (as the name of the property implies) a running sum of the charge calculation within the Detail section. As Access encounters each new row in the Detail section, it adds the current value of calculation to the previous accumulation and displays the result. Because you asked for the sum Over Group, Access resets the accumulating total each time it encounters a new group.

Next, let's use a little trick to generate a line number for each line in the Detail section. To make room for this line number, click the Facility label and FacilityName text box, and drag their left edge to the right side to reduce their width and create enough space for a small text control. (The Facility label and FacilityName text box controls should be about 1.71 inches in width and the Left property should be about .30 inch when you complete these steps.) Insert a small text box in the space you just created in the Detail section. Above this text box, create a label that displays # as its caption. (You can use the Format Painter button again to copy the format from one of the existing label controls to the new one.)

Remember that as Access formats each detail line, it takes the current value of the field (actually, the current value of the text box), adds it to the previous total, and displays the result. If you set the text box equal to any constant numeric value, Access uses that value for each detail line it produces. So, the trick is to set this text box equal to 1 (=1 in the Control Source property) and then set the Running Sum property. If you choose Over All for Running Sum, Access will number the first line 1, add 1 for the second line and display 2, add 1 for the third line and display 3, and so on throughout the report. If you choose Over Group, Access increases the number for each line but resets the number back to 1 when a new group starts. Select Over Group on the Running Sum property for this control to sequentially number all the reservations on the same date, as shown in Figure 18-24. Also set the Format property of the control to **0.** to place a period after each displayed value.

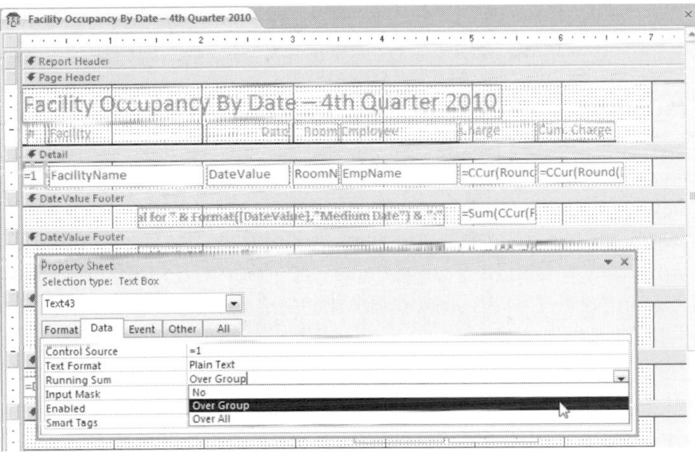

Figure 18-24 Use the Running Sum property to generate a line number.

If you switch to Print Preview, you can see the result of using Running Sum, as shown in Figure 18-25. The charge accumulates over each group and then resets for the next group. The line numbers start at 1 and also reset for each group. You can find this report saved as rptXmplFacilityDateOccupancyStep4 in the sample database.

Facility Occupancy By Date - 4th Quarter 2010

Facility Occupancy By Date – 4th Quarter 2010

#	Facility	Date	Room	Employee	Charge	Cum. Charge
1.	Main Campus Housing A	01-Oct-10	410	Sazanovich, Vadim	$36.43	$36.43
2.			507	Cheng, Yao-Qiang	$50.00	$86.43
3.			507	Fort, Garth	$50.33	$136.76
				Total for 01-Oct-10:	$136.76	
1.	Main Campus Housing A	02-Oct-10	209	Sanchez, Ken	$45.71	$45.71
2.			410	Sazanovich, Vadim	$36.43	$82.14
3.			507	Fort, Garth	$50.33	$132.47
4.			507	Cheng, Yao-Qiang	$50.00	$182.47
5.			802	Sneath, Timothy	$84.50	$266.97
				Total for 02-Oct-10:	$266.97	
1.	Main Campus Housing A	03-Oct-10	209	Sanchez, Ken	$45.71	$45.71
2.			507	Fort, Garth	$50.33	$96.04
3.			507	Cheng, Yao-Qiang	$50.00	$146.04
4.			802	Sneath, Timothy	$84.50	$230.54

Page: 1 No Filter

Figure 18-25 You can see the result of using Running Sum to produce a cumulative total for each group and a line number for each detail line.

Taking Advantage of Conditional Formatting

In Chapter 15, "Advanced Form Design," you learned how to define conditional formatting for a text box control on a client form. Access makes an identical facility available to you for reports. Let's say, for example, that you want to highlight any daily total that is more than $400 or any monthly total that is greater than $10,000. To do this, open the report from the previous example in Design view, select the Sum text box in the first DateValue Footer section that displays the sum of the charge, and then click the Conditional Formatting button in the Control Formatting group on the Format tab. Access displays the Conditional Formatting Rules Manager dialog box, as shown in Figure 18-26. In the Show Formatting Rules For combo box, Access lists the names of all the controls on the report that support conditional formatting. You can create, edit, and delete conditional formatting rules for the controls on your form by selecting the control name from this combo box, without having to close the dialog box to select a different control. In previous versions of Access, you were limited to three conditional formatting rules for each control. In Access 2010, you can have up to 50 conditional formatting rules for each control.

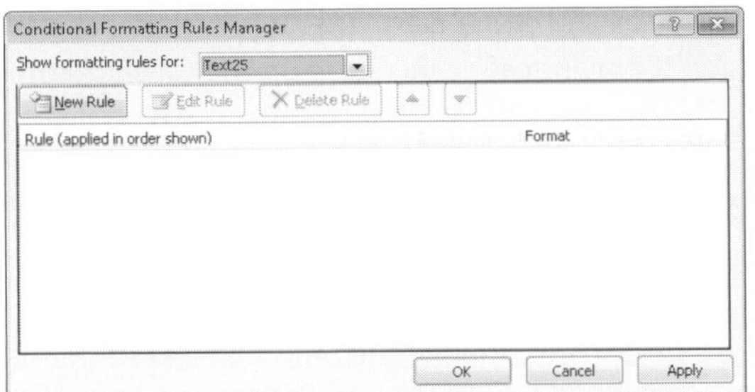

Figure 18-26 You can create, edit, and delete conditional formatting for controls using the Conditional Formatting Rules Manager dialog box.

To begin creating a new conditional formatting rule for the text box, select the control name, Text25 in this case, in the Show Formatting Rules For combo box (it should already be selected), and then click New Rule to open the New Formatting Rule dialog box, as shown in Figure 18-27. In Select A Rule Type, you can choose to create a conditional formatting rule that checks other values in the current record or use an expression. You can also choose to compare the value of this control with values in the same control for other records. When you select Compare To Other Records, Access creates a Data Bar conditional formatting rule. (You learned about data bars in Chapter 15.) For the control rule on this Sum text box in the first DateValue Footer section, select Check Value In The Current Record Or Use An Expression. Access displays a single blank condition rule under Edit The Rule Description.

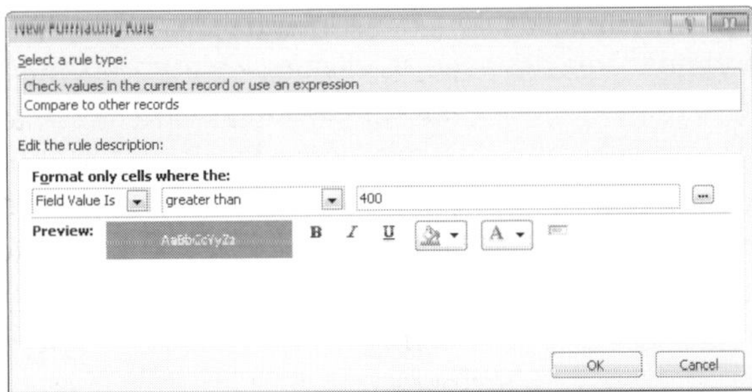

Figure 18-27 Set conditional formatting for the Sum text box in the first DateValue footer section.

In the leftmost list, you can choose Field Value Is to test for a value in the field or Expression Is to create a logical expression that can test other fields on the form or compare another field with this one. In this case, verify that Field Value Is appears in the first list, click Greater Than in the second list, and enter the value **400** in the box. Under the second list, click the Back Color button and select a dark color. Click the Fore Color button and select white. You can see a preview of your formatting color choices next to Preview. Click OK to save the new conditional format rule and return to the Conditional Formatting Rules Manager dialog box. You can specify a similar condition for the Sum text box in the second DateValue footer (by month) to test for a monthly total greater than 10,000. (You'll need to select DateValue from the Show Formatting Rules For combo box and then click New Rule to start creating the new rule.) After you create both condition formatting rules, click Apply in the Conditional Formatting Rules Manager dialog box to save your changes, and then click OK to close the dialog box.

Note

In the Detail section, you can reference any other field in the current row to create an expression. But when you create a conditional formatting expression in a grouping section, any field reference that you use in an expression uses the value of the current row. In a group footer, for example, the current row is the last row displayed in the previous Detail section.

Before viewing the report one more time, let's change the margins on the report to center the printed area left to right on the page. Assuming a standard U.S. paper width of 8.5 inches and with the report print area designed at 7 inches, we need a 0.75-inch margin on both sides. Click the Page Setup button in the Page Layout group on the Page Setup tab. Access opens the Page Setup dialog box, shown in Figure 18-28. On the Print Options tab, change the Top, Bottom, Left, and Right margins from .25 inch to .75 inch. Click OK to save your changes and close the Page Setup dialog box. When you switch to Print Preview, you can see the result, as shown in Figure 18-29. You can find this sample saved as rptXmplFacilityDateOccupancyStep5. (Page 40 in the sample report shows both conditional formats in action.)

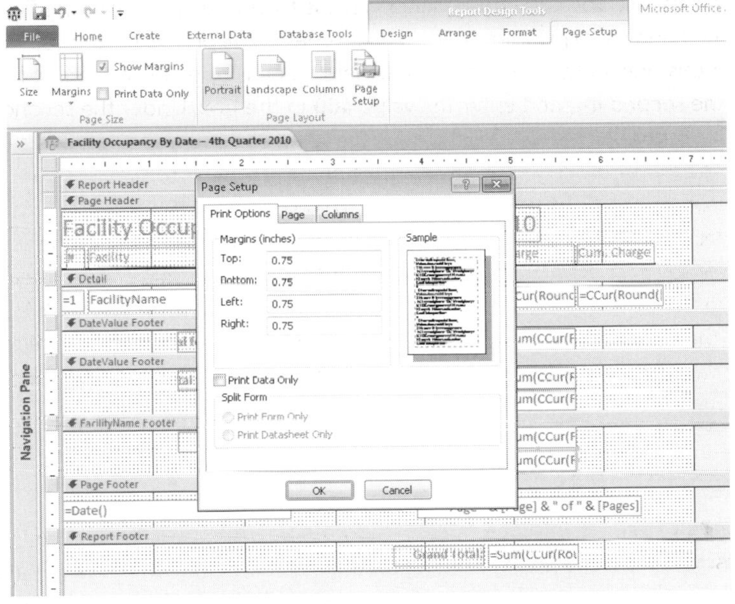

Figure 18-28 Change all the page margins to 0.75 inch.

INSIDE OUT

Make Sure Controls Are Not Transparent

If you have a text box control and set a conditional formatting rule that changes the background color, you must set the Back Style property of the control to Normal to see the formatting in Report view or Print Preview. If you have a text box control with the Back Style set to Transparent, you won't see the background color formatting when the conditions are met.

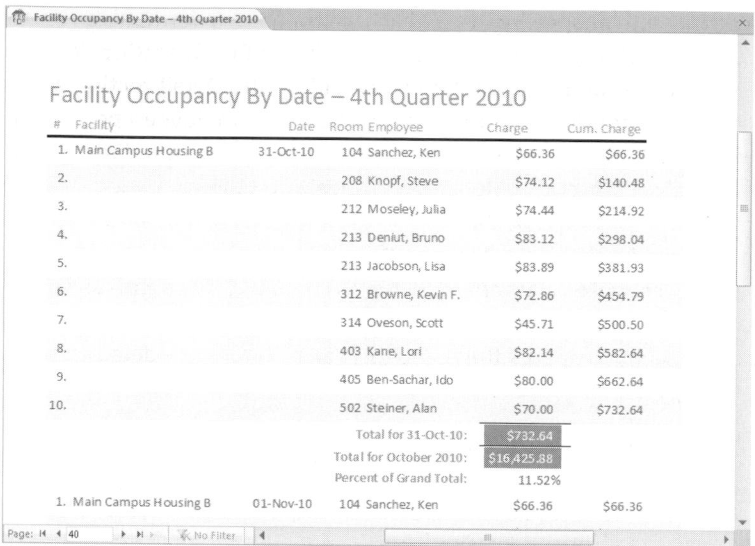

Figure 18-29 Here is the result of setting conditional formatting for the two Sum text boxes.

TROUBLESHOOTING

Why do my Data Bar conditional formatting rules not show anything when I view the report in Print Preview or Report view?

Data Bar conditional formatting rules use domain functions, specifically DMin and DMax, to calculate the Data Bar lengths. Access, however, supports only Domain functions on named table and query objects. If you have your report (or form) record source based on an embedded SQL statement, Access cannot display the Data Bar formatting. You should receive an error message when you try to save a Data Bar conditional formatting rule on a report or form that does not use a saved table or query object as its record source. You might also not see your Data Bar conditional formatting applied on controls that use expressions for their Control Source property if Access cannot calculate the DMin and DMax in the given context or expression.

To see a more complex example of conditional formatting in action, open rptEmployeeRes in the sample database. That report uses conditional formatting to check for overlapping reservation requests, highlight them, and reveal a warning label in the section header.

To see an example of applying more than one conditional formatting rule to the same control, open the web report rptPermitExpDates in the BOSSDataCopy2.accdb sample web database. The two permit expiration date fields in the Detail section of that web report each have three conditional formatting rules. If the employee's permit expiration is past due, the back color of the control shows red, if the expiration date is coming up within the next 30 days, the back color of the control shows yellow, and if the expiration date expires sometime later than the next 30 days, the back color of the control shows green. To see an example of a Data Bar conditional formatting rule, open the client report rptVendorPurchaseRecapSummary in the BOSSDataCopy2.accdb sample web database. The SubTotals field in the Detail section of that client report show Data Bars comparing the Subtotal amount against the grand total of all the invoice detail amounts.

Creating and Embedding a Subreport

In many of your reports, you will probably design the Detail section to display a single line of information from the underlying record source. As you learned earlier in this chapter, it's fairly easy to link several tables to get lots of detail across several *one-to-many* relationships in your database. You also saw how to use the Hide Duplicates property to display a hierarchy across several rows of detail.

However, as with forms and subforms, which you learned about in Chapter 15, you can embed subreports (or subforms) in the detail section of your report to display multiple detail lines from a table or query that has a *many* relationship to the one current line printed in the Detail section. You must use this technique when you want to display information from more than one *many* relationship on a single page. In the Conrad Systems Contacts database, for example, if you want to provide details about contact events and products owned by a contact, you must use subreports. You could create a very complex query that joins all the information, but you'd get one row for each unique combination of contact event and product. If a contact has 100 events and owns six products, each of the six product rows is matched with each of the 100 contact event rows. You'll get 600 rows for that contact in a query that joins the tblContacts, tblContactEvents, and tblContactProducts tables—each product record appears 100 times, and each contact event record appears six times.

Note

Subreports are not supported on web reports for Access Services. You can embed web reports into client reports as subreports, but you cannot embed subreports (client or web) into web reports. As you learned in Chapter 15, Access Services supports embedding web reports into web and client forms.

Understanding Subreport Challenges

Subreports present a unique challenge. Unlike a subform, where you can scroll through all available related rows in one window, a subreport has no scroll bar. The subreport expands to list all the related rows. If the rows won't fit on one page, it can be difficult to repeat the header information at the top of the subsequent pages. Although you can define a report header in a report that you use as a subreport, that header prints only once at the top of the subreport space on the page where the subreport starts.

To understand how this works, let's examine two approaches to listing department information in a report with related employee information in a subreport. In the HousingDataCopy2.accdb sample database, open rptDepartmentsWSubBad in Design view, as shown in Figure 18-30. When you drop a report onto the design of another report to create a subreport, Access sizes the subreport control to the height of one line from the report inside the control. The figure shows the subreport control expanded so that you can see the subreport inside it. We selected the control and dragged down the bottom edge, but you might find it easier to change the Height property in the Property Sheet window because the bottom sizing box is difficult to grab with your mouse pointer.

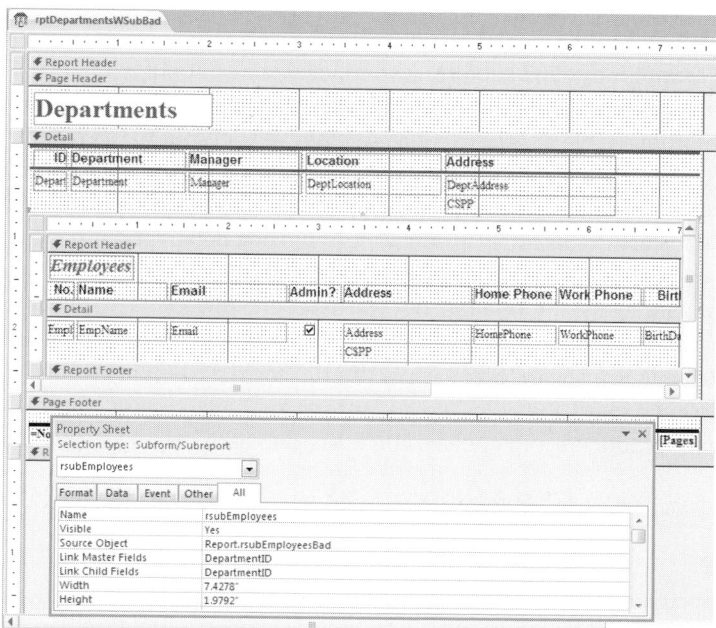

Figure 18-30 This report displays departments with related employees in a subreport.

The outer report, Departments, uses a query based on the tblDepartments and tblEmployees tables to provide information about each department and the department's manager. The report inside the subreport control, Employees, has another query on the tblEmployees table. The report looks simple enough—a heading for each department row and a heading inside the subreport to provide column headings for the employee information. You can also see that a subreport works just like a subform—you define the Link Master Fields and Link Child Fields properties of the subreport control to link the information from the two reports.

Now, switch to Print Preview and go to the fourth and fifth pages of the report, as shown in Figures 18-31 and 18-32, to see what really happens when a department has more employees than will fit on one page.

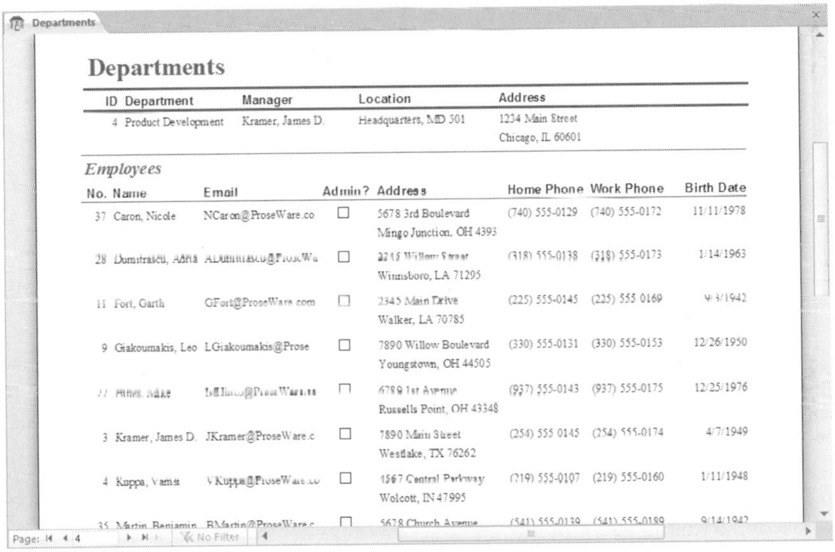

Figure 18-31 The top of the fourth page of the departments and employees report displays the header information.

Figure 18-32 The top of the fifth page of the departments and employees report has missing headers.

As you can see, the fifth page has nothing more than the page header to help identify the information being printed. The detail department information printed once on the fourth page, as did the report header from the subreport. When the subreport overflowed onto a second page, the column heading information from the report header defined for the subreport didn't print again.

To solve this problem, open rptDepartmentsWSub in Design view, as shown in Figure 18-33. Again, the figure shows the subreport control expanded so that you can see the subreport inside it.

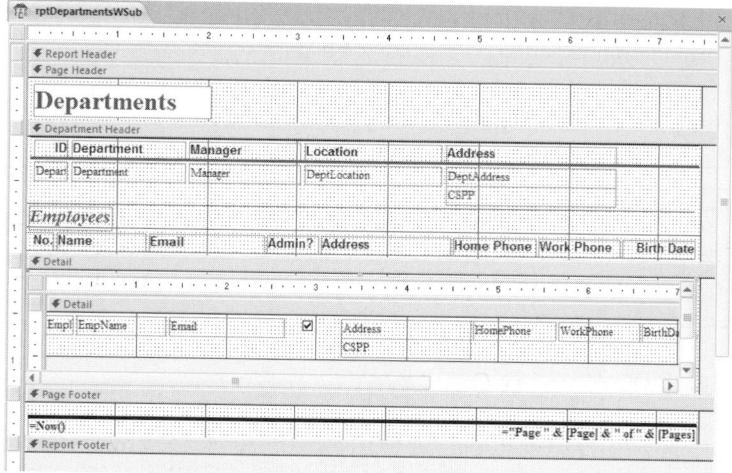

Figure 18-33 This design of a report and subreport handles the page overflow problem.

Can you figure out the difference? The secret is that the outer report has a group defined on department, even though there is only one detail row per department. All the department information and the headers for the columns in the subreport appear in this group header. Remember that you set the Repeat Section property of a group header to Yes to force it to appear again at the top of a page if the information in the Detail section overflows the page. The Detail section contains only the subreport, and the subreport has no headers. If you switch to Print Preview and go to the fifth page in this report, as shown in Figure 18-34, you can see that the appropriate headers appear again when the Product Development department overflows onto another page.

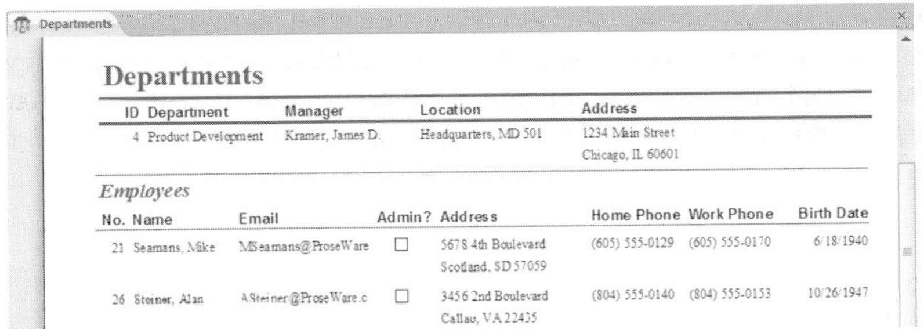

Figure 18-34 The top of the fifth page of the departments and employees report in this sample has headers correctly repeated.

Building a Client Report with a Subreport

The manager of Housing Administration has just asked you to produce a report that summarizes for each facility the revenue by month. You know the manager is someone who likes to see a visual representation as well as the data, so you need to design a report that will ultimately display a revenue chart as well. You'll learn how to add the PivotChart in the last section of this chapter.

Building the Subreport Query

If all you needed to do was display total revenue by facility and by month, you could build one totals query that joins the tblFacilities table with the tblReservations table and groups by facility. However, the need to add the chart means you'll need a subreport to calculate the monthly totals so that you can display the chart that graphically shows all the month values immediately below the numerical data. If you try to add a chart to the Detail area of a report that displays totals by month, the chart will show one graph point for the current month, not all months.

In the previous examples, you have been using a complex query to calculate revenue by day—an accounts receivable perspective. But guests in a hotel usually don't pay for their stay until the day they check out. So, to calculate actual revenue received for a month, you should use the check-out date and the total amount owed.

Start a new query on the tblReservations table. In the query design grid, include the FacilityID (you'll need this field to provide the link between the subreport and the main report), CheckOutDate, and TotalCharge fields. You could turn this into a totals query to sum the total charge by month, but it's just as easy to do that in the report. Your query should look like Figure 18-35. You can find this query saved in the sample database as qryXmplFacilityRevenue.

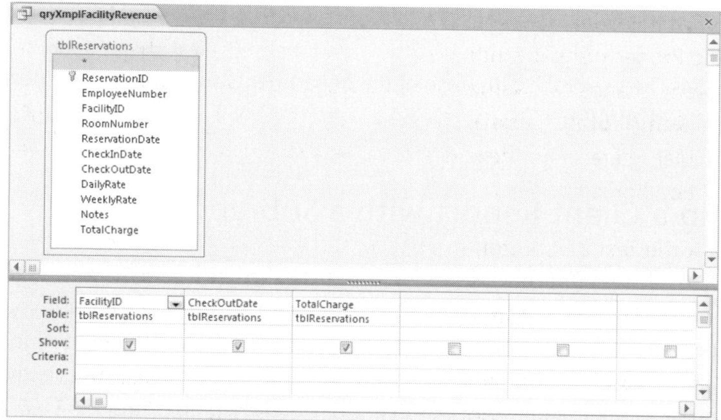

Figure 18-35 This query for the subreport calculates revenue by facility and month.

Designing the Subreport

The report you need for the subreport is very simple. Click the Report Design button in the Reports group on the Create tab to start designing your report. Remember from the discussion in the previous section that you'll see what's in the report header and report footer of a report that you use as a subreport, but Access never displays the page header or page footer. Right-click anywhere on the design grid and then click Page Header/Footer on the shortcut menu to hide the Page Header and Page Footer sections. Right-click on the design grid in the Detail section again and then click Report Header/Footer on the shortcut menu. You now need to bind this report to the qryXmplFacilityRevenue query (or the query you created earlier). Open the Property Sheet window, and set Record Source to qryXmplFacilityRevenue.

Open the Group, Sort, And Total pane by clicking the Group & Sort button in the Grouping & Totals group on the Design tab. Click Add A Group to start a new grouping specification. Select the CheckOutDate field in the Select box, click More to expand the option list, set the group interval to By Month, and then close the pane. Because you want the report to calculate and display totals by month only, close up the Detail section to zero height. Reduce the report design area to about 5.5 inches. Close up the Report Header section to zero height because you'll add the column labels to the outer report.

Draw a line across the top of the CheckOutDate Header section starting near the left edge and extending to about 5.1 inches wide. In the Property Sheet window, set the Border Width property to 1 pt. Underneath this line, about 1.5 inches from the left, drag the CheckOutDate field from the Field List window to the CheckOutDate Header section, and delete the attached label. In the Property Sheet window, set the Format to **mmmm yyyy** to display the month name and four-digit year, change the Border Style to Transparent, and change the Width to 1.5 inches. Drag the TotalCharge field from the field list to the CheckOutDate Header section about 3.75 inches from the left, and delete the attached label. In the Property Sheet window, expand the width to 1.2 inches, change the Border Style to Transparent, change the Name of the control to **TotalChargeSum**, and change the Control Source to **=Sum([TotalCharge])**. (Remember, you must change the name of the control to avoid a circular reference in the expression!) Line up the two text boxes in the CheckOutDate Header section horizontally.

Finally, click the Text Box button in the Controls group on the Design tab, and add a text box to the Report Footer section lined up under the TotalChargeSum text box. Set its Control Source to **=Sum([TotalCharge])**, change the font to Bold, change the Border Style to Transparent, and set the Format property to Currency. Change the caption of the attached label to **Grand Total**, change the font to Bold, and position it near the left edge of the Report Footer section. Your report should look something like Figure 18-36. You can find this report saved as rsubXmplFacilityRevenueByMonth in the sample database.

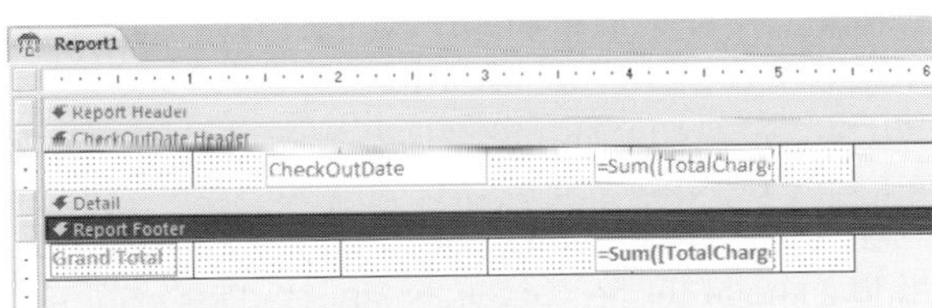

Figure 18-36 This is your subreport to summarize revenue by month.

Embedding a Subreport

You can find the query you need for the outer report saved as qryRptFacilities in the sample database. This query includes the FacilityID, FacilityName, and FacilityAddress fields. It also includes an expression (named FacilityCSPP) that concatenates the FacilityCity, FacilityStateOrProvince, and FaciltyPostalCode fields so that they display nicely on one line in the report.

Click the Report Design button in the Reports group on the Create tab to start your report design. Expand the report to 6.5 inches wide. Open the Property Sheet window, and enter **qryRptFacilities** in the Record Source property to bind the report to the saved query. Expand the Page Header section to 0.5 inch, add a label control to the Page Header section, and type **Facility Revenue** in the label. Change Font Size to 20, bold the text, size the label to fit, and position it in the upper-left corner of the Page Header section.

Open the Group, Sort, And Total pane by clicking the Group & Sort button in the Grouping & Totals group on the Design tab. Click Add A Group to start a new grouping specification. Select the FacilityName field in the Select box, click More to expand the option list, set the last column to Keep Header And First Record Together On One Page, and then close the pane. Expand the FacilityName Header section to about 1.3 inches high to give yourself some room to work. Select the FacilityName Header section, and in the Property Sheet window, set the Force New Page property to Before Section.

Drag all four fields one at a time from the Field List window to the FacilityName Header section of the report, as shown in Figure 18-37. Delete the attached label for the FacilityCSPP control, expand the width of the FacilityName text box to 1.6 inches, and expand the width of the FacilityAddress and FacilityCSPP text boxes to 3.2 inches. Change the Border Style to Transparent for the four text boxes you just added to the grid—FacilityID, FacilityName, FacilityAddress, and FacilityCSPP. Left-align the text in the FacilityID text box control. Bold the text of the three labels in the FacilityName Header section. Click the Label button in the Controls group on the Design tab, and place a label control under the FacilityCSPP text box control about 2.5 inches in from the left. Type **Month** in the label, and press Enter. (You can ignore the smart tag warning about an unattached label.) Add a second label control about 4.5 inches in from the left, type **Revenue** in the label, and press Enter. Line up the two labels horizontally, and bold their text. Click the Line Control button in the Controls group on the Design tab, and add a line at the top of the FacilityHeader section. In the Property Sheet window for this line, set the Border Style property to Solid, set the Border Width property to 1 pt, and set the Width property to 4.5 inches.

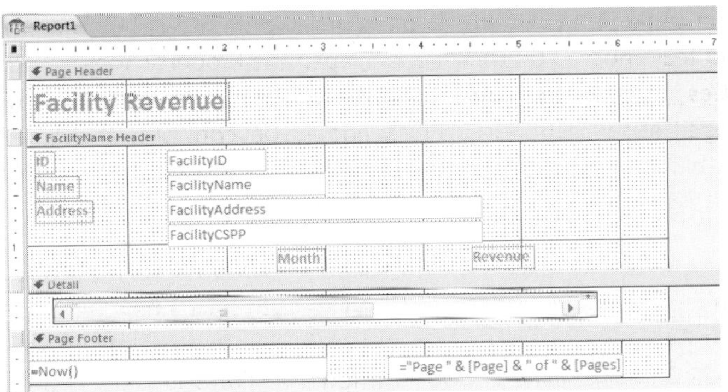

Figure 18-37 The design of your report now includes a subreport.

Expand the Navigation pane if it is collapsed, click the Navigation Bar at the top of the Navigation pane, click Object Type under Navigate To Category, and then click Reports under Filter By Group to display a list of reports in the sample database. Drag the report you created in the previous section (or the rsubXmplFacilityRevenueByMonth report) from the Navigation pane to the Detail section of the report into the upper-left corner about 0.25 inch in from the left edge. In the Property Sheet window, set the Link Child Fields and Link Master Fields properties to **FacilityID**. Delete the label that Access attached to the subreport control, and then reduce the height of the Detail section to about 0.36 inch.

As a finishing touch, you can add a date text box control and a page number text box control to the Page Footer section, as you learned to do earlier in this chapter. Also, you should change all the margins for the report to .25 inch for Top, .5 inch for Bottom, and 1 inch for Left and Right using the Page Setup dialog box and enter a caption of **Facility Revenue** for the report in the Property Sheet window. Your report should look something like Figure 18-37. You can find this report saved as rptXmplFacilityRevenue in the sample database.

Switch to Print Preview to see the result, as shown in Figure 18-38. If the Month and Revenue labels aren't correctly positioned over the columns in the subreport, switch to Layout view to easily make the adjustment.

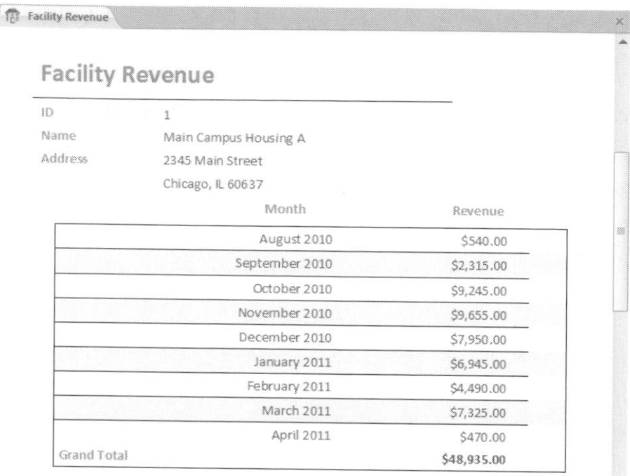
Facility Revenue

Facility Revenue

ID 1
Name Main Campus Housing A
Address 2345 Main Street
Chicago, IL 60637

Month	Revenue
August 2010	$540.00
September 2010	$2,315.00
October 2010	$9,245.00
November 2010	$9,655.00
December 2010	$7,950.00
January 2011	$6,945.00
February 2011	$4,490.00
March 2011	$7,325.00
April 2011	$470.00
Grand Total	$48,935.00

Figure 18-38 Your report now displays facility information with monthly revenue in a subreport.

Adding a PivotChart to a Client Report

You can now design a form in PivotChart view to graphically display monthly revenue data. Note that a report doesn't have a PivotChart or Pivot Table view, but it is perfectly legal to embed a form into a client report as a subreport.

Designing the PivotChart Form

When you built the subreport for the Facility Revenue report, you used a simple query on the tblReservations table. For the chart, you need to include the name of the facility—the ID won't make much sense in the legend for the chart. In the sample database, you can find a query named qryXmplChtFacilityRevenue that includes both the tblFacilities and tblReservations tables. The fields in the query are FacilityID and FacilityName from the tblFacilities table and CheckOutDate and TotalCharge from the tblReservations table.

To build the chart you need, select the query in the Navigation pane, click More Forms in the Forms group on the Create tab, and then click PivotChart from the drop-down list of form options. This command opens a new report object in PivotChart view.

Open the chart field list, and drag the FacilityName field to the Drop Series Fields Here area of the chart. Click the plus sign (+) next to the CheckOutDate By Month field to expand its list and drag Months to the Drop Category Fields Here area. Drag the Total Charge field to the Drop Data Fields Here area—the chart calculates a sum of this field for you. Click the Property Sheet button in the Tools group on the Design tab, and select Chart Workspace on the General tab in the Property Sheet window. Click both the Add Title and Add Legend buttons to add these elements to your chart.

Click the Chart Workspace Title element to select it. In the Property Sheet window, select the Format tab, and enter **Facility Revenue** in the Caption box. In the PivotChart, click the vertical Axis Title, and in the Property Sheet window, enter **Revenue** in the Caption box. In the PivotChart, click the horizontal Axis Title, and change its Caption to **Months**. Go back to the General tab, and select the Chart Workspace. On the Show/Hide tab of the Property Sheet window, clear all the options under Show By Default and Let Users View so that users cannot modify the chart. Your chart should now look like Figure 18-39. Switch back to Design view, and make sure Access set the Default View property to PivotChart. Be sure to save the form, and give it a name such as chtFacilitiesRevenue. You can find this form saved as chtXmplFacilityRevenue in the sample database.

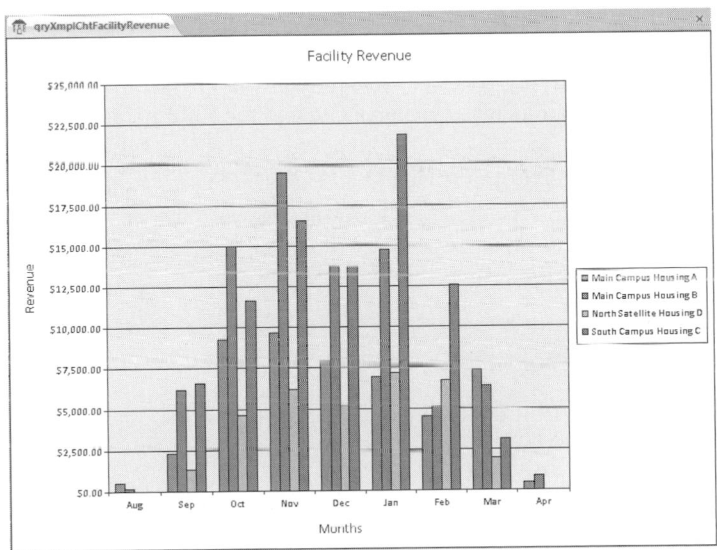

Figure 18-39 This PivotChart form displays facility revenue by month.

Embedding a PivotChart in a Client Report

The rest is easy. Go to the Navigation pane and select the report you created in the previous section to display facilities with revenue by month in a subreport. Open that report in Design view. (You can also open the sample rptXmplFacilityRevenue report.) Select the subreport control in the Detail section, and click the To Fit option under the Size/Space command in the Sizing & Ordering group on the Arrange tab to make sure the subreport is exactly one line high to give yourself some room to work. Don't worry about displaying all the lines in the subreport—when you dragged it to the report, Access set its Can Grow property to Yes. When you view the report, Access will expand the subreport control to display all the lines.

Expand the Detail section to about 5.5 inches high. Make sure the Use Control Wizards button in the Controls group is turned off, click the Subform/Subreport button in the Controls group on the Design tab, and finally draw the control in the Detail section under the previous subreport approximately 5.5 inches wide and 4 inches high. The size of the subreport control affects the resolution of the chart you're going to put inside it, so you want it big enough to be easily readable. Delete the label from the control. Move the subreport control up under the previous subreport control.

With the new subreport control selected, open the Property Sheet window and set the Source Object property to the PivotChart form you created earlier. (Alternatively, you can use the example chtXmplFacilityRevenue form in the sample database.) If you select the drop-down list for the Source Object property, you'll notice that Access precedes the form names with the word *Form* followed by a period and all the report names with the word *Report* followed by a period. If you manually type in the form name you want to use in the Source Object property, make sure you first type the word Form, a period, and then the name of the form. Set both the Link Child Fields and Link Master Fields properties to FacilityID. Your report design should now look like Figure 18-40. Notice that the subreport window shows you the Form view design of the form, not the chart.

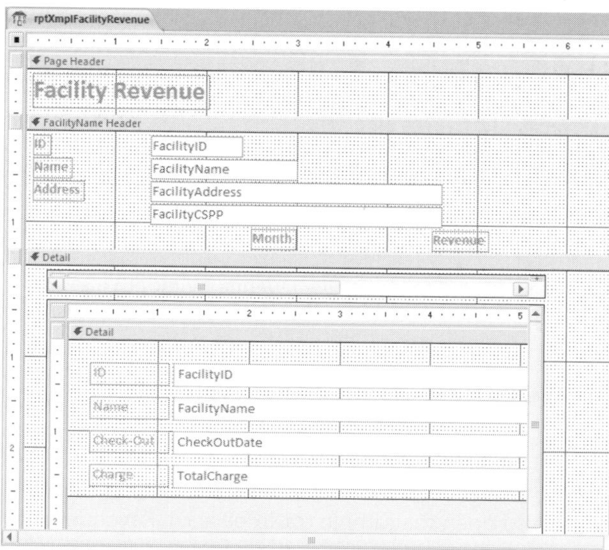

Figure 18-40 Your report now includes an embedded PivotChart form as a subreport.

Switch to Print Preview to see the result, shown in Figure 18-41. Now *that* layout should make the facilities manager happy! You can find the report saved as rptXmplFacilityRevenueChart in the sample database.

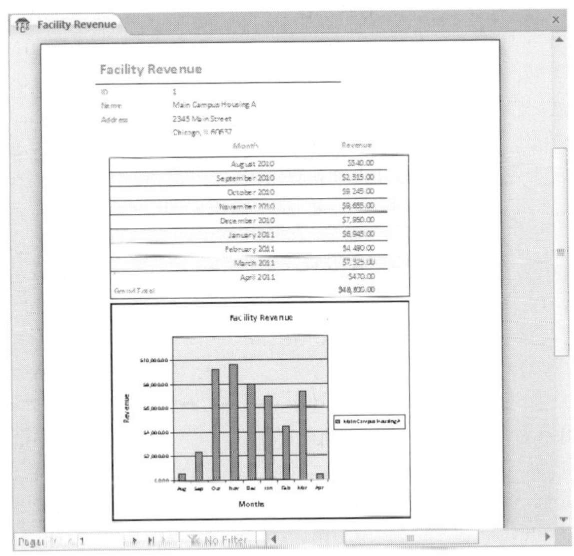

Figure 18-41 Here is your completed report with an embedded subreport and PivotChart in Print Preview.

At this point, you should thoroughly understand the mechanics of constructing client and web reports and working with complex formulas. Now, the fun begins. The next part of the book, "Automating an Access Application Using Macros," discusses how to capture events on your client and web forms and reports and how to make your application come alive with macros.

PART 6

Automating an Access Application Using Macros

CHAPTER 19

Understanding Event Processing

Although you can make Microsoft Access 2010 do a lot for you by setting properties when you design forms and reports, you really can't make your application "come alive" until you build macros or Microsoft Visual Basic procedures that respond to *events*. An event can be as simple as the user clicking a button—and your code responds by opening a related form or report. An event can also trigger complex actions, such as creating a booking record when the user selects an available room.

In this chapter, you'll first learn what event processing is all about—both in Windows and specifically within Access 2010. The second part of the chapter contains a comprehensive reference for all the events available within Access, a discussion of event sequence, and a list of the specific macro actions you can use to respond to events.

Access as a Windows Event-Driven Application

If you're reading this book, you're using Microsoft Office 2010 and Windows. You probably use Windows every day and don't give a second thought to how it actually works. Understanding Windows is essential to programming events in Access 2010.

Understanding Events in Windows

Windows is an event-driven and message-based operating system. When you start an application on your system, that application sends messages to Windows to tell Windows that it wants to respond to certain events. When an event occurs (such as moving your mouse over the application window or clicking somewhere), Windows sends a message to the application to notify it that the event happened. The message usually includes critical information, such as the location of the mouse pointer when the event occurred. The application then responds to the event, usually by sending a message back to Windows to act upon the event. Figure 19-1 shows you a conceptual view of this process.

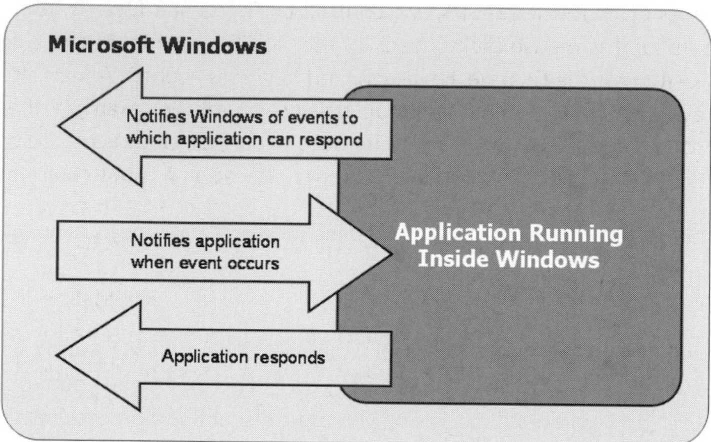

Figure 19-1 Applications running in Windows send messages and respond to events.

For example, when you have Windows Explorer open and click a file name, Windows sends a message to Explorer to tell it where you clicked. Explorer sends a message back to Windows to tell it to highlight what you selected. Another example is the clock applet that runs on your task bar. This utility starts when Windows initializes unless you've set a task bar option not to display the clock. When the utility starts, it asks Windows to notify it when the system clock time changes. When the clock utility receives a message from Windows that the system clock time has changed to a different minute, it sends a message back to Windows to tell it to change the characters displayed on the task bar.

The most important aspect of this entire process is that the user is in control of the applications that are running. As the user of your personal computer, you decide what you want the applications to do next. And because Windows can handle multiple messages at a time, you can start a process in an application (perhaps a search in Explorer for a file) and then switch to or start another application to do something else (such as playing a game of solitaire while you wait for the search to finish).

Using Access Events to Build an Application

If you think of forms and reports in your Access application as little applications running under Access, you have the right idea. When you set an event property (one of the properties on the Event tab in the Properties window) in a report, a form, or a control on a form or report that points to a macro or a Visual Basic procedure, you're notifying Access that you want to respond to that event. The code you write in your macro or Visual Basic procedure provides the response to the occurrence of the event.

Access passes on to forms, reports, and controls on forms and reports, some typical Windows events such as mouse clicks (the Click and DblClick events) or characters entered from the keyboard (the Change, KeyDown, and KeyPress events). Access also defines a wide range of events that are specific to the objects it supports. For example, the BeforeUpdate event signals that the value in a control is about to change or a record being edited in the form is about to be saved. You can perform data validation in your macro or Visual Basic code that responds to BeforeUpdate and have your macro or code send a message back to Access to cancel the save if some business rule is about to be violated.

Although events in Access occur in a specific sequence, you should keep in mind that other events can occur while any code you've written to respond to an event is running. Also, some events signal that an action is about to happen but might not have completed yet. For example, the form Open event signals that a command has been issued to open the form, but the form isn't displayed on the screen yet.

The next section gives you a comprehensive overview of all events in Access 2010 and describes how you can use them.

Summary of Form and Report Events

Access provides more than 60 different events on forms, form controls, and reports that can trigger macros or Visual Basic procedures. You indicate that you want to respond to an event by providing the name of a macro, a Visual Basic function (preceded by an equals sign), or the special settings [Event Procedure] or [Embedded Macro] as the setting of the event property in the Property Sheet window. When you specify [Event Procedure], Access looks for a Visual Basic procedure in the module stored with the form or report that has the name of the event. When the event property is set to [Embedded Macro], Access executes the related macro embedded in the form or report definition. For details about Visual Basic procedures, see Chapter 24, "Understanding Visual Basic Fundamentals," on the companion CD.

This section summarizes those events and organizes them in the following functional categories:

- Opening and closing forms and reports
- Changing data
- Detecting focus changes
- Detecting filters applied to forms
- Trapping keyboard and mouse events

- Detecting changes in PivotTables and PivotCharts
- Printing
- Trapping errors
- Detecting timer expiration

Each table of events also includes a column indicating whether the event is available for web forms or controls on web forms. (Web reports and controls on web reports do not support any events.)

Note

The event property names listed on the following pages are the names you will see in the property sheet in form or report Design view or Layout view. To reference an event property from a macro or a Visual Basic procedure, do not include the blanks in the name. For example, the On Load event property in a form property sheet is the OnLoad property of the form. The exceptions to this rule are the 18 events associated with PivotTables and PivotCharts. For those event properties, the name of the event property is the same as the name of the event, which might not match the property name you see in the Property Sheet window.

Table 19-1 Opening and Closing Forms and Reports[1]

Event Property (Event Name)	Description	Web Support
On Close (Close)	Runs the specified macro, Visual Basic function, or Visual Basic event procedure when the user or a close command in your code requests to close the form or the report but before Access clears the screen. Your code that responds to the event cannot cancel the Close event. For forms, the Close event occurs after the Unload event.	Not available for web forms.

Event Property (Event Name)	Description	Web Support
On Load (Load)	Runs the specified macro, Visual Basic function, or Visual Basic event procedure when Access loads a form or report and then displays the records in the recordset. Your code that responds to the event can set values in controls or set form, report, or control properties. The Load event occurs after the Open event and before the Resize event. Your code cannot cancel a Load event.	Available for web forms.
On Open (Open)	Runs the specified macro, Visual Basic function, or Visual Basic event procedure when the user or an open command in your code requests to open the form or the report but before Access displays the first record. To gain access to a control on the form or report, your code must specify a GoToControl action or SetFocus method to set the focus on the control. The Open event occurs before Access loads the form or report recordset, so your code that responds to the event can prompt the user for parameters and apply filters. Your code can also change the form or report record source in this event.	Not available for web forms.
On Resize (Resize)	Runs the specified macro, Visual Basic function, or Visual Basic event procedure when a form or report changes size. This event also occurs when a form or report opens, after the Load event but before the Activate event. Your code can use this event to force immediate repainting of the resized form or report or to recalculate variables that depend on the size of the form. This property has no effect when you are using the single-document interface (SDI) unless you have also set the Pop Up or Modal properties to Yes. When you open a report in Print Preview, this event occurs only when Access opens the report; the event does not occur again if the user resizes the window in Print Preview.	Not available for web forms
On Unload (Unload)	Runs the specified macro, Visual Basic function, or Visual Basic event procedure when the user or your code requests that the form or report be closed but before Access removes the form or report from the screen. Your code can cancel an Unload event if it determines that a form should not be closed.	Not available for web forms.

[1] These events occur for all views of forms and reports except Design view.

Chapter 19

Table 19-2 Changing Data[1]

Event Property (Event Name)	Description	Web Support
After Del Confirm (AfterDelConfirm)	Runs the specified macro, Visual Basic function, or Visual Basic event procedure after the user has requested that one or more rows on the form be deleted and after the user has confirmed the deletion. The AfterDelConfirm event also occurs if your code that responds to the BeforeDelConfirm event cancels the deletion. In a Visual Basic procedure, you can test a status parameter to determine whether the deletion was completed, was canceled by your code in the BeforeDelConfirm event, or was canceled by the user. If the deletion was successful, you can use the Requery action within your code that responds to the AfterDelConfirm event to refresh the contents of the form or combo boxes. Your code cannot cancel this event. In an Access Project (.adp), this event occurs before the Delete event.	Not available for web forms.
After Insert (AfterInsert)	Runs the specified macro, Visual Basic function, or Visual Basic event procedure after the user has saved a new record. Your code can use this event to requery a recordset after Access has inserted a new row. Your code cannot cancel this event.	Not available for web forms.
After Update (AfterUpdate)	Runs the specified macro, Visual Basic function, or Visual Basic event procedure after the data in the specified form or form control has been updated. See "Understanding Event Sequence and Form Editing," on page 1185, for details. Your code that responds to this event cannot cancel it. In the AfterUpdate event of a control, you can, however, use a RunCommand action to choose the Undo command from the Quick Access Toolbar, or execute the Undo method of the control. This event applies to all forms and to combo boxes, list boxes, option groups, text boxes, and bound object frames as well as to check boxes, option buttons, and toggle buttons that are not part of an option group.	Web forms do not support the AfterUpdate event on itself, but most controls on web forms do support this event.
Before Del Confirm (BeforeDelConfirm)	Runs the specified macro, Visual Basic function, or Visual Basic event procedure after Access has deleted one or more rows on the form, but before Access displays the standard confirmation dialog box. If your code cancels this event, Access replaces the deleted rows and does not display the confirmation dialog box. In a Visual Basic procedure, you can display a custom confirmation dialog box and then set a return parameter to suppress the standard confirmation dialog box. In an Access Project (.adp), this event occurs before the Delete event.	Not available for web forms.

Event Property (Event Name)	Description	Web Support
Before Insert (BeforeInsert)	Runs the specified macro, Visual Basic function, or Visual Basic event procedure when the user types the first character in a new record. This event is useful in providing additional information to a user who is about to add records. If your code cancels this event, Access erases any new data on the form. This event occurs prior to the BeforeUpdate event.	Not available for web forms.
Before Update (BeforeUpdate)	Runs the specified macro, Visual Basic function, or Visual Basic event procedure before Access saves changed data in a control to the form's record buffer or saves the changed record to the database. See "Understanding Event Sequence and Form Editing," on page 1185, for details. Your code that responds to this event can examine both the current and previous values of a control. Your code can cancel this event to stop the update and place the focus on the changed control or record. This event is most useful for performing complex validations of data on forms or in controls. This event applies to the same controls as the AfterUpdate event.	Not available for web forms.
On Change (Change)	Runs the specified macro, Visual Basic function, or Visual Basic event procedure whenever the user changes any portion of the contents of a combo box control or a text box control. Your code cannot cancel this event. See also the KeyDown and KeyPress keyboard events in Table 19-5.	Not available for web forms.
On Delete (Delete)	Runs the specified macro, Visual Basic function, or Visual Basic event procedure just before Access deletes one or more rows. This event occurs once per row being deleted, and your code that responds to the event can examine the data in each row to be deleted. Your code can provide a customized warning message. Your code can also provide automatic deletion of dependent rows in another table (for example, of all the orders for the customer about to be deleted) by executing a delete query. Your code can cancel this event to prevent individual rows from being deleted. (Cancel the BeforeDelConfirm event to cancel deletion of all rows.)	Not available for web forms.

Event Property (Event Name)	Description	Web Support
On Dirty (Dirty)	Runs the specified macro, Visual Basic function, or Visual Basic event procedure whenever the user first changes the contents of a bound control on a bound form (a form that has a record source). This event also occurs if your code changes the value of a bound control from a macro (SetValue) or a Visual Basic procedure. Your code that responds to this event can verify that the current record can be updated. Your code can cancel this event to prevent the update. After this event occurs, the Dirty property of the form is True until the record is saved.	Not available for web forms.
On Not In List (NotInList)	Runs the specified macro, Visual Basic function, or Visual Basic event procedure when the user types an entry in a combo box that does not exist in the current recordset defined by the Row Source property for the combo box. Your code cannot cancel this event. Your code can allow the user to create a new entry for the combo box (perhaps by adding a record to the table on which the Row Source property is based). You can also use the List Items Edit Form property to tell Access to open a form to add or edit the records in the recordset of the combo box. In a Visual Basic procedure, you can examine a parameter passed to the event procedure that contains the unmatched text. Your code can also set a return value to cause Access to display the standard error message, display no error message (after your code has issued a custom message), or requery the list after your code has added data to the Row Source property.	Not available for web forms.
On Undo (Undo)	Runs the specified macro, Visual Basic function, or Visual Basic event procedure when the user undoes a change in a form or a text box or combo box control that has been committed to the form's record buffer. See "Understanding Event Sequence and Form Editing," on page 1185, for details. The Undo event does not occur when the user chooses the Undo Typing command. Your code that responds to the event can examine both the current and previous values of the control and cancel the event if the change should not be undone.	Not available for web forms.
On Updated (Updated)	Runs the specified macro, Visual Basic function, or Visual Basic event procedure after the data in a form's object frame control changes. Your code cannot cancel this event. In a Visual Basic procedure, your code can examine a status parameter to determine how the change occurred.	Not available for web forms.

[1] These events occur for forms in Form view or Datasheet view. They do not apply to forms in Design, PivotTable, PivotChart, or Layout view.

CAUTION!

You can cause an endless loop if your code changes the contents of a control within the event procedure for the control's Change event.

Table 19-3 Detecting Focus Changes[1]

Event Property (Event Name)	Description	Web Support
On Activate (Activate)	Runs the specified macro, Visual Basic function, or Visual Basic event procedure in a form or a report when the Form or Report window receives the focus and becomes the active window. This event does not occur for pop-up or modal forms. This event also does not occur when a normal Form or Report window regains the focus from a pop-up or modal form unless the focus moves to another form or report. Your code cannot cancel this event.	Not available for web forms.
On Current (Current)	Runs the specified macro, Visual Basic function, or Visual Basic event procedure in a bound form or report when the focus moves from one record to another, but before Access displays the new record. Access also triggers the Current event when the focus moves to the first record as a form or report opens. This event is most useful for keeping two open and related forms synchronized. Your code cannot cancel this event. Your code can, however, use GoToRecord or similar action to move to another record if it decides that the form display should not move to the new record. This event does not occur for reports displayed in Print Preview.	Available for web forms.
On Deactivate (Deactivate)	Runs the specified macro, Visual Basic function, or Visual Basic event procedure when a form or a report loses the focus to a window within the Access application that is not a pop-up or modal window. Your code cannot cancel this event.	Not available for web forms.

Event Property (Event Name)	Description	Web Support
On Enter (Enter)	Runs the specified macro, Visual Basic function, or Visual Basic event procedure when the focus moves to a bound object frame, a combo box, a command button, a list box, an option group, or a text box, as well as when the focus moves to a check box, an option button, or a toggle button that is not part of an option group. Your code cannot cancel this event. This event occurs only when the focus moves from another control on the same form or report. If the user changes the focus to another control with the mouse, this event occurs after LostFocus and Exit in the current control and before the GotFocus, MouseDown, MouseUp, and Click events for the new control. If the user changes the focus to a control using the keyboard, this event occurs after the KeyDown, Exit, and LostFocus events in the control that previously had the focus but before the GotFocus, KeyPress, and the KeyUp events in the control that is receiving the focus. This event does not occur for reports displayed in Print Preview or forms displayed in PivotTable or PivotChart view.	Not available for web forms.
On Exit (Exit)	Runs the specified macro, Visual Basic function, or Visual Basic event procedure when the focus moves from a bound object frame, a combo box, a command button, a list box, an option group, or a text box, as well as when the focus moves from a check box, an option button, or a toggle button that is not part of an option group to another control on the same form or report. Your code cannot cancel this event. This event does not occur when the focus moves to another window. If the user leaves a control using the mouse, this event occurs before the Enter, GotFocus, MouseDown, MouseUp, and Click events in the new control. If the user leaves a control using the keyboard, the KeyDown and Exit events in this control occur, and then the Enter, KeyPress, and KeyUp events occur in the new control. This event does not occur for reports displayed in Print Preview or forms displayed in PivotTable or PivotChart view.	Not available for web forms.
On Got Focus (GotFocus)	Runs the specified macro, Visual Basic function, or Visual Basic event procedure when an enabled form or report control receives the focus. If a form or report receives the focus but has no enabled controls, the GotFocus event occurs for the form or report. Your code cannot cancel this event. The GotFocus event occurs after the Enter event. Unlike the Enter event, which occurs only when the focus moves from another control on the same form or report, the GotFocus event occurs every time a control receives the focus, including from other windows. This event does not occur for reports displayed in Print Preview or forms displayed in PivotTable or PivotChart view.	Not available for web forms.

Event Property (Event Name)	Description	Web Support
On Lost Focus (LostFocus)	Runs the specified macro, Visual Basic function, or Visual Basic event procedure when an enabled form or report control loses the focus. The LostFocus event for the form or report occurs whenever a form or report that has no enabled controls loses the focus. Your code cannot cancel this event. This event occurs after the Exit event. Unlike the Exit event, which occurs only when the focus moves to another control on the same form or report, the LostFocus event occurs every time a control loses the focus, including to other windows. This event does not occur for reports displayed in Print Preview or forms displayed in PivotTable or PivotChart view.	Not available for web forms.

[1] These events do not apply to forms or reports in Design view.

Table 19-4 Detecting Filters Applied to Forms and Reports[1]

Event Property (Event Name)	Description	Web Support
On Apply Filter (ApplyFilter)	Runs the specified macro, Visual Basic function, or Visual Basic event procedure when a user applies a filter on a form or report from the user interface or via the ApplyFilter command. Setting the form or report's Filter, OrderBy, ServerFilter, FilterOn, or OrderByOn properties from code does not trigger this event. Your code can examine and modify the form or report's Filter and Order By properties or cancel the event. Within a Visual Basic procedure, you can examine a parameter that indicates how the filter is being applied.	Not available for web forms.
On Filter (Filter)	Runs the specified macro, Visual Basic function, or Visual Basic event procedure when the user opens the Filter By Form or the Advanced Filter/Sort window. Your code can use this event to clear any previous Filter or Order By setting, set a default Filter or Order By criterion, or cancel the event to prevent the window from opening and provide your own custom filter form. Within a Visual Basic procedure, you can examine a parameter that indicates whether a user has asked to open the Filter By Form or the Advanced Filter/Sort window.	Not available for web forms.

[1] These events apply to forms in Form or Datasheet view and reports in Report view.

Table 19-5 Trapping Keyboard and Mouse Events[1]

Event Property (Event Name)	Description	Web Support
On Click (Click)	Runs the specified macro, Visual Basic function, or Visual Basic event procedure when the user clicks a command button or clicks an enabled form, report, or control. Your code cannot cancel this event. The Click event occurs for a form or report only if no control on the form or report can receive the focus.	Web forms do not support the Click event on itself, but most controls on web forms do support this event.
On Dbl Click (DblClick)	Runs the specified macro, Visual Basic function, or Visual Basic event procedure when the user double-clicks a bound object frame, a combo box, a command button, a list box, an option group, or a text box, as well as when the user double-clicks a check box, an option button, or a toggle button that is not part of an option group. The Click event always occurs before DblClick. That is, when the user clicks the mouse button twice rapidly, the Click event occurs for the first click, followed by DblClick for the second click. Access runs the macro or Visual Basic procedure before showing the user the normal result of the double click. Your code can cancel the event to prevent the normal response to a double click of a control, such as activating the application for an ActiveX object in a bound control or highlighting a word in a text box. The DblClick event occurs for a form or report only if no control on that form or report can receive the focus.	Web forms do not support the DblClick event on itself, but most controls on web forms do support this event.

Event Property (Event Name)	Description	Web Support
On Key Down (KeyDown)	Runs the specified macro, Visual Basic function, or Visual Basic event procedure when the user presses a key or a combination of keys. Your code cannot cancel this event. In a Visual Basic procedure, you can examine parameters to determine the key code (the numeric code that represents the key pressed) and whether the Shift, Ctrl, or Alt key was also pressed. You can also set the key code to 0 in Visual Basic to prevent the control from receiving keystrokes. If the form or report has a command button whose Default property is set to Yes (this indicates that the command button responds to Enter as though the button had been clicked), KeyDown events do not occur when the Enter key is pressed. If the form or report has a command button whose Cancel property is set to Yes (this indicates that the command button responds to the Esc key as though the button had been clicked), KeyDown events do not occur when the Esc key is pressed. See also the Change event. The KeyDown event occurs before KeyPress and KeyUp. If the key the user presses (such as the Tab key) causes the focus to move to another control, the control that has the focus when the user presses the key signals a KeyDown event, but the control that receives the focus signals the KeyPress and KeyUp events. If you set the form's KeyPreview property to Yes, this event also occurs for the form or report.	Not available for web forms.
On Key Press (KeyPress)	Runs the specified macro, Visual Basic function, or Visual Basic event procedure when the user presses a key or a combination of keys that would result in a character being delivered to the control that has the focus. (For example, KeyPress does not occur for the arrow keys.) Your code cannot cancel this event. In a Visual Basic procedure, you can examine the ANSI key value and set the value to 0 to cancel the keystroke. The KeyPress event occurs after KeyDown and before KeyUp. If the form or report has a command button whose Default property is set to Yes, the KeyPress event occurs for the form or report and the command button when the Enter key is pressed. If the form or report has a command button whose Cancel property is set to Yes, the KeyPress event occurs for the form or report and the command button when the Esc key is pressed. See also the Change event. If you set the form or report's KeyPreview property to Yes, this event also occurs for the form or report.	Not available for web forms.

Event Property (Event Name)	Description	Web Support
On Key Up (KeyUp)	Runs the specified macro, Visual Basic function, or Visual Basic event procedure when the user releases a key or a combination of keys. Your code cannot cancel this event. In a Visual Basic procedure, you can examine parameters to determine the key code and whether the Shift, Ctrl, or Alt key was also pressed. If you set the form or report's KeyPreview property to Yes, this event also occurs for the form or report. If the form or report has a command button whose Default property is set to Yes, the KeyUp event occurs for the form or report and the command button when the Enter key is released. If the form or report has a command button whose Cancel property is set to Yes, the KeyUp event occurs for the form or report and the command button when the Esc key is released.	Not available for web forms.
On Mouse Down (MouseDown)	Runs the specified macro, Visual Basic function, or Visual Basic event procedure when the user presses any mouse button. Your code cannot cancel this event. In a Visual Basic procedure, you can determine which mouse button was pressed (left, right, or middle); whether the Shift, Ctrl, or Alt key was also pressed; and the X and Y coordinates of the mouse pointer (in twips) when the button was pressed. (Note: There are 1440 *twips* in an inch.)	Not available for web forms.
On Mouse Move (MouseMove)	Runs the specified macro, Visual Basic function, or Visual Basic event procedure when the user moves the mouse over a form, a report, or a control. Your code cannot cancel this event. In a Visual Basic procedure, you can determine which mouse button was pressed (left, right, or middle) and whether the Shift, Ctrl, or Alt key was also pressed. You can also determine the X and Y coordinates of the mouse pointer (in twips).	Not available for web forms.
On Mouse Up (MouseUp)	Runs the specified macro, Visual Basic function, or Visual Basic event procedure when the user releases any mouse button. Your code cannot cancel this event. In a Visual Basic procedure, you can determine which mouse button was released (left, right, or middle); whether the Shift, Ctrl, or Alt key was also pressed; and the X and Y coordinates of the mouse pointer (in twips) when the button was released.	Not available for web forms.
On Mouse Wheel (MouseWheel)	Runs the specified macro, Visual Basic function, or Visual Basic event procedure when the user rolls the mouse wheel while the focus is on a form or report. In a Visual Basic procedure, you can determine whether rolling the wheel caused the form to display a new page and the count of rows that the view was scrolled. (When the user rolls the mouse wheel, the form scrolls up or down through the records in the form.)	Not available for web forms.

[1] These events apply to forms in Form or Datasheet view and to reports in Report view.

Table 19-6 Detecting Changes in PivotTables and PivotCharts

Event Property (Event Name)	Description	Web Support
After Final Render (AfterFinalRender)	In PivotChart view, runs the specified macro, Visual Basic function, or Visual Basic event procedure after all elements in the chart have been rendered (drawn on the screen). Your code cannot cancel this event.	Not available for web forms.
After Layout (AfterLayout)	In PivotChart view, runs the specified macro, Visual Basic function, or Visual Basic event procedure after all charts have been laid out but before they have been rendered. In a Visual Basic procedure, you can reposition the title, legend, chart, and axis objects during this event. Your code can also reposition and resize the chart plot area. Your code cannot cancel this event.	Not available for web forms.
After Render (AfterRender)	In PivotChart view, runs the specified macro, Visual Basic function, or Visual Basic event procedure when a particular chart object has been rendered. In a Visual Basic procedure, you can examine the drawing object and the chart objects and use methods of the drawing object to draw additional objects. Your code cannot cancel this event. This event occurs before the AfterFinalRender event.	Not available for web forms.
Before Query (BeforeQuery)	In PivotTable view, runs the specified macro, Visual Basic function, or Visual Basic event procedure when the PivotTable queries its data source. Your code cannot cancel this event.	Not available for web forms.
Before Render (BeforeRender)	In PivotChart view, runs the specified macro, Visual Basic function, or Visual Basic event procedure before an object is rendered. In a Visual Basic procedure, you can determine the type of rendering and the type of object that is about to be rendered. Your code can cancel this event if it determines that the object should not be rendered. This event occurs before the AfterRender and AfterFinalRender events.	Not available for web forms.
Before Screen Tip (BeforeScreenTip)	In PivotTable or PivotChart view, runs the specified macro, Visual Basic function, or Visual Basic event procedure before a ScreenTip is displayed. In a Visual Basic procedure, you can examine and change the text of the tip or hide the tip by setting the text to an empty string. Your code cannot cancel this event.	Not available for web forms.

Event Property (Event Name)	Description	Web Support
On Cmd Before Execute (CommandBeforeExecute)	In PivotTable or PivotChart view, runs the specified macro, Visual Basic function, or Visual Basic event procedure before a command is executed. In a Visual Basic procedure, you can determine the command to be executed and cancel the event if you want to disallow the command. This event occurs before the CommandExecute event.	Not available for web forms.
On Cmd Checked (CommandChecked)	In PivotTable and PivotChart view, runs the specified macro, Visual Basic function, or Visual Basic event procedure when the user has selected (checked) a command. In a Visual Basic procedure, you can determine the command selected and disallow the command by setting the value of the Checked parameter to False. Your code cannot cancel this event.	Not available for web forms.
On Cmd Enabled (CommandEnabled)	In PivotTable and PivotChart view, runs the specified macro, Visual Basic function, or Visual Basic event procedure when a command has been enabled. In a Visual Basic procedure, you can determine the type of command and disable it. Your code cannot cancel this event.	Not available for web forms.
On Cmd Execute (CommandExecute)	In PivotTable and PivotChart view, runs the specified macro, Visual Basic function, or Visual Basic event procedure after a command has executed. In a Visual Basic procedure, you can determine the type of command and issue additional commands if desired. Your code cannot cancel this event.	Not available for web forms.
On Data Change (DataChange)	In PivotTable view, runs the specified macro, Visual Basic function, or Visual Basic event procedure when the data fetched or calculated by the PivotTable has changed. In a Visual Basic procedure, you can examine the reason for the change, which could include changing the sort, adding a total, or defining a filter. Your code cannot cancel this event. This event often precedes the DataSetChange event.	Not available for web forms.

Event Property (Event Name)	Description	Web Support
On Data Set Change (DataSetChange)	In PivotTable view, runs the specified macro, Visual Basic function, or Visual Basic event procedure when the data source has changed. Your code cannot cancel this event.	Not available for web forms.
On Connect (OnConnect)	In PivotTable view, runs the specified macro, Visual Basic function, or Visual Basic event procedure when the PivotTable connects to its data source. Your code cannot cancel this event.	Not available for web forms.
On Disconnect (OnDisconnect)	In PivotTable view, runs the specified macro, Visual Basic function, or Visual Basic event procedure when the PivotTable disconnects from its data source. Your code cannot cancel this event.	Not available for web forms.
On PivotTable Change (PivotTableChange)	In PivotTable view, runs the specified macro, Visual Basic function, or Visual Basic event procedure when a field, field set, or total is added or deleted. In a Visual Basic procedure, you can examine the reason for the change. Your code cannot cancel this event.	Not available for web forms.
On Query (Query)	In PivotTable view, runs the specified macro, Visual Basic function, or Visual Basic event procedure when the PivotTable must requery its data source. Your code cannot cancel this event.	Not available for web forms.
On Selection Change (SelectionChange)	In PivotTable or PivotChart view, runs the specified macro, Visual Basic function, or Visual Basic event procedure when the user makes a new selection. Your code cannot cancel this event.	Not available for web forms.
On View Change (ViewChange)	In PivotTable or PivotChart view, runs the specified macro, Visual Basic function, or Visual Basic event procedure when the table or chart is redrawn. In a Visual Basic procedure, you can determine the reason for a PivotTable view change. When the form is in PivotChart view, the reason code is always –1. Your code cannot cancel this event.	Not available for web forms.

Table 19-7 Printing

Event Property (Event Name)	Description	Web Support
On Format (Format)	Runs the specified macro, Visual Basic function, or Visual Basic event procedure just before Access formats a report section to print. This event is useful for hiding or displaying controls in the report section based on data values. If Access is formatting a group header, your code has access to the data in the first row of the Detail section. Similarly, if Access is formatting a group footer, your code has access to the data in the last row of the Detail section. Your code can test the value of the Format Count property to determine whether the Format event has occurred more than once for a section (due to page overflow). Your code can cancel this event to keep a section from appearing on the report.	Server reports do not support events.
On No Data (NoData)	Runs the specified macro, Visual Basic function, or Visual Basic event procedure after Access formats a report that has no data for printing and just before the reports prints. Your code can cancel this event to keep a blank report from printing.	Server reports do not support events.
On Page (Page)	Runs the specified macro, Visual Basic function, or Visual Basic event procedure after Access formats a page for printing and just before the page prints. In Visual Basic, you can use this event to draw custom borders around a page or add other graphics to enhance the look of the report.	Server reports do not support events.
On Paint (Paint)	Runs the specified macro, Visual Basic function, or Visual Basic event procedure just before Access paints a formatted section of a form or report. If you open your report in Layout view or Report view, this event occurs instead of the Format or Print event. If you are using the Format event during printing or displaying your report in Print Preview, you might also need to use the Paint event to see the same result in Layout view or Report view. Your code cannot cancel this event.	Server reports do not support events.
On Print (Print)	Runs the specified macro, Visual Basic function, or Visual Basic event procedure just before Access prints a formatted section of a report. If your code cancels this event, Access leaves a blank space on the report where the section would have printed.	Server reports do not support events.

Event Property (Event Name)	Description	Web Support
On Retreat (Retreat)	Runs the specified macro, Visual Basic function, or Visual Basic event procedure when Access has to retreat past already-formatted sections when it discovers that it cannot fit a "keep together" section on a page. Your code cannot cancel this event.	Server reports do not support events.

Table 19-8 Trapping Errors

Event Property (Event Name)	Description	Web Support
On Error (Error)	Runs the specified macro, Visual Basic function, or Visual Basic event procedure whenever a run-time error occurs while the form or report is active. This event does not trap errors in Visual Basic code or macros; use the On Error statement in the Visual Basic procedure or macro logic instead. Your code or macro cannot cancel this event. If you use a Visual Basic procedure or macro to trap this event, you can examine the error code to determine an appropriate action.	Not available for web forms.

Table 19-9 Detecting Timer Expiration

Event Property (Event Name)	Description	Web Support
On Timer (Timer)	Runs the specified macro, Visual Basic function, or Visual Basic event procedure when the timer interval defined for the form or report lapses. The Timer Interval property defines how frequently this event occurs in milliseconds. If the Timer Interval property is set to 0, no Timer events occur. Your code cannot cancel this event. However, your code can set the Timer Interval property for the form to 0 to stop further Timer events from occurring.	Not available for web forms.

You should now have a basic understanding of events and how you might use them. In the next section, you'll see some of these events in action.

Understanding Event Sequence and Form Editing

One of the best ways to learn event sequence is to see events in action. In the WeddingMC.accdb sample database on the companion CD, you can find a special form that you can use to study events. Open the sample database and then open the WeddingEvents form, as shown in Figure 19-2. (The form's Caption property is set to Wedding List.)

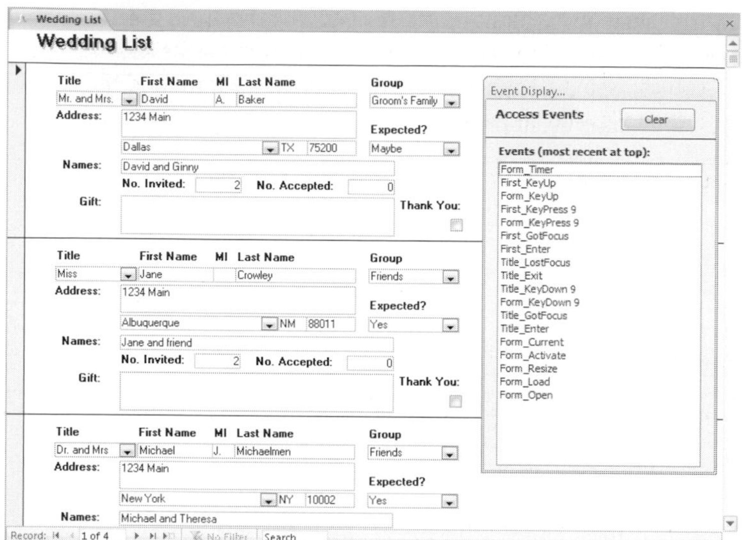

Figure 19-2 Use the WeddingEvents form to study event sequence.

When you open the form, it also opens an event display pop-up form that shows the events that have occurred. All the events (except the Mouse and Paint events, which fire so frequently that they would make it hard to study other events) are set to write the event name to the pop-up window. The pop-up window shows the most recent events at the top. When you open the form, the initial events are as follows:

1. **Form Open** This signals that the form is about to open.
2. **Form Load** This signals that the form is now open and the record source for the form is about to be loaded.
3. **Form Resize** The form's Auto Resize property is set to Yes, so this indicates that Access is resizing the window to show an exact multiple of rows. (The form's Default View property is set to Continuous Forms.)
4. **Form Activate** The form has now received the focus.
5. **Form Current** The form has now moved to the first row in the record source.
6. **Title Enter** The first control in the tab order has been entered.
7. **Title GotFocus** The first control in the tab order now has the focus.

After the form opened, we pressed the Tab key to move from the Title field to the First Name field. (The name of the control is First.) The form has its Key Preview property set to Yes, so you can see the keyboard events for both the form and the controls. The events occurred in the following sequence:

1. **Form KeyDown** The form detected that the Tab key (key code 9) was pressed.
2. **Title KeyDown** The Title combo box control detected that the Tab key was pressed.
3. **Title Exit** Pressing the Tab key caused an exit from the Title combo box control.
4. **Title LostFocus** The Title combo box control lost the focus as a result of pressing Tab.
5. **First Enter** The First text box control (First Name) was entered.
6. **First GotFocus** The First text box control received the focus.
7. **Form KeyPress** The form received the Tab key.
8. **First KeyPress** The First text box control received the Tab key.
9. **Form KeyUp** The form detected that the Tab key was released.
10. **First KeyUp** The First text box detected that the Tab key was released.

In Figure 19-2, you can also see a Form Timer event listed. The Timer Interval property for this form is set to 20,000 (the value is milliseconds), so you should see the timer event occur every 20 seconds so long as you have the form open.

You can have fun with this form, moving around and typing in new data. You'll be able to see each character that you enter. You'll also see the control and form BeforeUpdate and AfterUpdate events when you commit changed values. You can also switch to PivotChart or PivotTable view to watch events related to those views.

Figure 19-3 shows you a conceptual diagram of how editing data in a form works and when the critical Current, BeforeUpdate, and AfterUpdate events occur.

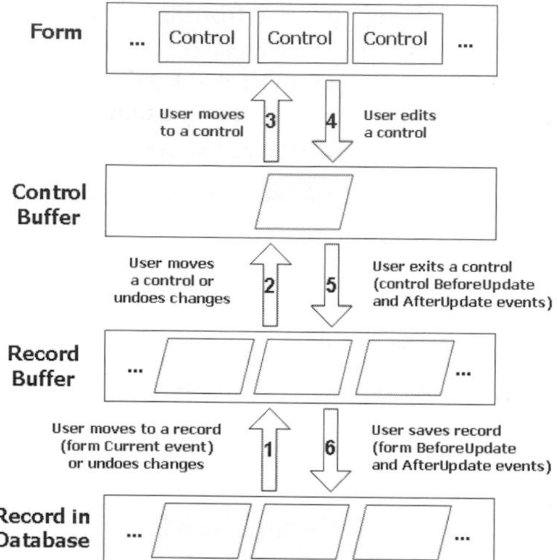

Figure 19-3 Many events occur behind the scenes when you edit data on a bound form.

Of course, the ultimate goal is to update data in your database table. When Access opens a form, it builds a special buffer to contain the contents of the current record displayed on the form. As you move from control to control on the form, Access fetches the field bound to each control from this record buffer and puts it into a special control buffer. As you type in the control, you're changing the control buffer, not the record buffer or the actual record in the table.

If you have changed the data in a control and then you move to another control, Access signals the BeforeUpdate event for the control. If you do not cancel the event, Access then copies the updated contents of the control buffer into the record buffer and signals the control's AfterUpdate event. Access then fetches into the control buffer the contents of the field bound to the control to which you moved from the record buffer and displays it in the control.

If you undo any edit, Access signals the appropriate Undo event and either refreshes the control buffer from the record buffer (if you undo a control) or the original record from the table into the record buffer (if you undo all edits). When you save a changed record, either by clicking the Save button in the Records group on the Home tab, moving to another record, or closing the form, Access signals the BeforeUpdate event of the form. If you do not cancel this event, Access writes the changed record to your table and signals the After-Update event of the form.

What Happened to Visual Basic?

You might be wondering why we are focusing on macros for automating your Access automation in the next two chapters, rather than discussing using Visual Basic code. For the Access 2010 product cycle, a sizeable portion of the Access team's development resources focused on feature areas in the new Access Services web database functionality. In deciding what features to cover for this edition of *Microsoft Access 2010 Inside Out*, there simply was not enough space to include a full discussion of all the new features included in Access 2010 and all the existing functionality in the printed pages alone. The two Visual Basic chapters are very in-depth and require many pages to adequately discuss how to automate your Access application using Visual Basic. We decided to move the two Visual Basic chapters to the companion CD to maximize space in the printed pages for the new features—specifically, creating and working with web databases and Business Connectivity Services.

So fear not; you don't need to interpret our decision to put the Visual Basic chapters on the companion CD to mean we think that macros are more important than Visual Basic. Macros and Visual Basic are two different tools to automate your applications, and we think it is best to study both of these tools. In fact, you can use only macros to automate web forms in a web browser, so it's important for you to learn macros if you are using a web database.

In Chapter 24, "Understanding Visual Basic Fundamentals," you'll be introduced to the Microsoft Visual Basic Editor and learn about variables, constants, and procedural statements. In Chapter 25, "Automating Your Application with Visual Basic," you'll learn how to use Visual Basic code to automate many common tasks in your applications.

Now that you understand events and event sequence, the remaining two chapters in Part 6 discuss client and web macros and how you can design macro actions to respond to form and report events.

CHAPTER 20

Automating a Client Application Using Macros

In Chapter 7, "Creating Table Data Macros," you learned about the new data macro feature in Microsoft Access 2010. Data macros are attached to table events or the table itself and interact only at the data layer. In this chapter and the next, you'll learn about user interface macros. In Access 2010, you can define a user interface macro to execute just about any task you would otherwise initiate with the keyboard or the mouse. The unique power of user interface macros in Access is their ability to automate responses to many types of events without forcing you to learn a programming language. The event might be a change in the data, the opening or closing of a form or a report, or even a change of focus from one control to another. Within a user interface macro, you can include multiple actions and define condition checking so that different actions are performed depending on the values in your forms or reports. For the remainder of this chapter and the next, we'll only use the term macros to refer to user interface macros.

Macros are particularly useful for building small, personal applications or for prototyping larger ones. Macros are also essential if you want to automate a web database and display the application in a web browser using Access Services and SharePoint 2010. (You'll learn how to automate a web database in Chapter 21, "Automating a Web Application Using Macros.") As you'll learn in Chapter 24, "Understanding Visual Basic Fundamentals," on the companion CD, you probably should use Microsoft Visual Basic for complex applications or for applications that will be shared by several users over a network. However, even if you think you're ready to jump right into Visual Basic, you should study all the macro actions first. You'll find that you'll use nearly all the available macro actions in Visual Basic, so learning macros is an excellent introduction to programming in Access in general.

Note

The examples in this chapter are based on the Wedding List Macro (WeddingMC.accdb) sample client database on the companion CD included with this book. The results you see from the samples in this chapter might not exactly match what you see in this book if you have changed the sample data in the files. Also, all the screen images in this chapter were taken on a Windows 7 system with the Access color scheme set to Silver. Your results might look different if you are using a different operating system or a different theme.

In this chapter, you will

- Learn about the various types of actions you can define in macros
- Tour the new Logic Designer and learn how to build both a simple macro and a macro with multiple defined actions
- Learn how to manage the many macros you need for a form or a report by creating submacros inside a macro object
- See how to add conditional expressions to a macro to control the actions that Access performs
- Learn about embedded macros, error trapping in macros, temporary variables, and macro actions that are not trusted
- Learn how to reference other form and report objects in macros
- Understand some of the actions automated with macros in the Wedding List Macro sample client database

Note

In Article 6, "Macro Actions," on the companion CD, you'll find summaries of the client macro actions and of the web macro actions. You might find that article useful as a quick reference when you're designing macros for your applications.

Uses of Macros

Access 2010 provides various types of macro actions that you can use to automate your application. With macros, you can

- Open any table, query, form, or report in any available view or close any open table, query, form, or report.
- Open a report in Print Preview or Report view or send a report directly to the printer.
- Send the output data from a report to a Rich Text Format (.rtf) file or a Notepad (.txt) file. You can then open the file in Microsoft Word 2010 or Notepad.
- Execute a select query or an action query. You can base the parameters of a query on the values of controls in any open form.
- Include conditions that test values in a database, a form, or a report and use the results of a test to determine what action runs next.
- Execute other macros or execute Visual Basic functions. You can halt the current macro or all macros, cancel the event that triggered the macro, or quit the application.
- Trap errors caused during execution of macro actions, evaluate the error, and execute alternate actions.
- Set the value of any form or report control or set selected properties of forms and form controls.
- Emulate keyboard actions and supply input to system dialog boxes.
- Refresh the values in forms, list box controls, and combo box controls.
- Apply a filter to, go to any record in, or search for data in a form's underlying table or query.
- Execute any of the commands on any of the Access ribbons.
- Move and size, minimize, maximize, or restore any window within the Access workspace when you work in multiple-document interface (MDI) mode.
- Change the focus to a window or to any control within a window or select a page of a report to display in Print Preview.

- Display informative messages and sound a beep to draw attention to your messages. You can also disable certain warning messages when executing action queries.
- Rename any object in your database, make another copy of a selected object in your database, or copy an object to another Access database.
- Delete objects in your database or save an open object.
- Import, export, or attach other database tables or import or export spreadsheet or text files.
- Start an application and exchange data with the application using Dynamic Data Exchange (DDE) or the Clipboard. You can send data from a table, query, form, or report to an output file and then open that file in the appropriate application. You can also send keystrokes to the target application.

Consider some of the other possibilities for macros. For example, you can make moving from one task to another easier by using command buttons that open and position forms and set values. You can create very complex editing routines that validate data entered in forms, including checking data in other tables. You can even check something like the customer name entered in an order form and open another form so that the user can enter detailed data if no record exists for that customer.

The Macro Design Facility—An Overview

In Chapter 7, you learned that Microsoft redesigned the macro design window in Access 2010 for Access developers to be more productive when creating macros in their applications. Although functional, the older macro design window was not the most intuitive interface to work with. For example, when you wanted to create a new action for a macro, you selected the action in the upper part of the window, but you entered the arguments in the bottom part of the window. The Arguments column in the upper part of the window was read-only, so you constantly needed to switch from the top window to the bottom window. You also could not create complex nested logic conditions for your macro execution and the readability of the macro elements was difficult to follow.

The following sections explain how to work with the macro design facility in Access 2010 in the context of user interface macros.

Working with the Logic Designer

Open the Wedding List Macro sample database (WeddingMC.accdb) from the folder where you installed the sample files. (The default location is \Microsoft Press\Access 2010 Inside

Out on your C drive.) As you'll discover later in this chapter, a special macro called Autoexec runs each time you open the database. This macro determines whether the database is trusted, opens an informational form for a few seconds, and then tells you which macro to run to start the application. We'll look at that macro in some detail later.

On the Create tab, in the Macros & Code group, click Macro. Access opens the new Logic Designer for creating macros, as shown in Figure 20-1.

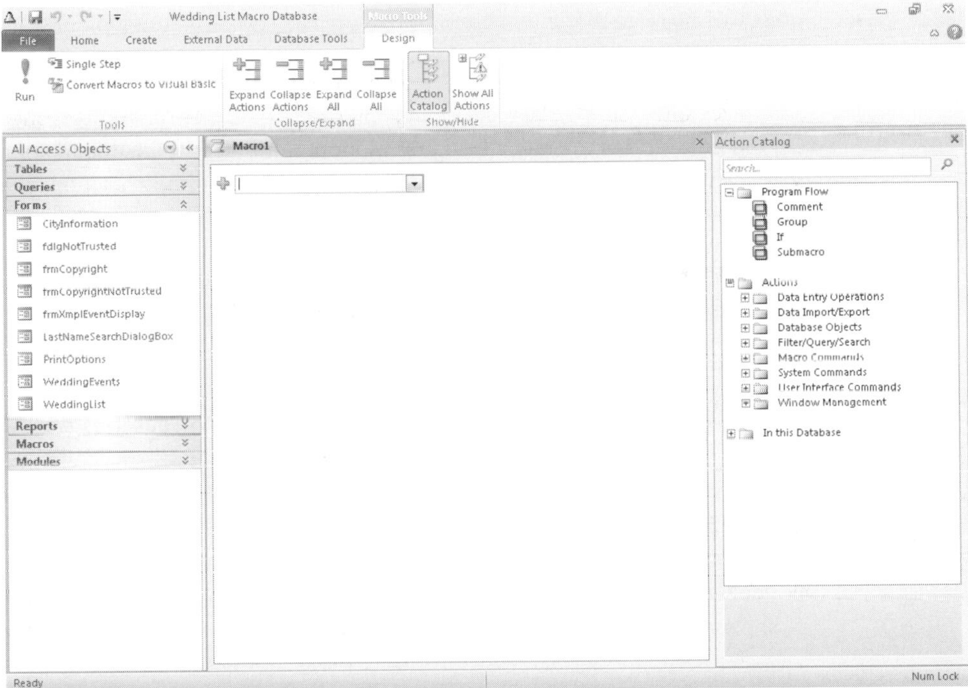

Figure 20-1 This is the new Logic Designer where you create data and user interface macros.

Whenever you need to create or edit data macros or user interface macros in Access 2010, this is the design surface that you use. When you're working with user interface macros, Access enables the commands in the Tools group and displays the macro actions available for user interface macros in the Action Catalog. You'll also notice that Access did not collapse the Navigation pane when you clicked the Macro command on the ribbon, as it does when you are working with data macros. When you are working with user interface macro objects—macros displayed in the Navigation pane—Access does not open the Logic Designer window modally, which means you can open other database objects while working on your macro. (You'll learn later in this chapter that Access opens the Logic Designer modally when you're creating embedded macros.)

As you can see in Figure 20-1, the new Logic Designer layout looks more like a Visual Basic code window. The Expand Actions, Collapse Actions, Expand All, and Collapse All buttons in the Collapse/Expand group selectively expand or collapse the actions listed in the macro designer surface. In the Show/Hide group on the Design tab, you can choose to hide the Action Catalog, shown on the right side of the Logic Designer window, by clicking the Action Catalog toggle button. When you're working with macro objects, Access does not display the Close group on the Design tab as it does for data macros. When you want to save your macro changes, you can click the Save button on the Quick Access Toolbar or press Ctrl+S. Note that if you attempt to close the Logic Designer window with unsaved changes, Access prompts you and asks if you want to save your changes before closing the window.

On the right side of the Logic Designer window is the Action Catalog. The Action Catalog shows a contextual list of the program flow constructs and macro actions that are applicable for user interface macros. If you are working with a client macro, Access displays macro actions available for client macros. Similarly, when you're working with a web macro, Access displays macros actions available for web macros. (We'll discuss the Action Catalog in more detail in the next section, and we'll discuss web macros in Chapter 21.)

INSIDE OUT Searching the Action Catalog Also Searches the Action Descriptions

When you type search criteria into the Action Catalog Search box, Access not only looks at the action name for a possible match, but it also searches all the action descriptions for any matching text. For example, if you type Query into the Search box, you'll see that Access returns other actions such as ApplyFilter and GoToRecord. Access shows those results because the word *query* exists in the descriptions for those actions.

In the middle of the Logic Designer window is the main macro designer surface, where you define your macro. You add program flow constructs, macro actions, and arguments to the designer surface to instruct Access what actions to take for the macro. If you have more actions than can fit on the screen, Access provides a scroll bar on the right side of the macro design surface so you can scroll down to see the rest of your actions.

In the lower-right corner of the Logic Designer window is the Help window. Access displays a brief help message in this window, which changes based on where the focus is located in the Action Catalog. (Remember: You can always press F1 to open a context-sensitive Help topic.)

To get you accustomed to using the Logic Designer for macros, let's create a simple macro that displays a message. You can use the MessageBox action to open a pop-up modal dialog box with a message in it. This is a great way to display a warning or an informative message in your database without defining a separate form. To begin, let's add a Comment block to the macro design surface. As you learned in Chapter 7, you'll find the Comment block especially useful for documenting large macros that contain many actions. Click on the word Comments under the Program Flow node in the Action Catalog, hold the mouse key down, drag the comment onto the macro design surface, and then release the mouse button, as shown in Figure 20-2. Note that in Figure 20-2, we collapsed the Navigation pane so you can see more of the macro design surface.

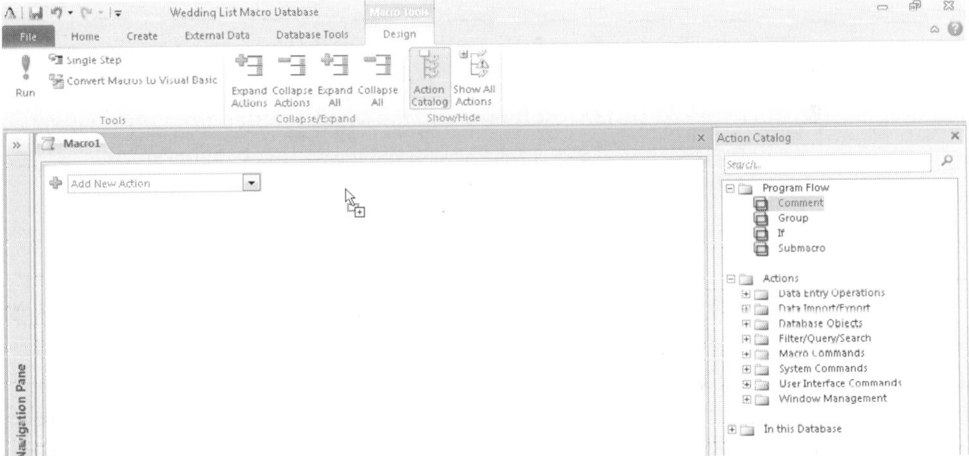

Figure 20-2 Drag the Comment program flow element from the Action Catalog onto the macro design surface.

Assume that this message will be a greeting, so click inside the Comment block and type **Greeting** message. Click outside the Comment block onto the macro design surface and Access collapses the size of the Comment block to just fit the text you typed and displays the text in green. As you learned in Chapter 7, the /* and */ symbols mark the beginning and end of a block of comments. Access designates anything written between those symbols as a comment and they are there only to provide information about the purpose of the data macro or particular action to follow.

Click in the Add New Action combo box on the macro design surface now and drop-down the list of macro actions. In the Add New Action combo box, you can specify any of the 84 client macro actions and four program flow constructs provided by Access 2010. Select MessageBox from this drop-down list. After you select an action such as MessageBox, Access displays argument boxes for the specific action you choose, as shown in Figure 20-3, in which you enter the arguments for the action.

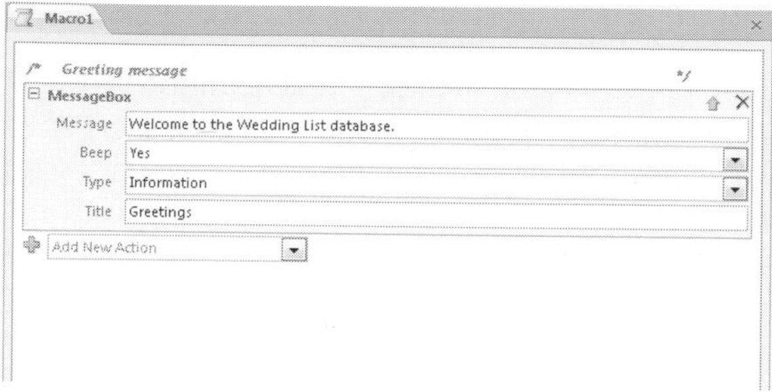

Figure 20-3 Enter arguments for a MessageBox action to display a greeting message.

Note

In Access 2010, Microsoft renamed the MsgBox action from previous versions of Access to MessageBox. If you have existing databases that use the MsgBox action, Access 2010 can still understand and execute the action.

You use the Message argument box to set the message that you want Access to display in the dialog box you're creating. The setting in the Beep argument box tells Access whether to sound a beep when it displays the message. In the Type argument box, you can choose a graphic indicator, such as a red critical icon, that will appear with your message in the dialog box. In the Title argument box, you can type the contents of your dialog box's title bar. Use the settings shown in Figure 20-3 in your macro.

TROUBLESHOOTING

Why doesn't the list include all the available macro actions?

Access 2010 includes 86 client macro actions, but not all these actions can run in a database that is not trusted. By default, Access displays only the macro actions that can run in a trusted database in the Action column. To see the complete list of client macro actions, click the Show All Actions button in the Show/Hide group on the Design tab. When you select an action that can run only in a trusted database, Access displays an exclamation point in the upper-left corner of the action block. If a macro in your application includes actions that can run only in a trusted database, your user must trust your database to be able to run the macro.

Saving Your Macro

You must save a macro before you can run it. Click the Save button on the Quick Access Toolbar, or click the File tab on the Backstage view and then click Save. When you do so, Access opens the dialog box shown in Figure 20-4. Enter the name **TestGreeting**, and click OK to save your macro.

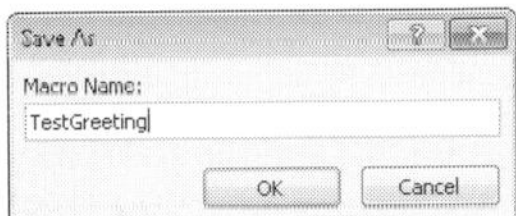

Figure 20-4 Enter a name for this test macro in the Save As dialog box.

Testing Your Macro

You can run some macros (such as the simple one you just created) directly from the Navigation pane or from the Macro window because they don't depend on controls on an open form or report. If your macro does depend on a form or a report, you must link the macro to the appropriate event and run it that way. (You'll learn how to do this later in this chapter.) However you run your macro, Access provides a way to test it by allowing you to single-step through the macro actions.

To activate single-stepping, right-click the macro you want to test in the Navigation pane and then click Design View on the shortcut menu. This opens the macro in the Logic Designer. Click the Single Step button in the Tools group on the Design tab. Now, when you run your macro, Access opens the Macro Single Step dialog box before executing each action in your macro. In this dialog box, you'll see the macro name, the action, and the action arguments.

Try this procedure with the TestGreeting macro you just created. Open the Logic Designer, click the Single Step button, and then click the Run button in the Tools group on the Design tab. The Macro Single Step dialog box opens, as shown in Figure 20-5. Later in this section, you'll learn how to code a condition in a macro. The Macro Single Step dialog box also shows you the result of testing your condition.

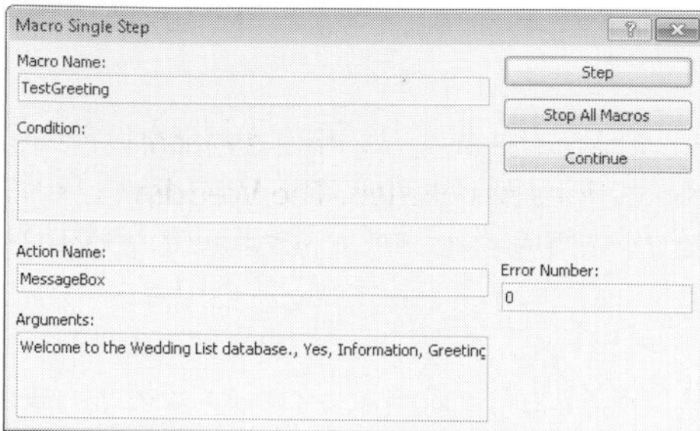

Figure 20-5 The Macro Single Step dialog box allows you to test each action in your macro.

If you click the Step button in the dialog box, the action you see in the dialog box will run, and you'll see the dialog box opened by your MessageBox action with the message you created, as shown in Figure 20-6. Click the OK button in the message box to dismiss it. If your macro had more than one action defined, you would have returned to the Macro Single Step dialog box, which would have shown you the next action. In this case, your macro has only one action, so Access returns you to the Logic Designer.

Figure 20-6 Access displays the dialog box you created by using the MessageBox action in the TestGreeting macro.

If Access encounters an error in any macro during the normal execution of your application, Access first displays a dialog box explaining the error it found. You then see an Action Failed dialog box, which is similar to the Macro Single Step dialog box, containing information about the action that caused the problem. At this point, you can click only the Stop All Macros button. You can then edit your macro to fix the problem. We'll discuss handling errors in "Trapping Errors in Macros," on page 1219.

Before you read on in this chapter, you might want to return to the Logic Designer and click Single Step again so that it's no longer selected. Otherwise, you'll continue to single-step through every macro you run until you exit and restart Access or click Continue in one of the Single Step dialog boxes.

Defining Multiple Actions

In Access 2010, you can define more than one action within a macro, and you can specify the sequence in which you want the actions performed. The Wedding List Macro database contains several examples of macros that have more than one action. Open the database if it is not open already. Click the Navigation menu at the top of the Navigation pane, click Object Type under Navigate To Category, and then click Macros under Filter By Group to display a list of macros available in the Wedding List Macro database. Right-click the macro named AutoexecXmpl, and then click Design View on the shortcut menu to open the Logic Designer. Figure 20-7 shows the macro.

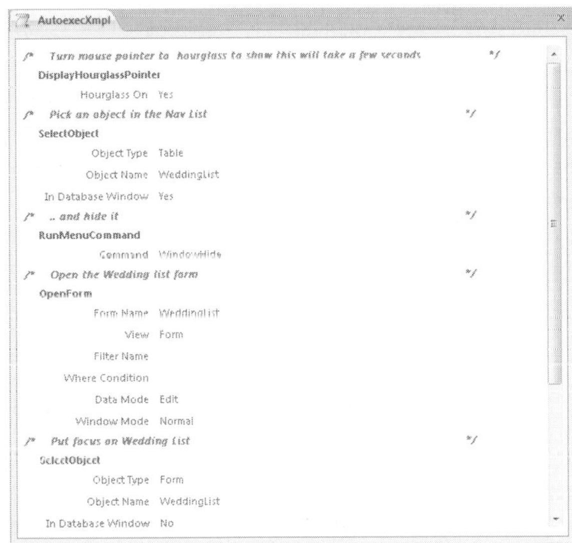

Figure 20-7 The AutoexecXmpl macro defines multiple actions that Access executes when you run the macro.

INSIDE OUT Autoexec Macros—A Special Type of Macro

If you create a macro and name it Autoexec, Access runs the macro each time you open the database in which it is stored. The preferred method to run start-up code is to define a start-up form in the Application Options section of the Current Database category in the Access Options dialog box. For details, see Chapter 26, "The Finishing Touches," on the companion CD.

In the Wedding List Macro sample database, the Autoexec macro examines the IsTrusted property of the CurrentProject object (CurrentProject defines all the executable code) to see whether the database is trusted. (You can trust the database by placing it in a trusted location.) If the database is not trusted, the macro opens a dialog form with instructions on how to create a trusted folder. If you open this database in a trusted location, the macro displays a copyright form followed by a message box telling you to run the AutoexecXmpl macro to start the application.

If this macro were named *AutoExec*, Access would execute each action automatically whenever you open the database. This sample macro is an example of a macro that you might design to start the application when the user opens your database.

We defined eight actions in this macro. First, the DisplayHourglassPointer action displays an hourglass mouse pointer to give the user a visual clue that the next several steps might take a second or two. It's always a good idea to turn on this visual cue even if you think the next several actions won't take very long. Next, the SelectObject action puts the focus on a known object in the Navigation pane, and the RunMenuCommand-WindowHide action hides the selected window (the Navigation pane).

The next action, OpenForm, opens the WeddingList form. As you can see in Figure 20-7, the OpenForm client action has six arguments that you can use to define how it should work. The Form Name argument indicates the form you want to open. The View argument tells Access what view you want. (The seven choices for the View argument are Form, Design, Print Preview, Datasheet, PivotTable, PivotChart, and Layout.) You can ask Access to apply a filter to the form when it opens either by specifying the name of a query that defines the filter in the Filter Name argument or by entering filter criteria in the Where Condition argument. You can click the Build button on the Where Condition argument to open the Expression Builder, which can help you create the filter.

Edit is the default for the Data Mode argument, which allows the user to add, edit, or delete records while using this form. The other choices for this argument are Add, which opens the form in data entry mode, and Read Only, which opens the form but does not allow any changes to the data. The default setting for the Window Mode argument is Normal, which opens the form in the mode set by its design properties. You can override the design property settings to open the form in Hidden mode, as an icon in the Icon mode, or in the special Dialog mode. When you open a form hidden, the user can reveal it only by adding the Unhide Window command to the Quick Access Toolbar and then clicking the command. When you open a form in Dialog mode, Access does not run further actions or Visual Basic statements until you close that form.

When you select the OpenForm action block on the macro design surface, you'll see an Update Parameters hyperlink in the lower-right corner of the action block. You can use this link to pass in parameters to the OpenForm action. For example, if the form you are going to open is based on a query that requires parameters, you can use this link to display text boxes beneath the Window Mode argument, where you can set the parameters necessary for the query. We'll discuss how to pass in parameters with macros in Chapter 21.

Access doesn't always wait for one action to complete before going to the next one. For example, an OpenForm action merely starts a task to begin opening the form. Particularly if the form displays a lot of data, Access might take several seconds to load all the data and finish displaying the form. Because you're running Windows, your computer can handle many tasks at once. Access takes advantage of this by going to the next task without waiting for the form to completely open. However, because this macro is designed to maximize the WeddingList form, the form must be completely open for this to work.

You can force a form to finish opening by telling Access to put the focus on the form. This macro does so by using the SelectObject action to identify the object to receive the focus (in this case, the WeddingList form), followed by the GoToControl action to put the focus on a specific control on the form. After the GoToControl action puts the focus on the control, the MaximizeWindow action sizes the active window (the window containing the object that currently has the focus) to fit the entire screen. The final action in the macro (the DisplayHourglassPointer again) restores the mouse pointer to let the user know that the macro is finished.

Note

Because macros might be used by inexperienced programmers, Access automatically restores Hourglass when it finishes running a macro. If it didn't do this, the mouse pointer would continue to show an hourglass. The user would think that Access is broken. However, it's good practice to always restore what you turn off, which is why the sample AutoExecXmpl macro includes Hourglass-No at the end, even though it isn't required. As you'll learn in Chapter 24, Visual Basic isn't quite so forgiving. If you turn the mouse pointer to an hourglass in a Visual Basic procedure and forget to turn it back on before your code exits, your mouse pointer will forever display an hourglass!

Learning to define multiple actions within a macro is very useful when you want to automate the tasks you perform on a day-to-day basis. Now that you've learned how to do this, the next step is to learn how to group actions by tasks.

Working with Submacros

You'll find that most of the forms you design for an application require multiple macros to respond to events—some to edit fields, some to open reports, and still others to respond to command buttons. You could design a separate macro saved with its own unique name in the Database window to respond to each event, but you'll soon have hundreds of macros in your application.

You can create a simpler set of more manageable objects by defining *submacros* within named macro objects. A submacro is a named collection of macro actions inside a macro object. One approach is to create one saved macro object per form or report. Another technique is to categorize macros by type of action—for example, one macro containing all the OpenForm actions and another containing all the OpenReport actions.

Let's take a look at a form that depends on submacros. Figure 20-8 shows the PrintOptions form from the Wedding List Macro database in Form view. This form contains two command buttons, Print and Cancel, each of which triggers a different submacro. The two submacros are contained within a macro object called DoReport.

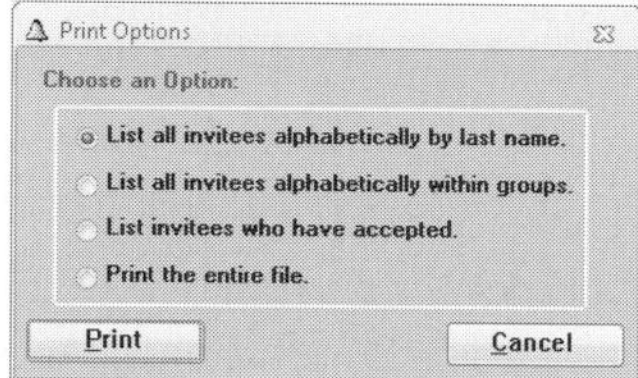

Figure 20-8 The two command buttons on the Print Options form run submacros.

To look at the macro object, right-click the DoReport macro in the list of macro objects in the Navigation pane, and then click Design view on the shortcut menu to open this macro object in the Logic Designer. Figure 20-9 shows the macro.

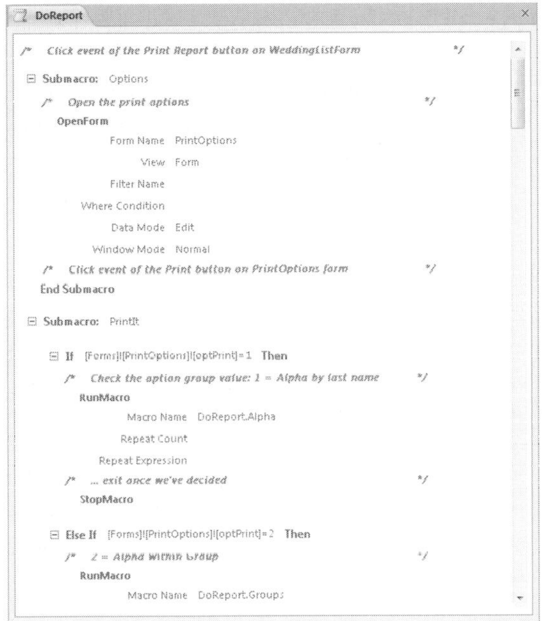

Figure 20-9 The DoReport macro group includes nine individual submacros.

To create a submacro within a macro object, you use the Submacro program flow construct in the Action Catalog. (You can also find the Submacro construct in the drop-down list of actions in the Add New Action combo box on the macro design surface. Access displays the four user interface macro program flow constructs—Comment, Group, If, and Submacro—first in the drop-down list.) You can create a series of actions at the beginning of the macro definition—not inside a submacro block—that you can reference from an event property or a RunMacro maccaction by using only the name of the macro object. As you saw earlier in the AutoexecXmpl macro, naming a macro object in a RunMacro action (without any qualifier) asks Access to run the unnamed actions it finds in that macro object.

To create a set of named submacros within a macro object, you can drag a Submacro construct from the Action Catalog to the macro design surface or select Submacro from the Add New Action combo box. You then need to provide a name for your submacro. Note that Access always places submacro blocks below macro actions on the macro design surface. You cannot place macro actions that are outside a submacro block beneath any submacros. To execute a named submacro within a macro object from an event property or a RunMacro action, enter the name of the macro object, a period, and then the name of the submacro. For example, to execute the PrintIt submacro set of actions in the DoReport macro, enter **DoReport.PrintIt** in the event property or the Macro Name parameter.

In the sample DoReport macro, there are nine submacros within the object. (You must scroll down to see the other submacros.) The first submacro, Options (triggered by the Print Report button on the WeddingList form), opens the Print Options form, and the second submacro, PrintIt, determines which report was selected. The next four submacros (Groups, Alpha, Accepted, and PrintF) display the appropriate report in Print Preview mode, based on the result of the second submacro. The Cancel submacro merely closes the Print Options form if the user clicks the Cancel button. The NoRecords submacro cancels opening a report when the report's record source has no data, and the ErrReport submacro handles errors. As you might have guessed, Access runs a submacro starting with the first action in the submacro block name specified and executes each action in sequence until it encounters a StopMacro action, another submacro, or no further actions. As you'll see later, you can control whether some actions execute by adding conditional tests in the macro. Note that you can click Collapse All in the Collapse/Expand group on the Design tab to collapse all the actions quickly and see the submacro names.

If you open the PrintOptions form in Design view (see Figure 20-10) and look at the properties for each of the command buttons, you'll see that the On Click property contains the name of the submacro that executes when the user clicks the command button. If you open the list for any event property, you can see that Access lists all macro objects and the named submacros within them to make it easy to select the one you want.

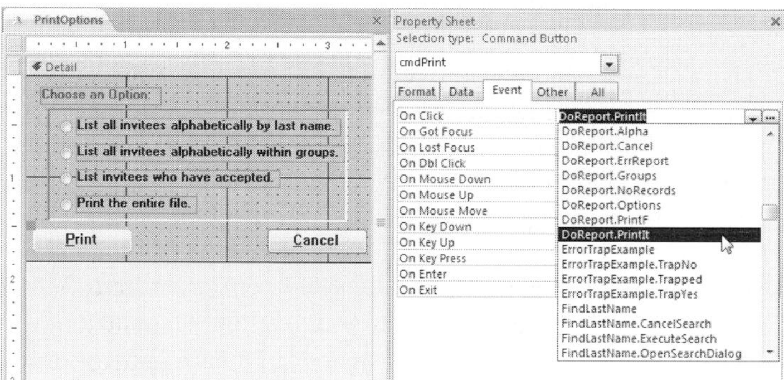

Figure 20-10 You can see that Access lists all macro objects and named submacros in the various event properties.

Remember, the macro name is divided into two parts. The part before the period is the name of the macro object, and the part after the period is the name of a specific submacro within the object. So, for the first command button control, the On Click property is set to DoReport.PrintIt. When the user clicks this button, Access runs the PrintIt submacro in the DoReport macro object. After you specify a macro name in an event property, you can click the Build button next to the property, and Access opens that macro in the Logic Designer.

Understanding Conditional Expressions

In some macros, you might want to execute some actions only under certain conditions. For example, you might want to update a record, but only if new values in the controls on a form pass validation tests; or you might want to display or hide certain controls based on the value of other controls. You can use an If block in macros to test conditions and then perform different actions based on the outcome of the conditional expression.

The PrintIt submacro in the DoReport macro group is a good example of a macro that uses conditions to determine which action should proceed. Right-click the DoReport macro in the Navigation pane, and then click Design View on the shortcut menu to see the Logic Designer, shown in Figure 20-11

As you saw earlier, this macro is triggered by the On Click property of the Print button on the PrintOptions form. This form allows the user to print a specific report by selecting the appropriate option button and then clicking Print. If you look at the form in Design view (see Figure 20-10), you'll see that the option buttons are located within an option group control on the form. Each option button sets a specific numeric value (in this case, 1 for the first button, 2 for the second button, 3 for the third button, and 4 for the fourth button) in the option group, which you can test using an If program flow construct.

As you learned in Chapter 7, when you include an If block in a macro, Access won't run the action on that line unless the condition evaluates to True. The text box next to If is where you type your conditional expression. Each condition is an expression that Access can evaluate to True (nonzero) or False (0 or Null). A condition can also consist of multiple comparison expressions and Boolean operators. If the condition is true, Access executes the action or actions immediately following the Then keyword. If the condition is false, Access evaluates the next Else If condition or executes the statements following the Else keyword, whichever occurs next. If no Else or Else If condition exists after the Then keyword, Access executes the next action following the End If keyword.

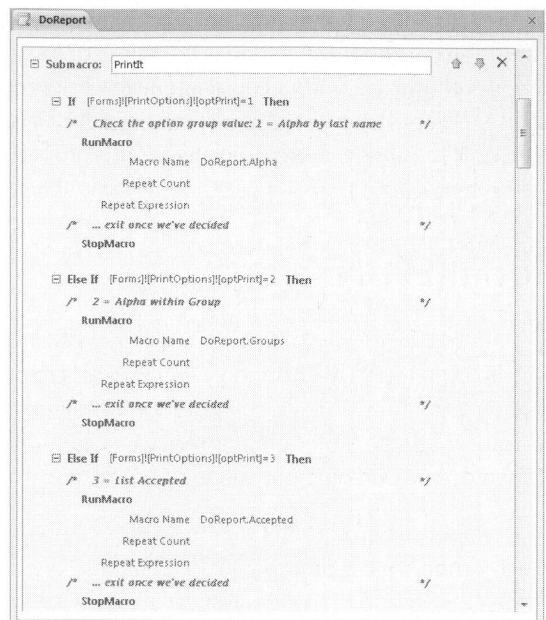

Figure 20-11 In the PrintIt submacro, you can see that we added an If block in the DoReport macro group.

In this particular example, the expressions next to If and the three Else If conditions in the PrintIt submacro test the value of the option group control on the form. You can reference any control on an open form by using the syntax

```
FORMS!formname!controlname
```

where *formname* is the name of an open form and *controlname* is the name of a control on that form. In this case, the direct reference is *[FORMS]![PrintOptions]![optPrint]*. (*optPrint* is the name of the option group control. You can see this in the Name property on the Other tab of the property sheet for this control.) See "Referencing Form and Report Objects," on page 1229, for more details about the rules for referencing objects in Access.

INSIDE OUT **When to Use Brackets**

If your object names do not contain any embedded blanks or other special characters, you don't need to surround *formname* or *controlname* with brackets when you use this syntax to reference a control on a form; Access inserts the brackets as needed.

After you understand how to refer to the value of a control on a form, you can see that the PrintIt submacro tests for each of the possible values of the option group control. When it finds a match, PrintIt runs the appropriate named submacro within the macro object to open the requested report and then stops. If you look at the individual report macros, you'll see that each runs a common submacro, DoReport.Cancel, to close the PrintOptions form (which isn't needed after the user chooses a report) and then open the requested report in Print Preview and put the focus on the window that displays the report.

Using Embedded Macros

Access 2010 includes a feature to create *embedded macros* in the event procedures for forms, reports, and controls. The macros you have been creating and opening thus far in this chapter are macro objects that you can access from the Navigation pane. You save embedded macros, however, within the event procedures for forms and reports. You cannot see or run these macros directly from the Navigation pane. You can think of embedded macros as similar to data macros in that data macros are not objects seen in the Navigation pane, they are attached to table events.

Editing an Embedded Macro

To edit an embedded macro, you must first open a form or report in Design or Layout view. The fdlgNotTrusted form in the Wedding List Macro database contains two embedded macros, each of which is attached to the Click event of one of the two command buttons. Select this form in the Navigation pane, and open it in Design view. Click the Property Sheet button in the Tools group on the Design tab to open the form's property sheet. Next, click the Print These Instructions command button or select cmdPrint from the selection list on the property sheet to view the properties for this command button, as shown in Figure 20-12.

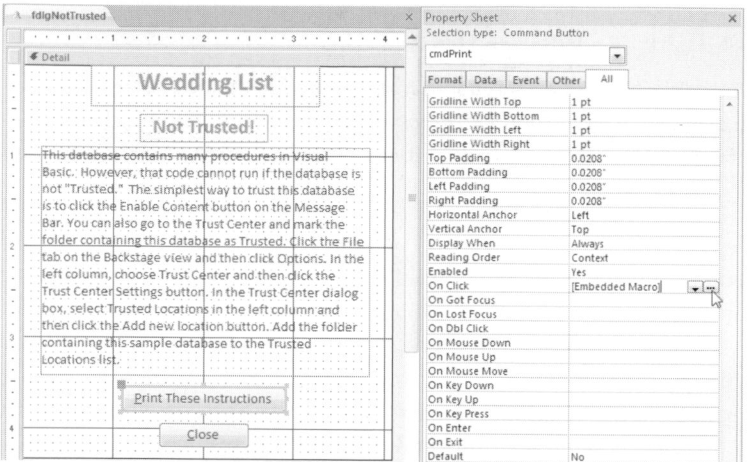

Figure 20-12 The property sheet lists any embedded macros attached to events.

Notice that [Embedded Macro] appears in the On Click property—this indicates that a macro is stored with the form design that responds to this event. To view and edit the macro attached to this event property, click the Build button on the right side of this property line. Access opens the Logic Designer, as shown in Figure 20-13. Notice that in the tab at the top of the macro design surface, Access displays the name of the form, the object name the embedded macro is attached to (in this case, the cmdPrint command button), and the specific event of the object that runs the embedded macro.

You'll notice Access automatically collapsed the Navigation pane to show you more of the macro designer surface. Access also opens the Logic Designer window modally when you are working with embedded macros, which means you cannot open any other database objects until you close the designer window.

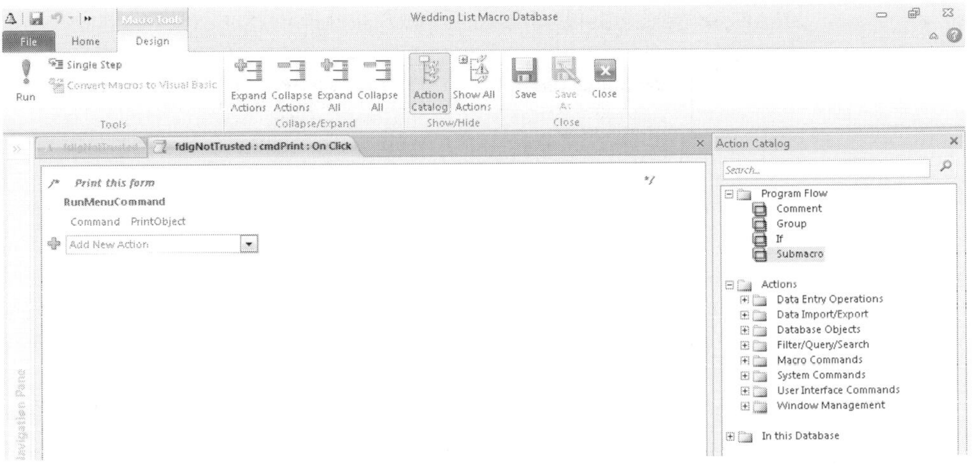

Figure 20-13 The Logic Designer shows the embedded macro that we created to respond to the Click event of the cmdPrint button on the fdlgNotTrusted form.

With the Logic Designer open, you can now view and edit the macro conditions (not used in this sample macro), actions, arguments, and comments. For the cmdPrint command button, you can see we attached a simple macro that executes the RunMenuCommand action. In the Command argument, we selected the PrintObject command, which tells Access to print the object that has the focus—in this case, the fdlgNotTrusted form. The application displays this form only if the database is not trusted. We provide this print button so that you can print the instructions for creating a trusted location displayed on the form.

Close the Logic Designer for this embedded macro by clicking the Close button in the Close group on the Design tab, and then click the Close command button on the form (or select cmdCancel from the selection list). You'll see [Embedded Macro] displayed in the On Click property for this command button. Click the Build button for this property to open the Logic Designer shown in Figure 20-14. This embedded macro uses the CloseWindow action to tell Access to close the fdlgNotTrusted form when the user clicks this command button.

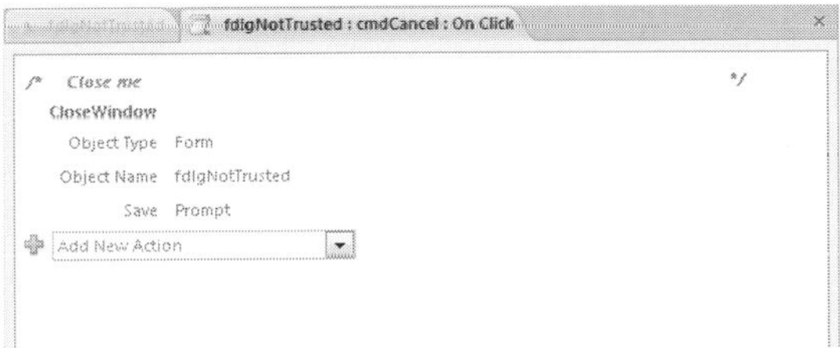

Figure 20-14 The Close button on the fdlgNotTrusted form executes an embedded macro to close the form.

We set the Save argument of the Close action to Prompt, which instructs Access to ask the user whether any changes to the form design should be saved on closing. (The form opens in Form view, so the user shouldn't be able to make any changes.) We selected this setting because choosing any other option causes the Close action to be not trusted. We'll discuss actions that are not trusted later in this chapter.

The two embedded macros you've seen on this form are simple macros with only one action each. You're not limited to using only one action in an embedded macro. You can create a very complex macro, such as the DoReport macro you saw previously in this chapter, with several macro actions using several conditions. However, there is one important difference when designing a complex embedded macro. If you create named submacros in an embedded macro, Access executes only the actions defined in the first submacro when the event to which this macro responds occurs. To execute the additional named submacros inside the embedded macro, you must create a call within the first set of actions to tell Access to execute the other submacros—as the DoReport macro object demonstrated earlier in this chapter.

INSIDE OUT **Embedded Macros Stay with Their Controls**

If you attach embedded macros to a specific control on a form or report, Access saves the macro with the control. If you cut or copy this control to the Clipboard and then paste it back on the form or report, Access keeps the embedded macro attached to the control.

Creating an Embedded Macro

Close the Logic Designer if you still have it open, and let's create a new embedded macro to display a message box when this form opens. From the list under Selection Type near the top of the property sheet, select Form to display all the properties of the form. Click the Event tab, and then click the On Open property. To create a new embedded macro, click the Build button at the right end of the property. Access opens the Choose Builder dialog box, as shown in Figure 20-15.

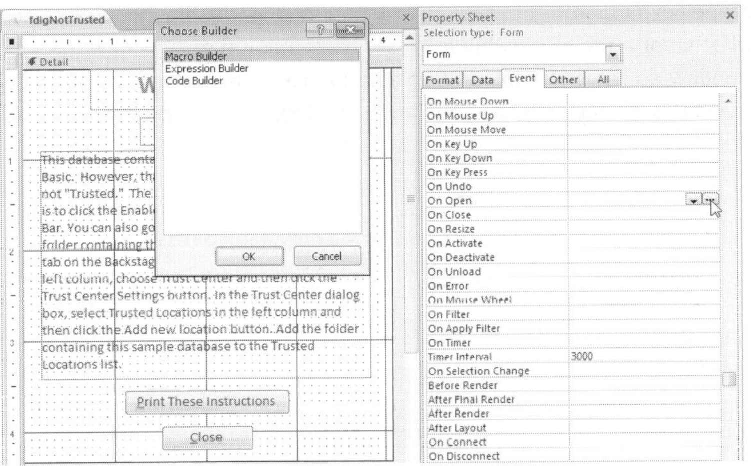

Figure 20-15 Select Macro Builder in the Choose Builder dialog box to create an embedded macro.

If you select the Macro Builder option, Access opens the Logic Designer window, where you can create your embedded macro. If you select Expression Builder, Access opens the Expression Builder dialog box, where you can build an expression to enter in the property. If you select Code Builder, Access opens the Visual Basic Editor, where you can write a Visual Basic code procedure for this event property. (We'll discuss Visual Basic in Chapter 24, "Understanding Visual Basic Fundamentals," and Chapter 25, "Automating Your Application with Visual Basic," on the companion CD.) Select the Macro Builder option, and then click OK to begin creating a new embedded macro.

To display a message box, select MessageBox in the Add New Action combo box. In the Message argument, enter the following text:

This database is not trusted, so it cannot execute all the code needed to automate this application. Please read and follow the instructions displayed in the form that opens after you close this message in order to have the application function properly.

In the Beep argument, leave the default setting Yes, and change the Type argument to Warning! to provide a visual cue that something is wrong and call attention to the message. In the Title argument, enter **Embedded Macro Test**. Your finished macro should look something like Figure 20-16.

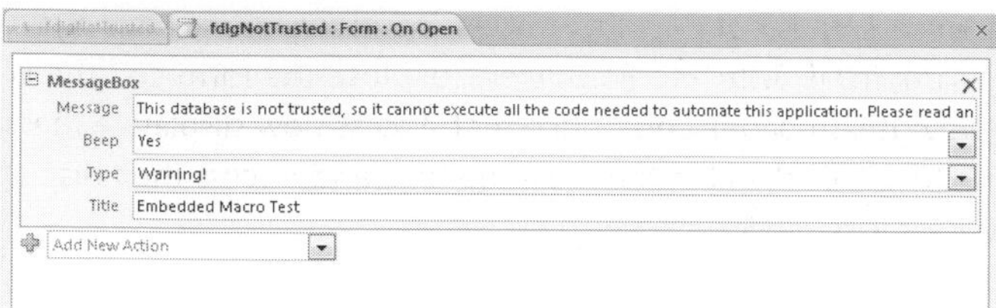

Figure 20-16 The MessageBox action displays a message box in Access.

INSIDE OUT Enabling the Choose Builder Dialog Box

In Chapter 24, you'll learn that you can select [Event Procedure] from the list in an event property and then click the Build button to open the Visual Basic Editor to create the appropriate procedure. Unfortunately, there is no corresponding [Embedded Macro] option that you could use in the same way to create a macro to respond to the event. You also cannot type [Embedded Macro] in the property and click Build. You must leave the property blank, click Build, and choose Macro Builder in the Choose Builder dialog box.

But there's a catch. To see the Choose Builder dialog box, you must not select the Always Use Event Procedures check box in the Form/Report Design View section in the Object Designers category of the Access Options dialog box. (The option is cleared by default.) If you select that check box, Access always opens the Visual Basic Editor window when you click the Build button in any event property. When you're working with client forms and client reports, the only way to create a new embedded macro is to select Macro Builder in the Choose Builder dialog box. If you intend to use embedded macros, you must leave the Always Use Event Procedures option cleared.

Click the Save button on the Quick Access Toolbar to save this new embedded macro, and then close the Logic Designer window. You'll notice that Access now displays [Embedded Macro] on the On Open property line. Note that if you don't click Save before closing the macro design window, Access prompts you to save the changes and update the property.

If you click No, Access does not save the embedded macro. Click Save again to save the changes to the form itself. Switch to Form view (or close the form and then open it in Form view from the Navigation pane), and notice that Access now displays a message box, as shown in Figure 20-17. Click OK in the message box, and Access then displays the not trusted form. Click Close to close the form.

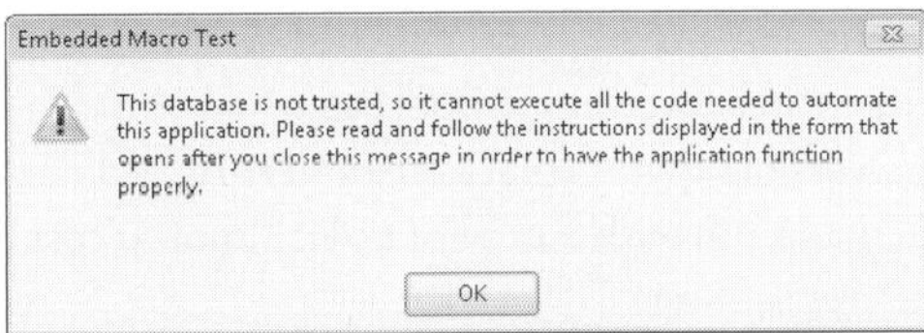

Figure 20-17 Your embedded macro now displays a message box before the form opens.

Deleting an Embedded Macro

If you need to delete a saved macro object, you can easily delete it in the Navigation pane. For embedded macros, however, you need to delete the contents in the specific property. Open the fdlgNotTrusted form again in Design view, and then open the property sheet for the form. To delete the message box embedded macro you just created, find the On Open property on the Event tab, highlight [Embedded Macro], and then press Delete to delete the embedded macro. Click the Save button on the Quick Access Toolbar to save your changes, and then close the form.

CAUTION!

Access does not warn you that it deletes the macro associated with an event property when you clear the property setting. You also cannot undo clearing the property to get the macro back. If you delete a complex macro that was previously saved in the form design, click the File tab on the Backstage view, and click Save Object As to save the form with a new name (or close the form without saving if you're willing to discard other changes). You can then open the original form in Design view to recover the macro. Remember that when you copy and paste a control from one form to another, Access also pastes any attached embedded macros, so you can copy the control and its macro from the old form to the new one to get the macro back in the new form.

INSIDE OUT **Embedded Macros Won't Work with Earlier Versions of Access**

If you create a database in the .mdb file format, Access 2010 allows you to create embedded macros for forms, reports, and controls just like you can in an .accdb file format database. But if you open the .mdb database with an earlier version of Access—2000, 2002, or 2003—the embedded macros do not function. In fact, you cannot see any [Embedded Macro] entries for event properties when you open an .mdb database with an earlier Access version. If you create an .mdb format database using Access 2010 that will be opened and run with a previous version of Access, do not create embedded macros for your application.

Using Temporary Variables

You can use a temporary variable in Access to store a value that can be used in other macros, event procedures, expressions, and queries. As you'll learn in Chapter 24, we use a variable to store the user name when you log into the Conrad Systems Contacts and Housing Reservations sample databases. Variables are very useful when you need Access to remember something for later use. You can think of a temporary variable in a macro as writing yourself a note to remember a number, a name, or an address so that you can recall it at a later time. All variables have a unique name. To fetch, set, or examine a variable, you reference it by its name. Temporary variables stay in memory until you close the database, assign a new value, or clear the value.

To see an example of using a temporary variable in the Wedding List Macro sample database, open the ValidateCitySetStateAndZip macro in Design view. We'll study this macro in more detail in "Validating Data and Presetting Values," on page 1239, but for now, we'll focus on creating a temporary variable. Creating a temporary variable in a macro is easy—Access creates the variable for you when you reference it for the first time in a SetTempVar action. In Figure 20-18, you can see that in the AskEdit submacro in the ValidateCitySetStateAndZip macro object, we created a new temporary variable called AddFlag and set its value to True in the Expression argument.

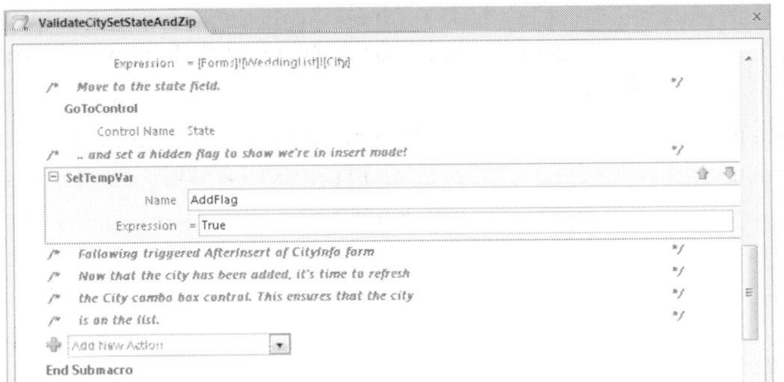

Figure 20-18 The AskEdit submacro in the ValidateCitySetStateAndZip macro uses a temporary variable to indicate that the CityInformation form has been opened in data entry mode.

The AskEdit submacro runs from the BeforeUpdate event of the City combo box on the WeddingList form when the user enters a new city name that isn't in the row source. The macro first executes a MsgBox function in the condition of the first action to ask the user whether the new city should be added. If the user clicks the Yes button in the dialog box displayed by the MsgBox function, the function returns the value 6. (We'll explain more about the MsgBox function later.) If the user clicks No, the macro halts. When the user clicks Yes, the submacro calls the IsFormLoaded custom Visual Basic function (in the modUtility module object) to determine whether the CityInformation form is open. If it is, the submacro closes it. The submacro then opens the CityInformation form in data entry mode and copies the new city name from the WeddingList form to the CityInformation form.

The application uses the AddFlag variable to let code in another macro know that this macro has closed and reopened the CityInformation form in data entry mode. The RefreshCityList submacro that executes in response to the AfterInsert event in the CityInformation form is also stored in the ValidateCitySetStateAndZip macro. The RefreshCityList submacro tests the AddFlag variable set in the AskEdit submacro. Scroll down the macro design surface until you come to the RefreshCityList submacro, as shown in Figure 20-19.

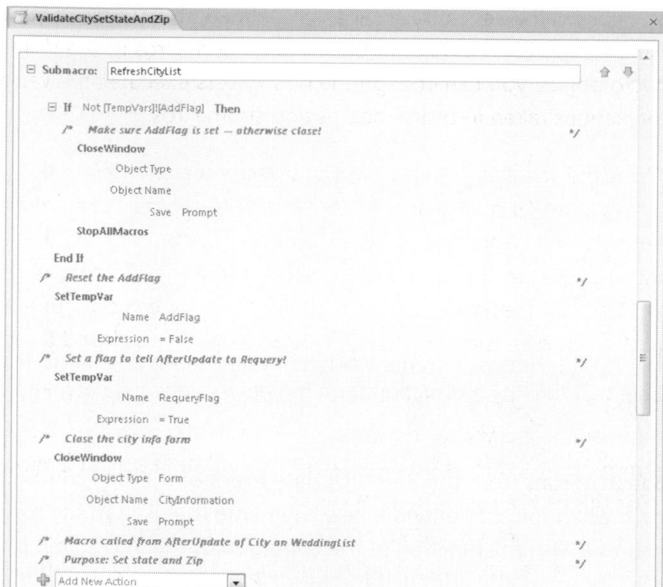

Figure 20-19 The RefreshCityList submacro in the ValidateCitySetStateAndZip macro tests and sets temporary variables.

In the If conditional expression for the first action in this submacro, you can see the following expression:

```
Not [TempVars]![AddFlag]
```

This test checks to see whether the AddFlag temporary variable has been set. If not, then the user must be using the CityInformation form to add a new record independent of the WeddingList form, so the submacro closes the form and stops (the StopAllMacros action). If the AddFlag temporary variable is true, the submacro resets the AddFlag temporary variable to False, sets another temporary variable, RequeryFlag, to let the macro that responds to the AfterUpdate event of the City combo box to do a requery, and closes the CityInformation form.

Note the special syntax you need to use to reference a temporary variable anywhere other than in an action specifically related to temporary variables. When you create a temporary variable in a macro, Access adds the variable to the special collection of the database called TempVars. When an object is a member of a collection (Access treats temporary variables as objects), you can reference the object by naming the collection, using an exclamation point separator, and then naming the object. So, to reference a temporary variable in macros, queries, event procedures, and even Visual Basic code, use the following syntax:

```
[TempVars]![<name of temporary variable>]
```

You can have as many as 255 temporary variables defined at any time in your Access 2010 database. By using temporary variables in the various submacros in the ValidateCitySet-StateAndZip macro object, you can change the way Access executes the various macro actions based on actions taken in other macros and submacros.

If you need to clear the value stored in a temporary variable and delete the variable, you can use the RemoveTempVar macro action. The RemoveTempVar action requires only one argument—Name—and it clears any value stored in the temporary variable of that name and then deletes the variable. If you need to delete all temporary variables from memory, you can use the RemoveAllTempVars action. This action requires no arguments because it clears all temporary variables, similar to what would occur if you closed the database.

Although removing a temporary variable technically deletes it from the TempVars collection, you won't get an error if you attempt to reference a temporary variable that doesn't exist. If you attempt to fetch the value of a nonexistent temporary variable, Access returns the value Null. For this reason, you should be careful when naming and using temporary variables. If you set a temporary variable in one macro and then think you're referencing the same variable in another macro but slightly misspell the variable name, you won't get the results you expect.

Note

Access 2010 allows you to create temporary variables in macros if you save your database in the .mdb file format. If, however, you open the .mdb database with an earlier version of Access—2000, 2002, or 2003—the temporary variables do not function, and you will receive error messages when your macros run. If you have users still using previous Access versions, do not use temporary variables created in macros for your application.

Trapping Errors in Macros

Access 2010 supports trapping and handling errors within macros. During the normal process of running your application, Access can (and most likely will) encounter errors. Access might encounter errors in your code that it cannot resolve—such as a syntax error in a predicate used to filter a form. In those cases, Access cannot proceed further. Other errors might occur that are not quite so catastrophic but happen in the normal processing of your application. For example, you might use the OnNoData event of a report to display a message box saying no records were found. If your code then cancels the report from opening, Access returns an error if a subsequent action attempts to reference the report that didn't open. If there's no error trap in the macro, Access displays an ugly and confusing dialog box to the user.

To see how error trapping works in Access 2010, close the ValidateCitySetStateAndZip macro and then open the ErrorTrapExample macro in Design view. We created this simple macro specifically to show you two things—how Access handles an unexpected error with no error trapping and how you can trap and respond to an error. In Figure 20-20, you can see some of the submacro names, conditional expressions, actions, and arguments for this example macro.

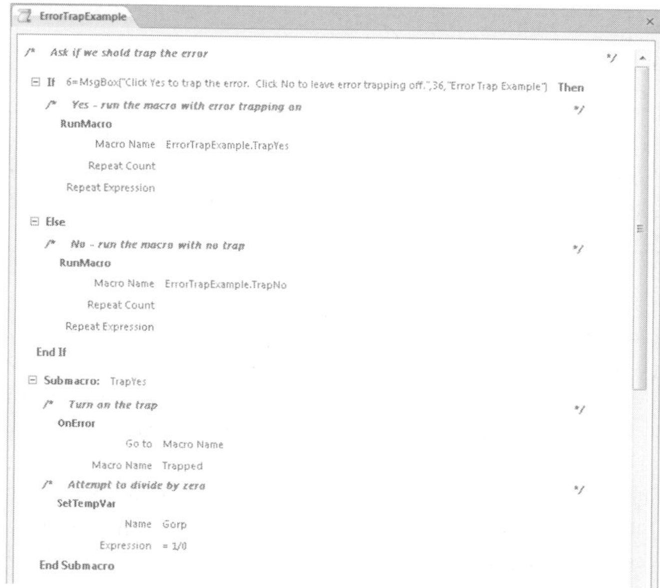

Figure 20-20 The ErrorTrapExample macro demonstrates error handling in Access 2010.

In the first action of the macro, we call the MsgBox function in the If conditional expression to ask whether you want to use error trapping. (You can learn more about the settings in the MsgBox function in Table 20-4 on page 1243.) If you click the Yes button in the dialog box displayed by MsgBox, the function returns the value 6. So when you click Yes, the condition is True, and the RunMacro action calls the TrapYes submacro. If you click No, the condition is False, so Access moves down to the Else block and executes the second RunMacro that calls the TrapNo submacro.

The first action in the TrapYes submacro uses the OnError macro action to tell Access how it should proceed if any error occurs. The OnError action has two arguments—Go To and Macro Name. The options in the Go To argument are Next, Macro Name, and Fail. If you select Next in the Go To argument, Access does not halt the macro when an error occurs—it simply goes on to the next action. If you select Macro Name in the Go To argument, Access runs the submacro you specify in the Macro Name argument. If you select Fail, you're basically turning error trapping off.

In all cases, Access records the error number and error description information in the MacroError object. If you have trapped the error by specifying Macro Name or Next, you can examine the error in an If conditional expression to determine what action, if any, to take. For simple errors (such as an OpenReport that might be canceled), you can choose Next and check to see whether an error has occurred in an If block on the next action. For more complex errors, you should go to another submacro that can test for several potential errors that you plan to handle. In this example, we tell Access to run the Trapped submacro if any errors occur.

Note

If you specify a submacro name in the Go To argument of the OnError action, the submacro must exist in the same macro object. You cannot reference a submacro in a different macro object when using the OnError action.

The next line in the TrapYes macro uses the SetTempVar action to create a temporary variable named Gorp and set it to an invalid mathematical expression of 1/0—dividing by zero will cause an error. Because we asked Access to trap any error, Access runs the Trapped submacro when the error occurs. Although we could have examined the error and perhaps taken some other action, for this simple example, we used a MessageBox action to tell Access to display a message containing the error number and description of the error. Scroll down the macro design surface, select this MessageBox action, and notice the following text in the Message argument:

```
="Error Trapped: " & [MacroError].[Number] & ", " & [MacroError].[Description]
```

All errors in Access have both a unique error number and a description. When an error occurs in a macro, the Number property of the MacroError object contains the error number, and the Description property of the MacroError object contains text describing the error associated with the number. The Message argument of the MessageBox action asks Access to fetch the Number and Description properties of the MacroError object and display them in the message.

Finally, the TrapNo submacro executes the assignment of an invalid value to a temporary variable without first setting an error trap. To see how this process works, click the Run button in the Tools group on the Design tab. Because the first action contains a call to the MsgBox function in the If conditional expression, Access displays the message box shown in Figure 20-21, asking whether you want to trap the error as part of evaluating the condition.

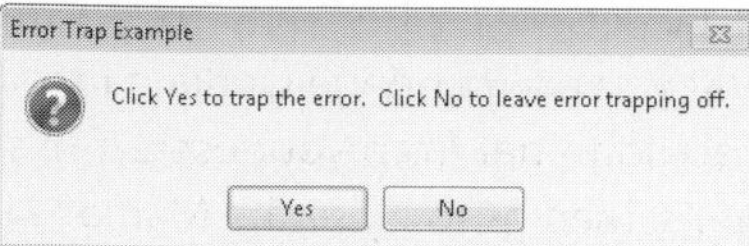

Figure 20-21 When you run the ErrorTrapExample macro, it first asks you whether you want to trap the error.

Click No to see what happens when the error isn't trapped. First, Access displays a message box telling you the nature of the error, as shown in Figure 20-22.

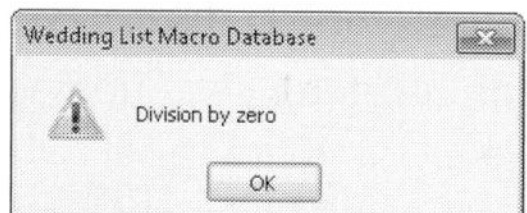

Figure 20-22 Access cannot divide a number by zero, so it displays an application error message.

Click OK in this error message, and then Access displays the Macro Single Step dialog box, as shown in Figure 20-23. Not very user friendly, is it? Access displays the Macro Single Step dialog box whenever it encounters an unhandled error while running a macro. Access displays the specifics of where the error occurred in the Macro Name, Condition, Action Name, and Arguments text boxes. Access displays the error number currently stored in the MacroError object in the Error Number text box—in this case, error number 11.

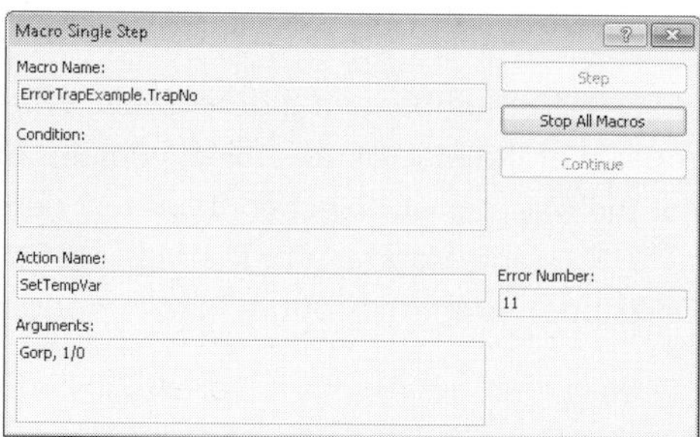

Figure 20-23 Access displays the Macro Single Step dialog box if it encounters an unhandled error.

The only button you can click in this dialog box is Stop All Macros. When you click this button, Access stops running the macro so that you can continue working in your application. You can imagine the support calls you're going to get from your users if this dialog box displays often in your applications. Click Stop All Macros to close the Macro Single Step dialog box.

Now, let's see what happens when the macro traps the error. Run the macro again, and click Yes when the code asks you whether you want to trap the error. This runs the TrapYes submacro (shown earlier in Figure 20-20), which executes OnError, followed by the SetTempVar action that generates an error. Access traps the error and executes the Trapped submacro as requested. That submacro asks Access to display another message box with the error number and description, as shown in Figure 20-24. Notice that Access displays the error number (11) and error description (Division By Zero) in the message text.

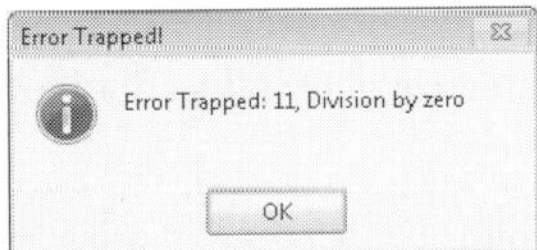

Figure 20-24 By trapping an error in a macro, you can display a helpful message to the user.

In a completed application, you probably would not need to display the error details to the user, but for debugging your application, the information in the MacroError object can be very useful. For a user, it could be more informative to display a message such as "While attempting to calculate a value, the application divided a number by zero. Please recheck the numbers you entered before proceeding."

Click OK in the message box, and notice what happens when you do trap the error—nothing! Because we trapped the error, Access does not display the confusing Macro Single Step dialog box.

Earlier in this chapter, you saw the DoReport macro that is used with the PrintOptions form. This macro also uses error trapping to handle the possibility that a report might not contain any records. Close the ErrorTrapExample macro, and then open the DoReport macro in Design view. In the Groups, Alpha, Accepted, and PrintF submacros, you can see that we used the OnError action just before each OpenReport action. Scroll down until you can see the PrintF submacro, as shown in Figure 20-25.

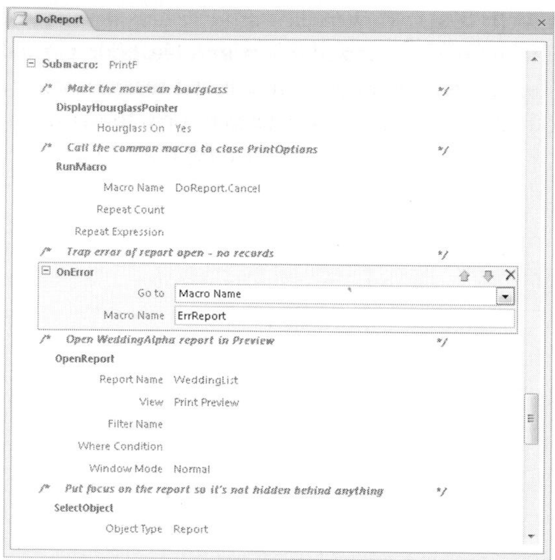

Figure 20-25 The DoReport macro uses the OnError action to handle the possibility that no records are returned in the report.

The first action of the submacro turns the mouse pointer into an hourglass. The second action calls the Cancel submacro that closes the PrintOptions form and puts the focus back on the WeddingList form. The third action sets the error trap. We selected Macro Name in the Go To argument and ErrReport in the Macro Name argument to tell Access to go to the ErrReport submacro if any errors occur. The fourth action attempts to open the report.

In each of the four reports in this sample database, the On No Data event property specifies the NoRecords submacro. When the report has no records, this macro executes the CancelEvent action to prevent the report from opening. If the report opening is canceled, Access encounters an error on the next action of our submacro—SelectObject. Access cannot put the focus on a report that isn't opened, so we need to plan for this possibility. Because we're trapping all errors, the user won't see the ugly Macro Single Step dialog box. Instead, the ErrReport submacro runs, and this submacro restores the mouse pointer and displays an informative message telling the user that the report requested has no records.

To test how this works, close the DoReport macro, and then open the WeddingList form in Form view. Click the Print button on this form to open the PrintOptions form. On the PrintOptions form, select List Invitees Who Have Accepted. Unless you have changed the sample data, this report should return no records. Click Print to run the PrintIt submacro in the DoReport macro group. This submacro looks at the option you chose on the PrintOptions form and runs the Accepted submacro. That submacro attempts to open the WeddingAccepted report with a filter to return only the records where the value in the Accepted field is greater than zero.

Because no records qualify, the NoData event in the WeddingAccepted report runs the NoRecords submacro and cancels the opening of the report. Next, the submacro attempts to set the focus on the WeddingAccepted report. Because the report is now closed, this causes an error—2489, if you're curious—that Access returns to the submacro that attempted to set the focus. Because we turned on error trapping, the ErrReport submacro displays a message to inform you that no records were found in the report, as shown in Figure 20-26.

Figure 20-26 The error handling in the DoReport submacro presents an informative message if the report contains no records.

If you want to see what happens when the error isn't trapped, open the DoReport macro object, scroll down to the Accepted submacro, and change the Go To argument to Fail for the OnError action so that the error trap isn't set, and save the macro. Try to run the report again from the WeddingList form, and you'll see the ugly error messages that result when you don't trap the error. Be sure to change the Go To argument back to Macro Name in the OnError action of the Accepted submacro and save it again so that the application works properly.

If you want to use macros in your application, you should add appropriate error handling using the OnError action. A well-designed Access application should always display helpful messages to users when errors occur.

INSIDE OUT **Clearing the MacroError Object**

The MacroError object contains only the information from the last reported error. Access retains this information in the MacroError object until either the macro stops running, another error occurs, or you run the ClearMacroError action. If you need to continue running your macro after an error is handled and expect to possibly test the MacroError object again (perhaps after setting OnError to Next), you can use the ClearMacroError action to clear the contents of the MacroError object. The ClearMacroError action requires no arguments.

Understanding Macro Actions That Are Not Trusted

Earlier in this chapter, we mentioned that Access 2010 has trusted and not trusted macro actions. As you might recall from Chapter 2, "Exploring the Access 2010 Interface," the Trust Center settings in the Access Options dialog box control whether Access disables certain content in your database. If your database is not trusted, Access might silently disable any potentially malicious macros or Visual Basic for Applications (VBA) code depending upon the Trust Center settings you enabled or disabled. So, what exactly is a malicious macro? In Microsoft's terms, a malicious macro runs an action that could potentially do harm to your computer or files, such as deleting a file.

Access 2010 separates client macro actions into two categories—those that will run in any database, even in a database that is not trusted (trusted macros), and those that can run only in a database that is trusted (not trusted macros). Note that if you select Enable All Macros in the Trust Center Macro Settings section (not recommended by Microsoft), Access treats all macro actions as trusted even when the database is not trusted. (In Chapter 21, you'll learn that all web macro actions are trusted.)

Note

If you are in a corporate network environment, you should check with your IT department to determine whether your company has established guidelines concerning enabling content in Access databases.

Access 2010 recognizes 27 client macro actions as potentially unsafe to run in a database that is not trusted. Seven of the actions are not trusted only when you select certain arguments. Table 20-1 lists the client macro actions that Access will run only when the database is trusted. The Comments column lists special cases that depend on the arguments you choose or an alternative trusted method you can use.

Table 20-1 Macro Actions That Are Not Trusted

Action	Comments
CloseWindow	Setting the Save argument to Prompt is trusted.
CopyObject	
DeleteObject	
Echo	
ImportExportData	
ImportExportSpreadsheet	
ImportExportText	
ImportSharePointList	
OpenForm	Setting the View argument to Design or Layout is not trusted.
OpenQuery	Setting the View argument to Design is not trusted.
OpenReport	Setting the View argument to Print, Design, or Layout is not trusted.
OpenSharePointList	
OpenSharePointRecycleBin	
OpenTable	Setting the View argument to Design is not trusted.
OpenVisualBasicModule	
PrintOut	
QuitAccess	Setting the Options argument to Prompt is trusted.
RenameObject	
RunApplication	
RunMenuCommand	Commands that affect objects in Design or Layout view are not trusted.
RunSavedImportExport	
RunSQL	
SaveObject	
SendKeys	
SetValue	Use the trusted SetProperty action instead of SetValue to change the Enabled, Visible, Locked, Left, Top, Width, Height, Fore Color, Back Color, and Caption properties of forms, reports, or controls.
SetWarnings	
ShowToolbar	

INSIDE OUT Using Older Macro Action Names

In Access 2010, some macro actions from previous versions of Access have been renamed. For example, the TransferText macro action is now named ImportExportText, and the MsgBox action is now named MessageBox. If you open a database created in an earlier version of Access in Access 2010, you'll see the new macro action name displayed on the macro design surface. If you type the older macro name in the Add New Action combo box and press Enter, Access displays the action on the macro design surface. However, you'll note that Access displays the new action name on the action block. Your existing macros created in previous versions will run in Access 2010, but you should use the new action names when designing new macros. See Article 6 on the companion CD for a list of older macro names and their new equivalents in Access 2010.

Note that when you select a client macro action or argument that is not trusted, Access displays an exclamation mark in the upper-left corner of the action block on the macro design surface. Access also displays an exclamation mark to the left of any untrusted action names displayed in the Action Catalog, as shown in Figure 20-27. When you're designing your macros, you can use these visual aides to easily see whether any of your client macro actions will not run in a database that is not trusted.

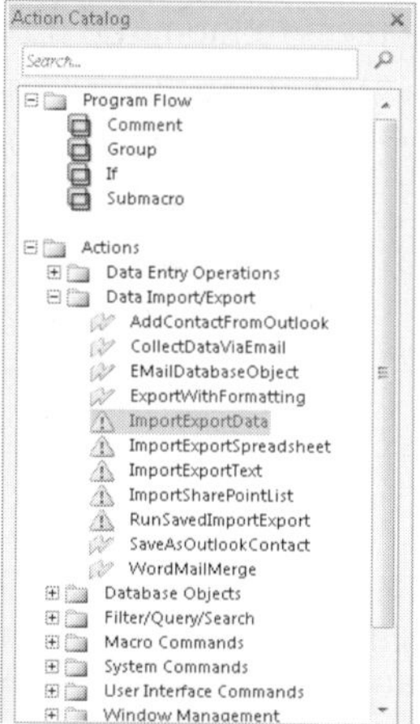

Figure 20-27 Client macro actions that are not trusted display an exclamation mark next to the action name in the Action Catalog.

Making Your Application Come Alive with Macros

Throughout this book, you've learned how to perform common tasks by using ribbon commands or by finding the object you want in the Navigation pane and opening it. In working with your database, you've probably also noticed that you perform certain tasks repeatedly or on a regular basis. You can automate these tasks by creating macros to execute the actions you perform and then associating the macros with various form or control events, such as the Current event of a form, the Click event of a command button, or the DblClick event of a text box. In the following sections, you'll use examples from the Wedding List Macro sample database (WeddingMC.accdb) to understand how macros can help automate your application.

Referencing Form and Report Objects

As you create macros to automate tasks that you repeat frequently, you'll often need to refer to a report, a form, or a control on a form to set its properties or values. Before we dig into some of the macros in the Wedding List Macro, you need to know how to code these references. You can find the syntax for referencing reports, forms, report and form properties, controls, and control properties in the following sections.

Rules for Referencing Forms and Reports

You can refer to a form or a report by name, but you must first tell Access which collection contains the named object. Open forms are in the Forms collection, and open reports are in the Reports collection. To reference a form or a report, you follow the collection name with an exclamation point to separate it from the name of the object to which you are referring. You must enclose an object name that contains blank spaces or special characters in brackets ([ ]). If the object name contains no blanks or special characters, you can simply enter the name. However, it's a good idea to always enclose an object name in brackets so that your name reference syntax is consistent.

For example, you refer to a form named WeddingList as follows:

```
Forms![WeddingList]
```

You refer to a report named WeddingList as follows:

```
Reports![WeddingList]
```

Rules for Referencing Form and Report Properties

To reference a property of a form or a report, follow the form or report name with a period and the property name. You can see a list of most property names for a form or a report by opening the form or the report in Design or Layout view and displaying the property sheet while you have the form or the report selected. With macros, you can change most form or report properties while the form is in Form view, or from the Print, Format, and Paint events of a client report as Access prints or displays it.

You refer to the Scroll Bars property of a form named CityInformation as follows:

```
Forms![CityInformation].ScrollBars
```

You refer to the Caption property of a report named CityInformation as follows:

```
Reports![CityInformation].Caption
```

> **Note**
>
> **The names of properties do not contain embedded blank spaces, even though the property sheet shows blanks within names. For example, BackColor is the name of the property listed as Back Color in the property sheet.**

Rules for Referencing Form and Report Controls and Their Properties

To reference a control on a form or a report, follow the form or report name with an exclamation point and then the control name enclosed in brackets. To reference a property of a control, follow the control name with a period and the name of the property. You can see a list of most property names for controls by opening a form or a report in Design or Layout view, selecting a control (note that different control types have different properties), and opening its property sheet. You can change most control properties while the form is in Design view.

You refer to a control named State on the WeddingList form as follows:

```
Forms![WeddingList]![State]
```

You refer to the Visible property of a control named Accepted on a report named WeddingList as follows:

```
Reports![WeddingList]![Accepted].Visible
```

Rules for Referencing Subforms and Subreports

When you embed a subform in a form or a report, the subform is contained in a *subform control*. A subreport embedded in a client report is contained in a *subreport control*. You can reference a subform control or a subreport control exactly as you would any other control on a form or a report. For example, suppose you have a subform called RelativesSub embedded in the WeddingList form. You refer to the subform control on the WeddingList form as follows:

```
Forms![WeddingList]![RelativesSub]
```

Likewise, you can reference properties of a subform or a subreport by following the control name with a period and the name of the property. You refer to the Visible property of the RelativesSub subform control as follows:

```
Forms![WeddingList]![RelativesSub].Visible
```

Subform controls have a special Form property that lets you reference the form that's contained in the subform control. Likewise, subreport controls have a special Report property that lets you reference the report contained in the subreport control. You can follow this special property name with the name of a control on the subform or the subreport to access the control's contents or properties. For example, you refer to the LastName control on the RelativesSub subform as follows:

```
Forms![WeddingList]![RelativesSub].Form![LastName]
```

You refer to the FontWeight property of the LastName control as follows:

```
Forms![WeddingList]![RelativesSub].Form![LastName].FontWeight
```

Opening a Secondary Form

As you learned in Chapter 12, "Using Forms in an Access Application," it's easier to work with data by using a form. You also learned in Chapter 15, "Advanced Form Design," that you can create multiple-table forms by embedding subforms in a main form, thus allowing you to see related data in the same form. However, it's impractical to use subforms in situations such as the following:

- You need three or more nested subforms to see related data.
- The main form is too small to display the entire subform.
- You need to see the related information only some of the time.

The solution is to use a separate form to see the related data. You can open this form by creating a macro that responds to one of several events. For example, you can use a command button or the DblClick event of a control on the main form to give your users access to the related data in the secondary form. This technique helps reduce screen clutter, makes the main form easier to use, and helps to speed up the main form when you're moving from record to record.

You could use this technique in the WeddingList form. It would be simple to create a macro that would respond to clicking the City Info button by opening the CityInformation form and displaying all records from the CityNames table, including the best airline to take and the approximate flying time from each city to Seattle, Washington. However, if you're talking to your friend Jane in Albuquerque, New Mexico, it would be even more convenient for the CityInformation form to display only Albuquerque-related data rather than the data for all cities. In the following section, you'll create a macro that opens the CityInformation form based on the city that's displayed for the current record in the WeddingList form.

Creating the SeeCityInformation Macro

Open the Wedding List Macro sample database (WeddingMC.accdb) if you've closed it. Click OK in the opening message so that no objects are opened. Click the Macro button in the Macros & Code group on the Create tab to begin creating a new macro object. When the Logic Designer window opens, collapse the Navigation pane. Figure 20-28 shows the macro you are going to create. (If you simply want to view the macro, it is saved as XmplSeeCityInformation in the sample database.)

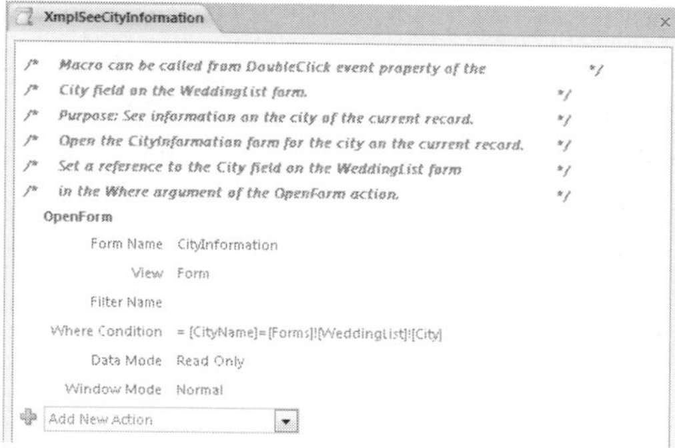

Figure 20-28 When triggered from an event on the WeddingList form, this macro opens the CityInformation form filtered on the city name.

The macro contains only one action, OpenForm. The OpenForm action not only opens the CityInformation form but also applies a filter so that the city that will be displayed matches the city currently displayed in the WeddingList form. Add an OpenForm action to the macro design surface by dragging the action from the Action Catalog or by selecting OpenForm in the Add New Action combo box. In the Where Condition argument, enter the following expression:

```
[CityName]=Forms![WeddingList]![City]
```

The Where Condition argument causes the OpenForm action to open the CityInformation form showing only the rows in the form's record source whose CityName field equals the value currently shown in the City combo box on the open the WeddingList form. (Later, you'll learn how to create a macro to synchronize these two forms as you move to different rows in the WeddingList form.)

Set the rest of the action arguments for the OpenForm action, as shown in Figure 20-28. After you finish creating the action for the macro, it's a good idea to add Comment blocks to the macro design surface to document your macro. Documenting your macro makes it easier to debug, modify, or enhance the macro in the future. It's also easier to read in English what each macro action does rather than have to view the arguments for each action line by line. Refer to Figure 20-28 and enter the information displayed into several Comment blocks. You can see that we've added comments about the macro in general and about the specific action the macro is designed to perform. Click the Save button on the Quick Access Toolbar, and save the macro as SeeCityInformation.

Next, you can associate the macro with the City combo box control on the WeddingList form. Click the WeddingList form in the Navigation pane, right-click the name, and click Design View to open the form in Design view. Click the City combo box control, and then click the Property Sheet button in the Tools group on the Design tab. When the property sheet opens, click the Event tab. You'll want to trigger the SeeCityInformation macro you just created from the DblClick event, so click the On Dbl Click property box, and select the macro from the On Dbl Click event property's drop-down list. You'll find a macro called SeeCityInfo already entered here, as shown in Figure 20-29. We created a slightly different version of the macro and saved it in the form so that the application is fully functional when you first open it. You can change the event property to your macro (SeeCityInformation) to test what you've built.

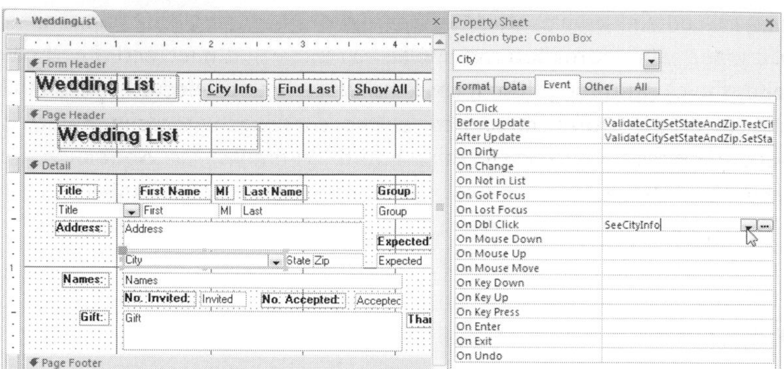

Figure 20-29 Select the macro you created for the DblClick event of the City combo box control.

You can also associate the macro with the City Info button by changing the button's On Click event property to point to the macro. To do this, click Save on the Quick Access Toolbar to save your changes and then switch to Form view. Scroll down one or two records, and double-click the City combo box. The CityInformation form opens, and the data displayed should be for the city in the current record in the WeddingList form. Your screen should look like Figure 20-30.

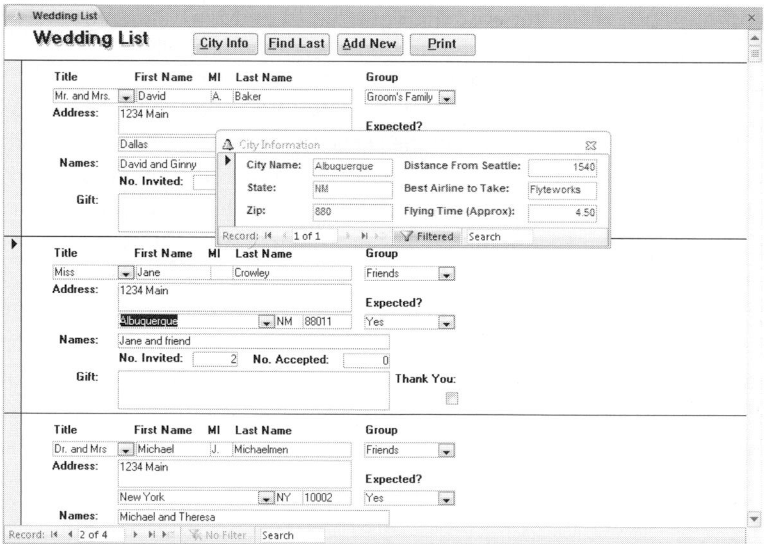

Figure 20-30 The CityInformation form displays a matching city in the WeddingList form.

Linking two related forms in this manner is very useful, but what happens to the data displayed in the CityInformation form when you move to a new record in the WeddingList form? Try scrolling through the records using the record selector. You'll find that the data in the CityInformation form changes as you move through records in the WeddingList form. The data changes because we've set one of the events on the WeddingList form to execute a macro that keeps the data displayed on the two forms synchronized. In the next section, you'll walk through the steps to re-create this macro yourself. Close the two forms that are currently open to continue with the next section.

Synchronizing Two Related Forms

In the previous section, you learned how to open a secondary form from a main form based on matching values of two related fields in the two forms. In the following sections, you'll create a macro that synchronizes the data in a companion form when the selected record changes in a main form.

Creating the SyncWeddingListAndCity Macro

Click the Macro button in the Macros & Code group on the Create tab to start creating a new macro object. Figure 20-31 shows the actions and arguments you'll create for this macro. Note that in Figure 20-31, we collapsed most of the actions so you can see all the macro logic. (You can find this sample macro saved as XmplSyncWeddingAndCity.)

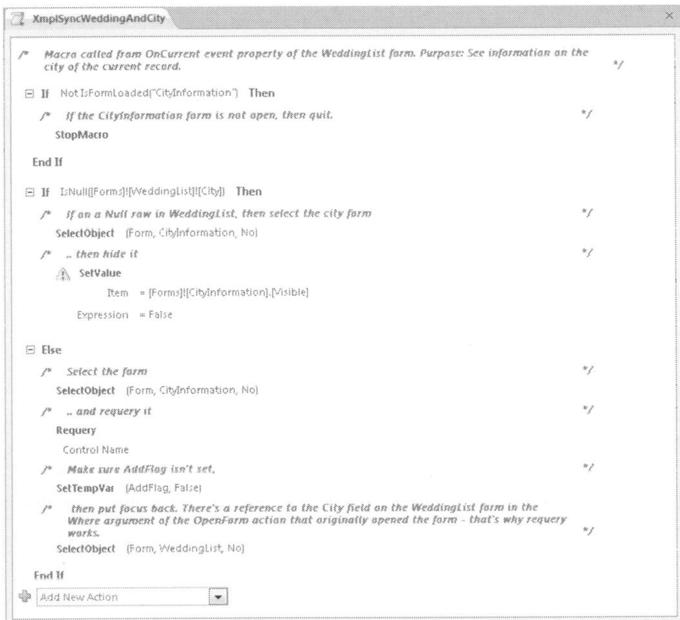

Figure 20-31 You'll create these conditions, actions, and comments for the SyncWeddingAndCity macro.

You'll create this macro in the same basic manner that you created the SeeCityInformation macro. Enter the needed conditional expressions into the two If blocks, and add the actions from the Action Catalog (listed in Table 20-2 in the Action column). Type the associated arguments options, listed in the Setting column in Table 20-2, into the action arguments on the macro design surface. (You can ignore typing in the comments for this example.)

> **Note**
>
> **Some code and expression examples in this chapter are too long to fit on a single printed line. A line that ends with the ➘ symbol means that the code shown on the following line should be entered on the same line.**

Table 20-2 Actions, Arguments, and Settings in SyncWeddingAndCity

If Condition	Action	Argument	Setting
Not IsFormLoaded➘ ("CityInformation")	StopMacro		
IsNull([Forms]!➘ [WeddingList]!➘ [City])	SelectObject	Object Type	Form
		Object Name	CityInformation
		In Database Window	No
	SetValue	Item	[Forms]![CityInformation]. [Visible]
		Expression	False
Else	SelectObject	Object Type	Form
		Object Name	CityInformation
		In Database Window	No
	Requery		
	SetTempVar	Name	AddFlag
		Expression	False
	SelectObject	Object Type	Form
		Object Name	WeddingList
		In Database Window	No

This macro has a couple of If block conditional expressions that determine which parts of the macro execute. The first If block condition uses the IsFormLoaded function, which is included in the modUtility module of the Wedding List Macro database. This function checks to see whether a form (whose name you've provided to the function) is currently open. (The form can be hidden.) The syntax for the function is IsFormLoaded("*formname*"), where *formname* is the name of the form in question. You must enclose the name of the form in double quotation marks for the function to work. The *Not* before the function expression tells Access to evaluate the converse of the True/False value returned from the function. So, this condition will be true only if the form is not loaded. If the companion CityInformation form isn't open, there's nothing to synchronize, so the macro action inside the If block—StopMacro—executes and the macro ends.

Now that we know the companion CityInformation is open, we need to decide whether the value on which that form is filtered is valid. Remember, when you created the SeeCityInformation macro that opens the CityInformation form, you included a Where Condition to filter what's displayed in the CityInformation form to match the city in the current record in the WeddingList form. However, it's a bad idea to reference an empty value in a Where Condition argument. In fact, in some cases you'll get an error message. When you move beyond the last row in the WeddingList form or click New Record under the Go To button in the Find group on the Home tab, you'll be in a new blank row in which the City field has no value. In this case, if you force the CityInformation form to refresh, it will go blank because it's a read-only form and there will be no rows returned if the filter compares to an empty value.

It probably makes more sense to test for an empty, or Null, value and hide the companion form if you're in a new row in the WeddingList form. The second If block conditional expression in this macro uses the IsNull built-in function to check for this condition. If City is Null, the macro hides the CityInformation form by using the SetValue action. We reference the CityInformation form's Visible property in the Item argument and use False in the Expression argument to hide the form. After the macro hides the CityInformation form, the macro ends because the rest of the macro actions exist inside the Else block. Note that the form is still open even though you can't see it. If you move back to a row in the WeddingList form that contains data, this macro executes again, but the actions to hide the CityInformation form will be skipped because the City field won't be Null anymore.

The CityInformation form displays the city details for the current record in the WeddingList form because your macro opened the CityInformation form with a filter pointing to the City control on the WeddingList form. However, the CityInformation form doesn't "know" when you move to a different record in the WeddingList form, so Access never reapplies the filter. Access does save the Where Condition argument you specified in the Filter property of the CityInformation form. To display the appropriate city information when the user moves to a new record in the WeddingList form, all you need to do is requery the CityInformation form to make Access reevaluate the filter. In the Else block of the second If condition, the macro selects the CityInformation form to make sure it has the focus (this also reveals the form if it was hidden) and then executes a Requery action with no value specified in the Control Name argument. With no control name specified, Access knows to requery whatever form or report has the focus.

Finally, the SetTempVar action sets a value that's tested by other macros, and the SelectObject action ensures that the form has the focus after setting the value of the AddFlag temporary variable. We'll explain more about using SetTempVar in "Passing Status Information Between Linked Forms," on page 1245.

After you have the synchronization macro you need, save it as SyncWeddingAndCity. The last step is to associate the macro with the Current event of the WeddingList form. To do that, right-click the WeddingList form in the Navigation pane, and click Design View to open the form in Design view. Click the Property Sheet button in the Tools group on the Design tab to open the property sheet for the form, and then click the On Current property box. Use the list to select your SyncWeddingAndCity macro. (You'll find the example XmplSyncWeddingAndCity macro set in this property in the form.) Your screen should look like the one shown in Figure 20-32.

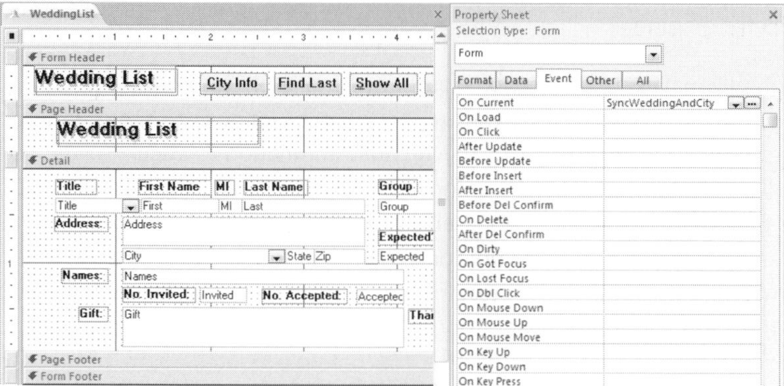

Figure 20-32 Associate the SyncWeddingAndCity macro with the On Current event property of the WeddingList form.

When you finish, save and close the form. Open the form in Form view, double-click the City combo box control and move to the second record. Your screen should look like the one shown in Figure 20-30 on page 1234, assuming that Jane Crowley's record is the current one.

Test the macro by moving through the records in the WeddingList form. As you move from record to record, the data in the CityInformation form should change to reflect the city displayed in the current record of the WeddingList form. If you move to the blank record at the end of the recordset, the CityInformation form disappears. Move back to a row containing data, and it reappears.

Using a macro to synchronize two forms containing related data is a technique that works well with almost any set of forms, and you can use it in a number of situations. In the next section, you'll learn how to create a more complex macro set of named submacros within a macro object. When you arrange submacros by task into macro objects, you'll see that this is a good way to organize your work and to keep from cluttering your database with dozens of macro objects.

Validating Data and Presetting Values

Two tasks you'll commonly automate in your applications are validating data that a user enters in a field and automatically setting values for specific fields. You'll now explore several macro objects saved in the sample database and learn how they perform these tasks on both the WeddingList form and the CityInformation form.

Validating Data

A problem you'll often encounter when you create database applications is ensuring that the data the users enter is valid. Three types of invalid data are unknown entries, misspelled entries, and multiple versions of the same entry:

- **Unknown entries** A good example of this error is an entry such as *AX* in a state field. No state name is abbreviated as AX, but a user who tries to enter *AZ* might accidentally hit the X key instead of the Z key.
- **Misspelled entries** This sort of error is quite common among users with poor typing or spelling skills and among very fast typists. In this case, you might see entries such as *Settle*, *Seatle*, or *Saettle* for Seattle.
- **Multiple versions** These errors are common in poorly designed databases and in databases that are shared by a number of users. You might see entries such as *ABC Company, Inc.*; *ABC Company, Incorporated*; *ABC Co., Inc.*; or *A B C Company Inc.*

You can use macros to validate data and help reduce errors. In the next section, you'll create a macro for the WeddingList form that validates the city that the user enters in the City field. If the city doesn't exist in the CityNames table, the macro then executes the following steps:

1. It displays a message indicating that the city is currently unlisted and asks whether the user wants to enter a new city name.
2. If the user wants to create a new city record, another macro runs that opens the CityInformation form in data entry mode and copies the city name that the user just typed.
3. If the user successfully saves a new row, a macro associated with the AfterInsert event of the CityInformation form sets a temporary variable.
4. Back in the WeddingList form, the city name gets revalidated, and if the city entry is a new one, a macro triggered by the AfterUpdate property of the City field sets the combo box to the new name. When the city name is validated, this macro also automatically enters the state name and the first three digits of the ZIP code.

Understanding the ValidateCitySetStateAndZip Macro

In the Navigation pane, find the ValidateCitySetStateAndZip macro and open it in Design view. Figure 20-33 shows the first submacro and its associated actions.

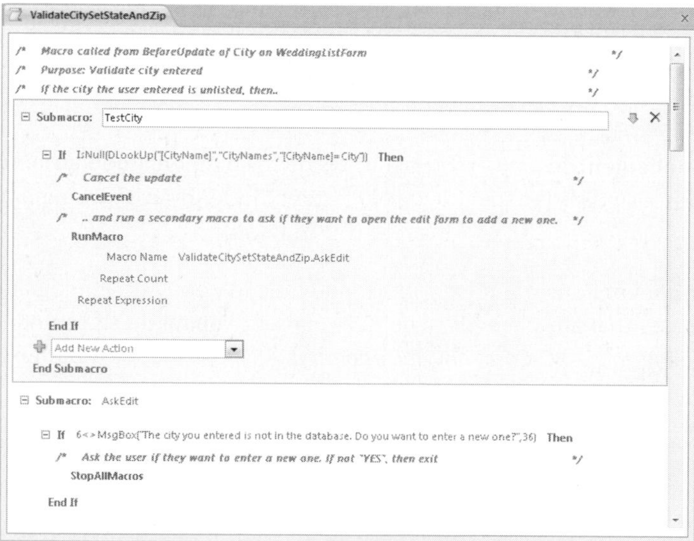

Figure 20-33 This figure shows the macro design surface for the first submacro in the ValidateCitySetStateAndZip macro object.

The first three lines of the macro are comments, and TestCity is the name of the first submacro in the object. You can see the actions for this submacro inside the If block listed in Table 20-3.

Table 20-3 Actions, Arguments, and Settings in the TestCity Submacro

Action	Argument	Setting
CancelEvent		
RunMacro	Macro Name	ValidateCitySetStateAndZip.AskEdit

To understand how this macro works, let's look at the conditional expression in the If block that validates the city name for the TestCity submacro. What we want to do is look up the name just entered in the CityName field to find out whether it exists in the CityNames table. If it doesn't exist, the first action inside the If block of the submacro executes a CancelEvent action. The second action then calls another macro that we'll examine later.

To see this conditional expression easily, click into the expression text box for the If block and then press Shift+F2 to open the expression in the Zoom box, as shown in Figure 20-34.

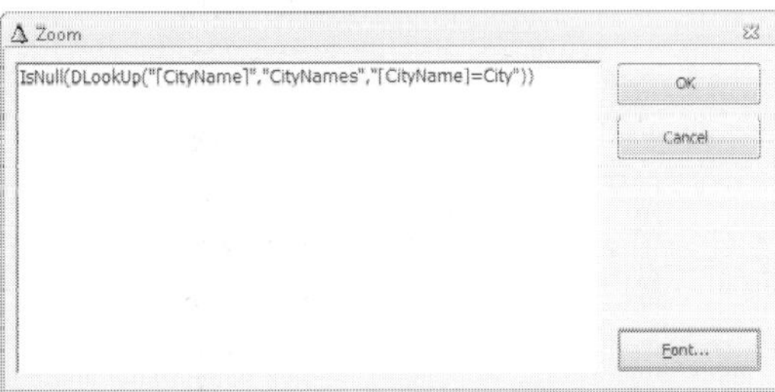

Figure 20-34 The conditional expression in the TestCity submacro If block uses the DLookup function to try to find the city in the CityNames table.

This conditional expression uses two built-in functions: DLookup and IsNull. The DLookup function looks up the city name in the CityNames table. The IsNull function checks the return value of the DLookup function. If the DLookup function doesn't find the city name, it returns a Null value. This causes the IsNull function to return a True value because the return value of the DLookup function is indeed Null. If no row in the CityNames table matches the current city name in the WeddingList form, Access then executes the actions inside the If block because the condition evaluated to True. In this case, the CancelEvent macro action tells Access not to store the new value in the City field. So if the city doesn't exist in the CityNames table, the RunMacro action inside the If block calls the AskEdit submacro, which we'll look at in a moment.

On the other hand, if the DLookup function does find the city name, it returns the city name to the IsNull function. The IsNull function then returns a value of False because the return value of the DLookup function is not Null. Access disregards running any actions inside the If block, and since there is no Else or ElseIf associated with this If block, the submacro ends without taking any further action.

What's the point of all of this? If you open the WeddingList form in Design view, click the City combo box, and look at its event properties, you'll find this macro "wired" into the Before Update property. If you remember from the previous chapter, you can use the BeforeUpdate event of a form or control to verify what's about to be saved. If the data is not valid, you can cancel the event to tell Access not to save the change. This is exactly what the CancelEvent action of this submacro is doing.

When you don't cancel a BeforeUpdate event on a control, Access accepts the changes and gives you a chance to look at the result in the AfterUpdate event. You don't want to use the AfterUpdate event to validate data because the data has already been saved, but it's perfect for filling in other fields on the form based on what the user just entered. As you'll see later, this application uses AfterUpdate on this control to fill in the correct state and part of the ZIP code.

INSIDE OUT

Why Aren't We Using the NotInList Event to Test for a New City Name?

The NotInList event occurs when the user types a name that's not in the row source of a combo box. The CityNames table is the row source of the City combo box, so NotInList seems to be an ideal choice to detect a name that's not in the CityNames table. But for NotInList to work properly, you need to be able to return a response code to the event to let Access know whether you've handled the problem and inserted a new city name. You can do that only in Visual Basic code, not in a macro. We set the Limit To List property of the combo box to No so that the NotInList event never happens. By trapping the problem in the BeforeUpdate event of the combo box, we can test the value and take appropriate action without having to return a response code to Access. As you'll learn later in the Visual Basic chapters, the NotInList event is a much better choice so long as you can return a response code.

So what happens if the user enters a city name that's not yet in the database? The AskEdit submacro runs, and the first step it takes is to evaluate the conditional expression in the first If block at the beginning of the submacro. The conditional expression for the first If block is as follows:

```
6<>MsgBox("The city you entered is not in the ➘
    database. Do you want to enter a new one?",36)
```

You've seen the MessageBox action before. This conditional expression uses a built-in function called MsgBox that's a lot more powerful. The MsgBox function lets you not only display a message but also specify what icon you want displayed, and it provides several options for buttons to display in the message box. You set these options by adding number selections and providing the result as the second argument to MsgBox. In this case, 36 is the sum of 32, which asks for a question icon, and 4, which requests Yes and No buttons. (Intuitive, isn't it?) You can find all the option settings by searching for MsgBox Function in Access Help. For your convenience, we've listed all the option settings for the MsgBox function in Table 20-4. In addition, the function returns an integer value that depends on the button the user clicks in the message box. If you look at the MsgBox Function help topic, you'll find out that when the user clicks Yes, MsgBox returns the value 6. Table 20-5 shows you the MsgBox return value settings. So if the user doesn't click Yes, the action inside the first block—a StopAllMacros action—executes, and the macro ends. If the user does click Yes, the rest of the submacro executes. Table 20-6 lists all the actions and arguments for this submacro.

Table 20-4 Option Settings for the MsgBox Function

Value	Meaning
	BUTTON SETTINGS (CHOOSE ONE)
0	OK button only
1	OK and Cancel buttons
2	Abort, Retry, and Ignore buttons
3	Yes, No, and Cancel buttons
4	Yes and No buttons
5	Retry and Cancel buttons
	ICON SETTINGS (CHOOSE ONE)
0	No icon
16	Critical (red X) icon
32	Warning query (?) icon
48	Warning message (!) icon
64	Information message (letter *i*) icon
	DEFAULT BUTTON SETTINGS (CHOOSE ONE)
0	First button is the default
256	Second button is the default
512	Third button is the default

Table 20-5 Return Values for the MsgBox Function

Value	Meaning
1	OK button clicked
2	Cancel button clicked
3	Abort button clicked
4	Retry button clicked
5	Ignore button clicked
6	Yes button clicked
7	No button clicked

Table 20-6 Actions, Arguments, and Settings in the AskEdit Submacro

Action	Argument	Setting
StopAllMacros		
Close	Object Type	Form
	Object Name	CityInformation
	Save	Prompt
OpenForm	Form Name	CityInformation
	View	Form
	Data Mode	Add
	Window Mode	Normal
SetValue	Item	[Forms]![CityInformation]![CityName]
	Value	[Forms]![WeddingList]![City]
GoToControl	Control Name	State
SetTempVar	Name	AddFlag
	Expression	True

The AskEdit submacro contains several actions that Access executes if the user enters the data for a new city name and responds by clicking Yes on the MsgBox that asks whether the user wants to add the new city. The submacro uses the IsFormLoaded function you saw earlier inside the second If conditional expression to determine whether the CityInformation form is open. If it is, the submacro instructs Access to close the form. Next, Access opens the CityInformation form in Add mode and copies the city name from the WeddingList form to the CityName field of the CityInformation form by using the SetValue action. (Note that SetValue has an exclamation mark icon on the macro design surface to the left of the action name indicating Access will not run this action in a database that is not trusted.) SetValue inserts the city name that the user typed for user convenience and to ensure that the user starts with the city name just entered. After the submacro copies the city name to the CityName field, it tells Access to move the focus to the State field using the GoToControl action. Finally, the submacro creates a temporary variable called AddFlag and sets the value to True to indicate that the CityInformation form is now opened in data entry mode. The submacro attached to the AfterInsert event checks this temporary variable to determine whether it should notify the AfterUpdate event of the City control on the WeddingList form to refresh its list.

Passing Status Information Between Linked Forms

As you just saw, the AskEdit submacro creates a temporary variable called AddFlag to tell the CityInformation form's AfterInsert event macro that the WeddingList form needs to know whether a new row has been added successfully. Likewise, when the user adds a new row using the CityInformation form, the submacro that runs in response to an AfterInsert event (the event that Access uses to let you know when a new row has been added via a form) needs to check the flag and pass an indicator back to the submacro that responds to the AfterUpdate event of the City combo box on the WeddingList form. You'll learn in later chapters that you can also do this sort of "status indicator" passing by using variables in Visual Basic procedures.

Figure 20-35 shows the submacro that you need to respond to the AfterInsert event of the CityInformation form. You might recall from Chapter 19, "Understanding Event Processing," that Access triggers this event right after it has saved a new row. You could save the row by clicking Save in the Records group on the Home tab, moving to a new row, or closing the form. The If block at the beginning of the RefreshCityList submacro has a conditional expression that tests to be sure that the user asked to add a new row. The conditional expression is as follows:

```
Not [TempVars]![AddFlag]
```

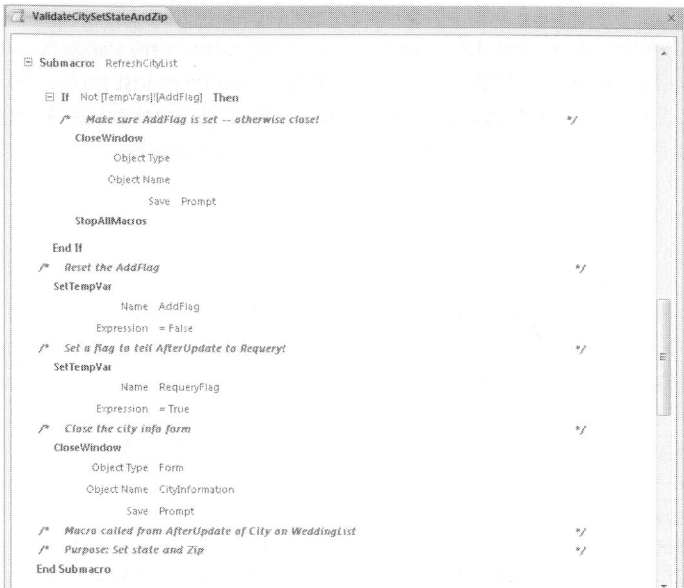

Figure 20-35 The RefreshCityList submacro sets a temporary variable to indicate that a requery is needed.

If the AddFlag temporary variable is not true, the actions inside the If block close the form, and then the StopAllMacros action causes the submacro to end. If the variable is true, the SetTempVar action creates another temporary variable called RequeryFlag and sets the flag to let the submacro that responds to the AfterUpdate event of the City combo box know that it must refresh the list in the combo box at its earliest opportunity. Finally, the submacro closes the CityInformation form. Remember that the AfterInsert event could be triggered as a result of clicking the form's Close button after entering new data. Normally, you would expect an error if you try to execute a Close command while the form is already in the process of closing (you will get an error in Visual Basic). Access does not generate any error from either of the Close actions in this submacro if this is the case.

If the user triggers the AfterInsert event by moving to another row, closing the form makes sense after adding the one row you need. If the user closes the form without entering any new data, the AfterInsert event won't happen. The user will be back in the WeddingList form with the unmatched city data still typed in the City combo box. If the user attempts to save the unmatched name again, the BeforeUpdate event runs the TestCity submacro that cancels the update when the city isn't in the CityName table. The user must either add the new value or enter a value in the list.

As a final touch, the SetTempVar action in the SyncWeddingAndCity macro that you created in Figure 20-31 (on page 1235) sets the AddFlag temporary variable to False when you move to a new row on the WeddingList form. When you have just moved to a new row, you clearly aren't worried about adding a new row to the CityNames table. Also, there's a SelectObject action in the macro to make sure the focus is back on the WeddingList form after the macro updates the temporary variable.

Presetting Values

Validating data is just one of the many ways you can ensure data integrity in a database. Presetting values for certain fields is another way. Although you can set the Default property of a field, sometimes you'll need to set the value of a field based on the value of another field in a form. For example, you'll want to set the values of the State field and the Zip field in the WeddingList form based on the value of the City field. You can accomplish this with a macro.

In this section, you'll examine actions in the ValidateCitySetStateAndZip submacros that set the values of the State and Zip fields in the WeddingList form based on the city entered. If you scroll down the macro design surface, you can see the additional actions, as shown in Figure 20-36.

Figure 20-36 The SetStateAndZip submacro uses SetValue actions to automatically fill in the State and Zip controls.

Table 20-7 lists the actions and arguments in this submacro.

Table 20-7 Actions, Arguments, and Settings in the SetStateAndZip Submacro

Action	Argument	Setting
SetValue	Item	[State]
	Expression	DLookup("[State]","[CityNames]","[CityNames].[CityName]=City")
SetValue	Item	[Zip]
	Expression	DLookup("[Zip]","[CityNames]","[CityNames].[CityName]=City")
GoToControl	Control Name	Zip
SetValue	Item	[Forms]![WeddingList]![Zip].[SelStart]
	Expression	255
Requery	Control Name	City
SetTempVar	Name	RequeryFlag
	Expression	False

When the user enters a valid city name, the first SetValue action uses the DLookup function to retrieve the matching State value from the CityNames table. If the value for State isn't blank or Null in the conditional expression for the first If block, the second SetValue action retrieves the first three digits of the ZIP code from the table, moves the focus to the Zip control with a GoToControl action, and sets the SelStart property of the Zip control to a high value (255) to place the cursor at the end of the data displayed in the control. Pressing the F2 key after you move to a control also places the cursor at the end of the data in the control, so you could use a SendKeys action here instead. However, setting the SelStart property is faster and more reliable. The user can now enter the last two digits of the ZIP code on the main form before moving on to the Expected field. The conditional expression in the first If block is as follows:

```
Not ([State]="" Or [State] Is Null)
```

The set of submacros in this macro object is now complete. You can see how these submacros help implement data integrity by validating data and presetting specific values. This decreases the likelihood that users will make errors. Now, you'll see how to associate these submacros with the appropriate events on the WeddingList form and the CityInformation form.

Right-click the WeddingList form in the Navigation pane, and click Design View to open the form in Design view. Click the City combo box control, and then click the Property Sheet button in the Tools group on the Design tab. After the property sheet opens, click the Event tab. You should see the ValidateCitySetStateAndZip.TestCity submacro associated with the BeforeUpdate event of the City combo box. Remember, this is the macro you should run to verify whether the user has entered a valid city name. The AfterUpdate event property should be set to ValidateCitySetStateAndZip.SetStateAndZip. This submacro automatically sets the matching State and Zip values whenever the user specifies a new City value. Figure 20-37 shows the result.

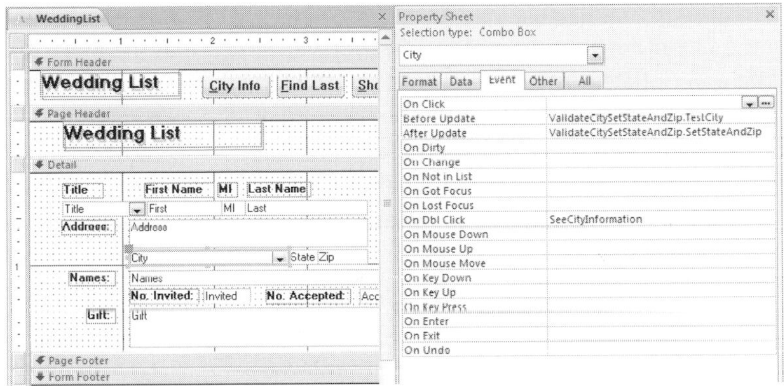

Figure 20-37 The Before Update and After Update event properties for the City control on the WeddingList form are set to run submacros in the ValidateCitySetStateAndZip macro.

Close the WeddingList form. Open the CityInformation form in Design view, and click the Property Sheet button in the Tools group on the Design tab to open the property sheet. The ValidateCitySetStateAndZip.RefreshCityList macro is set in the form's After Insert event property, as shown in Figure 20-38. Recall from Chapter 19 that you could also use the form's AfterUpdate event to see changed data. However, in this case, you don't care about existing rows that change. The AfterInsert event is more appropriate because Access fires this event only when a new row is saved, not when an existing row is saved.

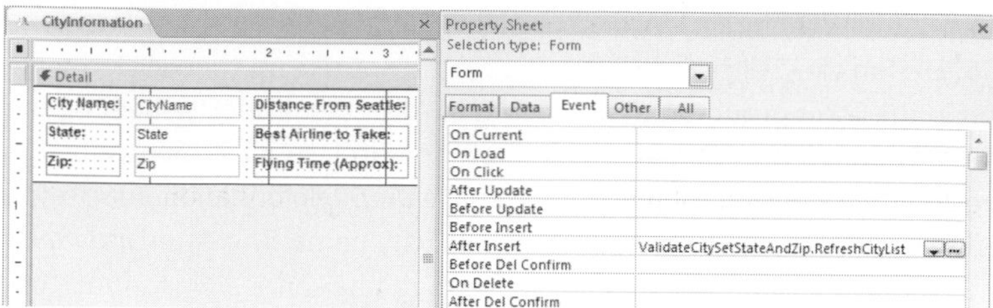

Figure 20-38 The ValidateCitySetStateAndZip.RefreshCityList submacro executes when the After Insert event of the CityInformation form occurs.

Close the CityInformation form. Now that you've verified that the macros are associated with the appropriate objects and events, you're ready to test how this works. Begin by closing all open objects, and then double-click the AutoexecXmpl macro in the Navigation pane to run the macro and open the WeddingList form. Move to a new record in the WeddingList form, and enter a title, a name, an address, and a group. When the cursor moves to the City combo box, enter **Miami**. After you press Enter or Tab, Access runs the ValidateCitySetStateAndZip.TestCity submacro. Because this city doesn't currently exist in the CityNames table, the AskEdit submacro runs, and Access displays the message box shown in Figure 20-39.

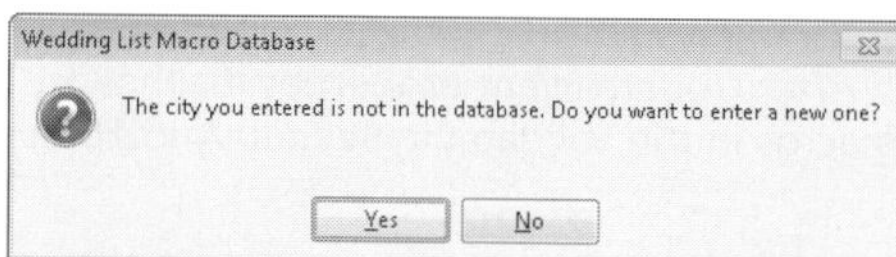

Figure 20-39 The AskEdit submacro displays a message box if you enter a new city.

After you click Yes, Access executes the remaining actions in the submacro. Access opens the CityInformation form in data entry mode, copies the city name to the City field of the form, and moves the cursor to the State field. Figure 20-40 shows the result of these actions.

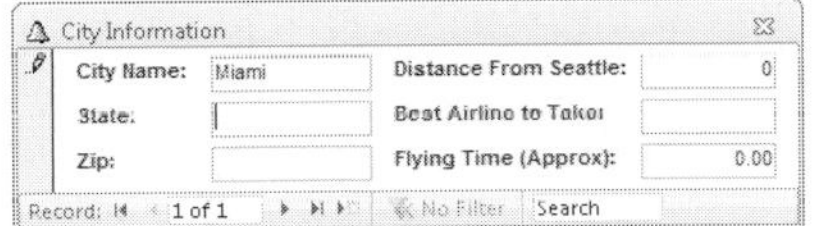

Figure 20-40 The AskEdit submacro then opens the CityInformation form, where you can enter the details of the new city.

After you enter information in the remaining fields and close the CityInformation form, the AfterInsert event of the form triggers the ValidateCitySetStateAndZip.RefreshCityList submacro. After the form closes, Access moves the focus back to the WeddingList form. When you finally leave the now valid City control, the macro triggered by AfterUpdate requeries the City combo box control and automatically updates the State and Zip fields.

In Chapter 25, we'll introduce you to some enhancements we made to the Wedding List sample database after we converted all the macros to Visual Basic. You can find this version of the database saved as WeddingList.accdb on the companion CD.

Article 6, on the companion CD, summarizes all the actions you can include in client and web macros. You'll find it useful to browse through that article to become familiar with the available actions and events as you automate your applications with macros.

CHAPTER 21

Automating a Web Application Using Macros

In Chapter 20, "Automating a Client Application Using Macros," you learned how to create user interface macros in a client database. You also learned how to create stand-alone macro objects (macros that appear in the Navigation pane), embedded macros attached to client forms, and use macro actions to automate different elements of your client application. Automating a web application is the same as automating a client application in many ways. You define macro actions in macro objects and embedded macros to help users navigate through the different parts of your application and perform automated tasks.

In this chapter, we'll focus on calling out specific differences you need to be aware of when creating web macros versus client macros. We'll help guide you around potential pitfalls you'll encounter when trying to automate web forms and offer tips to help you build a smooth interface for the users of your application. We'll also show you how to make user interface macros work with data macros to interact with the data layer.

Note

The examples in this chapter are based on the Back Office Software System data copy sample web database (BOSSDataCopy.accdb) on the companion CD included with this book. The results you see from the samples in this chapter might not exactly match what you see in this book if you have changed the sample data in the files. Also, all the screen images in this chapter were taken on a Windows 7 system with the Access color scheme set to Silver. Your results might look different if you are using a different operating system or a different theme.

In this chapter, you will

- Learn about the various types of actions you can define in web macros.
- Learn some new tips and tricks about the Logic Designer.
- Learn how to call data macros from the user interface level and use values returned from the data layer with ReturnVars.
- See how to work around potential pitfalls when working with web macros for web objects.
- Learn how to pass parameters when opening web forms and web reports using web macros. You'll also see how to display parameters from a web form on a web report section.
- Learn how to verify what group permissions a user has for your web application and take different actions based on their permission level.
- Learn how to conditionally run different actions based on whether a web form is open in Access client or in the browser.
- Understand some of the actions automated with web macros in the Back Office Software System sample web database.

In Article 6, "Macro Actions," on the companion CD, you'll find summaries of the client macro actions and the web macro actions. You'll also find a listing of the arguments you can use for web macros. You can use the article as a quick reference when designing web macros for your web applications.

Creating Web Macros

To create web macros, you need to be working in a web database. Although you can create both client and web macros in a web database, you can create web macros only in web databases, not client databases. Just like client macros, you can create stand-alone web macro objects and embedded web macros in objects; however, there are differences you should be aware of. First, web macros only support 26 macro actions, far less than their client counterparts. (You can review Article 6 for a complete list of the web macro actions available in Access 2010.) Second, several web macro actions have different arguments than the same client macro action. For example, in a client macro, the MessageBox action has four arguments—Message, Beep, Type, and Title. A MessageBox action in a web macro, however, has only one argument—Message. Third, all web macro actions are trusted actions, so you do not need to worry about enabling the content of the web database to run web macro actions. Finally, you cannot embed macros into web report events because web reports do not support events. You can create embedded web macros only in web forms.

To show you how to create a new web macro object, open the BOSSDataCopy.accdb sample web database found on the companion CD. Next, click Macro in the Macros & Code group on the Create tab, as shown in Figure 21-1. Notice that a web macro has the globe icon on the Macro button in the Macros & Code group. (If you want to create a client macro object in a web database, click Client Objects in the Macros & Code group and then click Macro from the drop down list of options.)

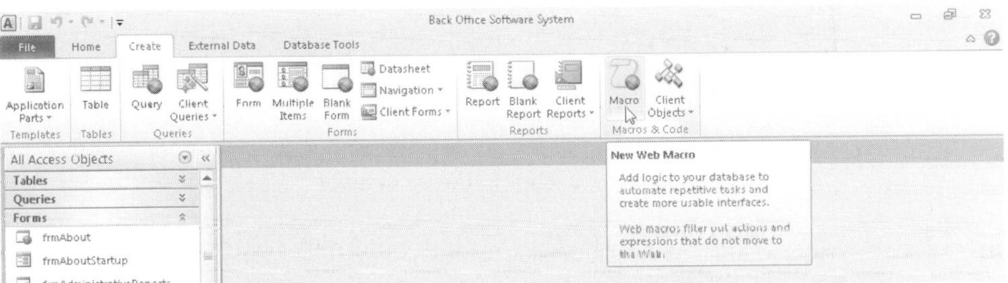

Figure 21-1 Click the Macro button in the Macros & Code group in a web database to create web macro objects.

After you click Macro, Access opens up the Logic Designer, as shown in Figure 21-2. As you can see in Figure 21-2, the Logic Designer elements, for the most part, are the same when you're designing a web macro as when you're designing a client macro. The main difference you'll see in the design surface for web macros is the list of actions available in the Action Catalog. Note that in Figure 21-2, we expanded one of the action categories in the Action Catalog so you can see some of the actions available to you when designing web macros. In the Logic Designer with Access 2010, you can create data macros, client macros, and web macros. The notable key feature of the Logic Designer is that Access presents to you only the elements applicable to the context of the macro you are creating.

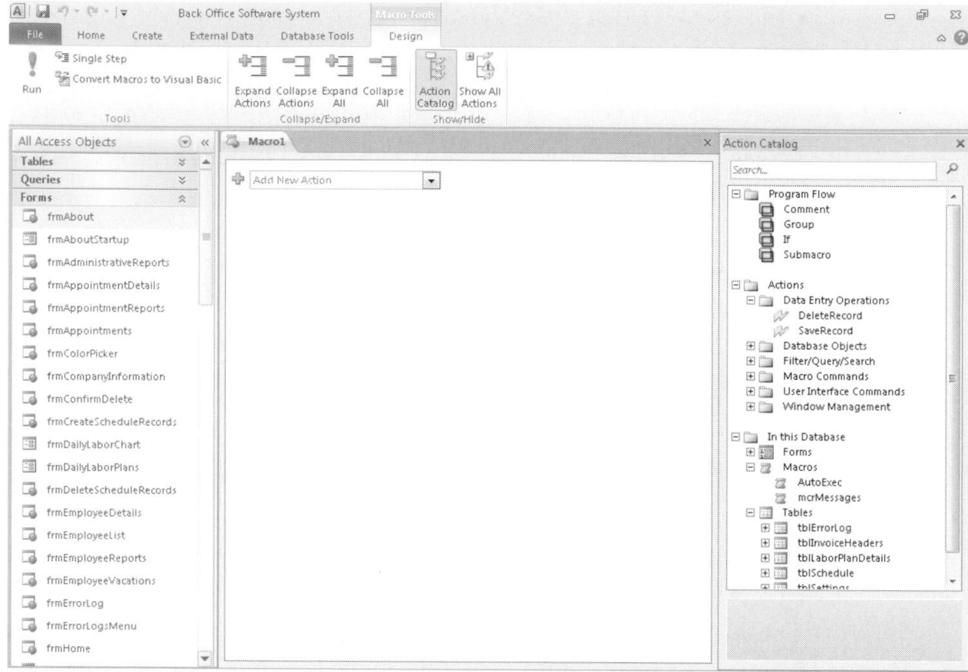

Figure 21-2 The Action Catalog in a web macro only displays actions supported for web objects.

If you expand the In This Database node at the bottom of the Action Catalog (also shown in Figure 21-2), you'll notice that Access displays three categories—Forms, Macros, and Tables. If you have any embedded macros attached to web form controls, Access displays a Forms node here with a list of the web forms and the embedded macros in a sub-node under Forms. If you have any saved macro objects, Access displays a list of the macro object names under the Macros node. If you have any named data macros attached to web tables, Access displays a list of the table names and their associated named data macros in a sub node under Tables.

In Chapter 20, you learned how to use the MessageBox action in a client macro to display a message to the users of your application. Let's create a similar message using a web macro in this web database. Click in the Add New Action combo box on the macro design surface and to drop-down the list of macro actions. In the Add New Action combo box, you can specify any one of the 26 macro actions and four program flow constructs provided by Access 2010 for web macros. Select MessageBox from the list of actions in this drop-down list. After you select an action such as MessageBox, Access displays argument boxes for the specific action you choose, as shown in Figure 21-3, in which you enter the arguments for the action.

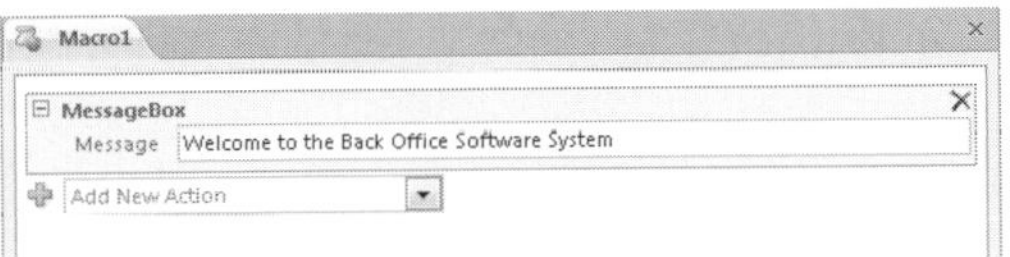

Figure 21-3 Enter text in the Message argument for a MessageBox action to display a greeting message.

You'll notice right away that there are fewer arguments available for the MessageBox action in a web macro; in fact, there is only one argument available for web macros—Message. You cannot make a beep sound, set a message type graphic, or set a custom message title when you're using the MessageBox action in a web macro. Enter a greeting message in the Message argument box. (You can use the example shown in Figure 21-3.) You must save a web macro object before you can run it, so click Save on the Quick Access Toolbar, or click the File tab on the Backstage view and then click Save. Enter a name for your new web macro object, such as **TestGreeting**, and click OK.

Note

In web macros, you cannot use the MsgBox function to display a message box and then evaluate the user's response. If you need this functionality in a web form, you'll need to create a custom web form that you display in Dialog mode and then evaluate the response from the user. You can see an example of using a custom form for this purpose by opening the frmLaborPlans web form. If you look at the embedded macro logic attached to the cmdDeleteRecord command button, you'll see we open a custom web form called frmConfirmDelete to ask the user if they want to proceed with the delete operation.

You can run web macro objects, such as the simple one you just created, directly from the Navigation pane or from the Logic Designer as with client macro objects, because they don't depend on controls on an open form. (If your web macro does depend on a form, you must link the macro to the appropriate event and run it that way.) To run your test web macro object, you can click Run in the Tools group on the Design tab, or double-click the web macro object in the Navigation pane if you closed the macro object. Access displays the greeting you defined earlier, as shown in Figure 21-4. You'll notice that Access uses the application title defined for the database under the Current Database category in the Access Options dialog box as the title of your web message box.

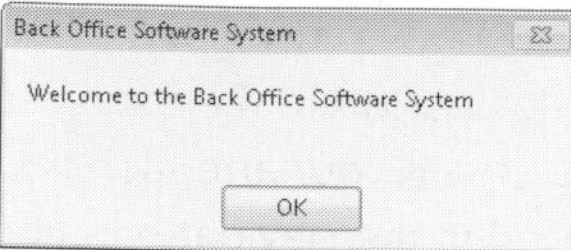

Figure 21-4 Access displays the dialog box you created by using the MessageBox action in the TestGreeting web macro.

> **Note**
>
> **You can link both client and web macro objects to client form and client report events, but you can link web macro objects only to web forms. You cannot use client macro objects with web forms, nor can you can assign macro objects to web reports because web reports do not support events.**

Using Macro Objects for Common Functionality

You can create embedded web macros in the event procedures for web forms and web form controls similar to client macros. As you'll recall from Chapter 20, you cannot see or run embedded macros directly from the Navigation pane. When you are working within Access, you can run a saved web macro object from the Navigation pane. However, as you'll learn in Chapter 22, "Using Web Applications in a Browser," you can run web macro objects only by calling them from event procedures when you're using your web database in a browser. As an application developer, this means you'll be working with web form events, web control events, and embedded web macros heavily as you automate your web database for use in a browser.

There are three approaches for defining web macro logic in a web application: You can define your web macro logic in saved macro objects and call them using the RunMacro action from within embedded macros; you can define all your web macro logic directly within embedded macros; or you can use a combination of the two techniques. There is no hard rule you must follow when using any of the design path choices because they each have advantages and disadvantages. If you define all your logic in web macro objects, it might be harder to determine where your application uses each macro object if you have a complex application. You might alleviate some of the confusion by creating a naming scheme for your web macro objects that helps determine where they are used. One advantage to using saved web macro objects is that you can call these macros and submacros within the macro objects from multiple places, including even from client objects. If you define all your logic directly within embedded macros, you cannot call any submacros defined in embedded macros from other places. This might mean you'll be duplicating similar actions in many different web forms. An advantage to using only embedded macros is that all the logic needed for the web form is contained within the form itself. If you need to change the logic for a specific web form, you can focus your attention just on the one object. You'll also have fewer macro objects displayed in the Navigation pane if you use embedded macros.

So which design should you follow? For our applications, we used a combination of the two approaches. We defined most of the macro logic within embedded macros in the Back Office Software System web database, so each web form can be independent of the actions the form depends upon. We also used saved web macro objects to define web macro actions that we want to call from multiple web forms. By centralizing common functionality within a saved web macro object, we can make a change to an action in one place and have that change available to many areas of the application.

To see an example of using a saved web macro object utilized by different web forms, open the web macro object called mcrMessages in Design view from the Navigation pane. Access opens the Logic Designer and displays the logic we defined in this web macro object, as shown in Figure 21-5. We use this web macro object to define many messages that we want to display to users of the application. In Figure 21-5, you can see that we use submacros and MessageBox actions to define the messages. From the various web forms in this web database, we can reuse the same submacro message instead of creating essentially the same action and message multiple times in different web forms. If we want to change the text for a specific message, we now need to change the message in only one location instead of trying to find all instances of the message in all the web forms.

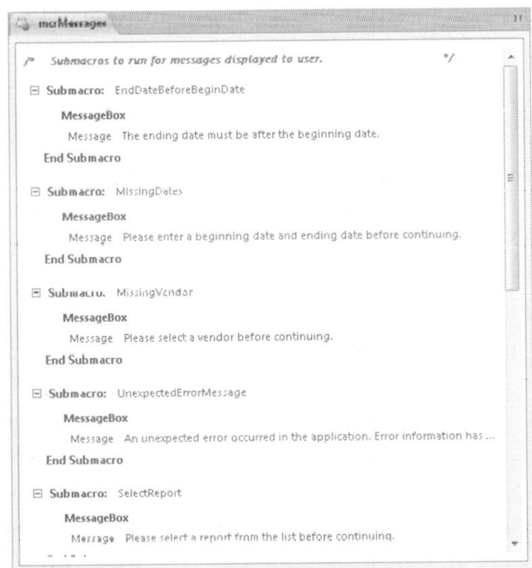

Figure 21-5 You can use web macro objects to define actions called from different web forms in your application.

INSIDE OUT **Using the In This Database Node to Create New Macros**

When you are creating a macro, you can expand the In This Database node in the Action Catalog and drag saved macro objects and embedded macros to the design surface. When you drag a macro object to the macro design surface, Access creates a RunMacro action and fills in the Macro Name argument with the name of the saved macro object. If you drag an embedded macro defined in a form event to the macro design surface, Access creates a copy of all the macro actions defined in the embedded macro to the macro design surface. Note that if you have any submacros defined in an embedded macro and drag that embedded macro onto the macro design surface, Access does not copy the submacros onto the macro design surface. To work around this limitation, you can double-click the embedded macro in the Action Catalog to copy all the actions and submacros defined in the embedded macro to the macro design surface.

You can copy an embedded macro under Forms in the In This Database node to add the actions for that embedded macro into your new macro. To do this, right-click an embedded macro in the Action Catalog, and Access displays an option called Add Copy Of Macro. If you click that option, Access copies all the macro actions, including submacros, defined in the embedded macro to the macro design surface. When you right-click a macro object in the In This Database node, Access displays two options—Add Copy Of Macro and Add RunMacro. If you click Add RunMacro, Access creates a RunMacro action and fills in the Macro Name argument with the name of the saved macro object.

Working with Web Form and Control Events

As you learned in Chapter 19, "Understanding Event Processing," web forms and controls on web forms support only a few events compared to client forms and controls on client forms. Web forms only support attaching macros to the OnCurrent and OnOpen events. In Table 21-1, you can see a list of events each web form control supports.

Table 21-1 Supported Web Form Control Events

Control	OnClick	AfterUpdate	OnDblclick	OnChange
Attachment	Supported			
Check Box		Supported		
Combo Box		Supported	Supported	

Control	OnClick	AfterUpdate	OnDblclick	OnChange
Command Button	Supported			
Image	Supported		Supported	
Label	Supported		Supported	
Tab Control				Supported
Text Box	Supported	Supported	Supported	

Note that Navigation Buttons, Navigation Controls, Subform Controls, Tab Pages, and Web Browser Controls do not support any events when you are working with web forms. When you have a web form open in Layout view, Access displays only the supported events for each control on the Property Sheet window.

TROUBLESHOOTING

Why don't I see any events in the Property Sheet window for my label control?

When you drop a text box control onto a web form in Layout view, Access also creates an associated label control for the new text box. Access does not display events in the Property Sheet window if a label is associated with a text box control. To display the two supported events for your web label control, you'll need to delete the associated Mondaylabel control and then drop in a new label control by itself. Remember that you can also create a new label control in an Empty Cell in Layout view by clicking in the Empty Cell and then typing a caption.

Passing Parameters to Forms and Reports

In Chapter 7, "Creating Table Data Macros," you learned how the Logic Designer displays parameter boxes when you create and use named data macros. If you use parameters in a query for a form or report record source, Access displays the parameters you defined in the query when you place an OpenForm or OpenReport action on the macro design surface. To show you an example of this behavior, open the frmInvoiceReports web form in Layout view. Open the Property Sheet window, select the command button called cmdPreviewReport from the Select box, and then click the Event tab. Next to the On Click event property line, click Build to open the Logic Designer and see the macro actions we defined for this command button, as shown in Figure 21-6.

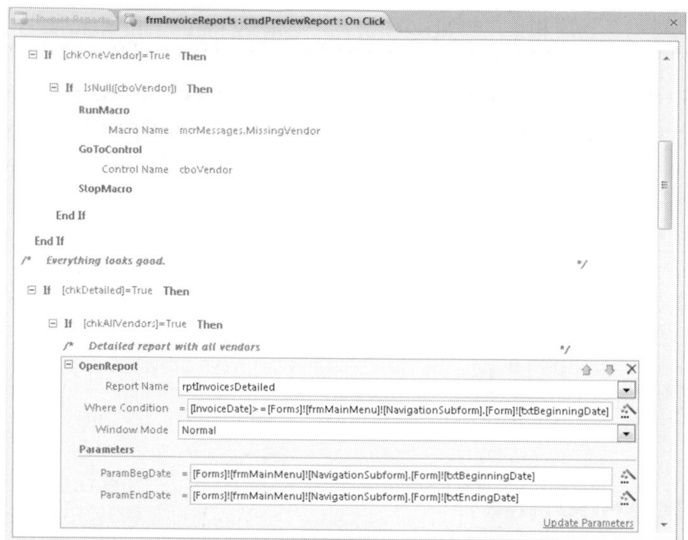

Figure 21-6 Access displays Parameter boxes on the macro design surface for OpenForm and OpenReport actions that require parameters.

Note

In Figure 21-6, you'll notice near the top of the displayed macro actions, we are using a RunMacro action to call one of the message submacros in the global mcrMessages web macro object. We discussed this web macro object in "Using Macro Objects for Common Functionality," on page 1258.

The first part of the logic defined for this embedded macro verifies the user entered beginning and ending dates for the report in the form controls. We also verify that the user did not enter an ending date that is before the beginning date. Scroll down the macro design surface until you see the first OpenReport macro action, as shown previously in Figure 21-6. This command button opens the rptInvoicesDetailed or rptInvoicesSummary web report based on the settings the user chooses on the web form. Both of these web reports use parameterized queries as their record source. Access displays the two parameters in the underlying query—ParamBegDate and ParamEndDate—as parameter boxes at the bottom of the action. You can enter a value you want to use for each parameter by typing the value into the parameter box or using an expression to derive that parameter value.

INSIDE OUT Drag Forms and Reports to the Macro Design Surface

If you are creating a macro object and drag a form or report object from the Navigation pane to the macro design surface, Access creates a new OpenForm or OpenReport macro action for you and fills in the name of the form or report in the Form Name or Report Name argument. Note that you can use this trick with both client and web macro objects, but you cannot use this trick with embedded macros because Access displays the Logic Designer modally when you're working with embedded macros.

In Chapter 20, you learned about referencing controls on subforms. In the Back Office Software System database you have open, nearly all our forms are presented to the user inside the navigation control found on the frmMainMenu web form or on the frmMainMenuClient client form. To properly reference the controls on the frmInvoiceReports web form you're currently working with, we need to reference the main form first (frmMainMenu), and then use the form's special Form property to access the controls on the subform container's Controls collection. In our case, we want to pass in the beginning and ending dates the user wants to use from the form controls on the frmInvoiceReports web form. For example, here is the expression we use for the ParamBegDate parameter:

```
[Forms]![frmMainMenu]![NavigationSubform].[Form]![txtBeginningDate]
```

When the user selects a beginning and ending date range in the date text boxes on the form and clicks the command button to open the report, Access passes in the values shown in the date controls to the query layer for processing. The query processor either in Access client or on the server can then use the parameter values for the report that were obtained from the form controls. Note that for the expression to work properly, you need to open the frmInvoiceReports web form within the frmMainMenu web form.

INSIDE OUT Click the Update Parameters Link to Update Query Parameters

If you add, edit, or delete parameters in the underlying query for a form or report record source, you can click the Update Parameters link on the OpenForm or OpenReport macro action block on the macro design surface to update the parameters. Access evaluates the parameters in the query and then refreshes the parameters boxes to match the parameters in the query.

For the rptInvoicesDetailed web report, it would be useful to display the beginning and ending dates the user selected on the frmInvoiceReports web form on the report itself. If you want to display parameter values in a web report, you can display parameter values in the Page Header, Detail, Report Footer, Group Header, and Group Footer sections. However, you cannot display parameter values in the Report Header or Page Footer sections on web reports. If you display the parameter values in the Report Header or Page Footer sections, the values display when you open the report in the Access client, but the report fails to load if you try to open the report in a web browser.

To show how the parameters look on the web report, close the Logic Designer you currently have open, close the frmInvoiceReports web form, and then open the frmMainMenu web form from the Navigation pane. (If you are prompted to save any changes to the macro or form when you attempt to close the objects, click No.) After the frmMainMenu form opens, click the Purchases top-level navigation button, and then click the Reports second-level navigation button to display the frmInvoiceReports web form inside the navigation subform. Enter **9/1/2010** in the beginning date control, enter **9/30/2010** in the ending date control, leave the report option and vendor option set on their defaults, and then click the Preview Report command button. Access opens the rptInvoicesDetailed web report and displays any invoice records within the date range you provided, as shown in Figure 21-7.

Home | Invoice Report

Saturday, May 15, 2010 6:10:57 PM

Purchase Recap Detailed Report

Includes invoices between 9/1/2010 and 9/30/2010

Vendor	Invoice Number	Invoice Date	Invoice Total
Adventure Works	EB574831	9/6/2010	$89.45
	Report Group	Account	Subtotal
	Dairy Products	4953	$89.45
			$89.45

Figure 21-7 Access displays the parameter values from the form in the report's Page Header section.

Near the top of this web report, you can see the beginning and ending dates you provided on the frmInvoiceReports web form displayed within the text in the report's Page Header section. By using parameters defined at the query level and binding a form or report to that query for its record source, Access can display the parameters needed for the form or report when you add an OpenForm or OpenReport action to the macro design surface. You can pass parameter values from form controls in your macro action to the form or report you want to open. You can then display those values, for example, on a report Page Header so the user can see the parameter values they selected.

TROUBLESHOOTING

Why do I get errors saying Access cannot find the field when I view the web form or web report in a browser, but not when I view the form or report in Access?

When you assign a record source to a form or report, Access can work with the data in every field of the record source, even if you do not bind a form or report control to every field on the form or report design surface. For example, if you want to apply filters and sorts to the records displayed on your web form, Access can identify and use the fields for those filters or sorts even if you don't have a control bound to those fields on the form or report design surface. You can also open a form or report using macros or Microsoft Visual Basic code with a WHERE condition for a field, and Access can read the field's data and display the correct records even if you don't have the field on the form or report design surface.

When you're working with web forms, web reports, and web macros to automate your application, you need to be aware that the server behaves differently. Access Services requires that you bind any fields to controls on the form or report design surface if you're sorting, filtering, or grouping with those fields using web macros. If you don't want to show those fields to the users of your application, you can set the visibility of those field controls to False. Access Services can use the data in any hidden fields on the form or report so long as a control is bound to those fields. Access Services can also use the data from fields in your record source if you use the field in an expression on the form or report. For example, if you use a field in an expression for a conditional formatting rule, Access Services can use the data when you view the web report in a web browser.

If you examine the web forms and web reports in the Back Office Software System sample web database, you'll notice we placed a lot of controls on the design surface, resized them to be small, and set their visibility to False because we didn't want to show the user the field values. We added these extra controls to the form and report objects so that we can filter, sort, or group on those fields even if we don't want to show the data to the user.

Exploring the Invoice Audit Web Form Macros

In the following sections, you'll explore one of the more complicated embedded web macros used in the Back Office Software System data copy sample web database (BOSSDataCopy.accdb) to understand how macros can help automate your web application. We'll show you a complex user interface macro that interacts with the data layer by calling named data macros and using return variables to display values returned back from the data layer to the users of the application. You'll also learn about the powerful SetProperty macro action and how to use it to dynamically change form control properties on your web forms while they are displayed onscreen. Close any objects you might have open and then open the frmInvoiceAudit web form in Form view, as shown in Figure 21-8. The purpose of this web form is to give application administrators an entry point to audit the invoice records stored in this restaurant management application. Before an application administrator runs an invoice report, he or she might want to verify that the invoice detail line item totals stored in the tblInvoiceDetails web table add up to the correct invoice amount total stored in the parent invoice record in the tblInvoiceHeaders web table.

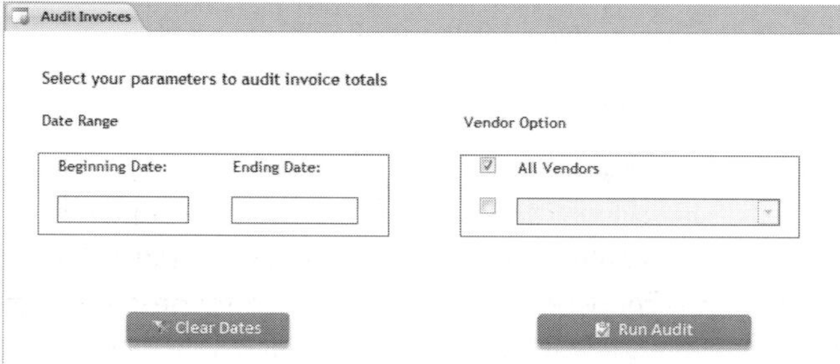

Figure 21-8 You can audit the invoice records in this database through the frmInvoiceAudit web form.

Using the SetProperty Action with Web Form Controls

When you're automating a web database, you'll probably find yourself using the SetProperty macro action quite often. The SetProperty macro action is a powerful action because it allows you to dynamically change several form control properties while the form is viewed in Form view in Access client or viewed in a web browser. You can also change the value of text boxes using the SetProperty action.

On the frmInvoiceAudit web form, shown previously in Figure 21-8, we provided two text boxes for the application administrators to enter a date range for invoices they want to audit. Under Vendor Option, the administrator can choose to audit the invoices from all vendors or from one specific vendor in the application. The Clear Dates command button quickly clears any selected dates in the text boxes. (We'll discuss the Run Audit command button in the next section.)

Switch to Layout View for this web form, open the Property Sheet window, select cmdClear-Dates in the Select box, click the Event tab in the Property Sheet window, and then click the Build button on the On Click event property line to see the following embedded macro logic behind this command button:

```
Comment Block: Clear any values stored in the beginning and ending date text boxes.
SetProperty
  Control Name: txtBeginningDate
  Property: Value
  Value:
SetProperty
  Control Name: txtEndingDate
  Property: Value
  Value:
GoToControl
  Control Name: txtBeginningDate
```

The SetProperty macro action has three arguments—Control Name, Property, and Value. For the Control Name argument, you provide the name of the control shown in the Property Sheet window (in our example, we used txtBeginningDate and txtEndingDate). In the Property argument, you can choose from one of seven control properties to change—Enabled, Visible, Locked, ForeColor, BackColor, Caption, and Value. Note that you cannot set all seven properties for any control type. (We'll discuss the supported properties for each control type in a moment.) In the Value argument, you can enter the value you want to set for the control property. Do not confuse the Value argument with the Value control property option for the Property argument. Although they are both named values, they have different purposes.

To set the Enabled, Visible, and Locked properties, you enter either **–1** or the word **True** when you want the Value argument to contain a True value. You can enter either **0** or the word **False** when you want the Value argument to contain a False value. If you enter **–1** or **0** in the Value argument, you'll notice Access displays the word *True* or *False* in the argument line after you save, close, and then reopen the macro. For the ForeColor and BackColor properties, you can enter a color value (such as #000000 for black) in the Value argument. For the Caption and Value properties, you can enter the text you want to use for the new control property in the Value argument. Note that if you want to use an expression for the Value argument, enter an equals sign (=) first in the Value box.

See Article 5, "Color Names and Codes," on the companion CD, for a reference guide to the color values you can use for the ForeColor and BackColor properties.

We used the control name for each of the two text boxes, selected Value for the Property argument, and left the Value arguments empty in the embedded macro attached to the cmdClearDates command button. By leaving the Value arguments empty, Access clears any values in the text box controls. Note that we used the GoToControl macro action as the last action in the macro to put the focus in the txtBeginningDate text box so users can immediately enter a new date if they want.

Web forms do not support option group controls and radio button controls, but you can simulate the behavior of those controls using check boxes and SetProperty macro actions. Close the Logic Designer for the embedded macro you have open and then switch back to Form view so you can see the form design surface. Under Vendor Option, you'll see two check boxes, a label control, and a combo box control, shown previously in Figure 21-8. If you select either of the two check boxes, you'll see Access clears the other check box, much like how radio buttons function inside an option group on client forms. You'll also notice that Access clears any values in the vendor names combo box control and selectively enables or disables the control to correspond to the selected check box. We accomplish all of this dynamic form control manipulation through SetProperty macro actions.

Let's examine the embedded macro logic behind one of these check boxes. Switch back to Layout view, open the Property Sheet window, select chkAllVendors in the Select box, click the Event tab on the Property Sheet window, and then click the Build button on the After Update event property line to see the following embedded macro logic behind this first check box:

```
If [chkAllVendors] = True Then
  Comment Block: Clear the check box for one vendor
  SetProperty
    Control Name: chkOneVendor
    Property: Value
    Value: False
  Comment Block: Clear any combo box values and disable the control
  SetProperty
    Control Name: cboVendor
    Property: Value
    Value:
  SetProperty
    Control Name: cboVendor
    Property: Enabled
    Value: False
```

```
Else
  Comment Block: Select the one vendor check box
  SetProperty
    Control Name: chkOneVendor
    Property: Value
    Value: True
  Comment Block: Enable the vendor combo box control and set focus to it
  SetProperty
    Control Name: cboVendor
    Property: Enabled
    Value: True
  GoToControl
    Control Name: cboVendor
End If
```

In the AfterUpdate event of this check box, we first check to see the current value of the chkAllVendors check box. If the check box is selected (True), we clear any value in the chkOneVendor check box, clear any value selected in the cboVendor combo box, and then disable the cboVendor combo box. If the chkAllVendors check box is cleared (False), the macro executes the actions after the Else keyword. Under Else, Access selects the chkOneVendor check box, enables the cboVendor combo box, and the sets the focus to the cboVendor combo box using the GoToControl action. If you examine the embedded macro logic behind the second check box on the form—chkOneVendor—you'll notice the macro logic is essentially the reverse of the macro logic behind chkAllVendors. Using SetProperty actions, we can effectively guide the user as they use the application forms and selectively hide, enable, or change form controls as needed.

Table 21-2 lists the SetProperty behavior for the seven web form control properties. If the cell in the table lists *Client*, Access changes the property of the control only when you view the form in client. When you view the web form in the browser and attempt to execute the action, you'll see a macro error message indicating the property is not supported. If the cell in the table lists *Web*, you can change the control property when you view the web form in the browser, but you'll receive an error message executing that action when you view the form in the Access client. If the cell in the table lists *Both*, you can change the property in both the Access client and the web browser. If the cell in the table is empty, you'll see a macro error message indicating that the property is unsupported if you execute that action when viewing the form in the Access client or in a web browser.

Table 21-2 SetProperty Action Behavior for Web Controls

Control	Enabled	Visible	Locked	ForeColor	BackColor	Caption	Value
Attachment	Both	Both	Both				
Check Box	Both	Both	Both				Both
Combo Box	Both	Both	Both	Client	Client		Both
Command Button	Both	Both		Both		Both	
Image		Both			Both		
Label		Both		Both	Both	Both	
Navigation Button	Both	Both		Both	Client	Both	
Navigation Control	Both	Client			Client		
Subform	Both	Both	Both				
Tab Control	Both	Both		Client	Client		
Tab Page	Both	Both		Web		Both	
Text Box	Both	Both	Both	Both	Both		Both
Web Browser	Client	Both					

INSIDE OUT Changing a Form Caption

You can dynamically change the Caption property of a form by using the SetProperty macro action. To set the Caption property of the form, leave the Control Name argument blank, select Caption for the Property argument, and enter the text you want to display in the Value argument. You can see examples of this technique in many of the detail forms for the Back Office Software System database. For example, you can study how we dynamically change the form caption in the Open event for the frmEmployeeDetails and frmInvoiceEdit web forms.

You can also check the current values of the control properties listed in Table 21-2 by referring to the control's properties collection in a conditional expression. You can verify a form's AllowAdditions, AllowDeletions, AllowEdits, and Dirty properties by referring to the form property in a conditional expression.

Calling Named Data Macros and Using Return Variables

In Chapter 7, you learned how to define return variables in named data macros. You also learned that you can call named data macros from table After events and then return data back to the calling table event by using return variables in the ReturnVars collection. In Access 2010, you can also call a named data macro from a user interface macro and then return data to the calling user interface macro for use in messages, forms, and reports.

On the frmInvoiceAudit web form you've been studying, the user first selects a beginning and ending date range to audit invoices and then selects to either edit all the vendors or a specific vendor within the given date range. The real magic for this web form, however, happens behind the Run Audit command button. If you have the Logic Designer still open from the previous section, close it, select the cmdRunAudit control from the Select box on the Property Sheet window, and then click the Build button on the On Click event property line to see the embedded macro logic behind this command button. Scroll down the macro design surface until you see the CheckRangeLimit Group block, as shown in Figure 21-9.

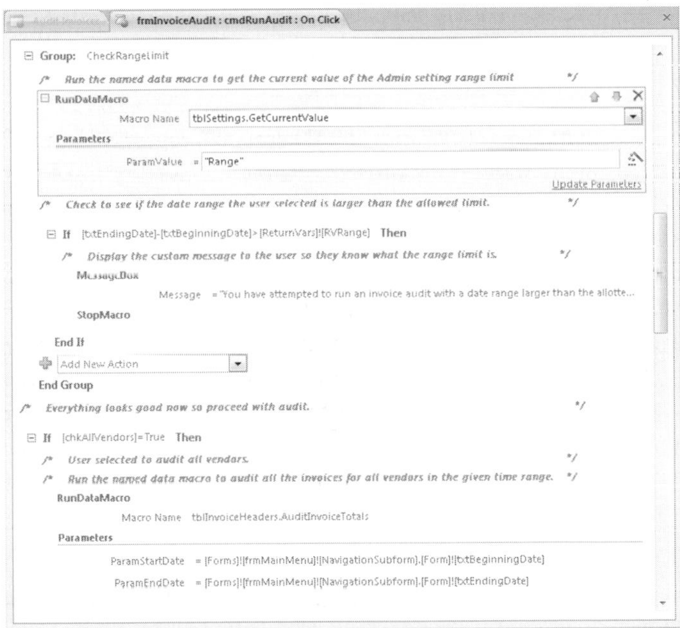

Figure 21-9 The macro logic behind the cmdRunAudit control calls named data macros.

The first part of this embedded macro (not shown in Figure 21-9) verifies the user entered a date range within the two text box controls, verifies the ending date is after the beginning date, and then verifies the user selected a vendor from the cboVendor combo box control if he or she chose to audit only one vendor. If any of the above conditions are false, the macro displays a message to the user indicating the error, and then the macro halts further execution. If the initial test conditions pass, Access proceeds to the Group block called CheckRangeLimit.

Auditing invoice records can be a time-consuming operation to perform, especially if you have many invoices and invoice detail records to verify within the database. We purposely created a field in the tblSettings web table that we could use to limit the number of days selected in a date range for different application operations. The default setting we defined in the tblSettings RangeLimit field is 7 days. Within the CheckRangeLimit Group block, you can see we use a RunDataMacro action to execute the named data macro called GetCurrentValue attached to the tblSettings web table. You previously studied this named data macro in Chapter 7 and learned that we use this named data macro to fetch values from the one record in the administrative table called tblSettings. In this embedded macro, we pass in the text value Range for the parameter value ParamValue needed for the GetCurrentValue named data macro. Access executes the named data macro and returns the value stored in the RangeLimit field to the user interface macro.

After the named data macro finishes executing, Access continues with the next action in the embedded macro. Before starting the process of auditing invoices, the embedded macro compares the number of days the user selected to the maximum value allowed in the RangeLimit field. We accomplish this test by subtracting the beginning date from the ending date and seeing if that value, in number of days, is greater than 7 days. Our conditional expression for this test in the If block is as follows:

```
[txtEndingDate]-[txtBeginningDate]>[ReturnVars]![RVRange]
```

You'll notice we can use the return variable RVRange just returned from the named data macro by referencing the ReturnVars collection. If the user selected a range of dates greater than our default of 7 days, the macro displays a custom message and then stops the macro. In Figure 21-9, you cannot see the entire expression we use for the custom message, so we've listed it here:

```
="You have attempted to run an invoice audit with a date range larger than the
  allotted number of days. Please restrict your date range to " &
  [ReturnVars]![RVRange] & " days."
```

Here again, we reference the RVRange return variable and display that value in a custom message. Users of this application have an easier time understanding why Access does not run the macro if they see a message that tells them exactly the maximum number of days they can select for the audit procedure.

If the user selected a date range less than or equal to our default of 7 days, Access continues with the remaining actions defined in the embedded macro. If the user selected to audit all vendors, Access executes the AuditInvoiceTotals named data macro attached to the tblInvoiceHeaders web table. (You can see this macro action at the bottom of Figure 21-9, shown previously.) If the user selected to audit only a single vendor, Access instead executes the AuditInvoiceTotalsOneVendor named data macro attached to the tblInvoiceHeaders web table. In both cases, we pass the beginning date and ending date as parameters to the named data macros. If the user selected only one vendor, we also pass in the VendorID from the cboVendor combo box to the AuditInvoiceTotalsOneVendor named data macro.

After the named data macro completes auditing the invoices, Access returns the number of unbalanced invoices found in a return variable called RVUnbalanced. Access could find either no unbalanced invoices or at least one unbalanced invoice within the given parameters. In Figure 21-10, you can see that we use an If conditional expression to test the value of this return variable. (Scroll down the macro design surface so you can see the macro actions we're discussing here.) If the return variable RVUnbalanced is 0, there are no unbalanced invoices so the macro displays a custom message indicating Access did not find any unbalanced invoices. The macro is effectively finished at this point if Access found no unbalanced invoices because the remaining actions are within an Else block.

The macro then uses another If condition expression to see if the return variable RVUnbalanced is 1. If the value is exactly 1, the macro displays a message to the user with a singular tone in the sentence structure for the message. If the value is not 1, this means Access found more than 1 unbalanced invoice, so the macro executes the actions in the Else block. Here again, we display a message to the user indicating the number of unbalanced invoices found, but in this case, we use a plural tone in the sentence structure. Finally, the macro browses to another web form to display the list of unbalanced records Access found after executing the named data macros. (You'll learn about browsing to another form in the next section.) As you can see, using the RunDataMacro macro action in conjunction with named data macros and return variables allows you great flexibility to pass data from the form level to the data layer and back.

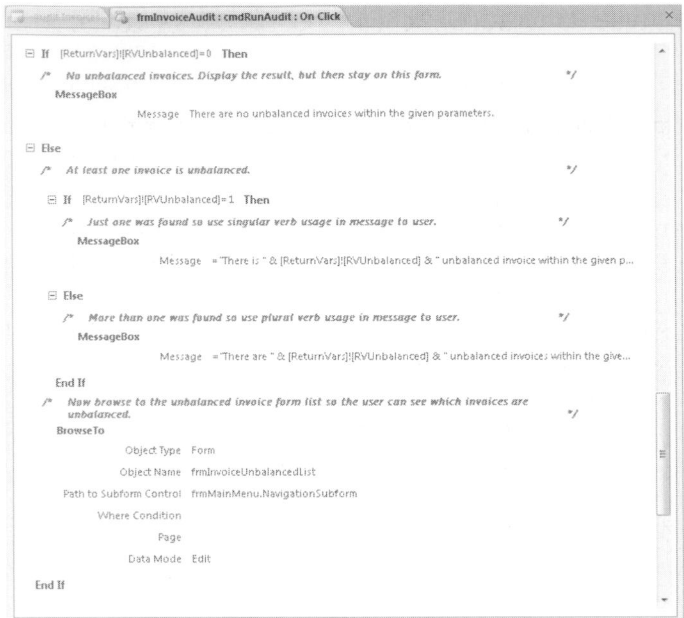

Figure 21-10 This macro uses return variables to display the number of unbalanced records found in message boxes.

INSIDE OUT Referencing Local Variables in User Interface Macros

In Chapter 7, you learned how to use local variables in data macros to store a value that can be used throughout the execution of the data macro. You can also use local variables in user interface macros by using the SetLocalVar macro action. You need to be aware, however, of one important difference when using local variables in the context of user interface macros. In data macros, you can refer to the value of a local variable by using only the local variable name in brackets. When you're referencing local variables in user interface macros, however, you must reference them by prefixing the LocalVars collection. For example, to reference a local variable called MyVariable within a user interface macro, use the syntax [LocalVars]![MyVariable] to retrieve the value correctly.

Using BrowseTo Macro Actions to Browse to Forms and Reports

Near the bottom of the embedded macro in the OnClick event of the cmdRunAudit command button you've been studying so far, you'll notice we use a macro action called BrowseTo. The BrowseTo macro action is a new macro action in Access 2010. You can use the BrowseTo action to browse to a different top-level form object or report object or you can browse to a different form or report displayed inside a subform control, such as a navigation control. As we've mentioned previously, nearly all the forms and reports in the Back Office Software System web database are displayed inside the frmMainMenu and frmMainMenuClient forms. Both of these forms contain a navigation control to allow users to easily click the navigation buttons and view different forms and reports, much as you see for website navigation. Behind the scenes, Access is essentially performing a BrowseTo macro action to swap out the object shown in the navigation subform container control.

Listed below are the BrowseTo macro action and argument values we use in the cmdRunAudit embedded macro:

```
BrowseTo
  Object Type: Form
  Object Name: frmInvoiceUnbalancedList
  Path To Subform Control: frmMainMenu.NavigationSubform
  Where Condition:
  Page:
  Data Mode: Edit
```

In the Object Type argument, you can choose to browse to either a form or report. In the Object Name argument, you provide the name of the form or report you want to browse to with this action. In the Path To Subform Control argument, you provide the path to the subform control you want the form or report to display in. (We'll discuss this argument in more detail shortly.) In the Where argument, you can use an expression to filter the records in the form or report. In the Page argument, you can enter the page number you want to display for a continuous form. (Continuous web forms have a Page Size form property—20 by default—that the server uses to know how many records to display on each page when you view the web form in a browser. You can also use the Page argument to browse to a specific page for your continuous web form.) In the Data Mode argument, you can choose to select Add, Edit, or Read Only. If you choose Add, Access browses to the form and displays a new record. If you select Edit, Access browses to the form and allows you to edit the data. If you select Read Only, Access browses to the form, but you cannot edit any data. The BrowseTo argument also allows you to pass parameters to the form or report you want to browse to, such as the OpenForm and OpenReport actions discussed previously.

Most of the arguments for the BrowseTo action are straightforward; however, the Path argument needs more clarification. The BrowseTo action functions quite differently based on the Path argument and where you initiate the macro action. For example, you could call the BrowseTo action from a top-level form—a form not contained with a subform control. You can also call the BrowseTo action from a form currently displayed within a subform container. Here are the possible results of using BrowseTo based on the context:

- If you call the BrowseTo action from a top-level form and leave the Path argument blank, Access opens (or browses to, as the term implies) the form or report specified in the Object Name argument. You can think of the BrowseTo, in this instance, as a hyperlink—Access closes the current form and then opens the other form or report.
- If you call the BrowseTo action from a form displayed inside a parent form's subform control and leave the Path argument blank, Access changes the subform Source Object property and displays the form or report specified in the Object Name argument. In this case, Access does not open or close a new parent form; Access merely swaps out one subform or subreport for another subform or subreport inside the subform container.
- If you call the BrowseTo action from a form displayed inside a parent form's subform control and provide a valid Path argument, Access allows you to change the Source Object property of any subform control currently displayed.

You might have noticed that in the BrowseTo action for our example, we provided a Path argument, but we also display the frmInvoiceAudit web from inside the subform control called NavigationSubform on the frmMainMenu web form. Our example doesn't seem to fit with the three results we just showed you, but we did that on purpose. Our example actually fits into the third category above. If we remove the Path argument `frmMainMenu.NavigationSubform`, we can still have the same functionality we want; Access swaps out the current form, frmInvoiceAudit, with the frmInvoiceUnbalancedList web form inside the NavigationSubform container displayed on the frmMainMenu web form. Our example Path argument works because we provide a valid Path argument that contains only the element for the subform container.

If you want to use the BrowseTo action to dynamically change the Source Object of any subform currently displayed, you can use syntax for the Path argument like the following:

```
MainForm.SubformControlOnMainForm>FormNameLoadedInsideMainForm.SubformControlName
```

Let's assume that for the Object Name argument, you provide a form name called MyForm. In the example Path argument above, Access loads the form called MyForm inside the SubformControlName subform control of the FormNameLoadedInsideMainForm form object. The form called FormNameLoadedInsideMainForm, in turn, is loaded inside the SubformControlOnMainForm subform control of the MainForm form.

The Path argument must be a series of valid FormName.SubformContolName with the greater than (>) symbol separating the pairs. You can think of the Path argument with the greater than symbol as the following: Access loads the form specified to the right of the greater than symbol into the subform control specified to the left of the greater than symbol. The first form name you specify in the Path argument must be a form currently loaded in the Access window or in your browser window. You can only use the Path argument to change the contents of a subform control that is currently open.

Note

When you enter the form, report, and subform container names in the Path argument for the BrowseTo macro action, do not include any brackets or quotation marks even if your object names contain spaces. If you include brackets or quotation marks, Access displays an error message indicating the Path argument is invalid when you execute the macro action.

If you'd like to see how this BrowseTo action works, close the Logic Designer if you still have it open, close the frmInvoiceAudit web form, and then open the frmMainMenu web form from the Navigation pane. (If you are prompted to save any changes to the macro or form when you attempt to close the objects, click No.) After the frmMainMenu opens, click the Purchases top-level navigation button and then click the Audit Invoices second-level navigation button to display the frmInvoiceAudit web form inside the navigation subform. Enter **9/6/2010** in the beginning date control, enter **9/12/2010** in the ending date control, leave the vendor option set on the defaults, and then click the Run Audit command button. Access runs the macro actions you just studied and then displays a message box indicating it found one unbalanced invoice (assuming you have not changed any of the sample data in this database). After you click OK in the message box, Access browses to the frmInvoiceUnbalancedList web form inside the subform container on the frmMainMenu web form and displays the one unbalanced invoice record, as shown in Figure 21-11. You'll notice that Access selects the Unbalanced navigation button on the navigation control.

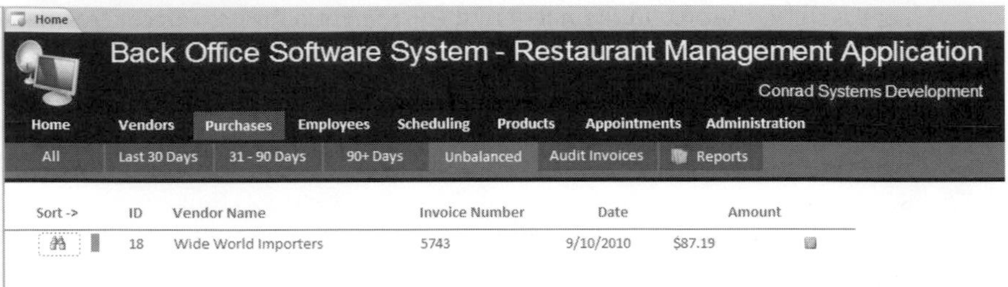

Figure 21-11 Access browses to the frmInvoiceUnbalancedList web form using the BrowseTo action defined in a different form.

> **When should you use BrowseTo instead of OpenForm?**
>
> **When you're working with web forms, you can only open forms in Dialog mode when you use the OpenForm web macro action. You cannot open forms in Normal mode for web forms as you can with client forms. What this means to you as a developer is that you cannot open multiple parent forms using the OpenForm action in web forms. If you use the OpenForm action in a web form, for example, you cannot open a main parent form and then close the one you just opened. If you need this type of automated interface functionality in web forms, you'll need to use the BrowseTo macro action to open (or browse, in the web context) a new main parent form and then close the parent form you just opened.**

Trapping Error Messages

In Chapter 7, you learned about the RaiseError data macro action and how you can specify your own error number for this error condition. In Chapter 20, you learned about trapping errors when running user interface macros. When you're automating your application with user interface macros and calling named data macros, Access (or the server, if you're running the web application in Access Services) could encounter an error at the user interface level or at the data level. You can trap for specific error message numbers you assign in RaiseError data actions at the user interface level exactly the same way as trapping other macro errors. You can add an If block in a submacro that tests the Number property of the MacroError object and perform different actions based on the error number returned.

On the frmInvoiceAudit web form you've been studying, we included an error handling submacro in the embedded macro logic attached to the cmdRunAudit command button. If you examine the error handling submacro logic attached to the cmdRunAudit command button, you'll see the macro first displays a message box to the user indicating an unexpected error occurred. The macro then calls a named data macro to record all the error details. We pass in the name of the form, the name of the control, the Macro Error number, the Macro Error description, the current user of the application, and the current computer time as parameters to the LogError named data macro. Note that in this specific case, we'll log all errors in this submacro, but we could just as easily trap for and possibly ignore specific errors or display different messages based on any errors raised during macro execution.

Checking SharePoint User Permission Group Levels

In the Back Office Software System sample web database, we verify the assigned group level for a user when the user navigates to the main web startup form in the browser. We then display one of two possible web forms based on the user's assigned group. We'll demonstrate how this functionality works in the browser in Chapter 22, but for now, we'll show you the macro logic and conditional expressions we use to check the Microsoft SharePoint group level.

Close any objects you might have open, right-click the web form called frmLoading in the Navigation pane, hold down the Shift key, and then click Layout view from the shortcut menu. Note that you must hold down the Shift key while opening this web form in Layout view to prevent the form's Load event from firing. If you don't hold down the Shift key, you won't see the frmLoading form open because the macro logic, which we'll discuss in a moment, opens a different form and then closes the frmLoading form.

Open the Property Sheet window, select Form from the Select box, click the Event tab on the Property Sheet window, and then click the Build button on the On Load event property line to view the embedded macro logic attached to this event, as shown in Figure 21-12.

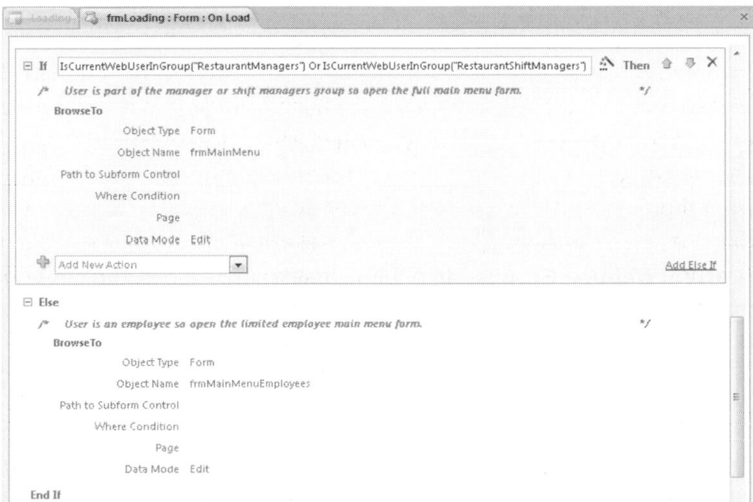

Figure 21-12 You can check the SharePoint group membership of a user by using the IsCurrentWebUserInGroup expression.

The first part of the macro logic in the form's OnLoad event (not shown in Figure 21-12), runs a named data macro to see if the Access Services site is available for use by checking a field value stored in the tblSettings web table. Next, the macro logic runs another named data macro to retrieve the version number of the application for use as a display value on the main form of the application. Finally, we use an If block to test the SharePoint group-level membership of the current user. In Figure 21-12, you can see that we use the following conditional expression for this test:

```
=IsCurrentWebUserInGroup("RestaurantManagers") Or
  IsCurrentWebUserInGroup("RestaurantShiftManagers")
```

You can use the *IsCurrentWebUserInGroup* expression to test for a specific SharePoint group name membership. This expression takes one argument—the name of a SharePoint permissions group. Note that you need to enclose the SharePoint group name in quotation marks. In published web applications, the IsCurrentWebUserInGroup expression returns a Boolean value indicating whether the user currently logged in is a part of the specified group. Note that if you use this expression in a client database, the expression always evaluates to false.

See Chapter 22 to learn how to create SharePoint permission groups and assign users to your groups.

In our example, if the user is a member of the RestaurantManagers or RestaurantShiftManagers SharePoint group, we browse to the frmMainMenu web form where all the administrative and application features are available. If the user is not in either of these SharePoint groups, the macro browses instead to the frmMainMenuEmployees web form where the employee can see their work schedule only. (We don't want employees other than managers to be able to view and edit administrative or confidential areas such as employee wages.) By using the IsCurrentWebUserInGroup Access Services web expression, we can display different forms depending which user is accessing the site. You can also selectively show, hide, enable, disable, or change form control elements by using this expression along with the SetProperty action you studied earlier in this chapter. For published web databases, you might also find the following two expressions useful:

- **CurrentWebUser** In published web applications, this expression returns a string representing the user currently logged in. This expression returns Null in client databases.

- **CurrentWebUserGroups** In published web applications, this expression returns a string listing the groups, separated by semi-colons, to which the user currently logged in belongs. This expression returns Null in client databases.

Performing Different Actions When Opening a Web Form in a Browser

When you're working with a web database, you might need to know whether a web form is currently open in Access client or in a web browser window. Close the Logic Designer if you still have it open, close any other open objects, and then open the web form called frmMainMenu in Form view from the Navigation pane. This web form is the main form we display to users when they are using the application. This web form also serves as an entry point to our main client form called frmMainMenuClient. If you double-click the image logo displayed at the top of the frmMainMenu web form, you'll notice that Access closes the frmMainMenu web form and then opens the frmMainMenuClient client form. This little trick serves as a unique entry point to the client forms that complement the web objects in our hybrid application.

Open the frmMainMenu in Layout view and let's take a look at how we test the form's current context using macros. Open the Property Sheet window, select imgLogo from the Select box, click the Event tab on the Property Sheet window, and then click the Build button on the On Dbl Click event property line to view the embedded macro logic attached to this event, as shown in Figure 21-13.

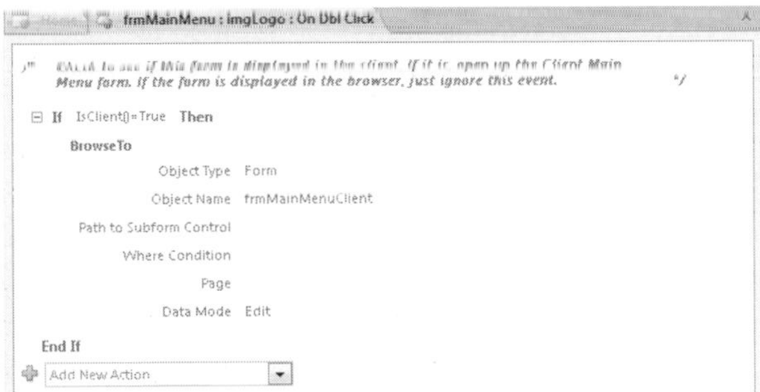

Figure 21-13 You can use the IsClient expression to test to see if your web form is open in client or in a browser.

In the conditional expression for the If block in this embedded macro, we use the IsClient web expression. The IsClient web expression returns true when evaluated on the client and returns false when evaluated on the server. If the user opens this web form in Access client and double-clicks on the image logo, Access runs this macro logic and determines the web form is open in Access client. Access then performs the BrowseTo macro action inside the If block and browses to the frmMainMenuClient client form. If the user double-clicks the image logo when the web from is open in a browser, Access evaluates the condition to false and, therefore, does not try to open the client form.

Note

You cannot perform client functionality, such as calling Visual Basic code or using client macro actions, on a web form using the IsClient expression; you are limited to using web macro actions available on web forms. You can, however, open client forms and reports even though Access does not list client form and report names in the drop-down list of object names for OpenForm, OpenReport, or BrowseTo web macro actions. If you want to open a client form or client report in a web macro, you'll need to manually type the object name in the Object Name argument for those actions.

INSIDE OUT **Using SetProperty under Different Form Contexts**

If you'd like to see another example of using the IsClient expression in the Back Office Software System sample web database, look at the embedded macro logic attached to the OnLoad event of the frmInvoiceEdit web form. When you view a form in Access client, you cannot perform a SetProperty macro action that changes the ForeColor property of a tab page. You can, however, change the ForeColor of a tab page when you view a web form in a browser window. We use the IsClient expression to test if the user opened the frmInvoiceEdit web form in client. If the expression evaluates to false, we know the form is currently open in the browser window so the macro dynamically changes the ForeColor of the tab page on the form to green or red depending upon the balanced status of the current invoice.

Avoiding Type Coercion Issues

One of the most challenging aspects you'll find in automating your web application is avoiding type coercion issues. Access client is generally correct when it needs to guess the data type of a value in a control used in a user interface or data macro. When you're viewing your web forms in a browser, however, Access Services does not always follow the client behavior. You might find that your macro actions on web forms function exactly the way you want when you work with the form in Access client, but the same macro actions result in different behavior, perhaps even displaying runtime error messages, when you work with the same web form in a browser.

In general, if you have a web form control bound to a field in a web table, or a field in a web query that is bound to a field in a table, the server can correctly identify the data type of the data displayed in the control when you use that value in user interface and data macro actions. You might, however, encounter errors when you use unbound text boxes on web forms displayed in the browser. By default, the server interprets an unbound text box as a string data type. If you're working with string values in the text box, this won't be an issue. If you're working with Number, Currency, or Date/Time values, you'll likely encounter unexpected results. Unfortunately, the server does not offer as many tools as client does to convert a value to another data type. For web forms, you can only use the CDbl function to convert a value in an unbound text box to a Double.

To work around the limitations of unbound controls, make sure you set the Format property of the unbound control to a format appropriate for the data type. If you set a Format property for the unbound control, the server uses that property to determine the data type of the data to use in your macro actions. For example, if you examine the unbound date controls on the web forms in the Back Office Software System, you'll notice we set the Format property to Short Date. If we have a text box control that displays a whole number value, we set the Format property to Standard and the Decimal Places property to 0. If we use an unbound combo box control that displays the ID and other values from a web table, we generally wrap the control value within a CDbl function inside macro action expressions before sending the data to other actions such as OpenForm, OpenReport, or RunDataMacro. If we want to display currency values, we set the Format property to Currency.

See Article 4, "Function Reference," on the companion CD, for a list of Access functions supported in web objects.

We've previously discussed the topic of Boolean values and web objects in Chapter 6, "Designing Web Tables," but the topic bears repeating here. SharePoint Boolean fields store True values as 1, unlike Access Boolean fields which store True as –1. To work around this disparity, you should only use check boxes to display Boolean fields in web databases. (When you create a Boolean field in a web table, you'll notice that Access only gives you the option to display check boxes.) If you attempt to use any restrictions, filters, or comparisons on the integer value of Boolean fields on web forms, you'll see a runtime error when you view the web form in a browser. Note that it is still possible to use the integer value of Boolean fields in restrictions, filters, and comparisons in Access client with data published to the server; however, we recommend you always use True and False constants when working with Boolean fields to ensure consistent behavior in both client and server.

If you need to concatenate a string value with other data types, you can use the FormatCurrency, FormatDateTime, FormatNumber, and FormatPercent functions to format the other data types to a string value. Earlier in this chapter, you saw how to display the date parameter values in the Page Header section of the rptInvoiceDetailed web report. If you examine the expression used for that unbound control, you'll see we used the FormatDateTime function to concatenate the message text with the Date/Time values as the following:

```
="Includes invoices between " & FormatDateTime([txtBegDate],2) & " and " &
  FormatDateTime([txtEndDate],2)
```

We recommend you thoroughly test your web application macros not only in Access client, but also in a web browser after you publish your web database to an Access Services site. The Web Compatibility Checker tool does not usually catch these type coercion issues, so it's in your best interest to carefully test your application end-to-end and verify everything works as you expect in both client and server. You'll save yourself a lot of support calls identifying and correcting these issues before distributing your application to other users.

In Chapter 22, you'll learn how to publish your web database to a server running SharePoint 2010 and Access Services and work with your application in the browser.

PART 7

Working with the Web

CHAPTER 22

Using Web Applications in a Browser

You've created your web tables, queries, forms, reports, and macros, and now you're ready to publish your web database to a server running Microsoft SharePoint 2010 and Access Services. The unique aspect of publishing a web database to an Access Services site is that everything about your application—the data, the web objects, the database properties, and even client objects—is stored on the SharePoint server.

Note

The examples in this chapter are based on the Back Office Software System sample web database (BOSS.accdb), the BOSSLogsForServer.accdb web database, and the ContactsMap.accdt web template on the companion CD included with this book. The results you see from the samples in this chapter might not exactly match what you see in this book if you have changed the sample data in the files. Also, all the screen images in this chapter were taken on a Windows 7 system using Windows Internet Explorer version 8 and the Access color scheme set to Silver. Your results might look different if you are using a different operating system, different browser, or a different color scheme.

In this chapter, you will learn how to

- Publish your web database to a server running SharePoint 2010 to create an Access Services site.
- Work with the forms and reports in your web application inside a web browser.
- Create SharePoint permission groups for your site and assign users to groups.
- Use the Recycle Bin to restore deleted records.

- Make changes to a published web application from Microsoft Access 2010 client and synchronize your changes with the server.
- Work offline with your web application from Access client.
- Remove your web application from the server.
- Instantiate a web template on the server to create an Access Services site.

Working with SharePoint

SharePoint 2010 is a web-based server product from Microsoft that enables companies to create a central repository for many types of information that can be viewed and updated by authorized users. SharePoint 2010 runs as a service on servers running Windows Server 2008 or later and uses Microsoft SQL Server to store and manage the shared data. Any company that needs a way to improve team collaboration should find SharePoint very useful.

A full discussion of SharePoint and all its features is beyond the scope of this book, so our goal in this chapter is to familiarize you with how to use Access Services in conjunction with SharePoint. Access Services is a set of services that runs on top of the SharePoint 2010 Enterprise Client Access License (CAL). Check with the information technology (IT) staff in your organization to see if they have installed Access Services and SharePoint 2010 so you can publish your Access web databases to the server and collaborate with other users. If your internal organization does not have Access Services, look for third-party companies, including Microsoft, who offer Access Services hosting services.

In this chapter, we assume you already have access to and appropriate permissions for a server running SharePoint 2010 and Access Services so you can publish your web databases. A full discussion of installing and configuring SharePoint 2010 to run Access Services is also beyond the scope of this book. For more information on installing and configuring SharePoint 2010, see *Microsoft SharePoint 2010 Administrator's Companion* (Microsoft Press, 2010).

Publishing Your Database to an Access Services Site

Throughout this book, you've studied different parts of the Back Office Software System sample web database. This web database is a restaurant management application used by owners of restaurants to help keep track of various aspects of their business. This database can function perfectly in Access client without ever being published. However, to fully appreciate the benefits of Access Services, it's time you published this database to a server running SharePoint. To show you how to publish this web database, hold down the Shift key while you open the BOSS.accdb sample web database found on the companion CD. (Holding down the Shift key bypasses the startup properties we defined for this web database. Access also displays the default ribbon and Backstage view instead of our custom ribbons.)

Assigning a Web Display Form

Before you publish your web database, it's a good idea to first assign a web form as your web display, or startup, form. As you'll learn later in this chapter, if you don't assign a web display form for your web database, Access Services displays a web page that resembles the Navigation pane, displaying a list of all your database objects, when you navigate to the site. There is no requirement that you first assign a web display form before publishing your web database because you can also change this setting after publishing your web database. However, we recommend that you assign a web display form before allowing other users to use your Access Services site.

To assign a web form as your display form for Access Services, click the File tab on the Backstage view, click Options, and then click the Current Database category in the Access Options dialog box. In the Web Display Form combo box, you can select a web form to use as the web display form, as shown in Figure 22-1.

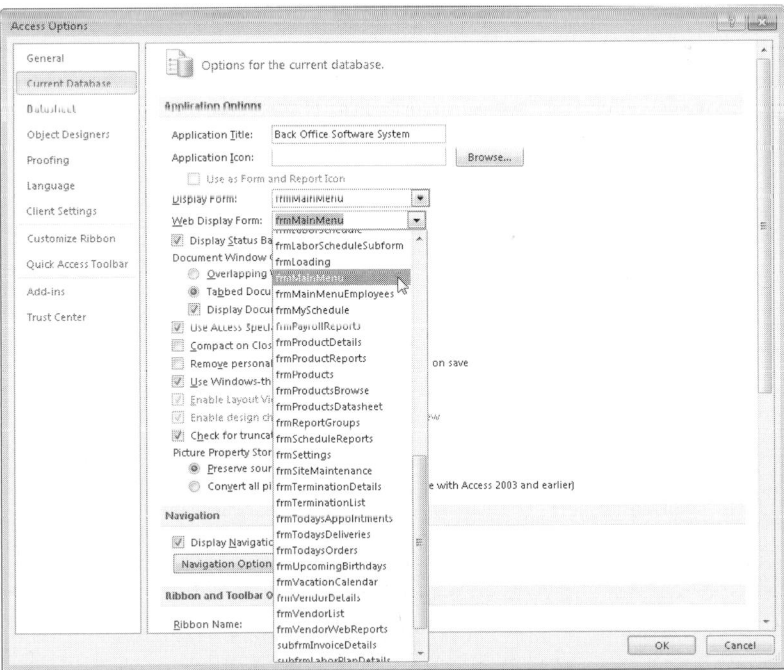

Figure 22-1 Select a web form as your web display form on the Access Options dialog box.

In Chapter 21, "Automating a Web Application Using Macros," you studied the web form called frmLoading. For this web database, we initially defined frmLoading as the display form for our Access Services application. When a user browses to our published site Uniform Resource Locator (URL), Access Services opens the frmLoading web form first and checks the permissions of the current user. We haven't defined permissions and set up SharePoint groups on the server yet, so for now, change the Web Display Form property to frmMainMenu by selecting frmMainMenu from the drop-down list, and then click OK to close the Access Options dialog box before proceeding to the next section. (You'll see how the frmLoading web form works in the browser later in this chapter.)

Understanding the Publish Process

To begin the publish process to the server, click the File tab on the Backstage view, click the Info tab, and then click Publish To Access Services. Access now displays the Save & Publish tab of the Backstage view with Publish To Access Services selected in the center pane of the Save & Publish tab, as shown in Figure 22-2.

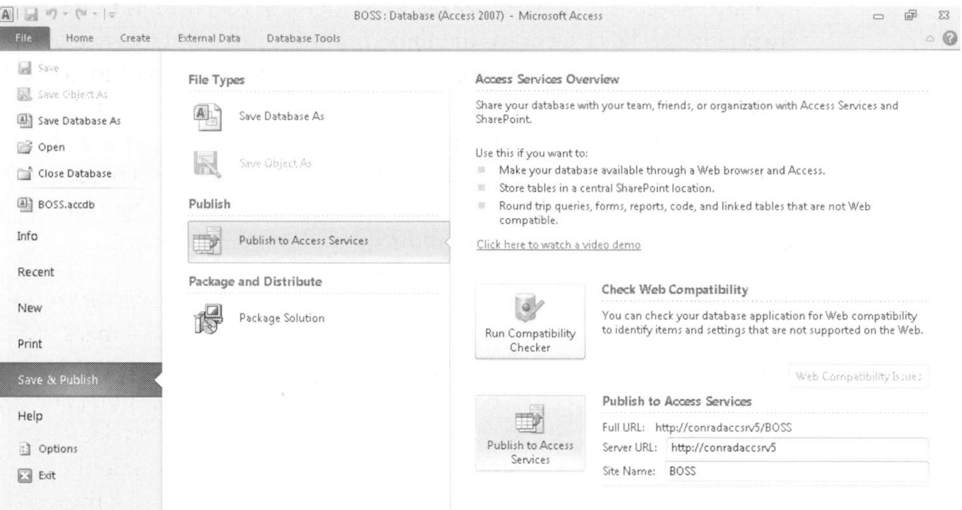

Figure 22-2 On the Save & Publish tab, enter the server and site name for your new Access Services site.

In the Server URL text box on the right side of the screen, enter the URL for your server running SharePoint and Access Services. If you are publishing to the root site of your SharePoint server, your URL might be something like *http://YourServerName* or *https://YourServerName*. In that URL example, *YourServerName* represents the name of your SharePoint server. If you are publishing to a sub-site on the SharePoint server, your URL might be something like *http://YourServerName/YourSubSiteName* or *https://YourServerName/YourSubSiteName*. If you are unsure of the URL to use, talk to your SharePoint server administrator. Note that if you do not include the *http://* prefix in the Server URL text box, Access adds it when you publish your web database. Access displays the full URL path that it will publish to above the Server URL text box. In the Site Name text box under Server URL, enter a name for your new Access Services site. Note that when you first open the Save & Publish tab on the Backstage view with this sample web database, the Site Name text box displays the text Back Office Software System. By default, Access fills in the Site Name text box with the Application Title found in the Current Database category of the Access Options dialog box. For brevity of a site name for your new test site in this example, enter **BOSS** in the Site Name text box, as shown previously in Figure 22-2.

Now that you've provided a location and name for your Access Services site, click Publish To Access Services on the right side of the screen. Access communicates with your SharePoint server and attempts to create a new empty Access Services site. Note that, at this point, you might be prompted for your login credentials to the server depending upon the security settings of the SharePoint server in your organization or the security settings of your third-party hosting provider. Enter your login credentials to continue the publish process. (If you have problems at this point with Access not accepting your login credentials for the SharePoint server you are trying to publish to, you'll need to talk with your internal SharePoint server administrator or your third-party hosting company for help with troubleshooting this issue.) If you attempt to create an Access Services site with the same site name as an existing site in the same location, Access stops the publish process at this point and informs you that an existing site with that name already exists. You cannot create an Access Services site with the same name in the same SharePoint location.

When Access successfully communicates with your SharePoint server and creates the new empty Access Services site, Access then closes the web database, makes a copy of your database in your Windows Temp directory, reopens the web database from that location, and then begins the publish process. Access next runs the Web Compatibility Checker tool on your web database. In Chapter 6, "Designing Web Tables," you learned that the Web Compatibility Checker checks the web compatibility of all the tables in a database as well as any web objects. This tool, however, does not check any data in the tables, nor does it attempt to check any client objects other than local tables. Access displays a progress bar as the Web Compatibility Checker scans your web database, as shown in Figure 22-3. If you click Cancel, Access stops the publish process and deletes the empty Access Services site it created earlier.

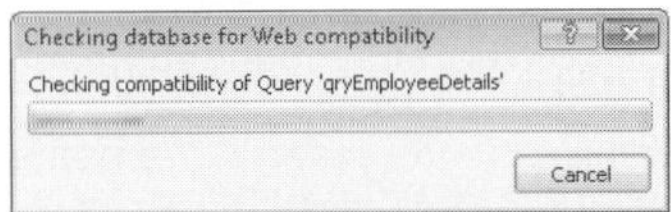

Figure 22-3 Before publishing your objects to the server, Access checks your web database for compatibility issues.

You can think of the Web Compatibility Checker tool as a gatekeeper, always making sure your objects are web-legal before you publish your database to the server, import objects into a web database, or make changes to existing objects and try to send those changes to the server. If the tool finds issues during this process, Access aborts the publish process and deletes the empty Access Services site. If the Web Compatibility Checker tool finds no issues with your web database, Access then begins the process of publishing your database objects to the server.

Access first creates a new SharePoint list for each one of your tables. In SharePoint terminology, a table is referred to as a list that stores information about a single subject. In a list, you have columns (fields) that contain the different kinds of information about the subject. Access creates columns for each list that match your Access web table fields. Next, Access uploads the data from your web tables into the appropriate SharePoint lists. Access then proceeds to upload all the client and web objects, such as queries, forms, reports, macros, and modules, as well as all shared images and form control images from your web database to the Access Services site. In Figure 22-4, you can see a snapshot of a few different points in time during the publish process with the Back Office Software System web database.

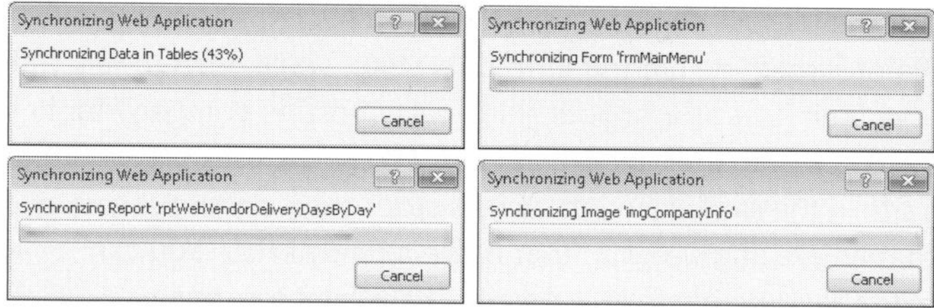

Figure 22-4 During the publish process, Access uploads all your database objects to the Access Services site.

INSIDE OUT Convert All Embedded Images in Client Objects to Shared Images in Web Databases

As you learned in Chapter 14, "Customizing a Form," if you are using a web database that includes client forms and reports, we recommend that you change all embedded images on client forms and reports to shared images. When you publish a web database to a SharePoint Server running Access Services, Access converts embedded images to text in client objects before sending to the server. Publishing and synching client objects with embedded objects can significantly increase the publish and sync time because the image is converted to text. If you convert all embedded images in client objects to shared images in web databases, you'll significantly decrease the amount of time it takes to publish and synch changes for your web database.

The entire publish process can take less than a minute, or it can take much longer, depending upon the number of objects in your web database and the amount of data in your web tables. For example, if you have thousands of records in your web tables, you can expect to see the publish process take much longer. Access should periodically update the Synchronizing Web Application progress bar with a percentage of data uploaded to the server. Your publish time also depends upon your connection speed. If your connection speed to the SharePoint server is slow, you can expect the publish time to take much longer to complete. If the publish process succeeds without any errors, Access displays a Publish Succeeded dialog box, as shown in Figure 22-5. Access displays a link to your completed Access Services site in this dialog box. If you click the link, Access opens your default web browser and navigates to your Access Services site. Click OK to close the dialog box.

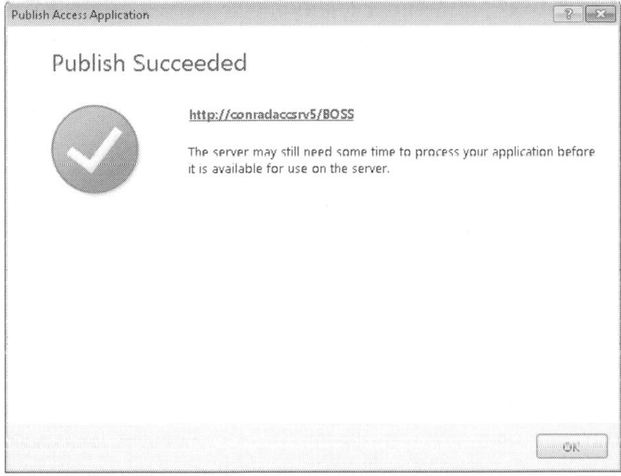

Figure 22-5 Access displays this message when the publish process succeeds.

> **Note**
>
> **After successfully publishing your web database to the server, Access appends the name of your original web database with *_Backup*. Access then moves the published web database from the Temp directory and places it in your original directory. You now have a published web database and a backup copy of your web database (before publishing) in the same directory. For example, if your file name is MyFile.accdb, Access creates a backup copy of your web database called MyFile_Backup.accdb in the same directory. MyFile.accdb is the published web database.**

Below the Publish Succeeded confirmation and hyperlink to your published application, Access displays a message indicating the server might still need more time to process your application before you can use the site. After Access sends up all the objects to the server, Access Services then compiles all the web objects. Access Services compiles the tables first (this includes any data macros attached to the tables) and then the queries, forms, reports, and web macros. If you browse to your completed site using the hyperlink on the dialog box shown in Figure 22-5, you might not be able to view your site objects until Access Services finishes the compile process. We'll discuss more about this process and what messages you'll see on the server later in this chapter. If you start to use your published web database within Access immediately after the publish process, you can encounter errors if Access Services has not finished compiling your site. For example, if you enter or edit data that triggers data macros, you might see an error message in Access if Access Services is still in the process of compiling those data macros on the server.

INSIDE OUT

Using a Shortcut to Your Published Application

After you publish your first web database to a server running SharePoint and Access Services, Access creates a new folder called Access Applications in your default database folder for new applications. If you're not sure of the location for your default database folder, you can open the Access Options dialog box and look for the path in the Default Database Folder text box on the General category page. In the Access Applications folder, you'll see a shortcut link to your published web database, as well as any other databases you previously published. Access uses the name of your Access Services site and the server name you published to as the name of this shortcut file. For example, if you used a site name *Test* and published to a server called *MyServer*, Access creates a shortcut file called *Test on MyServer.accdb*. Do not be confused by the file extension in the name. Your published .accdb file still resides in the directory folder from where you published; this shortcut file is just a pointer to that local copy of the published web database. If you double-click this shortcut file, Access opens the local copy of the published web application in Access client.

At this point, what you see in Access client is a local copy of your published web application. Your data is now stored in SharePoint lists, and you have linked tables in your local copy of the web application pointing to those lists. Your data and database object separation, in this sense, is really no different than having your data stored in a different data source such as SQL Server—you have linked tables to your data source and you work with that data using database objects stored locally. If you delete the local .accdb database file you just published from your computer, you haven't really lost anything. You can download an entirely new copy of your web application from the SharePoint server and see all your linked data and use all your database objects. You can have other users navigate to your published Access Services site and download a copy of the application to their computers as well. (We'll show you how to do that later in this chapter.)

Note

We don't recommend that you delete your local copies of published .accdb database files. In fact, we recommend that you always maintain good backups of all your Access client and web applications. Our comments in this section are merely to illustrate that you can obtain an entirely new copy of your published web application at any time by downloading it from your Access Services site. In good practice, the SharePoint server administrators should be conducting regular backups of their servers, which means your published Access Services applications should also be regularly backed up as well.

In Chapter 7, "Creating Table Data Macros," we showed you how to use the USysApplicationLog local table to analyze errors during data macro execution. During the publish process, Access deletes the USysApplicationLog local table, if one exists, because Access Services creates its own USysApplicationLog list as part of the site creation process. After you publish your web database to the server, you'll now have a link to the USysApplicationLog list stored in the Access Services site. If you need the data previously saved in the USysApplicationLog local table, you need to back up this data before publishing.

If the publish process completes successfully, Access Services compiles all the web objects on the server. If Access Services cannot successfully compile any objects, Access Services writes a record to the USysApplicationLog list for each object that fails to compile. (In practice, this should not occur very often.) You should periodically check this table when you're working with your Access Services site because this table contains information about data macro errors and object compilation errors.

After you publish your web database, you can open the USysApplicationLog table by clicking the File tab on the Backstage view. On the Info tab, Access displays a View Application Log Table button, as shown in Figure 22-6. Click this button to open the USysApplicationLog web table in Datasheet view. You'll notice in Figure 22-6 that Access displays a message indicating there are no new errors. If Access client or Access Services writes any new data to this table, Access displays the message, "Your application has new errors in the log," and highlights the Application Log area in red.

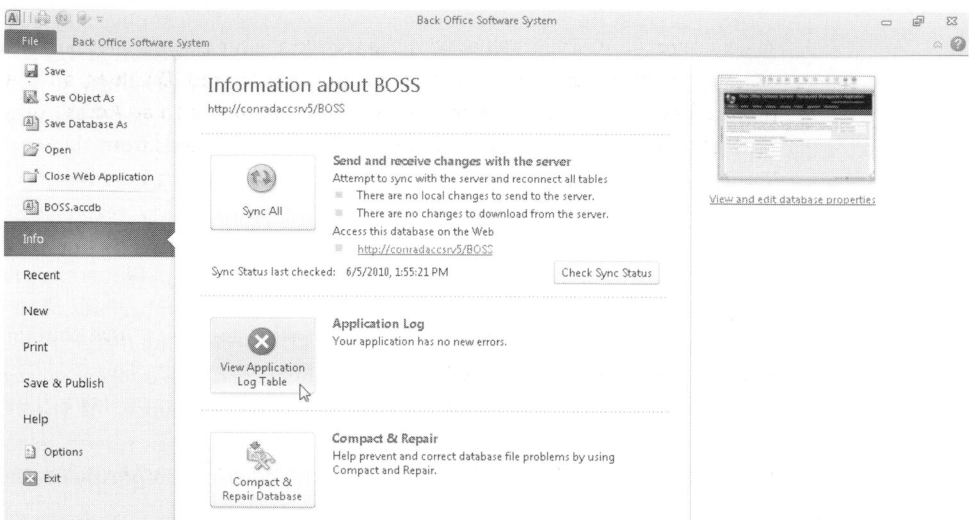

Figure 22-6 You can open the USysApplicationLog from the Backstage view.

ID Value Changes After Publish

After you publish a web database to an Access Services site, you'll notice that the ID values in your web table records might change. For example, if you have three records in a web table with ID values of 1, 3, and 5, and then publish that web table to an Access Services site, your ID values change to 1, 2, and 3. The reason your ID values change after publish is because the ID value in SharePoint lists behave like AutoNumber fields in Access. SharePoint increments the ID value automatically; you cannot set a SharePoint ID value programmatically to a specific value. When Access uploads the records to the SharePoint lists, SharePoint assigns an ID value to each record in sequential order. What this means is that if you have gaps in your ID values in Access before publishing, perhaps because you deleted records, you won't have gaps in the ID values initially after publish.

At first glance, you might be quite concerned about the ID values changing during the publish process, especially if you use those ID values as foreign keys in other web tables for lookup fields. The good news is that Access accounts for this issue by remapping any changed ID values in the parent web table to their respective child web table records during the publish process. For example, if your ID value in a parent web tables is 5 before publish and then is changed to 3 after publish, Access changes the ID value from 5 to 3 in any child table records that referenced that specific ID.

Access saves your old ID values with the web table in case you ever need them, although in most cases you never would. To see these old ID values, open a web table in Datasheet view in Access after publishing the database to an Access Services site, right-click any column heading, and then click Unhide Fields from the shortcut menu. You'll see a field called _OldID in the Unhide Columns dialog box. Select _OldID in this dialog box, click OK, and then you can see the ID value for this record before you published the database. You can safely delete this field if you want, or just leave it in the web database because the old ID value is irrelevant at this point.

If you're attaching any meaning to these ID values, such as for invoice numbers that cannot have gaps, you're using ID values incorrectly. The ID values in SharePoint lists, like AutoNumber fields in Access, should be thought of only as a unique record identifier.

Analyzing Publish Errors

So far in this chapter, we've discussed what happens when Access can successfully publish your web database to a SharePoint server running Access Services. But what happens when Access cannot successfully publish your web database? Even if the Web Compatibility Checker does not find any issues with your web database, you still might encounter publish errors. If Access cannot publish your web database to the server, you'll see a Publish Failed dialog box, as shown in Figure 22-7. When you click OK or close this dialog box, Access deletes the Access Services site it created at the beginning of the publish process.

Figure 22-7 You'll see this dialog box if Access cannot publish your web database to the server.

In the Publish Failed dialog box, Access informs you that it encountered problems during the publish operation. Access records any publish failure information in a local table called Move To SharePoint Site Issues. If you encounter this Publish Failed dialog box during a publish procedure, click the Move To SharePoint Site Issues link to close the dialog box and open the Move To SharePoint Site Issues table, as shown in Figure 22-8. Note that in Figures 22-7 and 22-8, we triggered this publish failure example by attempting to publish a table that included a Hyperlink data type field. In the data for this field, we included a URL that was more than 255 characters long, which is not supported in SharePoint lists. (The Web Compatibility Checker, as you recall from Chapter 6, does not check any data in tables, so if you run the tool on this example web table, the tool reports that everything is fine.) The structure might be fine, but the data is not, and you might not know this until you attempt to publish your web database to the server.

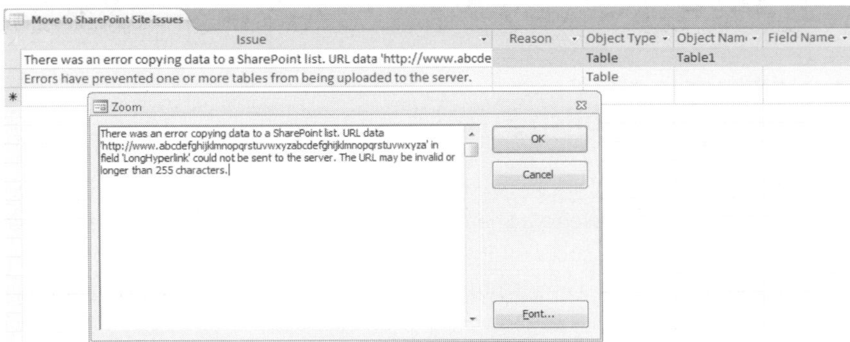

Figure 22-8 If you encounter publish errors, open the Move To SharePoint Site Issues table to examine the cause.

The Move To SharePoint Site Issues table includes five fields—Issue, Reason, Object Type, Object Name, and Field Name. In the Issue field, Access lists a detailed explanation of the specific publish failure. In the Object Type field, Access lists the type of object that it couldn't move to the server. In the Object Name field, Access lists the specific object name that it could not publish to the server. Note that Access does not enter any information in the Reason and Field Name fields in a publish failure scenario. In Figure 22-8, we tabbed into the Issue field and then opened the Zoom dialog box so you can see the error information Access created. You can see in the Zoom dialog box that Access could not copy the data to the server because the URL is invalid. If you encounter publish errors concerning data, you might need to run some client action queries before publishing to correct any data issues found in your web tables.

Working with Your Application in a Web Browser

Now that you're familiar with the publish process, let's learn how to work with your application in a web browser. If Access successfully publishes your web database to the server, Access displays the Publish Succeeded dialog box, shown previously in Figure 22-5. As we mentioned, Access Services needs to compile all your web objects after Access sends all the database information to the server. If you immediately browse to your Access Services site, you might see a Preparing Site page, as shown in Figure 22-9.

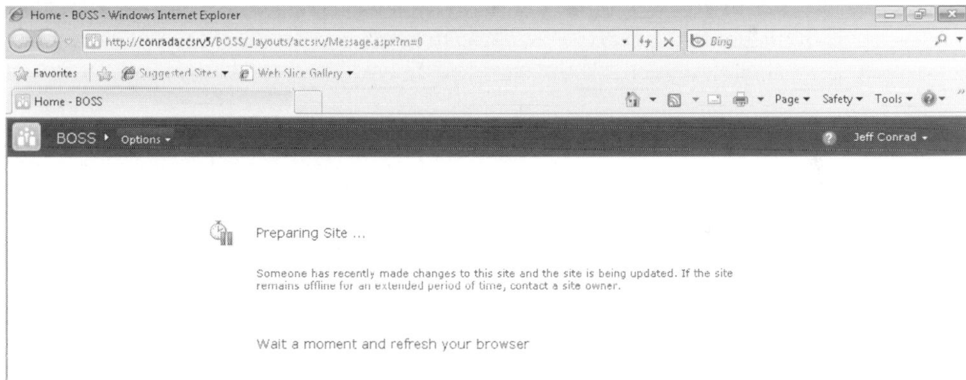

Figure 22-9 You'll see this web page when the server is compiling your Access Services site.

If you see the Preparing Site web page when you browse to your site, you'll need to wait a minute or two until Access Services finishes compiling all your web objects. The length of time for the compile process depends on the number of web objects in your web database; the more web objects you have, the longer the compile process takes to complete. You can refresh your browser (press the F5 key if you're using Internet Explorer) until Access Services displays the home page of your site.

Using Forms

After you publish the Back Office Software System sample web database earlier in this chapter to an Access Service site and the site finishes compiling, you'll see the main web form called frmMainMenu, as shown in Figure 22-10.

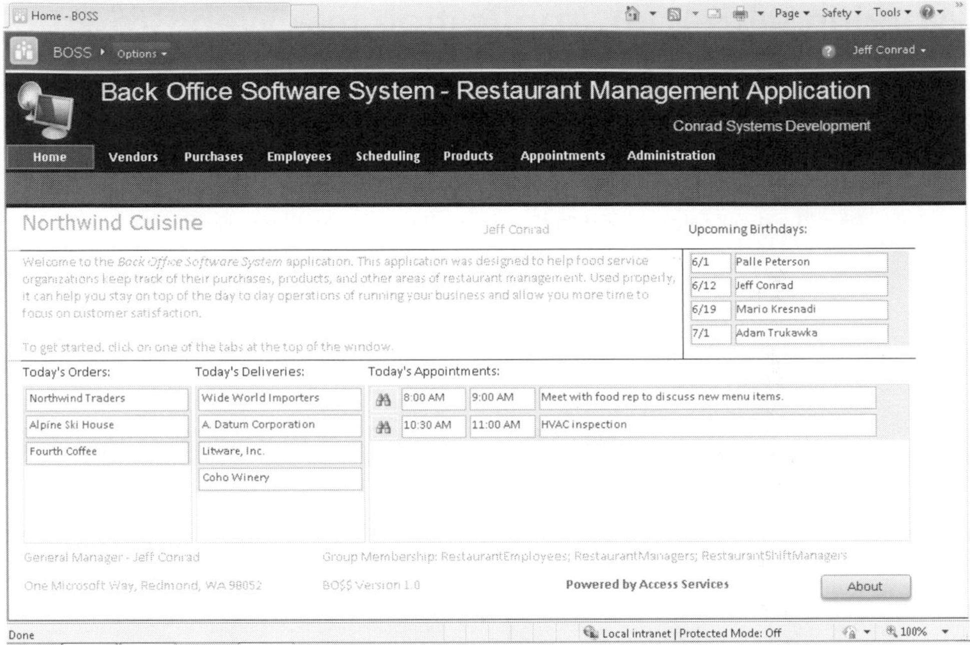

Figure 22-10 Access Services displays the main web form of the Back Office Software System after it compiles all your web objects.

INSIDE OUT Locating Your Published URL

If you cannot remember the URL to your Access Services site, but you have the published web database open in Access client, you can always find the URL on the Backstage view. Click the File tab on the Backstage view of a published web database and then click the Info tab. Access displays the URL as a link next to the Sync All button. Click this link to open your Access Services site in the web browser.

Navigating through the various web forms you've created in Access client should function the same way when you view your web forms in a browser. For example, if you click the navigation buttons on the main web form for the BOSS site, you'll notice that Access Services displays the correct subform in the navigation control. You can also open other forms, run user interface macros, close forms, call named data macros, and open reports by using macros you've attached to control events in the same way you work with the database in Access client. For example, click the Employees top-level navigation button, and Access Services displays the correct subform in your browser, as shown in Figure 22-11.

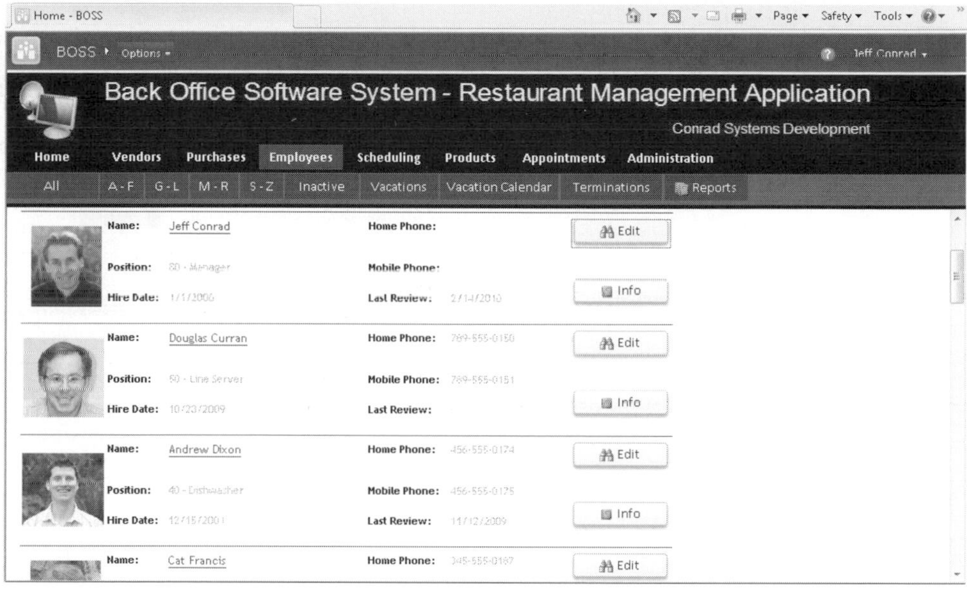

Figure 22-11 The navigation control functions the same way in the browser as it does in Access client.

Click the Edit command button for one of the employee records (we clicked the record for Jeff) and Access Services opens the frmEmployeeDetails form in Dialog mode, as shown in Figure 22-12. When you open a form in Dialog mode using the OpenForm web macro action, Access Services displays the form on top of other windows, in much the same way that Access client renders forms in Dialog mode. Notice, in Figure 22-12, that Access Services also dims the form displayed underneath the form opened in Dialog mode. You cannot interact with any form elements on any forms displayed underneath other forms open in Dialog mode. To close a form opened in Dialog mode, you can create a CloseWindow macro action attached to a control event (perhaps for a command button's Click event) or use the X (Close) button displayed in the upper-right corner of the form window. Close this frmEmployeeDetails form by clicking the X (Close) button in the form window or by clicking the OK or Cancel command button on this form.

Figure 22-12 Access Services displays forms opened in Dialog mode on top of other browser windows.

INSIDE OUT Receiving Feedback on Validation Rule Failures

When you define a field validation rule on a table field, Access Services can provide a visual cue when you enter data that won't pass the field validation rule on a bound web form. For example, if you enter a negative amount in the Pay Rate text box on the frmEmployeeDetails web form shown in Figure 22-12 and then tab out of the text box, Access Services changes the border color of the control to red as a visual cue that the data you entered won't pass the field validation rule we defined for the PayRate field in the tblEmployees web table. If you tab back into the Pay Rate text box, Access Services displays our custom field validation message as an alert message beneath the control. When you change the data in the Pay Rate text box control to a positive number and then tab out of the control, Access Services removes the red border around the text box.

If you make data changes to a record in any type of web form and then attempt to close the browser window or browser tab without saving those changes, Access Services displays a Confirmation dialog box, as shown in Figure 22-13. If you click Yes, Access Services discards any uncommitted data changes and closes the browser window. If you click No,

Access Services cancels the close request and keeps the web form open but does not commit the record changes. Note that if you click the X (Close) button on this dialog box, Access Services saves any pending record changes, dismisses the dialog box, and cancels the close request for the web form. If Access Services cannot save your changes, possibly because the data won't pass field or table level validation rules, Access Services displays a Record Not Saved dialog. You'll need to change your data to pass the validation rules in order to commit your record changes.

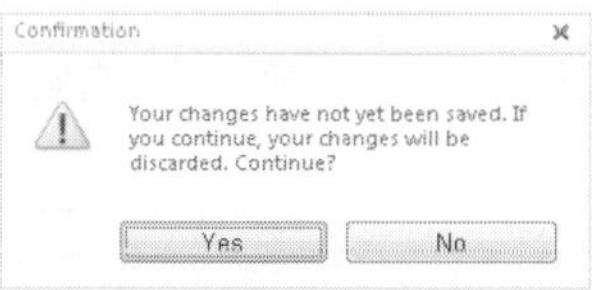

Figure 22-13 Access Services displays this message if you attempt to close a web form with uncommitted data changes.

When you clicked the Employees top level navigation button earlier, we designed the continuous form shown in the navigation subform to display all the active employees. By default, Access Services displays only 20 records in a continuous form page. If you scroll down to the bottom of this continuous form, you'll see that Access Services displays navigation buttons in the lower left corner of the form window, as shown in Figure 22-14. These navigation buttons in the web browser function similar to the built-in navigation buttons displayed on forms viewed within Access client. Access Services displays the current record number and the number of records in the form's record source on the left. Access Services also displays First, Previous, Next, and Last buttons, which you can use to navigate to different pages displayed in the web form. If your form is a single record form, the navigation buttons navigate you through each record because each record is essentially a new page. If your form is a continuous form, the navigation buttons navigate you through each page of records. In the Current Page/Record box, you can enter a page number you want to display, press Enter, and Access Services navigates to that page of records. On the right side, you can click New Record to begin creating a new record or click Save Record to save any changes to the current record.

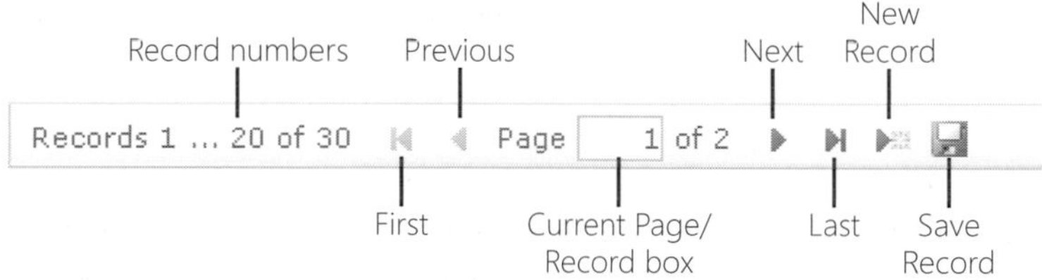

Figure 22-14 Access Services displays navigation buttons so you can navigate to other records.

> **INSIDE OUT** **Adjusting the Page Size Form Property**
>
> **You can display more records per page in a continuous form viewed in the browser by adjusting the Page Size form property in Access client. You'll see this form property listed only in the Property Sheet window for continuous forms, not for single record or datasheet forms. Keep in mind that your form takes longer to load in the browser when you display more records.**

Using Reports

Navigate to the second page of employee records by clicking the Next or Last navigation button. Access Services now displays the second page of employee records. Access Services loads the second page of records, but the focus remains at the bottom of the page. Scroll up the second page until you see the employee record for John Viescas, and then click the Info command button next to his record. Access Services opens a report showing John's employee information, as shown in Figure 22-15. Attached to the Click event of this command button, we have an OpenReport web macro action to open a web report showing the selected employee's personal information. You'll notice that Access Services opens the report in a new browser window. Access Services displays the report's Caption property—Personal Report, in this example—in both the browser tab and the upper-left corner of the browser window.

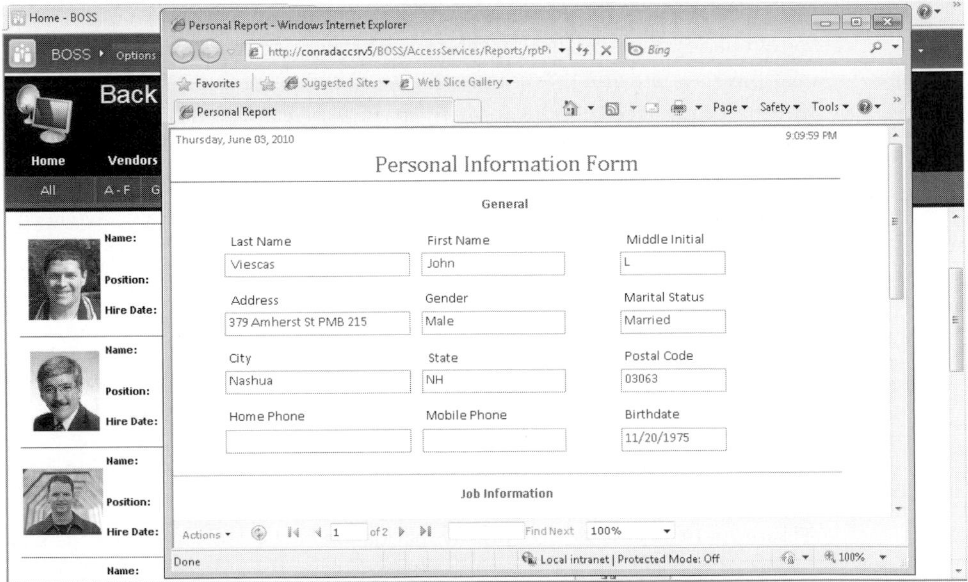

Figure 22-15 When you open a web report using the OpenReport macro action, Access Services opens the report in a new browser window.

At the bottom of the report browser window, you'll see a toolbar that contains buttons, as shown in Figure 22-16. These buttons are similar to the navigation buttons you saw previously for web forms. For web reports, you'll see additional options next to the First Page, Previous Page, Page Number Box, Next Page, and Last Page elements. On the left side of the web report toolbar is the Actions button, which you can use to select options to print or export your report to different formats. (We'll discuss these options in more detail in just a moment.) Next to the Actions button is the Refresh button. Click Refresh when you want Access Services to refresh the data shown in the report and display the most recent data changes. To the right of the Last Page button is the Find Text In Report box. Enter data you want to find in the report in this text box, press Enter or click the Find link, and Access Services searches the entire report, including data displayed in label controls, for the first instance of that search criterion. The Find Text In Report feature is very useful when you need to search for specific information in a report that contains a lot of data. For example, if you enter **03063** in this text box and click the Find link, Access Services highlights the data in the Postal Code field for John's record on the report. You can click the Next link, and Access Services continues to search for the next instance of 03063. In this case, because there is no other data that matches that criterion, Access Services displays a message box indicating that the entire report has been searched. To the right of the Next link is the Zoom box. You can adjust the zoom level of the report by clicking the zoom level options in this drop-down list.

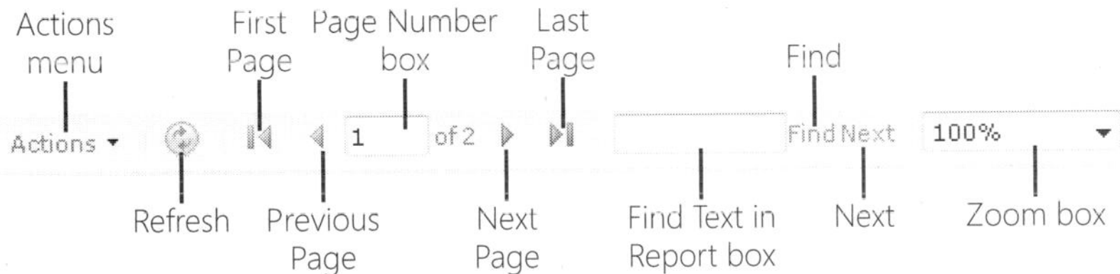

Figure 22-16 Access Services reports can display a navigation toolbar.

INSIDE OUT Hiding or Repositioning the Web Report Toolbar

When you open a web report by itself (not contained within a subform/subreport control) in a web browser, Access Services always displays the web report toolbar. If you display the web report inside a subform/subreport control, you can control whether to show or hide the web report toolbar in the browser. Open the web form that contains the subform/report control in Layout view in Access client, select the subform/subreport control, and then find the Show Toolbar property on the Property Sheet window. Select None, and Access Services will not display the web report toolbar when you view the form and embedded subreport in a web browser. Select Top to display the toolbar at the top of the report window or select Bottom, the default, to display the toolbar at the bottom of the report window.

Click the Actions button on the web report toolbar to see the Actions menu, as shown in Figure 22-17. If you click Print, Access opens the Print dialog box, where you can select the printer that you want to print to and adjust any printer preferences. Note that the first time you click Print, you'll see a prompt at the top of your browser window indicating you need to install the SQL Server Reporting Services 2008 add-in to print the report. Click this prompt and install the add-in to open the Print dialog box and print the web report. When you click Export on the Actions menu, you can select to export the web report to Excel (.xls), PDF (.pdf), or Word (.doc) format. Access Services exports the report and then prompts you for a location to save the file. You do not need to install Microsoft Excel, Microsoft Word, or Adobe Acrobat to export the web report because the server exports the file. You do, however, need to install Excel, Word, Acrobat, or Reader if you want to view the exported report on your computer.

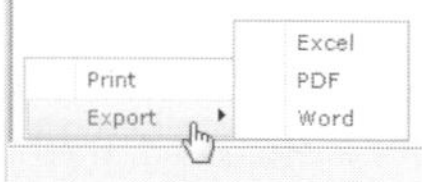

Figure 22-17 You can print your web report or export it to other formats by clicking the options on the Actions menu.

Using Datasheet Forms

Close the web report browser window currently open so you can see the main menu navigation form again. Click the Products top-level navigation button and then click the Datasheet View second-level navigation button to see a datasheet form displaying all the active products in the web application, as shown in Figure 22-18. Across the top of the datasheet form, you'll see column headers for each column of data. If you hover over the column header, Access Services displays a down arrow on the right side. Click the arrow button to open the AutoFilter menu. You can see that in Figure 22-18, we clicked the column header above the Inventory Location field to display the AutoFilter menu options available for this column.

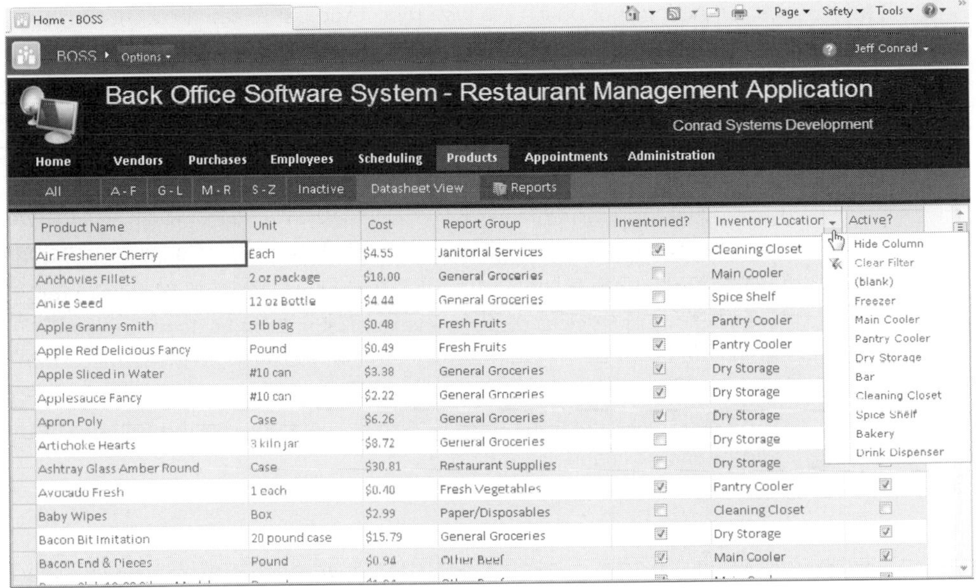

Figure 22-18 Access Services displays AutoFilter menu options for datasheet forms.

At the top of the AutoFilter menu, you can click Hide Column, and Access Services hides the column from view. Note that this change to the datasheet form is not permanent. If you refresh the browser or close the datasheet form and then reopen it, Access Services displays the column again. Beneath Hide Column, you can click Sort Ascending or Sort Descending (not shown in Figure 22-18) to sort the records in ascending or descending order by that column. You can click one of the filter options to filter the records displayed in the datasheet form to just the records that match that filter criterion. You can filter by more than one option by dropping the AutoFilter menu down again and clicking another option. Click (Blank) when you want to filter the data to show records where no value exists in that column. Click Clear Filter near the top of the AutoFilter menu to clear the filters and see all the data again.

You won't see all the options available in the AutoFilter menu, depending upon the data type of the column. For Memo fields formatted as Rich Text and Multi-Value Fields that look up data in a table, Access Services displays only the Hide Column option in the AutoFilter menu. When you have a Hyperlink field, you won't see any filter options. When you have a Lookup field that looks up data in a table, you won't see the sorting options.

INSIDE OUT Resize and Move Columns in Datasheet Forms

You can resize the width of the columns and reposition columns when you view datasheet forms in a web browser. To resize a column, position your mouse on the right edge of the column header until your cursor becomes a two-sided arrow. Click and drag the column header to the left to decrease the width of the column, or drag the column header to the right to increase the width of the column. To move a column, position your mouse over the column header until your cursor becomes a four-sided arrow. Click and drag the entire column header to the left or right to reposition the column. Access Services displays a vertical I-Bar to indicate where it will place the column when you release the mouse. Note that resizing and moving columns when you view the datasheet in a web browser is not permanent. If you refresh the browser or close and then reopen the form, Access Services displays the columns at their original widths and positions.

Datasheet forms displayed in the browser function very much like datasheet forms displayed in Access client. If you've enabled additions, edits, and deletions on the web form, you can create new records, make changes to the data, and delete records within the browser window. To create a new record in a datasheet form, you'll need to scroll to the bottom of the datasheet form window until you see the new record line and then enter your data on the new datasheet record. To delete a record, right-click the row selector on the left side of the datasheet form and then click Delete on the shortcut menu to remove the record. To edit data, you can click in a cell and edit the data. If you don't want to overwrite the existing data, you can press F2 after selecting a cell to go into edit mode, which positions your cursor at the end of the existing data. If you want to cancel any changes to the data in the cell, press Escape. You can use the Tab and arrow keys to move around the datasheet and press Enter to move down a column. When you move to a new record, Access Services automatically attempts to save the record. (You'll see this same behavior with continuous forms, too.) When Access Services successfully saves any record changes, you'll see a Record Updated message displayed briefly in the upper-right corner of the browser window, as shown in Figure 22-19.

Figure 22-19 You'll see a Record Updated message when Access Services saves your record changes.

Waiting for Server Processing

In the normal use of your web application, you might need to execute data macro operations that take a long time to complete. For example, you might run a named data macro from a user interface macro that needs to edit many records in a web table. When you call that named data macro, perhaps from an embedded macro attached to a Click event of a command button, Access Services sends the request to execute the action and then waits until the action completes. During this execution time, Access Services provides a visual cue to indicate a processing request is currently underway.

To see an example of a server processing message, click the Scheduling top-level navigation button on the main menu of the Back Office Software System and then click the Copy Schedules second-level navigation button. The form you see displayed in the navigation subform allows you to create new employee schedule records by copying data from a labor template, copying existing records from a specific date, or by copying existing records from a selected date range. In the Select Labor Plan combo box, select one of the two saved labor plan templates, enter a date into the Date To Apply text box, and then click the Create Schedule command button to run a named data macro to create new schedule records. Access Services dims the browser window to let you know it is currently running a data macro operation. If the data macro takes more than a few moments to run, you'll see a processing message. After a few more moments, Access Services displays another processing message, indicating that you can press Escape to return to the application, as shown in Figure 22-20. Note that if you press the Escape key, Access Services continues to run the data macro until completion or until it encounters an error. You might not see all your expected data additions, edits, and deletions if you press Escape before Access Services finishes running your data macro.

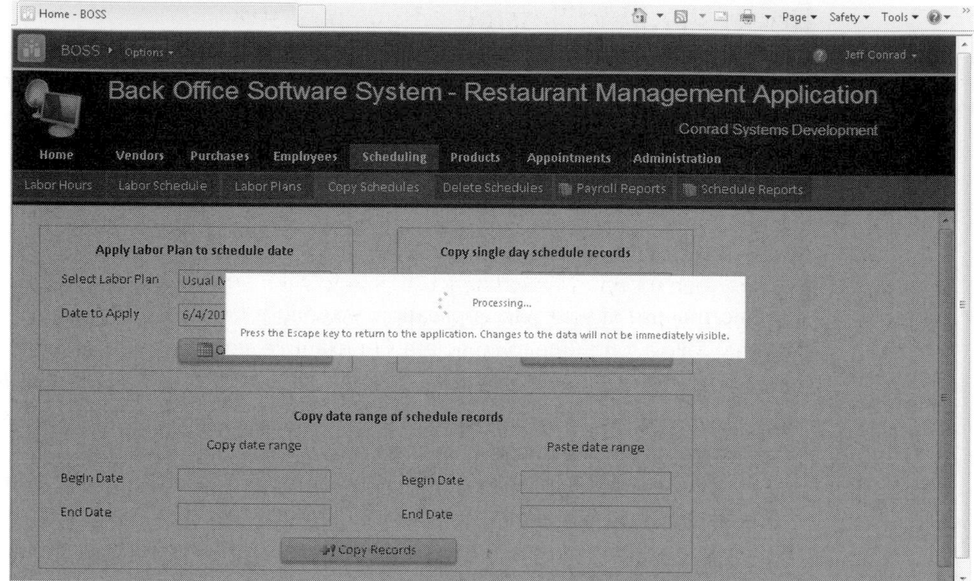

Figure 22-20 You'll see this message when Access Services is processing a data macro operation.

The first time you execute a specific data macro after publishing your web database to the server, Access Services takes slightly longer to complete the operation than it does on subsequent attempts. The reason for this is because Access Services needs to compile each data macro and perform setup work the first time you try to run that data macro. You'll notice it takes less time on subsequent attempts to execute the same data macro because Access Services does not need to perform the extra setup work. If you change the data macro, Access Services needs to recompile the data macro again on the first run.

Note

If you run a data macro in a published web application when you are working in Access client, you'll see a similar server processing message. In Access client, the message says "Please wait for server processing."

Understanding Session Management

One important and noticeable difference you'll encounter when working with an Access Services application in a web browser involves session timeout. When you are working with a client database in Access client, you generally don't have to worry about session time-out. If, for example, you are not using your computer for an extended period of time with uncommitted record changes or a database object open, you won't see error messages in Access client when you resume work on your computer. If, however, you leave your browser window open for an extended period of time without making any changes to a web form and then attempt to add, edit, or delete records, Access Services displays a session timeout message in the upper-right corner of your browser window and in some cases, also in a message box, as shown in Figure 22-21. When you see a session timeout message, you'll need to refresh your browser to continue working with your Access Services application. Note that if you have uncommitted record changes, you'll lose these changes when you refresh your browser. In this case, you might want to copy your record changes to the Clipboard or another program before refreshing your browser if you don't want to lose your uncommitted data.

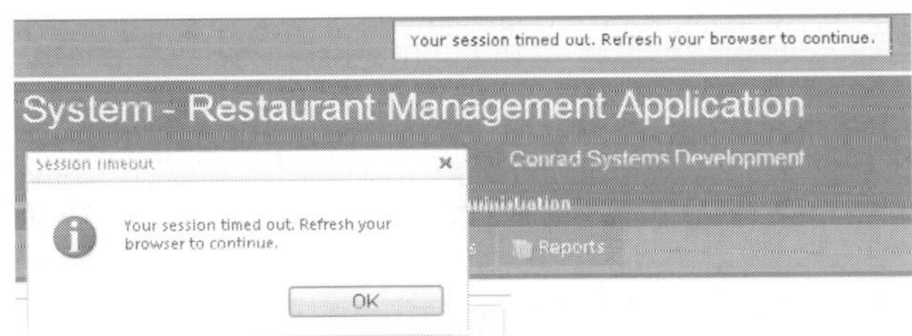

Figure 22-21 You'll see this message in your browser window if your session times out.

Access Services has several configurable server settings concerning session management that you should be aware of when working with your application in a web browser. By default, Access Services times out after 25 minutes of inactivity and you can have only 10 sessions per user. Each browser window or browser tab that displays an Access Services form uses one session. By default, this means you can actively work with only 10 browser windows or tabs pointing to the same Access Services site at the same time. Table 22-1 summarizes the server session management settings with a description of each setting and the default values. If you want to adjust the default values, you'll need to talk with your SharePoint server administrator because these settings affect all Access Service applications in the entire SharePoint server farm and not just each individual Access Services site. If you are using a hosted service for your Access Services applications, you'll need to talk with the hosting company about adjusting these settings.

Table 22-1 Server Settings for Session Management

Setting	Description	Default Value	Range
Maximum Request Duration	The maximum duration (in seconds) allowed for a request from an application.	20	–1 (indicates no limit); 1 through 2073600 (24 days).
Maximum Sessions Per User	The maximum number of sessions allowed per user. If a user has the maximum number of sessions and starts a new session, the user's oldest session is deleted.	10	–1 (no limit); 1 to any positive integer.
Maximum Sessions Per Anonymous User	The maximum number of sessions allowed per anonymous user. If this maximum is reached, the oldest session will be deleted when a new session is started.	25	–1 (no limit); 1 to any positive integer.
Cache Timeout	The maximum time (in seconds) that a data cache can remain available, as measured from the end of each request for data in that cache.	1500	–1 (indicates no limit); 1 through 2073600 (24 days).
Maximum Session Memory	The maximum amount of memory (in megabytes) that a single session can use.	64	0 (disable) through 4095

INSIDE OUT **Viewing Access Services Application Settings**

If you have sufficient permissions to your server running SharePoint and Access Services, you can view all the application settings applicable for Access Services applications. Navigate to the SharePoint 2010 Central Administration page on your server. Next, click the Manage Service Applications link under Application Management. Finally, click the Access Services link on the Service Applications page to view all the configurable administration settings for Access Services applications.

Exploring the Access Services Shell

Above your web form pages, you'll see a few hyperlinks and buttons that appear on every page of your Access Services site—the name of your published Access Services site, the Options button, the Help button, and your login name, as shown in Figure 22-22. These elements are referred to as the *shell* of your Access Services site. In the upper-left corner, you'll see the name of your Access Services site—BOSS, in our example. Click this hyperlink to return to the default page (your web startup form) at any time. Click Options, and Access Services displays four options in a drop-down list—Open In Access, Site Permissions, Settings, and Navigate Up. You can use the options in this menu to open a copy of the web application in Access client, navigate to a page to edit site permissions for your Access Services site, navigate to other pages of your Access Services, or to navigate to the parent site of your SharePoint server. We'll discuss these options in more detail in the next section.

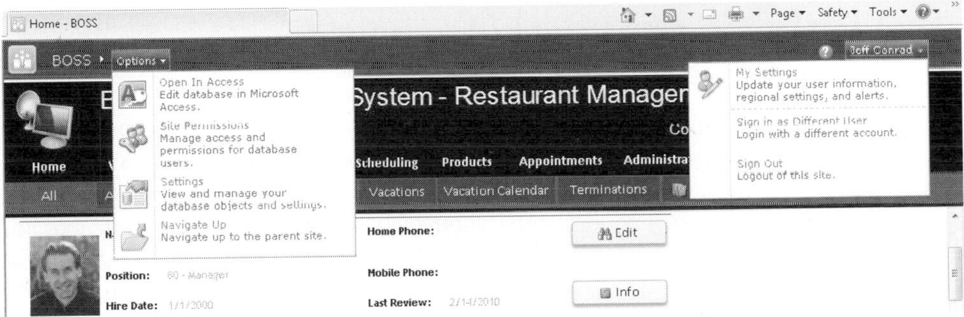

Figure 22-22 In the Access Services shell, you can access options to view different areas of your application and sign out of your application.

Click the Help button in the upper-right corner of the shell to open a Help web page on SharePoint 2010 topics. Click your login name and Access Services displays three options in a drop-down list—My Settings, Sign In As Different User, and Sign Out. You can use these options to update your personal information, sign in to your Access Services site as a different user, or sign out of the Access Services site. Click My Settings to open the User Information page, and then click My Regional Settings to modify settings such as locale, time zone, and default calendar. (In Figure 22-22, we combined two figures so you could see both option menu drop-down lists. Under normal use, you cannot access two drop-down lists at the same time.)

Note

Not all the options shown beneath your login name in Figure 22-22 are available depending upon how your SharePoint administrator configured the SharePoint server and what web page you might be viewing. For example, Access Services sites cannot use the Personalize This Page option shown on some web pages. If you click that option, you'll see an error message on the web page.

Downloading a Web Application Back into Access

Click the Options button in the Access Services shell, and then click Open In Access. Access Services opens the File Download dialog box, as shown in Figure 22-23. Click Open and Access Services downloads—or *rehydrates*—a copy of your Access Services web application to your computer and opens the application in Access client. Click Save to download an Access Web Application shortcut to your local computer. An Access Web Application shortcut has an .accdw file extension. This shortcut is merely a pointer to the published Access Services web application URL. You can send this .accdw file via email to other people that need to work with your published Access Services site from within Access client. When a user double-clicks the .accdw file, Access opens, downloads a copy of the web application to his or her local computer and synchronizes any server changes with their local copy of the application. Note that if the user has a local copy of the web application already, Access opens the existing local application and *synchronizes* any server changes into that copy. During this synchronizing process with the server, Access checks to see if there are any changes from the server that need to be sent to your local web database. If Access determines there are updates to any objects on the server that don't exist in your local copy of the published web application, Access retrieves those changes from the server and applies them to your local web database. (We'll discuss the synchronization process in more detail later in this chapter.) Click Cancel on the File Download dialog box to close the dialog box.

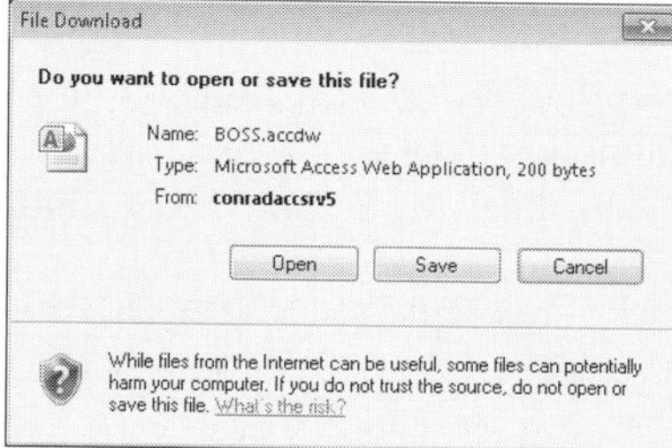

Figure 22-23 In the File Download dialog box, you can open the web application from within Access client or save a shortcut to the web application.

When you click Open, Access opens the local copy of this published web application on your computer and synchronizes any server changes to the local copy. If you have not opened the specific Access Services web application from your computer, Access Services downloads a copy of the application to your computer with all the latest changes.

Setting Site Permissions

You must grant other people appropriate permissions to access your site for them to use your Access Services application. To create, edit, and delete site permissions, click the Options button in the Access Services shell and then click Site Permissions. Access Services opens the Permission page, as shown in Figure 22-24. Note that the command options and groups on the SharePoint ribbon for this page can vary based on how your internal organization's SharePoint server administrator or third-party hosting services company configured the server you are using. For example, your Access Services site might inherit permissions from the parent site, (or from the hosting server's site) in which case you might see fewer command options in the ribbon.

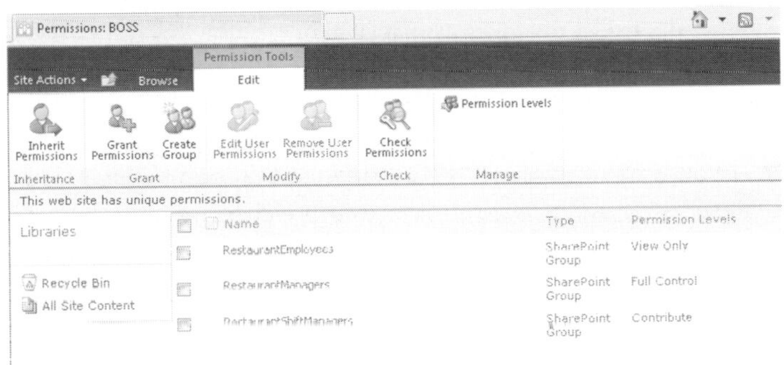

Figure 22-24 On the Permissions Tools page, you can edit the user and group permissions for your Access Services site.

For our BOSS Access Services site, we created three SharePoint groups—RestaurantEmployees, RestaurantManagers, and RestaurantShiftManagers. We assign each user of the Access Services site to one of these groups. It's not a requirement that you create your own custom groups because SharePoint includes several built-in groups. However, we wanted to have the additional level of control by defining our own custom groups. To create a new SharePoint group, click the Create Group button on the SharePoint ribbon. You'll then see the Create Group page, partially shown in Figure 22-25. In the Name box at the top of the page, you need to provide a unique name for your custom group. At the bottom of the Create Group page, you can specify the permission level that members of this group will have on your site. For the RestaurantManagers group, we selected Full Control (shown in Figure 22-25), for the RestaurantShiftManagers group, we selected Contribute, and for the RestaurantEmployees group, we selected View Only. Click Create to save your new custom SharePoint group and return to the Permissions page. Note that you might need to create new SharePoint groups at the parent site level, depending upon how your SharePoint server administrator or third-party hosting services company configured the server you are using.

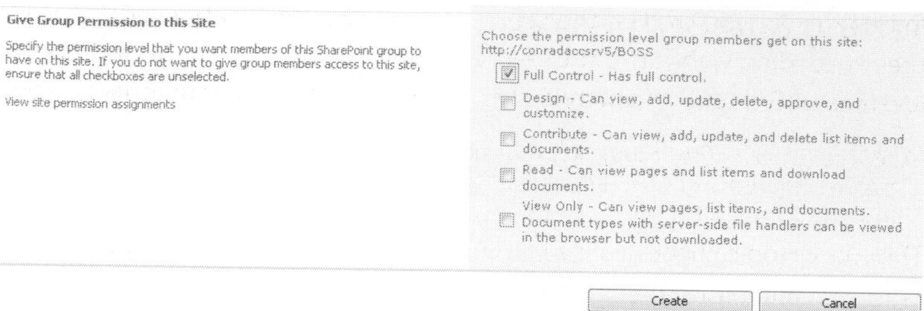

Figure 22-25 You can create new SharePoint groups on the Create Group page.

To assign a user to a custom group, click Grant Permissions on the SharePoint ribbon. SharePoint opens the Grant Permissions dialog box, as shown in Figure 22-26. In the Select Users box, enter the name of a user you want to give access to your site. Under Grant Permissions, you can add a user to one of the built-in SharePoint groups or one of the custom groups you created. Select the Grant Users Permission Directly radio button if you want to assign a user to a specific permission level. Note that you'll have an easier task managing permissions for everyone that uses your Access Services site if you assign users to groups instead of assigning permissions directly to each individual user. Click OK to save your changes.

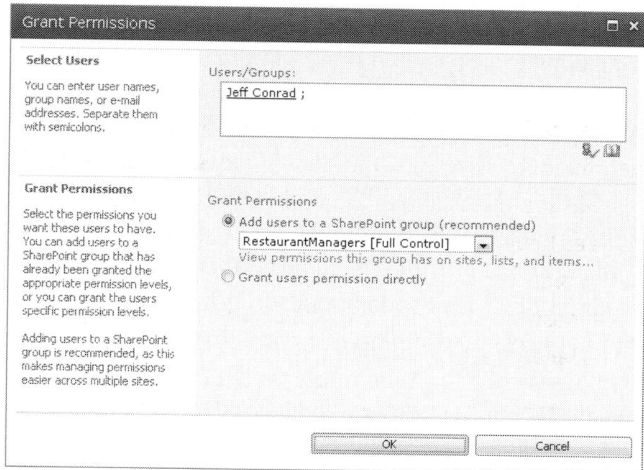

Figure 22-26 On the Grant Permissions dialog box, you can assign users to SharePoint groups or specific permission levels.

In Chapter 21, you studied the user interface macro logic attached to the OnLoad event of the frmLoading web form. You learned that we use an If block to test the SharePoint group level membership of the current user with the following conditional expression:

```
=IsCurrentWebUserInGroup("RestaurantManagers") Or
  IsCurrentWebUserInGroup("RestaurantShiftManagers")
```

This macro logic checks to see if the current user is a member of the RestaurantManagers or RestaurantShiftManagers SharePoint custom groups. If they are a member of either of those two groups, the macro logic uses the BrowseTo action to browse to the frmMain-Menu web form, where all the administrative and application features are available. If the user is not in either of these SharePoint groups, the macro browses instead to the frm-MainMenuEmployees web form, where the employee can see their work schedule only. (We don't want employees other than managers to be able to view and edit administrative or confidential areas, such as employee wages.)

At the start of this chapter, we had you change the Web Display Form property for this web database from frmLoading to frmMainMenu in Access client. Now that you've defined the appropriate SharePoint groups and permissions, change this property back to frmLoading in Access client. To do this, click the File tab on the Backstage view, click Options, and then click the Current Database category in the Access Options dialog box. In the Web Display Form combo box, select frmLoading and then click OK to save your change. Note that you'll synchronize this change to the Access Services site later in this chapter.

Note

For the Back Office Software System web database, we added this group-level test only to the frmLoading web form. If regular restaurant employees browse to the Access Services site URL, they will see the appropriate limited main menu for their group. However, if the employees browse to a specific form or report, they will be able to view the form or report in the web browser. In a production environment, we would want to add a similar group level test in the OnLoad or OnOpen event of every form or report for a higher level of interface control.

INSIDE OUT Preventing Users from Downloading Your Web Application

By default, all users of your Access services application can click Open In Access in the Options menu on the Access Services shell and download a copy of the web application. You can set appropriate permissions to each list to prevent users from viewing data you don't want them to view, but if you want to prevent users from downloading the web application, you'll need to a create a custom permission group.

To do this, click Site Actions on the parent site and then click Site Permissions. Next, click the Permission Levels command in the Manage group on the SharePoint ribbon. On the Permission Levels page, click Add A Permission Level. In the list of permissions, select all the same options that exist for a Contributor. Note that we used the Contributor options as a base for the permissions, but you could select more or less restrictive permissions to start. Next, make sure you clear the Use Remote Interfaces option. If you leave this option selected, any user with rights to the Access Services site can click the Open In Access option and rehydrate the web database into a compatible version of Access 2010. If you clear this option, any users with this permission level cannot make any external web service calls. As a result, when the user clicks the Open In Access option, they are blocked from rehydrating the published Access Services application into Access client. If you clear the View Application Pages settings, you can also prevent a user from viewing all SharePoint application pages (Settings Page, Permissions Page, etc.) as well as the default SharePoint view pages. Finally, save your changes and assign the appropriate users to this group.

There is one caveat when clearing the Use Remote Interfaces permission level. When users are prevented from using Remote Interfaces, they cannot view any reports in the web browser. Access Services uses SQL Reporting Services to render reports and SQL Reporting Services relies on making Simple Object Access Protocol (SOAP) requests. If the users assigned to this permission level do not need to view reports, this should not be a problem. However, if those users do need to view reports in the browser, you will either need to display the data in forms for them to view or not use this approach.

Reviewing the Modify Application Page

Each Access Services site includes a web page that resembles the Navigation pane found in Access client, where you can see a list of all the database objects in your application. Click the Options button in the Access Services shell and then click Settings. Access Services opens the Modify Application page, as shown in Figure 22-27. This web page lists the tables, queries, forms, reports, and macro objects in your web application. You can scroll down this page to see the object names in alphabetical order grouped by object type. (Note that in Figure 22-27, we're showing only a few of the web table names for the BOSS Access Services site.) Next to the name of each object, you can see the date and time when the object was last changed and by whom. Access Services does not list any Module objects on this page, but they are stored on the server. You can use any procedures and functions defined in Modules when you work with the published application from within Access client.

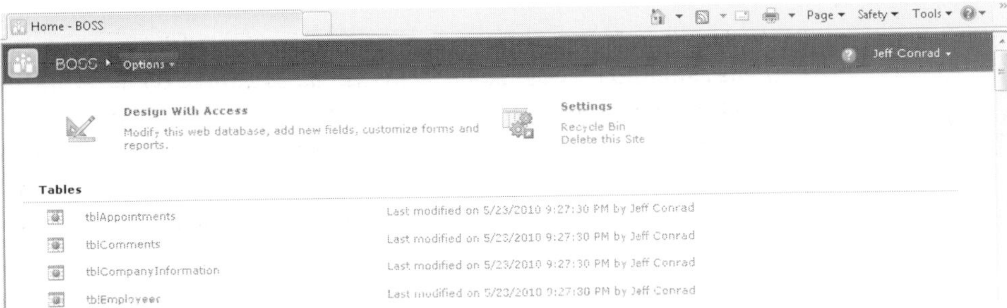

Figure 22-27 On the Modify Application page, you can see a listing of all the objects in your web database.

Across the top of the Modify Application page, you'll see a link under Design With Access called Modify This Web Database, Add New Fields, Customize Forms And Reports. When you click this link, Access opens the File Download dialog box you saw previously in Figure 22-23. Click this link if you want to open the web application in Access client. Under Settings in the upper-right corner of the Modify Application page, you'll see two additional links—Recycle Bin and Delete This Site. Click the Recycle Bin link to open the SharePoint Recycle Bin page, where you can restore deleted records from your application. (We'll discuss the Recycle Bin in more detail later in this chapter.) Click the Delete This Site link to open a web page where you can delete your entire Access Services site.

Note

If you do not assign a web display form for your web database, Access Services navigates you to the Modify Application page directly when you browse to your published site URL. You'll also see a yellow Alert message saying that you have not selected a default web display form. We recommend that you assign a web display form before allowing other users to use your Access Services site.

The name of each database object displayed on the Modify Application page is essentially a link that you can click to see a list of options. In Figure 22-28, we combined several screenshots into one figure to show you the options available for all the database object types. When you click a table, you'll see options to modify the table and export the table to Excel. If you click the modify option, Access Services opens the File Download dialog box, where you can open the web application in Access client or download an .accdw shortcut file. If you click Export To Excel, Access Services opens a different File Download dialog box, where you can open the web table in Excel or download a Microsoft Excel Web Query File (.iqy) file. Note that your browser might prompt you about downloading a file before seeing the File Download dialog boxes.

Figure 22-28 You can click a database object name to see additional options.

When you click a web form or web report name, you'll see options to modify the web object and view the object. If you click the modify option, Access Services opens the File Download dialog box, where you can open the web application in Access client or download an .accdw shortcut file. If you click the option to view the object, Access Services opens the web form or web report in your browser window. Note that you can open only web forms and web reports for a published Access Services site in a web browser. When you click web queries, web macro objects, or any client objects, you can see only the option to modify the object, which opens the web application in Access client. If you look closely in Figure 22-28, you'll notice that all web objects have a globe icon to indicate that they are web objects. Client objects are stored on the server for rehydration back into Access client, but they do not run in a web browser.

INSIDE OUT Using ACCDW Shortcut Files

When you click the option to modify a specific object on the Modify Application page, you can download an .accdw shortcut file to your computer. If you double-click this shortcut, Access opens, downloads a copy of the web application to your local computer, synchronizes any server changes with your local copy of the application, and then opens the specific object. If you clicked to open a table, for example, Access opens the table in Datasheet view, and if you clicked a form, Access opens the form in Layout view. If you open an .accdw file in Notepad, you can see the Extensible Markup Language (XML) for the shortcut. You'll see XML tags for the object name, type, and mode to open the object. In Chapter 23, "Using Business Connectivity Services," you'll learn how to use XML.

Working with the Recycle Bin

One of the great advantages to having your data stored in an Access Services site is the site Recycle Bin. In most cases, if you delete something in an Access client database, it is deleted permanently. If you delete one record (or a thousand) by mistake and then close the database, those records are lost. In some situations, it is possible to retrieve deleted client database elements using professional recovery services, but retrieval is not always guaranteed, and those services can be costly. If you're fortunate, you might have a backup of your database that you can use to restore deleted records, but you still might lose some very important data, depending upon when you made the last backup.

SharePoint has a built-in Recycle Bin, where you can easily recover deleted records. Suppose, for example, we accidentally delete an invoice record in our application that we have been working on. In our web table setup, we have a Cascade Delete relationship between the tblInvoiceHeaders and tblInvoiceDetails web tables. If you delete an invoice from the application, all related child invoice detail records also get deleted. We can navigate to the Recycle Bin on our Access Services site and recover these records. The Recycle Bin in SharePoint works in much the same way as the Recycle Bin in Windows. The one difference is SharePoint empties deleted items more than 30 days old automatically.

To navigate to the site Recycle Bin, Click Options on the Access Services shell to open the Modify Application page. Now, click the Recycle Bin link in the upper-right corner of this page. Access Services opens the Recycle Bin page, as shown in Figure 22-29. In Figure 22-29, you can see an invoice record we previously deleted. SharePoint shows the type of object deleted (in this case a record), the ID of the deleted record, the original location of the list from which the record was deleted, who created the record, when the record was deleted, and the size of the record. To restore the invoice record, select the check box next to the invoice record and then click Restore Selection. SharePoint restores the parent invoice record and all related child invoice detail records.

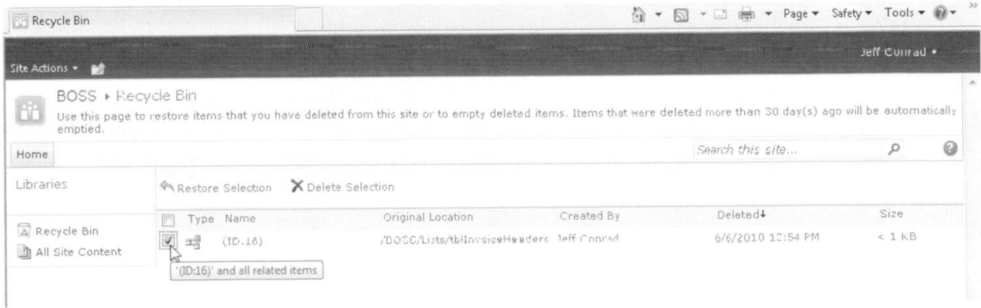

Figure 22-29 You can restore records from the Recycle Bin on the Access Services site.

TROUBLESHOOTING

Why can't I restore my record from the Recycle Bin?

If you have a data macro attached to the BeforeChange event of a web table, you cannot restore records back into that table from the Recycle Bin. If you want to recover the deleted records, you'll need to temporarily remove any data macro logic attached to the BeforeChange event for the web table from within Access client, save the changes to the server, restore the deleted records, and then reattach any data macro logic to the BeforeChange event. To facilitate this process, you could copy the data macro logic to Notepad and then paste the XML back into the BeforeChange event after restoring the deleted records.

Extending Your Access Services Application

When you publish a web database to a server running SharePoint and Access Services, all your data is stored in SharePoint lists. The SharePoint platform offers a wealth of possibilities for extending your application beyond just what you can do from Access client. A full discussion of all the possibilities you can do with your data in SharePoint lists is beyond the scope of this book, but we'll show you one way that you can capitalize on the gains of using SharePoint to store your data.

SharePoint includes a feature that allows you to create a calendar view of your list data. The tblVacations web table in the Back Office Software System is a perfect candidate to build a calendar view. If you still have the Recycle Bin page open, click the All Site Content link on the left side of the web page. If you're not currently on the Recycle Bin page, you can get there by clicking the Options button on the Access Services shell and then clicking the Recycle Bin link on the Modify Application page. You should now see the All Site Content page for your Access Services site, as shown in Figure 22-30. Under Document Libraries, you can see two lists that store the shared images and web report definitions—AppImages and Report Definitions. You should see a list for each one of your published web tables under Lists.

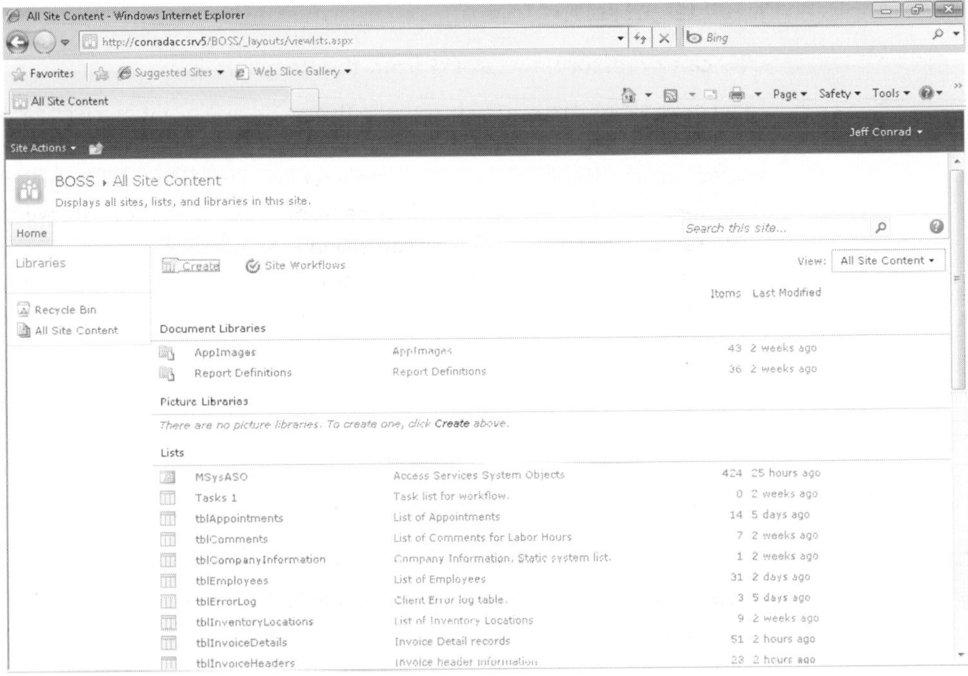

Figure 22-30 You can see the structure of your Access Services site on the All Site Content page.

CAUTION

Do not attempt to modify any of the system lists that control your Access Services site on the All Site Content page. If you modify any of these objects, you could cause damage to your Access Services site, and you also might encounter problems working with the web application from within Access client. If you need to make changes to your table schema, you should always make the changes in Access client and then synchronize your changes with the server.

Scroll down this page and then click the tblVacations link. You'll now see a SharePoint datasheet view of the tblVacations list, as shown in Figure 22-31. There are four records already saved in this list for the Back Office Software System web database.

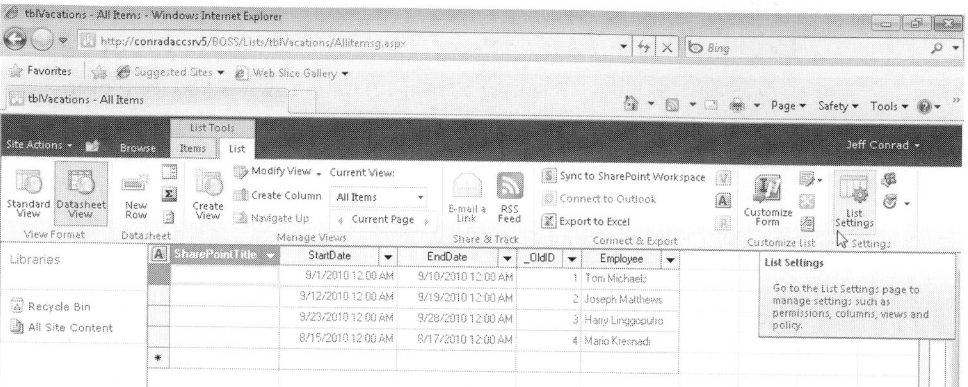

Figure 22-31 Click List Settings to view the definition for the tblVacations list.

Click List Settings in the Settings group on the List contextual SharePoint ribbon tab to view the definition of this list. Access opens the List Settings page for the tblVacations list, as shown in Figure 22-32. On the List Settings page, you can access several links to control the various settings of each list in your Access Services list. If you need to make schema changes to your web tables in an Access Services site, we recommend that you always make those changes from within Access client. If you make changes to the list definition here, you could make changes that Access client cannot understand.

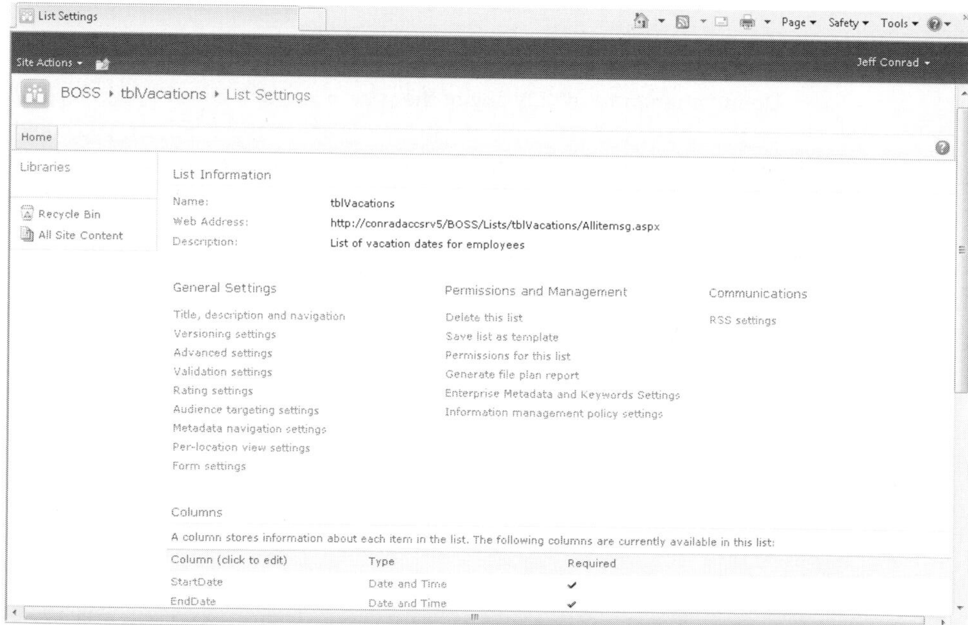

Figure 22-32 You can set many options for your list on the List Settings page.

INSIDE OUT Assign Permissions to Each List for Greater Security

You can use the IsCurrentWebUserInGroup function at the user interface layer to control which users can open forms and reports. However, for tighter security, you should set permissions for each list in your Access Services site. You can set permissions for each list by clicking the Permissions For This List link on the List Settings page.

Scroll to the bottom of the List Settings page and click the Create View link to open the Create View web page, as shown in Figure 22-33. On this page, SharePoint shows several links you can click to create different view of your list data. To create a calendar view of the data in the tblVacations list, click the Calendar View link.

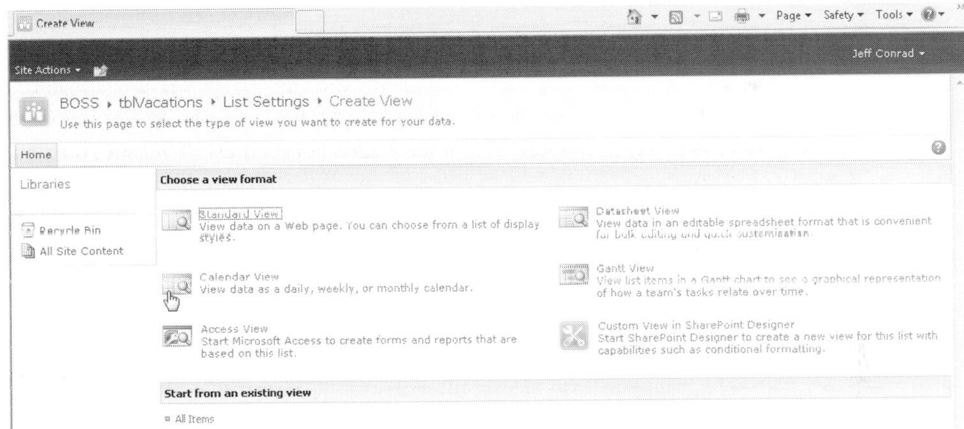

Figure 22-33 Click the Calendar View link on the Create View page.

You should now see the Create Calendar View page, as shown in Figure 22-34.

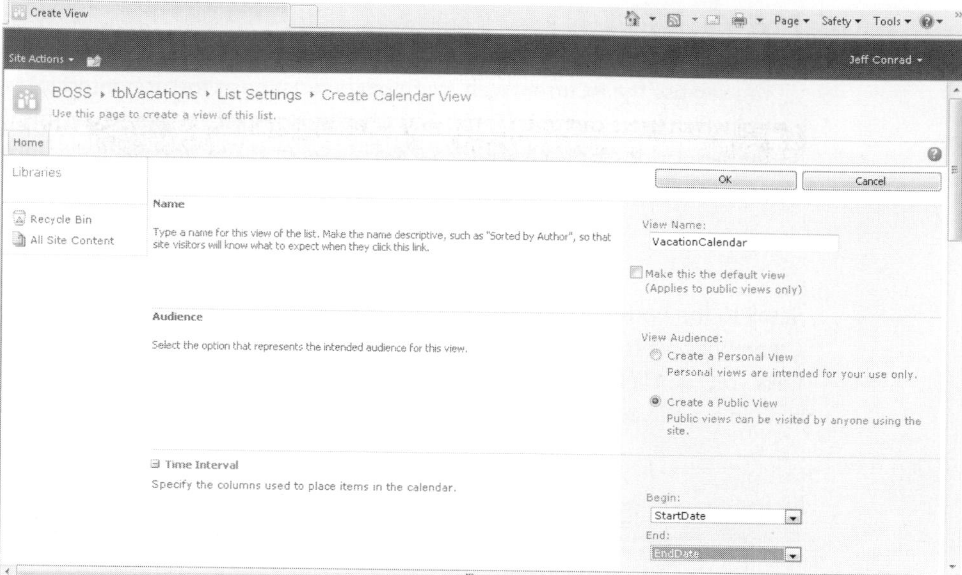

Figure 22-34 You can set options for the calendar view on the Create Calendar View page.

Perform the following steps to make a calendar view of the tblVacations list:

1. In the View Name text box, enter **VacationCalendar** for the name of the view.
2. In the Time Interval section, select the StartDate field in the Begin combo box and select the EndDate field in the End combo box.
3. In the Calendar Columns section, select the Employee field for the Month View Title, Week View Title, and Day View Title combo boxes.
4. Click OK at the bottom of the page to save your changes.

You can now see a nice graphical calendar view of the data in the tblVacations list, as shown in Figure 22-35. If you navigate the calendar to September 2010, you should see the employee names and start and end dates for their vacations that we created in the sample web database.

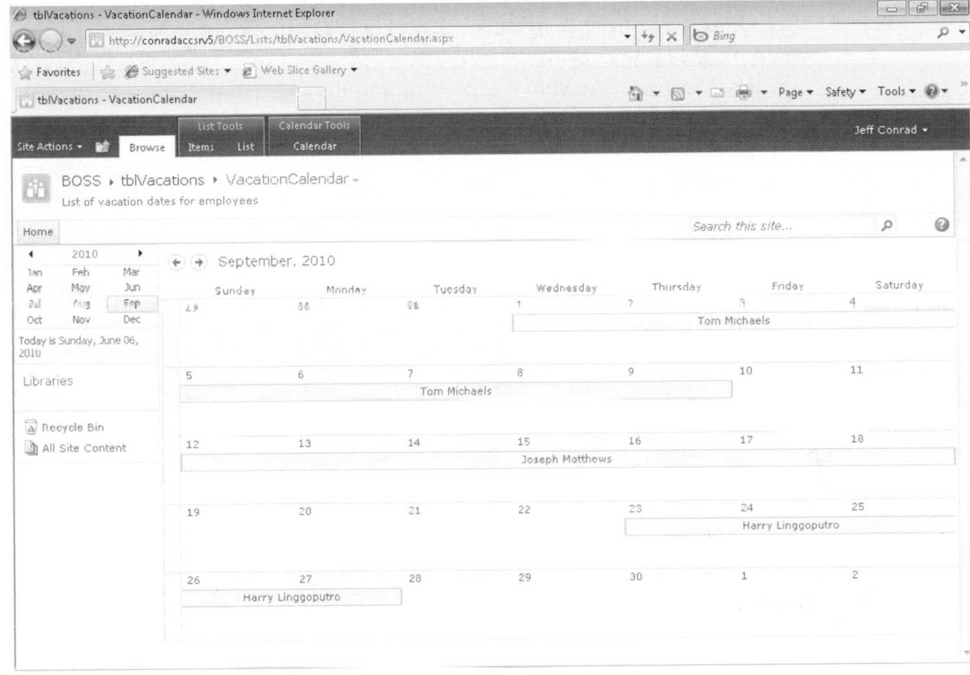

Figure 22-35 You can see a graphical representation of the employee vacations in a calendar view.

INSIDE OUT Link the Vacation Calendar to the Main Menu

In the main menu for the Back Office Software System web database, we provided an entry point to the calendar view you just created for the tblVacations list. Copy the URL for the VacationCalendar view to the Clipboard. (You can see an example of the URL in the Address Bar shown previously in Figure 22-35.) Next, navigate to the main menu page of the site by clicking the BOSS link in the upper-left corner of the browser window. Click the Administration top-level navigation button on the main menu and then click the Settings second-level navigation button. Paste the URL to the Vacation-Calendar view page in the Vacation Calendar text box on the settings form, and then click the Save Changes command button to save the record changes. Finally, click the Employees top-level navigation button and then click the Vacation Calendar second-level navigation button on the main menu. You should now see the calendar view page you created earlier shown in the subform web browser control.

Using Your Published Web Database in Access

Now that you've seen what happens during the publish process and understand how to work with your Access Services site in a web browser, let's show you what happens when you open a published web database in Access client. If you still have the BOSS.accdb published web database open from the start of this chapter, close the database. Note that if you click the File tab on the backstage view, Access displays Close Web Application instead of Close Database. You can use this option to close the application or click the Close X button in the upper-right corner of the application window to close the database and Access. Open your published web database and you'll notice that Access displays the dialog box shown in Figure 22-36.

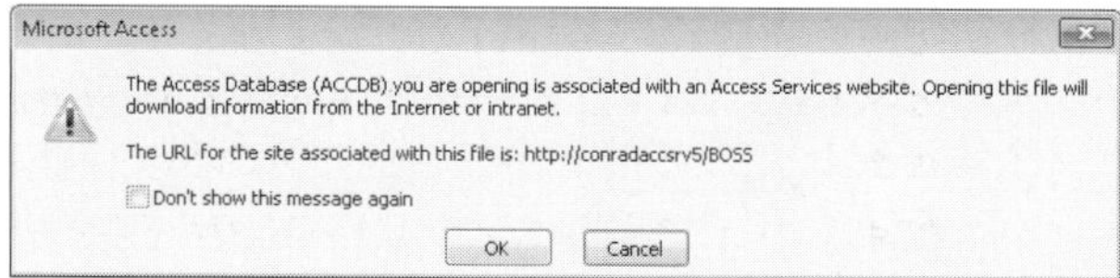

Figure 22-36 Click OK in this dialog box and Access opens your published web application.

When you open a local copy of a published Access Services web application, Access prompts you that it needs to communicate with the Internet or intranet. Access informs you that this is a published web application and displays the URL for your application in the dialog box. If you click OK, Access opens the local copy of the web database and then synchronizes your application with the server. If you click Cancel in this dialog box, Access stops the process of opening the local web database and then displays the New page of the Backstage view. Select the Don't Show This Message Again check box if you do not want Access to prompt you again before opening any published web applications.

INSIDE OUT Re-enabling the Prompt When Opening Published Web Databases

If you select the Don't Show This Message Again check box in the dialog box when opening a published web application and then click OK, you cannot change that option in any entry point in the Access user interface. If you want to display this dialog box again, you'll need to edit the Registry for your computer. In the Registry Editor, navigate to the following registry folder:

[HKEY_CURRENT_USER\Software\Microsoft\Office\14.0\Access\Settings]

There are two registry keys that control showing this dialog box, one for .accdw files and the other for published .accdb files:

```
"Show Accdw Warning"=dword:00000000
"Show Accdb Web Application Warning"=dword:00000000.
```

You can either change their values to 1 or delete these keys.

Note that you should use extreme caution when editing any registry keys because you could inadvertently cause damage to your computer applications. We recommend that you make a backup of your registry first if you need to change or delete these values.

Click OK to open your local copy of the published Back Office Software System sample web database. Access synchronizes any server changes with your local copy of the published web database and then opens the main menu form of the application, as shown in Figure 22-37. If you expand the Navigation pane and then hover over one of the web table names, you'll notice Access displays a tooltip that contains the URL to your Access Services site. In a published web database, Access also displays a Status Bar message in the lower-right corner of the application window, indicating you are working online with a SharePoint site.

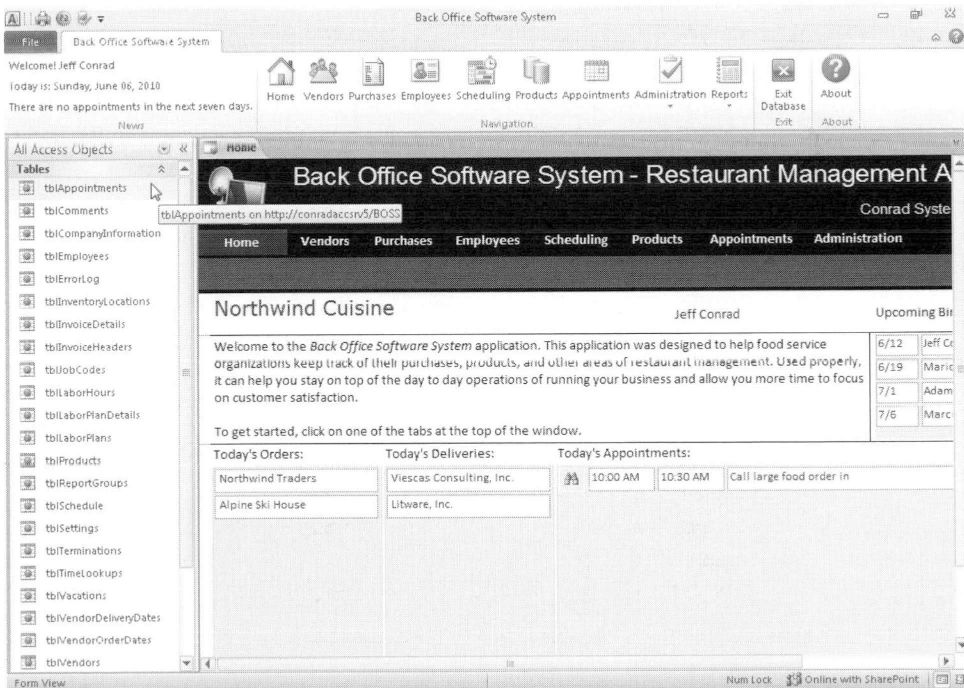

Figure 22-37 In a published web application, you can see the URL for your site if you hover over a web table object.

The BOSS.accdb uses custom ribbons and a custom Quick Access Toolbar to help control what users can view when they open the application in Access client. For the next sections of this chapter, we'll use commands on the built-in Access ribbon, so you'll need to change the Access Options so that it does not show the custom ribbon. To do this, click the File tab on the Backstage view, click Options, click the Current Database category, remove the rbnMain text from the Ribbon Name option, click OK to save your changes, and then close and reopen your web-published web database. You can now see the default Access ribbons.

INSIDE OUT **Using SharePoint Fields**

After you publish a web database to an Access Services site, you can use the built-in SharePointEditor, SharePointAuthor, SharePointModifiedDate, and SharePointCreatedDate fields that exist in all SharePoint lists. For example, if you create a new query, you'll notice that Access displays these fields in the query design window. You can reference these fields in both client and web objects in your published web application.

Making Changes to a Published Web Application

There is no requirement that you must have your web database completely finished with all the objects you think you'll ever need before publishing it to a server running SharePoint and Access Services. You could, in fact, publish nothing more than a one-field table to the server, although that wouldn't be of much practical use. Access Services is designed to be flexible, allowing you to add, edit, delete objects, or make changes to the table schema as your application needs change. You can even have multiple people changing database objects and synchronizing their changes to the server in a collaborate environment.

Let's show you an example of how to add and edit objects in your published web application and then synchronize those changes to the Access Services site. Earlier in this chapter, as well as in Chapter 6, you learned about the USysApplicationLog table that records data macro execution errors and compile errors on the server. Unfortunately, you cannot have database objects bound to this table before you publish the web database to the server, because the Web Compatibility Checker prevents you from publishing if you have objects bound to this table. The good news, however, is that you can bind database objects to the USysApplicationLog linked table after you publish. In the BOSS.accdb sample web database, we've created an entry point in the main menu to see the data in the USysApplicationLog linked table, both in Access client and the browser. On the companion CD, you'll find a web database file called BOSSLogsForServer.accdb that contains a web form and web report that we can import into our published application and then use in both Access client and the browser to easily view any data recorded in the USysApplicationLog table. Note that you can also create new objects and edit existing objects in your published application and send those changes to the server, but for our example, it was easier to have these web objects already created for you.

To add this web form and web report into your published application, perform the following steps:

1. Close any database objects you might have open.
2. Click the Access button in the Import & Link group on the External Data ribbon tab.
3. In the Get External Data – Access Database dialog box, browse to the folder where you installed the sample files and select the BOSSLogsForServer.accdb file. Select the option to import objects and then click OK.
4. In the Import Objects dialog box, select frmErrorLogServer on the Forms tab and rptErrorLogServerWeb on the Reports tab. Click OK to import those two web objects into the published web application. Click Close in the dialog box after the import process completes.
5. Open the web form called frmErrorLogsMenu in Layout view. Select the Server Log –TBD navigation button on this web form. Change the Caption property of this navigation button to **Server Log**. In the Navigation Target Name property, select Form.frmErrorLogServer from the drop-down list of object names. The navigation subform on the frmErrorLogsMenu form should now be showing the frmErrorLogServer form. The command buttons on the frmErrorLogServer web form open the rptErrorLogServerWeb web report so you can print the data in the USysApplicationLog table. Note that the form might be blank if there are currently no records in your USysApplicationLog table on the server.
6. Save your changes to the frmErrorLogsMenu web form and then close the form.

TROUBLESHOOTING

Why do I not see any controls on my form in Layout view?

When you open a web or client form in Layout view, you won't see any controls displayed on the form surface if there are no records in your form's record source and the form's Allow Additions, Allow Deletions, and Allow Edits properties are all set to No. To see and edit your form controls on the design surface, you can temporarily add a record to the form's record source.

Now that you have the new completed web form and web report in your local published web database, you need to synchronize these changes with the server. To synchronize your local changes with the server, click the File tab on the Backstage view. Access displays the Info tab for a published web application, as shown in Figure 22-38. Next to the Sync All button, Access displays a message indicating that there are local changes that have not been sent to the server. Beneath that message, Access displays a message indicating that there are no changes on the server. Access also displays a hyperlink that you can click to open the Access Services site in your web browser. Beneath the Sync All button, you'll see the date and time when Access last checked the synchronization status between the client and the server. If you click Check Sync Status, Access checks to see if there are any pending local changes that need to be sent to the server, checks to see if there are any changes on the server that have not been downloaded to the local copy of the published application, and then updates the three messages. If there are changes on either client or the server, Access colors the section around the Sync All button in red.

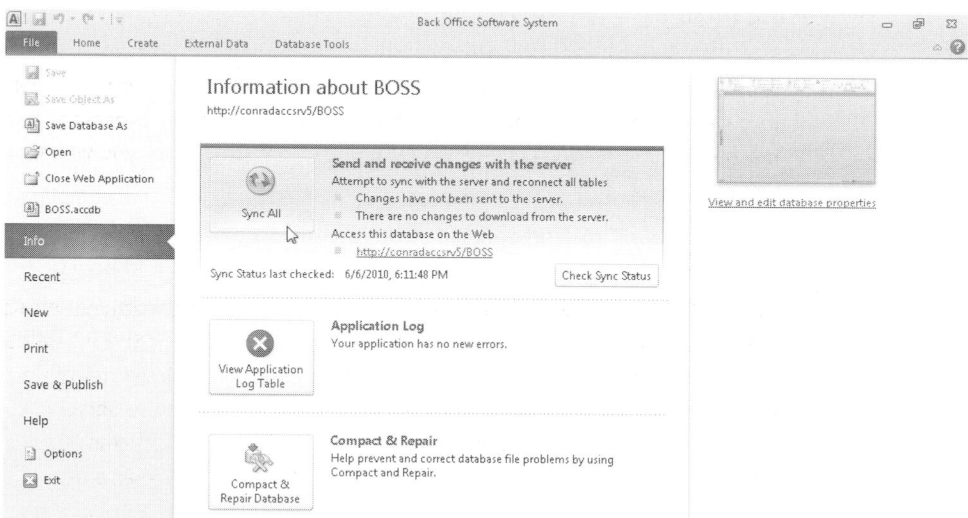

Figure 22-38 You can check the synchronization status and synchronize changes with the server on the Info tab.

To send your local changes to the server, click Sync All. Access first synchronizes any changes from the server into your local copy and then runs the Web Compatibility Checker on your database. If the tool finds issues during this process, Access aborts the remaining synchronization process. You can check the Web Compatibility Issues table to see what caused the failure and then correct the issues. If the Web Compatibility Checker finds no issues with your web database, Access begins the process of synchronizing your local changes with the server. Access sends up any changes from the local copy of the database to the server. These changes could be new objects, changes to existing objects, or database properties (such as the Web Display Form database property we had you change earlier). Access Services then compiles your changes.

Note

If you click Sync All when there are no changes in either client or the server, Access displays a message box indicating that your application is already in sync with the server.

INSIDE OUT Working with Larger Web Databases

Whenever you synchronize your changes with the server, the Web Compatibility Checker needs to scan all the web objects. When you are working with a web database that has many web objects, this process can add up to lots of extra time waiting for the tool to complete the scan each time. You might consider dividing your web application into smaller test group applications during the development process and then importing the completed objects into the master web database after you've completed your testing of new objects.

Navigate to your Access Services site in the browser, refresh the main menu page if you still have the browser window open from the previous section, click the Administration top-level navigation button, and then click the Error Log second-level navigation button. You should see the new web form and web report when you click the Server Log navigation button on the left side. You've now successfully added new elements to your web application and synchronized those changes with the server. Anyone else using the site in the browser will see these changes as well.

INSIDE OUT Add the Sync All Command to your Quick Access Toolbar

When you are working with a published web application and making many changes to the database objects, you might find it useful to add the Sync All command to your Quick Access Toolbar. To do this, click the down arrow on the right side of the Quick Access Toolbar, and then click Sync All on the Customize Quick Access Toolbar drop-down list. You should now see the Sync All command listed on your Quick Access Toolbar.

When you synchronize new or changed web objects to the server, Access Services needs to recompile those objects. If there are other objects that depend on the new or changed web object, Access Services needs to recompile those objects as well. During the compilation phase, Access Services locks the site, which means you might see the Preparing Site web page shown earlier in Figure 22-9. You might not be able to view some objects in the browser until the site compilation process completes.

When you are making changes to any objects within Access to your published web application, Access does not synchronize those changes with the server until you click Sync All. When you make changes to web tables, however, Access sends up those changes to the server immediately. For example, if you change the Caption property of a table field in a published application, Access sends up that change to the server immediately. If you change another field property, Access sends up that change immediately, and so on.

As a result of this setup, there are two things you should be aware of when making schema changes to a published web database. First, you cannot make schema changes in a published web application if you are not currently connected to your Access Services site. Second, your Access Services site will be compiling quite often when you are making schema changes because each change forces the web table on the server to recompile, which in turn forces dependent objects to recompile as well. If you have users using your Access Services site in the browser, they will likely encounter messages stating that the site is unavailable and record saving error messages because the data macros are recompiling. We recommend that you make schema changes to your published web application during times of low activity so as not to interrupt people using your Access Services site. You might want to schedule a specific time to work on schema changes and inform users of this schedule.

If a web table, web query, or web macro fails to compile to the server, Access Services locks the site and prevents you from opening any objects in a web browser. If you navigate to the Access Services site in the browser, you'll see a Site Is Down web page, as shown in Figure 22-39. Click the Click Here To View The Errors In Microsoft Access link to open the File Download dialog box, where you can open or save the .accdw file to view the error in Access client. If you have the web application open in Access, you can open the USysApplicationLog table to help analyze the compilation errors. Access Services creates a new record in this table for each object that failed to compile. The SourceObject field lists the name of the object that filed to compile. In the Category field, you'll see the word Compilation. The Object Type field lists the type of object that failed to compile. In the Description field, you'll see information detailing the cause of the compilation failure. You'll need to fix these issues in Access and synchronize your changes to the server to use your Access Services application in the browser.

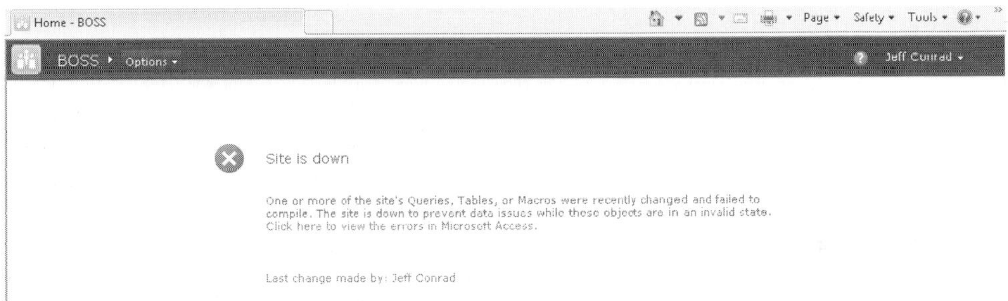

Figure 22-39 Access Services displays this web page if it could not compile a table, web query, or web macro object.

Resolving Synchronization Conflicts

If multiple people are editing objects in an Access Services web application from their own computers using Access client, you might encounter a synchronization conflict when you attempt to synchronize your local changes to the server. A synchronization conflict occurs when two or more people modify the same database object and attempt to synchronize their changes. For example, suppose a user—User 1—makes a change to the web macro object mcrMessages in the Back Office Software System published web application from his copy of Access client, saves his changes, and then synchronizes the changes with the server. Another user—User 2—also makes a change to the mcrMessages web object from her own local copy, saves her changes, and then synchronizes the changes with the server. If User 1 synchronized his changes first, User 2 will see a synchronization conflict message when she attempts to synchronize her changes with the server, as shown in Figure 22-40.

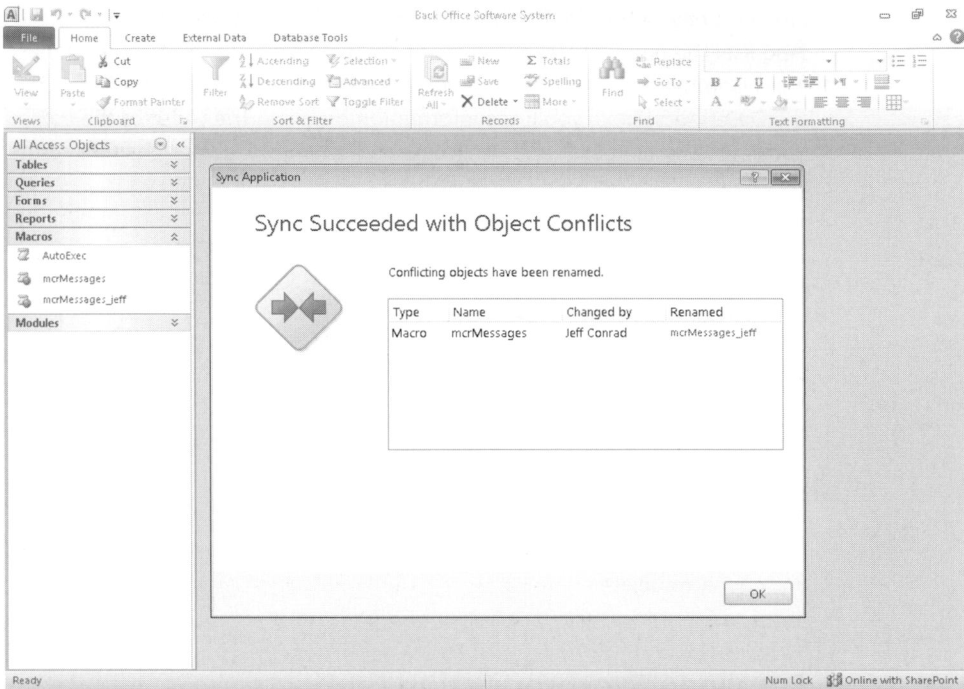

Figure 22-40 Access displays this dialog box when you have an object synchronization conflict.

In the Sync Application dialog box, Access informs User 2 that it successfully synchronized changes from the server but encountered a synchronization conflict with at least one object. Access displays the object type (Macro, in this example), the name of the object (mcrMessages), which user changed the object (Jeff Conrad), and the new name Access gave the conflicting object (mcrMessages_jeff). User 2 also sees the mcrMessages object in the Navigation pane, as well as a new object called mcrMessages_jeff.

In this scenario, User 1 does not see any synchronization conflict messages. User 1 synchronized his changes first, so the mcrMessages object stored on the server contains the changes made by User 1. When User 2 attempts to synchronize her changes with the server after User 1, the Access program on User 2's computer notices that the mcrMessages object in the local copy needs to be sent to the server. But the same object also has a newer version on the server and needs to be brought down to the local copy. For User 2, Access renames the local copy of the mcrMessages object to mcrMessages_jeff. (Access appends the SharePoint user name to the name of the object so the object is renamed mcrMessages_jeff in our example.) Access then brings down the server copy of the mcrMessages object into the local copy of User 2's database.

User 2 now has the ability to see the changes made by User 1 by opening mcrMessages in her local copy and comparing the changes in that object with her own changes in the mcrMessages_jeff object. User 2 has to resolve these object conflicts. If User 2 wants to keep the changes made by User 1, User 2 can delete the mcrMessages_jeff object from the Navigation pane. If User 2 wants to keep her changes and discard the changes made by User 1, User 2 can delete the mcrMessages object from her Navigation pane, rename the mcrMessages_jeff object to mcrMessages again, and then synchronize her changes with the server. If User 2 wants to keep both changes, User 2 can manually merge the changes between the two objects (possibly in the mcrMessages object), delete the other object, and then synchronize her changes with the server. One key point to remember when synchronizing changes with the server is that the object on the server is always the latest version.

Working Offline

We've shown you how to work with your published web application in a browser, but what happens when the server running your Access Services site is unavailable or you have network connectivity issues? You have the ability to work with a published web application within Access client in *offline mode*—without a connection to the Access Services site. If Access detects that it cannot communicate with the server, you'll see a message in the Status Bar indicating that the SharePoint tables are disconnected, as shown in Figure 22-41.

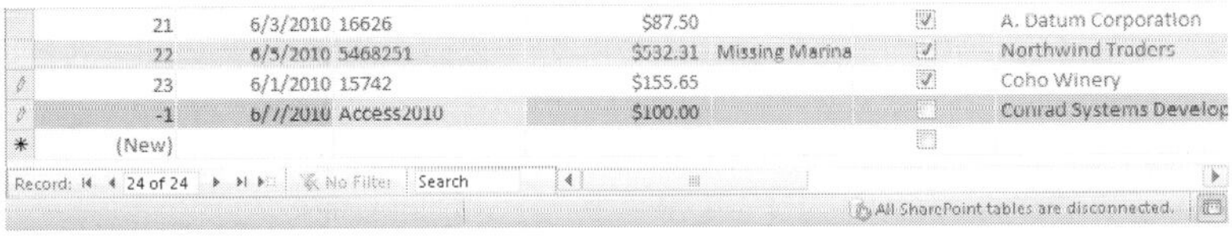

	21	6/3/2010 16626	$87.50		☑	A. Datum Corporation
	22	6/5/2010 5468251	$532.31	Missing Marina	☑	Northwind Traders
✎	23	6/1/2010 15742	$155.65		☑	Coho Winery
✎	-1	6/7/2010 Access2010	$100.00		☐	Conrad Systems Develop
*	(New)				☐	

Record: 24 of 24 No Filter Search

All SharePoint tables are disconnected.

Figure 22-41 Access displays a notification on the Status Bar if you are offline and caches data changes locally.

When you are offline, you can continue to add, edit, and delete records, but these changes are only cached locally on your computer. Access temporarily assigns the ID value a negative number to new records you create in offline mode. Access also displays a dimmed pencil icon in the record selector for any new or changed records. In Figure 22-41, you can see that we edited an existing record (record ID 23) and created a new record in the tblInvoiceHeaders web table. You can see the dimmed pencil icon next to both of these records and the negative ID value for the new record.

> **Note**
>
> **In Access 2007, if you had links to lists in a SharePoint site, you could manually disconnect from the server using the Work Offline command. This command is no longer available in Access 2010. You cannot force Access to disconnect from the SharePoint server except by manually disconnecting your network connection.**

If you are working in offline mode, Access displays the Reconnect Tables section on the Info tab of the Backstage view, as shown in Figure 22-42. If you click Reconnect All Tables, Access synchronizes cached data changes only to the server. (The synchronization process fails if Access still cannot communicate with the Access Services site, though.) If you click Discard All Changes, Access displays a dialog box indicating that all data changes made in disconnected tables will be permanently discarded. If you click OK in this dialog box, Access deletes all cached data changes you've made while in offline mode. Note that clicking OK does not delete any object changes made in offline mode. Click Cancel to keep your changes and dismiss the dialog box. To the right of the Reconnect All Tables button, Access lists the names of any tables that have cached local changes not uploaded to the Access Services site and a status of the current communication with the site. When the connection is reestablished, Access displays the text "Ready To Be Reconnected" next to each table name.

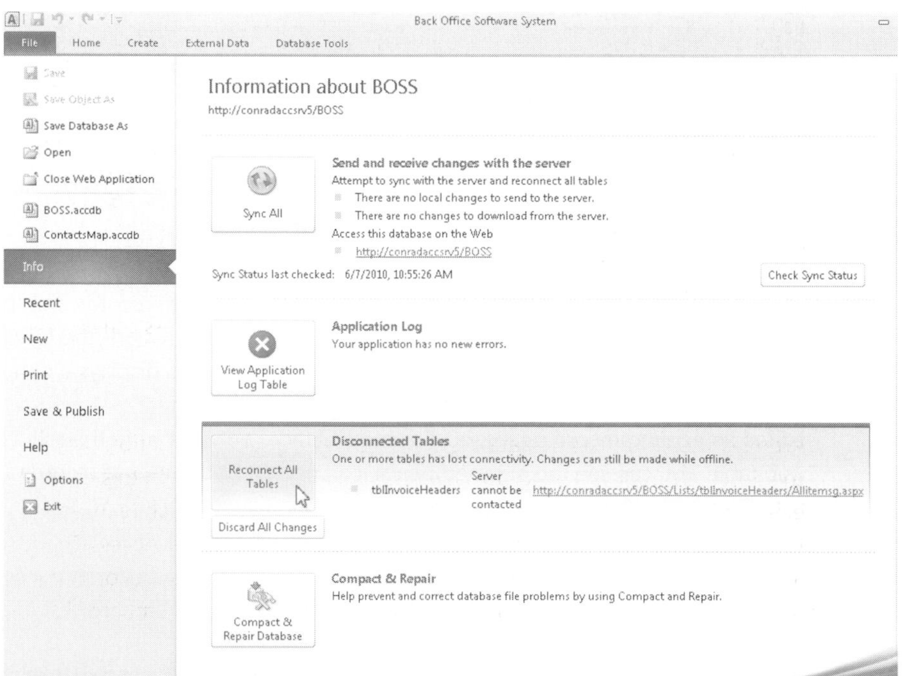

Figure 22-42 Access displays options to reconnect with the server or discard any cached data changes on the Info tab.

While you are working in offline mode, Access checks to see if it can connect with the Access Services site every 30 seconds (this setting cannot be changed). When Access successfully communicates again with your Access Services site, Access displays the Reconnect To SharePoint Server message bar and a Status Bar message indicating that one or more tables are available for reconnect, as shown in Figure 22-43. To synchronize your data with the Access Services site, you can click either the Synchronize button on the Reconnect To SharePoint Server message bar or the Reconnect All Tables button on the Info tab of the Backstage view.

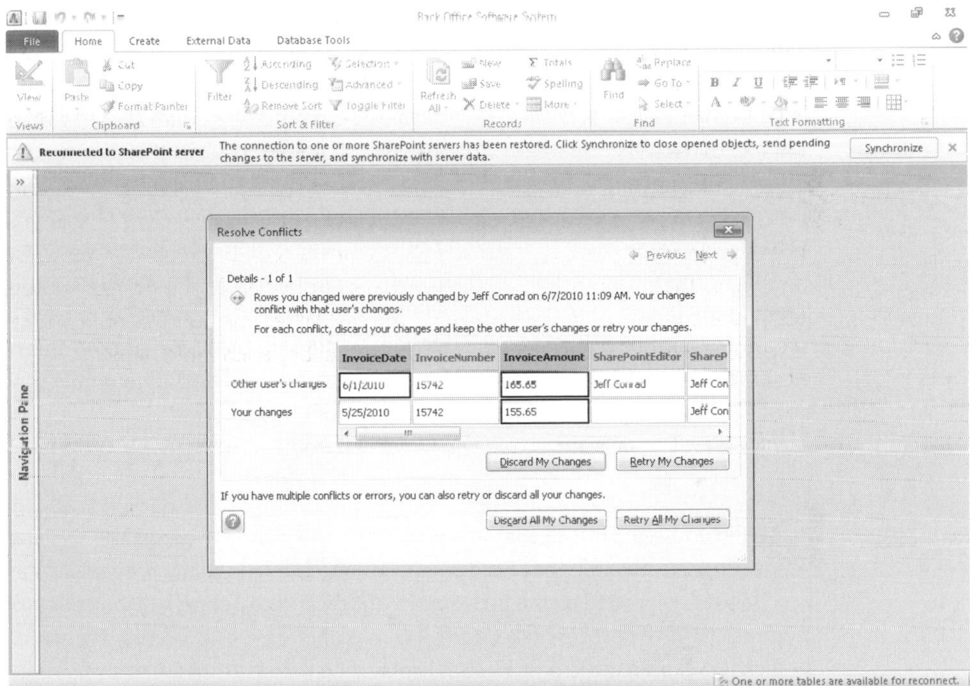

Figure 22-43 Access displays a message bar indicating that Access can communicate with the Access Services site again.

When you encounter any data conflicts during the synchronization process, Access displays the Resolve Conflicts dialog box, also shown in Figure 22-43. In this example, we edited an existing invoice's amount (record ID 23) within Access client while in offline mode. On a different computer, we opened a web browser, navigated to the Access Services site, entered a different invoice amount for the same record, and saved the record changes. Access correctly identifies that this record has data conflicts during the synchronization process.

The Resolve Conflicts dialog box has Previous and Next buttons in the upper-right corner. You can use these buttons to move back and forth between the records that have data conflicts. (These buttons appear dimmed if only one conflict is found in a table.) Access displays the number of conflicts it finds near the top of the dialog box. In our example, Access shows a message of "Details – 1 of 1"—one record has data conflicts. The Resolve Conflicts dialog box also shows who changed the data on the server and the date and time it was changed. In the middle of the dialog box, Access displays all the fields in the list, highlights what the other user changed in the record on the Access Services site, and the changes you made to the same record. In our example, you can see that the InvoiceAmount field was changed to 165.65 on the server and we changed it to 155.65 in our local copy of the data while in offline mode.

If you want to keep the record changes that the other user made, click Discard My Changes. Click Retry My Changes if you want to keep the changes you made to the record. For each record conflict (if you have more than one), you need to decide whether you want to keep your changes or discard them. If you want to discard all your data changes, click the Discard All My Changes button at the bottom of the dialog box. If you want to keep all your record changes, click Retry All My Changes. If you have additional data conflicts in other tables, you'll need to resolve those conflicts as well. As you might recall, we added one new record to the tblInvoiceHeaders table. Access had no problems adding this record to the Access Services tblInvoiceHeaders list because there were no data conflicts. We want to keep all the changes we made, so click Retry All My Changes.

Note

When you synchronize a large amount of data changes back to the server after reconnecting, it's possible that Access Services needs to run many data macros as the record changes get added to the lists. You might cause the data synchronization process to time out if the process takes too long to complete. If this occurs, Access opens the Resolve Conflicts dialog box and displays the records that failed to be committed. You can click Retry All My Changes to try to commit the remaining records.

Here is a summary of other Access behavior that you should be aware of when working in offline mode:

- You cannot make design changes to any web tables in offline mode, but you can make design changes to other database objects. This means you also cannot modify any data macros in offline mode because data macros are attached to tables.
- All data operations—insert, edit, and delete—function normally. Your changes are stored locally until you synchronize your changes with the server.

- Any RunDataMacro actions fail when you are in offline mode. This might cause web forms that call named data macros to fail when you're working in offline mode.
- If you have data macro logic attached to Before table events, those events fire immediately in Access client as you add, edit, or delete data. After you reconnect to the server and synchronize your data changes, Access Services also runs the Before event on the server as it commits the data changes. If another user changes the data macro logic before you reconnect, you might encounter errors committing all your data changes if the new logic conflicts with your data updates.
- If you have data macro logic attached to After table events, those events do not fire in Access client as you add, edit, or delete data. After you reconnect to the server and synchronize your data changes, Access Services runs the After event data macro logic as it commits the data changes.

INSIDE OUT **Caching Data Locally**

When you work with a published web application in Access client, Access caches data in the tables only when you use the data. For example, if you open the tblInvoiceHeaders web table in Datasheet view, run a query, or open a form or report that uses the data in that table, Access caches the data locally. However, if you don't use the data in the tblAppointments web table, Access does not cache the data locally for that table. To guarantee that you have a cached copy of all the data in your Access Services site, you can open each table individually and move to the end of the datasheet. You can also write Microsoft Visual Basic code that opens a recordset on each table. If you want to clear the cache whenever you close the published web database, click the File tab on the Backstage view, click Options, click the Current Database category, and then select Clear Cache On Close under the Caching Web Service And SharePoint Tables category. This option is cleared by default. Select Never Cache in client databases if you do not want to cache any data from linked SharePoint lists. Note that you cannot select the Never Cache option in published web databases.

Saving a Web Application as a Local Database

If you want to remove your Access Services site, navigate to the Delete This Site web page for your web application in a browser. You cannot delete a published web application from within Access client. Before you consider deleting your Access Services, we recommend that you first save a copy of your published web application as a local database. Throughout the last sections of this chapter, you've been working with a published web application that stores the data in SharePoint lists in an Access Services site. While it's true you have a copy of all the database objects right now on your computer, your data is stored on the server. If you delete the Access Services site, your data, except for what might be cached locally, is deleted.

When you save a copy of your published web application as a local database, you are essentially reversing the publish process. In this procedure, you'll not only bring down a copy of all the objects in your web database but all the data as well. To do this, click the File tab on the Backstage view, click the Save & Publish tab, click Save Database As under File Types, and then double-click Save As Local Database. Access opens the Save As dialog box, where you can browse to a location to save the file. Click Save, and Access starts the process of downloading the entire application with data to your download location. When you open the database after this process, you'll notice the web tables are local tables again and contain all your data.

Now that you have a copy of the Access Services site saved locally, you can safely delete your Access Services site. To do this, click the Options button on the Access Services shell, and then click Settings to open the Modify Application page. Click the Delete This Site link to open the SharePoint Delete This Site page. Click the Delete button on this page to delete your Access Services site.

Instantiating an Access Services Template

In addition to publishing a web database from Access client, you can create an Access Services site by instantiating a template on a server running SharePoint 2010 and Access Services. In Chapter 6, you learned how to create a web database by instantiating one of the five built-in web templates shown in the Backstage view. You can also instantiate web templates on a server running SharePoint 2010 and Access Services.

Using an Installed Web Template

The five built-in Access Services web templates—Assets, Charitable Contributions, Contacts, Issues, and Projects—are preinstalled on a server running SharePoint 2010. You can instantiate one of these web templates on the server, even if you don't have Access installed on your local computer. To instantiate one of these installed web templates, open your web browser and navigate to your server running SharePoint 2010. Note that you might need to navigate up to the parent site of your SharePoint server if you are currently viewing an existing Access Services site in your web browser. Next, click Site Actions in the upper-left corner of the SharePoint page and then click New Site from the drop-down list of options. SharePoint opens the Create dialog box, as shown in Figure 22-44.

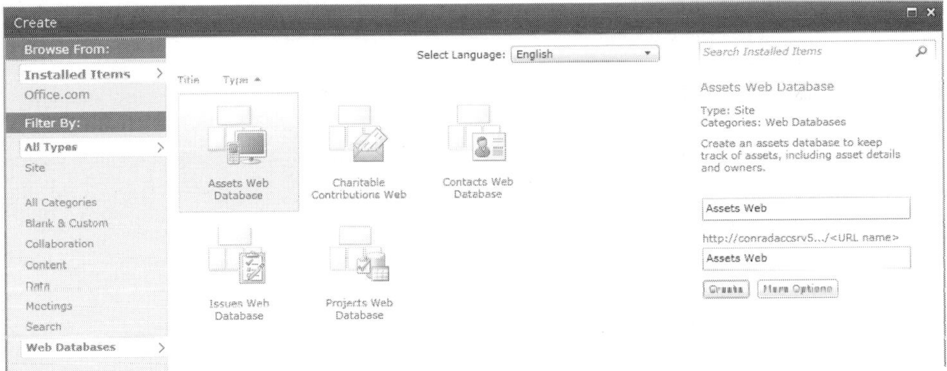

Figure 22-44 You can instantiate one of the five built-in web templates from the Create page.

Click the Web Databases link on the left side of the dialog box under Filter By. Select one of the five built-in web templates to instantiate, enter a site name on the right side, enter the URL name to use for your application, and then click Create. Note that if you want to set additional options for your Access Services site, click More Options before clicking Create. You'll see a Processing screen for a minute or two while SharePoint instantiates the web template, creates an Access Services site based on this web template, and then compiles the site. When SharePoint is finished compiling the site, SharePoint automatically takes you to your completed Access Services site, as shown in Figure 22-45. Your site is ready to be used in a web browser, or you can open the completed Access Services application within Access client if you have it installed on your computer.

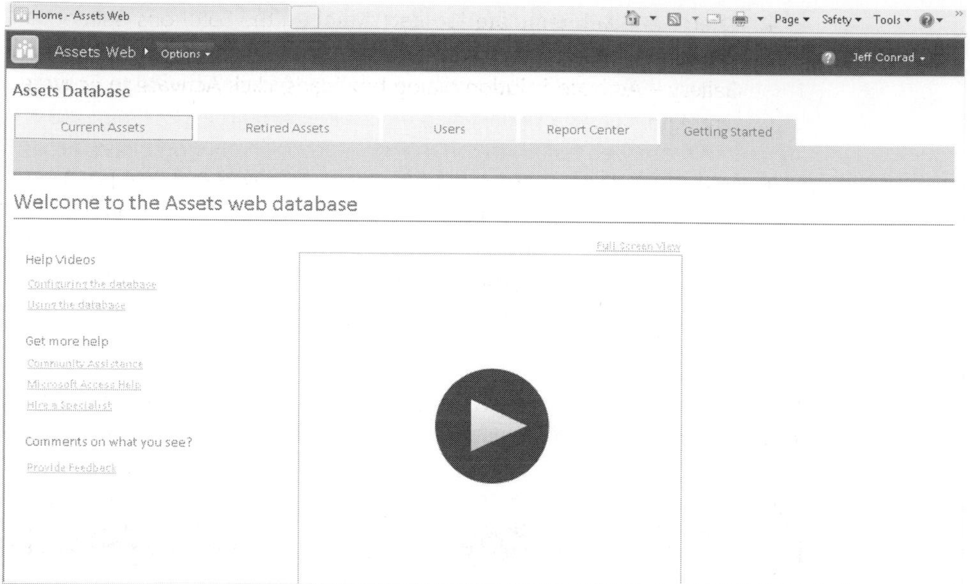

Figure 22-45 You now have a complete Access Services site created from a built-in web template.

Instantiating a Custom Template

In addition to instantiating one of the five built-in web templates on a server running SharePoint 2010, you can upload your own custom web template and instantiate it on the server to create a new Access Services site. In Chapter 27, "Distributing Your Application," on the companion CD, you'll learn how to create a template (.accdt) from an Access database file. You'll also find a sample web template called ContactsMap.accdt on the companion CD, which you can use to follow along with the next section. To upload, activate, and instantiate your own custom web template, perform the following steps:

1. From the main page of your SharePoint server, click Site Actions in the upper-left corner of the SharePoint page, and then click Site Settings from the drop-down list of options. On the Site Settings page, click the Solutions link.
2. SharePoint navigates you to the Solutions Gallery page. Click the Upload Solution button in the New group on the Solutions ribbon tab.
3. On the Upload Document dialog box, browse to the location where you installed the sample files and select the ContactsMap.accdt file. Click OK to upload the .accdt file to the Solutions Gallery.

4. Select your web template (ContactsMap) on the Solutions Gallery page and then click Activate in the Commands group on the Solutions ribbon tab. When the Solution Gallery – Activate Solution dialog box loads, click Activate to activate the web template.

5. Click Site Actions in the upper-left corner of the SharePoint page and then click New Site from the drop-down list of options. Click the Web Databases link on the left side on the Create dialog box, and then select the ContactsMap custom web template that you previously uploaded and activated. Enter a site name on the right side, enter the URL name to use for your application, and then click Create.

After a minute or two of processing time, you'll see your completed Access Services site instantiated on the server from a custom Access web template, as shown in Figure 22-46.

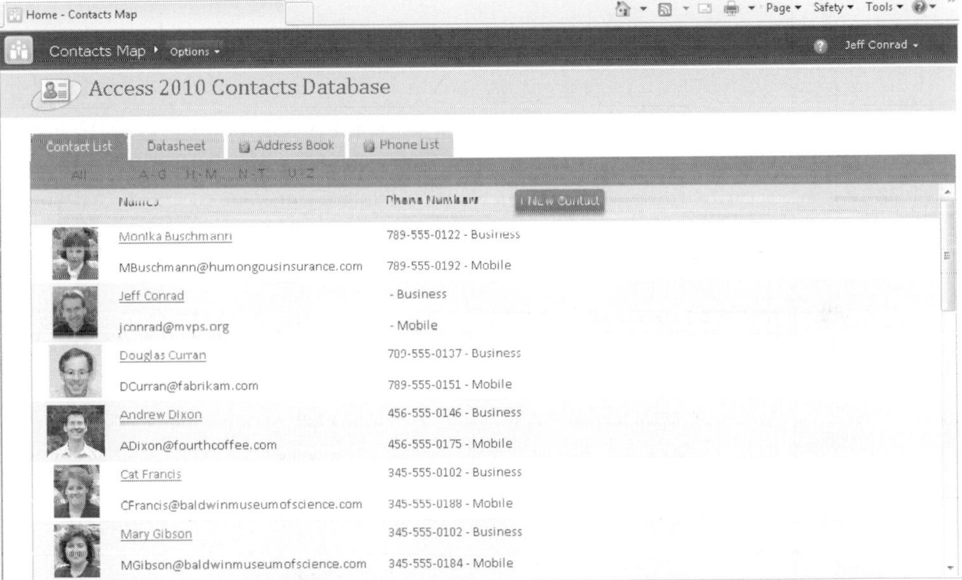

Figure 22-46 You can use a custom web template to create an Access Services site.

You now have a better understanding of how to publish and instantiate a web database to create an Access Services site on a server running SharePoint 2010. You also know how to work with your application in a web browser and make changes to your application. In Chapter 23, you'll learn how to work with Business Connectivity Services using SharePoint Designer 2010 and Access 2010.

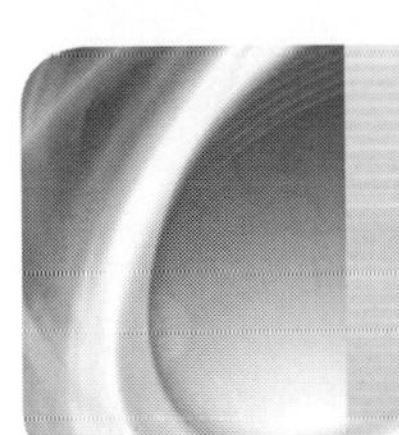

CHAPTER 23

Using Business Connectivity Services

As you've learned in previous chapters, Microsoft Access 2010 can connect to a wide variety of data sources such as Microsoft SharePoint and Microsoft SQL Server. Web services are quickly becoming one of the most common ways to expose and use data in all types of applications. In Access 2010, you can now create a Data Service linked table to a Simple Object Access Protocol (SOAP)–based web service. When you create a Data Service linked table in Access, you can view the data returned from the web service and use expressions to make calls to the web service. This chapter shows you how to:

- Create a Business Connectivity Services model definition file using Extensible Markup Language (XML).
- Use SharePoint Designer to generate and export a Business Connectivity Service model definition.
- Import a model definition into Access to create a linked table to a web service.

Note

The examples in this chapter are based on the supporting files you can find in the Web Services folder on the companion CD. The results you see from the samples in this chapter might not exactly match what you see in this book if you have changed the sample data in the files.

Understanding Web Services

At their heart, web services exchange data encoded as XML over the Web. Many websites today are simply *mashups*—websites created by combining multiple web services into one application. Web services are generally categorized in two ways—public web services and enterprise web services. Public web services expose data that is unrestricted to all computer users with Internet access. Some examples of public web services are Amazon's E3 web service, eBay's marketplace web service, and many Really Simple Syndication (RSS) feeds. Figure 23-1 shows you a conceptual diagram of a public web service.

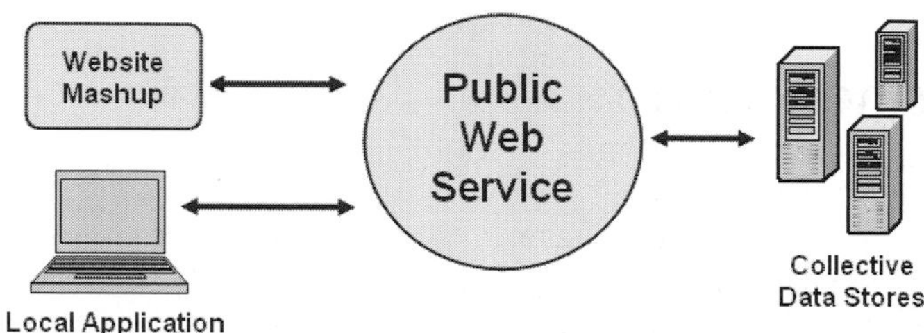

Figure 23-1 Public web services expose data to the public over the Internet.

In Figure 23-1, you can see the public web service acting as a bridge between the data stores of a company and the local applications accessing the data from the Internet. The web service created by the company exposes data that client and web applications can manipulate.

Enterprise web services are used to create a common interface across multiple data sources, as well as to provide a security model to control access to the data. For example, if your enterprise stores data stored in SQL Server and Oracle databases, you can create web services on top of each data store. Information Technology (IT) applications can then easily communicate to each of their respective web services. This method of exposing data in enterprises through common web service endpoints is referred to as a *Service Oriented Architecture (SOA)*. Enterprise web services often tend to be smaller and simpler than large public web services, although there can be wide deviations within both categories. A conceptual diagram of an enterprise web service is shown in Figure 23-2.

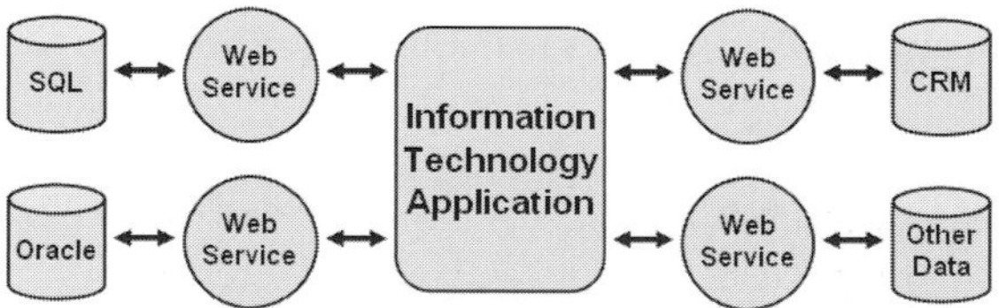

Figure 23-2 Enterprise web services can create interfaces across different data sources.

In Figure 23-2, you can see an IT-developed application that relies on multiple data stores such as SQL Server databases, Oracle databases, Customer Relationship Management (CRM) data, and other sources. In this case, the application does not need to have separate interfaces for the data sources but only needs to interface with the standardized web services that sit on top of these data stores.

Introducing Business Connectivity Services

In Microsoft Office SharePoint Server 2007, Microsoft introduced a mechanism, called the Business Data Catalog (BDC), for utilizing back-end data sources in SharePoint applications. In SharePoint 2007, you could connect to data through Open Database Connectivity (ODBC) connections, Web Services, and SQL Server databases. The data connections in SharePoint 2007, however, were read-only, and you could communicate to *protocols* only through *protocol shims* that were developed by and shipped with the BDC. You can think of a protocol as a description of formats and rules for exchanging electronic messages and a protocol shim as a means for the BDC to talk different protocols.

With the SharePoint 2010 release, Microsoft renamed the BDC service to Business Connectivity Services (BCS) and made significant improvements to the architecture. Here are some of the new BCS features with SharePoint 2010:

- BCS now has extensible protocol shim architecture. For example, a .NET developer can write a custom shim for speaking to any back-end protocol such as RSS, Atom-formatted web feeds, Java Script Object Notation (JSON), and Representational State Transfer (REST).
- BCS supports full Create, Read, Update, Delete, and Query (CRUDQ) operations on data sources.
- BCS can expose data sources directly into SharePoint as virtual lists. These virtual lists appear and behave the same as traditional SharePoint lists.
- BCS Virtual Lists can be accessed from within Microsoft Outlook 2010.

In Figure 23-3, you can see a conceptual diagram showing how Access 2010 interacts with the BCS client to display enterprise web service data within Access client.

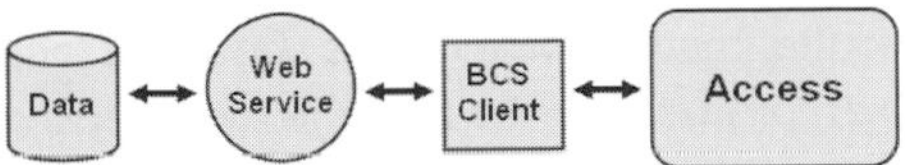

Figure 23-3 Here, you can see a conceptual diagram of BCS integration in Access.

The functional unit in BCS is the *entity*. Entities describe the connections and transform for a given data source. On a high level, entities are meant to represent conceptual objects. For example, you could define a BCS entity which represents a customer, which is connected to data from one or more web services. Using the BCS interface, you can then perform standard CRUDQ operations with that customer entity. Entities are contained in a BDC model definition file, also known as a *metadata* file. Metadata files are typically XML documents that describe a data structure. Access 2010 can use entities by installing the BCS model definition files. Before we begin our study of BCS metadata XML files, we need to discuss in more detail the topic of XML.

Using XML

Today's modern companies are increasing productivity and cutting costs by finding ways to share more and more information online. When data can be shared in a universal format, it doesn't matter whether an employee is down the hall, across the street, or thousands of miles away. The online sharing of information also makes it easier for companies to expand into global markets. Customers half a world away can explore a company's products and services and place orders online. Companies can tap into vendors worldwide to find the best products at the best price.

The World Wide Web has certainly been an enabling technology for increasing productivity and expanding markets. The web works because of the universal acceptance of protocol and language standards. Hypertext Markup Language (HTML) enables a web page to be displayed on any computer and in any browser anywhere in the world. As an adjunct to HTML, XML defines a standard and universal way to share data files or documents. SharePoint Server 2010 uses both these technologies to provide an enhanced web-based data and information sharing mechanism to help companies increase productivity.

Exploring XML

The current XML standard is based on an International Organization for Standardization (ISO) standard, but the most commonly used version is the one maintained and published by the World Wide Web Consortium (W3C). Because a file in XML format contains not only the data but also a description of the structure of the data, XML-enabled receiving systems know exactly how to process the data from the information included in the file.

An XML document can contain data from a single table or from an entire database. An XML document can also have supporting files that describe details about the table schema (for example, field properties and indexes) or that describe how the recipient should lay out (format) the data for display (for example, fonts and column sizes).

Like HTML, XML uses tags to identify descriptive elements. Examples include the name of a table or the name of a field in an XML data file, the names of table properties or index properties in an XML schema file, and the size and color of a border or the name of a style sheet template in an XML layout file. However, where most browsers are forgiving of errors in HTML, such as a missing end tag in a table row, most software that can process XML insists that the tags in an XML file be very precise and follow strict rules. An XML document or set of documents that contain precise XML are said to be well formed.

Well-Formed XML

Although you can create most XML documents using a program such as Access 2010 that always creates well-formed XML, you might occasionally need to view and edit XML files that you receive from outside sources. You should understand the following rules that apply to well-formed XML:

- Each XML document must have a unique root element that surrounds the entire document.
- Any start tag must have an end tag. Unlike HTML, which supports stand-alone tags (such as <br>), XML requires all tags to have explicit ends. However, some tags within XML are self-contained. For example, you code an object definition tag within a schema file like this (the /> characters at the end of the string define the end of the tag):

  ```
  <od:object-type attributes />
  ```

- Tags cannot overlap. For example, you cannot start the definition of one table field and then start the definition of a second table field without ending the first one.
- When you need to include certain characters that are reserved for XML syntax (such as <, &, >, ", ') within the data portion of an element, you must use a substitute character sequence. For example, you indicate a single quote within data using the special sequence *&apos*.
- All tags in XML are case-sensitive. For example, </tblcustomers> is an invalid end tag for the start tag <TBLCustomers>.

As you examine the XML examples in this chapter, all XML samples you encounter should be well formed.

Working with BDC Model Definition Files

Now that you have a better understanding of XML, let's look at the basic XML file structure of a BDC model definition file at a high level. Listed here is an example of a BDC model definition file:

```
<Model>
 <LobSystems/>
  <LobSystem>
   <LobSystemInstances/>
    <Entities>
     <Entity>
      <Methods>
       <Method>
        <Parameters/>
        <MethodInstances/>
       </Method>
      </Methods>
     </Entity>
    </Entities>
  </LobSystem>
 </LobSystems>
</Model>
```

A *LOBSystem*, short for line-of-business system, in the XML document loosely correlates to a single data source, such as Amazon web service or an SQL database. LOBSystems contain properties that describe how to connect to and authenticate the data source. Within a LOBSystem, there are multiple entities, each representing the grouping of various web service methods into a single conceptual object. Each entity contains a *method* with a corresponding *method instance*. Methods map to web service function calls, while method instances map methods to one of the BCS method *stereotypes*. The stereotypes represent categories of interaction into which a given web service can fall. The only BCS stereotype Access can use is the Finder stereotype. The Finder stereotype can take input parameters and produce a table of entity type.

INSIDE OUT Using Visual Studio to Create BDC Model Definition Files

If you use Microsoft Visual Studio to manually create or modify a BDC model definition file, you can use IntelliSense to help show you the attributes and elements available within each element context. To construct a new BDC model definition file in Visual Studio, start by creating a new XML document. In the Properties section of the new XML file, under Schemas, you can point to the bdcmetadata.xsd schema file. You can locate the schema file in the following folder, assuming you have installed Office 2010 in the default folder on a Windows 32-bit operating system:
C:\Program Files\Microsoft Office\Office14\bdcmetadata.xsd

If you install the 32-bit version of Office 2010 on a Windows 64-bit operating system, you can find the schema file in the following default folder:

C:\Program Files (x86)\Microsoft Office\Office14\bdcmetadata.xsd

On the companion CD in the Web Services folder, you can find an example of a BDC model file, called BCSFullDemo.xml, containing three entities—Customers, Orders, and Order-Types. Listed here is a portion of that BDC model file showing the Customers entity:

```
<?xml version="1.0" encoding="utf-16" standalone="yes"?>
<Model xmlns:xsi=http://www.w3.org/2001/XMLSchema-instance
  xsi:schemaLocation="http://schemas.microsoft.com/windows/2007/BusinessDataCatalog
  BDCMetadata.xsd" Name="BCSDemo"
  xmlns="http://schemas.microsoft.com/windows/2007/BusinessDataCatalog">
<LobSystems>
 <LobSystem Type="Wcf" Name="BCS Demo">
 <Properties>
  <Property Name="WsdlFetchAuthenticationMode"
   Type="System.String">PassThrough</Property>
  <Property Name="WcfMexDiscoMode" Type="System.String">Disco</Property>
  <Property Name="WcfMexDocumentUrl"
   Type="System.String">http://conradaccsrv5:55653/service1.asmx?WSDL</Property>
  <Property Name="WcfProxyNamespace" Type="System.String">BCSServiceProxy</Property>
  <Property Name="WildcardCharacter" Type="System.String">*</Property>
 </Properties>
 <LobSystemInstances>
  <LobSystemInstance Name="BCS Demo">
  <Properties>
   <Property Name="WcfAuthenticationMode" Type="System.String">PassThrough</Property>
   <Property Name="WcfEndpointAddress"
    Type="System.String">http://conradaccsrv5:55653/service1.asmx</Property>
   <Property Name="ShowInSearchUI" Type="System.String"></Property>
  </Properties>
  </LobSystemInstance>
 </LobSystemInstances>
 <Entities>
  <Entity Namespace="http://conradaccsrv5" Version="1.1.0.0"
   EstimatedInstanceCount="10000" Name="EntityCustomers"
   DefaultDisplayName="Customers">
   <Identifiers>
    <Identifier TypeName="System.String" Name="ID" />
   </Identifiers>
   <Methods>
    <Method IsStatic="false" Name="GetCustomer">
     <Parameters>
     <Parameter Direction="In" Name="ID">
      <TypeDescriptor TypeName="System.String" IdentifierName="ID" Name="ID" />
     </Parameter>
     <Parameter Direction="Return" Name="GetCustomer">
```

```
      <TypeDescriptor TypeName="BCSServiceProxy.Customer, BCS Demo"
       Name="GetCustomer">
       <TypeDescriptors>
        <TypeDescriptor TypeName="System.String" Name="FirstName" />
        <TypeDescriptor TypeName="System.String" Name="LastName" />
        <TypeDescriptor TypeName="System.String" Name="PhoneNum" />
        <TypeDescriptor TypeName="System.String" Name="StreetAddress" />
        <TypeDescriptor TypeName="System.String" Name="City" />
        <TypeDescriptor TypeName="System.String" Name="State" />
        <TypeDescriptor TypeName="System.String" Name="ZIP" />
        <TypeDescriptor TypeName="System.String" Name="ProductsOrdered" />
        <TypeDescriptor TypeName="System.String" ReadOnly="true" IdentifierName="ID"
         Name="ID" />
       </TypeDescriptors>
      </TypeDescriptor>
     </Parameter>
    </Parameters>
    <MethodInstances>
     <MethodInstance Type="SpecificFinder" ReturnParameterName="GetCustomer"
      Default="true" Name="GetCustomer" DefaultDisplayName="GetCustomerItem">
      <Properties>
       <Property Name="LastDesignedOfficeItemType"
         Type="System.String">None</Property>
      </Properties>
     </MethodInstance>
    </MethodInstances>
    </Method>
     <Method IsStatic="false" Name="GetCustomers">
      <Parameters>
       <Parameter Direction="Return" Name="GetCustomers">
        <TypeDescriptor TypeName="BCSServiceProxy.Customer[], BCS Demo"
         IsCollection="true" Name="GetCustomers">
         <TypeDescriptors>
         <TypeDescriptor TypeName="BCSServiceProxy.Customer, BCS Demo"
          Name="GetCustomersElement">
         <TypeDescriptors>
        <TypeDescriptor TypeName="System.String" Name="FirstName" />
        <TypeDescriptor TypeName="System.String" Name="LastName" />
        <TypeDescriptor TypeName="System.String" Name="PhoneNum" />
        <TypeDescriptor TypeName="System.String" Name="StreetAddress" />
        <TypeDescriptor TypeName="System.String" Name="City" />
        <TypeDescriptor TypeName="System.String" Name="State" />
        <TypeDescriptor TypeName="System.String" Name="ZIP" />
        <TypeDescriptor TypeName="System.String" Name="ProductsOrdered" />
        <TypeDescriptor TypeName="System.String" ReadOnly="true" IdentifierName="ID"
         Name="ID" />
       </TypeDescriptors>
      </TypeDescriptor>
     </TypeDescriptors>
    </TypeDescriptor>
   </Parameter>
  </Parameters>
```

```
  <MethodInstances>
  <MethodInstance Type="Finder" ReturnParameterName="GetCustomers" Default="true"
   Name="GetCustomers" DefaultDisplayName="GetCustomerList">
   <Properties>
    <Property Name="UseClientCachingForSearch" Type="System.String"></Property>
    <Property Name="RootFinder" Type="System.String"></Property>
   </Properties>
   <AccessControlList>
    <AccessControlEntry Principal="NT AUTHORITY\Authenticated Users">
     <Right BdcRight="Edit" />
     <Right BdcRight="Execute" />
     <Right BdcRight="SetPermissions" />
     <Right BdcRight="SelectableInClients" />
    </AccessControlEntry>
   </AccessControlList>
  </MethodInstance>
 </MethodInstances>
</Method>
</Methods>
</Entity>
  <!-- Other Entities defined after this point -->
  </Entities>
  </LobSystem>
 </LobSystems>
</Model>
```

In this specific example, when you call the GetCustomers method on the Customer entity, BCS makes the appropriate web service call and returns the data in the Customer entity.

Generating Entities

As you've seen from the previous example, BDC model definition files can be very complex. Thankfully, there are tools that allow you to point to a web service and then generate and export a BDC model definition. Once you've created a definition file for the first time, you can then share the definition file throughout an enterprise or even on public communities and forums. Other users can then use the definition file to connect to the specific web service.

One of the tools you can use to generate and export a BDC model definition file of a web service is SharePoint Designer 2010. You can download a free copy of SharePoint Designer 2010 from Microsoft's website. If you need the 32-bit version of SharePoint Designer 2010, go to *http://www.microsoft.com/downloads/details.aspx?displaylang=en&FamilyID=d88a1505-849b-4587-b854-a7054ee28d66*. If you need the 64-bit version, go to *http://www.microsoft.com/downloads/details.aspx?displaylang=en&FamilyID=566d3f55-77a5-4298-bb9c-f55f096b125d*.

You can find an example web service called WebService1 in the Web Services folder on the companion CD. Note that this section assumes you have a web service available and running.

Setting Up the Sample Web Service

If you'd like to follow the steps outlined in the next section using your own server running SharePoint 2010, you'll need to install the sample web service. You might need to enlist the help of your SharePoint server administrator to install this sample web service.

On the SharePoint server, you first need to open the Internet Information Services (IIS) Manager and add a new website. We named our sample website Service1 and used port 55653 so as not to interfere with any other services running on the server. You then use Windows Explorer to navigate to the *C:\inetpub\wwwroot* folder and look for the Service1 folder. If there is no folder present in that directory, you can create one.

On the companion CD, navigate to the Web Services folder. Open the WebService1 folder inside the Web Services folder and then copy the *Service1.asmx* and *Web.config* files from the WebService1 folder to your *C:\inetpub\wwwroot\Service1* folder on your server computer. Now, copy the Bin folder (this folder contains two files) from inside the WebService1 folder on the companion CD to the *C:\inetpub\wwwroot\Service1* folder as well.

Now that you have the web service files copied, you'll need to make sure the BDC Service is running on your SharePoint server. Click Start on your Windows taskbar, click Programs, click Microsoft SharePoint 2010 Programs, and then click SharePoint 2010 Central Administration to open the Central Administration page for your server running SharePoint. Click Manage Services On Server under the System Settings category to view a list of all the services and their status on your SharePoint server. Verify that BDC Service lists the word *Started* under the Status column. If the status currently reads Stopped, click the Start link in the Action column to start the service.

If you've installed everything correctly, you'll be able to see the sample web service by navigating to a Uniform Resource Locator (URL) similar to this on your SharePoint server: *http://YourServerName:YourPortNumber/service1.asmx*.

Note

You are not required to use SharePoint Designer to create or use BDC model files—we've used it here because SharePoint Designer makes the creation experience easier. You can find third-party tools from other software developers for building BDC model definition files.

To create a BDC definition file using SharePoint Designer 2010, follow these steps:

1. Open SharePoint Designer 2010 and then click Open Site on the Sites tab of the Backstage view. In the Open Site dialog box, enter the URL for your server running the web service. Note that you might need to enter the port number, such as *http://ServerName:PortNumber,* in the URL to connect to your server. Once you've connected to the server, click External Content Types in the Navigation pane under Site Objects, as shown here.

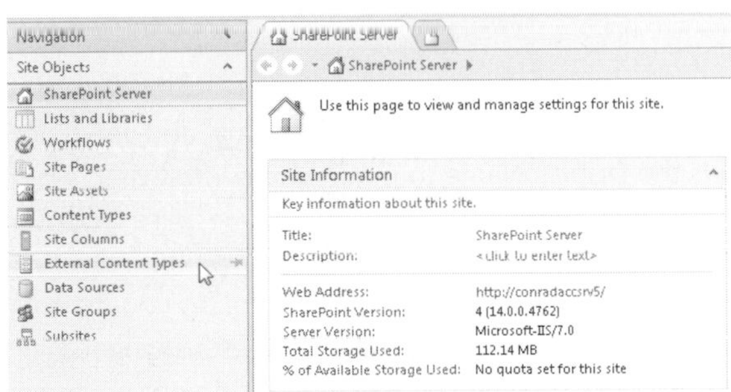

2. BCS data sources in SharePoint and SharePoint Designer, as well as Outlook, are called External Content. Access uses the term *Data Services* to differentiate BCS from other external data types available in Access. An External Content Type is just another name for a BCS entity. Click External Content Type in the New group on the External Content Types tab, as shown here.

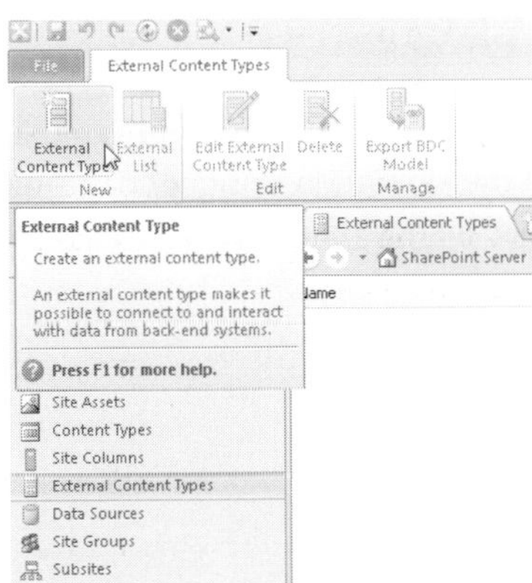

3. Under External Content Type Information, click the New External Content Type link next to Name and type **Order** as the name for your new External Content Type, as shown here.

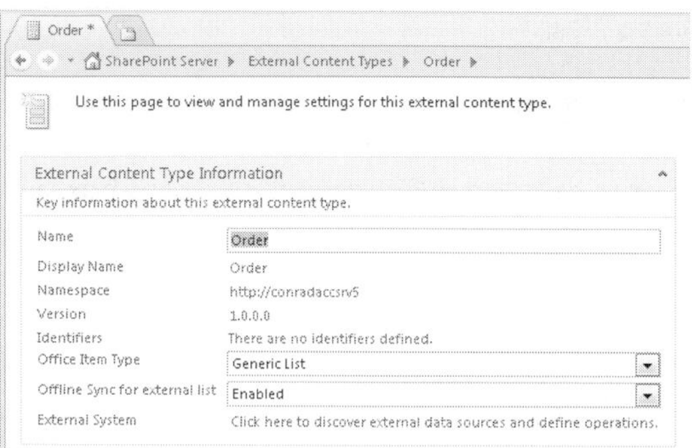

4. Tab out of the control to commit your new name, and you'll notice SharePoint Designer sets the Display Name to match the name *Order*, which you just created. SharePoint Designer automatically sets the Namespace (your server name) and Version fields for you under External Content Type Information. SharePoint uses the Version value to track this External Content type, so you do not need to change this value. Next to Identifiers, SharePoint Designer lists any identifiers for the entity. We don't want to set any identifiers at this time, so do not enter anything for this setting. In the Office Item Type combo box, SharePoint Designer displays five complex types—Generic List, Appointment, Contact, Task, and Post. Note that Access can only read Generic List, so make sure that option is selected in the Office Item Type field. (Generic List is the default option.) The Offline Sync For External List option allows an entity to be synched with offline clients such as Outlook or SharePoint Workspaces. You can choose Enabled, the default option, or Disabled to prevent sync operations. Access does not require this option to be set for the entity to operate correctly in Access, so leave this option set to Enabled.

5. Next to External System, click the Click Here To Discover External Data Sources And Define Operations link to open the Operation Designer page. Click Add Connection on the Operation Designer Page, as shown here.

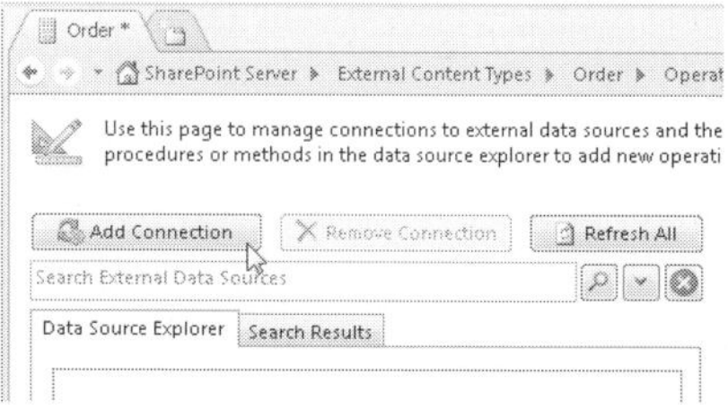

6. SharePoint Designer displays the External Data Source Type Selection dialog box, shown here. In the Data Source Type combo box, you can choose .NET Type, SQL Server, or WCF Service. Select WCF Service for this new connection and then click OK.

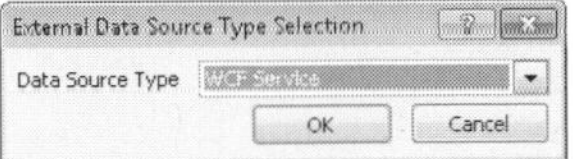

7. SharePoint Designer opens the WCF Connection dialog box, as shown here. In the Service Metadata URL field, enter the URL address to the Web Service Description Language (WSDL) for the web service on your server. In the Metadata Connection Mode field, you can choose between WSDL and Metadata Exchange. Select WSDL from the drop-down list because this is a SOAP service. Enter the URL address, including the http:// prefix, to your web service in the Service Endpoint URL field. The Name field is optional, but we recommend adding a readable reference name for your connection within SharePoint Designer. In our example, we named our WCF connection **Order Info Service**. Leave all other options set at their defaults on this dialog box, and then click OK to save your changes and continue.

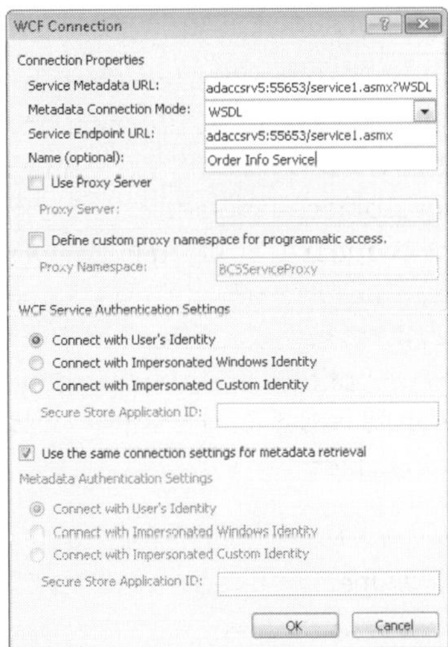

8. SharePoint Designer takes a few moments to test your connection and then displays your Order Info Service connection information on the Data Source Explorer tab. Click the plus symbol (+) next to Order Info Service to expand the various nodes. You'll see that under Web Methods, SharePoint Designer displays all the exposed functions of the web service. This example web service exposes methods that map to three different entities—Orders, Customers, and OrderTypes, as shown here.

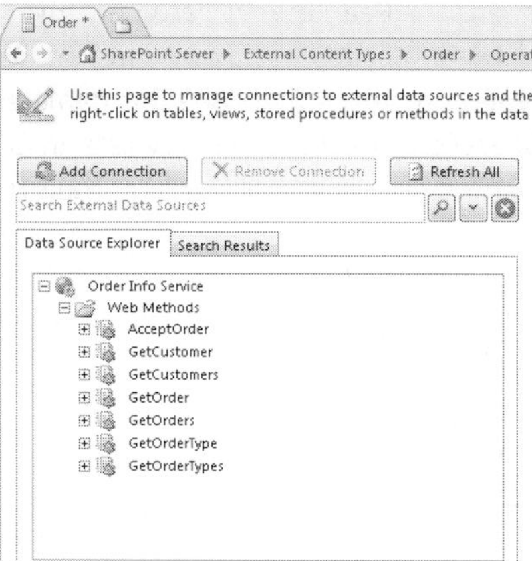

9. For this example, we'll focus on the Order entity. Let's map these web service methods to the appropriate method stereotypes for our new entity. Right-click the GetOrder method to open the shortcut menu. You'll notice the shortcut menu displays data actions that we can map to this web service, such as read, create, update, and delete operations. (*Read item operation* is another term for the BCS Specific Finder method stereotype.) Click New Read Item Operation from the shortcut menu, as shown here.

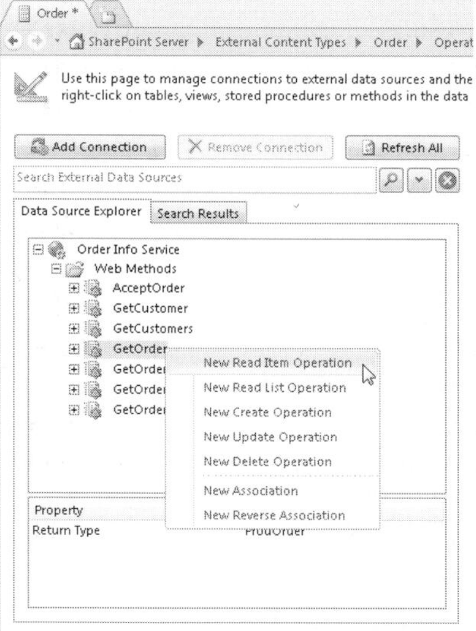

10. SharePoint Designer now opens the Read Item wizard, as shown here. On the first page of the wizard—Operation Properties—you can enter an Operation Name and Operation Display Name. Note that you will not see this name exposed in the Access user interface. By default, SharePoint Designer already lists an Operation Name and Operation Display Name for you. Leave the names set at their default, and click Next to continue.

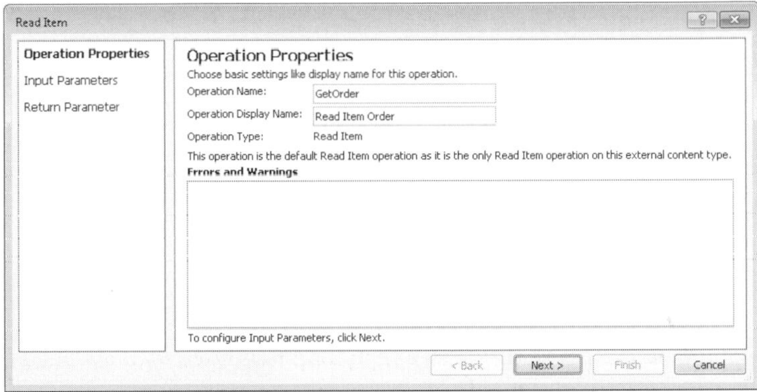

11. On the second page of the Read Item wizard, Input Parameters, you can configure input parameters for each operation, as shown here. Select OrderNum under Data Source Elements in the middle pane of this wizard page. (The GetOrder web method takes an OrderNum as input. This OrderNum maps to the identifier for the Orders external content type we're creating.) Under the Properties section, Element references the name of the input variable as it appears in the web service definition. The .NET Type is the type of variable defined in the web service definition. Select the Map To Identifier field, cleared by default, since we want OrderNum to act as the ID for this external content type. In the Identifier field, select OrderNum from the drop-down list as the identifier for the input of this method. The Display Name is the name by which the input variable will be exposed in the entity definition. In the Default Value field, you can define a default value for this input in the entity definition. An example might be to set the OrderNum to 0 so no value is specified when this method of the entity is executed, but for our purposes, this value should be left to the default, <<None>>, as shown here. Click Next to continue to the last page of the wizard.

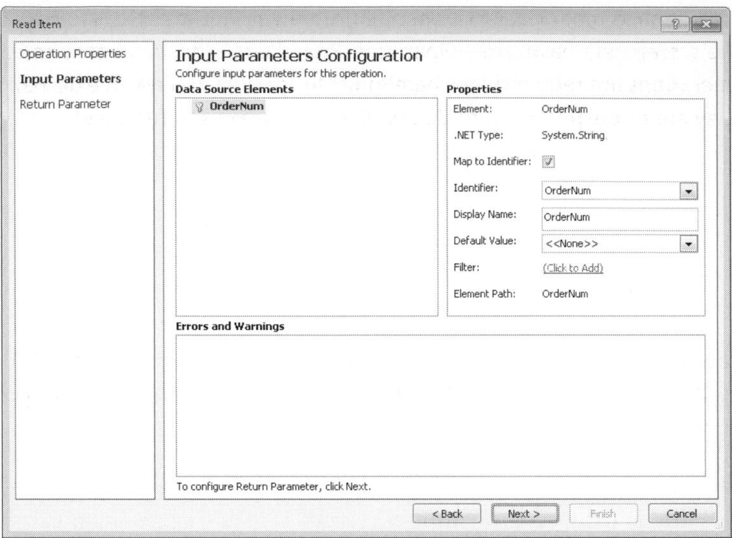

12. On the last page of the wizard, Return Parameter, you can configure return parameters for the data source elements, as shown here. You can define Display names and set the return values to be required or read-only. Select OrderNum in the left panel, and then select the Map To Identifier checkbox in the right panel to map the OrderNum identifier. Click Finish to save your changes and exit the wizard.

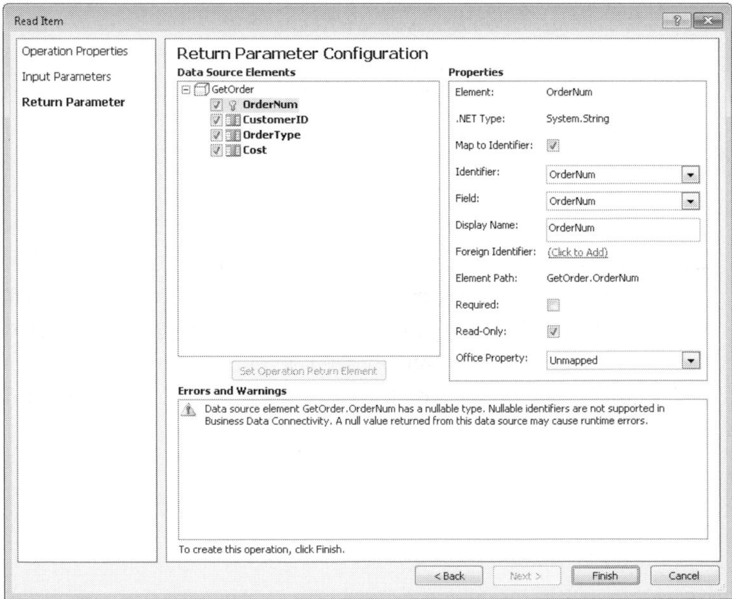

You'll notice that under the External Content Type Operations header on the right side of the screen, you have a new Read Item called GetOrder, as shown here. Note that Read Item operations are required for SharePoint Designer to define an external content type, but they are not exposed in the Access Data Services user interface.

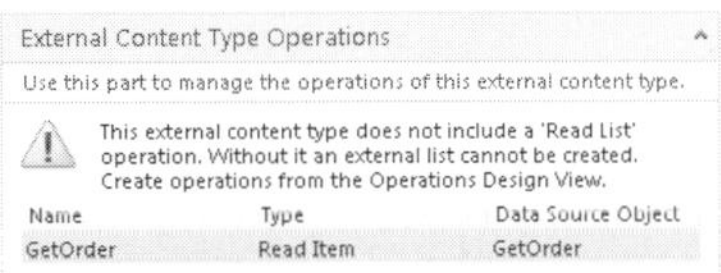

You've finished making the Read Item operation, but now you need to map the Finder method that Access uses for reading lists of data. In SharePoint Designer, Finder methods are called Read List operations. To map the Finder method, follow these steps:

1. Right-click the GetOrders web method under Order Info Service, and then click New Read List Operation from the shortcut menu, as shown here.

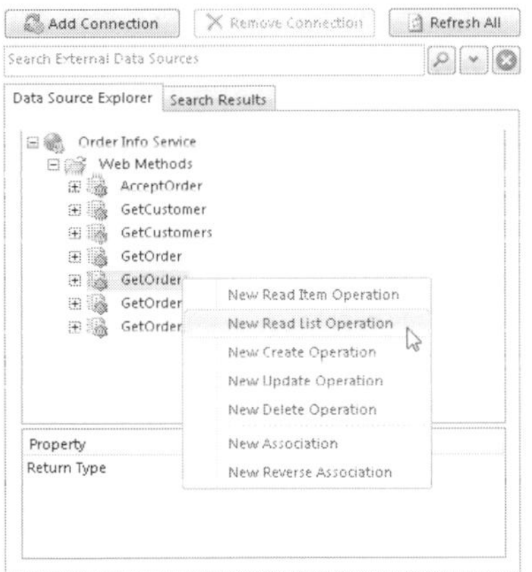

2. On the first page of the Read List wizard, provide a name for the operation in the Operation Name text box (you can use the default name of **GetOrders**). Click Next to proceed to the next page of the wizard. On the Input Parameters page of the wizard, select Location under Data Source Elements. Under Properties on the right side of the Input Parameters page, click the Click To Add link next to the Filter option, as shown here.

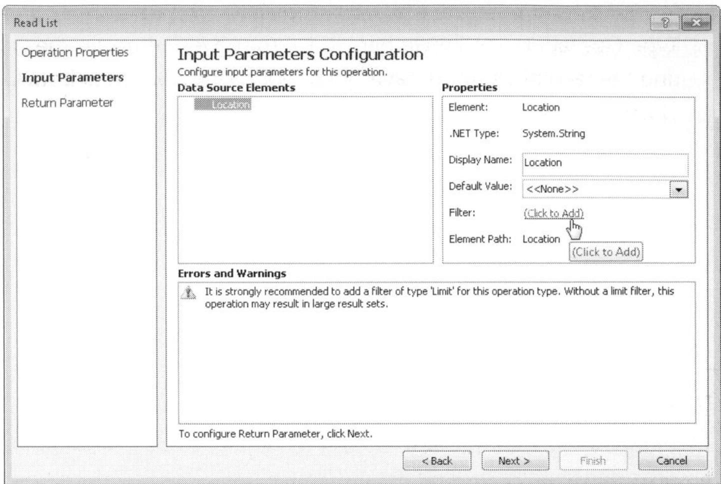

3. SharePoint Designer opens the Filter Configuration dialog box shown here. You can use the dialog box to assign a filter for the return results you get when you request a list of data. In the New Filter text box, type **Location** for the name of this filter. (You can view this filter name within Access.) In the Filter Type and Operator options, you can leave these set at their defaults of Comparison and Equals from the drop-down lists of options. Setting these options means that when we pass an input filter in from Access, the entity returns all values where Location equals the value you specify. Leave the other options set on their defaults as well, and then click OK to close the dialog box.

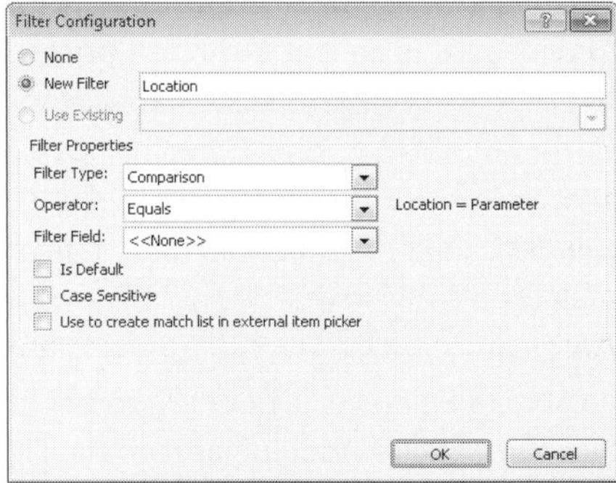

4. SharePoint Designer returns you to the Input Parameters page of the Read Item wizard. Click next to move to the last page of the Read Item wizard, called Return Parameter. Select OrderNum in the left panel and then select Map To Identifier, as you did with the GetOrder method in the previous section. Click Finish to save your changes and exit the wizard.

5. You'll now see both the GetOrder and GetOrders operations under External Content Type Operations, as shown here. Click the Save button on the Quick Access Toolbar, and SharePoint Designer saves your work to the Business Data Connectivity Metadata Store.

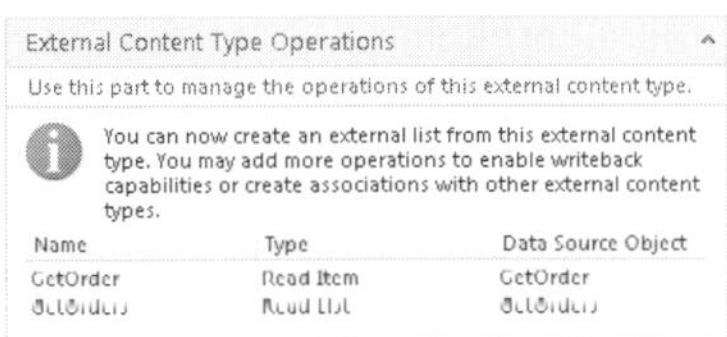

> ## Note
>
> **Although Access does not use method types, SharePoint Designer requires that each entity contain a Specific Finder or Read Item Operation method type. You can certainly create an entity definition without a Specific Finder included, but you'll need to use a different tool besides SharePoint Designer or create the entity definition by hand.**

You've now defined a BCS Entity using SharePoint Designer. You can use this entity to interact with your web service data on SharePoint sub-sites and applications. In our example, we want to use this entity within Access, so we need to export the entity to an XML file that we can import into Access. To export the entity to an XML file, follow these steps:

1. Navigate to the External Content Types listing by clicking External Content Types in the SharePoint navigation bar. SharePoint Designer displays a list of BCS entities on the server. You'll see the Orders entity you created in the previous section listed here. Right-click the new Orders entity and then click Export BDC Model on the shortcut menu, as shown here. (You can also click the Export BDC Model button in the Manage group on the ribbon to export a BDC model file.) Note that you can export multiple entities in the same BDC model file; select all the entities you want to export, right-click, and then click Export BDC Model from the shortcut menu. When you import a model file into Access with multiple entities, Access displays all the entities.

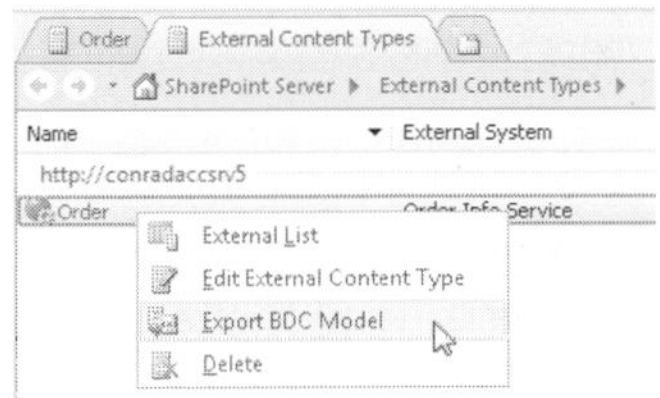

2. SharePoint Designer now opens the Export BDC Model dialog box shown here. To create a BDC model that contains your entity and connection information, you need to supply a name in the BDC Model Name field. Enter **OrderModel** for the name, and then select Client from the Settings field drop-down list. If you select the other option—Server—in the Settings field, SharePoint Designer prepares the entity definition to instantiate on another SharePoint 2010 server but Access client cannot import the definition. Click OK, browse to a location to save the file, and then click Save in the File Save dialog box to save your BDC model file.

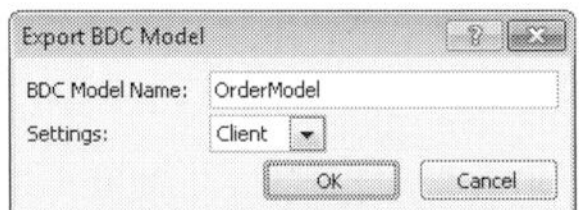

3. SharePoint Designer exports the BDC Model file with a .bdcm file extension. For Access to import this model, you need to change the file extension to .xml. Using Windows Explorer, navigate to the BDC Model file you just saved. Right-click the BDC Model file, click Rename from the shortcut menu, and then change the file extension to .xml before proceeding further.

You've now completed your first BDC model file, also known as a BDC metadata file. Creating the BDC model files is the most challenging step of using the BCS components in Access 2010. If you're fortunate, another developer might have already written a BDC model file for a web service you can use. After you or someone else exports a BDC model file, you don't need access to the SharePoint server from that point on—BCS, in Access, connects directly to the data source. Once someone takes the time to map a web service to BCS, they can easily share and distribute their work with other Access and SharePoint developers. If you are in a business or enterprise that includes SharePoint developers, there's a good chance other developers have already defined BCS entities that you could export and use in your Access projects. You can also find BDC model files posted on public sites for communicating with various public web services, such as Data.gov.

Connecting Data Services in Access

Now that you have a usable BDC model definition XML file, let's import it into Access. As we discussed previously, Access understands how to expose Read List Operations or Default Finder of a BCS Entity. Behind the scenes, Access loads a small managed Dynamic Link Library (DLL), which is the BCS client. Access sends the BCS client the BDC model file and asks for the Finder method. The BCS handles the communications, authentication, and authorization with the remote data source, all according to the specifications in the BDC model file.

Let's take a look at how Access creates these linked lists from a BDC model file in a new Access database file. Start Access, click Blank Database on the New tab of the Backstage view, provide a name for your new database in the File Name text box, and then click Create. After Access creates your new database, close and don't save the default Table1 table that Access initially displays. Click More in the Import & Link group on the External Data tab and then click Data Services on the drop-down list of options beneath the More command, as shown in Figure 23-4.

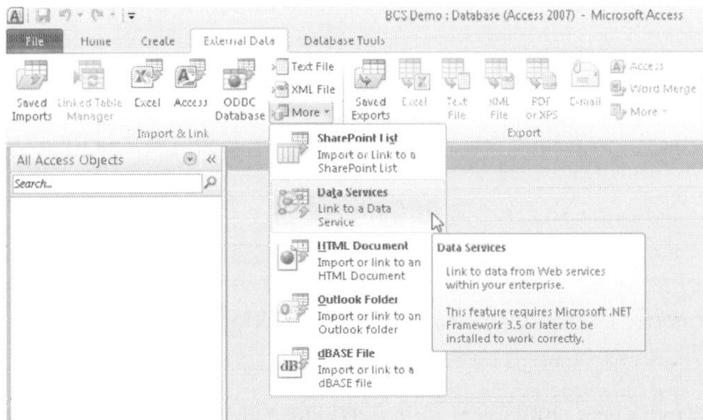

Figure 23-4 Click Data Services to start importing your BDC model definition file.

TROUBLESHOOTING

Why is the Data Services option disabled on the ribbon?

When you're connecting to web services data using the BCS client, Access requires Microsoft .NET Framework 3.5 or later to be installed on your computer. If you are missing this component, Access disables the Data Services button on the ribbon. You'll need to download and install .NET Framework 3.5 or later to import BDC definition files into Access.

Access opens the Create Link To Data Services dialog box, as shown in Figure 23-5. To start importing your BDC model file, click Install Connection in the lower-left corner of the dialog box.

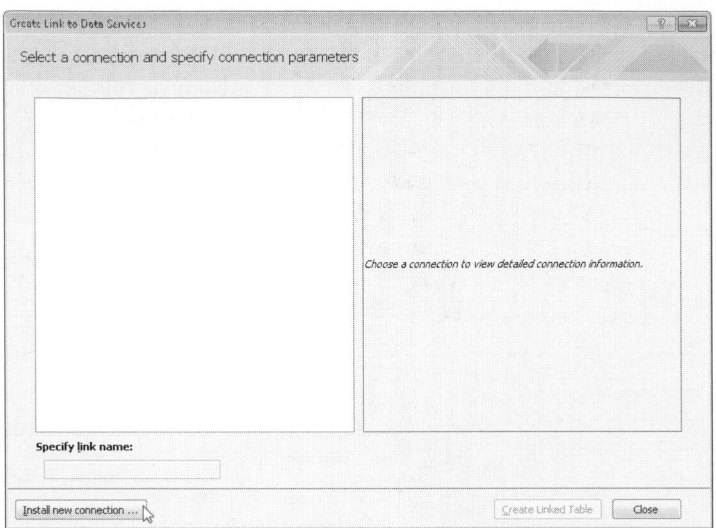

Figure 23-5 Click Install New Connection to create a connection to your web service.

Access opens the Select A Connection Definition File dialog box, where you can browse to the location you exported your BDC model file from SharePoint Designer in the previous section. Browse to the BDC model file, select it, and then click OK. (You can use the Order-ModelSample.xml file found in the Web Services folder on the companion CD, but you'll need to adjust the model file to point to the web service running on your server.) Access examines the XML file and then loads the model in the left pane on the Create Link To Data Source dialog box. After Access installs the new data services connection, expand the Order Info Service system name and select the underlying Order entity, as shown in Figure 23-6. Note that if there are multiple Finder methods in an Entity definition, Access exposes only the default Finder method.

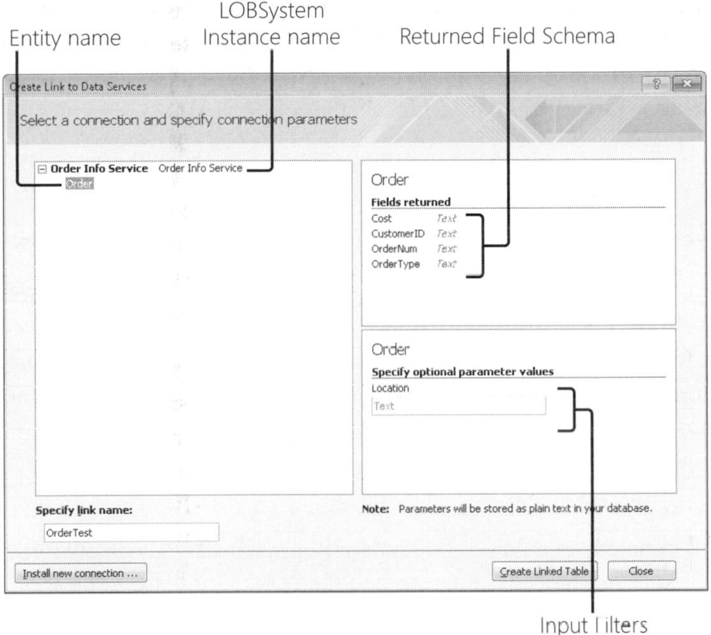

Figure 23-6 You can specify your connection parameters on the Create Link To Data Services dialog box.

The four main elements shown in Figure 23-6 are as follows:

- **LOBSystem Instance name** Maps to the name of the web service that you gave when you defined the connection in SharePoint Designer.
- **Entity name** Maps to the display name of the External Content Type you gave when you generated the entity in SharePoint Designer. Note that if an entity doesn't appear in the Create Link To Data Services dialog box, the entity doesn't contain a finder stereotype method.
- **Returned Field Schema** Lists columns (name type) that make up the return table. Note that once you define the schema of an entity, it can be altered only by modifying the original entity definition, exporting the definition file, and then importing into Access again.

- **Input Filters** Lists entities that can take input into their finders. This is usually used to filter down the returning result set, but it can be used for any input to the underlying web method, depending on the mapping. Once these values are set for a linked table, they cannot be changed for that linked table.

INSIDE OUT Save BDC Model Files for Future Use

When you install a BDC model file, Access installs all the contained entities into your current database and stores the definitions with your Access database, even if you copy the file to another location. If you want to use a BDC model file in a different database, you'll need to reinstall the BDC model file into that database. We recommend that you save those model files in a location that uses regular backup procedures.

If you want to delete an entity or LOBSystem from your database, right-click the item in the Create Link To Data Services dialog box and then click Delete from the shortcut menu. You will no longer be able to use any existing Data Services links in your database that depend on these items.

For this example, type **OrderTest** in the Specify Link Name text box to name this linked table and then click Create Linked Table. You'll notice a new linked table in the Navigation pane, as shown in Figure 23-7. You can distinguish Data Services linked tables from other linked table types by the blue spherical objects in the lower-right corner of the linked table icon.

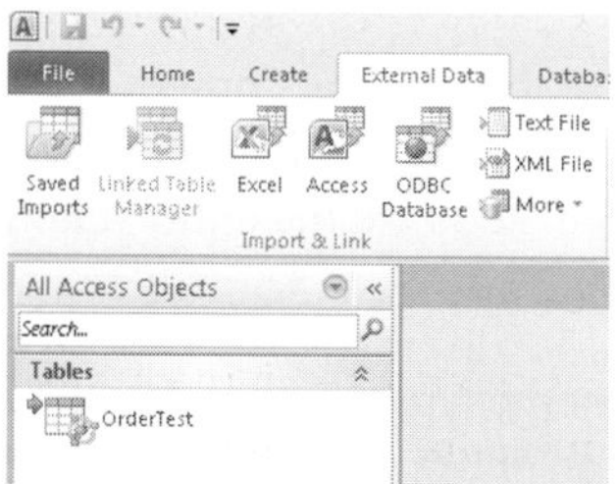

Figure 23-7 You can see your new Data Services linked table in the Navigation pane.

Note

You might need to add an AccessControlList tag to your BDC model file if you receive a permissions error message opening your Data Services linked table. In the OrderModel-Sample.xml sample on the companion CD, we included the following AccessControlList tag information:

```
<AccessControlList>
 <AccessControlEntry Principal="NT AUTHORITY\Authenticated Users">
  <Right BdcRight="Edit" />
  <Right BdcRight="Execute" />
  <Right BdcRight="SetPermissions" />
  <Right BdcRight="SelectableInClients" />
 </AccessControlEntry>
</AccessControlList>
```

You can look at our sample XML file to see where you need to place this tag.

Web service lists of data are displayed in Access as read-only linked tables. You can use these tables linked to the web services data in Access like other linked data sources, except that you can only view the data. For example, you cannot directly change the data in a table datasheet. You can, however, create queries, forms, and reports that reference these linked tables, and you can use Microsoft Visual Basic code to call the web service methods. In addition, you can refresh the data in the linked table to show the latest changes by clicking the Refresh All button in the Records group on the Home tab on the ribbon. Access caches the data in the linked tables when you disconnect from the data source, which means the data is still available to use. The sample web service we've used does not filter data but returns the entire set of data for the Orders entity. In a real-world web service, for example, we could supply a ZIP code to the Location filter to display all orders from within a specific ZIP code.

INSIDE OUT Updating BDC Model Files

If you have a new version of a BDC model file, you can install it in your current Access database. Access overwrites any LOBSystems or entities with the same name, and your linked tables continue to function as before. Be aware, however, that if the changes involve the return schema for entities, then any linked tables in Access based on those entities need to be recreated.

If you have a BDC model file that contains a scalar method type, Access exposes that method as an expression. You can see what expressions are available by browsing the Web-Services tree in the Immediate Window of the Visual Basic Editor. An example of this Visual Basic code is the following:

```
WebServices.LOBSystem("WebServiceName").Entity("EntityName").Operation("MethodName")
  .Execute("PARAM_NAME1=<string>;PARAM_NAME2=<string>")
```

You can use the following Visual Basic code stored in a public module to list the names of all web services, entities, and operations in a database:

```
Public Sub ListWebServices()
Dim ws As WebService
Dim ent As Entity
Dim op As Operation
' Loop through the WebServices and list
' out the names, entities, and operations
 For Each ws In WebServices
  Debug.Print "WebService Name: " & ws.Name
   For Each ent In ws.Entities
    Debug.Print " Entity Name: " & ent.Name
     For Each op In ent.Operations
      Debug.Print "  Operation Name : " & op.Name
     Next
   Next
 Next
End Sub
```

This code loops through each installed web service and then prints out the name to the Immediate Window using the Debug.Print command. Next, the code loops through the Entities in each web service and prints their names to the Immediate Window. Finally, the code loops through the operations for a given entity and prints out their name to the Immediate Window. In Chapter 24, "Understanding Visual Basic Fundamentals," on the companion CD, you'll learn about working with Visual Basic, the Visual Basic Editor, and the Immediate Window.

Note

To see additional example data services links to the Customers, Orders, and OrderTypes entities for our sample web service, you can open the Create Link To Data Services dialog box again, and then install the BCSFullDemo.xml sample found in the Web Services folder on the companion CD. You can create a separate link to each of the three entities we defined for our sample web service and open the links to see the sample data. Note that you'll need to manually adjust the model file to point to the web service running on your server.

This concludes the printed chapter portion of *Microsoft Access 2010 Inside Out*. However, you'll find four additional chapters on the companion CD. In Part 8, "Automating an Access Application Using Visual Basic," you'll learn about Visual Basic for Applications (VBA) and see many examples of how we automated the sample databases using Visual Basic code. In Part 9, "After Completing Your Application," you'll learn how to create custom ribbons for your applications, create database templates, understand how run-time mode works, as well as many other topics. The companion CD also includes six reference articles that you'll find essential for increasing your knowledge about building applications using Access.

APPENDIX

Installing Your Software

This book assumes you have installed Microsoft Access 2010 as part of Microsoft Office Professional Plus 2010. To install Office and related software for a single user, you need a Microsoft Windows–compatible computer configured as follows:

- A Pentium 500 megahertz (MHz) or faster processor (Pentium III is recommended as a minimum), and 1 gigahertz (GHz) is required for Microsoft Outlook with Business Contact Manager.
- Microsoft Windows XP with Service Pack (SP) 3 (32-bit), Windows Vista with SP1 (32-bit or 64-bit), Windows Server 2003 R2 (32-bit or 64-bit) with MSXML 6.0 installed, Windows Server 2008 (32-bit or 64-bit), or Windows 7 (32-bit or 64-bit). Terminal Server and Windows on Windows (WOW), which allows installing 32-bit versions of Office 2010 on 64-bit operating systems, are supported.
- At least 256 megabytes (MB) of random access memory (RAM); 512 MB is recommended.
- A hard drive with at least 527 MB of free space for a minimum installation when your network administrator has set up an install package for you on a server. When you perform a local installation, you need up to 3.5 gigabytes (GB) on your primary hard drive for the installation files and programs. At the end of the Office system install, you have the option to leave some of the installation files on your hard drive, which requires up to an additional 240 MB of free space.
- A CD-ROM or DVD-ROM drive. (A DVD-ROM is recommended.) If you are installing over a network, no disc drive is required.
- A mouse or other pointing device.
- A 1024 × 768 or greater monitor display.

Other options required to use all features include the following:

- A multimedia computer for sound and other multimedia effects.
- Dial-up or broadband Internet access.
- Certain inking features require running Windows XP Table PC edition or later. Speech recognition functionality requires a close-talk microphone and an audio output device. Information Rights Management features require access to a Windows Server 2003 with SP1 or later running Windows Rights Management Services.
- Connectivity to Microsoft Exchange 2000 Server or later is required for certain advanced functionality in Outlook 2010. Instant Search requires Windows Desktop Search 3.0. Dynamic Calendars require server connectivity.
- Microsoft Internet Explorer 6 or later, 32-bit browser only. Internet functionality requires Internet access (fees might apply).
- Connection to an Internet service provider or a local copy of Microsoft Internet Information Services (IIS) installed.
- 512 MB of RAM or higher recommended for Outlook Instant Search. Grammar and contextual spelling in Microsoft Word 2010 is not turned on unless the computer has 1 GB memory.

Installing the Office System

Before you run the Office system setup program, be sure that no other applications are running on your computer.

If you're installing from the Office Professional Plus 2010 CD-ROM or DVD-ROM, insert the first disc. On most systems, the Office system setup program starts automatically. If the setup program does not start automatically, click the Run command on the Start menu. In the Run dialog box, type **x:\setup.exe** (where x is the drive letter of your CD-ROM drive), and click OK. If you see the User Account Control dialog box and you're logged on as a non-administrative user, specify the user name and password for an administrative account, and click Continue. If you're logged on as an administrator, click Continue.

To install from a network drive, use Windows Explorer to connect to the folder in which your system manager has placed the Office system setup files. Run Setup.exe in that folder by double-clicking it. If you're installing the Office system from a Master License

Pack, click Run on the Start menu, and include a PIDKEY= parameter and the 25-character volume-license key in the open box, as in the following example:

```
x:\setup.exe PIDKEY=1234567890123456789012345
```

Note that the setup program might take several minutes after it displays its opening screen to examine your computer and determine what programs you currently have installed—be patient! If you didn't supply a license key on the command line, the setup program asks for a valid product key. If you're installing from a CD or DVD, you can find the product key in the materials included with the Office 2010 release installation package. Enter a valid key, and click Continue to go to the next page. The setup program asks you to confirm that you accept the license agreement. Select the I Accept The Terms Of This Agreement check box, and then click Continue. The setup program asks whether you want to install now or to customize your installation.

Choosing Options When You Have No Previous Version of the Office System

When you install the Office 2010 release on your computer, you can choose between two options—Install Now or Customize, as shown in Figure A-1. If you click Install Now, the setup program installs all the programs and components that Microsoft considers most useful to the majority of users. The fastest way to complete an install is to click Install Now. If you don't want to tailor the installation to your specific needs by clicking Customize, click Install Now to include Access 2010 so that you can work through the examples in this book.

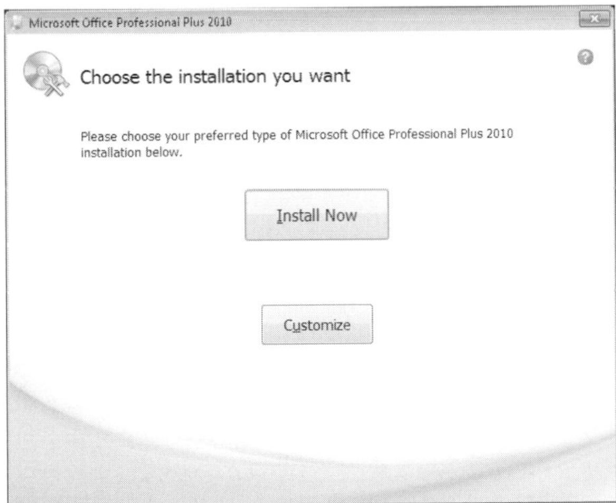

Figure A-1 Click Install Now to install the default Office Professional Plus 2010 programs.

We like to click Customize to pick the options we need. The Customize install option allows you to choose only some applications or include additional features that Microsoft considers optional. When you click Customize, the setup program displays a window with three tabs—Installation Options, File Location, and User Information, as shown in Figure A-2.

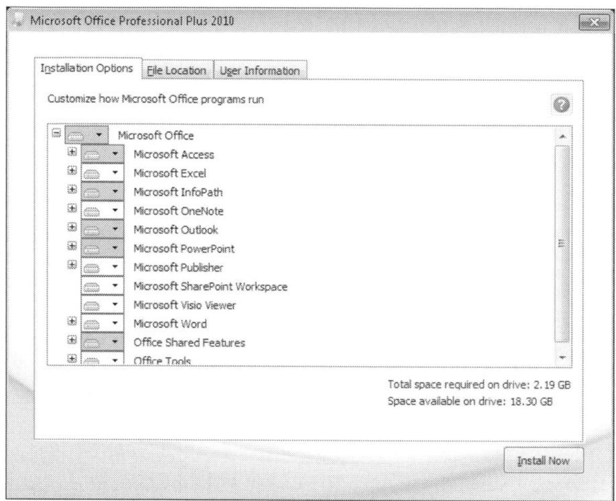

Figure A-2 The Installation Options tab allows you to choose which programs and options to install.

The setup program shows you the available options for the Office system and each program in a hierarchical view. By default, the setup program selects all programs, but it selects only some of the features for several of the programs. Click the plus sign (+) next to any category to expand it and see the options in subcategories. When you see a category that interests you, click the arrow next to the disk drive icon to choose options for all items in that category and its subcategories. To work through all the examples in this book, you should select the Run All From My Computer option for Microsoft Access, as shown in Figure A-3. Choosing this option selects the Run From My Computer option for all subcategories. Note that when you select this option, the setup program installs the Package Solution Wizard add-in, which helps you create installation files that include your database application, the runtime modules necessary to run your application, and any supporting files (such as ActiveX controls or icons). The wizard creates a standard Windows Installer setup file (.msi). When you select Installed On First Use, the installation program creates a shortcut for the program on your Start menu, but you'll be prompted to install the application when you select the shortcut the first time. Choosing Not Available causes the installation program to neither install the program nor provide a shortcut.

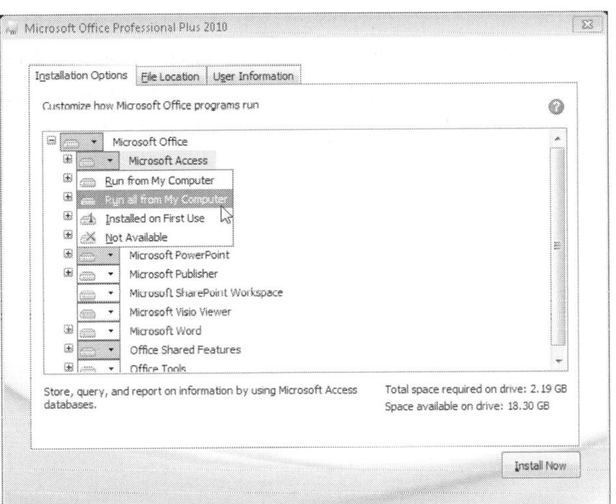

Figure A-3 Choose Run All From My Computer to have the setup program install Access 2010 components.

We personally like to begin by selecting the Run All From My Computer option for the top-level item, Microsoft Office. We then go through each of the major categories and selectively choose Installed On First Use or, for options that we do not want, Not Available. For example, you might want to go to the Office Shared Features category and remove some of the extra fonts under International Support. If you're unsure about any option, you can click the title of the option to see a brief description in the lower part of the window.

On the File Location tab, you see a box with a default location chosen, as shown in Figure A-4. You can enter a different program file location or click Browse to select a location on your hard drive. We recommend that you keep the default location. You'll see summary information on how much space is required and available on your hard drive in the middle of the window.

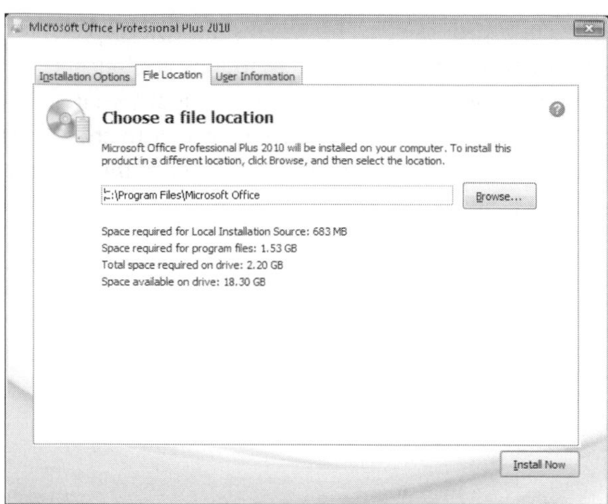

Figure A-4 Select an installation folder on the File Location tab.

On the User Information tab, you can enter personal information about yourself and your company, as shown in Figure A-5. Type your name in the Full Name text box, your initials in the Initials text box, and your organization or company name in the Organization text box. (Note, if you do not fill in these boxes here, the first Office system program you open after installation prompts you for your full name and initials.)

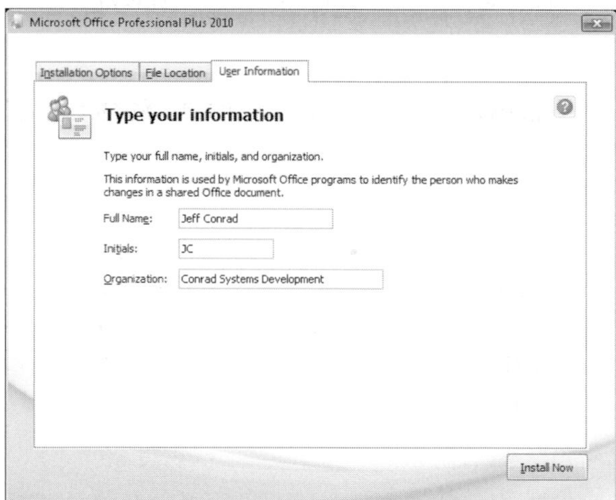

Figure A-5 Enter your personal information on the User Information tab.

After you have finished making your selections, click Install Now to proceed. If you're not sure, you can click any of the three tabs to verify the options you selected. When the setup program finishes, it shows you a setup completed window, as shown in Figure A-6. In this final window, you can select options to open your web browser to check for additional updates. You can click the Help icon in the upper-right corner of the window to display information registering your copy of the Office 2010 release. Click Close to close the setup program window.

Figure A-6 The setup program displays this message when the installation process completes.

Choosing Options to Upgrade a Previous Version of the Office System

When you have a previous version of any of the Office system programs installed on your computer, the setup program shows you different options after you accept the license agreement, as shown in Figure A-7. If you click Upgrade, the setup program installs all the programs and components that Microsoft considers most useful to the majority of users and removes any previous versions of the Office system programs. The fastest way to complete an install is to click Upgrade.

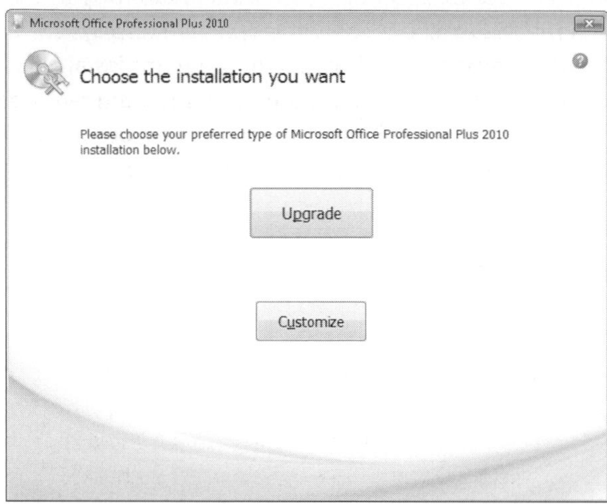

Figure A-7 When you have previous versions of the Office system programs installed, you can choose either Upgrade or Customize.

We like to click Customize to pick the options we need. The Customize install option allows you to choose only some of the applications to install and to not remove previous versions. When you click Customize, the setup program displays a window with four tabs—Upgrade, Installation Options, File Location, and User Information, as shown in Figure A-8.

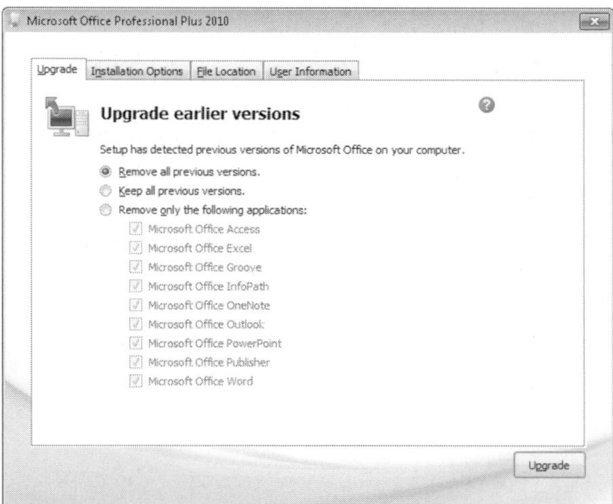

Figure A-8 On the Upgrade tab, you can choose to keep or remove existing Office system programs.

The Installation Options, File Location, and User Information tabs display the same options you learned about in the previous section. The setup program displays the Upgrade tab only when you have previous versions of Office system programs installed on your computer. If you select Remove All Previous Versions, the setup program removes any existing Office system programs before installing the Office 2010 release programs. If you select the Keep All Previous Versions option, the setup program does not remove any existing Office system programs before installing the Office 2010 release programs. Notice that you cannot choose to keep a previous version of Outlook if you have chosen to install Outlook 2010. If you select Remove Only The Following Applications, you can choose which existing Office system programs to keep.

As professional Access developers, we keep several versions of Access installed on our primary development computers so that we can continue to support older applications that we wrote. You might also want to keep an older version of Microsoft Excel, Microsoft PowerPoint, or Word. To keep an older version, you must clear the appropriate check box for the application under Remove Only The Following Applications.

As you learned in the previous section, you can change which of the Office 2010 release components are installed on the Installation Options tab, change the installation folder on the File Location tab, and specify your user name information on the User Information tab. After clicking Upgrade, the setup program proceeds and displays the Setup Completed window in Figure A-6 on page 1381 when it is finished. You can click the Help icon in the upper-right corner of the window to display information registering your copy of the 2010 Office release. Click Close to close the setup program window.

Converting from a Previous Version of Access

Access 2010 (version 14 of Access) can work with the data and tables in a database file created by Access version 2, version 7 (Access for Windows 95), version 8 (Access 97), version 9 (Access 2000), version 10 (Access 2002), version 11 (Access 2003), and version 12 (Access 2007). For version 2, you can only import the tables and queries in the old database into a new database that you create using Access 2010. Depending on the complexity of the application, you might be able to open and run a version 7 or version 8 database application with version 14, but you won't be able to modify any of the objects in the database. You can open a version 9, version 10, version 11, or version 12 database with version 14 and modify any of the objects in the database.

You can convert a version 7 or version 8 database file to either the Access 2000 format (version 9), the Access 2002-2003 format (versions 10 and 11), or the Access 2007 .accdb format (version 12 and version 14). Before you begin the conversion process, make sure all Access Basic or Microsoft Visual Basic for Applications (VBA) modules are compiled in your earlier version database. If you want to convert your database to the .accdb file format, start Access 2010, click the File tab on the Backstage view, click Save & Publish, and then click Access Database (*.accdb) under Save Database As. Access opens the Save As dialog box. You must specify a different file name or location for your converted database because Access won't let you replace your previous version file directly. Click Save to convert the database. If you want to convert your database to the Access 2000 or Access 2002–2003 format, start Access 2010, click the File tab on the Backstage view, click Save & Publish, and then click either Access 2000 Database (*.mdb) or Access 2002-2003 Database (*.mdb). Access opens the Save As dialog box. You must specify a different file name or location for your converted database because Access won't let you replace your previous version file directly. Click Save to convert the database.

If you open a version 2, version 7, or version 8 database in Access 2010, you will see a dialog box offering to convert the database to the current version or attempt to modify the database for shared use between versions. For these versions, we recommend that you attempt to convert them rather than modify them for shared use. You won't be able to convert a database that contains anything other than tables and queries. You must create a new Access 2007/2010 format database and import tables and queries from a version 2 database that has forms, reports, macros, or modules. You can also convert an earlier-version database by creating a new Access 2007/2010 format database and then importing all the objects from the older version database.

Conversion Issues

Access 2010 reports any objects or properties that it is unable to convert by creating a table called Convert Errors in your converted database. The most common problems you're likely to encounter are Microsoft Visual Basic libraries that were available in a previous version but not in Access 2010, and obsolete code that you created in a user-defined function.

Other changes that might affect the conversion of your application code or how your converted application runs include the following:

- In versions 7 and earlier, you had to use macros to construct custom menus. Access 2010 continues to support macros for custom menus, but you might want to rebuild custom ribbons using Extensible Markup Language (XML).

- As of version 8, DoMenuItem is no longer supported. The conversion utility replaces this command in all macros with the equivalent RunMenuCommand action or method. The DoMenuItem method in Visual Basic code is still supported for backward compatibility, but you should locate and change these statements after converting your database.

- In version 8, you could create a formatted Windows dialog box with the MsgBox action or function, separating the sections of the message with the @ character. Version 9 and later no longer support this feature. You should remove the @ character used in this way in code you wrote for version 8.
- Versions 7 and 8 supported the Microsoft DAO 2.5/3.x compatibility library for databases converted from previous versions. Version 9 and later no longer support this library. You will need to replace the reference to this library to the Microsoft Office 14.0 Access Database Engine Object Library after you convert the database, and you might need to change old Visual Basic statements that depended on the older version of Data Access Objects (DAO).
- If you convert a database by importing its objects, your new database might not compile or execute properly. The problem is most likely a reference to an obsolete Visual Basic code library. You can correct this by opening any module in the Visual Basic Editor and then clicking Tools, References. Remove any libraries marked MISSING and attempt to compile the project.
- Unless you also have Office 2003 installed on your computer, you won't be able to edit any data access pages that you created in Access 2003.

Installing the Office 64-Bit Version

The Office 2010 applications are also available in 64-bit versions. Before you run the Office system setup program, be sure that no other applications are running on your computer. Note that you can install the 64-bit versions of Office 2010 only on a computer running a 64-bit Windows operating system.

If you're installing from the Office Professional Plus 2010 CD-ROM or DVD-ROM, insert the first disc. On most computers, the Office system setup program starts automatically. By default, the Office setup program wants to install the 32-bit versions of the Office 2010 applications. To install the 64-bit versions, you need to exit the default setup program. Using Windows Explorer, browse to your CD-ROM or DVD-ROM drive, open the x64 folder on the install disc, and then double-click the Setup.exe file located inside the x64 folder. If the setup program does not start automatically, click the Run command on the Start menu. In the Run dialog box, type **y:\x64\setup.exe** (where y is the drive letter of your CD-ROM drive), and click OK. If you see the User Account Control dialog box and you're logged on as a non-administrative user, specify the user name and password for an administrative account, and click Continue. If you're logged on as an administrator, click Continue.

If you have any previous 32-bit versions of Office applications already installed on your computer, you'll see the Setup Error dialog box shown in Figure A-9. You must uninstall all 32-versions of Office applications on your computer before you can install the 64-bit versions of Office 2010 applications. Note that this rule also applies even if you have 32-bit versions of Office 2010 applications installed. You cannot have mixed versions of 32-bit and 64-bit Office applications installed on the same computer.

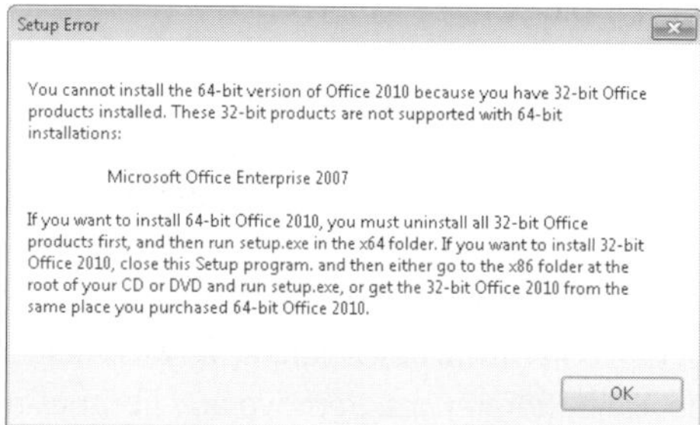

Figure A-9 You must uninstall all previous versions of 32-bit Office programs before installing 64-bit versions of the Office 2010 applications.

The setup procedures for installing the 64-bit Office 2010 applications after this point are the same as the 32-bit versions of Office 2010. You can follow the steps outlined in the previous sections for customizing the application options you'd like to install.

Here are some caveats to using the 64-bit version of Access 2010 that you should be aware of before deciding to install the 64-bit version:

- Existing 32-bit ActiveX controls will not work with the 64-bit version of Access 2010. If you open a form or report that contains a 32-bit ActiveX control, you'll see a red "X" within the box where the control should be. You'll need to update those 32-bit ActiveX controls to work within 64-bit environments.
- Microsoft did not update the ComCtl collection of controls to work within 64-bit environments. If you open a form or report that contains a ComCtl control, you'll see a red "X" within the box where the control should be. You'll need to update those 32-bit ComCtl controls to work within 64-bit environments.
- Existing 32-bit Access add-ins will not work in 64-bit Access 2010. You'll need to obtain a version of the add-in that works in 64-bit environments from the supplier of the add-in.

- Existing Access .mde and .accde files compiled with 32-bit versions of Access will not work with the 64-bit version of Access 2010. You'll need to create a new .mde or .accde from the original database and compile it in the 64-bit version of Access 2010.
- You'll need to update some existing VBA code for it to work within the 64-bit version of Access 2010. In Chapter 25, "Automating Your Application with Visual Basic," on the companion CD, you'll learn what changes you need to make to your VBA code so that your application runs within a 64-bit environment.

For all the reasons mentioned above, Microsoft recommends using the 32-bit version of Access 2010 unless you have a specific reason for using the 64-bit version of Office 2010. The main reason for using the 64-bit versions of Office 2010 is the capacity to work with very large workbooks in Excel and very large projects in Microsoft Project. The maximum database size for Access 2010—2 GB—is identical for both the 32-bit and 64-bit versions of Access 2010.

Installing the Sample Files

To install the sample files from the companion CD, you'll first need to create a new folder on your C drive called Microsoft Press. Next, navigate to the folder called Sample Files on the companion CD using Windows Explorer. Inside the Sample Files folder you'll find another folder called Access 2010 Inside Out. Finally, copy that entire Access 2010 Inside Out folder and all its subdirectories to the Microsoft Press folder. You should now have a folder structure like this on your C drive:

C:\Microsoft Press\Access 2010 Inside Out

Inside the Access 2010 Inside Out folder, you'll see additional subfolders that contain supporting files, as well as the main sample databases used throughout the book. After you have your files copied over from the companion CD onto your computer, make sure you set the Microsoft Press folder and all its subdirectories as a trusted location to enable all the content in the sample databases. See the section, "Enabling Content by Defining Trusted Locations," on page 55, for information about creating trusted locations.

Note

All the sample applications in this book were created and tested using a 32-bit installation of the Office 2010 applications. The sample database files included on the companion CD are most likely not compatible with a 64-bit version of Access 2010.

Index

Symbols and Numbers

All index entries for page 1449 onward refer to content on the companion CD.

A

B

C

D

E

J

K

L

N

O

P

Q

S

T

U

V

W

X

Y

Z

About the Authors

Jeff Conrad started working with Access when he saw a need at his full-time position for a database solution. He bought a book on Access (should have been one of John's books) and began teaching himself how to use the program to solve his business's needs. He immediately became hooked on the power and ease of working with Access long after John had written several books on the program.

Jeff found a home in the Microsoft Access newsgroups asking questions as he was learning the ins and outs of Access and database development. He now enjoys giving back to a community that helped him when he was first learning how to use Access. He has been an active participant for many years in the Access newsgroups, where he is best known as the Access Junkie.

Jeff also was awarded Microsoft's Most Valuable Professional award from 2005 to 2007 for his continual involvement with the online Access community. He maintains a website with a wealth of information and resource links for those needing guidance with Access (*http://www.AccessJunkie.com*). He co-authored *Microsoft Office Access 2007 Inside Out* with John Viescas. Jeff is currently employed by Microsoft as a Software Design Engineer in Test working with the Access development team.

John Viescas has been working with database systems for most of his career. He began by designing and building a database application for a magazine and paperback book distributing company in Illinois in 1968. He went on to build large database application systems for El Paso Natural Gas Company in his hometown in the early 1970s. From there, he went to Applied Data Research in Dallas, where he managed the development of database and data dictionary systems for mainframe computers.

Before forming his own company in 1993, he helped market and support NonStop SQL for Tandem Computers in California. Somewhere along the way (would you believe 1991?), he got involved in the early testing of a new Microsoft product that was code-named "Cirrus." The first edition of *Running Microsoft Access* was published in 1992. Since then, he has written four more editions of *Running*, co-authored the best-selling *SQL Queries for Mere Mortals*, wrote *Building Microsoft Access Applications*, and is pleased to be writing about Access from the "Inside Out" for this book. If you hang out on the Web, you can find him answering questions about Access in the newsgroups. John has been named a Microsoft MVP every year since 1993 for his continuing help to Access users' community. You can reach John via his website at *http://www.viescas.com*.